FOURTH EDITION

LITERACY

assessment & intervention

FOR CLASSROOM TEACHERS

Beverly A. DeVries

SOUTHERN NAZARENE UNIVERSITY

Holcomb Hathaway, Publishers
Scottsdale, Arizona

Library of Congress Cataloging-in-Publication Data

DeVries, Beverly A.
    Literacy assessment & intervention for classroom teachers / Beverly A. DeVries, Southern
Nazarene University. — Fourth Edition.
        pages cm
    Rev. ed. of: Literacy assessment and intervention for K-6 classrooms, 2008.
    ISBN 978-1-62159-020-0 (Print) — ISBN 978-1-62159-021-7 (Ebook)
    1. Reading (Elementary)   2. Reading (Elementary)—Ability testing.   3. Literacy.   I. DeVries,
Beverly A., Literacy assessment and intervention for K-6 classrooms.   II. Title.   III. Title:
Literacy assessment and intervention for classroom teachers.

    LB1573.D445 2015
    372.4—dc23

                                                                2014030010

I dedicate this book to my husband, Merlyn, who is my cheerleader when the going gets tough.

Poetry Credits/Acknowledgments. The following materials may not be reproduced in any form or by any means without the prior written permission of the cited publisher: **Pg. 83:** Excerpt from "My Tooth Ith Loothe," copyright © 1995 by George Ulrich. Reprinted with permission. • Excerpt from "My Family of Dinosaurs," copyright © 1998 by Helen Ksypka. Reprinted from *Miles of Smiles* with permission from Meadowbrook Press. • Excerpt from "Kangaroos," copyright © 1998 by Kenn Nesbitt. Reprinted from *Miles of Smiles* with permission of Meadowbrook Press. **Pg. 84:** Excerpt from "Mr. Backward" in *BING BANG BOING*, copyright © 1994 by Douglas Florian, reprinted by permission of Houghton Mifflin Harcourt Publishing Company. All rights reserved. **Pg. 85:** From *Miss Spider's New Car* © David Kirk and Calloway Arts and Entertainment. All rights reserved. • Excerpt from *In the Haunted House* by Eve Bunting, illustrated by Susan Meddaugh. Text copyright © 1990 by Eve Bunting. Reprinted by permission of Clarion Books, an imprint of Houghton Mifflin Harcourt Publishing Company. All rights reserved. **Pg. 273:** From *COME ON, RAIN* by Karen Hesse. Scholastic Inc./Scholastic Press. Copyright ©1999 by Karen Hesse. Reprinted by permission.

Please note: The author and publisher have made every effort to provide current website addresses in this book. However, it is inevitable that some of the URLs listed here will change following publication of this book.

Holcomb Hathaway, Publishers, Inc.
8700 E. Via de Ventura Blvd., Suite 265
Scottsdale, Arizona 85258
480-991-7881
www.hh-pub.com

10 9 8 7 6 5 4 3 2

Print ISBN 978-1-62159-020-0
Ebook ISBN 978-1-62159-021-7

Printed in the United States of America.

Photo credits: *front cover,* Carline Bonami/123 RF *(main),* Tyler Olson/123 RF *(top left),* Cathy Yeulet/123 RF *(center),* Cathy Yeulet/123 RF *(bottom left); back cover,* Syda Productions/123 RF *(main),* Lisa Young/123 RF *(left),* Cathy Yeulet/123 RF *(center),* Rimma Zaytseva/123 RF *(right); page iii,* Dmitriy Shironosov/123 RF; *page xiv,* kzenon123 RF; *page xvii,* Dmitriy Shironosov/123 RF; *page xviii,* Petro Feketa/123 RF; *page 1,* goodluz/123 RF, Dmitriy Shironosov/123 RF; *page 19,* Dmitriy Shironosov/123 RF, Cathy Yeulet/123 RF; *page 37,* Petro Feketa/123 RF, auremar/123 RF; *page 73,* Inspirestock International/123 RF, Lyubov Kobyakova/123 RF; *page 99,* Zlatan Durakovic/123 RF, Hongqi Zhang/123 RF; *page 121,* Dmitriy Shironosov/123 RF, Cathy Yeulet/123 RF; *page 145,* Cathy Yeulet/123 RF, Inspirestock International/123 RF; *page 173,* Ilka Erika Szasz-Fabian/123 RF, Inspirestock International/123 RF; *page 211,* Tyler Olson/123 RF, kzenon/123 RF; *page 259,* Tyler Olson/123 RF, Matthew Antonino/123 RF; *page 283,* goodluz/123 RF, Cathy Yeulet/123 RF; *page 329,* Dmitriy Shironosov/123 RF, Dmitriy Shironosov/123 RF; *page 351,* Dmitriy Shironosov/123 RF, Lisa Young/123 RF; *page 367,* Jasmin Merdan/123 RF, Cathy Yeulet/123 RF; *page 613,* Dmitriy Shironosov/123 RF; *page 633,* Wavebreak Media Ltd/123 RF; *page 638,* Jim Scolman

contents

Intervention Strategies & Activities   xi

Preface   xiv

Acknowledgments   xvii

About the Author   xviii

1 **Forming a Personal Philosophy About Literacy Assessment and Intervention   1**

INTRODUCTION   2

The Importance of Literacy   2

Theories Related to Literacy   3

Constructivist Theory   3

Zone of Proximal Development   3

Hierarchy of Human Needs   4

Critical Literacy Theory   4

Reading Models   5

Part-to-Whole Model   5

Whole-Part-Whole Model   6

Comprehensive Approach   6

Which Method Is the Most Effective?   9

English Learners   9

English Language Development   9

Effective Practices for English Learners   11

Forming Your Teaching Philosophy   12

Reflect on Assessing Reading Problems   12

Personal Philosophy of Intervention and Instruction for Struggling Readers   12

Historical Overview of Reading Reforms   13

Elementary and Secondary Education Act of 1966   13

The America Reads Challenge Act   13

The National Reading Panel Report   13

No Child Left Behind Act   13

Common Core State Standards   13

BOX *What Does "Scientifically Based Research" Mean?   14*

Response to Intervention   14

New Literacies   16

Concluding Thoughts   17

REFLECTIVE LEARNING Diverse Learners   18

2 **The Literacy Event   19**

INTRODUCTION   21

Teachers   21

Motivation   22

Students   26

Knowledge of General Information   26

Literacy Knowledge   26

Language Systems Readers Use   28

Learning Styles   28

Multiple Intelligences   29

Text   29

Levels of Readability   29

Leveled Books   31

Dimensions of Text Complexity   33

BOX *Readability Software Programs and Formulas   33*

Context   34

Task   34

Concluding Thoughts   35

REFLECTIVE LEARNING At-Risk Students   35

3 Assessment 37

INTRODUCTION 39
Defining Assessment 39
Standards for Assessment 40
Formal/Standardized Assessment Instruments 41
Individual and Group Intelligence Tests 41
BOX *Examples of Individual Intelligence Tests* 41
Achievement Tests 42
Diagnostic Tests 44
Informal Assessment Instruments 45
Emergent Reading and Writing Instruments 46
Informal Reading Inventories 47
Miscue Analysis 48
Retrospective Miscue Analysis 51
Running Records 51
Cloze Tests 54
Maze Tests 56
Anecdotal Records 56
Checklists 57
Rubrics 59
Portfolios 60
Informal Assessment for English Learners 63
Personal Interest Surveys 64
Attitude Surveys 66
Literacy Self-Perception Scales 66
Student Self-Assessment 66
Book Logs 66
Skill Logs 66
Reflection Logs 68
Accomplishment and Goal-Setting Logs 68
Technology and Assessment 70
Concluding Thoughts 71
REFLECTIVE LEARNING Testing 71

4 Phonemic Awareness 73

INTRODUCTION 75
Definitions 75
Dimensions of Phonemic Awareness 76
Phonemic Awareness and English Learners 77
What Teachers Should Know 78
Is Phonemic Awareness Necessary for Students to Become Proficient Readers? 78
How Do Children Become Aware of Phonemes Within Words? 79
Is Phonemic Awareness Addressed in the Common Core State Standards? 79
Assessment 80
Assessing a Student's Level of Phonemic Awareness 80
Assessing a Student's Growth in Phonemic Awareness 81
Introducing Students to the Wonderful Sounds of Our Language 81
Songs 82
Nursery Rhymes and Poems 82
Jump Rope Jingles 84
Tongue Twisters 84
Children's Literature 84

intervention STRATEGIES & ACTIVITIES 86
Activities Emphasizing Syllables 87
Activities Emphasizing Initial Sounds 88
Activities Emphasizing Rhymes 90
Activity Emphasizing Oddity 91
Activities Emphasizing Blending 92
Activity Emphasizing Segmenting 93
Activities Emphasizing Deleting 94
Activities Emphasizing Manipulating 95
Phonemic Awareness & Technology 96
Concluding Thoughts 96
REFLECTIVE LEARNING Phonemic Awareness 97

5 Phonics 99

INTRODUCTION 100
Definitions 101
BOX *Phonics at a Glance* 101
What Teachers Should Know 103
How Students Learn Phonics 103
English Spelling Patterns 104
English Learners and the Graphophonic System 106
Phonics and the Common Core State Standards 107
Principles of Phonics Instruction 107
Principle One: Base Instruction on What Students Know 107

Principle Two: Provide Systematic Phonics
Instruction   108

Principle Three: Use Appropriate Texts   108

Principle Four: Embed Instruction in Meaningful
Contexts   108

Assessment   109

Informal Assessment   109

Formal Assessment   111

intervention STRATEGIES & ACTIVITIES   111

Activities Emphasizing Initial Consonant Sounds   112

Activities Emphasizing Onset and Rime   114

Activities Emphasizing Rhyme   115

Activities Emphasizing Word Patterns   116

Activities Emphasizing Sounds Within Words   117

Phonics and Technology   119

Concluding Thoughts   120

REFLECTIVE LEARNING English Learners   120

6   Word Recognition   121

INTRODUCTION   122

What Teachers Should Know   123

The Four Cueing Systems   123

Components of Word Recognition   124

BOX *High-Frequency Words   126*

Word Recognition and the Common Core State
Standards   128

Sequence of Word Study for English Learners   128

Assessment   128

Informal Assessment   128

Formal Assessment   132

intervention STRATEGIES & ACTIVITIES   133

Small Group Activity for Teaching Word Recognition
Skills   134

INSIDE THE CLASSROOM *A Guided Reading Session   135*

Activities Emphasizing Receptive and Expressive
Vocabularies   135

Activities Emphasizing Sight Words   136

Activities Emphasizing Sight Vocabulary   137

Activity Emphasizing Context Clues   139

Activity Emphasizing Visual Analysis of Monosyllabic
Words   140

Activities Emphasizing Blending Polysyllabic Words
and Structural Analysis   140

Word Recognition and Technology   143

Concluding Thoughts   144

REFLECTIVE LEARNING English Learners   144

7   Vocabulary Building   145

INTRODUCTION   147

What Teachers Should Know   147

The Relation Between Vocabulary and Reading   147

Vocabulary Development   148

Categories of Words   148

Features of Words   148

Vocabulary and the Common Core State
Standards   149

Increasing Students' Vocabulary   149

Life Experiences   149

Vicarious Experiences   149

Explicit Instruction   151

BOX *Semantic Complexities of English   152*

Meeting the Vocabulary Needs of Struggling
Readers   154

Meeting the Vocabulary Needs of English
Learners   155

Accepting Students' Limited Vocabulary   156

Assessment   156

Informal Assessment   156

Formal Assessment   158

intervention STRATEGIES & ACTIVITIES   159

Vocabulary Building and Technology   171

Concluding Thoughts   172

REFLECTIVE LEARNING Vocabulary Building   172

8   Comprehension of Narrative Text   173

INTRODUCTION   175

**Reading Narrative Text and the Common Core
State Standards   176**

Reading Skills   176

Decoding   176

Fluency   177

Vocabulary   177

Close Reading of Complex Narrative Text   177

Reading Comprehension Strategies   179

Before Reading Strategies   179

During Reading Strategies   181

After Reading Strategies   185

Teaching Comprehension Strategies   186

Comprehension and Critical Literacy   186

Critical Literacy Themes and Topics   186

BOX *Helping Students to Comprehend Historical Fiction Picture Books   187*

Questions to Encourage a Critical Stance   187

English Learners and Narrative Texts   188

Instructional Recommendations   188

Selecting Narrative Texts   188

Skilled Versus Unskilled Comprehenders   189

Assessment   190

Informal Assessment   190

INSIDE THE CLASSROOM *Using Think-Alouds for Assessment   191*

Formal Assessment   193

intervention STRATEGIES & ACTIVITIES   193

Strategies and Activities to Use Before, During, and After Reading   194

Strategies and Activities to Use Before Reading   197

Strategies and Activities to Use During Reading   198

Strategies and Activities to Use After Reading   201

Comprehension of Narrative Text and Technology   208

Concluding Thoughts   210

REFLECTIVE LEARNING Critical Literacy   210

9   Comprehension of Informational Text   211

INTRODUCTION   212

Reading Informational Texts and the Common Core State Standards   213

Helping Students Comprehend Informational Texts   214

Teach Strategies Specific to Comprehending Informational Text   214

Help Students Understand an Author's Use of Technical Words and Word Choice   215

Help Students Understand Diagrams and Graphics in Informational Text   215

Model Close Reading of Complex Texts   215

INSIDE THE CLASSROOM *Discussing How an Author's Word Choice Shapes Meaning   216*

INSIDE THE CLASSROOM *Comprehending Complex Text   217*

Teach the Skills Needed to Navigate the New Literacies   217

Factors Affecting the Comprehension Process   217

BOX *Language Arts Teachers as Advocates   218*

Factors Within the Reader   218

Factors Within the Reader's Environment   219

Factors Within the Text   220

Organizational Structure of Informational Text   221

Persuasive Passages   221

Chronology or Sequence   222

Description or Enumeration   222

Listing   223

Classification or Hierarchy   223

Comparison/Contrast   223

Cause/Effect   224

Problem/Solution   224

Sequence for Teaching Expository Text Organizational Patterns   224

Analysis of Informational Texts   224

Visual Appeal   225

Traditional Book Features   225

Electronic Text Features   227

Use of Technical Vocabulary   227

Author's Assumption of Readers' Background Knowledge   228

Readability   228

English Learners and Informational Text   229

Instructional Recommendations   229

Selecting Informational Text   231

Developing Critical Literacy with Informational Texts   231

Assessment   232

Informal Assessment   232

Formal Assessment   234

intervention STRATEGIES & ACTIVITIES   236

Strategies and Activities to Use Before, During, and After Reading   236

BOX *Active Learning   240*

Strategies and Activities to Use Before Reading   249

Strategies and Activities to Use During Reading   250

Strategies and Activities to Use After Reading   252

Comprehension of Informational Text and Technology   254

Concluding Thoughts   256

REFLECTIVE LEARNING English Learners   256   ■
Reading Comprehension   256

10   Fluency   259

INTRODUCTION   260

What Is Fluency?   261

Components of Fluency   262

Rate   262

Automaticity/Accuracy   264

Phrasing or Prosody   264

Comprehension   268

What Teachers Should Know About Fluency Instruction   268

Fluency and the Common Core State Standards   268

Research-Based Guidelines for Fluency Instruction   269

Fluency Instruction for English Learners   270

Assessment   270

Informal Assessment   270

Formal Assessment   272

intervention STRATEGIES & ACTIVITIES   272

Strategies for Tutoring (One-on-One) Settings   272

Strategies to Use with Small Groups   275

Fluency and Technology   282

Concluding Thoughts   282

REFLECTIVE LEARNING Reading Speed and Comprehension   282

11   Writing   283

INTRODUCTION   285

The Reading–Writing Connection   285

Similarities in Reading and Writing Cognitive Processes   286

Similarities in the Goals of Reading and Writing   286

Differences Between Reading and Writing   286

What Teachers Should Know About Writing Instruction   286

Components of Writing   287

Stages of Emergent Writing   288

Writing Stages of Bilingual Spanish–English Writers   292

Writing and the Common Core State Standards   293

BOX Modeling a Think-Aloud   295

The Writing Process and Writing Workshop   301

Prewriting Stage   301

Drafting   302

Revising   302

Editing   303

Publishing   303

6 + 1 Trait® Writing Model of Assessment and Instruction   306

The Traits   306

Teaching the 6 + 1 Traits   307

Assessing Writing with the 6 + 1 Traits   307

Connecting Writing Instruction and Assessment   307

Assessment   307

Informal Assessment   307

Formal Assessment   310

intervention STRATEGIES & ACTIVITIES   310

Using Computers for Authentic Writing Tasks   324

Writing and Technology   327

Concluding Thoughts   328

REFLECTIVE LEARNING Reluctant Writers   328

12   Spelling   329

INTRODUCTION   331

Spelling Instruction   331

What Teachers Should Know About Spelling   332

Developmental Stages of Spelling   332

Patterns of English Spelling   337

BOX Complex Patterns of English Spelling   338

Spelling and the Common Core State Standards   338

Good Versus Poor Spellers   338

Assessment   338

Informal Assessment   338

Formal Assessment   343

intervention STRATEGIES & ACTIVITIES   343

Spelling and Technology   349

Concluding Thoughts   349

REFLECTIVE LEARNING Stages of Spelling Development   349
- Improving Spelling   350

13 Identifying and Working with Students with Diverse Needs   351

INTRODUCTION   352

Response to Intervention   353
Guiding Principles   353
The RTI Process   353
RTI and the Common Core State Standards   355

Differentiating Instruction   355

Tutoring   356
Successful Tutoring Programs   357
Planning and Conducting the Tutoring Session   357
Tutoring Sessions for English Learners   360
Intervening with the Tutee During Reading   363

Tutoring and Technology   365

Concluding Thoughts   365

REFLECTIVE LEARNING Differentiated Instruction: Gifted Students   365   ■   RTI, English Learners, and Tutoring   366

14 Teachers, Caregivers, and the Community Working in Collaboration   367

INTRODUCTION   369

The Importance of Understanding Students' Home Lives   369

Benefits of Parental Involvement   370

Engaged Parents   371

Ways to Communicate with Parents   371
Introductory Letters   371
Introductory Parent–Teacher Conference   372
Newsletters   372
Bulletin Boards   373
Parents' Nook   373
Telephone Calls or E-mails   373
Happy Grams   373
Weekly Student Letter to Caregivers   374
Portfolios with Personal Notes   374
Daily Welcome   374
Family–Teacher Conference   374
Family Literacy Programs   375

Parental Involvement That Makes a Difference   376
General Suggestions to Share with Parents   376
Suggestions for Establishing a Home–School Literacy Connection   376

Working with Challenging Parents   378
Parents Who Do Not Seem to Value Education   378
Parents Who Seem Highly Critical   378
Parents Who Seem Not to Accept Their Child's Academic Difficulties   379

Community Volunteers/Tutors   379

Caregiver Involvement and Technology   380
Backpack Project with Audio Books   380
Technology Nights   380
Technology Classes for Parents   380
Technology in the Home   380

Concluding Thoughts   381

REFLECTIVE LEARNING Parent Volunteers   381

For Appendices and Activities Contents, see the following pages

References   613
Author Index   633
Subject Index   638

appendices

A Resources   383

A.1 NCTE/IRA Standards for the Assessment of Reading and Writing   384

A.2 Commercial Informal Reading Inventories   387

A.3 Alphabet Books   387

A.4 Poetry Collections and Mother Goose Books   387

A.5 Wordless Books   388

A.6 Wordless (or Almost Wordless) Picture Books for Content Area Learning   389

A.7 Books with Rhyme, Phonograms, Alliteration, and Other Language Play   389

A.8 Suggested English–Spanish Bilingual Concept Books   390

A.9 Suggested Bilingual English–Spanish Narrative Picture Books   391

A.10 Suggested Multicultural Picture Books   391

A.11 Audio Chapter Books   392

A.12 Software Options That Promote Comprehension and Problem Solving   392

B Lists and Guides   393

B.1 Comparison of Five Book-Leveling Systems   394

B.2 Most Common Word Families   396

B.3 Consonant Pronunciation Guide   399

B.4 Vowel Diphthongs, Digraphs, and Variants with Examples and Utility of Each   401

B.5 High-Frequency Word List   402

B.6 Dolch Word Lists   403

B.7 The Fry Phrase Lists   404

B.8 Frequently Used Suffixes and Prefixes   407

B.9 Greek and Latin Word Roots with Definitions and Examples   408

B.10 Generalizations About Word Spellings   417

B.11 Complex Patterns of English Spelling   418

C Assessment Devices   419

C.1 DeFord Theoretical Orientation to Reading Profile   421

C.2 Checklist for Assessing Students' Multiple Intelligences   422

C.3 Applying the Fry Readability Formula   425

C.4 Concepts of Print Checklist   427

C.5 Concepts of Writing Checklist   428

C.6 Miscue Analysis Grid   429

C.7 Grandma's Garden Student Story   430

C.8 Miscue Analysis Grid for Grandma's Garden   432

C.9 Johnny's Birthday Student Story   434

C.10 Miscue Analysis Grid for Johnny's Birthday   436

C.11 Running Record Form   438

C.12 Blank Checklist for Assessing Progress for Use with Any Standards   439

C.13 Checklist for Observations of Progress Toward the CCSS ELA CCR Anchor Standards for Reading   440

C.14 Observational Checklist of Literacy Habits: Early Emergent Literacy Stage   442

C.15 Observational Checklist of Literacy Habits: Emergent Literacy Stage   443

C.16 Observational Checklist of Literacy Habits: Beginning Reading and Writing Stage   444

C.17 Observational Checklist of Literacy Habits: Nearly Fluent Stage   445

C.18 Observational Checklist of Literacy Habits: Fluent Reading and Writing Stage   446

C.19 Personal Interest Survey   447

C.20 Reading Attitude Survey for Primary Students   448

C.21 Writing Attitude Survey for Primary Students   450

C.22 Scoring Sheet for Attitude Surveys   452

C.23 Reading Attitude Survey for Older Students   453

C.24 Writing Attitude Survey for Older Students   454

C.25 Reader Self-Perception Scale   455

C.26 Writer Self-Perception Scale   457

C.27 Reading Log for Primary Students   460

C.28 Reading Log for Intermediate Students   461

C.29 Reading Reflection Log   462

C.30 Quick Phonemic Awareness Assessment Device   463

C.31 Pre-Assessment for Phonemic Awareness   464

C.32 Post-Assessment for Phonemic Awareness   468

C.33 Checklist for Phonemic Awareness for Primary Grades   472

C.34 Checklist for Progress Toward the CCSS ELA Reading: Foundational Skills Phonological Awareness Standards for Kindergarten   473

C.35 Checklist for Progress Toward the CCSS ELA Reading: Foundational Skills Phonological Awareness Standards for Grade 1   474

C.36 Phonics, Word Recognition, and Fluency Checklist Based on the CCSS ELA Reading: Foundational Skills Standards for Grade 3   475

C.37 Checklist of Known Letter Names and Sounds   476

C.38 Phonics Mastery Survey   478

C.39 Scoring Sheet for Word or Phrase Lists   481

C.40 Vocabulary Growth Checklist Based on the CCSS ELA Standards for Language for Grade 8   482

C.41 Rubric for Narrative Reading Comprehension Based on the CCSS ELA Reading: Literature Standards for Grade 5   483

C.42 Interest Inventory for Informational Texts   484

C.43 Observation Checklist of Student's Informational Text Reading   485

C.44 Rubric for Informational Text Comprehension Based on the CCSS ELA Reading: Informational Texts Standards for Grade 6   486

C.45 Informational Text Reading Rubric   487

C.46 Checklist of Basic Online Skills   488

C.47 Fluency Questions for Self-Evaluation   489

C.48 Fluency Checklist   490

C.49 Fluency Checklist for Narrative Text   491

C.50 Oral Reading Fluency Rubric   492

C.51 Student Checklist for Evaluating the Presentation of an Argument   493

C.52 6 + 1 Trait® Writing Assessment   494

C.53 Rubric for Assessing the Writing Process of Writers in Primary Grades   496

C.54 Rubric for Assessing the Writing Process of Third Graders   498

C.55 Rubric for Writing Stories for Grade 4   500

C.56 Rubric for Writing a Research Paper for Grade 4   501

C.57 Rubric for Story Writing   502

C.58 Research Report Rubric for Grades 5/6   503

C.59 Multimedia Group Project Rubric   505

C.60 Writing and Spelling Self-Assessment   506

C.61 Bear, Invernizzi, Templeton, & Johnston Qualitative Spelling Inventory   507

C.62 Recording and Analyzing Spelling   508

D   Instruction Materials   509

D.1 Qualitative Dimensions of Text Complexity (Chapter 2)   511

D.2 Lesson Plan for English Learners (Chapter 13)   512

D.3 Directions for Creating Game Boards and Picture/Word Cards (Chapter 4)   513

D.4 How Many Syllables in the Zoo? Game Board and Picture Cards (Chapter 4)   514

D.5 Remember the Beginning Sound Picture Cards (Chapter 4)   517

D.6 Initial Sound Picture Bingo Cards (Chapter 4)   530

D.7 Toss the Cube Art (Chapter 4)   540

D.8 Go Fish Picture Cards (Chapter 4)   549

D.9 Humpty Dumpty Game Board and Picture Cards (Chapter 4)   556

D.10 Listen for the Initial Consonant Blend Sound Game Board and Picture Cards (Chapter 5)   561

D.11 Word Dominoes (Chapter 5)   567

D.12 Concentration Word Cards (Chapter 5)   571

D.13 Blank Bingo Card (Chapter 5)   575

D.14 Listen for the Vowel Sound Board and Game Pieces (Chapter 5)   576

D.15 Dolch List Bingo Word Cards (Chapter 6)   582

D.16 Templates for Morphology Rummy Cards (Chapter 6)   588

D.17 Vocabulary Bookmark Template (Chapter 7)   590

D.18 Cognate Sort (Chapter 7)   591

D.19 Multiple Meaning Racetrack Board (Chapter 7)   592

D.20 Questions to Consider When Previewing Features of Historical Fiction Picturebooks (Chapter 8)   593

D.21 Text Mapping Form (Chapter 8)   594

D.22 Narrative E-Book Evaluation Form (Chapter 8)   595

D.23 Textbook and Trade Book Evaluation Checklist (Chapter 9)   596

D.24 Template for a Chart Comparing Multiple Sources for a Topic (Chapter 9)   598

D.25 Template for a K-T-W-L-E Chart (Chapter 9)   599

D.26 Informational E-Text Evaluation Form (Chapter 9)   600

D.27 Record, Check, Chart (Chapter 10)   601

D.28 Fluency Log (Chapter 10)   602

D.29 Readers Theater Sample Script (Chapter 10)   603

D.30 Graphic Organizer for an Argument (Chapter 11)   605

D.31 Graphic Organizer for Prewriting an Argumentative Essay (Chapter 11)   606

D.32 Matrix Aligning Elements of Writing Instruction and Assessment (Chapter 11)   607

D.33 Mt. Plot (Chapter 11)   608

D.34 Lesson Plan for Tutors (Chapter 13)   609

D.35 Log Sheet of Strategies (Chapter 13)   610

D.36 Log Sheet of Books Read (Chapter 13)   611

D.37 Postcard for Children Reading Books with Oral Reading and Comprehension Scaffolding (Chapter 14)   612

intervention | STRATEGIES & ACTIVITIES by chapter

CHAPTER 4 PHONEMIC AWARENESS

Clapping Syllables to Familiar Songs and Rhymes   87

Clapping Syllables to Multisyllable Words   87

Let's Make Music   87

How Many Syllables in the Zoo?   87

Sound Boxes   88

Alphabet Sound Booklets   89

Spanish/English Concept Books   89

Remember the Beginning Sound!   89

Initial Sound Bingo   89

Toss the Cube   90

Go Fish   90

Tongue Twisters   90

Identifying Rhyming Words in Poetry   90

Humpty Dumpty Board Game   91

Clowning Around with Rhyming Words   91

Odd-Card Out!   92

Children Are Sounds   92

Blending with Puppets   92

Onset and Rime Blending Card Game   93

Blending Individual Sounds Card Game   93

Segmenting Individual Sounds (Card Game)   93

Pop Off The Beads!   94

Children and Sounds   94

Moving the Tiles   95

Attending to Differences Between What They Expect to Hear and What They Actually Hear   96

CHAPTER 5 PHONICS

Word Sorting with Pictures   112

Word Sorting with Pictures for English Learners   112

Listen for the Initial Consonant Blends   112

Word Walls   112

Personalized Word Family Dictionary   113

Alphabiography   113

Alliteration   113

Dominoes   113

Word Family Word Walls   114

Find the Mystery Word   114

Flip Books   114

Word Family Concentration   115

Rhyming Word Concentration   115

Predictable Rhyming Texts   115

Yankee Doodle Poetry   116

Short Vowel Bingo   116

The Magical E!   117

Listen to the Vowel Sounds   117

Collecting Vowel Sounds Made with Different Spellings   118

Word Sorting with Words   118

Change Hen to Fox   118

Word Ladders   119

CHAPTER 6   WORD RECOGNITION

Guided Reading   134

Wordless Books   136

Picture Books   136

Using Pictures to Enhance the Expressive Vocabulary of Middle School Students   136

Match the Word   137

Dolch List Bingo   137

Unscramble the Sentence   137

Personalized Flash Cards   137

Personal Word Walls   138

Unscramble the Word   138

Technical or Domain-Specific Terms   138

Cloze Passages   139

Toss the Cube   140

Compound Words   140

Affixes Word Study   140

Personalized Word-Part Dictionaries: Affixes and Roots   141

Morphology Rummy   141

CHAPTER 7   VOCABULARY BUILDING

Vocabulary Bookmarks   159

Language Gestalts   159

Morphology Tic-Tac-Toe or Bingo   160

Example of Meaning   160

Word Box   161

Figurative Speech   161

Language Experience Approach (LEA)   162

    Wordless Books   162

    Science Experiment   162

    Listening Walk   163

    Schoolyard Safari   163

Total Physical Response   163

Categorizing   164

Possible Sentences   165

Analogies   165

Origin of Words   166

Crossword Puzzle   166

Synonym/Definition Concentration   167

Cognate Picture Cards   169

Multiple Meaning Racetrack   169

Lexical and Structural Riddles   169

Word Expert Cards   170

Collaborative Activities   170

    Picture Puzzlers   170

    Music Puzzlers   170

    Matching Game   171

    Two Cube Game   171

    Pictionades   171

    Action Jeopardy   171

CHAPTER 8   COMPREHENSION OF NARRATIVE TEXT

The Memphis Comprehension Framework   194

Repeated Interactive Read-Aloud   196

Alternate Writing   197

Directed Listening–Thinking Activity (DL–TA)   197

Directed Reading–Thinking Activity (DR–TA)   197

Text Mapping   198

Reciprocal Questioning   198

Think-Aloud for Narrative Text   199

"And This Is the Rest of the Story"   200

Teacher-Made Audiobooks   200

Text-Talk   201

Wordless Books for Developing Inferential Reading   201

Repeated Readings   201

Multiple Perspectives: Diary Entries   202

Painting Mental Pictures   203

Spin the Discussion   204

Graphic Organizers for Narrative Text   204

Retelling with Puppets   206

Question Connect Transform (QCT) for Narrative Text   206

Character Perspective Chart   206

Venn Diagrams for Narrative Text   207

Character Sketch   208

Solving Mysteries   208

Comprehending Visual Images   208

CHAPTER 9   COMPREHENSION OF INFORMATIONAL TEXT

Textmasters   236

Multiple Source Chart for Close Reading and Citing
   Evidence   237

Pairing Nonfiction and Fiction Texts   238

Science Experiments, Crafts, and Math Games   239

Read-Alouds   240

Partner Reading and Content Too (PRC2)   241

Graphic Organizers for Expository Text Structures   242

Lesson Cycle   246

Questioning Technique for Struggling Readers   246

K-T-W-L-E   246

Inference Training   248

Question–Answer Relationships (QARs)   248

Survey of Text Features   249

Pre-Reading Plan (PReP)   249

Think-Aloud for Informational Text   250

Checklist   251

Request   251

Scanning   252

Learning Logs   252

Collaborative Approach   253

Question Connect Transform (QCT) for Informational
   Text   253

Dramatizing Informational Texts   254

CHAPTER 10   FLUENCY

Echo Reading   272

Preview-Pause-Prompt-Praise (PPPP) Strategy   273

Oral Recitation Lesson (ORL)   274

Carbo Recorded-Book Method   274

Record, Check, Chart   274

Fluency Development Lesson (FDL)   275

Speech Reading   276

Telling Jokes   276

Supported-Reading Strategy   277

Dyad Reading   277

Repeated Readings   277

Fluency Idol Contest   277

Readers Theater   278

Choral Reading   279

Rhythm Walks   281

CHAPTER 11   WRITING

Interactive Writing ("Sharing the Pen")   311

   Variation for English Learners   311

Quick Writes (Writing on Demand)   311

   POW   311

   TREE   311

Read, Flip, Write   312

Activities for 6 + 1 Traits of Writing   312

Writing Interviews   314

Using Concrete Examples of Authors' Writing   315

Guided Writing   316

Mt. Plot   317

Expository Frames   317

Sequels   318

Modeling Professional Writers' Picture Books   318

Writing Parodies   319

Acrostic Poems   319

Cinquain Poems   320

Diamante   320

Biopoems   321

Fibbin Poems   322

Friendly Letters   322

Wordless Books   323

Classroom Alphabet Books   323

Creating Brochures   324

Sentence Combining   324

Using Computers for Authentic Writing Tasks   324

   Blogs   324

   Wikis   325

   International Pen Pals   325

   Connecting with Authors   325

   Digital Storytelling   326

CHAPTER 12   SPELLING

Magnetic Letters   343

Think-Aloud on Word Patterns   344

Personal Spelling Dictionary   345

Foam Board Letters   346

Mnemonics, Memory Aids   347

Spelling in Parts (SIP)   347

World Walls Related to Content   347

preface

As I wrote this new edition, the following thought was the foundation of my work: in today's world, we cannot over-emphasize the importance of literacy, in its many forms. Students who struggle with reading and writing and other aspects of literacy require and deserve more instructional time than other students. This text will help future and in-service classroom teachers recognize and assess particular problems and provide effective interventions to help students in grades preK–8, including English learners and those who struggle with reading, writing, and other aspects of literacy. It is intended for use by undergraduates majoring in elementary or middle school education, for graduate students as they tutor, and for classroom teachers as they work with struggling readers and writers; it may also be used by reading specialists who provide staff development for their districts and by coordinators of volunteer community tutoring programs.

Since the prior edition of this book was written, many states have adopted the Common Core State Standards (CCSS) and other states have rewritten their standards to reflect the more complex reading that is required for college, career, and citizenship. But regardless of which educational standards are applied, it is imperative that teachers understand, first, how to assess students' literacy skills and, second, how to implement strategies to help students accomplish goals set by the standards.

This book reflects the interconnected aspects of literacy: writing supports the growth of reading ability and reading supports writing ability, and both of these are intricately linked with success in the other language arts—speaking, listening, viewing, and visually representing. Teachers encounter many types of literacy problems when working with students. Some students may struggle with word recognition, comprehension, or fluency while others may need help understanding letter–sound relationships, writing or reading informational text, or spelling. This book focuses on the major areas of literacy, including phonemic awareness, phonics, word recognition, comprehension (of both narrative and informational text), vocabulary, fluency, writing, and spelling.

The book is organized as follows. Chapters 1 and 2 help literacy educators understand the qualities of effective teachers, learning theories that affect reading, reading models, special literacy needs of English learners, reading reforms, new literacies, and the teacher's role in motivating students. These chapters also give readers (whether education majors or practicing educators) an opportunity to reflect on personal experiences and opinions that may affect their interaction with students and then use this reflection to formulate a teaching philosophy. I believe formulating such a philosophy helps each of us to become a more effective teacher.

Chapter 3 discusses formal and informal assessment, providing a variety of clear, concrete examples. It reviews the various types of standardized tests and explains how to administer informal literacy assessments such as informal reading inventories, miscue analyses, running records, cloze/maze tests, and checklists and rubrics that are based on the Common Core or other state standards. Also included is a short discussion of next-generation assessments designed to measure the depth of knowledge and skills described in the standards. Because the goal of this book is intervention based on informed assessment, Chapter 3 acts as an important foundation for the book.

The next nine chapters of this text (Chapters 4–12) are devoted to the major areas of literacy mentioned earlier. I believe that comprehension is the primary purpose of reading and that the other areas aid comprehension; therefore, two chapters of this book are devoted to comprehension—one focuses on comprehension of narrative texts and the other on comprehension of informational texts. These chapters are separate because readers use differing approaches to comprehend, analyze, and evaluate these distinct types of texts.

Chapter 13 discusses identifying and working with diverse learning needs, including response to intervention (RTI) and differentiating instruction. Many struggling readers and English learners benefit from the one-on-one instruction provided by tutoring; therefore, I've included a sample tutoring session (based on a successful tutoring program) with adaptations for English learners.

Throughout the text, I emphasize the importance of teachers partnering with students' parents and caregivers. In Chapter 14, I discuss types and levels of parental involvement and how teachers can work effectively with families.

Chapters in this text offer a four-part approach to their topics. This four-part approach includes the following aspects:

- **Scenario:** Previewing the chapter topic, each chapter opens with a scenario in which an elementary or a middle school teacher encounters a real-life literacy challenge in the classroom. The vignettes are followed by guiding questions to tie the scenarios to chapter content and provide a purpose for reading.
- **Research:** Each chapter discusses research studies and theories relevant to the particular topic highlighted in the chapter to help readers understand when and why particular assessments and interventions are effective.
- **Technology:** Most chapters include a section on using technology, including annotated app and website recommendations, to increase students' skills in the particular areas being discussed. Where relevant, technology is also incorporated in selected intervention strategies and activities, allowing readers to see its use in context.
- **Ending Scenarios:** Finally, chapters close with additional classroom scenarios accompanied by questions for readers to answer and discuss with others as they review and apply what they learned while reading.

In addition, the nine chapters covering the major areas of literacy include the following three sections:

- **Foundational knowledge:** This section presents background information teachers need to provide effective assessment and instruction in each area of literacy, including information on how the CCSS address that area.
- **Diagnosis and assessment:** I discuss possible assessment instruments for diagnosing and assessing problems and growth in the literacy area being discussed.
- **Intervention:** This section offers a wide variety of research-supported intervention activities and strategies, recognizing that different students benefit from different strategies. Many of the activities can help students meet various CCSS requirements. The activities in these intervention sections also call for students to read a wide variety of materials including narrative and informational texts in print and digital formats.

Finally, teachers of every experience level will benefit from the multitude of resources, assessment devices, and instructional materials included in Appendices A through D of this book. The book's table of contents gives a complete list of these resources and tools.

NEW TO THIS EDITION

T his edition has been substantively revised and updated. Here are some of the changes:

- Readers now have access to www.hhpcommunities.com/literacyassessment, a website designed specifically for and unique to this text. This valuable site includes
  - a portfolio of student work samples from which readers can gain experience in assessing and determining interventions for students.
  - materials for projection onto interactive whiteboards.
  - note-taking capability so readers can prepare for in class discussions of the chapter opening and closing scenarios.
  - an interactive glossary so readers can check and review their knowledge of key concepts.
  - links to instructive videos so readers can view lessons and strategies described in the book in actual classrooms.
- This edition discusses important shifts that have occurred in teaching the major areas of literacy, resulting from the CCSS and evolution of state standards. These shifts include a focus on students reading complex text, performing close readings of a variety of texts and genres to understand the author's stance and possible biases, balancing the reading and writing of informational and narrative texts, learning to cite evidence when speaking or writing, understanding academic and domain-specific vocabulary, writing opinion/persuasive passages, and using multimodal texts for gaining and sharing information during oral and written communication.
- I've included many new intervention strategies and activities, some with a technology component, as well as new assessment devices and student samples.
- The makeup of classrooms across the United States continues to change. Throughout this edition, I address the need for teachers to (1) understand the development stages of English learners and (2) learn how to scaffold these students as they become literate in English.
- As mentioned, this edition reflects the importance of using technology and online resources to aid students as they work with word recognition, phonics, phonemic awareness, vocabulary, and all components of literacy. In Chapters 4 through 12, I share student-friendly websites and apps to help motivate readers as they engage in the literacy activity being discussed.

ABOUT THE EBOOK

T he ebook version of this text includes active links for all URLs cited in the text and instant access to cross-reference links between chapters; for example, readers can link directly to (and from) tools and resources in the appendices as they are discussed. If you wish your students to have both the print book and the ebook, suggest they purchase the cost-effective "bundle" from the Holcomb Hathaway website, www.hh-pub.com.

acknowledgments

s before, I wish to express sincere thanks to my editor and the staff at Holcomb Hathaway for making this edition reader friendly, for encouraging the use of vignettes, and for enhancing the book's eye appeal. I also want to thank my past and present students, who continue to find and share new websites with me and who give me honest feedback on what changes need to be included. Thanks also to Jo Dorhout and Betty Lou Thompson, whose encouragement allowed me to finish this text and make it far better than it would have been otherwise.

It is my pleasure to thank the many individuals who have reviewed this book in manuscript stage, for this and previous editions. I appreciate their constructive comments, which have helped me to improve the text. *For this edition, those individuals are:* Diane Campfield Youngs, Indiana University South Bend; Jeanne Clidas, Roberts Wesleyan College; JaneMarie Dewailly, Arkansas State University; Deborah Duval, University of Central Florida–Ocala; William L. Edwards, Jr., Missouri Southern State University; Katrina Hall, University of North Florida; Kerry Holmes, University of Mississippi; Lijun Jin, Towson University; Michelle Kelley, University of Central Florida; Angie Madden, Eastern Kentucky University; DiAnn McDown, University of Central Oklahoma; Jerilou J. Moore, University of Mississippi; Linda Murphree, Wayland Baptist University; Tamara Ogletree, University Of West Georgia; Helen J. Robbins, Florida International University; Stephan Sargent, Northeastern State University; Rebecca Short, Georgia Southwestern State University; Susan Stewart, Ashland University; Janell Uffelman, Concordia University, Nebraska; Betsy VanDeusen-MacLeod, Central Michigan University; Beth Walizer, Fort Hays State University; Carol Wickstrom, University of North Texas; Cynthia Walters, University of Central Florida–South Lake; and Debra Weingarth, Jacksonville State University. *For earlier editions:* Diane Allen, Julie Ankrum, Suzanne Bell, Leonard Breen, Carol Bunch, Donna Harkins, Ginny Helwick-Jackson, Charlene Hildebrand, Peter B. Hilton, G. Peter Ienatsch, Jennifer Kagan, Dixie Keyes, Rebecca A. Maloy, Susan McGowan, Adriana Medina, Kouider Mokhtari, Kathleen A. J. Mohr, Jacqueline K. Peck, Timothy Rasinski, Jennifer Rasmussen, Monica Riley, Elizabeth Rowell, Patsy Self, Martha Sheppard-Mahaffey, Maureen V. Spelman, Christina Walton, Janell Uffelman, Min Zou, and Vassiliki Zygouris-Coe.

Beverly DeVries, Ed.D., has been teaching at Southern Nazarene University in Oklahoma since 1993. She teaches reading diagnosis and remediation and primary and elementary literature/language arts. In all of her courses, she demonstrates how teachers can use authentic assessment and instruction, using quality children's literature. When mentoring her students as they work with struggling readers, she finds that no two students approach reading in exactly the same manner, each reader responding uniquely to any specific strategy. This observation has helped DeVries formulate her teaching and intervention strategies and is a vital part of this book.

DeVries is presently on the Standards and Ethics Committee of the International Reading Association (IRA) and is the reading specialist on the Oklahoma Commission Program Advisory Board. She also is an auditor for the CAEP/IRA program review process. DeVries presents workshops on Writing Successful Reading Program Reports at the state and national levels. She also conducts workshops on various components of reading to classroom teachers.

DeVries received her doctorate in education from Oklahoma State University. Before beginning her college teaching career, she spent most of her years in the middle school, teaching composition and reading. It was during those years that she recognized the importance of early literacy intervention, and realized that struggling primary and middle school students benefit greatly from one-on-one instruction.

1

Forming a Personal Philosophy About Literacy Assessment and Intervention

To teach is to learn twice.

JOSEPH JOUBERT

scenario

On the first day back to school, Ms. Hillerton, a veteran teacher of thirty years, overheard two of her third-grade teammates, Ms. Box and Mr. Armstrong, complain about the new state standards, which are based on the national Common Core State Standards (CCSS).

"What don't you like about them?" asked Ms. Hillerton.

"I liked our old standards that dictated exactly what skills my students needed to know by the end of the third grade. I knew exactly what I had to teach in order for them to do well on the state tests," replied Mr. Armstrong.

"I agree," Ms. Box chimed in. "The new state standards seem so vague that I'm worried about what the state test will require my students to know."

"Well," Ms. Hillerton said, "I welcome the change because the new standards require me to engage students in higher-level thinking instead of merely focusing on skills."

"But, what about all this I hear about close reading, citing evidence, text complexity, and domain-specific vocabulary?" complained Ms. Box.

"I'm sure we'll figure it out," said Ms. Hillerton. "I have been teaching so long that one thing I have learned—there will always be changes, and I have found that it is better to embrace the changes and see how I can change my teaching with them. Now, let's go to our staff development meeting. Today's topics are close reading and text complexity, so that should give us some idea about what our students will need to know."

As you read this chapter, consider the following questions:

guiding questions

1. Why does Ms. Hillerton believe that the new state standards based on the CCSS will require her students to engage in higher-level thinking skills?

2. If you were the presenter at the staff development meeting, what sources would you recommend for learning more about each term?

3. What other aspects of the Common Core State Standards would you want the teachers at the meeting to know?

introduction

Education is always changing and evolving. Research findings and new local, state, and federal mandates result in continual changes in schools and classrooms. Like the three teachers in the scenario, all teachers need to read professional journals and attend professional development courses and conferences in order to stay current with new teaching approaches, learning theories, research-based practices, and mandates. This chapter will introduce you to learning theories and reading models that will help you develop your literacy philosophy; explore issues surrounding the literacy development of English learners; encourage you to reflect on personal literacy experiences and views of reading instruction; provide a familiarity with recent reading initiatives; and finally, discuss the new literacies and how they have affected the teaching and learning of literacy.

THE IMPORTANCE OF LITERACY

For many of us, reading is enjoyable and effortless. Realistic fiction makes us laugh, cry, and empathize with the protagonist. Mysteries make us bite our nails or draw the blinds. Novels about far-flung parts of the world help us appreciate other cultures. Historical fiction and nonfiction about the plights of nondominant cultures prompt us to take action. In addition to providing relaxation and pleasure, reading is a skill necessary to be a productive citizen in today's global society. Each day we are bombarded with text, both printed and electronic, that we must read in order to function: warnings on medication and household cleaning products, disclaimers on television commercials, information on computer screens, directions on microwave dinners, nutritional information on packaged foods, road signs, application forms, instructional manuals, and the list goes on. The more advanced our society becomes, the higher the literacy level we need to complete everyday literacy activities. Figure 1.1, for example, lists the reading

Reading levels of daily reading materials.

Help-wanted ads	6th–7th grade
Front-page newspaper stories	9th–12th grade
Information on medication	10th grade
Directions on frozen dinners	8th grade
Directions on 1040 income tax forms	9th–10th grade
Articles in romance, TV, and movie magazines	8th grade
Life insurance policies	12th grade
Articles by professionals on Wikipedia	College sophomore level

Sources: S. McCormick, S. (2010) / K. Anderson (2012). / http://scholarlykitchen.sspet.org/2012/09/24/wikipedias-writing-tests-show-its-too-sophisticated-for-its-audience/

grade levels required for various tasks. This information makes it obvious that children must become proficient readers in order to perform daily tasks. Classroom teachers must be prepared to teach reading and other literacy skills—such as writing, speaking, listening, viewing, and visually representing—and detect both students who struggle with these skills and those who need an extra challenge so they do not become disenchanted with school.

Readers not only need to read at an advanced level for everyday tasks, they also must be able to read with discernment. The Internet holds a wide array of information. Responsible readers analyze their sources, synthesize complex text from multiple sources, and tap into their existing knowledge base in order to accurately evaluate the "information" presented.

Writing is also a necessary skill in today's society. Children must become fluent in expressing their ideas, opinions, and feelings. From a very young age, children need to understand that writing is a key means of communication and that its most important aspect is the message. They need to value using standard spelling and grammar so readers will understand their intended message. Students also need to learn how to write for different audiences and purposes and in different genres. All skills associated with writing must begin to be developed in the early grades.

Elementary and middle school teachers face great challenges and are frequently pressured by principals and school districts to achieve higher student performance. They cannot merely try a number of instructional strategies, hoping one will do the trick. Instead, they need to help every student become a proficient reader and writer. To do this, teachers must know

how to assess literacy problems, match interventions to particular problems, teach students to use reading strategies effectively, and reflect on the effectiveness of their own pedagogic practices.

THEORIES RELATED TO LITERACY

Before developing your philosophy about how children learn to read and write, consider the learning theories you have studied in your other education courses and how they relate to literacy assessment and instruction. The following are some of the most important, relevant learning theories.

Constructivist Theory

All students make sense of new learning situations by linking what they know with what they are being taught. Through accommodation and assimilation, they build on their prior knowledge (Piaget & Inhelder, 1969). They categorize information by hypothesizing how it differs from and is similar to their existing knowledge (Bruner, 1960; Anderson, 2013). Teachers provide authentic learning experiences for students, help them build connections, and provide background knowledge for students who have not yet acquired it. As proficient readers construct meaning, they activate prior knowledge and select the strategies necessary to complete the task. Teachers must help struggling readers build their background knowledge and explicitly teach strategies until the students become proficient readers. For example, suppose a student reads this sentence from Seymour Simon's *Whales* (1989): "A whale has a tail with horizontal flukes, which are different from the vertical tail fins of fish." If she does not know *horizontal* from *vertical* and *flukes* from *fins,* the student will not comprehend the information.

Zone of Proximal Development

Students construct meaning and validate new information and processes by interacting with someone who already knows the information and processes (Vygotsky, 1962). Vygotsky uses the phrase **zone of proximal development** to describe "the distance between the [child's] actual development as determined by independent problem solving and the level of potential development as determined through problem solving under adult guidance or in collaboration with more capable peers" (1978, p. 86). Furthermore, he argues that "what the child can do in cooperation today he can do alone tomorrow" (1962, p. 104). His ideas suggest that teachers can play a key role in young students' development by providing the necessary **scaffolding** (i.e., the support students need until they are able to work independently). This is why teachers demonstrate the skill or reading strategy, provide guided practice, maximize opportunities for peer modeling, and schedule time for independent practice.

Hierarchy of Human Needs

Psychologists suggest that all humans have a wide variety of needs, some of which are essential for physical survival and others that are necessary for psychological well-being. Maslow (1987) proposes that humans have the following basic needs:

1. *physiological:* oxygen, water, food, shelter, and so on
2. *safety:* security in one's present environment
3. *love and belonging:* acceptance by others
4. *esteem:* feeling good about oneself and having the respect of others
5. *self-actualization:* knowledge that one has fulfilled one's potential

Maslow contends that the most basic needs (food and shelter) must be satisfied before needs further up on the hierarchy can be addressed. Therefore, most schools now provide free or reduced-cost breakfasts and lunches because children cannot concentrate if they are hungry. State departments of education are likewise concerned about students feeling safe at school. Most states now have laws requiring all visitors to sign in and wear badges so they are readily identifiable to administrators. Schools are also likely to have on file a list of individuals authorized to sign each student out of the building and with whom the student may leave after dismissal. Teachers may help each child experience a sense of belonging in the "classroom family" by forming students into small groups and having a teacher's helper for the day or a featured "star" for the week. Effective teachers also seek ways to build self-esteem by ensuring that all students experience some measure of success. For example, they involve students in readers theater so everyone gets to practice their lines before a performance. They know each student has different abilities, strengths, and weaknesses and provide specialized instruction accordingly. When schools and teachers support students through the lower levels of Maslow's hierarchy, they help make it possible for individuals to eventually reach the self-actualization stage and attain their full potential.

Critical Literacy Theory

Critical literacy has implications for action (Behrman, 2006). Teachers who embrace this theory view literacy as more than being able to accurately and fluently read a text in order to answer literal and inferential questions. Their goal is for students to develop literacy skills that will enable them to actively engage with text in order to understand the potential for abuse of power and other forms of inequality and injustice among races, cultures, genders, sexual orientations, and social systems and then to engage students in appropriate social action (Beck, 2005; Cervetti, Pardales, & Damico, 2001; Lewison, Flint, & Van Sluys, 2002; Coffey, 2010; Behrman, 2006). Critical literacy advocates focus on sociopolitical issues as expressed in all types of literacy, such as movies, lyrics of popular songs, advertisements, and, of course, books. Teachers of critical literacy expose students to texts that "lead them to new ways of understanding the world" (Labadie, Mosley-Wetzel, & Roger, 2012, p. 119) and encourage students to find their voice and then take action against the social injustice in our society (Beck, 2005).

There is a difference between critical reading and critical literacy. **Critical reading** encourages students "to use elements of logical analysis—that is, they examine claims of validity and reliability to better understand how these texts function in society" (Cervetti, Pardales, & Damico, 2001, p. 3). To test validity and reliability, teachers facilitate students as they examine authors' credentials, intentions, political interests, and their powerful ways of manipulating language in all forms of writing. Teachers encourage students to understand both the author's perspective and the perspective of those highlighted in the passage (Morgan & York, 2009). For example, students reading a story about Ruby Bridges, the first African American child to attend an all-white elementary school in the South, may question the author's credentials as follows: Is the author knowledgeable? Does the author live in the same town? Is the author attempting to paint an honest picture, or color the text to reflect his or her ideals? Although students realize that only Ruby Bridges can explain what her experience was really like, they can attempt to walk in Ruby's shoes and reflect on how they would feel if they attended a school where they were the only student of their race: Would they be afraid? Do they think Ruby was afraid? Would they wish to be in a school with their neighborhood friends? Did Ruby? These are examples of the types of questions teachers use to help students read critically.

Critical literacy, however, is more than critical reading; it requires students to act on what they have read and analyzed. Classrooms in which critical literacy is taught are "places in which students should come to understand how and why knowledge and power are constructed" (Lloyd, 2003, p. 1). Teachers using critical literacy facilitate students as they begin to understand the historical, political, cultural, and economic context of their world (Labadie, Mosley-Wetzel, & Roger, 2012). These teachers encourage students to think critically about issues and become agents of social change

(Coffey, 2010). Critical literacy focuses on getting students to understand that "language is never a neutral account of the world" (Beck, 2005, p. 393), and that it can contain the social, cultural, and ideological viewpoints of the dominant society. Although critical literacy makes students aware of the biases in language, it also uses literacy for "the potential to transform and assist in preparing students for participation in a democratic society" (Lloyd, 2003, p. 1). Note, however, that not every lesson needs to include a critical literacy component and not every text needs to be read from a critical literacy perspective. Critical literacy strategies will also be discussed in Chapters 8, 9, and 11.

Successful teachers not only draw on learning theories, but they also understand reading models that will aid them in reading instruction. The following section reviews three important reading models.

READING MODELS

There are many points of view on how children learn to read. These perspectives can be grouped into three major reading models: (1) the part-to-whole approach, often called the skills or phonics approach, (2) the whole-part-whole approach, often referred to as the socio-psycholinguistic approach (Weaver, 2002), and (3) the comprehensive approach, which integrates skill instruction with literature-based reading and process writing (Kaufman, 2002; Reutzel & Cooter, 2011; Routman, 2002). A teacher's philosophy about how children learn to read usually reflects one of these approaches, and it shapes the way he or she assesses and assists struggling readers. Figure 1.2 compares the three models.

Part-to-Whole Model

The **part-to-whole model** emphasizes the importance of students first learning letter names and sounds, followed by simple words that are easily decoded, and then reading stories that consist of these easily decoded words (Adams, 1990; Chall, 1983; Stanovich, 1991; Vellutino, 1991). Phonics concepts are taught in isolation. The part-to-whole model represents three approaches to teaching reading—phonics approach, linguistic approach, and sight word approach.

Phonics approach

The **phonics approach** emphasizes learning the names of each letter of the alphabet and the various sounds associated with the letters (e.g., the short and long vowel sounds, the two sounds of c and g). Blends (cl, br, gr, etc.), vowel digraphs (oa as in road and ea as in sea), consonant digraphs (ck as in back and ch as in cheese), and diphthongs (oi as in oil, oy as in toy) are also studied out of their linguistic context. In phonics programs, students learn phonic rules along with the exceptions to these rules.

Commercial phonics programs differ; in general, however, phonics lessons are systematic and explicitly taught. Many manuals for these programs are scripted, indicating what teachers are to say and which student responses are correct. Students are usually instructed in one concept at a time and then complete worksheets based on that concept. Mastery in one concept is typically expected before students proceed to the next concept. Skills are often taught in isolation, and teachers frequently do not integrate them with the texts used during shared reading.

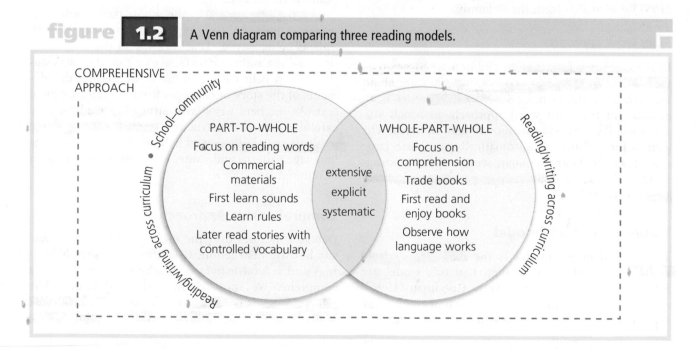

figure 1.2 A Venn diagram comparing three reading models.

Readers who are struggling often receive a heavy dose of phonics and/or instruction in word recognition (Weaver, 2002). Phonics-oriented teachers usually believe that struggling readers need to understand the simplest linguistic units (the sound of letters) before they can progress to single words and later to sentences composed of easily decoded words. These students often spend their reading time doing worksheets instead of actually reading.

Linguistic approach

In the linguistic approach, another part-to-whole approach, the emphasis is on identifying patterns in words. Proponents of this approach believe it is easier for children to learn words when they focus on two distinctive parts of each word (the onset and rime) instead of on individual letter sounds. Onset is "the part of the syllable that precedes the vowel." Rime is "the vowel and any consonants that follow it in a syllable" (Savage, 2001, p. 21). For example, in the word *three, thr* is the onset and *ee* is the rime. (Terms related to onset and rime include phonogram, word families, and word patterns.) The rime is taught first and then children add onsets to create different words. For example, students learn the rime *at*, and then add the /s/ to create *sat*, /h/ to create *hat*, and so on, until they know *fat, bat, cat, mat, pat, Nat*, and *rat*. Simple stories are then created from each word family. An example of a linguistic story might be: "Pat sat on a flat hat. Cat sat on a flat hat." The *Bob Books* by Lynn Maslen and John Maslen are an example of the linguistic approach. Many trade books also use word families. For example, Dr. Seuss's *Green Eggs and Ham* (1960) uses many words from the *am* family, and *The Cat in the Hat* (1957) uses words from the *at* family.

Sight word approach

In the sight word approach, children are first taught the words that will appear in a story they are about to read. The once-popular *Dick and Jane* series is an example of the sight word approach, in which students use flash cards to memorize lists of words. The goal is for children to automatically recognize large sets of words. With the sight word approach, struggling readers spend much of their reading time memorizing flash cards.

Whole-Part-Whole Model

The second major model is the whole-part-whole model. Some of the proponents of this model are Kenneth Goodman (1996), Yetta Goodman (1996), and Constance Weaver (2002). Teachers who use this model begin reading instruction with a reading activity known as shared reading or a shared book experience (Holdaway, 1986). Shared reading begins with teachers reading a story with the children. With young children, teachers often use a big book so the students can follow along as teachers read and point to the words. The initial emphasis is on enjoying the plot, characters, and language of the story, and relating the story to their lives. During repeated readings, children begin to chime in on the parts of the story they know, such as the repeated phrases. Later, the teacher and students discover and discuss rhyming words, word endings, new vocabulary, and mechanics such as punctuation. For example, after multiple readings of Lorinda Bryan Cauley's (1992) *Clap Your Hands*, a book with many rhyming words, students are guided to discover words that rhyme because they end in the same letters, such as *sand* and *land*. After they find *down, clown, and frown*, they discover with the teacher that these words end in *own*. Later, they find other rhyming words such as *toes* and *nose* and discover that they rhyme even though they do not end with the same letters. Children become aware of letter sounds as they talk about words in these stories. The teacher then returns to a discussion about the characters, plot and/or theme, or concepts in an informational book.

Teachers using the whole-part-whole method often appreciate the importance of phonics instruction and plan stories around a specific letter sound or word family. The phonics instruction in the whole-part-whole model is also explicit, systematic, and extensive; however, these teachers tend to avoid commercial phonics programs. Instead, they teach the phonics concepts their students require, using texts they enjoy (Cunningham, 2012).

Struggling readers in the whole-part-whole programs receive the same type of instruction through individual tutoring. Teachers spend their tutoring time reading authentic texts, working on the parts students need help with, and finally discussing the elements of the story or concepts from the informational text. As teachers work with struggling readers, they carefully plan the instruction, building on concepts students already know and helping them discover new language patterns and strategies to aid comprehension (Cunningham, 2004).

Comprehensive Approach

Debate continues over the merits of skills-based versus holistic instruction. Given recent research findings and federal mandates, teachers recognize that a comprehensive approach to reading is needed. The comprehensive approach (Routman, 2002) integrates skills with literature-based reading and process-writing instruction. Teachers generally show students how language works by utilizing authentic texts and authentic writing tasks. They instruct students to identify small chunks within words as they attempt to pronounce unknown words. Teachers show students how to use the prefix, suffix, and root part of a word to understand the meaning of unfamiliar words. They teach fluency strategies when reading from trade books and how to organize new information obtained from multiple sources. Teachers usually impart these strategies while students are enjoying narrative texts, but also when they are reading informational texts and during science and social studies lessons. A comprehensive approach focuses on reading and writing for meaning, while recognizing that systematic instruction is essential to meet the needs of individual learners.

The comprehensive approach is "a complex and unified system" (Rasinski & Padak, 2004) in which all parts of the curriculum are interrelated. Reading and writing are important aspects of social studies, science, health, art, and music. During literacy instruction, teachers using the comprehensive approach consider (1) the amount of time for various tasks, (2) the instructional grouping, (3) the types of text, (4) the cognitive and affective components of learning, (5) the importance of reading to writing and writing to reading, and (6) the relationship between school and home.

The comprehensive approach requires more than giving equal amounts of instructional time to learning literacy skills and reading authentic texts. Teachers need to understand students' individual needs and engage them in tasks that will develop their literacy skills. All students do not need an equal amount of time to understand a skill. It is meaningless for students who recognize all of the words on the Dolch word list (see Appendix B.6) to sit through ten minutes of flash cards. For other students, ten minutes may not be enough time to master these words. Teachers using the comprehensive approach should plan the literacy time so every student engages in tasks that will help him or her grow as a reader.

In the comprehensive approach, students are grouped differently for various tasks. Teachers recognize that whole-group instruction is not the most effective form of reading instruction. Likewise, if struggling readers are always grouped together, they never hear fluent readers and begin to see themselves as poor readers. When students of mixed abilities read in unison, the struggling reader has an opportunity to be successful. Other times, students of varying reading abilities can practice a readers theater selection and perform it for the rest of the class. Teachers can also form groups with similar skills to provide

direct instruction so all students will develop a needed skill. Instructional groups are flexible.

With the comprehensive approach, students read all types of materials. They are exposed to stories, informational texts, biographies and autobiographies, magazines, poetry, newspapers, websites, wikis, blogs, and e-texts. These materials are either at the individual's instructional level in small group instruction or at her easy reading level during independent reading time when she is reading something of her choice.

Teachers using the comprehensive approach understand that students' affective learning domain is interrelated with their cognitive learning domain (Rasinski & Padak, 2004). They know that students who enjoy reading will read more; and the more students read, the better they will read. They assist students in selecting materials that suit their interests and reading level. If texts are too difficult, students, like adults, will feel defeated and quit reading. Successful teachers know the importance of choosing materials that interest students and creating a classroom library that has a wide choice of texts in all formats encompassing many different topics and reading levels. New texts are continually added to the collection via the Internet, the school library, and the public library. The teacher's goal is to have all her students become lifelong readers.

Reading and writing carry equal weight in the comprehensive approach (Rasinski & Padak, 2004) and should be integrated. Students respond to their readings in journals, logs, poems, and in other written forms. They are challenged to read to get ideas for their compositions. Students become better writers through reading, and they become better readers through writing.

Teachers using the comprehensive approach understand that students spend the majority of their time away from school, so they make sure students take texts home to share with their parents and caregivers. Even if the caregivers are not literate, teachers encourage them to provide quiet time at home and listen to their children read. Good teachers will let students know about literacy events at the local library and will see that children who cannot get to the library are exposed to additional texts.

Teachers also model reading and writing. Often during independent reading time, teachers too will pick up a book or magazine that interests them so students see them as readers. They also share with students their favorite books and poems, and will share compositions they have written. Regardless of the content they teach, it is important that teachers have a positive disposition toward reading and writing.

Figure 1.3 lists strategies found in classrooms that embrace the comprehensive approach.

figure 1.3   Classroom strategies used in the comprehensive approach.

BUDDY READING
- Older students share love of books with younger students.

COLLABORATIVE PROJECTS
- Students do authentic research and writing with other students in the classroom, the United States, and the world.

INDEPENDENT READING
- All students in school read books of their choice for 15 to 30 minutes.

E-PALS
- Students do authentic writing to form new friends around the world.

EBOOKS
- Students follow along as computer reads books.
- Students hear fluent reading.
- Students are introduced to new vocabulary words.

ONLINE RESEARCH PROJECT
- Students share research projects with other students around the world.

GUIDED READING
- Teachers work with homogeneous groups to teach reading skills.
- Teachers teach phonics, word analysis, vocabulary, etc.
- Students read under teacher's supervision.
- Students read graded books on their instructional level.

GUIDED WRITING
- Teachers work with homogeneous groups to teach writing skills.
- Teachers teach phonics, word analysis, vocabulary, etc.
- Students practice skills under teacher's supervision.

INTERACTIVE WRITING (e.g., MORNING MESSAGE)
- Teachers do majority of writing, and students "share the pen" when they know letters/words.
- Teachers explicitly teach phonics, word patterns, and other spelling skills.

JOURNAL WRITING
- Students express themselves personally.
- Students write for authentic purposes.

LANGUAGE EXPERIENCE APPROACH (LEA)
- Students express themselves while teacher acts as scribe.
- Students recognize words in print they use in their speech.

LITERACY CLUB
- Students who share interest in same book/author read and discuss books.

PUPPET SHOW
- Students work in small groups.
- Students improve expression and fluency.
- Students perform for audience.

READERS THEATER
- Students work in small groups.
- Students improve expression and fluency.
- Students perform for audience.

READING WORKSHOP
- Students choose genre and topics.
- Students share favorite books with peers.

Mini-lessons
- Teachers share with class information about authors and genres.
- Teachers instruct class on reading skills.

Conferences
- Peers read to each other.
- Teachers give explicit instruction on skills to individuals.

Share time
- Students share favorite sections or passages.
- Students share new vocabulary words.

SHARED READING
- Teachers share good literature that is at higher reading level.
- Students hear advanced vocabulary.
- Teachers and students discuss elements of stories.
- Teachers and students discuss information given in passage.

THINK-ALOUDS
- Teachers model reading strategies.
- Teachers teach metacognition skills.

WORD WALLS
- Teachers display words in categories to help students automatically recognize words.
- Students learn patterns within words.
- Students increase their vocabulary.

WRITING WORKSHOP
- Students choose genre and topics.
- Students share writing with peers.

Mini-lessons
- Teachers give explicit instruction on writing skills to class.
- Teachers share types of writing with class.

Conferences
- Peers help with revising and editing.
- Teachers give explicit instruction on writing skills to individuals.

Share time
- Students share finished product with class.

Which Method Is the Most Effective?

As a preservice teacher, you may wonder which method is best for a classroom of students with diverse abilities and cultural backgrounds. How will you teach reading and writing to students who do not speak English? How will you teach reading and writing to an autistic child? How will you challenge a student who has been identified as gifted but struggles with reading and writing? How will you work with students who have learning disabilities? Finally, how will you work with students who lack motivation?

Those who study literacy practices and their impact on diverse populations often disagree about the most effective way to ensure that all students learn to read. Remember that no one method suits everyone. As you form your philosophy of reading instruction, understand that teachers teach children; they do not teach methods or materials (Allington, 2011). Always consider the strengths of each individual student first, and then assess the needs of the student. Some children need to isolate small "parts" in order to understand the "whole," while other children are confused by many small parts and must first understand the whole (Carbo, 2007). There is no perfect method to use for all students; effective teachers "understand the physical, psychosocial, and cognitive characteristics of their students" (Manning, 2002, p. 225) so they can choose a method that fits each student's strengths and needs.

ENGLISH LEARNERS

Between 1947 and 2003, the U.S. population of school-aged children increased 19 percent; however, during that same period the English-learner student population increased 124 percent (National Center for Education Statistics, 2005). In 2004, 20 percent of U.S. students lived in homes where English was not the native language. In 2007, 5 percent of K–12 students were English learners, and in 2010–2011, 10 percent were English learners (Center for Public Education, 2013). By 2050, this percentage is expected to increase to 40 percent (International Reading Association, 2001). In the 2010–2011 school year, there were approximately 4.7 million English learners in grades K–12. Spanish speakers are the fastest growing group of English learners. In 2007, the Hispanic population of the United States (21.1 percent) was larger than the African American population (16.6 percent) (Center for Public Education, 2010). Some researchers argue that English learners must first learn to read in their native language before they learn to read in English (Krashen, 2004/2005; Weber, 1991). Others believe this is not necessary and merely delays academic progress for English learners (Fitzgerald & Noblit, 1999; Rossell, 2004/2005).

Regardless of your thoughts on this issue, you must remember that English learners have different educational backgrounds and thus different needs. Some English learners have had strong academic schooling in their native country and are literate in their native language and perhaps a number of other languages. Others have had limited formal schooling and are not literate in their native language. Some English learners have parents who are university graduates and can read and speak English fluently, while other students' parents are illiterate in their native language and cannot speak English (Short & Echevarria, 2004/2005).

Cummins (1979) distinguishes between English learners' **basic interpersonal communicative skills** (**BICS**) and their **cognitive academic language proficiency** (**CALP**). BICS refers to English learners' ability to be fluent in personal conversation, while CALP refers to their ability to read and write at the academic level of their peers. Most English learners achieve conversational English skills in about two years; however, they may not have the literacy skills for academic studies for five to seven years (Cummins, 1979; Otaiba & Pappamihiel, 2005). Yet in the classroom these students are expected to grasp the language well enough to understand new concepts.

Complicating the academic progress of English learners is the fact that many are not in the United States during the vital period of kindergarten and first grade. Some enter U.S. schools in upper-elementary or high-school classes, where they do not understand the language and yet are expected to learn new, advanced concepts presented in English. For this reason, all teachers must have some background knowledge on English learners' literacy development and must choose effective strategies to make these students feel welcome in the classroom community and enable them to work toward academic success.

English Language Development

Otaiba and Pappamihiel (2005) classify the stages of English language development as (1) the silent stage, (2) the early production stage, (3) the productive language stage, and (4) the intermediate fluency language stage. They identify some observable characteristics of each stage, and provide appropriate instructional strategies for each (see Figure 1.4). Teachers must remember that some English learners in the silent stage may be in upper elementary or even middle school. However, the older silent stage learners may stay in the silent stage for a shorter period of time than the younger silent stage learners.

figure **1.4**   Progressive stages of English language development.

SILENT STAGE (ALSO KNOWN AS PREPRODUCTION)

Characteristics	Appropriate Instructional Strategies
Key characteristic: Communication with peers is very limited, which in turn hampers development of social language proficiency.	**Particular instructional focus:** Help children adapt to the classroom culture and establish instructional routines.
Student may continue speaking in his or her first language (L1).	Tutors are responsible for up to 90% of conversational burden.
Student is processing language, but oral communication is limited or nonexistent.	Use pictures, props, manipulatives, and other hands-on materials to ensure active student involvement.
This period may last longer in very young students than students in later elementary.	Use simplified language that focuses on key concepts and the repetition of essential vocabulary.
	Use total physical response (TPR).

THE EARLY PRODUCTION STAGE

Characteristics	Appropriate Instructional Strategies
Key characteristic: Students tend to use imitation and repetition (formulate phrases or speech patterns such as *I goed to lunch*) to become part of the social fabric of the class.	**Particular instructional focus:** Provide basic tools for immediate use including explicit instruction in vocabulary and social communication.
Student begins to develop aspects of social English that will become building blocks of English proficiency.	Tutors are responsible for up to 50%–60% of conversational burden.
Students' social skills in English are based on highly contextualized language.	Ask *who, what, where,* and *either/or* questions, labeling activities and questions that can be answered formulaically.
The student may decode print, but struggles to comprehend.	Use TPR with responses—verbal and nonverbal, role-playing activities.

THE PRODUCTIVE LANGUAGE STAGE

Characteristics	Appropriate Instructional Strategies
Key characteristic: Students begin to manipulate language on their own, rather than relying on formulaic phrases (e.g., *I goed to lunch*).	**Particular instructional focus:** Modeling, scaffolding, providing guided instruction with academic language. Increased support for reading to learn versus learning to read and for building content-area knowledge.
Students may begin to overgeneralize language rules and may appear to regress.	Tutors are responsible for up to 40% of conversational burden.
Students begin to develop academic skills in English.	Use language experience approach, ask *how* and *why* questions, and increase social interaction.
Students may appear to have fairly complete fluency because they can handle most social situations, but academic English development is still critical.	Emphasize increased problem solving, predicting, comparing, describing, labeling, listing. Provide graphic organizers that include more text.

THE INTERMEDIATE FLUENCY LANGUAGE STAGE

Characteristics	Appropriate Instructional Strategies
Key characteristic: Students struggle with reading comprehension and other advanced literacy skills although overall English skills appear fluent.	**Particular instructional focus:** Teachers should continue scaffolding academic skills and advanced critical thinking skills, providing motivation for wide reading.
Social English is well established and the student appears fully proficient in English to an outside observer. However, student will continue to struggle/develop higher-level academic English.	Tutors are responsible for up to 10% of conversational burden.
Students may become frustrated with what they perceive to be their own language limitations.	Use scaffolded writing process activities that use graphic organizers, analyzing charts and graphs, more complex problem solving and evaluating, research and support questions, literary analysis.
Note that at all stages, tutors should support native language retention.	

Effective Practices for English Learners

To be effective with English learners, teachers must strive to do the following (Bouchereau-Bauer & Manyak, 2008; Yaden et al., 2000):

1. Understand the families and culture of English learners.
2. Base lessons on students' interests.
3. Use collaborative learning groups as much as possible.
4. Provide tutoring by well-qualified tutors.
5. Connect tutoring lessons to classroom instruction.
6. Provide meaningful, challenging learning tasks.
7. Respect students' cultures and intellectual abilities.
8. Teach in both the native language and English when possible.
9. Be flexible in permitting students to use their native language.
10. Give English learners opportunities to talk and ask questions in a risk-free environment.
11. Display cognates on the word wall so English learners can see the comparison. This also aids native speakers in learning a second language.
12. Provide social settings so English learners can learn from authentic communication with peers, just as they did when learning their native language.

Vaughn, Mathes, Linan-Thompson, and Francis (2005) found a number of additional practices in effective English-learner programs. Teachers use repetitive routines so students can readily become members of the class. They also use language that is slightly above the students' current level. Krashen (1981) calls this the **I + 1 Theory**, which states that English learners acquire language when they interact with language that is one level above their current stage of competency. They can comprehend new information when they receive only one or two new vocabulary words or concepts at any given time. Visual scaffolding—showing an image of what is being explained—is particularly beneficial to English learners. For example, when a teacher refers to vowels and points to a list of vowels, an English learner quickly associates the word *vowel* with the letters.

The **total physical response (TPR)** approach is another effective practice. In TPR, students recite key vocabulary words, spell them, and act out their meaning so that they comprehend the difference between similar-sounding words such as *ship* and *skip* (see Chapter 7). Effective teachers model new information, rather than merely explaining it. They use paralinguistic communication (hand gestures, body movements, and facial expressions) as much as possible to

help students understand routines and new concepts and encourage students to dialogue with them as well as with peers.

The **sheltered instruction (SI)** model is another practice that, according to Echevarria and Short (2007), helps English learners achieve significantly. The SI model is "an approach to teaching content in a strategic manner so that concepts are comprehensible and ELLs will develop English skills" (Echevarria & Short, 2007, p. 2). SI is a way of scaffolding English learners as they learn the social skills of the classroom, such as taking turns, waiting for one's turn, sharing classroom equipment, and not "sharing" answers (cheating).

In SI, teachers may do the following:

1. Adjust their speech by paraphrasing, giving examples, using hand gestures and facial expressions, elaborating on students' responses, and speaking more slowly.
2. Pre-teach new vocabulary words by acting them out.
3. Use visual aids such as demonstration graphic organizers to show relationships.
4. Use small groups and tutoring.
5. Use the native language, if possible, to explain content.
6. Provide a risk-free environment and encourage English learners to talk.
7. Connect concepts to students' life experiences.
8. Engage students at all times; no student sits passively.
9. Support students while they work.
10. Provide supplementary materials such as computer-based resources and trade books that are on the topic, but written at a lower grade level.

Several other specific instructional strategies are effective. Choral reading, interactive writing, language experience approach (LEA), audiobooks, and shared reading are all strategies that work with English learners (Drucker, 2003).

- In **choral reading**, the students and teacher read the text together so that English learners can hear the pronunciation and be actively involved in the reading process (see Chapter 10).

- In **interactive writing**, the teacher and students share the pen. Teachers do most of the writing; however, when they recognize that a student knows the initial letter or the spelling of the entire word, the student writes the letter or word (see Chapter 11).

- In the **language experience approach (LEA)**, the student dictates to the teacher. The teacher is the scribe, writing down the exact words the child says. The student reads it back to the teacher so he can identify text that does not make sense or realize words are missing. LEA uses either short captions under pictures that the student draws or longer texts such as stories (see Chapter 7).

■ During shared reading in the elementary grades, the teacher uses large books as much as possible and discusses a story with a small group. Instead of quizzing the students at the end of the story, students are encouraged to ask questions during and after the reading. Through the discussion, teachers can explain the setting, the background, and key words that will help the students as they listen to the story. Reading stories or folk tales that relate to the students' cultures is advantageous (Alyousef, 2005; Drucker, 2003). Of course, teachers must ensure that such books do not reinforce stereotypes.

■ Many audiobooks are available through publishers such as Scholastic and Libraries for the Blind. However, some of the best audiobooks are those created by the teacher or other fluent readers who read a little slower than normal so English learners can follow along better (see Chapter 10).

■ Also helpful are ebooks with highlighted text. English learners can easily follow along and click on unknown words for the correct pronunciation and definition (see Chapter 7).

Additional strategies for use with English learners will be described throughout this book.

FORMING YOUR TEACHING PHILOSOPHY

Your personal teaching philosophy is important. You must understand how young people learn and which factors affect their learning. Elementary and middle school teachers should also have a specific literacy philosophy. They must understand the processes of reading and writing, types of problems, methods of assessment, and strategies of instruction that will strengthen their students' literacy. For example, Ms. Rea's philosophy of reading instruction is that reading is learning to read words correctly. She believes the root of all reading problems is the failure to pronounce words correctly and automatically. She assesses her students by having them read word lists, and she spends many hours each week teaching them phonics rules. Mr. Garcia has a contrasting philosophy. He believes that reading involves bringing one's background knowledge to the reading event in order to comprehend the passage. He also knows that the students' personal vocabulary, both receptive and expressive, affects their ability to read text. He assesses what readers do while reading a passage that is at their instructional level. Mr. Garcia uses a variety of word

walls (science words, social studies words, puns, "found an interesting word," and others) and draws from an array of instructional strategies to help readers become proficient. Both teachers have a philosophy of reading instruction, and both assess students and provide strategies based on their philosophies. Your philosophy may be completely different from both Ms. Rea's and Mr. Garcia's.

Reflect on Assessing Reading Problems

As you formulate your philosophy of reading instruction, consider your interpretation of reading errors. Ask yourself: "Do all of the reading errors I make while reading orally or silently disrupt comprehension?"

Proficient and struggling readers constantly make reading miscues (errors). Not all miscues, however, are bad if they do not hinder comprehension (Goodman, Watson, & Burke, 1996). Some miscues indicate that the reader is reading for meaning instead of merely pronouncing words correctly. When assessing students' reading, teachers should be able to discern which miscues hinder comprehension and which do not.

Personal Philosophy of Intervention and Instruction for Struggling Readers

The DeFord Theoretical Orientation to Reading Profile (TORP) is designed for teachers to reflect on their personal views of reading and reading instruction. Complete the DeFord TORP found in Appendix C.1. The abbreviation SA means "strongly agree"; SD means "strongly disagree." There are no right or wrong answers. After completing the inventory, discuss your responses with your peers. When disagreement arises, explain the reason behind your response. You can also share the TORP with a practicing teacher whom you consider to be an effective reading teacher. After each of you completes the inventory, discuss your responses.

To score the inventory, first add your responses from numbers 1, 2, 3, 6, 8, 9, 10, 12, 13, 14, 16, 19, 20, 21, 22, 24, 25, and 28. If the sum of these responses is low (18–45), it indicates that you view reading as a set of skills. You probably also believe that students must be taught phonics and other skills in order to read complete passages. Next, add your responses from numbers 4, 5, 7, 11, 15, 17, 18, 23, 26, and 27. If the sum of these responses is low (10–25), it indicates that you view reading as a holistic event. You would likely teach skills using stories that students have read and enjoyed. If your scores were neither low nor high on these sets, you probably have not given much thought to how you would teach and assess reading.

The DeFord inventory presents opposing points of view. For example, statement 5 is in direct contrast to statement 20, and statement 6 is in direct contrast to statement 15. If you strongly agree that early reading materials should be written in natural language (statement 5), you will strongly disagree that early reading materials should have controlled vocabulary (statement 20).

HISTORICAL OVERVIEW OF READING REFORMS

Teachers must be aware of the political issues surrounding the teaching of reading. Current federal mandates require teachers to provide quality instruction that ensures that all children, regardless of race, gender, or ability, will reach their potential. This section reviews recent legislation that greatly impacts elementary classroom teachers.

Each state is responsible for providing a free education to all of its young people. However, in the last few decades federal government officials have become concerned with how U.S. students rank among their peers in other countries. These concerns persist despite the fact that in 2011 the National Center for Education Statistics (NCES) found fourth-grade reading scores from 2009 to 2011 were unchanged; however, when viewed over a longer period of time—from 1992 to 2011—they were four points higher. For example, while the eighth-grade reading scores from 2009 to 2011 rose one point, the scores rose 5 points higher from 1992 to 2011. High school reading scores were also higher in 2011 than in 2009 (National Center for Education Statistics, 2013). The federal government has also been concerned with the continued lag among minorities and lower socioeconomic groups, but in 2011, scores were higher than in 2009 for Black, Hispanic, and White eighth-grade students, while the Asian students' scores did not change significantly during the same two-year span.

Elementary and Secondary Education Act of 1966

The Elementary and Secondary Education Act of 1966 (ESEA) earmarked Title I monies to fund supplementary reading instruction for students in high-poverty schools. Monies were used to purchase materials and tests and to pay certified reading specialists who provided extra instruction outside the regular classroom. The instruction, however, was seldom related to the reading tasks that students were asked to perform in the regular classroom. Schools submitted comprehensive plans for the use of these federal monies and then documented how the funds were used and the tests administered to gauge growth. Title I monies could only be used to provide reading instruction in high-poverty schools. Some of you may have heard about or attended one of these Title I schools.

The America Reads Challenge Act

In 1997 President Bill Clinton signed into law another act that influenced reading instruction: the America Reads Challenge Act. It mandated that all students would read at grade level by the end of the third grade and inaugurated many new community-based tutorial programs. These programs provided all struggling students in kindergarten through third grade with extra help in reading to ensure that they could read at the third-grade level before they entered fourth grade.

The National Reading Panel Report

Also in 1997 Congress commissioned the director of the National Institute of Child Health and Human Development and the U.S. Secretary of Education to form the National Reading Panel (NRP). The panel released a two-volume report titled *Teaching Children to Read: An Evidence-Based Assessment of the Scientific Research Literature on Reading and Its Implications for Reading Instruction*. The panel concluded that effective reading instruction included systematic, explicit instruction in five essential components of reading: phonemic awareness, phonics, vocabulary, comprehension, and fluency.

No Child Left Behind Act

Based on the NRP's report, President George W. Bush signed into law the No Child Left Behind Act of 2001 (NCLB). This act mandated that all students must show adequate yearly progress (AYP) in the five areas of reading identified by the NRP: phonemic awareness, phonics, vocabulary, comprehension, and fluency. It also outlined specific, detailed requirements with which schools must comply and sanctions for failing to do so and required that all materials purchased with federal funds be backed by scientific research.

Common Core State Standards

In 2010, the National Governors Association Center for Best Practices (NGACBP) and the Council of Chief State School Officers (CCSSO) released the Common

What Does "Scientifically Based Research" Mean?

In the years since passage of NCLB, the emphasis on scientifically based research has remained steadfast. What does the term **scientifically based research** mean? According to the National Institute for Literacy (2006), such research must:

- employ systematic, empirical methods that draw on observation or experiment;

- involve rigorous data analyses that are adequate to test the stated hypotheses and justify the general conclusions;

- rely on measurements or observational methods that provide valid data across evaluators and observers, and across multiple measurements and observation; and

- be accepted by a peer-reviewed journal or approved by a panel of independent experts through a comparatively rigorous, objective, and scientific review. (p. 1)

Given this emphasis, today's reading materials often are promoted as being "scientifically research based." Teachers are advised, however, to investigate who conducted the research and how it was conducted in order to be aware of possible bias and to determine if a rigorous scientific research method was indeed used.

master by the end of each grade (K–12). The English language arts anchors include standards for reading, writing, speaking and listening, and language. The grade-level English language arts standards include reading literature; reading informational text; reading foundational skills, such as print concepts, phonological awareness, phonics, word recognition, and fluency; writing; speaking and listening; language; and range, quality, and complexity of text standards. This text addresses the literacy standards, especially the reading and writing standards.

The CCSS emphasize that being literate is more than having the foundational skills of literacy that have been emphasized in many previous state tests. According to the Introduction to the CCSS for the English Language Arts,

> Students who meet the Standards readily undertake the close, attentive reading that is at the heart of understanding and enjoying complex works of literature. They habitually perform the critical reading necessary to pick carefully through the staggering amount of information available today in print and digitally. They actively seek the wide, deep, and thoughtful engagement with high-quality literary and informational texts that builds knowledge, enlarges experience, and broadens worldviews. They reflexively demonstrate the cogent reasoning and use of evidence that is essential to both private deliberation and responsible citizenship in a democratic republic. (NGACBP & CCSSO, 2010, p. 3)

Figure 1.5 presents the key themes reflected in these standards: an emphasis on text complexity, close reading, domain-specific and academic vocabulary, citing evidence, and informational text.

A unique aspect of these standards is that they integrate all the language arts. When students are asked to cite evidence when responding to a text they have read, they are either writing or speaking. When writing, students are asked to "[d]raw evidence from literary or informational text to support analysis, reflection, and research" (NGACBP & CCSSO, CCRA Writing, 2010, p. 18); that is, they need to read first. When speaking, students are asked to "[m]ake strategic use of digital media and visual displays of data to express information and enhance understanding of presentations" (NGACBP & CCSSO, CCRA Speaking & Listening, 2010, p. 22).

Response to Intervention

In addition to emphasizing scientifically based research and more robust literacy standards, legislation has also specified how to identify students who need special services. The Individuals with Disabilities Education Act 2004 (IDEA 2004) requires dis-

Core State Standards (CCSS) to establish a framework of educational standards for kindergarten through twelfth grade for English language arts and math and standards for grades six through twelve for literacy in history/social studies, science, and technical subjects. "The standards are designed to ensure that students graduating from high school are prepared to enter credit bearing entry courses in two- or four-year college programs or enter the workplace" (NGACBP & CCSSO, 2010, p. 1).

Even though the CCSS document was authored by the NGACBP and the CCSSO, many teachers, parents, and community leaders contributed to the development of the standards, which were designed to provide students "with high-quality education" (NGACBP & CCSSO, 2010, p. 1). The standards, which include the College and Career Readiness Anchor (CCRA) Standards as well as grade-level standards, can be found at www.corestandards.org; they are also available as an app.

The anchor standards give an overview of the standards, and then specific grade-level standards guide teachers in determining what students must

figure   **1.5**   Key themes of the Common Core State Standards.

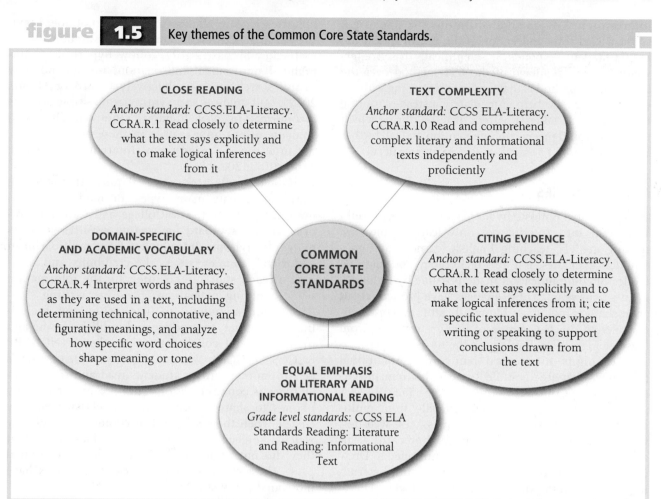

CLOSE READING

Anchor standard: CCSS.ELA-Literacy. CCRA.R.1 Read closely to determine what the text says explicitly and to make logical inferences from it

TEXT COMPLEXITY

Anchor standard: CCSS ELA-Literacy. CCRA.R.10 Read and comprehend complex literary and informational texts independently and proficiently

DOMAIN-SPECIFIC AND ACADEMIC VOCABULARY

Anchor standard: CCSS.ELA-Literacy. CCRA.R.4 Interpret words and phrases as they are used in a text, including determining technical, connotative, and figurative meanings, and analyze how specific word choices shape meaning or tone

COMMON CORE STATE STANDARDS

CITING EVIDENCE

Anchor standard: CCSS.ELA-Literacy. CCRA.R.1 Read closely to determine what the text says explicitly and to make logical inferences from it; cite specific textual evidence when writing or speaking to support conclusions drawn from the text

EQUAL EMPHASIS ON LITERARY AND INFORMATIONAL READING

Grade level standards: CCSS ELA Standards Reading: Literature and Reading: Informational Text

Source: www.corestandards.org/other-resources/key-shifts-in-english-language-arts/

tricts to use a **response to intervention (RTI)** method for this identification. RTI is a framework for identifying students with diverse needs and for providing instructional services with a multi-tiered system of support. The concept of RTI is for all students to "first be considered general education students" (International Reading Association, 2009c, p. 1). In order for students to be identified with a special need, teachers must engage in a "process that incorporates both assessment and intervention so that immediate benefits come to the student" (Mesmer & Mesmer, 2009, p. 287). Prior to IDEA, however, other laws attempted to identify students with diverse needs and determine appropriate interventions for them. Some of these contributed to the development of RTI.

In 1975 after Congress passed the Education for All Handicapped Children Act, all children with learning disabilities became eligible for special education. A child with a learning disability was defined as one with a "severe discrepancy between achievement and intellectual ability" (U.S. Department of Education, 1977, p. G1082). When IDEA was signed into law in

1990, it was intended to close the gap between the achievements of students with disabilities and what was required of them.

For both acts the most widely used method of identifying students with disabilities was the IQ–achievement discrepancy method, which is the difference between a student's IQ and his or her achievement. However, this resulted in over-identification and disproportionate representation of minority children. The number of students who were labeled as having a learning disability skyrocketed.

When IDEA was reauthorized in 2004, the law stated that "a learning disability may be present when a student's performance is not adequate to meet grade-level standards when provided with appropriate instruction and research-based interventions" (Mesmer & Mesmer, 2009, p. 281). This means that schools no longer need to use the discrepancy between a student's achievement and IQ when attempting to determine if a student is eligible for special services. Instead, schools use the RTI approach, which identifies diverse needs by observing how a student responds to research-based intervention. This method abandons the sole use of standardized tests and endorses the use of measuring how a student responds to scientifically based intervention. The advantage of the RTI method over the discrepancy method is that students struggling with literacy skills receive help immediately instead of waiting until they have taken a battery of tests, during which time they would receive no intervention and fall further behind. Chapter 13 discusses RTI in greater detail.

NEW LITERACIES

A personal philosophy for teaching literacy should take into account not only learning theories, reading models, teaching English learners, and government mandates, but also technology and multiple modes of communication made possible by technology in recent years. These changes have brought about great changes in literacy. Many educators and researchers refer to the new forms of literacy resulting from these changes in technology as the **new literacies.**

Reading is much more than reading traditional print texts that are "bounded spaces that remain static overtime" (Coiro & Moore, 2012, p. 552). Today's reading includes reading electronically from multiple sources such as ebooks, text messages, websites, wikis, blogs, movies, advertisements, billboards, visual arts, songs, drama, and various multimedia. Drew (2012/2013) found that the majority of students' reading takes place in one of these new literacies. Therefore, teachers need to understand the reading process of these new literacies, how to assess students' needs, and how to provide activities that will increase students' skills in this area.

Some of the cognitive processes for traditional texts and the new literacies are the same. Both, for example, require that the reader has ability to read and comprehend the text, to make inferences, to summarize, to evaluate, and to connect background knowledge to new information. Literacy, however, has become deictic, a term linguists use for words "whose meanings change rapidly as their context changes" (Leu, Kinzer, Coiro, Castek, & Henry, 2013, p. 1150). In other words, the meaning of literacy changes as the context changes: "Thus, to have been literate yesterday, in a world defined primarily by relatively static book technologies, does not ensure that one is fully literate today where we encounter new technologies," requiring a new definition of literacy and being literate (Leu, Kinzer, Coiro, Castek, & Henry, 2013, p. 1150). The new literacies are a "part of a dynamic and unfounded information system that changes daily in structure, form, and content" (Coiro & Moore, 2012, p. 552) as we interact with new technologies to gain information. New

literacies require readers to navigate nonlinear text, sift through extraneous materials (Karchmer-Klein & Harlow-Shinas, 2012), follow hyperlinks, comprehend multimodal information, understand how to use search engines effectively (Coiro & Moore, 2012), and analyze and synthesize multiple sources of information. New literacies require teachers and students to not only read from these new literacies, but to also write using them (International Reading Association, 2009b).

Our technological society requires that students learn to navigate many types, or modes, of communication. In fact, one College and Career Readiness Anchor standard for writing requires students to "gather relevant information from multiple print and digital sources, assess the credibility and accuracy of each source, and integrate the information while avoiding plagiarism." Another writing standard requires students to "use technology, including the Internet, to produce and publish writing and to interact and collaborate with others" (NGACBP & CCSSO, CCRA Writing, 2010, p. 18). In today's classroom one can see students read and respond to all types of communication. They *text* on their smartphones to share information with classmates; they *Google* when they want to learn some fact; and they *watch* a YouTube video to understand a concept that they did not understand when reading the printed page. These evolving modes of communication have motivated many students.

Understanding and producing **multimodal communication** involves four basic literacies: technological literacy, visual literacy, media literacy, and informational literacy (Sylvester & Greenidge, 2009 **Technological literacy** is the ability to read and manipulate all types of digital resources, such as computers, interactive whiteboards, tablets, e-readers, printers, scanners, MP3 players, video cameras, and other electronic devices. **Visual literacy** includes the ability to read, interpret, and create images and icons on tool bars, videos, photographs, graphs, charts, and maps. **Media literacy** requires students to read, create, manipulate, analyze, and evaluate messages conveyed through images, narration, text, and music in a variety of media modes. **Informational literacy** refers to the ability to find, evaluate, analyze, and synthesize information from multiple sources, including the Internet. Besides developing these literacies, students must learn about copyright laws and how to give credit for any copyrighted materials they use (Sylvester & Greenidge, 2009).

Research has found that students are motivated to develop these skills because technology fosters interaction among peers. For example, a small group of students collaborates on an online research project. Each member researches one part of the topic and then the group puts all the parts together to create a presentation they share with the class (Coiro & Moore, 2012; Mouza, 2005). Traditional print sources often leave students isolated at a desk, reading from stationary pages with static pictures. Multimodal communication frequently involves interacting and collaborating with a small group of peers on tasks they find interesting. Learning becomes social, which is how humans learn best (Vygotsky, 1978). Mouza (2005) also found that collaborative and interactive programs work well because they encourage students "to wonder, explore, create, hypothesize, problem-solve, and interact with other children" (p. 515). Social networking tools (e.g., blogs, wikis, Facebook) that students may use out of school can become tools for collaborative learning in schools. For example, when a class is learning facts about the International Space Station, teachers can set up a class blog so students can post information they learn while watching an educational channel at home in the evenings or on weekends. They can share information even when they are not in the classroom. Spence (2009) found that English learners became motivated by partnering with peers to create a website based on their family's heritage. Students interviewed family members and then worked with peers to create pages about foods, stories, and jokes shared by the family. The pages also featured the Spanish alphabet, Spanish phrases, and the family's favorite places to visit in Mexico. As peers worked together they developed literacy, drawing, and technology skills, as well as creative, abstract, and complex thinking skills. Spence reported the project's greatest benefit was in building school–family relationships with parents who had not felt they were an integral part of their child's education. Parents were naturally drawn into their child's schooling as they shared family stories and jokes for the project, and they were proud when they viewed the websites their child had created. This activity built a school–family relationship that lasted throughout the year.

In another example, Sox and Rubinstein-Avila (2009) used WebQuest, an interdisciplinary learning unit they posted online. As middle school English learners worked with WebQuest, they developed reading skills by analyzing and synthesizing information from various websites. They developed writing skills by responding to tasks and problem-solving skills instead of memorization skills as they learned content material. They developed higher-order thinking skills as they persuaded peers to adopt their point of view when a group consensus was required. They developed technology skills as they produced a multimodal product. WebQuest projects also helped these middle-school English learners to develop oral skills during the collaboration process. WebQuest provided that zone of proximal development necessary for optimal learning conditions (Vygotsky, 1978).

Chandler-Olcott (2009) found that when middle school students edited Wikipedia articles, not only did their editing skills become more sophisticated, but they also became motivated by the social process. Students editing Wikipedia focused not on mechanical errors, but on factual information. Correcting factual errors encouraged students to check different sources and use key social skills so that other readers accepted their changes.

Not only do the new literacies require that students develop a wide array of literacy skills in elementary and middle grades, they also help them become active learners as they work collaboratively with peers. Throughout this text, you will learn how to use technology to develop a variety of literacy skills, including phonics, phonemic awareness, vocabulary, comprehension, fluency, writing, and spelling.

CONCLUDING THOUGHTS

This chapter has given you an opportunity to reflect on theories related to literacy; reading models; reading practices; teaching learners with diverse needs; federal, state, and local mandates; and new literacies. Effective teachers constantly examine how they are impacting student learning, and they continuously study the effective use of technology to enhance literacy skills. Teachers must formulate and revise their own opinions regarding reading instruction, assessment, and remediation through research and working with children.

So what should you, as a teacher, do with this information? First, you must understand the era in which you are entering the teaching profession. Currently, knowledge of the Common Core State Standards is essential, including the CCSS's emphasis on close reading, complexity of text, domain specific vocabulary, citing evidence, and informational texts. You will learn more about each of these as you learn strategies to teach them. Second, you must strive to help all students to grow in their reading ability. For example, teachers must understand how English learners acquire English in order to help them. Third, you must develop your own philosophy of teaching through study, observation, and practice. Fourth, you must be knowledgeable about learning theories and reading models so you know how to assess reading problems, match interventions to particular problems, teach all students to use reading strategies effectively, and reflect on the effectiveness of your own pedagogic practices.

reflective learning

The end of each chapter presents a scenario that describes a dilemma or challenge that you may encounter as a teacher. Read each scenario and answer the questions that follow it. Then, discuss the scenario and questions with classmates.

DIVERSE LEARNERS. Mr. Opp is a first-year seventh-grade language arts teacher in a large urban school. He is responsible for teaching all components of language arts: reading, writing, speaking, listening, viewing, and visual representing and incorporating the new state standards, which reflect the Common Core State Standards, in his teaching. His class is very diverse, and he is amazed at his students' wide range of reading ability: Three of his students qualify for the gifted and talented program; four students have a learning disability; one student is from Kenya and speaks Swahili; one is from Ethiopia and speaks Arabic; and three are from Mexico and speak Spanish. Mr. Opp is fluent in Spanish and is not concerned about helping those students. But how can he help the other English learners, the gifted students, and the students with learning disabilities?

questions

1. How do you think Mr. Opp should organize his class time to provide optimal learning for all students? Why?

2. Are there any federal mandates that Mr. Opp must consider? If so, which ones?

3. Building on all you have learned in your other professional education classes, write three suggestions you could give Mr. Opp to help him organize his class time.

4. Using an academic database, find three peer-reviewed articles about teaching English learners and summarize their findings so Mr. Opp would benefit from your information.

2

The Literacy Event

Teaching reading IS
rocket science.

LOUISA MOATS

scenario

Ms. Young is the principal at Rockwell Elementary, a large school with eight fourth-grade classrooms. She is pleased with all her teachers, but every time she walks past Miss Brooke's fourth-grade room, she notices a hum of student activity; neither Miss Brooke nor the students are ever sitting still. Students are reading together, designing graphic organizers together, or searching for information on the Internet together. Throughout the school year, Ms. Young becomes familiar with Miss Brooke's idea of active learning.

One day in early fall, Ms. Young notices that a number of Miss Brooke's parents have checked into the school. She finds them in the school pit, a small amphitheater, where they are watching the students perform fairy tales with unique twists. The skits are hilarious, and the children are wearing paper plate masks. The students later tell Ms. Young that after reading *The True Story of the Three Little Pigs*, Miss Brooke invited them to write their own modern fairy tales. The students were so pleased with their fairy tales they asked Miss Brooke if they could turn them into scripts and then perform them for the parents. Miss Brooke tells Ms. Young that she had used the humorous story to engage her students in a critical literacy activity. It would be perfect, she believed, to illustrate how most stories can be told from a different perspective.

Just before Thanksgiving break, Ms. Young witnesses Miss Brooke and her students visiting Ms. Hackler's first-grade classroom. Miss Brooke says to the first graders, "Each of my students has recorded a book that they think you will enjoy, and we're here to give you copies of the books and show you how to listen to the stories online. We found the books at garage sales, and you can keep them. My students worked hard to read the books with expression and they added background music to fit the story. Each student will read the name of his or her book and place it in your listening center."

As the fourth graders introduce their books, their pride is obvious.

In January Ms. Brooke's class invites the second graders to the school pit and performs their own versions of familiar songs. They have written funny rhyming lyrics to such tunes as "London Bridge" and "On Top of Old Smokey." They teach the second graders some of the words and have them sing along.

A few weeks later Ms. Young walks past Miss Brooke's room and sees students in pairs around the computers, scanning in photos, writing essays and poetry, recording audio, and creating slideshow presentations. Ms. Young asks a student what they are doing and he explains, "We took pictures around our neighborhoods and wrote poems and essays about them. Now we're putting them into a slideshow with sound and we're going to critique them, revise them, and share them with our pen pals in Florida. They don't know what the desert looks like." Ms. Young asks them to invite her to see the slideshow presentations.

Yet another time Ms. Young observes groups of Miss Brooke's students browsing through newspaper advertisements. Each group is planning a party and trying to find the cheapest food and party favors from the ads, add up the cost, and see which group can give the grandest party for the least amount of money. Miss Brooke will use the winning group's list to buy items for the party, which is to reward the class for reading 2,000 pages during independent reading time, both in and out of school. Miss Brooke has documented the titles of the books and the number of pages read by each student.

When Ms. Young walks past the room in the spring, she notices another buzz of excitement. All the students are dressed in white tee-shirts that look like lab coats and the room is set up like a science fair. At each desk, or "station," are materials necessary for an experiment and colorful brochures illustrating how to perform it. The students have searched the Internet and Miss Brooke's science experiment books and each has selected an experiment to perform at his or her station. They have each designed and printed a brochure so the other visiting fourth graders can do the experiment at home. For the afternoon, Miss Brooke's students are scientists performing experiments for their visitors.

In addition to all these activities, several times throughout the year Ms. Young observes Miss Brooke's class headed to the kindergarten and first-grade classrooms—books in hand—to read to their buddies. They are always greeted with a flutter of excitement. When the state reading and writing test scores are announced at the end of the year, it is no surprise to Ms. Young that Miss Brooke's class has outscored all the other fourth-grade classes in the district.

As you read this chapter, consider the following questions:

1. What practices does Miss Brooke use to motivate her students to read and write?
2. What other recommendations do you have to ensure that her students remain engaged in various activities?
3. In your opinion, what are the primary reasons Miss Brooke's students' scores were high?
4. What qualities and teaching practices make Miss Brooke an effective teacher?

guiding questions

introduction

Miss Brooke is an effective teacher. She creates a learning environment that engages students in challenging activities. She welcomes their ideas and is willing to try them. She understands that learning is social and that students learn from and encourage one another; thus, she chooses projects that involve cooperation and interaction, such as the skits. She is interested in what books her students enjoy reading and is willing to read them herself. Unlike many fourth graders, her students do not experience the fourth-grade slump. They remain excited about the variety of reading and writing activities she introduces them to. They strive to be fluent readers so their reading buddies will enjoy story time each week. They know that reading involves more than trade books and textbooks; they read from many different sources—the Internet, magazines, newspapers, and song lyrics. They understand the importance of editing their writing because an audience—pen pals or other fourth graders—will be reading their projects. Reading and writing always have a purpose in Miss Brooke's classroom.

Teachers such as Miss Brooke understand how five essential components—teacher, student, text, context, and task—come together to create a meaningful learning experience. This chapter examines the role of these five components in the reading event.

TEACHERS

We all remember good and bad teachers, and most of us can list a number of qualities our good teachers possessed. The list may include descriptions such as fair, consistent, sense of humor, made learning fun, organized, knowledgeable, caring, did not waste time, and even-tempered.

Just as much has been written about effective teachers in general, much has also been written about effective literacy teachers in particular. The International Literacy Association, formerly the International Reading Association, compiled a list of six critical qualities of knowledge and practice that excellent literacy teachers possess (IRA, 2000):

1. "They understand reading and writing development, and believe all children can learn to read and write.
2. They continually assess children's individual progress and relate reading instruction to children's previous experiences.
3. They know a variety of ways to teach reading, when to use each method, and how to combine the methods into an effective instructional program.
4. They offer a variety of materials and texts for children to read.
5. They use flexible grouping strategies to tailor instruction to individual students.
6. They are good reading 'coaches' (that is, they provide help strategically)." (p. 1)

Effective literacy teachers also continuously assess students' abilities and adjust their instruction accordingly (IRA, 2000).

Allington (2002) contends that teachers are more influential in the literacy learning process than in any other curriculum or strategy. After a decade of observing exemplary elementary classroom teachers, Allington

(2002) concluded that "enhanced reading proficiency rests largely on the capacity of classroom teachers to provide expert, exemplary reading instruction—instruction that cannot be packaged or regurgitated from a common script because it is responsive to children's needs" (p. 740). He further concluded that "no research existed then, or exists now, to suggest that maintaining fidelity to a core reading program will provide effective reading lessons" (2013, p. 523). Instead, the expertise of the teacher is what makes the difference in reading programs. Allington (2002) reported that all effective literacy teachers exhibit similar characteristics:

1. *Time:* Students are engaged in reading or writing authentic passages; they do not spend time filling out worksheets.

2. *Text:* Students spend time on texts they find interesting and can read successfully.

3. *Teaching:* Teachers do more than assign and assess; they spend time demonstrating and modeling strategies that will make students successful readers and writers.

4. *Talk:* Teachers foster communication skills by posing higher-level thinking questions; they encourage students to ask questions and to discuss ideas with their peers.

5. *Tasks:* Students have a choice of tasks that require them to integrate reading, writing, thinking, speaking, and listening.

6. *Testing:* Teachers grade process as well as product through the use of rubrics.

Effective literacy teachers (as well as teachers in other subjects) also expect students to succeed. These teachers challenge student thinking instead of relying on scripted commercial lesson plans, which "stultify and deaden the mind" (Applegate & Applegate, 2010, p. 233). Instead of asking closed-ended questions, they lead students into thoughtful reflection by asking open-ended questions that have no right or wrong answers. Examples of such questions may be "What do you think the character's motive was?" or "How did you do or think of that?" or "What other way could have the character responded?" (Applegate & Applegate, 2010; Johnston, Ivey, & Faulkner, 2011/2012). For informational text, questions might include "How do you think the immigrants felt when they left their homeland?" or "Do you think it was advantageous for them to leave their communities? Why or Why not?"

Figure 2.1 lists other common traits and activities of effective literacy teachers.

Motivation

Before reading this section, discuss the following two quotes with classmates, colleagues, and/or effective teachers: "Motivation frequently makes the difference between learning that is temporary and superficial and learning that is permanent and internalized" (Edmunds & Bauserman, 2006, p. 414), and "The failure to align school curricula with students' interests and outside-of-school competencies is thought to be behind the general erosion of engagement in reading and learning" (Brozo, 2010, p. 279). How do these statements relate to your own life? What concepts or skills have you learned that will stay with you forever? Why will you remember these concepts and skills? Conversely, what have you read recently that was difficult to comprehend? What kept you plugging away until you succeeded?

If we have a personal goal or a difficult task to accomplish, we will invest much time and energy on it because we are highly motivated. So it is with children learning to read (Shenton & Beautyman, 2012).

Effective teachers know that students will accomplish a particular reading task if they have reason to do so or believe that they can. Children enter kindergarten and first grade eager to learn to read. Somewhere between the first and fourth grades, however, their motivation to read declines. Decreased motivation results in students reading less, and by the time students reach middle school, motivation to read independently is very low. Why do students who enter school so eager to learn lose that desire only three or four years later?

Reasons for the decline in the motivation to read

Edmunds and Bauserman's (2006) study of 831 students in pre-K through fifth grades found that the greatest decline in motivation to read comes between the first and fourth grades. They suggest three reasons for the decline: (1) self-consciousness about reading proficiency, (2) emphasis on competition, and (3) lack of interest in assigned reading. All of these reasons result in some students not reading as much as their peers, which leads to even poorer reading skills. The following sections discuss how teachers can address these three reasons for decline in motivation and engagement.

Self-consciousness about reading proficiency. Early in first grade, some students become aware that their peers can read better than they can. They hear themselves reading slowly, stumbling over many words, and are unable to discuss in detail what they have read. Then they hear many of their peers read fluently, discuss what they have read, and even question some of the things they have read. In sports, if children become aware that they lack hand–eye coordination and struggle to hit a baseball, they will find reasons not to play. So it is with reading. Those who know their reading is not fluent or who pronounce words incorrectly will become self-conscious and shy away from reading in front of peers. The reading experience will no longer be enjoyable and they will lose their motivation.

figure **2.1**   Traits and activities of effective literacy teachers.

EFFECTIVE TEACHERS . . .

1. Teach letter sounds using big books.
2. Model sound activities.
3. Stress the importance of writing for an audience beyond the teacher.
4. Engage in interactive writing with students.
5. Avoid published materials for handwriting practice; instead, have students copy favorite poems.
6. Use whole texts for teaching concepts, instead of worksheets.
7. Teach the parts of speech through poetry study and composition.
8. Teach specific language features in the wider context of writing activities.
9. Teach fast-paced lessons.
10. Use large blocks of time (as much as 90 minutes) for literacy activities.
11. Set time limits for tasks.
12. Model writing extensively through the use of flip charts, posters, and chalk or white boards.
13. Demonstrate and explain the thought process behind reading or writing.
14. Model how to write dialogue.
15. Teach students how and when to skim and scan.
16. Model expressive reading.
17. Emphasize rhyme and word patterns through the study of poems.
18. Emphasize good diction by studying authors' word choices.
19. Use a wide range of higher-level thinking questions and ask students to provide reasons for their answers.
20. Hold students responsible by requiring them to submit a report of the work they accomplish in each literacy time block.
21. Teach metacognitive strategies.
22. Understand that no single strategy works best for all students.
23. Demonstrate to students when and where to use a particular strategy.
24. Instruct students to monitor their own performance.
25. Engage and challenge all students in constructing new knowledge.
26. Make modifications in instruction and materials as needed.
27. Provide explicit instructions for use with authentic reading and writing activities.
28. Understand the uniqueness of each student.
29. Respond to and provide feedback on students' assignments while they work.

Sources: Wray, D., Medwell, J., Fox, R., & Poulson, L. (2000). The teaching practices of effective teachers of literacy. Educational Review 52(1), 75–85. / Schmidt, R., Rozendal, M., & Greenman, G. (2002). Reading instruction in the inclusion classroom. *Remedial and Special Education 23*(3), 130–141. / Rankin-Erickson, J., & Pressley, M. (2000). A survey of instructional practices of special educational teachers nominated as effective teachers of literacy. *Learning Disabilities Research and Practice 15*(4), 206–226.

To prevent this dilemma, make sure all students are reading texts that are not too difficult for them, especially when reading in front of others. Additionally, avoid having children read in front of the whole class too frequently. Divide students into groups of two or three, and tailor your teaching strategy to the needs of the group in order to increase their reading proficiency.

To build confidence in students' reading ability, initiate choral reading in somewhat larger groups (five to six students) so struggling readers become part of a successful reading experience. Readers theater, in which the struggling reader practices his line repeatedly before performing in front of classmates, is another technique. See Chapter 10 for more information on both activities.

A third way to build reading confidence is through buddy reading. For example, an eighth-grade teacher can partner with a fourth-grade teacher, having the older students buddy read with younger students. In buddy reading, the older student selects a book on the younger student's reading level and practices it so he can read it fluently to his buddy. The older student has a reason to practice an easy book, and this builds self-esteem. Chapter 13 includes more details about setting up a successful book buddies reading program.

Emphasis on competition for extrinsic rewards. Some students lose their motivation to read because instruction emphasizes competition. Teachers may give out rewards such as paper ice cream scoops on a paper ice cream cone or paper gumballs from paper gumball machines. They applaud the students who earn many scoops of ice cream or gumballs, but may provide little encouragement to those who collect fewer rewards.

Instead of extrinsic rewards that emphasize competition in the elementary classrooms, teachers should lead students in thoughtful reflections that challenge their thinking (Applegate & Applegate, 2010; Johnston, Ivey, & Faulkner, 2011/2012). Asking open-ended questions that have no right or wrong answer leads to thoughtful inquiry. Some open-ended questions that teachers may consider asking are:

- "What did you notice about the author's and illustrator's techniques?
- "What was your favorite part?"
- "What new information did you learn from that book?"
- "You said it was the best book you ever read. What made it the best book for you?"
- "I haven't read this book. Why do you think I might like it?"
- "I see you're reading a mystery—what clues have you come across? Is it a scary story? What makes it so scary?"
- "I see you stopped reading that book. What did you not like about it?"

All of these are questions adults ask each other about the books they read. They are not quiz-type questions, but curiosity-type questions. It is important with this type of questioning that teachers not judge students' responses (Johnston, Ivey, & Faulkner, 2011/2012).

Lack of interest in assigned reading. Lack of interest in required texts is the third reason for declining motivation to read. If students are given more choice of texts early in their reading experiences, will they stay interested in books? Yes, say those experienced with struggling readers (Allington, 2013; Cooter & Perkins, 2011; Gambrell, 2011; Parsons & Ward, 2011; Shenton & Beautyman, 2012). If students are given texts that expand their knowledge on topics that interest them, they will enjoy reading even if the text is somewhat difficult (Allington, 2013). A student interested in snakes, for example, who is provided with a text on her reading level about different types of snakes, their habitats, and eating habits and then is encouraged to share her newfound knowledge with classmates, may desire to read more books about snakes. A student who loves humorous stories or scary stories can select texts on his reading level from those genres and will likely stick with reading longer than if he is required to read stories that are neither humorous nor scary. If students find stories interesting, they will want to share them with classmates. All children feel good when they can enlighten or entertain their classmates.

Edmunds and Bauserman (2006) found that fourth graders are interested in reading narrative text if stories relate to their interests; if the book's cover is exciting or enticing; if they like the story's genre, such as humor or adventure; and if they can select the book. The study also revealed that students become interested in expository text if they learn information they can share with others, if they choose the book, and if they are interested in the topic. The researchers asked students who were motivated to read how they find good books. Most say they find them in the school library, their teacher recommends them, they find them in the classroom library, or their parents or peers recommend or give them the titles (Edmunds & Bauserman, 2006).

Teaching recommendations to increase motivation

Research shows that students become engaged when they are interested in a concept or activity and that engaged students perform better academically (Brozo & Flynt, 2008; Gambrell, 2011; Parsons & Ward, 2011; Patterson, Schaller, & Clemens, 2008; Shenton & Beautyman, 2012). Disengagement, on the other hand, is the root of many students' learning problems (Edmunds & Bauserman, 2006). Disengaged readers are easily distracted and often unaware of what is going on. Teachers will often find that disengaged students fake reading, get out of their seats frequently, daydream, flip pages without reading, distract others, waste time finding a book, or constantly switch books (Kelley & Clausen-Grace, 2009).

Effective teachers understand that they must always focus on keeping students engaged. But how do teachers accomplish this task? Gambrell (2011) offers teachers the following seven principles for literacy engagement. She posits that engaged readers are intrinsically motivated to read and write.

1. Give students reading and writing tasks that are relevant to their lives. This motivates students to accept the challenge of reading. For example, consider the fourth graders in the chapter's opening scenario who were clipping advertisements out of fliers and newspapers in order to find the cheapest party items. They understood that they would get more for their money if they could find the store with the lowest prices. They were motivated to find this information by reading.

2. Provide students with a wide range of reading materials. They should have access to many different genres, magazines, Internet sites, newspapers, and other sources of reading material. Many times students find a particular author or genre and that is the only thing they want to read. Teachers can give quick commercials for books; the commercials should pique students' interest to read the book. Students want control over their reading materials (Cooter & Perkins, 2011; Dozier, Garnett & Tabatabai, 2011).

3. Allow time for sustained reading when students read authentic texts of their choice. Allington (2013) agrees with Gambrell that struggling readers need to spend time reading authentic texts instead of completing worksheets during the reading block. Too often struggling readers are completing worksheets during reading time instead of reading material that interests them (Allington, 2013; Turgescent, 2004).

4. Provide students with choices or options of what they read. Adults want choices about the foods they eat, the movies they watch, the sports they play, the music they listen to, and the books they read. Some

of us prefer science fiction and others historical fiction, newspapers or magazines that cover current events, or other informational texts. Children and young adults also have preferences. In my many years of working with reluctant and struggling readers, I have found that many of these students prefer informational texts. They want to learn something when they read.

5. Allocate time for students to interact socially. When students read a good book or find some interesting facts, they want to share them with classmates (Cooter & Perkins, 2011). Gambrell suggests that after sustained silent reading time, teachers provide time for students to turn to their partners and discuss what they have read.

6. Give students reading choices that are challenging but not overwhelming. Many researchers and educators agree with Gambrell that students should be given text that they can read with 98 percent to 100 percent accuracy (Allington, 2013; Cooter & Perkins, 2011; Ehri, Dreyer, Flugman, & Gross, 2007; O'Connor et al., 2002). Even adults do not enjoy reading a passage in which six to ten words per one hundred are unfamiliar. It is too mentally taxing to read such difficult material.

7. Provide incentives that "reflect the value and importance of reading" (Gambrell, 2011, p. 176). Teachers need to acknowledge students' accomplishments with sincere words, not with undeserved praise.

Teachers should also foster a mastery orientation versus a performance orientation to increase engagement. In **achievement goal theory**, both orientations are related to motivation. According to this theory (Alderman & Green, 2011), more students succeed in academic activities when the task has a mastery orientation instead of a performance orientation. In the **performance orientation**, students focus on performing tasks or engaging in behaviors that will earn the teacher's approval. They want to be recognized by the teacher as being "smart." If they have a high performance orientation, they are usually motivated to be engaged and work hard; however, if they have a low performance orientation, they usually become disengaged and often do not try to perform a task. Classrooms that focus on competition tend to foster a performance orientation in students.

In a classroom where teachers foster a **mastery orientation**, students compete only with themselves. Teachers usually focus on creating an atmosphere where the joy of learning is the goal, not earning a high score. Teachers celebrate with all students when they succeed; they ask students to explain to them what they are doing and learning and are excited when they learn from their students. Students with a mastery orientation usually persist in quite challenging tasks and frequently choose a challenging task over a mundane task. They develop a lifelong love of learning. To promote a mastery orientation, teachers should (1) create meaningful, challenging, open-ended, inquiry-based tasks; (2) provide private evaluation and recognition and praise effort over ability; and (3) invite students to participate in the decision-making process (Ames, 1992; Alderman & Green, 2011).

Edmunds and Bauserman (2006) offer the additional recommendations listed in Figure 2.2 for motivating students, which can be implemented in all elementary and middle school classrooms.

Guthrie and Davis (2003) offer additional ideas that work particularly well in motivating middle school students. Figure 2.3 lists these characteristics;

figure 2.2

Recommendations to motivate student reading.

1. Let students select their texts from a large collection of texts that are on their reading level.

2. Give all students ample time for silent independent reading, even struggling students.

3. Create a three-piece kit for each student, stored in a large, resealable plastic bag. Each kit should contain an informational text, a narrative text, and a poem on a topic that interests the student.

4. Suggest particular texts, both narrative and informational, that interest the student.

5. Permit students to visit the school library after completing their work. Let the librarian know that when your student is wearing a tag that says "I completed my work and I am here to find another GREAT book!" he will know you expect the student to quietly and independently find a text and check it out.

6. With the librarian's permission, provide one afternoon a month for parents and students to use the library to browse and read.

7. Read aloud every day to students. Make sure your selections include informational text on topics that will interest students and narrative books of various genres, as well as multimodal texts. Read both humorous and serious poems.

8. Have a large selection of texts, both informational and narrative, on a wide range of topics and reading levels in the classroom library. Consistently refresh the collection with titles from the public library.

9. Construct a bulletin board display titled "Texts We Recommend as an Excellent Read!" near the classroom library where students can post the name of the text, the author's name, and one or two brief comments about the book's content. For example, one student may write, "This books gives details about the differences between poisonous and non-poisonous snakes." Another may write, "This book is a funny story about some rabbits that outwitted a lazy bear."

figure   2.3   Motivators for middle school students.

1. Students pose their own questions on a topic and read to answer those questions. In science, this may involve reading about how to set up an experiment and then performing it with others or in front of their peers. In social studies, it may include reading about a particular time period or person in history and reenacting the era or presenting a monologue of the historical figure.

2. Teachers provide many trade texts about the topic being studied in any subject, and the trade texts cover a wide range of reading levels.

3. Students choose the text they want to use and how they will present what they learn. They even get to construct the rubric used to grade their work.

4. Teachers introduce strategies for comprehending certain texts and then model how to use those strategies. Next, students practice the strategy while the teacher supervises.

5. Students form groups to work on a project. Each member selects an aspect of the project to complete. Students are free to help each other so the project is exemplary. All students receive credit for the final project.

notice that some are identical to the motivators of elementary students.

Research shows that (1) students who are motivated to read will read more (Allington, 2013; Alderman & Green, 2011); (2) when students spend more time reading, their reading ability increases (Gambrell, 2011); and (3) good readers become lifelong readers (Gambrell, 2011; Alderman & Green, 2011).

Those who work with children know that motivation and self-interest make any task easier and more enjoyable. So it is with reading. Students with a reason for reading a text and who have a choice in what they read are more apt to read. Ultimately, the more they read, the better readers they become.

STUDENTS

Figure 2.1 listed "Understand the uniqueness of each student" as the next-to-last trait. Uniqueness is what makes teaching so enjoyable and challenging. As stated earlier, the National Center for Education Statistics reported that the average national reading score for fourth graders remained the same from 2009 to 2011. While 33 percent scored below the basic reading level, 67 percent were at or above basic level, and 33 percent were at or above the proficient level. These numbers in 2011 are the same as in 2009.

Despite the variation in students' reading proficiency, the Individuals with Disabilities Education Act (IDEA) states that regular classrooms are the most appropriate placement for all students, even those with disabilities. Thus, each classroom is home to students with a wide range of differences, and prudent teachers learn as much as possible about all of them. Students differ in (1) their background knowledge of subjects and in how they integrate new information; (2) their literacy knowledge; (3) the language systems they use; (4) their learning styles; and (5) their types of intelligences.

Knowledge of General Information

Some students enter school with a wide array of experiences beyond their families and communities. They may have visited zoos, museums, fire stations, mountains, oceans, rural areas, cities, or other countries and discussed these experiences with their parents and other adults. These students have a rich aural and oral vocabulary, which enhances their literacy skills. Research demonstrates that all students, both native language learners and English learners, have prior knowledge that aids them as they construct meaning through literacy activities (Carrell, 2010; Shaughnessy, 2010). Other students lack a variety of early experiences and, as a result, have limited vocabulary and background knowledge related to many topics studied in school. Effective teachers will either activate or provide background knowledge, depending on the needs of individual students. They also understand that some students may rely too much on background knowledge when they read. Teachers need to help all students learn how to synthesize new information with prior knowledge.

Literacy Knowledge

This section requires an understanding of five terms—skills, strategies, metacognition, self-efficacy, and epistemic knowledge. **Skill** refer to one's ability to perform a task. Strategies are the plans or methods used to accomplish a task. **Metacognition** is the ability to explain what and how one knows. Self-efficacy is believing that one can reach his or her goals. **Epistemic knowledge** refers to knowing what knowledge is important, along with where and how to find it. For example, professional golfers have the *skills* to drive a ball straight down the fairway, chip a ball onto the green, and putt a ball into the cup. In addition, they have *strategies* for performing each step—a specific stance depending on the position of the hole;

a type of swing based on the number of yards to the pin; and a particular chip depending on the slope and conditions of the green. Despite how golfers were taught these strategies, they practiced different methods to decide which ones worked for them. *Metacognition* refers to the thought process a golfer uses as he decides which swing, chip, and putt to use and his explanation for why he chose them. *Self-efficacy* is the belief that the golfer can win the round of golf or at least will do better than his/her last game. *Epistemic knowledge* is when the golfer knows key facts about a particular situation, such as the direction of the wind at the moment and whether this particular course features a lip around the hole. The same five capacities apply to readers.

Literacy skills

Students' backgrounds with text greatly affect their literacy development. Some students enter kindergarten with rich language backgrounds and advanced literacy skills because their parents or others have read and discussed stories and informational texts with them. These children understand the conceptual organization of written material in English. They know that text is read from top to bottom and left to right. They know where a book begins and ends and the difference between letters and words. They know that some books convey good stories and other texts provide information about the world. Many of these students enter kindergarten knowing letter names and how to form them.

Other students may not have these skills because they have had limited reading experiences with adults. They do not understand narrative forms or that one reads top to bottom and left to right. They have little knowledge of letters and words, and they have a limited vocabulary. Students with these different skill levels are a challenge to teachers when they are in the same class. Those with limited literacy experience need guidance to become skilled readers. The teacher's responsibility is to understand the strengths and weaknesses of each reader's literacy skills.

Reading strategies

Teaching **reading strategies** explicitly helps students become more proficient when they read by themselves. The three types of reading strategies are those used (1) *before* reading, which activate their prior knowledge; (2) *while* reading, which improve their comprehension and skills; and (3) *after* reading, which help them analyze and remember what they read (Walker, 2004). Effective teachers equip students with strategies for all three parts of a reading event. These strategies will be discussed in Chapters 8 and 9.

When teaching a strategy, be explicit in explaining its process, model it, and then monitor students while they practice it. For example, students need to know what to do when they encounter an unfamiliar word. You might instruct them to do the following:

1. Skip the word and read to the end of the sentence.
2. Look at the picture for clues.
3. Think of a word that would make sense in context.
4. Check to see if the letters of that word correspond to those of the word in the passage.
5. If the letters do not correspond, think of a different word that fits the context.

For example, in the book *The Wobbly Tooth* from the Oxford Reading Tree series, the teacher comes to the word *humungous*. She models the strategy above by first skipping over the word and reading to the end of the sentence. Then she says, "The picture looks like the girl has a *big* smile," and asks, "Would *big* make sense here?" As she reads the sentence with the word *big,* she agrees with the students that big makes sense; however, big begins with a *b* and the word in the book begins with an *h*. She asks, "What word means big, but begins with an *h*? Do any of you know of a word?" One student exclaims, "Humungous! My brother always says he wants a humungous hamburger!" The teacher then checks to see if the letter and sounds correspond by spelling out *humungous* on the whiteboard and comparing it to the word in the text. "Yes," she says, "the word is *humungous*." She then continues reading.

The teacher guides them as they practice this strategy the next few times they encounter an unfamiliar word. The goal is for the students to use the strategy automatically when they read by themselves.

Teaching appropriate strategies is demanding for teachers because they must constantly assess students as they read, demonstrate the appropriate steps, and teach students how and when to use them. They can teach reading strategies to large groups, small groups, or to individuals. Effective teachers teach reading strategies when the students need them, in the context of authentic reading or writing activities (Allington, 2013; Dozier, Garnett, & Tabatabai, 2011; Fountas & Pinnell, 2006b; Parsons & Ward, 2011).

Metacognition

Poor readers lack metacognitive strategies. Metacognition involves a person's awareness of his or her own thinking and the conscious effort to monitor this awareness. Afflerbach and colleagues (2013) argue that readers need metacognition in order to become skilled readers. Students with metacognition are proactive. They set goals for themselves, they select strategies that work for them, they self-monitor, and they have a purpose for reading a particular text.

One way to enhance students' metacognition is for a teacher to use a "think-aloud" to demonstrate her metacognitive process as she monitors her own reading. For example, when reading a passage on Abraham Lincoln, she might comment, "It says here that Abe Lincoln had very little schooling by the time he was 16. That doesn't seem right. It seems like he should have had more by that age in order to be president. I need to reread to see how old Lincoln was when he began school in order to confirm this fact." The teacher then invites the students to read with similar awareness; when they encounter a puzzling fact, she asks them questions to guide them through the process. Eventually, students will use metacognitive strategies independently to monitor their reading processes and comprehension.

Self-efficacy

Struggling readers may lack self-efficacy because they never experience success or no adult has ever believed that they can succeed. Students with self-efficacy have likely had some adult in their past who believed they could complete a task and scaffolded them until he or she was successful. Success breeds success. Once individuals have experienced success, they begin to believe in their ability to succeed. They also tend to "view problems as challenges to be conquered and they put forth effort when challenged" (Afflerbach et al., 2013, p. 446).

Epistemic knowledge

As students progress to higher grades, they are bombarded with information. Some readers continue to be able to determine what is important knowledge and what are unimportant details. They also know where to locate information. They know that certain books such as atlases, encyclopedias, and thesauri provide different types of information. When looking for information online, they understand the importance of checking the author's credentials; when they think a writer is biased, they perform a close, critical read. They seek credible sources such as those sites created by professional organizations. Students that engage in the above are demonstrating epistemic knowledge of reading.

Language Systems Readers Use

Readers use four cueing systems—syntactic, semantic, graphophonic, and pragmatic—as they make sense of written text. The **syntactic cueing system** refers to the grammar of sentences: Does it sound right? Most words in English-language sentences must appear in a particular order. "Mary had a little lamb" is accept-

able, but "Had little a lamb Mary" is not. Very young children learn the accepted syntax of their native language when they begin to talk. The **semantic cueing system** refers to the meaning of words and sentences: Do they make sense? For example, a writer conveys two very different ideas with the following two sentences: "I went to visit England" and "I went to conquer England." A change of one word results in two drastically different sentences. The **graphophonic cueing system** refers to letter–sound relationships: Does it look right? When students do not produce the correct vowel sounds, they can easily mix up words (e.g., *dig* becomes *dog*, *cut* becomes *cat*, and *bag* becomes *big*). Obviously, students who misread *dog* for *dig* will misunderstand the meaning of the sentence. The *pragmatic cueing system* refers to the situational context of the passage; it reflects the social and cultural aspects of language. Teachers support the use of this cueing system by showing how different forms of language are appropriate in different situations. Some texts, such as emails to friends, are less formal than business letters, for example, and different forms of language are appropriate for each.

Understanding which language systems your students use when they read is important (Clay, 1993c; Fountas & Pinnell, 2012/2013; Walker, 2004). Some students use syntax clues to figure out unknown words. Syntax involves the study of grammar—the rules by which sentences are formed and ordered. Students who use syntactic clues recognize when a sentence does not "sound" right based on their knowledge of the common sentence patterns in English. Other readers use context clues; they recognize from the surrounding words, phrases, sentences, or paragraphs that a sentence does not make sense. Still other students use visual clues; they recognize the difference between *frog* and *toad* because frog begins with an /f/ sound, while toad begins with a /t/ sound. Once teachers understand which clues students use, they can demonstrate how to use the other clues. Proficient readers can explain what language systems and strategies they use when the reading process breaks down.

Learning Styles

Effective teachers determine all they can about students' learning preferences, not to label them but to provide the environment most conducive to their learning style (Hall, 2006).

Two opposing learning styles that frequently affect reading instruction are the **analytical** and the **global** styles of learning (Carbo, 1996b). Analytical readers are auditory learners and process information in logical, sequential steps. Because phonics programs are logical and sequential, analytical readers often learn to read best when first presented with phonics and then proceed to whole text with decodable words. Global processing is accomplished when students are first presented with an overview of the information and then taught to analyze the parts. Global readers tend to learn best if they first read the text and then learn skills in the context of the passage (Carbo, 1996c). Poor readers usually have an approach that is more global than analytical (Carbo, 1996b). Remember that both analytical and global readers need to read whole text and require explicit phonics and word study (Stahl & Kuhn, 1995). They just need them presented in a different order. For this reason, homogeneous groupings of students with similar learning styles may enhance instruction.

Multiple Intelligences

Howard Gardner's **theory of multiple intelligences** (1983, 1993) is relevant to teaching literacy skills. This theory states that all humans possess nine different intelligences; however, one (or more) tends to be dominant in each person. Figure 2.4 lists the nine intelligences with a brief description of each. Some of Gardner's critics argue that the ninth intelligence is learned (i.e., people learn to understand philosophies and theories) and therefore is not an intelligence.

Consider the following examples of multiple intelligences: Joey, a third grader with musical ability, stays on task when background music is played. When he is asked to retell a story, he likes to make up a jingle about the plot. Juan, another boy in the same class, learns best when manipulating objects and likes to create intricate models. When Juan is asked to retell a story, he likes to retell it by creating a diorama. The more teachers know about their students' unique intelligences, talents, abilities, and learning styles, the better they can cater lessons and learning environments to fit the students' needs.

Gardner did not initially develop the multiple intelligences theory for education, but many educators have written curricula based on it. Keep in mind, however, that teachers teach children, not curricula. Therefore, the theory of multiple intelligences is helpful inasmuch as it assists teachers in understanding the differences among learners. For example, students with a dominant musical intelligence, such as Joey, may be able to clap syllables while singing a song. Students with a dominant spatial intelligence may be able to relate concepts from informational text by creating drawings and graphs. Students with a dominant interpersonal intelligence may be able to provide effective organization for group activities, such as skits and readers theater, because they know how to motivate others to work as a group.

Figure 2.5 illustrates Armstrong's (2000) concise overview of eight of the nine intelligences to indicate how students with each dominant intelligence think, what they like to do, and what they need. Remember that Gardner believes that *all* intelligences must be developed; therefore, begin with the student's natural strength and gradually encourage him or her to develop other areas.

Armstrong (2000) created a checklist for teachers to use to assess their students' multiple intelligences. Use this checklist as you observe a student in the classroom as he interacts in big groups and small groups and works independently. See Appendix C.2.

TEXT

The third element of the reading event is the text. Effective teachers know that giving students texts that are too difficult or too easy causes frustration for all types of readers. However, the Common Core State Standards (CCSS) hold teachers in all grades responsible for students reading more complex text than under previous standards. It can be a balancing act for teachers to give students texts that are challenging but not so difficult that students become overwhelmed. Teachers need to find texts that are suitable for students to read by themselves and some challenge texts that they can read with the help of the teacher's instruction. This section discusses the three different reading levels, how texts are leveled so teachers can aid students as they choose books, and the dimensions of text complexity.

Levels of Readability

Readability levels are based on the percentage of words students read correctly. Educators consider three different levels: independent, instructional, and frustration.

figure 2.4

Howard Gardner's multiple intelligences.

1. Linguistic: Ability to use and manipulate languages.
2. Logical–Mathematical: Ability to understand causes and effects, to calculate easily, and to think abstractly.
3. Spatial: Ability to represent the spatial world in one's mind.
4. Kinesthetic: Ability to use one's body.
5. Musical: Ability to hear rhythms and melodies.
6. Intrapersonal: Ability to understand oneself.
7. Interpersonal: Ability to interact with and understand others.
8. Naturalistic: Ability to discriminate among the parts of nature.
9. Existential: Ability to understand philosophies and theories.

figure **2.5**   Summary of the eight multiple intelligences with example teaching materials and strategies.

INTELLIGENCE	TEACHING ACTIVITIES (EXAMPLES)	TEACHING MATERIALS (EXAMPLES)	INSTRUCTIONAL STRATEGIES
Linguistic	lectures, discussions, word games, storytelling, choral reading, journal writing	books, audio recorders, stamp sets, audio books	read about it, write about it, talk about it, listen to it
Logical–Mathematical	brain teasers, problem solving, science experiments, mental calculation, number games, critical thinking	calculators, math manipulatives, science equipment, math games	quantify it, think critically about it, put it in a logical framework, experiment with it
Spatial	visual presentations, art activities, imagination games, mind-mapping, metaphor, visualization	graphs, maps, video, LEGO sets, art materials, optical illusions, cameras, picture library	see it, draw it, visualize it, color it, mind-map it
Bodily–Kinesthetic	hands-on learning, drama, dance, sports that teach, tactile activities, relaxation exercises	building tools, clay, sports equipment, manipulatives, tactile learning resources	build it, act it out, touch it, get a "gut feeling" of it, dance it
Musical	rhythmic learnings, rapping, using songs that teach	audio recorder, audio collection, musical instruments	sing it, rap it, listen to it
Interpersonal	cooperative learning, peer tutoring, community involvement, social gatherings, simulations	board games, party supplies, props for role plays	teach it, collaborate on it, interact with respect to it
Intrapersonal	individualized instruction, independent study, options in course of study, self-esteem building	self-checking materials, journals, materials for projects	connect it to your personal life, make choices with regard to it, reflect on it
Naturalistic	nature study, ecological awareness, care of animals	plants, animals, naturalists' tools (e.g., binoculars), gardening tools	connect it to living things and natural phenomena

Source: Multiple Intelligences in the Classroom, 2nd ed. (pp. 4–6), by Thomas Armstrong, Alexandria, VA: ASCD. © 2000 by ASCD. Reprinted with permission of Association for Supervision and Curriculum Development via CCC. Learn more about ASCD at www.ascd.org.

• *Independent reading level.* When reading independently, a student reads this passage with 95 to 100 percent accuracy. This means that in a passage of 100 words, the reader makes five or fewer errors and has a comprehension level of 90 percent or better. The student can read these passages at an appropriate rate, with correct phrasing and expression that conveys the meaning of the passage.

• *Instructional reading level.* When reading at an instructional level, a student reads this passage with 90 to 94 percent accuracy and with a comprehension level of 60 percent or better. Thus, in a 100-word passage the reader makes no more than 10 errors. At the instructional level, the reader can comprehend most of the unknown words quickly and accurately.

• *Frustration reading level.* At this level, a student reads the passage with less than 90 percent accuracy and a comprehension level of 50 percent or less. This means that in a 100-word passage, he makes more than 10 errors. If the passage is at his frustration level,

he cannot comprehend unknown words quickly. His pace is slow and he reads words instead of phrases.

When reading independently, students should work with texts they can read easily. To become proficient independent readers, they must spend substantial time reading books successfully. Children become motivated to read when they read easy material that interests them (Allington, 2013; Cooter & Perkins, 2011; Clay, 1993c; Fountas & Pinnell, 2012/2013). When working with a teacher or other adult, however, students need to be challenged with a text at their instructional reading level, which means that the text offers a minimum of new words and concepts (Fountas & Pinnell, 2006b). Frustration-level texts are discouraging to children as well as adults.

Effective teachers give students a wide variety of reading materials. They expose students to historical fiction, biography, mysteries, folklore, science fiction, and poetry. They also use materials other than books, such as magazines and websites. All of these materials need to be at the student's easy reading level for independent reading and at the instructional level when students are working with teachers or paraprofessionals (Allington, Johnston, & Day, 2002).

Follow these criteria for selecting both easy and instructional reading texts for your students:

1. Select texts that students enjoy and find interesting.
2. Be certain texts present accurate information.
3. Choose texts with accurate and diverse multicultural representations.
4. Use texts from a range of genres (e.g., poetry, stories, drama, and nonfiction exposition).
5. Use many texts at each reading level.
6. Choose texts with high-quality illustrations and complementary texts and illustrations.
7. Select texts of a length appropriate for the desired reading level.
8. Use instructional reading–level texts that are challenging but not discouraging.
9. Include easy reading–level books to build fluency.
10. Use easy reading–level texts to allow readers to build comprehension rather than focusing on deciphering words.

Leveled Books

Over the last two decades, a number of techniques to divide books into different levels have emerged. These may be confusing to caregivers and teachers who are unfamiliar with the system assigned to a given book.

Age leveling

The publisher assigns an intended age for which the book was written and lists it on the cover. The age levels often refer to the interest level of the story or the amount and depth of information given. Many books for infants and toddlers have designated age levels.

Grade leveling

Another way publishers level books is according to grade. The formulas used to calculate grade levels are based on sentence length and the number of syllables in a sentence.

The Accelerated Reader program, used in many schools in the United States, classifies books according to grade level. Renaissance Learning, which levels books and quizzes for the Accelerated Reader program, assigns levels to thousands of books. Teachers can readily find a book's grade level by visiting their website (www.renlearn.com). Once at the website, click on "Order Quizzes" and then "Reading." Type in the book's title, and

the grade level will appear. Titles used by more than one author (e.g., *The Mitten*) will give the reading level for each. Here are two websites for locating books for particular grade levels:

> www.ofcs.net/docs/Leveled%20Book%20List%20O-T.pdf
>
> www.scholastic.com/bookwizard/

Two problems exist with this type of leveling. First, sentences can be short with single-syllable words, but the syntax may be awkward and difficult for students to comprehend. For example: "With his hat, map, pen, and pouch in hand, leaped the man." Second, not all children read at grade level; therefore, teachers cannot assume students in the first grade will be able to read and comprehend first-grade books.

Lexile leveling

A third system for leveling is the Lexile scale, which ranges from 450L to 1355L. This scale has been realigned with the CCSS. The bands have been adjusted upward so "that all students should be reading at the college and career readiness level by no later than the end of high school" (Finn, 2013, p. 1 of 3). Figure 2.6 shows the original band with the "stretch" band that aligns with the CCSS. The bands were stretched so that beginning in the second grade students are required to read more complex texts.

At one time the Lexile scale, like many other reading level scales, was calculated based on the number of words and number of syllables in each sentence. Basing a scale on these factors is problematic for two rea-

figure 2.6

Comparison of the original Lexile bands with the Stretch Lexile bands.

GRADE BAND	ORIGINAL LEXILE BAND	"STRETCH" LEXILE BAND
K–1	N/A	N/A
2–3	450L–725L	450-790
4–5	645L–845L	770-980
6–8	860L–1010L	955-1155
9-10	960L–1115L	1080-1305
11–CCR	1070L–1220L	1215-1355

Sources: http://lexile.com/using-lexile/lexile-measures-and-the-ccssi/text-complexity-grade-bands-and-lexile-ranges / National Governors Association Center for Best Practices & Council of Chief State School Officers (2010). Common Core State Standards for English, Language Arts, Appendix A (Additional Information). Washington, DC: NGACBP, CCSSO, p. 8.

sons. The same multisyllable words may appear many times in the text, thus giving it a higher Lexile level than one with words with fewer syllables that are not repeated. Conversely, some texts have short sentences and one-syllable words, but they may actually be harder to understand because the one-syllable words are technical terms. To correct this, the psychometricians who determine Lexile levels incorporated the use of technology to determine word frequency in a text. **Word frequency** is how "rare" a word is in comparison to all the words in a given word bank. In determining Lexile levels, "The average frequency of all words in a particular text . . . is established in comparison with all the words in an extensive database" (Hiebert, 2013, p. 461). In general, texts with lower frequency words have higher Lexile levels while those with higher frequency words have lower Lexile levels. When the frequency of words is considered during the leveling process, the texts with a similar number of lesser/more frequency words reflect a similar level of difficulty.

The purpose of the Lexile framework is to provide a measure of students' reading (Lexile) level and then to match them with appropriate reading materials. A student's Lexile level is determined through the Scholastic Reading Inventory (SRI). Other tests (Iowa Tests of Basic Skills, SAT-10, SAT-9, SDRT-4) and some norm-referenced tests (North California End-of-Grade Tests and Texas Assessment of Knowledge and Skills) also provide the Lexile level. Teachers can readily find a list of appropriate books for a student by entering his Lexile range at www.lexile.com.

Gradient leveling

A fourth way books are leveled is called **gradient leveling**. Some publishers (the Wright Group, Rigby, and Sundance) publish books with fine gradient texts for teachers to use for instructional purposes. Gradient-leveled books differ from grade-leveled books in that gradient-leveled books reflect minute shifts in difficulty between the levels. The following criteria determine the level:

1. Length and number of words in the book.
2. Size and layout of the print. First levels have a larger print size with the text on the same part of each page.
3. Vocabulary and concepts. First levels begin with vocabulary and concepts found in children's oral language.
4. Language structure. First levels can begin with a single word or simple phrases and continue to simple sentences.
5. Text structure and genre. First levels have a single incident or concept.
6. Predictability and pattern of language. First levels follow a single linguistic pattern.

7. Illustration support. The illustrations in the first levels thoroughly support the text.

Reading Recovery (see Chapter 13), a tutoring intervention program for first graders used in more than 6,000 U.S. school districts, and guided reading, a small-group classroom-based instructional strategy (see Chapter 6), use gradient-leveled books.

Reading Recovery books have a finer gradient than the books used for guided reading. Reading Recovery uses numbers and guided reading, based on Fountas and Pinnell's (2006a) scale, and uses the alphabet for leveling purposes. Appendix B.1 compares the Lexile, AR (Accelerated Reader), DRA (Developmental Reading Assessment), Guided Reading, and Fountas and Pinnell's leveling systems. This chart allows teachers who use these scales to see how they relate to age and grade levels.

Fountas and Pinnell's (2006a) guided reading books are leveled from A to Z. The following discussion gives brief examples of several levels, but more in-depth descriptions can be found in the Fountas and Pinnell text *Guided Reading: Good First Teaching for All Children* (2006b). Level A books are short and simple and demonstrate a "direct correspondence between the text and the pictures" (p. 117). Pages contain one to four lines of text on a page, and the words are spaced far enough apart so students can point to them as they read. Level F books feature varied placement of the text and proportionately smaller text. The stories have plots with a beginning, a middle, and an end, and the informational texts have more than one detail on a page. Level J signifies short chapter books that still include pictures but offer a wider vocabulary. Level L books represent a significant shift in reading material, including chapter books with few illustrations, more complex characterization and involved plots, or detailed information in expository texts. Word spacing is narrower in Level L books, which presents a challenge to many students. Fountas and Pinnell name *Cam Jansen and the Mystery of the Monster Movie* by David Adler as a Level L book. Level P books, such as Jean Fritz's *George Washington's Breakfast* and Eloise Greenfield's biography *Rosa Parks,* are longer chapter books that take more than one sitting to complete, requiring readers to recall information from the previous sitting. Levels Q through Z offer challenging vocabulary and still more complex plots, characterization, and integrated concepts in informational texts. Readers need to use many strategies to comprehend the text. As an example of a Level Q book, Fountas and Pinnell (2006a) cite Dick King-Smith's *Babe the Gallant Pig,* and as a Level Z book, *The Hobbit* by J. R. R. Tolkien.

All books are categorized according to guided reading levels. Figure 2.7 lists publishers of leveled books used in reading recovery and guided reading.

figure 2.7

Publishers of leveled books.

Celebrations Press, www.celebrationspress.com

Creative Teaching Press, www.creativeteaching.com

Houghton Mifflin, www.eduplace.com

National Geographic, www.nationalgeographic.com

Newbridge Educational Publishing,
    www.newbridgeonline.com

Rigby, www.hmhco.com/shop/education-curriculum/
    reading/guided-reading/pm-books

Sadlier-Oxford, www.sadlier-oxford.com

Scholastic, www.scholastic.com

Scott Foresman, http://books.atozteacherstuff.com/
    leveled-books

Sundance, www.sundancepub.com

McGraw-Hill, www.mheonline.com

Dimensions of Text Complexity

As stated in Chapter 1, the CCSS emphasize that students be able to "Read and comprehend complex literary and informational texts independently and proficiently" (NGACBP & CCSSO, CCRA Reading, 2010, p. 10). The NGACBP and CCSSO understand that when selecting appropriate texts for students that teachers must attend to three **dimensions of text complexity**: the quantitative dimensions, the qualitative dimensions, and the reader and task considerations. The diagram and explanation can be found at www.corestandards.org/assets/Appendix_A.pdf.

Quantitative dimension

The **quantitative dimension of text complexity** uses the stretch Lexile Band reading scale (see Figure 2.6). This scale is used to ensure that graduating high-school seniors are prepared to comprehend college

texts and other career materials; students in lower grades are working toward this goal. Once teachers know a student's Lexile range using the Scholastic Reading Inventory (SRI) or other tests mentioned earlier, they can visit the Lexile site (www.lexile.com) and find a long list of books in the student's range categorized by topic. If teachers have specific books for which they want to determine the reading levels, they can find the information at the Accelerated Reading website (www.renlearn.com) or at the Fountas and Pinnell Leveled Books website (www.fountasandpinnellleveledbooks.com). The Accelerated Reading website is free; however, there is a yearly subscription fee for the Fountas and Pinnell site.

Qualitative dimensions

The **qualitative dimensions of text complexity** for literature and informational text consider "levels of meaning or purpose; structure; language conventionality and clarity; and knowledge demands" (NGACBP & CCSSO, Appendix A, 2010, p. 5). For literature, the levels of meaning refer to the multiple levels of meaning a story can have. For example, satire has an underlying meaning that may not be comprehended on the first reading. Satire is more difficult to understand than other humorous texts. Allegories are also more difficult to understand because there is a underlying meaning, typically a moral or political one. For informational texts, the levels of meaning consider if the author explicitly states the information or if there is "an implicit hidden, or obscure purpose" (NGACBP & CCSSO, Appendix A, 2010, p. 5).

Another qualitative dimension refers to the structure of a text. Chronological stories, for example, are easier to comprehend than those with flashbacks and flash-forwards. Informational texts that use one of the common structural organizations, (e.g. chronological order, compare/contrast, problem/solution, or description) are easier to comprehend than those that contain multiple expository structures or that include detailed graphics that add information to the text. These graphics must be read in conjunction with the related text

Readability Software Programs and Formulas

BOX

Occasionally, you may not know the reading level of a book. In these cases, readability software programs are available online. Readability Calculations (see www.micropowerand light.com/rd.html) provides nine formulas for calculating a readability score. Other online readability calculators are also available; for example, Readability-Score.com uses the Flesch–Kincaid Reading Ease formula for calculating readability. With either calculator, teachers can type the passage into a text file or merely cut-and-paste it. The program then calculates the reading level of the passage.

The Fry Readability formula can also give teachers an estimate (plus or minus one year) of a text's readability. Appendix C.3 includes a sample passage, the Fry Readability graph, and directions for estimating the reading level of a text.

and understood accurately in order to fully comprehend the concepts of the text.

A third qualitative dimension is the language of the text. "Texts that rely on literal, clear, contemporary and conventional language tend to be easier to read than texts that rely on figurative, ironic, ambiguous, purposefully misleading, archaic or otherwise unfamiliar language" (NGACBP & CCSSO, Appendix A, 2010, p. 5). Informational texts that have many academic terms without their definitions are more difficult to read than passages that use fewer technical terms and define any terms that the author may think are new to readers.

The final qualitative dimension is the knowledge demands placed on the reader, including life experiences, cultural/literary knowledge, and content/discipline knowledge. Texts in which the authors take into consideration their audience and the common background knowledge most of them are likely to have are much easier to read than texts in which authors do not consider the background knowledge of the readers. For example, stories set during the 1950s and 1960s with plots involving the civil rights movement or the Cold War are more complex than those involving aspects of typical family life.

See Appendix D.1 for more information on the qualitative dimensions.

Reader and task considerations

The third dimension of text complexity involves reader and task considerations. During this step, teachers consider all aspects of the readers in the class. Have they had many experiences outside their community? Have students read this genre before? Is the topic of the text sensitive to many students? Is the book one of the first chapter books that students must read independently? Teachers must also consider the task of the reading assignment. Is she going to read the book during shared reading or are students going to read it independently? Teachers know they can read aloud books that surpass students' independent reading levels and students will still comprehend them. Teachers must also consider if students will respond orally or in written form and how much time they will allow students to complete these tasks.

CONTEXT

The context of the reading event is the climate of the classroom. Consider the scenario at the beginning of this chapter and think about the classroom context. The context includes teacher and student beliefs, type of literary event or interaction, student groupings, and other factors. Teachers' beliefs about teaching and learning are essential for creating an effective learning environment. Teachers who believe all students can be successful tend to focus on students'

strengths instead of their weaknesses. They provide unison reading for all students so struggling readers can be a part of fluent reading experiences. They permit students to practice short poems or passages before they read in front of their classmates. They effectively use readers theater by giving long, difficult passages to fluent readers and short, repetitive passages to struggling readers. With these three types of reading experience, all readers achieve success in front of their peers.

Effective teachers understand the social aspects of literacy. Students need time to expand their ideas through discussion with peers. From those discussions they encounter different points of view and new ideas. Students often connect that information to some aspect of their own lives. Thus, effective teachers use discussions instead of simple questions to engage students in higher-level thinking activities. Teachers may ask students to consider whose voice was not presented in the story, or what information was not given in the passage, or how different the story would be if told from the antagonist's point of view.

As a teacher, create opportunities for frequent, sustained, and consistent literary discussion (Johnston, Ivey & Faulkner, 2011/2012). Use an array of class groupings, including homogeneous and heterogeneous small groups. One small homogeneous group setting is guided reading (see Chapter 6). Frequently change groupings, and shift heterogeneous groups so that struggling readers can listen to many different fluent readers. Give students opportunities to discuss stories and informational texts with many different thinkers. Change homogeneous groups based on the need; one group may comprise all those who need to be taught a particular skill. Groups will change frequently because students' needs change frequently.

TASK

Allington (2013) reports that effective literacy teachers engage students in reading or writing for 50 percent of the school day! Many of these teachers assign large blocks of time to literacy activities, usually 90 minutes. This reading block includes all types of interesting and authentic tasks—independent reading, reading along with audiobooks, paired reading, or guided reading. Students do not complete worksheets; instead they read a variety of texts—stories, mysteries, poems, plays, informational texts, and so on. Reading extends beyond books; they also read websites and other online resources, children's magazines, newspapers, other students' stories, and posters. Not all students read the same text at the same time.

Foster higher-level thinking tasks through teacher–student and student–student exchanges. In such discussions, you should ask higher-level thinking questions that have no simple, correct answer. This permits students to think and express themselves logically. It also encourages students to question the authors and seek answers that will improve their comprehension.

Personalize tasks by responding to students' interests, needs, strengths, and weaknesses (Allington, 2013; Brozo, 2010; Johnston, Ivey, & Faulkner, 2011/2012; Parsons & Ward, 2011). Exercise control over tasks the students need to accomplish, but give them a choice of many texts to accomplish them. For example, if a struggling reader needs to improve her fluency, the teacher might provide 10 selections of easy reading material from which she is instructed to choose one or two.

Also engage students in longer tasks that integrate reading, writing, thinking, and listening, and give students opportunities to choose from a suggested list of activities. Make sure all tasks are meaningful and challenging enough so all students are developing and refining their literacy skills. This will help ensure that by the time they reach the end of high school, they are ready for the literacy tasks of college and the workplace.

Students also require time for silent reading. Silent reading and oral reading make different demands on students. During oral reading, students must pronounce words correctly, read with expression, and comprehend. During silent reading, students must remain focused in order to comprehend.

Independent reading allows students to master the tasks of skimming, abandoning, and scanning in selecting texts. When selecting a book for independent reading, students should skim the first page and the illustrations to see if they find the book interesting. If the book is not interesting or they find the first page too difficult, they should know that abandoning it is a legitimate strategy. If they miss one word in ten, then the book is probably too difficult for them to read independently. They need to learn to scan for specific information. They must identify capital letters quickly if they are trying to locate the name of a person or other proper noun, or numbers if they are locating dates.

During small group reading instruction, the class should be set up so that students not working in the small group can work independently, with a tutor (see Chapter 13), or with a volunteer (see Chapter 11). This enables teachers to concentrate on the needs of the students in the small group without interruption from other students. Afterward, the teacher may allow the students to complete some literacy tasks independently (Fountas & Pinnell, 2013). These tasks may include:

1. Reading self-selected texts and writing in a journal or logbook.
2. Listening to audiobooks and responding to questions, with or without a partner.
3. Reading in pairs.
4. Reading from a poem box and drawing a picture based on the poem.
5. Reading ebooks or online articles.
6. Buddy reading.
7. Rehearsing for readers theater.
8. Reading riddles that are posted on the bulletin board and writing answers.
9. Reading texts the class has written together.

CONCLUDING THOUGHTS

Reading is a complex cognitive process, and becoming proficient in it requires a lot of practice. Your responsibility as a teacher is to create a setting in which all students can be successful. In order to accomplish this, consider (1) your own effectiveness, (2) the uniqueness of each student, (3) multifaceted strategies that will fit readers' needs, (4) methods of motivating and engaging students, (5) appropriate use of a variety of texts, including those at a variety of reading levels and complex texts, (6) the context of the reading event, and (7) creating an environment conducive to learning and assigning meaningful and appropriate tasks. To be effective you will also need an understanding of (1) the reading process, (2) various assessment instruments, and (3) how and when to teach reading strategies so students will know how and when to use them independently. Finally, remember to have fun with language so your literary passion will be infectious!

reflective learning

AT-RISK STUDENTS. It is the end of May and Mr. Glass has just completed his first year of teaching. He teaches eighth-grade language arts at a school in a low socio-economic neighborhood. This year, as is usual, his classes were racially diverse, each with three to four students who were English learners. Most students came from single-parent homes in which the parent worked one or two jobs to support the family. None of these parents had attended college, and many did not complete high school. His students did not enjoy learning and often did not complete assignments. Their test scores at the end of the year indicated adequate yearly progress on the reading comprehension and writing test, but only by a small margin.

Mr. Glass is not content; he realizes he failed to motivate his students. He knows that you are in a teacher education program and asks you to help him compile a list of five to eight principles that he can embrace his second year so his next students will enjoy reading and become lifelong learners. He wants his students to dream of going to college.

questions

1. After reading this chapter, compile a list of principles that will help Mr. Glass or any teacher motivate students to learn.
2. Discuss the scenario with classmates and seasoned teachers and ask them to share their lists. Do the comments from classmates differ from those of seasoned teachers?

3 Assessment

The important thing is not so much that every child should be taught, as that every child should be given the wish to learn.

JOHN LUBBOCK

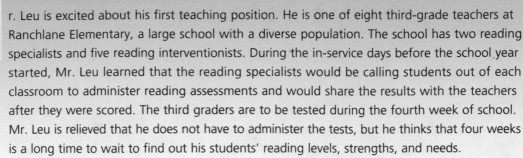

scenario

Mr. Leu is excited about his first teaching position. He is one of eight third-grade teachers at Ranchlane Elementary, a large school with a diverse population. The school has two reading specialists and five reading interventionists. During the in-service days before the school year started, Mr. Leu learned that the reading specialists would be calling students out of each classroom to administer reading assessments and would share the results with the teachers after they were scored. The third graders are to be tested during the fourth week of school. Mr. Leu is relieved that he does not have to administer the tests, but he thinks that four weeks is a long time to wait to find out his students' reading levels, strengths, and needs.

During the first two weeks of school, Mr. Leu becomes aware of the wide range of reading abilities in his class and realizes he cannot wait for the test results from the reading specialists. He feels he needs to do some in-class assessments to immediately address his students' needs.

During one of his university reading classes, Mr. Leu had tutored a struggling third-grade student from the university lab school. He had been required to administer two miscue analyses as pre- and post-tests and to take a running record over the passage a student reread. He found both of those assessments were great tools in helping him understand the student's reading needs. He remembered that during the first miscue analysis his tutee, Alice, had enjoyed filming herself reading a passage using the computer's photo booth software program. Alice liked watching and hearing herself read the passage. After that session, Mr. Leu used the Photo Booth software during each tutoring session to motivate Alice to determine if she misread any words and if she read with expression. Mr. Leu thought that his third-grade students would enjoy using Photo Booth as well. As a bonus, it would also allow him to later listen to and analyze the students' reading. He also decided to take a running record from one student during each guided reading session. During the course of one week, he would have a running record and one other passage from each student that he could analyze.

Using an interactive whiteboard and his laptop, he demonstrated to the students how to use the photo booth program. He read a short passage without expression and made a couple of errors. He played it back and asked the students for comments. Many students noticed the errors, and one student commented that he sounded like he was not interested in the passage because his voice was monotone. Mr. Leu complimented them on their observations.

Mr. Leu explained that they would all have a chance to read a passage into Photo Booth during center time and would be able to self-assess their reading. He laminated short passages of texts at different reading levels. Students were instructed to record the passage and then listen to it. As they listened, they used a Visa pen to circle words they misread and commented on their expression. On a separate piece of paper they were asked to write a short summary and then to comment if they would or would not recommend the passage to a classmate and why. Mr. Leu was pleased to have the students learn to assess themselves. The photo booth exercise allowed him to immediately begin tailoring instructional interventions to his students' strengths and needs. Of course, he was also eager to get the test results from the reading specialists.

As you read this chapter, consider the following questions:

guiding questions

1. Do you think it was prudent of Mr. Leu to assess his students informally before he received the results from the reading specialist? Defend your stance.

2. What other methods could Mr. Leu have used to assess his students?

3. What reading assessments do you remember from elementary and middle school?

4. What is the difference between formative and summative assessments and between formal and informal assessments?

5. What are the possible strengths and weaknesses of each of the different formal and informal reading assessments?

introduction

Mr. Leu understands the importance of assessing students. He and all classroom teachers can choose from many different assessment instruments, but he used two that he knew how to administer and analyze. This chapter discusses a variety of formal assessments, usually summative, which are used to evaluate a program, overall growth in student ability, and/or teacher effectiveness; and informal assessments, usually formative, which are used to drive instruction.

The Buros Institute publication *Reading* (2002) identifies 102 different assessments that measure reading competencies and attitudes toward reading. The list includes inventories, achievement and aptitude tests, comprehension tests, decoding tests, and oral tests. With so many tests available, teachers must analyze the data from several tests to determine their students' strengths and needs. For example, teachers administer a wide variety of tests mandated by their particular state and school district, and they must review the results of these tests. In addition, teachers analyze the results of informal assessments used in developing instructional plans for their students.

The purpose of this chapter is not to debate the pros and cons of testing, but rather to (1) define terms associated with assessment; (2) describe the characteristics of standardized tests, including the differences between intelligence tests, achievement tests, and diagnostic tests; (3) list commonly used standardized tests; (4) look at a variety of reading assessments that indicate student growth in particular areas of reading; and (5) discuss in detail how to administer and score the various informal assessments used to help teachers make sound judgments for ongoing instruction This chapter will primarily focus on informal assessment because these tests are beneficial to classroom teachers in identifying students' strengths and weaknesses and making plans for instruction. The many assessment procedures discussed in this chapter will help teachers to meet the increasing demands they face for accountability of student learning. Always keep in mind that assessments drive instruction.

DEFINING ASSESSMENT

Assessing students' performance to guide instruction is a long-standing practice of classroom teachers and reading specialists (Mokhtari, Hutchison, & Edwards, 2010; Risko & Walker-Dalhouse, 2010; Roskos & Neuman, 2012).

Assessment is the "process of gathering data in order to better understand the strengths and weaknesses of student learning, as by observation, testing, interviews, etc." (Harris & Hodges, 1995, p. 12). School districts and classroom teachers use two basic types of assessment, formal and informal. **Formal assessments** are **standardized tests** given under controlled conditions so that groups with similar backgrounds can be compared. **Informal assessments** are not standardized; rather, they record observations using anecdotal records, checklists, rubrics, portfolios, informal reading inventories, running records, and miscue analysis. Figure 3.1 presents various assessment types.

figure 3.1   Categories of assessments.

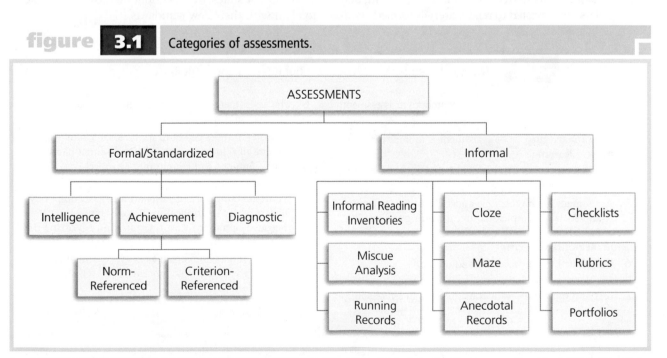

You will assess students using both formative and summative assessments. **Formative assessments** are "all about forming judgments frequently in the flow of instruction" (Roskos & Neuman, 2012, p. 534) in order for teachers to provide daily feedback to students so they know what to do in order to improve. **Summative assessments**, on the other hand, are given at the end of a designated time period and used to assess student growth and assign grades. Both kinds of assessments provide teachers with valuable information around which to plan instruction.

STANDARDS FOR ASSESSMENT

The National Council of Teachers of English (NCTE) and the International Literacy Association (ILA) collaboratively wrote the 11 *Standards for the Assessment of Reading and Writing,* which can be used as a guide when planning assessment of your students' literacy. Figure 3.2 lists these standards, and Appendix A.1 provides a short explanation of each.

In addition, many states use the Common Core State Standards (CCSS) as a basis for their assessments, while other states are adopting CCSS-aligned assessments. The goal of these **next generation assessments** is to go beyond the usual multiple-choice and short-answer questions to measure the full breadth and depth of knowledge and skills described in the standards. As discussed in Chapter 1, the CCSS have students reading more complex text and more informational texts. The Lexile bands have been stretched so second graders are now expected to read proficiently materials that were identified as third-grade materials under the old leveling system, and third graders are expected to read materials formerly considered fourth-grade materials. Another focus is on students being able to cite evidence for their answers and/or stance. Students are also expected to use computers during testing; therefore, they must know how to use word processors and use such features as copy and cut and paste. The new tests reflect these expectations as well as other emphases of the standards.

Two consortiums have developed tests based on the CCSS. They are the SMARTER Balanced Assessment Consortium (SBAC) (www.smarterbalanced.org) and the Partnership for Assessment of Readiness for College and Careers (PARCC, www.parcconline.org). PARCC assesses students' ability to (1) comprehend complex texts, (2) analyze sources in writing, (3) conduct and report on research, and (4) speak and listen, while the SBAC assesses the ability to (1) critically read complex literacy and information texts; (2) produce writing for different purposes and for different audiences; (3) employ speaking and listening skills for a variety of audiences and purposes; and (4) engage in investigating topics and analyze, integrate, and present information (SBAC, 2011). Both SBAC and PARCC provide year-end summative assessments. PARCC is developing interim formative assessments for grades K–2 that can be used to monitor progress during the year, while SBAC provides interim and formative assessments for all grades. One of the purposes for the CCSS is to provide a degree of continuity among states so that if a student moves to another state, he or she will be able to jump in roughly where he or she left off. Some states have joined with one or the other consortium to develop assessments for their students that align with the CCSS. Other states are designing their own assessments to align with their new standards.

figure 3.2   NCTE/ILA Standards for Assessment of Reading and Writing.

1. The interests of the student are paramount in assessment.
2. The teacher is the most important agent of assessment.
3. The primary purpose of assessment is to improve teaching and learning.
4. Assessment must reflect and allow for critical inquiry into curriculum and instruction.
5. Assessment must recognize and reflect the intellectually and socially complex nature of reading and writing and the important roles of school, home, and society in literacy development.
6. Assessment must be fair and equitable.
7. The consequences of an assessment procedure are the first and most important consideration in establishing the validity of the assessment.
8. The assessment process should involve multiple perspectives and sources of data.
9. Assessment must be based in the local school learning community, including active and essential participation of families and community members.
10. All stakeholders in the educational community—students, families, teachers, administrators, policymakers, and the public—must have an equal voice in the development, interpretation, and reporting of assessment information.
11. Families must be involved as active, essential participants in the assessment process.

From *Standards for the Assessment of Reading and Writing* by the International Reading Association and the National Council of Teachers of English, Copyright © 2009 by the International Reading Association and the National Council of Teachers of English. Visit www.ncte.org/standards/assessmentstandards for the complete standards.

The websites for both organizations offer sample questions based on the standards. For example, on the PARCC end-of-the-year reading assessment for third grade, students read the passage "How Animals Live." They must then answer a question about the main idea and a question about the details from the passage that support their response to the question about the main idea. It is prudent for teachers to know if their district uses one of these consortiums or if their state has developed their own assessments.

FORMAL/STANDARDIZED ASSESSMENT INSTRUMENTS

Figure 3.1 lists the three types of standardized tests: intelligence, achievement, and diagnostic. There are also standardized tests for English learners. Most schools administer standardized tests, and classroom teachers who suspect a student has a reading problem should use the student's standardized test score as a starting point for recommending individual reading tests.

Standardized tests have advantages and disadvantages. Two advantages of standardized tests are that (1) they indicate whether an individual student needs additional screening, and (2) they are designed for validity and reliability. **Validity** means the test measures what it claims to measure; **reliability** means it does so on a consistent basis.

Standardized tests have two primary disadvantages. First, because many questions are in a multiple-choice format, the student can guess the answer, which results in an inaccurate score. Second, students may be able to answer some questions without comprehending the passage. This is especially true for literal questions, which use the exact language of the passage. Consider

this example: The passage the student reads includes the following sentence: "A favorite main dish in Louisiana is gumbo, a type of soup." One of the multiple-choice questions that follows the short passage is: "Gumbo is a type of (A) bread, (B) fish, (C) soup, (D) none of the above." Students may deduce that they merely need to find the word *gumbo* in the passage and look at the surrounding words to complete the answer.

Individual and Group Intelligence Tests

Intelligence tests determine the scholastic aptitude of students. While it is important for classroom teachers to understand students' potential, teachers must remember that some students with low IQ scores do not struggle with reading and some students with high IQ scores do (Barry, 1998). Intelligence test scores must be used with great caution because scores may differ depending on students' exposure to schooling and other cultural experiences.

The classroom teacher, who closely follows the script found in the testing manual, may administer intelligence tests to a group or class of children. The teacher does not score these tests, but he or she can interpret the scores if instructed. One example of a group intelligence test given by the classroom teacher is the California Test of Mental Maturity. Because most students do not perform as well on group tests as they do on individual tests (Miller, 1988), most intelligence tests used in school are individual tests.

School psychologists or guidance counselors usually administer individual intelligence tests because of the complexity of administering and scoring the tests. Examples of individual intelligence tests are given in the box below.

Examples of Individual Intelligence Tests

BOX

1. Wechsler Intelligence Scale for Children, for students ages 6–17, and Wechsler Adult Intelligence Scale (WAIS) provide a verbal intelligence quotient (IQ), a performance IQ, and a full-scale or overall IQ. The Verbal Scale includes the following subtests: (1) general information, (2) comprehension, (3) arithmetic, (4) similarities, (5) vocabulary, and (6) digit span, which tests the individual's ability to recite digits forward and backward. The Performance Scale includes subtests for (1) picture completion; (2) picture arrangement or sequencing; (3) block design, a task that resembles a jigsaw puzzle; (4) object assembly; (5) coding, which involves making associations; (6) mazes; and (7) symbol search, which measures ability to process novel information.

2. Stanford–Binet Intelligence Scale for ages two through adulthood measures students' intelligence in verbal reasoning,

quantitative reasoning, abstract/visual reasoning, and short-term memory. The subtests include vocabulary, comprehension, verbal absurdities, pattern analysis, matrices, paper folding and cutting, copying, number series, equation building, memory for sentences, memory for digits, memory for objects, and bead memory.

3. Peabody Picture Vocabulary Test—Revised, for grades pre-K through 12, provides information about students' receptive vocabulary based on life experiences. This test can be useful with English learners because it assesses receptive vocabulary.

4. Slosson Intelligence Test (SIT) for children and adults measures the overall mental ability of both children and adults, but has no subtest scores. The test is a set of 10 graded word lists. The score is based on the student's ability to pronounce words at different levels of difficulty.

Achievement Tests

Achievement tests measure the current level of a student's performance in a variety of areas, including reading, language arts, mathematics, science, and social studies. Each of these main areas has subtests; for example, the reading tests may include comprehension, vocabulary, phonics, and so on. There are two different types of standardized achievement tests—norm-referenced and criterion-referenced. All of these tests assess student achievement and are given under standardized conditions; however, their goals differ.

Norm-referenced tests

Norm-referenced tests are assessment instruments developed by publishers who administer them to large populations of students from different geographic locations and socioeconomic backgrounds in order to develop norms. The norms are the average scores of the large population of students in each age group and grade level who take the test. That average score becomes the "measuring stick," or norm, by which to gauge the performance of other students who take the test. A norm-referenced test permits teachers to compare their students against the students used in the standardization sample.

The scores of norm-referenced tests provide a comparison of each student's achievement level to national norms. Results are reported in the form of **grade equivalent scores**, **stanine scores**, **percentile ranks**, and **standard scores**. Teachers need to accurately interpret and communicate the test scores for parents. Figure 3.3 explains the different types of scores. Figure 3.4 lists standardized, norm-referenced achievement tests with their reading subtests.

Norm-referenced tests exist for a variety of subjects, including reading, mathematics, social studies, and science. The reading sections of such tests often include subtests for word recognition, vocabulary, comprehension, reading rate, and study skills.

Criterion-referenced tests

Criterion-referenced tests allow teachers to compare a student's performance to a predetermined goal and assess the degree to which the student has achieved mastery of that goal. These tests do not compare students to others with similar backgrounds. Criterion-referenced tests help teachers determine whether a student has met the necessary criteria for mastery in a particular area or achieved competency on a specific reading subskill, for example. One advantage of these tests is that they help teachers identify areas of student weakness so they can plan instruction based on the students' needs. Teachers should realize, however, that subtests divide reading into fragments and do not approach it as a holistic process.

figure 3.3

Types of standardized test scores.

■ **Standard scores** are transformed from raw scores using the standard deviation. The standard deviation is the number (usually ±1, 2, or 3) used to refer to the variability in the scores indicated by their distance from the mean, or average. Converting scores from raw scores to standard scores allows teachers to make comparisons between two dissimilar measures.

■ **Grade equivalent scores** reflect the median raw score for a grade level. For example, a raw score of 126 with a grade equivalent of 6.4 indicates that the students used in setting the norm, whose median raw score was 126, were in the sixth grade, fourth month.

■ **A percentile ranking** compares the student to other students her age. For example, if Jane has a percentile rank of 65 percent, it indicates that 35 percent of all students Jane's age had better scores than Jane, while 64 percent had worse scores than Jane.

■ **Stanine scores** are much like percentiles; however, the stanine scores range from one through nine. Stanine scores are more general than percentile scores. Scores of four through six are average scores. For example, if Joe has a stanine of six, it indicates that his score is average when compared to all students at his same grade level who were used for establishing the norm. To find a stanine score for a particular test, the teacher needs to calculate the overall score and use the test's chart to convert the raw score into a stanine score. If the tests are graded by a testing company, the stanine score is given.

figure 3.4

Standardized norm-referenced achievement tests.

1. Iowa Test of Basic Skills (Grades K–8).
   Subtests: vocabulary, comprehension, listening, word attack, spelling, study skills.
2. Stanford Achievement Tests (Grades K–13).
3. Gates-MacGinitie Reading Tests (Grades K–12).
   Subtests: vocabulary and comprehension.
4. Metropolitan Achievement Tests–Reading (Grades K–12).
   Subtests: primer = listening for sounds; primary = word knowledge, word analysis; grades 1–12 = vocabulary and comprehension, spelling.
5. Comprehensive Test of Basic Skills, U and V (Grades K–12).
   Subtests: vocabulary, comprehension, word attack.
6. California Achievement Tests–Reading (Grades K–9).
   Subtests: vocabulary, comprehension, listening, spelling.

State-designed criterion-referenced tests. As mentioned previously, many states have adopted the CCSS or have developed their own standards that reflect the higher-level thinking and reading of more complex texts, especially informational texts as emphasized in the CCSS. As a result, some state departments of education have decided to use PARCC or the Smarter Balanced Assessments, which are criterion-referenced tests in that they reflect students' mastery of standards such as close reading and citing evidence. Other states have designed criterion-referenced tests that are aligned with their state standards (also called benchmarks or competencies in some states) or the CCSS.

State-designed criterion-referenced tests for English learners. In January 1974 the U.S. Supreme Court ruled in *Lau v. Nichols* that students who were not native English speakers had to receive instruction that they could understand. States are required "to have in place standards and assessments for the English language proficiency (ELP) of ELLs as well as having the capacity to ensure that these students meet the same challenging state academic content and student academic achievement standards as all students. Ensuring that ELLs are ready to meet this challenge requires standards and assessments that are rigorous and demanding but also sensitive to the linguistic and cultural backgrounds of this diverse group of students" (National Clearinghouse for English Language Acquisition, 2010). Some states have their own standards for English learners, other states use or adapt the standards of Teachers of English to Speakers of Other Languages (TESOL), and still other states use assessments aligned with the CCSS, which include language standards, so these students are also prepared for the challenge of college and career literacy requirements. Figure 3.5 lists the TESOL standards.

Making sure English learners meet these standards is a challenging mandate for classroom teachers, because it includes assessing the growth not only of English learners' oral or social language, but also their growth in the main subject areas. School districts use standardized tests to determine if English learners are meeting these standards and if their programs are meeting the needs of English learners.

Familiarize yourself with the difficulties English learners encounter when they take standardized state and district tests. When assessing an English learner via these tests, take into consideration the student's background. For example, did she have a formal education in her native country? Did her native country use standardized tests? How long has she been in the United States? You can provide some accommodations for English learners when they take teacher-designed tests; however, for state standardized tests, accommo-

figure 3.5

English Language Proficiency Standards.

Standard 1: English language learners communicate for social, intercultural, and instructional purposes within the school setting.

Standard 2: English language learners communicate information, ideas, and concepts necessary for academic success in the area of language arts.

Standard 3: English language learners communicate information, ideas, and concepts necessary for academic success in the area of mathematics.

Standard 4: English language learners communicate information, ideas, and concepts necessary for academic success in the area of science.

Standard 5: English language learners communicate information, ideas, and concepts necessary for academic success in the area of social studies.

Source: Pre-K–12 English language proficiency standards. Copyright © 2006 by Teachers of English to Speakers of Other Languages.

dations may be more limited and monitored closely. O'Loughlin and Haynes (2004) recommend the following:

1. Make the language understandable.
2. Give English learners more time to take the test.
3. Give the test orally by reading the test to the student and permitting them to respond orally, or permit them to record their responses.
4. Give tests in the student's native language, if possible, to assess their content knowledge.
5. Allow the student to use spellcheck on essay tests.
6. On multiple-choice tests, reduce the number of choices to two from the four or five on the original test.
7. On fill-in-the-blank tests, provide a word bank from which to choose.
8. If idioms are on standardized tests, interpret the idiom for the student.
9. Simplify directions and make sure the student understands them.
10. Use a peer interpreter to read the test to the student.

Three tests widely used to measure English learners' oral, reading, and writing skills are Pre-Language Assessment Scales–2000, Language Assessment Scales–Oral (LAS–O), and Language Assessment Scales–Reading/Writing (LAS–R/W). The Pre-Language Assessment Scales–2000 uses games, pictures, and stories to assess the pre-literacy skills of children ages four to six. The LAS–O and LAS–R/W (both group-administered tests) measure five areas of language development: sound/phrase recognition, sound/phrase reproduction, vocabulary, comprehension, and storytelling. The LAS–O is for preschoolers and up, while the LAS–R/W is for grades two and up. Because oral language development is crucial to developing reading skills (Helman and Burns, 2008), it is important that teachers monitor the oral language skills of English learners.

Informal assessments that are particularly helpful for literacy teachers to use with English learners will be discussed later in this chapter.

Diagnostic Tests

Diagnostic tests are standardized, but they differ from achievement tests in that they determine a student's strengths and weaknesses. In most school districts, primary students who score one year below grade level on achievement tests and intermediate students who score two or more years below grade level are given diagnostic tests.

Diagnostic reading tests include many subtests that cover a wide range of skills—visual and auditory discrimination, phonics skills, sound blending, word recognition, structural analysis, syllabication, scanning, skimming, contextual analysis, vocabulary, and comprehension. All of these subtests indicate a student's strengths and weaknesses, but none identifies the causes for the weaknesses.

Like all tests, diagnostic tests have advantages and disadvantages (Calkins, Montgomery, Santman, & Falk, 1998). The advantages include: (1) the fact that because they are standardized they are more valid and reliable than running records, miscue analyses, maze tests, and cloze tests; (2) they identify the student's reading level; (3) most are normed tests that can compare a student to others with similar characteristics; and (4) they identify a student's weaknesses. Disadvantages to diagnostic tests include: (1) they must be administered and scored by trained teachers; (2) the individual tests are time consuming to administer; (3) the tests may discriminate based on cultural differences; (4) some tests use nonsense words to evaluate a student's word recognition skills, which may frustrate younger students; and (5) they are timed, which requires students to perform on-demand (Murphy, 1995).

Diagnostic tests can be given to groups or individuals, and all group tests can be administered to individuals. Even though classroom teachers do not administer the tests, they should be familiar enough with the reading diagnostic subtests to know the tasks they measure.

Oral reading tests

Oral reading tests assess an individual student's rate, accuracy, fluency, and comprehension (see examples in Figure 3.6). They are usually reserved for struggling readers because of the time it takes to administer them. Oral tests consist of graded passages that range from first- through eighth-grade levels. The student reads the passages until she reaches a ceiling level, which is called her frustration reading level. The teacher checks oral errors, which include substitutions, mispronunciations,

figure 3.6

Individual and group diagnostic tests.

INDIVIDUAL DIAGNOSTIC TESTS

1. Gilmore Oral Reading Test: evaluates the reader's accuracy, comprehension, and rate.

2. Gray Oral Reading Test: evaluates accuracy and comprehension, but not rate.

3. Woodcock Reading Mastery Test (Grades 1–12).
   Subtests: letter identification, word attack skills (with nonsense words), word comprehension (analogies), and passage comprehension. This test is easy for classroom teachers to administer and score.

4. Durrell Analysis of Reading Difficulties (Grades K–6).
   Subtests: pre-reading phonics inventories, auditory analysis of words and word elements, visual memory of words, pronunciation of word elements, listening, vocabulary, and spelling.

5. Gates-McKillop-Horowitz Tests (Grades K–6).
   Subtests: auditory discrimination, phonics analysis, structural analysis, vocabulary, and spelling.

6. Diagnostic Reading Scales (Grades 1–7).
   Subtests: 12 subtests on phonics analysis, word recognition, oral reading, and silent reading.

7. Sipay Word Analysis Test.

All subtests evaluate word recognition or phonics analysis skills.

GROUP DIAGNOSTIC TESTS

1. Stanford Diagnostic Reading Test; Red Level, Green Level, Brown Level, and Blue Level. (Levels range from primary grades through high school.)
   Subtests: auditory vocabulary, auditory discrimination, phonetic analysis, structural analysis, and comprehension.

2. Iowa Silent Reading Test (Grades 6–adult).
   Subtests: comprehension, vocabulary, reading efficiency, work–study skills.

3. Nelson-Denny Reading Test (Grades 9–adult).
   Subtests: vocabulary, comprehension, rate.

omissions, insertions, repetitions, and hesitations, while the student reads. During this process the teacher learns the types of errors a student makes and how she handles unknown words. The teacher also notes the reader's expression and prosody, two aspects of fluency.

Diagnostic tests that assess foundational reading skills

The CCSS include Reading Foundational Skills standards for grades K through 5. Kindergarteners and first graders' standards include concepts of print, phonological awareness, phonics, word recognition, and fluency. Students are expected to master concepts of print and phonological awareness by the end of first grade so the standards for grades 2 through 5 only include phonics, word recognition, and fluency. Some diagnostic tests that assess these foundational skills are the Basic Early Assessment of Reading™ (BEAR®);

the Dynamic Indicators of Basic Early Literacy Skills (DIBELS); aimsweb; the Children's Progress Academic Assessment (CPAA); Developmental Reading Assessment, Second Edition, Plus (DRA2+); easyCBM; Group Reading Assessment and Diagnostic Evaluation (GRADE); and i-Ready.

Figure 3.7 lists the foundational skills components assessed in many tests for grades K–3.

INFORMAL ASSESSMENT INSTRUMENTS

Informal assessments are not standardized or normed, and they do not compare one student to another. Rather, they serve the following purposes:

1. Gauge what an individual student can do as a reader and writer.
2. Diagnose reading problems.
3. Check the student's reading level.

figure 3.7 Matrix of K–3 assessments on foundational skills, comprehension, spelling, and listening.

TEST	aimsweb	CPAA	DIBELS	DR1+	Easy CBM	GRADE	i-Ready	BEAR	Literacy First	Measures of Academic Progress for Primary	CLASS: DIBELS	STAR Early Literacy	Woodcock Reading Mastery Tests
SKILL													
Phonemic Awareness	X	X	X	X		X	X		X	X	X	X	X
Phonics	X	X	X	X		X	X	X	X	X	X	X	X
Word Identification	X	X	X	X		X			X	X	X	X	X
Fluency	X		X		X			X	X		X	X	X
Comprehension	X	X	X		X	X		X	X	X	X	X	X
Spelling	X	X						X	X	X			X
Writing	X									X			X
Listening		X						X		X			X
Vocabulary		X	X	X		X	X			X	X	X	X
Letter Naming		X						X				X	
Reading Engagement					X								
Concept of Print								X					
Grammar										X			
Mechanics										X			
Conventions										X			
Visual Discrimination												X	
Structural Analysis												X	

4. Analyze which cueing systems students use when making sense of print.

5. Highlight a student's interests and attitudes toward reading and writing so teachers can find materials that interest the student.

6. Monitor growth.

7. Allow a student to reflect on literacy accomplishments.

8. Provide an opportunity for the student to set realistic goals.

9. Help a teacher plan for instruction.

Commonly used informal tests include emergent reading and writing instruments, informal reading inventories, miscue analyses, running records, cloze tests, maze tests, anecdotal records, checklists, rubrics, portfolios, interest and attitude surveys, and student self-assessments. All of these informal assessment instruments aid a teacher as she gains insight into her students' literacy processes. Informal assessment instruments differ "significantly from all other commonly used diagnostic and evaluative instruments in that the resulting analysis of reading proficiency is qualitative as well as quantitative" (Goodman, Watson, & Burke, 1987, p. 4).

Because the classroom teacher is usually the first to detect a student's struggle with reading, writing, speaking, listening, or visual literacy, it is advantageous for the teacher to administer and score the informal literacy tests so she can observe the student as he engages in literacy processes.

It is also helpful to discuss authentic assessment in relation to informal assessment. **Authentic assessment** measures literacy behavior in real-life situations (e.g., in the community or workplace). For example, an authentic assessment may measure a student's ability to comprehend the directions when constructing a model airplane. "Authentic assessment practices . . . hold enormous potential for changing what and how we teach and how children come to be readers and writers" (Allington & Cunningham, cited in Fountas & Pinnell, 2006b, p. 89).

Using these and other classroom-based assessments effectively depends on the teacher's ability to select assessments based on instructional goals, frequently and systematically collect data, and immediately implement instructional interventions based on analysis of that data (Roskos & Neuman, 2012).

Emergent Reading and Writing Instruments

Informal literacy assessment begins with young children. Many preschoolers and kindergarten children are assessed on their concepts of print. These assessments are administered individually to see what the child understands about reading and writing. One of the first instruments used to assess a child's concepts

of print was Marie Clay's *Sand* (1993a), followed by her *Stones* (1993b), *Follow Me, Moon* (2000a), and *No Shoes* (2000b). The print size of these books is appropriate for young children and is intended to be used as a basis for asking questions about print. The books begin with the text and pictures written correctly and progress to pages with the words written upside down and with high-frequency words spelled incorrectly. As the adult shares the book with a child, the following print concepts are assessed (Los Angeles County Office of Education, 2000):

1. Does the child know which is the front of the book? Does she hold a book correctly?

2. Does the child know that the words, not the picture, is what is read when asked, "Where do I start to read?"

3. Does the child know that one reads from the top of the page to the bottom?

4. Does the child know that one reads the left-hand page and then the right-hand page? Can he point to where you go after completing the left-hand page?

5. Does the child know the return sweep concept? (Where do I go when I come to the end of a line?)

6. Can the child point from word to word?

7. Does the child know the difference between a word, a letter, and a sentence?

8. Does the child know that letter order is important and different in each word? (Does she recognize the misspelled words?)

9. Can the child identify the first and last letters in words?

10. Does a child recognize the difference between various end marks? Does she know the purpose of a period, question mark, and exclamation mark?

The child's answers to these questions reveal her depth of knowledge about print. As you can see, some questions are more advanced than others. For example, a child who can recognize when the text is written upside down or who can locate misspelled words is more advanced than one who merely knows how to hold the book correctly. See Figure 3.8 for traits of emergent and beginning readers. Teachers can assess most of the concepts of print by using any picture book along with the checklist in Appendix C.4, although most picture books do not have upside down text or misspelled words.

Although many reading concepts overlap with writing, Clay (2006) used the following concepts and principles to assess early writing:

1. *Sign concept:* Child understands that writing conveys a message.

2. *Message concept:* Child understands that what is spoken can be written down.

figure 3.8 Traits of emergent and beginning readers.

EMERGENT READERS

1. Understand that print carries meaning.
2. Understand directionality such as left to right, top to bottom, and front of book to back of book.
3. Use picture clues for meaning when pretend reading.
4. Use story-like language when pretend reading (e.g., "Once upon a time" or "There once was a").
5. Mime a reader's intonation.
6. Recognize environmental print.
7. Expect books to be enjoyable.
8. Can retell stories.

BEGINNING READERS

1. Understand that words are made up of letters and each letter makes a sound.
2. Understand that text has a space between words.
3. Read word by word.
4. Point to words when reading.
5. Can successfully read books with uncomplicated, monosyllabic words, such as Dr. Seuss's *Hop on Pop* (1963) and *One Fish, Two Fish, Red Fish, Blue Fish* (1960b).
6. Successfully read books with patterns.

3. *Copying principle:* When first learning to make letters, a child closely observes all of the lines, circles, and details of letters and words by copying them.
4. *Flexibility principle:* Child learns how to change a letter's form while retaining its identity.
5. *Inventory principle:* Child lists what he knows about writing.
6. *Recurring principle:* Child writes repeatedly so producing patterns becomes habitual and the child feels competent.
7. *Generating principle:* Child combines or arranges elements of print in an inventive manner.
8. *Directional principle:* Child writes from left to right and from top to bottom.
9. *Reversing the directional pattern:* Child has not learned the importance of left versus right on a page.
10. *Contrastive principle:* Child can distinguish the differences between the shapes, meanings, and sounds in letters and words.
11. *Space concept:* Child understands that a space is needed between words.
12. *Page and book arrangement:* If necessary, child ignores directionality to use up leftover spaces.
13. *Abbreviation principle:* Child understands that letters construct words.

The checklist in Appendix C.5 assesses a child's concepts about writing based on Clay's principles, and the observational checklists in Appendices C.14 and C.15 assess a child's literacy habits at the early emergent and emergent literacy stages.

Informal Reading Inventories

Informal reading inventories (IRIs) are individual tests given by a classroom teacher. They general-ly include lists of leveled words or sentences and sets of graded reading passages with accompanying questions. Commercial IRI passages range from 50 to 250 words, depending on the grade level; thus, they take little time to administer. The passages, together with the retelling of main points and/or questions, measure the readers' comprehension and recall ability. Most commercial IRIs have three equivalent passages for each grade, accompanied by graded word lists. Two passages are narrative text and the third is expository text. This permits a teacher to use one of the narrative passages to test oral reading comprehension and the other for silent reading comprehension.

During an IRI, students are first asked to read words from a graded word list of the most frequently used words for the intended grade level. Word lists assess students' ability to read words out of context. After reading the word list, students silently read a short story or informational passage. Teachers are encouraged to give both a narrative and an expository passage so they can determine if the students comprehend one type of passage better than the other. After silent reading, the students retell the story or all they remember about the information. Teachers assess the silent reading by determining how many of the questions that accompany each story the students answer during the retelling. If the students do not answer many of the questions, the teacher asks questions to determine whether the students forgot to include the information or did not comprehend the passage. After the retelling, the students read the story orally. Teachers then ask the students if they remember anything else about the passage. If so, the students may still be at the stage of reading aloud in order to comprehend stories and information. Although many commercial IRIs suggest that teachers record the students' reading so they can analyze it later, some teachers do it while the student reads. While analyzing miscues (using the process discussed later), teachers determine the strengths and weaknesses of each student.

A teacher can also use the IRI to determine the student's comprehension score. The comprehension score is based on the reader's retelling. In the retelling, students should include an account of *who, what, where, when, why,* and *how.* A teacher determines how many of these six items were included in the retelling and then calculates the comprehension score. For example, if Joey recounts only *who* and *what* in his retelling of the story "The Pumpkin Man for Piney Creek" (by Darleen Bailey-Beard, 1995), he receives a comprehension score of 33 percent. The story is at Joey's frustration reading level. Figure 3.9 lists sample scoring criteria from the Ekwall/Shanker Reading Inventory (2013), which defines the three reading levels for retelling.

Appendix A.2 lists commercial IRIs. Commercial IRIs also include forms used during a miscue analysis.

Miscue Analysis

Miscue analysis, designed by Yetta Goodman and Carolyn Burke (1972), is based on Kenneth Goodman's *Taxonomy of Reading Miscues* (1969). Goodman developed this taxonomy "by analyzing the degree to which unexpected responses or miscues change, disrupt, or enhance the meaning of a written text" (Goodman, Watson, & Burke, 1987, p. 5). He used the word *miscues* instead of *errors* "to eliminate the pejorative connotations of words such as *error* and *mistake* and to underscore the belief that all reading is cued by language and personal experience and is not simply random, uncontrolled behavior" (Goodman, Watson, & Burke, 1987, p. 5).

Types of miscues

When analyzing **miscues**, a teacher focuses on what type(s) of miscues—substitutions, mispronunciations, repetitions or insertions, and omissions—the reader makes.

Substitutions. There are many different types of substitutions. Sometimes a substitution is a word that does not resemble the written word, but it may mean nearly the same thing as the word in the text. For example, a student may read *frog* for the word *toad.* This type of substitution may occur if the student uses picture clues to help with unknown words; in this case the miscue reveals the student is reading for meaning. Other times, substitutions may not resemble or mean anything approximating the original word. For example, a student reads *cookie* for the word *catalog.* Obviously, when this occurs the student is not reading for meaning. A third type of substitution is a reversal. The text may read "Dad said" but the student recites "said Dad." The meaning remains intact despite the reversal of the two words.

Mispronunciations. Mispronunciations often reflect a student's dialect. For example, the student may pronounce *specific* as *pecific,* or *spaghetti* as *pashetti* or *breakfast* as *breafest.* Mispronunciations caused by dialects are not considered miscues (Goodman & Burke, 1972). Other times, a student's mispronunciations may result from accenting the wrong syllable. For example, "He will re*cord* his voice" becomes "He will *record* his voice." This type of miscue may indicate that the student is unfamiliar with the use of the word in its verb form and that he does not comprehend the passage.

Repetitions/insertions. Repetitions are words the student repeats, and insertions are words the student adds to a text. The text may read, "The fisherman was hungry after his long day of fishing," but the student may say, "The fisherman was very hungry after his long long day of fishing." Many times the student is reading for meaning and adds words for effect. Insertions of this type are miscues; however, they do not disrupt meaning.

Omissions. Omissions are words that the student drops from the text. Sometimes the student may not know the word and merely skips it. These types of omissions disrupt meaning. Other omissions may involve the elimination of commas and end marks. These also hinder comprehension. One omission that does not always hinder comprehension is the skipping of explanatory words in dialogue. For example, in the following sentence the student may omit *asked Dad:* "Will you," asked Dad, "please mow the lawn for me?" This type of miscue indicates a proficient reader (Goodman & Burke, 1972).

Figure 3.10 provides the unified set of conventions used for miscue analysis.

Preparing and administering a miscue analysis

A teacher can administer a miscue analysis using any text; however, as stated previously, commercial IRIs include passages and grids to facilitate the process. Advantages of using commercial miscue analyses include: (1) they have graded passages for both narrative and expository

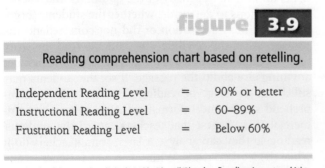

figure 3.9

Reading comprehension chart based on retelling.

Independent Reading Level	=	90% or better
Instructional Reading Level	=	60–89%
Frustration Reading Level	=	Below 60%

Source: Shanker, J. & Ekwall, E. (2013). *Ekwall/Shanker Reading Inventory* (4th ed.). Boston: Allyn & Bacon.

figure 3.10   Conventions used for miscue analysis.

1. **Substitutions:** Write substituted word above actual word.

    frog
The toad leaped down the path.

2. **Mispronunciations:** Write mispronounced word above actual word.

    countent
I was content with my B on the test.

3. **Omission:** Circle omitted word.

    Jane walked into the (huge) store.

4. **Insertion:** Use caret to show point of insertion; write word above.

    new
I want to go to the ∧ movies.

5. **Repetition:** Underline repeated words.

    Dan's pet is a monkey.

6. **Long pauses:** Use "P" to show where pause occurred.

    Molly wants a new P dollhouse.

7. **Self-corrections:** Use symbol and underlining as shown.

    ⓒ
Molly wants a (new) doll.

8. **Sounding-out words:** Write out approximate version of sounded-out word.

    A–All–Al–i–ga–tors
Alligators live in swamps.

---

texts; (2) they have graded word lists; and (3) they provide the passage from which the students read and a prepared script with a grid for the teacher's use. A drawback to commercial miscue analyses is the fact that the short passages lack the elements of a well-developed story or expository text. Weaver (2002) found that students make fewer miscues after reading approximately 200 words because they become familiar with the author's vocabulary and style. Teachers who would like to use longer passages to analyze their struggling readers can prepare and administer a miscue analysis on any story using the following steps:

1. Select an interesting story that has all of the elements of good literature or an expository passage taken from a well-written trade book. The story or passage should be at least 600 words in length and challenging to the reader, but not so difficult as to cause frustration.

2. Prepare the script using the blank form found in Appendix C.6.

3. Prepare a number of questions based on the story's setting, characters, and main events or the expository passage's main topic, supporting details, and key vocabulary.

4. Prepare a quiet reading station with the chosen selection (it can be the original text or a photocopied script) and a recording device.

5. Instruct the student to read the selection silently.

6. Ask the student to retell the story in as much detail as he can. Note which of your prepared questions the student answers in his retelling.

7. Have the student read the selection orally into the recorder. Inform her that you will not help; she must try to figure out the words or skip them and continue.

8. Ask the student to retell the story or passage again. Take notes on the prepared questions the reader answers in this retelling. (This step helps teachers determine whether a student's comprehension increases with oral reading.)

9. Dismiss the student and listen to the recorded selection, marking the miscues on the prepared grid. For example, if the miscue is an omission, mark an X in the "Omission" column. If the miscue makes sense grammatically, mark an X in the "Syntax acceptable" column. If the miscue disrupts meaning, mark an X in the last column.

10. Total the number of miscues in each column, making note of which type of miscue the student most often makes.

11. Calculate the total number of miscues that disrupt meaning and summarize the reading and retelling.

12. Decide which reading strategy you will teach first in order to increase the student's reading comprehension.

Figure 3.11 is a short example of an eighth grade student's reading of *The Jungle Book* (1894) by Rudyard Kipling. For experience performing a miscue analysis, you may use the two sample stories and the grids provided in Appendices C.7–C.10. Both stories can be used with students; alternatively for Grandma's Garden, use the video of a student reading the story

figure **3.11**   Grid for miscue analysis.

TEXT	Substitution	Mispronun-ciation	Insertion	Omission	Repeats	Self-correction	Syntax acceptable	Meaning disrupted
SC six It was seven o'clock of a (very)				✓		✓	✓	
night warm evening in the	✓						✓	
See won Seeonee hills when Father		✓					✓	
wake Wolf woke (up) from his day's	✓			✓			✓ ✓	
stretched rest, scratched himself,		✓						✓
loudly yawned and spread out his			✓				✓	
paws one after the other to								
very get rid of the sleepy feeling			✓				✓	
in their tips. Mother Wolf								
lay with her big gray nose								
dropped across her four								
tumbling, squealing cubs,								
shined and the moon shone into	✓						✓	
the mouth of the cave								
where they (all) lived.				✓			✓	
TOTAL MISCUES:	3	2	2	3	0	1	9	1

Notes: One miscue disrupted meaning.

Source: Text from Rudyard Kipling, *The Jungle Book* (1894).

at **www.hhpcommunities.com/literacyassessment** to complete the analysis. The website also contains additional stories and grids for your use.

Quantitative scoring

To obtain the quantitative score, the teacher calculates the number of words read correctly (words that do not disrupt meaning). The quantitative score is calculated using the following steps:

1. Count the number of words in the passage.
2. Count the number of miscues that disrupted meaning.
3. Subtract the number of miscues that disrupted meaning from the total number of words in the passage.
4. Divide the number of words read correctly by the total number of words in the passage.
5. Multiply quotient by 100 to get the percentage of the reading score.
6. Use the Reading Level Chart in Figure 3.12 to determine the reading level of that passage for the student.

For example, if Joey reads a passage of 500 words and makes 30 miscues that disrupt meaning, he reads 470 words correctly. To calculate the score, divide 470 by 500 and multiply by 100 to get 94 percent. Joey scores a 94 percent on the oral reading, which means the passage is at Joey's instructional level. This passage would be appropriate to use when teaching Joey new reading strategies. The criteria for the three reading levels are found in Figure 3.12.

figure 3.12	
Reading level chart based on correct word recognition.	
Independent Reading Level	=	99%
Instructional Reading Level	=	90–98%
Frustration Reading Level	=	Below 90%

Scores set by the International Reading Association. Source: Harris, T., & Hodges, R. (Eds.) (1995). *The Literacy Dictionary: The Vocabulary of Reading and Writing.* Newark, DE: International Reading Association.

Qualitative analysis

The quantitative score of a miscue analysis may help a teacher determine the student's instructional reading level. However, the main purpose of a miscue analysis is to evaluate a reader's miscues "based on the degree to which the miscue disrupts the meaning of the written material" (Goodman, 1972/1997, p. 534). It is important for a teacher to assess a reader's strategies when encountering unknown words or those he uses to correct a miscue. This qualitative analysis of miscues "provides specific information regarding readers' strengths and weaknesses, which can be used to plan a personalized reading program" (Goodman, 1972/1997, p. 534).

In a qualitative analysis, teachers ask the following questions about the students' miscues and use the following strategies to address them:

1. *Does the student insert or omit words?* Instruct him to point to words as he reads to avoid additions and deletions.

2. *Does the student guess at words by looking only at the initial letter sound?* Have her work on analyzing the entire word.

3. *Does the student read too fast or too slow?* Echo read with him. In echo reading, a teacher reads a phrase or sentence, and the student repeats the phrase or sentence using the same speed and intonation as the teacher.

4. *Do the miscues disrupt meaning?* If so, repeat the phrase or sentence as the student read it, and ask if it made sense. Some students can determine whether a sentence makes sense when they hear it read by another person.

5. *Does the student pause for commas and periods?* If not, echo read or have the students snap their fingers each time they see a comma and clap their hands each time they see a period.

6. *Does the student have good intonation?* If the student reads in a monotone voice, ask her how she would say a particular sentence if she were talking to you. Or read a sentence to the student using correct intonation and have the student repeat it.

Retrospective Miscue Analysis

Retrospective miscue analysis, designed by Yetta Goodman and Ann Marek (1996), contains all the steps of a miscue analysis and adds steps following the recorded oral reading of a passage. The teacher finds a portion of the written passage with a number of miscues representative of the reader's miscues in general. She then cues the recording to that portion of the passage and asks the student to listen to his reading while following the script. The purpose is to determine if the student can locate his miscues—omissions, insertions, and so on—and articulate what type of miscues they are. The teacher and student then discuss the miscues and the ways the student can improve his reading. The teacher records this second session in a separate recording for further analysis. Retrospective miscue analysis is more than assessment; it becomes a powerful instructional tool when the student listens for his errors and attempts to understand if the error disrupts the intended message. When he listens to his reading, he also determines if he has read at an appropriate rate and if he has made the same type of errors throughout the passage (Goodman & Marek, 1996).

Running Records

Running records, designed by Marie Clay (2000c), are another type of informal assessment. The purpose of the running record is to give a teacher the opportunity to observe, score, and interpret a student's reading behaviors. As the name suggests, this tool provides a running record of the student's oral reading. The process involves three steps:

1. Recording the student's oral reading through check marks and other conventions.

2. Examining each error and determining which of the three cueing systems—syntactic, semantic, or graphophonic—the student used when making the errors.

3. Determining if the passage is at the student's independent, instructional, or frustration reading level.

Unlike the miscue analysis, a running record does not require the teacher to use a prepared script or a recording device. The only tools needed are a copy of a book for the student to read from, a pen or pencil, and a blank sheet of paper. In a running record, all words read incorrectly are called *errors* instead of *miscues*.

The goals of the running record and the miscue analysis are different. In the miscue analysis, the goals are to determine if the miscue disrupts the intended meaning of the text and if the student comprehends what he reads. The goals of the running record are to (1) determine a student's instructional level, (2) analyze cues used and cues neglected during oral reading, (3) analyze the student's strategic processing of a text through the teacher's interpretation of the strategies used during oral reading, and (4) use the results to guide individual instruction.

Quantitative analysis of running records

The marking conventions used for the quantitative analysis of running records are somewhat different from those used in a miscue analysis. The teacher makes a check mark ✓ for each word the student reads correctly. Figure 3.13 lists the conventions used to record a reader's oral reading, with examples. Each error is recorded above the word that appears in the text with a horizontal line separating the two words. In order for the teacher to relate the running record to the text, he makes the check marks on the record in the same pattern as the words on the page. For example, if the first page of the passage has three lines, with five words on each line, the teacher makes five check marks (if the student reads all words correctly) on three different lines. To keep track of page numbers, the teacher draws a line across the page for every new page and records the page number in the left column.

When scoring a running record, calculate the errors in the following manner:

1. Substitutions, omissions, insertions, and "tolds" (teacher tells student the word) each count as one error.
2. Multiple attempts count only as one error.
3. Self-corrections do *not* count as errors.
4. Repeats are *not* errors.

The percentage of correct words read correctly is calculated by (1) subtracting the number of errors from the total number of words in the reading, (2) dividing that remainder by the number of words in the passage, and (3) multiplying the answer by 100. For example, a passage has 200 words, and Jodi has 20 errors.

$$200 - 20 = 180$$
$$180 / 200 = .9$$
$$.9 \times 100 = 90\%$$

Jodi reads 90 percent of the words correctly. Figure 3.14 provides a conversion table for a running record, and Figure 3.15 lists the reading levels for the percentage of words read correctly. The passage that Jodi reads is at her instructional level.

Qualitative analysis of running records

The quantitative analysis of a running record identifies the reading level of the passage for a particular student, while the qualitative analysis determines which of the cueing systems—semantic, syntactic, and gra-

---

figure 3.13 **Running record conventions.**

Correct reading	=	✓ ✓ ✓	
Omission (one error)	=	Child / text	— / very
Insertion (one error)	=	Child / text	very / —
Repeats (no error)	=	R (one repeat), R2 (two repeats)	R2 / The house
Self-corrections (no error)	=	misread sc / text	want/went / went
Appeal	=	— |A / Text |	"What's that word?" / hurricane
Teacher told (one error)	=	— | / Text | T	long pause | / hurricane |(teacher gives word)

Try that again [TTA]: one error for the entire confusion (if a reader jumps a line or really gets confused).

figure 3.14 Conversion table for running records.

EASY READING LEVEL		INSTRUCTIONAL READING LEVEL		DIFFICULT READING LEVEL	
Error Rate	Percentage (%) Accuracy Rate	Error Rate	Percentage (%) Accuracy Rate	Error Rate	Percentage (%) Accuracy Rate
1:200	99.5	1:17	94	1:9	89
1:100	99	1:14	93	1:8	87.5
1:50	98	1:12.5	92	1:7	85.5
1:35	97	1:11.75	91	1:6	83
1:25	96	1:10	90	1:5	80
1:20	95			1:4	75
				1:3	66
				1:2	50

Source: Adapted from Schulman, M., & Payne, C. (2000). *Guided Reading: Making It Work.* New York: Scholastic.

figure 3.15

Reading levels for percentage of words read correctly.

95–100%	=	Easy level
90–94%	=	Instructional level
Below 90%	=	Frustration level

phophonic (note the pragmatic system is not analyzed during a running record)—the student uses when encountering an unknown word, as shown in Figure 3.16, and whether she self-corrects and monitors her reading. The quantitative analysis lets the teacher know if the reading material was too easy, too hard, or perfect for the instructional purpose, while the qualitative analysis helps a teacher decide which reading strategies to teach the student.

Thus, when determining which cueing system the student is using, the teacher asks three questions: "Does it make sense?"; "Does it sound right?"; and "Does it look right?" During instructional time, the teacher prompts the reader to ask herself these three questions when encountering unknown words. Note that when administering a running record, the teacher focuses on the specific cueing system that the reader uses.

The teacher uses the acronym MSV (Meaning, Structure, Visual) to represent the three cueing systems. Notice the four columns marked E, SC, E, and SC on the right side of the scoring sheet in Figure 3.17. In the first E column, the teacher records the number of errors the reader makes in each line. In the first SC column, the teacher records the number of self-corrections the reader makes in each line. In the second E column, the teacher writes an MSV for each error the reader makes in each line. If a reader makes three errors in one line, the teacher writes three MSVs on that line and circles the cueing system the reader used for each error. Many

figure 3.16 The cueing systems used during reading when encountering an unknown word, as assessed using a running record.

SEMANTIC SYSTEM. If the student uses the semantic cueing system, the sentence will still make sense. The teacher asks herself, "Does this error make sense in the sentence and passage? Is the meaning the same?" If a student reads *house* instead of *home* in the following sentence, the meaning remains almost exactly the same: "We moved to a new home last fall."

SYNTACTIC SYSTEM. When the student uses the syntactic system, the error sounds correct in the sentence. The question the teacher asks is, "Does that sound right in the sentence?" The student who reads, "I got a valentine *for* my grandmother"

instead of "I got a valentine *from* my grandmother" is using the syntactic cueing system. The reader changes the meaning of the sentence; however, the error fits the sentence structure.

VISUAL OR GRAPHOPHONIC SYSTEM. A student uses the graphophonic system when the word he reads erroneously resembles the word in the text. The error may share the same initial letter as the word in the text, or it may share other letters of the word in the text. The question the teacher asks is, "Does the error look like the word in the text?" For example, if Jodi reads *cap* instead of *cape,* she is using the visual cueing system.

figure 3.17 Running record of *Just Juice* by Karen Hesse.

TEXT	RUNNING RECORD	Number E	Number SC	System Used E	System Used SC
PAGE					
12 While I stand in the raggedy	When/While ✓ ✓ ✓ ✓ r – r / raggedy	2		M S Ⓥ / M S Ⓥ	
road, my sisters start walking	✓ ✓ s–sis/sc sister ✓ walk/sc walking		2		M S Ⓥ / M S Ⓥ
to school without me, shoulder	✓ ✓ with/without ✓ show/shoulder	2	0	M S Ⓥ / M S Ⓥ	
to shoulder, closing up the	✓ shoulder ✓ ✓ ✓	1	0	M S V	
little space where I had been	✓ s–sp/sc space ✓ ✓ ✓ ✓	0	1		M S Ⓥ
in the middle. Half of me	✓ ✓ mind/middle ✓ ✓ ✓	1	0	M S Ⓥ	
wishes I was going down	✓ ✓ ✓ ✓ ✓	0	0		
that raggedy road with them.	✓ raggedy ✓ ✓ ✓	1	0	M S V	

M = meaning (semantic system); S = structure (syntactic system); V = visual (visual/graphophonic system); E = errors; SC = self-corrections

Source: Hesse, K. (1998). *Just Juice,* p. 12. New York: Scholastic. Reprinted with permission.

times the reader uses more than one cueing system for each error. In those cases the teacher circles each letter that represents a cueing system used by the reader. In the second SC column, the teacher writes an MSV for each self-correction and circles the cueing system the reader uses for each self-correction. Figure 3.17 is a sample record for a student's reading of *Just Juice* (1998) by Karen Hesse. The story's original text is provided in the left column. For experience in using running records, you may use the stories in Appendices C.7 and C.9 as well as the blank running record form in Appendix C.11. Alternatively, use the video at **www.hhpcommunities.com/literacyassessment** of a student reading Grandma's Garden. The website also contains additional stories you can use to administer running records with students.

Once a teacher determines which cueing system(s) a student uses when deciphering an unknown word, he can use these findings during instruction. For example, when Jodi, a struggling sixth-grade reader, reads *Just Juice* (Figure 3.17), she uses visual cues to self-correct. With two of the three self-corrections, she sounds out the word. During instructional time, the teacher will help Jodi develop strategies to use the other cueing systems that she currently does not use,

such as reading to the end of the sentence and then going back to insert a word that makes sense. The student must determine if the inserted word begins with the same sound as the printed word. For example, the student may provide the word *winding* for *raggedy,* which makes sense, but the printed word begins with an *r.* The teacher prompts the student to use other clues to decode "raggedy."

As previously stated, running records can be tallied on a sheet of plain paper. However, for beginning teachers and tutors, the blank form in Appendix C.11 may prove helpful. The top of the form includes spaces for the reader's name, the name of the story, the quantitative score, and some general notes about the reading. As mentioned earlier, you can use the blank form together with the videos at **www.hhpcommunities.com/literacyassessment** for experience administering a running record.

Cloze Tests

The **cloze test** is another informal reading assessment. The purpose of the cloze test is twofold—for informal assessment and for instruction. When used for assessment, the cloze test helps a teacher to (1) understand how readers use context and background knowledge to figure out unknown words, and (2) determine if a text is too easy or too difficult for a particular reader. When used for instruction, the cloze test shows students how to use context clues and background knowledge to decipher unknown words. A cloze passage can be taken from any text and is 125 to 500 words long, depending on the reader's grade level. To construct a cloze test, delete every fifth word in the passage, while keeping the first and last lines intact. To calculate the reader's score, divide the total number of correct suggestions for missing words by the total number of blanks. For example, if there are 100 missing words and the student provides 80 correct responses, the student's final score is 80 percent.

The most valid scoring system for diagnostic purposes is to accept only the exact word from the original passage (Ruddell, 1964). When using the cloze test for instructional purposes, however, synonyms are acceptable (Gillet & Temple, 2004). When determining the reading level, the following scale is used:

Individual reading level = 60–100%
Instructional reading level = 40–59%
Frustration reading level = Below 40%

Later chapters will discuss in detail and provide examples of how to use cloze tests in instruction.

Figure 3.18 provides a short example of a cloze test from Chapter 1 of *Little Men: Life at Plumfield with Jo's Boys* by Louisa May Alcott (1913). Because the reader has only 12 correct responses—approximately 46 percent—the passage is at the reader's instructional level. Because most of the responses make sense, the teacher concludes that student reads for meaning and will be able to comprehend the passage with some instructional help. If the teacher observes the student during the reading, she will be able to detect the strategies the student uses.

figure 3.18   Sample cloze test.

CHAPTER 1

"Please, sir, is this Plumfield?" asked a ragged boy of the man who opened the great gate at which the omnibus left him.

"Yes; who sent you?"

"__1__ [Hello] Laurence. I have got __2__ [a] letter for the lady."

"__3__ [All] right; go up to __4__ [the] house and give it __5__ [to] her; she'll see to __6__ [it], little chap."

The man __7__ [talked] pleasantly, and the boy __8__ [walked] on, feeling much cheered __9__ [by] the words. Through the __10__ [new] spring rain that fell __11__ [on] sprouting grass and budding __12__ [flowers], Nat saw a large __13__ [green] house before him—a __14__ [big] house, with an old-fashioned __15__ [porch], with wide steps, and lights __16__ [on] in many windows. Neither __17__ [curtains] nor shutters hid the __18__ [shiny] glimmer; and, pausing a __19__ [second] before he rang, Nat __20__ [saw] many little shadows dancing __21__ [on] the walls, heard the __22__ [cheerful] hum of young voices, __23__ [and] felt that it was __24__ [just] possible that the light __25__ [and] warmth and comfort within __26__ [would] be for a homeless "little chap" like him.

"I hope the lady will see to me," he thought; and gave a timid rap with the great bronze knocker, which was a jovial griffin's head.

ANSWERS:

1. Mr.	2. a	3. All	4. the	5. to	6. you
7. spoke	8. went	9. by	10. soft	11. on	12. trees
13. square	14. hospitable-looking	15. porch	16. shining	17. curtains	18. cheerful
19. moment	20. saw	21. on	22. pleasant	23. and	24. hardly
25. and	26. could				

Source: Excerpt from *Little Men: Life at Plumfield with Jo's Boys,* by Louisa M. Alcott. Copyright © 1913, Little, Brown, & Co.

Does he read to the end of the sentence to figure out the missing word? Does he read past the sentence to figure out the missing word? Based on observation, the teacher introduces the strategies not used by the student.

Maze Tests

The **maze test** is much like the cloze test in purpose and construction. Its purpose is to allow younger students to demonstrate what context clues and background knowledge they use when they encounter unknown words. Like the cloze test, the maze test can be used for diagnostic and for instructional purposes. To construct a maze test, again delete every fifth word while keeping the first and last sentences intact. However, instead of leaving a blank, give students three choices. One choice is correct; one fits the sentence's syntax; and the third choice does not fit the sentence in any way. Figure 3.19 presents a short example from Paula Danziger's (2001) *A Is for Amber: It's Justin Time, Amber Brown*. The maze test works best when the teacher observes the student during the process and notes whether the student rereads sentences, reads beyond the word choice, or reads beyond the sentence to figure out the word.

Anecdotal Records

Anecdotal records refer to notes a teacher makes about student behavior. Anecdotal records follow no criteria or standards; they are merely a teacher's observations about a student's habits, attitudes, or abilities. A teacher may record changes in attitude for one student and changes in the reading strategies for another. The notes can be taken in a number of ways. Some teachers keep anecdotal records in a file folder for each student; some use a three-ring notebook; and others maintain a digital record. Each teacher should select a method that is compatible with her organizational style, begin taking notes at the start of the school year, and continue until year's end.

Mr. Jackson, a first-grade teacher, and Mr. Green, a second-grade teacher, both keep anecdotal records for their students. At the beginning of the year Mr. Jackson notes that Ali is shy and appears to have neg-

figure **3.19**   Maze test for *A Is for Amber: It's Justin Time, Amber Brown* by Paula Danziger.

I, Amber Brown,

am one very excited six-year,

364-day-old kid.

I am so excited

      1.   2.

(which, that, too) I am dancing with (your, two, my) toy gorilla.

        3.

He is (a, that, for) two-year,

364-day-old gorilla.

      4.   5.

I (have, got, by) him on my fourth (school, built, birthday).

          6.

Tomorrow, July 7, is our (fun, birthday, bottle).

          7.

Last year I was (seven, five, six) on July 7.

        8.   9.

Next year (I, we, too) will be eight on (August 3, birthday, July 7).

This year I will be seven on July 7. (p. 5)

ANSWERS:

| 1. that | 2. my | 3. a | 4. got | 5. birthday |
| 6. birthday | 7. six | 8. I | 9. July 7 | |

Mr. Jackson's anecdotal record.

STUDENT: Ali   GRADE: 1st

DATE: COMMENTS

9-10   Ali readily went to the back of the group rug during shared book reading when other children pushed her. During the reading of the story, she did not pay attention and offered no comments to the class discussion.

9-12   Ali sat right in the middle of the horseshoe table during guided reading, facing me. She pointed to each word as we read in unison. She contributed to group discussion. She appears to have a speech impediment.

9-13   During guided reading, she sat at the end of the horseshoe table, next to me. She did not follow along with her finger. She did not read in unison with group and gave no comments during discussion.

9-17   During shared reading, she sat right in front of me and chimed in on "Catch me if you can." She added comments during discussion. She definitely has a speech problem. I referred her to Ms. Wilson, the speech teacher.

9-18   Ms. Wilson reported that Ali has a hearing problem. She called her mother. Ali reads lips.

9-19   During guided reading, Ali sat directly in front of me so she could hear and read my lips. She participated in unison reading and discussion. She told me she gets to go to the hospital to get her ears fixed.

9-24   Ali had tubes put into her ears.

10-1   During guided reading, she sat at the end of the table and participated. She told me she can hear now!

10-2   During shared reading, she sat at the back of the rug and chimed in and discussed questions with the group.

ative feelings about reading. As you read the anecdotal records for Ali in Figure 3.20, note how Mr. Jackson detects the problem that hinders Ali from becoming engaged in the reading activities. Figure 3.21 displays Mr. Green's digital notes about Rosa, whose native language is Spanish. His notes are based on Rosa's reading habits. Mr. Green records the instructional strategies he uses to help Rosa become a more proficient reader. Notice that Mr. Green's notes are very detailed. Not all anecdotal records need to be as thorough.

Checklists

Checklists allow teachers to gauge students' literacy gains throughout the year. A checklist includes all traits the teacher expects students to display by the end of the school year. Each observation is dated; the checklist may include a column to mark "yes" if the trait is observed or "no" if it is not. Symbols may be used to show consistency of a trait (e.g., a plus sign means "always observed," a check means "sometimes

Mr. Green's anecdotal record.

observed," and a zero means "seldom observed"). Symbols may also be used to indicate degrees of mastery of a trait (e.g., a plus sign means "target," a check means "acceptable," and a zero means "unacceptable").

The objective of a checklist is threefold: (1) to assist a teacher as he observes a student's behavior or performance; (2) to assist a teacher as he plans for instruction; and (3) "to compare evidence of behavior over time and thus help determine student progress" (Cooper & Kiger, 2005, p. 31). To design a checklist, a teacher includes a list of competencies—often based on national or state standards or benchmarks—that all students are expected to attain by the end of the school year. The checklist may be used at the end of each quarter so the teacher can analyze which students are meeting the standards and which students need more instructional time and practice.

To illustrate the design of a checklist based on CCSS foundational reading phonics and word recognition skills, Figure 3.22 shows a partial checklist that was completed after the first grading period. Using this tool, the teacher can see which students are progressing and who needs extra help. Appendix C.12 provides a blank checklist for observing students' progress that can be used with any standards.

This checklist in Figure 3.22 gives the date and the names of the students. The plus sign (+) indicates that the student performs the task all the time, an X indicates that the student performs the task sometimes, and a zero (0) means that the student does not perform the task. As you can tell, this type of assessment also provides a general assessment of the class. From this assessment, the teacher can readily note which standards no one in the class has met and thus need to be addressed.

Another checklist, based on the CCSS ELA CCR Anchor Standards for Reading, is provided in Appendix C.13. This checklist is specific to one student and records the context in which each behavior was observed. The teacher may use this type of checklist to show the student and his caregivers his progress in meeting national standards. Checklists that do not include the context are more subjective and serve as general guidelines for teachers.

The Literacy Habits checklists in Appendices C.14–C.18 are intended for use with early emergent through proficient readers. A teacher may need to use two consecutive checklists to get accurate records of the student's behavior. Later chapters will discuss other checklists for assessing specific aspects of literacy.

figure 3.22 Partial checklist for second grade, based on the CCSS Foundational Reading Skills for phonics and word recognition.

TEACHER Mr. Reinhart   Grading Period ① 2   3   4

+ = always   x = sometimes   0 = seldom/never

STANDARD	Kourtlyn	Kim	Gillian	Quinton	R. J.	Arielle	Coy	Zachary	Rosa	Alexis	Gabrielle	Mat	Blake	Taylor	Teagan	Josh	Zeb	Tyler
1. Distinguish long and short vowels when reading regularly spelled one-syllable words.	+	X	X	+	+	X	O	O	+	+	+	X	X	+	+	+	X	O
2. Know spelling–sound correspondences for additional common vowel teams.	X	O	X	+	+	O	O	O	+	X	+	X	O	+	+	+	O	O
3. Decode regularly spelled two-syllable words with long vowels.	+	O	X	+	O	O	O	O	O	X	+	O	O	O	+	+	O	O
4. Decode words with common prefixes and suffixes.	X	O	O	+	O	O	O	O	O	O	+	O	O	O	+	+	O	O

Source: Standards based on CCSS (2010), English Language Arts Standards, Reading: Foundational Skills, Grade 2. Washington, DC: NGACBP, CCSSO, p. 16.

Rubrics

A **rubric** "describes the knowledge and skills a particular project or performance demonstrates, based on specific criteria for quality work" (Fiderer, 1999, p. 5). Like checklists, rubrics list competencies that students are expected to master. Unlike checklists, rubrics are *scoring guides* for particular assignments or for an evaluation period within the school year. Most rubrics describe three or four levels of achievement or performance. Each level gives a detailed explanation of the degree of mastery and/or a numerical score. Often the same rubric is used for similar assignments throughout the year so it can document student growth in a particular area. The rubric in Figure 3.23, used at the end of each grading period, gives a detailed explanation of degrees of mastery for the CCSS Reading: Informational Texts standards for second grade.

The rubric in Figure 3.23, which closely reflects the CCSS, helps the teacher focus on each item in the standards. Note that the rubric's target degree of mastery (4–5 points) corresponds with the CCSS; the other two degrees of mastery—acceptable (2–3 points) and unacceptable (0–1 point)—represent the degree to which the student has met the standard.

If the teacher uses the same rubric each quarter, she can document each student's progress in reading comprehension. If the entire class is weak in one or two areas, she can readily tell which part of the standard she needs to emphasize with the class. The rubric will also identify the weaknesses of individual students.

Figure 3.23 presents Victor's rubric at the end of the first grading period, completed by his teacher after viewing Victor's running records and miscue analyses for nine weeks. Obviously, at the end of the first grading period, no second grader would have reached the target degree of mastery in each part of the standards; therefore, Victor will not score a 100 percent (50 points) for the grading period. One goal for the next nine weeks to improve Victor's learning from his reading would be to have him complete a graphic organizer as he reads or after he reads a section of a text. Before reading a text,

figure 3.23 Rubric for reading informational texts based on the CCSS, Second Grade Reading: Informational Texts standards.

STUDENT: *Victor*   GRADING PERIOD ①2 3 4   TOTAL SCORE: *16*

TRAIT	TARGET (4–5 POINTS)	ACCEPTABLE (2–3 POINTS)	UNACCEPTABLE (0–1 POINT)
1. W Questions	Ask and answer *who, what, where, when, why, how* questions to demonstrate understanding of key details in text. _____	Answers *who, what, where, when* questions to demonstrate understanding of main details. _____	Answers only *who* and *what* questions. _X_
2. Main Topic	Identify the main topic of a multi-paragraph text as well as the focus of specific paragraphs within the text. _____	Identify the main topic of multi-paragraph text. _____	Cannot identify main topic of paragraphs. _X_
3. Connection among concepts	Describe the connection between a series of historical events, scientific ideas or concepts, or steps in technical procedures in a text. _____	Describe the connection between one or two series of historical events, scientific concepts, or technical procedures in a text. _____	Cannot make connections between ideas in a text. _X_
4. Vocabulary	Determine the meaning of words and phrases in a text relevant to a grade 2 topic or subject area._____	Can determine the meaning of most technical words in a text relevant to grade 2 topic or subject area. _X_	Cannot determine the meaning of technical words in a text relevant to grade 2 topic or subject area. _____
5. Text Features	Know and use various text features (captions, bold print, subheadings, glossaries, indexes, electronic menus, icons) to locate key facts or information in a text efficiently. _____	Knows and uses most text features (captions, bold print, subheadings, glossaries, indexes, electronic menus and icons) with scaffolding from teacher or another adult. _X_	Forgets the importance of using text features in a text. _____

(continued)

figure **3.23** Continued.

TRAIT	TARGET (4–5 POINTS)	ACCEPTABLE (2–3 POINTS)	UNACCEPTABLE (0–1 POINT)
6. Main purpose of author	Identify the main purpose of a text, including what the author wants to answer, explain, or describe. _____	Identify the main purpose of a text, including what the author wants to answer or explain with scaffolding from teacher or another adult. _____	Finds it difficult to identify the main purpose of text, including what the author wants to explain, answer, or describe. _X_
7. Explanation of visuals	Explain how specific images (diagrams) contribute to and clarify a text. _____	With scaffolding from teacher, can explain how specific images contribute to and clarify a text. _X_	Cannot explain how specific images contribute to and clarify a text. _____
8. Support of points	Describe how reasons support specific points the author makes in a text. _____	With scaffolding from teacher can describe how reasons support specific points the author makes in a text. _____	Cannot describe how reasons support specific points the author makes in a text. _X_
9. Compare/ contrast points of two texts on same topic	Compare and contrast the most important points presented by two texts on the same topic. _____	With scaffolding from teacher, can compare and contrast the most important points presented by two texts on the same topic. _____	Cannot compare and contrast the most important points presented in two texts on the same topic. _X_
10. Reading complex text independently	Comprehend informational texts, including history/social studies, science and technical texts, in the grades 2–3 text complexity band proficiently with scaffolding as needed at the high end of the range. _____	With support can comprehend informational texts, including history/social studies, science and technical texts, in the grades 2–3 text complexity band in the middle range. _____	Cannot comprehend informational text in the grades 2–3 text complexity band even with much scaffolding from teacher. _X_

TEACHER COMMENTS: Victor is an auditory learner who has much background knowledge that he has learned from watching educational television programs. Therefore, he knows most technical terms and is quick to look at pictures in a text. During class, he often reads captions of pictures and charts. However, he has a difficult time learning from texts that he reads.

Source: Standards based on CCSS (2010), English Language Arts Standards, Reading: Informational Text, Grade 2. Washington, DC: NGACBP, CCSSO, p. 13.

he should be encouraged to read to answer the following questions: *where, when, why,* and *how?*

Rubrics for a variety of subjects can be accessed at http://Rubistar.4teachers.org. The rubrics at this site fall into eight main categories—oral projects, research/writing, work skills, multimedia, science, math, music, and art. There are rubrics in English, Spanish, and Dutch. The user can modify the rubrics to fit a particular assignment. More rubrics are available on the PARCC website to help teachers prepare their students for the PARCC assessments. Figure 3.24 has the expanded scoring rubric for analytic and narrative writing for grades four and five.

Portfolios

Portfolios are collections of students' work from the school year. They are useful tools to organize materials, document growth, and display exemplary work. Portfolios can be file folders, three-ring binders, or electronic files. It is helpful for each portfolio to include a log to record the title of the composition or passage read and the date it was completed. There are three types of portfolios—working portfolios, best-work portfolios, and growth portfolios. Any of these can be in an electronic rather than a physical format.

figure **3.24**   PARCC Condensed Scoring Rubric for Prose Constructed Responses, Grades 4–5.

CONSTRUCT MEASURED	SCORE POINT 4	SCORE POINT 3	SCORE POINT 2	SCORE POINT 1	SCORE POINT 0
READING Comprehension of Key Ideas and Details *Notes: The type of textual evidence required is grade and prompt specific and included in the scoring guide.		—The student response provides an accurate analysis of what the text says explicitly and inferentially and references the text explicitly to support the analysis, showing full comprehension of complex ideas expressed in the text(s).	—The student response provides a mostly accurate analysis of what the text says explicitly and inferentially and references the text to support the analysis, showing extensive comprehension of ideas expressed in the text(s).	—The student response provides a minimally accurate analysis of what the text says and may reference the text showing limited comprehension of ideas expressed in the text(s).	—The student response provides an inaccurate analysis or no analysis of the text, showing little to no comprehension of ideas expressed in the text(s).
WRITING Written Expression		—The student response addresses the prompt and provides effective and comprehensive development of the topic and/or narrative elements by using clear reasoning, details, and/or description; the development is consistently appropriate to the task, purpose, and audience. —The student response demonstrates effective coherence, clarity, and cohesion and includes a strong introduction and conclusion. —The student response uses language well to attend to the norms and conventions of the discipline. The response includes concrete words and phrases, sensory details, linking and transitional words, and/or domain-specific vocabulary effectively to clarify ideas.	—The student response addresses the prompt and provides effective development of the topic and/or narrative elements by using reasoning, details, and/or description; the development is largely appropriate to the task, purpose, and audience. —The student response demonstrates coherence, clarity, and cohesion, and includes an introduction and conclusion. —The student response attends to the norms and conventions of the discipline. The response includes concrete words and phrases, sensory details, linking and transitional words, and/or domain-specific vocabulary to clarify ideas.	—The student response addresses the prompt and develops the topic and/or narrative elements minimally by using limited reasoning, details, and/or description; the development is limited in its appropriateness to the task, purpose, and/or audience. —The student response demonstrates limited coherence, clarity, and/or cohesion, and may or may not include a clear introduction and/or conclusion. —The student response shows limited awareness of the norms of the discipline. The response includes limited descriptions, sensory details, linking and transitional words, or domain-specific vocabulary to clarify ideas.	—The student response is under-developed and therefore inappropriate to the task, purpose, and/or audience. —The student response demonstrates a lack of coherence, clarity, and cohesion. —The student response shows little to no awareness of the norms of the discipline. The student response lacks the descriptions, sensory details, linking and transitional words, or domain-specific vocabulary needed to clarify ideas.

(continued)

figure **3.24** Continued.

CONSTRUCT MEASURED	SCORE POINT 4	SCORE POINT 3	SCORE POINT 2	SCORE POINT 1	SCORE POINT 0
WRITING Knowledge of Language and Conventions	—The student response demonstrates command of the conventions of standard English consistent with effectively edited writing. Though there may be a few minor errors in grammar and usage, meaning is clear throughout the response.	—The student response demonstrates command of the conventions of standard English consistent with edited writing. There may be a few distracting errors in grammar and usage, but meaning is clear.	—The student response demonstrates inconsistent command of the conventions of standard English. There are a few patterns of errors in grammar and usage that may occasionally impede understanding.	—The student response demonstrates limited command of the conventions of standard English. There are multiple errors in grammar and usage demonstrating minimal control over language. There are multiple distracting errors in grammar and usage that sometimes impede understanding.	—The student response demonstrates little to no command of the conventions of standard English. There are frequent and varied errors in grammar and usage, demonstrating little or no control over language. There are frequent distracting errors in grammar and usage that often impede understanding.

NOTE:

- The reading dimension is not scored for elicited narrative stories.
- Per the CCSS, narrative elements in grades 3–5 may include: establishing a situation, organizing a logical event sequence, describing scenes, objects, or people, developing characters' personalities, and using dialogue as appropriate.
- The elements of organization to be assessed are expressed in the grade-level standards W1–W3 and elucidated in the scoring rules for each individual PCR.

Coded Response (all coded responses are scored with a 0 on the rubric):

A = No response

B = Response is unintelligible or undecipherable

C = Response is not written in English

D = Response is too limited to evaluate

Note—additional codes may be added after the tryout or field testing of tasks.

Source: www.parcconline.org/sites/parcc/files/Grade4-5-ELACondensedRubricFORANALYTICANDNARRATIVEWRITING.pdf

Working portfolios

Working portfolios organize a student's work-in-progress. For example, a working portfolio for reading may contain a recording that the student is using to increase reading expression, rate, or fluency. If a student is writing a research report, the working portfolio may contain prewriting graphic organizers; notes taken from sources; a list of sources; all drafts and revisions; the editing copy; and the final copy. After the teacher has assessed and discussed the process and result of the project, the final copy of the composition, poem, or report is placed in the growth portfolio.

Growth portfolios

Teachers usually have one growth portfolio for reading, one for writing, and another for math or other subjects. The **growth portfolio** contains final copies of the student's work along with their scoring rubrics.

Because they contain samples of a student's work over time, growth portfolios are valuable assessment tools for documenting achievement in reading and writing. For example, a growth portfolio may include an audio recording of the student's monthly reading. With each reading, the teacher includes a miscue analysis, a running record, and/or anecdotal records, as well as checklists and rubrics used to assess the student's reading ability. The teacher then uses the recording to (1) discuss reading strengths and weaknesses with students and parents, (2) plan for future instruction, and (3) encourage readers' abilities.

Teachers can share the growth portfolios during parent–teacher conferences to illustrate the particular literacy skills the students are developing or need to develop. It will also help the teacher and caregiver identify the areas in which the student may need extra help. For example, if a second-grade student cannot retell a story in the correct sequence by the end of the third grading period, the teacher and caregiver know that they need to give the student opportunities to develop that skill. Portfolios are tools to encourage the caregiver and the student about the student's growth.

Best-work portfolios

If the student believes that an item represents his best work, he places a copy of it in his **best-work portfolio**. The best-work writing portfolio may contain poems, stories, reports, and newspaper articles, each accompanied by a self-assessment sheet explaining why the student believes it is one of his best works. The best-work reading portfolio may include selections from the student's favorite stories, poems, and other passages. The student reviews each selection and chooses to keep it as a favorite story, poem, or passage.

Electronic portfolios

The contents of electronic portfolios are usually the same as the file-folder and three-ring binder versions, but items are saved digitally. The electronic portfolio contains scanned forms, student writings, audio versions of students' readings, digital photographs, and videos. The material is stored electronically. Teachers and students use equipment such as scanners, digital and video cameras, audio recorders, and portfolio software to create and organize the contents.

One flexible software program is the *Scholastic Electronic Portfolio*. The program permits the teacher to store text, record a student's readings, and make slide shows and videos. The program comes with a detailed manual for teachers.

Another software program that can be used in primary and middle school is *The Portfolio Assessment Kit,* produced by Super School Software. This program is designed for the Mac but can be transferred to PCs. It allows student writing to be stored and viewed easily; teachers can use it to scan rubrics, checklists, logs, and anecdotal records that can be shared with caregivers during conferences. All records can be viewed on the screen and printed out. A third software program, useful to elementary and middle school teachers, is *The Portfolio Builder for PowerPoint,* produced by Visions-Technology in Education. This program permits users to create graphics, sound, and video in addition to text.

Study the capabilities of several portfolio programs before you purchase one. Ask yourself, (1) What do I want to accomplish with the program? (2) Is it complicated and time consuming to operate? (3) Can students readily learn how to use it?

INFORMAL ASSESSMENT FOR ENGLISH LEARNERS

The two assessments for English learners discussed earlier, the LAS–O and LAS–R/W, measure general growth, but they are not diagnostic-oriented (Kuhlman, 2005). Classroom teachers, especially in grades four and up, require additional methods to measure English learners' literacy development in teacher-designed, subject-area tests such as science, social studies, math, and health education. Lenski, Ehlers-Zavala, Daniel, and Sun-Irminger (2006) suggest authentic performance assessments for this purpose.

Lenski et al. (2006) use Hurley and Blake's (2000) six guiding principles for teachers as they consider authentic performance assessments. They are:

1. Assessment activities should help teachers make instructional decisions.
2. Assessment strategies should help teachers find out what students know and can do . . . not what they cannot do.
3. The holistic context for learning should be considered and assessed.
4. Assessment activities should grow out of authentic learning activities.
5. Best assessments of student learning are longitudinal . . . they take place over time.
6. Each assessment activity should have a specific objective-linked purpose. (Lenski et al., p. 25)

Depending on the information teachers seek about an English learner, they can choose from several types of authentic assessments. The first type of authentic assessment measures an English learner's knowledge base. Teachers determine this knowledge base by interviewing the student, family members, former teachers, and any community worker who may have assisted in the student's literacy development. From these sources teachers determine what type of formal education (if any) the students have had or are receiving in their native language, including whether the students currently attend literacy classes in their native language. This assessment aids the teacher's understanding of the student's background. Never assume that all English learners with the same first language have had similar experiences.

The second type of authentic assessment permits students to demonstrate what they know using non-language methods. These include Venn diagrams, charts, drawings, slide presentations, or other multimodal methods. See Chapters 8 and 9.

The third type of assessment is observation. Teachers observe students' abilities and willingness to participate in literacy discussions and small group circles and work with their peers.

The **language experience approach (LEA)** is an instructional strategy that can also be used for assessment. The teacher writes the text as the student dictates the "experience"; then the teacher informally assesses the student each time he reads it back. The teacher assesses the correct pronunciation of words, the prosody, and fluency. The student may also note syntax errors that he made in the initial dictation.

To encourage students to self-monitor their development, teachers may have them write reflections on the LEA. Students may reflect how the content connects to another subject or how one story reminds them of another.

Teachers can also authentically assess English learners by modifying a teacher-created test. The following modifications from Lenski et al. (2006) are in addition to those listed earlier in the chapter:

1. Give the test orally. Assess content knowledge by reading the test to students and permitting them to answer orally. If the teacher wants to assess the student's reading ability, the student can read the text and answer the questions orally. Often students' reading (receptive) skills are stronger than their writing (expressive) skills. Letting them answer orally bypasses their weaker writing skills but allows the teacher to assess their stronger reading skills.

2. Give the test in small segments. English learners may read more slowly than other students and process information in their native language before answering in English. This takes more time than reading, thinking, and answering in English. Dividing the test into small segments will keep students from becoming exhausted and giving up on the task.

3. Use as many visuals as possible. The visuals can include photos, drawings, charts, diagrams, or any type of graphic organizer.

4. Permit students to use glossaries in English or in their native language.

5. Simplify vocabulary and sentence structures by using synonyms and simple sentences.

6. Simplify directions so English learners understand how to complete the assessment.

7. Write tasks instead of questions, using imperative statements. For example, instead of "Who signed the Declaration of Independence?" state: "Write the names of the men who signed (wrote their names at the bottom of) the Declaration of Independence."

8. Permit students to take breaks during the assessment. Tests in middle school often last the entire 45- or 50-minute period; allowing a small break for students to stretch or rest their eyes will prevent them from becoming exhausted and rushing to finish the task.

9. Give double grades on essay tests, one for correct responses and another for grammatical correctness.

One free website designed to informally assess English learners in many different subject areas is http://world-english.org. This site has online assessment tests in vocabulary, grammar, reading comprehension, listening, writing, literature-based quizzes on Shakespeare and novels, and WebQuests that assess world-content knowledge. The grammar tests assess student's knowledge in Standard English usage, while the reading comprehension tests require the student to read a passage and answer the questions. All these assessments begin at an easy level and become more difficult if the student's answers are correct. With some of the multiple-choice tests, if the student answers incorrectly, the same question appears later with the answers given in a different order. The computer indicates immediately if the answer is correct, and the student receives her score at the end of the test.

As discussed above, teachers and districts can use both formal and informal or authentic assessments to determine the individual literacy development of English learners and whether or not the district's literacy program is meeting these students' needs.

PERSONAL INTEREST SURVEYS

As I discussed in Chapter 2, students' motivation highly affects their reading. If you know each student's interests, you can provide them with more effective, individualized reading and writing opportunities that will motivate them to engage in the activities. Figure 3.25 is a personal interest survey for young students. The teacher should be the scribe so the student will express what he really likes without worrying about spelling or grammar. Try extending the interest inventory if the student expresses interest in things not on the survey. To illustrate how the interest survey can provide the student with more meaningful literacy experiences, Figure 3.25 suggests that Grey enjoys spending time with his grandpa. His teacher can then look for stories about grandparents, such as Tomie dePaola's *Tom*.

Personal interest surveys are also useful for older students. Some may enjoy informational books or magazines but dislike funny stories. Others may not like informational books but enjoy mysteries or graphic texts. Older students should complete the surveys themselves to ensure honest responses. If they give their responses verbally, they may tend to give what they believe is the "correct" answer, rather than an honest answer. Use the completed surveys to find materials that interest the students. Figure 3.26 contains a partially completed personal interest survey for older students; Appendix C.19 contains the full survey.

figure 3.25 Personal interest survey for young students.

MY FAVORITES!
By Grey

Foods:
  pizza
  grandpa's waffles

Snacks:
  apples
  grapes

Hunt for bugs

Swim by
grandpa's house

Sleep over by
grandpa's house

Read:
  about snakes, bugs,
  wild animals

Don't like to write!

I am a star at _____Rollerblades._____

I like to _____read_____ alone.

I like to _____play video games_____ with friends.

I like to _____ride bike_____ with my family.

My favorite things to do on Saturday and Sunday are _____rollerblade in the park with grandpa._____

figure 3.26 Partial personal interest survey for older students.

NAME: LaVonda   GRADE: 6   QUARTER: 1st

List more than one item for each category if you have more interests. Explain why you gave each response. For example, why do you enjoy researching (*your favorite topic*) on the Internet?

1. My favorite subjects in school are _____music and art because I like to sing and draw_____.

2. My least favorite subject in school is _____science because it is hard_____.

3. My favorite topic to research on the Internet is _____art galleries to learn about them_____.

4. My favorite topic to study in science is _____weather because it is interesting_____.

5. My favorite foreign country to study is _____Italy because I would like to go there_____.

ATTITUDE SURVEYS

Teachers must gain insight into their students' attitudes. Some are quite happy when someone else reads to or writes for them, but they dislike reading aloud or writing of any kind. When students have strong dislikes for reading and/or writing, attempt to understand why. They may find it boring or too hard, or they may be afraid of failure. You need to help students change these negative attitudes so they will not avoid these crucial activities. Once you understand what reading and writing events a student dislikes and why, you can help him build a more positive attitude.

Appendices C.20–C.24 include Reading and Writing Attitude Surveys for primary and older students. The scoring sheet found in Appendix C.22 can be used for the primary reading and the primary writing attitude surveys. The pre- and post-test scores are recorded on this sheet. To score them, the teacher gives four points for each circled happy character, three points for each circled somewhat-happy character, two points for each neutral character, and one point for each unhappy character. The higher the score, the more interest the student has in reading or writing.

"Collecting data about students is an empty exercise unless the information is used to plan instruction" (McKenna & Kear, 1990, p. 627). With any attitude survey, the quantitative score is not as important as the information the student shares about each statement. According to the criteria above, a score of 20 indicates that a student does not have a positive attitude toward any kind of writing, while a score of 80 indicates the opposite. However, one teacher discovered that one of her students circled the happy character only because it seemed friendlier than the others. Thus, teachers should take time to discuss the survey. The conversation may indicate that the student likes to write about himself or his pets, but dislikes composing letters to authors, thank-you notes, poems, or riddles.

It is also important to remember that attitude surveys do not indicate the sources of poor attitudes, nor do they give suggestions about instructional techniques that will change them (McKenna & Kear, 1990).

These surveys are effective pre- and post-tests. After a student is tutored by a teacher, paraprofessional, or adult volunteer, the surveys will hopefully reflect a change in attitude.

LITERACY SELF-PERCEPTION SCALES

Literacy self-perception scales provide a picture of how students feel about themselves as readers and writers. The Reader Self-Perception Scale (RSPS; Henk & Melnick, 1995) and the Writer Self-Perception Scale (WSPS; Bottomley, Henk, & Melnick, 1998) have been validated systematically. Teachers conducting experimental studies and needing validated assessment instruments may find these useful. Both surveys, with the directions for administering, scoring, and interpreting them, are found in Appendices C.25 and C.26.

STUDENT SELF-ASSESSMENT

Assessment by a teacher is important, but self-assessment by students can also increase self-esteem and the motivation to read and write.

Book Logs

When students log the texts they read and indicate their likes and dislikes, they see themselves as having a voice in the reading process. These logs also help them determine their preferences for informational or narrative text, genre, and authors. The log in Figure 3.27 (also found in Appendix C.27) allows primary students to record their reading habits. At the end of a grading period they can check how many texts they read and note their favorite authors and illustrators.

Even young children have a preference for certain authors and illustrators over others. They can simply circle the face that fits their attitude toward the text. Figure 3.28 (also found in Appendix C.28) has a similar log form for more advanced readers. They also record the genre and how long it took them to read each text. In the comments column, they can indicate if they would recommend the text to others or if they liked a particular character. This column is not intended to be used as a book report.

Skill Logs

When students log their skills, they have a repository of strategies to turn to when they struggle with a passage. For younger students, you can record the strategies taught during a teacher–student conference. Older students can record what they learned in the conference with the teacher, with a peer, or by themselves.

When stumped on a task, students can then look back at the strategies in their log for help. It also gives them a record of what they have learned over a period of time. These sheets are also helpful during home–school conferences to show caregivers what a student has learned. Logs also let students list information about different genres and authors. The form in Figure 3.29 is a sample form for a second-grade reader. The form in Figure 3.30 is designed for older students to record details about genres and authors.

figure 3.27 Book log for primary school student.

RECORD OF BOOKS _____Chao_____ READ   GRADE: __2__

Circle the face that best shows how you feel about the book.

BOOK	AUTHOR/ILLUSTRATOR	COMMENTS
The Little Red Hen Makes Pizza	Philemon Sturges/Amy Walrod	☺ ☺ ☹
Raccoons	Melvin & Gilda Berger	☺ ☺ ☹
Gumbrella	Barry Root	☺ ☺ ☹
26 Fairmount Avenue	Tomie dePaola	☺ ☺ ☹
Chipmunks	Melvin & Gilda Berger	☺ ☺ ☹
Here We All Are	Tomie dePaola	☺ ☺ ☹
Fables from Aesop	Tom Lynch	☺ ☺ ☹
Deer	Melvin & Gilda Berger	☺ ☺ ☹

figure 3.28 Book log for older student.

BOOKS THAT _____Kalee_____ READ   GRADE: __5__   QUARTER ① 2 3 4

TEXT	AUTHOR	GENRE	DATE STARTED/ENDED	COMMENTS
Mister and Me	Kimberly Willis Holt	Realistic fiction	8/24–8/26	Very easy reading. My mom is dating too and I know how Jolene felt.
Choosing Up Sides	John Ritter	Realistic fiction	9/1–9/5	I recommended this to Jack because his dad is a preacher.
Don't You Know There's a War On?	Avi	Realistic/Historical fiction	9/10–9/12	It was so funny! I loved it!
Graveyard Girl	Anna Myers	Historical fiction	9/13–9/14	Loved it! But it was so sad! I cried.
We've Got a Job: The Birmingham Children's March	C. Levison	Informational text	9/18–9/19	It showed the courage of children.
Surviving the Hindenburg	L. Gester Verstraete	Informational text	9/21	Short! Excellent details
Beyond Courage:	D. Rappaport	Informational text	9/25–9/26	I learned many new facts I never read before

My favorite book I read this quarter was ___Mister and Me___

because ___my mom is dating again and I treat my mom badly too.___

figure 3.29 Skills list for primary school student.

FOR QUARTER   1 ② 3 4

Things that _____Syndee_____ learned to do as a reader.

1. Stop at the periods (.)
2. Point to every word as I read it.
3. Raise my voice with questions (?)
4. Get excited when I see !
5. Read to the end of the sentence when I come to a word I don't know. Then ask, "What word would make sense?" Also look at pictures.

figure 3.30 Skills list for older student.

FOR QUARTER   1 2 ③ 4

Things that _____Hayley_____ learned to do as a reader.

1. Sometimes authors don't use explanatory words.
2. Authors can use flashbacks like movies do.
3. Authors use first person—you only know what that person thinks.
4. Authors use some real information in fiction.
5. Stories are interesting when authors use dialect.
6. Information follows a basic organizational structure (e.g. compare/contrast).
7. Details are new and presented in an interesting manner.
8. The photographs support the text.
9. The Index makes it easy to find key concepts.
10. The Table of Contents helps me locate chapters that interest me.

Reflection Logs

Teach your students to think about their reading habits. At the end of each quarter have them complete a form to summarize their thoughts, such as the one Sheila uses in Figure 3.31. (A blank form is in Appendix C.29.)

In the primary grades, the teacher confers with each student and writes the student's response to each statement. Older students write their responses before they meet with the teacher. Forms such as "My Thoughts About My Reading" challenge students to become lifelong reflective readers. Proficient readers reflect on aspects of texts they liked or disliked and think about why they prefer certain reading materials to others.

Accomplishment and Goal-Setting Logs

After students reflect on their reading habits and understand their preferences, they need to set literacy goals for themselves. Setting such goals gives students an active role in their literacy development. With the teacher's guidance, students should set realistic goals and determine how to accomplish them. A teacher can fill out the form with young students, while older students can fill out the form themselves and then discuss it with the teacher. Allowing students to set their own goals empowers them and makes them more likely to strive for the goal than if they had no voice in the process. Encourage your students to reach their goals by discussing them periodically throughout the grading period. Figure 3.32

figure 3.31 Reflection log.

MY THOUGHTS ABOUT MY READING

NAME ___Sheila___   GRADE: __6__   QUARTER ① 2 3 4

1. The informational books I read were about ___Composers and their compositions.___
2. The novels I read were mostly (realistic, (historical,) biographies, autobiographies, mysteries, science fiction, fantasy, folktales).
3. My favorite author is ___Avi.___
4. The best book I read was ___Don't You Know There's a War Going On?___
5. When I dislike a book, ___I put it back on the book shelf.___
6. My favorite place to read is ___on my bed.___
7. My reading habits at home are: ___I always read before I go to bed.___
8. I do not enjoy reading books ___that are science fiction.___
9. The book I recommended to my friends was ___Don't You Know There's a War Going On?___
10. After I read a book, I like to ___talk about it with Megan.___

figure 3.32 Accomplishment and goal-setting log.

ACCOMPLISHMENTS AND GOALS FOR READING

NAME ___India___   GRADE: __5__   QUARTER ① 2 3 4

ACCOMPLISHMENTS	GOALS	WAYS TO ACHIEVE GOALS
I read 2 chapter books. Both—realistic fiction. I re-read almost all the poems from A Light In the Attic.	Read at least 3 books— historical fiction.	Read at least 30 minutes each night and 1 hour on Sat. and Sun.
I also read 2 folktales on the "Starfall" website.	Read 2 comic strips from "Starfall" website.	Don't read books that are too hard for me.
I looked up three different topics for science class on the National Geographic website.	Read two e-texts about the Revolutionary War (our social studies topic for the next 9 weeks) so I learn to compare information from different authors.	Read a book that someone else recommends so I know it's good.
I read two picture books on the planets Mercury and Venus.	Read informational texts that are not story picture books.	Ask my teacher if I can go to the computer lab during independent reading time to search for more information on planets.

TEACHER'S COMMENTS:

Student's Signature _____

Teacher's Signature _____

is a form that Ms. Walker uses with her fifth-grade students to record their accomplishments and goals. It clearly shows that India has been working on becoming a faster reader so she can read more books and that she knows how to accomplish that goal.

TECHNOLOGY AND ASSESSMENT

Reluctant readers often are motivated to tackle any task—even tests—on the computer because it is different from paper and pencil tests. The Internet provides free resources for teachers to assess students in various literacy areas. Some free sites include:

Vocabulary Test, www.vocabtest.com. Offers vocabulary quizzes for grades six through AP senior level.

World-English, http://world-English.org. As mentioned earlier in this chapter, offers assessments in many literacy areas; students receive direct feedback and scores.

Apps: Assessment

Record of Reading (Free, Grades 1–3). Developed at Clemson University, this app assists in recording, administering, and analysis of running records. Using a stylus, a teacher can annotate the running record form (see Figure 3.33). Student records can be replayed, stored, reviewed, shared through email, and printed. The app is also integrated with Dropbox. Formulas in the app calculate a reader's accuracy and self-correction rates.

Reading Comprehension Prep ($2.99, Grades K–3). This app includes 12 passages, both fiction and nonfiction, with a variety of questions about each reading selection. It also offers the ability to create your own lessons with your own passages and assessments.

Kids Reading Comprehension Level 1 ($.99, Grades K–3). This app features short passages with brief assessments at their conclusion. The app allows tracking of up to four readers and provides progress reports about each student within the app.

Fluency Finder ($6.99, Grades 1–5). Although focused on grades 1–5, this app can also be used for kindergarten students who are more fluent readers and middle grade students who are struggling with reading. Students read from the passages provided while you tap buttons to record mistakes and self-corrections. The app enables you to assess your students' reading fluency and store the data for analysis of fluency growths or setbacks.

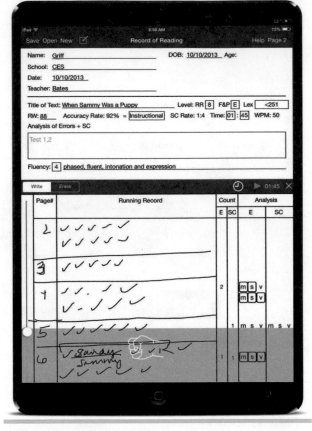

figure 3.33

Sample scored running record from the Record of Reading app.

Source: http://recordofreading.com/about/

Fountas & Pinnell Reading Record ($14.99, Grades K–8). This app allows you to code reading records in the *Fountas & Pinnell Benchmark Assessment* and *Leveled Literacy Intervention* systems. It provides oral reading rate, accuracy rate, self-correction ratio, and fluency and comprehension scores. The app also enables you to record the assessment conference.

Read With Me Fluency ($2.99, Grades 1–8). The app allows users to administer an informal reading inventory. It has a built-in library of three passages per grade level for grades 1–8. Users may also add their own passages. Students can be recorded while reading the passages, and the app has many options for analyzing and presenting the data.

Throughout the text, I will discuss other websites and apps that assess different aspects of literacy, including phonemic awareness, phonics, comprehension, vocabulary, and spelling, through game-like activities.

CONCLUDING THOUGHTS

Assessment instruments come in many varieties. Teachers use formative assessments on a daily basis to drive instruction and summative assessments at the end of each quarter to gauge whether students are reaching their end-of-the-year goals. Both formative and summative assessments show teachers which students are in need of more intensive individualized instruction.

Assessments can also be either formal or informal. Formal tests are standardized, which means they are given under controlled conditions. Formal tests include intelligence, achievement, and diagnostic tests. Achievement tests measure the achievement level of the student and can be either norm-referenced or criterion-referenced. Norm-referenced tests compare the performance of a student to the group on which the test was standardized. Criterion-referenced tests measure a skill that the student is expected to have mastered. Diagnostic tests have many subtests that assess a student's strengths and weaknesses in particular areas.

Teachers use informal assessment instruments to (1) diagnose reading problems, (2) check the reading level of a student, (3) analyze which cueing systems students use when making sense of print, (4) understand student attitudes toward reading and writing and help identify materials that interest them, (5) monitor student growth, (6) provide opportunities for students to reflect on literacy accomplishments, (7) help students set realistic goals, and (8) develop plans for instruction.

Formal and informal assessments are both useful for measuring students' literacy skills. Formal test scores indicate general abilities in various areas of literacy. Informal assessments, administered by classroom teachers, permit those teachers to observe students' behaviors while they make sense of print.

Rubrics, checklists, and anecdotal records serve as indicators of certain aspects of students' growth that cannot be measured on a test. Throughout this chapter and other chapters in this text, I have included checklists and rubrics for specific types of reading and writing activities. Many of the checklists, rubrics, surveys, and logs are designed to help you assess the entire reading process, which encompasses students' skills, attitudes, and interests. When you diligently assess the entire reading process, you can truly *teach the student and not the method!* All of the checklists and rubrics in this text are provided only as suggestions. You can create your own checklists and rubrics based on your curriculum and students' needs.

reflective learning

TESTING. After teaching first grade for a number of years, Grace Cho stayed at home with her son for several years. Last May Ms. Cho's family moved to a small town and she decided to return to teaching, since her son was older and she wanted to become involved in the community. She was excited when Mr. Day, the principal, told her she had the first-grade job, because the school has only one classroom per grade and she knew others had applied for the position. The interview had been brief because Mr. Day said her former school had recommended her highly. They never discussed new trends in education or testing.

Excited to teach again, Ms. Cho sets up her classroom the week before teacher orientation week. During teacher orientation, she keeps hearing about the Common Core State Standards and DIBELS—terms new to Ms. Cho. There is no other first-grade teacher to help her understand how these items impact teachers, and she is hesitant to ask the other teachers for fear of appearing unqualified.

During the first week of school, Principal Day hands Ms. Cho a set of the standards and DIBELS and tells her he wants the test administered, scored, and analyzed by the end of the third week so he can decide if he needs to hire a reading specialist that year. In reading the DIBELS instructional manual, she realizes the test needs to be administered individually. She is overwhelmed because she already has her curriculum planned for the first month.

questions

1. Should Ms. Cho seek help from Mr. Day or from another teacher?

2. How can she learn about the impact of adequate yearly progress and tests like DIBELS?

3. What are your recommendations for classroom management as she administers the individual tests?

4 Phonemic Awareness

To learn to read
is to light a fire:
every syllable that
is spelled out
is a spark.

VICTOR HUGO

scenario

Ms. Reyes is a kindergarten teacher who knows it is crucial to understand what each child knows about letters and their sounds at the beginning of the year. She plays a game to identify students who appear unable to distinguish sounds. The game format is ideal because most students perceive games as fun. Last year Ms. Reyes's students enjoyed playing various versions of the "train" game, with students listening carefully as the list grew longer and longer.

During the first week of school, Ms. Reyes gathers a group of six on the rug and explains that they are going to play a sound game. She says, "I will announce one sound of the alphabet, for example /d/, and I will begin with the sentence 'I know that *dog* begins with /d/.'" (Note: Ms. Reyes says the /d/ sound, not the letter name.) "I want the student next to me to repeat my sentence and my word, and then give another word with that sound. For example, the first student might say, 'I know that *dog* and *dirt* begin with /d/.' The second might say, 'I know that *dog, dirt,* and *dad* begin with /d/.'"

She encourages each student to listen carefully so he or she can remember the words that have already been said. When Ms. Reyes is sure they understand the game, she begins with the following: "I know that *milk* begins with /m/." After one round and a few errors, the students say, "Let's do it again." In the first round some students repeat the same word as a classmate, but everyone except Brandon gives a correct response.

"Ok," Ms. Reyes says, "let's do it again with /b/." She begins, "I know that *bag* begins with /b/." The second round goes much better; however, Brandon is again the only student who gives an incorrect response.

During center time Ms. Reyes asks Brandon to join her for a game. She lays out picture cards of a clock, bell, and duck, and asks Brandon to pick up the card that begins with the /k/ sound. He picks up the bell card. She repeats the process two more times and each time Brandon is unable to pick up the correct card. (See Appendix D.5 for picture cards.)

When Brandon's eighth-grade buddy comes to read with him, Mrs. Reyes gives Brandon and his buddy several old magazines and invites them to make their own alphabet book. She provides 10 index cards and one card with a big "B" on the front. She begins with "B" because it is the first letter of his name.

Brandon's job is to find pictures in the magazines that begin with the sound of his name and glue them onto the cards. Ms. Reyes instructs the eighth grader to emphasize the initial sound of the pictures to help Brandon determine if it begins with the same sound as his name. If the picture does not begin with the /b/ sound, the buddy is to say "Brandon" and the incorrect picture word (e.g., *cake*) and really emphasize the beginning sound, such as "C-C-C-C-Cake" and then "B-B-B-B-Brandon," so the initial sound of the word is exaggerated.

After a half hour, the eighth grader reports that at first Brandon had a difficult time choosing correct picture cards; but once he had Brandon say the words while exaggerating the beginning sound, he was able to choose quickly the last four picture cards correctly.

Ms. Reyes thanks the buddy and makes Brandon his own personal /B/ alphabet book. As you read this chapter, consider the following questions:

guiding questions

1. Which dimensions of phonemic awareness are the focus of Ms. Reyes's lessons?

2. What assessments could Ms. Reyes use to measure Brandon's growth in phonemic awareness?

3. From your observations in classrooms or your own kindergarten days, what are some other game-like activities Ms. Reyes could do with Brandon? What are some activities she could do with the entire class?

4. Choose several activities from the chapter and think about how you would modify these activities for English learners.

introduction

"Filling children's heads with rhyme is one of the easiest and most natural ways to focus their attention on the sounds of the English language."

BEAR, INVERNIZZI, TEMPLETON, & JOHNSTON, 2008, P. 111

Young children become aware of differing and similar sounds within words by enjoying the alliteration, rhyme, rhythm, and onomatopoeia found in songs, nursery rhymes, poems, and children's literature. The teacher's responsibility is to provide opportunities for children to experience joy in using the English language. One way to fulfill this responsibility is to encourage children to play with language as they sing, chant, and read.

This chapter discusses a number of different topics surrounding phonemic awareness: (1) its definition, (2) its seven dimensions, (3) phonemic awareness and English learners, (4) what teachers should know about it, (5) methods teachers can use to introduce children to the sounds of our language, (6) types of phonemic awareness assessments, and (7) activities that help children become sensitive to the sounds within words.

As an adult who spends hours reading and writing, you may think phonemic awareness is a simple skill for younger children to develop. However, as you read this chapter, take time to reflect on the intricate characteristics of phonemic awareness to gain awareness of why some young children struggle with written language.

DEFINITIONS

Phonological awareness is the ability to identify and manipulate various units of sound in speech, including syllables, onsets, and rhymes, as distinct from their meaning. Although **phonemic awareness** also involves an understanding of the ways that sounds function in words, it focuses only on manipulating individual sounds (phonemes). A **phoneme** is the smallest unit of sound in spoken words that affects a word's meaning (e.g., /l/, /m/, /b/, /sh/, /ch/, and so on). Technically, phonemic awareness is only one aspect of phonological awareness, although the terms are often used interchangeably. This text uses the more commonly used term *phonemic awareness* to describe both skill sets.

According to the IRA (ILA) and the National Association for the Education of Young Children (1998), phonemic awareness is "a child's understanding and conscious awareness that speech is composed of identifiable units, such as spoken words, syllables, and sounds" (p. 4). Yopp and Yopp (2000) elaborate on this definition by characterizing phonemic awareness as "the ability to generate and recognize rhyming words, to count syllables, to separate the beginning of a word from its ending (e.g., the *st* from the *op* in *stop*), and to identify each of the phonemes in a word" (p. 30). Linguists disagree on the actual number of phonemes in the English language; this disagreement stems from distinct dialects, accents, and individual speech patterns. Figure 4.1 lists the 44 phonemes on which most linguists agree.

Phonemic awareness is not the same concept as **phonics**, which is the understanding that letters represent certain sound(s). Phonemic awareness tasks are aural and oral, while phonics focuses on written letters

figure 4.1 The 44 most common phonemes.

VOWEL SOUNDS

/a/	cat	/ā/	game	/ə/	aloft	/ô/	all
/e/	bed	/ē/	see	/ōō/	spoon	/û/	bird
/i/	it	/ī/	I	/ŏŏ/	look	/â/	air
/o/	odd	/ō/	hole	/ou/	mouse	/ä/	far
/u/	under	/ū/	use	/oi/	toy, oil		

CONSONANT SOUNDS

/b/	boy	/k/	key	/s/	sun	/ch/	church
/d/	dad	/l/	log	/t/	tent	/sh/	shadow
/f/	fish	/m/	man	/v/	vest	/th/	thumb
/g/	game	/n/	nose	/w/	wagon	/th/	the
/h/	hat	/p/	pipe	/y/	yellow	/wh/	wheel
/j/	judge	/r/	rake	/z/	zipper	/zh/	pleasure
						/ng/	sing

Source: Adapted from W. Blevins (2001). *Teaching Phonics and Word Study in the Intermediate Grades.* New York: Scholastic.

and the aural process. Students do not need to know letter names and their sounds in order to merely hear the sounds in a word. However, if they do know the letter names, teachers can facilitate their learning by highlighting the letters in their instruction.

DIMENSIONS OF PHONEMIC AWARENESS

According to Cavanaugh (2007), Blevins (2006), and Yopp (2005), phonemic awareness consists of various dimensions; nevertheless, it is important to note that "there is no research to suggest that there is an exact sequence of acquisition of specific sounds" (Cunningham et al., 1998, p. 3). The following are seven dimensions of phonemic awareness:

1. The ability to hear syllables within a word. To assess children's ability to hear syllables, have them first clap one-syllable words or names (e.g., Jim, Jane, Kim), and then progress to two-, three-, and four-syllable words (e.g., Ste-ven, Gin-ger, Kim-ber-ly, In-di-a, Ok-la-ho-ma).

2. The ability to hear initial letter sounds or recognize alliteration. This includes listing words like those Ms. Reyes asked her students to name. Most children enjoy adding to a list of words that begin with the same sound. For example, the teacher may say, "'Sally sells seashells' all begin with the /s/ sound. What other words, can you think of that begin with the /s/ sound?" Children with phonemic awareness will respond with such words as *silly, summer,* and *sun.*

3. The ability to distinguish rime and rhyme. The concepts of **rime** and **rhyme** are often confusing not only to students but also to educators. Words in the same rime family always end with the same letters (e.g., *sit, hit, fit*), while words with rhyme share the same sound but do not necessarily share the same ending letters (e.g., *great/late* or *bear/care*). Words in the same rime family also rhyme since they have the same ending (*fat, bat, sat*); however, words that rhyme are not necessarily part of the same rime family since they may end differently.

Words with rime have two parts—**onset** (the consonant or consonant blend at the beginning of the word), and rime (the ending letters that are shared). For example, in the words *cat* and *bat,* the *c* and the *b* are the onsets and the *at* in each of the words is the rime. Words with the same rimes are often referred to as **word families.**

The concepts of rime and rhyme may be difficult for some children to distinguish, but a wide array of books introduce them. (See Appendix A.7 for a list of books that highlight rime and rhyme.) Like many authors, Guarino (1989) emphasizes both rime and rhyme in her book *Is Your Mama a Llama?*:

> "Is your <u>mama</u> a <u>llama</u>?" I asked my friend Clyde. (rime, which also happens to rhyme)
>
> "No, she is not," is how <u>Clyde</u> <u>replied</u>. (rhyme)

4. The ability to distinguish oddity. Children's ability to identify words that begin with a different sound from the other words that the teacher pronounces is their ability to distinguish oddity. For example, the teacher might pronounce *man, money,* and *cat* and ask the children to listen and identify which word begins with the different sound.

5. The ability to blend sounds together orally to make a word. For this dimension, the teacher should again first work with onset and rime because they are larger units of sound. Students are able to control larger units of sound before smaller units or phonemes (Blevins, 2006; Yopp, 2005). When working with blending, say the first sound (the onset) of a word (e.g., /s/) and have the students repeat it. Then say the rime (e.g., *at*), and ask them to repeat it. Then ask them to blend the two parts into one word. You may wish to work with one word family (e.g., the *at* family) before moving on to another family. Appendix B.2 contains a list of word families commonly used in instruction.

Another aspect of the fifth phonemic awareness dimension is children's ability to blend individual sounds to form a word. With this task, the teacher begins with three-letter words that have the consonant–vowel–consonant (CVC) pattern, such as *big, fun, bat,* and so on. (Notice these words are members of word families, but at this point you are working with individual letters and not the onset, rime, or rhyme.) Articulate each sound separately, ask the student to repeat each sound, and then ask her to blend the three sounds together to form a word. An example of such an activity would be the following exchange:

> Teacher: /s/
>
> Student: /s/
>
> Teacher: /a/
>
> Student: /a/
>
> Teacher: /t/
>
> Student: /t/
>
> Teacher: Now blend all three sounds together.
>
> Student: *sat*

If students already know the names of the letters and the sounds of some letters, Ransom, Santa, Williams, and Farstrup (1999) recommend the teacher work with magnetic letters because this helps children's visual and auditory processes. If they do not know letter names, the teacher can simply emphasize the sounds within the words. Blending may be difficult for some children because this task involves working with language in an unnatural form, a form in which they have not heard words spoken (Smith, 2005). The section on phonemic awareness instruction later in this chapter will explain in greater detail why this task is difficult for many students.

6. The ability to segment words orally. Segmenting is different from blending. In blending, the task is to put sounds *together* to make a word *before* hearing the entire word. In segmenting, however, the task is to pull sounds apart *after* hearing the entire word. In segmenting, the teacher says the entire word—for example, *man*—and asks the children to say all three sounds in the word. An example of such an exercise is the following:

> Teacher: I'm going to say a word that has three sounds in it. I want you to tell me the three sounds you hear. For example, in *cat*, I hear /c /, /a /, and /t/. Now I want you to tell me which three sounds you hear in *man*.
>
> Student: /m/ . . . /a/ . . . /n/.

7. The ability to manipulate sounds orally to create new words. This task can be difficult for some children because they must focus on small parts of a word (Smith, 2005). **Manipulating sounds** involves the task of either substituting or deleting. **Substituting** is the act of replacing one sound for another sound in a word. For example, in substitution, the teacher says the word *Sam,* asks children to put an /h/ sound in place of the /s/ sound, and then asks them to pronounce the new word *(ham).* **Deleting** is the act of removing a sound from a word to create a new word. The sound can be either an initial or an ending sound. An example is to pronounce the word *beat* and then omit the /t/ sound to get *be.* Or, you could pronounce *beat* and then omit the /b/ sound to get *eat.*

According to Blevins (2006) children should master the first three of the seven dimensions of phonemic awareness by the end of kindergarten and the last four dimensions by the end of first grade. This does not mean, however, that one dimension needs to be mastered before working on the next.

PHONEMIC AWARENESS AND ENGLISH LEARNERS

When working with the seven dimensions of phonemes, be aware that phonemes differ from one language to another. As the number of English learners in U.S. schools grows dramatically each year, many classrooms have English learners from many different countries, while some schools have large populations of English learners from one country, particularly Mexico. All of these students must learn to produce the 44 most common phonemes of the English language to become fluent English speakers.

Many languages (e.g., Spanish, Italian, or Romanian) have fewer phonemes than English (Bear et al., 2007). Some English phonemes are unique to the English language, while other phonemes are unique to other languages. "A phoneme not present in one's native language is more difficult to hear and, in turn, produce" (Helman, 2004, p. 454). If you have ever attempted to say a phrase in Thai, Japanese, Korean, or Chinese, you may have struggled because Asian languages have many phonemes that are not part of the English language. You may have wondered how to place your tongue and lips to produce the unfamiliar sound. Similarly, many non-English speakers have difficulty producing phonemes that are unique to English. For example, Asian speakers have difficulty with the English phonemes that are produced with the tongue and lips (e.g., /v/, /f/, /p/, /d/) because they do not use the lips and tongue to produce phonemes when speaking their native language.

Native Spanish speakers, the largest group of second-language learners in the United States, have difficulty with phonemes because English has 44 phonemes and Spanish has only 24. Spanish speakers, therefore, must learn to produce at least 20 new sounds. Figure 4.2 shows English phonemes that are not found in Spanish as well as Spanish vowels and their pronunciation.

Many of the consonant blend phonemes are not Spanish phonemes. Any phoneme that is unique to English speakers may be difficult for native Spanish learners. Think of how difficult the following sentence would be for a native Spanish speaker (phonemes not found in Spanish are underlined): <u>R</u>obert <u>sp</u>illed <u>j</u>elly on <u>R</u>uth's trea<u>s</u>ure. When working with Spanish speakers, begin not with phonemes that are uncommon in Spanish, but rather with phonemes that are common in English and Spanish. Figure 4.3 shows the phonemes, represented by the English grapheme, common to Spanish and English. In Chapter 5, you

figure 4.2

Differences between English and Spanish vowel sounds.

ENGLISH VOWEL SOUNDS NOT FOUND IN SPANISH:
schwa vowels, *r*-controlled vowels, short /i/, short /u/

SPANISH VOWELS:
/i/ = keep; /e/ = make, vet; /a/ = cot; /u/ you; /o/ sew

Source: Goldstein, B. A., (2004). *Bilingual Language Development and Disorders in Spanish–English Speakers.* Baltimore: Paul H. Brooks Publishing.

will learn that even though some phonemes are common in both languages, the same letters may not represent the same phonemes. For example, the long /a/ phoneme is spelled with the letter *e* in Spanish, but in English the long /a/ is spelled many different ways (e.g., *cake, eight, they*).

Figure 4.4 lists English phonemes not found in Chinese, French, Greek, Italian, Japanese, and Native American languages. Notice how many languages do not have the schwa, /th/, /dg/, and /oo/ phonemes. As with Spanish speakers, when working with other non-English speakers always begin with the phonemes that are common in English and the student's native language, while being aware of why they may struggle with other phonemes.

Not only do languages have unique phonemes, but every language also has different phoneme placements within words. For example, phoneme placement within words varies between English and Spanish. In English all consonant phonemes, except /ng/ and the /h/, are placed anywhere within a word. However, in Spanish only five consonant phonemes (/l/, /r/, /d/, /n/, and /s/) are ever heard as ending sounds (Helman, 2004). Think of the difficulty native Spanish students

have when repeating this sentence: *The cat and dog ate from the same dish*. Again, begin with words that have common placement of phonemes in the two languages, and progress to those with unfamiliar placement.

WHAT TEACHERS SHOULD KNOW

Teachers often have several questions about phonemic awareness as they prepare to teach young children to read. These include: (1) Is phonemic awareness necessary for students to become proficient readers? (2) How do children become aware of the phonemes within words? and (3) Is phonemic awareness addressed in the CCSS?

Is Phonemic Awareness Necessary for Students to Become Proficient Readers?

Wood, Mustian, & Ya-yu (2013), Ashby et al. (2013), Cavanaugh (2007), and IRA/NAEYC (1998) argue that students must be aware that words are made up of distinct sounds if they are to become proficient readers and writers. IRA/NAEYC (1998) indicate that when children approach unfamiliar words, they learn to read

figure 4.3 Phonemes, represented by the English graphemes, common in English and Spanish.

/b/	/d/	/f/	/g/	/k/	/l/	/m/	/n/	/p/	/s/	/t/	/w/
/y/	/ch/	long /a/		long /e/		long /i/		long /o/		/u/ as in *June*	
/pl/	/pr/	/bl/	/br/	/tr/	/dr/	/cl/	/cr/	/gl/	/gr/	/fl/	/fr/

Sources: Helman, L. A . (2004). Building on the sound system of Spanish: Insights from the alphabetic spellings of English-language learners. *The Reading Teacher, 57*(5), 452–460. / Bear, D., Helman, L., Templeton, S., Invernizzi, M., & Johnston, F. (2007). *Words their way with English learners: Word study for phonics, vocabulary and spelling instruction* (4th ed.). Upper Saddle River, NJ: Pearson.

figure 4.4 English phonemes not found in the Chinese, French, Greek, Italian, Japanese, and Native American languages.

LANGUAGE	SOUNDS NOT PART OF THE LANGUAGE							
Chinese	dg	long /a/		th	v			
French	ch	long /e/		j	ng	oo	th	
Greek	aw	long /e/		i	oo	schwa		
Italian	a	ar	dg	h	I	ng	th	schwa
Japanese	dg	f	I	th	oo	v	schwa	
Native American (some dialects)	l	r						

Source: Cecil, N. L. (2015). *Striking a Balance: A Comprehensive Approach to Early Literacy* (5th ed.). Scottsdale, AZ: Holcomb Hathaway.

them by understanding that they contain individual sounds and that every word is different. Otherwise, each new word must become a sight word—a word they automatically identify. Writing, they also suggest, requires that children understand words are composed of individual sounds. These experts do not conclude that children need to master all the phonemic awareness dimensions before they begin to read, only that they are able to detect beginning sounds to learn initial letter–sound relationships.

Many elementary teachers believe phonemic awareness instruction is important for reading achievement. These teachers emphasize the importance of the following elements of phonemic awareness, in which the student must:

1. Understand that a word is a series of speech sounds.
2. Be able to isolate a sound in a word.
3. Be able to blend individual sounds to form a word.
4. Be able to substitute sounds in a word to produce new words.
5. Be able to recognize common rhymes.
6. Be able to recognize syllables within words.

Lane and Pullen (2004) also argue that proficient readers need to understand how phonemes—the sounds of spoken language—are connected to the printed word.

IRA/NAEYC (1998) suggest that literacy does not develop naturally, and careful instruction in phonemic awareness is necessary for students to become literate. Cunningham et al. (1998) conclude that different children need different amounts and forms of phonemic awareness instruction. They find some children benefit when teachers combine text with phonemic awareness instruction, while others respond better when engaged in oral language experiences such as nursery rhymes, songs, chants, and other language play. The key is that a teacher engages the student while manipulating sounds within words. Cunningham et al. conclude that "instruction with print with explicit attention to sound structure in spoken words is the best vehicle toward [language] growth" (p. 3).

To date, no longitudinal study documents the effectiveness of intense, sustained phonemic awareness activities. However, the National Reading Panel conducted a quantitative meta-analysis evaluating the effects of phonemic awareness instruction on learning to read and spell (Ehri et al., 2001) and found that it:

1. Impacts children's awareness of sounds in letters.
2. Impacts children's reading comprehension and decoding.
3. Impacts most children's spelling, but not the spelling of readers with a disability.

4. Is more effective when taught with letter names.
5. Is more effective when only one or two skills are taught in a session, instead of multiple skills.
6. Is more effective when conducted in small groups, rather than individually or in classroom settings.

How Do Children Become Aware of Phonemes Within Words?

Most researchers and educators agree that when students are actively engaged and involved in literacy activities, they become aware of the sounds within words (Bear, Invernizzi, Templeton, & Johnston, 2011; Cunningham et al., 1998; IRA/NAEYC, 1998). These activities include linguistic awareness games (such as those found in the last section of this chapter), nursery rhymes, poems, songs, rhythmic activities such as jump-rope jingles, and stories that use rhyme and onomatopoeia. Because phonemic awareness develops over time and through sustained exposure, students should have opportunities to develop it every day. Cunningham et al. (1998) found an estimated 80 percent of students develop phonemic awareness by the middle of first grade. The other 20 percent benefit from one-on-one language activities with an adult who actively engages the student in play with word sounds. These types of activities are found in the Intervention section of this chapter.

Is Phonemic Awareness Addressed in the CCSS?

With so much emphasis on the new reading and writing requirements of the Common Core State Standards, teachers may not be aware that the CCSS also include foundational reading skills standards that address phonemic awareness for kindergarten and first grade (see Figure 4.5), as well as phonics, word recognition, and fluency for grades K through 5.

Of course, if a first grader cannot perform the tasks required of kindergarteners, first-grade teachers must be sure to work individually with him or her. Unlike kindergarteners, first graders need to recognize if a word has a long or short vowel sound. For example, they need to understand that *dime* and *cone* have long vowel sounds. To assess if students can distinguish these sounds, teachers can create a list of words with long or short sounds. After students indicate mastery of that skill, then teachers can advance to a more difficult task by giving students a set of three words, two of which will be short and the third word will be long. Students must tell which one has the long vowel sound. First graders also need to be able to blend the

figure | **4.5** | CCSS ELA Reading: Foundations Skills standards that address phonemic awareness.

KINDERGARTEN

CCSS.ELA-Literacy.RF.K.2 Demonstrate understanding of spoken words, syllables, and sounds (phonemes).

CCSS.ELA-Literacy.RF.K.2.a Recognize and produce rhyming words.

CCSS.ELA-Literacy.RF.K.2.b Count, pronounce, blend, and segment syllables in spoken words.

CCSS.ELA-Literacy.RF.K.2.c Blend and segment onsets and rimes of single-syllable spoken words.

CCSS.ELA-Literacy.RF.K.2.d Isolate and pronounce the initial, medial vowel, and final sounds (phonemes) in three-phoneme (consonant–vowel–consonant, or CVC) words. (This does not include CVCs ending with /l/, /r/, or /x/.)

CCSS.ELA-Literacy.RF.K.2.e Add or substitute individual sounds (phonemes) in simple, one-syllable words to make new words.

GRADE 1

CCSS.ELA-Literacy.RF.1.2 Demonstrate understanding of spoken words, syllables, and sounds (phonemes).

CCSS.ELA-Literacy.RF.1.2.a Distinguish long from short vowel sounds in spoken single-syllable words.

CCSS.ELA-Literacy.RF.1.2.b Orally produce single-syllable words by blending sounds (phonemes), including consonant blends.

CCSS.ELA-Literacy.RF.1.2.c Isolate and pronounce initial, medial vowel, and final sounds (phonemes) in spoken single-syllable words.

CCSS.ELA-Literacy.RF.1.2.d Segment spoken single-syllable words into their complete sequence of individual sounds (phonemes).

Source: National Governors Association Center for Best Practices (NGACBP) & Council of Chief State School Officers (CCSSO). (2010). English Language Arts Standards, Reading: Foundational Skills, Kindergarten and Grade 1. Washington, DC: NGABP, CCSSO, p. 15.

sounds in words that have more than the CVC pattern. For example, first graders must be able to blend words such as *flat, street, fox* (a word that ends in /x/), *hill, black,* and *truck*. Of course, students will not pronounce two /l/ sounds in *hill* or two /k/ sounds in *black* and *truck*.

ASSESSMENT

Assessing a Student's Level of Phonemic Awareness

The first step in assessing phonemic awareness occurs during the "kid watching" that takes place during small-group language activities. For example, in the opening scenario Ms. Reyes notices while she is working with small groups that Brandon does not have the ability to clap the syllables of names or to recognize words that have the same beginning sounds. Following this observation, she assesses Brandon individually, using commercial and informal assessment instruments. Commercial phonemic awareness assessments available to teachers, based on the seven dimensions of phonemic awareness, include:

1. Lindamood-Bell Auditory Conceptualization Test (LAC). Hingham, MA: Teaching Resources Corporation.

2. Test of Phonological Awareness (TOPA-2+). Austin, TX: Pro-Ed.

3. Scholastic Phonemic Awareness Kit. New York: Scholastic.

4. Yopp, H. K. (2005). A test for assessing phonemic awareness in young children. In S. J. Barrentine & S. M. Stokes (Eds.). *Reading Assessment* (pp. 262–271). Newark, DE: IRA (ILA). This assessment is also available online at http://teams.lacoe.edu. A short video demonstrates how to administer it.

5. Basic Early Assessment of Reading™ (BEAR®). Rolling Meadows, IL: Riverside Publishing.

6. Dynamic Indicators of Basic Early Literacy Skills (DIBELS). Longmont, CO: Sopris West Educational Services.

One easy informal phonemic assessment is the Quick Phonemic Awareness Assessment Device (Cecil, 2015; see Appendix C.30). Appendices C.31 and C.32 feature two assessments, one to use as a pretest before one-on-one time with the student, and the other as a post-test after spending individualized time with the student. Five correct responses for each task indicate the child has mastered the skill. Three or four correct responses indicate that he is developing the skill, and only one or two correct responses indicate he is having difficulty with the tasks. Remember, this is only an informal assessment to indicate a student's knowledge about the individual sounds within words. Not all seven of the dimensions of phonemic awareness need to be mastered before children can read, nor does a teacher need to assess all students. Only those children who would benefit from the assessment and instruction in the strategies need to complete it. It only measures children's capacity for hearing small units of sound within words. In addition, a teacher can easily make his or her own informal assessment by having students complete activities based on each of the seven dimensions.

Because most states require schools to document growth in phonemic awareness, primary teachers are advised to keep a class checklist based on the seven dimensions of phonemic awareness. Using this checklist, the teacher can monitor class growth in each area during each grading period. She can also use the checklist to form small groups based on the children's strengths and weaknesses. The checklist in Figure 4.6 reflects results at the end of the first quarter. It shows that Reed is competent in all seven dimensions; Erin and Stacey are weak in all areas; and most of the students cannot manipulate sounds or delete an ending sound. A blank checklist is provided in Appendix C.33. Appendices C.34 and C.35 contain checklists for progress toward the CCSS Reading Foundational Skills Phonological Awareness Standards for kindergarten and first grade.

Assessing a Student's Growth in Phonemic Awareness

After a semester of reading to students in small groups, with an emphasis on listening to the sounds of our language, and after introducing various language activities, most students will show signs of growth in phonemic awareness. To assess their growth, you may use one of the assessment instruments listed above or you may use the post-test informal assessment instrument found in Appendix C.32. The scoring on the post-test is the same as the pretest. To document the phonemic awareness growth of the class, use the Phonemic Awareness checklist found in Figure 4.6 or design one that fits your needs.

INTRODUCING STUDENTS TO THE WONDERFUL SOUNDS OF OUR LANGUAGE

Jongsma (2000) points out that the building materials and tools of the English language are the eight parts of speech—adjectives, adverbs, verbs, pronouns, conjunctions, prepositions, nouns, and interjections—which are themselves filled with many wonderful sounds that add color and luster to our speech. She believes a teacher must help students develop an ear for the sounds within words. One way to do this is through language play. Teachers can engage students in language play through songs, nursery rhymes, poems, jump-rope jingles, riddles, jokes, tongue twisters, and stories because they are filled with words and phrases that emphasize the sounds

figure 4.6 Checklist for phonemic awareness based on the seven dimensions, primary grades.

TEACHER Jones   DATE 10/12

+ = always   x = sometimes   0 = seldom/never

DIMENSION	Cooper	Cy	Reed	Melinda	Jami	Scott	Rebecca	Tim	David	Erin	Marie	Lori	Stacey	Terri	Aubree	Alea	Darci	Janelle
1. Ability to hear syllables within words.	X	+	+	X	+	X	+	X	+	O	+	+	O	+	+	X	+	+
2. Ability to hear initial sounds or recognize alliteration.	X	+	+	X	+	X	+	X	+	O	+	+	O	X	+	X	+	+
3. Ability to hear rhyming words.	X	+	+	X	+	X	+	X	X	O	+	X	O	X	+	X	X	+
4. Ability to distinguish oddity.	X	O	+	O	X	O	X	O	X	O	+	X	O	O	X	O	X	+
5. Ability to blend words orally.	O	O	+	O	X	O	X	O	X	O	X	X	O	O	X	O	X	X
6. Ability to segment words. * Drop beginning sound * Drop ending sound	O	O	+	O	O	O	O	O	O	O	O	O	O	O	O	O	O	O
7. Ability to manipulate sounds orally to create new words.	O	O	+	O	O	O	O	O	O	O	O	O	O	O	O	O	O	O

and rhythms of our language. These words and phrases may fall into one of the following categories:

- **alliteration** (sentences or phrases that begin with same letter sound; e.g., *Silly Sally shines seashells*).
- **assonance** (sentences or phrases that have repeated vowel sounds; e.g., *Aunt Bea flees when she sees bees*).
- **onomatopoeia** (words that sound like their meanings; e.g., *crackle, pop*).
- **nonsense words** (made up words e.g., *jabberwocky*).

Language learning begins with oral language; children first hear and speak words they will later learn to read and write. Children of all ages, beginning with the very young, should have many opportunities to play with language orally—to enjoy the sounds of words through alliteration (*Peter Piper picked a peck of pickled peppers*), rhymes (*Humpty Dumpty sat on a wall / Humpty Dumpty had a great fall*), and onomatopoeia (*Snap, Crackle, Pop!*) before they are asked to analyze words (Hadaway, Vardell, & Young, 2001). Because language learning occurs when teachers engage students in language play (Taylor, Pressley, & Pearson, 2000; Thomas, 2012), students should have many opportunities to engage in play-based aural and oral language activities.

Songs

Language activities can include singing, because many songs are filled with alliteration and rhyme (Thomas, 2012). Teachers may want to develop a repertoire of songs that emphasize the sounds within words. Words and phrases such as "fid-dle-ee-fee," "chimney chuck, chummy chuck," and "swishy, swashy" in the delightful "Barnyard Song" (adapted by Glazer, 1973) delight young children. "Hush, Little Baby" (traditional) allows children to make up their own rhyming verses after they sing the first few. Following the seventh verse of "Hush, Little Baby," for example, you may make up your own verse (something like the eighth verse given below), and then invite the children to create their own.

7TH VERSE:

If that dog named Rover don't bark,
Papa's gonna buy you a horse and cart.

8TH VERSE:

If that horse and cart won't run,
Papa's gonna buy you the golden sun.

There are many books of children's songs. *Wee Sing: Children's Songs and Fingerplays* (2005) by Pamela Conn Beall and Susan Hogan Nipp includes classic children's songs with fingerplay directions and a CD (in case a teacher does not feel comfortable leading children in singing). *The Big Book of Nursery Rhymes and Children's Songs* (Hal Leonard Corp. 2004), *A Children's Treasury of Songs* (Black, 2006), *You Are My Sunshine* (Davis, 2011), and *A Children's Treasury of Lullabies* (Beck, 2006) are books with a wide variety of songs for young children. *The Great Family Songbook: A Treasury of Favorite Show Tunes, Singalongs, Pop, and Blues* (Fox, Weissman, & Wilkins, 2010) has various types of songs for all ages. Hilda Jackman's *Sing Me a Story! Tell Me a Song!* (1999) includes creative curriculum activities with many songs for young children, which are grouped into thematic units.

Nursery Rhymes and Poems

Children are often introduced to poetry through nursery rhymes chanted by their parents or caregivers. Continue to model the joy of hearing the sounds, feeling the rhythms, and telling the stories found in nursery rhymes. They abound with wonderful rhythm, rhyme, and onomatopoeia; think of the musical sounds in the words "Hickory, Dickory, Dock." The rhythm of the three words is triplet, triplet, quarter note, with an accent on the beginning of each word. To assist children in feeling the rhythm, add actions, such as the following:

"Hick" (right hand up) "ory" (right hand down)

"Dick" (left hand up) "ory" (left hand down)

"Dock" (both hands up in a v-shape and then down again)

"The mouse ran up the clock" (run fingers up the imaginary clock)

"The clock" (draw a circle with finger) "struck one" (hold up index finger)

"The mouse ran down" (run fingers down the imaginary clock)

"Hick" (right hand up) "ory" (right hand down)

"Dick" (left hand up) "ory" (left hand down)

"Dock" (both hands up in a v-shape)

"Humpty Dumpty" is another favorite nursery rhyme that evokes many characters and story lines in rhythmic rhyme. Again, body actions can help the children feel the beat of the syllables:

"Hump" (bounce once so the accent and syllable can be felt) "ty"

"Dump" (bounce once) "ty"

"Sat" (crouch in a sitting position) "on a wall."

"Hump" (bounce once) "ty"

"Dump" (bounce once) "ty"

"Had a great fall." (fall down)

"All the King's horses,"

"And all the King's men,"

"Couldn't put Humpty together again." (stay sprawled out)

In the introduction to *Mary Engelbreit's Mother Goose* (Engelbreit, 2005), Engelbreit describes Mother Goose rhymes as those that are "fun to say, and fun to hear" (Introduction). Teachers can demonstrate the joyful language of nursery rhymes with the following:

- "Handy-Spandy" with rhyming words such as *Handy-spandy, Jack dandy.*
- "To Market to Market," with such words as *jiggety-jig.*
- "Horsie, Horsie," with words such as *clipetty-clop, swish, giddy-up.*
- "From Wibbleton to Wobbelton." The repetition of the two words in the title makes it a tongue twister.

Nursery rhymes and poetry are more enjoyable when the author emphasizes the sounds of words as spoken by children. Sometimes these sounds are different from standard pronunciation. An example is George Ulrich's poem "My Tooth Ith Loothe" (1995), which envisions how a child might speak with a loose tooth:

My tooth ith looth! My tooth ith loothe.
I can't go to thcool, that'th my excuthe.
I wath fine latht night when I went to bed
But today it'th hanging by a thread! (p. 6)

Continue to use poems with first and second graders. Read them aloud, emphasizing the rhythm and engaging students in the sounds of the words and rhymes. In many of Jack Prelutsky's *Zoo Doings: Animal Poems* (1983), he uses words that are enjoyable to hear and even more fun to roll off the tongue. "Yickity-yackity yickity-yak, the yak has a scriffily, scraffily back!" begins one delightful poem about a yak. Later in the same poem, Prelutsky uses the phrase, "Sniggildy-snaggildy, sniggildy-snag." Children can have fun with these words and even change the beginning consonant to form a new tongue twister. Try changing the y in "yickity-yackity yickity-yak" to *j* or *l* or *s*, and the *scr* in "scriffily, scraffily" to a *tw* or *th*. Model these transformations to help children become aware of the sounds within words.

"The Giggling Gaggling Gaggle of Geese," in Prelutsky (1983), uses the title phrase 10 times in a five-verse poem. The words are as noisy as the geese and twist the tongue if the reader attempts to read them with speed. Again, you might change the beginning sound of "giggling, gaggling gaggle of geese" to a *ch* and say it fast!

Many poems use onomatopoeia, which naturally emphasizes the sounds of words. *Noisy Poems*, collected by Jill Bennett (1987), contains many delightful poems that emphasize the noisy sounds of the English language. As you read them, take visible pleasure in their alliteration, assonance, onomato-

poeia, rhyme, and rhythm. You can model how these sounds evoke laughter and other emotions by substituting different initial sounds for some words and by emphasizing how sounds create different moods. The following few lines of "Jazz-Man" from *Noisy Poems* demonstrate how the poet Eleanor Farjeon uses onomatopoeia:

Crash and
Clang!
Bash and Bang!
And up in the road the Jazz-Man sprang . . .
. . . Toot and
Tingle!
Hoot and
Jingle!
Oh, what a clatter! How the tunes all mingle! (unpaged)

Onomatopoeia, alliteration, rhythm, and rhyme are also found in classic children's nursery rhymes, such as "Horsie, Horsie":

Horsie, horsie, don't you stop,
Just let your feet go clippety clop;
Your tail goes swish, and the wheels go round—
Giddy-up, you're homeward bound!

Poets also play with language by coining names and words to indicate the characteristics of people. One such poem is Helen Ksypka's "My Family of Dinosaurs," in *Miles of Smiles: Kids Pick the Funniest Poems*, Book #3 (1998) edited by Bruce Lansky:

My sister, finkasaurus,
is a tattletaling shrew.
My brother, Slobasaurus,
doesn't quite know how to chew.
My mother, rushasaurus,
Finds it hard to be on time. (p. 85)

To emphasize how the name of the person fits the personality, you might change the poem to read: "My mother, flowerasaurus / Grows flowers of every kind." Or, "My mother, jogasaurus / Jogs both day and night." After you model some of these improvisations, encourage students to add their own.

Kenn Nesbitt's "Kangaroos," also from Lansky (1998), contains more coined words:

If a person has four babies
You would call them all quadruplets.
If a kangaroo does likewise,
Should you call them Kangaruplets? (p. 89)

Many poems are written in couplets—two lines that rhyme—which make it easy for children to hear the rhymes. An easy way to introduce children to couplets is through the nonsense poem "Mr. Backward" by Douglas Florian, in Lansky (1998). Read six lines and then ask students to insert a word that rhymes. It does not matter if the word is different from the original word used in the poem because the poem is full of nonsense:

Mr. Backward lives in town

He never wakes up; he always wakes down.

He eats dessert before his meal.

His plastic plants and flowers are real.

He takes a bath inside his sink

And cleans his clothes with purple ____ (ink). (p. 98)

By permitting the students to fill in the blank, you engage them in language play and emphasize the enjoyable nature of rhyme.

"The Walrus" by Jack Prelutsky, found in the *National Geographic Book of Animal Poetry: 200 Poems with Photographs that Squeak, Soar, and Roar* (Lewis, 2012), likewise engages children with language play. This poem has alliteration (e.g. "widdly, waddly walrus"; "flippery, floppery feet," rhyme (e.g., feet/ eat; hide/tide), onomatopoeia (e.g., "thundery," "flippery," and some great vocabulary (e.g., "elegant," "debonair").

A list of poetry and Mother Goose books is in Appendix A.4. Other books with rhyme are presented in Appendix A.7.

Jump Rope Jingles

Jump rope jingles (or chants) are full of rhythm and rhyme. They cater to kinesthetic learners because the children jump in rhythm with the syllables. Straight jumping, which is most appropriate for very young children, requires they jump once for every beat or syllable. Jump rope jingles also lend themselves to the addition of more rhyming verses by the children. A good example of this is the following jingle found on the Traditional Jump Rope Rhymes page at buyjump ropes.net:

Benjamin Franklin went to France

To teach the ladies how to dance.

First the heel, and then the toe,

Spin around and out you go (Greil, 2013, p. 3 of 15)

You can model adding to the jingle with lines such as the following:

Benjamin Franklin went to Greece

To buy the ladies some soft fleece.

or

Benjamin Franklin went to Maine

To sell his goods and get some fame.

Also on this website is "Postman":

Postman, Postman,

Do your duty,

Send this letter

To my cutie.

Don't you stop

Nor don't delay.

Get it to her

Right away. (Donius, p. 11 of 15)

Have fun with jump rope jingles and with improvising verses. This activity should take place in a safe environment and children should feel comfortable adding their own verses. A safe environment means that the teacher and the children accept all student suggestions, even nonsense words, because they are a legitimate part of many jingles.

Tongue Twisters

Tongue twisters are a natural way to introduce students to alliteration. Not all the words in a twister need to begin with the same initial sound, but most of them should. An example of alliteration in a tongue twister is, "Peter Piper picked a peck of pickled peppers." Remember to emphasize the repeated initial sounds so students will develop an ear for words beginning with the same sound.

Challenging tongue twisters are found in *Ready . . . Set . . . Read!* (1990) compiled by J. Cole and S. Calmenson. One of these tongue twisters is "Fran fried five flat fishes" (p. 124). You can extend this tongue twister by adding to the sentence: "Fancy, frilly Fran fried five flat fishes on Friday." Another of the book's easily expanded tongue twisters is, "Sue saw sheep in shoes" (p. 125). Add the following words and attempt to say it really fast: "Silly Sally and sad Sue saw sheep in shoes and snakes in sneakers." More books with alliteration and language play are listed in Appendix A.7. After practicing tongue twisters with students, encourage them to create and share their own with their classmates.

Children's Literature

Engage students in additional language play by reading texts that feature rhyme, alliteration, and onomatopoeia. The teacher's responsibility is to focus on the sounds within words so students become engaged in the activity. Listening to these sounds should be an everyday activity for children. Do not be concerned if students do not hear all the intricate sounds of a particular passage at first; focus on making these language experiences positive so they look forward to more texts. Phonemic awareness will develop over time with continued exposure to and engagement in diverse language experiences (Cunningham et al., 1998).

Many of Dr. Seuss's books are filled with humor and rhymes, with the story line often taking a back seat to the sounds of the text. *Green Eggs and Ham* (1960) is filled with rhymes. Notice the rhymes are all couplets so the children can hear them easily.

> I do not like them in a box.
> I do not like them with a fox.

The more you read the story and encourage students to participate, the more fun they will have as the words roll off their tongues. You can always permit them to add their own verses, such as the following:

> I do not like them in the mall.
> I do not like them with y'all. (In a nice Southern accent!)
>
> *or*
>
> I do not like them on a log.
> I do not like them with a frog.
>
> *or*
>
> I do not like them in a tree.
> I do not like them with a bee!

Some authors use couplets in stories in which the primary emphasis is on plot; the rhyme adds to the tone of the story. Robert Kinerk in *Clorinda* (2003) uses couplets that enhance the tone of the adventure as Clorinda seeks fame in New York City with her ballet moves:

> Sparkling and whirling, the dancers took flight.
> The music, the costumes, the dazzling light. (unpaged)

Kinerk also introduces readers to the many technical terms of ballet, such as "pirouetting," "corps," and "*en barre*," and uses onomatopoeia:

> She crashed and she smashed,
> and she crushed and she smushed. (unpaged).

Other books with rhyme, alliteration, and language play are listed in Appendix A.7.

Many authors use multiple language elements to create a story's mood. Some use onomatopoeia, alliteration, and assonance, which add a range of sounds and moods to a story. A favorite board book of many young children is *Miss Spider's New Car* (1999) by David Kirk. The verbs and interjections are filled with onomatopoeia, which are written in brightly colored capitals. Here are a few sample lines:

> It mustn't SCREECH (written in bright orange) or GROWL (written in blue) or WHINE! (written in green)
> CHA-HISS! (written in orange) This speedster's charged with steam.
> VA-ROOM! (written in bright pink) Slow down, I'm going to scream!

Students enjoy when you exaggerate the sounds of a car.

Eve Bunting's *In the Haunted House* (1990) uses couplets with alliteration, assonance, and carefully chosen words to conjure a scary setting:

> There's a coffin-shaped tub, claw-footed and deep
> and in it's a vampire who smiles in his sleep.
> Ghosts swim in the hallway
> Three witches appear
> Bats hang by their feet
> From the cracked chandelier . . . .
> At the basin a werewolf is washing his snout
> Sucking in water and spouting it out.

Emphasize the alliteration and assonance and discuss with the students how the sounds of the words add to the story's scary mood. For example, you might emphasize the clicking /k/ and /t/ sounds in *coffin-shaped, tub,* and *claw-footed* to mimic the eerie sounds of the haunted house. (Notice how an exaggerated /h/ sound in *haunted house* echoes the hollow sounds of the house!) Heighten the devious mood by drawing out the long /i/ sound in *vampire* and *smiles.* Forming your mouth into a wide smile on the long /i/ also adds to the mood. In the next setting, the alliteration of the /w/ in *werewolf washing* might evoke a feeling of fear or woe, and the /s/ sound in *washing, sucking,* and *spouting* suggests the hissing of the werewolf. These playful sounds help the students become conscious of sounds within words and to realize that the sounds of words in a story or poem help set the mood just as much as the illustrations do.

In *Zin! Zin! Zin! A Violin* (1995), Lloyd Moss uses couplets, alliteration, and onomatopoeia to introduce orchestral and musical terms to young readers. Notice the light, high-pitched, flute-like sounds in the following passage:

> Flute, that sends our soul a-shiver,
> Flute, that slender, silver sliver.
> A place among the set it picks
> To make a young sextet—that's six.

In many books, characters' names have magical or musical sounds. Younger children enjoy the rhyming names of the different characters in Joan Powers's *Henny Penny* (1988): Cocky Locky, Ducky Lucky, Turkey Lurkey, Foxy Loxy, and Goosey Loosey. You can substitute other sounds to make your own names, such as Turkey Murkey or Ducky Mucky. The more you manipulate word sounds while reading stories, the more the students will become aware of the sounds in language.

Jan Brett's *Berlioz the Bear* (1991) also uses sounds to suggest the musical instruments played by the characters. Notice the /z/ sounds of the bass as the story begins:

> Zum. Zum buzz. Zum. Zum. Buzz. Berlioz had been practicing for weeks, and now just when the orchestra was going to play in the village square for a gala ball, a strange buzz was coming from his double bass. (unpaged)

Authors are using poetry in a growing number of informational books. Kesler (2012) reveals that through the recursive reading process, children move from the efferent (reading for information) to aesthetic reading (reading for enjoyment). With informational texts that use poetry, the students may learn new facts the first time they read it. When they reread it, however, they may notice the author's word choice and figurative language. In *Mississippi*, Siebert (2001) uses rhythm and rime to describe the Mississippi River:

> I am the river
>
> Deep and strong,
>
> I sing an, old enduring song
>
> With rhythms wild, and rhythms tame. (unpaged)

As teachers read this lilting poem, children are learning facts about the Mississippi River, including its origin and path to the Gulf of Mexico. During rereads, children begin to appreciate how the author has the river speaking to the reader and how the river believes it is not only deep, but also strong. Children also realize that the river is telling the reader that it is sometimes rough and at other times calm, but the author tells it as if the river is a singer. Other informational books written in poetry are listed in Figure 4.7.

What more needs to be said about the wonderful language in children's songs, chants, poems, tongue

Figure 4.7 Informational books in poetry.

Dawson, N. (2010). *Tracks of a Panda*. Illus. Y. Rong. Candlewick.

Hill, L. (2011). *Dave the Potter, Artist, Poet, Slave*. Illus. B. Collier. Little Brown Books.

Levenson, G. (2008). *Bread Comes to Life*. Illus. S. Thaler. Tricycle Press.

Nelson, M. (2009). *Sweethearts of Rhythm*. Illus. J. Pinkney. Dial Books.

Patz, N. (2003). *Who Was the Women Who Wore That Hat?* Illus. N. Patz. Dutton Juvenile.

Rappaport, D. (2009). *Eleanor: Quiet No More*. Illus. G. Kelley. Hyperion Books.

Sanders, N. (2011). *D Is for Drinking Gourd*. Illus. E. B. Lewis. Sleeping Bear Press.

Sidman, J. (2011). *Dark Emperor and Other Poems of the Night*. Illus. R. Allen. HMH BOOKS.

twisters, riddles, and stories? Take advantage of it by reading with expression and playing with word sounds. Drawing attention to the sounds within words while taking pleasure in reading these texts is the best way to develop children's phonemic awareness. Language play should take place in small groups or with individual students who lack a rich language background. Most of the activities described here can be conducted with such students. They will need extra one-on-one experience with an adult who engages them while they play with language.

intervention

STRATEGIES & ACTIVITIES

T he following section includes a number of activities that correspond to the seven dimensions of phonemic awareness. You may believe it is not necessary for students to develop all seven dimensions. However, some students, especially English learners and those who are inattentive in a large group, may benefit from these language activities, especially one-on-one or in a small group, which gives them more intensive exposure to language sounds (Hadaway, Vardell, & Young, 2001; Taylor et al., 2000). Many children become aware of the sounds of the English language through game-like activities and sustained exposure to singing and rhymes. Remember that games are a part of childhood play and meant for entertainment, not direct instruction. Therefore, the emphasis should not be on teaching phonemic awareness, but rather on playing with language in an enjoyable, relaxed manner. Instructions written for small groups can be modified for use with individuals and vice versa.

As mentioned earlier, some English sounds are not found in other languages. Also, because some sounds (e.g., /t/ and /d/; /b/ and /p/) are confusing even for native speakers, it is a good idea to present them several weeks apart (Vaughn et al., 2005). It is recommended that high-frequency sounds be introduced early (see Figure 5.5, p. 106, and Appendix B.5).

Activities Emphasizing Syllables

When introducing activities that focus on the sounds within words, start with syllables because they are a larger part of a word than single sounds. During small group work, you may observe some students having difficulty clapping out the syllables in their names or keeping up with similar activities. If you administer a phonemic awareness pre-assessment and the student cannot complete the first task (clapping out syllables), engage him in one of the following activities to emphasize listening to syllables. For these activities, the student may benefit from a one-on-one tutoring setting.

Clapping Syllables to Familiar Songs and Rhymes   GRADES K–2   A C T I V I T Y

Teach the children the following rhymes, then have them clap their hands or slap their knees for each syllable. All of the following rhymes can be found in *My Very First Mother Goose* (1996), edited by Iona Opie and illustrated by Rosemary Wells.

- "Jack and Jill Went up the Hill." (Most words have one syllable.)
- "Little Boy Blue, Come Blow Your Horn." (Most words have one syllable.)
- "Hey Diddle, Diddle." (Many two-syllable words.)
- "Humpty Dumpty." (Many one- and two-syllable words.)
- "Down at the Station, Early in the Morning." (A great combination of one- and two-syllable words.)

Clapping Syllables to Multisyllable Words   GRADES 3–6   A C T I V I T Y

Older students also need to hear syllables within words as they analyze multisyllable words and write them. For this age group, find multisyllable words in poems that you read together. You say the multisyllable word and the student taps his fingers as he repeats the word. For example, *streptococcus* is a fun word in "My Brother Doesn't Like to Share" (Lansky, 2000). Say the word and have the student tap as he pronounces *strep-to-coc-cus*.

Let's Make Music   GRADES K–1   A C T I V I T Y

When the child can sing the following songs by heart, have her beat each syllable with a rhythm instrument as she sings. Choose instruments that produce a distinct beat, such as rhythm sticks, drums, triangles, and sand blocks. Shaking instruments such as maracas are not as good because the beat is not as distinct. All of the following songs can be found in Pamela Beall and Susan Nipp's *Wee Sing* (2005) songbook:

"The Eentsy Weentsy Spider"   "This Old Man"
"Rain, Rain Go Away!"   "Teddy Bear"
"Twinkle, Twinkle, Little Star"   "Bingo Was His Name-o"

How Many Syllables in the Zoo?   GRADES K–1   A C T I V I T Y

Using the game board and picture cards found in Appendix D.4 and the directions for using them in Appendix D.3, have the student select a picture card from the stack. She says the word and claps the number of syllables. If she claps the correct number, she moves forward that number of spaces on the game board. If she claps the number of syllables incorrectly, she moves backward that number of spaces. You may need to help the student with unfamiliar animals.

Activities Emphasizing Initial Sounds

Listening for initial sounds in words is best developed when a teacher models writing during morning message and other writing experiences (Bear, Invernizzi, Templeton, & Johnston, 2011). However, if a student cannot distinguish the difference between sounds when most of his peers can, or if he cannot tell which two words begin with the same sound (task #2 on the pre-assessment phonemic awareness instrument), the following activities may prove helpful.

ACTIVITY   **Sound Boxes**   GRADES K–3

Sound boxes, developed by Elkonin (1973), demonstrate how words are made up of smaller pieces. When working with sound boxes, begin with three-letter words in the consonant–vowel–consonant (CVC) pattern.

1. Fold up the bottom of a large sheet of construction paper to make a pocket and staple the ends. (See Figure 4.8.) Use different colors of paper to represent different sounds, although the same color does not always have to match a particular sound.

2. Place three different colored slips of paper in the pocket, one over "Beginning," one over "Middle," and one over "End." Because the focus is on sounds and not letter names, it is not necessary to put the letters on the slips of paper.

3. Select words systematically. McCarthy (2008) suggests teachers choose first from level one words, which are the easiest for young students to dictate, to level three words, which are a little more difficult.

   a. Level 1: words with three phonemes that begin with /s/, /f/, or /m/ because the "flow of breath is not constricted" (p. 347) as these sounds are made.

   b. Level 2: words with three phonemes that begin with /d/, /k/, or /t/. These phonemes are "stop-consonant sounds" that feature a distinct break between these initial phonemes and the next phoneme.

   c. Level 3: words that begin or end with a consonant blend, such as /gr/ and /mp/. Blends are so closely connected that young students have a difficult time segmenting them.

4. After sharing a song, poem, or book with rimes, select one word with the CVC pattern, such as *sun*. Bear et al. (2011) suggest singing the following song to the tune of "Are You Sleeping, Brother John?"

   > Beginning, middle, end; beginning, middle, end.
   > Where is the sound? Where is the sound?
   > Where's the *ssss* in sun? Where's the *ssss* in sun?
   > Let's find out. Let's find out. (p. 123)

5. After singing this verse, the child selects the position of the sound by selecting the first card. This activity can also be used when listening for final consonant sounds by changing the third line appropriately.

figure 4.8

Sound boxes.

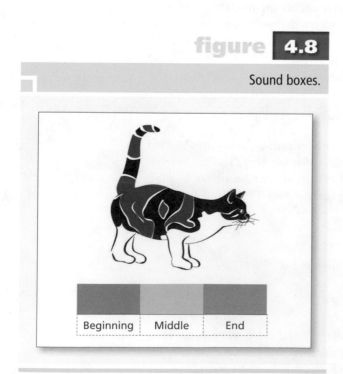

| Beginning | Middle | End |

Alphabet Sound Booklets

1. Give the child a magazine and have her find three or four pictures that begin with a designated consonant.
2. Have the child tear or cut out the pictures and glue them onto 3 x 5 index cards.
3. Put the letter on an index card and use it as a cover for the booklet.
4. Make a booklet for each consonant by using a comb binding to secure the pages.

Spanish/English Concept Books

Many concept books (books that help children discriminate among letters, numbers, colors, shapes, and other concepts by featuring illustrations of the concept) are bilingual (Spanish and English). These books are great to use when tutoring, because most authors use objects that have phonemes common to both English and Spanish.

Recommended concept books are presented in Appendix A.8. You may pair two native Spanish speakers, one who knows some English and another who knows very little English. Instruct the student who knows some English to look at the pictures and pronounce both the English and Spanish words for the images, and then to have his buddy say the word in English. Explain to the "student teacher" how important it is for him to pronounce the English word to the best of his ability because he is helping his classmate.

Remember the Beginning Sound!

This activity is played like the popular game of Memory or Concentration.

1. The picture cards (see Appendix D.5) are placed face down on the table or floor.
2. The teacher and student take turns turning over two cards at a time. The player says the words on the cards; if the two words begin with the same sound, the player must isolate the beginning sound by saying it.
3. If the player recognizes that the words do begin with the same sound, the player keeps the two cards.
4. If the player does not pick up two cards that begin with the same sound or if the player does not recognize that the words begin with the same sound, the player turns the cards back over in their places.
5. The objective is for the players to collect as many cards as possible. Begin the first game with cards of two different letters and then proceed to cards with three and four different letters.

Initial Sound Bingo

Make copies of the picture bingo cards provided in Appendix D.6 and laminate them. Make more than one set if a large group is going to play. Call out words from the following list. Each participant puts a marker on any image of a word that begins with the same letter sound. Participants try to get five in a row in a vertical, horizontal, or diagonal line.

WORD LIST

basket	kick	tip	doughnut	potato
cards	love	very	farmer	rooster
dad	move	want	game	Santa
first	no	yell	jelly	telephone
go	pick	zip	lace	water
hard	rise	bump	mom	yellow
jump	stand	camel	nice	zap

Note: Because the game focuses on initial sounds, accept responses that confuse *c* and *k* words.

ACTIVITY   **Toss the Cube**   GRADES K–2

Using cubes like those found in Appendix D.7, students toss a cube, say the sound the letter makes, and name one word that begins with that sound.

ACTIVITY   **Go Fish**   GRADES K–1

For kinesthetic learners in the semi-phonemic stage, Go Fish reinforces initial sounds of words. First, using pictures of objects known to students as "fish," attach a magnetic strip on the back. Place the fish on a large piece of blue butcher paper. Have the students use the fishing pole (a stick attached to a piece of string, with a magnet as a hook) to fish for a word. Students then say the initial sound and name the first letter of the word. Appendix D.8 has templates of fish for each letter of the alphabet.

ACTIVITY   **Tongue Twisters**   GRADES 2–3

For older students having difficulty distinguishing words with the same initial sound, reciting tongue twisters with the teacher often helps. Focus on saying them, not writing them. Most older students are familiar with "She sells seashells down by the seashore." You can improvise a tongue twister based on your name and then invite the student to create one based on his name. The focus is on hearing initial sounds, not identifying the letter names. For example, you might improvise, "Cute Katie Cauthrin couldn't cut carrot cake."

Activities Emphasizing Rhymes

Many students have a difficult time hearing rhymes. A teacher who is a good "kid-watcher" will be able to identify these students as she reads poems and stories; they will either not respond or will give incorrect responses. They often cannot complete the third task on a phonemic awareness pre-assessment instrument. The following activities emphasize rhyme.

ACTIVITY   **Identifying Rhyming Words in Poetry**   GRADES 1–8

One useful activity for any age students who cannot hear rhyme is for you to read an age-appropriate poem to students and ask them to listen for rhyming words. An example in "My Grandma's Teeth" (Lansky, 2000) uses rhyme (*bright/night*) and similes: Teeth like stars that are "sparkling bright," and teeth like stars that "come out at night" (p. 27).

Using poetry to help middle school students listen for rhyme can aid their spelling skills. Choose short poems intended for adolescents and instruct them to listen carefully for words that sound the same at the end. For example, "Good Models," a poem in Bagert (1997), is appropriate for older students because it references Elizabeth Browning, Emily Dickinson, and Walt Whitman. It includes the rhymes *frowning/Browning, change/strange, weird/beard,* and *rule/school.*

Verify that the student understands the rhyme by asking for another word that rhymes with *rule*. Then use one of Bruce Lansky's poems, whose humor appeals to middle school students, and ask the student to identify the rhyming words. Here are a few suggested poems, all from Bruce Lansky's *My Dog Ate My Homework!* (2009) collection. Each of these poems has the ABCB pattern.

- "My Dog Chewed Up My Homework"
- "Measles"
- "There's a New Cook in the Cafeteria"
- "Confession"
- "A Bad Case of the Giggles"

Humpty Dumpty Board Game

After reading "Humpty Dumpty," assemble the game board provided in Appendix D.9 and follow these directions.

- The game is for two participants.
- Turn all Humpty Dumpty halves upside down.
- Assign one side of the board to each participant.
- Decide who goes first.
- The first participant picks up a Humpty Dumpty half, pronounces the word, and checks to see if there is a half on her side of the wall that rhymes with it. If the participant has a rhyming picture and can correctly match it with its half on her side of the board game, she receives another turn. If she does not have a match or cannot identify the matching piece, her half is again turned upside down and put back in the playing pack.
- The objective for players is to get all the matches on their side of the wall.

Clowning Around with Rhyming Words

Using the picture word cards in Appendix D.5 from the "Remember the Beginning Sound" activity, lay out the pictures for the following words:

dog	pig	boat	fan	king	ham	bat	cow
coat	sun	cat	fish	duck	nose	cake	ball
goat	hand	top	fox	box	frog		

The student picks up the card and names the picture. He then must name any word that rhymes with the picture. For example, if he picks the picture of the pig, he can say any word that rhymes with *pig*, such as *big* or *fig*. With each correct response, add one section of the clown (as shown in Figure 4.9) until the entire clown is complete.

figure 4.9 Steps for clown drawings.

Activity Emphasizing Oddity

To emphasize oddity, pronounce three words, two of which begin with the same sound and one that does not (e.g., *milk, mom, table*). Ask the students which word is different. Those who have a difficult time with this tend to listen to the entire word rather than focusing on the initial sound. Students who do this may think that all the words are different. One-on-one time with the teacher, in which you emphasize the beginning sounds of the two similar words and then point out the beginning sound of the word of the different word, will help. Working with manipulatives, such as in the following activity, may make the task easier.

Odd-Card Out!

Using the picture cards from "Remember the Beginning Sound" (Appendix D.5), place three cards in front of the student. Two begin with the same initial sound, and the other is the "odd" picture card. The student must pick out the picture card that does not begin with the same initial sound as the other two.

As an example, place the cards with a picture of a fish, boat, and bat in front of the student. She must pick out the fish card as the "odd" card. Work with any particular sounds that give the student trouble.

Activities Emphasizing Blending

B lending is a skill that is needed when students begin to decode and encode unknown words. Most will learn to blend onsets with rime as the teacher plays with language in small groups. However, some students have difficulty blending because when decoding words, they often look for smaller parts within a word and then put the parts together. These children often struggle to complete the fifth task on the pre-assessment for phonemic awareness. The following activities emphasize blending.

Children Are Sounds

Some students learn best through kinesthetic activities. This activity will help both kinesthetic and visual learners; it is designed for small- or whole-group learning.

1. Call three students to stand in a straight line in the front of the group. You then stand behind them.
2. Assign each student a sound (e.g., first child is /h/; second child is a short /a/; and the third child is /t/).
3. Tell the group each student's sound, and then ask them to say the sounds as you point to each student. Point slowly at first and repeat a few times. Go faster each time.
4. Ask the group what word (e.g., *hat*) the three students represent.
5. Ask the group to say the three sounds again while you point, then give a swooping gesture to have the group say the word.
6. Repeat with other students and other words.

Blending with Puppets

This activity works well with young English learners in the shy, silent stage, who may be reluctant to speak for themselves but willing to talk through a puppet (refer back to Figure 1.4; Vaughn et al., 2005). The activity works best with one child at a time, but can be performed with a small group of up to five students.

1. Put on three finger puppets (any puppets will do) and explain to the student(s) that the puppets can only say sounds, no words.
2. Instruct the student(s) to listen carefully as the puppet says its sound. For example: Puppet #1 is /p/, Puppet #2 is a short /a/, Puppet #3 is /n/.
3. Have the student(s) repeat the sound as each puppet says its sound.
4. Repeat steps 2 and 3 a little faster each time.
5. Then ask the student(s) what word the three puppets make together (*pan*).

Onset and Rime Blending Card Game

GRADES 1–3   A C T I V I T Y

Use the words listed below from the picture cards provided in Appendix D.5. Place three cards in front of the student; for example, the cards with pictures of the fish, cat, and hat. Then say the onset and the rime for one of the cards. For example, say, "I see a /k/ plus *at*." The student must pick up the cat card and say the word. Continue the activity by placing a new card with the fish and hat cards; for example, the bed card.

PICTURE CARDS TO USE

ball	cat	frog	key	net	rake	top
bag	cup	gate	king	nose	rat	vase
bat	dog	goat	lock	pail	ring	vest
bed	fan	ham	log	pan	rug	web
bee	fin	hand	map	pen	sink	well
box	fish	hat	mouse	pig	socks	wing
cake	fork	jar	nest	pin	sun	wig

Blending Individual Sounds Card Game

GRADES 1–3   A C T I V I T Y

Use the picture cards named below from Appendix D.5. Draw two cards and place them in front of the student. For example, the two cards may be the pictures of the bell and the bat. Ask, "Which picture is /b/ plus /a/ plus /t/?" (say each sound separately, but do not distort the sounds). The student must say the word and select the correct card.

PICTURE CARDS TO USE

ball (/b/ + /a/ + /l/)	cat	gate	log	pig	top
bat	coat	goat	lock	pin	tub
boat (/b/ + /o/ + /t/)	cup	gum	map	pipe	tie
bell	dog	ham	moon	rat	web
bed	dime	hat	net	rake	wig
bag	duck	jet	nose	road	zoo
box	fan	jug	nut	rope	
bee	fin	kite	pan	rug	
cake	five	key	pen	sun	

Activity Emphasizing Segmenting

Being able to segment sounds within words is an important skill as students begin to write. They pronounce the entire word as they start writing it, and then segment the sounds as they write each letter. When working in small groups, you may find a student who cannot detect individual sounds in words. Administer a phonemic awareness pre-assessment to determine her ability to segment words. If she cannot complete the sixth task, she may benefit from the following activity.

Segmenting Individual Sounds (Card Game)

GRADES 1–3   A C T I V I T Y

Use the same picture cards from Appendix D.5. The student draws a card from the deck and segments each sound of the word. For example, if she draws the picture card of the pig, she must say, "/p/ plus /i/ plus /g/."

Next, reverse roles with the student. Draw a card and say each individual sound. The student must determine if you are correct. Try making some errors to see if the student recognizes them.

Activities Emphasizing Deleting

Most students will be able to delete sounds as they participate in small group activities with the teacher. Use the sound box described earlier in this section and choose three-letter words in which the rime is a word by itself (e.g., *hit, fan, sat, Sam*). Place a "word" (three different colors of paper) in the sound box and review with the small group the sound for each slip of paper (e.g., first slip: /b/ sound, second slip: short /a/ sound, and third slip: /t/ sound). Then, remove the first slip of paper (the /b/ sound) and ask the group to pronounce the new word. During this activity watch closely for children who do not understand the concept, and conduct it again with them on an individual basis if necessary.

A C T I V I T Y   **Pop Off the Beads!**   GRADES K–1

Perform this activity using different colored pop beads with those who need one-on-one help deleting sounds from words. Each bead represents one sound within a word. When the child completes the activity successfully with manipulatives, try conducting it orally.

If the word has three sounds, give the student three connected pop beads. Say to her, "I'm going to say a word and ask you to take off one sound from the word. I want you to first say the entire word, and then I want you to pop off a bead and say the new word. For example, here are three beads. The three beads are the word *bat*. The first red bead is the /b/, the middle yellow bead is the short /a/ sound, and the last green bead is the /t/. Now I am going to take off the /b/ bead, and I have the word *at*. Now, I am going to let you do it." You can use any three-letter words from the following lists. When the child is comfortable working with three-letter words, you can add one bead and work with four-letter words.

SET #1	SET # 2	SET # 3
Late; take off /l/	Harm; take off /h/	Bin; take off /b/
Meat; take of /m/	Burn; take off /b/	Send; take off /s/
Ball; take off /b/	Cup; take off /k/	Hand; take off /h/
Bat; take off /b/	Chair; take off /ch/	Ledge; take off /l/
Ham; take off /h/	Fear; take off /f/	Wax; take off /w/
Beat; take off /b/	Bus; take off /b/	Pant; take off /p/
Bill; take off /b/	Nod; take off /n/	Mask; take off /m/
Sit; take off /s/	Link; take off /l/	Cash; take off /k/
Boar; take off /b/	Ditch; take off /d/	Dan; take off /d/
Cart; take off /k/	His; take off /h/	Fact; take off /f/

You can make more sets by using the rimes from the list above and adding new onsets.

A C T I V I T Y   **Children and Sounds**   GRADES K–1

This activity is similar to "Children Are Sounds" and is good for kinesthetic learners. It also has students delete sounds.

1. Choose a three-letter word, such as *bat, sit,* or *ham,* and assign one letter sound to each child. For example, Carolyn is the /b/ sound, Victor is the short /a/ sound, and Juan is the /t/ sound.

2. Line up the three children in a row in the correct order: *b a t.*

3. Ask them the following set of questions.
   - What sound is Carolyn?
   - What sound is Victor?
   - What sound is Juan?
   - What word do the three sounds make?
   - Now let's have Carolyn sit down.

- What word do Victor and Juan make?
- Now let's have Carolyn stand back up. What word do we have now?

This activity can be done with any word in which one letter can be deleted to form another word (e.g., *sand, ball, Jill, sit, meat*). Words such as *right* and *sound*, of course, do not work.

Activities Emphasizing Manipulating

Learning to manipulate sounds within words aids students when they later need to find patterns within words to decode unknown words and spell new ones. Manipulating activities can be done in small groups. The following small group activity uses the sound box, discussed earlier in this chapter.

1. Assign a sound to each of the three slips of paper in the pocket (e.g., /f/ + /a/ + /n/), and pronounce the word with the students.
2. Remove the first slip of paper, the /f/ sound, replace it with another colored slip of paper, and call it the hard /c/ sound.
3. Ask the children what word the three sounds make. Take out the "c" slip of paper, replace it with yet another colored slip, and call it the /m/ sound. Have the children name the new word.

For those who do not respond correctly and also cannot complete the eighth task on the pre-assessment for phonemic awareness instrument, work with the students to complete the following activities during one-on-one time.

Moving the Tiles   GRADES 1–3   A C T I V I T Y

1. Cut seven 2 x 3 x 2 tiles from seven different colors of poster board. You can laminate the pieces so they can be used over a period of time.
2. Lay out three different colored tiles in front of the student (e.g., blue, red, and yellow). Assign a letter sound to blue (e.g., the /b/ sound), another sound to the red tile (e.g., the short /a/ sound), and a third sound to the third yellow tile (e.g., the /t/ sound).
3. Ask him to say the word that the tiles make.
4. Remove the blue tile and replace it with a white tile, calling it the /f/ sound. Again ask the student to pronounce the new word. Do this activity first with three tiles and later add the fourth tile to form four-letter words.

The following are lists of suggested words. Note that the child is to replace the initial sound of each of the words in the list with the sound of the letter that is on top of the list.

S	M	B	P	H
pat	late	late (bait)	sat	sat
pit	neat	meat	meat	pit
neat	ball	call	ball (Paul)	meat
ham	bat	sat	bat	Sam
boar	bake	cake	ham	late
bake	fan	fill	bill	neat
ring	cart	sit	sit	ball
round	night	soar	cart	cart (heart)
right	round	turn	cup	fill
		pear	bear	farm
		wig	wig	fair
		site		night (height)

ACTIVITY   **Attending to Differences Between What They Expect to Hear and What They Actually Hear**   GRADES K–1

In a small group, so you can do some "kid-watching assessment," read familiar rhymes out loud, but occasionally reverse, substitute, or swap words (Adams, Foorman, Lundberg, & Beeler, 2013). Assess whether students are listening carefully to what you are saying. Here are a few examples (be sure students are familiar with the original rhymes):

> Baa Baa sheep black
> Old Queen Cole was a merry ole soul
> Mary had a little dog
> Dub-a-dub-rub
> The five little kittens who mittens their lost

If students do not catch the word reversal or substitutions, they may not be listening carefully. Poor listening may result in students not hearing phonemes, so be sure nothing is distracting students from the task at hand.

PHONEMIC AWARENESS AND TECHNOLOGY

Research indicates that computer-assisted tutoring of phoneme segmentation can increase students' ability to hear phonemes (Wood et al., 2013). Many interactive websites encourage students to listen for phonemes. The following resources will assist you as you help students build phonemic awareness:

- www.learningtoday.com/curriculum/phonemic-awareness/ Includes lessons in listening for oddity, blending phonemes, listening for rhyming sounds, and identifying individual sounds.
- http://teacher.scholastic.com/clifford1/flash/phonics/index.htm Emphasizes isolation of letter match, isolation of sound match, and blending of phonemes to make words.
- www.sadlier-oxford.com/phonics/teacher.cfm Emphasizes isolation of phonemes, rhyming words, and identifying sounds.
- www.readwritethink.org/classroom-resources/grade/kindergarten/ Emphasizes isolation of word family sorts, and blending of phonemes to make words.
- www.pbskids.org/games Some games emphasize isolation of phonemes and blending of phonemes.

Apps: Phonemic Awareness

Beginning Sounds Interactive Game ($.99, Grades PreK–1). Students match words that share the same beginning sound, dropping each picture ball into the correct spot on the board.

ABC Magic 4 (Free, Grades PreK–1). This app will help students associate each letter with its most commonly occurring sound. Students use touch-activated sound features to match pictures to the correct letters.

ABC Magic Phonics (Free, Grades PreK–1). This app will help students learn the sounds of the letters of the alphabet, matching a photo with each letter.

Phonics Awareness, 1st Grade (Free, Grade 1). This app, which uses bugs to peak student interest, is highly interactive and provides instant feedback on how students are doing.

CONCLUDING THOUGHTS

Phonemic awareness is the ability to distinguish oral sounds and syllables within words. Children with this ability can distinguish initial sounds, determine how many sounds are in a word, manipulate sounds to create new words, delete sounds from a word to create a new word, and determine the number of syllables within a word. Most researchers and educators agree that proficient readers and writers need these skills; however, how teachers should facilitate these skills is open for debate. Some believe children must receive explicit instruction in phonemic awareness, while others believe that teaching phonemic awareness breaks language into too many parts, which makes language difficult for children.

Learn as much as you can about phonemic awareness and enjoy the wonderful sounds in the English language. Then, as you work with your students, you can instill in them the fun of listening to and manipulating sounds in words.

reflective learning

PHONEMIC AWARENESS. Mr. Ross is certified to teach early childhood and elementary grades. After teaching fifth grade for three years, he is offered a kindergarten position and is thrilled to have a new challenge. Even though many of his students have spent time in day-care, he will be their first formal teacher because the district has no four-year-old program.

When Mr. Ross meets with the other kindergarten teachers in the fall, he is surprised to learn about the district's emphasis on phonemic awareness and that teachers are required to assess kindergarteners on it. The other kindergarten teachers tell him the principal, a former kindergarten teacher, is motivated to demonstrate that kindergarten students make adequate yearly progress in building phonemic awareness and that she will question him regularly on what he is doing to achieve that goal.

The results of the initial DIBELS assessment indicate that most of his students cannot clap syllables, many cannot give words that begin with the same initial sound, and no student can delete or manipulate sounds. Mr. Ross knows he needs to spend time helping students build their awareness of phonemes; however, he knows of no strategies to help build phonemic awareness.

questions

1. What should Mr. Ross do first?

2. Do you think Mr. Ross should spend time each day with explicit instruction in phonemic awareness? Explain why or why not, as though you are addressing the parents of children in Mr. Ross's class.

3. What types of activities are most appropriate for kindergarten children, and which should Mr. Ross use?

4. Where should Mr. Ross go to find creative activities in all the five areas of phonemic awareness?

5. Is there a particular sequence of the five areas that Mr. Ross should use? Or should he engage the students in all five areas each day?

Phonics

My father told me once
that words and letters hold
the secrets of the universe.

ELIZA, *THE BEE SEASON*

scenario

At the beginning of the fall semester at Neil Armstrong Middle School, reading interventionist Mr. Spearhead is assigned to work with Jesus, a seventh-grade English learner. Jesus has lived in the United States for four years and attended nine different schools before his father found steady work and enrolled Jesus at the school. During their first session, Mr. Spearhead observes the boy reading a short poem, "Bring Your Own Lunch" (Lansky, 2009), which has mainly one-syllable words recognizable to most seventh graders. The poem also has rhyming words (e.g., *lick/sick* and *ill/will*). When Jesus is unable to identify the rhyming words, Mr. Spearhead has Jesus tell him about his family, their favorite family activities, and his other schools. This allows Mr. Spearhead to assess Jesus's oral language, which he finds adequate for a fourth-year English learner.

During his second session with Jesus, Mr. Spearhead works with riming words. He reads three words (e.g., *hall, jump, fall*) and asks Jesus to repeat the words that rime. He cannot, so Mr. Spearhead writes *hall* and *fall* on a whiteboard and underlines the *all* in each word. Jesus catches on quickly and soon adds to the list with *mall, ball, call,* and *tall.* Mr. Spearhead begins with onset and rimes because there are 37 rimes that create nearly 500 words (Stahl, 1998), and Jesus recognizes analogies between shared rime spelling.

As you read this chapter, consider the following questions:

guiding questions

1. What do you know about phonics generalizations? Can you remember any jingles you learned about phonics?

2. What generalizations will be important for Mr. Spearhead to teach Jesus?

3. What principles of phonics instruction is Mr. Spearhead using with Jesus?

4. If you had a student with Jesus's abilities, what would you do to assess his knowledge of phonics?

5. In what specific additional activities would you engage your student?

introduction

Reading researchers and educators agree that phonics is important for readers as they learn how the sounds of language create words (Bear, Invernizzi, Templeton, & Johnston, 2011; Cunningham, 2012; Fountas & Pinnell, 2003; Smith, Walker, & Yellin, 2004). In 2003, the International Reading Association declared that explicit and systematic phonics instruction has long-lasting positive effects on students' reading ability (International Reading Association, 2003).

The big question that teachers face is, "What is the most effective way to help students as they learn the letter–sound relationships?" Camilli and Wolfe (2004) contend that direct phonics instruction may aid some struggling young readers, "but only if embedded in a print-rich comprehensive literacy program and delivered in brief, individualized lessons" (p. 28). They found whole-class phonics instruction ineffective because some students already know and use the concept being presented, and other students lack the background knowledge to understand the concept. Dombey (2011) argues that if teachers focus on reading as learning and applying phonics rules, the enjoyment of reading and engaging with a text is lost.

Another debate is whether phonics instruction is needed for older students. Ivey and Baker (2004) argue that it is not. Instead, older students need strategies to develop vocabulary and make sense of text, not to understand letter–sound relationships. However, older English learners, such as Jesus in the above scenario, can benefit from explicit phonics instruction if it is not part of their background knowledge.

Teachers should approach phonics with the same enthusiasm that they approach phonemic awareness; the study of these foundational skills should be like an adventure, solving the puzzle of the unique way English words are formed. Consider this puzzle:

- begin with the word *in*, add the letter *k* at the end of *in* (ink),
- add two letters to the beginning of *ink* (think), change one letter within the new word (thank),

- drop the beginning letter (Hank), change the ending letter (hand),
- drop the beginning letter (and),
- drop the ending letter (an),
- drop one more letter (a) to form a single-letter word.

Doing fun puzzles such as this with elementary students makes learning fun and helps them see how uniquely words are formed. After giving students some of these puzzles, invite students to create their own puzzles for their classmates.

Phonics should be an engaging activity, not simply a process of learning rules and completing worksheets. Teachers can also point out fundamental skills during a shared reading experience so students understand that phonics is not separate from reading and writing. Phonics is a brain tool that readers and writers use when engaging in authentic tasks.

These questions and other topics related to phonics instruction are addressed in this chapter, including (1) what teachers need to know about phonics, (2) how students learn phonics, (3) how to teach phonics, (4) types of phonics assessments, (5) effective intervention strategies and activities for teaching phonics, and (6) websites and apps that reinforce phonics.

DEFINITIONS

The **graphophonic system** is the relationship between the letters and their sounds. Recall that a phoneme is the smallest unit of speech sound (e.g., /l/, /m/, /b/, /sh/, /ch/, and so on). A **grapheme** is the written representation of the phoneme. A grapheme may be one letter or a cluster of letters. For example, the word *wish* includes four letters, three phonemes (/w/, /i/, and /sh/), and three graphemes (*w, i,* and *sh*). The cluster /sh/ makes one distinct sound. Our English alphabet is complicated because some letters have more than one sound. For example, each vowel has a long sound, a short sound, a schwa sound (a vowel sound that is articulated with the tongue in a neutral position, e.g., *a* in *a-gree,* and *e* in *chil-dren*), and a controlled *r* sound (the letter *r* follows a vowel and alters the vowel sound, e.g., *art* and *term*). Sometimes more than one letter represents the same sound. The /k/ sound can be represented by a *k* (kite) or a *c* (cake), and sometimes the *k* is silent (know). Because all elementary teachers work with struggling readers at some point during their teaching career, they should understand terms such as *grapheme* and *schwa* as well as other basic phonics terms. Terms associated with phonics are listed in the following box.

Phonics Glossary at a Glance

BOX

Accent: The vocal emphasis applied to syllables in words. In *ac-cent,* the first syllable *ac* is accented.

Affix: Meaning units (prefixes and suffixes) that are added to root or base words.

Analytic phonics: An inductive approach to analyzing a word. The whole word is first read, then each letter sound is analyzed to determine the pronunciation of the word.

Base: Also called the root part of the word. The part to which affixes are added.

Blend: Two or three consonants with closely related but separate sounds. Also called consonant clusters. (Two examples: /br/, /fl/.)

Closed syllable: Syllable that ends with a consonant sound. (Example: first syllable of *but-ter.*)

Cluster: See **blend.**

Compound word: Two words joined together to form a new word. (Example: *butterfly.*)

Consonants: The letters *b, c, d, f, g, h, j, k, l, m, n, p, q, r, s, t, v, w, x, y, z.*

Consonant cluster: Two connecting consonants that when blended together make a unique sound:

/br/	as in	*brick*	/cr/	as in	*crib*
/dr	as in	*drink*	/fr/	as in	*frog*
/gr/	as in	*grape*	/pr/	as in	*prize*
/tr/	as in	*tree*	/bl/	as in	*block*
/cl/	as in	*clock*	/fl/	as in	*flag*
/gl/	as in	*glue*	/pl/	as in	*plane*
/sl/	as in	*slime*	/sc/	as in	*scar*
/sk/	as in	*skate*	/sm/	as in	*small*
/sn/	as in	*snail*	/sp/	as in	*spoon*
/st/	as in	*star* and *mist*		and	*crisp*
/scr/	as in	*screen*	/sw/	as in	*swan*
/str/	as in	*stream*	/squ/	as in	*squirrel*
/spl/	as in	*splash*	/spr/	as in	*spring*
/nt/	as in	*ant*	/thr/	as in	*throne*
/rd/	as in	*card*	/pt/	as in	*slept*
/sk/	as in	*ask*	/rk/	as in	*park*

(continued)

Phonics Glossary at a Glance, continued

Consonant digraphs: Two connecting consonants that make one sound:

> /sh/   as in   *sheep*
>
> /th/ (voiced) as in *the*
>
> /th/ (voiceless) as in *third*
>
> /ch/   as in   *cheese*
>
> /zh/   as in   *pleasure*
>
> /wh/   as in   *wheel*
>
> /ng/   as in   *ring*

Decoding: The process of identifying words by attaching appropriate sounds to corresponding letters or letter sequences.

Derivational suffixes: An affix at the end of the word that changes the word's syntactic category and/or its meaning. (Example: -*ly*.)

Digraph: Two letters that represent one sound. (Examples: /ch/ in *church*, and /oa/ in *road*.)

Diphthong: Two connecting vowels that make a distinct sound, unlike either of the two vowels. Examples:

> /ou/   as in   *cloud*   /ow/   as in   *now*
>
> /oi/   as in   *oil*   /oy/   as in   *boy*

Encoding: The process of attaching appropriate letters to sounds when writing.

Fricative consonants: When pronounced, they cause friction in the mouth (/f/, /v/, /th/, /z/, /s/, /zh/, /sh/).

Grapheme: Unit of writing that represents a phoneme.

Inflectional endings: A letter or letters at the end of a base word that change its grammatical properties within its syntactic category. (Examples: -*s* and -*es*.)

Nasal consonants: When pronounced, the air is forced through the nose (/n/, /m/, /ng/).

Onset: The part of a word that precedes the vowel. (Examples: *p* in *pat* and *str* in *street*.)

Open syllable: Syllable that ends in a vowel sound. (Example: *ba* in *ba-by*.)

Phoneme: The smallest unit of sound. (Example: *fly* has three phonemes, /f/, /l/, and /y/.)

Phonetics: Study of speech sounds and the way these sounds are made.

Phonics: A way of teaching reading and spelling that stresses symbol–sound relationships.

Phonemic awareness: Awareness that spoken language consists of a sequence of phonemes.

Phonogram: The vowel and any letter that follows the beginning consonant. (Example: *am* in *Sam*.) Words that share the same phonograms are often called word families.

Phonological awareness: The ability to identify and manipulate various units of sound in speech, including syllables, onsets and rhymes, as distinct from their meaning.

Plosive consonants: When pronounced, these consonants produce a burst of air (/b/, /p/, /d/, /t/, /k/, and /g/ as in *gate*).

Rhyme: Sound elements that consist of the same sound combination. (Examples: *fly* and *by*, *fox* and *socks*.)

R-controlled vowel: When the letter *r* follows a vowel and alters the vowel sound. (Examples: *art, term, girl, fort, burp*.)

Rime: The vowel and any letter that follows the beginning consonant. (Example: *am* in *Sam*.) Also called phonogram.

Schwa: Vowel sound that is articulated with the tongue in a neutral position. (Examples: /a/ in *a-gree*, /e/ in *chil-dren*, /i/ in *e-dit*, /o/ in *ed-i-tor*, /u/ in *un-load*.)

Short vowel: Vowel sounds that occur in words like *hat, men, fit, hop, but*.

Silent letters: Letters that make no sound. (Example: *k* in *knit*.)

Syllable: Combination of phonemes that creates larger sound units within words. All syllables have a vowel sound. (Example: *clut-ter* has two syllables.)

Synthetic phonics: Stringing isolated letter sounds together to create words. (Example: /c/ + /a/ + /t/ = cat.)

Vowels: These letters of the alphabet: *a, e, i, o, u* and sometimes *y* and *w*.

Vowel digraph: Two connecting vowels that make one sound. Examples:

ai	as in	*mail*	*ee*	as in	*see*
ea	as in	*break*	*oa*	as in	*road*
ay	as in	*day*	*ey*	as in	*they*
ie	as in	*die*	*ei*	as in	*receive* or *eight*

Whole word approach: Learning new words by memorizing the entire word.

WHAT TEACHERS SHOULD KNOW

In 1995 Louisa Moats surveyed teachers' backgrounds in linguistics. She found that about 50 percent of the surveyed teachers could benefit from additional training in linguistics, especially phonics. Specifically, she determined that teachers with a basic understanding of linguistics could help struggling readers in the following ways:

- Interpret and respond to readers' errors.
- Provide clear and simple examples for decoding and spelling.
- Organize and sequence instruction.
- Explain spelling patterns.
- Integrate language instruction.

Remember that students may become confused by educational jargon and terms such as *consonant blends, clusters, digraphs,* and *diphthongs* (Cunningham, 2012). Therefore, much of the information in this section is designed to help you gain a better understanding of phonics, but the terms and "rules" are not intended to be taught to struggling readers, because they may be overwhelming or intimidating.

How Students Learn Phonics

English spelling has three layers: alphabetic, pattern, and meaning. *Alphabetic* refers to spelling words letter by letter from left to right. *Pattern* refers to understanding the major patterns of letters: CVC (*hat*), CVCe (*hate*), CVVC (*road*), and so on. *Meaning* refers to different spellings for the different forms of words, for example, *music* and *musical.* Children learn about these three layers through decoding (reading), encoding (writing), and teacher modeling.

Decoding words

The human brain detects patterns (Bear et al., 2011; Cunningham, 2012). Therefore, young readers learn new words more easily by analyzing onset and rime than by attempting to make letter–phoneme correspondences. For example, it is easier for young readers to read *Sam, ham,* and *jam* when they recognize the rime *am* and add the onsets *s, h,* and *j*. When the rimes become longer than two letters, it is even easier for children because they see two parts instead of four or five. Take the *ound* rime in *found, sound, round,* and *mound* as an example. *Ound* is rather complicated to sound out as individual letters; however, if students know *ound* as one sound, they merely add the onsets— *f, s, r,* and *m*—to create the four words.

Young readers also use analogies to pronounce unknown words (Moustafa & Maldonado-Colon, 1999). For example, if beginning readers know that the letter

m makes the /m/ sound in *mom*, they know they need to make the /m/ sound when they see the word *milk* for the first time.

Students learn to read by focusing on onset, rime, and the initial letter, and by considering the length of words (Cunningham, 2012). Emerging readers can recognize their classmates' names by looking at initial letters; when two names begin with the same letter, they can identify which name sounds longer. For example, they know that when they pronounce *Jill,* it is shorter than when they pronounce *Jeremy*. Therefore, when they see *Jill* and *Jeremy* in print, they can determine which word is *Jill* and which one is *Jeremy*.

Students learn decoding skills when the skills are introduced, taught, practiced, and reinforced within a context that is meaningful to them (Cunningham, 2012; Dombey, 2011; Reedy, 2011). When a teacher reads a text that interests students, they see "real" words at work and not nonsense words. When reading, you can help students discover simple examples of the various phonics concepts. Hiebert (1999) found that "[p]honics instruction disconnected from texts that children read contributes little to children's use of phonics strategies in recognizing words" (p. 556).

Encoding words

As students write their own texts, they learn to listen to the sounds within words when they break up words to encode them. They also learn (1) to read/write from left to right, (2) to read/write from top to bottom, and (3) that words have spaces between them. During this process students should write meaningful texts, not strings of nonsense words. Their words do not need to be spelled correctly; they will make approximations of correct spellings as they develop writing skills. Students who listen to sounds and make approximations as they write become better decoders when they read (Cunningham, 2012).

Teacher modeling

Students also learn phonics by observing teachers model and talk about their writing. Ask students to talk about the initial sounds, ending sounds, medial sounds, and the patterns within words as you write the morning message. Effective teachers choose texts that use rhyme. For example, Ms. Synder might choose Ludwig Bemelmans's *Madeline and the Gypsies* (1986) to emphasize the word families for words such as *side, land, bring,* and *went*. After the class reads the book, Ms. Synder writes these words one at a time on the board or flip chart and asks the students to think of other words that rhyme with them. As Ms. Synder writes the rhyming words, she notes how they share the same ending letters. She may also demonstrate how some words rhyme even though they do not have the same ending letters. For example, in the same story, Bemelmans uses the following rhyming words: *more/door, blue/new, girls/curls,* and *bread/bed.* Ms. Synder writes *more* on the board or flip chart and asks the students to recall other words in the book that rhyme with *more.* She writes them down and discusses the different spellings with her students in this guided discovery of rhyme.

English Spelling Patterns

English is "a complex system that is basically phonetic, but also relies upon patterns and meaning to provide an optimal system" (Johnston, Bear, & Invernizzi, 2005).

Consonants

Many struggling readers and English learners have a difficult time distinguishing consonant sounds because they do not know the proper mouth position for each. Teachers who understand the position of the mouth and tongue for each sound can help students who struggle with correct pronunciation and spelling of words. Appendix B.3 provides detailed information about each consonant of the alphabet. Elementary students should not memorize or recite this information, but you may consult it in your effort to aid struggling readers. For example, after determining which letter sounds are problematic for a student, recite a word containing that letter sound to show the proper shape of the mouth as the sound is formed. The better you understand the English language, the more help you can offer struggling readers and English learners as they make sense of print.

Struggling readers may attempt to pronounce each sound of a **consonant cluster**—two connecting consonants that make a unique sound—separately. For example, they may separate the /s/ and the /t/ in *stop* or *post* rather than blending them together fluidly. Help these students recognize consonant clusters (e.g., /st/, /str/, /tr/, etc.) as distinct sounds. The same is true of **consonant digraphs**, which are two connecting consonants with one sound (e.g., *sh* in *sheep,* or /f/ in *phone*). Students need to recognize these digraphs as having one sound, instead of two distinct sounds.

Teachers working with struggling readers must also be aware of **allophones,** which are the slight variances of each phoneme. Allophones are caused by co-articulation. For example, the /m/ has a more distinct nasal sound in *mum* than in *most.* This is caused by the mouth positioning itself for the letter after the /m/.

Blevins (2006) found the nine consonant generalizations listed in Figure 5.1 have 95 to 100 percent utility.

Vowels

The vowels *a, e, i, o,* and *u* represent 19 different phonemes. This presents a challenge for struggling read-

figure 5.1

Ten useful consonant generalizations.

1. Only one consonant is heard when two of the same consonants are side by side (*merry, ladder*).
2. *C* has the /k/ sound when it is followed by *a* or *o* (*cat, cot*).
3. *C* has the /s/ sound when followed by *e, i,* or *y* (*cent, city, cycle*).
4. The digraph *ch* is usually pronounced /ch/, not /sh/ (*chair, chocolate*).
5. When *c* and *h* appear next to each other, they always are a digraph.
6. When a word ends in *ck*, it produces the /k/ sound (*buck, shock*).
7. *G* has the /j/ sound when followed by *e, i,* or *y* (*gem, giant, gymnasium*).
8. When *ght* appear together, the *gh* is always silent (*light, might*).
9. When *kn* appears at the beginning of a word, the *k* is always silent (*knee, know*).
10. When *wr* appears at the beginning of a word, the *w* is always silent (*write, wren*).

Source: From *PHONICS FROM A TO Z,* 2/E by Wiley Blevins. Scholastic, Inc./ Teaching Resources. Copyright © 2006, 2009 by Wiley Blevins. Reprinted by permission.

ers because with every vowel they encounter they must determine which sound it makes. Notice what happens to the sound of *o* as a different letter is added to *ho*:

hoe	hop	hoop	house
hope	hour	horse	hook
hoist	how		

It has at least nine distinct sounds. For this reason, synthetic phonics (teaching new words by adding one sound on to the next) may not be the best way to teach phonics.

The letter *y* is also used as a vowel when it appears at the end of a syllable or word. It usually has the long /i/ sound at the end of a syllable (*cycle*) or a one-syllable word (*by, fly*), and usually has the long /e/ sound at the end of a polysyllabic word (*funny, silly*). The letter *w* is also a vowel when it is used with another vowel (*low, now*).

Vowel sounds can be written many different ways. Figure 5.2 lists the possible spellings of the long vowel sounds and vowel diphthongs.

When working with English learners, help them understand how vowels are articulated in the mouth. Demonstrate the positions by first saying these long vowel words in this order—*beet, bait, bite, boat, boot*—in which the articulation is from front to back. When

figure 5.2 Various spellings for long vowels and diphthongs.

LONG /A/ SOUND	LONG /I/ SOUND	DIPHTHONG /OI/ SOUND	VARIANT /OO/ SOUND
a – came	i – bite	oi – oil	oo – food
ue – bouquet	ey – geyser	oy – boy	ui – fruit
ay – say	igh – sight		
ey – they	ie – lie	**DIPHTHONG /OU/ SOUND**	**VARIANT /OO/ SOUND**
ai – rain	ei – seismic	ow – how	oo – foot
ei – eight		ou – house	
	LONG /O/ SOUND		**VARIANT /O/ SOUND**
LONG /E/ SOUND	o – hope	**CONTROLLED R**	au – haul
e – be	oa – road	ar – arm	aw – saw
ee – see	ow – know	er – fern	
ea – eat		ir – girl	
ey – key	**LONG /U/ SOUND**	or – for	
ei – receive	u – use	ur – turtle	
ie – chief	ew – flew		

teachers talk about articulation of vowels, they also need to "describe the shape of the mouth, the openness of the jaw, and position of the tongue" (Bear et al., 2007, p. 145). Next, demonstrate short vowels by pronouncing these words in this order—*bit, bet, bat, but, bah.* Note the short /o/ is represented with an *ah.* The diagram in Figure 5.3 depicts where the vowels are articulated in the mouth.

Vowel diphthongs are two vowels placed "together in a word that produce a single glided sound"

(Reutzel and Cooter, 2011). When pronouncing a diphthong, the mouth changes positions as the sound is produced. Common diphthongs are /oi/, spelled *oi* (*oil*), *oy* (*boy*), and /ow/ (*owl*), /ou/ (*loud*), and /ai/ in *aisle.* Many Southerners transform their vowels into diphthongs; hence the dialect known as a Southern drawl. Appendix B.4 includes common diphthongs with an example and utility of each.

Vowel digraphs are two vowels placed together, but only the long sound of one of the vowels is heard. Examples include *rain* and *steam.* Many children are taught that "When two vowels go a-walking, the first one does the talking." Gates and Yale (2011) view this rule as not very helpful because it has so many exceptions. Appendix B.4 lists common vowel digraphs with an example and the utility of each. The struggling reader should try different possibilities to see which one works or sounds best. When *r* follows a vowel, the vowel takes on an *r*-controlled sound. All five vowels can be controlled by the *r* (*care, fern, girl, corn, turn*).

Other common variant vowels are (1) /oo/ (*food*), (2) /oo/ (*book*), (3) /au/ (*caught*). Generalizations about vowels that are helpful to struggling readers are listed in Figure 5.4.

Common spelling patterns in English words

Because the English language relies upon regular patterns of letters, teachers need to be familiar with these patterns to help readers discover them (Cunningham, 2012; Fountas & Pinnell, 2008; Helman, Bear, Templeton, Invernizzi, & Johnston, 2011). Figure 5.5 lists 37 high-frequency spelling patterns.

figure 5.3

Articulation of vowel sounds.

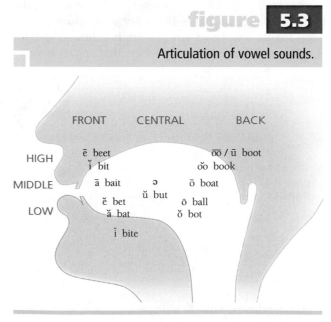

Source: Words their way: Word study for phonics, vocabulary, and spelling instruction (4th ed.) by Bear/Invernizzi/Templeton/Johnston, © 2006. Reprinted by permission of Pearson Education, Inc., Upper Saddle River, NJ.

figure 5.4

Seven generalizations about vowels.

1. If a single vowel is followed by one or two consonants, it usually is short (*cat, cent, hop, cut*).
2. If the letter a comes before *l, u,* or *w,* it usually has the /ô/ sound (*ball, caught, crawl*).
3. In the vowel digraphs *ai, ay, ee,* and *oa,* the first vowel is long (*bait, day, bee, road*).
4. The *y* usually represents the long /i/ sound in one-syllable words (*by, fly*).
5. The *y* usually represents the long /e/ sound at the end of a two-or-more syllable word (*happy, merry, sensibly*).
6. Some vowel spellings are used to distinguish word meanings (*meat/meet, red/read, beet/beat*).
7. In the word pattern (VCe) the *e* is often silent (*gave, time, cape*).

Source:: From *PHONICS FROM A TO Z,* 2/E by Wiley Blevins. Scholastic, Inc./Teaching Resources. Copyright © 2006, 2009 by Wiley Blevins. Reprinted by permission.

figure 5.5

High-frequency spelling patterns.

ack	(black)	ay	(tray)	ip	(ship)
ail	(pail)	eat	(meat)	it	(hit)
ain	(train)	ell	(shell)	ock	(sock)
ake	(cake)	est	(nest)	oke	(Coke)
ale	(whale)	ice	(rice)	op	(mop)
ame	(game)	ick	(brick)	ore	(store)
an	(pan)	ight	(night)	ot	(hot)
ank	(bank)	ill	(hill)	ound	(round)
ap	(cap)	in	(pin)	uck	(truck)
ash	(trash)	ine	(nine)	ug	(bug)
at	(cat)	ing	(king)	ump	(jump)
ate	(skate)	ink	(pink)	unk	(skunk)
aw	(claw)				

Source: From Cunningham, Patricia M., *Phonics They Use: Words for Reading and Writing,* 3rd Ed. Copyright © 2000, pp. 63, 94. Reprinted by permission of Pearson Education, Inc., Upper Saddle River, NJ.

English Learners and the Graphophonic System

Learning the sounds of English is not easy for English learners because English, like French, is a deep orthography. This means that the letter–sound relationship is not consistent (Helman, Bear, Invernizzi, & Templeton, 2008; Bear et al., 2007; Perez-Canado, 2005). For example, some consonants have two sounds (e.g., *c* and *g*), some phonemes can be represented by more than one grapheme (e.g., /f/ in *from* and *phone*; long /a/ in *maid, eight,* and *they*), and some consonants are silent if they precede a certain letter (e.g., *w* is silent when it precedes *r,* as in *write* and *wren,* and *k* is silent when it precedes *n* at the beginning of a word, as in *knee* and *know*). Other languages, such as Spanish, Italian, and Portuguese, are shallow or translucent orthographies, which means that their letter–sound relationships are quite consistent (Bear et al., 2007). The fact that it is a deep orthography is what makes learning to read English so difficult for English learners. And of course it takes longer for English learners whose native languages do not share our alphabet (e.g., Chinese, Vietnamese, Arabic, and Korean).

Because the largest population of English learners in the United States is composed of native Spanish speakers, you will likely have Spanish speakers in your classroom. Note that Spanish, like English, has three deviations. First, some phonemes are represented by more than one letter. For example, the /g/ is written g before the vowels *a, o,* and *u* and is written *gu* before the vowels *e* and *i.* The /k/ sound can be written as *c, k,* or *qu* (Perez-Canado, 2005). Second, one letter can have more than one sound. For example, the letter c has a /k/ sound before *a, o,* and *u,* and the /s/ sound before the vowels *e* and *i* (Perez-Canado, 2005). Third, some words share the same pronunciation. For example, *sac* and *saq* are both pronounced /sak/. As discussed in Chapter 4, some phonemes are common in both English and Spanish; however, some of these phonemes are represented with different graphemes. For example, the short /o/ sound in *top* is the letter *a* in Spanish (e.g., *ajo*). Figure 5.6 shows vowel sounds common to both English and Spanish and the letters that create them.

figure 5.6

Vowel sounds common to English and Spanish.

ENGLISH VOWELS	SIMILAR VOWEL SOUND USED IN A SPANISH WORD	EXAMPLE SPELLING ERROR
a as in cake	e as in h<u>e</u>cho	shek (shake)
e as in bean	I as in <u>i</u>do	spic (speak)
i as in like	ai as in <u>ai</u>re	nait (night)
o as in hope	o as in <u>o</u>cho	flout (float)
o as in top	a as in <u>a</u>jo	jab (job)
u as in June	u as in <u>U</u>sted	flut (flute)

Source: Helman, L. A. (2004). Building on the sound system of Spanish: Insights from the alphabetic spellings of English-language learners. *The Reading Teacher, 57*(5), 452–460.

Phonics and the Common Core State Standards

With the adoption of the Common Core State Standards and other new state standards, many professional development sessions have focused on such topics as close reading, domain-specific vocabulary, and citing evidence. But because phonics is a foundational skill, the CCSS includes standards addressing these skills for the early grades. Figure 5.7 lists the CCSS foundational phonics standards for grades K–2. Take time to consider the progression of these foundational skills. Like any other form of learning, teachers build on what the student knows so they are familiar with the skills from preceding grades. For example, if a student in third grade cannot automatically distinguish between long and short vowels in one-syllable words, the teacher must instruct her in that skill even though the standards indicate it should have been mastered in second grade. Also, note that if a first grader knows the spelling–sound correspondences for common consonant digraphs, she should not spend time continuing to work on the skill. This chapter, together with Chapters 4, 6, and 7, presents ways to teach to the CCSS reading foundational skills standards and assess whether students are progressing toward them.

PRINCIPLES OF PHONICS INSTRUCTION

Four key principles underlie phonics instruction:

1. Base instruction on what students know (Piaget & Inhelder, 1969).
2. Provide systematic instruction (International Reading Association, 2003).
3. Use appropriate texts.
4. Embed instruction in meaningful contexts (Bear et al., 2011; Cunningham, 2012; Gates & Yale, 2011; International Reading Association, 1997).

Principle One: Base Instruction on What Students Know

Effective teachers assess what students already know and build on that knowledge. Take the same approach with phonics instruction—begin with what students know. Assess students' knowledge during shared reading, interactive writing, and other literacy activities. Closely observe ("kid watch") what the students know about words. (In addition, you may use one of the other methods described in the informal assessment section of this chapter, such as word sorts or an IRI.)

Once you have a basic idea of students' literacy knowledge, place them in homogenous groups in order to provide appropriate instruction for each. The instruction for each group should be embedded in a meaningful context. Carefully select texts that permit students to examine both known words and new words appropriate for their developmental stage. As students examine a text, encourage them to make generalizations about groups of words. Subtly guide students to articulate a "phonics rule" behind their generalization; their "rules" may be similar to the generalizations in Figures 5.1 and 5.4. Note that students may also find exceptions to these generalizations.

---

figure 5.7   CCSS Reading: Foundational Skills standards that address phonics.

KINDERGARTEN

CCSS.ELA-Literacy.RF.K.3.a Demonstrate basic knowledge of one-to-one letter–sound correspondences by producing the primary or many of the most frequent sounds for each consonant.

CCSS.ELA-Literacy.RF.K.3.b Associate the long and short sounds with common spellings (graphemes) for the five major vowels.

GRADE 1

CSS.ELA-Literacy.RF.1.3.a Know the spelling–sound correspondences for common consonant digraphs.

CCSS.ELA-Literacy.RF.1.3.b Decode regularly spelled one-syllable words.

CCSS.ELA-Literacy.RF.1.3.c Know final –e and common vowel team conventions for representing long vowel sounds.

CCSS.ELA-Literacy.RF.1.3.d Use knowledge that every syllable must have a vowel sound to determine the number of syllables in a printed word.

CCSS.ELA-Literacy.RF.1.3.e Decode two-syllable words following basic patterns by breaking the words into syllables.

CCSS.ELA-Literacy.RF.1.3.f Read words with inflectional endings.

GRADE 2

CCSS.ELA-Literacy.RF.2.3.a Distinguish long and short vowels when reading regularly spelled one-syllable words.

CCSS.ELA-Literacy.RF.2.3.b Know spelling–sound correspondences for additional common vowel teams.

Source: National Governors Association Center for Best Practices (NGACBP) & Council of Chief State School Officers (CCSSO). (2010). English language arts standards, reading: Foundational skills, grades K, 1, and 2. Washington, DC: NGACBP, CCSSO, p. 16.

Principle Two: Provide Systematic Phonics Instruction

Systematic phonics instruction means teaching phonics in a planned sequence, using one of several approaches:

1. *Analytic phonics.* Teachers begin with students' sight words, known words developed from authentic reading, and then guide the students to analyze patterns and identify the phonics generalizations.

2. *Synthetic phonics.* Students convert letters into sounds and then blend the sounds to form a word.

3. *Phonics-through-spelling.* Students transform sounds into letters as they write; thus, they are engaged in many writing activities.

4. *Analogy phonics.* Students use parts of already-known words to identify unknown words.

5. *Phonics in context.* Students use sound–letter correspondences along with context cues to identify unknown words. This approach relies on students' knowledge of letter–sound relationships and patterns in words.

6. *Onset and rime phonics instruction.* Students recognize rimes and add the onset when reading new words. See the section on decoding words earlier in this chapter.

Commercial phonics programs teach a sequence of concepts in each grade. Some phonics programs begin with a pair of voiced and unvoiced consonants, such as *b* and *p*. Other commercial programs begin with consonants that are distinctly different from one another, beginning with *l*. Gates and Yale (2011) suggest a sequence that teachers can use without purchasing a commercial phonics program. The CCSS presented in Figure 5.7 also offer a guide for the skills students should acquire each year, and a suggested sequence is available at **www.hhpcommunities.com/literacyassessment.**

Principle Three: Use Appropriate Texts

"At the earliest stages of reading acquisition—particularly with students who are first introduced to book reading in school—careful attention needs to be paid to the text of instruction" (Hiebert, 1999, p. 555). For example, texts used during shared reading events should meet the following criteria:

- Include predictable text
- Have a small amount of text on each page
- Use large illustrations that support the text
- Appeal to children
- Be conceptually appropriate (i.e., they support a concept the teacher is introducing, such as the topic for a unit, author study, or illustrator study)

In addition, reading researchers have found that during shared reading, authentic children's literature is most effective with text that (1) is predictable, (2) uses **phonograms** (rhymes following onsets), and (3) includes riming words (Cunningham, 2012; Fountas & Pinnell, 2006b):

1. *Predictable text.* Children enjoy stories with predictable text, such as *When Pigs Fly* (Coulman, 2001) and *Rap a Tap Tap: Here's Bojangles* (Dillon, 2002). Students chime in as soon as they know words and refrains.

2. *Phonograms.* Books that emphasize phonograms help students see patterns within words. For example, *Snowmen at Night* (Buehner, 2002) uses phonograms: "One wintry day I made a snowman / very round and tall. / The next day when I saw him / he was not the same at all" (unpaged) as does *How Many Fish?* (Cohen, 2000): "How many fish? How many fish in the bay? Where do they go? Where do they go? Six little fish on their way" (unpaged). As you read and discuss stories with students, they discover words that have the same letter patterns. Dr. Seuss has written many books highlighting phonograms. Appendix A.7 lists others.

3. *Rhyming words.* Rhyming texts also draw attention to the sounds in words. Words that rhyme do not necessarily share the same letter pattern, as phonograms must (thus, *socks* and *fox* are rhyming words with different rimes). Draw attention to the difference between phonograms and words that rhyme. Appendix A.7 lists books that feature alliteration, phonograms, and rhymes.

Conversely, there is no research regarding the exclusive use of decodable texts for beginning reading instruction (Cunningham, 2012). Decodable texts, such as the *Books to Remember Series* by Flyleaf Publishing, are those written with words that closely follow phonetic rules or that feature words from one word family (e.g., "Dan can fan Nan").

Principle Four: Embed Instruction in Meaningful Contexts

Reading, writing, listening, and speaking activities that focus on meaningful tasks create meaningful contexts. Carefully select texts that children enjoy, have predictable patterns, and use words that help teach phonics concepts. Cunningham (2012) suggests engaging in the following series of activities to provide meaningful context:

1. Choose a book with predictable text that both the teacher and the students will enjoy.

2. Read and enjoy the text!

3. Act out the story or put on puppet shows. (Acting caters to kinesthetic learners and develops oral language skills.)

4. Have students discuss what they notice about words. (E.g., ask "Which ones begin with same letter?")

5. Play word games based on the story.

6. Add words from the story to the word walls.

7. Find rhyming words and words that end with the same spellings.

8. Have students write creative extensions of books that use predictable patterns. (For example, "I went walking. What did I see? I saw _____ looking at me.")

Another activity that teaches phonics in a meaningful context is to have students reread favorite predictable texts and then ask them to point to words that begin with certain sounds. Next, ask them to create a list of words that begin with that same sound. You may also give students words on index cards and ask them to match them with words in the text.

Students also learn phonics when they write meaningful messages (Bear et al., 2011; Cunningham, 2012). They learn to break up words and listen for all the sounds when they write riddles, notes to friends, stories, and log observations from experiments. Effective teachers model "stretching out words" as they write morning messages and involve students in interactive writing. Students are less likely to listen for sounds in words when performing rote exercises such as copying words correctly. Writing skills are discussed in greater detail in Chapter 11.

ASSESSMENT
Informal Assessment

Ideally, phonics assessment is conducted in natural settings as you observe students making sense of letter–sound relationships as they read and write. However, for those who must record growth throughout the school year, a number of informal assessment instruments can help, including checklists, surveys, word sorts, rubrics, running records, miscue analyses, and informal reading inventories.

Checklists

Teachers need to know exactly which phonics skills their students need to acquire by the end of each school year. One way to keep track of students' needs is to create a checklist with the CCSS or your state standards and use it to assess your students throughout the school year. When teachers identify a small group of students with the same needs, they can work with the group on a particular skill. Remember to make sure students master these skills through meaningful activities and not by completing worksheets. The partial checklist in Figure 5.8 is based on the first

figure 5.8 Checklist for letter–sound relationships based on the CCSS Reading: Foundational Skills for the first grade.

TEACHER M. Francis   PERIOD 1 ② 3 4

+ = always   x = sometimes   0 = seldom/never   8-27 (Beginning of school)

SUBSTANDARD / STUDENTS	Eric	Leah	Coby	Vanessa	Jocelyn	Hayden	Blake	Erin	Lindsay	Lesley	Cole	Shona	Ryan	Shannon	Casey	Warren	Brooke	Marsh
CCSS RF.1.3a Know the spelling–sound correspondences for common consonant digraphs.	+	+	+	+	+	+	X	X	+	+	+	+	+	+	X	+	X	+
CCSS RF.1.3b Decode regularly spelled one-syllable words.	+	+	+	+	+	+	X	X	+	+	+	+	+	+	X	+	X	+
CCSS RF.1.3c Know final –e and common vowel team conventions for representing long vowel sounds.	+	0	X	X	X	0	0	0	+	X	X	X	X	0	0	X	0	+
CCSS RF.1.3d Use knowledge that every syllable must have a vowel sound to determine the number of syllables in a printed word.	0	0	0	0	0	0	0	0	0	0	0	0	0	0	0	0	0	0

Source: Standards from CCSS (2010), English Language Arts Standards, Reading: Foundational Skills, Grade 1. Washington, DC: NGACBP, CCSSO, p. 16.

grade CCSS reading foundational skills that relate to phonics. A complete checklist, based on the entire phonics, word recognition, and fluency standards for the third grade, is located in Appendix C.36. If your state uses different standards, you can easily create your own checklist using the blank form in Appendix C.12 and share it with the team for your grade level.

Another type of checklist that can be used with very young children is the Checklist of Known Letter Names and Sounds (see Figure 5.9 for a partially filled-out example). Two copies (one typeset and one in cursive) of the Master Card of Letter Names and Sounds, along with the score sheet, are located in Appendix C.37. The checklist assesses a student's knowledge of letter names, letter sounds, and words with these sounds. The student reads from the Master Card, while the teacher records the responses on the checklist. The student is asked (1) the names of the uppercase letters, (2) the names of the lowercase letters, (3) the names of the script letters, if appropriate, (4) the sound of each letter, (5) a word that begins with that sound, and (6) a word that ends with that sound. To measure your students' progress, use the blank checklist in Appendix C.12, filling in the above six criteria, or the one at **www.hhpcommunities.com/literacyassessment** that already includes the criteria for assessing students' knowledge at the beginning of the year. Then use it to record students' growth throughout the school year.

Surveys

The Phonics Mastery Survey (Cecil, 2015) is an informal instrument for assessing various phonics elements. I do not advocate using nonsense words when teaching letter–sound relationships to students, but I do believe that using nonsense words to assess students tells me what they know about particular sounds of letters and how to blend those sounds. However, do not use this survey to assess students' sight word ability.

The Phonics Mastery Survey is designed to assess a student's ability to recognize (1) consonant sounds, (2) rhyming words, (3) consonant digraphs, (4) long vowel sounds, (5) words with CVC patterns, (6) consonant blends, (7) other vowel sounds, and (8) syllables in words. The scoring and answer sheets for this survey are in Appendix C.38. This assessment is also appropriate for middle school students. Too often middle school teachers assume that all students know letter–sound relationships and can hear rhyme. This survey is easy to administer and does not include pictures that would make middle school students think it is too elementary for them.

Word sorts

Having a student perform a word sort task is another informal phonics skills assessment. When assessing a student's ability to sort words by initial, ending, or medial sounds, use picture cards that prevent the student from looking at the letters. When the student cannot see the words, you can determine if she knows letter–sound relationships. Give the student pictures beginning with two, three, or four different letters, identify the letters for her, and ask her to sort the picture cards according to the initial letters. As a pretest, you may choose letters that have not been formally introduced; for a post-test, you may choose letters that have been explicitly taught. You can also assess a student's knowledge of ending sounds or medial sounds

figure 5.9 Partial sample checklist of known letter names and sounds for a student at the beginning of the year.

STUDENT: Dustin   DATE: 8–27

LETTER	UPPERCASE NAME	LOWERCASE NAME	SCRIPT NAME	SOUND	WORD WITH INITIAL SOUND	WORD WITH ENDING SOUND
K	✓	✓				
N	✓					
E	✓					
J	✓	✓				
A	✓					
T	✓	✓				
B	✓			✓	✓	
S	✓	✓		✓	✓	

such as long and short vowel sounds. Appendix D.5 contains a set of picture cards.

Scholastic Phonics Inventory (SPI)

This computer-based assessment is applicable for grades 3 through 12. It assesses students on sight words, letter recognition, and nonword decoding (nonwords that follow English language conventions and are decodable but cannot be read from memory). Because it is computer-based, this assessment is one that teachers can use with upper-grade students who appear to lack phonics skills.

Informal reading inventories

The informal reading inventory, running record, and miscue analysis are excellent devices to assess a student's ability to approach unknown words. As the student reads an unfamiliar text, observe what cueing systems he uses and what types of miscues he makes. Although these informal assessments take time to administer and analyze, they provide valuable information about students' phonics skills. (See Chapter 3 for a detailed discussion of these instruments.)

Qualitative Spelling Inventories 1 and 2

The Bear et al. (2008) Qualitative Spelling Inventories 1 and 2 assess students' capacity for encoding letter sounds. They test what students know about letter sounds as they write words. Chapter 12 describes the inventory and Appendix C.61 includes the two lists.

Formal Assessment

A number of standardized tests include phonics subtests; many of these use nonsense word lists. Remember, nonsense words will help you understand what the student knows about the sounds of letters and how to blend the sounds together, but they do not assess student's sight vocabulary. Figure 5.10 lists standardized tests with phonics subtests. Chapter 3 includes detailed descriptions of many of these tests.

figure 5.10 Standardized tests with phonics subtests.

1. Iowa Test of Basic Skills
2. Stanford Achievement Tests
3. Metropolitan Achievement Test–Reading
4. Comprehensive Test of Basic Skills, U and V
5. Phonics Criterion Test
6. Prescriptive Reading Performance Test
7. Stanford Diagnostic Reading Test–Red Level, Green Level
8. Woodcock Reading Mastery Test
9. Durrell Analysis of Reading Difficulties
10. Gates–McKillop–Horowitz Tests
11. Diagnostic Reading Scales
12. Sipay Word Analysis Test
13. Basic Early Assessment of Reading™ (BEAR®)
14. Dynamic Indicators of Basic Early Literacy Skills (DIBELS)

intervention   STRATEGIES & ACTIVITIES

Students learn about letter–sound relationships and patterns within words most effectively when they read and discuss books that interest them and engage in other meaningful literacy tasks. As you work with small groups and individual students, remember the four principles of phonics instruction (see page 107). Therefore, base the following intervention activities on texts students have enjoyed and on words they have encountered in print.

Instruction must always be based on the student's needs. The following activities are systematic; they start with initial consonant sounds, move to onset and rime, and finish with word patterns. However, if a student masters initial consonant sounds but struggles with onset and rime, emphasize onset and rime activities. Students can perform these activities with a teacher, a trained tutor, an older book buddy, or a peer (see Chapter 13).

Activities Emphasizing Initial Consonant Sounds

During group time, if you notice a student who cannot name three or four words that begin with the same sound, engage her in one of the following activities in a tutoring setting or have a trained tutor who understands these activities work with her. Do not merely engage the student in the activity, but also determine why the student has a difficult time distinguishing initial sounds. You may find she has an auditory problem. Usually, however, you will find that young children who cannot distinguish initial sounds lack linguistic experience and simply need time with an adult to develop the skill.

The following activities focus on listening to the initial sounds of words.

A C T I V I T Y   **Word Sorting with Pictures**   GRADES K–1

Beginning readers need practice relating letters to their sounds. Word sorting with picture cards emphasizes letter–sound relationships.

1. Place two magnet letters on the desk.
2. Have the student sort pictures according to the initial letter sounds using the picture cards found in Appendix D.5. Work up to three or four letters with their corresponding cards when he demonstrates progress.
3. If a student continues to confuse two letter sounds (e.g., the /d/ and /t/ sounds), continue working with only those two letters.
4. Later, set out magnet letters that correspond to the ending sounds and ask the student to sort the pictures accordingly.

A C T I V I T Y   **Word Sorting with Pictures for English Learners**   GRADES 4–8

English learners enter U.S. schools in all grade levels. English learners, like native speakers, need time to learn letter–sound relationships. One of the first skills to focus on is listening for the initial sound of a word. Using the picture cards found in Appendix D.4 and D.5, have students sort the cards different ways. For example, first give the student pictures of objects that begin with two different letter sounds and ask her to sort the words into two piles according to the initial sounds. Next, give her pictures of objects that begin with three different letter sounds and have her sort the words into three piles according to the initial sounds. Have the student name the object each time; this will also increase her vocabulary.

A C T I V I T Y   **Listen for the Initial Consonant Blends**   GRADES 1–3

1. Using the picture cards and game board in Appendix D.10, turn all picture cards upside down in a pile. Decide which person should begin.
2. The first player picks up a picture card, pronounces the word for the picture, and correctly places the picture on the consonant blend space that corresponds to the initial consonant blend of the word.
3. If the player cannot place a card on the correct consonant blend space, the card is placed on the bottom of the pile.

The goal is for students to fill all of the consonant blend spaces.

A C T I V I T Y   **Word Walls**   GRADES 1–2

Create a word wall featuring all the letters of the alphabet. On a poster board or butcher paper, write all of the letters of the alphabet and add words that children want to remember or will use in writing or reading. In a tutoring setting, write the letters of the alphabet in order on slips of paper, place them in a file folder, and have the tutee add words she wants to remember below the appropriate letters.

Personalized Word Family Dictionary

Arrange a personalized dictionary with two major sections. The first section contains a page for each letter of the alphabet. The second section contains a page for each of the following common word families: *ack, age, ake, an, am, at, ight, ound, all, it, in, ill, ig, ell, ed, ead, ot, op, og, ad, ap*. The top of each page includes either a letter (in upper- and lowercase) or the name of the word family; for example:

Aa	**ack (back)**
after	lack
about	Jack
around	sack
alligator	smack

Students can add words as they find them in texts or hear them in conversation.

Alphabiography

Alphabiography is described on the website ReadWriteThink.org (International Reading Association, 2010). This activity encourages middle school students to connect their personal lives with the alphabet. Students create an alphabet book by thinking of one event, object, friend, or attribute associated with their lives. They need one word for each letter of the alphabet. They can have the one word on the page and add narrative to make the booklet meaningful to share with classmates. For example, Juan may create a picture book about his new friends in the United States. For the letter "A," he may write, "My friend Ben likes apples." For the letter "B," he may write, "My friend Ben plays basketball." For the letter "C," he may write, "My friend Carl likes to play cards." For each letter, he writes a sentence based on his ability. More advanced students will write longer sentences. This activity can be found at: www.readwritethink.org/classroom-resources/lesson-plans/alphabiography-project-totally-937.html.

Alliteration

In this activity, either you or the student can do the writing.

1. Share some familiar tongue twisters such as *Sally sells seashells down by the seashore,* or *Peter Piper picked a peck of pickled peppers,* and then share some not-so-familiar tongue twisters such *Peter Potter splattered a plate of peas on Patty Platt's pink plaid pants* (Rosenbloom & Artell, 1999, p. 219).
2. Create your own original tongue twisters, perhaps based on the student's name.
3. Ask what sound the student hears at the beginning of the words.

Some of these sentences will result in amusing tongue twisters that also help the student with articulation, such as *Happy, hungry Harry has hundreds of hamburgers* or *Brave Beverly Beaver blew blue bubbles.*

Dominoes

This activity is designed to help struggling readers focus not only on the initial sounds, but also on the ending sounds of words. Using the domino cards from Appendix D.11, participants match the ending consonant sound (not the letter) of one domino with the initial sound of the next word. For example, if one player lays out the cat domino, the next player must lay down a domino picture that begins with a /t/ sound. Play the game with the students or observe as they play together. Through observation, you will determine which letter sounds are troublesome for which students.

Activities Emphasizing Onset and Rime

Often a teacher will observe a student "sounding out" phonograms letter-by-letter, instead of recognizing the pattern within the phonograms. For example, the student may read this passage in the following manner: "Mike put his h-h-a-a-n-n-d hand in the s-s-a-a-n-n-d sand." This student would benefit from tutoring sessions with some of the activities presented in this section, which emphasize the recognition of onset and rime. Helping a student recognize onset and rime will result in quickly gaining a large bank of recognizable words. For young readers, begin with texts that have word families with two letters in the rime (e.g., the *an*, *at*, *am*, *up*, or *op* families), because they only need to recognize those two letters. Later, choose texts that have word families with more letters in the rime, such as the *ound* and *ight* families.

ACTIVITY   **Word Family Word Walls**   GRADES 1–3

A separate word wall can be used for all phonograms students discover in texts. Word walls with phonograms draw students' attention to patterns within words. Appendix B.2 lists common phonograms. Figure 5.11 shows a sample word wall.

figure 5.11   Phonogram word wall.

at	all	an	and
bat	ball	ban	band
cat	call	can	sand
fat	fall	fan	land

ACTIVITY   **Find the Mystery Word**   GRADES 1–2

Use the word wall in your classroom for this activity, which is appropriate for whole group, small group, or individual instruction. The goal is for students to listen to the teacher for sound clues, put the sounds together, and name the word from the word wall. At the beginning of the year, use easy clues (initial sound, followed by medial sound, followed by ending sound). Later, try giving the sounds in a mixed order. Here is a mixed order example:

1. Instruct students to look at the word wall and to think, not say, the mystery word.
2. Give clues to the mystery word by saying, "I see a word that has a short /a/ sound." (Say the sound, not the letter name.) "This word begins with a /b/ sound. This word ends with a /g/ sound. If you know the word, whisper the word to your neighbor. What was the word, Robert?"
3. As the word wall grows, use words that have silent sounds or digraphs.

ACTIVITY   **Flip Books**   GRADES 1–2

Struggling readers often do not see the common rime within word families. Show these students how the rime is a common factor in the entire "family" and how the onset changes the words. Explicit instruction in word families encourages readers to look for known parts within words. Again, use word families from texts that have been read in a tutoring or small group session. For example, after reading Dr. Seuss's *The Cat in the Hat,* have readers construct a flip book of all the *at* words.

1. To construct a flip book using sentence strips, neatly print *hat* on a strip and cut the word off the sentence strip.

2. Using the rest of the sentence strip, write the letters *b, c, f, h, m, p, r, s, v.*

3. Cut them up and staple them on top of the *h* in *hat.* Because *at* is a word, the top sheet should be blank.

See Figure 5.12 for an example. Using *The Cat in the Hat,* you can also construct a flip book for the *ump* family. Put the letters *h, c, gr, d, j, l, p, r, st,* and *th* on the pages. Because *ump* is not a word, the top page must have a letter.

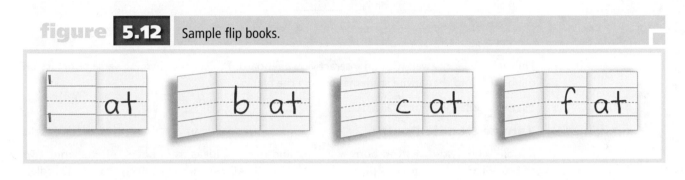

figure 5.12 Sample flip books.

Word Family Concentration

GRADES 2–5   A C T I V I T Y

Concentration is a game that teaches students to focus and remember. Cards can be based on any text the struggling reader enjoys. Work with the student to decide which words she wants to learn and remember. Make two cards of the same word. If the book has phonograms, make the activity more challenging by having the student match phonograms (e.g., the *hat* card with the *cat* card). Participate in the activity with the student in order to understand what letter sounds or words are troubling her. Appendix D.12 contains two examples. The first, based on Nancy Shaw's *Sheep Out to Eat* (1992), is built on a number of different word families. The second is built on other homophones. It is not recommended that you use all the cards in each activity.

Activities Emphasizing Rhyme

Eventually students discover that not all rhyming words end with the same letter (e.g., *know/go, blue/shoe*). The following two activities focus on students writing their own rhyming verses.

Rhyming Word Concentration

GRADES 6–8   A C T I V I T Y

Concentration is a game that middle school students can also enjoy. Many poems by Shel Silverstein and Bruce Lansky are humorous and include rhymes. After reading Lansky's (2009) "New Year's Resolutions" and "Someone's Toes Are in My Nose" have the student write each of the rhyming words—*better/letter, looking/cooking, stairs/chairs, sorrow/tomorrow, me/be, understand/band, truck/stuck, mad/had*—on an index card. Then turn the cards over and challenge the student to find the matches as quickly as possible, or play the game according to the traditional rules.

Predictable Rhyming Texts

GRADES 1–2   A C T I V I T Y

Smith, Walker, and Yellin (2004) suggest that teachers encourage students to write their own rhyming verses by using a template. First, teachers share any book with a predictable text, such as *Here Are My Hands* (Martin & Archambault, 1998). After finding the rhyming words, provide a template that eliminates some of the words. Have students brainstorm words that could fit in each blank, then write a verse or two with them. Finally, invite students to write their own verses. Here is an example:

"Here are my eyes
For seeing and crying.
Here are my ears
For washing and drying." (Martin & Archambault, 1998, unpaged)

Template:

Here are my _____

For _____ and _____.

Here are my _____

For _____ and _____.

This activity works well with an interactive whiteboard. Project the rhyming verse template on the board, and then invite students to fill in the blanks.

ACTIVITY   **Yankee Doodle Poetry**   GRADES 6–8

Middle school students can borrow writing and rhyming ideas from poets. After sharing two of Bruce Lansky's humorous poems from *My Dog Ate My Homework!* (2009), "Yankee Doodle's Monkey Ride" and "Yankee Doodle's Turtle Ride," invite students to brainstorm with you to write hilarious versions of this four-line verse. Write one or two together, then have them write their own and share them with the class. To add a technology component to the activity, have the students provide illustrations for their poems and post them on a class wiki or website.

Activities Emphasizing Word Patterns

S ome students will continue to have difficulty recognizing word patterns, despite explicit demonstrations. You will identify these students by observing how they approach an unknown word; often they will sound out unknown words letter-by-letter. Students who have learned to recognize word families may tend to believe that all words will have onset and rime. Again, you will identify them by observing how they read. When they approach an unknown word, they will often sound out the first letter and then attempt to put all the other letters together. For example, they will attempt to sound out *hope* as *h– op*. Both these types of students will benefit from some individualized sessions working on word patterns.

The following activities are designed to help a student see patterns within words. The first pattern, consonant–vowel–consonant (CVC), is also found in many phonograms. However, the emphasis is now on the short vowel sound that is found in most CVC words. Some exceptions to this pattern that students may notice are words like *cow, how, few,* and *sew.*

ACTIVITY   **Short Vowel Bingo**   GRADES 1–3

Play short vowel bingo with readers who struggle with short vowel sounds.

1. Duplicate the blank bingo card in Appendix D.13.
2. Write a list of 25 words with short vowel sounds on the board.
3. Instruct the students to write the words on their bingo cards in any order, leaving the free space blank.
4. Write the words on index cards, draw one from the stack, and read it aloud.
5. Have the students place a marker on the word.

The goal is for a student to fill five spaces in a row, vertically, horizontally, or diagonally. If you laminate the cards before students write on them, the cards can be used for many different bingo games. (You may want to use erasable pens or pencils.) The following word list is from Kristen Hall's *A Bad, Bad Day* (1995) and Rex Schneider's *That's Not All!* (1993). Both are books for beginning readers.

bad	dad	bed	hit	what	can
bus	got	not	that	bug	rug
has	pet	let	hen	pen	den
cat	rat	dog	hog	bat	hat
pig	wig	run	fun		

The Magical E!

The following activity builds on the CVC pattern and introduces the CVCe pattern. Using the cards shown in Figure 5.13, have the student first pronounce the short vowel word. Then have him move the "e" card to the end of the word and pronounce the new word, which has a long vowel sound. Choose words that are familiar to the student. Versions of the cards are available at www.hhpcommunities.com/literacyassessment.

figure **5.13**   Magical E! cards.

Activities Emphasizing Sounds Within Words

Students should learn to recognize long, short, controlled-*r*, and schwa vowels as well as the subtle differences between /b/ and /p/, /m/ and /n/, /f/ and /v/, and /t/ and /d/ sounds. You may notice that when some students approach unknown words, they cannot determine whether a vowel sound is long, short, schwa, or controlled by the letter *r*. Other students may consistently write a *t* when the correct letter is a *d*, or a *p* instead of a *b*. These students will benefit from tutoring sessions that feature some of the following intervention activities.

Listen to the Vowel Sounds

1. Create a board game by gluing a page of vowel squares (Appendix D.14) on each side of an opened file folder so both players can view the vowels right-side up.
2. Using the picture cards in Appendix D.14, place them face down in a pile.
3. Decide which student will begin.
4. The first player picks up a picture card, pronounces the word for the picture, listens to the medial vowel sound, and matches the picture with the correct vowel space.
5. If the player cannot place the card on the correct vowel space, the card is placed on the bottom of the pile.

The game is over when students fill all the vowel spaces.

Collecting Vowel Sounds Made with Different Spellings   GRADES 1–8

This activity will help students understand that a vowel sound may have different spellings (e.g., the long /a/ sound can be spelled *a, ue, ay, ey, ai,* or *ei*). Have students find words in their texts that use various spellings to represent the same letter sounds. One way to have students keep track of the words is by giving them one index card for each specified vowel sound. For example, you might begin with all the spellings of the long /a/. Figure 5.14 shows a sample long /a/ card.

figure 5.14   Sample long /a/ card.

Long /a/ Sound			
ey words	ay words	a words	ai words
they	day	came	rain
grey	say	gave	main
	play	made	pain
		mane	
ve words	ei words		
bouquet	eight		
croquet			

Word Sorting with Words   GRADES 1–5

Word sorts can be done with words as well as pictures. Write 15 to 20 words on sentence strips and cut the strips into single-word sections. Let the students sort the words however they choose, by the number of syllables, initial sound, ending sound, vowel sounds, or shared sounds (rhymes). Ask students to explain their sorting strategy to you. The cards found in Appendix D.12 from the Concentration activity can be used for this, or you can use any words students find in their reading.

Technology alternative: Have students use the interactive word family sort online at www.readwritethink.org/classroom-resources/student-interactives/word-family-sort-30052.html.   In this activity, students select a vowel (e.g., "a"). They are then shown a chart with the words representing the word families related to the vowel (e.g., "cat," "man," "cap," "back"). Students drag and drop words at the top of the chart into the column of the proper word family.

Change Hen to Fox   GRADES 1–4

This activity, created by Cunningham (2004), is based on *Hattie and the Fox* (1987) by Mem Fox, but it can be played with different words.

1. Instruct the students to write *hen* on the top line of their paper.
2. Have them change *hen* to *pen* on the next line.
3. Have them continue to change words using this sequence: *pen* to *pet* to *pit* to *sit* to *six* to *fix* to *fox*.
4. Have them discuss how changing one letter creates a new word each time. For example:

   hen   pen   pet   pit
   sit   six   fix

For a variation on this activity, write a word on the board (e.g., *lost*), and announce the class is going to change one letter at a time to get from *lost* to *find*. For example, write *lost* and directly below it write *los__*. Ask the students what letter will complete this word. Give students one word at a time so that they cannot look to the next line for the answer. Continue in this fashion until you reach the target word.

> lost
>
> los__
>
> lo__e
>
> l__ne
>
> __ine
>
> min__
>
> __ind

The answers are *lose, lone, line, mine, mind, find.*

Word Ladders

Rasinski (2005a, 2005b) creates a more difficult version of Hen to Fox by having students add, delete, rearrange, or substitute letters to create words that correlate to a definition. The following activity encourages students to see how changing one or two letters results in a new word. This activity is based on the *ing* sound.

> Write down *think.*
>
> Delete two letters to create a word that refers to something used to write. *(ink)*
>
> Add one letter to create a word that refers to what a person may do with his/her eye. *(wink)*
>
> Change one letter to create a word that names a part of a bird. *(wing)*
>
> Add one letter to create a word that names a favorite piece of playground equipment. *(swing)*
>
> Delete one letter to create a word that refers to a rock star's talent. *(sing)*
>
> Add one letter to create a word that refers to the action of a bee. *(sting)*
>
> Add one letter to create a word that refers to a part of tennis shoes. *(string)*

PHONICS AND TECHNOLOGY

Macaruso and Rodman (2011) conducted two studies with preschool children and kindergartners to determine if they would benefit from computer-assisted instruction in phonological awareness and phonics. They used a pretest/post-test format with a control class that received no treatment. The preschool study included phonemic awareness, visual skills, verbal concepts, picture categories, and listening comprehension. The kindergarten study emphasized awareness of print (e.g., recognizing question marks, capital letters), letter recognition, selecting the same word as the target word, identifying the sentence that was read, connecting phoneme to grapheme, and selecting the word that was spoken. The results of their study indicated that overall both groups benefited from "intensive" use of computer-assisted instruction programs as assessed by the pretest and post-tests.

Websites: Phonics

Many websites offer computer-assisted instruction. One of my favorite interactive websites for K–2 students is ReadWriteThink.org, designed by the ILA and the National Council of Teachers of English. The site permits teachers to type in literacy terms, such as *phonics* or *rhyme,* and click "interactive" to allow students to work on a particular phonics, rhyme, or other literacy skill. The six interactive phonics pages are ideal for helping K–2 students construct words, create an alphabet organizer, match pictures, play a word family sort and ABC match, and participate in word wizard. The pages are simple enough for young students to navigate.

Another site that has multiple phonics games is PBSKids.org. This site includes music, animated characters, and voice instructions that guide students as they play the games. The site also has an application for use with tablets (see the next section). Remember to monitor students as they use these sites; some young students just click without attending to the task. Monitoring students helps to ensure that they are learning all the unique aspects of building words.

An online search for phonics reveals even more sites that feature useful lessons for building skills. Some other favorite sites include:

www.learningtoday.com/corporate/reading-games.asp

www.starfall.com

http://teacher.scholastic.com/clifford1/flash/phonics/index.htm

www.learningplanet.com

Apps: Phonics

A to Z for Kids (Free, Grades K–2). This app features games that focus on improving phonics and spelling for younger audiences. Images of animals, fruits, birds, and flowers are provided along with their spelling and pronunciation. Games ask users to spell out each individual word once it has been displayed, accompanied by sounds to improve memorization.

abc PocketPhonics ($6.99, Grades K–1). This app uses a set of games to teach sound formation based on letter combinations, and letter writing tutorials accompanied by the sound of each letter. Options for student profiles along with individual and class-based progress tracking allow students to continue where they left off and move at their own pace.

SUPER WHY Phonics Fair (PBS Kids) ($2.99, Grades K–1). This app, based on the PBS KIDS series SUPER WHY, features sounds organized into 30 word families and provides five related games. Progress is motivated and rewarded with stickers that can be used for decoration within the game. The app offers progress tracking for parents. Additionally, 30 more complex word families can be purchased for the app for $0.99.

Smarty Pants School (Free, Grades K–3). This app, which can be used with and track progress for multiple students, assesses and helps develop early reading skills. After taking a brief assessment, students are directed to activities that match their skill level and developmental needs, in five categories: letter knowledge, phonemic awareness, phonics, phonetic words, and sight words.

CONCLUDING THOUGHTS

All teachers need to understand the graphophonic system that links letters with sounds. Insight into the unique sound structure of the English language will help you assess specific reading problems. Remember, phonics instruction must be based on what students know, and it should be systematic. Strive to find appropriate texts and to teach phonics concepts in a meaningful context.

reflective learning

ENGLISH LEARNERS. After teaching for five years in her hometown, a rural community in Ohio, Ms. Synder moved to a large city in Texas. Anticipating that she would have Spanish-speaking students in her eighth-grade language arts class, she got out her college Spanish textbook and CDs over the summer to brush up on her skills. Although she was prepared for the new challenges of the position, she was still overwhelmed by the number of native Spanish speakers in her class. Five had been in the school system since first grade; three had been at the school for two years, and eight had moved to the United States during the summer. Ms. Synder determined the five students who had been in the system since first grade were on grade level in all subjects; the three students who had been at the school only two years had weak literacy skills and struggled to read stories, poems, and informational text. The eight new students had few English literacy skills, and she was not sure if they were literate in Spanish.

questions

1. What assessments should Ms. Synder give the eight students?

2. What type of help should she give the three students with weak literacy skills?

3. What type of literacy instruction should she give the eight students, considering they are eighth graders and not first graders?

4. What should she do with the English learners when the class is reading a novel?

6 Word Recognition

A teacher is one who brings us tools and enables us to use them.

RALPH WALDO EMERSON

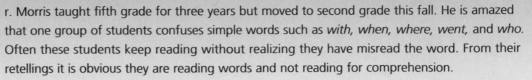

scenario

M r. Morris taught fifth grade for three years but moved to second grade this fall. He is amazed that one group of students confuses simple words such as *with, when, where, went,* and *who.* Often these students keep reading without realizing they have misread the word. From their retellings it is obvious they are reading words and not reading for comprehension.

Another group of students looks at him when they do not know a word. They expect him to say the word or they simply skip it. Often these words have more than one syllable, such as *together, mountain, vacation,* and *important.* Mr. Morris knows both groups need extra help. The first group needs help learning simple sight words, and the second group needs help learning to recognize syllables within polysyllabic words and other strategies that will help them when they encounter an unfamiliar word when engaging in independent reading. The second-grade teachers in his building have high school interns who are planning to be teachers, and Mr. Morris is fortunate to have three interns working with him for an hour each day. Mr. Morris decides that he will ask these interns to read and write with the students who are working at grade level, while he works with the struggling readers. For the students who do not recognize their reading errors, he makes a set of flash cards with the Fry phrases and sentences (see Appendix B.7). He sorts the cards into groups of five, beginning with the first five phrases. He keeps track of which words the students have learned. He has these students read some books that are easy for them; he also reads more difficult books with them so they understand that reading entails more than recognizing words.

For the students who do not attempt to pronounce unknown words, Mr. Morris makes a set of cards with compound words such as *butterfly, mailbox, backpack, piggyback, backyard, downtown,* and *homework.* He helps the students look for two small words in the longer word. Mr. Morris also makes a set of cards for them, each featuring one element of a compound word. The cards include these words: *butter, fly, box, mail, pack, back, yard, piggy, down, town, work,* and *home.* Students are instructed to put two cards together to make one longer word. Mr. Morris also teaches students how to read to the end of a sentence to see what word would make sense (both in terms of meaning and the part of speech).

Mr. Morris knows what both groups need in order to become fluent readers. He also knows that it is wiser to have interns read with proficient readers than to have them work with struggling readers who need more guidance.

As you read this chapter, consider the following questions:

guiding questions

1. Do you think it is necessary that young readers recognize simple words automatically?

2. How would you assess a student's ability to recognize sight words?

3. What other activities could Mr. Morris use to help the students needing work in learning sight words?

4. What other activities could Mr. Morris used to help those needing work in learning to recognize syllables in polysyllabic words? What are some generalizations about polysyllabic words that could aid in his students' visual analysis of them?

introduction

Although Mr. Morris understands the role of **word recognition** in reading, he also knows the purpose of reading is not just to read words correctly but to comprehend texts. One reads stories for entertainment, newspapers for current events, menus to satisfy appetites, poetry to feed the soul, informational texts to learn about interesting topics, instruction manuals to assemble items or operate tools, and text messages to communicate with friends.

In order to comprehend texts and enjoy reading, students should be able to instantaneously recognize a large bank of words and effortlessly analyze unknown words. This automaticity requires the brain to process both visual and nonvisual information (Smith, 2005). Every time a reader identifies a letter or word, the brain is involved in a decision, "and the amount of information required to make the decision depends on the number of alternatives there are" (Smith, 1978, p. 24).

Smith's (2005) research on the brain's role in the reading process reveals that the brain is capable of identifying only four or five random letters (e.g., *w, x, q, e, j*) per second. This is because when one letter is presented, the brain has 26 letters from which to choose. Thus, the brain takes approximately two seconds to identify five to eight random letters.

When letters are organized into a random list of words (e.g., *basket, board, sneeze, Iowa*), the brain approaches them as chunks of information, which permits a reader to identify two or more words (the equivalent of 10 to 12 letters) in one second (Smith, 2005). When the words are organized into grammatically correct sentences (e.g., *I love to read*), the brain can process four times the amount it can handle when identifying random letters. This gain occurs because readers make use of nonvisual information already stored in the brain. Readers' prior knowledge reduces the amount of information required to identify entire words. Being able to automatically identify words and being able to comprehend texts depend "on using visual information economically and using as much non-visual information as possible" (Smith, 1978, p. 33). "Tunnel vision," a state of incomprehension when faced with a text, occurs when the brain is overloaded with visual information. Beginning readers often find themselves paralyzed by tunnel vision because they read too slowly, attempting to sound out each word letter by letter. Tunnel vision also often occurs when readers lack background knowledge or when reading materials are too difficult. When readers encounter too many unknown words, they pay attention to the visual aspects of reading (the letters within words), which prompts the brain to process all of the letters separately.

It is imperative that students have the automatic word recognition and word analysis skills to comprehend text. Struggling readers find reading unpleasant because the task is laborious and embarrassing when they must read aloud in front of peers. Thus, they spend little time on it and do not receive enough practice to become fluent. Like any other skill, word recognition requires practice. It is best if students develop this skill with a teacher who can assess their reading problems, teach appropriate strategies, and provide engaging activities. However, teachers do not have time to spend long periods of time with one child. Therefore, like Mr. Morris, teachers can have interns or others assist with proficient readers so they can spend more time with students who are struggling.

In order for reading to become more pleasurable for struggling readers, they must develop the ability to automatically recognize a large bank of words, known as **sight words** (words immediately recognized as a whole unit, e.g., *at, the, of, have*). According to Pinnell and Fountas (2007), word recognition includes the following elements:

- Recognizing words without conscious attention
- Recognizing words without attending to every letter
- Using parts of words to quickly identify new words
- Connecting unknown words to known words (analogies)
- Connecting spelling with word meaning (homonyms, plurals, tenses, etc.)

Students achieve automatic word recognition when they read full texts, not when they spend hours on drills with isolated word lists (Clay, 1991; Pinnell & Fountas, 2007).

To identify words in full text, proficient readers use all four cueing systems—syntactic, semantic, pragmatic, and graphophonic—along with context clues and their receptive vocabulary. A good goal for corrective reading instruction is to have struggling readers (1) learn how to use the four cueing systems, (2) learn the components of word recognition, and (3) increase their range of strategies for analyzing words.

Before you assess and assist struggling readers, you need to understand some basic concepts about the role of word recognition in reading.

WHAT TEACHERS SHOULD KNOW

S tudents do not become proficient readers simply by memorizing lists of words or learning all of the combinations of letter–sound relationships. Instead, they "use visual information for print and graphics; put together the information to gain the literal meaning of the text; [and] remember it while reading, thinking beyond the text" (Pinnell, 2006, p. 79). Proficient readers simultaneously use their knowledge of the four cueing systems—syntactic, semantic, pragmatic, and graphophonic. Here is a brief recap of the concepts discussed in Chapter 2, related to their roles in word recognition.

The Four Cueing Systems

1. Syntactic system. The syntactic language system is often described as the system of grammar and sentence structure. The sentence structure of English is unique. For example, when translating a sentence from German to English, you cannot simply substitute English words for German words to produce a meaningful, well-formed sentence. From birth, native English speakers automatically acquire the flow of English syntax when they communicate with adults. When reading, most children automatically use the syntactic system to identify familiar words and learn new ones. For example, even if proficient readers do not know the word *track*, they can use syntax to help them make sense of the sentence, "The train sped down the track." They will know that any verb such as *trampled, tried*, or *tackled* will not be appropriate here, because the determiner "the" is not followed by a verb. Proficient readers may not be able to explain the grammatical rule, but their prior knowledge of syntax will tell them that a verb does not make sense at the end of that sentence. Struggling readers, on the other hand, do not automatically use syntax in this way.

English learners know only the syntax or grammar of their native language and must learn a new syntax. Because no foreign language can be translated word-for-word into English, English learners cannot use context clues as readily as native English-speaking students. For this reason, English learners need to hear books read to them so they become familiar with the English syntax.

2. Semantic system. Semantic refers to the meanings of words, sentences, and longer passages in language. Many words have multiple meanings. For example, *run* can be a verb ("Run as fast as you can!"), a noun ("The ski run is fast and challenging."), or a root word for a number of other words (*runny, runner, running*). In each instance, *run* has a different meaning. Struggling readers may recognize the word when it stands by itself, but they may have a problem recognizing *runner* and *runny* in a word list. However, if they read each of these words in a sentence, the context will help them identify the word. For example, most students would easily recognize *runner* in the following sentence because of the context: "As the race was about to begin, the runner waved to his dad." Also, most students would recognize *runny* in the following sentence because of the context: "The sick baby had a runny nose."

Homonyms are words that are pronounced the same but have different spellings, such as *blew/blue* and *grate/great*. **Homographs** are words with identical spelling, but they differ in meaning and sometimes pronunciation (such as *bass* fish and a *bass* singer). **Heteronyms** are words that are spelled the same but have different pronunciations and meanings in differing contexts. The words *minute, wind, read*, and *tear* are pronounced differently and carry different meanings in the following sentences.

The minute hand on the clock was stuck on seven.

The minute glove was too small for the giant's hand.

I love to feel the soft wind on my face.

Please wind the alarm clock.

You need to read two chapters tonight.

I read that book three times.

The child's tears cascaded down her face as the balloon floated above the roof.

Please do not tear any pages of the library book.

Readers know the correct pronunciation and intended meaning of these words only when they are used in context.

3. Pragmatic system. The pragmatic system refers to the situational context of a word, sentence, or passage. Readers' prior knowledge and previous experiences impact the pragmatic system because all readers' experiences are different. For example, students who live in the southern United States and who have never visited the northern plains might not appreciate a description of the bone-chilling winds of a blizzard as much as students who live in North Dakota. In fact, a southern student may lack a whole range of sights, sounds, and feelings that a North Dakota student associates with a blizzard. When a student from the South reads a story set in a blizzard, she may not automatically identify words such as *blizzard, parka*, and *toboggan* with the same ease as students in the North.

4. Graphophonic system. The graphophonic system refers to relationships between letters and their sounds. Chapter 5 contains a detailed discussion of this cueing system.

Proficient readers use these four cueing systems automatically, and teachers should encourage early readers to use all cueing systems when they read (McKenna & Cournoyer-Picard, 2006).

Components of Word Recognition

Automaticity is not only the ability to recognize a large bank of words by sight and to quickly decode unfamiliar words, it is also the ability to comprehend words in their context and thus comprehend passages. Both knowledge and skills are needed for automaticity. Students must know words and be able to use word analysis skills. See Figure 6.1.

Word knowledge

Students must have good receptive and expressive vocabularies. They need to know frequently used sight words (words that do not conform to pronunciation rules). They also need an extensive sight vocabulary, a large bank of words they recognize instantaneously.

figure 6.1

The main components of word recognition.

WORD KNOWLEDGE

Receptive vocabulary: a bank of words a student can understand during conversation; listening vocabulary

Expressive vocabulary: vocabulary students use during speech or writing

Sight words: words that do not conform to pronunciation rules

Sight vocabulary: words that students recognize in half a second or less

WORD ANALYSIS SKILLS

Context clues: rhetorical knowledge, schema, and picture clues that a student can use to figure out unknown words

Visual analysis of monosyllabic words: the ability to break words into smaller known parts to figure out unknown words

Blending polysyllabic words: the ability to blend the smaller parts (single syllables) of words together to make whole words

Structural analysis: the ability to distinguish frequently used prefixes and suffixes from root words and the knowledge of how they affect the meaning of words

Morphemic structure: Understanding how root words with different affixes (prefixes and suffixes) form different parts of speech (e.g., music, musician, musical/magic, magician)

Receptive and expressive vocabularies. Readers' vocabularies consist of two parts—their receptive vocabulary and their expressive vocabulary. Receptive vocabulary consists of the words students know in conversation and while reading texts. Students' receptive vocabulary is a result of their past experiences, conversations, and reading. Oral language in home and daycare experiences are the primary sources of students' receptive vocabulary (Molfese, Modglin, & Molfese, 2003; Kieffer & Lesaux, 2007; Wasik, 2006; Rasinski, Padak, Newton, & Newton, 2008). Because a large receptive vocabulary is essential for successful reading and writing in school and all through life, it is essential that preschool children are immersed in environments where they interact with adults during play and reading/writing activities. Quality children's literature is a great source to increase students' receptive vocabulary.

Because receptive vocabularies are developed orally (in conversation and listening to quality literature), students need to be able to distinguish between phonemes that have fine gradations. Some of these phonemes include /b/ and /p/, /f/ and /v/, or short /i/ and short /e/. Wolf (2009) found that some of her students with oral- and written-language learning disabilities

(OWL–LD) heard something quite different from what the teacher dictated. For example, when Wolf dictated "Rome wasn't built in a day," the student wrote "Row mustn' bill tinted a." When she dictated "Always be polite," the student wrote "Al waits beep a light." To determine if older students can distinguish sounds with close gradations, dictate short sentences that are appropriate for their writing ability.

Students' **expressive vocabulary** is often smaller than their receptive vocabulary and has two parts—one used in speech and one used in writing. Their oral expressive vocabulary is usually larger than their written vocabulary.

When students encounter new words in text and attempt to identify them, they are aided by their receptive vocabulary and their expressive oral vocabulary. If the unknown words are not part of either vocabulary, they will not recognize words as they attempt to pronounce them. Too often struggling readers have limited receptive and expressive oral vocabularies. These struggling readers are often students "who live in poverty and are exposed to fewer experiences than their middle-class counterparts" (International Reading Association, 2002).

Sight words. As stated previously, sight words are those that are immediately recognized as a whole unit; identification of sight words does not require word analysis. Sight words appear often in simple text (e.g., *the, to, you, there, one, once*). There are many sight word lists. See Appendix B.6 for Dolch's (1948) list. Cunningham's (2004) list of high-frequency words (see the box and Appendix B.5) also includes many sight words. As stated earlier, students learn words in context. For this reason, it is beneficial to use phrase lists made up of sight words. The Phrases and Short Sentences for Repeated Reading Practice list (Rasinski, 2003) is based on the Fry Instant Word List (2003) and is presented in Appendix B.7. I will refer to this list as the Fry phrase list. Shanker and Ekwall's (2002) list of sight word phrases is another example.

Students should be introduced to sight words when they begin reading. Gunning (2001) contends that sight words are best learned using the whole-part-whole approach as demonstrated in the following activity. Note that the teacher and students first enjoy the poem as a whole, then work with individual sentences, phrases, and words, and finally put the words and sentences back together.

1. Using a short poem that students will enjoy, the teacher selects four or five sight words.
2. The teacher points to the words as he reads the poem.
3. The teacher reads the poem again, inviting the students to "chime in" on words or phrases they know.

4. After a number of readings, students are invited to read the poem independently.

5. The teacher writes each sentence of the poem on a separate sentence strip.

6. Students are asked to read the sentence strips and put them in order.

7. The teacher cuts the sentence strips into single words and ask the students to put the sentences back together.

The teacher might focus on four or five sight words and add them to the class word wall. When students write, they should be expected to correctly spell the words that appear on the wall.

Sight vocabulary. Readers' **sight vocabularies** are the words they recognize in half a second or less (Fry & Kress, 2006). Each reader's sight vocabulary is unique because his or her experiences differ from everyone else's (Heath, 2004).

Native speakers and English learners develop their sight vocabularies in three ways (August & Shanahan, 2006; Helman & Burns, 2008; Nilsen & Nilsen, 2004):

1. *Known to unknown.* Alice may know the simple word *walk* and learn *walking* when it appears in a sentence. Alice is learning unknown words by focusing on the part of the word she does know.

2. *Simple to complex.* Dameon knows the word *volcanoes* and learns more complex scientific terms such as *lava* and *magma* when reading the text and captions under photographs on a website about this subject.

3. *Literal to metaphorical.* Jeremy understands what it is to cry tears and what rain is. When he reads the sentence "The clouds cried for hours yesterday," he

understands and appreciates the personification of the cloud and rain.

Word analysis skills

When students encounter words that are not part of their sight vocabulary, they must be able to use context clues to figure them out. They need skill in visual analysis and blending, and they need the ability to distinguish affixes and root words.

Context clues. When readers come to unknown words, they use the context clues known as rhetorical knowledge, schema, and picture clues. Rhetorical knowledge is readers' knowledge about story grammar, the structure of expository text, paragraphs, and so on. Schema refers to readers' knowledge of the world. Readers' background knowledge (or schema) is closely related to their receptive vocabularies (Wasik, 2006; International Reading Association, 2002). If the reader has background knowledge on the reading topic, unknown words will be easier to recognize. For example, if the teacher mentions that a passage is about pioneers, readers who know a bit about this topic will begin to think of prairies, mud houses, covered wagons, buffalo, and so on. When readers sound out these words they have never encountered in print, their background knowledge helps them. Picture clues, illustrations that help readers identify unknown words, are another type of context clue used by proficient readers. For example, readers may not recognize the word *iguana* in the text, but a picture may help them associate the word with the object. To aid struggling readers, teachers often use vocabulary words that will be found in the text during a pre-reading discussion of the pictures.

Visual analysis of monosyllabic words. When words cannot be determined from context clues, readers can use visual analysis. This skill involves breaking syllables into smaller, known parts. Proficient readers look for parts they know. For example, as discussed in Chapter 5, they will look for a rime within the syllable and then add the onset (e.g., *ight* + *fl* = *flight*). (See Appendix B.2 for common word families, or phonograms.)

For monosyllabic words that are not part of a word family, proficient readers look at the whole word, automatically say the sound of the vowel or vowel cluster, and then add the beginning and ending consonants (e.g., *ie* + *shr* + *k* = *shriek*). Struggling readers, however, tend to mechanically sound out the word from left to right (Rasinski & Padak, 2003). This may cause problems because the sound of certain letters changes as more letters are added to a syllable. For example, with the word *knee*, readers encounter a problem if they first sound out the /k/ in *knee*, because the *k* is silent when followed by *n*.

High-Frequency Words

"One hundred words account for almost half of all the words we read and write. Ten words—*the, of, and, a, to, in, is, you, that,* and *it*—account for almost one-quarter of all the words we read and write" (Cunningham, 2004, p. 54). Many **high-frequency words** are difficult for readers because they represent abstract concepts. However, students need to recognize these words automatically when they read and to spell them instantaneously when they write. Displaying these words on a word wall keeps them available to students as they read and write.

Appendix B.5 features the list of high-frequency words compiled by Cunningham (2004). Appendix B.6 includes the Dolch word list, a collection of high-frequency words.

Visual analysis also involves knowing how polysyllabic words are divided into syllables. This knowledge aids students with pronunciation and spelling of words (Blevins, 2001).

The concepts listed in Figure 6.2 are consistent 95 to 100 percent of the time; thus they are valuable concepts to teach students to help them visually analyze words.

Blending polysyllabic words. Once readers recognize the smaller parts (single syllables) of words, they need to quickly blend these parts to make whole words. Accurate, quick blending is necessary for pleasurable reading. Struggling readers may recognize the parts but lack the skill to quickly blend the

pieces back together (Bear et al., 2011). Instruction in blending should begin with word endings, such as -ed, -ing, -ly, -er, and -est, because readers frequently need to recognize only the base word and the ending. Next, introducing compound words helps readers understand that longer words often consist of smaller words. Words such as *butterfly, mailbox, tablespoon,* and *teacup* are long words to sound out letter by letter; however, quickly recognizing the smaller words within the longer ones and blending them together will enable students to identify these longer words automatically. After working with inflectional endings and compound words, students can work with other polysyllabic words.

Structural analysis. Young readers and writers first become aware of endings that are added to words, such as *s* to make plural nouns, and *ed* and *ing* to change verb tenses. As they begin to use more polysyllabic words, familiarize them with frequently used prefixes, suffixes, and root words. Recognizing these parts helps them see the structure of words. If students enter fourth grade with a limited receptive and expressive vocabulary, they are likely to struggle in content subjects (Chall & Jacobs, 2003; RAND Reading Study Group, 2002; Biancarosa & Snow, 2004). Kieffer and Lesaux (2007) suggest that in order for these students to be successful, teachers should focus on **morphology** (the study of **morphemes,** the smallest units of words, such as prefixes, suffixes, and root words). They propose four principles of teaching morphology:

1. "Teach morphology in context of rich, explicit vocabulary instruction." Morphology study should be an important component of vocabulary study that includes explaining the meaning of words found in content areas and teaching word learning strategies, such as dictionary skills and using context clues.

2. "Teach students to use morphology as a cognitive strategy with explicit steps." Students must learn how to analyze words by finding the affixes and root, attaching the meaning of each of these parts, and then hypothesizing the meaning of the word in the context of the passage being read.

3. "Teach the underlying morphological knowledge needed in two ways—both explicitly and in context." Students should learn the meaning of common prefixes and suffixes by teachers teaching them explicitly. Students should also learn them through reading activities such as word hunts. During word hunts, students look for words with prefixes, suffixes, and root words and add them to the classroom word wall or their personalized dictionaries. Teachers also need to explain how words are transformed from one part of speech to another by changing the suffix (e.g., *necessary/necessitate; negate/negative*).

figure 6.2

Generalizations concerning words that aid visual analysis.

1. Syllables have one vowel sound, even though there may be more than one vowel. (*bat, boat*)

2. Words with CVC or CVVC patterns are one syllable.

3. Words with multiple syllables have one syllable that is accented.

4. Compound words are broken between the two identifiable words.

5. Vowels in unaccented syllables have the schwa sound. (le-mon, a-bove)

6. When the first vowel in a word is followed by *th, ch,* or *sh,* these symbols are not broken when the word is divided into syllables, and they may go with either the first or second syllable. (e.g., fa-ther)

7. If the last syllable of a word ends in *le,* the consonant preceding the *le* usually begins the last syllable. (e.g., ta-ble)

8. In most two-syllable words that end in a consonant followed by *y,* the first syllable is accented and the last is unaccented. (ba-by)

9. In most two-syllable words that end in a /r/ sound, the second syllable is unaccented. (teach-er)

10. When *tion* or *ture* is the final syllable in a word, it is unaccented. (e.g., va-ca-tion)

11. Consonant and/or vowel diagraph and diphthongs are never separated. (*black-mail, speed-way, em-ploy-ment, sur-round*)

12. Inflectional endings (*ly, ing, er*), prefixes (*pre-, be-*), and suffixes (*-tion, -ant, -able*) are often syllables.

13. When one consonant is found between two vowels (e.g., *o-pen*), the word is divided after the first vowel. The vowel in the first syllable is often long.

Source: Adapted from *TEACHING PHONICS AND WORD STUDY IN THE INTERMEDIATE GRADES* by Wiley Blevins. Scholastic, Inc./Teaching Resources. Copyright © 2001 by Wiley Blevins. Reprinted by permission.

4. "For students with developed knowledge of Spanish, teach morphology in relation to cognate instruction." Comparing the spelling of cognates (words from the same original word or root) aids Spanish-speaking English learners in comprehending English text (Kieffer & Lesaux, 2007, pp. 139–142). For example, when the student reads *metropolitan,* she may recall the Spanish word *metropolitano* and recognize the meaning of the English word from the Spanish.

Pacheo and Goodwin (2013) suggest yet another way to teach morphology by placing students in small groups, giving them a morpheme such as *sphere,* and having each group write as many words with *sphere* as they can. They also suggest that when reading text, students solve word meanings by looking at the morphemes and context of the word. Focusing on morphemes also helps those English learners whose native language is based on Latin and Greek morphemes to identify cognates their native language shares with English.

Word Recognition and the Common Core State Standards

The authors of the CCSS understand the importance of students having a large bank of words that they recognize automatically. The Foundational Skills Reading Standards for kindergarten through fourth grade list items that directly address word recognition (see Figure 6.3). Notice that in kindergarten the word recognition standards highlight high-frequency words; by the second grade, the standards highlight structural analysis (prefixes and suffixes), and by the fifth grade they highlight roots and affixes. Throughout the elementary grades word recognition standards progress from emphasizing high-frequency words to Latin root and affixes.

SEQUENCE OF WORD STUDY FOR ENGLISH LEARNERS

English learners also need to break down long words into smaller chunks and syllables (Kieffer & Lesaux, 2007; Bear et al., 2007). Figure 6.4 provides a suggested sequence for teaching syllables and affixes to English learners.

ASSESSMENT

Because reading comprehension depends on automatic word recognition and oral vocabulary among other factors, you must know how to assess the readers' oral vocabulary, their ability to identify unfamiliar words, and their sight vocabularies using both informal and formal assessment instruments.

Informal Assessment

As discussed earlier, students' receptive vocabularies, their sight vocabularies, their ability to use context clues, their ability to use visual analysis in monosyllabic words, their ability to blend, and their knowledge of

---

figure 6.3   CCSS English reading foundational skills standards that address word recognition.

KINDERGARTEN

CCSS.ELA-Literacy.RF.K.3.c Read common high-frequency words by sight (e.g., *the, of, to, you, she, my, is, are, do, does*).

CCSS.ELA-Literacy.RF.K.3.d Distinguish between similarly spelled words by identifying the sounds of the letters that differ.

FIRST GRADE

CCSS.ELA-LITERACY.RF.1.3.G Recognize and read grade-appropriate irregularly spelled words.

SECOND GRADE

CCSS.ELA-Literacy.RF.2.3.d Decode words with common prefixes and suffixes.

CCSS.ELA-Literacy.RF.2.3.e Identify words with inconsistent but common spelling–sound correspondences.

CCSS.ELA-Literacy.RF.2.3.f Recognize and read grade-appropriate irregularly spelled words.

THIRD GRADE

CCSS.ELA-Literacy.RF.3.3.a Identify and know the meaning of the most common prefixes and derivational suffixes.

CCSS.ELA-Literacy.RF.3.3.b Decode words with common Latin suffixes.

CCSS.ELA-Literacy.RF.3.3.c Decode multisyllable words.

CCSS.ELA-Literacy.RF.3.3.d Read grade-appropriate irregularly spelled words.

FOURTH GRADE

CCSS.ELA-Literacy.RF.4.3.a Use combined knowledge of all letter–sound correspondences, syllabication patterns, and morphology (e.g., roots and affixes) to read accurately unfamiliar multisyllabic words in context and out of context.

FIFTH GRADE (same as Fourth Grade)

Source: National Governors Association Center for Best Practices (NGACBP) & Council of Chief State School Officers (CCSSO). (2010). English Language Arts Standards, Reading: Foundational Skills. Washington, DC: NGACBP, CCSSO, pp. 16–17.

figure 6.4   Suggested sequence for teaching syllables and affixes to English learners.

1. Inflectional ending *ing*
   a. For some single-syllable words that end in a consonant and the vowel is short, the consonant is doubled before adding the *ing* (*hopping, sitting*).
   b. For some single-syllable words with a short vowel that end in a consonant, only the *ing* is added (*walking*).
   c. For some single-syllable words ending in silent *e*, the *e* is dropped (*hope = hoping*).
   d. For one-syllable words with a long vowel sound, only the *ing* is added (*sleeping*).

2. Inflectional ending/suffix *ed* can have different sounds: /d/ as in *died*, /t/ as in *laughed*, or /ed/ *wanted*

3. Plural endings (*s* or *es* have three possible pronunciations: /s/ as in *plants*, /z/ as in *zoos*, and /ez/ as in *faces*)

4. Compound words, such as *backpack, notebook*

5. Unusual plurals (*wives, children, oxen*)

6. Simple prefixes (*re, un, dis, mis*)

7. Diphthongs in one-syllable words (*oil, boy, doubt, cow*)

8. Familiar vowel patterns in accented syllable: long vowel sound in accented syllable (*a-**lone***), and the short or schwa sound in unaccented syllable (*a-**lone***)

9. Less familiar and ambiguous vowels in two-syllable words (*mountain, powder*)

10. Final unaccented syllable with *er, or, ar* (*reporter, doctor, sugar*)

11. Initial hard and soft *c* and *g*: these letters followed by *a, u, o* are hard (*cat, cut, cot, gate, guy, go*); these letters followed by *e, i, y* are soft (*cent, city, cycle, gem, ginger, gym*)

12. Simple suffixes (*er, est, ier, iest, y, ly*)

13. Less frequent one-syllable homophone/heterographs (*cruise/crews*) and two-syllable homophones/heterographs (*principal/principle*). These sets of words are homophones because they have the same pronunciation and are heterographs because the two words are spelled differently.

14. Less frequent one-syllable homographs (*bow/bow; wind/wind*)

15. Two-syllable homographs (***pre**sent/pre**sent***)

16. Spelling-meaning connection (*music/musical*)

17. Concrete and frequently occurring Greek and Latin word roots (*spect, struct, tele*).

Source: Bear, Donald R.; Helman, Lori; Invernizzi, Marcia R.; Templeton, Shane; Johnston, Francine R., *Words Their Way with English Learners: Word Study for Spelling, Phonics, and Vocabulary Instruction,* 1st ed., © 2007. Adapted by permission of Pearson Education, Inc., Upper Saddle River, NJ.

word parts all affect their capacity to automatically identify words. Informal assessments in evaluating students' abilities in each of these areas include the following.

Checklists

At the beginning of the school year, familiarize yourself with your state's literacy standards, especially those that address word recognition. To ensure that all students become competent in these standards, design a checklist to informally assess each student's growth in this area. You may assess knowledge at the beginning of the year and at the end of each quarter. Students who lag behind the others should receive extra help in word recognition. Students who are competent in all areas should perform other activities when the rest of the class is focused on word recognition. The partial checklist in Figure 6.5 is based on CCSS foundational reading skills for the third grade. This chart was completed by Ms. Henderson after the first quarter. From her review of this checklist, she realizes that Rosa and R.J. need more time working on all areas of word recognition. Kim is competent in all areas; therefore, she gives him other reading materials during guided reading time. The entire checklist based on the CCSS ELA Reading: Foundation Skills for phonics, word recognition, and fluency for third grade is reproduced in Appendix C.36.

Assessing receptive vocabulary

A student's receptive vocabulary consists of words he recognizes when listening to speakers. The context for the conversation often helps him grasp the meaning. One way you can informally assess a student's receptive vocabulary is by having him read a passage at his instructional level. If he decodes a word and does not realize he has mispronounced it, the word may not be a part of his receptive vocabulary. For example, imagine that Jacob has never heard the word *signature*; when he encounters it in a text, he may pronounce it "sign-a-ture," with emphasis on the *sign*, with a long /i/, and never realize that he has mispronounced the word.

Assessing sight words

Many word lists are available to help you informally assess readers' sight words. The Dolch Basic Sight Vocabulary (see Appendix B.6) is commonly used, especially with first graders. The Fry phrase list (Rasinski, 2003; see Appendix B.7) is a good informal assessment tool because it consists of phrases. Many basal readers also have graded word lists for students to master by the end of the school year. You may use the list as a pretest at the beginning of the school year and as a quarterly assessment instrument through-

figure 6.5 Checklist for word recognition skills based on the CCSS ELA Reading: Foundational Skills standards for third grade.

TEACHER Ms. Henderson   DATE 10/30

+ = always   x = sometimes   o = seldom/never

STANDARD   STUDENTS

STANDARD	Kourtlyn	Kim	Gillian	Quinton	R. J.	Arielle	Coy	Zachary	Rosa	Alexis	Gabrielle	Mat	Blake	Taylor	Teagan	Josh	Zeb	Tyler
1. Identify and know the meaning of the most common prefixes and derivational suffixes.	X	+	X	O	O	X	X	O	O	O	X	O	X	X	X	O	O	X
2. Decode words with common Latin suffixes.	+	+	X	X	O	+	X	+	O	X	+	+	X	X	X	X	+	X
3. Decode multisyllable words.	+	+	+	X	O	+	X	+	O	X	+	+	X	X	X	+	X	X
4. Read grade-appropriate irregularly spelled words.	X	+	X	X	O	X	X	X	O	X	+	+	X	O	X	X	X	X

Source: Standards based on CCSS (2010), English Language Arts Standards, Reading: Foundational Skills, Grade 3. Washington, DC: NGACBP, CCSSO, p. 17.

out the year. Decide which list is appropriate for your struggling readers.

To use these lists as informal assessment tools, print the words or phrases on individual index cards. Number the cards in order of difficulty on the back, with number one corresponding to the easiest word or phrase. Prepare a scoring sheet that lists the words or phrases in order. Figure 6.6 includes a partial sample based on the Fry phrase list. Appendix C.39 has a complete form that can be used for any list. The Fry phrase list can also be entered into a tablet, and the assessment can be administered using such a device. The tablet allows teachers to go through the list at the rate students are reading the words (see the video at **www.hhpcommunities.com/literacyassessment**). Mark all correctly pronounced items with a plus sign (+) on the scoring sheet and missed items with a minus sign (−). If you are using a phrase list, all words in the phrase must be read correctly or the student receives a minus.

To administer the Fry phrase list, you may also have the student read the list into a recording device as you flash one card every two seconds. If a student misses five consecutive words, pause the exercise. You may also use the program found on the Reading Center site at http://np.harlan.k12.ia.us/reading_center. htm, which flashes the cards in two-second intervals. The following website exposes each word for three seconds: https://sites.google.com/site/mrsfullenkamp/

fry-words. The goal is for every student to read each list that is appropriate for her grade with 90 percent accuracy (Shanker & Ekwall, 2002). The following commercial informal reading inventories have graded word lists. They can be used in the same way as the Fry phrase list; however, they provide a scoring sheet and a list from which the students can read. Note that not all of the words on these lists are sight words.

- Burns, P., & Roe, B. (2011). *Informal Reading Inventory* (8th ed.). Boston: Houghton Mifflin.
- Shanker, J., & Ekwall, E. (2014). *Reading Inventory* (6th ed.). Boston: Allyn and Bacon.
- Silvaroli, N., & Wheelock, W. (2011). *Classroom Reading Inventory* (12th ed.). New York: McGraw-Hill.

Assessing sight vocabulary

Informally assess struggling readers' sight vocabularies by having them read a passage at their instructional level. If their sight vocabulary is weak, they will read word by word or laboriously sound out every word to the point that they won't know what word they have read by the time they get to the last sound.

You can also informally assess each struggling reader's sight vocabulary by designing a personalized speed test. To do this:

1. Write three words of equal difficulty on a line.

figure 6.6   Scoring sheet for a sample phrase list using the Fry phrase list (Rasinski, 2003).

STUDENT _Tyler_   GRADE _2nd_

+ = yes   − = no

WORDS	BEGINNING OF YEAR	1st QUARTER	2nd QUARTER	3rd QUARTER	4th QUARTER
The people	+				
By the water	−				
You and I	+				
He called me	+				
What did they say?	+				
No way	+				
One or two	+				
More than the other	−				
How many words?	+				
This is a good day	+				
Sit down	−				
But not me	+				

2. Repeat this process to make at least 10 different lines. The first line should have the easiest words and the last line the most difficult ones.

3. Pronounce one of the words from the first line two times for the student.

4. Within five seconds, the student must circle the word you pronounced.

5. Repeat this process for the remaining lines.

Figure 6.7 provides a sample list for this activity. Remember that sight vocabulary assessment must be quick and accurate. The following graded word lists can also be used for sight vocabulary assessment:

1. ESA (Early School Assessment) Word List by Shepard, Kagan, and Wurtz

2. *Basic Elementary Reading Vocabulary* by Harris and Jacobson

3. *DLM's Word Radar,* software by Chaffin, Maxwell, and Thompson

Assessing context clues

Students' background knowledge impacts their ability to use context clues. You can informally assess readers' background knowledge in a number of ways. The first way is to ask the student to "read" the pictures in a text. While discussing the pictures, listen to his tech-

figure 6.7

Sight vocabulary assessment.

1. Mars	planet	meteor
2. skyscraper	train	traffic
3. experiment	hypothesis	conclusion
4. mystery	clues	investigator
5. cello	violin	guitar
6. moth	caterpillar	butterfly
7. circus	clown	ringmaster
8. answer	animal	world
9. every	earth	never
10. example	important	together
11. children	river	second
12. mountain	enough	idea

nical vocabulary. If he does not use any specific terms and relies on words like *things* or *whatchamacallit,* you can assume the reader is not familiar with the topic.

You can also assess a reader's ability to use context clues through a cloze test. When completing a cloze test, readers read for meaning and to recognize the missing word. (To construct a cloze test, see the instructions in Chapter 3.) A cloze test should be administered orally so you can analyze the reader's ability to fill in the blank correctly and ask why she chose a particular word. If the reader makes wild guesses, you can infer that she is not using context clues.

The running record (also discussed in Chapter 3) is another way to assess if and how students use context clues. Use it to determine if readers use picture clues or context clues to help them with unknown words.

Assessing visual analysis

One informal way to assess readers' ability to analyze monosyllabic word parts is to give them a list of words that highlight onset and rime. Pronounce either the onset or the rime of each word, and allow five seconds for students to circle the word part you pronounced. Figure 6.8 presents a small sample list for the reader and a list of sample answers.

To informally assess readers' visual ability to analyze polysyllabic words, ask yourself the following questions while observing how they analyze unknown words:

- Do the readers attempt to sound out the words letter-by-letter?
- Do they segment the words into syllables?
- Do they segment the word into the correct syllables?

Assessing blending

To assess a reader's ability to blend word parts, first assess auditory blending skills by saying two parts of a word and having the reader put the two sounds together. You might begin with monosyllabic words by pronouncing *fl* and then *ight*. The reader should pronounce *flight*. Proceed to two-syllable words (e.g., *pic + nic = picnic*), then progress to three- and four-syllable words.

Next, assess students' visual blending abilities by writing the parts of words on separate cards and having the students push the cards together and pronounce the word. For example, with monosyllabic words, one card might have a c and another card an *at*. Students move the cards together and pronounce *cat*. With polysyllabic words, each card displays a syllable of the word; one card has *moun* and the other has *tain*. Students put the cards together and pronounce *mountain*. See the Intervention section of this chapter for sample cards.

Assessing structural analysis

To informally assess readers' ability to analyze word structure, observe as they encounter words with prefixes and suffixes. Does the reader automatically pronounce the prefix and suffix as separate syllables? For example, on the word *unending,* does the reader automatically pronounce *un*, or does she attempt to sound out the *u* and then the *n*? Does the reader pronounce *ing* as one syllable?

You can also give the student a list of words with prefixes and suffixes (Rasinski, Padak, & Newton, 2013). See Figure 6.9 for an example. Pronounce either the prefix, suffix, or root of the word and allow five seconds for the student to circle that part. Allow no more than five seconds because word recognition must be instantaneous.

Formal Assessment

Figure 6.10 lists diagnostic tests that include subtests that assess oral language, phonic skills, structural analysis, blending, visual and auditory discrimination, sight word recognition, and syllabication skills.

---

figure 6.8   Words with onset and rimes for assessing visual analysis.

LIST FOR READER

1. bill	6. found	11. top	16. sand	21. man
2. light	7. pup	12. see	17. hay	22. pack
3. ham	8. flat	13. hill	18. sound	23. stop
4. land	9. fan	14. might	19. cup	24. bee
5. may	10. back	15. clam	20. hat	

UNDERLINED PART PRONOUNCED

1. b<u>ill</u>	6. <u>f</u>ound	11. <u>t</u>op	16. s<u>and</u>	21. <u>m</u>an
2. <u>l</u>ight	7. p<u>up</u>	12. s<u>ee</u>	17. ha<u>y</u>	22. p<u>ack</u>
3. ha<u>m</u>	8. f<u>l</u>at	13. h<u>ill</u>	18. <u>s</u>ound	23. st<u>op</u>
4. <u>l</u>and	9. <u>f</u>an	14. <u>might</u>	19. c<u>up</u>	24. <u>bee</u>
5. <u>may</u>	10. <u>b</u>ack	15. cl<u>am</u>	20. h<u>at</u>	

figure 6.9 List of words with prefixes and suffixes for assessing word structure analysis.

LIST FOR READER

1. recalls	5. smiled	9. smallest	13. unopened	17. jumpy
2. unless	6. hopeless	10. bigger	14. unnecessary	18. weakness
3. before	7. careful	11. friendly	15. prettiest	19. reading
4. coming	8. running	12. quicker	16. unfriendly	20. teacher

UNDERLINED PART PRONOUNCED

1. rec<u>alls</u>	5. smil<u>ed</u>	9. small<u>est</u>	13. <u>un</u>opened	17. jump<u>y</u>
2. <u>un</u>less	6. hope<u>less</u>	10. bigg<u>er</u>	14. <u>un</u>necessary	18. weak<u>ness</u>
3. <u>be</u>fore	7. care<u>ful</u>	11. friend<u>ly</u>	15. prett<u>iest</u>	19. read<u>ing</u>
4. com<u>ing</u>	8. runn<u>ing</u>	12. quick<u>er</u>	16. <u>un</u>friendly	20. teach<u>er</u>

figure 6.10 Diagnostic tests used to assess sight words.

1. Diagnostic Reading Scales (individual test): Decoding skills and word recognition.
2. Gates McKillop-Horowitz Reading Diagnostic Test: Word recognition, phonics, syllabication, producing letter sounds, letter naming, blending, word analysis, and use of context clues.
3. Gray Oral Reading Tests: Word recognition in context.
4. Gilmore Oral Reading Test: Word recognition in context.
5. The Durrell Analysis of Reading Difficulty: Word analysis in isolation and in context.
6. Diagnostic Reading Scales, Revised: Word analysis in isolation and in context.

intervention STRATEGIES & ACTIVITIES

Word recognition skills should not be taught through isolating worksheets (Bear et al., 2008; Bloodgood & Pacifici, 2004; Pinnell & Fountas, 2007; Rasinski & Padak, 2003), but rather in context—for example, while reading good literature or writing a letter. A primary goal of teaching word recognition skills is to help struggling readers gain automatic word recognition. "The best way to develop fast and accurate perception of word features is to engage in meaningful reading and writing, and to have multiple opportunities to examine those same words out of context" (Bear et al., 2011). Having struggling readers memorize lists of words is fruitless. Rather, help them learn how to think about words by looking for familiar parts within words. Many words can be identified as part of a word family, and sometimes there are familiar short words in longer words, such as *chimpanzee,* which contains *pan,* or *scare,* which contains *s + care.* When segmenting a longer word, the result is sometimes several smaller, connected words. Consider *attendance,* which segments into *at + ten + dance.* In this word and others like it, the smaller words must be blended together quickly to form the longer word. When teaching word recognition skills, incorporate reading and writing activities. During the editing portion of the writing process, examine spelling patterns and spelling–meaning relationships (Bloodgood & Pacifici, 2004). All of the strategies and activities discussed in this section can be used in small group settings. However, it is strongly recommended that these activities be primarily used in tutoring sessions so teachers can focus on what each individual student knows about word recognition. All instruction should take place while working with authentic literature and writing tasks. Use the suggested texts for these activities, or choose those that interest the struggling readers. Assisting students to discover patterns within monosyllabic words and morphological relationships helps them unlock pronunciation, spelling, and meaning of words (Blevins, 2001).

The activities in this section are divided into the following categories: (1) small group activity for teaching word recognition skills; (2) activities emphasizing receptive and expressive vocabularies; (3) activities emphasizing sight words; (4) activities emphasizing sight vocabulary; (5) activity emphasizing context clues; (6) activities emphasizing visual analysis of monosyllabic words; and (7) activities emphasizing blending polysyllabic words and structural analysis. First assess struggling readers as they read and write, then emphasize the specific skills that meet their particular needs. The first activity is designed for small groups; the others can take place either in small groups or during one-on-one instruction.

Small Group Activity for Teaching Word Recognition Skills

During the first benchmark tests at the beginning of the year, you may identify students who are below benchmark and could benefit from word recognition activities. To use your classroom time effectively, teach concepts to small groups who need to develop similar skills. Observe and assess what each student does when faced with unknown words during these sessions and modify your instruction as needed. Guided reading is a popular small group instructional strategy designed for teachers to work with students of similar strengths.

ACTIVITY   **Guided Reading**   GRADES 1–6

In **guided reading** the teacher works with a small group of students who read at the same level and use similar reading processes (Fountas & Pinnell, 2006b; Fountas & Pinnell, 2013). For these activities, use leveled books that offer a minimum of new concepts to learn, and take time to teach one or two new concepts in each session. The premise of guided reading is for students to experience new texts that they can read at once with minimal support. Your role is to teach strategies and skills and how to use them successfully during independent reading.

The guided reading lesson follows a specific format:

1. Select a text that offers one or two new concepts. The text may be in a large book format so that all students in the group can see it clearly.

2. Introduce the book by talking through the pictures, using the vocabulary of the text. For example, if the story is about a humungous bear but the students use the word *big* in the discussion, introduce the word *humungous* during further discussion.

3. After you talk through the entire text, give each student a copy of the book. Instruct them to look at the pictures again, and perhaps ask them to find a particular word on a particular page.

4. Next, instruct the students to read the book aloud quietly to themselves. Watch for words they find difficult.

5. After the reading, make a list on a whiteboard of words they found difficult. Now teach them an appropriate word recognition skill (e.g., structural analysis) and ask them to apply it to the given word.

6. Read the text in unison with the students.

INSIDE THE CLASSROOM | A Guided Reading Session   BOX

Mr. Francis is supervising a small group activity in which students are quietly reading aloud to themselves Meish Goldish's *Step Inside the Rain Forest* (1993). He notes the children struggle with the word *sloth*, an unfamiliar animal, and *chimpanzee*, a longer word for this group of readers. When the students use picture clues for this word, some say, "ape," while others say, "monkey." When they have completed the story, Mr. Francis writes *sloth* on the whiteboard.

Mr. Francis: What parts do you see in this word?

Students: A *sl* and a *th*.

Mr. Francis: Good. What sound does *sl* make?

Students: /sl/.

Mr. Francis: Good! What sound does the *th* make?

Students: /th/.

Mr. Francis: Good! Do you think the *o* makes a short or long sound?

Carla: A short sound because there is no *e* at the end of the word.

Mr. Francis: Now let's blend the three parts together.

Students: /sl/ . . . /o/ . . . /th/.

Mr. Francis: A little faster now.

Students: *Sloth* (as Mr. Francis quickly moves his finger under the letters).

Mr. Francis: Now turn to page 11 and let's read that page together.

Students: A sloth—it doesn't walk on the ground.

Mr. Francis: Great! We also know that monkeys and apes are incorrect words because these animals can walk on the ground. Now let's look at this word. (He writes *chimpanzee* on the board.) Again, some of you read *ape* and some of you read *monkey.* The animal on page 13 looks like a monkey or ape. But let's look at the letters of the word. What sound does *monkey* start with?

Students: /m/.

Mr. Francis: Correct! This word (pointing to *chimpanzee* on the board) does not begin with the /m/ sound or the letter *m*. What sound does *ape* begin with?

Carla: A long /a/ sound.

Mr. Francis: Correct! These letters (points to the *ch*) do not make the long /a/ sound. What word do you see in this long word?

Colin: I see *pan*. (He points to it.)

Brian: It's *chimpanzee!* A chimpanzee is like a monkey, and that has *pan* in it. Listen, *chim pan zee.*

Mr. Francis: Great job! Let's read that page together.

Students: Bats and snakes and chimpanzees.

Colin: Mr. Francis, you spelled it wrong. It has an *s* on the end.

Mr. Francis: Thanks for catching that, Colin. What does that *s* mean?

Colin: That there are more than one.

Mr. Francis: Great job! Colin saw a smaller word in *chimpanzee* and Brian, you recalled that a chimpanzee is like a monkey. Today, boys and girls, you learned how to find smaller parts in words, like in *sloth* and in *chimpanzees*. Now, let's read the entire book together.

7. Sometimes you might invite students to respond to the book to assess their comprehension. Other times you may include writing, drama, multimedia, or art extensions to complement the book. However, not every book works with such extensions.

8. Ask a student to stay so you can make a running record of his reading.

Read the scenario in the accompanying box and examine how Mr. Francis teaches several word recognition skills during a guided reading session.

Fountas and Pinnell's *Guided Reading: Good First Teaching for All Children* (2006b) offers more detail on how to conduct a guided reading session.

Activities Emphasizing Receptive and Expressive Vocabularies

During discussions you may observe a student whose receptive and expressive vocabularies are very limited. The student may use general terms such as *thing* for common objects, like the wheel of a car. Or she may not know the specific names of familiar animals. Take time to discuss books and pictures with her, using specific words and prompting her to join in. The following two activities should be conducted in a tutoring session so you or the tutor can adapt the activity to the student's individual needs.

ACTIVITY **Wordless Books**   GRADES 1–8

"Reading" a wordless book is one way to build a struggling reader's receptive vocabulary and schemata. The "reading" becomes a discussion when a teacher also comments on the pictures, using specific terms or a more advanced vocabulary than a reader has. Appendix A.5 presents a list of wordless books that encourage this kind of discussion, and Appendix A.6 presents some appropriate material for content area learning. Some of the books in the list are intended for younger students, while some, especially those in Appendix A.6, are complex enough for middle school students. One example is the complex wordless book *Zoom* (1995) by Istvan Banyai, in which the illustrations involve multiple shifts in perspective. After viewing the first picture in the book, a middle school student may say that it depicts a bird. As the student turns to the second page, you may agree but say that it is a rooster because of the colorful crown. As you continue through the book, if the student calls the cruise ship a boat, you can explain the difference. As you discuss the pictures, write each specified word on an adhesive label and stick it to the appropriate page so the student can later go through the book and read these words back to the tutor.

ACTIVITY   **Picture Books**   GRADES 1–3

Jan Brett's books have detailed pictures and borders. Often the borders are stories within the main plot or details that supplement it. Using one of Brett's books, you can help a struggling reader "read" the pictures before tackling the text. Use specific vocabulary so she hears potentially challenging words before she attempts to read. For example, while discussing the pictures in Brett's *Armadillo Rodeo* (1995), use words such as *lizard, hand-tooled, chili, arena, jalapeno,* and *fiddles,* which may be unfamiliar to the student. When she reads the book, she will refer to the discussion and picture clues to help decode the unfamiliar words. Additional titles by Jan Brett are listed on her website (www.janbrett.com), and she includes many useful ideas for using her books with students.

ACTIVITY   **Using Pictures to Enhance the Expressive**   GRADES 6–8
Vocabulary of Middle School Students

Brod Bagert's (2006) *Hormone Jungle: Coming of Age* poetry book has a drawing on each page that can assist middle school students in enhancing their expressive vocabulary. Read the title of the poem and then invite the student to explain the drawing, many of which are abstract. For example, the poem "The Gap" features a drawing of the right half of one face and the left half of another. The right-half face has a heart drawn over it. Ask the student to explain why she thinks the artist drew that picture for that poem. (This poem is written from a female's perspective so this activity works best with a female student.) As you ask "why" questions, the student will be developing an expressive vocabulary as she tries to explain herself. An appropriate poem for boys is "The Girl-Crazy Alien Body Snatcher," featuring a drawing of an alien-looking male with four wings; one wing has a mask of a devil and one wing has three moons on it. The male has his hand up in the air as if he is in a dilemma. Ask "why" questions such as, "Why do you think the illustrator drew an alien-looking male?" and "What is meant by the four wings?" Give him time to find words to express his thoughts.

The wordless book *Ben's Dream,* which includes illustrations of famous places such as the Leaning Tower of Pisa and Big Ben in London, may also be used with middle school students. Ask students to describe the places in as much detail as they can. If students are unfamiliar with these places (they are listed on the book's final page), encourage them to use the place name as a search term and read more about it online.

Activities Emphasizing Sight Words

Sight words do not follow phonetic rules, yet they are found in every story. Students who do not recognize sight words quickly fall behind the rest of the class. If you notice some students who continue to struggle with sight words such as *the, of,* and *once* during group time, schedule one-on-one time with them. The goal is enabling each student to recognize sight words automatically. If a student needs more time than others to gain proficiency at the task, have her work with a tutor.

Match the Word

1. After reciting a poem or song with sentence strips, place them in a pocket chart.
2. Give the student a card with one of the sight words from the text.
3. Ask the student to place the card over the correct word in the sentence strip. This will be easy for most, but some will not take enough time to examine the letters within words.

This activity can also be used with big books by writing the sight word on a sticky note and asking the student to place it over the word in the book. Later, you can say a sight word and ask him to point to the word in the text.

Dolch List Bingo

The bingo cards in Appendix D.15 use the words from the Dolch word list. When playing bingo, call out each word twice and allow only five seconds between each word. Remember, automaticity is the goal with word recognition.

Activities Emphasizing Sight Vocabulary

As you observe students in small groups, you will notice some struggle with words that are not difficult for others. These words are frequently necessary to understand a particular passage. For example, when reading about natural disasters, students need to quickly and automatically recognize words such as *hurricane, volcano, tornado,* and *earthquake.* Students who cannot do this may become frustrated and give up. These students will need one-on-one time for activities that will help them develop their sight vocabularies. The following activities should be conducted in tutoring sessions.

Unscramble the Sentence

Read a short poem and then write each line on a separate sentence strip. After reading "Perfect Children" (1997) by Brod Bagert, for example, write the following four lines on four separate sentence strips:

1. | We | children | are | sweet. |

2. | We | children | are | nice. |

3. | We | always | say | "please." |

4. | At | least | once, | maybe | twice. |

After the student can comfortably put the four lines in the correct order and read each sentence while pointing to each word, cut each line into individual words and have her put the sentences back in the correct order.

Personalized Flash Cards

As you and a student read books that contain topic-specific vocabulary, he may encounter difficult words that he sounds out every time they appear. For middle school students, these words will be found in the content materials. Have a stack of index cards handy to write down words that the reader needs to remember. Create no more than 10 to 12 of these cards. The goal is for the reader to recognize those words quickly by sight. When these words are mastered, place them in the "known" stack. Students find it satisfying to see their stack of "known" words grow. Students can also enter their personal lists on a class computer or tablet using a slideshow program or app.

A C T I V I T Y **Personal Word Walls**   GRADES 1–5

To help a struggling reader create a meaningful word bank, create personalized word walls on card stock or a piece of paper. One of Mr. Morris's students created the following list as she read various books about birds, adding words that she found tricky: *bulbul, extinction, emu, ganets, molting, osprey, preening, plumage.*

A C T I V I T Y **Unscramble the Word**   GRADES 1–2

1. After reading a book with the student, select some nouns from the text that the student wants to remember or that are new vocabulary for him.
2. Write out the words, using half-inch squares for each letter, and cut them out.
3. Give the student the squares for one word and have the student unscramble it.
4. Repeat for all the words.

This activity is useful for assisting tactile learners. The sample cards found in Figure 6.11 are based on *First Discovery: The Universe* (Jeunesse & Verdet, 2005).

figure 6.11   Unscramble the letters.

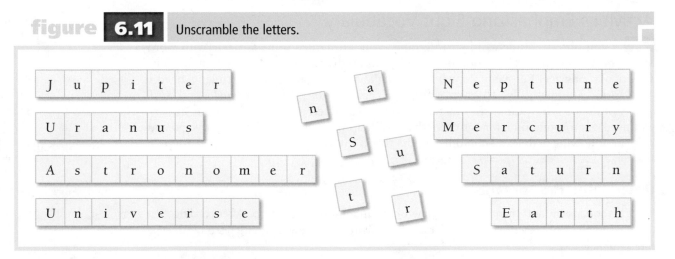

A C T I V I T Y **Technical or Domain-Specific Terms**   GRADES 2–8

Many concept books feature vocabulary words that are specific to the book's topic. Many educators refer to these terms as *domain-specific,* as used in the CCSS, because the words are used when discussing a particular concept in a particular subject. To familiarize a student with this specialized vocabulary, first ask her what she knows about the topic. Then create a word-web for the book's key terms. This will aid the student as she learns to recognize the words before reading the text. The web in Figure 6.12 was drawn by Ms. Inoue for her second grader, Ben, as they discussed his knowledge of the rain forest. She asks him if he has seen TV shows about the rain forest or if he has read about the rain forest at home. After Ms. Inoue marks down the words that Ben contributes, she adds a few more she knows he will encounter in the text. After the discussion, she has Ben read the words in the web. This gives him an opportunity to see these potentially difficult words in print before he reads the text.

Jon, an eighth grader, is very interested in Greek mythology, but when he begins researching mythological figures online, he is surprised to find so many categories. With the help of a high school buddy, he creates the web organizer found in Figure 6.13.

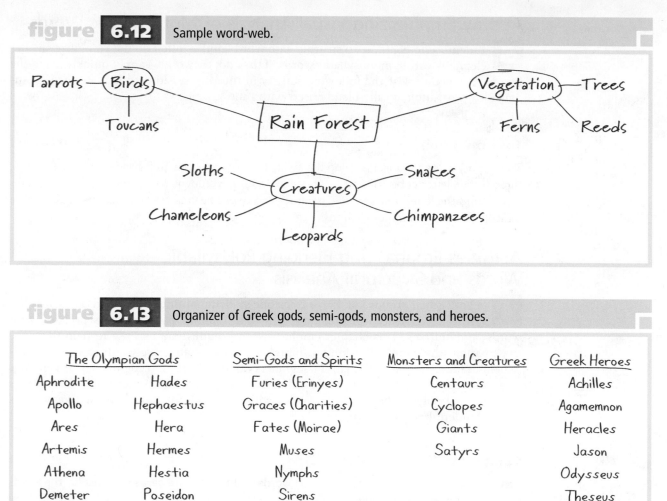

figure 6.12 Sample word-web.

figure 6.13 Organizer of Greek gods, semi-gods, monsters, and heroes.

The Olympian Gods		Semi-Gods and Spirits	Monsters and Creatures	Greek Heroes
Aphrodite	Hades	Furies (Erinyes)	Centaurs	Achilles
Apollo	Hephaestus	Graces (Charities)	Cyclopes	Agamemnon
Ares	Hera	Fates (Moirae)	Giants	Heracles
Artemis	Hermes	Muses	Satyrs	Jason
Athena	Hestia	Nymphs		Odysseus
Demeter	Poseidon	Sirens		Theseus
Dionysus	Zeus			

Source: www.greek-gods.info

Activity Emphasizing Context Clues

While emphasizing context clues during guided reading sessions, you may observe students who still do not use the text or illustrations to decode unfamiliar words. Reinforce that reading for meaning is more important than simply reading words correctly.

Cloze Passages   GRADES 1–8   A C T I V I T Y

Using books at the struggling reader's instructional level, select a key word in a sentence and cover it with a sticky note. Instruct the student to read on to the end of the sentence. Then ask him to choose a word that makes sense in the context of the sentence. If the student has no suggestions, prompt him to look at the pictures for clues. (Choose a book with vivid illustrations to help younger students.) If you are working with an older student and the book has no illustrations, simply have him read to the end of the paragraph to determine the correct word. After the student selects a word, he can take off the label and see if he was correct.

For a variation on this activity, photocopy a short passage at the student's instructional level. Delete every fifth word or every key word and have the student fill in the deleted words. As you observe the student, look for context clues to help her select the correct word.

Activity Emphasizing Visual Analysis of Monosyllabic Words

S tudents who continue to struggle with word families often do not recognize smaller elements within monosyllabic words; if they do, they often cannot quickly blend the two parts together. Use the following activity in tutoring sessions to help struggling students learn to automatically blend onsets with rimes.

A C T I V I T Y   **Toss the Cube**   GRADES 1–3

This activity helps a student develop the ability to create words with a given set of letters. Using three to five letter cubes (found in Appendix D.7), the student tosses the cubes and creates words from the letters. He gets one point for each word he creates. To make the activity more difficult, set a time limit for each toss.

Activities Emphasizing Blending Polysyllabic Words and Structural Analysis

I n your small groups you may notice one student continues to sound out words letter-by-letter instead of breaking them into familiar parts, such as prefixes, root words, and suffixes. This chapter emphasizes techniques you can use to help them see these parts within words. Working with prefixes, suffixes, and base words can be extremely helpful for a struggling student. First graders can benefit from recognizing word endings (e.g., *ing, ed, ly, er,* and *est*), while older students, especially middle school students encountering polysyllabic words, can work with prefixes, root words, and suffixes. Assess what a student knows and continue to develop the skills she needs for success.

A C T I V I T Y   **Compound Words**   GRADES 2–4

Read a book with a variety of compound words and then create cards that display the words that make up each compound word. These cards will help students to see how many compound words they can form by putting the cards together. Time students to make this exercise more challenging. One book that features many compound words is *The Jolly Postman* (2001) by Janet Ahlberg. Some words that relate to the postal service are found in Figure 6.14. Another book with many compound words is *Once There Was a Bull . . . (frog): Adventures in Compound Words* (2011) by Rick Walton.

figure 6.14   Compound words that correlate with *The Jolly Postman,* by Janet Ahlberg.

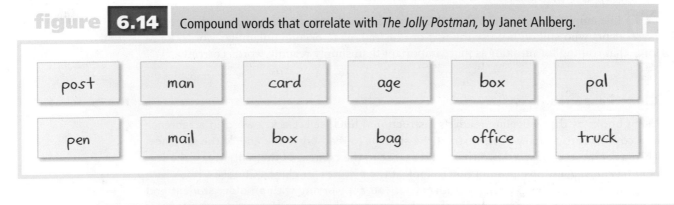

| post | man | card | age | box | pal |
| pen | mail | box | bag | office | truck |

A C T I V I T Y   **Affixes Word Study**   GRADES 1–2

Select texts with words that have a number of affixes. First read the book for enjoyment and then discuss the words that have affixes. When selecting texts for English learners, refer to the sequence for teaching syllables and affixes to English learners (Figure 6.4). The list progresses from most commonly found suffixes to words with Greek and Latin bases. A good example for this exercise is Sam McBratney's *Guess How Much I Love You* (1994), because it uses many past tense verbs and *ing* verbs: *listening, stretching, reached, swinging, laughed,* and *touched.* Notice these words have endings that do not share letters with the base word (e.g., *listen* + *ing; swing* + *ing*). At first exclude words with double consonants and words in which the base word and the suffix ending share letters. For example, words such as *hopping* and *tumbled* should be avoided because in *hop,* the *p* is doubled to form *hopping,* and in *tumbled* the root word (*tumble*) and ending (*ed*) share the *e.*

In the building blocks activity, write all of the base words, suffixes, and prefixes from a passage on sentence strips of different colors. For example, write all root words on orange strips, prefixes on green strips, and suffixes on blue strips. Then cut up the words and affixes and have the readers form as many words as possible by putting the pieces together. Figure 6.15 presents a sample list of words and affixes.

figure 6.15 Root words and affixes.

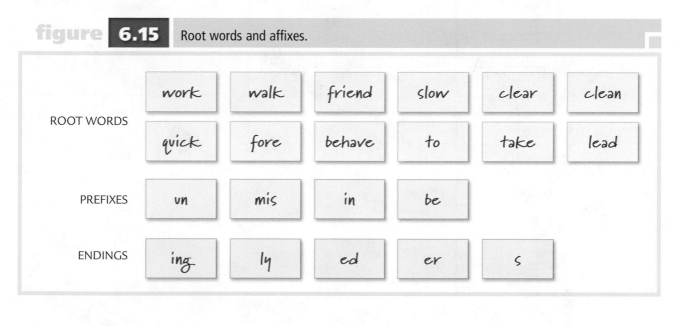

Personalized Word-Part Dictionaries: Affixes and Roots GRADES 3–8 ACTIVITY

When working with older students, help them see the parts as well as the definition of each part. Using Appendices B.8 and B.9, have students make personalized dictionaries that are divided into three sections—one for prefixes, one for suffixes, and one for root words. Give each affix and root word a half page so there is room for students to add new words. This personalized dictionary, like all dictionaries, must include the definition of each affix and root word. When reading, students need to be encouraged to add words to their dictionaries. For example, when a student comes across the word *irresponsible* in a story, he can add the word to the *ir-* page and put the definition in his own words.

Morphology Rummy GRADES 6–8 ACTIVITY

The following morphology rummy games are adapted from *Homophone Rummy* (Bloodgood & Pacifici, 2004). Using the template provided in Appendix D.16, make 20 copies of the entire page, giving you 60 root cards, 60 prefix cards, and 60 suffix cards. Before cutting the cards apart, fill in (or have your students fill in) 30 root words on the two diagonal corners, so the cards resemble playing cards (see Figure 6.16). Then, fill in the definitions of the 30 root words on separate cards. Thus, the original card may have *bio* on its diagonal corners, while its mate has the definition *life* on its corners. Do the same for prefixes and suffixes. Cut the cards apart and create three 60-card rummy decks: roots, prefixes, suffixes.

You or your students may make more cards, but be sure each root, prefix, or suffix card has a matching definition card. The object for student players will be to find as many matches

figure 6.16 Sample morphology rummy cards.

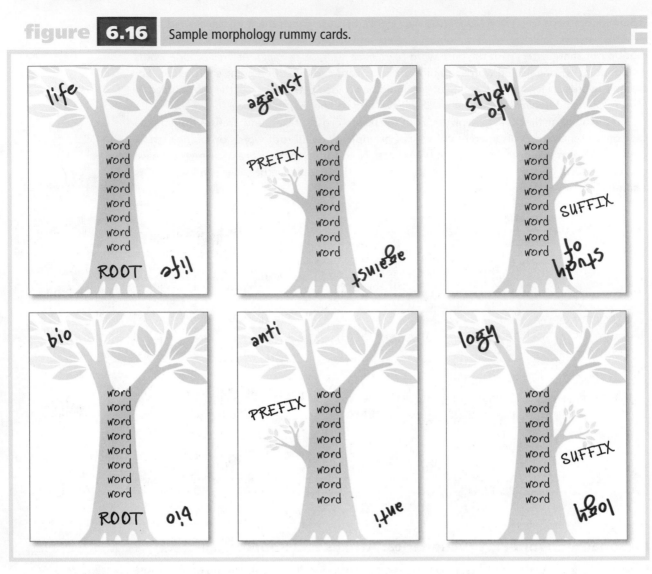

(a root word card and its definition card) as possible. When two cards are matched, the player discards them. The goal is to be the first player to discard all his or her cards.

Directions:

1. Give each player five to seven cards, depending on the number of cards and players.
2. Place the remaining cards in a draw pile, with the top card lying face up next to the pile. The upturned card is the discard pile. (Subsequent discards should be placed so that each previous discard is still partially visible because students can pick up more than one discard during their turns.)
3. The player to the left of the dealer draws a card from the draw pile or the discard pile. If the card from the discard pile is chosen, the player must have a match for it. For example, if a player draws a root word card, then she must have the card with the root word's meaning in her hand. The same procedure is followed for the prefix or suffix cards.
4. Players lay down any matching pair in their hand when it is their turn.
5. When players make a match they must say the root word, prefix, or suffix, read the definition, AND give a word that uses that root word, prefix, or suffix. If the player cannot give a word, the player to the left of the player may attempt to give a word. If that second player can give a word, he keeps the match; if he cannot give a word, the match is placed on the discard pile.

6. If the player has no match, the player discards a card from his or her hand by placing it on the discard pile.

7. Players can challenge a word at any time by consulting a dictionary.

8. If the discard pile contains a card a player needs in order to create a match for a card he has in his hand, he must pick up all the discarded cards on top of the one he wants and keep them. At the end of his turn, he must discard one card.

9. The game is over when one person gets rid of all his or her cards.

10. The winner is the person with the most matches.

WORD RECOGNITION AND TECHNOLOGY

Computer activities motivate many students to read, and a number of interactive books are available to aid students in word recognition. Some books, for example, allow students to click the mouse once to hear the pronunciation of unknown words and twice to hear the definition.

Wanderful (www.wanderfulstorybooks.com) offers a wide selection of interactive books that help students master unknown words. Text is highlighted in phrases so readers can follow along. Students control the turning of each page so they do not become lost. Additionally, We Give Books (www.wegivebooks.org) offers a wide variety of award-winning online narrative and informational books at no cost.

Listening to an audiobook while following a printed text is an excellent way for students to increase their ability to identify unknown words. See Chapter 8 for a thorough discussion of using audiobooks.

Scholastic offers the following CDs/DVDs with interactive books and strategies to increase students' word recognition skills:

- *Phonics Readers.* Includes 72 interactive books on 12 CDs.
- *Phonics Booster.* Offers interactive books on 16 CDs.
- *Let's Go Read 1.* 175 lively lessons build a love for reading.
- *Let's Go Read 2.* Nine interactive stories.
- *Dinosaur Adventure 3-D.* Learn facts about dinosaurs while solving puzzles.
- *I Spy Spooky Mansion* ("Mystery Bins"). Offers challenging riddles.

Websites: Word Recognition

The ReadWriteThink.org site offers three lesson plans related to word recognition:

1. Learning Vocabulary Down by the Bay
2. Active Reading Using *The Enormous Watermelon*
3. Word Sorts for Beginning and Struggling Readers

Many websites allow students to read books online. Some sites are programmed with digitized speech so the student can place the cursor over a word and hear its pronunciation.

My favorite interactive websites to help build word recognition skills include:

www.readingrockets.org

www.funbrain.com

www.prongo.com

www.starfall.com

www.pbskids.org

One site (www.candohelperpage.com, click on "Sight Vocabulary") helps students learn sight words in the context of sentences rather than as isolated words. Words from the Fry Instant Word List (2003) are embedded in simple sentences. The word appears both in a box and in a simple sentence below it. Digitized speech is available to help with pronunciation. A sample page from the site is found in Figure 6.17.

figure 6.17

Screenshot of a website that helps students learn sight words in the context of short sentences.

Fry Words-First Hundred-1 to 15

the

Did you see the dog?

help   next   stop

Source: www.candohelperpage.com.

Be sure students know how to operate programs so they do not waste time. Continue to browse publisher websites and catalogs to stay current on educational software. When your school considers new hardware, be sure any existing media you still want to use will work with the new equipment.

Apps: Word Recognition

Pocket Wally Sightwords ($.99, Grades K–3). Students hear sentences containing Dolch sight words and are asked to correctly identify five in a row. Sentences change so students are exposed to new material.

ABC MAGIC READING (Free, Grades K–2). This app helps students, including English learners, develop word analysis, including segmenting and blending, and prereading skills.

Mad Libs (Free, Grades 1–3). Students fill in the blanks of a story with words they choose, and they can share the stories via an email feature. Includes four stories; additional stories are available for $3.99 per collection of 20 or more.

Quik Tap Words ($.99, Grades PreK–3). This app teaches Dolch sight words using flashcards and games, sorted by grade level.

See Read Say ($1.99, Grades K–2). This app also teaches the Dolch sight words, which are sorted by grade level and frequency. Students read the words aloud and can self-track their progress. Up to four users can use the app at one time.

CONCLUDING THOUGHTS

Automatic identification of words is a necessary skill for reading comprehension. Many readers struggle with sight words and others lack vocabulary to read about specific topics. To address these problems, teachers must (1) help students see patterns in words rather than having them memorize long lists; (2) help struggling readers recognize onset, rime, prefixes, suffixes, and root words to increase their sight vocabularies; and (3) help students use context clues when they encounter unknown words, because many words are not phonograms and do not have prefixes or suffixes.

Throughout this chapter the emphasis has been on the importance of students automatically recognizing a large bank of words, especially those found most frequently in a given text. Read and reflect on the following scenario and answer the questions. Then discuss the scenario with classmates and, if possible, a reading specialist who works with English learners.

reflective learning

ENGLISH LEARNERS. For five years Mr. Perez has taught fourth grade in a small Midwestern town. Last January a new company moved into town, along with many families who were not native English speakers. Mr. Perez had no English learners in his first five years of teaching. However, this year he has five. Two students' native language is Mandarin, and three students' native language is Spanish. During the summer, all five students attended a reading camp that focused on the alphabet, its sounds, and nouns and verbs used in daily conversations. When they started school in August, all five could identify the letter names, give the common sound for each letter, give at least one target word that began with the sound (e.g., b = /b/ and *bat* begins with *b*), and read and write common nouns and verbs used in daily conversation (e.g., types of foods and verbs such as *run, walk, smile*). However, Mr. Perez realizes they struggle with common words such as *with, went, off, the, is, was,* and *saw.*

questions

1. What type of assessment should Mr. Perez give these five students to assess their ability to read sight words?

2. What type of small group instruction should Mr. Perez give these students?

3. What type of individual strategies should he teach these students?

4. Because his time is limited, what do you suggest he does to give these students the maximum help they need?

7 Vocabulary Building

The limits of my language are the limits of my mind. All I know is what I have words for.

LUDWIG WITTGENSTEIN

scenario

Mrs. Lopez, the principal of an urban school, overhears some of the fifth-grade teachers in the lounge discussing their students' difficulties in reading and understanding science materials. She reminds the teachers how readers' vocabularies affect their comprehension. At the fifth-grade team meeting, Mrs. Lopez gives the teachers the following passage from her old music harmony textbook:

> If the root of a triad remains stationary while its third and fifth rise one degree and return, a six-four chord is formed. This type differs from the appoggiatura type in that it is weak rhythmically and the sixth and fourth must enter from below in the manner of auxiliary tones. A simple analysis of one root for all three chords is always possible, the sixth and fourth being nonharmonic tones. (Piston, 1962, p. 108)

Then Mrs. Lopez asks them to write a short summary of this passage, explaining it in their own words. The teachers object, saying they cannot complete the task because they have little background knowledge about music and are not familiar with the terms *root, triad, six-four chord,* and *appoggiatura*. Ms. Ling comments that she is not even sure of the paragraph's main topic. Mrs. James surmises the topic is music because of two words: *tone* and *rhythmically*.

Next, Mrs. Lopez gives the teachers this paragraph:

> The French system was an extension of Franconian principles. The long, the breve, and the semibreve could each be divided into either two or three notes of the next smaller value. The division of the long was called mood, that of the breve time, and that of the semibreve prolation; division was perfect if it was triple, imperfect if duple. (Grout, 1964, p. 79)

Again, the teachers do not comprehend what they have read. No one knows the word *prolation*. At first Mrs. James thinks the paragraph is about the French government because of the words *Franconian, system,* and *principles.* However, the word *notes* in the second sentence convinces her this paragraph must also be about music. She has no idea that it, in fact, has to do with rhythm, because she does not know the terms *quarter note* and *eighth note*. Mr. White, who has a strong background in phonics instruction, thinks the paragraph has to be about marking vowels in words because of the term *breve*. Finally, Mrs. Lopez explains the reason for the exercise: She has heard the teachers complain about students not being able to comprehend science texts. She reminds them that science texts are dense with new vocabulary and with common words that have multiple meanings. When students encounter many new vocabulary words and do not have background knowledge of the topic, they may struggle to comprehend the text. She suggests that they, as a school community, focus on building students' vocabulary. She asks volunteers to find strategies that have proven successful for large group instruction, small group instruction, and tutoring. She also asks for ideas about ways to motivate students to learn new words. The volunteers will share the activities with the entire faculty at their meeting in September. After reading the passages with unfamiliar vocabulary words, the teachers understand the importance of vocabulary building, and 15 teachers volunteer.

As you read this chapter, consider the following questions:

guiding questions

1. If you were one of the teachers in Mrs. Lopez's school, what strategies would you recommend for large group instruction? For tutoring sessions?

2. In the scenario, what words are domain-specific?

3. Would you recommend that a list of vocabulary words be assigned each week? If so, why?

4. How would you recommend that teachers select the vocabulary to teach?

5. What specific vocabulary building strategies would you recommend for the English learners at Mrs. Lopez's school?

6. What would you recommend that your fellow teachers do to motivate students to become interested in new words?

introduction

Between 2008 and 2011, the *Concise Oxford English Dictionary* added 400 new words and revised the entries of 1,900 other words (Oxford University Press, 2013). Have you learned that many new words within the last couple of years? Out of the words you have learned recently, how many do you use in conversational speech and how many are specific to your course work?

The CCR Anchor Standards for Reading specifically state that students are to "[i]nterpret words and phrases as they are used in a text, including determining technical, connotative, and figurative meanings, and analyze how specific word choices shape meaning or tone" (National Governors Association Center for Best Practice and Council of Chief State School Officers, 2010, p. 10). With this mandate it is important for teachers to energize the classroom's verbal environment and to nurture students' vocabulary growth so that students are curious about words (Kucan, 2012). Teachers must consider how they are going to get students excited about learning technical (i.e., domain-specific) words so they are ready for college and career level texts. Reading passages closely so they understand the connotative meaning of words and various forms of figurative language is essential. Teachers will also need to know how to help students unravel the author's intent by examining the author's word choice. Teachers will need to model a love of learning new words and model using a rich vocabulary.

To really comprehend the meanings of words, students need to process the words "deeply and repeatedly" (Richek, 2005) in different contexts. Students need to "own" the word in order to understand and use it in different contexts. Townsend (2009) contends that in order for middle-school students, including middle-school English learners, to "own" words they need less memorizing and more meaningful, engaging, collaborative learning experiences that cater to their social needs. Vocabulary building must be an activity that is enjoyable for students of all ages so they will find joy in learning new words and will be looking for new, "spicy, tasty words" (Baumann, Kame'enui, & Ash, 2003) that roll off the tongue.

Therefore, it is imperative for teachers (1) to understand how proficient readers naturally enrich their vocabulary, (2) to explicitly teach vocabulary, (3) to meet the vocabulary needs of English learners, and (4) to assess struggling readers' vocabulary. This chapter examines these issues and discusses various interventions to use with elementary and middle school students.

WHAT TEACHERS SHOULD KNOW

Have you ever listened to a student read a list of words perfectly? You compliment him on pronouncing all the words correctly; however, when you ask him what a particular word means, he has no idea and cannot use it in a sentence. Focusing on having a student recognize and read aloud a list of words is useless if he does not know their meanings. Knowing a word's meaning includes knowing its multiple definitions and variants and being able to use them in conversation and for written communication. Facilitating students as they build vocabulary skills along with word recognition should be a goal of all teachers.

The Relation Between Vocabulary and Reading

Research indicates a strong correlation between readers' vocabulary knowledge and their reading comprehension (Armstrong, 2004; Blachowicz & Fisher, 2005a; Cooper, 2006; Juel & Deffes, 2004). Baumann, Kame'enui, and Ash (2003) conclude that students' knowledge of words is the single greatest predictor of their reading comprehension. Whether students are learning language arts, math, science, or social studies concepts, comprehension of content depends on word knowledge. In addition, according to August and Shanahan (2006) and August, Carlo, Dressler, and Snow (2005), vocabulary knowledge is an important precursor for literacy skills for bilingual students.

Heilmann, Miller, and Dunaway (2010) found a relationship between children's vocabulary and narrative organizational skills, which includes telling the three main parts of a story—the problem, attempts to solve the problem, and the outcome. In a study with four-year-olds and kindergarten students, Puccelli and Paez (2007) found that Spanish-speaking kindergarten students' Spanish and English oral language and vocabulary knowledge affected their storytelling ability in kindergarten and first grade. Oral language skills of preschool children predict reading skills in later years (Dickinson & Porche, 2011; Wasik & Iaunote-Campbell, 2012/2013), and students who scored high in kindergarten on the picture vocabulary subtests of the Woodcock Language Proficiency Battery–Revised 1991 scored higher on the beginning reading scores in first grade compared to students who scored low on the same test.

Proficient readers tend to have a large working vocabulary; therefore, comprehension comes easily for them. However, students who have a limited vocabulary often struggle with reading because even when they decode words correctly, they do not understand them. Consider the following scene: A student reads the following sentence fluently: "When the lion glared at the boy, the boy turned and ran." However, when the teacher asks why the boy turned and ran away, the child has no idea because he did not know the meaning of the word *glared*. Just because students can pronounce words does not ensure that they know their meanings.

Vocabulary Development

Environment affects children's vocabulary development. By age three, children from privileged families (those with higher than average incomes and parental education) have heard 30 million more words than children from underprivileged families (those with lower than average income and parental education) (Hart & Risley, 2003). Linguistically advantaged children enter first grade knowing approximately 20,000 words, while linguistically disadvantaged children know only 5,000 words (Juel & Deffes, 2004). Parents in a higher socioeconomic status usually have a postsecondary education and know the importance of reading to and discussing books with their children; they take their toddlers and preschoolers to story time at the public library or local bookstore and model good reading habits. These same parents have a robust oral vocabulary, which they impart to their children through everyday activities, including reading. Students whose parents have read to them at an early age have a more advanced vocabulary than children who did not have books read to them (Childress, 2011).

Children who have conversations with adults who have a rich vocabulary naturally learn a wide range of words, whereas children who lack such an environment have fewer opportunities to hear and use new words. Compare the different conversational environments of the two young children in the sample sentences below:

Adult speaking to Susie: "I need to inflate the balloon."

Adult speaking to Mary: "I need to blow up the balloon."

Adult speaking to Susie: "Watch the yellow duckling go swoosh as it submerges its head into the water."

Adult speaking to Mary: "Watch the yellow ducky put its head into the water."

Adult speaking to Susie: "Listen to the chirping of the cardinal."

Adult speaking to Mary: "Hear the bird singing?"

Adult speaking to Susie: "I appreciate the daisies you gave me."

Adult speaking to Mary: "I love the flower you gave me."

In a meaningful context, Susie is learning words such as *duckling, submerge, appreciate,* and *chirping,* and specific names for birds and flowers. In contrast, even though Mary is conversing with adults, she is not developing an advanced vocabulary.

Categories of Words

Beck, McKeown, and Kucan (2013) defined three word tiers. **Tier one words** are common words used in everyday conversation (e.g., *house, car, run, sleep*). **Tier two words** are less frequent but interesting words (e.g., *persuade, parched, exhausted*) and include **academic words** that are used across content areas (e.g., *summarize, describe, analyze, synthesize, compare,* and *contrast.*) In classroom conversations, teachers should explicitly teach and use tier two words so students begin to own them and use them in their conversations and written communications. In contrast to tier two words, **tier three words** are those usually learned when studying specific content area subjects through explicit instruction. The preface to the Common Core State Standards refers to tier three words as **technical words** or **domain-specific words**.

Features of Words

Knowing a word involves more than merely recognizing it when it is spoken. Kucan (2012) posits that there are five features that can help students know a word; teachers should teach all five features in order to facilitate student learning. The features are (1) semantic representation, (2) phonological representation, (3) orthographic representation, (4) morphology, and (5) syntax.

The **semantic representation** of a word refers to the meaning(s) of a word in various contexts. The **phonological representation** refers to the pronunciation of the word; if students cannot pronounce the word they will never use it. The **orthographic representation** refers to the spelling of the word. Students must learn to spell the word so they can use it in their written responses and work. As discussed in Chapter 6, **morphology** refers to the study of the different morphemes (the smallest unit of meaning in words, such as prefixes, suffixes, and roots). Because 60 to 80 percent of words used in middle-school texts are morphologically complex, teachers should engage students in morphological word studies (Flanigan, Templeton, & Hayes, 2012; Kucan, 2011; Pacheo & Goodwin, 2013). Finally, the fifth feature of knowing a word is the syntax, which refers to how it is used in a sentence. Many words can be used in different ways, depending on the sentence. For example, in the sentence "Mary gave me a present" the word *present* is pronounced differently than in the sentence "I will present the award to the winner." In the first sentence *present* is used as the direct object (noun) in the sentence, while *present* is used as the action (verb) in the second sentence.

In addition to understanding the five features of a word, it is also important to teach students how a word is related to other words (Brabham, et al., 2012; Pollard-Durodola, Gonzalez, Simmons, Davis, Simons, & Nava-Walichowski, 2011/2012). Recognizing that *hexagon, quadrangle,* and *parallelogram* are all geometric figures can help students learn the meanings of these words.

Vocabulary and the CCSS

The CCSS recognize the importance of student's vocabulary acquisition and use. The CCR Anchor Standards for Language strand includes the standards presented in Figure 7.1.

figure 7.1

The CCR Anchor Standards for Language related to students' vocabulary acquisition and use.

CCSS.ELA-Literacy.CCRA.L.4 Determine or clarify the meaning of unknown and multiple-meaning words and phrases by using context clues, analyzing meaningful word parts, and consulting general and specialized reference materials, as appropriate.

CCSS.ELA-Literacy.CCRA.L.5 Demonstrate understanding of figurative language, word relationships, and nuances in word meanings.

CCSS.ELA-Literacy.CCRA.L.6 Acquire and use accurately a range of general academic and domain-specific words and phrases sufficient for reading, writing, speaking, and listening at the college and career readiness level; demonstrate independence in gathering vocabulary knowledge when encountering an unknown term important to comprehension or expression.

Source: National Governors Association Center for Best Practices (NGACBP) & Council of Chief State School Officers (CCSSO) (2010). English Language Arts Standards, College and Career Readiness Anchor Standards for Language. Washington, DC: NGACBP, CCSSO, p. 35.

INCREASING STUDENTS' VOCABULARY

 he average high-school senior has a vocabulary of approximately 40,000 words (Nagy & Herman,

1987). This means that from grades 1 through 12, students learn approximately 2,700 to 3,000 new words a year, or seven words a day (Snow, Burns, & Griffin, 1998).

Researchers refer to children's awareness of new words and their desire to learn and use them in speaking and writing as "word consciousness" (Graves & Watts-Taffe, 2002). The major avenues of students' vocabulary growth are life experiences in and out of school, vicarious experiences, and explicit instruction, which includes activities involving word play (Fezell, 2012; Goodwin, Lipsky & Ahn, 2012; Kucan, 2012; Pacheo & Goodwin, 2013).

Life Experiences

Students learn the meanings of words that are frequently used in their communities. Students from rural areas understand terms such as *barn, silo, harvester,* and *corncrib;* students from urban areas understand words such as *skyscraper, taxi,* and *subway.* They learn these words through daily interaction with people in their communities. Students from different communities also learn different meanings for the same words. To rural students, an elevator may be a large tower used to store grain, while to the urban student an elevator is a boxlike enclosure that carries passengers between different floors in a building.

Children and adults constantly learn new words through new experiences. On a person's first visit to a Mexican restaurant, he learns the differences between a *taco, burrito, quesadilla,* and *tortilla.* A trip to the ocean introduces children to the terms *low tide, high tide,* and *sandbar.* Cooking helps them understand the difference between *creaming, grating,* and *blending.* A trip to a large department store introduces children to different categories of products and the various items found in each department. In all these experiences, adults need to draw young people's attention to the words and their meanings so they become conscious of the new words. As mentioned earlier, students immersed in vocabulary-rich environments naturally take ownership of a broad spectrum of words.

Vicarious Experiences

The second way students' vocabulary increases is through vicarious experiences. Such experiences might include viewing educational programs and reading a variety of texts, including those on the Internet. These forms of media take students places they have not visited in person.

Educational programs increase students' vocabulary by explaining concepts in technical terms. Many movies and most television shows, however, do not increase students' vocabulary, because they usually focus on everyday life issues that only reflect what students already know (Rasinski & Padak, 2004).

Researchers have found that students' vocabulary develops through reading (Mason, Stahl, Au, & Herman, 2003; Yopp & Yopp, 2007; Beauchat, Blamey, & Walpole, 2009; Nagy & Scott, 2004). High-quality poems and books offer a great opportunity to learn new words because the "authors choose vocabulary that is rich and interesting—words that create a particular mood, feel, or texture" (Rasinski & Padak, 2004, p. 138). When listening to stories and poems above their reading level, students will increase their vocabularies because they hear new words in context and become familiar with their pronunciation and meaning (Yopp & Yopp, 2007; Rasinski & Padak, 2004).

Poems have especially rich language. Jack Prelutsky (1990) introduces readers to vivid vocabulary in many of his humorous poems. In "The Turkey Shot Out of the Oven," he uses phrases such as "partly *demolished* a chair," "It *ricocheted* into a corner," "completely *obscuring* the room," "It *blanketed* every appliance," and "thought with *chagrin* as I mopped." Readers easily grasp these italicized terms and add them to their vocabularies. In another poem, "Floradora Doe" (1984), Prelutsky introduces the reader to many synonyms for *talked*, including *recited, chatted, murmured, yammered, babbled, lectured, whispered, tittered, gossiped, prattled,* and *regaled.*

Trevor Harvey, in his poem "The Curse of the Foul-Smelling Armpit" (1998), also uses a rich vocabulary to explore the odor of the infamous armpit. In this short poem, Harvey introduces students to seven useful words—*lurks, unsuspecting, despair, frantic, foul, performance,* and *grungy*—that are easily understood in the context of the poem. Of course, poetry is read for more than increasing students' vocabulary, but discussing a poet's diction is a crucial part of understanding how poets select word choice to shape meaning or tone, which is the fourth standard of the CCRA for Reading.

Authors of stories and novels also use a rich, descriptive language to paint scenes for readers. In Chapter 7 of *26 Fairmount Avenue*, Tomie dePaola (1999) talks about "driving on the sea of mud" and "squishing through all the muddy water." In the same chapter, he introduces the reader to the concepts of *guardian angels* and *nor'easters.* In *Beauty*, Bill Wallace (1988) carefully chooses the following words to describe a rat: "A huge, gigantic rat was hiding under the sack. He glared up at me with his beady, ratty eyes. His scaly, ratty tail was curled up behind him" (p. 83). The words *gigantic, glared, beady,* and *scaly* provide a disturbing word picture of this creature. After reading short passages such as these with your students, explain unfamiliar words and discuss how the author's word choice contributes to the mood of the story and creates a vivid picture in the reader's mind.

In her books on the parts of speech, Ruth Heller also uses distinctive vocabulary to create pictures in the reader's mind. *Many Luscious Lollipops* (1989) includes the words *star-spangled, asteroidal, mesmerizing, soggy, remarkable,* and *regal.* In *A Cache of Jewels* (1987), she introduces students to new words or words used in new ways:

Cache of jewels (Students may be familiar with the homophone *cash.*)

Batch of bread

School of fish (Students may only be familiar with the *school* house.)

Gam of whales

Bevy of beauties

Muster of peacocks (Teachers may need to explain the difference between *muster* and *mustard.*)

Host of angels

Kindle of kittens

Pod of peas

Parcel of penguins (Students may recognize *parcel* as a package.)

Coven of witches

Drift of swans (Students may be familiar with *drift* used as a verb.)

Brood of chicks

Clutch of eggs

Pride of lions (Students may be familiar with *pride* used as an adjective.)

Lock of hair (Students may be familiar with "Lock the door" or "The lock on the door.")

Army of ants

In *Some Smug Slug* (1996), P. D. Edwards also uses evocative vocabulary to introduce young readers to alliteration. Words include *sauntered, slithered, snickered, sapphire, swooshing, shrieked,* and *scurrying.* As students hear the words in context, they become familiar with their pronunciations and meanings. You can explain these words by acting them out and then inviting students to do the same so they remember the word. After sharing these books and discussing the words, invite the students to "saunter and not scurry in the hall" instead of commanding them to "walk in the hall."

The Internet introduces students to new vocabulary words, just as traditional sources do. The level of vocabulary varies with the type of passage they are reading. If students are researching how animated movies are created, they will learn words such as *optical illusion, footage, flip book,* and *stop motion.* When teachers use these new words in daily conversation, students begin to use them in their own conversations. Learning new words should be an adventure for students and not a boring task!

Explicit Instruction

Lehr, Osborn, and Heibert (2005) estimate that students learn approximately 3,000 new words each year through life experiences and vicarious experiences, but other research shows students' vocabulary also grows through explicit instruction (Manyak & Bouchereau-Bauer, 2009; Carlo et al., 2004; Townsend, 2009; Flynt & Brozo, 2008). Most students can easily learn eight to ten words each week through explicit instruction. So, which eight to ten words should be taught and how should they be taught?

Selecting vocabulary for explicit instruction

Staudt (2009) suggests that teachers ask the following questions when choosing words for study:

1. Does the word have multiple meanings? (E.g., Please sit on that *chair*. I was asked to *chair* the meeting.)
2. Does it function as multiple parts of speech? (E.g., Please *present* your gifts to the queen. I love the *present* I got from my sister.)
3. Does it have an affix or root word that will help the student segment the word (e.g., *unpredictable*)?
4. Does the word have an affix or root base that the student knows (e.g., *audio* from the base *aud*, which means *hear* or *listen*)?
5. Can the word be easily confused with another word (e.g., *fleece* and *fleas*)?
6. Does the word have a common onset and rime (e.g., *fright/flight*)?
7. Is the word an adjective or the comparative or superlative degree of that adjective (e.g., *happy/ happiest*)?
8. Is there a synonym or antonym the student knows (e.g., *happy for exuberant*)?
9. Is the word used figuratively? (E.g., Heaven's tears fell softly on my cheek.)

Teachers should also teach the content (domain-specific) words necessary for students to understand the concepts they are studying and other general words that students must know as they read more difficult texts (Kucan, 2012; Neuman & Roskos, 2012). Many researchers and educators also suggest that teachers teach tier two words—those that are not connected to a specific content area but that are words that literate, educated people know (Fezell, 2012; Graves & Watts-Taffe, 2008; Kucan, 2012; Neuman & Roskos, 2012).

Guidelines for explicit instruction of vocabulary

As mentioned before, vocabulary words are best learned naturally through direct experiences (Rasinski & Padak, 2004). However, many domain-specific (tier three) words cannot be conveyed in an everyday setting. Most new concepts students learn in school are introduced through textbooks and trade books, and each new concept includes a set of vocabulary words. Consider a few of the terms associated with the geologic concepts of volcanoes and caves: *eruption, lava, magma, stalactite,* and *stalagmite.*

When teaching new words explicitly in the context of the topic being studied, be a cheerleader as students pronounce new words, learn their meanings, and use them in different situations. Because words with multiple syllables are often difficult to pronounce, provide many opportunities for students to practice fluent pronunciation. Have them pronounce the new word a number of times so it flows smoothly off their tongues. I have found that having students tap out syllables with their fingers as they pronounce a new word helps break it into smaller pieces. When students can pronounce the word, explain it by naming a familiar synonym or by linking it to a concept the students understand. After students grasp the meaning of the new word, explain how it is used in different situations.

Flynt and Brozo (2008) give teachers six guidelines for introducing tier three (domain-specific) vocabulary words from various content subjects:

1. Selectively choose words students need to know to understand the content.
2. Expose students to these selected words multiple times and use them in discussion. Require students to use vocabulary when they discuss the content.
3. Teach students to infer word meaning by looking for context clues and word parts (affixes and root words).
4. Use vocabulary maps and word association to demonstrate the relationships among words.
5. Teach students how to do a morphemic analysis on words.
6. Teach students multiple meanings of words.

Marzano and Pickering (2010) suggest that when you encounter tier two words with your students as you read passages together, teach the words using these steps:

1. Give an explanation or example of the word, but do not give a dictionary definition. Also, determine what students already know about the word and provide information about the term's prefix, suffix, and/or root word.

2. Have students give a description or an example different from yours. From their responses, determine if they understand the word.

3. Ask students to draw an illustration that depicts the word. Emphasize that an elaborate illus-

tration is not necessary; it should simply indicate that they understand the word. The picture can be used later to help them remember the word.

4. Have students add the words to their personal academic notebook or dictionary. Their entries should note any prefixes, suffixes, root words, synonyms, antonyms, and categories to which they can relate the word. Categories could include "happy words" such as *ecstatic,* "talking words" such as *mumbled,* or "walking words" such as *meandered.* Also include time for students to think about the word and its meaning, to find a partner to share or compare their meanings, and then to share their understanding with the entire class.

5. Have students participate in game activities to reinforce "knowing" the word so they begin to use it in daily conversation.

After using the this process, give students time to play with new words in a risk-free environment. "Jazz-Man," a poem by Eleanor Fargeon in *Noisy Poems* (Bennett, 1987), features a number of challenging words—*mingle, accordion,* and *pandemonium.* You can encourage students to repeat the word *mingle* as they demonstrate mingling with their classmates in the room. Next, have students repeat the word *accordion* as they act as if they are playing the accordion. Finally, have them keep repeating the word *pandemonium* as they create a scene of pandemonium. I suggest students repeat the word as they act it out so they become fluent in the word's pronunciation. Too often we do not cater our lessons to the kinesthetic learners. Any action within a lesson keeps all students alert.

Use explicit instruction not only to teach new words, but also to teach word-learning strategies, such as how to use morphological knowledge, how to use a dictionary to find the origin of words and their multiple meanings, and how to collect new words that they have heard or read. Students should also receive explicit instruction in context clues, word hierarchies, and language concepts, which will be discussed in more detail in the next sections.

No matter what activity you use, always collect the grouped words and display them on posters around the room so students can add to the list and be surrounded with words (Goodwin, Lipsky & Ahn, 2012; Flanigan, Templeton, & Hayes, 2012; Kucan, 2012; Pacheo & Goodwin, 2013). Consider creating brightly colored posters with prefix, suffix, and root families, and when students encounter a word with a particular word part you can add it to the poster. Figure 7.2 is an example of a poster with the EXCESS family of prefixes.

figure 7.2

Sample poster with the EXCESS family of prefixes.

EXCESS FAMILIES: OVER, SUPER, OUT		
OVER-	SUPER-	OUT-
Overtime	Superior	Outlandish
Overweight	Superhero	Outrageous
Overbearing	Supermarket	Outstanding
Overcome	Superfine	Outgrow
Overconfident	Superimpose	Outdoing

Semantic Complexities of English

Because 60 to 80 percent of the words middle-school students encounter in their texts are morphologically complex (Pacheo & Goodwin, 2013), prudent teachers in elementary and middle school teach the meanings of common Latin and Greek root words, prefixes, and suffixes. As you can tell from the long list in Appendices B.8 and B.9, it would be a monumental task to memorize them one by one, so teaching these morphemes in groups is advantageous (Flanigan, Templeton, & Hayes, 2012; Kucan, 2012; Pacheo & Goodwin, 2013; Goodwin, Lipsky, & Ahn, 2012). One way to group them is by teaching "families" of suffixes, which can be grouped in the following manner (Goodwin, Lipsky, & Ahn, 2012; Kucan, 2012):

1. Inflectional plurals (-s, -es)
2. Inflectional tenses (-ed, -ing)
3. Inflectional comparatives (-er, -est)
4. Derivational adverbs (-ly, -er, -or, -ist)
5. Derivational nouns (-ion, -tion, -ition, -ness, -ment)
6. Derivational adjectives (-ible, -able, -al, -ship, -ent, -ant, -ous, -y, -en, -ful, -less, -sh).

Flanigan, Templeton, and Hayes (2012) suggest teachers teach common roots that are found in different content areas, for example, for *syn and sym,*

- in math, the words *symbol* and *symmetry,*
- in science, the words *syndrome* and *synapse,*
- in English, the words *syntax* and *synthesis,* and
- in social studies, crime *syndicate.*

Older elementary and middle-school students need to understand that words and word phrases can have more than one meaning. Encourage students to reflect on the semantic complexities of English as they play with ambiguous language (Sterling-Honig, 2007; Zipke, 2008). Consider the double meanings of the following sentences:

1. Kids make nutritious snacks (Zipke, 2008).
2. When a clock is hungry, it goes back four seconds.
3. A chicken crossing the road is poultry in motion.
4. A bicycle cannot stand alone because it is two tired.
5. What is the definition of a will? It is a dead give-away.
6. Bakers trade bread recipes on a knead-to-know basis.
7. A boiled egg in the morning is hard to beat. (Sterling-Honig, 2007, p. 600)

Share these examples with your students to illustrate the multiple meanings of English words.

Explicit instruction in context clues

One way to teach students how to learn the meaning of words is to focus on contextual clues (see Chapter 6). Start by teaching them to read to the end of the sentence and then guess what the word may mean. Sometimes they may need to read to the end of the paragraph to get the meaning of the word. Point out that many authors define words in the text by including a synonym or definition of the new term in the sentence. Figure 7.3 lists various examples of how authors share the meanings of unknown words with the reader. You should explain the different ways authors may define words in their texts by using specific examples from the students' reading. Many ebooks and websites provide the definition of words. Show students when and how they can click on the word to receive its pronunciation and definition.

As an example of teaching a student to use context clues, consider the word *brusque*. It may be new to fifth graders; however, they can get a good idea of its meaning when reading the following paragraph:

> "What's wrong with Joan?" Lynn asked.
>
> "I don't know. Why?" Deena replied.
>
> "Last night she was so brusque. When I saw her in the grocery store and asked her how she was, she replied, 'None of your business!' and stomped away."

After reading this short passage to the students, ask them what they think the word means. Most students will guess that it means "rude." By affirming their guesses, you will teach them that readers often learn new words from the context of the passage without using the dictionary. Repeat this procedure with examples from the material the students are currently reading. Once the students can pronounce a word and understand its meaning, invite them to use it in a sentence to demonstrate their understanding. This process gives students a sense of ownership.

Explicit instruction in word hierarchies

In all content areas, especially social studies and science, students need to understand the hierarchy of words that organize most informational materials. Some words are headings and other words fit under those headings. Still other words make up subheadings and individual topics. In teaching this concept to students, begin with an idea they already understand, such as departments within a department store. Through games and team activities, students can have fun learning about word hierarchies. The Intervention section of this chapter discusses game-like activities involving categorization. The purpose of these exercises is to help students understand the hierarchy of concepts that will later help them with vocabulary building in various subjects.

Explicit instruction in language concepts

Understanding some basic language concepts is advantageous for students as they build their vocabularies. Give students direct instruction in all of the concepts found in Figure 7.4, and explain more about them when they encounter them in texts. After that encourage them to find examples as they read and use them as they write their own texts. Figure 7.5 lists texts that emphasize many of the concepts defined in Figure 7.4. Direct instruction in these concepts should take place in a fun environment so students learn to enjoy language and vocabulary building.

figure 7.3

Ways that authors define words within texts.

Definition in an appositive phrase: The *waif, a homeless child,* longed for a ten-speed bicycle.

Definition within the sentence: A *vagabond who wanders from place to place* is also called a tramp.

Synonym: Mary does not *procrastinate* because she never *postpones* her assignments.

Antonym: After the storm, the *wild* sea became *serene*.

Situation: Juan will be the *valedictorian* speaker because he *ranks first* in the senior class.

Ann is so *vain*; she is constantly *bragging* about her excellent grades and good looks.

figure 7.4 Language concepts and examples.

Synonyms: Words that have the same or nearly the same meaning.
raven and *black*

Antonyms: Words that have opposite meanings.
mingle and *separate*

Homophones: Words that sound the same but may be spelled differently and have different meanings.
would and *wood; which* and *witch*

Neologisms: New words that enter our vocabulary through extensive usage or for new inventions.
bytes, silicon

Portmanteaus: New words formed by combining two existing words and omitting some of the letters.
breakfast + lunch = brunch; smoke + fog = smog

Acronyms: Words formed from initials of other words.
NATO = North Atlantic Treaty Organization

Euphemisms: A more pleasant sounding word used in place of a word with negative connotations.
administrative assistant instead of *secretary*

Oxymoron: Two contradictory words or ideas used together in a word or phrase.
jumbo shrimp; awfully good; plastic silverware

Regionalisms: Words associated with particular geographic regions.
couch or *sofa; pop* or *soda; griddle cakes* or *pancakes*

Puns: Humorous expressions that highlight the multiple meanings of a word or two words that sound alike.
Fruit *flies* like a banana.

Onomatopoeia: Words that sound like their meanings.
Sploosh went the fish through the water!

figure 7.5 Books emphasizing various language concepts.

VOCABULARY

A Cache of Jewels and Other Collective Nouns by R. Heller (1987). (Nouns; vocabulary building)

A Mink, a Fink, a Skating Rink: What Is a Noun? by B. Cleary (1999). (Nouns; vocabulary building)

Four Famished Foxes and Fosdyke by P. D. Edwards (1995). (Alliteration; vocabulary building)

Hairy, Scary, Ordinary: What Is an Adjective? by B. Cleary (2000). (Adjectives; vocabulary building)

Many Luscious Lollipops: A Book About Adjectives by R. Heller (1989). (Adjectives; vocabulary building)

Some Smug Slug by P. D. Edwards (1996). (Alliteration; vocabulary building)

HOMONYMS AND PUNS

A Chocolate Moose for Dinner by F. Gwynne (1976).

A Little Pigeon Toad by F. Gwynne (1988).

The King Who Rained by R. Gwynne (1970).

IDIOMS

Amelia Bedelia series by P. Parish. (Also emphasizes homonyms and puns)

In a Pickle and Other Funny Idioms by M. Terban (1983).

Mad as a Wet Hen! And Other Funny Idioms by M. Terban (1987).

Punching the Clock: Funny Action Idioms by M. Terban (1990).

OTHER

A Word Wizard by C. Falwell (1998). (Anagrams)

Donavan's Word Jar by M. DeGross (1998). (Rich vocabulary)

Frindle by A. Clements (1998). (Coined words)

Guppies in Tuxedos: Funny Eponyms by M. Terban (1988). (Eponyms)

Jackalope by J. Stevens & S. Stevens-Crummel (2003). (Puns)

Little Mouse's Big Book of Fears by E. Gravett (2008). (Phobia words)

Max's Word by K. Banks (2006). (Rich vocabulary)

Miss Alaineus: A Vocabulary Disaster by D. Frasier (2007). (Rich vocabulary)

Noisy Poems edited by J. Bennett (1987). (Onomatopoeia)

Opposites by M. Novick & S. Harlin (2001). (Synonyms and antonyms)

The Boy Who Loved Words by R. Schotter (2006). (Rich vocabulary)

The Tale of Despereaux by K. DiCamillo (2006). (Definition in text)

What's a Frank Frank? Tasty Homograph Riddles by G. Maestro (1984). (Homographs)

What's Mite Might? Homophone Riddles to Boost Your Word Power! by G. Maestro (1986). (Homophones)

Meeting the Vocabulary Needs of Struggling Readers

Struggling readers often have a limited vocabulary, which may be a result of limited early language experi-ences. Blachowicz and Fisher (2005b) note the vocab-ulary disparity between young children who come from homes rich in conversation, experiences, and lap reading, and children who come from less language-rich home environments. When students with under-developed language enter school, it is the teacher's responsibility to immerse them in rich language experiences. To help these students acquire the vocabulary necessary for academic success, Blachowicz and Fisher suggest teachers include four practices in their vocabulary instruction:

1. Develop a love of words through word play. Permit students to post interesting words on a bulletin board and have them explain to the class where they encountered the words and what they mean. Also, play word games and provide age-appropriate crossword puzzles.

2. Deliver rich instruction by teaching words they need to know to understand a passage, discussing the words with the students, revisiting the words often.

3. Teach strategies so students can decipher new words as they encounter them. Teach word parts (prefix, suffix, root word) and how to use dictionaries or glossaries.

4. Engage students actively in a wide range of texts by providing literature circles, guided reading groups, shared reading, and book clubs. Also, allow the students to show the meanings of words, such as the difference between *surprised* and *stupefied*.

Graves and Watts-Taffe (2008) suggest teachers use books that focus on the play of words. For example, after sharing Debra Frasier's (2007) *Miss Alaineus: A Vocabulary Disaster,* in which a student's mistakes in spelling and defining a word inspire her to organize a vocabulary parade, students can have their own vocabulary parade. After sharing *Little Mouse's Big Book of Fears* (Gravett, 2008), teachers can invite students to create their own book of other phobia words. Figure 7.5 lists these and other books that play on words.

Other experiences that create a language-rich environment include, but are not limited to, experiments, field trips, videos, the Internet, and audiobooks or ebooks. During the field trips and after viewing videos, conversation between adults and students is important. Be sure to use the pertinent technical terms and invite students to pronounce the words with you. Lev Vygotsky's (1962) theory of the zone of proximal development stresses the importance of students interacting with someone who thoroughly understands the concept being taught. As discussed in Chapter 1, the "zone" is the gap between what students know or can express on their own and what they know when working and talking with an informed adult. According to Vygotsky, what students understand today when working with an adult, they will understand by themselves in the future. For this reason, it is important that during and after all of the learning events listed here, students are given ample opportunity to ask questions and discuss new concepts.

Meeting the Vocabulary Needs of English Learners

The vocabulary needs of English learners must also be addressed in the classroom, as the English learner population continues to grow. The Center for Public Education (2010) reported that in 2009, 21 percent of the K–2 population were English learners who spoke a language other than English at home. Five percent of these students did not know enough English to function in a regular classroom. English learners are often diagnosed as learning disabled when, in fact, they may only lack the vocabulary to read grade-level texts (August, Carlo, Dressler, & Snow, 2005; Carlo et al., 2004). Research indicates that many English learners lack the depth of understanding and the vocabulary they need to comprehend grade-level texts (August, Carlo, Dressler, & Snow, 2005; Puccelli & Paez, 2007). These students, however, do not need to spend vocabulary-building time memorizing definitions of words; they need learning experiences that are engaging and meaningful. They need games that are fun and collaborative because students are social and enjoy activities with peers. Teamwork provides English learners a risk-free environment because they are not evaluated individually. They also benefit from studying words that appear in various content materials. When students reach the upper grades, such words often have multiple meanings, but with "specific meanings in different contexts" (Townsend, 2009, p. 243). For example, *function* has one meaning when referring to a computer, but has a totally different meaning when referring to a school activity (e.g., a school *function*). The Intervention section of this chapter discusses engaging, fun strategies for middle-school English learners.

English learners from high socioeconomic status (SES) families tend to outperform English learners from low SES families, and they perform as well or better than native English-speaking students from low SES families (Krashen & Brown, 2005). This indicates that SES correlates with students' vocabulary and success in school more so than whether they are English learners. Schools cannot change the SES of their students, but teachers can provide all students, both native speakers and English learners from all socioeconomic levels, with a literacy-rich environment in order to narrow the achievement gap between all students.

Manyak and Bouchereau-Bauer (2009) outlined the following ways teachers and schools can help English learners acquire in-depth word knowledge:

1. Schools must implement vocabulary instruction that builds from one grade to the next.

2. Teachers must teach high-frequency words in phrases so students are introduced to the way they will encounter new words.

3. English learners also need to learn higher-level or academic English words.

4. English learners must learn strategies that help them infer word meanings.

5. English learners benefit when teachers use real objects, visual images, graphic organizers, and drama to teach new words and their definitions.

6. Teachers should read informational books and engage students in activities that will help them learn new words. Some strategies will be discussed in the Intervention section of this chapter.

Furthermore, in vocabulary instruction with English learners, effective teachers use many gestures and facial expressions, and they encourage students to ask questions so they can clarify the meaning (Vaughn et al., 2005). Like all students, English learners need repeated exposure to the words and benefit from acting out the words. For example, they can demonstrate with their body the difference in such verbs as *melt, shrink, stretch,* and *bounce.* (See the Total Physical Response activity in the Intervention section of this chapter.) When students are emotionally engaged, they are more likely to understand and remember the words. As stated earlier, knowing a word is more than pronouncing it correctly. It implies the user knows its literal meaning, connotations, part or parts of speech, synonyms and antonyms, and multiple forms (e.g., *music* = noun; *musical* = adjective). In addition, English learners must understand how words relate to one another (the relationship between *helmet* and *football,* for example) and how words differ from one another (such as the difference between *chilly* and *cold*) (Brabham, Buskist, Henderson, Paleologos, & Bough, 2012; Kucan, 2012). Brabham et al. suggest that teachers share a semantic gradient word chart such as the one found in Figure 7.6 to help students understand the gradient of words. They also must know how to use the words in oral and written expressions.

Another way to help English learners build vocabulary is to examine the cognates—words with similar spellings and meanings across languages—that their language shares with English (Puccelli & Paez, 2007; Carlo et al., 2004). For example, when working with Spanish-speaking students, you can examine the overlap between the spelling and pronunciation of words such as *coincidencia* and *coincidence, industrioso* and *industrious,* and *afortunado* and *fortunate.* Write the English word on one side of an index card and the Spanish word on the other. On the Spanish side have the student draw a picture to depict the word's meaning or write its meaning in Spanish. See also the activity in the Intervention section of this chapter.

Accepting Students' Limited Vocabulary

When working with students who have underdeveloped oral language skills, accept their vocabularies and be patient as they learn new words. Also, work on simultaneously developing their oral and aural language abilities and their reading skills. Students with weak language experiences should not be isolated from their classmates but instead be included in small and large group situations so they can hear words in meaningful contexts. Always provide these students with special help in a risk-free environment that focuses on their strengths and successes and minimizes their weaknesses. This chapter includes strategies that can be used in these tutoring settings.

ASSESSMENT

Much vocabulary assessment is initiated by teachers closely observing students' oral language capabilities in conversation and in small groups and when reading new passages. When teachers detect students with limited oral vocabularies, they can choose from a number of assessment instruments.

Informal Assessment

You can frequently determine a pre-reader's weak vocabulary through conversation. Pre-readers with limited vocabulary often do not use specific terms in conversation. They may call any form of money—nickels, dimes, and quarters—just *money.* Sedans, SUVs, and dump trucks are all *cars.*

figure 7.6 Semantic gradient word chart.

WORD	JUST A LITTLE	SOMEWHAT	DEFINITELY	VERY	EXTREMELY	VIOLENTLY
hot	tepid	warm	sizzling	blazing	scorching	searing
big	large	huge	enormous	gigantic	mammoth	colossal

When assessing students' vocabulary, be mindful that knowing a word means more than simply reciting its definition. It means being able to use the word and explain it to others. Informational books are dense with domain-specific terms. The goal is to encourage students to "own" a word so they can use the specific term instead of the phrase, "this thing." According to Dale, O'Rourke, and Bamman (1971), there are four levels of knowing a word:

1. I've never seen or heard the word before.
2. I've heard it, but don't know what it means.
3. I recognize the word in context.
4. I know and can use it.

Dale, O'Rourke, and Bamman (1971) suggest four methods a teacher can use when assessing readers' vocabulary knowledge:

1. Ask students to give the definition in their own words orally or in writing.
2. Have students complete a multiple choice exercise.
3. Have them complete a matching exercise.
4. Ask students to check words they know in a list.

For the first method choose a list of new words from a passage. The readers then explain the terms in their own words and then use the terms in a sentence. From their definition and use of the new words, you can determine readers' level of understanding.

Try not to use the second and third methods—multiple choice and matching exercises—because readers may resort to guessing. In the fourth method, students are merely indicating whether or not they know the meaning of the word. If this is done as a pre-reading task, take time to explain the words that are needed to comprehend the passage. If this exercise is done as a post-reading task, evaluate how well readers comprehended the concepts.

Another assessment if you detect a weak vocabulary in a student is to use pictures from magazines mounted on construction paper. The pictures might be of different types of vehicles (cars, pickups, semi-trucks, recreational vehicles, and so on), various types of workers (firefighter, police officer, farmer, nurse, doctor, dentist, and so on), or numerous kinds of animals or plants. Prepare a checklist of the objects and then either name the object and ask the student to point to the word, or invite her to name all the different items in the category (e.g., *tulips, sunflowers, roses, daisies*) that she knows. If the student is weak in naming specific objects, arrange for a tutor to take time to talk with her about pictures in books or about more mounted magazine pictures labeled with specific terms. Later, she can go through this picture collection and practice reading the names.

Other informal vocabulary assessment instruments are the cloze test for older students, maze tests, zip tests, synonym tests for younger students, and checklists based on state standards.

Cloze tests, discussed in Chapter 3, indicate whether students have the requisite vocabulary background for a particular passage. The test allows teachers to determine if students know specific terms related to the topic or if they merely know general ones. For example, in a passage about the jungle, the teacher might delete the word *panther*. The rest of the sentence indicates the animal is a panther and not a lion; however, the student's response is *lion*. The teacher concludes the student's vocabulary lacks the word *panther*.

In maze tests, also discussed in Chapter 3, students are given three possible answers to fill blanks in sentences. Teachers list one general term and specific term as choices for the blank, and the third choice is not associated with the topic. Teachers can then determine if students are familiar with the specific term. For example, a passage might be about a farm with horses and include pictures of horses. The maze sentence reads "Mary wanted to ride the (animal, horse, zebra)." The synonym cloze test is another form of maze test. A synonym is added above the deleted word and three choices are provided for each deleted word. The synonym gives readers an excellent clue, but teachers can still assess students' technical vocabulary. The following is an example:

hungry
The basketball player was (ravenous, exotic, zealous) after the game.

The zip test, designed by Blachowicz and Fisher (2005a), can be used for assessment as well as instruction. In this test the words chosen for deletion are masked with blank labels. The readers attempt to supply the word and then "zip" off the label to receive immediate feedback. This permits teachers to assess students' vocabulary and students to continue reading with a sense of understanding.

Checklists based on the CCSS or your state standards can help you assess students' vocabulary growth throughout the year. Use this type of checklist at the beginning of the year to assess what they know and at the end of each quarter or semester to assess which students need extra help with vocabulary. The partial checklist in Figure 7.7 is based on the CCSS ELA Language strand standards for eighth grade and on data from Ms. Lorenz's eighth-grade class. It appears from the checklist that after the first quarter most students in the class know domain-specific words and tier two words. However, most students struggle with figurative language. The complete checklist is in Appendix C.40.

figure 7.7 Vocabulary growth checklist based on the CCSS ELA Language standards for the eighth grade.

TEACHER Ms. Lorenz   Date 10–7

+ = always   x = sometimes   o = seldom/never

STANDARD	Amy	Leigh	Marisa	Lauren	Candace	Kas	Kirby	Katie	Carly	Faith	Summer	April	Hunter	Logan	Brett	Zachary	Allie	Andy
1. Can determine meaning of domain-specific words.	+	+	X	X	X	X	X	X	X	+	X	+	+	+	+	X	+	+
2. Can determine meaning of tier two words, appropriate for eighth grade.	+	+	X	X	+	+	+	X	X	+	X	+	+	+	+	X	+	+
3. Understands figurative language in texts.	X	O	X	X	O	O	O	X	O	O	X	+	+	+	+	X	X	X
4. Can identify rich word choices in texts.	+	+	X	X	X	+	+	X	X	X	X	+	+	+	+	X	+	+

Source: Florida Department of Education, www.floridastandards.org/Standards/FLStandardSearch.aspx

Formal Assessment

Most formal vocabulary assessments are multiple choice tests. Some require students to match a word with its definition. Others ask students to choose the one word out of three that best fits the sentence (e.g., "John took the [escalator, generator, mobile] to the third floor in the department store.").

The Peabody Picture Vocabulary Test–Revised (Dunn & Dunn, 1997), discussed in Chapter 3, is an individual test that assesses students' receptive vocabulary. The test has four pictures on a page. The teacher says the word corresponding to one of the pictures and the student must point to the correct picture. The test begins with simple noun pictures that most students know—words such as *car, ball, money,* and *mail.* The test becomes progressively more difficult through the use of words such as *attire, incisor, convergence,* and *bumptious.* The Expressive Vocabulary Test (Williams, 1997) assesses students' expressive vocabulary. Figure 7.8 lists some other formal reading tests that have vocabulary subtests.

WIDA (www.wida.us) provides assessments that measure the developing English of English learners in kindergarten through twelfth grade. The tests are based on the English learner proficiency (ELP) standards in the areas of listening, speaking, reading, and writing skills. Teachers who are specially trained to give and analyze the WIDA instruments use them to identify, place, and measure the growth of individual students. Since the assessments require special training, a classroom teacher can request the English language teacher in the district to administer the test to ensure that the student is doing work that is at his or her ability.

figure 7.8

Formal reading tests with vocabulary subtests.

STANDARDIZED ACHIEVEMENT TESTS

Iowa Test of Basic Skills (Grades K–8)

Stanford Achievement Tests–Ninth Edition (Grades K–13)

Gates-MacGinitie Reading Tests (Grades K–12)

Metropolitan Achievement Tests (Grades K–12)

Comprehensive Test of Basic Skills, U and V (Grades K–12)

California Achievement Tests (Grades K–9)

GROUP DIAGNOSTIC TESTS

Stanford Diagnostic Reading Test (Grades 1–12)

Iowa Silent Reading Test (Grade 6–Adult)

Gates-MacGinitie Reading Tests (Grades 1–9)

Nelson-Denny Reading Tests (Grade 9–Adult)

INDIVIDUAL DIAGNOSTIC READING TESTS

Woodcock Reading Mastery Test (Grades 1–12)

Durrell Analysis of Reading Difficulties (Grades K–12)

Gates-McKillop-Horowitz Tests (Grades 1–12)

intervention

STRATEGIES & ACTIVITIES

Teachers need to use a wide variety of strategies to prevent students from becoming complacent about word study. Teachers should also enjoy word study and make it engaging for students (Brabham et al., 2012; Fezell, 2012; Graves & Watts-Taffe, 2011). As noted earlier in this chapter, learning words in an isolated context is rarely beneficial. The practice of giving students 10 vocabulary words on Monday and testing them on Friday often leads to frustration and no sense of personal ownership of the words. Words learned in the context of a social studies or science unit or from stories and poems are words students will use and remember. All of the strategies explained in this section should be associated with topics being studied.

Vocabulary Bookmarks

GRADES 4–6   **ACTIVITY**

Draw students' attention to new vocabulary words as they listen to a teacher read and as they read independently. One strategy to increase upper elementary students' expressive and receptive vocabulary is to have them "collect" interesting words and make a bookmark with the words and definition (Baumann, Ware, & Carr-Edwards, 2007). This activity should help students develop independence in acquiring vocabulary knowledge, as specified in the CCR Anchor Standards for Language.

During shared reading and independent reading, invite students to note descriptive verbs such as *saunter, slithered,* and *lollygag.* Then have them create a bookmark that includes the information seen in Figure 7.9.

Alternately, during independent reading students can create a specific vocabulary bookmark that they keep with the book and refer back to as they continue reading. See Appendix D.17 for a template.

figure 7.9

Sample vocabulary bookmark.

> Name: Kaylee   Date: January 15
>
> **VOCABULARY BOOKMARK**
>
> Title: Ruby Holler
>
> Author: Sharon Creech
>
> Word: Worrywart
>
> Definition: Someone who worries unnecessarily about some small incident that <u>might</u> happen.
>
> Sentence: "Listen to us," Sairy said. "A couple of worrywarts."

Language Gestalts

GRADES 1–8

Use a language gestalt activity when teaching groups of words. **Language gestalts** are clusters of words; for example, tier two words (those that students should know, but are not domain-specific) or tier three words (domain-specific) that are related (Brabham et al., 2012) and/or words unique to the unit of study. For example, a language gestalt for primary students studying reptiles could have the following tier three words: *habitats, prey, predator, python, anaconda, black mamba, cobra, alligator, crocodile, gecko, chameleon, iguana, lizard, tortoise, turtle,* and any other words associated with reptiles. A gestalt for middle school students studying the various types of figurative language could have the following words: *personification, metaphor, similes, onomatopoeia, oxymoron,* and *hyperbole.* Language gestalts for tier two words could be grouped as happy words (e.g., *exuberant, ecstatic*) and speaking words (e.g., *whisper, stuttered*). To help students learn clusters of words, create colorful posters of the word groups and display them around your classroom. The purpose of gestalt word posters is to brighten the classroom with words!

Morphology Tic-Tac-Toe or Bingo   GRADES 3–8

As you introduce students to prefix, suffix, and root families, review the definitions of the word parts through a game of tic-tac-toe or bingo. For primary students, use tic-tac-toe cards so the game moves quickly; for upper grades use bingo cards, which have more spaces. Both games help students learn to analyze word parts as specified in the CCR Anchor Standards for Language.

figure **7.10**

Example morphology tic-tac-toe card.

emit	submit	commit
permit	transmit	omit
intermittent	remit	admit

To play either game, put a list of words that have been studied on the board. Provide at least 12 to 15 words per tic-tac-toe card (Figure 7.10), and 30 per bingo card (Figure 7.11). Have students choose words from the board to fill in the spaces of their card, in any order they choose. Then call out the meaning of word parts; for example, for the word *emit*, say "out," and for the word *transmit*, say "across" and "send." Students who have the words on their cards will mark them. In either game the winner is the first student who fills in a row, column, or diagonal. Appendix D.13 provides a blank template for the bingo game.

figure **7.11**   Example morphology bingo card.

B	I	N	G	O
phobia	claustrophobia	acrophobia	aquaphobia	postpone
component	opponent	proponent	expose	impose
deposit	posture	position	expound	impound
sentiment	consent	resent	dissent	sentimental
sense	sensation	sensitive	sensory	dissension

Example of Meaning   GRADES 6–8

As stated earlier, Kucan (2012) encourages teachers to consider five features (semantics, phonological, orthographic morphology, and syntax) of a word when studying vocabulary. To focus on semantics, generate situations, context, or examples of a word to get students to learn the context in which it can be used. Begin by giving students three words they have been studying and three sentences presenting situations, a context, or examples of the word. For example, you may select the words *dignity, audacious, indignant* and provide the following three sentences.

1. The coach's face turned bright red when his top player missed the free throw at the end of the game.

2. James walked over to the opponent, shook his hand, and said, "Congratulations," even though he lost the tennis match.

3. Maggie walked boldly into the principal's office with glaring eyes, determined to argue with the principal that she did not deserve detention even though she knew she broke the rule.

Students match the sentence with the word that best describes what the sentence communicates.

After modeling a few examples, have students pair up and create descriptive sentences about the vocabulary words they are studying. Students can challenge their classmates with their sentences.

Word Box

GRADES 4–8   A C T I V I T Y

In order to keep students aware of new, interesting words they encounter during their independent reading time or during conversation at home, create a word box for the classroom (Fezell, 2012).

1. Label a box as "word box'" and place a stack of 3 x 5 cards by it.

2. Throughout the week, instruct students to collect words and write the word with the sentence in which they found the word, the source (e.g., book/author, conversation with family member), and their name on a 3 x 5 card.

3. At the end of the week, go through the words, and select five tier two words to teach the following week.

4. On an index card, write the word, an explanation/definition that students can understand, the sentence in which the word was found, the source/author, and the name of the student who added the word. Put the index cards on the chalk tray rail or other ledge in your classroom.

5. On Monday, introduce the words and discuss them with the class.

6. On Tuesday, using a flip chart or whiteboard, write a different sentence in a different context than the one the student provided on the card.

7. On Wednesday and Thursday, engage students in various activities to "play" with the words.

8. On Friday, prepare questions for 10 words (the five for the week and five from previous weeks).

9. Give each student a set of small red, green, and yellow cards. Call on one student to answer each question and ask the other students to hold up one of three cards—red for the wrong answer, green for the correct answer, or yellow for not sure. Alternatively, with older students, use a polling app such as Poll Everywhere (www.polleverywhere.com), and have your students respond using their cell phones. Students can then see their responses in real time via a computer and projector.

10. From the display of cards, assess students' understanding of the words. If the majority of the students did not have the correct answer, discuss the word.

11. Discuss any words that were added to the word box but not chosen for the exercise with the students who submitted them. This keeps all students interested in participating.

Figurative Speech

GRADES 4–8   A C T I V I T Y

Authors spice up their narratives and poems with many types of figurative language. Introduce figurative language, give examples, write original examples, and encourage students to find all of the following in the text they are reading: synonyms, antonyms, homophones, alliteration, slang, similes, metaphors, hyperbole, idioms, oxymorons, homographs, acronyms, and personification. Create a word wall where students can add their original creations or ones they find in books. Christopher Paul Curtis' books *Bud, not Buddy* (1999), *The Watsons Go to Birmingham—1963*

(1995), and *Elijah from Buxton* (2007); and Richard Peck's *A Long Way from Chicago* (1998) have many slang words and examples of figurative speech that pique students' interest. For example, in *Elijah,* Curtis describes Ma's reaction to the toady-frog on her lap this way: "[she] jumped straight out of the rocker. Yarn and needles and buttons and the toady-frog and the half-knit sweater flewed all over the stoop like your guts do after you been hoop snake bit! Ma's knitting spectacles jumped partway up her forehead and she started hopping up and down and slapping at her skirt like it's afire" (2007, p. 14). This activity can help students understand figurative language and how an author's word choice can influence the tone and meaning of a text, both specified in the CCSS related to vocabulary.

LANGUAGE EXPERIENCE APPROACH (LEA)   GRADES K–3

The language experience approach (LEA) can be traced back to the late 1930s (Lamoreaux & Lee, 1943). LEA was widely used in New Zealand in the late 1960s and 1970s (Ashton-Warner, 1963; Holdaway, 1979) as an effective technique to introduce children to their oral vocabulary in written form. In the 1970s Roach Van Allen (1976) used it as an approach to teaching literacy in the United States. Today, LEA is used in many different contexts. LEA views reading, writing, and the other language arts as interrelated, and it uses students' experiences as the basis for reading materials.

For example, after you and your students share an experience, such as a science experiment or a schoolyard safari focused on environmental noise or identifying types of trees, flowers, or insects, discuss what you have seen. If you use technical terms, then the students will begin to use them as well. Facilitate the creation of a word-web about the experience. Next, have a student think of a sentence about the experience and write it down exactly as the student says it. Have the student read the passage aloud. If the student thinks the sentence does not sound right, he may change it to be more grammatically correct. When used for vocabulary instruction, the purpose of the LEA is for a student to dictate a passage that includes words from his expanding vocabulary and then read it back to the teacher. This activity can also be done with a small group of students, and it is especially good for English learners.

The following four ideas are variations of the LEA and can be performed with individual struggling readers. The teacher acts as the scribe for each activity, while the student reads and rereads the passage.

Wordless Books   GRADES 1–8

Wordless books are useful for students with limited language experiences and students who are learning English (see Appendices A.5 and A.6 for title lists). Some wordless books, such as *Deep in the Forest* (1976) by Brinton Turkle and *The Bear and the Fly* (1976) by Paula Winter, are appropriate for younger children, while older children enjoy *Freefall* (1988), *Tuesday* (1991), *Sector 7* (1997), *Flotsam* (2006), and *The Three Pigs* (2001) all by David Wiesner. (Wiesner's books appeal to upper elementary and middle school students because of their more developed plots.) When using wordless books, talk through the book a number of times with the student. During these discussions, point out different aspects of the pictures while introducing new words to the student. Then have the student dictate the story to you. Using adhesive notes, post the text on each page. Finally, have the student read her story a number of times in order to learn the new vocabulary words in print.

Science Experiment   GRADES 1–3

After reading *The Empty Pot* (1990) by Demi, help your students plant lima beans in clear plastic cups. Each day have them dictate notes on their observations and discuss them with you. Use technical terms such as *soil* (instead of *dirt*), *seed* (instead of *bean*), *sprout, embryo,* and *root.* Each day the students should read their previous entries. Note: lima beans grow quickly so students with short attention spans see results fast.

Listening Walk

After reading *The Listening Walk* (1961) by Paul Showers, take a walk on the playground or in the school hallways with your students and discuss what you hear. Strive for vivid descriptions so their vocabulary is enriched (e.g., *chatter* of voices, *squeaky* wheels, *screeching* tires, *whirling* water sprinklers, and so on). Put each idea into a sentence so the text becomes predictable. For example, in the school you can begin each sentence with "In the hallway, I hear _____ and _____." Out on the playground, the sentence pattern can be: "Outside my school, I hear _____ and _____."

Schoolyard Safari

In the fall or spring during the changing seasons, take your students outside and write a book based on the following pattern. Encourage vivid use of adjectives (e.g., *decomposing* leaves, *howling* winds, *multicolored* hues, or *budding* blossoms).

> On the playground, I see _____, _____, and _____.
> On the playground, I hear _____, _____, and _____.
> On the playground, I smell _____, _____, and _____.
> On the playground, I feel _____, _____, and _____.

Total Physical Response

As the name suggests, Total Physical Response (TPR), developed by James Asher (1982), is a strategy that emphasizes using the body to act out a word or phrase so that it is easy for English learners to understand its meaning. If a student has limited English skills, use TPR to demonstrate the meaning of common commands the student must know. TPR steps include the following:

1. Pronounce the vocabulary word and then use actions to demonstrate its meaning.
2. Repeat the word and actions.
3. Invite the students to perform the action simultaneously with you.
4. Say the word or phrase without performing the action but have the group do it.
5. Say the word or phrase and ask an individual student to perform the action.

The following is an example of a teacher using TPR with a small group of kindergarten English learners who have never cut with scissors. The key vocabulary concepts the teacher wants the students to grasp are *scissors, cut,* and *kite.*

> Teacher: Take a scissors. (*Action: takes a scissors from the center of the table.*)
> Teacher: Take a scissors. (*Action: repeats taking a scissors from the center of the table.*)
> Teacher: Take a scissors. (*Action: teacher and students each take a scissors from the table.*)
> Teacher: Take a scissors. (*Action: the students, without the teacher, take a scissors from the table.*)
> Teacher: Juan, take a scissors. (*Action: Juan takes a scissors from the table.*)
>
> Teacher: Take a scissors and paper and cut the paper. (Students already know the word *paper.*) (*Action: teacher takes scissors and paper and cuts a blank sheet of paper.*)
> Teacher: Take a scissors and paper and cut the paper. (*Action: teacher takes scissors and paper and cuts the paper.*)
> Teacher: Take a scissors and paper and cut the paper. (*Action: teacher and students take scissors and paper and cut the paper.*)
> Teacher: Take a scissors and paper and cut the paper. (*Action: students, without the teacher, take scissors and paper and cut the paper.*)
> Teacher: Marie, take a scissors and paper and cut the paper. (*Action: Marie takes a scissors and paper and cuts the paper.*)

Teacher: Take a scissors and a paper with a picture of a kite and cut out the kite. (*Action: teacher takes a scissors and a piece of paper with a picture of a kite and cuts out the kite.*)

Teacher: Take a scissors and a paper with a picture of a kite and cut out the kite. (*Action: teacher takes a scissors and another piece of paper with a picture of a kite and cuts out the kite.*)

Teacher: Take a scissors and a paper with a picture of a kite and cut out the kite. (*Action: teacher and group of students take a scissors and a piece of paper with a picture of a kite and cut out the kite.*)

Teacher: Take a scissors and a paper with a picture of a kite and cut out the kite. (*Action: group of students, without the teacher, take a scissors and another piece of paper with a picture of a kite and cut out the kite.*)

Teacher: Rose, take a scissors and a paper with a picture of a kite and cut out the kite. (*Action: Rose takes a scissors and a piece of paper with a picture of a kite and cuts out the kite.*)

Once the students know a number of commands or phrases, the teacher can assess their knowledge of the words by saying all of the words or phrases and asking the students to perform the task.

ACTIVITY   **Categorizing**   GRADES 2–8

Older students especially need practice in categorizing to connect known words to unknown words so they can learn relationships among words. This activity provides main headings of areas students have studied and asks them to name as many items as possible for each category. Figure 7.12 offers examples.

figure **7.12**   Categorizing.

Name as many items as possible for each category.

AIR TRANSPORTATION	WATER TRANSPORTATION	ROAD TRANSPORTATION	DOGS
airplane	ship	bike	Collie
hot air balloon	boat	car	Retriever
space ship	wave runner	truck	Labrador
helicopter	sail boat	RV	Poodle
	ocean liner		

POETS	AUTHORS	GENRE	MINERALS
Bruce Lansky	Avi	poetry	iron
Shel Silverstein	Gary Paulsen	science fiction	nickel
Brod Bagert	Anna Meyer	realistic fiction	zinc
	Richard Peck	historical fiction	copper
	Sharon Creech	drama	
	Lois Lowry	biography	
	Linda Sue Parks	autobiography	

VEGETABLES	FRUITS	CARBOHYDRATES
carrot	apple	bread
potato	orange	rice
squash	banana	pasta
pea	peach	cereal
corn	pear	

Possible Sentences

This activity, designed by Moore and Moore (1986), is a strategy to preview new words from a story, concept book, or informational text.

1. Create a list of six or seven new words to the students and explain them.
2. Give them another list of six or seven words they already know.
3. Have them write sentences, each containing one or more words from each list.
4. After they read the passage you have been previewing, have them decide which of their sentences are "true" in regard to word usage.
5. Ask them to change the sentences so all information is correct.

Figure 7.13 shows an example of words and sentences appropriate for Tomie dePaola's *Clouds* (1984). Both Nathaniel and Anton are applying what they know about clouds, and both will need to modify their sentences after they read the book.

figure 7.13 Possible sentences based on new vocabulary.

NEW VOCABULARY WORDS	KNOWN WORDS
cumulus	clouds
stratus	rain
cirrus	weather
nimbostratus	thunder

Nathaniel's sentences: We can tell what kind of weather is coming by looking at the clouds. Cumulus and stratus clouds bring us rain. Cirrus and nimbostratus clouds bring us thunder and storms.

Anton's sentences: Some clouds do not bring bad weather, but other clouds do bring us bad weather. Cumulus clouds are just white, pretty clouds that come on sunny days. Stratus clouds look like rib cages and bring us rain. Cirrus and nimbostratus clouds are black clouds that bring us thunder and hurricanes.

Analogies

Standardized tests often assess students' vocabulary through analogies; therefore, it is advantageous to introduce struggling readers to the types of analogies they will encounter in these tests. Analogies are written as *A : B :: C : D* (say, "A is to B as C is to D"). Analogies display the ways that words are related. Following are six relationships that elementary students are asked to complete on standardized tests:

1. Part to whole: *Leaf* is to *tree* as *hand* is to *human*.
2. Synonym: *Black* is to *raven* as *red* is to *crimson*.
3. Antonym: *Black* is to *white* as *up* is to *down*.
4. Action: *Bird* is to *fly* as *fish* is to *swim*.
5. Cause and effect: *Hurricane* is to *wind* as *blizzard* is to *snow*.
6. Geography: *London* is to *England* as *Washington, D.C.* is to the *United States*.

Once students are familiar with analogies, they can write their own. Writing analogies helps students understand words at a deeper level. Students must be able to justify each analogy by explaining the relevant relationship. The following are examples of analogies written by fourth graders who were studying analogies before they took standardized tests. The teacher knew that if students could write their own, they would better understand how to complete them on the test.

> Cloud is to sky as dew is to _____ (grass or earth).
>
> Seed is to apple as pit is to _____ (cherry, peach, apricot).
>
> Barn is to cow as _____ is to bird (nest).

This next set would be appropriate as samples to use with middle school students.

> Fragrance is to stench as sour is to _____(sweet).
>
> Plankton is to microscopic as redwood is to _____(gigantic).
>
> Football is to touchdown as hockey is to _____(goal).

ACTIVITY   **Origin of Words**   GRADES 3–8

Exploring the origin of words with struggling readers interests them in new vocabulary, especially if you choose familiar words with interesting origins. Students and teachers may find it fascinating that candy is named after the seventeenth-century Prince Charles de Conde (pronounced con-DAY), who loved sugary treats. His chef glazed bits of meats and vegetables with egg whites, sugar, and nuts so the young prince would eat the "healthy" foods. Older struggling readers may enjoy learning how the bikini swimsuit got its name, and younger children may enjoy learning how hamburgers and sandwiches got their names. *Guppies in Tuxedos: Funny Eponyms* (1988) by Marvin Terban explains the origins of many words that are familiar to all students.

Often schools are named after national or state heroes. Exploring the background of these heroes can also be fun. For instance, many schools named after heroes in the Oklahoma City area have some interesting stories—Angie Debo Elementary, Cooper Middle School, Gene Autry Elementary, Sequoyah Middle School, and Cheyenne Middle School. Encourage students to learn about local heroines or heroes and create books about them. You might also encourage them to research the origins of words that interest them and write their own booklets. "Exploring the origin of words with students helps them develop indelible memories as they link specific words with stories of the words' origin" (Rasinski & Padak, 2003, p. 147).

ACTIVITY   **Crossword Puzzle**   GRADES 2–8

Many students enjoy making and doing crossword puzzles. Crossword puzzles most often focus on definitions or synonyms; however, you can construct them using antonyms. The best crossword puzzles are those based on words found in books that students have read. A useful resource for integrating vocabulary learning with books students are reading is *Hooked on Caldecott Award Winners! 60 Crossword Puzzles Based on Gold Medal Books* (1986) by Marguerite Lewis. Each puzzle helps familiarize students with the vocabulary used in a specific book, and each is shaped like the book's main topic. For example, the puzzle for *Tuesday* (1991) by David Wiesner is in the shape of a frog, which is the book's subject.

Many online resources allow you to create crossword puzzles easily. To create your own simple puzzle, select the words from a topic or text being studied that are important for students to remember, identify shared letters among them, and assemble them in the form of a puzzle. For example, a few of the words needed by students to comprehend Avi's *City of Orphans* (2001) are *murky, jumble, reeks,* and *warped.* Using large-ruled graph paper makes this task easier. Then assign numbers to the blanks and write the definitions based on the numbers in the puzzle. See Figure 7.14 for a completed crossword puzzle using the language terms from Figure 7.4 (created using www.discoveryeducation.com/free-puzzlemaker). This puzzle is for fifth-grade students.

figure **7.14** Crossword puzzle based on literary terms.

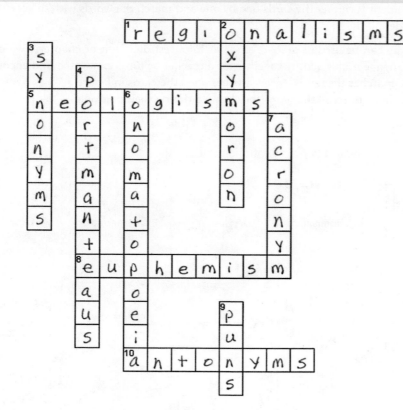

ACROSS

1. Words associated with particular geographic regions.

5. New words that enter our vocabulary through extensive usage or for new inventions.

8. A more pleasant sounding word used in place of a word with negative connotations.

10. Words that have opposite meanings.

DOWN

2. Two contradictory words or ideas used together in a word or phrase.

3. Words that mean the same or nearly the same.

4. New words formed by combining two existing words and omitting some of the letters.

6. Words that sound like their meaning.

7. Word formed from the initial letters of other words.

9. Humorous expressions that highlight multiple meanings of a word or two words that sound alike.

Synonym/Definition Concentration

GRADES 2–8   **A C T I V I T Y**

For this activity first read and discuss with students a story or informational book that includes new vocabulary. The purpose of this version of Concentration is to have students match the word with its definition or its synonym.

1. During the reading, explain any vocabulary word that students do not understand.

2. After reading the book, choose 10 to 15 important words from the text and write them on square cards.

3. Create an equal number of cards with a synonym or concise definition of each word.
4. Turn all 20 to 30 cards face down.
5. Have a student turn over the cards one by one and match the words with the correct synonym or definition.

   This activity can be used to prepare students for a test on a unit or chapter. Two or three students can engage in this activity together, or a teacher or tutor can watch and encourage a student as she matches the terms. Mr. Watts designed the cards in Figure 7.15 as a way for his sixth-grade students to recall the terms they learned during their unit on mythology.

figure 7.15 Sample synonym/definition Concentration cards.

Achilles	Amazon	Agamemnon	Atlas	Cassandra	Electra
Helen of Troy	Hercules	Jason	Muses	Odysseus	Paris
Pegasus	Penelope	Phoenix	Priam	Prometheus	Saturn
Greek warrior who could be killed only by a wound to the heel.	Female Greek warriors who were powerfully built and ferocious.	Greek king who led his men in the Trojan War.	Giant who could hold earth and sky on his shoulders.	Prophet in Troy whom no one believed.	Agamemnon's daughter, who helped kill her mother.
Daughter of Zeus and Leda.	Son of Zeus and Alcmene, who showed his strength doing the impossible.	Greek hero who found the golden fleece of a magical ram.	Nine daughters of Zeus and Mnemosyne, each representing a different art.	Greek, also called Ulysses.	He killed Achilles with an arrow.
Winged horse that flew above the earth.	Wife of Odysseus; symbol of fidelity.	Bird that could set itself on fire.	King of Troy.	Giant who stole fire from gods and gave it to humans.	Father of Jupiter.

Cognate Picture Cards
(Adapted from Bear et al., 2007)

GRADES 1–5   A C T I V I T Y

As stated previously, one way to help build English learners' vocabulary is to have them examine cognates their languages share with English. The following activity uses picture cards of several common cognates in various languages, including Spanish, German, Italian, French, Norwegian, and Dutch.

1. Use the picture and cognate cards for a bank, musical notes, a park, a train, a computer, and a telephone, found in Appendix D.18.
2. Have the students sort the cards, placing the cognates together with the appropriate picture card. Because the words are similar in spelling, students should be able to correctly match the words and pictures.
3. Help students practice pronouncing the various words.
4. Ask them what they notice about the words and discuss how cognates can help them as they learn new languages.
5. Have them perform an online search to hunt for the cognates for *bank, music, park, train, computer,* and *telephone* in other languages. They may also search for other cognates, such as *coincidence, industrious,* and *fortunate.*

Multiple Meaning Racetrack

GRADES 2–5   A C T I V I T Y

Multiple Meaning Racetrack highlights the multiple meanings of commonly used words. The goal is for struggling readers to provide as many definitions as possible for a set of words.

1. Duplicate the racetrack in Appendix D.19 on card stock and laminate it.
2. Make a list of words that have multiple meanings and have been introduced to the students in various texts. Your list might include:

run	box	wind	chair	grate
bow	tire	hanger	frog	wing
exhaust	ring	minute		

3. Write the words on index cards.
4. Have players draw cards from the deck and give as many definitions as possible. Players move their game pieces one space for each correct definition. If a player gives an incorrect definition, he must move one space backward.
5. As on any racetrack, drivers may encounter other obstacles!

Lexical and Structural Riddles

GRADES 5–8   A C T I V I T Y

Zipke (2008) states that it is important for older students to understand that words and phrases can have more than one meaning. Riddles manipulate language by relying on words' multiple meanings, metaphors, and idioms.

Zipke designs two kinds of riddles with humorous answers. The first, lexical riddles, are those in which one word of the answer is a homonym. For example, "Why are fish so smart? Because they swim in schools" (p. 131). The second type is the structural riddle, in which the reader must decipher the non-preferred meaning in the question. For example, "How do you make a hot dog stand? You take away its chair" (p. 131). For English learners and struggling readers, you can draw a picture of a person attempting to make a hot dog stand upright to make sure students understand the riddle's humor.

To have students write their own riddles, Zipke (2008) gives the following steps. She suggests that teachers walk through the steps with a small group of students first to monitor their comprehension of the concept.

1. Collect all words associated with a topic that interests students (e.g., baseball).

2. Have students generate a list of words associated with baseball (e.g., bats, ball, diamond, coach).

3. Instruct students to look for homonyms in the list (e.g., *bats* can be a stick or a flying creature; *diamond* can be a field on which baseball is played or a precious gem).

4. Have the group write a riddle for each homonym: Write a question that is about one meaning of the word, and an answer that is about the other meaning of the same word. (E.g., "Why do spiders like baseball? They are good at catching flies.")

After students understand the steps, invite the students to write and share riddles based on vocabulary in their content area subjects.

ACTIVITY   **Word Expert Cards**   GRADES 6–8

Word expert cards (Richek, 2005) encourage students to become an expert in a word and then teach the word to peers.

- Before reading a story, novel, or informational text, choose new key words and assign one or two words to each student.

- Have students look up each word's definition, state it in their own words, find synonyms and antonyms, and use the word in a sentence.

- After approving their answers, give each student a 4 x 6 index card and instruct them to fold it in half so it resembles a booklet.

- On the cover, have them write the word in large print and illustrate it. Inside they write the definition, synonym, antonym, and the sentence. On the back they write their name and the title of the novel, story, or content area passage.

- Then ask students to teach their words to classmates. An effective method is to form groups of three students with each taking turns. Then they rotate to different groups until everyone has taught his or her word to the entire class.

- *Alternative:* Have students create a slideshow presentation with a voiceover of their word booklets.

ACTIVITIES   **COLLABORATIVE ACTIVITIES**

Middle-school English learners need less memorizing of academic (content area) word lists and more meaningful, engaging learning experiences (Townsend, 2009). Middle-school students are social and enjoy being with friends; capitalize on this preference by choosing collaborative activities. Picture puzzlers and the following activities are especially good for middle-school English learners. To effectively monitor students' development, divide them into small groups.

Picture Puzzlers   GRADES 6–8 ENGLISH LEARNERS

For picture puzzlers (Townsend, 2009), select pictures that represent abstract terms. For example, the word *function* is an abstract term. Find pictures of objects that have a function, such as a computer, desk, notebook, and screwdriver. The small group discusses the function of each of the pictures. Then students add the word to their personalized dictionary using their own words and an illustration.

Music Puzzlers   GRADES 6–8 ENGLISH LEARNERS

To play music puzzlers (Townsend, 2009), select several songs the group likes and discuss a tier two word found in multiple disciplines. For example, in many classes students are asked to interpret, compare, or contrast different topics. For the word *interpret,* students interpret the song; for the word *contrast,* students explain how the song is different from another song; and for *compare,* they compare the song to another song.

Matching Game

In the matching game (Townsend, 2009), put selected words on individual 2 x 3 cards. Write the definitions of the words on a second set of cards and a sentence with a blank where a word fits in on a third set of cards. For example:

Word: Octagon

Definition: An octagon is a shape that has eight sides and eight angles.

Sentence: A stop sign is in the shape of a(n) _____.

Distribute the word cards, definition cards, and sentence cards among the students. The goal is for them to find the matches for their card. Then each trio with a set of matching cards performs a skit to dramatize their word, and the rest of the class guesses the word. Other times the small group can draw a picture instead of acting out the word. For variation, the game can be played in silence, or a word card can be taped to a student's back and she must determine what it is by asking questions of the others in the group. These variations will prevent students from becoming tired of playing the "same old game again."

Two Cube Game

When playing the two cube game (Townsend, 2009), create two cubes using the template in Appendix D.7. Tape target words on each side of one of the cubes, and instructions on each side of the other cube, such as "draw a picture," "write a sentence," "act it out," and so on. A small group of students rolls the cubes and performs the action while the class tries to decipher the word.

Pictionades

Pictionades (Townsend, 2009) is a combination of Pictionary and charades. Divide students into two teams. A student from team A draws a word card from a pile. The student acts out the word and draws a picture of it so his team can guess the word in one minute or less. Then a student from team B draws a word card and acts it out and draws a picture for her team. The team that guesses the most words wins the game. You can also play the game without making it a competition.

Action Jeopardy

In Action Jeopardy (Townsend, 2009), set up a game board, which can be a large poster board divided into five columns and four or five rows. Label the columns with the following categories: definition, synonym, antonym, sentences, and context. In each row write a definition, a synonym, an antonym, a sentence with a blank that needs to be filled in with the focused word, and the topic in which the word would be found. Each row becomes more difficult and the points increase, just like on the *Jeopardy* TV game show. Students work in teams of three as they choose the answer and state the question in one minute or less. Use words students need to learn for their content areas. The following websites offer free game boards to simplify the set-up:

http://quizboxes.com

http://www.goalbrecht.com/jeopardy/

Some sites enable you to post the game board on an interactive whiteboard, and some allow you to include images or MP3 files in the game.

VOCABULARY BUILDING AND TECHNOLOGY

Many ebooks feature verbal word pronunciations and definitions as students read along. Acha (2009) conducted research in which second-language third and fourth graders read a story from a computer program in which 12 new concrete nouns were presented in three ways: verbal annotation, visual annotation, or verbal and visual annotation. Results on both the immediate post-test and the delayed post-test given two weeks later indicated that students had better recall when words were given only in verbal annotation. Acha concluded that processing multiple visual cues simultaneously may be an overload on students' cognitive abilities. Thus, use ebooks with visual annotation cautiously, making sure students are reading the text and not merely clicking on objects. With proper teacher guidance and monitoring, some ebooks can facilitate vocabulary growth.

A helpful website for building English learners' vocabulary is www.languageguide.org/english/. It features categories (e.g., human body, foods, family, time) with many familiar words in each. The student places the cursor over the image and receives the spelling and pronunciation of the word. This is a good program to use at a center so English learners can practice their pronunciation and build their vocabulary of common words.

Finally, you should always encourage students to use a rich vocabulary in their writing. A handy thesaurus can be found at www.thesaurus.com. But caution students to evaluate the synonyms carefully before choosing since not all synonyms fit the meaning of the sentence.

Apps: Vocabulary Learning

The Opposites ($2.99, Grades 3–12). This app helps students learn words and their corresponding antonyms. Students match up pairs of opposing words, working up to increasingly difficult levels. Students learn the importance of word context. The app includes a dictionary option in a user-friendly format.

Opposite Ocean (Free, Grades 2–6). In this app, Luna and Leo strive to master the magic of words by correctly choosing the antonym of the given keyword. Students earn pearls when they drag the correct bubble word to the enchanted clam. Developed in association with the Virginia Department of Education.

Same Meaning Magic ($0.99, Grades 2–6). In this app, students help Luna and Leo, young students at magic school, drag the word stones with the best synonyms into the wishing well to earn gold coins and jewels.

Same Sound Spellbound ($0.99, Grades 2–6). This app is designed to help students understand homophones. Luna and Leo use a spell book to bring animal statues to life. Students must correctly identify the homophone that best completes the puzzle sentence. If the chosen word is correct, the animal statue comes to life. If it is incorrect, the statue crumbles.

CONCLUDING THOUGHTS

Research indicates that readers' vocabulary knowledge is strongly correlated with their reading comprehension, which makes assessing and facilitating students' vocabulary growth essential. The CCSS require that students be able to interpret technical words and phrases, interpret figurative language, and determine how authors create mood through their word choices.

Students build their vocabulary through life experiences, vicarious experiences, and explicit instruction. Many students' vocabularies are weak because they lack life experiences and vicarious experiences, which leaves them without the vocabulary necessary to comprehend grade-level texts. Work with these students in a meaningful context, focusing on building their vocabularies. Discuss topics using domain-specific (technical) terms. In order for students to "own" a word, they must know all its features. This includes its semantic representation (meaning), phonological representation (pronunciation), orthographic representation (spelling, discussed in Chapter 12), morphology (affixes and roots) and syntax (part of speech as used in the sentence). Remember that many students love to play games with peers; therefore, turning vocabulary building into a game makes learning fun.

reflective learning

VOCABULARY BUILDING. Mr. Stone teaches sixth-grade science in an urban Iowa school. Each year, many of his students struggle with the assigned textbook because of their limited vocabularies. It is August and he has just received his four class lists for the year. Because he considers himself a reading teacher as well as a science teacher, he checks his new students' scores for the reading and vocabulary subtests on the Iowa Basic Skills Test. He discovers a wide range of scores on the reading comprehension subtest, but most scores on the vocabulary subtest are below grade level. Only 5 percent of the students have scored at or above grade level on the vocabulary subtest.

QUESTIONS

1. Mr. Stone understands that his students' vocabulary skills are low. What large group activities would be appropriate to motivate them to learn the words necessary to comprehend the science concepts?

2. What small group activities would you suggest Mr. Stone use, and how would you manage the classroom so all groups remain engaged during the entire period?

3. What individual activities would you suggest Mr. Stone use to engage students to build their vocabulary?

8

Comprehension of Narrative Text

It is better to read a little and ponder a lot than to read a lot and ponder a little.

DENIS PARSONS BURKITT

scenario

I n past years Mr. Simon's second graders did not understand how, through the course of a story, a character may change and that the author and illustrator cleverly craft the text and illustrations to depict this change. Sometimes the change is subtle, while other times a major event causes the change. However, with the state adopting the Common Core State Standards, Mr. Simon realizes that he needs to carefully select books that will help his second graders understand how authors use text and illustrations to depict character growth. He has always used Kevin Henkes's books because students can identify with the main characters, and he will continue to do so because Henkes's protagonists exhibit the type of change that will facilitate literary understanding. He begins with *Julius: The Baby of the World* (Henkes, 1995) because the change is abrupt and obvious, and students should be able to find support in the text for this character growth. Mr. Simon also has decided to teach this lesson in small groups of four or five so all students have a chance to share their ideas.

After reading the story and sharing the pictures, he begins the discussion with these questions about the main character Lilly.

Mr. Simon: At the beginning of the story, what was Lilly's attitude toward the baby?

April: Lilly did not like him.

Ty: No, that's not right. Mr. Simon, turn back to the first page, it says she liked him.

Mr. Simon: What makes you say that Lilly likes Julius? Be sure to cite evidence from the story to support your point of view.

Ty: (Pointing to the words) It says she gave him things, told him secrets, and sang lullabies. Oh, and here it says Lilly was the best big sister. So at the very beginning of the story, Lilly liked Julius.

Mr. Simon: What do you think, April, is Ty right?

April: I guess, but she only likes him before he is born. Afterward, she doesn't like him.

Justine: In fact, she does mean things to him. I like the picture where Lilly is counting wrong and saying the ABC's in the wrong order. That was mean because Julius will learn them the wrong way.

Mr. Simon: Natasha, did you see anything else in the text or illustrations that shows that Lilly did not like Julius after he was born?

Natasha: I liked it when Lilly kept saying *disgusting* after the parents talked about his wet nose. That meant that she really doesn't like him at all.

Damon: I like how you read that word, Mr. Simon, *DISGUSTING* (said with great emphasis).

Mr. Simon: How does Lilly feel about Julius at the end of the story?

Natasha, April, and Ty: She loves him!

Damon: Turn to the page when Lilly's cousin says Julius is disgusting. See, right here, it says: "Lilly's nose twitched. Her eyes narrowed." That means that she doesn't like what her cousin said about her brother.

Ty: She also says here (pointing to the text), "For your information..." When my dad says that, I know he means business and wants me to pay attention to what he is going to say.

April: I like how she said here (pointing to the text), "Kiss! Admire! Stroke! Lilly commanded." I am sure she said it like this: "KISS" (long pause), "ADMIRE" (long pause), "STROKE."

Ty: Look here, the author made these words all big: "JULIUS IS THE BABY OF THE WORLD!"

In previous years, Mr. Simon had never taught such a lesson in small groups. He was pleased with the first lesson, believing that his students gained some appreciation for how an author can show character change in a story and the way they could point to specific text and illustrations to support their stance about the way Lilly changed.

As you read this chapter, consider the following questions:

guiding questions

1. Did Mr. Simon choose an appropriate book for this lesson? Why or why not?

2. Could he have chosen a better one? If yes, what book would you suggest?

3. Reread the discussion. Could Mr. Simon do a better job of directing students' attention to how the author changed the protagonist's attitude toward her brother?

4. As you read this chapter, think of other ways Mr. Simon could teach this lesson and what book you would choose after this one.

5. What writing assignment could Mr. Simon add in order for students to write their responses?

introduction

Comprehension is a complex, cognitive process that results in readers making "connections between what they know (prior knowledge) and what they are reading (the text)" (McLaughlin, 2012). It is an active process that requires complex, higher-level thinking skills, and in the case of narrative text, it "is based on the ability to encode and retrieve the basic building blocks (propositions) of sentences and relate the meaning within them to scenes and stories from a text" (Rose, Parks, Androes, & McMahon, 2000, p. 4). Research indicates that readers use the following strategies to comprehend text: draw inferences, predict, self-monitor, retell and summarize, draw conclusions (McLaughlin, 2012; Stricklin, 2011), activate prior knowledge (Harvey & Goudvis, 2013), and visualize before, during, and after reading (McLaughlin, 2012). Readers also need to generate their own questions such as *I wonder if...? How? Why? What is the big idea or theme?* (Stricklin, 2011; Hollenbeck & Saterus, 2013). To comprehend more complex texts on a deep level—one goal specified in the CCSS—students need to have the background knowledge (McLaughlin, 2012) as discussed in this chapter, adequate vocabulary (Blachowicz, Fisher, & Watts-Taffe, 2011; Goodwin, Lipsky, & Ahn, 2012) as discussed in Chapter 7, and motivation (Back, 2009) as discussed in Chapter 2.

Comprehending a text goes beyond the literal level; it includes being able to read critically. In order to comprehend text at a critical level, students need to have an appropriate vocabulary, be able to visualize times and places beyond their present world, and consider the author's perspective and the voices of those not represented in a story. To help students comprehend at this level, teachers, especially in primary grades, must read and discuss stories with their students that are conceptually challenging, so they can help students actively construct knowledge (Harvey & Goudvis, 2013).

Most students can have these discussions in a large or small group setting and learn from both activities. Others, however, require a one-on-one setting in which such stories are read to them. These may be students who have few opportunities at home to read and discuss stories with adults, so they may be lacking a narrative vocabulary or a sense of story grammar. Other students, including many who have attention deficit disorder (ADD) or attention deficit hyperactivity disorder (ADHD), have a difficult time focusing in a large group. Therefore, teachers should scaffold struggling students as they begin to decode and comprehend text. Like all readers, struggling readers need to experience success as they engage with texts (Allington, 2011).

For students to develop reading comprehension skills, they need long periods of time for independent reading of texts that interest them and are on their reading level (Ivey & Fisher, 2005). They also need to read more complex texts independently and closely so when they complete high school they have the reading skills needed for college and their careers (NGACBP & CCSSO, 2010). Teachers of all grades should help students find their reading level and provide a wide range of narrative texts. Effective teachers encourage readers to be adventurous and try different genres and texts that are a little more difficult than their present level. No matter their reading level, students should always be permitted to read texts of their choice during independent reading time.

Upper elementary teachers focus on comprehension strategies, such as making inferences, visualizing, and setting a purpose for reading, to help students become more proficient. However, they should never teach such strategies in isolation (Afflerback, et al., 2013), because even older students cannot transfer strategies taught in isolation to reading full texts (Rhodes, 2002).

As noted earlier, comprehension has many elements and is intertwined with other reading knowledge and skills—decoding, vocabulary, fluency, and prior knowledge. This chapter discusses the complex process of reading comprehension by examining (1) the relationship of comprehension to other reading skills, (2) reading comprehension strategies, (3) critical literacies, (4) the characteristics of poor versus good comprehenders, (5) informal and formal diagnostic and assessment instruments, (6) English learners and narrative text, and (7) intervention strategies and activities to aid comprehension. The focus of this chapter will be primarily on the skills and strategies needed to deeply comprehend complex narrative text, while Chapter 9 focuses on skills and strategies that are unique to comprehending informational text.

Both types of text require many of the same skills, and those skills are discussed in this chapter.

READING NARRATIVE TEXT AND THE CCSS

One of the goals of the CCSS is to ensure that students are exposed to a variety of narrative texts (as well as informational texts, which will be discussed in Chapter 9) that become increasingly complex as they progress from one grade to the next. To ensure this goal is met, the CCSS provide Anchor Standards for Reading as well as grade level standards for Reading: Literature and Reading: Informational Text. The grade level standards for narrative text encompass four areas: key ideas and details, craft and structure, integration of knowledge and ideas, and range of reading and level of text complexity. For a comparison of standards in the range of reading and level of text complexity for a few grade levels, see Figure 8.1.

To view the 10 standards in the CCR Anchor standards for Reading strand as well as the grade level standards, visit www.corestandards.org/ELA-Literacy/. Additional discussion of the reading standards for narrative text is threaded throughout the chapter.

READING SKILLS

Comprehension of narrative text is complex, just like a car is complex. Readers require fundamental skills to comprehend text, just like a car requires fundamental parts in order to move down a road. A car requires four tires, an engine, a steering wheel, and a chassis; readers need decoding skills, fluency skills, and an adequate vocabulary. With the CCSS and other new state standards in place, it is important that teachers model these skills so that students use them naturally when they read independently.

Decoding

Recognizing familiar words automatically and decoding unknown words quickly are essential skills for comprehending text (Guccione, 2011; Blachowicz, Fisher, & Watts-Taffe, 2011). If students focus all their energy and concentration on decoding, they have no energy left for comprehending. A reader's decoding ability helps him pronounce terms automatically that may be part of his aural vocabulary. When he hears himself say these words, he understands them. Struggling readers who cannot effectively decode do not have the benefit of hearing the word. Also, because decoding a word takes so long, struggling readers become discouraged by the length of time it takes to read each assigned passage.

Decoding skills include the knowledge of letter–sound relationships, consonant blends, consonant digraphs, vowel digraphs, and diphthongs. Equally important is the ability to analyze words, because many technical terms have multiple syllables. Readers who can easily break words into syllables and who know the meanings of basic prefixes, suffixes, and root words read faster and become less discouraged than readers who lack these skills. For example, the word *transferable* may be a long word for a third-grade reader. However, if she can readily recognize the prefix (*trans*) and the suffix (*able*) and identify the meanings

---

figure 8.1   Comparison of the CCSS ELA Reading: Literature Range of Reading and Level of Text Complexity strand standards for Grades K, 1, and 3.

KINDERGARTEN
CSS.ELA-Literacy.RL.K.10 Actively engage in group reading activities with purpose and understanding.

FIRST GRADE
CCSS.ELA-Literacy.RL.1.10 With prompting and support, read prose and poetry of appropriate complexity for grade 1.

THIRD GRADE
CCSS.ELA-Literacy.RL.3.10 By the end of the year, read and comprehend literature, including stories, dramas, and poetry, at the high end of the grades 2–3 text complexity band independently and proficiently.

Source: National Governors Association Center for Best Practices (NGACBP) & Council of Chief State School Officers (CCSSO). (2010). English Language Arts Standards, Reading: Literature, Grades K, 1, and 3. Washington, DC: NGACBP, CCSSO, pp. 11, 12.

of each part, she can easily figure out the meaning of the entire word.

Chapter 6 discusses in detail how readers learn to recognize and decode words. That chapter also provides strategies to help struggling readers with decoding.

Fluency

Fluency implies a reader can accurately and automatically recognize a large bank of words; read at an appropriate rate, which is about 75 words per minute with 98 percent accuracy (Rasinski & Padak, 2003); and read with expression. However, students with these traits do not necessarily comprehend everything they read (DeKonty-Applegate, Applegate, & Modla, 2009). Some studies show that growth in fluency correlates with growth in comprehension (Flood, Lapp, & Fisher, 2005; White & Swanson, 2007); however, in most of these studies comprehension was measured by standardized multiple-choice literal questions (Keehn, 2003; O'Connor, White, & Swanson, 2007) or on retellings (Keehn, 2003). As discussed earlier, we know that comprehension goes beyond the literal level. Chapter 10 discusses the components of fluency at length.

Vocabulary

A large listening vocabulary is necessary for comprehension (Nagy & Scott, 2013; Flanigan, Templeton, & Hayes, 2012; Beck, McKeown, & Kucan, 2013). When students attempt to decode written words already in their listening vocabulary, they recognize and grasp their meanings more quickly (Beck, McKeown, & Kucan, 2013).

As stated in Chapter 7, the CCSS require students to determine "technical, connotative, and figurative meanings, and analyze how specific word choices shape meaning" (NGACBP & CCSSO, CCRA Reading, 2010, p. 35). With this in mind, when teachers select fiction to read aloud to students, they should select passages with rich vocabulary, including figurative and technical language.

Poetry is filled with figurative language. Joyce Sidman (2009) in *Red Sings from Treetops: A Year in Colors* describes spring as "Red squirms on the road after rain" (unpaged). After reading the section on spring, teachers can go back to the first page and ask students what Sidman is describing in that phrase. Teachers then can guide students to read carefully, and reread if necessary, phrases of poetry so they can visualize the picture that the poet is trying to create with words.

Technical words can be found in fiction as well as in nonfiction. For example, in *Chrysanthemum* (Henkes, 1991), the music teacher leads the students in singing scales. At this point in the story, the teacher may discuss what a musical scale is.

Shanahan (2012) suggests that a teacher not teach unknown words before she reads a story, but after reading, she can ask students what they think certain words mean. Returning to the *Chrysanthemum* example, after reading the story, a teacher can reread the scene in which Chrysanthemum's parents are attempting to make her feel better after her friends made fun of her name:

> "Oh pish," said her mother. "They're just jealous."
> "And envious and begrudging and discontented and jaundiced," said her father.

After reading this passage, the teacher can ask students what they think *jealous, envious, begrudging, discontented,* and *jaundiced* mean. Understanding these words is important for readers to interpret the parents' responses as supportive and comforting to Chrysanthemum, not as criticism of her. After modeling such a lesson, teachers should encourage students to always try to figure out the meaning of the word by its context. Whichever strategy teachers want their students to use when reading independently should be modeled during read-alouds.

Chapter 7 discusses strategies for building struggling readers' vocabularies.

Close Reading of Complex Narrative Text

The CCSS requires students to "[r]ead and comprehend complex literary and informational texts independently and proficiently" (NGACBP & CCSSO, CCRA Reading, 2010, p. 10). You may ask what makes a narrative complex? In Chapter 2, I discussed how the Lexile levels for each grade have increased so that by the end of the senior year in high school, students are ready for reading expected of them in college, career, and life. In addition to this quantitative dimension of text complexity, Chapter 2 also discusses the qualitative dimension that includes five specific aspects of texts the teacher should also consider as described in Appendix A of the CCSS (see also Appendix D.1). Following is a discussion of the five aspects applied to narrative text:

1. *The level of meaning of the text.* Any story with a single level of meaning is easier to comprehend than stories with multiple levels of meaning, such as allegories or fables.

2. *The structure of the story.* Are the events of the story in chronological order, or are there flashbacks, such as in *The Day Jimmy's Boa Ate the Wash* (Noble, 1992) and flash forwards? Does the story follow traits that are common to the genre, or is it difficult for readers to determine if it is an adventure or a mystery? Do the illustrations complement or augment the text, or do

the illustrations include an entire new story, such as in *Green Snake Ceremony* (Watkins, 1997)?

3. *The clarity of the language.* Does the story use mostly literal language or is it full of figurative or ironic language? Is the language contemporary and conversational or archaic?

4. *The demands on the readers' past experiences.* Is there one simple theme or are there multiple themes? Is the story based on everyday experiences or is it clearly fantasy? Also consider the author's perspective: Is it like the reader's or is it significantly different from that of most readers?

5. *The cultural/literary demands placed on the reader.* A text that takes place in a familiar time and place and/or has low intertextuality is easier than a story that involves another culture and/or has many allusions to other stories.

Comprehending complex narrative texts will usually require students to perform a close reading to fully understand it. Recall from Chapter 1 that CCRA Standard 10 states that students must be able to "Read closely to determine what the text says explicitly and to make logical inferences from it" (NGACBP & CCSSO, p. 10). In order for students to be able to read closely on their own, teachers will need to scaffold them. Teachers can introduce students to close reading through "an instructional routine in which students critically examine a text, especially through repeated readings" (Fisher & Frey, 2012, p. 179). This instructional routine includes:

- examining the organizational structure of informational texts;
- understanding the literal and connotative meaning of the vocabulary;
- examining the author's intent, perspective, and background;
- connecting new information with known information; and
- reading critically to determine the perspective that is not given.

Note how the above routine aligns with aspects of the qualitative dimension of text complexity. Note also that close reading is not necessary for all texts. Some texts are simple and the entire meaning is clear to the reader with one reading.

To begin teaching students how to do a close reading of a narrative text, teachers may want to have students examine and discuss multiple levels of meaning in a single literary quote. Some quotes from classic literature that lead to discussion of different levels of meaning are the following:

"A full belly is little worth where the mind is starved." (Mark Twain, *The Prince and the Pauper*)

"A little nonsense now and then is cherished by the wisest men." (Roald Dahl, *Charlie and the Chocolate Factory*)

"I do not know everything; still many things I understand." (Madeline L'Engle, *A Wrinkle in Time*)

"Most people believe almost anything they see in print." (E. B. White, *Charlotte's Web*)

"I don't understand it, and I don't like what I don't understand." (E. B. White, *Charlotte's Web*)

More recent fiction also offers quotes that can lead to stimulating small group discussions:

"Humans waste words. They toss them like banana peels and leave them to rot." (Katherine Applegate, *The One and Only Ivan*)

"You have to pick which battles are worth fighting." (Christopher Paul Curtis, *The Mighty Miss Malone*)

"I don't like to be unhumble, but anyone could see I have great taste in picking my friends." (Christopher Paul Curtis, *The Mighty Miss Malone*)

Of course, these statements and the context in which they are made must be considered. Teachers can choose a short piece of narrative text that has multiple or underlying meanings and read and discuss it with students over several lessons to unravel the author's intent (Brown & Kappes, 2012). For example, teachers can scaffold younger students in finding hidden humor in a text or discovering a sentence that states a fact about human nature in *The Mouse with the Question Mark Tail* (Peck, 2013). When sharing the book, stop after reading: "But for a mouse, curiosity might open many doors. And some of those doors might just have cheese on the other side" (p. 7). When encountering such a statement, teachers can encourage students to consider and discuss what the author is attempting to say about human nature or life in general. Peck has many humorous lines tucked in this book, but if students quickly read over this statement and others throughout the book, they will miss the humor and commentary on human nature. As students read the text, they should be encouraged to find other subtle bits of humor about human nature.

With older students, teachers can use a book such as *The Other Side* (Woodson, 2001), which is set in the South in the 1960s. On the last page Woodson writes, "'Someday somebody's going to come along and knock this old fence down,' Annie said. And I nodded, 'Yeah,' I said. 'Someday'" (unpaged). Annie makes this statement because her mother told her she cannot go over the fence to play with some African American children. Teachers can ask students to consider the meaning of these two statements by examining the literal and connotative meaning of the words; the author's intent, perspective, and background; and the culture of the place and time. This discussion can help students realize that Woodson is making a statement about the senseless "rules" adults had in the 1960s based on the color of one's skin. Teachers can then lead students to recognize the ambiguity of the narrator's response about whether the "fence" will ever come down so they understand that the author is making a statement about life. Through this demonstration of close reading and discussion, teachers can expose students to the more complex levels of meaning related to the author's perspective, the cultural issues, and the language used in the story.

To scaffold students in closely reading a book with complex literary demands, select a book that will require them to have background knowledge necessary to fully comprehend its allusions. For example, in the picture book *Interrupting Chicken* (Stein, 2010), readers need to be familiar with the fairy tales *Hansel and Gretel, Little Red Riding Hood,* and *Chicken Little* in order to grasp the author's humor. This is because the Little Red Chicken interrupts Papa at the crucial points in his storytelling, like when Hansel and Gretel are about to follow the old woman into the forest, when Little Red Riding Hood is about to follow the wolf into the woods, and when Chicken Little is about to warn her friends that the sky is falling. Students will find these interruptions funny only if they already know what is about to happen in Papa's stories.

One important aspect of Anchor Standard 10 is that students must engage in close reading with complex texts "independently and proficiently." Many of the comprehension strategies, such as making inferences, text-to-text, and text-to-world connections discussed in the next section will help students to closely read narrative texts independently. See also the Strategies and Activities section for additional ideas to develop close reading skills.

READING COMPREHENSION STRATEGIES

Reading comprehension requires many strategies (see Figure 8.2). A reader needs all of these strategies and each strategy depends on the others; all must work concurrently for the reader to attain comprehension. When teaching each of these strategies, teachers should aim for students to use the strategies during independent reading (Broyles, 2012/2013).

Before Reading Strategies

Comprehension strategies that come into play before reading include predicting and setting a purpose.

Predicting

Predicting is a higher-level thinking skill that requires readers to perform many different tasks simultaneously. Students who predict draw on background knowl-

figure 8.2

Strategies for comprehension.

- Finding main ideas/story elements
- Predicting
- Making inferences
- Setting a purpose
- Self-monitoring
- Generating visual images
- Drawing conclusions
- Summarizing
- Retelling
- Comparing and contrasting
- Interrelating ideas
- Connecting appropriate background knowledge to new information
- Understanding characters' motives
- Sequencing events
- Self-questioning
- Analyzing text for story elements—character, plot, setting, theme, style, point of view
- Synthesizing
- Retaining information from one reading to the next
- Elaborating on author's intent
- Understanding purpose

Sources: Doty, Popplewell, & Byers (2001); Dowhower (1999); Duffy-Hester (1999); Manning (2001); NEA Today (2001); Rose, Parks, Androes, and McMahon (2000); Vaughn et al. (2000).

edge, supply details, and then try to determine whether their prediction was correct. Good readers make predictions automatically, while struggling readers often make no attempt to predict what will happen next in the story (Hurst, 2000; Santoro, Chard, Howard, & Baker, 2008; Oster, 2001). Teachers must model for students how to make predictions when they are reading aloud so students can use prediction as a way to comprehend text when they are reading independently (Brown & Kappes, 2012). Introduce a new text to students by previewing the title, author, and illustrator to decide if they have read texts with similar topics or by the same author or illustrator. For example, a teacher who has shared Kevin Henkes' *Lilly's Purple Plastic Purse* (1996) and *Julius: The Baby of the World* (1995) shows the students *Lilly's Big Day* (2006) and asks them what they think Lilly will do in this book. One way to encourage struggling readers to predict is to have them look at the cover illustration (without reading the title) and ask what they think the story is about. Predictions may include details that are not in the story, which later gives students an opportunity to evaluate and adjust their predictions with the benefit of hindsight. For example, the teacher is about to read *The Old Woman Who Lived in a Vinegar Bottle* (Mac-Donald, 2005), a book in which a fairy grants the old lady of the title her wish for a bigger house each time the fairy visits her, the conversation may go as follows:

(Note: the cover of the book features an elderly woman with white hair pulled back in a bun, looking into a large bottle. Also on the cover are a small fairy and a chicken.)

Teacher: Who do you think this story is about?

Student: An old lady, a fairy, and a chicken.

Teacher: Why do you think the lady is old? (Nudge the student to make inferences.)

Student: Because her hair is white and she has it pulled back like the old lady who lives in my building.

Teacher: Do you think she is happy?

Student: No.

Teacher: Why not?

Student: Because I think she wants a chicken.

Teacher: Do you think she will get a chicken?

Student: Yes, I think the fairy will give her one.

Teacher: Let's see if you are correct. The title of the book is *The Old Woman Who Lived in a Vinegar Bottle*.

Student: See! I was right! She is an old lady. But why would she want to live in a vinegar bottle? It must be a big bottle!

Teacher: Yes, you are right; she is an old lady. Let's find out why she lives in a vinegar bottle, and let's see if it is a large bottle.

Predicting engages students in the reading task. The idea that the old woman wants a chicken is incorrect, but the fairy does make the old woman happy. This is an excellent book to read while students continue to confirm predictions and make new ones. The book has repetitive text and a plot that is easy to follow: The woman constantly asks the fairy for bigger houses, but is not content until the fairy returns her to the vinegar bottle.

If your students depend too much on a picture book's illustrations for their predictions, merely read the title without revealing the cover and ask them what they think may happen in the story (Brown, 1999/2000). With younger students this may be a hard task because they enjoy the illustrations and rely on them for help with comprehension. In these discussions, always ask "why" questions and ask students to support their answers. Keep in mind that simply reading the title of the book *The Old Woman Who Lived in a Vinegar Bottle* while not allowing students to see the illustrations may elicit an entirely different conversation.

Teacher: This book is called *The Old Woman Who Lived in a Vinegar Bottle*. What do you think the story is about?

Student: A woman who lives in a vinegar bottle. (A very literal answer to a very literal question.)

Teacher: Why do you think she lives in a vinegar bottle?

Student: What's a vinegar bottle? (Good! The child recognizes her lack of prior knowledge.)

Teacher: Vinegar is a sour liquid used to make pickles.

Student: Phew! Does it stink like pickles?

Teacher: Vinegar doesn't smell very good. So why do you think the woman lives in the vinegar bottle?

Student: Because she was old and mean and someone didn't like her so they first made her drink the vinegar and then they made her small and then they put her into the bottle so she couldn't be mean anymore.

This student has a complete but inaccurate plot in mind. However, that is fine because she will change her predictions as the story unfolds. The teacher has engaged the student in the thinking process, which is the purpose of predicting.

Predicting helps readers interrelate ideas through the reading of a story. They begin to understand that reading is more than just reading words correctly. Begin this activity with stories having simple, predictable plots in order to give students a better chance of success with their predictions (McLaughlin, 2012). The goal is to get students to make predictions when they read independently. Stories with repetitive text are helpful because students can join in on repeated phrases and learn to recognize unfamiliar words. Appendix A.7 has a list of books with repetitive texts and predictable plots.

Middle-school teachers can also use the book's cover and title to get students to predict what it may be about. For example, a discussion of *Chains* (Anderson, 2008) may go like this:

Teacher: From the title and illustration on the cover, can you predict what the novel will be about?

Student 1: I think it is about a young slave in the South.

Student 2: It may be, but look at the birds; one looks like it is an American flag and the other looks like a British flag.

Student 3: I do not think it has anything to do with slavery because Laurie Halse Anderson writes about problems that teens face today. I read three of her other books.

Student 1: Good point. I read *Speak* and that book takes place in the present time.

Student 2: I still think it is about slavery because the young girl has her wrists together and "Chains" is written across her wrists.

Student 1: But why are the birds dressed in American and British flags?

Student 4: Are there some chapter titles so we can get a better idea?

Teacher: No there are no chapter titles, but let's read the first page and see if we can tell if any of your predictions are correct.

Through this discussion, the teacher enables students to build on each other's thinking and background knowledge about the author. The teacher did not give any information about the book, but merely promoted the strategy of prediction that students can use when they read independently.

Setting a purpose

Setting a purpose is an important part of reading comprehension that occurs before reading (Shanahan, 2012). After reading the title of a text, readers should ask themselves what genre the text belongs to. The primary purpose of reading narrative text is to find out who did what, when, where, how, and why. In both fantasy and realistic fiction, readers usually attempt to understand the protagonist's conflict and how the conflict is resolved. In historical fiction, readers attempt to answer the same questions while learning more about the time and place in which the story is set. In a mystery, readers usually attempt to find clues in the text about how the protagonist will identify a criminal or resolve a problem.

During Reading Strategies

During reading comprehension strategies include making inferences, self-monitoring, visualizing, understanding vocabulary including figurative language, and connecting prior knowledge to text. Santoro et al. (2008) suggest that teachers use a consistent strategy to discuss the text until students become proficient in using it. Students can then use the strategy during independent reading.

Making inferences

According to Cooper, Kiger, Robinson, & Slansky (2012), one of the most significant strategies for comprehension is the ability to make **inferences**. Making inferences is the process of judging, concluding, or reasoning indirectly from the information available. Most of the information needed for making inferences comes from students' background knowledge (Santoro et al., 2008). To model the skill of making inferences, teachers can pose questions that will activate students' knowledge and prompt them to make inferences, for example, "Have we ever read about a similar plot in another story?" "Have you ever experienced a similar incident?" "Have any of you ever visited this country in which the story takes place?" These ques-

tions help students make three types of connections: text-to-text, text-to-self, and text-to-world (Santoro et al., 2008). By answering these questions they connect their prior knowledge to the events of the story. This connection helps students make inferences. It is easy to see that inferring is a higher-level thinking skill that involves close reading, a goal of the CCSS. Proficient readers readily combine their prior knowledge and then draw conclusions that are not stated in the text. Struggling readers often find this task difficult (Cooper et al., 2012).

Many teachers understand inferential thinking but find it difficult to formulate inferential questions. May (2001) suggests that teachers "listen within our heads to the author and infer the messages left between the lines" (p. 114). May contends that authors "subconsciously leave empty slots for your imagination to fill in" (p. 114), and teachers need merely look for what the author omitted when they attempt to devise inferential questions. For example, a middle-school teacher, after reading with her class Chapters 1 and 2 of *Mockingbird* (Erskine, 2010), can ask the question, "What do you learn from the following two short passages on page 5?": "They want to help you deal with life, Caitlin . . . without Devon" and "I wish I could hide in Devon's room but I'm not allowed in there now. Not since The Day Our Life Fell Apart and Dad slammed Devon's door shut and put his head against it and cried and said, *No, no no no no*" (Erskine, 2010, p. 5). When students are discussing their ideas, always ask them to explain why they arrived at their conclusions. The teacher may point them to the unique way the author uses capital letters, incomplete sentences, and italics and ask students if the author is revealing to readers something about the character who is telling the story.

Readers can make inferences before and after reading a story, but they must also make inferences about how characters feel based on how they act or what they say. At other times, readers make inferences about characters from what other characters say about them. Authors invite inferences because they want to show, not tell, readers about a character or a scenario and want them to use their imaginations. Teachers can facilitate students' ability to make inferences by asking open-ended questions. Katie Couric gives many opportunities for readers to imagine what kind of character Lazlo is in *The Brand New Kid* (2000). While reading this story to a struggling reader, you might ask him how Lazlo feels when he is ignored. The story does not explicitly describe Lazlo's feelings. Stop reading from time to time and ask inferential questions. The reader may need to draw on personal experience to infer how Lazlo feels when he is ignored. The following presents a passage from the book, followed by possible inferential questions.

. . . all morning long, they kept shooting him looks.

They headed to gym class, a quick softball game.

When they went to pick teams, no one mentioned his name. (unpaged)

What do you think it means that other students "shoot him looks"?

What kind of looks are they?

What happens earlier in the story to let you know how Lazlo feels?

Can you shoot me that type of look?

What does it mean when the narrator states that "no one mentioned his name"?

Do you know how it feels when no one calls your name to be on the team?

How did that make you feel?

Do you think Lazlo feels the same way?

Reading books such as this one with and to students and discussing the implicit aspects of characterization, setting, and plot can help students who are struggling with inferential strategies. This approach prompts them to connect their own knowledge to what they learn from the text. Ask probing questions that will help readers grasp characters' motives and elicit their empathy or understanding. Always ask students why they have particular reactions to characters or events; the "why" questions give readers a chance to practice their higher-level thinking skills and to cite evidence in the text to support their answers. More activities for increasing readers' ability to make inferences will be discussed in the Intervention section of this chapter.

Self-monitoring

Self-monitoring is yet another important strategy of reading comprehension (Santoro et al., 2008). According to Fountas and Pinnell (2007), **self-monitoring** is the ability of readers to figure out if something sounds right. Good readers can hear whether each word they read fits the syntax of the sentence. They automatically stop when it does not sound correct. Struggling readers, on the other hand, may pronounce words that are not real words or they may grasp at words that do not make sense in the sentence. By helping struggling readers to self-monitor these simple tasks, you help them notice their errors. Stop such a student at the end of a sentence, reread the sentence the way the student read it, and ask, "Did that sound correct? What word doesn't sound right or make sense?" These prompts help readers understand that what they read must match the print and make sense.

The main goal of self-monitoring is to make sure readers are making sense of what they have just read and are connecting previously read information to the current passage. Therefore, periodically stop a student and ask him to retell what they just read. If the reader cannot do this accurately, have him read the passage again and retell it. If this fails, read the passage aloud and ask the student to retell it. If he can then retell, this suggests that he may be spending too much energy on decoding, which is causing comprehension to break down. When this happens, choose an easier text or spend more time reading stories to them, discussing the story as it unfolds.

A student may add information to a retelling that is not in the story. In such cases, ask her where in the story she found the information. If it came from the story's illustrations, you may conclude this reader used illustrations to comprehend. However, if she cannot locate the source of the information, find out if the student is making an inference from background experience or knowledge. The goal is to help students focus on the events of the particular story that is being read. Modeling the think-aloud strategy (see the discussion below and the activity in this chapter's Intervention section) is one way to help students with self-monitoring.

With longer chapter books, readers should self-monitor their comprehension from one sitting to the next. Sometimes a day or two will pass before they resume reading. Or, as with the popular Harry Potter series, the reader may take a break between reading one volume and the next. With longer texts or series, readers need to relate ideas from chapter to chapter and book to book. For example, in the Harry Potter series, the Dursleys are introduced at the beginning of the first book, but they do not return again until the second book. Readers learn some new information in the second book about how Harry differs from the Dursleys. Readers need to be able to interrelate all of this information in order to understand the characterization and the plot of the series. Struggling readers often have trouble relating information from one chapter or book to the next.

Visualizing

Visualizing the imagery and events of the story as it unfolds is another critical strategy necessary for comprehension (Fountas & Pinnell, 2007; Gregory & Cahill, 2010). Readers should visualize the scene so vividly that they can almost hear the surrounding noises and smell the scents. They should imagine what each character looks like, how he or she walks or runs, and how the character speaks. Is the character's voice nasal or sweet? Husky or weak? For example, in *The Brand New Kid* (2000), the narrator describes the lunchroom in the following manner:

As Lazlo was leaving the line with his tray

Someone tripped him, his food it went every which way.

The students all froze as they saw Lazlo's face

With French fries and ketchup all over the place. (unpaged)

After reading this passage and without revealing the pictures, ask the struggling readers questions regarding details the author leaves to the reader's imagination:

What kind of tray was he carrying, plastic or metal?

Were there any items besides French fries and ketchup on the tray?

Do you think Lazlo fell to the floor or did he just stumble and drop his tray?

Describe the mess on the floor.

How do you think they looked?

What smells are in the cafeteria?

What type of floor did the cafeteria have?

Good readers will visualize Lazlo falling or stumbling and can imagine the entire scene because good readers can visualize the details of a story. Struggling readers have trouble with visualization. Gregory and Cahill (2010) suggest teachers ask these students "I wonder" questions. For example, while sharing *Epossumondas Saves the Day* (Salley, 2006), the teacher may ask: "I wonder what sodysallyraytus does for a birthday cake"; "I wonder what a hissy fit looks like"; "I wonder what it would look like if a snapping turtle really ate a person"; or "I wonder what kind of gifts a possum would get for his birthday." After modeling some "I wonder" questions, encourage students to ask similar questions as other books are shared.

Connecting prior knowledge to texts

Connecting background knowledge to the text you are reading is another strategy for comprehension. There are three types of background knowledge: (1) literary background, or text-to-text connection; (2) world knowledge, or text-to-world connection; and (3) life experiences, or text-to-self connection (Gregory & Cahill, 2010). Each of these is discussed below.

Literary knowledge or text-to-text connection. Literary knowledge includes what readers know about story elements—setting, characters, plot, climax, resolution, point of view, style, and theme. Struggling students often need help understanding these elements as they learn to become independent readers (Fountas & Pinnell, 2007; Gregory & Cahill, 2010; Staal, 2000). One way to help struggling readers discover story elements is by reading stories and completing story webs with them. Staal's Story Face strategy (2000) is a web technique that helps readers identify the main elements of the story. One eye on the "face" represents the story's setting, with eyelashes composed of adjectives that describe the setting. The other eye is the main character(s), with eyelashes composed of adjectives that describe these character(s). The nose is the conflict. The events are arranged in the shape of a mouth, which forms a smile if the story has a happy ending and a frown if it has a sad ending. See Figure 8.3 for an example.

Literary knowledge also includes an understanding of various genres and how they are similar and different from one another. The CCSS require that by the end of fifth grade students should have read fables, folktales, myths, all types of stories, drama, and poems from different cultures (NGACBP & CCSSO, Reading: Literature, Grade 5, 2010). These genres differ in many ways. For example, the fantasy genre often includes talking animals and stories that begin with "Once upon a time." Young proficient readers may not always know the names of different genres, but their previous exposure helps them recognize the components of a fantasy, a mystery, realistic fiction, or historical fiction. Struggling readers, on the other hand, will not know to look for clues when reading a mystery; when reading historical fiction, they will often not be able to separate historical facts from fictitious details the author has added to enhance the plot. They may also find it difficult to differentiate between fantasy and realistic fiction because in fantasy, animals and objects often exhibit human behaviors and emotions. Help readers recognize the differences between fantasy and realistic fiction by having them complete a Venn diagram that shows the commonalities between the two genres and the conventions that are unique to each.

Another facet of literacy knowledge is making connections between texts. By the end of second grade, the CCSS require that students "[c]ompare and contrast two or more versions of the same story by different authors or from different cultures" (NGACBP & CCSSO, Reading: Literature, Grade 2, 2010, p. 11). Proficient readers can easily make connections from one text to another (Gregory & Cahill, 2010). For example, if second-grade teachers share *Pretty Salma: A Little Red Riding Hood Story from Africa* (Daly, 2006) and *Little Red Riding Hood: A Newfangled Prairie Tale* (Campbell-Ernst, 1994), most children readily see the comparison between these two versions of the folktale; for example, both feature a girl on her way to her grandmother's house who is tricked by a predator with sharp teeth.

As students progress through the grades, the CCSS require them to make more complex comparisons between texts. The standards specify that fourth graders, for example, be able to "[c]ompare and contrast the treatment of similar themes and topics (e.g., opposition of good and evil) and patterns of events (e.g. the quest) in stories, myths, and traditional literature from different cultures" (NGACBP & CCSSO,

figure 8.3 "Sad" story face.

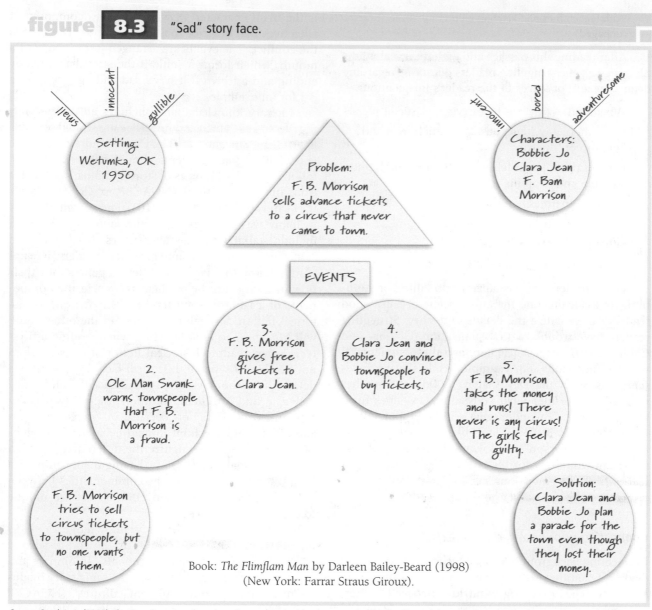

Setting:
Wetumka, OK
1950

small *innocent* *gullible*

Problem:
F. B. Morrison
sells advance tickets
to a circus that never
came to town.

Characters:
Bobbie Jo
Clara Jean
F. Bam
Morrison

innocent *bored* *adventuresome*

EVENTS

3.
F. B. Morrison
gives free
tickets to
Clara Jean.

4.
Clara Jean and
Bobbie Jo convince
townspeople to
buy tickets.

2.
Ole Man Swank
warns townspeople
that F. B.
Morrison is
a fraud.

5.
F. B. Morrison
takes the money
and runs! There
never is any circus!
The girls feel
guilty.

1.
F. B. Morrison
tries to sell
circus tickets
to townspeople, but
no one wants
them.

Solution:
Clara Jean and
Bobbie Jo plan
a parade for the
town even though
they lost their
money.

Book: *The Flimflam Man* by Darleen Bailey-Beard (1998)
(New York: Farrar Straus Giroux).

Source: Staal. L. A. (2000). The Story Face: An adaptation of story mapping that incorporates visualization and discovery learning to enhance reading and writing. Adapted from a graphic by Paula Clifford and Doug Ritsema. *The Reading Teacher, 54* (1), 26–31.

Reading: Literature, Grade 4, 2010, p. 12). For example, after the class has read Gratefully Yours (Buchanan, 1997) and Mister and Me (Holt, 1998), teachers may ask students to consider how these two short novels are similar. The stories, settings, and characters are very different, but both are based on the theme of change and acceptance.

World knowledge or text-to-world connection. The second aspect of background knowledge is readers' knowledge of the world. This knowledge enables readers of historical fiction, for example, to understand the plight of the characters. To comprehend *Freedom Summer* (Wiles, 2005), students need to understand the conditions of African Americans during the 1950s.

In many historical fiction stories, the setting plays a pivotal role in the problem. Think-alouds (discussed below and in the Intervention section of this chapter) help struggling readers by providing background knowledge about settings beyond their communities.

Life experience or text-to-self connection. The third component of background knowledge is one's life experience in terms of family, community, and other social interactions. All these experiences help readers construct meaning when they encounter new stories. A reader whose family member has suffered a stroke will have a better understanding of Tomie dePaola's *Now One Foot, Now the Other* (1981). Readers who have watched a parent struggle with depression or who have lived in a foster home may have a richer appreciation for Patricia MacLachlan's *Mama One, Mama Two* (1982).

All readers have previous life experience, but proficient readers are able to make connections between their personal experiences and the story. For example, J. W., who is a poor reader and whose grandfather recently suffered a stroke, reads about Bob's stroke in *Now One Foot, Now the Other* and asks, "Why is Bob sick just because he cannot move his arms and legs? Why can't he talk? Why wouldn't Bob know who Bobby is?" From these questions, J. W.'s teacher knows he is not connecting his background family knowledge to his reading, because J. W. often talks about his grandpa's inability to walk, talk, and recognize him. Poor readers such as J. W. often miss connections that will seem obvious to proficient readers.

On the other hand, readers may encounter comprehension problems if they rely too much on personal experiences (Beck, McKeown, & Kucan, 2013). Both types of reading problems—not connecting previous experiences or relying too much on such experiences—make comprehension difficult. In such cases, teachers can use text-talks (Beck & McKeown, 2001). Text-talks are described in the Intervention section of this chapter. When readers depend too much on previous personal experiences, teachers ask students to find the sentences in the text that support their comments.

After Reading Strategies

Comprehension strategies after reading include retelling, drawing conclusions, and elaborating the author's intent.

Retelling story elements

Retelling is more than listing the events in a story. Retelling is the readers' ability to name the main characters, state the problem, and relate events that lead to the climax and resolution. This process requires students to (1) understand the vocabulary and language in order to comprehend the meaning, (2) apply decoding skills for unknown words, (3) understand the chronological order of events, and (4) understand the author's intended message (Mills, 2009; Lapp, Fisher, & Johnson, 2010). Proficient readers are good at retelling stories.

Unskilled readers, on the other hand, may be able to tell who did what, but not in the correct sequence of events. They may relate the climax first and then what leads up to it. Often they cannot remember where and when the story takes place. For example, Cloe, a struggling reader retelling Paula Danziger's *It's Justin Time, Amber Brown* (2001), states that Amber Brown gets a watch and a walkie-talkie for her birthday. Cloe does not relate that it is Amber's seventh birthday and she wants the watch so she can tell how late Justin is when he comes over to play. Cloe also fails to relate that Justin is late the day before Amber's birthday because he is writing a card and wrapping her gift—the walkie-talkie. Cloe only relates what gifts Amber receives. A more skilled reader would relate the story from beginning to end, summarizing the main points of the plot.

When students struggle to relate the plot in sequence, construct a set of four index cards with one of these questions on each card: "Where?", "When?", "Who?", and "Did what?" Display each card in order after reading a story. Use this technique for a period of time, then remove the cards and ask the students to retell the story. Retelling events in sequence is an important skill in exploring fiction, and it will also serve students later when relating scientific phenomena and historical events.

Drawing conclusions

Drawing conclusions demonstrates a student's ability to answer higher-level thinking questions. The main conclusion question is "Why?" The answers to these questions are not stated in the story, but students who comprehend the stories draw conclusions based on textual clues or previous experiences. Struggling readers will have trouble doing this because they cannot find the answer stated in the text. For example, while retelling Linda Sue Park's *A Single Shard* (2001), the proficient reader will be able to explain why Tree-ear is faithful in delivering the delicate celadon ware for Min even though the journey is dangerous. The proficient reader realizes Tree-ear does this because Min's destiny will be determined by his delivery of the ware, and because of the lessons his friend Crane-man has taught him. The struggling reader, when asked why Tree-ear is faithful to his task, may say, "because Min tells him to do it."

Elaborating on the author's intent

After reading a story discuss the author's intent. Did the author write the story to make readers laugh, inspire them, teach a lesson, relate historical information, or explore another culture? Teach students to consider the author's perspective as well as other perspectives by examining stories written from opposing points of view. One way to get students to understand different viewpoints is to read and discuss *The True Story of the Three Little Pigs as Told by A. Wolf* (Scieszka, 1995) or *Twice Upon a Time: Rapunzel: The One With All the Hair* (Mass, 2005). In *The True Story of the Three Little Pigs,* the wolf attempts to convince readers that he had a cold and his sneezes were the cause of the pigs' houses falling down; of course, after that he could not let good pork go to waste. In *Twice*

Upon a Time, the story shifts between the voices of the Prince and Rapunzel. Even young students recognize that both these stories have perspectives different from those of traditional fairy tales. After discussing these stories, invite students to choose another fairy tale and rewrite it from a different perspective.

Teaching Comprehension Strategies

Studies show that teaching comprehension strategies to students directly enhances reading comprehension (Harvey & Goudvis, 2007; Lewin, 2009). Therefore, effective teachers know many strategies and match them to the needs of each struggling reader.

Before examining activities to use with struggling readers, consider the following question: Is explicit instruction in comprehension strategies necessary? The answer differs for good comprehenders and poor comprehenders. Swanson and De La Paz (1998) concluded that good comprehenders know which strategies to use without recalling having learned them. However, struggling readers do not necessarily know when to use the strategies they have been taught. A teacher's duty is to demonstrate how and when students need to apply strategies, explaining which strategies to use before, during, and after reading. First explain and then demonstrate a strategy while engaging in a text. Next, guide the students through passages as they read and use the strategy until they demonstrate proficiency in it (Flynt & Cooter, 2005; Lapp, Fisher, & Johnson, 2010). Then monitor the students as they use the strategy during independent reading. Focus on one instructional strategy for a minimum of three weeks. Instead of peppering students with a different strategy with every new passage, you need to "marinate students in the new skill if it is to become permanent knowledge" (Flynt & Cooter, 2005, p. 775). Stress to students that although they are learning one strategy at a time, readers often use multiple strategies to comprehend a text.

When teaching comprehension strategies to struggling readers, remember the following:

- Teach in context.
- Use simple, easy-level reading material.
- Individualize! (This is the most important factor.)
- Choose an appropriate strategy for that material.
- Teach the strategy explicitly.
- Model the use of the strategy.
- Have the reader practice it under your supervision.
- Give appropriate feedback.
- Provide numerous opportunities for the student to practice the strategy so he or she can self-regulate.
- Don't present multiple strategies at one time.

- Have the student verbalize the steps of the strategy, explaining when it should be used.

The Intervention section later in this chapter includes a number of activities to be used before, during, or after reading with students who struggle with comprehension. Remember that comprehension strategies should be explicitly taught (Ciardiello, 1998).

COMPREHENSION AND CRITICAL LITERACY

As stated previously, comprehending a text goes beyond the literal level; it includes being able to read critically. It means understanding the possibly biased language authors sometimes use, the author's perspective and use of figurative language, and a willingness to take action if the reader is moved by the author's message. Comprehending at this level refers to the critical literacy theory (DeKonty-Applegate, Applegate, & Modla, 2009) and is the type of close reading required by the CCSS.

Critical literacy was introduced in Chapter 1 as a theory that focuses on sociopolitical issues of our society. Its goal is for teachers to "encourage students to recognize connections between their lives and the lives of real or imagined story characters . . . [and] to explore authors' possible biases, and to reflect on how to take social action to create a more compassionate world" (Richards, 2006, p. 193). Critical literacy helps students "develop a critical awareness that texts represent particular points of view while often silencing other views" (Ciardiello, 2004, p. 138). Nieto (1996) believes that if teachers do not engage their students in critical literacy, "they receive only a partial and biased education" (p. 312).

Critical Literacy Themes and Topics

Teachers can examine six themes with students as they comprehend text at this deeper level. According to Ciardiello (2004, 2010) and Soares & Wood (2010), the themes are:

1. Recognizing social barriers, or ways that barriers have been broken, between race, age, religions, ethnic groups, social classes, and gender.
2. Examining multiple perspectives of historical events throughout history.
3. Examining authentic voice by critically looking at the language of the text and exploring how different cultural groups can use language to change situations.
4. Juxtaposing two contrasting texts.
5. Finding one's identity by discussing differences within the classroom and examining ways to overcome any existing prejudices.
6. Finding ways to take action.

Helping Students to Comprehend Historical Fiction Picture Books   BOX

Many historical fiction picture books lend themselves to teaching students how to read both text and images critically. When reading these picture books, readers must "simultaneously process written text, visual images, and elements of design to construct meaning" (Serafini, 2011, p. 342). Quality historical fiction picture books tell the story through text and pictures.

Serafini (2011) suggests that teachers facilitate students' comprehension of pictures in historical fiction picture books by drawing their attention to composition, perspective, and visual symbols. Composition refers to the placement of objects and characters on a page. Artists consider the size of objects in proportion to one another and foreground the object that is the main focus of the work. Perspective refers to "[h]ow close or far away the viewer is positioned relative to the objects and participants in an image" (Serafini, 2011, p. 346). **Visual symbols** refer to visual elements that are used to represent something else. For example, red may represent anger, and green may represent envy.

When engaging students in reading historical fiction picture books, ask questions to get students to consider what the author or illustrator is conveying through the pictures and from whose perspective. Labadie, Wetzel, and Rogers (2012) suggest using the following prompts:

1. Which illustrations highlight the characters and their emotions? What did the illustrator do to the lines in the faces to show different emotions? Is the character looking at the reader or at other characters? Is the protagonist in the foreground? How is the dimension of the protagonist in proportion to the other part of the picture?

2. What does the illustrator tell you about the setting of the story? Do the illustrations help readers place themselves in the story? Does the color of the setting create a mood or complement the mood of the text?

3. Do the illustrations support the point of view of the text?

4. What technique did the illustrator use? How does he or she use lines, shapes, colors, and space to create mood?

Authors and illustrators of historical fiction, including picture books, must ensure that all the information in the text and the details of the illustrations accurately portray the era in which the story is set. Serafini (2011) suggests a list of questions, found in Appendix D.20, to ask students when reading historical fiction picture books with them.

Possible topics to be read and discussed with students are (1) westward expansion by white Americans from the point of view of native tribes; (2) Chinese immigrants detained on Angel Island during the early 20th century; (3) slavery in the United States; (4) Native American children taken from their homes and enrolled at white-run boarding schools; (5) the civil rights movement; (6) the fight for the vote in the early 20th century by women and minorities; (7) internment of Japanese Americans during World War II; and (8) outsourcing of U.S. jobs in the late 20th and early 21st centuries. These are only a few of the many possible topics from which to choose. You may find additional topics for critical literacy units through an Internet search; many sites suggest unit plans.

Teachers engage students in reading about and discussing these critical literacy topics so they become citizens who empathize with others through their actions. The Intervention section of this chapter includes specific activities that encourage such discussions and actions.

Questions to Encourage a Critical Stance

Critical literacy "is a dynamic process that examines relationships, expands our thinking, and enlightens our perceptions as we read the word and the world—as we read from a critical stance" (McLaughlin & DeVoogd, 2004, p. 55). When students read from a critical stance, they not only understand the words, but they are also "'reading the world' and understanding a text's purpose so [they] will not be manipulated by it" (McLaughlin & DeVoogd, 2004, p. 53).

To encourage upper elementary and middle school students to take a critical stance, pose the questions presented in Figure 8.4 after reading a novel, short story, traditional text, e-text, song lyric, or poem. Consider these questions as springboards. Always encourage students to raise questions about a story or novel.

Scaffold students' discussions as they consider these questions. Prompt them to use a variety of comprehension strategies, such as predicting, connecting background knowledge to present text, using the correct meaning of words, and self-questioning. Also encourage students to read additional stories with similar themes so they are exposed to a variety of perspectives. It is important to guide the discussions, listen to all students' ideas, encourage students to listen and respond to other classmates' ideas, and not force opinions on the students. Remember, this type of deep reading is for all students, not just gifted students.

figure 8.4   Example questions to encourage students to take a critical stance.

1. Is the setting integral to the story?
2. Does the plot present a problem that is unique to a particular race, ethnic group, or gender? If so, whose perspective does the author give? Is any group's voice silenced? If so, how do you think they would tell the story?
3. Is the story or novel a work of historical fiction? If so, whose perspective does the author give? Could the story be told from a different perspective?
4. What seems to be the primary purpose for the story? To entertain? To inform? To help readers understand a particular problem of a group of people? Or some other purpose?
5. From what point of view is the story told? If it were told from a different perspective, would the story change drastically?
6. Is there any language, figurative or literal, that persuades readers to "feel" any particular way?
7. Does the story provoke you to take action for or against a cause? If so, what are some appropriate ways to take action?

ENGLISH LEARNERS AND NARRATIVE TEXTS

Instructional Recommendations

The reading development of English learners differs from that of English speakers and requires modified instruction. It should be explicit, in-depth, conducted at a slower pace, and provide many opportunities for discussion and physical response (see the discussion of TPR in Chapters 1 and 7). When sharing a picture book, teachers should browse the book by "reading" the pictures and allowing these students ample time for discussion so they develop their oral language skills concurrently with their comprehension skills. They should participate in collaborative conversations about stories they have heard or read (Beckman-Anthony, 2008). Collaborative conversations occur when English learners are able to discuss open-ended questions in small groups where the teacher is an observer and not the leader. These open-ended questions may include:

- "What do you think about . . . ?"
- "Have you ever had the same problem as in the story?"
- "What other action could the main character have taken to solve the problem?"

When English learners discuss these open-ended questions in risk-free small groups, they comprehend the story on a deeper, more meaningful level than the literal level (Beckman-Anthony, 2008; Bouchereau-Bauer & Manyak, 2008).

Selecting Narrative Texts

Choosing the appropriate text is also an important element when working with English learners. First, choose texts that are age appropriate and interesting to the students. Second, the texts must be quality literature with intriguing plots and well-developed characters. Because English learners' reading abilities are as varied as those of English language readers, teachers must have books for all reading levels accessible in the classroom. Picture books are great for English learners because they are written on many grade levels and cover topics interesting to all ages.

Vardell, Hadaway, and Young (2006) provide the following guidelines when choosing texts for English learners:

1. Provide texts based on the students' cultures. Topic familiarity will help them identify with the characters and comprehend the story line. Figure 8.5 lists the traits of quality multicultural books.
2. Choose texts with chronological story lines. Flashbacks are more difficult to follow.
3. In the beginning avoid stories with idioms and other colloquial expressions; however, when the student is ready, begin to incorporate stories with figurative language and help them understand what they mean as you read with them.
4. Choose themes that are based on (a) fitting in, (b) adjusting to a move, (c) being different, or (d) finding one's niche in society, if they seem appropriate for the student.
5. Choose texts that address "survival" topics, such as days of the week, months, foods, weather, types of clothing, occupations, and family members.
6. Choose predictable story lines so students can guess what will happen with each turn of the page.
7. Choose texts with illustrations that advance the story.
8. Because the CCSS are intended for ALL students, teachers need to teach English learners how to read more complex stories (Brown & Kappes, 2012). See Chapter 2 for a discussion about selecting complex texts.

See Appendix A.8 for a list of suggested bilingual English–Spanish narrative picture books and Appendix A.9 for a list of multicultural picture books.

figure **8.5**

Traits of quality multicultural books.

1. Exhibit high literary quality
2. Contain no distortions or omissions of history
3. Contain no negative or inaccurate stereotypes of minorities
4. Free from derogatory overtones (e.g., words such as *savage* or *primitive*)
5. Portray genuine, complex lifestyles
6. Contain dialogue that represents oral tradition, if appropriate to the culture
7. Confirm that all groups can be successful
8. Portray roles of females, elders, and families accurately
9. Free from situations anyone might find embarrassing or offensive
10. Written and illustrated by members of the group represented, or by those qualified to represent the culture
11. Contain illustrations depicting genuine individuals
12. Portray minorities as leaders who can solve their own problems
13. Present heroines and heroes whose struggles for justice are appropriate to their culture
14. Written no earlier than the late 1970s

Source: Johnson-Higgins, J. (2002, January). *Multicultural children's literature: Creating and applying an evaluation tool in response to the needs of urban educators.* New Horizons of Learning. Retrieved from http://education.jhu.edu/PD/newhorizons/strategies/topics/multicultural-education/multicultural-childrens-literature/.

SKILLED VERSUS UNSKILLED COMPREHENDERS

What is the difference between a skilled reader and an unskilled reader? First, skilled readers have a purpose for reading, such as for information, enjoyment, adventure, or to understand historical eras. Second, skilled readers know how to accomplish goals through creating story maps or journaling. Third, as they read, they monitor themselves and use effective strategies, such as those discussed earlier, when comprehension breaks down. This comes so naturally that they are not even aware they are using strategies. Finally, at the end of reading, they determine whether they accomplished their goal. Skilled readers use higher-level thinking skills to interpret, analyze, and evaluate the text as they read.

Skilled readers also have the ability "to provide sequenced explanations, logical arguments, grounded interpretations, and abstract analysis" (Jacobson et al., 2001, p. 2). Figure 8.6 summarizes behaviors and characteristics of proficient readers, and Figure 8.7 summarizes some common habits of struggling readers. It is important for teachers to be able to assess readers' strengths and weaknesses.

figure **8.6**

Behaviors and characteristics of proficient readers of narrative text.

1. Have a positive attitude toward reading.
2. Understand the conventions (e.g. punctuation marks, grammar, word meanings) when they read.
3. Make predictions.
4. Select main ideas.
5. Understand important details and omit unimportant details.
6. Make inferences.
7. Use background knowledge to comprehend.
8. Know purpose for reading (enjoyment, to answer questions, retell).
9. Stay focused for the entire passage and don't "zone out."
10. Visualize.
11. Look for meaning.
12. Determine the theme of the story.
13. Adjust reading rate when necessary.
14. Use a variety of strategies when comprehension breaks down.
15. Read from aesthetic or efferent stances.
16. Understand that different genres require different reading strategies (mysteries look for clues).
17. Choose books that fit their reading level.

Sources: Garan, E. M. (2002). *Resisting reading mandates: How to triumph with the truth.* Portsmouth, NH: Heinemann. / Kamil, M. L., Mosenthal, P. B., Pearson, P. D., & Barr, R. (Eds). (2000). *Handbook of reading research (Vol. 3)* Mahwah, NJ: Erlbaum. / North Central Association for Accreditation and School Improvement (2010, February 9). *Characteristics of good readers.* Retrieved from www.ncacasi.org.

figure **8.7**

Behaviors and characteristics of a poor reader.

1. Focuses exclusively on pronouncing words.
2. Remembers small, unimportant details.
3. Relies too much on picture clues.
4. Lacks appropriate background knowledge.
5. Has a limited vocabulary.
6. Doesn't recognize failures of comprehension.
7. Doesn't connect prior knowledge to text.
8. Has difficulty drawing inferences.
9. May lack decoding skills. (Some poor comprehenders have good decoding skills.)

Source: Richek, M. A., Caldwell, J., Jennings, J., & Lerner, J. W. (2006). *Reading problems: Assessment and teaching strategies* (5th ed.). Boston: Allyn & Bacon.

The next section discusses formal and informal assessments of comprehension.

ASSESSMENT

A ny oral assessment of comprehension is beneficial to teachers because they can observe what readers do during the reading process. Good inflection, appropriate pace, and adherence to punctuation and dialogue indicate comprehension (Vaughn et al., 2000). You can also observe what readers do when they encounter unknown words. Comments made by students during reading or during retelling indicate their level of comprehension.

There are formal (standardized) comprehension tests and many types of informal tests. I recommend the informal tests in order to get a deeper understanding of readers' methods of comprehending texts.

Informal Assessment

Informal reading inventories

An informal reading inventory (IRI) determines a student's reading level. However, IRIs can also be used to compare the student's silent reading skills to her oral reading comprehension. First have the student read a passage silently and then retell the story; next have her read a grade-equivalent text orally and retell that story. Most commercial tests have questions that should be answered by the student in the retelling. Compare the number of questions answered in the retelling after the reading of each story. After the retelling, ask her the questions she left unanswered to determine whether she comprehended that aspect of the story.

Miscue analysis

Miscues are oral divergences from the written text (Goodman et al., 1987). The major question concerning each miscue is, did it disrupt meaning for the reader? When working with a student, analyze which type of miscue most often disrupts meaning and then work with him to eliminate that miscue. Miscues that disrupt meaning will most certainly hinder comprehension. See Chapter 3 for instructions on how to administer a miscue analysis.

Appendices C.7 through C.10 provide two sample stories and corresponding miscue analysis grids; photocopy and use these to practice a miscue analysis with a student who is reading at the grade level indicated on the story sheet. Alternatively, for "Grandma's Garden," use the video of a child reading the story as provided on the website (**www.hhpcommunities.com/literacy assessment**) to complete the analysis. The website also contains additional stories and grids for your use. You may choose to compare your grid with a partner's so you can compare your markings and your analysis.

Retrospective miscue analysis

The retrospective miscue analysis (RMA) can be used for instructional purposes and assessment (Goodman & Marek, 1996). During the RMA session, a student listens to a recording of his or her reading while following along in the text. The teacher asks the student if her miscues disrupt the story's meaning.

The RMA "seeks to empower readers to view reading miscues as repeated attempts to predict meaning and to make sense of text" (Moore & Aspegren, 2001, p. 2). Use the RMA to analyze critically and constructively the entire reading process—in other words, to analyze what students do when they recognize their miscues (Goodman, K., 1996; Martens, 1998; Moore & Aspegren, 2001).

Running records

Running records can also be used to assess comprehension when used for more than cueing errors. The purpose here is to analyze the errors to determine which language system—syntax (sentence sense), semantics (meaning), or graphophonic (visual)—students use (Clay, 2000c). If the analysis indicates that a student uses only visual clues, the student will need instruction in developing the skills to read for meaning. You may also use running records to help determine whether a student's inflection and pace hinder or aid comprehension. For example, proficient first-grade readers raise their voices when they read questions, they make a slight pause for commas, and they read at least 75 words per minute, which is considered to be a good reading rate. See Chapter 3 for instructions on how to administer and analyze running records. For experience in using running records, use the stories in Appendices C.7 and C.9 and the blank running record form in Appendix C.11. As mentioned above, you may also use the video of a child reading "Grandma's Garden" at **www.hhpcommunities.com/literacyassessment**.

Retelling

Retelling, the act of relating the most important events of the story, is an important indicator of reading comprehension (Harvey & Goudvis, 2013; Hollenbeck & Saterus, 2013; McLaughlin, 2012; Stricklin, 2011). Retelling can be used for assessment and instruction. (See the description of retelling in the "After Reading Strategies" section earlier in this chapter.) Retellings give you insight into readers' thinking and sequencing skills and their ability to restate the main points of the story. Retellings give students opportunities to reflect and discuss the complete text, rather than merely answer questions that cover one aspect of the story.

Think-alouds

Jongsma (1999/2000) suggests that think-alouds "offer excellent opportunities for teachers to assess students' developing comprehension processes" (p. 310) because they help teachers gain insight into how students process texts. Although teachers commonly use think-alouds as a strategy to model how students should make sense from text, once teachers have modeled the process, student think-alouds can also be used for assessment. For example, Ms. Jones has Jenny complete a think-aloud of Janet Stevens's (1999) *Cook-a-Doodle-Doo!* to assess Jenny's ability to make predictions from text, sound out unfamiliar words, and understand puns. See the In the Classroom box for Ms. Jones's analysis of Jenny's think-aloud. The text from the book is in italics and Jenny's think-aloud is in bold.

Use a think-aloud for assessment to determine if students (1) understand a text's vocabulary, (2) predict upcoming actions, (3) visualize settings, characters, and events, (4) make inferences, and (5) self-monitor when comprehension breaks down.

Cloze and maze tests

As discussed in Chapter 3, cloze and maze tests can be used to determine whether a passage is at a student's easy, instructional, or frustration reading level. Cloze and maze tests are also good tools for diagnosing and assessing reading comprehension (Gillet & Temple, 2004).

Gillet and Temple (2004) found cloze tests to be particularly worthwhile for assessing comprehension because they require readers to focus on the entire meaning of the passage in order to fill in missing words. Teachers can observe students in action as they construct meaning in the cloze test. Questions to ask while observing students complete this activity include:

1. Does the reader give up when he or she does not know the word?
2. Does the reader make wild guesses?
3. Does the reader go back to the beginning of the sentence to fill in the blank?
4. Does the reader read to the end of a sentence before filling in the blank?
5. Does the reader read to the end of a paragraph and then come back to the blank to fill in the word?

The Intervention section in this chapter includes a discussion on how to use the cloze test to teach comprehension.

Rubrics

Rubrics, especially those based on standards, are another way to ensure that all students are attaining the competencies needed for the criterion-referenced tests that many states use to document reading growth. The partial rubric in Figure 8.8 is based on the CCSS ELA Reading: Literature standards for grade 5. Notice in this example that Joshua, a fifth grader at the end of his second quarter, can only make inferences, determine a theme, and provide the overall structure of a chapter book without much assistance from an adult. He cannot compare/contrast two or more characters or stories from the same genre, nor give meaning of words and phrases even with the help of an adult. Joshua's scores on this rubric indicate that he needs some extra help in reading and interpreting stories. Appendix C.41 contains a blank version of the complete rubric found in Figure 8.8.

INSIDE THE CLASSROOM | Using Think-Alouds for Assessment

Jenny's Think-Aloud

Ms. Jones listens to Jenny as she reads from the text and thinks about what she is reading. Jenny's "think-aloud" comments are in brackets and **boldface**:

"Rooster put a big bowl on the table. 'What's our first ingredient?' he asked."

["I think an ingredient is something you put into a recipe like butter."]

"'The recipe says we need flour,' said Turtle."

["Ah, I was correct! The ingredient was something like flour or butter."]

"I can do that!' said Iguana. He dashed outside and picked a pet-un-i-a, pe-tun-ia."

["What is a petunia? Oh, I bet it is this flower."]

Jenny looks at the picture. ["Oh no! Iguana was thinking of the wrong flour. He thought it was a plant, not the white stuff that goes into cookies. That's funny!"]

Ms. Jones's Analysis

In analyzing Jenny's think-aloud, I can tell that she is reading for meaning. Jenny predicts what she thinks an ingredient is. I am surprised that Jenny can pronounce the word and am happy to know that Jenny predicts and then confirms her surmise. At the beginning of the school year, Jenny never made predictions. I'm also glad to hear Jenny sound out the word *petunia*. Previously, Jenny expected me to pronounce any unfamiliar word; however, now she sounds them out herself. Jenny is able to (1) predict the meaning of a term and then confirm her prediction; (2) make attempts to sound out an unfamiliar word; and (3) understand a pun without any prompting.

8.8   Rubric for narrative reading comprehension based on the
CCSS ELA Reading: Literature standards for grade 5.

STUDENT: _Joshua_   GRADING PERIOD: 1 ② 3 4

TRAIT	TARGET (4–5 points)	ACCEPTABLE (2–3 points)	UNACCEPTABLE (0–1 point)	SCORE
CCSS RL.5.1	Quotes accurately from a text when explaining what the text says explicitly and when drawing inferences from the text.	With the assistance of an adult, quotes accurately from a text when explaining what the text says explicitly and when drawing inferences from the text.	Cannot quote accurately from a text when explaining what the text says explicitly and when drawing inferences from the text.	2
CCSS RL.5.2	Determines a theme of a story, drama, or poem from details in the text, including how characters in a story or drama respond to challenges or how the speaker in a poem reflects upon a topic; summarize the text.	With the assistance of an adult, determines a theme of a story, drama, or poem from details in the text, including how characters in a story or drama respond to challenges or how the speaker in a poem reflects upon a topic; summarize the text.	Cannot determine a theme of a story, drama, or poem from details in the text, including how characters in a story or drama respond to challenges or how the speaker in a poem reflects upon a topic; summarize the text.	2
CCSS RL.5.3	Compares and contrasts two or more characters, settings, or events in a story or drama drawing on specific details in the text (e.g. how characters interact).	With the assistance of an adult, compares and contrasts two or more characters, settings, or events in a story or drama drawing on specific details in the text (e.g. how characters interact).	Cannot compare and contrast two or more characters, settings, or events in a story or drama drawing on specific details in the text (e.g. how characters interact).	1
CCSS RL.5.4	Determines the meaning of words and phrases as they are used in a text, including figurative language such as metaphors and similes.	With the assistance of an adult, determines the meaning of words and phrases as they are used in a text, including figurative language such as metaphors and similes.	Cannot determine the meaning of words and phrases as they are used in a text, including figurative language such as metaphors and similes.	1
CCSS RL.5.5	Explains how a series of chapters, scenes, or stanzas fits together to provide the overall structure of a particular story, drama, or poem.	With the assistance of an adult, explains how a series of chapters, scenes, or stanzas fits together to provide the overall structure of a particular story, drama, or poem.	Cannot explain how a series of chapters, scenes, or stanzas fits together to provide the overall structure of a particular story, drama, or poem.	2
CCSS. RL 5.6	Describes how a narrator's or speaker's point of view influences how events are described.	With the assistance of an adult, describes how a narrator's or speaker's point of view influences how events are described.	Cannot describe how a narrator's or speaker's point of view influences how events are described.	1
CCSS. RL 5.7	Analyzes how visual and multimedia elements contribute to the meaning, tone, or beauty of a text (e.g. graphic novel, multimedia presentation of fiction, folktale, myth, poem).	With the assistance of an adult, analyzes how visual and multimedia elements contribute to the meaning, tone, or beauty of a text (e.g. graphic novel, multimedia presentation of fiction, folktale, myth, poem).	Cannot analyze how visual and multimedia elements contribute to the meaning, tone, or beauty of a text (e.g. graphic novel, multimedia presentation of fiction, folktale, myth, poem).	3
CCSS. RL 5.9	Compares and contrasts stories in the same genre (e.g. mysteries and adventure stories) on their approaches to similar themes and topics.	With the assistance of an adult, compares and contrasts stories in the same genre (e.g. mysteries and adventure stories) on their approaches to similar themes and topics.	Cannot compare and contrast stories in the same genre (e.g. mysteries and adventure stories) on their approaches to similar themes and topics.	1

figure 8.8   Continued.

TRAIT	TARGET (4–5 points)	ACCEPTABLE (2–3 points)	UNACCEPTABLE (0–1 point)	SCORE
CCSS. RL 5.10	By the end of the year, reads and comprehends literature, including stories, dramas, and poetry at the high end of the grades 4–5 text complexity band independently and proficiently.	By the end of the year, with the assistance of an adult, reads and comprehends literature, including stories, dramas, and poetry at the high end of the grades 4–5 text complexity band independently and proficiently.	By the end of the year, cannot read and comprehend literature, including stories, dramas, and poetry at the high end of the grades 4–5 text complexity band independently and proficiently.	NA
			TOTAL SCORE:	13

Source: National Governors Association Center for Best Practices (NGACBP) & Council of Chief State School Officers (CCSSO). (2010). English Language Arts Standards, Reading: Literature, Grade 5. Washington, DC: NGACBP, CCSSO, p.12.

Computer programs as assessment tools

Software tutorial programs can be used to assess students' current reading level and track their progress. These programs also define the level of text appropriate for students' independent and instructional reading and save teachers time by providing summaries that can be shared with parents. Such software programs include the following:

1. Accelerated Reader program, distributed by Renaissance Learning (www.renlearn.com/ar/) is aligned with some of the emphases of the CCSS and uses the ATOS readability formula mentioned in Appendix A of the Standards. The site also includes the academic benchmarks for each state. The program is available online or as an app.

2. Scholastic Reading Inventory program, distributed by Scholastic (http://www.scholastic.com/education/assessment/literacy/sri-index.htm), provides teachers with students' Lexile reading levels, as mentioned in Appendix A of the CCSS.

3. Istation (www.istation.com) is a computer-based assessment and intervention program that measures and provides instruction in vocabulary, comprehension, and other skills such as spelling and fluency.

Effective teachers administer a variety of informal assessments in order to evaluate a struggling reader's skills and weaknesses. They then demonstrate an appropriate strategy and permit the individual reader to practice the strategy while they watch. Teachers must be knowledgeable about a variety of reading strategies in order to choose strategies that will help a particular reader. Many of the activities in the Intervention section focus on teaching various comprehension strategies.

Formal Assessment

Standardized achievement tests measure the current level of students' performance in a variety of areas including reading comprehension. However, because many achievement tests are group tests, they are not designed to diagnose individuals (Gillet & Temple, 2004). Nonetheless, teachers can look at student reading subtest scores to get a benchmark level for how an individual student scored in comparison to his grade level. Some commonly used achievement tests are the current edition of the Metropolitan Achievement Test, the Comprehensive Test of Basic Skills, the Iowa Tests of Basic Skills, and the Stanford Achievement Test. See Chapter 3 for a complete list of formal student comprehension assessments.

intervention   STRATEGIES & ACTIVITIES

T he International Literacy Association and the National Council of Teachers of English deem it important that all readers, including struggling readers, be able to apply a wide range of strategies for comprehension (IRA/NCTE, 1996). In the 1960s and 1970s, the trend was to teach subskills through direct instruction and then have students master each subskill while reading a short passage. However, research now indicates it is more effective to teach skills to students in context, at moments when they can make an active choice to use them to aid comprehension of that particular text (Beck, McKeown, & Kucan, 2013; Fountas & Pinnell, 2006b). The comprehension strategies in this section should be taught in context when struggling readers need them. Each strategy should be explicitly explained and demonstrated by the teacher using the story that is being read.

Some of the activities presented in this section extend through all of the stages of reading, while others are intended for a specific stage. Make sure you are familiar with many types of activities, that you understand the needs and interests of the students, and then apply the activity that best fits the need of each reader. Many of these activities can be used in large or small groups. However, it is suggested that these activities be used in a tutoring setting so they fit the needs of individual struggling readers.

Strategies and Activities to Use Before, During, and After Reading

ACTIVITY   **The Memphis Comprehension Framework**   GRADES 4–6

The Memphis Comprehension Framework is a research-based process shown to be effective with grades 4 through 6 (Flynt & Cooter, 2005). In this framework, teachers use fiction and informational books to teach concepts. The framework has three steps:

1. Preplanning: Select an age-appropriate comprehension skill or strategy and use it for a minimum of three weeks.

2. Focused read-aloud and discussion: Read a story based on a concept once a week, and read informational texts based on a topic twice a week. Teach unfamiliar vocabulary words before, during, and after each reading. All readings should be 10–15 minutes daily. Follow each read-aloud with a group discussion that encourages higher-level thinking (see Figure 8.9 for examples of questions to start such discussions); encourage students to justify their comments. During discussion, create a graphic organizer to show relationships among concepts. Chart unfamiliar vocabulary words on the graphic organizer to show relationships between words and the topic.

3. Engage in a three-level retelling:
   - Level 1 is a guided oral retelling in which students are encouraged to retell the information in a logical sequence.
   - Level 2 is a graphic organizer retelling in which students use the graphic organizer that was created during the focused read-aloud and discussion time.
   - Level 3 is a written/graphic retelling in which the students create their own graphic organizers and write a summary.

The following pages show example materials from a seventh-grade unit on the Holocaust. For the unit, Mr. Greenberg selected fiction and nonfiction in the form of both picture and chapter books with a range of reading levels. He selected these books because they were set in Germany, Poland, France, Switzerland, and Czechoslovakia. See Figure 8.10 for a list of the books he selected. One of Mr. Greenberg's students, Michelle, created the graphic organizer and retelling depicted in Figure 8.11.

figure 8.9

Higher-level discussion questions for the unit on World War II.

1. We have read as a class a number of fiction books about World War II. Compare and contrast the experiences of Milkweed, living in Poland, and Sevrine, living in France. Which of the main characters had a harder time surviving daily life? Give evidence for your stance.

2. Ann in *When Hitler Stole Pink Rabbit* had very different experiences than did the children in *The Story of Friedl Dicker-Brandeis*. Explain how their experiences were different and give some reasons why you think this was so.

3. *Every Day Lasts a Year: A Jewish Family's Correspondence from Poland* is nonfiction, and *Milkweed*, also set in Poland, is fiction. Do you think Jerry Spinelli used accurate information in *Milkweed*? Why or why not? Explain.

figure 8.10   Fiction and nonfiction books for a seventh-grade unit on the Holocaust.

FICTION

Kerr, J. (1971). *When Hitler Stole Pink Rabbit*. New York: Putnam & Gosset Group.

Polacco, P. (2000). *The Butterfly*. New York: Philomel Books.

Spinelli, J. (2003). *Milkweed*. New York: Alfred Knopf.

NONFICTION

Browning, C. R., Hollander, R. S., & Tec, N. (Eds.) (2007). *Every Day Lasts a Year: A Jewish Family's Correspondence from Poland*. New York: Cambridge University Press.

Glick, S. (2003). *Heroes of the Holocaust*. San Diego, CA: Lucent.

Gross, E. B. (2009). *Elly: My True Story of the Holocaust*. New York: Scholastic.

Krinitz, E. N., & Steinhardt, B. (2005). *Memories of Survival*. New York: Hyperion Books for Children.

Rubin, S. G. (2000). *Fireflies in the Dark: The Story of Friedl Dicker-Brandeis and the Children of Terezin*. New York: Holiday House.

figure 8.11   Michelle's graphic organizer and retelling of Patricia Polacco's The Butterfly (2000).

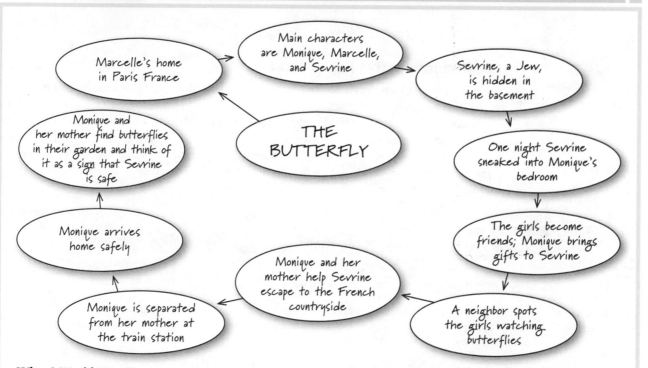

When? World War II.

Where? France, at Marcelle Solliliage's home, an underground safe haven for Jews escaping to freedom.

Who? Monique (young French girl), Marcelle (her mother), Nazi soldiers, Sevrine (a Jewish girl hiding in Monique's basement).

Main Problem: Jews were being taken from homes and shipped to "camps."

Sequence: Monique noticed Sevrine one night in her bedroom.

Monique kept taking things, including butterflies, to Sevrine to enjoy.

Neighbor spotted the two girls at the bedroom window.

Marcelle and husband, dressed like a nun and priest, fled on foot with the girls to the French countryside.

Another family met them on the way and took Sevrine to another place.

At the train station Monique was separated from her mother.

Monique made it back to her house without her mother.

Her mother found her safe at home.

Climax: Monique and her mother spotted butterflies in their garden in the spring; they saw it as a "sign" that Sevrine was safe.

(continued)

figure 8.11   Continued.

Retelling: Monique and her parents lived in Paris during World War II. They provided a hiding place for a Jewish girl who was the same age as Monique. First, Monique did not know who Sevrine was, but her mother told her Sevrine was hiding in a secret room in their basement. Monique and Sevrine became friends and loved to watch the butterflies from Monique's bedroom window.

One day a hateful neighbor spotted two girls at the window (he knew his neighbor had only one girl). Monique told her mother, and that night they fled on foot to the countryside where another friendly person helped Sevrine get to Switzerland. When Monique and her mother were returning to Paris, they became separated in the crowd at the train station.

Monique took the train to Paris and walked the two miles to her home. Later her mother arrived home too.

The next spring, Monique and her mother found hundreds of butterflies one day in the garden. They saw that as a good sign that Sevrine was safe.

ACTIVITY   **Repeated Interactive Read-Aloud**   GRADES PRE-K–8

This strategy aligns with the CCSS goal that students be able to perform a close read of a complex text. It is a research-based approach that aids students in pre-K through eighth grades. One story or book is read three different times. Each read-aloud includes analytic talk, which involves students making predictions and "inferences that explain a character's motivation or connect events from different parts of the story" (McGee & Schickedanz, 2007, p. 742). With each reading the talk is more in-depth. Figure 8.12 is a framework of a repeated interactive read-aloud based on three readings.

figure 8.12   An example repeated interactive read-aloud.

	FIRST READING	SECOND READING	THIRD READING
Introduction of Book	By looking at title and book cover, predict what story is about.	Have students talk about the characters and what they did in the story.	Have students tell you what the problem was and how it was resolved.
Reading of Book	Focus on new vocabulary words or words that are important to the story. Comment on what the protagonist is thinking and feeling throughout the story. Ask students why they think the character is thinking or feeling that.	Using the same vocabulary words, review meanings and give more verbal definitions. Comment on what other characters are thinking or feeling throughout the story. Ask students why they think these characters are feeling or thinking that way.	Before reading a double page, ask the students to retell what has happened on that page. Point out the focused vocabulary words in the text. Ask students to think of other times they hear that word.
Discussion After Reading	Ask "why" questions and be sure students explain. Use follow-up questions if necessary to get students to explain their stance.	Ask other "why" questions or "What would have happened if . . . .?"	Ask a different "why" question, or "What would have happened if . . . ?" Get students to extend their explanations.

Adapted from McGee, L. & Schickedanz, J. (2007). Repeated interactive read-alouds in preschool and kindergarten (p. 747). *The Reading Teacher, 60*(8), 742–751.

Strategies and Activities to Use Before Reading

Alternate Writing

This strategy combines reading and writing. Alternate writing creates a story written by a teacher and a struggling reader. It helps students acquire knowledge of story elements, such as setting, characters, conflict, climax, and resolution, and thus aids comprehension. Alternate writing is a pre-reading activity that helps readers understand the beginning, middle, and end of stories. Use paper or a computer as you complete the following steps:

1. Agree with the student on a topic and a title for her story.
2. Write the first sentence of the story.
3. Have the student read your sentence and then add a sentence.
4. Then, you read the first two sentences and add the third sentence. Take turns writing sentences until the story is complete.
5. Discuss story elements with the student as she writes her sentences.

All good stories begin with a setting and a problem and include roadblocks as well as a resolution. The focus throughout the writing process should be on comprehension, not correct spelling.

The following is an example of an opening sentence for an alternate writing story. Note that the teacher does not name the frog. This permits the student to write a sentence about the frog's name or to begin describing the place.

Once upon a time, in a far away place, there lived a sad frog.

Directed Listening–Thinking Activity (DL–TA)

A directed listening–thinking activity (DL–TA) is used before (and during) the reading, with the teacher doing the reading. You may use this strategy in two ways. One way is as follows:

1. Read the title without showing the cover picture to the students.
2. Ask them to predict what will happen in the story.
3. Read a little of the story and have the students validate the prediction.
4. Ask the students to predict what will happen next.

These steps continue to the end of the text. The second way to use this strategy is the following:

1. Show the picture on the cover without reading the title.
2. Have the students predict what will happen in the story.
3. Read the title, turn to the first page, show the pictures on the first page, and ask the students to make predictions about what will happen on that page.
4. Read that page as the students validate predictions.

These steps continue to the end of the book. Note that the activity can also be performed using an ebook and an interactive whiteboard.

Directed Reading–Thinking Activity (DR–TA)

Directed reading–thinking activity (DR–TA) is used before (and during) reading. It differs from the DL–TA in that here the students do the reading. Students look at the cover of the book, read the title, and predict what will happen in the story. Students then read to validate their predictions. This cycle continues as students read the book, using chapter titles, illustrations, and so forth to make predictions.

With the DR–TA you can also cover up the words of a picture book and allow readers to make predictions based solely on the pictures. Then they expose the words and find out whether their predictions were accurate.

Strategies and Activities to Use During Reading

ACTIVITY **Text Mapping**   GRADES 6–8

Lapp, Fisher, and Johnson (2010) believe students must become proficient in one comprehension strategy and able to use it independently before they learn a new strategy. Text mapping improves and expands students' comprehension and oral retells. First, teachers model filling in the map as they read and discuss a passage with students. Then they guide students to complete a map by themselves. Later, students complete maps while reading with no guidance from teachers. See Figure 8.13 for an example. Appendix D.21 is a blank version of this form.

figure 8.13 Text mapping example.

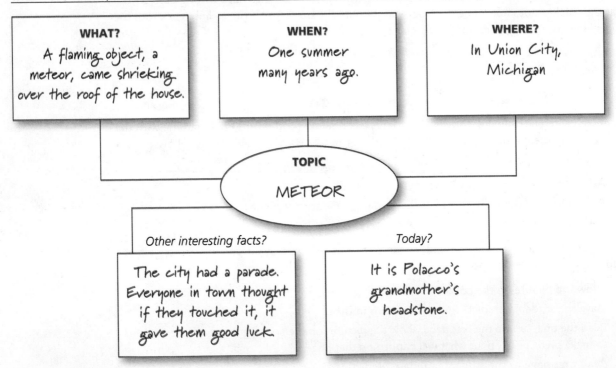

TITLE: Meteor! Patricia Polacco

WHAT?
A flaming object, a meteor, came shrieking over the roof of the house.

WHEN?
One summer many years ago.

WHERE?
In Union City, Michigan

TOPIC
METEOR

Other interesting facts?
The city had a parade. Everyone in town thought if they touched it, it gave them good luck.

Today?
It is Polacco's grandmother's headstone.

From *TEACHING PHONICS AND WORD STUDY IN THE INTERMEDIATE GRADES* by Wiley Blevins. Scholastic, Inc./Teaching Resources. Copyright ©2001 by Wiley Blevins. Reprinted by permission.

ACTIVITY **Reciprocal Questioning**   GRADES 1–6

In this strategy the student and teacher take turns asking each other questions. After you and the student read to a certain point in the story, instruct the student to ask you a literal or inferential question. You then ask the student a literal or inferential question in return. Next, read another section of the story and repeat the process. Because most children ask literal questions, you can model higher-level thinking by asking inferential and evaluative questions. See Figure 8.14 for an explanation of the different kinds of questions.

figure 8.14   Types of questions.

1. **LITERAL QUESTIONS.** Literal questions can be found on the page; the purpose of a literal question is to check a reader's ability to recall information stated in the book. For example, a literal question from *Mr. Lincoln's Way* (Polacco, 2001) is to ask students is "On page one, the text told readers what Mr. Lincoln did with students that made students think he was really cool. Looking at the illustration, what else did Mr. Lincoln do with the students?" The answer is clearly illustrated; he played jump rope with students.

2. **INFERENTIAL QUESTIONS.** The answers to inferential questions are not written verbatim in the text. In order to answer inferential questions, a student needs to read between the lines. For example, in *Mr. Lincoln's Way,* on the last page after Mr. Lincoln told Eugene that he showed the ducklings the way out to the water, Eugene states: 'Hey, you showed me the way out, Mr. Lincoln.' What did Eugene mean by that statement?" The answer is not stated directly in the story; however, there is an answer implied in the text that students can cite, and a reader who comprehends the story will understand what Eugene means by that statement. Teachers can also ask inferential questions concerning the illustrations. An example of such a question is when a teacher asks: "On pages 11–12, Mr. Lincoln is attempting to understand Eugene and to draw him into a project. Examine Mr. Lincoln's appearance in the illustrations, and explain how in the illustration Polacco gets readers to understand Mr. Lincoln's approach to getting Eugene to accept the offer of helping with the project."

3. **CRITICAL QUESTIONS.** Critical questions require a reader to analyze and synthesize in order to give a correct answer. A critical question may require a student to gather information from a number of books or from her personal experiences. For example, a critical question to ask students after sharing *Mr. Lincoln's Way* would be "Why didn't Mr. Lincoln get angry and discipline Eugene after he called the two students from Mexico 'brown-skinned'?" This type of question will get students to think about their own reaction to incidents in which others bully them.

A critical question to ask students that will require them to think beyond the story and illustrations is the following. "On page pages 13–14, the text tells readers that Mr. Lincoln and Eugene made a list of plants, shrubs, grains, and seeds to buy for the atrium. What type of vegetation, grains, and seeds would they buy to attract birds? Explain your answer. "

4. **EVALUATIVE QUESTIONS.** Evaluative questions have no right or wrong answer. A reader gives his own opinions, but must provide sound reasoning. One example of an evaluative question about *Mr. Lincoln's Way* is "How different would the story end if Mr. Lincoln became angry at Eugene calling the Mexican students 'brown-skinned'?" To get students to think critically how illustrators use their art to expand the story, ask students, "Why do you think Polacco drew the illustration opposite the title page when the story is not about students swinging together? Explain your answer."

Critical and evaluative questions require a student to read past the words on the page.

From *TEACHING PHONICS AND WORD STUDY IN THE INTERMEDIATE GRADES* by Wiley Blevins. Scholastic, Inc./Teaching Resources. Copyright ©2001 by Wiley Blevins. Reprinted by permission.

Think-Aloud for Narrative Text

GRADES 1–5   A C T I V I T Y

Although a think-aloud can be used for assessment, it can also be used first by you to verbalize your thoughts and then by students as they read and make sense of a text. When you verbalize your thoughts while reading, you permit the students to understand the strategies you use to comprehend texts. As you read, you can comment on or question the text, bringing your "prior knowledge to bear, or making inferences or predictions" (Oster, 2001, p. 64).

Before class, select a passage from the class's current reading that provides opportunities for using one or more comprehension strategies, such as using background knowledge, inferring, or predicting. Read through the passage and identify places that invite questioning. Script a comment or a question that demonstrates the use of a strategy. Write these on sticky notes and place in the text to ask as you are reading the passage. You then have the students practice the strategy as you observe and scaffold their thought processes as necessary. Be sure to model a think-aloud using a book that is conceptually challenging to the readers. The following is an example of a teacher modeling a think-aloud, using Patricia MacLachlan's *Mama One, Mama Two* (1982). The teacher's think-aloud thoughts are presented in italics.

Maudie heard the baby cry in the middle of the night. *[I wonder how old Maudie is and how old the baby is. I wonder if the baby is sick.]* She got up and walked through the moonlit hallway to the room. *[I wonder if she is angry that the baby woke her up.]* The baby reached out and curled his fingers around hers. *[I see the baby is a boy and that he likes Maudie.]* "Are you awake, too?" asked Katherine in the doorway. *[I wonder who Katherine is. From the picture, I think she is Maudie's mother. However, if it is Maudie's mother, she probably wouldn't be called Katherine.]* She held the baby's night bottle of milk. *[I guess the baby is hungry, not sick.]*

Later in the story we read:

"Tell me the story again," said Maudie, "the story about Mama One, Mama Two." *[I wonder what Maudie means. Is she talking about Katherine? Is Katherine not her real mother? Who are Mama One and Mama Two?]*

This process demonstrates to struggling readers that the teacher also asks questions as she reads and makes and confirms predictions. After you have modeled this strategy, give struggling readers an opportunity to practice it with a book on their instructional level they have not yet read. This will reinforce the strategy so it becomes second nature when they are reading independently.

ACTIVITY   ## "And This Is the Rest of the Story"   GRADES 3–5

In this strategy a teacher reads the story and stops at a critical point, such as the climax. The student then tells the rest of the story. For the student's ending to be plausible, he must have comprehended the story up to that point and be able to make inferences as he thinks about the ending. After he predicts the ending, the teacher finishes the story. The student finds it enjoyable to compare his ending to the author's. Good stories to use with this strategy include:

Cloudy with a Chance of Meatballs (1978) by Judi Barrett

Show and Tell (1991) by Elvina Woodruff

The Popcorn Shop (1993) by Alice Low

The Vanishing Pumpkin (1996) by Tony Johnston

Strega Nona's Magic Lessons (1982) by Tomie dePaola

A variation of this strategy is called "What If?" Instead of having the students write their own ending, they read to the end of the story and write a different ending by asking, "What if such and such happened?"

ACTIVITY   ## Teacher-Made Audiobooks   GRADES 1–3

Marie Carbo (1996a) suggests creating read-along audiobooks that allow you to record the story at a pace slightly slower than normal. These are especially useful for English learners and struggling readers. Students are invited to read along with the audiobook. To create a read-along audiobook, do the following:

1. Select a story or passage that is at the student's instructional level.
2. Record only one short selection into an audio file. Do not put more than one story in a file even if the passage is very short, because students must be able to quickly find the starting point.
3. Read the story at a pace that allows the reader to point to each word and read along.
4. Be sure to include a turn-the-page signal with a pause long enough to allow the reader to turn the page.

Teacher-made audiobooks have many advantages. You can create them to fit a particular reader's interest and read them at a pace that allows the student to follow along. Audiobooks can transcend the mere read-along when you add cues that prompt students to stop and respond to reflective questions. If two children listen together, they can stop the recording after each question and discuss the question together. If they disagree on an answer, have them replay the audiobook until they can discern who is correct.

If you do not have time to create read-along audiobooks, Figure 8.15 lists companies that sell them.

figure 8.15   Publishers of read-along audiobooks, with examples of available titles.

Newbridge	Sundance	Scholastic
www.newbridgeonline.com	www.sundancepub.com	www.scholastic.com

Newbridge
www.newbridgeonline.com
1. *Spinning a Web*
2. *Out of Space*
3. *A Butterfly Is Born*
4. *Amazing Water*
5. *Sink or Float?*
6. *An Apple a Day*

Sundance
www.sundancepub.com
1. *Making Friends with Samson*
2. *The Fine Line*
3. *Two Hours with Tilly*
4. *Sticky Fingers*
5. *Mug Shots*
6. *Chocolate Chuckles*

Scholastic
www.scholastic.com
1. *Caps for Sale*
2. *City Mouse–Country Mouse*
3. *Henny Penny*
4. *Little Rabbit's Loose Tooth*
5. *More Spaghetti, I Say!*
6. *Is Your Mama a Llama?*

Text-Talk

GRADES 2–5   A C T I V I T Y

First introduced by Beck and McKeown (2001), text-talks require a specific kind of text and talk. Beck and McKeown suggest all texts should be "conceptually challenging to require grappling with ideas and taking an active stance toward constructing meaning" (p. 10), and all talk or discussion between the teacher and reader should require the reader "to make sense of ideas that are about something beyond the here and now" (p. 10). Text-talks require the following steps:

1. Read a section of the story without showing the pictures.
2. Pose open-ended questions that focus on text ideas and encourage inferential thinking. The open-ended questions should encourage language development.
3. Have the student attempt to answer the questions.
4. If necessary, scaffold the student's thinking by posing more open-ended questions using the language of the book. Scaffolding is an important process because you provide information that the student has not provided.
5. Show pictures of that section of the story to encourage more discussion.
6. Repeat steps 1–5 with each section of the story until you reach the end.

Using the language of the story during text-talks will encourage students to use the story's vocabulary later in retellings and summarizations.

Wordless Books for Developing Inferential Reading

GRADES 2–6   A C T I V I T Y

While "reading" wordless books, students need to make inferences about characters, plot, and motives. They need to connect sets of pictures to make a story. Drawing inferences and connecting information to previously read information are two components of comprehension.

To use this strategy, read the title and have the student skim each page of the entire book. Then, have the student start from the beginning and "read" each page. If the story does not make sense, ask her to "read" the page again. Use wordless books to develop inferential reading skills by asking students to add more detail to their stories. For example, concerning *Tuesday* (1991) by David Wiesner, you may ask what the man who is eating the midnight snack is thinking when he sees frogs flying past the window, or why the old lady did not wake up when the frogs watched her television.

Appendices A.5 and A.6 offer lists of wordless books that can be used for this strategy.

Strategies and Activities to Use After Reading

Repeated Readings

GRADES 2–6   A C T I V I T Y

Repeated readings by both the teacher and the struggling reader have been shown to increase comprehension. The close reading of complex texts, a goal of the CCSS, may also involve repeated readings. Rereading a passage is a common task of postsecondary students as they grapple with fiction that has multiple layers of meaning. Students in the lower grades also need to be taught that rereading is sometimes necessary in order to fully comprehend a story. Repeated readings by the teacher give such readers an opportunity to understand how to unravel the multiple layers of meaning in favorite stories. Through these readings and the discussions that follow, readers begin to make inferences about characters' motives and how the setting affects the action. They consider the point of view and the author's perspective. They also think about the words the author chooses to create a mood. Repeated readings allow students to focus less on decoding words and more on comprehending the story (Brown, 1999/2000; Pearson & Fielding, 1991), but also remember that not all stories require repeated readings.

ACTIVITY   **Multiple Perspectives: Diary Entries**   GRADES 4–8

Some narrative texts are embedded with multiple meanings. Teachers need to guide students to draw conclusions about the author's perspective, position, and power (Clarke & Whitney, 2009).

Clarke and Whitney (2009) found that this strategy facilitates students' abilities to comprehend multiple perspectives by reading about an historical account often omitted in history books. For example, students in the upper grades have learned about Columbus's voyages to the New World; however, Jane Yolen's (1992) *Encounter,* a story told from a Taino Indian boy's perspective, introduces students to the Native Americans' point of view about the white man coming to their land. For example, Greg is a sixth grader involved in a collaborative social studies and language arts unit on Columbus. After Greg's class has read *Encounter,* Mr. Grigg, his language arts teacher, invites them to write diary entries representing different perspectives. Greg, a shy student, writes a diary entry of Whitecloud, a young Taino Indian, and Christopher Columbus. Figure 8.16 shows examples of Greg's diary entries.

figure 8.16   Diary entries of Whitecloud and Christopher Columbus.

Whitecloud's Diary	Columbus' Diary
October 10, 1492 I had a bad dream last night during the thunder storm. Three winged birds rode the wild waves in our bay.	October 10, 1492 We need to find land soon. So many of my people are sick. Our food is low and getting stale and rotten.
October 11, 1492 I had the same bad dream last night. This time I heard the winged birds' voices. I think this is a bad omen. I even saw their sharp white teeth.	October 11, 1492 I looked through my spy glass today and I saw land in the distance! I think we have finally sailed to India! I told my people! There was great happiness! I told them to gather the gifts that we had taken with us to give to these people.

figure 8.16 Continued.

October 12, 1492

I again had a restless night, and when I left my hammock to walk the beach, I saw a great canoe with white sails. I went to tell our chief not to welcome the strangers, but he told me that it is our custom to welcome all who come to our village.

All the strangers looked like parrots with their bright clothes. They did not look human with their ivory skin.

I warned my people not to welcome them because funny sounds came from their mouths.

They gave us strings with smooth balls, with many colors on them. We gave them spears so they could fish. During the feast that we shared with them, I looked into their chief's eyes and they looked threatening. His smile was a wicked smile; I again went to my chief to warn him, but he pushed me aside because I was only a child. I remembered my dream and left the feast to pray to my zemis.

October 12, 1492

We landed today on the shores where people with very dark skin welcomed us! But we do not understand them; they speak a different language. But they appear friendly enough because we exchanged gifts. We got spears and bouncy balls for the beads we had given them. They made a feast for us of orange potatoes, bread and fish. They gave us tobacco leaves to smoke, but they were strong and caused many of us to cough. This was a GOOD day!

October 13, 1492

I was taken with four other young boys to the stranger's canoe. They are taken us to far away. I MUST escape even if I have to jump into the cold waters! I MUST get back to my people! I knew these strangers were bad people! What is going to happen to me?

October 13, 1492

I am taking five of these young boys with me as we continue to search these strange shores. I am taking these young boys because they are healthy and they will be able to talk to any other of these people on this strange land that is not India like I thought it would be.

Painting Mental Pictures   GRADES K–2 **A C T I V I T Y**

This activity is based on research suggesting that comprehension requires readers to visualize the characters, setting, and action of a story (Gregory & Cahill, 2010). Teachers read a picture book without showing the pictures and then invite students to share a mental picture from the story with a classmate. After they share their mental pictures, they draw those pictures. Finally, the students compare their pictures with the book's illustrations.

figure 8.17

Sample spinner for prompting narrative text discussions.

Spin the Discussion   GRADES 1–8

In lieu of using literal questions, use prompts to discuss books, allowing students to learn from others and demonstrate their comprehension of a story (Blum, Koskinen, Bhartiya, & Hluboky, 2010). First, make a spinner with the following prompts in the four sections (Figure 8.17 shows a miniature version, but yours should be approximately 6 inches across):

1. Synopsis (The student tells in his words what happened.)
2. Rich language (The student gives examples the author used, e.g., metaphors, personification, alliteration, and so on.)
3. Point of view (The student explains the point of view from which the story is told.)
4. Theme (The student explains the theme conveyed in the text.)

After reading a book to a small group, invite one student to flick the spinner to begin a discussion. Other students can add to that discussion or take a turn with the spinner to start a new discussion.

A C T I V I T Y   **Graphic Organizers for Narrative Text**   GRADES 2–8

The general term *graphic organizer* includes all types of story maps, charts, webs, diagrams, or any visual representation of a story's content. Although graphic organizers usually do not promote a deep analysis of a story, they do help struggling readers comprehend and demonstrate a basic understanding of a story. Some graphic organizers chart the beginning, middle, and ending of the story. Most include the setting, characters, problem, main events, and resolution. Previously in this chapter, we discussed the Story Face by Staal (2000). Figure 8.18 includes examples of three types of graphic organizers. When selecting one for a struggling reader, consider her age, her reading ability, and the purpose for using the strategy. For each one of these organizers, first model how to fill in the structure and then monitor the student as she begins to use it.

figure 8.18   Types of graphic organizers.

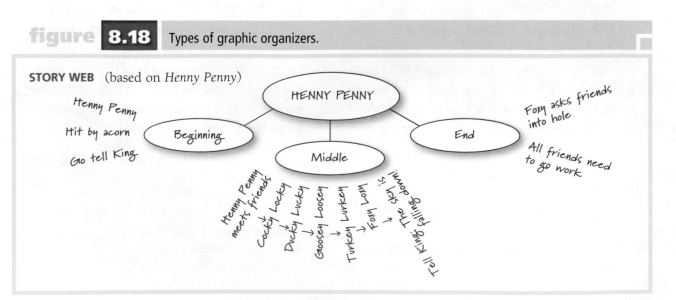

figure **8.18**   Continued.

STORY MAP   (based on *Luba and the Wren* by P. Polacco)

Setting:	Time	Place
	Long ago	Ukraine

→

Characters:	Luba
	Luba's parents
	The wren w/magical powers

Problem: Wren will grant any wish to Luba. Luba doesn't want anything. However, her parents want a bigger farm, but are never content.

Action: Wren gives Luba's parents each of the following after her parents become unhappy:

1. Bigger house on fertile land
2. Manor with large estate
3. Palace and rulers of the Ukraine
4. Become Tsar & Tsarine of all Russia
5. Become Emperor & Empress of the world
   They want to become Gods.

Outcome: Wren knows that Luba does not like her parents' last wish. Wren returns them to their former poor dacha on a small piece of poor land. — But they are happy!

Source: Basic story map adapted from J. David Cooper, *Literacy, Helping Children Contract Meaning,* 4th ed. Copyright © 2006 by Houghton Mifflin Company.

MT. PLOT   (based on *The Old Woman Who Lived in a Vinegar Bottle* by M. R. MacDonald)

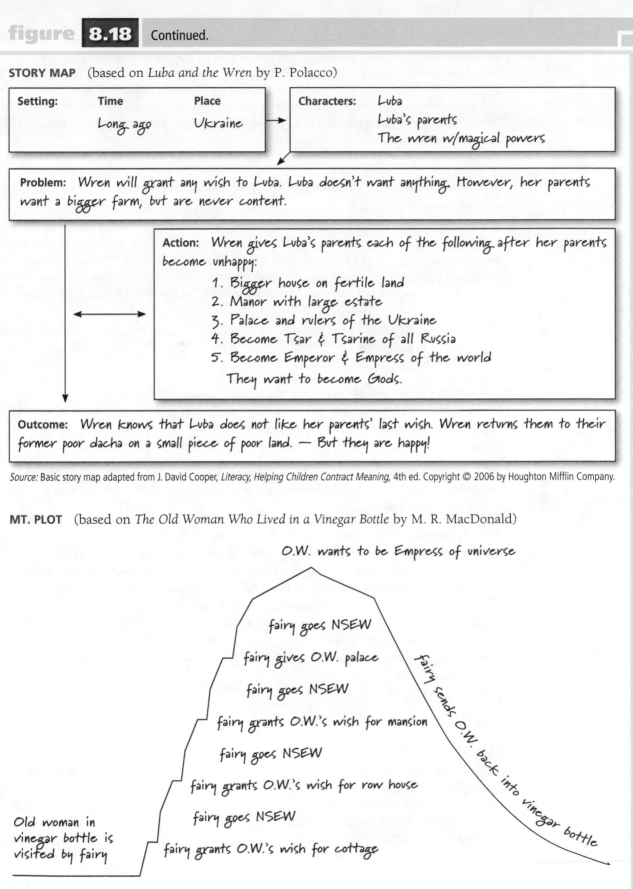

O.W. wants to be Empress of universe

fairy goes NSEW

fairy gives O.W. palace

fairy goes NSEW

fairy grants O.W.'s wish for mansion

fairy goes NSEW

fairy grants O.W.'s wish for row house

fairy goes NSEW

fairy grants O.W.'s wish for cottage

Old woman in vinegar bottle is visited by fairy

fairy sends O.W. back into vinegar bottle

ACTIVITY   **Retelling with Puppets**   GRADES 1–4

Retelling a story using simple stick or sack puppets helps readers with sequencing and recalling main points. When students act out the story, they draw inferences about a character's vocal quality and motives, and puppets facilitate this process. Create a puppet for each character and have students manipulate all the puppets in the retelling. One enjoyable story for young children to retell with puppets is *The Little Old Lady Who Was Not Afraid of Anything* (1986) by Linda Williams, but many of students' favorite stories can be retold with puppets.

ACTIVITY   **Question Connect Transform (QCT) for Narrative Text**   GRADES 6–8

Richards (2006) developed this critical literacy strategy to help middle-school students "enhance their critical literacy abilities" (p. 194). After reading an historical story or novel, engage the students in questioning (Q) "the moral and ethical dimensions of issues presented in the historical fiction" (p. 194). Second, ask the students to connect (C) the story to their lives. Finally, ask the students to think how they might transform (T) any inequities that were presented in the novel and are still prevalent in today's society. See Figure 8.19 for a student example.

figure 8.19   Student journal using QCT with Katherine Paterson's *Lyddie* (1991).

Questioning the moral issue: I question why Lyddie's employer had her and other employees work for low wages in deplorable working conditions at the mill. I also question how the owner got away with forcing the girls into having sex with him and then firing them if they became pregnant.

Connecting the story to my life: I never had to work in such deplorable conditions, but I do remember when men were paid more than women for teaching the same grade.

Transforming the unjust wages: I could have told a judge about the deplorable working conditions and demand he make the owner install air vents so the girls did not have to breathe the textile dust. I could have gone to other places of employment to see if the wages were similar to the ones in the mill. I could have gone to a pastor to explain how the owner was sexually abusing the girls and asked him to confront the owner. I could have gone to the local newspaper and submitted a letter to the editor about the deployable working conditions, low wages, and the owner's abuse of the employees.

ACTIVITY   **Character Perspective Chart**   GRADES 4–6

Many stories depict conflict between the goals of two characters. For example, in Anna Harwell Celenza's *The Farewell Symphony* (2000), Joseph Haydn and his 22 musicians have a goal to return to their families in Austria after spending a long summer in Hungary providing music for Prince Nicholas. Prince Nicholas's conflicting goal is to remain at his Hungarian summer palace long into the fall and have the musicians play at all of his parties. Shanahan and Shanahan (1997) introduce the Character Perspective Chart, which follows a story map from two characters' points of view. Shanahan and Shanahan believe this type of chart helps readers draw inferences about the goals of each character. Figure 8.20 features a character perspective chart of *The Farewell Symphony*.

figure 8.20 Character perspective chart for *The Farewell Symphony*.

Haydn & Musicians	**MAIN CHARACTER**	Prince Nicholas
Palace in Hungary	**SETTING**	Palace in Hungary
Haydn and musicians want to return to Austria.	**PROBLEM**	Nicholas wants to stay in Hungary.
Go back to Austria	**GOAL**	Stay in Hungary
Musicians ask to go home.	**ATTEMPTS**	Prince says later.
Musicians beg for their families to join them.		Prince says there is no room in the palace.
Musicians say they are going home.		Prince says he will fire them if they do.
Haydn writes the Farewell Symphony to show Prince the anger of the musicians.		Prince was upset with the angry music.
Musicians play with passion.	**OUTCOME**	Prince is filled with compassion and permits them to go home.
Reward awaits those who are faithful.	**THEME**	Think of others' feelings.

Venn Diagrams for Narrative Text

GRADES 2–6   **A C T I V I T Y**

One goal of the CCSS is being able to compare and contrast information. Venn diagrams are often used for this task. This strategy has been effectively applied to fairy tales that have been retold by various authors and illustrators. You and a student may read two versions of the same tale and then compare the versions by completing a Venn diagram. Figure 8.21 shows a diagram comparing Jan Brett's *The Mitten* (1989) and Alvin Tresselt's *The Mitten* (1964).

figure 8.21 Venn diagram comparing two versions of *The Mitten*.

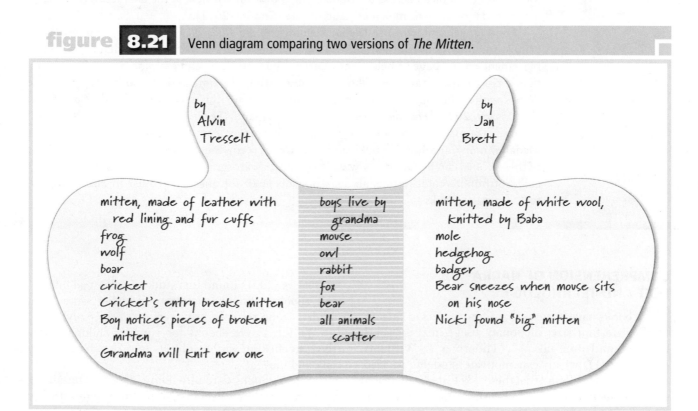

by Alvin Tresselt | by Jan Brett

mitten, made of leather with red lining and fur cuffs
frog
wolf
boar
cricket
Cricket's entry breaks mitten
Boy notices pieces of broken mitten
Grandma will knit new one

boys live by grandma
mouse
owl
rabbit
fox
bear
all animals scatter

mitten, made of white wool, knitted by Baba
mole
hedgehog
badger
Bear sneezes when mouse sits on his nose
Nicki found "big" mitten

ACTIVITY   **Character Sketch**   GRADES 3–5

This strategy encourages readers to visualize a story's characters by providing graphically inclined students an opportunity exercise their artistic abilities. To use this strategy, read a story to students without showing the pictures and then have them draw a picture of the characters. Ask them to explain the reasons for their depictions to better understand their level of thinking and comprehension of the story.

ACTIVITY   **Solving Mysteries**   GRADES 3–5

Sherlock Bones and the Missing Cheese (Stevens-Crummel, 2012) is a mystery based on the nursery rhyme "The Farmer in the Dell." Students need to read closely to find the story's clues. This activity encourages close reading, group discussion, and stating opinions as students attempt to convince their small group that their clue is correct. In this mystery, Sherlock Bones uses his five senses to find the special cheese. Read the text, which parodies "The Farmer in the Dell" song familiar to most children, while sharing the illustrations. Ask students to listen and watch for clues. Have them write their clues as they hear or see them, and then before reading the end of the story, have students form groups of three to share their clues. Challenge the groups to identify which of their clues they agree on as a group, and then have them share their consensus on the clues with the class.

ACTIVITY   **Comprehending Visual Images**   GRADES 2–8

Students comprehend at a deeper level when they read and study both text and illustrations. When introducing or sharing a book, draw attention to how authors, illustrators, and publishers construct meaning through the endpapers, cover, title page, dedication, book jacket, author's note, fonts, orientation of the book (e.g., landscape, square, portrait design, etc.), borders, type of art (e.g., folk, modern, realistic, surrealistic, etc.), colors, lines, space, picture format (e.g., full bleed across the double pages or framed), view of the characters (e.g., looking at reader or away from reader), and texture (Serafini, 2011).

For younger children, use Denise Fleming's *In the Tall, Tall Grass* (1991) and *Beetle Bop* (2007) to show how authors, illustrators, and publishers use font, book shape, and word placement on the page to help create stories. Older students can examine books from a particular era to understand how illustrators must study the time period in order to get all the details within the illustrations correct. Good books for this technique include *Goin' Places* (McKissack, 2001), *Freedom Summer* (Wiles, 2005), and *The Other Side* (Woodson, 2001). All of these take place before or during the civil rights movement. Also keep a stack of Caldecott Medal–winning and honor books on hand, which recognize picture book illustrators. A list of these books can be found at www.ala.org/alsc/awardsgrants/bookmedia/caldecottmedal/caldecotthonors/caldecottmedal. See Appendix D.20 for questions to use in discussing historical picture books.

COMPREHENSION OF NARRATIVE TEXT AND TECHNOLOGY

E books have features that allow readers to "manipulate font size, dictionary usage, text-to-speech features, and note-taking" (Thoermer & Williams, 2012, p. 441), which can motivate students to read. Allington (2013) found that these text features increased students' fluency and comprehension. Doty, Popplewell, and Byers (2001) found that students who read interactive ebooks "obtained significantly higher scores than students who read the print version of the storybooks" (p. 3). Interactive ebooks for younger children allow them to click on various objects to make characters to talk and move.

Select ebooks carefully. Some are so entertaining that students may become overly involved with the animation and may not follow the story line. Other ebooks are not engaging, and students will lose interest. When selecting ebooks, make sure the book aids student learning, particularly for struggling readers and English learners. Quality ebooks scaffold students by providing them the opportunity "to master tasks that they would not be able to accomplish independently" (Shamir & Korat, 2006, p. 2). A good ebook allows students to build on their present knowledge through active involvement with the story. Scaffolding is accomplished if the ebook both provides narration and permits students to turn off the narration, as well as when it pronounces unknown words and gives definitions when students click on the words. Ebooks help students build knowledge by permitting them to click on pictures to demonstrate an action or a character's mood and when they engage users in open-ended activities. The narrative ebook form in Appendix D.22 will help you evaluate particular features of ebooks. Shamir and Korat (2006) suggest a score of 69 out of 92, or 75 percent, makes an ebook acceptable.

The following sites offer free e-texts. Some of them feature e-texts with digitized speech. Others allow students to click on an unfamiliar word and hear its pronunciation and definition. Still other sites are text only.

- **www.wegivebooks.org** This free site, established by Penguin, offers many titles, and each time the student completes a text, they get to choose a charity organization and the foundation donates a book to that organization.
- **http://kids.nypl.org** Access to any book in the library for those with a New York City Public Library card.
- **www.starfall.com** Leveled books for students that allow readers to click on unfamiliar words and hear the correct pronunciation.
- **www.brainpop.com** Teaches students how dialogue is written in novels, comics, and movie and TV scripts.
- **www.mightybook.com** Over 800 animated stories and songs for students to read.
- **www.roythezebra.com** A reading website that can be used on a whiteboard with the class.
- **http://bygosh.com/childrensclassics.htm** Includes many favorite classics such as *Peter Rabbit* and *Alice in Wonderland,* with first edition illustrations.

As stated earlier, the ReadWriteThink.org site, created and maintained by the International Literacy Association and the National Council of Teachers of English, includes many wonderful literacy activities for students of all ages. One activity that encourages students to consider multiple perspectives of a story is "Fractured Fairy Tales," in which students create an alternate version of a popular fairy tale. Teachers may complete this activity with struggling readers to help develop their critical thinking skills, or small groups of students can create a fairy tale and then share it with the class.

If a school has extra funds, e-readers or tablet computers are great for expanding classroom libraries. Books purchased online for these devices may be less expensive than the printed copies.

Apps: Comprehending Narrative Texts

Professor Garfield Fact or Opinion (Free, Grades K–2). This app helps students distinguish between facts and opinions, particularly in regard to the online sources. Garfield's friend Nermal receives an "F" on his report for using opinions instead of facts, and "Professor G." helps explain the difference between fact and opinion, how to read with a questioning mind, and how a fact can be verified. This app offers a comic book style story mode as well as a game mode to test the skills learned from the app. Developed by the Virginia Department of Education.

Minimod Fact or Opinion Lite ($3.99, Grades 2–5). This app helps students learn to distinguish between fact and opinion. After reading passages aligned with the CCSS, students answer questions based on the passages. When students answer successfully, they place a marker on a bingo-like board. The goal is to get five marks in a row. Students can play in practice mode or in game mode against the computer.

Minimod Reading For Details Lite ($3.99, Grades 2–6). This app helps students build detail oriented reading skills. After reading a short passage about an inventor or invention, students are asked a series of questions based on the who, what, where, when, and why of the passage. When students answer successfully, they place a marker on a bingo-like board. The goal is to get five marks in a row. Students can play in practice mode or in game mode against the computer.

Alice for the iPad ($8.99, Grades 2–8). This digital version of the classic book *Alice's Adventures in Wonderland,* by Lewis Carroll, offers both an abridged and a full version. The app has been praised for its vivid and animated content, and students are encouraged to read the story and explore illustrations and animations that bring it to life.

Question Builder ($5.99, Grades K–5). This app teaches students how to answer abstract questions based on inference. When given a question and a related picture, students must select from a list of choices regarding what is happening in the picture. The app uses optional audio clips for questions and answers to reinforce concepts.

Aesop's Quest ($0.99, Grades 2–6). In this app, based on Aesop's Fables, students must remember a variety of story elements in order to progress. At the end of each story segment, students are asked questions ranging from story details and sequence to analogies and figurative language, based on their grade level. When successful, students are rewarded with pieces to a puzzle. Once the story and puzzle are complete, the student moves on to the next story. Developed in association with the Virginia Department of Education.

(Visit www.readingrockets.org/teaching/reading101/comprehension/literacyapps_comprehension/ for more information about additional comprehension apps.)

CONCLUDING THOUGHTS

Comprehension of narrative text is a skill needed by students in all grades. Most students are able to achieve comprehension by listening to and reading stories written at their instructional level. However, some students struggle with narrative comprehension.

After reviewing your students' standardized test scores, you will likely notice those who struggle with comprehension. You can administer a number of different informal reading inventories to help you understand the causes of each student's struggle. After determining the strengths and weaknesses of a student, choose from a number of strategies to engage him in authentic reading and writing tasks. You can also engage students in higher-level thinking and reading skills as you guide them through various critical thinking activities.

reflective learning

CRITICAL LITERACY. Ms. Williams teaches fifth grade in a small rural town with a student population that is 99 percent Caucasian and one percent African American. She has only two African American students in her class. This is her first year at this school, but she previously taught for five years in a diverse urban school. She always taught a unit on the Newbery winner Christopher Paul Curtis in her previous school and wants to do so again. Because she has heard some racial comments around the small town, she thinks this will be a great unit to introduce her students to the inequalities that many Americans endure, but she does not know how to approach the subject. She does not want to be didactic, and she really wants her students to think for themselves about the injustices that African Americans continue to suffer. When she introduces Christopher Paul Curtis, no one has read any of his books or heard of him.

questions

1. Considering the students and their parents may have some racial prejudices, would you advise Ms. Williams to teach this unit? Give reasons for your stance.
2. Assume she does teach the unit. What activities would you suggest Ms. Williams use to meet her goals of avoiding didacticism and having her students discover for themselves the injustices perpetrated upon African Americans throughout history?
3. What opening activity would you suggest Ms. Williams use to motivate students to read Curtis's books?
4. Which of Curtis's novels do you think Ms. Williams should assign? Why?
5. What other books on the same topic might you suggest Ms. Williams use with this unit? Why would these books be good for fifth graders?

9 Comprehension of Informational Text

A book is the most effective weapon against intolerance and ignorance.

LYNDON B. JOHNSON

scenario

ason is a fourth-grade student in Mr. Weatherspoon's class. Mr. Weatherspoon is concerned about Jason's comprehension of informational text. When the class discusses stories, Jason contributes many ideas; however, when the class discusses informational text, Jason remains silent. During independent reading time, Mr. Weatherspoon asks Jason to come to the reading table to read orally the following short passage taken from *Owls* (Morgan, 2006).

Owls Under Threat

All around the world, owls are under threat. The main cause is the destruction of their habitat, as forests are cleared for timber or new farmland.

Many owls are poisoned by chemicals that farmers use to protect their crops. When the owls eat rats, mice, and other animals that have been killed by pesticides, they too become poisoned and die. Owls are also under threat because some people steal owls' eggs, even though it is illegal to do this in many countries This means the eggs never hatch and the owl population declines. (p. 28)

During the reading, Jason struggles only with the word *pesticides*. He reads the rest of the passage fluently, including the title. Afterward, he and Mr. Weatherspoon have the following conversation:

Mr. Weatherspoon: Jason, what is the main idea of the passage?

Jason: Owls.

Mr. Weatherspoon: Any particular aspect of owls?

Jason: Pesticides kill them.

Mr. Weatherspoon: Are there any other reasons for owls being under threat?

Jason: I'm not sure.

From this short discussion, Mr. Weatherspoon realizes that Jason does not get the main idea of this short passage, which is that owls are under threat for various reasons.

As you read this chapter, consider the following questions.

guiding questions

1. What possible reasons would cause Jason's inability to give the main idea of the short passage?

2. Why is it important for Mr. Weatherspoon to work with Jason so he can comprehend informational texts?

3. What specific strategies would you recommend Mr. Weatherspoon use to help Jason understand the main idea of the passage and list the various threats to owls?

introduction

You may have heard of the "fourth-grade slump." This is the year the students' undeveloped vocabulary, weak comprehension skills, and lack of motivation begin to affect content-area reading (RAND Reading Study Group, 2002). Many teachers in grades 1 through 3 tend to use narrative texts instead of informational texts to help students develop such reading skills as decoding, word recognition, and vocabulary (Malock & Horsey, 2013). Then in fourth grade when students are expected to read to learn new concepts, they, like Jason, are unfamiliar with the organizational structure of informational text and may lack fundamental skills needed to read and comprehend more complex content area texts. Reading becomes a difficult task and they enter a "reading slump" as their underdeveloped skills leave them ill-prepared to learn dense new content material. For these students to be successful, they must continue to learn reading strategies that help them with decoding, vocabulary, and other skills as their teachers motivate and engage them in content reading (Duke, 2003; Malock & Horsey, 2013).

Young readers who have only had stories read to them may find informational text confusing because there are no characters, setting, or a plot. However, kindergarteners can comprehend informational text if they are taught strategies such as connecting prior knowledge to new information, predicting, visualizing, inferring, and asking questions (Gregory & Cahill, 2010). Students also need strategies to understand the visuals such as illustrations, diagrams, charts, and maps (McTigue & Flowers, 2011). To comprehend informational text students must also be able to understand technical terms and ask *how* and *why* (Stricklin, 2011).

Beginning in kindergarten, teachers can motivate students by providing an abundance of interesting informational texts at various reading levels, allowing struggling readers to learn content while reading texts at their independent reading level. When reading informational books at their appropriate reading level, students expend their energy learning the content instead of decoding words. Malock and Horsey (2013) posit that young students who are curious about the world will be motivated to read informational text if teachers encourage them to collaborate as they seek answers on topics that interest them. After students have read various books about the same topic, teachers can encourage them to collaborate and learn from one another.

Fortunately, many teachers supplement an assigned textbook with informational trade books and online reading. Both can be more engaging and also more challenging than textbooks. They are engaging because they provide detailed information about a topic and use photographs or detailed illustrations to explain it. They are more challenging for a number of reasons. First, trade books often include excerpts from primary sources, such as personal letters, newspaper articles, and diaries. Poor comprehenders find these primary sources challenging because they frequently contain unfamiliar words and writing styles. Second, trade books and online reading can be challenging because they may present conflicting information, forcing students to evaluate the writers' credentials. Third, the diagrams, flowcharts, and other graphics may be confusing to students because they are abstract (McTigue & Flowers, 2011), and the hyperlinks readers encounter may distract them from their primary task. Finally, when readers gather information from multiple sources, they must synthesize it (Afflerbach & VanSledright, 2001; Malock & Horsey, 2013).

READING INFORMATIONAL TEXTS AND THE CCSS

When the NGACBP and CCSSO wrote the CCSS, their mission was to design standards that would be "robust and relevant to the real world, reflecting the knowledge and skills that our young people need for success in college and careers" (Common Core State Standards Initiative, Mission Statement, n.d.). These two groups understood the disconnect between the tasks high school students were required to perform in school and the requirements they would face when entering college or the workplace. Most college reading, for example, involves informational text—history, science, psychology, business, and so on.

One goal of the CCSS is that students in early grades be exposed to more informational texts. By fourth grade, 50 percent of students' reading should be informational text. By eighth grade, 55 percent of the students' reading should be informational texts, and by the twelfth grade 70 percent should be informational reading (National Assessment Governing Board, 2008). In order to meet this fourth-grade objective, teachers need to introduce students to informational text in kindergarten (Marinak & Gambrell, 2009).

Some teachers question whether kindergarteners like to read informational text. In a study of kindergarteners, Correia (2011) found her students usually chose nonfiction or informational text over fiction for their independent reading time. Duke (2003) found that even preschool children, when given the opportunity, enjoy informational texts. Mohr (2003) found that 89 percent of her first graders chose informational text over fiction, and Schiefele, Krapp, and Winteler (1992) found that young struggling readers prefer informational texts.

When young students are exposed to informational text, they gain world knowledge and a technical vocabulary. They also learn that the information conveyed by photographs, diagrams, and charts is as important as the text. When a teacher shares how to find particular information by using the table of contents and the index in informational texts with students, they learn that reading informational text is nonlinear (Duke, 2003). All of these skills align with the CCSS. As stated in Chapter 8, the CCSS provide Anchor Standards for Reading as well as grade level standards for Reading: Literature and Reading: Informational Text. Like the grade level standards for narrative text, the standards for informational text encompass four areas: key ideas and details, craft and structure, integration of knowledge and ideas, and range of reading and level of text complexity. For a comparison of Reading: Informational Text standards in the range of reading and level of text complexity for a few grade levels, see Figure 9.1.

To view the 10 standards in the CCRA reading strand as well as the grade level standards, visit www.corestandards.org/ELA-Literacy/. Additional discussion of the reading standards for informational text is threaded throughout this chapter.

figure 9.1

Comparison of the CCSS ELA Reading: Informational Text Range of Reading and Level of Text Complexity Standards for Grades K, 3, and 6.

KINDERGARTEN

CCSS.ELA-Literacy.RI.K.10 Actively engage in group reading activities with purpose and understanding.

THIRD GRADE

CCSS.ELA-Literacy.RI.3.10 By the end of the year, read and comprehend informational texts, including history/social studies, science, and technical texts, at the high end of the grades 2–3 text complexity band independently and proficiently.

SIXTH GRADE

CCSS.ELA-Literacy.RI.6.10 By the end of the year, read and comprehend literary nonfiction in the grades 6–8 text complexity band proficiently, with scaffolding as needed at the high end of the range.

Source: National Governors Association Center for Best Practices (NGACBP) & Council of Chief State School Officers (CCSSO) (2010). English Language Arts Standards, Reading: Informational Text, Kindergarten, Grades 3 and 6. Washington, DC: NGACBP, CCSSO, pp. 13–14, 38–39.

HELPING STUDENTS COMPREHEND INFORMATIONAL TEXTS

What are teachers' responsibilities in helping students comprehend informational text so that by the end of each grade they "[r]ead and comprehend complex . . . informational texts independently and proficiently" (NGACBP & CCSSO, CCRA for Reading, 2010, p. 10)? Many of the responsibilities are the same as those required when helping students comprehend narrative texts. First, teachers must approach the text with the same enthusiasm as they approach a favorite story or novel. They must select high quality informational text on topics that interest students. When discussing the texts, teachers should permit students to ask questions and discuss any new concepts that the author introduces. Finally, teachers must provide many informational texts at different reading levels in their classroom library so students can read them during independent time.

Other responsibilities teachers have in helping their students read informational text are specific to this type of text. Teachers should demonstrate how to use the table of contents and index to find information about a particular aspect of the main topic and tell students that it is all right to read only that section of the book. They must convey the concept that informational books do not need to be read in a linear fashion. When studying a unit, in addition to using the textbook, teachers should introduce trade books on that topic from their classroom library, the school library, and the community library and display them in a special area of the classroom so students can readily use them. To supplement these texts, teachers should bookmark several safe and appropriate websites on the topic for student use. Readings from newspapers and magazines—either print or online—can augment students' understanding of how these texts are structured. If information conflicts between the various texts, teachers can demonstrate how to access a third or even a fourth text to determine which is correct.

The following sections suggest additional ways teachers can help students comprehend informational text.

Teach Strategies Specific to Comprehending Informational Text

Reading informational texts requires more than decoding skills and literal comprehension. Using a variety of informational text materials requires students to (1) synthesize information, (2) analyze authors' credentials, and (3) apply critical thinking skills when confronted with conflicting information. Struggling readers are often not expected to use these higher-level thinking skills. Too often they are asked to perform only lower-level thinking tasks because teachers are convinced they are incapable of higher-level thinking. Yet this is not true; struggling readers need only the opportunity to develop these skills. One way to help them develop is to teach them specific strategies that researchers have found are used by proficient readers when reading informational texts. These strategies are

- asking questions,
- inferring by connecting new information with background knowledge,
- synthesizing information from the beginning of passage to the end of the passage,
- synthesizing information from multiple sources,
- using one's schema to make sense of the information,
- visualizing the information, rereading information when confused,
- developing an awareness of the important information,
- checking the credentials of the author or organization,
- reading and studying visuals (e.g. photographs, diagrams, charts, maps, and so on),

- summarizing the information, understanding the perspective of author, and

- understanding one's personal perspective. (Harvey & Goudvis, 2013; Hollenbeck & Saternus, 2013)

Harvey & Goudvis (2013) propose that comprehension peaks when students actively use the knowledge gained from reading, such as when they use it to make presentations or use it in their daily lives. For example, Carrie, a fourth grade student, reads an article about toxic waste in rivers and lakes that is harmful to fish. She loves to eat fish, especially the fish her grandfather catches in a nearby lake. This first passage prompts her to find more information on the Internet about toxic waste in lakes. She finds a second article that highlights information on the types of water pollution and a third one that specifically explains how debris in lakes kill fish. During her multimodal presentation, Carrie not only presents the facts about water pollution, she also encourages her classmates not to throw any type of debris in lakes, rivers, and oceans. Teachers can encourage all students, like Carrie, to find more than one passage about a topic that interests them, critically read each one, and then synthesize the information in a presentation to their classmates. If students find conflicting information, teachers should guide them into checking the credentials of the author or organization.

Help Students Understand an Author's Use of Technical Words and Word Choice

When new technical or domain-specific terms are encountered, stop and explain how the author gives the definition, whether it is in a phrase, parentheses, a box, an illustration, etc. Encourage students to pronounce the word; if students cannot pronounce technical terms they will not use them when discussing the topic. If necessary, create a graphic organizer that helps students understand how technical concepts are related. Also make sure students understand terms that are academic but not domain-specific, such as *analyze, synthesize, explain, summarize, evaluate,* and *cite evidence.*

In discussing a text's vocabulary, teachers can show how the author uses words to shape the meaning of the text. They can also discuss the author's point of view and how she may use her point of view to sway readers' opinions. See the box on p. 216, which offers short passages from Dorothy Hinshaw Patent's (2002) *The Lewis and Clark Trail: Then and Now* and a question that Mr. Bradley, a middle-school teacher, poses to encourage his students to explore and understand how authors use words to convey a point of view.

Help Students Understand Diagrams and Graphics in Informational Text

Many teachers believe graphics help students understand the concepts explained in texts. This is true if the graphics are not complex. When viewing graphics, students must (1) determine the order in which the graphics must be studied; (2) decipher the pertinent from the superfluous; (3) decide how the information and text are related; and (4) integrate the information from the graphics with the information presented in the text (Hannus & Hyona, 1999). Since graphics in informational text can be complex, students benefit from explicit instruction about how to interpret them. McTigue and Flowers (2011) suggest the following steps:

1. Talk through the graphics, explaining the order, for example, in which one reads flowcharts.

2. Do a think-aloud when reading text and graphics so students understand how to connect the information from the two sources.

3. Assess understanding of a graphic by asking students to explain it. During the explanation, redirect students' thinking, if necessary, by asking specific questions.

4. Provide multiple different visual representations (e.g. illustrations, photographs, diagrams, charts, flowcharts, and so on) of a particular concept and have students explain similarities and differences among the representations. Ask the evaluative question, "Which representation do you think better explains the concept and why?"

5. Have students explain what they have learned about the concept and have them cite evidence from the text and visuals.

6. Assess students' understanding by asking them to draw their own visual of a concept represented in a graphic so classmates will be able to understand it.

McTigue and Flowers (2011) report that on "the U.S. state science tests for grades 4–8, more than half of the questions included graphical representation and 80% of those graphics contained essential information" (p. 579). Besides helping students understand the organizational structure of informational texts, teachers must help them comprehend the visuals found in informational texts, especially science textbooks.

Model Close Reading of Complex Texts

Previous chapters discussed *close reading* and *complexity of text,* two themes emphasized by the CCSS and associated with getting students ready for postsecondary reading materials. As explained in Chapter

INSIDE THE CLASSROOM

Discussing How an Author's Word Choice Shapes Meaning

In preparation for a discussion on author word choice, Mr. Bradley and his class read together a two-page excerpt from *The Lewis and Clark Trail: Then and Now* (Patent, 2002). Then Mr. Bradley chooses the following two short excerpts for the purpose of demonstrating how students need to read carefully to determine how an author uses words to shape the meaning or establish the tone of a passage, an emphasis of the CCSS. For example, ELA Reading: Informational Text standard 4 for grade 7 requires that students "Determine the meaning of words and phrases as they are used in a text, including figurative, connotative, and technical meanings: analyze the impact of a specific word choice on meaning and tone" (NGACBP & CCSSO, 2010, Reading: Informational Text, Grade 7, p. 39).

> Not far upriver the expedition came upon an island densely packed with white pelicans. The birds were gathered together while they molted. . . . It was these molted feathers that had formed the three-mile-long blanket. . . . The birds were so tightly packed, however, that a random shot killed one. Even though much of the land along the lower Missouri River today is prone to flooding and therefore sparsely populated, white pelicans have become a rare sight in the area. (p. 22)

> The buffalo was the basis of the Plains Indian cultures. The Indians used every part of the animals— for food, tools, clothing, and tepee construction . . . [until] commercial hunters slaughtered all the buffalo they could find, almost wiping them out. (p. 23)

Mr. Bradley: What is the author trying to tell the reader?

Juan: That once there were many white pelicans and buffalo.

Grace: I think that the one shot was heard round the world.

Damon: Grace, are you saying that that first shot was the beginning of killing off all the pelicans?

Grace: Yeah, I'm sure that there were no laws protecting the pelicans.

Juan: I also think the author wants us to understand that the Indians used all parts of the buffalo when they killed them because it says here that "Indians use every part of the animal—for food, tools, clothing, and tepee construction."

Grace: I think when the author used the word *slaughter,* she was trying to get the reader to take her side. *Slaughtered* has the connotation that it was ruthless and unnecessary.

Damon: I agree with you, Grace. I also think when the author described the pelicans as a three-mile-long blanket that it was a pretty sight, not something ugly. To me a blanket is a positive thing.

Juan: I think the author is letting us know that the Lewis and Clark expedition did not have all positive results.

Mr. Bradley: Great discussion! I like all your insights. Now as you continue to read the next section of the book, try to find other words and phrases that the author uses to persuade you to take her point of view.

Damon: The author is pretty subtle. I like that.

Mr. Bradley believes in small group discussion so all students' voices can be heard. Once he asked the opening question, he remained silent because he knew the students were getting the point he wanted to teach. Do you think Mr. Bradley's approach was a good one? If not, how could he have improved the way students explored how the author used words and phrases to persuade the reader?

2, the level of difficulty for text needs to increase in order for students to be ready for this. As you know, college students are required to read and comprehend vast amounts of text on concepts that may be new to them. The groups that drafted the CCSS understood this demand, and thus created standards requiring that students throughout the primary and secondary grades be able to read and comprehend complex literary and informational texts (NGACBP & CCSSO, CCRA for Reading, 2010). An important part of this standard is that students must read complex information books independently and proficiently. Close reading of complex texts should be modeled in order for students to learn to do it automatically when they read independently.

Consider the following short passage from *Mercury and Venus: Become a Space Explorer* (Mist, 2008), which is rated as appropriate for fourth graders.

> Venus is the second planet from the Sun. It orbits the Sun between Mercury and Earth. Venus is about the same size as Earth, but looks very different. Like Mercury it is a planet without a moon. (p. 14)

Now read the following box, which shows how Mr. Weatherspoon helped his students comprehend this complex text.

INSIDE THE CLASSROOM   Comprehending Complex Text

Mr. Weatherspoon and his students are engaged in a unit on planets, and he plans to use the passage above to model how to do a close reading. He considers all the important information that his students will need to process in this short passage: the position of Venus in relationship to the Sun, Mercury, and Earth. They must understand the meaning of *orbits*. They must remember what they read previously about the size of Earth, and they must infer how Venus could possibly look different from Earth. The illustrations on the page include one of Venus and another of a spinning sphere. He also considers the students' past experiences with informational text on the planets to determine how much additional discussion is needed to comprehend the text.

Then after he and his students have read the passage, he begins a discussion of the text by asking students if there is any information on previous pages that will help them understand the position of Venus in relationship to the Sun, Mercury, and Earth. If students cannot find the page, he directs them to turn back to page 5 to view the illustration that shows the relationship between the planets' positions. Next, Mr. Weatherspoon asks his students what *orbit* means. If they cannot remember, he again refers them back to page 4, which explains the word's meaning.

Because this book contains no information about Earth, Mr. Weatherspoon directs his students to a different book in this series. He reads the pages from the book that describes the size and other features of Earth, and then redirects students' attention back to the present book. Next, he reads the inserted the Star Fact from the book and the insert that explains how to find Venus in the night and morning skies.

As you can see, close reading of a text involves much more than correctly reading the words on the page. Mr. Weatherspoon's students need to be able connect previously read pages with the present page and also synthesize information from a different text with information about the Earth in their current reading. Mr. Weatherspoon makes sure his students understand the technical term *orbit*.

Since this is scientific information, Mr. Weatherspoon also wants his students to consider whether it is accurate. One way he has his students check the trustworthiness of the information is to evaluate the credentials of the author. On the book's copyright page are photograph credits from NASA and Johns Hopkins University Applied Physics Laboratory/Carnegie Institute of Washington. The book provides no credits for the author, Rosalind Mist, but does mention the person with whom she consulted. Mr. Weatherspoon then discusses all this information with students and lets them decide if the author is credible. Another way his students check for the accuracy of the information is to consult another text about Venus. If students find conflicting information between the two texts, Mr. Weatherspoon will demonstrate how they can read the third and even the fourth text to see which information is correct.

Teach the Skills Needed to Navigate the New Literacies

In recent years, the term *new literacies* has been widely discussed in educational journals. As mentioned in Chapter 1, the new literacies are "unique cognitive processes required to communicate with information communication technologies (ICT)" (Karchmer-Klein & Shinas, 2012, p. 289). One basic difference between the reading and writing skills needed for traditional texts and those needed for new literacies is that students use inquiry-based learning when using ICT; this means that students must proactively ask questions and seek answers. This type of learning requires certain skills. Some of the skills needed to navigate ICT are

1. knowing how to effectively use search engines,

2. understanding nonlinear text,

3. evaluating credentials of all links,

4. determining important material and ignoring unimportant information,

5. inferring meaning,

6. communicating through blogs, wikis, instant messaging, and other forms of electronic text,

7. understanding social responsibilities when participating in online communities, and

8. synthesizing information from multiple sources (Karchmer-Klein & Shinas, 2012).

FACTORS AFFECTING THE COMPREHENSION PROCESS

Recall from Chapter 2 that factors from three distinct sources affect the comprehension process of informational text. These sources are (1) factors within the reader, (2) factors within the reader's environment, and (3) factors within the text. Understanding the complexity of these factors gives teachers a better understanding of why some readers may struggle with reading in general and informational text in particular.

Language Arts Teachers as Advocates

As a teacher, you will be an advocate for strong literacy programs. Oftentimes teachers whose students have strong reading scores are asked to share some strategies with their team or colleagues. Language arts teachers should volunteer to conduct informal (or formal) seminars on particular strategies. Only one or two helpful strategies should be shared and modeled during one seminar; if teachers are overwhelmed with information they will not want to attend future seminars. During these seminars, language arts teachers can share the various graphic organizers described later in this chapter. Other times, they can share some of the vocabulary building strategies shared in Chapter 7. If one's schedule permits, a language arts teacher in the middle school can ask social studies teachers what units they are teaching. He can then find historical fiction that complements the unit and have students in his language arts class read the texts. The CCSS require that middle-school teachers collaborate so students reach all standards for each grade level.

Factors Within the Reader

Basic reading skills are necessary to comprehend all types of informational text. These basic skills include

* knowledge of organizational patterns in expository text.
* adequate background knowledge of the topic being read.
* knowledge of domain-specific terms associated with the topic as well as academic terms.
* ability to read diagrams, flowcharts, and other graphics so they comprehend the information given in each graphic.
* ability to analyze the author's purpose and credentials.
* ability to synthesize similar information from various sources.

Other factors that affect a reader's ability to comprehend informational text are her prior knowledge and experiences and her personal attitudes and interests.

Prior knowledge and experience

Prior knowledge includes all of life's experiences—walks with adults through woods and parks or trips to a zoo, a museum, or the ocean. All experiences that take students out of their immediate surroundings help them develop a broader view of the world in which they live. Through many such experiences, they are introduced to new concepts in a natural setting. This knowledge aids reading comprehension (August & Shanahan, 2006; Richek, 2005; Richardson & Morgan, 2011). Some students enter school never having left their local community. Their background knowledge gained through firsthand experience is limited. Consider the contrast between Sally, who has never been outside her community, and George, who has traveled with his family to a wide variety of places in his home state, across the United States, and to other countries. These trips have afforded George many different firsthand experiences, all of which have enriched his vocabulary and knowledge of the world.

When George and Sally's fifth-grade social studies class studies the Middle Ages, George has an advantage over Sally and the other students. The teacher, Mr. Black, asks his students what a moat is. Sally, who knows about castles from fairy tales featuring queens, kings, princes, and princesses, predicts that a moat is someone who works for the royal family. However, George has visited castles and knows that the moat is the water—sometimes natural, sometimes man-made—that surrounds the castle and protects its inhabitants from outside invaders. George is able to picture new information about the Middle Ages more readily than the other students. George's interest in the Middle Ages is also likely greater than the other students' because of his experiences.

Because prior knowledge is based on all of one's personal experiences, it includes one's experience with informational text. Students who have had a parent or other adult read and discuss informational texts with them understand that not all books tell a story. They understand that some texts teach them about the world or provide important information for everyday use. When children are read concept books, they are introduced to technical vocabulary that is unique to the particular topic. Obviously, these children have an advantage over their peers who have never had informational texts read to them. Richardson and Morgan (2011) suggest that students with a broad background and understanding of the world will have an easier time comprehending texts than students with a more limited background.

Interests and attitudes

A positive attitude toward learning and reading, which often originates in the home, is key to being a successful lifelong learner. If students are interested in snakes and bugs, the teacher should find texts on those topics and read them with the students. Teachers in the primary grades need to expose their students to informational text just as they expose them to fiction. As mentioned earlier, many struggling readers prefer reading materials from which they learn new concepts. Teachers can encourage informational reading by eliciting students' interests through discussions of what they do in their spare time and what they would like to do when they become adults. Teachers may want to expose their students to *Time for Kids*, a kid-friendly version of *Time* magazine that features stories on current topics. Reading this magazine will draw students' attention current events that affect them.

Viewing videos on YouTube and on sites such as National Geographic Kids (http://kids.nationalgeographic.com) can also pique students' interest in reading an informational book on a particular topic. Once teachers detect a student's interest in a particular topic, they can help him select books from the classroom and school libraries. The Assessment section of this chapter discusses how to assess reader interests, and Appendix C.42 contains an interest inventory that will aid you in learning more about your students' interests.

Many factors affect readers' comprehension of informational texts. Figure 9.2 lists some characteristics of skilled and unskilled expository readers.

Factors Within the Reader's Environment

Home

Of the three environments most students inhabit—home, community, and school—the home most affects reading comprehension and provides the foundation upon which attitudes toward reading are built. Richardson and Morgan (2011) argue that students who are good comprehenders have parents who read and discuss many different types of texts with their students, and have books, magazines, and other informational materials available in their home. The parents also view and discuss videos, articles on the Internet, and educational TV programs with their children. They make good use of the community's library by checking out informational videos and trade books, and by using the Internet in the library if they do not have access at

---

figure **9.2**   Characteristics of skilled and unskilled readers of informational texts.

SKILLED READERS

1. Know the purpose for reading (e.g., to find comparisons, understand details).
2. Know whether their purpose for reading was fulfilled.
3. Recognize a large bank of words automatically.
4. Analyze technical words with ease.
5. Possess background knowledge of many topics and make use of it when reading.
6. Have an advanced vocabulary about many topics.
7. Make inferences about information in the passage.
8. Use fix-up strategies when comprehension breaks down.
9. Are flexible in the use of strategies.
10. Paint mental pictures of the topic.
11. Recognize the organizational structure of text (e.g., cause/effect, comparison/contract, sequence, definition).
12. Build relationships between larger units of text (e.g., relate information among chapters or books).
13. Know where to go for more information if passage is not clear (e.g., go to Internet, databases, or other books).
14. Use appropriate graphic organizers to summarize and to remember text.

UNSKILLED READERS

1. Are often poor decoders.
2. Give up when the passage is not clear.
3. Lack word analysis skills.
4. Have limited background knowledge.
5. Do not relate limited background knowledge to the passage.
6. Have limited vocabulary.
7. Cannot monitor comprehension.
8. Cannot make inferences.
9. Do not create mental pictures of the passage's topic.
10. Do not recognize the organizational structure of text.
11. Do not build relationships between larger units of text.
12. Have poor summarizing skills.
13. Do not acquire strategic strategies; must be taught how, when, and where to consistently use appropriate comprehension strategies.

Sources: Anders & Lloyd (1996); Bos & Vaughn (2011); Gipe (2013); Kletzien (1991); Oakhill & Patel (1991); Richardson, Morgan, & Fleener (2011); Swanson & De La Paz (1998); Symons & Pressley (1993); Winn, Graham, & Prock (1993).

home. Many parents model the love of learning new things by reading, viewing, and discussing complicated ideas and facts with their children; these children have a great source of prior knowledge from which to draw when reading informational texts.

Community

The second environment that affects reading comprehension is that of the community. Consider two fictional communities with contrasting financial resources—Educationwise and Noread. The leaders of the little town of Educationwise love to learn new things and want their young people to learn about the world in which they live. After all, their wheat crops are exported to all parts of the world. Educationwise's community library is a great source of information because the community leaders understand the importance of providing funds for the library. This library has a vast selection of books, ebooks, audiobooks, DVDs, and online resources. Its many computers offer free access to the Internet. This library also has many Saturday and after-school programs, such as story time, and focused studies on particular topics, authors, and genres. The Educationwise Public Library also provides classes that teach a range of crafts and skills from different cultures. The library staff welcomes children and young adults and encourages them to hang out in the library. The community also provides summer day camps and free art and musical events in the local parks. The young people from Educationwise have access to a great library and many community programs, thus affording them many opportunities to develop a rich vocabulary and background knowledge on many topics.

Noread is in the same state as Educationwise. Noread has town leaders who do not see the importance of widening their children's horizons; thus, even when funding is available they choose to allocate it elsewhere. This town's library is in a small, dilapidated building and houses outdated books. It has no computers or DVDs. It provides no Saturday or after-school programs. The community also has no summer day camps for its children to explore nature. In fact, it does nothing to entice young people to come and explore its paltry resources. The children and young adults from Noread have few opportunities for outside enrichment. Its leaders do not understand how this lack of resources affects young people's reading, their academic achievement, and success in life.

A community can provide many resources that support the public schools and students' learning. All of these resources enrich background knowledge and encourage them to read more about the topics that interest them.

School

The third influential student environment is the school, and the most important aspect of the school is the classroom. Furthermore, the most important aspect of the classroom is the teacher. A successful teacher is one who:

1. models a love of reading and learning new things.
2. expects all students to succeed.
3. accepts all students as they are and does not assign blame for a student's lack of skills.
4. encourages risk-taking.
5. asks higher-level thinking questions in addition to literal questions with correct answers.
6. uses a variety of activities to teach students how to read informational text (see the Intervention section of this chapter for example activities).
7. provides materials for all reading levels.
8. reads some of the same informational texts as well as fictional texts as the students.
9. bookmarks safe websites with information at appropriate reading levels on the classroom computers.
10. shares informational texts for students to read during independent reading times.

Effective, positive teachers provide a wide variety of learning materials on a wide variety of topics. Their classrooms contain programs and software that appeal to many interests and do more than simply enhance skills. Hands-on stations allow students to conduct experiments. Old appliances (with electrical cords cut off) are disassembled and reassembled so students can figure out for themselves how they work. These teachers understand that hands-on experiences enhance the background knowledge students use to comprehend informational texts. They also understand that many struggling readers first need hands-on experiences to entice them to read about the topic.

Factors Within the Text

Teachers now include more quality nonfiction trade books, computer programs, and online resources in their classrooms than in past decades. In 2006, the Cooperative Children's Book Center reported a 200 percent increase of published informational texts in the prior decade (Marinak & Gambrell, 2009).

The following sections examine the organizational structure of informational text and then discuss how to analyze informational trade and textbooks to select the best ones for your class.

ORGANIZATIONAL STRUCTURE OF INFORMATIONAL TEXT

Informational text may be challenging for some students who have little difficulty with narrative text because its organizational structure is different. When reading fictional stories, students become familiar with settings, characters, and plots, and focus on conflicts that need to be resolved. Informational texts omit many elements of fictional narratives, so students must develop a new schema to grasp how the information is organized. The CCRA for Reading require students to "analyze the structure of texts, including how specific sentences, paragraphs, and larger portions of the text (e.g. a section, chapter, scene, or stanza) relate to each other and the whole" (NGACBP & CCSSO, CCRA for Reading, 2010, p. 10). The eight commonly used organizational patterns in expository texts are chronology or sequence, description or enumeration, listing, classification or hierarchy, comparison/contrast, cause/effect, problem/solution, and persuasion.

Authors of informational text use key words for the various text structures. Knowing these key words can help students understand how the text is organized. Figure 9.3 lists words associated with various text structures. Graphic organizers also help students understand the organizational patterns in expository text. The Intervention section of this chapter contains an activity for creating graphic organizers and sample organizers for the various organizational patterns.

Persuasive Passages

Persuasive passages are different from other types of informational texts in that the authors' main goal is to persuade the readers or audience to agree with their point of view. Authors of persuasive texts follow a certain pattern and use these specific elements when attempting to persuade readers of their point of view:

- Establish facts that support their argument.
- Prioritize the facts in a sequence that best supports the argument, deciding if they can make a stronger statement by prioritizing facts from most important to least important or by building facts from least important to the most important.
- Give the sources for the facts. If the sources are unknown to readers, they will state the credits for each.
- Clarify the relevance of their topic to the audience. For example, if the topic is bullying, the author will explain why it is relevant to the readers.
- Acknowledge other point(s) of view and any possible "hot buttons" that trigger emotions, so the reader understands that the author is knowledgeable about the other point(s) of view. In some cases, the author may refute the opposing viewpoint.
- Give passionate concluding statements by choosing words that will persuade the audience to accept the author's argument.

figure 9.3   Key words associated with text structures.

DESCRIPTION (ENUMERATION)	TIME FRAME (CHRONOLOGY)	COMPARE/CONTRAST	CAUSE/EFFECT & PROBLEM/SOLUTION	PERSUASION/ ARGUMENT
to begin	on a specific (date)	however	because	consequently
first	not long after	but	since	specifically
secondly	now	as well as	therefore	first reason, second reason, etc.
next	as	on one hand/on the other hand	consequently	another reason why
then	before	not only/but also	as a result	next
finally	after	either/or	leads to	one last reason why
most important	when	while	nevertheless	finally
also	following	although	accordingly	therefore
in fact	soon	unless	if/then	because
for instance	later	similarly	thus	in the final analysis
for example	finally	yet	thereby	in conclusion
				you can see why

Sources: Neufeld, P. (Dec. 2005/Jan. 2006). Comprehension Instruction in Content Area Classes. *The Reading Teacher, 59*(4), 302–312. / Swartz, R. J., & Parks, S. (1994). *Basic transition words.* Retrieved from www.syracusecityschools.com/tfiles/folder717/persuasive_writing_transition_words.pdf. / NGACBP & CCSSO (2010). English Language Arts Standards, Writing, Grade 5, p. 20.

Teachers usually will need to point out to struggling readers how authors attempt to persuade them. As you recall from the discussion in Chapter 1 on critical literacy, teachers can guide students to consider the author's point of view and language in persuasive texts about a particular topic. You can also advise students to consider other possible points of view. For example, some authors attempt to change readers' thinking about environmental issues such as offshore oil drilling, logging, and protecting wildlife. To do this they will use vivid adverbs, adjectives, and other powerful words, or offer a personal assessment of the topic. Notice Todd Wilkinson's persuasive technique in *Bison for Kids* (1994). The underlined words are examples of subtle persuasion; the last sentence, however, is emphatic rather than subtle.

> What happened after that is a sad story. People killed millions of buffalo for food and hides. Settlers slaughtered them to make room on the Great Plains for cattle. One of the most famous bison hunters was William "Buffalo Bill" Cody, who delivered mail for the Pony Express and shot bison to feed railroad workers. He killed thousands of bison. As a result of the over hunting, only a few hundred wild buffalo were left in the United Stated at the end of the 1800s. Bison needed to be protected fast! (pp. 15–16, emphasis added)

Sometimes authors use more forceful techniques to persuade readers to accept their point of view. Point out these techniques to your students.

Propaganda is a persuasive technique that involves the distortion of facts or manipulation of readers. Propaganda is prevalent in advertisements, so smart readers understand these techniques. Listed below are seven propaganda techniques accompanied by brief descriptions.

- *Name calling*: denouncing one product or person to promote another.
- *Card stacking*: giving one side of the story or telling half-truths. Note: advertisements for prescription medications now are required to list negative side effects as well as benefits in order to combat this technique.
- *Plain folk*: using ordinary people to promote a product.
- *Glittering generalities*: stating a list of positive attributes without giving any specific details.
- *Testimonial*: using a popular person to promote a product that he or she uses.
- *Transfer*: using a popular person to promote a product that is not associated with his or her job or ability.
- *Bandwagon*: convincing consumers that "everyone is doing it, so you should too."

Teachers in upper elementary and middle school can use any campaign speech to illustrate how politicians convince voters why they should be elected. One source with famous speeches in www.americanrhetoric.com.

Chronology or Sequence

A text that presents information in a chronological or sequential pattern features events that happen in a particular order, and this order is important to understanding the information. In chronological texts, the information is often organized around dates. Usually the dates are explicitly stated, but sometimes the author gives only the number of years between events. With this type of text, students must make inferences to attach dates to the events. David Adler, in *A Picture Book of Benjamin Franklin* (1990), includes dates and phrases that represent the passage of time. Following are some examples:

> Benjamin Franklin was born in Boston, Massachusetts, on January 17, 1706.
> Benjamin began school when he was eight years old.
> When Benjamin was ten, he began to work in his father's soap-and-candle shop.
> When he was twelve, his father put Benjamin to work in a print shop. (unpaged)

From this information, the student can infer the following facts:

- 1706   Benjamin Franklin was born.
- 1714   He began school.
- 1716   He quit school and began working in soap-and-candle shop.
- 1718   He began working in a print shop.

Description or Enumeration

If the organizational structure of the text is description, the author explains an event, an object, or a phenomenon in detail so the reader can better understand it. Notice how Seymour Simon describes the sperm whale in *Whales* (1989):

> The sperm whale is the only giant among the toothed whales. It is the animal that comes to mind when most people think of a whale. A sperm whale has a huge, squarish head, small eyes, and a thin lower jaw. All the fist-sized teeth, about fifty of them, are in the lower jaw. The male grows to sixty feet long and weighs as much as fifty tons. The female is smaller, reaching only forty feet and weighing less than twenty tons. (unpaged)

Simon paints a picture with words, and it is the reader's responsibility to transform those words into a mental picture. In this example, the reader must draw a mental picture of a square head with a thin lower jaw and small eyes in order to understand what a sperm whale looks like. The reader also needs to picture teeth the size of human fists. Proficient readers will do this without assistance. They may use a specific strategy, such as slowing down or rereading the passage, in order to create the picture in their minds (Bos & Vaughn, 2011). Struggling readers often read the words without picturing these images. Teachers should assist them in painting these mental pictures. Strategies for this kind of visualization are discussed later in the chapter.

In the following example from Philip Steele's *I Wonder Why Castles Had Moats and Other Questions About Long Ago* (1994), the author paints a picture so that readers can imagine the events and images of a Japanese Noh play: "*Noh* are Japanese plays in which actors wear masks and move very slowly, telling story-poems through mime and dance" (p. 27).

As discussed earlier, background knowledge is very important for comprehension of informational texts. It is clear here that readers will benefit from background knowledge about mime and story-poems in attempting to learn about Noh plays. Writers who use description and enumeration expect readers to bring the background knowledge to the reading event, because it is cumbersome to explain every concept in detail. Teachers may need to demonstrate mime and read a story-poem in order for struggling readers to understand the author's description of Noh theater.

In enumeration, an author states a concept and then elaborates on it. In the text *Frogs* (1996), written for young readers, Carolyn MacLulich explains how a frog makes a croaking sound: "Male frogs make a croaking sound. They puff up the vocal sac under their chin, which makes the sound louder" (p. 13).

Texts for older readers have more detailed descriptions. Notice how Seymour Simon enumerates the process by which the mother whale feeds her calf:

> The mother squirts milk into the young calf's open mouth forty times a day. The milk is rich in fat and energy. Each feeding is very brief, because the baby must surface for air. But in a few seconds, the baby drinks two or three gallons of milk. In one day, a baby whale drinks more than 100 gallons of milk and may gain as much as 200 pounds. (unpaged)

Listing

In this third type of organizational structure, authors may merely list all of the things that fall into a particular category. In *Frogs* (1996), Carolyn MacLulich lists all of the things frogs eat: "Frogs eat insects, spiders and worms. Some frogs eat larger animals, such as lizards, mice or even other frogs" (p. 12).

In the emergent reader book *Who Lives in the Rainforest?* (1998), Susan Canizares lists the inhabitants of a rainforest. Each type of creature is pictured on its own page with a simple two-word phrase. The text begins with the question "Who lives in the rainforest?" The following are some of the answers to this question:

> Iguanas do.
>
> Snakes too.
>
> Jaguars do.
>
> Pumas too.

This simple list with the colorful photographs of each creature intrigues even the emergent reader to find more information about rainforest creatures.

Classification or Hierarchy

Scientific texts often use classification to show relationships among concepts. Notice how Mary Cerullo explains the categorical relationships among dolphins, whales, and humans in *Dolphins: What They Can Teach Us* (1999):

> Dolphins are small, toothed whales. They belong to the group known as cetaceans (from the Latin word *cetus,* meaning large sea animals), which includes all whales, dolphins, and porpoises . . . Dolphins and humans have a lot in common; we are both mammals. (pp. 4–5)

This text requires higher levels of thinking because readers need to see the main classification with the families under it. Struggling readers will need help to understand how whales, dolphins, porpoises, and humans are related to each other.

Comparison/Contrast

In a comparison/contrast text, authors explain a concept by showing how one event, subject, or object is similar to or different from another. Comparison/contrast helps readers better understand concepts when authors directly present the similarities and differences between the two items. Sandra Markle, in *Outside and Inside Sharks* (1996), explains how sharks differ from fish:

> Look at the reef shark and the soldier fish. They are both fish. They both need oxygen, a gas in air and water, to live. And they both have special body parts called gills that carry oxygen from the water into their bodies. But there are differences between sharks and other fish. A shark's gills are in separate pouches with slits opening to the inside and outside of its body. The soldier fish, and other fish like it, have gills grouped in one chamber. . . . A shark's tail usually has a top part that is longer than the bottom. Other fish usually have tails with two equal parts. But the biggest difference between sharks and other fish is on the inside. (p. 5)

Cause/Effect

Cause/effect passages are often found in science texts to explain what causes natural phenomena. For example, Jenny Wood, in *Caves: Facts and Stories and Activities* (1990), explains how caves form:

> The process of making a cave takes thousands of years. It starts when surface water trickles down through tiny cracks in the rock. The water contains a gas called carbon dioxide which is absorbed from the air and this forms a mild acid that eats away the limestone. As it travels underground, the water continues to eat away some of the rock, forming passages and caves. (p. 4)

In *Volcano: The Eruption and Healing of Mount St. Helens* (1986), Patricia Lauber explains what causes a volcano to erupt.

> Beneath the crust is a region called the mantle. It is made of rock that is very hot. Rock of the mantle can flow, like thick tar. The crust floats on the mantle. . . . The plates are in motion, moving a few inches each year. . . . There are places where plates pull away from each other. Here molten rock wells up and sometimes volcanoes erupt. (pp. 51–52)

Notice that in both of these passages, readers need to be able to mentally picture the action as it happens. Struggling readers who cannot do this will have great difficulty with cause/effect texts. These readers should be taught to recognize the signal words authors use to indicate relationships between causes and effects.

Problem/Solution

Another organizational structure commonly found in expository texts is problem/solution. Often the explanation of a problem will expand for a number of pages before the solution is stated. In *Children of the Dust Bowl: The True Story of the School at Weedpatch Camp* (1992), Jerry Stanley devotes the first chapter to naming all of the problems the Okies endured during the 1930s before he offers a possible solution to the Okies' problems—moving to California. With this text, it is useful for teachers and students to make a list of all the problems that Oklahoma faced during the 1930s. In this way, the students will better understand why much of the state's poorer population migrated to California. The text explores the following problems in detail:

- Small farms
- Great Depression
- No irrigation
- Low wheat prices
- No reservoirs or canals
- Dust storms
- No rain

- Bankruptcy
- Crops shriveled
- Mortgages foreclosed; evicted from homes

Finally, the text offers the solution many Oklahomans chose by describing how they loaded their possessions on trucks and moved to California, seeking a better life for their families.

Sequence for Teaching Expository Text Organizational Patterns

When introducing an informational text pattern to students, you can use the following sequence of instruction (adapted from Tompkins, 2002):

1. Introduce the organizational pattern (e.g., comparison/contrast or sequence) by explaining when and why writers choose this particular structure.
2. Point out the key words associated with the structure (e.g., *because, therefore, as a result, first, next, after that*) and share an example of text using these key words. (Refer to Figure 9.3.)
3. Model ways students can determine text structures when key words are not used (e.g., look at the table of contents and headings).
4. Introduce a graphic organizer for the pattern.
5. Read aloud a section of a book illustrating the text structure.
6. Ask students to listen for and identify the key words in the selection.
7. Using a whiteboard or projector, have the class complete a graphic organizer illustrating the pattern type.
8. Ask students to work in pairs to locate an example of the structure in other informational texts.
9. Have students identify the key words and create a graphic organizer for their informational text.

ANALYSIS OF INFORMATIONAL TEXTS

A great variety of nonfiction trade books are available for all reading levels. Teachers and publishers find that even young students enjoy learning about their world. When selecting nonfiction books for the classroom, review these lists of award-winning titles:

Orbis Pictus Award, www.ncte.org/awards/orbispictus

Sibert Medal, www.ala.org/awardsgrants/robert-f-sibert-informational-book-medal

Children's Choices, http://www.literacyworldwide.org/get-resources/reading-lists/childrens-choices-reading-list

When analyzing any type of informational text—trade books, textbooks, e-texts, or websites—consider a number of elements: visual appeal, text features, author's writing style, use of technical vocabulary, and assumptions about readers' background knowledge (Gill, 2009).

Visual Appeal

When examining a text or a website, do the same thing students do when they first look at a book—thumb or scroll through it to see if it looks interesting. Visual appeal is an important characteristic of informational texts; attractive books and websites entice students to read (Stephens, 2008; Gill, 2009). An appealing text has the following traits:

- Appropriate print size for grade level
- Generous margins and white space
- Attractive, up-to-date graphics and photographs that represent both genders and different ethnicities
- Charts that are easy to read
- Pages or screens with the appropriate amount of text with pictures, graphs, and so on (Those filled with text scare young readers!)
- Many subheadings so no passage is too long
- No more than 7 or 12 words per line so the readers' eyes do not make unnecessary movements
- Not too many different ideas on one page so readers are not overloaded with information

- Graphics are located near the corresponding text (Hindes, 2007)

Traditional Book Features

Good textbooks have specialized features that aid reader comprehension, and many trade books also have these features: a table of contents, a glossary, questions at the beginning and end of each chapter, and highlighted vocabulary words. Examine these features to see if they will be useful to readers.

The table of contents should give an overview of the text and depict the relationships among the various topics and the progression of one topic to the next. For example, a table of contents for a history book should indicate whether the text is organized chronologically or by topic. Figure 9.4 shows a table of contents for one chapter of a science textbook. Notice how the subheadings support the main topic of the chapter: Changes in the Earth's Surface. Also notice how each "Lesson" topic is presented in the form of a question. Good readers will infer from these questions that volcanoes, earthquakes, and wind cause changes in the Earth's surface. You may need to read a table of contents with your struggling readers so they learn how to make inferences about terms and headings. Asking the struggling student questions about these items also will activate his or her background knowledge.

figure 9.4   Sample table of contents.

Unit C   Earth Science

	SCIENCE AND TECHNOLOGY	C2
CHAPTER 1	**Changes in the Earth's Surface**	C4
EXPLORE ACTIVITY	**Exploring Rocks Formed from Molten Rock**	C6
READING FOR SCIENCE	**Identifying the Main Idea**	C7
LESSON 1	**How Do Volcanoes and Earthquakes Change the Earth?**	C8
LESSON 2	**What Landforms Are on the Earth's Surface?**	C14
INVESTIGATE ACTIVITY	**Making a Model of a Landform**	C18
LESSON 3	**How Do Water and Wind Change the Earth's Surface?**	C20
LESSON 4	**How Can Living Things Affect the Earth's Surface?**	C24
	Chapter Review	C28

Many textbooks and trade books have a glossary and an index. The glossary gives readers the definitions of words as they relate to the text. The index helps readers locate the pages that include discussion about particular concepts or vocabulary words. A good informational book highlights new vocabulary terms, either by defining new terms in the margin or using boldface or italics within the body of the text and embedding its definition. See Figure 9.5 for an example from the same science textbook.

Good textbooks for elementary and middle-school grades include some thought questions at the beginning and end of each chapter. These questions should include literal, inferential, and critical/evaluative questions (see Chapter 8). For example, in *Bison for Kids* a literal question is, "What are wisents?" The answer is stated in the text, which provides a definition of wisents. An inferential question is, "Why was it not possible for bison and cattle to live on the Great Plains together?" A critical/evaluative question is, "Was it wrong for settlers to kill bison for food and hides? Support your answer."

Figure 9.6 has an example from the same science textbook that presents main questions with supporting questions under each main heading. Figure 9.7 pro-

---

figure   9.5   Sample definition of terms.

How Volcanoes Form

Hot, melted rock and gases are bursting out of the volcano in the picture. A **volcano** is a special type of mountain with an opening, or vent, at its top. Thousands of years ago, this volcano did not exist. So what happened to form this volcano?

> **GLOSSARY**
>
> volcano (vol kā´ nō), a type of mountain that has an opening at the top through which lava, ash, or other types of volcanic rock flows
>
> Glossary

---

figure   9.6   Pre-reading questions from a textbook.

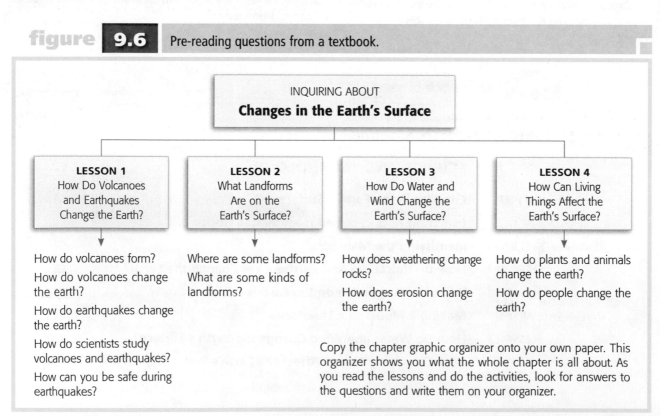

INQUIRING ABOUT
Changes in the Earth's Surface

LESSON 1 How Do Volcanoes and Earthquakes Change the Earth?	**LESSON 2** What Landforms Are on the Earth's Surface?	**LESSON 3** How Do Water and Wind Change the Earth's Surface?	**LESSON 4** How Can Living Things Affect the Earth's Surface?

How do volcanoes form?

How do volcanoes change the earth?

How do earthquakes change the earth?

How do scientists study volcanoes and earthquakes?

How can you be safe during earthquakes?

Where are some landforms?

What are some kinds of landforms?

How does weathering change rocks?

How does erosion change the earth?

How do plants and animals change the earth?

How do people change the earth?

Copy the chapter graphic organizer onto your own paper. This organizer shows you what the whole chapter is all about. As you read the lessons and do the activities, look for answers to the questions and write them on your organizer.

figure **9.7**   End of chapter questions.

LESSON 1 REVIEW

1. How does a volcano erupt?
2. How do volcanoes change the earth?
3. How do earthquakes change the earth?
4. How do scientists study earthquakes and volcanoes?
5. What are some ways to stay safe during an earthquake?
6. **Main Idea**   Read the material on page C10. What is the main idea of this material?

vides an example of the questions often found at the end of a chapter. Take time to evaluate the questions in a text. Are all three types of questions represented?

Electronic Text Features

Electronic texts, including online texts and ebooks, have features that differ from those of traditional texts, and students may need help in using these features. Whether accessed online or on an e-reader, mobile device, or computer, electronic texts typically contain hyperlinks to related material that supports the topic or provides more in-depth information.

Many electronic texts permit readers to click on vocabulary words; clicking provides an audio pronunciation of the word and its meaning for that context. Some electronic texts have audio and/or videos to help explain concepts.

Many websites provide informational texts for all reading levels. These electronic texts give students access to a wide variety of topics; however, they may need more guidance as they read online. Walk students through a website, showing them electronic text features and demonstrating how to use the back button. A good website for such a demonstration is the National Geographic Kids site mentioned earlier. The home page gives students a list of possible activities and topics to explore. The reading level is for upper elementary or middle school students. Figure 9.8 shows the opening page. Preview as many Internet sites as possible so you know whether they are at your students' reading level.

figure **9.8**

National Geographic Kids website.

Source: www.kids.nationalgeographic.com/kids

Use of Technical Vocabulary

In addition to a complex writing style, the academic and domain-specific vocabulary used in informational texts may be overwhelming for struggling readers. If you recall, Chapter 7 discussed the three tiers of words, and domain-specific words are tier three words.

Expecting students to learn new words, especially academic and domain-specific words, from context may be tricky (McKeown & Beck, 2004) if students are not given explicit instruction about the context clues found in informational text. Struggling readers are especially unlikely to learn words from context; however, all readers benefit by having teachers explain the ways new technical words may be defined within an informational passage. Authors sometimes give a definition first and then state the vocabulary word. For example, in *Bison for Kids* Wilkinson explains wisents in this manner: "Huge ancestors of the modern bison, known as the wisent (VEE-SENT), roamed far and wide" (p. 12). Wilkinson even indicates how the word is pronounced by using parentheses and capital letters. Simon uses the same technique in *Whales* by setting off the technical term in commas: "A whale's nostril, called a blowhole, is at the top of its head. A whale breathes through its blowhole" (unpaged).

Authors sometimes introduce a term and then set off the definition in commas: "Dolphins are remarkable mimics, copying others' behavior and sounds" (Cerullo, 1999, p. 18). Others provide definitions by setting them off with a dash: "This humpback whale is breaching—jumping almost clear out of the water and then crashing down in a huge spray of foam" (Simon, 1989, unpaged).

Most authors use a mix of techniques. In the following example, Philip Steele in *I Wonder Why Castles Had Moats* (1994) uses a sentence to describe one term, an appositive phrase to describe another, and a participial phrase to explain the last term:

> Minarets are the tall slender towers on mosques, the building where Muslims pray to God. They, too, point to heaven. At the top of the minaret is a balcony, where a man called a muezzin stands to call people to prayer. (p. 13)

Like many authors, in *Caves: Facts and Stories and Activities* (1990), Wood uses boldface to draw attention to new words and then states definitions immediately after: "Another group of scientists who are interested in caves are **geologists.** Geologists study caves, rocks, soil, mountains, rivers, oceans, and other parts of the Earth" (p. 23). Watt (1993) uses boldface to indicate that the word is included in the glossary at the back of the book.

You must explicitly teach struggling readers about the techniques authors use to define new words, because they do not necessarily recognize them on their own (Fisher, Frey, & Lapp, 2008).

Author's Assumption of Readers' Background Knowledge

Authors tend to choose words that will best describe an event, an action, or a phenomenon; however, unfamiliar vocabulary may make the passage difficult for struggling readers. Be on the lookout for words that may cause problems for readers with a limited vocabulary. In the following sentence, struggling readers may not create the appropriate mental picture of the swimming dolphins because they do not know the words *proportioned* and *penetrate:* "You have to watch a dolphin swim for a few seconds to see that it is perfectly proportioned to penetrate the wave" (Cerullo, 1999, p. 10). In the next sentence, readers' comprehension may break down because they cannot pronounce *Cetaceans* and *cetus;* they will probably not know that *Cetaceans* is a classification based on the Latin root *cetus.* Teach-

ers should explain these facts to struggling readers: "[Dolphins] belong to the group known as Cetaceans (from the Latin word *cetus,* meaning large sea animal), which includes all whales, dolphins, and porpoises" (Cerullo, 1999, p. 4).

Authors may assume readers have sufficient background knowledge to fully comprehend the text and visualize its images. In the following passage, readers need to know the location of several countries to know what is meant by the word *ring* in the phrase *Ring of Fire.*

> Some of these volcanoes are on the ocean floor. Others are on land. Most of the land volcanoes circle the Pacific Ocean. They run from South America to Alaska to Japan, Indonesia, and New Zealand. Together they are known as the Ring of Fire. (Lauber, 1986, p. 51)

Some authors do not provide enough illustrations, graphs, charts, and photographs to explain the text. The paragraph above would be easier to comprehend if the author had included a map of that area with the ring of volcanoes clearly marked.

Authors can aid readers' comprehension by organizing materials in a cohesive manner, using clear diagrams and charts, and writing literate sentences. Figure 9.9 presents considerate versus inconsiderate characteristics of textbook styles. As you critique textbooks, you may want to add to the list. In addition, you may use the checklist provided in Appendix D.23 for textbook evaluation.

Readability

Readability is often determined by formulas that approximate the reading level of texts. Many of the formulas are based on the number of syllables and the sentence length within passages. However, as discussed in Chapter 2, the Lexile scale uses technology to determine which words are repeated most often in a short passage and whether the repeated terms are familiar to most readers. This is important because readers may know certain four- and five-syllable words and not know some one- or two-syllable words. For example, consider the words *hippopotamus* and *rhinoceros* and the words *brusque* and *crux.* According to a readability formula, *hippopotamus* and *rhinoceros* would make the passage's reading level higher than the passage with the one-syllable words. Yet students are more likely to be familiar with the animals but not the other two words. The Lexile scale takes these factors into consideration (see Chapter 2 for more information about the scale). Teachers also understand that concrete words such as *butterfly* and *astronaut* are easier to understand than abstract words such as *transformation* and *prejudice.* A *butterfly* and *astronaut* can be seen and felt, while a *transformation* and a *prejudice* cannot. When determin-

figure 9.9   Considerate and inconsiderate textbook styles.

CONSIDERATE	INCONSIDERATE
1. Organization of text's structure is clear to reader	1. No logical text structure
2. Concepts are logically, clearly explained	2. Ungrammatical sentence structure
3. Main ideas are explicitly stated	3. Sentence length is long
4. Subtopics relate and support main idea	4. Lack of pictorial aids
5. Appropriate signal words are used for each type of text (e.g., sequence = *first, second*)	5. No use of subordinating conjunctions to show relationships
6. Clear pronoun/antecedent agreement	6. Ambiguous pronouns
7. Necessary background information is provided	7. Assumption of advanced background knowledge
8. Definition of new term is clearly stated	8. New vocabulary is not defined
9. New concepts are clearly and concisely explained	9. Information presented in encyclopedic fashion
10. Visual aids complement text	10. Pages of text without visual aids

Sources: Armbruster, B. (1996), Considerate text. In D. Lapp, J. Flood, & N. Farman (Eds.), *Content Area Reading and Learning: Instructional Strategies* (2nd ed.), pp. 47–58. Boston: Allyn & Bacon / Olson, M. W. & Gee, T. (1991), Content reading instruction in the primary grades: Perceptions and strategies, *The Reading Teacher, 45*, 298–307 / Palmer, R. & Stewart, R. (1997), Nonfiction tradebooks in content area instruction: Realistic and potential, *Journal of Adolescent and Adult Literacy, 40*(8), 630–642 / Richardson, J. & Morgan, R. (2011), *Reading to Learn in the Content Areas* (3rd ed.), Belmont, CA: Wadsworth Publishing Co.

ing the readability of a text, teachers can check the online Lexile scale (http://lexile.com) and use the checklist found in Appendix D.23.

ENGLISH LEARNERS AND INFORMATIONAL TEXT

Instructional Recommendations

English learners deserve special consideration when reading from informational books. They first need to understand the academic vocabulary in order to comprehend the information. You will need to scaffold these students as they read informational books. First work on building their vocabulary. English learners should know the word, implying they should be able to pronounce it correctly, give a definition in their own words, and use the word in multiple ways. Technical terms often have multiple syllables, so these students may need time to hear and practice the pronunciation. You may need to read the text with these students while they discuss the information and pictures. The pictures will help them with comprehension. Use as many visuals as possible; the visuals can be pictures, gestures, pantomime, and facial expressions. Give English learners opportunities to ask questions and restate the information. It is also advantageous for teachers and students to read the text in unison so the students can practice phrasing and intonation.

English learners should also receive small group instruction "to assist . . . in building and extending vocabulary and improving their listening comprehension and oral expression" (Vaughn et al., 2005,

p. 63). Base small group instruction on regular classroom materials to prevent a disconnect between small group and large group topics. You may choose easier books so the English learners can more readily grasp the concepts. Divide the passage into small sections of about 200 to 250 words and read only one section a day. The rest of the small group time should be used to discuss the passage—each student should be given an opportunity to discuss or explain the concept presented in their reading. This practice builds their confidence so they are later willing to express their ideas in the larger group.

Consider the following small group session between Mr. Chung and four of his third-grade English learners. The third graders are studying a unit on creatures of the seas. Mr. Chung is sharing Melvin and Gilda Berger's information book *Sharks* (2003) with the group because it is short, with only one or two sentences per page, but very interesting to third graders.

> Mr. Chung: The book we are going to read is *Sharks* (pointing to the word on the cover) by Melvin and Gilda Berger (pointing to the names on the cover). Look at the shark's big mouth (pointing to the shark's mouth) and big eye (pointing to the shark's eye). Let's read this book together.
>
> Mr. Chung and group: "Here comes a shark."
>
> Mr. Chung: What do you see?
>
> Juan: Shark big mouth.
>
> Mr. Chung: The shark does have a big mouth. (Notice how Mr. Chung extends Juan's sentence.)
>
> Mr. Chung: Now turn the page (as he turns his page). Let's read.

Mr. Chung and small group: "Fun Fact: If sharks stop swimming, they sink."

Mr. Chung: Do you know what *stop swimming* means?

(He can tell from their facial expressions that they do not understand.) Moving his arms as if he is swimming, he says, "I am swimming." Then he stops moving his arms and says, "I stop swimming. Do you understand?"

The students nod their heads and move their arms and repeat: "I am swimming." They stop moving their arms and repeat: "I stop swimming."

Mr. Chung: Do you know what *sink* means?

They shake their heads "No."

Mr. Chung fills a large glass with water and puts a paper clip into the water and says, "The paper clip sinks." He then puts a small square piece of paper in the water and says, "The paper floats." He points to the paper clip and says, "Sink" and then to the paper and says, "Float."

The small group says both words, "Sink! Float!"

Mr. Chung moves his arms as if he is swimming. Then he reads: "If the sharks stop swimming, they sink." (Mr. Chung stops moving his arms and falls to the floor.)

The group mimics Mr. Chung and repeats the sentence.

Mr. Chung knows that for students to comprehend the information in the book, he has to act out the words and have the students model the actions. Because they are in a room by themselves, Mr. Chung is not embarrassing any of the students in front of their peers. He continues reading and discussing each page, because he wants each student to comprehend the information and not just read the words.

English learners need to develop vocabulary and reading skills in content areas to be successful in school. Too often teachers focus only on reading the material to the students, which results in the struggling readers and English learners not getting practice in reading this type of material (Ogle & Correa-Kovtun, 2010). To develop skills in reading informational texts, they have to read materials on their independent level or instructional level so they can focus on the information, not on the decoding. They also need ample opportunity to discuss materials so they learn to pronounce the words and internalize the information. Like all students, when English learners verbalize the information, they solidify the material in their minds (Ogle & Correa-Kovtun, 2010; Mills, 2009; Wolf, Crossen, & Resnick, 2004). They also need to be in small groups, as Mr. Chung knows, where they are free to discuss the topic and activate prior knowledge. Small groups enable them to make inferences, create mental pictures, and ask questions, instead of just answering questions with the group (Mills, 2009). Encourage them to ask questions when they do not understand a concept. Just like all students, they need

explicit instruction in using many text features (captions, graphs, table of contents, glossary, and index). English learners also need to read and think critically by being encouraged to state their point of view concerning material that impacts their lives.

English learners in middle school are attempting to learn advanced concepts and pass state-mandated tests while still learning the language. Sheltered instruction (see Chapter 1 for a detailed discussion on sheltered instruction) is "specially designed academic instruction in English" (Marino-Weisman & Hansen, 2007, p. 181). The goal of sheltered instruction is to teach content and academic language simultaneously to a small group. The teacher speaks slowly and uses gestures or pantomime as Mr. Chung did in the previous example when explaining new concepts. Because middle-school textbooks use complex sentences that may be written in the passive voice, teachers and students should create graphic organizers of the information as they read. This will help English learners see the relationship between concepts. It is important to keep English learners engaged during instructional time, so students can also create a graphic organizer as the teacher creates it. After reading, discussing, and creating a graphic organizer related to a passage, invite the small group of students to role-play the concepts. This allows them to practice the vocabulary and gives the teacher an opportunity to informally assess their English growth and understanding of the concepts.

For example, if students are studying the life cycle of a seed, the teacher and students can first draw a graphic organizer showing the cycle (for example, see Figure 9.16, later in this chapter). Then the teacher can role play how the tiny seed sprouts through the earth and becomes a small plant. She starts in a crouching position with her head between her knees and slowly raises her head up. Next, she role plays how the plant grows, blossoms, and becomes a fruit. She slowly stands up, stretches out her arms with fists clutched, and then finally opens her palms and fingers wide. Then through pantomime a student pretends to pick the fruit, cut it open, find a new seed, and plant that seed in the ground.

Many content area vocabulary words are abstract; for example, social studies introduces *liberty, responsibility, democracy, freedom,* and *government.* Reading selections usually offer no visual clues to help English learners understand these abstract concepts. Therefore, introduce only the words needed for that day's lesson instead of all the words for the unit. However, one fun way to engage students in reviewing all the vocabulary words for a unit is to play Jeopardy. (Build your own game board for free at http://jeopardylabs.com.) You can have students work in teams of two; middle-school students enjoy collaborating.

Singing "enhances personal expression, builds community, and connects reading and writing" (Bintz, 2010b, p. 683). Singing helps facilitate phonics, phonemic awareness, rhymes, memorization, and vocabulary; therefore, it is a wonderful tool to help English learners (and others) to learn and remember science or social studies concepts. Bintz (2010b) suggests that teachers write parodies of songs with content information. For example, while teaching about clouds, he wrote a song to the tune of "London Bridge Is Falling Down" with a verse about cirrus clouds:

> Cirrus clouds are made of ice
>
> Seen before, rain or snow,
>
> Cirrus clouds are made of ice
>
> Clouds, thin and wispy (p. 684).

English learners are absorbing concepts, vocabulary, and English as they have fun singing with their classmates. Teachers can pair English learners with native speakers and have them write their own songs based on a concept they are studying.

Selecting Informational Text

What should a teacher consider when choosing informational texts for English learners? First, the books must be quality literature; they must contain accurate information, define technical terms, and feature illustrations that complement the text. Second, the books must be age appropriate and fit with the students' comprehension level. Because some English learners may not have the language skills to read or comprehend classroom science and social studies textbooks that feature technical information and vocabulary terms, you may want to choose trade books that deal with the same topic. Many authors write on a given subject, but for different grade levels. This makes it easy for teachers to choose books on a particular subject that accommodate a wide variety of reading levels. For example, when presenting a unit on weather, you can choose Gail Gibbons's *Weather Words and What They Mean* (1992) and *Weather Forecasting* (1993). Gibbons delivers the information in cartoon-style pictures. Her colorful and detailed illustrations help students comprehend the concepts. Tomie dePaola's *Clouds* (1984) also is written in the cartoon style with explanations that are easy to comprehend. Franklyn Branley's *Flash, Crash, Rumble, and Roll* (1999) and *Down Comes the Rain* (1997) are also written for young children. If you have students with a more advanced vocabulary and comprehension level, select Seymour Simon's *Storms* (1992), *Tornadoes* (2001), and *Hurricanes* (2002). His books are written at a high reading level, but his illustrations clarify the information.

Vardell, Hadaway, and Young (2006) provide the following guidelines for selecting informational trade books for English learners. They should:

1. Have reference aids (glossary, index, table of contents).
2. Be well organized (utilizing sequence, cause/effect, problem/solution, enumeration, and so on).
3. Have charts, graphs, diagrams, photographs, or illustrations with useful captions.
4. Fit the students' background knowledge, focusing on appropriate vocabulary and reading level.
5. Contain plentiful white space; some information books with pages full of text are written for advanced grade levels.
6. Introduce new vocabulary words in boldface type or highlighted text.

DEVELOPING CRITICAL LITERACY WITH INFORMATIONAL TEXTS

Chapter 8 discussed how students' critical literacy must be developed because "critical literacy challenges status quo and clarifies connections between knowledge and power" (Soares & Wood, 2010, p. 488). In this section I will discuss how critical literacy can be developed using informational texts in social studies, because "it is through the content of social studies that students make sense of their lives" (Soares & Wood, 2010, p. 487). Social studies gives students the opportunity to look at current events critically by questioning "truths, sources, and evidence" (Soares & Wood, 2010, p. 487). As students read about current and historical events they need to discuss the political, sociocultural, historical, and economic forces that affect their lives— and then question them—in order to become aware of their social responsibilities (Soares & Wood, 2010). Your goal is to prompt students to respond to information rather than be passive consumers of it.

After reading an informational text with students, lead a discussion that considers the following five aspects central to a critical literacy focus:

1. Does the author present the dominant or the minority's point of view and what is the author's intent?
2. Is the language biased? What words are used to sway the readers' opinions?
3. What assumptions are formed about the different groups? Are these assumptions unfair and harmful to society?
4. Are there any races represented in your classroom but not in the text? How do students of the unrepresented race feel?
5. What can the class do as a call to action?

ASSESSMENT

Reading informational text takes the same skills needed to read narrative texts. Readers must have a large bank of words they recognize on sight. They must have good decoding skills for encountering technical terms. They need to understand letter–sound relationships, digraphs, diphthongs, consonant blends, and syllabication for decoding. If a reader struggles with decoding, the teacher should determine what aspect of decoding is the problem. (Refer to Chapters 5 and 6 for ways to assess a reader's decoding and word analysis skills.) After assessment, teachers assist the readers as they build the necessary skills to master informational texts.

Informal Assessment

Informal reading inventories

As mentioned in Chapter 8, informal reading inventories (IRIs) can be used to assess oral and silent reading comprehension. IRIs include expository as well as narrative passages that can be used to assess a student's comprehension of informational text. Chapter 3 has more information about IRIs.

Rubrics

Designing rubrics based on the CCSS or other state standards helps teachers monitor individual student growth in comprehending informational text. The partial rubric in Figure 9.10 is based on the sixth-grade CCSS, and a blank copy of the complete rubric is in Appendix C.44. Notice that at the end of the second quarter, Wade sometimes uses effective strategies to comprehend expository text and sometimes can determine the main idea and how it is conveyed through supporting details; however, he cannot determine an author's point of view.

Running records and miscue analysis

Using informational texts for running records and miscue analyses will help you determine if a student uses different cueing systems than she does for narrative text. A reader may use the same cueing systems for both, or she may approach informational text in a different way. For example, she may use more visual clues, such as dividing words into parts, instead of using semantic clues, such as relying on background information. Chapter 3 discusses how to administer, score, and analyze both of these assessment instruments. Many commercial miscue analyses have one informational passage for each grade level.

Cloze and maze procedures

Often teachers find that most students are able to read a book or passage; only one or two students struggle with the text. There are two other ways to determine whether a text is at the easy level, the instruction level, or the frustration level for a student: the cloze test and the maze. Each of these assessments helps determine the appropriateness of a particular book for a particular student. See Chapter 3 for detailed description of these two tests.

figure 9.10 Partial rubric for reading comprehension based on the CCSS ELA Reading: Informational Text standards for sixth grade.

STUDENT _Wade_   TOTAL SCORE: _14_   GRADING PERIOD   1 ② 3 4

LEVEL OF MASTERY

TEXT	TARGET (4–5 POINTS)	ACCEPTABLE (2–3 POINTS)	UNACCEPTABLE (0–1 POINT)	SCORE
Citing evidence.	Always cites evidence to support analysis of what the text says explicitly as well as inferences drawn from the text.	Cites evidence to support analysis of what the text says explicitly but cannot cite evidence from inferences drawn from the text.	Struggles to cite evidence to support analysis of what the text says.	2
Determining central theme.	Always determines a central idea and how it is conveyed through particular details; provides a summary of the text distinct from personal opinions or judgments.	Can usually determine a central idea and how it is conveyed through particular details; however, struggles to provide a summary of the text distinct from personal opinions or judgments.	Cannot determine the central theme and struggle to provide a summary of the text.	2

figure 9.10 Continued.

TEXT	TARGET (4–5 POINTS)	ACCEPTABLE (2–3 POINTS)	UNACCEPTABLE (0–1 POINT)	SCORE
Analyzing details.	Analyzes in detail how a key individual, event, or idea is introduced, illustrated, and elaborated in a text.	Gives brief analysis of how a key individual, event, or idea is introduced, illustrated, and elaborated in a text.	Struggles in analysis of key details.	3
Determining meaning of words.	Determines the meaning of words and phrases as they are used in a text, including figurative, connotative, and technical meanings.	Determines the meaning of most words as used in a text, but struggles with figurative, connotative, and some technical meanings.	Struggles with meaning of words as used in a text.	3
Understanding overall structure of text.	Analyzes how a particular sentence, paragraph, chapter, or section fits into the overall structure of a text and contributes to the development of the ideas.	Analyzes how a particular sentence and paragraph contributes to the small section of the text, but struggles to understand how they fit into the overall structure.	Cannot explain how a particular sentence, paragraph, chapter, or section fits into the overall structure of a text.	3
Determining point of view.	Determines an author's point of view or purpose in a text and explains how it is conveyed in the text.	Determines author's point of view or purpose, but struggles to explain how it is conveyed in the text.	Cannot determine the author's point of view.	1

Source: Standards based on National Governors Association Center for Best Practices (NGACBP) & Council of Chief State School Officers (CCSSO). (2010). English Language Arts Standards, Reading: Informational Text, Grade 6. Washington, DC: NGACBP, CCSSO, pp. 38–39.

Assessing reading interests

When working one-on-one with a struggling student, attempt to get him "hooked on reading." The student may enjoy stories but dislike informational books. Choosing a topic that interests him is essential; when possible let him choose the topic. First make sure the book is on the reader's instructional reading level. If the student is a reluctant and struggling reader, try choosing a book that is on his easy reading level so he experiences success. Determine a student's interests by developing an interest inventory that prompts him to think about his personal interests. Figure 9.11 shows a partially completed interest survey that will help a teacher select appropriate informational texts. Appendix C.42 has a blank survey.

Assessing background knowledge

Teachers must assess students' background knowledge to determine whether they are comprehending informational material. One way to assess this aspect of reading is to give students a list of major concepts from a passage, and ask them what they know about each. Another way to assess background knowledge is by using a K-T-W-L-E chart (refer to Figure 9.23 on p. 247).

Talking drawings is another informal assessment used with kindergarten and first-grade students to assess their prior knowledge (Paquette, Fello, & Renck-Jalongo, 2007). Most kindergarten and first-semester first graders cannot take a paper-and-pencil test. From this assessment, teachers learn what prior knowledge students have about a topic and any misconceptions they might have. Teachers can also assess students' listening skills as they listen to their peers explain their drawings and students' oral vocabulary as they explain their own drawings. Talking drawings require the following steps:

1. Tell students the topic that they are going to study, such as farm animals.
2. Invite them to draw a picture depicting what they know about the topic. For example, students may be invited to draw pictures depicting objects they would find on a farm.
3. Have students share their drawings with peers.
4. Read the text(s), using the directed-reading-thinking activity.
5. After the reading, have students draw a new picture or modify their first drawing. Encourage students to label parts of their drawing. Offer

figure 9.11 Sample interest survey.

STUDENT: _Rami_   GRADE: _5_   DATE: _9/20_

WHAT INTERESTS YOU?

These questions will help me learn about your interests! (You can give more than one answer for each question.)

1. If you could choose a book about science or history, which would you choose? _science_

2. What is your favorite topic to study in science? _space and the ocean_

3. Do you have a favorite time in history that you like to read about? _not really_

4. What sport would you like to read about? _baseball_

5. Are you interested in any specific animals? _whales and sharks_

6. What would you like to learn about this animal? _If they are alike_

7. Do you watch any nature or discovery shows on TV? If so, are they about
   animals, space, history, different places in the world, or other topics? _sharks and space_

Source: Adapted from S. McCormick (2010), p. 170.

assistance with spelling if the student insists on correct spelling.

6. After all students have completed their drawings, again ask them to share with their peers the differences between the two drawings and explain what they learned from the text(s).

Assessing readers' growth

The most accurate assessment of students' growth in reading informational text comes through careful observation over a long period of time in a variety of settings—one-on-one tutoring, independent reading, and large and small group participation. The assessments must include all types of informational reading materials—textbooks, trade books, computer programs, age-appropriate Internet sites, magazines, and instructions (e.g., for board games, science experiments, arts and crafts projects).

When struggling readers do not recognize their own miscues, they continue to plod along. The goal for every reader is to become self-monitoring. One way to assess readers' self-monitoring growth is to have a student read a passage of expository informational text into a recording device and have the student play it back and identify her own errors. Teachers should be silent observers, allowing the student to find her own errors. The goal is for her to recognize reading miscues as she makes them.

However, many students are critical of themselves and have a poor self-concept. For these students to find their own errors may be counterproductive. In such cases, first record a passage that is at the reader's level and include some deliberate miscues. Then the student can listen to the recording while following the script, listening for your errors. When you make the recording, read a little slower than normal and very distinctly, so students can hear the errors. Closely observe them during this activity, and then discuss the miscues afterward. When students are comfortable with this procedure, they can then record their own readings.

To record struggling students' reading growth throughout the school year, use the recordings and a checklist similar to the one found in Appendix C.43 or the rubric found in Appendix C.45. Remember to date the checklist so there is a record of when the readers accomplished each task. The checklist can also help you write short-term goals for readers if it is used once a week or every other week.

Formal Assessment

Two types of standardized tests that assess students' reading comprehension are achievement tests and criterion-referenced tests. Many of the reading subtests that measure comprehension have informational passages as well as stories. As you will recall from Chapter 3, achievement tests measure the current level of students' performance in a variety of areas, including reading. There are three different types of standardized achievement tests—reading readiness, norm-referenced, and criterion-referenced. Only norm-referenced and criterion-referenced tests have comprehension subtests with informational passages. The following is a list of norm-referenced and criterion-referenced tests with comprehension subtests.

STANDARDIZED NORM-REFERENCED ACHIEVEMENT TESTS

1. Iowa Test of Basic Skills (Grades K–8)
2. Stanford Achievement Tests (Grades K–13)
3. Gates-MacGinitie Reading Tests (Grades K–12)
4. Metropolitan Achievement Tests–Reading (Grades K–12)
5. Comprehensive Test of Basic Skills, U and V (Grades K–12)
6. California Achievement Tests–Reading (Grades K–9)

STANDARDIZED CRITERION-REFERENCED TESTS

1. Comprehensive Test of Basic Skills–Reading, Expanded Edition (Grades K–12)
2. Phonics Criterion Test (Grades 1–3)
3. Prescriptive Reading Performance Test (Grades 1–12)

States that have adopted the CCSS are adjusting their state tests to align with these standards. As discussed in Chapter 3, two consortiums have developed state tests aligned with the CCSS: the Smarter Balanced Assessment Consortium and the Partnership for Assessment of Readiness for College and Careers (PARCC). Figure 9.12 is an informational text example from PARCC's online sample questions for third graders. They first read the passage "How Animals Live" by Lisa Oram and then answer the questions. Notice that the second question asks students to cite evidence for the answer they gave on the first question. Smarter Balanced website's sample question includes an informational passage with students responding in essay form. Both of the sites indicate that the tests are computer based.

If teachers engage their students in critical literacy, they should also assess students' critical thinking skills (interpretation, inference, evaluation, analysis, self-regulation, and deductive and inductive reasoning), because these are the skills used in critical literacy studies. Most critical thinking tests are not subject specific, but rather assess students' general critical thinking skills, such as the ability to interpret and make inferences, engage in deductive and inductive reasoning, evaluate arguments, and evaluate if arguments are consistent. A few critical thinking tests are appropriate for elementary and middle school students.

The James Madison Test of Critical Thinking Form B (Critical Thinking Company) is intended for middle-school students and above. This test assesses a wide range of students' critical thinking abilities, including interpreting complex texts; clarifying issues and arguments; distinguishing issues, claims, conclusions, and premises; evaluating whether an argument is strong or weak; evaluating claims for consistency and relevance; evaluating whether a deductive argument is valid; and discerning whether pairs of claims are consistent, contrary, contradictory, or paradoxical. All of these skills are needed as students engage in critical literacy as they read informational books. This test is available as software that tracks students' scores.

The California Critical Thinking Test MIB (Insight Assessment) assesses students in grades 3 through 5, while the California Critical Thinking Test M20/M25 assesses students in grades 6 through 9. Both assess students' inductive and deductive reasoning skills as well as their ability to analyze, draw inferences, and evaluate everyday situations. These tests are available in print and computerized versions.

The Cornell Critical Thinking Test, Level X and Level Z, for grades 5 through 12 (Critical Thinking Company) assesses students' critical thinking ability. Level X tests inductive reasoning, deductive reasoning, and ability to identify assumptions. Level Z assesses students' semantic ability and ability to make predictions for planning. The test is a software package that self-times, self-grades, and keeps records for the teachers.

Because each of these assessments measures different aspects of critical thinking, you must determine what skills you want your students to develop and then choose an assessment based on those goals.

figure 9.12 Sample informational text question from PARCC third-grade state test.

Read all parts of the question before responding.

PART A

What is one main idea of "How Animals Live"?

- a. There are many types of animals on the planet.
- b. Animals need water to live.
- c. There are many ways to sort different animals.
- d. Animals begin their life cycles in different forms.

PART B

Which detail from the article best supports the answer to Part A?

- a. "Animals get oxygen from air or water."
- b. "Animals can be grouped by their traits."
- c. "Worms are invertebrates."
- d. "All animals grow and change over time."
- e. "Almost all animals need water, food, oxygen, and shelter to live."

Source: www.parcconline.org/sample/items-tasks-prototypes.

intervention

You must explicitly teach reading strategies, model using them (Fisher, Frey, & Lapp, 2008; McLaughlin, 2012), and guide students as they become "marinated" in them (Flynt & Cooter, 2005) so using them during reading becomes automatic. In a recent study of students in grades 3 through 8, Fisher, Frey, and Lapp (2008) identified 25 effective teachers. These teachers used shared readings to model four categories of strategies: comprehension and vocabulary strategies, understanding text structure strategies, and using text features strategies. For comprehension strategies, teachers modeled how they activate prior knowledge, summarize, infer, predict, clarify, question, visualize, synthesize, evaluate, monitor, and connect passages to the world, other text, and personal experiences. When they modeled vocabulary strategies, they looked at word parts (affixes, roots, cognates, word families), used context clues, and used other resources, such as peers, dictionaries, a glossary, or the Internet. To model understanding text structure, they and their students created graphic organizers to illustrate relationships between ideas in compare/contrast, problem/solution, cause/effect, sequencing, and descriptive texts. Finally, to model how to use text features they explained in detail how to read headings and captions; how to study illustrations, charts, tables, and graphs; how to review bold or italic words as important vocabulary; how to use the table of contents to predict main ideas and supporting ideas; and how to use the index to find a word in the text.

The following activities will help students develop strategies for reading informational text.

Strategies and Activities to Use Before, During, and After Reading

ACTIVITY   **Textmasters**   GRADES 4–8

Textmasters (Wilfong, 2009) brings literature circles to textbook reading. These textbook circles can be formed in a regular classroom or used by reading specialists as they work with groups of four upper-elementary or middle-school struggling readers. Like literature circles with fiction, a teacher assigns one task to every member of the group. One student is the discussion director, who is responsible for formulating discussion questions. The second student, the summarizer, is responsible for summarizing the passage. The third student, the vocabulary "enricher," finds important words and gives definitions for each. The fourth student, the webmaster, is responsible for creating a graphic organizer of the information.

The students have 20 minutes to read the passage silently and complete their assigned task. Then the group spends the next 20 minutes discussing each task and questioning and challenging each other. The final 10 minutes is used for self-reflection on how they and their peers performed for the day.

If this activity is completed in the classroom, each group thinks of unique ways to present its material (e.g., dramatic performance, song, multimedia or art project, Jeopardy game) to the whole class or another audience. Wilfong (2009) found the following advantages to this strategy when used in the classroom:

1. Social learning caters to middle-school social needs; students learn from each other especially during discussion and performance time.
2. Students are engaged because they have a duty to perform for their group.

3. Students learn to do different tasks for each session; they learn to take on different leadership roles with peers.

4. They understand the responsibility of being a member of a group.

5. Scores can go up during the research project. For example, Wilfong (2009) found the average score was 86 percent on the first chapter. On the second chapter the scores rose to 89.3 percent.

6. Students take responsibility for their learning instead of expecting teachers to lecture to them.

Multiple Source Chart for Close Reading and Citing Evidence

The first CCR Anchor Standard for Reading requires students "[t]o read closely to determine what the texts says explicitly and to make logical inferences from it; cite specific textual evidence, when writing or speaking to support conclusion drawn from the text" (p. 10) and Standard 8 requires students to "[a]nalyze how two or more text address similar themes or topics in order to build knowledge or to compare the approaches the authors take" (NGACBP & CCSSO, 2010, CCRA for Reading, p. 10).

To facilitate students as they acquire these skills, help them organize their thoughts and the information by giving them a graphic table in which to record information. The table shown in Figure 9.13 is based on a study of polar wildlife in which students are asked to research and report on two species from polar regions. After students have completed their reading and filled out the table, have them present their findings in writing and orally. (The blank template for this chart can be found in Appendix D.24.)

This chart can be used anytime students are asked to read about a topic from multiple sources. The completed sample chart in Figure 9.13 is intended for fourth graders, and you may share it as a model. Some possible topics for older students could be oil spills, hurricanes, tornadoes, Jackie Robinson, Rosa Parks, Black Wall Street, the Great Depression, the civil rights movement, Japanese internment camps during World War II, the Trail of Tears, space exploration, or any appropriate topic that may interest the student. This chart is also useful when students are researching multiple online sites.

figure　9.13　Chart for comparing multiple sources for a topic.

TOPIC	FACTS	SOURCES	PAGE #/URL
Polar Bears' Habits	They travel many miles in the Arctic to find food.	Polar Bears by N. Rosing (2010). Photographs by R. Rosing. A Firefly Book.	p. 17
		Polar Bears by G. Gibbons (2002). Illus. M. Lloyd. Holiday House.	Unpaged
Polar Bears' Food	Seals, walruses. Small whales, fish, other sea life, musk, oxen, caribous, and seabirds.	Polar Bears by G. Gibbons (2002). Illus. M. Lloyd. Holiday House.	Unpaged
		Polar Bears by N Rosing (2010). Photographs by R. Rosing. A Firefly Book.	pp. 29–40

(continued)

figure **9.13**   Continued.

TOPIC	FACTS	SOURCES	PAGE #/URL
Polar Bears' Dens	Single room about 6 by 10 feet and 4 feet high; There is a long tunnel that leads to the den.	Polar Bears by G. Gibbons (2002). Illus. M. Lloyd. Holiday House.	Unpaged
		The World of the Polar Bear by N. Rosing (2006). Photographs by N. Rosing. Firefly Books.	p. 9
Penguins' Habits	They live in the sea except when they breed.	Polar Wildlife by K. Khanduri (1992). Scholastic.	p. 8
		Penguins! by G. Gibbons (1998). Illus. by G. Gibbons. Holiday House.	Unpaged
Penguins' Food	Krill and other sea creatures.	Emperor Penguins by C. Hughes, online.	p. 6 www.kids.nationalgeographic.com/kids/animals/creature feature/emperorpenguin/
Penguins' Huddles	To stay warm, they huddle close together and take turns standing in the middle where it is warmest. They live in Southern Hemisphere	Penguins, by J. Arlington & S. Langdon (2009). Gareth Stevens Publishing.	p. 27
		Penguins! by G. Gibbons (1998). Illus. G. Gibbons. Holiday House.	unpaged

ACTIVITY   **Pairing Nonfiction and Fiction Texts**   GRADES 3–8

When students read fiction based on historical facts, some students may not be able to distinguish which are real facts and which are fiction. To help students distinguish between the two, build comprehension by creating units in which you first read aloud nonfiction texts to provide background information about a topic that appears in a story or novel that students will read next (McTigue, Thornton, & Wiese, 2013). If students have the background knowledge (the facts) about a topic discussed in a story, they can then become critical readers of historical fiction. McTigue et al. (2013) recommend that students read nonfiction books, primary sources, and multimedia sources to get the facts. For example, middle-school students who first read *Chinese Immigrants 1850–1900* (Olson, 2001) will have the background knowledge to understand Yin's *Coolies* (2001). For younger students, you may share Charles Micucci's *The Life and Times of the Ant* (2003) before reading *Two Bad Ants* (Van Allsburg, 1988).

After reading aloud a nonfiction text, read aloud the fiction text and discuss how authors of fiction use facts to shape their story by asking questions such as the following:

- How did the author describe the geographical setting?
- Is the author's depiction of the characters plausible for the era?
- Is the book's theme one from that era?
- Are the historical facts accurate?
- What is the author's perspective?
- What is the reader's perspective?

Through discussion of both books, students are able to better discern fact from fiction.

Santoro, Chard, Howard, and Baker's (2008) research confirms that this read-aloud strategy was effective with English learners. They incorporated comprehension strategies and vocabulary building strategies as they conducted read-alouds with science and social studies informational and narrative text with first graders. They found that using the two types of text in tandem built background information about many social studies and science topics. For example, during a science unit on reptiles they used *A True Book: Sea Turtles* (Lepthien, 1997) and *Albert's Impossible Toothache* (Williams, 2004). For a social studies unit, they used *I Am Rosa Parks* (Parks & Haskins, 1999) and *Daisy and the Doll* (Medearis & Medearis, 2005). While reading both fiction and informational books, teachers used the following during, before, and after reading strategies, shown in Figure 9.14.

figure 9.14 Before, during, and after reading instructional strategies used while reading fiction and informational texts (Santoro et al., 2008).

BEFORE READING

- Identify the purpose for reading; is it fiction or nonfiction?
- Review the title, author, and illustrator and decide if students have read similar books or books by the same author or illustrator.
- Predict with students what the book may be about by looking at the title, and pictures. With young children, do a picture walk/talk of the entire book.
- Describe any key vocabulary words that are needed to understand the text.

DURING READING

- Use a consistent strategy to discuss the text until students become proficient in using it (e.g., story elements such as main characters, supporting characters, setting, problem, attempts at solving problem, climax, resolution; and K-W-L (or K-T-W-L-E) charts for informational books).
- Use open-ended questions.
- Make connections for students, such as text-to-text, text-to-self, and text-to-world, and encourage them to make their own.
- Have students make inferences based on background knowledge.
- Have students self-monitor by going back or slowing down when comprehension breaks down.
- Look for new vocabulary and talk about meaning as used in the text.

AFTER READING

- Have students retell the main points—characters, setting, main points of plot, ending of fiction, and two or three main points of nonfiction.
- Review and extend new vocabulary found in text.

Science Experiments, Crafts, and Math Games   GRADES 2–5   A C T I V I T Y

One way to show struggling readers the importance of reading informational text accurately and interpreting it correctly is to have them read about and perform simple science experiments, craft and art projects, or math games. You may use the Personal Interest Inventory (see Appendix C.42) to see which area interests the students most. Often struggling readers are tactile and kinesthetic learners, and experiments, crafts, and games meet their need to move around and use their hands. Reading directions emphasizes the importance of being able to read and comprehend accurately. Permit students to perform the experiment, craft, or game just as they understand it from reading the directions, so they learn by trial and error the importance of reading directions correctly. Provide inexpensive and safe materials so any possible misinterpretations of directions is not harmful. Science experiments are also wonderful ways to incorporate writing, because students can make predictions and keep a log of changes throughout the experiments. Read the accompanying factual reports of experiences college tutors had when working with tutees. All names are fictitious.

An excellent book to use for science experiments is Rebecca Gilpin and Leonie Pratt's *The Usborne Big Book of Science Things to Make and Do* (2008); those interested in astronomy may enjoy Kathi Wagner and Sheryl Racine's *Everything Kids Astronomy Book* (2008), which features facts, trivia, and puzzles. Florence Tempo's *Origami Magic* (1993) is a great book to use for origami. For struggling readers with a love for math, find math learning games that students must read carefully in order to play. Two good books for this are Eric Yoder and Natalie Yoder's *One Minute Mysteries: 65 Short Mysteries You Solve with Math!* (2010) and Mark Illingworth's *Real-Life Math Problem Solving, Grades 4–8: 40 Exciting, Classroom-Tested Problems with Annotated Solutions* (2000). Read the vignettes in the box below to see how science experiments can be used to motivate reluctant readers.

BOX

Active Learning

VIGNETTE 1

As part of a course requirement, Mary, an elementary education major, was assigned to work with Joe, a third grader, twice a week. Each tutoring session was 50 minutes long. Mary was encouraged to use science experiments with Joe, so she found a recipe to make slime. Mary was convinced Joe would love the experiment because he loved science and working with his hands. Mary made sure the steps for the recipe were written a little below Joe's reading level to ensure success.

Joe was excited and carefully read and followed each step. However, he misread the amount of water he had to add. Mary remembered from the discussion in her college class that it was important for the student to perform the experiment based on his interpretation of the instructions if he was to learn the importance of reading instructions carefully. Therefore, Mary let Joe proceed. Needless to say, Joe's slime did not come out with the desired consistency.

However, desirable learning did occur. On his own Joe said, "Wow! I must have read something wrong! Let's reread the directions." When he got to the step for adding water he realized he read the amount incorrectly. He said, "Man, I'm not ready to be a rocket scientist if I make a mistake on something so simple!" Joe was not discouraged. He made a plea: "I promise to read the directions better if you let me do this again." Of course, Mary did. The small amount of white glue and borax powder Joe wasted was worth the learning experience.

VIGNETTE 2

Bob, an elementary education major, was assigned to work with George, a very active third-grade reader. George could not sit still for any length of time. In fact, in the middle of a paragraph he would stand up as he continued to read. Because of his constant movement, George often omitted words or even lines, which resulted in poor comprehension. Bob also noticed that George's fingers were in constant motion as he read and that George's drawings were very detailed and advanced for a third grader. George indicated on an interest survey that he loved art. Bob decided to try some origami with George.

Wanting George to be successful, Bob wrote the directions for constructing an origami frog at George's easy reading level. George carefully read and reread the directions as he meticulously followed each step. The frog was neatly constructed, and it jumped! Afterward George asked, "Where did you get these directions? I want to do more of these." Bob showed George the book. George picked up another piece of paper, read the directions from the book (which Bob thought were too difficult for George to read), and made a box that could be inflated. Throughout the semester, George wanted to do origami during every session. He did not care that he had to read the instructions in order to correctly construct each object.

Bob also used George's interest to help his writing skills. George did not like to write. However, when Bob invited George to write in his own words some of the instructions for his favorite origami structures so he could share them with friends, George readily agreed. Through the writing experience, George learned the importance of writing directions clearly so others could understand them.

ACTIVITY   **Read-Alouds**   GRADES K–6

All teachers, especially those who teach grades K–3, should give students more access to informational texts. One way to do this is through read-alouds. During a read-aloud, a teacher can show students how informational texts differ from narrative text and what strategies she uses to make sense of expository text.

First, write on the board any new vocabulary words related to the topic that the students will hear in the text. Pronounce the words and give the students ample time to repeat them until their pronunciation is correct. If necessary, give a short explanation of the word. Also before reading, you can activate students' prior knowledge by creating a K-T-W-L-E chart (see the explanation later in this section). While making the K-T-W-L-E chart, encourage students to generate questions about the topic and list things they would like to learn.

Next, while reading the informational text, show your students how the pictures, charts, and figures are used to explain concepts and to give additional information. Also explain that with informational text you do not need to start at the beginning and read each page. Demonstrate how to use the index to find and read only relevant pages. Also show how on some pages the information is given in boxes and that the order in which one reads them does not matter.

Read-alouds should not be limited to trade books—newspapers, magazines, or websites can pique students' curiosity of current events. Demonstrate how you find an article that interests you, and how you connect the new information to your prior knowledge. *The Washington Post's* "KidsPost," available online at www.washingtonpost.com/lifestyle/kidspost/, features current events and other related articles that interest students in grades 3–8.

Magazines with useful read-aloud articles include the following Scholastic publications:

1. *Clifford the Big Red Dog* (PreK–K): an interactive magazine that promotes development of early learning skills.
2. *Let's Find Out* (K): articles about science, social studies, and language arts topics that reinforce the five reading components of phonemic awareness, phonics, vocabulary, comprehension, and fluency.
3. *Let's Find Out Spanish* (PreK–K)—the Spanish version of *Let's Find Out.*
4. *Scholastic News Magazine* (different magazine for each elementary grade from 1–6): each issue has high-interest articles about current events.
5. *Scholastic News Bilingual* (different magazine for each elementary grade from 1–6): each issue of this Scholastic magazine is bilingual; students read a page in English and flip the magazine upside down to read the same article in Spanish. Each month has two issues— one issue focuses on science topics and one issue focuses on social studies.
6. *Storyworks Magazine* (3–6): each issue is composed of fully illustrated, original children's literature that has engaging reading and writing activities based on the issue's story.

Magazines for students ages 9 to 14 include:

1. *FACES Magazine:* explores the people, places, and cultures of the world.
2. *Cobblestone Magazine:* features articles about American historical events.
3. *Dig:* features articles about archaeology.
4. *Cricket:* includes quality fiction and nonfiction and invites students to submit poetry and essays for different contests.

After reading an informational text selection, help students create graphic organizers to show the relationships between the concepts and help them remember the facts (see Figures 9.15–9.22).

Partner Reading and Content Too (PRC2)   ENGLISH LEARNERS GRADES 4–8   A C T I V I T Y

English learners need practice reading informational texts that include technical vocabulary. Partner Reading and Content Too (PRC2) is a strategy in which two English learners collaborate on reading a text together. The teacher is the silent observer and cheerleader.

First the partners preview the book or passage by discussing the pictures and their captions. Then the partners read a two-page spread silently. Then each partner rereads his page (his side of the text) again and writes two questions to ask his partner. After both have completed reading and writing their questions, the first partner reads his page orally and asks his questions. The two students discuss the information and answer the questions. Then the second partner reads his page orally and they discuss that information and answer his questions. At the end of each two-page spread, they write down important vocabulary terms in their personal notebook and write definitions in their own words.

Graphic Organizers for Expository Text Structures

"Mapping is thinking: constructing and creating the organizational design of ideas, selecting the information that is relevant and sorting this into its proper place, relating all facts to the whole and relating facts to other facts, and finally responding with personal reaction to the material" (Hanf, 1971, p. 229). Graphic organizers map how ideas are connected in an informational text. Heubach (1995) found that graphic organizers helped poor readers comprehend the material, which improved their attitude about informational books. Of course, educators know that when readers' attitudes improve, they will spend more hours reading.

As discussed earlier in this chapter, informational text is usually organized in specific patterns, and graphic organizers show how the information within a particular passage is related. Each expository pattern has a different type of graphic organizer. Mosenthal (1994) found that direct instruction in text organizational patterns before, during, and after reading improves comprehension and aids contextual understanding.

Note that all graphic organizers should be concise, clearly depict relationships, and be free of clutter. At first you should model how to construct the correct type of organizer and map the information. Later you can construct the organizer and have the student map the information. Graphic organizers can be used as a pre-reading strategy to see what a student already knows about the topic. During reading, the information can be filled in as the reader learns new facts. After reading, the student can use it for recalling the information. Figures 9.15 through 9.22 show graphic organizers that can be used for various organizational patterns.

- *Chronology or sequence.* The timeline in Figure 9.15 is based on David Adler's *A Picture Book of Benjamin Franklin* (1990). The graphic organizer in Figure 9.16 depicts the butterfly's life cycle.

- *Description or enumeration.* Figure 9.17 is based on William George's *Box Turtle at Long Pond* (1989).

- *Classification.* A graphic organizer used to show classification should clearly indicate the hierarchy of various categories. Figure 9.18 depicts the three levels of government.

- *Comparison/contrast.* Various organizers may be used to show comparisons and differences between two entities. Venn diagrams are often used for this purpose (refer back to Figure 1.2, p. 5), while Figure 9.19 shows a different type of organizer to compare and contrast.

- *Cause/effect.* Figure 9.20 depicts the events that result in the eruption of a volcano. The information is taken from Fiona Watt's *Earthquakes and Volcanoes* (1993).

- *Problem/solution.* The problem/solution graphic organizer in Figure 9.21 is based on Jerry Stanley's *Children of the Dust Bowl: The True Story of the School at Weedpatch Camp* (1992).

- *Persuasion.* You can use any advertisement from a magazine or newspaper to show how corporations persuade consumers to buy their products. The graphic organizer in Figure 9.22 is based on a Tums advertisement and is an example of card stacking.

figure 9.15 Graphic organizer: Timeline.

Born in Boston	Went to school	Worked in soap-and-candle shop	Worked in brother's print shop	Opened own print shop	Got married	Published *Poor Richard's Almanac*	Represented colonies in England	Represented colonies in France	Helped write peace treaty	Delegate to Constitutional Convention	Died in Philadelphia
1706	1714–1716	1716–1718	1718–1723	1728	1730	1732–1758	1765–1775	1776–1785	1782	1787	1790

Timeline based on Adler, D. (1990). *A Picture Book of Benjamin Franklin.* New York: Trumpet Club.

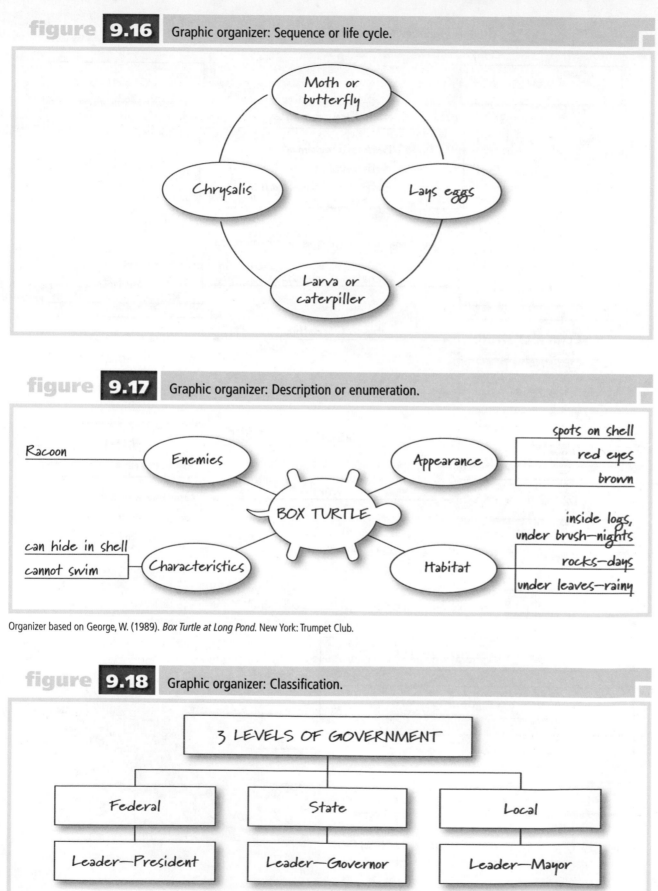

figure 9.16 Graphic organizer: Sequence or life cycle.

Moth or butterfly

Lays eggs

Larva or caterpiller

Chrysalis

figure 9.17 Graphic organizer: Description or enumeration.

Racoon

Enemies

Appearance

spots on shell
red eyes
brown

BOX TURTLE

can hide in shell
cannot swim

Characteristics

Habitat

inside logs, under brush—nights
rocks—days
under leaves—rainy

Organizer based on George, W. (1989). *Box Turtle at Long Pond*. New York: Trumpet Club.

figure 9.18 Graphic organizer: Classification.

3 LEVELS OF GOVERNMENT

Federal

State

Local

Leader—President

Leader—Governor

Leader—Mayor

figure 9.19   Graphic organizer: Comparison/contrast.

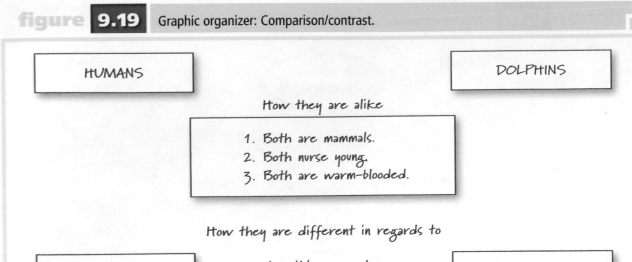
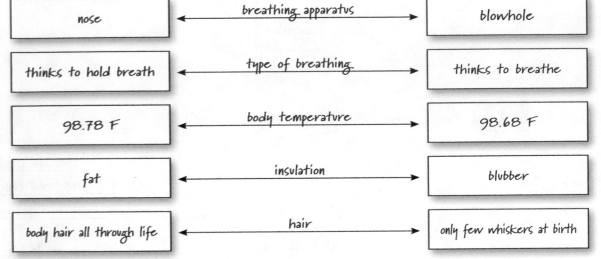

| HUMANS | | DOLPHINS |

How they are alike

1. Both are mammals.
2. Both nurse young.
3. Both are warm-blooded.

How they are different in regards to

HUMANS		DOLPHINS
nose	breathing apparatus	blowhole
thinks to hold breath	type of breathing	thinks to breathe
98.78 F	body temperature	98.68 F
fat	insulation	blubber
body hair all through life	hair	only few whiskers at birth

Organizer based on Cerullo, M. (1999). *Dolphins: What They Can Teach Us.* New York: Scholastic.

figure 9.20   Graphic organizer: Cause/effect.

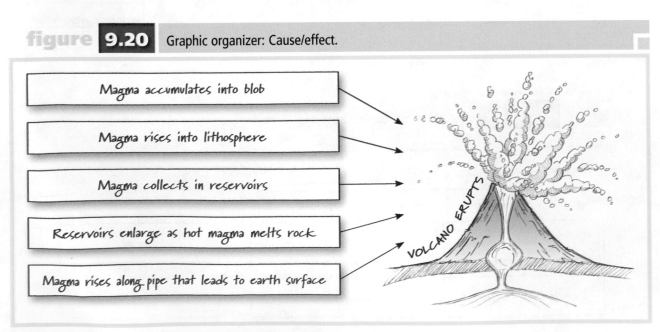

Magma accumulates into blob

Magma rises into lithosphere

Magma collects in reservoirs

Reservoirs enlarge as hot magma melts rock

Magma rises along pipe that leads to earth surface

VOLCANO ERUPTS

Organizer based on Watt, F. (1993). *Earthquakes and Volcanoes.* New York: Scholastic.

figure **9.21** Graphic organizer: Problem/solution.

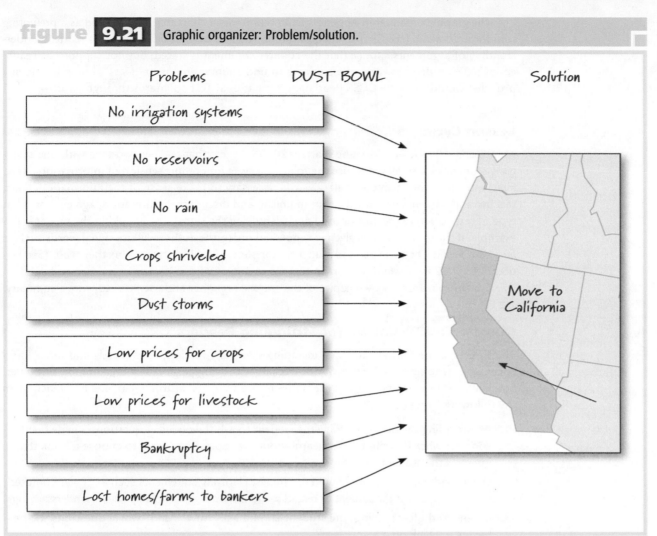

Organizer based on Stanley, J. (1992). *Children of the Dust Bowl: The True Story of the School at Weedpatch Camp.* New York: Trumpet Club Special Edition.

figure **9.22** Graphic organizer: Persuasion.

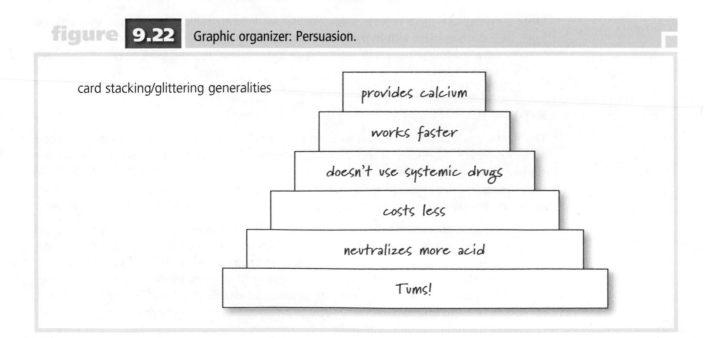

The graphic organizer in Appendix D.30 represents a chart that can be used as a prewriting tool for arguments (see Chapter 11), but it also can be used to demonstrate a reader's understanding of arguments. Notice that the counter argument is stated, but not supported. Teachers of older students may require students to find counter argument "facts"; however, the one provided would meet the CCSS Reading: Informational Text standards through grade 4.

ACTIVITY   **Lesson Cycle**   GRADES 5–8

Montelong, Herter, Ansaldo, and Hatter (2010) suggest that teachers working with one struggling student or a small group use the following cycle for comprehension of informational text. First, introduce the main vocabulary words necessary to make sense of the information. Next, teacher and students read the passage in unison and discuss the information, agreeing on what type of text structure the author used and identifying the signal words used in the passage. For example, if the information is given in sequential order, the author will use signal words such as *first, next, finally*. Then teacher and students complete a graphic organizer as they read. (See Figures 9.15–9.22 for examples of organizers for each type of text.)

Students create their own copies of the graphic organizer and use them to write a summary.

ACTIVITY   **Questioning Technique for Struggling Readers**   GRADES 3–8

The CCSS require that all students, including struggling readers, read closely and make inferences while reading complex text. When working with struggling readers on a one-on-one basis, Stricklin (2011) suggests that you use books at the students' instructional level and teach them the following strategies:

1. After reading the title, encourage the student to ask "I wonder..." questions. Guide him to consider what he would like to learn about the topic. Remember to choose a book that interests the student.
2. While reading, the student should use honest clarifying statements such as "I was confused when . . . ." Direct the student to reread sections that may help clarify any misunderstandings.
3. During and after reading, the student should ask "how?" and "why?' questions so she begins to think on a higher level.
4. After reading the student should ask: "So what is the big idea?" This will help her summarize the main ideas and not get hung up on unimportant facts.

Once students use these strategies successfully for informational texts at their instructional level, they can use them with more complex texts. Allington (2013) posits that if students are initially given reading materials at their easy or instructional reading level, they will ultimately be successful readers.

ACTIVITY   **K-T-W-L-E**   GRADES 2–6

The K-W-L method was developed by Donna Ogle (1986) as an aid to help students become active readers of informational text. This modification of the K-W-L addresses the CCSS anchor standard stating that students must "cite specific textual evidence" (NGACBP & CCSSO, CCRA for Reading, 2010, p. 10). The K-T-W-L-E is often used in classrooms, but it is also a useful strategy to use individually with a struggling reader. Here are the steps involved in using the activity:

1. Construct a chart by dividing a piece of paper into five columns as in Figure 9.23. Label the first column K, which stands for "what I KNOW about the topic." Label the second column T, for "what I THINK I know about the topic." Label the third column W, for "what I WANT to learn about the topic." The fourth column, labeled L, stands for "what I LEARNED about the topic." The fifth column, labeled E, stands for "EVIDENCE I found in the text." In this column, the student provides the source and page number or URL of where the information was found.

2. Write the topic across the top of the chart and ask the student to dictate everything she knows about it. Perform the role of scribe for young children so they do not withhold information due to spelling concerns. During the discussion, find out where and when the student learned the information. That way you will know if a struggling reader has learned about bats, sharks, or whales from viewing educational programs on TV or from listening to books read by an adult.

3. In the second column ask the student what she thinks she knows about the topic and ask her why she is not sure about the information. Again let the student dictate as you transcribe her thoughts.

4. Using the third column, have the student tell you everything she wants to learn about the topic. From this step you may find that although the text matches the student's reading level, it may not contain any new information and thus bore her. In such cases, find more appropriate materials for the reader at her instructional level.

5. After reading the passage(s) have the student tell you what she learned.

6. In the last column, help her locate the page in which the information was found. If you begin with only one book or website, you can write the source on the bottom of the chart; however, if you read from more than one text, write the source and page number or URL in the fifth column.

7. Now go back to the first column to see if all the background knowledge is accurate. Then refer to the second column to see if the student learned everything she wanted to. If not, the two of you may want to seek another source on the same topic.

Later, consider having the student fill out the K-T-W-L-E chart herself, permitting her to use inventive spelling or look up the words. K-T-W-L-E is a helpful strategy to use with a struggling reader because it helps you determine the student's background knowledge. K-T-W-L-E also actively involves the student in the reading process by encouraging her to think about what she would like to learn. Finally, K-T-W-L-E indicates if the student comprehended the material. As a variation to keep young students interested in this widely used activity, create the chart in the shape of the topic being discussed (e.g., a whale, tree, building). Figure 9.23 has a short sample of a K-T-W-L-E constructed by a teacher and a student, and Appendix D.25 contains a blank form.

figure 9.23   Sample of a K-T-W-L-E chart completed by a teacher and student.

NAME: Kita   DATE: 10/13

TOPIC: Penguins

K	T	W	L	E
Penguins are black and white They live up north	I think they lay eggs I think they are always in the water	Where they live If they lay eggs What they eat What fish eats them	They live in Antarctic (South), South America, southern tip of Africa and southern tip of Australia.	Map, p. 9
			Some penguins have more colors than black and white	pp. 6—7
			On land, they live in colonies	p. 10

Based on Morgan, S. (2005). *Penguins.* Laguna, CA: QEB.

Inference Training   GRADES 2–5

If a struggling reader does not connect book knowledge with everyday experiences, then learning seems irrelevant. Inference training stresses the importance of a student relating the information to her personal life (Anthony & Raphael, 1996). The following is an example of a teacher and a student engaging in inference training:

> Teacher: Today we are going to read about hurricanes. Do you know anything about a hurricane?
>
> Student: No.
>
> Teacher: Have you ever heard of a tornado?
>
> Student: Oh yes! My grandpa's house blew away in a tornado!
>
> Teacher: What caused his house to blow away?
>
> Student: Really strong wind!
>
> Teacher: Well, a hurricane is somewhat like a tornado. Both have strong winds and both are natural disasters, meaning that nature causes them and not humans. Today we are going to read about the hurricane named Andrew. Look at the pictures and tell me where you think it took place.
>
> Student: Some place by an ocean and where there is this kind of tree (pointing to a picture of a palm tree).
>
> Teacher: That's correct. Do you know what this tree is called?
>
> Student: No.
>
> Teacher: A palm tree.
>
> Student: Oh, I think they are in places where it is hot all year long.
>
> Teacher: Yes, they are. Where do you think the Andrew hurricane was?
>
> Student: I think it was in Texas because it is hot there all the time and I think it is on the ocean.
>
> Teacher: It is hot in Texas most of the year, but we will have to read and see if Andrew was a hurricane in Texas. When do you think Andrew happened?
>
> Student: I think it was in the 1800s; long before there were weather people.
>
> Teacher: That is an interesting observation; we'll have to read about it and see if that is true. Do you think it was a bad one?
>
> Student: It looks like everything was destroyed and some people were killed (as she looks at the pictures).

The student reads the passage to the teacher, affirming or changing predictions as she reads. The student will learn that many aspects of her predictions were incorrect, but she was correct about some people dying.

After reading the passage, the teacher relates the information to the student's personal experience. Students from the Midwest can distinguish hurricanes from tornadoes by looking at the endurance of the storms, the wind speeds, and the rainfall.

Question–Answer Relationships (QARs)   GRADES 3–8

Kinniburgh and Shaw (2009) expanded Raphael's (1986) question–answer relationship strategy in science class by having students classify questions into four categories: (1) literal questions for which answers are found in one place in the text; (2) literal questions for which answers are found in the text but require students to search several places; (3) inferential questions whose answers require students to use the text and their background knowledge; and (4) inferential questions that students can answer only by using their background knowledge. Make four columns on a whiteboard, poster board, or sentence pockets for younger students, and write questions for the four categories you will ask before, during, and after the reading. During each phase, read the questions and ask students to decide in which category the question should be placed. Then they answer the question. If the answer is found in the text, students must state where they found the answer. After all the questions are discussed, assign another passage from the Internet or another book and have the students write questions for each category. Kinniburgh and Shaw (2009) found that students were able to answer more questions correctly because they were required to determine if the question was literal or inferential and if the answer was found in the text or if they had to use their background knowledge (refer back to Figure 8.16).

The following are some example questions based on the online article "Far-Out Foods" (http://ngexplorer.cengage.com/pathfinder/1011/pdf/pa_teachersguide_1011.pdf):

- Literal question, found in one place: "What is an anthropologist?"
- Literal question, found in a number of places: "What insects are good for people to eat?"
- Inferential question, using the text and background knowledge: "Are termites nutritious?"
- Inferential question, using only background knowledge: "Is it possible that Americans consume insects without even knowing it? If so, when or how?"

The Question Builder app described later in the chapter can also be used to help students answer inferential questions.

Strategies and Activities to Use Before Reading

Survey of Text Features   GRADES 1–8   A C T I V I T Y

This strategy allows you to help a student examine the features of a textbook to predict what he will learn. (Some trade books have the same features.) First, encourage him to look for the text features that aid the reader. Using the table of contents, for example, helps struggling readers sort out main ideas from unimportant details (Bluestein, 2010). It can also help them to identify and follow the text's organizational structure. By looking at a detailed table of contents, you can help students create timelines if the information is given in chronological order. For chapters organized descriptively, comparatively, or according to some other system, you and your students can create graphic organizers gleaned from the headings and subheadings (see Figures 9.15–9.22). Next, ask the student to predict what he thinks he will learn from reading the selected passage. Activate his prior knowledge by asking if he knows anything else about the topic. If the book contains a glossary or index, convey to the student how helpful these can be. If he cannot figure out the definition of a term from context clues while reading, he simply needs to check the glossary for a definition or look in the index to see where else that topic is discussed.

Then turn to a selected chapter and help the student read the captions of the pictures. Again, the purpose is to generate interest and activate prior knowledge. Sometimes by talking about a picture, you introduce vocabulary that will be a part of the reading material. A student will then have heard the terms in context before reading the passage. After previewing the pictures, help the student read chapter headings and subheadings to predict how they are related to one another. Lastly, read with the student any questions at the start of the chapter. If there are none, then the student should read the questions at the end of the chapter. This will help the student focus on the main points of the chapter. Reading all of the text features will help a struggling reader to become familiar with vocabulary and the topic before he attempts to read.

Pre-Reading Plan (PReP)   GRADES 2–6   A C T I V I T Y

The pre-reading plan (PReP) is a questioning strategy used to activate prior knowledge and to develop a student's interest in the topic (Anthony & Raphael, 1996). The following is an example of a discussion between teacher and student before they read a book about caves:

Teacher (asking general questions about caves): Have you ever heard of stalactites and stalagmites?

Student: I think so.

Teacher: What do you think they are?

Student: I think they are the icicles that are in caves.

Teacher: Do you know anything else about them?

Student: I think the stalagmites hang from the cave and the other ones come out of the floor of the cave.

Teacher: Where did you learn all that?

Student: I saw a show on TV about going down into a cave. It was really cold and dark in it.

Teacher: That sounds interesting. I think the stalagmites come out of the cave's floor and the stalactites hang from the ceiling. But let's read and find out for sure which is correct.

Student: I think you are right. I remember the man hit his head on a stalactite and it was hanging from the ceiling.

PReP is especially helpful to correct a student's misconceptions about a particular topic.

Strategies and Activities to Use During Reading

ACTIVITY   **Think-Aloud for Informational Text**   GRADES 2–5

The purpose of the think-aloud strategy is for you to model what proficient readers do to make sense of a text (Davey, 1983). In this strategy, choose a passage that has new vocabulary and unfamiliar information, and then perform the following steps:

1. Read the title or heading of the passage and make predictions about the topic. "I think this will be about _____"; or "I think I will learn_____"; or "This subheading tells me I will also learn_____."

2. Describe the images that come to mind as you read the passage. For example, "I can almost feel (or hear or see or smell) _____."

3. Give analogies that relate the material to your personal life. "I (saw/heard/tasted/felt) _____ that is very similar to (topic of passage)."

4. Verbalize passages or phrases that you don't understand. This helps the student understand that proficient readers do not need to know everything to succeed.

5. Demonstrate the strategy you use to understand the passage (e.g., rereading, looking at a diagram or picture, looking up a word in the glossary, or reading ahead to see if the concept is explained).

Figure 9.24 is an example of a think-aloud using the section "Running Rivers" (pp. 30–31) in John Farndon's book *All About Planet Earth* (2000).

After you model a think-aloud, have the student do a think-aloud while you observe. The think-aloud should become a regular habit for struggling readers.

figure 9.24   Think-aloud based on John Farndon's *All About Planet Earth.*

1. The title "Running Rivers" tells me I will maybe learn why rivers run, where they come from, and where they go.

2. I could almost hear the noise of the "Thundering Water."

3. It reminds me of noise at Niagara Falls. I could not even hear my sister talking to me when we went to Niagara Falls even though we were standing right by each other. It also smelled like rain water as it roared over the ledge.

4. I still don't understand why a river winds. I would think that the closer it got to the sea, it would just go straight. I wonder if I can find out some more information about why rivers wind instead of going straight.

5. This diagram helps me better understand the three reaches of a river and how it becomes broader. I am surprised that many rivers don't become so broad in the lower reaches that they become lakes.

Based on Farndon, J. (2000). *All About Planet Earth.* New York: Anness Publishing.

Checklist

The checklist strategy allows students to see reading as an active process, in which they constantly analyze what is being read. You can model the process for students using the following steps:

1. Prepare statements about a passage that are either true or false.
2. Together with students read the statements before beginning to read the passage.
3. As you read, place a (+) before each true statement.
4. At the end of the reading, go back and reword the false statements to make them true. If necessary, you and the students should reread the material.

Figure 9.25 is a checklist that a teacher and student completed while reading "Into the Bat Cave" from Jenny Wood's *Caves: Facts and Stories and Activities* (1990).

figure **9.25** Checklist for *Caves* by Jenny Wood.

+ 1. Bats live in colonies.		**CORRECTION OF FALSE STATEMENTS**
+ 2. Bats live in caves.		3. Bats sleep during the day.
– 3. They sleep during the night.		4. Bats have excellent hearing.
– 4. Bats are almost deaf.		5. Bats are almost blind.
– 5. Bats have excellent eyesight.		9. Glowworms trap insects with sticky threads that they have spun.
+ 6. Echolocation is continuous high-pitched sounds.		
+ 7. Glowworms are found in New Zealand caves.		
+ 8. A glowworm's rear end gives off light.		
– 9. Glowworms trap flying insects in their mouths.		

Request

ReQuest is a good strategy for struggling readers because you and the students reverse roles. The students ask you the questions, and you provide the answers. The following steps are used with ReQuest:

1. Together with students, silently read a paragraph.
2. Have the students ask you a question that can be answered after reading the passage. It is the students' responsibility to clearly state the question. If it is not clearly stated say, "I don't understand the question."
3. If the question cannot be answered from the material read, ask students to help you find the answer.

This strategy is especially enjoyable for students if you occasionally give an incorrect response. You, of course, are checking the students' comprehension. This activity teaches students to formulate good questions and that the answers to some questions are right there in the book, while others demand they "read between the lines." Ciardiello (1998) found that when students formulate questions, they internalize new information and use higher-level thinking skills.

Strategies and Activities to Use After Reading

ACTIVITY   **Scanning**   GRADES 3–5

Provide opportunities for students to practice scanning while they find answers to textual questions. Too often struggling readers begin looking for an answer by reading from the beginning of the passage. This is time consuming and unnecessary. Teach them instead to check headings to determine if the answer can be located in a particular section. If the question asks for a date teach students to scan the page for numerals, such as 1776 or 2002. If the question asks for a name, the students should be taught to scan the page for the capital letters of proper nouns. Struggling readers need to remember that definitions can often be located by boldface or italic text. These dates, names, and definitions are easy for the eye to locate when scanning the printed page. Demonstrate to struggling readers what to do when looking for dates, names, and definitions. Then have them practice the strategy with you.

ACTIVITY   **Learning Logs**   GRADES 2–6

Learning logs are an after-reading strategy that connects reading and writing and are associated with all types of informational texts, including textbooks, trade books, computer programs, Internet sites, and magazines. With learning logs, students recall what they have read and then articulate it in a concise summary. After you have read and discussed a text with students, have them close all reading materials and write about what they have learned. Carefully analyze what the students write to see if they recall the main ideas or get stuck on unimportant details. Determine if the students can explain concepts in logical order and if they can summarize. As an additional task, have the students exchange logs with a partner to share information. Figure 9.26 presents a learning log entry and the teacher's analysis. This student has just read *Octopus' Den* (1997) by Deirdre Langeland. Figure 9.27 is a science log of a second-grade student.

figure 9.26 Learning log entry and analysis.

March 1: Octopus

An octopus eats crabs and glass. He has funny eyes. He squirts ink. He eats snakes and apples. I learned how to draw a circle with lines.

Teacher Analysis

The following information is incorrect. The octopus does not eat glass or snakes. The text states: "When he is sure it is safe, Octopus snakes an arm toward the piece of glass and snatches it back to the safety of the rock. For a moment he investigates it, the suckers on his arms tasting [not eating] the new object and feeling its shiny-smooth surface."

The last statement in the log is also incorrect. The text states: "The tiny opening is the size of an apple." The octopus does not eat apples.

Obviously, this reader reads concrete words and paints mental pictures of those objects, which causes the reader to see the octopus eating snakes and apples. It is apparent that the reader is not aware that these words have multiple meanings and uses.

(From the student's final statement, the teacher also realizes that the child does not know the term *graphic organizer*.)

figure **9.27** Sample science log, second grade.

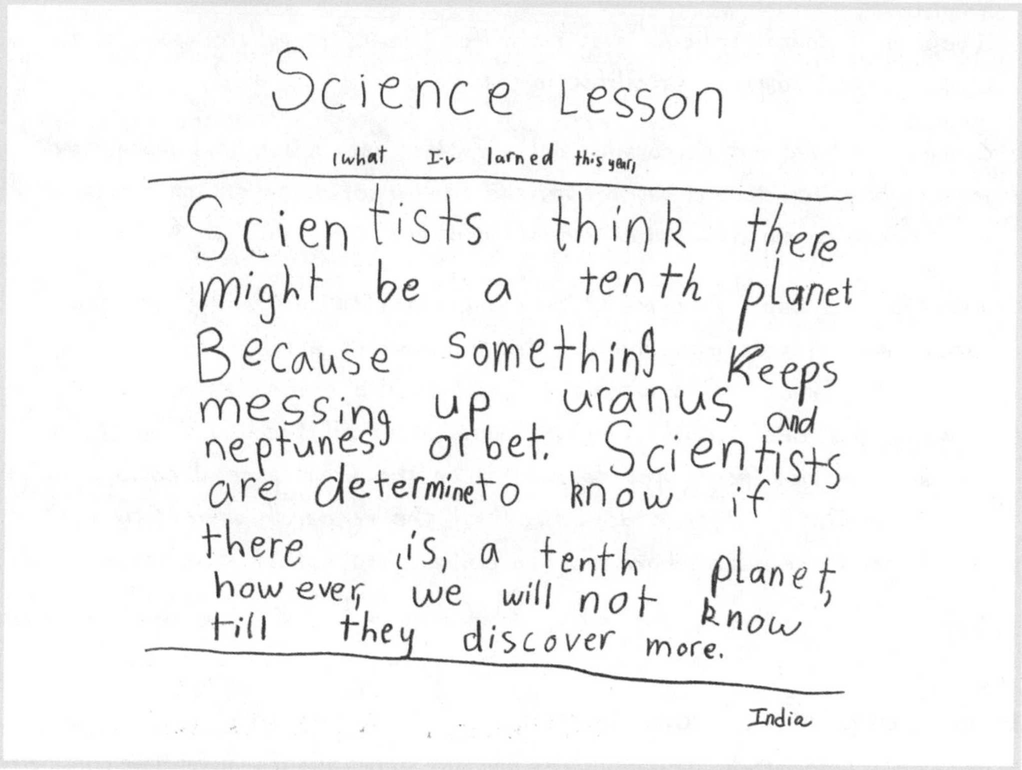

Science Lesson
(what I'v larned this year)

Scientists think there might be a tenth planet Because something keeps messing up uranus and neptunes orbet. Scientists are determine to know if there is, a tenth planet, however, we will not know till they discover more.

India

Collaborative Approach

GRADES 3–8   A C T I V I T Y

Meyer (2010) suggests the reading workshop format used with fiction reading should also be used with informational texts. This strategy is based on Vygotsky's (1978) social learning theory and the evidence-based approach of the QAR (Raphael & Au, 2005; see the activity earlier in this chapter). In the reading workshop, all students read the same informational text—from either a trade book or an online source—based on the topic they are studying in the textbook, such as natural disasters or the U.S. Civil War. Students write three types of questions on three different sticky notes after they have read the passage. The first is a "burning question," maybe a question about the definition of a word or clarification of the text. The second is a "wondering question," which begins with "Perhaps . . . ," "Could . . . ," "I wonder . . . ," "What could?", or "What if . . . ?" The third is a clever connection thought. These statements begin with "This reminds me of"; "I remember when"; "Another text like this is"; "I didn't realize that"; or "Aha!"

After all the sticky notes are posted to a board that has three columns, students discuss their questions, answer them, or find answers to them.

Question Connect Transform (QCT) for Informational Text

GRADES 6–8   A C T I V I T Y

This instructional strategy (Richards, 2006) was introduced in the Intervention section in Chapter 8, but it can also be used with informational text. In this technique, you guide the students to question the moral issue of a text. The students then connect that issue to their own lives and write about how they can take action to help transform society.

For example, after reading an online article about space junk, Ms. Snyder asked her students to write about the moral issues raised in the article. Figure 9.28 shows Dan's response to the three-part QCT.

figure 9.28 Sample response to QCT.

Question: I do not believe it is right for humans to pollute space with rockets used to place satellites in space.

Connect: I have not personally shot a rocket into space, but many times my neighbor has tossed paper cups and hamburger wrappers on our lawn. It is messy so my dad makes me clean it up.

Transform: I can write my U. S. Congress members and share the ideas from this article and ask them to write a bill to eliminate unnecessary rockets so we do not add to the space trash that is already up there. I could write a poem about all the space waste and ask our local newspaper to print it on the front page. I could also write our state's science department at the research university and ask them to research how we can collect trash that is in space.

A C T I V I T Y   **Dramatizing Informational Texts**   GRADES 2–7

Many teachers associate dramatizations with narrative stories and may never have considered having students dramatize a concept. For example, young students can act out how a tiny caterpillar eventually becomes a butterfly. Older students can act out the digestive system or the functions of the heart, or a part of Lewis and Clark's journey across the plains. McLaughlin (2012) encourages dramatizing concepts as a type of comprehension assessment in order to give kinesthetic learners an opportunity to display what they know.

COMPREHENSION OF INFORMATIONAL TEXT AND TECHNOLOGY

Our increasingly global world makes Internet proficiency mandatory. Students must be able to comprehend and respond to informational text found on the Internet, and doing so requires different reading comprehension strategies. Henry (2006) found that students using the Internet should know how to:

1. Locate materials.
2. Identify important questions.
3. Use search engines and select search words.
4. Refine search words so they are as specific as possible.
5. Read and evaluate the short descriptions found in search engine results and then use only the sites that address their topic.
6. Evaluate the site's or author's credibility, because anyone can post information on the Internet.
7. Use the "back" button to return to a previous page.
8. Read and comprehend the text. Often, Internet text is too advanced for elementary students.
9. Take notes from the sites, including what is needed for the citation.
10. Synthesize material from the various sites.
11. Cite sources.

Another important skill is the ability to sift through extraneous material without losing focus (Karchmer-Klein & Harlow-Shinas, 2012). Appendix C.46 contains a checklist based on Henry's findings that you can use to assess a student's basic Internet skills.

In addition to assessing basic skills, teachers can assess students' online reading comprehension to determine which students need additional assistance. Online reading comprehension assessments (ORCAs) are one method for measuring students' ability to comprehend online resources. ORCAs are curriculum-based measurements that capture "'real-time' online reading skills and strategies" (Coiro, 2009, p. 60). They present reading passages accompanied by multiple questions in a web-based environment. Using software programs such as Camtesia or I Show U, teachers can record a student's actions and comments as she reads the passage and completes the questions. They can then use online tools such as Survey Monkey to compile student responses and review the videos to determine how their students are reading online. If teachers wish to create their own ORCAs, Coiro recommends they construct short challenges using an online quiz format that requires students to:

- Use a search engine to locate information
- Check information with another source
- Evaluate the information's accuracy
- Determine the author's or website's purpose and how it influences the information provided

Websites: Informational Text

If the assessments indicate your students need work in navigating and comprehending online material, one method for teaching online skills is the Internet scavenger hunt. A good source for any beginner is Scavenger Hunts: Searching for Treasures on the Internet (www.education-world.com/a_curr/curr113.shtml)

Because websites are not objectively evaluated by trusted experts, you must also teach students how to evaluate the information they find. Teach your students to compare their background information about the topic and information found in other sources with the information found on the particular site. They can determine whether the site's information is current by checking the date on which the information was posted. Students should find out who the author is and with what organization, if any, the author is affiliated. You teach critical-thinking skills as you help students find biases in the information. The Library of Congress website, www.loc.gov, and its America's Story website, www.americaslibrary.gov, are excellent sources for accurate information.

Karchmer (2001) found that most reputable websites include the following:

1. The author's credentials with an e-mail address.
2. If the website is posted by an organization, its address, telephone number, and e-mail address.
3. Complete citations of quoted material.
4. Endorsements from organizations.
5. Links only to reputable sites.

Of course, when using the Internet, you must caution students about inappropriate sites. Many schools use blocking software to keep the Internet safe for students. Some teachers pre-screen sites and permit students to use only those they pre-screen.

Many informational ebooks are available on topics that interest elementary students. Use these with struggling readers to encourage problem solving and comprehension skills. Because choosing appropriate ebooks is not always an easy task, use the evaluation form in Appendix D.26. Some excellent online sites for informational texts are:

www.timeforkids.com

www.nasa.gov/kidsclub

www.nasa.gov/audience/forstudents/index.html

National Geographic Kids, http://kids.national geographic.com/

Kids Biology, www.kidsbiology.com

Read Write Think, www.readwritethink.org

Brain Pop Science, www.apples4teachers.com/science

http://www.apples4theteacher.com/science.html

Kids Know It Network, www.kidsknowit.com

The following associations and agencies award or identify high-quality children's and young adult books, many of which cover content areas.

The American Institute of Physics Science Communication Awards, https://www.aip.org/aip/awards/science-communication/children.

The ALA's Association for Library Service to Children Robert F. Sibert Medal page, www.ala.org/alsc/awardsgrants/bookmedia/sibertmedal.

The *Boston Globe*–Horn Book Awards, http://www.hbook.com/boston-globe-horn-book-awards/.

The California Department of Education Recommended Literature List, http://www.cde.ca.gov/ci/cr/rl//.

National Council for the Social Studies, Notable Social Studies Trade Books for Young People, www.socialstudies.org/notable.

National Council of Teachers of English, Orbis Pictus Award for Outstanding Nonfiction for Children, www.ncte.org/awards/orbispictus.

National Science Teachers Association, Outstanding Science Trade Books, www.nsta.org/publications/ostb.

Society of Children's Book Writers and Illustrators Awards, www.scbwi.org/awards/.

The Concepts of Comprehension Assessment (COCA) website (http://msularc.educ.msu.edu/what-we-do/projects/mai-coca) contains an assessment of informational reading comprehension designed for first and second grade students. It measures four factors: comprehension strategy use, vocabulary strategy use and knowledge, knowledge of informational text features, and comprehension of graphics in the context of text. Also recommended is the Intelligent Tutoring for Structure Strategy (ITSS). Online searches will locate resources available to apply ITSS; for example, a tutorial for teaching students how to use a passage's expository structure as an aid to comprehension.

Apps: Comprehension of Informational Texts

Apps available to help students with comprehension of informational texts include the following examples.

Skill: Fact & Opinion ($3.99, Grades 2–5). This bingo-style game helps students learn to determine whether a passage is based on fact or opinion. For each correct answer the student places a marker on their card; five markers in a row wins. Allows for single and multiple players.

Professor Garfield Fact or Opinion (Free, Grades K–2). This app helps students learn to distinguish between fact and opinion. The app is part cartoon, part game, and part online safety lesson. When Garfield's friend receives an "F" on his report about goats for using opinions instead of facts, Professor Garfield steps in to explain the differences between a fact and an opinion, how to read with a questioning mind, and how a fact can be verified. Developed by the Virginia Department of Education.

Question Builder ($5.99, Grades K–5). This app is designed to help students learn to answer abstract questions and create responses based on inference. Question formats include why, what, where, when, and random. Use of audioclips improves auditory processing for children with autism spectrum disorders or sensory processing disorders. Audio clip reinforcement can be turned on or off for children who do not have special needs.

CONCLUDING THOUGHTS

This chapter introduced assessment and reading strategies to aid in students' comprehension of informational text. Teachers are responsible for using these assessments regularly and explicitly teaching such strategies to struggling readers based on their assessment results. Reflective teachers must also analyze which strategies are best for each particular reader. Teachers must also engage their students in critical literacies as they read informational text.

reflective learning

ENGLISH LEARNERS. Hiroki, a fifth-grade student from Japan, arrived in the United States with his parents at the beginning of the school year. Hiroki's father is working on an advanced degree at the local university and reads and speaks English fluently. Hiroki's mother is literate in Japanese, but does not read English. Hiroki understands some oral English, and his father says Hiroki can read second-grade English materials. Ms. Johnson, his teacher, knows it is important for Hiroki to learn science and social studies concepts in addition to increasing his literacy skills. Hiroki's father has told Ms. Johnson that Hiroki is very interested in outer space and in studying inventors.

questions

1. What assessment could Ms. Johnson administer to determine Hiroki's reading level?
2. What can Ms. Johnson do to help Hiroki develop his literacy skills?
3. What strategies can Ms. Johnson use to teach the content area concepts to Hiroki?
4. What small group activities would benefit Hiroki?
5. What websites would you recommend Ms. Johnson show Hiroki so he can research his two areas of interest—outer space and inventors?

READING COMPREHENSION. As a teacher, you will often ask a student to read a passage. In some cases, even though the student may read the passage fluently, when you ask him to tell you what he read, he may struggle to retell the passage or answer questions about it.

Figure 9.29 contains a short passage from *Snakes* by Sally Morgan that Kara, a struggling fourth grader, reads for her teacher.

After Kara's silent reading, the teacher asks some questions. Here is their discussion.

Teacher: What was the main idea of this passage?

Kara: Snakes.

Teacher: What did you learn about snakes?

Kara: Snakes do not have any feet.

Teacher: Why do you think this passage is called "Predators"?

Kara: Because it's about that kind of snake?

Teacher: Can you explain what a "predator" type of snake looks like or eats?

Kara: I think they eat spiders.

Using your knowledge of reading comprehension, respond to the following questions. First try to answer the questions by yourself and then discuss your answers with classmates to compare your ideas.

questions

1. What causes Kara not to comprehend the passage?
2. Cite two specific examples (give quotes) of the student's responses to the text that support your answer to question 1.
3. Describe two different intervention activities to help address the need you have identified.
4. Explain why these strategies would help Kara.

figure 9.29

Excerpt from *Snakes,* by Sally Morgan (2005).

Predators

Snakes are predators, which means they kill other animals for food. Many snakes hunt a range of animals, from insects and worms to lizards and mice. Others hunt only one kind of animal. For example, hook-nosed snakes eat only spiders.

It is not just small animals that get eaten by snakes. Big animals, like deer, goats, and even people, get swallowed up by snakes like giant boa constrictors and pythons.

The Babon viper's color and pattern helps it hide among fallen leaves while it waits to ambush prey.

Snakes do not have any feet, so they can't hold their food and bite chunks out of it. Instead, snakes swallow their prey in one piece, usually head first.

Snakes can open their mouth very wide, because their lower jaw is loosely joined to the bottom of their skull. This means even large animals can fit through. The common egg-eater snake swallows bird eggs that are up to four times the size of its head. That's like a person swallowing a car tire.

Snakes have backward facing teeth to stop their prey from escaping.

Source: Morgan, S. (2005). *Snakes.* Laguna Hills, CA: QEB Publisher.

10 Fluency

So it is with children who learn to read fluently and well: They begin to take flight into whole new worlds as effortlessly as young birds take to the sky.

WILLIAM JAMES

scenario

"Will's life was the American dream.

He was rich in friendship, fortune, and fame.

But he always loved people—all people—

With a grin on his face and a smile in his heart.

'I never met a man I didn't like.'" (n.p.)

Thus ends Zach's flawless, fluent reading of *Will Rogers* (Keating, 2001). Abby, his tutor, is perplexed because Zach's mother said he needed help in reading. She explained to Abby that the fourth grader was getting poor grades in science and social studies, and his teacher said it was because of his reading. So when he finishes the book, Abby compliments him on his excellent reading. However, when she asks him what the book was about, he says, "Will Rogers."

"What did you learn about Will Rogers?" Abby prompts.

"He must be a cowboy because of the picture on the front cover."

"Is there anything else you remember?"

"Not really."

Abby reads the first page to Zach and then asks what he knows about Will Rogers.

"He traveled all over the world and he never met a man he did not like." This is exactly all the information shared on page one.

"Great! Now you reread the second page and let's see what we learn."

Again Zach reads the page without any errors, but he cannot provide any details about the information.

Abby knows some students read fluently without comprehending a passage. She figures this is the case with Zach and knows she has hard work ahead of her.

As you read this chapter, consider the following questions:

guiding questions

1. Do you believe that all fluent readers comprehend what they read?

2. Why would it be important to assess Zach in not just rate but in all components of fluency? What assessments would you recommend Abby use for this purpose?

3. Do you know what strategies to teach Zach so he not only reads fluently but also comprehends what he reads?

introduction

Fluency, the ability to read with automatic word recognition, expression, and meaning, is a critical component of reading instruction (Deeney, 2010; DeKonty-Applegate, Quinn, & Applegate, 2008; Rasinski, 2012; Rasinski & Lenhart, 2007; Stahl, 2011). Since the release of the National Reading Panel Report (NRP, 2000), the reauthorization of the Individuals with Disabilities Education Act (IDEA) in 2004, and the mandate to use the Response to Intervention (RTI) framework to identify students that need special services, fluency assessments and instructional strategies have received wide atten-

tion (Dekonty-Applegate, Applegate, & Modla, 2009; Moore & Hinchman, 2006; Rasinski & Padak, 2005; Valencia et al., 2010). Additionally, the CCSS identify fluency skills in the standards for Reading: Foundational Skills.

Despite all the attention given to fluency, teachers report that some of their most fluent readers do not comprehend what they read, as is the case with Zach in the opening scenario (Deeney, 2010; Marcell & Ferraro, 2013; Rasinski, 2012; Stahl, 2011). How can this be? In part, the answer may be that the number of words read correctly per minute (WCPM) has commonly been used to show student growth in fluency. The assessment typically used to measure growth in students' WCPM is one-minute readings. Because high WCPM scores are often equated with fluent reading, some educators may have had the misperception that fluency has been achieved; however, fluency involves much more than reading rate (Deeney, 2010; Marcell & Ferraro, 2013; Rasinski, 2012; Stahl, 2011).

Reading ability for both children and adults is measured by fluency—but what does fluency entail? According to *The Literacy Dictionary* (Harris & Hodges, 1995) fluency is "freedom from word-identification problems that might hinder comprehension . . . ; automaticity" (p. 585), and a fluent reader is "any person who reads smoothly, without hesitation, and with comprehension" (p. 85). Listeners recognize fluent readers because they read at a good pace, attend to the punctuation in sentences, raise their voices for question marks, pause for commas, and increase in volume for exclamation marks. Fluent readers recognize words automatically and quickly decode unknown words; they slow down when needed to emphasize a phrase, metaphor, or personification in order for the listeners to comprehend what is being read. Audiences enjoy listening to fluent readers because they interpret the text with expression.

When struggling readers read in a slow, staggering, monotone voice, audiences have a difficult time listening to and comprehending the text. Disfluency is not only a problem for the audience, however; it also causes comprehension problems for the reader. Disfluency causes readers to become self-conscious of their reading, and they soon learn to avoid reading in public. Readers who are not fluent also read less because it takes them longer than proficient readers to read a passage (Allington, 2013). Because reading takes so much time, they become discouraged and avoid it altogether.

Comprehension is the main purpose for all reading, and fluency is important for comprehension. This chapter presents two definitions of fluency and the four main components of fluency that are recognized by most researchers and educators: rate, automaticity or accuracy, prosody, and comprehension (Deeney, 2010; Marcell, 2011/2012; Marcell & Ferraro, 2013; Rasinski 2012; Valencia et al., 2010). The chapter also presents information teachers should know about fluency instruction, various instruments used to assess fluency, and numerous strategies that have proven to be effective with individual struggling readers and small groups.

WHAT IS FLUENCY?

The NAEP defines **fluency** as the ease or naturalness of reading. The key elements include:

1. grouping or **phrasing** of words as revealed through the intonation, stress, and pauses exhibited by readers;

2. adherence to author's **syntax**; and

3. **expressiveness** of the oral reading—interjecting a sense of feeling, anticipation, or characterization.

Figure 10.1 presents the NAEP fluency scale. Students at levels 3 and 4 are generally considered to be fluent, and those at levels 1 and 2 non-fluent.

Two other aspects of oral reading measured in the NAEP assessment are **accuracy** and **rate**. **Accuracy** is determined through an analysis of students' oral reading deviations from the words in the text (misread words), and **rate** is measured in terms of words-per-minute. The most important element of fluency, however, is comprehension. If students read with great expression, read all words accurately with good rate, but cannot explain what they read, they are not fluent readers! Comprehension is the goal of all reading and is certainly the goal of fluent reading.

Stahl (2011) puts fluency on a continuum with all other reading skills. On the left side of the continuum are **constrained skills**—skills easy to master and quantitatively assess such as writing one's name, reciting

figure 10.1

NAEP's oral reading fluency scale.

LEVEL 4

Reads primarily in larger, meaningful phrase groups. Although some regressions, repetitions, and deviations from text may be present, these do not appear to detract from the overall structure of the story. Preservation of the author's syntax is consistent. Some or most of the story is read with expressive interpretation.

LEVEL 3

Reads primarily in three- or four-word phrase groups. Some smaller groupings may be present. However, the majority of phrasing seems appropriate and preserves the syntax of the author. Little or no expressive interpretation is present.

LEVEL 2

Reads primarily in two-word phrases with some three- or four-word groupings. Some word-by-word reading may be present. Word groupings may seem awkward and unrelated to larger context of sentence or passage.

LEVEL 1

Reads primarily word-by-word. Occasional two-word or three-word phrases may occur—but these are infrequent and/or they do not preserve meaningful syntax.

Source: U.S. Department of Education, Institute of Education Sciences, National Center for Education Statistics, National Assessment of Educational Progress (NAEP), 2002 Oral Reading Study.

the alphabet automatically, and reading high frequency words. On the right side of the continuum are **unconstrained reading skills**; these skills are difficult to quantitatively assess because they continue to develop over one's life span. Examples of unconstrained skills include comprehension and vocabulary. In terms of fluency, Stahl identifies the component of accuracy as constrained and the component of comprehension as unconstrained. The constrained skills need to be mastered at levels of automaticity in order for the unconstrained to be attained. Stahl believes "[i]t is alarming to think about the ways that measures of reading rate are used to make decisions related to teacher accountability, general reading ability, and instruction" (p. 54). I concur with Stahl and other reading researchers and educators (Deeney, 2010; Marcell, 2011/2012; Rasinski, 2012) who believe that all four components need to be addressed. The next section discusses the four main components of fluency mentioned above and recognized by most researchers and educators (Deeney, 2010; Marcell & Ferraro, 2013; Rasinski, 2012; Stahl, 2011; Valencia et al., 2010).

COMPONENTS OF FLUENCY

In order for students to become fluent readers, teachers need to help them develop rate, automaticity or accuracy, prosody, and comprehension. Furthermore, to develop automaticity readers must master four categories of subskills: (1) phonological, (2) word recognition, (3) word analysis, and (4) semantic. Allington (2013) and Fountas and Pinnell (2006b) describe the traits of fluent readers versus disfluent readers. They are summarized in Figure 10.2.

Rate

A slow rate is one of the most common indicators of inefficient reading, and rate has been the most assessed element for determining student growth in fluency (Marcell, 2011/2012; Rasinski, 2012). As mentioned above, students are often given the words correct per minute (WCPM) assessment to determine fluency. In an effort to increase students' reading rate, some educators may ask students to complete repeated readings of these short passages. This may result in misleading WCPM rates and also may cause many students to equate fast reading with fluent reading (Marcell, 2011/2012; Rasinski, 2012; Stahl, 2011). Instead of emphasizing fast reading, teachers should focus on appropriate reading rates. Reading researchers have varying opinions about what constitutes an appropriate reading rate.

Hasbrouck and Tindal (2006) collected data from school districts in 23 states regarding students' fluency scores as measured by words correct per minute for students in grades 1 through 8 during three different times of the year—fall, winter, and spring—because oral reading fluency increases throughout the school year. Figure 10.3 shows the scores for each grade at each scoring time, with students categorized into 10th, 25th, 50th, 75th, and 90th percentiles. Teachers can use these norms as a way of diagnosing students' reading rates in comparison to the norm for their grade and time of the year (fall, winter, or spring). Obviously, if a student's reading rate is in the 10th percentile, he will need intervention. Remember, though, these norms reflect only students' correct words per minute and do not reflect their prosody and comprehension at those reading rates.

figure 10.2   Traits of fluent readers versus disfluent readers.

FLUENT READERS	DISFLUENT READERS
1. Use knowledge of language to keep reading.	1. Lack knowledge of language skills.
2. Use an appropriate reading rate.	2. Read word-by-word.
3. Slow down to solve problems.	3. Think fast reading is good reading.
4. Have automatic word recognition.	4. Have a poor bank of sight words.
5. Have automatic word analysis skills.	5. Lack word analysis skills.
6. Use intonation to convey meaning.	6. Lack expression.
7. Adhere to punctuation cues.	7. Omit punctuation.
8. Use knowledge of story structure and expository text to keep reading.	8. Lack prior knowledge of story structure and expository text structure.
9. Reproduce the natural phrasing of the text.	9. Lack the ability to phrase text appropriately.

Sources: Allington, R. L. (2006). *What Really Matters for Struggling Readers: Designing Research-based Programs.* (2nd ed.). Boston: Pearson/Allyn & Bacon / Fountas, I. D., & Pinnell, G. S. (2006b). *Guided Reading: Good First Teaching for All Children.* Portsmouth, NH: Heinemann.

figure 10.3 — Oral reading fluency norms, grades 1–8.

GRADE	PERCENTILE	FALL WCPM	WINTER WCPM	SPRING WCPM	GRADE	PERCENTILE	FALL WCPM	WINTER WCPM	SPRING WCPM
1	90	N/A	81	111	5	90	166	182	194
	75	N/A	47	82		75	139	156	168
	50	N/A	23	53		50	110	127	139
	25	N/A	12	28		25	85	99	109
	10	N/A	6	15		10	61	74	83
	SD		32	39		SD	45	44	45
Count [Students]			16,950	19,434	Count [Students]		16,212	13,331	15,292
2	90	106	125	142	6	90	177	195	204
	75	79	100	117		75	153	167	177
	50	51	72	89		50	127	140	150
	25	25	42	61		25	98	111	122
	10	11	18	31		10	68	82	93
	SD	37	41	42	Count [Students]		10,520	9,218	11,290
Count [Students]		15,896	18,229	20,128	7	90	180	192	202
3	90	128	146	162		75	156	165	177
	75	99	120	137		50	128	136	150
	50	71	92	107		25	102	109	123
	25	44	62	78		10	79	88	98
	10	21	36	48		SD	40	43	41
	SD	40	43	44	Count [Students]		6,482	4,058	5,998
Count [Students]		16,988	17,383	18,372	8	90	185	199	199
4	90	145	166	180		75	161	173	177
	75	119	139	152		50	133	146	151
	50	94	112	123		25	106	115	124
	25	68	87	98		10	77	84	97
	10	45	61	72		SD	43	45	41
	SD	40	41	43	Count [Students]		5,546	3,496	5,335
Count [Students]		16,523	14,572	16,269					

WCPM: Words correct per minute   SD: Standard deviation   Count: Number of student scores

Source: J. Hasbrouck and G. Tindal (2006). Oral reading fluency norms: A valuable assessment tool for reading teachers. *The Reading Teacher, 59*(7), 636–644. Reprinted with permission from the International Reading Association via Copyright Clearance Center.

Oral reading rate is calculated by counting how many words the student reads in 60 seconds. To find the most accurate rate for a student, have the student read at least three timed passages on the same easy reading level, and then average the reading rates. The silent reading rate is calculated by multiplying the total number of words read by 60 and then dividing that number by the total number of seconds it takes the student to read the passage.

Silent reading: $\dfrac{\text{Number of words read} \times 60}{\text{Number of seconds to read}} = \text{WPM}$

When working with struggling readers, select reading material that is at the student's easy reading level at first and at the instructional level later. As illustrated in the opening scenario, comprehension is the purpose for reading; therefore, a fast reading rate can never substitute for comprehension. Teachers must help struggling readers understand that proficient readers slow down when the passage is difficult to comprehend and speed up when the text is easy to comprehend.

Automaticity/Accuracy

Rate and fluency depend on **automaticity**, which is "the ability to engage and coordinate a number of complex subskills and strategies with little cognitive effort" (Allington, 2006). One of the reading theories associated with fluency and its importance to comprehension is **automatic information processing theory** (LaBerge & Samuels, 1974). This theory proposes that when young readers need to give all their cognitive energy to decoding words, they have no energy for deeper, comprehensive reading. LaBerge and Samuels argue that readers who recognize words effortlessly can devote all of their mental energies to comprehension, while readers who struggle to decode words and interpret punctuation have fewer cognitive resources available to process meaning. Readers who struggle with word recognition spend much of their mental ability on remembering letter–sound relationships or on breaking words into smaller chunks.

Recognizing common words

One of the subskills of automaticity is the ability to recognize common words, often referred to as *sight words,* that appear in almost all texts (see Chapter 6). Some examples of sight words are *have, done, live,* and *come.* Chapter 6 has more information on sight words and strategies for a reader to develop a bank of them.

Associating letter/letter combinations with their sounds

A second subskill of automaticity is the ability to associate letters or letter combinations (e.g., /sh/, /wr/, /oi/) with their sounds. For example, fluent readers recognize the /sh/ in *shake* as one sound, while too often disfluent readers will attempt to sound out the word letter by letter: /s/ + /h/ + /a/ + /k/ + /e/. This subskill includes familiarity with the various sounds the vowels make and when the various vowel sounds are used. The proficient reader quickly recognizes that adding an *e* to *cap* makes the *a* into a long *a* sound and changes the word to *cape.* They quickly recognize the subtle differences between the two vowel sounds of the words *pin* and *pen.* They understand and recognize vowel digraphs, diphthongs, and consonant clusters (see Chapter 5).

Recognizing chunks/syllables within words

A third subskill of automaticity is the ability to quickly analyze unknown words by recognizing chunks—or syllables—within words, such as onset and rime, prefixes, suffixes, and root words. When readers recognize onset and rime, they quickly combine two sounds instead of sounding out three or more sounds. For example *hat* = /h/ + /at/ for readers who recognize onset and rime, while disfluent readers sound out the three letters: /h/ + /a/ + /t/. Readers who see the syllables within unknown words also cut down on reading time. For example, readers who recognize *transportation* as *trans + por + ta + tion* have a faster reading rate than readers who attempt to sound out every letter (*t + r + a + n + s + p + o + r + t + a + t + i + o + n*). With a polysyllabic word such as *transportation,* readers take such a long time to sound out each letter that they often forget the beginning sound by the time they get to the last letter. It is very difficult to remember the sounds of 14 letters and then blend them back together. In fact, with the word *transportation,* readers produce the wrong sounds if they sound out the individual letters of the last syllable. They need to recognize *tion* as /shun/ instead of /t/ + /i/ + /o/ + /n/. For more information on prefixes, suffixes, root words, and blending, see Chapter 6.

Recognizing the meanings of words

A fourth subskill of automaticity is the ability to recognize the main meaning of words as well as the multiple meanings of these words. Readers who know the meaning of *crimp* read on when they encounter it in this sentence: "Fisherman Joe's job was to crimp the fish as Fisherman Mike tossed them to him." Some readers may be able to pronounce *crimp,* but do not know its meaning. They will slow down their reading rate when they get to the word because their comprehension breaks down.

Knowing multiple meanings of common words is also a part of this subskill. For example, take the multiple meanings of *frog.* When students read, "Mother has a frog in her throat," they must realize that Mother is hoarse—she does not have a green creature in her throat. If they do not realize that Mother has a sore throat, comprehension breaks down, which also hinders the reading rate. Chapter 7 has more information on building readers' vocabularies.

Phrasing or Prosody

Another component of fluency is a reader's ability to recognize phrases instead of seeing each word in isolation. Some readers recognize words quickly and have a good understanding of multiple meanings, but others are cautious and read words instead of grouping them into phrases. Recognition of phrases, also called **prosody**, greatly increases readers' fluency. Consider the following two readings of the same sentence. The first reader reads the sentence word by word.

The . . little . . girl . . with . . the . . pink . . bow . . was . . playing . . with . . her . . new . . doll.

The second reader automatically recognizes prepositional and other phrases and reads the sentence as follows:

The little girl
with the pink bow
was playing
with her new doll.

Reading word-by-word may be a result of struggling readers receiving poor instruction. Struggling readers often spend more time reading orally than proficient readers who mostly read silently—which is faster than oral reading (Allington, 2011). Struggling readers are also interrupted more quickly and more often than proficient readers when reading aloud (Allington, 2011). Struggling readers are taught to stop when they do not know a word, which, of course, slows down their reading process. The teacher or a classmate may provide the unknown words instead of sharing strategies for figuring them out.

Other teachers get in the habit of affirming each word a struggling reader says correctly. These students learn to wait for confirmation after each word (Allington, 2011). Consider the different length of time it takes two different students to read the following two sentences:

Student #1: The

Teacher: un-hunh.

Student #1: elephant

Teacher: Yes.

Student #1: was

Teacher: un-hunh.

Student #1: the

Teacher: un-hunh.

Student #1: first

Teacher: Good.

Student #1: animal

Teacher: Right!

Student #1: in

Teacher: un-hunh.

Student #1: the

Teacher: mm-hmm.

Student #1: parade.

Teacher: Good. Read on.

Student #2: The elephant was the first animal in the parade.

Be conscious of your actions when working with struggling readers. Instead of giving them an unknown word, have them skip it, read to the end of the sentence, and then go back to see what word makes sense in the blank. The student confirms the word is correct by seeing if her choice matches the spelling of the word in the text.

Parsing phrases

Students who read words instead of phrases need to be taught to parse phrases correctly. You may conduct a number of activities to help with phrasing. First, you can give students texts written at their easy reading level that are composed of natural phrases. For younger students, you can use many of Dr. Seuss's books, which are formatted in short, readable phrases. For example, *I Can Read with My Eyes Shut!* (1978) features phrases written in a natural, conversational form. Teaching students to group words in phrases increases their rate of reading and helps them comprehend connected thoughts.

For older students, choose short poems written in a natural style. Notice how each line of the poem "My Grandma's Teeth" (Lansky, 2000), found in Figure 10.4, is a natural phrase. Later, teachers can mark texts with arches to represent phrases, or put phrases within slash marks. See Figure 10.5 for an example. You can then model the phrasing and have students

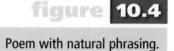

Poem with natural phrasing.

My grandma's teeth are like the stars.

She keeps them sparkling bright.

And like the stars up in the sky

her teeth come out at night. (p. 27)

Source: "My Grandma's Teeth." © 2000 by Bruce Lansky. Reprinted from *If Pigs Could Fly* with permission from Meadowbrook Press, www.meadowbrookpress.com.

Sample poem with marked phrases.

"Momma's sewing machine / clanked all week long. / Sometimes I woke up / and heard the Singer / before the morning sawmill whistle blew. / And sometimes / I fell asleep at night / listening to the rhythm / of the foot pedal / hitting the floor. But tonight was Friday / and we were going / to the picture show./ So Momma tucked the machine away / in a corner / like a broom / waiting to be used again."

Source: From *Mister and Me* by Kimberly Willis Holt, illustrated by Leonard Jenkins, copyright © 1998 by Kimberly Willis Holt, text. Used by permission of G.P. Putnam's Sons, a division of Penguin Young Readers Groups, a member of Penguin Group (USA) Inc., 345 Hudson St., New York, NY 10014. All rights reserved.

echo it. After the echo reading, students practice reading the text with the marked phrases on their own until they become comfortable (see the Intervention activity on echo reading later in this chapter). You can mark longer phrases after students learn to read the short ones.

Expressive reading

Expressive reading is another aspect of prosody. Reading with expression is about making written words sound like speech. Many young children enjoy hearing the deep voice of Papa Bear, the melodic voice of Mama Bear, and the high, squeaky voice of Baby Bear in "Goldilocks and the Three Bears." Older children enjoy hearing ghost stories from a storyteller with a scary voice. An expressive voice makes a story come alive! Fluent readers distinguish the various voices in dialogue and are able to "project the natural pitch, stress and juncture of the spoken word" (Richards, 2000, p. 534). When you read a good novel silently, you can probably hear the characters' voices. Some are weak, some are loud, and others may have a Southern twang. When reading orally, fluent readers are able to reproduce the different characters' voices as they hear them internally. Moreover, fluent readers not only read orally with expression; when they read silently, they hear themselves read fluently (Rasinski, 2012). Disfluent readers, on the other hand, do not distinguish between various voices in dialogue; instead they read every word in the same tone without expression. Note that expressionless, monotonous readers often read words correctly, but may not be comprehending the passage. Anyone who reads: "Ouch! You pinched my finger in the door!" in a monotone voice does not comprehend the passage.

When fluent readers express the tone and message of a passage, they emphasize important words, slow down for suspenseful passages, and change volume to convey the mood. Those who read with expression indicate they comprehend the author's intended message. Read the following passage from *Daisy Comes Home* (2002) by Jan Brett two different ways: first in a monotone voice and then with the intended expression, responding to the exclamation marks, the italics, and the two speakers. Notice the difference in the meaning between the two readings.

> The fisherman ran after them, furious. "Stop!" he yelled at Mei Mei. "That's *my* hen!"
>
> "Finders keepers!" Mei Mei called over her shoulder.

To teach expressive reading, first model this skill and then assist struggling readers through echo reading and unison reading. Readers' comprehension, rate, prosody, and expression increase through teacher modeling, large group choral reading, discussion of the text to unravel meaning, and paired reading (Calo, Woodlard-Ferguson, & Koitz, 2013; Marcell & Ferraro, 2013; Paige, 2011; Rasinski, 2012).

Selecting appropriate material for expressive reading is crucial. During the teacher-directed lessons, the material should be at the instructional level of the student, and during individual practice reading time the material should be at the reader's easy level. Appropriate materials include short passages from a text, readers theater scripts, poetry, monologues, dialogues, song lyrics, speeches, jokes, riddles (Calo, Woodlard-Ferguson, & Koitz, 2013; Cahill & Gregory, 2011; Rasinski, 2012), and informational text (Paige, 2011). When modeling, be sure to select materials that have lots of expressive dialogue or suspenseful narration.

Linda Williams's *The Little Old Lady Who Was Not Afraid of Anything* (1986) has excellent passages to model expression for younger children. The beginning of the story presents the peaceful scene of the Little Old Lady leisurely walking through the forest at night, when "Suddenly she stopped!" (Long pause) "Right in the middle of the path were two big shoes. And the shoes went CLOMP! CLOMP!" When you model this short passage, use appropriate expression and then discuss what you did with your voice to make the story interesting. Then invite students to read it with you using the same expressions. After they can imitate your expressions, have them practice it individually.

With older students, take passages from chapter books that have dialogue. Dialogue works well because most struggling readers can imagine the voices of different people. First, model reading the passage with appropriate expression and then invite students to read it in unison with you. If the passage has dialogue with two characters, assign the two characters' parts to two groups of students while you read the explanatory words and narrative.

Figure 10.6 features a short selection from Karen Hesse's (1998) *Just Juice*. The passage is divided into three parts—for the teacher, Group 1, and Group 2. This selection, like all selections used for beginning expressive instruction, does not have difficult vocabulary. This particular selection needs to be read with expression in order to convey first the encouragement and then the despair of the father (Group 2), and first the fear and then the kindness and encouragement of Juice (Group 1).

Readers theater scripts also provide good practice for developing expression and are excellent for grouping strong readers with struggling readers, because they get to practice their part before they perform for the class. See the Intervention section of this chapter for more information and resources for using readers theater in the classroom.

figure 10.6 Selection for expressive instruction from Karen Hesse's *Just Juice.*

TEACHER:	I hang out at the door to Pa's shop awhile, then hop over the timber frame and come in.
GROUP 1 (Juice):	"You think Ma had trouble with the truck?"
TEACHER:	I ask.
GROUP 1:	"You think she got stuck in the mud?"
TEACHER:	Pa takes his cap off and rubs his head.
GROUP 2 (Pa):	"I don't think so, honey. She'll be back soon. Don't worry."
TEACHER:	But I am worried.
GROUP 1:	"Were they mean to you at the town offices, Pa, when you were there?"
GROUP 2:	"They were nice enough. But they thought I was some stupid because of not reading those letters. I guess they were right, too. I am stupid."
GROUP 1:	"You're not stupid, Pa. No more than I am. Miss Hamble says some of us are wired up different inside our brains. You and me, we just have a different kind of wiring. You know?"

(pp. 129–130)

Source: Adapted from *Just Juice* by Karen Hesse. Scholastic Inc./Scholastic Press. Copyright © 1998 by Karen Hesse. Reprinted with permission.

Punctuation

Another topic related to prosody and reading with expression, punctuation helps writers convey their message and readers to interpret it. Students who read fluently understand and respond to punctuation marks. Notice how punctuation changes the message of the following sentences:

> Woman without her man is nothing!
>
> Woman: without her, man is nothing.
>
> Slow children playing.
>
> Slow! Children playing.

Many struggling readers do not read commas or end marks (Fountas & Pinnell, 2006b). Without observing these punctuation marks, their comprehension breaks down. Notice the differences between the following two sentences. The first reader omits the commas and believes that the author is asking for two kinds of juice. The second reader understands that the author is referring to three kinds of juice.

> Reader #1: Please give me cranberry apple and orange juice.
>
> Reader #2: Please give me cranberry, apple, and orange juice.

When readers omit periods, comprehension and reading rate also quickly deteriorate. Once comprehension breaks down, the student reads words and not complete thoughts. The following passage is from Jan Brett's *Daisy Comes Home* (2002). The punctuation has been dropped to indicate how it might sound to a reader who omits punctuation.

> Dawn broke over the Gui Mountains as the basket drifted along the river branches brushed against it fish swam silently by and birds flew overhead suddenly Daisy felt a thump. (unpaged)

How difficult was it to grasp the meaning of the passage? Did you have to read the passage twice to comprehend what was happening?

When fluent readers encounter ellipses, they know it indicates a pause for emphasis. Consider the sentence from *The Old Woman Who Lived in a Vinegar Bottle* (1995) by Margaret MacDonald: "There sat the old woman . . . complaining." The ellipses tell the reader that the author intends a pause between the words *woman* and *complaining* to emphasize the action, complaining.

Parentheses indicate less important material, which may suggest that readers pause and read the words with a lowered voice. Notice in the following sentence how the author uses parentheses to help readers understand the term *readers theater*. The phrase is set off with a pause after *theater* and the phrase is read in a lowered voice.

> Readers theater [pause, and with lowered voice] (conveying drama through vocal expression rather than acting), [pause and return to natural voice] is a great activity to develop fluency.

When teaching students to respond to punctuation, explain the purpose of punctuation marks and model the pauses and vocal inflections when "reading" them. For many beginning and older students, echo reading and unison reading are good strategies to help develop an awareness of punctuation marks. As you can see, prosody includes many different, yet related, skills.

Comprehension

Researchers and educators understand the connection between fluency and comprehension. Reciprocal theory suggests the relationship between fluency and comprehension is give-and-take rather than unidirectional. Correlation studies conducted on fluency and comprehension indicate that when fluency increases, comprehension increases and vice versa (Flood, Lapp, & Fisher, 2005; Griffith & Rasinski, 2004; O'Connor, White, & Swanson, 2007).

However, when DeKonty-Applegate, Applegate, and Modla (2009) conducted a study with 60 primary grade students, 57 intermediate students (grades 4–5), and 54 middle school and high school students (grades 6–12) to determine if there is a correlation between a high level of fluency and a high degree of reading comprehension, they found that one third of students who were classified as fluent readers struggled with comprehension. They discovered that many students were assessed on fluency based only on their rate, accuracy, and prosody; their fluency scores did not reflect their comprehension. In other words, these students were not as fluent as their scores indicated.

As mentioned earlier, many schools have been assessing students' fluency by having them read for one minute from a commercial test or a classroom text. Researchers and educators have determined that when students read while the teacher looks at a stopwatch, the students begin to believe that fast reading is fluent reading and that this type of fluent reading is more important than comprehension (Deeney, 2010; Marcell & Ferraro, 2013; Rasinski, 2012; Stahl, 2011). A study done by Valencia et al. (2010) with students in grades 2, 4, and 6 compared these one-minute assessments with assessments designed to measure combined aspects of fluency, such as rate, accuracy, prosody, and comprehension. The results indicated that fluency assessments that "include multiple indicators of oral reading fluency provided a finer-grained understanding of oral reading fluency and fluency assessment, and a stronger predictor of general comprehension" (p. 270).

Chapters 8 and 9 discuss the many subskills of comprehending narrative and expository texts.

WHAT TEACHERS SHOULD KNOW ABOUT FLUENCY INSTRUCTION

As mentioned earlier in this chapter, the poor instruction given to struggling readers may be a source of their disfluent reading. Often teachers give a different type of instruction to fluent readers than they do to disfluent readers. Although this is not intentional, teachers' lack of expertise in working with struggling readers may be the cause of this discrepancy (Allington, 2006). Figure 10.7 compares characteristics of instruction typical for fluent readers to the instruction typical for disfluent readers.

Fluency and the Common Core State Standards

As stated previously, the CCSS recognize fluency in the grade-level standards for Reading: Foundational Skills. For children in kindergarten, the fluency standard emphases comprehension; students are required to "read emergent-reader texts with purpose and understanding" (NGACBP & CCSSO, CCSS ELA Reading: Foundational Skills, Kindergarten, 2010, p. 16). In first through fifth grades, the emphasis in the fluency standard is on reading "with sufficient accuracy and fluency to support comprehension" (NGACBP & CCSSO, CCSS ELA Reading: Foundational Skills, 2010, pp. 16–17). The CCSS fluency standards for grades 1 through 5 use the same sub-skills and are presented in Figure 10.8.

figure 10.7 Typical instruction given to fluent and disfluent readers.

INSTRUCTION OF FLUENT READERS	INSTRUCTION OF DISFLUENT READERS
1. Given materials that are easy or on their instructional reading level.	1. Given materials that are too difficult.
2. Given time to read silently.	2. Asked to read orally, which slows down rate.
3. Are expected to self-monitor.	3. Interrupted more often.
4. Taught strategies to see groups of letters within words.	4. Encouraged to sound out words letter by letter.
5. Are expected to self-correct; only interrupted at end of sentence.	5. Interrupted when error is made.
6. Asked to cross-check when they misread.	6. Given words with no strategies.

Source: Adapted from Allington, R. L. (2006). *What Really Matters for Struggling Readers: Designing Research-based Programs.* (2nd ed.). Boston: Pearson/Allyn & Bacon.

figure 10.8

The CCSS fluency standard subskills for grades 1 through 5.

4.A Read grade-level text with purpose and understanding.

4.B Read grade-level text orally with accuracy, appropriate rate, and expression on successive readings.

4.C Use context to confirm or self-correct word recognition and understanding, rereading as necessary

Source: National Governors Association Center for Best Practices (NGACBP) & Council of Chief State School Officers (CCSSO). (2010). English Language Arts Standards, Reading: Foundational Skills, Grades 1–5. Washington, DC: NGACBP, CCSSO, pp. 16–17.

Research-Based Guidelines for Fluency Instruction

In order for teachers to avoid poor instructional practices, they must understand what reading researchers have discovered regarding specific types of instruction and the kinds of materials to use with struggling readers. Figure 10.9 lists some research findings related to fluent reading.

Rasinski (2012) suggests that students be given time to develop reading skills that are both wide and deep. "**Wide reading** refers to the common classroom practice of reading a text once followed by discussion, response, [and] instruction aimed at developing some specific reading strategies and skills" (pp. 517–518). **Deep reading** refers to repeated reading to develop prosody, i.e., using one's voice to convey meaning. Using prosody indicates that students have compre-

figure 10.9   Research related to fluent reading.

FINDINGS

1. "Guided repeated oral reading and repeated reading provide students with practice that substantially improves word recognition, fluency, and—to a lesser extent—reading comprehension" (National Reading Panel, pp. 3–20).

2. Assisted reading at the appropriate rate increases word recognition and fluency.

3. Fluency affects comprehension.

4. Dyad reading increases fluency.

5. Readers theater exercises improve fluency.

6. Choral reading improves fluency.

7. Prosodic instruction improves fluency.

8. Guided reading is an effective instructional practice to increase fluency.

9. Specific instruction in fluency is beneficial for readers in all grade levels.

10. Instruction focused on semantic and syntactic cues helps readers with the interpretation of an author's intended meaning.

11. Instruction in morphological strategies (e.g., recognizing affixes and root words) aids automaticity.

12. Instruction in self-monitoring (analyzing one's own rate, accuracy, and expression) increases fluency.

13. Readers' rate affects comprehension.

14. Unison reading is effective instruction for English learners.

STUDIES

1. Cahill & Gregory, 2011; Marcell & Ferraro, 2013; Marcell, 2011/2012; Rasinski, 2012

2. Deeney, 2010; Marcell, 2011/2012

3. Deeney, 2010; Rasinski, 2012; Marcell & Ferraro, 2013; Stahl, 2011

4. Marcell & Ferraro, 2013

5. Cahill & Gregory, 2011; Paige, 2011; Rasinski, 2011

6. Rasinski, 2012; Paige, 2011; Marcell & Ferraro, 2013

7. Deeney, 2010; Rasinski, 2012

8. Paige, 2011

9. Rasinski, 2012; Paige, 2011; Marcell & Ferraro, 2013

10. Marcell & Ferraro, 2013

11. Marcell & Ferraro, 2013

12. Calo, Woodlard-Ferguson, & Koitz, 2013; Cahill & Gregory, 2011; Deeney, 2010

13. Marcell, 2011/2012; Deeney, 2010; Rasinski, 2012

14. Rasinski, 2012; Paige, 2011; Cahill & Gregory, 2011

hended the text at an inferential level because they can understand which words to emphasize to reflect the text's meaning.

Other guiding principles for fluency instruction include the following:

1. Teachers need to model fluent reading.
2. Teachers need to provide direct instruction in fluency and feedback.
3. Students need support while reading. Support can be unison reading or reading along with an audio recording.
4. Students need opportunities to repeat readings. However, all repeated readings need a purpose or goal! Some benefits of repeated readings are that (a) readers increase their comprehension, (b) readers increase rate and accuracy, and (c) readers better understand phrasing.
5. Students need specific instruction to learn phrasing skills.
6. Students need easy reading to practice fluency, but the end goal of the practice should be expressive reading reflecting comprehension, not timing to get a better rate.
7. Disfluent students should not be embarrassed by being forced to read in front of peers.

Fluency Instruction for English Learners

English learners need support not only as they learn new words, but also as they strive to become fluent readers. When instructing English learners in fluency, follow these steps.

1. Read a short passage to the student that is on her instructional level.
2. You and the English learner read the passage together.
3. The English learner reads the same passage by herself so you can assess her progress.
4. The English learner practices to increase rate and improve intonation.
5. The English learner listens to a recording of his reading to self-assess. (See Appendix C.47 for a checklist the student can use.)

ASSESSMENT

Teachers need to recognize which of the subskills is causing problems for a struggling reader's fluency. You can use both informal and formal assessment instruments to diagnose fluency. The following are some formal and informal assessments. Listening to students and using the informal assessment instruments are the most useful ways to diagnose fluency

problems. However, many school districts require the use of formal assessment instruments for the student to receive help from federally funded programs.

Informal Assessment

Teachers can informally assess fluency through observation and anecdotal records. It is easy to detect disfluent reading by watching and listening to a reader: They often point to each word; they tend to read word-by-word; they read at a slow pace and lack intonation. They often reread words and phrases and do not recognize when they mispronounce words. They often mumble because they lack confidence to articulate. Readers who fall 20 to 30 percent below the average rate (refer back to Figure 10.3) usually require additional instruction (Rasinski, 2003).

Checklists

The checklist found in Appendix C.48 shows four stages of reading fluency. If the checklist is used throughout the school year, the progression from one stage to the next should be evident. Students can also assess their own fluency using a simple checklist like the one in Appendix C.47 (Cecil, 2015; Rasinski, 2003). Go over the questions with your students first. Then, the student can read a passage into an audio recorder and play back his reading while answering questions in the checklist. Alternately, students can take turns assessing each other using the form during partner reading.

Running records and miscue analysis

Running records and miscue analyses, both discussed in detail in Chapter 3, are also used to analyze fluency. The purpose of both of these informal reading assessments is for teachers to examine the graphophonic, semantic, and syntactic clues the reader uses. The teacher calculates what type of errors or miscues the reader most often makes. Mispronunciations indicate that readers lack graphophonic knowledge or word analysis skills. Substitutions for words indicate that readers lack the basic vocabulary needed for that text. Students who do not read punctuation or read in a monotone voice are most often disfluent readers. By administering the running record and miscue analysis, teachers can target the fluency skill the reader lacks and teach strategies that will aid him.

Retrospective miscue analysis

The retrospective miscue analysis discussed in Chapter 3 helps a student assess her own fluency. As the student listens to her reading, have her check for accuracy and expression. If the reading is not accurate, have her practice reading the passage and record it again to see if there are fewer errors. The student should also be taught to analyze her expression and phrasing while listening to the recording by considering such questions as, "Did I have different tones for different characters?" and "Did I sound excited or did I read it in a monotone (uninteresting) voice?" The Fluency Checklist for Narrative Text found in Appendix C.49 is simple enough for students in grades 2 through 8 to use to assess their own reading.

Rubrics

Applegate, Quinn, and Applegate (2008) designed a rubric that rates several aspects of fluency including oral reading, intonation, punctuation, and pacing. The rubric is found in Appendix C.50.

Rubrics based on state standards are yet another useful way for teachers to assess a student's fluency and rate. For the states that have adopted the CCSS or have revised their state standards to reflect stan-dards, Figure 10.10 presents a rubric based on the CCSS Reading: Foundational Skills fluency subskill standards for grades 1 through 5. As evident from this example rubric, Jake reads at-grade-level text; how-ever, he has no expression. Next term Jake needs to work on reading with expression by recording himself and listening to it so he can hear his expressionless tone. With his teacher, Jake should do echo reading on short passages, record the echo reading, and then lis-ten to the recording so he can determine if he imitates the teacher's reading.

Informal commercial assessments

The Reading Fluency Monitor, published by Read Nat-urally, is an instrument that permits teachers to assess students' progress during the school year. Read Natu-rally recommends that teachers assess students three times a year—fall, winter, and spring. It includes grade-level passages for grades 1–8. A software program allows teachers to easily report and keep records.

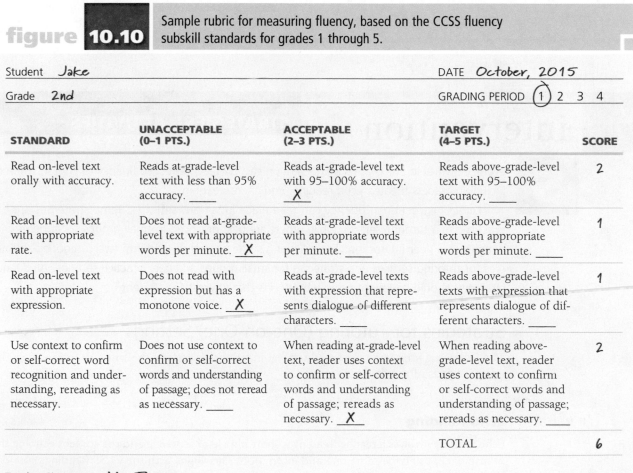

figure 10.10 Sample rubric for measuring fluency, based on the CCSS fluency subskill standards for grades 1 through 5.

Student _Jake_   DATE _October, 2015_

Grade _2nd_   GRADING PERIOD ⑴ 2 3 4

STANDARD	UNACCEPTABLE (0–1 PTS.)	ACCEPTABLE (2–3 PTS.)	TARGET (4–5 PTS.)	SCORE
Read on-level text orally with accuracy.	Reads at-grade-level text with less than 95% accuracy. ____	Reads at-grade-level text with 95–100% accuracy. _X_	Reads above-grade-level text with 95–100% accuracy. ____	2
Read on-level text with appropriate rate.	Does not read at-grade-level text with appropriate words per minute. _X_	Reads at-grade-level text with appropriate words per minute. ____	Reads above-grade-level text with appropriate words per minute. ____	1
Read on-level text with appropriate expression.	Does not read with expression but has a monotone voice. _X_	Reads at-grade-level texts with expression that repre-sents dialogue of different characters. ____	Reads above-grade-level texts with expression that represents dialogue of dif-ferent characters. ____	1
Use context to confirm or self-correct word recognition and under-standing, rereading as necessary.	Does not use context to confirm or self-correct words and understanding of passage; does not reread as necessary. ____	When reading at-grade-level text, reader uses context to confirm or self-correct words and understanding of passage; rereads as necessary. _X_	When reading above-grade-level text, reader uses context to confirm or self-correct words and understanding of passage; rereads as necessary. ____	2
			TOTAL	6

Teacher Signature _Ms. Thomas_

Source: Based on English Language Arts Standards, Reading: Foundational Skills, Grades 1–5. Washington, DC: NGACBP, CCSSO, p. 16.

Formal Assessment

Diagnostic tests, which are norm-referenced and standardized, are given to students who show signs of reading difficulty. There are a number of diagnostic tests that measure fluency by calculating rate and/or accuracy. Figure 10.11 lists formal reading tests that have fluency subtests. One negative aspect of these formal assessments is that they assess only rate and accuracy. Informal assessment allows the teacher to analyze all four components of fluency: comprehension, rate, automaticity, and prosody/expression, which gives them a more complete measure of a student's fluency.

---

figure 10.11   Formal reading tests with fluency subtests.

1. **Stanford Diagnostic Reading Test.** Levels four and up measure rate.
2. **Gray Oral Reading Tests.** This test focuses on oral accuracy and speed, and results in an oral reading quotient.
3. **Gilmore Oral Reading Test.** This test measures reading rate separately from comprehension.
4. **The Durrell Analysis of Reading Difficulty.** This test assesses oral fluency by counting the oral reading miscues. Rate is not measured.
5. **Diagnostic Reading Scales.** This test assesses oral fluency by counting the oral miscues. Rate is also measured.
6. **Woodcock Reading Mastery Test.** The three subskills of fluency measured in this test are word identification, word attack, and passage comprehension. Rate is not measured.
7. **Testing of Reading Fluency (TORF).** The student is timed as he reads for one minute, and the teacher calculates the number of words read correctly. The score is the average of three readings.
8. **AIMS Standard Reading Assessment Passages (RAPs).** Teachers can use this assessment with grade-leveled passages to assess students' oral reading fluency. RAPs is field-tested and validated. Internet-based software allows teachers to collect and report data.

---

intervention   STRATEGIES & ACTIVITIES

Several activities in this chapter's Intervention section teach effective fluency to English learners, including readers theater, echo reading, and choral reading.

Direct instruction in fluency can take place in various settings. Some strategies are best practiced in a tutoring setting, while others are best practiced in small groups so students can benefit from peer interaction. The following strategies are divided into two categories—strategies for tutoring settings and strategies for small groups and peer practice settings. All fluency strategies should be taught using whole texts that interest the student.

Strategies for Tutoring (One-on-One) Settings

The following strategies, designed for use in tutoring sessions, permit you to focus on the unique needs of the disfluent reader.

ACTIVITY   **Echo Reading**   GRADES K–4

Echo reading involves a teacher reading a short phrase or sentence and the student echoing the phrase back, using the same rate and intonation. This aligns with the CCSS Reading: Foundational Skills fluency subskill standard that emphasizes students' ability to read with appropriate rate and expression. It is important for the teacher to interpret the passage with the author's intended meaning. To introduce echo reading, choose a short poem or passage that presents natural phrases on single lines. For example, Nancy White Carlstrom's *Guess Who's Coming, Jesse*

Bear (1998) for younger students and Karen Hesse's *Come On, Rain!* (1999) for older students both use poetry to tell their stories. To echo read these books, you read a line and emphasize the underlined words, and the student echoes it using your rate and intonation. The slashes indicate where you stop and allow the reader to echo.

Echo reading is especially effective with English learners because they see the words and hear the correct intonation. Stress correct intonation when English learners echo the phrases and sentences.

Guess Who's Coming, Jesse Bear

Wednesday /

I <u>count</u> and <u>look</u> and then <u>sit</u> down. /

She <u>knows</u> she <u>never</u> will be <u>found</u>. /

At <u>hiding</u> Sara is the <u>best</u>. /

It gives us <u>both</u> a little rest. /

(unpaged)

Come On, Rain!

"Is there <u>thunder</u>?" Mamma asks. /

"No <u>thunder</u>," I say. /

"Is there <u>lightning</u>?" Mamma asks. /

"No <u>lightning</u>," Jackie-Joyce says. /

"You <u>stay</u> where I can <u>find</u> you," Mamma says. /

"<u>We will</u>," I say. /

"<u>Go on</u> then," Mamma says, /

<u>lifting</u> the glass to her <u>lips</u> to take a <u>sip</u>. /(unpaged)

Echo reading can be enjoyable for both you and the students when you practice small segments of passages that you both enjoy.

Preview-Pause-Prompt-Praise (PPPP) Strategy

The preview-pause-prompt-praise (PPPP) strategy developed by Topping and Ehly (1998) can be used by teachers, reading specialists, adult volunteers, and trained paraprofessionals.

1. During the *preview* segment, ask the reader to predict what will happen in the story based on the title and book cover.

2. Begin reading in unison with the student until she taps the desk to indicate that she wishes to read by herself.

3. When the student makes an error, *pause* three seconds or wait until the student gets to the end of the sentence.

4. If the student does not self-correct in three seconds or by the end of the sentence, give two *prompts:* "Let's read that again." If the student still does not self-correct, tell her the word.

5. Begin again to read with the student until she taps the desk.

6. If the student does self-correct after three seconds, *praise* her, and read with her again until she taps the desk.

7. After she completes the passage, talk about her favorite parts and ask if her predictions were correct.

This strategy focuses on fluency because the teacher reads along with the student, and it focuses on comprehension by emphasizing predictions before reading and in discussion afterward. It also aligns with the CCSS Reading: Foundational Skills fluency subskill that emphasizes students' ability to self-correct and reread as necessary.

ACTIVITY   **Oral Recitation Lesson (ORL)**   GRADES 2–5

The oral recitation lesson (ORL) developed by Reutzel and Hollingsworth (1993) was designed for a classroom setting with second graders. However, you can modify this strategy to work with any struggling reader who lacks comprehension and prosody skills. Choose material at the student's instructional level. Passages with repeated refrains, cumulative episodes, rhyming patterns, or poetry are good. The ORL has two major components: the first is direct instruction by the teacher; the second is indirect instruction. The following are the steps for the direct instruction:

1. Read and discuss the story with the student completing a story map (see Chapter 8).
2. Ask the student to write a summary using the story map.
3. Model expressive reading.
4. Have the student practice by reading chorally with you.

The indirect instruction occurs when the student practices the short passage in a "soft reading voice" while you check progress in accuracy and fluency. After the student has "polished" the passage, he can perform it for a small group or for the class.

ACTIVITY   **Carbo Recorded-Book Method**   GRADES K–3

Research indicates that children benefit from assisted reading. Reading along with audiobooks increases a reader's fluency, word recognition, and comprehension (Allington, 2006; Carbo, 1998; Koskinen et al., 1999). However, too often commercial read-along audiobooks proceed too quickly for most struggling readers to follow along. The Carbo Recorded-Book Method is a technique for using teacher-produced audio texts. The teacher selects interesting reading material that is at or a little above the reader's reading level. The passage is recorded (1) at a slow pace, (2) in short, natural phrases, and (3) with excellent expression.

The purpose of this method is to produce recordings that permit the disfluent reader to read along successfully. After reading along with them at school, the students take the recordings home for more practice and to involve their parents in the learning process. See Chapter 8 for a discussion of teacher-made recordings.

ACTIVITY   **Record, Check, Chart**   GRADES 2–8

Record, Check, Chart, designed by Allington (2006), is a type of repeated reading that students can use independently to improve their accuracy. The student reads from a photocopy of a passage, which is either a story or a poem, and performs the following steps:

1. The student reads the passage into a recording device.
2. While following the text, the student listens to the recording and marks each word read in error with a black pen.
3. Without replaying the recording, the student reads the same passage into the recording again.
4. While following the text, the student listens to a second reading and checks each error with a green pen.
5. Without replaying the recording, the student reads the same passage into the recording device.
6. While following the text, the student listens to the third reading and checks each error with a blue pen.
7. Using the chart found in Appendix D.27, the student tallies the number of errors for each reading. Figure 10.12 is a partially completed example of Amy's reading of *Secret Soup* (1989) by Jenny Hessell. The little book has 51 words.

figure 10.12 Record, check, chart.

STUDENT Amy

Story	1st reading errors	2nd reading errors	3rd reading errors	Teacher's comments
1. Secret Soup	☰☰ /// 8	☰☰ 5	/ / / 3	Had difficult time w/mushroom and lunch

Teacher Overall Comments:

Even though Amy had fewer errors with each reading, Secret Soup was not her easy (independent) reading level. Her next book must be one or two levels lower than Secret Soup.

The student's goal is to make fewer errors with each repeated reading. You can check the accuracy by listening to the three recordings. If the student misses some of the errors, listen to the recording with him, stop it when you hear an unmarked error, and ask him to listen closely as he follows the text. The student can take the chart and recording home in order for his parents or caregivers to listen to it with him.

Strategies to Use with Small Groups

Many fluency strategies are designed for use with a small group because by practicing together, students encourage and support each other's fluency. Teach the following strategies to a small group and then give the group ample time to practice the strategy. Encourage members to support each other in order to create a safe reading environment.

Fluency Development Lesson (FDL)   GRADES 1–3   A C T I V I T Y

One strategy to use with a small group is the fluency development lesson (FDL), designed by Rasinski et al. (1994), who found that nearly all students who used this strategy three to four times a week developed fluency. The lesson is 10 to 15 minutes in length. Choose short passages of 50 to 185 words that are at the students' instructional level. Then complete the following steps:

1. Give a copy of the passage to each student.
2. Read the passage while the students follow along.
3. Discuss story content and the quality of your reading (e.g., reasons for pausing or changing rate).
4. With small groups of students, read the passage chorally (in unison) or antiphonally (you read a phrase or sentence, and the students echo it).
5. Group the students in pairs and have each student read the passage three times to his or her partner.
6. Ask individuals or small groups to volunteer to perform the passage for the class.
7. Have students take the passage home and read it to their parents. Appendix D.28 can be sent home with the student in order for the parents to log the child's fluency. Figure 10.13 is a partially completed example.

figure 10.13 Sample fluency log.

Books I Can Read By ___Jeff W.___

	TITLE	AUTHOR	PARENTS' COMMENTS	START DATE	NUMBER OF TIMES READ
1.	Fox on Stage (250 words)	James Marshall	We worked on expression. But book was too long.	9/8	1
2.	Get-up Machine (115 words)	Sunshine Book	I read a phrase and he repeated it (1st time). 2nd time he read by himself.	9/10	2
3.	Henry, Mudge, & the Long Weekend (250 words)	Cynthia Rylant	He loved the book and wanted to practice it w/expression.	9/12	4
4.	How to Make Salsa (192 words)	Book Shop	Information book was more difficult to get expression. He read words.	9/15	1

ACTIVITY   **Speech Reading**   GRADES 6–8

Allow students to practice a monologue, famous speech, or poem and then perform it for an audience. Having students practice reading famous speeches, such as President Kennedy's inaugural address ("Ask not what your country . . .") or Martin Luther King, Jr.'s "I Have a Dream" speech, gives them opportunities to develop their fluency and public speaking skills. Fluency is more than reading at a fast pace (Paige, 2011; Marcell & Ferraro, 2013; Rasinski, 2012). Speed was not the goal of either President Kennedy or Dr. King; they used varying rates, pauses, and intonation to convey ideas they hoped would spur listeners to action. The website www. americanrhetoric.com includes the top 100 political speeches of the 20th century and hundreds more speeches spanning several centuries by presidents, politicians, and major cultural figures. The site includes transcripts for most speeches and videos for some. You and your students can use this site to locate speeches and to analyze the oratory techniques of famous Americans.

ACTIVITY   **Telling Jokes**   GRADES 5–8

Telling jokes helps students develop correct prosody so listeners get the punch line (Ness, 2009). Prosody includes the ability to (1) emphasize appropriate words, (2) use appropriate intonation, (3) use punctuation appropriately, (4) interpret characters' emotions, and (5) pause at phrase boundaries. In order to tell a joke effectively, readers need to have good delivery so listeners get the humor. Readers of jokes must adhere to punctuation, intonation, and phrasing (Ness, 2009). Collect books of jokes and help students with intonation, punctuation, pause, and interpretation and then let them read the jokes to friends in small groups. These are great for struggling readers because jokes are short and they can practice before they read them to peers. Joke books with appropriate humor for students include:

Brewer, P. (2003). *You Must Be Joking! Lots of Cool Jokes, Plus 17 1/2 Tips for Remembering, Telling, and Making Up Your Own Jokes.*

Dahl, M. (2002). *The Everything Kids Joke Book.*

Elliot, R. (2013). *Knock-Knock Jokes for Kids.*

Harwood, J. (2013). *A Joke Book for Kids: Clean Jokes for Kids.*

National Geographic. (2012). *National Geographic Kids Just-Joking: 300 Hilarious Jokes, Tricky Tongue Twisters and Ridiculous Riddles.*

Rosenbloom, J. (1981). *Gigantic Joke Book.*

Terban, M. (2007). *Eight Ate: A Feast of Homonym Riddles.*

Weitzman, I. (2006). *Jokelopedia: The Biggest, Best, Silliest, Dumbest Joke Book Ever.*

Supported-Reading Strategy

GRADES 2–3   A C T I V I T Y

Morris and Nelson (1992) found the following supported-reading strategy increased second graders' reading ability when used three days a week for six months. In this strategy, instructional-level reading material is used in a three-day cycle. The focus is on comprehension first, expression second.

DAY 1

a. Read and discuss story elements (setting, characterization, plot, climax, resolution, theme, style, point of view) with students.

b. Echo read segments of the passage with students, focusing on expression.

DAY 2

a. Have students read in pairs with each student reading alternate pages.

b. Have the pairs practice a short passage of their choice, focusing on expression.

c. Partners read their passages to each other and critique each other's expression. Partners may use the fluency checklist used for retrospective miscue analysis that is in Appendix C.49.

DAY 3

a. Ask individuals to read to you while you check for accuracy and expression.

Dyad Reading

GRADES 2–3   A C T I V I T Y

Another type of paired reading exercise that focuses on fluency is dyad reading. Dyad reading is unison reading with a buddy. The buddies share the same copy of text. One reader is usually somewhat stronger than the other. The readers sit side-by-side and take turns reading aloud, rotating after every paragraph. When a reader finishes a paragraph she summarizes it for the listener, who adds details not mentioned by the reader. Then the reader and listener switch roles. Dyad reading is most effective with reading material two grade levels above the reader's instruction level (Oliver, Wilcox, & Eldredge, 2000). The lead reader is responsible for setting the pace and pointing to each word while the buddies read.

Repeated Readings

GRADES 1–8   A C T I V I T Y

Many of the strategies already discussed include repeated readings. Studies show that repeated readings increase students' fluency (Allington, 2011; Rasinski, 2012; Samuels, 1979/1997) and accuracy (Samuels, 1979/1997). However, in order for repeated readings to be effective, they need to have a clear purpose (e.g., to increase rate, to increase accuracy, to improve phrasing, to increase comprehension). Repeated readings can be performed with an individual reader or with a small group of readers. Readers theater and choral reading also provide purposeful repeated readings and are effective for any grade.

Fluency Idol Contest

GRADES 2–6   A C T I V I T Y

Poems are a wonderful way to help students develop fluency. They are short, and students need to comprehend them to communicate their message to an audience. A good way to foster a love of poetry in the class is to hold a Fluency Idol Contest (Calo, Woodlard-Ferguson, & Koitz, 2013), in which students read a favorite poem they have practiced. Suggested steps for the contest are as follows:

1. On Monday, demonstrate how not to read a poem (in a monotone voice) and how to read a poem (with appropriate expression and correct pauses and rate so the audience understands its essence).

2. Next, hand out a copy of the poem-for-the-week.

3. Have students read and discuss the poem so all students understand it, explaining any words, phrases, or figures of speech that students do not understand.

4. Model reading the poem with correct expression and then invite the class to chorally read the poem with you.

5. Each day, have students practice the poem in small groups and in pairs.

6. On Friday, randomly select three contestants, providing them with a toy microphone to use as they perform the poem.

7. Advise all other class members that they are the judges who will choose the "Idol" through a secret ballot.

8. Give all three contestants a "Certificate of Performance."

9. Record the performers so students can view their performances. Have students self-assess their performances using the rubric in Appendix C.47.

10. Throughout the semester, keep track of performers so all students get an equal number of times to perform.

Most elementary students enjoy the humorous poems of Shel Silverstein, Jack Prelutsky, and Bruce Lansky. Some collections of my favorites include:

- Shel Silverstein's *Where the Sidewalk Ends* (1974), *A Light in the Attic* (1981), *Falling Up* (1996)
- Jack Prelutsky's *The New Kid on the Block* (1984), *Something Big Has Been Here* (1990), *A Pizza the Size of the Sun* (1994)
- Arnold Lobel's *The Book of Pigericks* (1983)
- Jill Bennett's *Noisy Poems* (1987)
- Brod Bagert's *Rainbows, Head Lice and Pea-Green Tile* (1999)
- David Roessel and Arnold Rampersad's *Poetry for Young People: Langston Hughes* (1994)
- Mary O'Neill's *Hailstones and Halibut Bones* (1961)
- Patrick Lewis' *A Hippopotamustn't* (1990)
- Bruce Lansky's (editor) *Miles of Smiles: Kids Pick the Funniest Poems, Book 1, Book 2, Book 3* (1996, 1997, 1998), and *If Pigs Could Fly . . . and Other Deep Thoughts* (2000).

See Appendix A.4 for a list of poetry anthologies.

ACTIVITY   **Readers Theater**   GRADES 1–8

Rasinski (2012), Marcell and Ferraro (2013), and Paige (2011) use readers theater to develop fluency. Young and Rasinski (2009) conducted a study with 29 second graders in a Title I school, which included nine English learners. The study researched whether readers theater instruction (1) motivated students to perform for others, (2) increased students' prosody, (3) instilled confidence in students as they performed, (4) built social skills among students as they practiced and encouraged each other to use correct expression, and (5) helped struggling readers learn to read with meaning. The study revealed a 20 percent overall improvement in students' ability to read with expression that reflected the meaning of the text. The readers theater was a part of a balanced literacy program. Readers theater also helps students meet the CCSS Reading: Foundational Skills fluency subskill of reading with expression and understanding.

The following websites offer free scripts to use for readers theater.

Fiction Teachers, www.fictionteachers.com/classroomtheater/theater.html

The Reading Lady, http://thereadingladyonline.com/blog/

Timeless Teacher Stuff, www.timelessteacherstuff.com

Teaching Heart, www.teachingheart.net/readerstheater.htm

Tim Rasinski, www.timrasinski.com/presentations/readers_theater_1-4.pdf

Aaron Shepherd, www.aaronshep.com/rt/index.html

You may also invite students to write their own readers theater scripts. Appendix D.29 offers one based on the familiar "The Three Little Kittens" nursery rhyme; however, in this script these naughty little kittens have grown into mischievous cats. Have students use this script as a model for writing their own scripts.

Readers theater is appropriate for all ages (Larkin, 2001), but especially for older students (Moore & Hinchman, 2006) and for English learners (Vaughn et al., 2005). As mentioned earlier, readers theater is excellent for grouping strong readers with struggling readers because they can practice their part before they perform for the class. You may assign parts with longer segments to more proficient readers and shorter segments to struggling readers.

For the strategy to aid fluency development, schedule time for the group to discuss how they want to interpret the script. Then give them ample time to practice their lines by themselves and then with the group. Set aside blocks of time over a period of a couple of days for the group to work on expression and fluency. All readers theater activities should result in performances. The performance can be for other classmates, other classes, or parents.

Choral Reading

GRADES K–8   A C T I V I T Y

Like readers theater, choral reading is a group activity. Unison reading, a form of choral reading in which students speak the same lines together, is especially effective with English learners. English learners hear other students pronounce the words, allowing them to practice rapid and accurate reading without fear of failure. Choral reading selections, however, do not transform texts into scripts. The purpose of choral reading is to read the selection with the interpretation intended by the author or poet. The passage is divided among a number of readers. Each reader is responsible for using vocal expression to communicate the meaning of the selection to the listeners. Poems are often used for choral reading because they come alive when read aloud. When conducting a choral reading, use the following format:

1. Read the poem to the students.

2. In a second reading, have the students echo read, using your rate and expression.

3. Read the selection in unison with the students.

4. Discuss the meaning of the selection, noting rhyming words, word patterns, and word meanings.

5. With the help of students, arrange the selection as a choral reading.

You can make an audio or video recording of any choral reading activity and share it with parents online. As an example, listen to the following: A Poetic Podcast, "The Dragon Who Ate Our School" from the Bishops Waltham Junior School in Hampshire, England at www.radio-anywhere.co.uk/displayStory.php?story=2252. You can also use this performance to discuss with your students how the use of sound effects, rhythm, and voice fluctuation can create an interesting interpretation of the poem.

Choral reading is also effective when used in the content areas and with informational texts. Consider *An Ordinance,* written by the state of South Carolina when they wanted to dissolve their ties with the Union. The language is archaic, but it is clear to readers that it was written with passion as the phrase "declare and ordain" is repeated twice: "We the People of the State of South Carolina, in Convention assembled, do declare and ordain, and it is hereby declared and ordained . . . " (Haskins, 1995, p. 5). You may first read the piece aloud and then discuss with students the terms that may be unfamiliar to them: *ratified, repealed, subsiding, dissolved.* After the students understand the background of the ordinance and the language used, they can first read it chorally, and then practice it individually so that it can be declared with confidence and passion. A copy of the ordinance can be found in Jim Haskins's *The Day Fort Sumter Was Fired on: A Photo History of the Civil War* (1995) and at www.teachinghistory.org.

Figure 10.14 shows an example of a poem arranged as a choral reading.

Impress reading is a type of unison reading that involves both teacher and student. Use a passage at the student's instructional level. When the two of you begin reading the passage, your voice should be dominant. As the student becomes more familiar with the vocabulary and the style of the passage, speak softer and allow the student's voice to become dominant.

Those new to choral reading may wish to begin this activity with poems written for two or more voices, such as Paul Fleischman's Caldecott-winning *Joyful Noise* (1988), which features poems about insects, and *I Am Phoenix* (1985), which features poems about birds. His book *Big Talk: Poems for Four Voices* (2000) is uniquely formatted, using four different colors to depict the four voices. The poems can be read with four individual voices or four groups. Theoni Pappas's unique poetry book *Math Talk* (1991) is written for two voices and presents poems about easy mathematical concepts, including numbers, circles, and fractions, as well as more advanced concepts, such as radicals, tessellations, and infinity.

Some poems suitable for choral reading are the following:

Sara Holbrook's "Copycat" and "The Dog Ate My Homework."

Douglas Florian's "Delicious Wishes," "School Cafeteria," and "Twins."

Carol Diggory Shields' "Clock-watching."

Janet Wong's "Face It."

Karla Kuskin's "The Question."

Websites that focus on poetry and have poems that are suitable for choral reading include:

The Electronic Poetry Center, www.wings.buffalo.edu/epc

Poets & Writers, www.pw.org

Poetry Magazine, www.poetrymagazine.com

Potato Hill Poetry, http://potatohill.com

figure 10.14   Example of choral reading.

The First Two Verses of "SPAGHETTI, SPAGHETTI!" by Jack Prelutsky

ALL VOICES:	Spaghetti! Spaghetti!
VOICE 1:	You're WONDERFUL (draws out the word) stuff,
VOICE 2:	I LOVE (draws out the /ah/ sound) you, spaghetti.
VOICE 3:	I can't get enough.
VOICE 4:	You're covered (voice rises and falls as if covering) with sauce,
VOICE 5:	and you're sprinkled (staccato voice) with cheese (draws out the /e/ sound)
ALL VOICES:	Spaghetti! Spaghetti!
	Oh, give me some more, please (in a plaintive voice).
ALL VOICES:	Spaghetti! Spaghetti!
VOICE 1:	Piled (draws out the long /i/) high (voice moves up in pitch) in a mound,
VOICE 2:	you wiggle (makes hand wiggle) you wriggle (makes body wriggle),
VOICE 3:	you squiggle (shaky voice) around.
VOICE 4:	There's slurpy (draws out the /slur/) spaghetti
VOICE 5:	all over my plate,
ALL VOICES:	Spaghetti! Spaghetti!
	I think you are GREAT! (emphasize *great*)

Books that feature action explained by narrators also make good choral reading selections. Books that have a question and answer format, such as *Mama, Do You Love Me?* (1991) by Barbara Joosse, are excellent for two groups or for two voices. Small groups give younger, struggling students the support they need to build confidence. Struggling readers should be placed with more proficient readers. Here is a short example of choral reading using *Mama, Do You Love Me?*

GROUP 1:   Mama, do you love me?

GROUP 2:   Yes, I do, Dear One.

GROUP 1:   How much?

GROUP 2:   I love you more than the raven loves his treasure, more than the dog loves its tail, more than the whale loves his spout. (unpaged)

Zin! Zin! Zin! A Violin (1995) by Lloyd Moss can also be divided into a number of voices, with each playing the part of a different instrument. The poem for each instrument gives students an opportunity to develop expression and fluency. Phrases such as "soaring high and moving in with Zin! Zin! Zin!" invite readers to change the pitch of their voices with each Zin! The evocation of the low trombone's "mournful moan" encourages the reader to draw out these words in a soft, low voice. Later, the same reader might raise and lower the pitch of his voice when "high notes go low." To choral read this text, first model the change of pitch, volume, and rate for each instrument and invite the students to echo read. Demonstrate how varying the rate, pitch, and volume helps you interpret the meaning of the selection.

Like all repeated readings, choral readings must be practiced in an environment that is enjoyable and relaxing. The materials for choral reading must be (1) engaging and inviting for students to use expressive voices, (2) manageable at the instructional level of the students, and (3) short enough so students can repeat their readings a number of times during one reading session.

Choral readings increase fluency and comprehension because the repeated readings have a clear purpose. The short-term purpose is having fun with language, and the long-term purpose is performance. Choral readings also encourage cooperation in small groups. Remind participants to help each other with fluency so the result is entertaining for the audience and instructive for the performers.

Rhythm Walks

GRADES 1–4   A C T I V I T Y

Many struggling readers need motivation because reading is a daunting task for them. Rhythm walks are collaborative, kinesthetic, fun ways to get students engaged by moving around as they read cards taped to the floor (Peebles, 2007).

1. Choose a short poem, story, or informational passage.

2. Analyze the text for natural phrases.

3. Laminate large pieces of rectangular card stock paper.

4. Using an erasable marker, write phrases on the rectangular pieces. The letters on the card should be at least 1.5 inches tall so students can easily read them while walking.

5. Place the rectangular pieces in curvy order around the room, about one step from the other.

6. Students line up.

7. One student reads the first card, then moves on to read the second and third cards. When she gets to the fourth card, the second student begins on the first card. The second student proceeds to the second, third, and fourth cards before the third student starts, and so on. The students' reading will resemble a musical round.

8. Encourage students to read each card with expression, such as using a soft voice and tiptoeing on *whisper* and using a loud voice and stomping on *shout*.

9. After a number of rhythm walks on a passage, students can read in unison from the original text.

FLUENCY AND TECHNOLOGY

Students can listen to audiobooks to build fluency by either following along with the text or reading along with the narrator. The Living Books and Discis Books series feature a wide variety of titles. Read-along radio drama kits, published by Balance Publishing Company (www.balancepublishing.com/deluxekits.htm), are intended for small group reading. The kits include CDs of radio plays performed by a professional cast that include sound effects like those used in old-time radio dramas. They also come with read-along scripts and a variety of student activities. The dramas help students develop comprehension by requiring them to visualize the action. After listening to these, students can produce their own radio dramas with accompanying sound effects.

The following websites offer short passages, readers theater scripts, monologues, dialogues, poems, song lyrics, speeches, and jokes/riddles to use in class.

Reading A–Z, www.readinga-z.com

Aaron Shepherd's Readers Theater Editions, www.aaronshep.com/rt/RTE.html

Reading Lady, http://thereadingladyonline.com/blog/

Teaching Heart Readers Theater Scripts and Plays, www.teachingheart.net/readerstheater.htm

Apps: Fluency

K12 Timed Reading (Free, Grades K–4). The free version includes 25 short, engaging stories, including both fiction and nonfiction; the $1.99 upgrade allows tracking for the entire class and offers over 250 brief stories leveled from grades K through 4. Track words per minute and percent above or below average reading rates.

Red Apple Readers—Island Adventures ($0.99–$4.99 depending on version, Grades K–3). Students can practice reading skills using brief, decodable illustrated stories (including fiction and nonfiction); they can touch any word to hear the pronunciation. Stories progress with increasingly challenging phonics skills.

FluencyCoach (Free, Grades 4–8). This software application uses Altered Auditory Feedback technology to simulate the effects of "Choral Speech" (speaking simultaneously with another person).

CONCLUDING THOUGHTS

Fluency is an important aspect of reading and is composed of four major components: rate, automaticity/accuracy, prosody, and comprehension. Research indicates a correlation between comprehension and fluency; therefore, teachers should not rely solely on a student's WCPM to measure fluency but instead use assessments that measure the multiple components of fluency. You can use fluency-enhancing strategies that are designed for individuals or for small groups. First model the strategy and then provide ample time for the individual or group to practice it. Many of these strategies result in a performance for peers, other classes, or for parents.

reflective learning

READING SPEED AND COMPREHENSION. Mr. Gonzales is a reading specialist in a large urban middle school. He is assigned to work with sixth-grade students who are below grade level in reading comprehension. At the beginning of the year he works with small groups of eight, but after the first quarter another reading test determines that four of the students are still two grade levels behind. Each of the four now come in for individual sessions.

The first time he asks Sage to read, he reads very quietly (almost mumbling) and very fast. Mr. Gonzales is not sure Sage read accurately because his voice is so soft. After Sage reads a short passage on vampire bats, Mr. Gonzales asks him what he thinks makes a good reader. Sage says that Kimberly, a girl in his class, is a good reader and she reads really fast.

Mr. Gonzales then asks Sage to retell the passage. Sage says it is about bats but gives no more information. Mr. Gonzales asks what he learned about the bats, but Sage cannot relate any facts.

questions

1. What strategies should Mr. Gonzales teach Sage? Explain why you think these strategies would be appropriate.
2. How can Mr. Gonzales get Sage to understand that fast reading is not necessarily good reading?
3. What specific strategies would you use with Sage to get him to comprehend the text?

11 Writing

Writing is an exploration.
You start from nothing
and learn as you go.

E. L. DOCTOROW

scenario

Mr. Burns is an eighth-grade language arts teacher who loves to write, and his goal each year is to get his students to love writing too. He uses the writing workshop as his framework, and his students always produce some interesting tall tales, stories, poems, plays, research reports, and persuasive pieces. However, he is baffled each year when his students do not perform well on the state-mandated writing test. After the second year of lower-than-expected scores, he analyzes the situation and comes up with a solution. He looks at what the students are required to do on the PARCC writing test, the test his state uses, and realizes that the test asks students to complete tasks they never do in the writing workshop. If students must respond to narrative text, they may be required to read a poem and a short story and explain how the two texts are similar. Or after reading three short stories, they may be asked to compare and contrast how the three authors developed the main characters. If students must respond to informational text, they may be required to synthesize information from two or three different sources; or they may be required to analyze how the charts, diagrams, and photographs develop the main topic of the passage. He now knows he has to prepare his students for that type of writing—writing on demand without conferencing with peers and the teacher!

During the summer he turns to his professional journals to find a strategy to help his students gain higher scores on the test. He feels the test scores do not reflect their ability to write, because his students never write under those conditions in the classroom; he always requires them to conference with peers and with him. In the *Journal of Adolescent and Adult Literacy,* he reads an article about Quick Writes (Mason, Benedek-Wood, & Valasa, 2010). He decides to use two Quick Write strategies mentioned in the article, the POW strategy and the TREE strategy (see the Intervention section of this chapter for details) for 15 minutes every Wednesday. Before the school year starts, he talks with the school's social studies and science teachers and tells them about his plan. He asks them to provide two or three short passages each week related to what the students are studying. Some passages need to include opposing points of view for the TREE strategy, which requires students to choose a point of view and persuade readers to support it. He will create prompts from those topics and have the students write for 15 minutes.

Mr. Burns introduces the POW strategy at the beginning of the year and has the students use it for nine weeks. Then he introduces the TREE strategy and uses it for nine weeks. During the second semester, he switches them again. He shares the students' writings with the science and social studies teachers. They are amazed at how much the students have improved with these Quick Writes over the year. They are not surprised when they see the state test results; the writing scores are greatly improved over the previous year's scores.

As you read this chapter, consider the following questions:

guiding questions

1. What writing skills do Mr. Burns's students learn from participating in writing workshops? What skills do they learn from the Quick Write strategies?

2. If Mr. Burns wants to incorporate more technology in his writing workshops, what recommendations would you suggest?

3. For the English learners in his class, what practices should Mr. Burns incorporate in his writing instruction?

4. How might the 6 + 1 Trait Writing Assessment and Instruction Framework help his students with expository writing? With narrative writing?

introduction

Mr. Burns believes that students should love writing as much as reading. He also understands that students need time to engage in various types of writing activities so they develop this love and do well on state-mandated tests. In 2011, the first national computer-based writing assessment was given to eighth and twelfth graders. At both grade levels, 24 percent of students performed at the proficient level, 54 percent of eighth graders and 52 percent of twelfth graders performed at the basic level, and only 3 percent of both eighth and twelfth graders performed at the advanced level (National Center for Education Statistics, 2012, p. 1). The basic level indicates only "partial mastery of prerequisite knowledge and skills that are fundamental for proficient work at each grade" (p. 7). The proficient level indicates a solid academic performance level that demonstrates "competency over challenging subject matter" (p. 7), and the advanced level indicates superior performance. These results reveal that teachers have a major task ahead of them and that they cannot ignore the importance of writing instruction. Since these tests as well as future writing tests will require students to use the computer, elementary teachers need to teach students to compose, revise, and edit on the computer.

Even though teachers must understand the importance of writing assessments such as those discussed above, their goal for writing instruction should be not only high performance on required exams, but also to inspire students to express themselves in a variety of written genres so they can entertain, inform, and persuade an audience that extends beyond the walls of the classroom.

Recent research indicates that reading and writing enhance one another (Anderson & Briggs, 2011; Borgia & Owles, 2011; Graham & Hebert, 2010; Williams & Pilonieta, 2012). Effective teachers understand, however, that good writing does not "just happen" because students read and reflect. Learning one skill does not guarantee that a student will automatically learn the other. Therefore, effective teachers include in their class schedules extended periods of time for students to write. Many use the writing workshop model that Mr. Burns uses and which is described later in this chapter. They also understand that writing is a process and students deserve a choice of topic and genre; they explain the writing process and expect their students to use it during writing workshop.

Teachers must take English learners' special needs into consideration as they plan their writing instruction. English learners acquire writing skills in the same manner that native learners do (Williams & Pilonieta, 2012; Zhang, 2013); however, most English learners acquire oral communication skills in about two years, and it takes five to seven years for most English learners to develop skills in academic reading and writing (Cummins, 1981). Teachers must understand the developmental writing stages for all students and have a wide variety of strategies that will help them become fluent writers. Research shows that English learners, like native English students, use the writing process to express themselves and that interactive writing and the writing workshop provide safe environments in which they can develop their writing skills (Dworin, 2006; Rubin & Carlan, 2005; Williams & Pilonieta, 2012).

Writing instruction for all students has changed because of the CCSS requirements for writing. The note to the CCR Anchor Standards for Writing states that students need "to learn to use writing as a way of offering and supporting opinions, demonstrating understanding of the subjects they are studying, and conveying real and imagined experiences and events" (NGABP, CCSSO, 2010, p. 18). To view the 10 standards in the CCR Anchor writing strand, visit www.corestandards.org/ELA-Literacy/CCRA/W. To meet these goals, teachers will need to make sure that their students write often and write in a variety of formats for a variety of purposes and to a variety of audiences.

The Internet has also brought changes to writing instruction. No longer are students writing only with paper and pencils and sharing their work only with their classmates. Today's students use computers to create compositions that include art, photographs, and/or music, and they recognize their audience can span the globe when they post their writing online.

In this chapter, discussion focuses on (1) the similarities and differences between reading and writing; (2) what teachers need to know about writing instruction; (3) tips for helping struggling writers during the five steps of the writing process; (4) using the 6 + 1 Trait writing model for assessing, discussing, and organizing writing; (5) connecting elements of writing instruction and assessment; and (6) assessment and intervention strategies and activities.

THE READING–WRITING CONNECTION

Why is writing instruction so important? Research studies reveal that "[e]arly writing is one of the best predictors of children's later success" in reading and writing (Cabell, Tortorelli, & Gerde, 2013, p. 651), and writing promotes the "foundational literacy skills that serve as necessary precursors to conventional reading" (Cabell, Tortorelli, & Gerde, 2013, p. 651). Writing helps students organize the knowledge that they have learned through a variety of sources, such as from a discussion, text, or video. As they write, they explore new thoughts and refine their ideas about what they have learned from these interactions (Harris, Graham, Friedlander, & Laud, 2013). Writing about passages that they have read has a positive impact on reading; and, of course, reading improves writing skills when students analyze writings of professionals (Harris et al., 2013).

Similarities in Reading and Writing Cognitive Processes

Reading and writing are complex cognitive developmental processes with aspects that occur before, during, and after each distinct reading or writing task (Anderson & Briggs, 2011; Borgia & Owles, 2011; Cabell, Tortorelli, & Gerde, 2013; Graham & Hebert, 2010; Harris, Graham, Friedlander, & Laud, 2013; Read, 2010; Sweeny, 2010). When students read and write, they use cognitive processes such as gathering ideas, questioning, and hypothesizing. Reading requires students to gather background knowledge and connect it to the new information they are processing. Writing requires they synthesize their thoughts to articulate a message in print. Readers question the author in order to better understand the passage, and writers question whether their thoughts are clearly articulated. Readers need to hypothesize as they read. A substantial part of comprehension involves inferring what the author implied in a passage or predicting what is coming next in a passage. Writers also hypothesize about what their audience will know or want to know regarding the topic of their work and what they will write next.

Reading and writing depend on the same cognitive systems—semantic, syntactic, graphophonic, and pragmatic. Earlier chapters discussed these systems as they relate to reading. Their relationship to writing is presented later in this chapter.

Similarities in the Goals of Reading and Writing

Reading and writing not only share many of the same cognitive processes, they also share many of the same goals or skills. Pinnell (1999) compiled the following list of seven goals/skills for young students as they read and write:

Goal/Skill 1: Automatically recognize or write words without conscious awareness.

Goal/Skill 2: Read and write words without focusing on every letter.

Goal/Skill 3: Connect unknown words to known words.

Goal/Skill 4: Focus on chunks of words.

Goal/Skill 5: Use root words to help determine meaning.

Goal/Skill 6: Connect spelling with meaning (e.g., homophones).

Goal/Skill 7: Focus on the main purpose of reading and writing, which is to communicate meaning.

Differences Between Reading and Writing

There are three big differences between reading and writing. First, reading is considered a **receptive language art** because it involves receiving a message; writing is considered an **expressive language art** because it involves creating and conveying a message. Second, readers must comprehend what others have written; writers must know their audience, choose the genre that best expresses their ideas, choose words that will allow the audience to understand the message, and choose how to share their writing. A third difference is that readers decode words; writers encode words automatically so they can spend their energy on expressing themselves, not on spelling words correctly.

WHAT TEACHERS SHOULD KNOW ABOUT WRITING INSTRUCTION

As stated earlier, the National Center for Educational Statistics (2012) reported that less than one-third of students who took the computer-based writing test mastered writing at the proficient or at grade level. In order to reverse this statistic, all teachers at every grade level must see themselves not only as reading teachers, but also as writing teachers. Writing instruction must begin in kindergarten. VanNess, Murnen, and Bertelsen (2013) propose that kindergarten students write on the first day of school, with teachers focusing on getting children to know that writing is putting their words on paper. On this day, the teacher can show children how to make the letter "I." She then can write and invite children to write what they like. Each time when they want to tell readers another thing that they like, they start a new line with the letter "I." Of course, the teacher can encourage pictures, scribbles, and other letter-like marks. Every teacher in the elementary grades should have students writing on the first day of school! Most teachers understand the importance of students reading every day, but many do not understand the importance of students writing every day.

In addition to writing every day, intermediate and middle-school students need advanced writing skills. Sweeny (2010) compiled the following list of these advanced skills:

1. Use critical thinking skills to solve problems and express them in written communication.

2. Lead and influence their audience by collaborating across networks.

3. Adapt to many different types of writing tasks and be agile in all types of writing.

4. Communicate effectively by being concise and using language that "hooks" the reader.

5. Access and analyze information from a wide number of sources and then synthesize the information.

6. Use their curiosity and imagination to engage the intended audience.

Outside of school, teenagers write complex, sophisticated texts in a variety of activities. These texts often tell stories, build community, or call for social activism (Kinney, 2012). For example, Weinstein (2002) found that marginalized teens could gain positive respect from their peers by expressing themselves in graffiti. Yemeni-American girls used "secular, religious, and Arabic texts to negotiate different identities" (Kinney, p. 396) that they experience in home and school. Harlem adolescents found their voice while writing their life stories; African American girls during a summer institute expressed themselves and explained that during the school year they had to "mask" their identity so they could be politically correct (Muhammad, 2012).

Teachers need to build on the type of writing all students engage in outside of school to interest them in expressing themselves in school writing. One suggestion is to invite students to enter writing contests (DeFauw, 2013). Contests get students to write for a distant audience so students learn to be very specific in word choice and explicit with information and opinions. The web offers many types of writing contests such as essays, narrative and persuasive pieces, and poetry. To get started with contest writing, teachers and students should take time to read award-winning pieces so they can analyze the "authors' use of leads, endings, details, word choice, and other writing techniques" (DeFauw, 2013). They can also discuss the required prompts (topics), and rules about length, citations if any, and due dates. Figure 11.1 lists 10 websites teachers can use to get their students started on writing for a contest.

As stated in the introduction, national assessments, the requirements of the CCSS, and technology have changed writing instruction in recent years. Sophisticated writing is required; therefore, it is pertinent that teachers help all students, especially those who struggle. How can teachers help students become more sophisticated writers? Zumbrum and Krause (2012) contend that "[t] hrough passion and enthusiasm for writing, as well as their own writing practice, teachers can show students that writing is valuable and important" (p. 351). They also state that effective writing instruction:

1. Motivates and engages students in meaningful writing experiences.

2. Begins with the goal for the end of the year and makes sure that all writing lessons work toward that goal.

3. Includes substantial blocks of time for writing each day because writing is a skill that demands daily practice.

4. Includes scaffolding the writing of individual students and responds to them in class.

figure 11.1

Websites offering writing contests.

www.poeticpower.com For 3rd–12th graders; three contests a year: February, August, and October.

www.thegrannieannie.org Family stories for 4th–8th graders.

www.legacyproject.org/contests/ltal.html Stories of a grandparent's life, for 8- to 18-year-olds.

http://www.read.gov/letters/ For 4th–10th graders, personal letters to a living or dead author whose book influenced their life.

www.magicdragonmagazine.com Contests for 1st–8th graders; poems, essays, or artwork.

http://pbskids.org/writerscontest Contests for K–3rd graders featuring a story with five illustrations.

https://clubs2.scholastic.com/?fileName=contests-and-programs On the website and in the magazine *Scope and Storyworks*, a variety of different contests.

www.writingconference.com Contests for poetry, narration, and exposition for elementary, middle, and high school students.

These principles can be added to the list:

5. Recognize and celebrate individual progress.

6. Give students choice so they are invested in the topic and writing for a purpose.

7. Advise students that just as a book can be abandoned, so can a writing piece that is not going anywhere.

The following discussion of writing instruction first describes the language systems that writers use. Then it reviews the developmental writing stages of emergent writers and English learners and the requirements of the CCSS for writing. Finally, it addresses the different forms of writing students need to engage in to become more sophisticated writers.

Components of Writing

Students use five aspects of language when they write—graphic, semantic, graphophonic, syntactic, and pragmatic (which relates to audience) (Zecker, 1999). Note that the graphic component is a language system unique to the writing process.

Graphic. The **graphic** aspect of writing involves knowledge about forming the 26 letters of the alphabet. Students need to form letters correctly and write in order for others to understand their writing. Some emergent and even older students struggle with letter formation, along with the directionality and the spacing of letters and words.

With the use of computers and other hand-held technologies, many students—even first graders—learn keyboarding skills. Some schools understand the importance of good keyboard skills and have added keyboarding to the elementary curriculum. Correct keyboard skills prevent students from falling into the habit of typing with one or two fingers, which slows down their ability to transform their thoughts into text.

Semantic. Language is symbolic. Words, made up of letters, represent objects, actions, and abstract ideas. Very young children sometimes think big objects call for big words. They make large scribbles for a cow because it is a big animal, and they make small scribbles for an ant because it is small. As they learn letters, they may string many letters together for the word *horse,* and only a few letters for the word *mosquito* because of the physical size of each creature (Zecker, 1999). The concept that letters form words, which represent ideas, is quite complex for young children.

As students progress in their writing, they are not concerned about the length of the words but about the use of vivid verbs, adjectives, and adverbs, which make it easier for readers to understand the intended message. They also learn that figures of speech used appropriately make their writing more interesting.

Graphophonic. Students need to learn letter–sound relationships and how one sound may be written in a number of ways (e.g., the long /a/ sound can be written as *a, ey, ay,* and *ei*). Learning all the possible letter–sound relationships is a complex cognitive process. They sound out the word for encoding by learning about patterns within words and how to break multisyllabic words into smaller parts (Bear, Invernizzi, Templeton, & Johnston, 2011; Fountas & Pinnell, 2002). Struggling writers often have trouble with irregular spellings and require explicit instruction in common word patterns (Bear, Invernizzi, Templeton, & Johnston, 2008; Cunningham, 2012).

Syntactic. Writers, especially English learners, have a lot to learn about how to write a good sentence. They must learn to be concise and how to organize ideas into paragraphs. They need to know how to structure a composition or story so it is enjoyable for the reader and how to organize expository material in the appropriate text structure (e.g., cause and effect, enumeration, etc.). They need to understand the different forms of various genres. Many writers struggle with these tasks and need practice with immediate feedback from teachers (Spence, 2010).

Pragmatic. Pragmatic is the "social" setting of a composition. For example, is the piece an informal email, a formal business letter, a humorous story, or an informational piece? The style of writing and the writer's tone differ depending on the type of writing; thus, students need to be aware of their purpose and the intended audience when the write.

Stages of Emergent Writing

In an effort to understand the very beginning stages of writing, Zecker (1999) studied young children and found seven stages of emergent writing. Most children pass through these stages at different rates and different ages. Some young children are given writing utensils and taught how to form letters early in life. These children have an advantage over those who do not receive these opportunities before entering school. Zecker found that children who are taught to listen to sounds within words and to connect sounds with letters will also advance through the stages faster than those who have not had such opportunities.

The seven stages of the emergent writer are listed and described in Figure 11.2, and Figure 11.3 presents a sample of each stage.

Because writing is a skill, it can be developed. Therefore, teachers need to understand everything they can about the writing stages and how to aid struggling writers as they attempt to develop better skills. Writing activities should be developmentally appropriate for each student. A number of different activities are pro-

figure 11.2

Zecker's seven stages of emergent writing.

1. *Drawing:* Pictures that represent the word; child can tell stories that fit pictures.
2. *Scribbling:* The lines and marks do not resemble the forms of any letters; no directionality to the writing.
3. *Letter-like forms:* Lines and marks resemble letters.
4. *Letter strings:* "Words" have repeated patterns or include letters that the child knows. Letters do not correspond to any text.
5. *Copying:* The child copies from environmental print.
6. *Invented spelling:* The child begins to connect letters to some of the sounds heard in words. (See Chapter 12 for the various stages of inventive spelling.)
7. *Conventional spelling:* Students spell most words correctly and use the correct format for each genre.

Source: Zecker, L. (1999). Different texts, different emergent writing forms. *Language Arts, 76*(6), 483–490.

figure **11.3**   Graphic examples of writing stages.

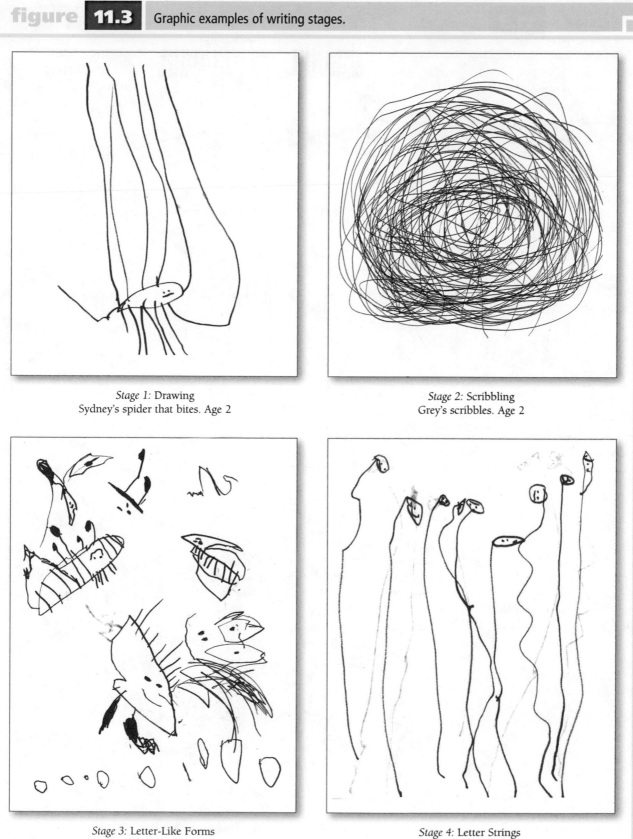

Stage 1: Drawing
Sydney's spider that bites. Age 2

Stage 2: Scribbling
Grey's scribbles. Age 2

Stage 3: Letter-Like Forms
Sydney's bugs. Age 3

Stage 4: Letter Strings
Sydney's snakes. Age 3

(continued)

figure **11.3**   Continued.

Stage 5: Copying
Grey copying from Hide-and-Find. Age 5

Stage 6: Invented Spelling
Grey's scorpion. Age 5

Stage 7: Conventional Spelling
India's story of the Four Princesses. Age 7

vided in the last part of this chapter. The following paragraphs describe activities appropriate for the drawing, invented spelling, and conventional stages of writing.

Activities appropriate for the drawing stage

When students are in the drawing stage, teachers may ask them to "read" their stories aloud and then write a short caption for the student, preferably a sentence, under the picture. Teachers can then read the sentence to the student, pointing to each word as it is spoken.

Activities appropriate for the invented spelling stage

For students in the invented spelling stage, teachers can write interactively with them. **Interactive writing** is an event in which teachers and students "share the pen" (Cabell, Tortorelli, & Gerde, 2013; Clay, 1993c; Fountas & Pinnell, 2002; VanNess, Murnen, & Bertelsen, 2013; Williams & Pilonieta, 2012). It is based on Vygotsky's (1978) theory of the zone of proximal development, which states that what students can do with an adult today, they can do independently in the future. See the activity in the Intervention section of this chapter for the interactive writing procedure.

Most students are successful when interactive writing is conducted in small groups. However, others need one-on-one interactive writing sessions with the teacher. It is important that students generate the ideas for the writing exercise. Young students need to know the focus of writing is composing content, not spelling words or filling in blanks. Interactive writing is also an appropriate strategy to use with English learners because the writing task is shared (Wall, 2008).

Activities appropriate for the conventional stage

As struggling students progress to the conventional writing stage, teachers can use the Reading Recovery method with sound boxes (Clay, 1993c). In Reading Recovery, students write a "story" (usually only one or two sentences) on the bottom section of a double folded slip of paper. The top section of the paper is reserved for students to try out possible spellings of unknown words. For example, Billy has visited his grandpa over the weekend and wants to write: "My grandpa said his dog Bo was ornery when he got out of the backyard." Billy notes how his grandpa said *ornery,* and he likes that word. Ms. Grimes, his teacher, knows the sentence will challenge Billy because he does not know how to spell *ornery* or *grandpa.* Ms. Grimes aids Billy as he writes his "story." Their writing task is explained in Figure 11.4. Notice that on the top half of the paper, Ms. Grimes draws the sound boxes for *grandpa* and *ornery.* She asks Billy what sounds he hears. Billy has learned how to

figure 11.4 Billy's writing task.

| g | r | a | n | d | p | a | | o | r | n | e | r | y |
| 1 | 4 | 5 | 2 | 6 | 3 | 7 | | 4 | 1 | 2 | 5 | 3 | 6 |

"My grandpa said his dog Bo was ornery when he got out of the backyard."

1. Billy knows *my* and writes it correctly.
2. Billy does not know *grandpa,* so Ms. Grimes suggests they draw a blank line and come back to it later.
3. When Billy attempts to write *said,* he quickly refers back to the book they have just read because he knows that *said* was in the story.
4. Billy sounds out *his* and knows that it is an /h/ sound before *is.*
5. Billy has no problem with *dog.*
6. Billy correctly sounds out *Bo,* but does not capitalize it. But with Ms. Grimes's question, "What do you do with the first letter of names?" Billy quickly made the *b* a capital letter.
7. Billy has no problem with *was.*
8. When he gets to the word *ornery,* Ms. Grimes again suggests that he draw a long line and come back to that word.
9. When Billy comes to the word *when,* he consults his personal word wall and finds *when* on it.
10. Billy has no problems with "he got out of the."
11. Billy writes *backyard* as two words. Ms. Grimes explains that *backyard* is a compound word and was one big word. Billy is pleased with the big word he now writes correctly.
12. After the sentence is complete, they return to the word *grandpa.* Ms. Grimes draws the sound boxes and helps Billy spell it correctly.
13. Then they return to Billy's new word and use the sound boxes to spell it correctly. By drawing out the sounds as he says the word, Billy is able to hear the sounds and spell *ornery* correctly. He decides to add that "fun" word to his word list. He also decides to add *grandpa* because he says he will be writing more stories about grandpa.

draw out the sounds of words as he listens for each letter sound. The numbers under each box indicate the order in which Billy hears the sounds. When Billy gets to the word *ornery,* Billy gives an *e* for the final *y,* so the teacher asks Billy what other letters can stand for the long /e/ sound at the end of words. With the teacher's prompting, Billy spells the word *ornery* correctly.

Billy puts significant effort into his "story" because he has a personal interest in it. Notice all the strategies Billy used to write his sentence. When he came to the two new words, Ms. Grimes taught him to draw a line and continue to write the words he did know so he would not lose his train of thought. When spelling *his,* he used his previous knowledge of patterns within words. When spelling *said,* he referred to a book where he had read the word. When he spelled *when,* he consulted his personal word wall. Ms. Grimes has taught Billy several strategies he can use when he writes independently. Ms. Grimes also understands that he still needs prompting so he does not become discouraged.

Activities that connect reading and writing are also appropriate during the conventional stage of writing. When students clarify and question their writing content, they become more critical readers and better writers (Kara-Soteriou, Zawilinski, & Henry, 2007; Mason, Benedek-Wood, & Valasa, 2010; Frye, Trathen, & Schlagal, 2010). Explore and evaluate texts with students so they understand how published authors write. Encourage students to use some of the same techniques their favorite authors use. Some reading–writing ideas for the conventional writing stage include the following:

1. Read poems that follow a pattern (e.g., acrostic, diamante, cinquain, haiku, or tanka) and write a poem based on that pattern.

2. Write a play based on a short favorite scene in a story or a fable. The plot is already organized for the student.

3. Write text for wordless books.

4. Use graphic organizers to summarize informational texts. (This makes it more difficult for students to plagiarize when they write summaries.)

These tasks should first be completed with a teacher, then students should be encouraged to engage in them during writing workshop.

Writing Stages of Bilingual Spanish–English Writers

In an effort to understand writing development in English learners and how it compares to that of English-speaking students, Rubin and Carlan (2005) analyzed 100 samples obtained from Spanish–English bilingual students. Students ages 3 to 10 were asked to draw a picture, explain the picture to their tutor, and then to write in both Spanish and English an explanation of the picture. When they compared the developmental writing stages of English-speaking students (Gentry, 1982; Rubin & Carlan, 2005) to that of the Spanish-speaking students (Ferreiro & Teberosky, 1979, 1982), Rubin and Carlan discovered unique developmental writing stages for bilingual Spanish–English students. Figure 11.5 shows the relationship among the three groups of writers.

Rubin and Carlan were amazed to learn that during the **precommunicative stage**, the bilingual Spanish–English students wrote the same string of letters for the English text as they wrote for the Spanish text; however, they read their sentences in Spanish and then in English, using the correct words.

During the **semiphonetic stage**, the bilingual Spanish–English students used both vowels and consonants for syllables, even though Ferreiro and Teberosky found Spanish-only writers used a vowel for each syllable. In this stage, some bilingual Spanish–English students wrote the same letters for the English text as they did for the Spanish text, while some students started to use different letters for the two languages.

In the **phonetic stage**, bilingual Spanish–English writers knew that words are written differently in English and Spanish. Like English-only writers, they omitted silent letters (e.g., *lam* for *lamb*) and sounds that are difficult to hear (e.g., *stad* for *stand*). In this stage the bilingual students used their knowledge of Spanish spelling. For example, the letter *i* in Spanish makes the long /e/ sound. They might write *si* for *sea* or *bi* for *bee.* They would often write *do* for *the* because the Spanish language does not use the initial /th/ sound. These bilingual students also confused the /v/ and /b/ because the /v/ in Spanish is similar to the English /b/.

During the **transitional stage**, bilingual Spanish–English students often put the adjective after the noun instead of in front of the noun like most English writers do. This again shows how these students used their knowledge of Spanish to write English text. Also in this stage, students insert Spanish words when they cannot think of the English equivalent. Perez-Canado (2005) found this to be a common writing habit of bilingual Spanish–English writers.

Based on the developmental writing stages of bilingual students, teachers should incorporate the following practices suggested by Rubin and Carlan (2005):

1. Provide extended periods of time to write and allow a personal choice of topic and genre.

2. Encourage students to use both languages so you can understand the student's development.

3. Emphasize that students should write original thoughts, not copy words or worry about spelling.

| | Summary and comparison of stages of writing development among English-speaking, Spanish-speaking, and bilingual children. |

Monolingual English speakers' stages of writing development (Gentry, 1982, 2007)	Monolingual Spanish speakers' stages of writing development (Ferreiro & Teberosky, 1979, 1982)	Bilingual Spanish-English speakers' stages of writing development
Precommunicative stage Know the difference between writing and drawing. Write with scribbles, mock letters, and real letters unconnected to sounds.	Levels 1 & 2 Know the difference between writing and drawing. Write with scribbles, mock letters, and real letters unconnected to sounds.	Generally the same as monolingual English and Spanish, except some children will write the same letter symbols in both languages but read them differently in English and in Spanish.
Semiphonetic stage Letters are written to represent some of the sounds in words.	Level 3 Each syllable in a word is usually represented by a vowel.	Generally similar to monolingual English, except some children will write the same words in both languages but read them differently in English and Spanish.
Phonetic stage Letters are written to represent most sounds in words.	Level 4 Letters are written to represent most sounds in words.	Generally similar to monolingual English and Spanish. Some errors exist because of different letter–sound relationships in the two languages.
Transitional stage Letters are written according to common spelling patterns and include silent letters.	No corresponding level.	Similar to English monolingual stage with some errors caused by different letter–sound relationships in the two languages. Vocabulary and sentence structure become more complex.
Conventional stage Writing is generally correct.	Level 5 Writing is generally correct.	Writing is generally correct. Vocabulary and sentence structure become more complex.

Source: Rubin, R., & Carlan, V. G. (2005). Using writing to understand children's literacy development. *The Reading Teacher, 58*(8), 728–739. Reprinted with permission of the International Reading Association via Copyright Clearance Center.

4. Have students read to you what they have written so you can help them develop their English vocabulary.

5. Value what bilingual students write, even if it is not lengthy.

6. Have bilingual students explain how they write and choose topics so you can understand their thinking.

7. Encourage students to use background knowledge when writing.

8. Teach spelling patterns within words and show students where to find correct spellings (e.g., on the classroom's word walls, online, or in books) instead of having students memorize spelling lists.

9. Assess growth by looking at all student writing samples and then praise them for the progress they are making.

In addition, interactive writing is an effective instructional method to use with English learners.

English learners may require extra time to complete a composition even though their finished piece may be shorter than the other students' pieces. When writing expository text, English learners should:

■ have more time to read and study the sources.

■ be permitted to read sources in their native language when possible.

■ write while they are learning English.

■ be able to choose their topics.

■ learn to write for a variety of purposes.

■ have opportunities to write about their families and cultures (Spence, 2010).

When analyzing English learners' compositions, teachers should ask some or all of the following questions:

1. What voices are represented in the piece?

2. What did I learn about the student as a person?

3. What did I learn about the student as a writer?

4. What instruction does this student need to develop his strengths and address some weaknesses?

Writing and the Common Core State Standards

The NGABP and CCSSO (2010) recognized the importance of high school graduates having the writing skills necessary for postsecondary education and the workplace. To meet this goal, the CCR Anchor Standards for

Writing emphasize academic writing that includes writing from sources, citing evidence, argument/persuasive writing, informational writing, narrative writing, and writing using technology. The following sections discuss how these emphases will help students become more sophisticated writers.

Academic writing

The introduction to the CCSS English Language Arts Standards for Writing for grades 6 through 12 states that "Each year in their writing, students should demonstrate increasing sophistication in all aspects of language use, from vocabulary and syntax to the development and organization of ideas, and they should address increasingly demanding content and sources" (NGACBP & CCSSO, Introduction to CCSS for Writing, Grades 6–12, 2010, p. 19). This suggests that students need to engage in **academic writing**. In the past, teachers emphasized using the writing process, choosing concise vocabulary, avoiding plagiarism, avoiding mechanical errors, and sharing their writing with classmates. Now, however, teachers also need to encourage their students to show "evidence of deep connections with content through academic discourse" (Wolsey, Lapp, & Fisher, 2012, p. 714). Academic writing is the type of writing found in professional books and uses a particular **register,** a term that refers to "linguistic features that are used in a particular situational context" (Scarella, 2003, p. 19). Some elements of **academic register** are using standard English grammar, writing in the active voice, consulting an adequate number of sources to understand what others have written about the topic, synthesizing other authors' thoughts, using technical vocabulary, and situating their own point of view "within the work others have done" (Wolsey, Lapp, & Fisher, 2012, p. 715).

Authors understand that all academic writing is a dialogue between writer and reader. Kesler (2012) gives the following tips for all writing, which are, of course, also applicable to academic writing:

1. Know your purpose for writing the piece.
2. Know your audience.
3. Know the main message you want to convey.
4. Know what has already been written on the topic.
5. Know your stance compared to that of your audience.

Citing Evidence

Anchor Standard for Writing 9 requires that students "[d]raw evidence from literary or informational texts to support analysis, reflection, and research" (NGACBP & CCSSO, Anchor Standard for Writing, 2010, p. 18). Think how often a friend or colleague informs you of something and you ask, "Where did you read that? I never heard of that before." That is exactly what this part of Reading Anchor 1 requires; writers and speakers must cite the source of their information. For example, first-grader Jon writes in his report that a jellyfish can grow bigger than a person and notes that the source of the information is page 8 of the book *Jellyfish* (Lindeen, 2005). Jon's classmate Jeremy does not believe Jon's report until he picks up Lindeen's book and reads page 8 for himself. Teachers need to instruct students to cite sources for their facts.

Arguments

In the past, most teachers engaged their students in narrative and expository writing but may not have emphasized argumentative writing. The first of the CCR Anchor Standards for Writing requires that students write arguments and support their stance with credible evidence. Of course, primary students will not have the skills to present a strong piece of argumentative writing; however, the CCSS requires that even kindergarten students express their opinions in writing through **opinion pieces** (NGACBP & CCSSO, CCSS for Writing, Kindergarten, 2010, p. 19). Kindergarteners can learn to express their opinions about a book, the type of animal that makes the best pet, and other topics appropriate for this age.

Thus, beginning in kindergarten, teachers need to give students many opportunities to develop the skill of writing opinion pieces by modeling how to write them. For example, after reading a number of Rosemary Wells's Max and Ruby books, a kindergarten teacher can encourage students to name their favorite Max and Ruby book. After the students share their opinions, the teacher models how she writes an opinion piece about her favorite book. As she writes she can do a think-aloud similar to the one in the accompanying box.

Once students reach first grade, the CCSS require that they be able to state their opinions and then give two or three reasons for their stance. If stating an opinion about a book, their reasons can be statements about the funny antics or kindness of a character, the intriguing plot, or the illustrations. By the end of second grade, students are expected to "supply reasons that support the opinion; use linking words (e.g. *because* and *also*) to connect opinion and reasons, and to provide a concluding statement or section" (NGACBP & CCSSO, Writing, Grade 2, 2010, p. 19). An example of a second grade opinion piece about a favorite book is found in Figure 11.6.

Students in these early grades as well as older students benefit from teachers sharing model book reviews found online. Allyn (2014) suggests that teachers together with their students analyze how the reviewers write specific "I like" statements or "I dislike" statements about the book and then persuade others to read

Modeling a Think-Aloud

Ms. Short says, "My favorite Max book is *Max's Dragon Shirt.*"

She then turns to the big flip chart and says, "I am going to start at the top of the paper. I am going to write: My favorite Max book is *Max's Dragon Shirt.*" She begins to write saying, "I need to begin my sentence with a capital letter." As she writes, she sounds out each word, puts a finger down when she is going to begin a new word, and puts an end mark.

She knows not all her students are capable of writing a complete sentence, so she invites students to draw a picture of their favorite Max and Ruby book. She explains that for her book she will draw Max in his new dragon shirt.

Ms. Short monitors the children as they write, and writes a sentence for students who can only draw a picture. By the beginning of the second semester, she encourages all students to copy her sentence: "My favorite Max book is..." Then they can find the book in the classroom library to copy the title. This type of writing should start early in the year and continue to the end of the year.

their position. The website www.spaghettibookclub.org offers reviews written by students about books that are appropriate for elementary and middle school. The site allows teachers to choose a review of a book or an author she and the class have read. Project the review on a screen so all students can read, analyze, and discuss it. Engaging students in writing opinion pieces may be one way to encourage reluctant students to express their opinions (Sweeny, 2010).

As students progress through the elementary grades, the CCSS writing standards continue to emphasize the writing of opinion pieces. Starting in grade 6, however, the standards require students to write arguments. To write **arguments**, writers must establish themselves as the voice of authority. To establish this voice, they need to be able to state a claim clearly and present evidence to support it—facts, statistics, or quotes from credible sources. They must know that their sources are credible and that they are experts in the subject area. As writers put their thoughts down, they must appeal to the audience's logic and emotions, meaning that writers must know their audience. They must also know the counter argument(s) to their claim and be able to refute the counter claim(s). Lapp and Fisher (2012) suggest that writers use the following steps when writing an argument:

1. Introduce your precise claim as well as the counterclaim(s).
2. Develop the claim with facts, statistics, and quotes, stating the sources for each.
3. Build relationships between claims and reasoning; between reasoning and evidence; and between claims and counterclaim(s).
4. Maintain a formal style and an objective tone.

or not read a book. The reviewers usually give specific examples about the character, setting, plot, theme, word choice, or text structure (e.g., graphic novel, picture book). In these opinion pieces, writers get the readers' attention with an opening statement. These statements can be a question, a quote from the text, or a short summary. After writers give two or three reasons for their stances, they provide an ending statement that restates

figure 11.6 Sample second grade opinion piece.

My favorite Arthur book is <u>Arthur Lost in the Museum</u> because I really like the illustrations Marc Brown used to show readers the museum. My second reason this book is my favorite Arthur book is because I also got lost on our field trip to the zoo when I went to get a drink. I was as scared as Arthur was in this book. This also is my favorite Arthur book because I thought Marc Brown drew a scary skeleton of the dinosaur so I know why Arthur was scared. Of all the Arthur books, this one is my favorite.

5. Provide a concluding statement or section that supports the argument.

As with all writing, students need to first research a topic before they write an essay in which they are presenting a point of view that has an opposing point of view. Marcus White, a fifth-grade Oklahoma student, passionately wants Oklahoma to adopt a bottle bill similar to Michigan's, the state from which he moved. Figure 11.7 is an organizer that he used as a prewriting tool, and Figure 11.8 is his essay. Also see Appendices D.30 and D.31 for blank graphic organizers for arguments.

After writing an argument, students can use the checklist in Appendix C.51 to evaluate their passages. Figure 11.9 offers a partial completed checklist based on Marcus White's essay.

---

figure **11.7**   Graphic organizer for an argument.

Position of Reader:			Counter Position:
Thesis: Our state should pass a bottle-deposit law on cans and bottles.			Thesis: Our state should not pass a bottle-deposit law on cans and bottles.

Reason #1: Our state would have less litter and pollution.	**Reason #2:** Bottle-deposit laws provide financial incentives for recycling.	**Reason #3:** Deposits promote recycling jobs.	
Supporting Details: 1. The 10 states that do have bottle-deposit laws have cleaner roadsides. (www.durangoherald.com, July 15, 2010) 2. Landfills take large amounts of space that could be used for farmlands and recreational areas. (www.durangoherald.com, July 15, 2012; www.bottlebill.org; www.Michigan.gov) 3. Bottles and cans pollute our state's rivers, lakes, and streams, which kills fish. (www.bottlebill.org)	**Supporting Details:** 1. Michigan collected 443.9 million dollars in deposits in 2002 (www.michigan.gov) and all 10 states that have deposit bills collect 66 to 96 percent for beverage containers. (www.durangoherald.com) 2. It is unlawful for Michigan residents to throw bottles and cans in the garbage; therefore all are returned for deposit from customers or from recycling bins. (www.Michigan.gov). 3. All unclaimed deposits that revert back to the state can be used for cleanup and redevelopment fund to clean up contaminated sites within the state. (www.Michigan.gov)	**Supporting Details:** 1. People are needed to manage the deposit stations. (www.bottlebill.org) 2. People are needed to recycle cans and bottles; thus promoting much needed jobs. (www.durangoherald.com July 15, 2012) 3. Truck drivers are needed to take bottles to recycling locations. (www.bottlebill.org)	

Reader's Conclusion:
Oklahoma must adopt a bottle-deposit law to keep our state from creating more landfills, to provide jobs, and to help raise state funds to clean up contaminated areas.

Sources:

Smedley, M. (July 15, 2012). Bottle-deposits could open can of worms. Online: www.durangoherald.com, July 15, 2012. Retrieved: December 27, 2013.

Container Recycling Institute. Benefits of Bottle Bills. Online: www.bottlebill.org. Retrieved: December 27, 2013.

Michigan Department of Treasury. (2013). Michigan Bottle Deposit Law Frequently Asked Questions. Online: www.michigan.gov. Retrieved: December 17, 2013.

figure 11.8 Example of a fifth grade argumentative essay.

Why Oklahoma Should Adopt Deposits on Beverage Containers
By Marcus White, Fifth Grade

Oklahoma claims it is a progressive state; however, it lags over forty years behind Oregon who adopted the first Bottle-Bill (Profita 2013), and behind nine other states who have had a Bottle Bill for a couple of decades (Smedley). Oklahoma should join the ten states that have adopted Bottle Bills, which requires citizens to pay deposits on all aluminum, plastic, and glass beverage containers. When the citizens return the containers to a retail store, a redemption center, or a reverse vending machine, they get their deposit back; it does not cost citizens any money if they return the containers. The ten states—California, Connecticut, Hawaii, Iowa, Maine, Massachusetts, Michigan, Oregon, Vermont, and Guam—report four positive results after adopting Bottle Bills. They boast that the bill reduces litter and landfills, increases recycling incentives, creates jobs, and conserves natural resources (Container Recycling Institute). Oklahoma must adopt a Bottle Bill so we can experience the same four benefits.

Did you know that plastic water bottles take 700 years to decompose (Environmental Media Association, EMA)? Did you know that Americans use 2,500,000 plastic bottles every hour, and 80,000,000,000 aluminum soda cans every year (EMA)? In 2003, 55.47 percent of American's municipal waste was solid waste such as beverage cans, plastic bottles and glass bottles. This was equal to 2.46 pounds of waste per person per day (Keep America Beautiful, KAB). Oklahomans are a part of this monumental problem of litter and waste because we do not have a Bottle Bill. In the ten states that have Bottle Bills, they have reduced litter and cut down on the amount of solid waste in landfills (Container Recycling Institute). New York reduced their roadside litter by 70 percent (Department of Environmental Conservation), and Oklahoma can do the same. Adopting a Bottle Bill in Oklahoma would not be a hassle as opponents state, but having such a bill will reduce litter and cut down on the amount of solid waste in Oklahoma landfills.

The ten states that have a Bottle Bill boast that the bill has increased recycling. Did you know that New York recycled 90 billion containers, which equals 6 million tons of materials that were not put into landfills (Department of Environmental Conservation). The ten states that do have a Bottle Bill average a recycling rate from 66 to 96 percent (Container Recycling Institute). Most states have a five to ten cents deposit, but Oregon has increased the deposit because five cents does not have the same value it did in 1971, the year they implemented the bill (Profita). Other states are considering raising the deposit also so it is worth citizens' effort to recycling (Container Recycling Institute). Oklahoma should begin with a 15-cent deposit on all nonalcoholic aluminum, plastic, and glass containers and a 20-cent deposit on alcoholic containers.

The third reason that Oklahoma should adopt a Bottle Bill is that it will create jobs (Container Recycling Institute). Workers are needed to manage the redemption centers. Workers are need in the factories that make the reverse vending machines. Workers are needed to truck empty containers back to the bottling companies so they can be recycled. Additional workers will be needed to work the machines that recycle the containers. Some opponents of a Bottle Bill may think Oklahoma has a low unemployment rate; however, this will make it even lower!

There are three primary reasons for Oklahoma to adopt a Bottle Bill. First, such a bill will reduce litter and keep solid waste out of our landfills. Second, a deposit will increase recycling incentives. Third, a Bottle Bill will create jobs for Oklahomans. Finally, such a bill will conserve our precious natural resources. Join me in writing a letter to your state representative to create and adopt a Bottle Bill!

Sources:

Container Recycling Institute. (2013). Benefits of Bottle Bills. Online: www.bottlebill.org. Retrieved December 27, 2013.

Department of Environmental Conservation. (2013). New York's Bottle Bill. Online: www.dec.ny.gov/chemical.8500.html.

Environmental Media Association, EMA. (2013). Oklahoma City Sustainability. Online: www.okc.gov/sustain/tips. Retrieved: December 29, 2013.

Keep America Beautiful. (2013). Oklahoma City Sustainability. Online: www.kab.org. Retrieved December 29, 2013.

Michigan Department of Treasury. (2013). Michigan bottle deposit law frequently asked questions. Online: www.michigan.gov. Retrieved: December 27, 2013.

Profita, C. (February, 2013). Three big changes to Oregon's famous bottle bill. Online: www.opb.org/news. Retrieved: December 28, 2013.

Smedley, M. (2012). Bottle-deposit could open a can of worms. Online: www.durangoherald.com. Retrieved: December 27, 2013.

figure **11.9** Partial checklist used for students' evaluation of their presentation of an argument.

EVALUATING THE POWER OF MY ARGUMENT

Introducing My Persuasive Claim and the Counterclaim(s)

___X___ My clearly stated claim is ... *that bottled water sales are increasing each year and contributing to the waste in landfills.*

___X___ My authority of my claim has been established by ... *the Container Recycling Organization (www.container_recycling.org/index.php/issues/bottled-water).*

___X___ The counterclaim to my claim is ... *people are drinking fewer carbonated drinks and more water which is healthier for individuals.*

Supporting My Claim and Refuting the Counterclaim

___X___ Evidence is included to support my claim. The evidence is ... *that between 2002 and 2005 water bottle sales doubled from 15 billion bottles sold to 29.8 billion (Container Recycling Organization, www.container_recycling.org/index.php/issues/bottled-water).*

Source: Adapted from D. Lapp and S. Fisher (2012). Persuasion = Stating and arguing claims well. *Journal of Adolescent and Adult Literacy, 55*(7), 641–644.

Informational text

Another emphasis of the CCSS is on writing informational texts. The second CCR Anchor Standard for Writing requires students to write informational texts that present complex ideas clearly and correctly (NGACBP & CCSSO, CCRA for Writing, 2010, p. 18). An effective way to teach informational writing to young students is to share quality informational texts with the class and then discuss what the author did to make the information easy to understand. For example, in kindergarten and primary grades, teachers can use one of Gail Gibbons's books. She is a prolific author of children's informational text, and her illustrations help explain the content. Using the reading/writing workshop format, teachers can share one of her books by reading and closely examining the details and labels in the illustrations. After sharing, for example, *My Soccer Book* (2000), *Basketball* (2000), *Football* (2000), and/or *Baseball* (2000) with first graders, teachers can invite their students to write information they have learned in their journal and draw and label a picture of what they wrote. Because the CCSS require students to collaborate on writing projects, teachers can group students together based on the sport they chose.

Another way to have students collaborate on writing informational text is to have them write and illustrate an alphabet book about their state after a unit on state history. Teachers can share the many different alphabet books written about different states. For example, *S Is for Sooner: An Oklahoma Alphabet* (Scillian, 2003) features different parts of Oklahoma, its heroes, and major historical events. Each page focuses on a letter of the alphabet and has text that explains the place and other information. For example, the "C"

page mentions Choctaw and Cherokee, two towns in Oklahoma, and Francisco Vasquez de Coronado, one of the first Europeans to explore the territory that later became Oklahoma (Scillian, 2003). After sharing the books, each student can choose one letter of the alphabet, find a point of interest that corresponds to it, and research it. They can write a short paragraph and draw an illustration that supports their fact. For example, Jack, a fourth-grader in Stillwater, Oklahoma, began his C page with "C is for Cowboys, the best basketball team in the state." He researched the team's statistics for the past 50 years to find out how many national titles they had won and which Cowboys got drafted by the NBA. It became a favorite page for the boys in his class. See the Intervention & Activities section for additional ideas for integrating content area material and writing and illustrating alphabet books.

State tests based on the CCSS require students to write expository responses to narrative text (Cummins & Quiroa, 2012). This task differs from the way students used to write story summaries. Instead of writing a summary, students may be asked to explain how a character's personality changed from the beginning to the end of the story and what caused this change. To enable students to write this type of response, primary teachers can use some of Kevin Henkes's books that display a character going through a drastic change. As mentioned in Chapter 8, a good book for such a writing assignment would be *Julius: The Baby of the World* (Henkes, 1995), because young students can readily see the character's change and its cause. You will need to pay close attention to students' written responses to make sure they are answering the right questions and not merely providing a summary of the book. As students become more fluent with these types of responses, you can require students to cite evidence, which may include statements the character makes, something revealed by the illustrations, or what other characters say to or about the protagonist.

Donavan and Smolkin (2011) shared a framework for informational report writing in elementary grades. As you read about each step in Figure 11.10, keep in mind that as a student becomes fluent in one step, you may need to nudge students to the next level of development.

Narrative text

Writing stories is a time-honored instructional practice in all grades. The third CCR Anchor Standard for Writing requires narrative writing. As with all writing, teachers and students should analyze quality literature together to understand how authors create humor, suspense, or mysteries. Studying the word choice in different genres increases students' awareness of what creates a good story. Analyzing leads, endings, and other techniques further makes them aware of quality writing (DeFauw, 2013). For example, if you want your students to use a new technique, such as writing stories that include a flashback, first share books that have flashbacks. Some choices include *Cloudy with a Chance of Meatballs* (Barrett & Barrett, 1978), *Why Epossumondas Has No Hair on His Tail* (Salley, 2004), and *The Day Jimmy's Boa Ate the Wash* (Noble, 1992). Then students and teachers should examine how the author began the flashback. For example, Salley begins the story with Epossumondas asking his mother why he does not have a bushy tail like other animals, and his mother relates that his great-great-grandpa Papapossum had a fluffy tail, but he got himself into trouble and lost his tail. At this point in the story, Salley begins the flashback by first stating: "And this was one of those times . . ."; then the mother proceeds to tell the story of how the great-great-grandpa lost his tail. Once teachers analyze techniques like flashbacks with students, they can encourage students to try the technique using a style similar to the author's or a style of their own.

Parodies are another form of narrative writing that teachers and students can analyze and then students can reproduce on their own. To engage young students in narrative parody writing, use a repetitive book such as *I Went Walking* (Williams, 1996) or *Brown Bear, Brown Bear, What Do You See?* (Martin, 1996) as a template. Intermediate elementary students enjoy the tall tales of Paul Bunyan, Thunder Rose, Pecos Bill, and Mike Fink and enjoy writing parodies of these stories. The Intervention & Strategies section includes a tall tale parody writing activity.

Middle-school educators understand the importance of motivating students to write narratives. Borgia and Owles (2011) suggest that teachers permit boys and girls to read different books to which they can relate. Two suggested titles that contain personal narratives are *Guys Write for Guys Read* (Sciezka, 2006) and *Every Girl Tells a Story* (Jones, 2002). After students read these books, have them write a personal narrative about a similar incident that happened to them.

When engaging students in narrative writing, remember to use the steps of the writing process and encourage the use of the 6 + 1 Writing Traits. The writing process and the 6 + 1 Writing Traits are explained later in this chapter.

Multimodal text

Standard 6 of the CCR Anchor Standards for Writing calls for students to "Use technology, including the Internet, to produce and publish writing and to inter-

---

figure 11.10 Framework of informational report writing of elementary students.

Phase 1: Students label their drawings: "This is my house."

Phase 2: Students give fact statements: "My house is yellow."

Phase 3: Students list facts: "My house is big. My house has a flag hanging on it. My house has an upstairs."

Phase 4: Students write couplets that show relationships: "My house has a flag on it because my dad is in the army."

Phase 5: Students give a fact list that contains more information than the list in phase three, but it is not a developed paragraph: "My house is a big, yellow house with an upstairs. My grandpa's house is white and has no upstairs. My friend has a small little blue house with cute little windows."

Phase 6: Students expand couplet collection by giving additional information and adding supporting explanation. "My house is big because I have one sister and one brother. We each have our own bedroom, and my mom and dad have a bedroom."

Phase 7: Students write unordered statements. All sentences support the topic, but they are not logically sequenced. "I live in a big place. The yard is big. My bedroom is blue with basketballs on the wall. The yard has a swing set. My sister has a yellow room."

Phase 8: Students write more complex paragraphs with some ordering. "I live in a big house. The backyard has a swing set and a small kiddie swimming pool. My bedroom is small and blue. My sister has a room that is yellow and large."

act and collaborate with others" (NGABPC & CCSSO, 2010, p. 18). Teachers have always engaged students in the various steps of the writing process, and many have invited students to sit in the author's chair and read their writing to the class. However, they may not have stressed the use of technology for sharing writing, even though most adolescents participate in social networking (Lenhart, Madden, Smith, Purcell, Zickuhr & Rainie, 2011). The sixth CCSS Writing Standard requires that even kindergarteners "[w]ith guidance and support from adults, explore a variety of digital tools to produce and publish writing, including in collaboration with peers" (NGABP & CCSSO, 2010, p. 19). By the end of the eighth grade, students are required to "[u]se technology, including the Internet, to produce and publish writing and present the relationships between information and ideas efficiently as well as to interact and collaborate with others" (NGABP & CCSSO, p. 43). Whether writing narrative or informational texts, students can use technology to enhance them.

A few years prior to the development of the CCSS, the National Council of Teachers of English (2005) wrote a position paper explaining why today's students need to write multimodal stories. Toward that end, teachers can encourage students to create multimodal graphic novels about their lives, using photographs or illustrations and speech bubbles to tell their story. They can invite English learners to tell their immigration story or that of their parents through graphic stories. Hughes, King, Perkins, and Fuke (2011) encourage classroom teachers to invite the art teacher or a local artist to teach students about splash pages, overlapping panels, floating panels, full-page panels, location of action in each box, the point of view of the main character in relationship to the reader, and the placement of speech bubbles. After students have created their own texts, permit students to collaborate with others to add photographs and illustrations.

In terms of informational writing, the eighth CCSS requires that first graders "[w]ith guidance and support from adults recall information from experiences or gather information from provided sources to answer a question," as well as to use technology in producing and publishing their writing (NGACBP & CCSSO, CCSS Writing, Grade 1, 2010, p. 19). Around Halloween time, first grade teachers can involve students in researching and writing multimodal informational text by reading one or two stories about bats and then sharing informational resources about bats. Figure 11.11 has a list of possible resources. After reading and discussing each text, teachers can model note taking by creating a web as found in Figure 11.12. Notice that the organizer is limited to the main topics of habitat, types, diet, size, and unique traits. After creating the graphic organizer as a class, students can create their own fact presentations about bats, using text, photos, illustrations, and audio/

figure 11.11

Resources on bats.

FICTION

Lies, B. (2006). *Bats at the Beach.* Boston: Houghton Mifflin.

Lies, B. (2008). *Bats at the Library.* Boston: Houghton Mifflin.

Lies, B. (2010). *Bats at the Ballgame.* Boston: Houghton Mifflin.

NONFICTION

Carney, E. (2010). *National Geographic Readers: Bats.* Photographs by National Geographic. National Geographic Children's Books.

Earle, A. (1995). *Zipping, Zapping, Zooming Bats.* Illus. H. Cole. New York: Harper Collins.

Fenton, M. B. (2001). *Bats.* Photographs. Checkmark Books.

Gibbons, G. (2000). *Bats.* Illus. G. Gibbons. New York: Holiday House.

Iorio, N. (2005). *Bats!* New York: Harper Collins.

WEBSITES

Defenders of Wildlife, www.defenders.org

National Geographic for Kids, http://kids.national geographic.com/

video. The presentations can then be posted on a class website and shared with family and friends.

Once students have progressed to the eighth grade, the CCSS require the writing of informational text to become more involved. By the time students are in middle school they should be collaborating with classmates and creating multimodal informational pieces that challenge them to use higher level thinking skills. The standards also require that students be able to "[g]ather relevant information from multiple print and digital sources, using search terms effectively; assess the credibility and accuracy of each source; and quote or paraphrase the data and conclusions of others while avoiding plagiarism and following a standard format for citation" (NGACBP & CCSSO, CCSS Writing, Grade 8, 2010, p. 44).

Spires, Hervey, Morris, and Stelpflug (2012) describe a middle-school project based on topics about which students are curious and that have social importance. Possible topics for such a project can include air pollution, foreign sweatshops, global warming, immigration laws, off-shore drilling, or any topic that is being discussed in science or social studies. Once students have chosen their topics, they gather information from a number of sources, taking notes and remember-

figure 11.12   Graphic organizer of bat facts.

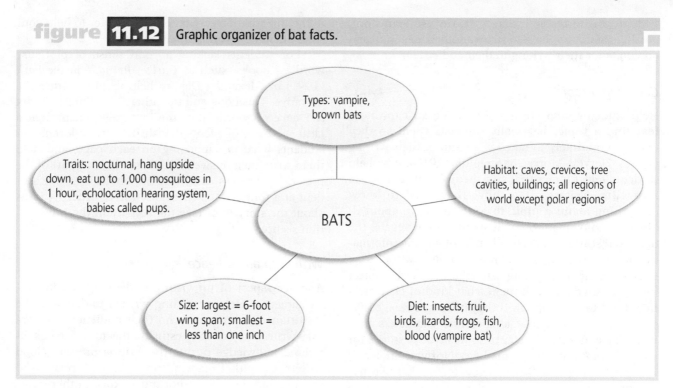

ing to write down references. After they have conducted the research, they creatively synthesize the information into a multimodal presentation that includes text, illustrations, music, voice, and a final slide that cites all the resources used to collect the information, the images, and the music. In projects of this kind, it is important that teachers assess not only the accuracy of the informational presentation and the credibility and use of citations, but also the creativity of the multimodal elements. For more information on assessing multimedia projects, see the Assessment section.

THE WRITING PROCESS AND WRITING WORKSHOP

Many teachers understand the process of writing as described by Graves (1990, 1991, 1994); the stages of this process will be discussed below. Because writing is a process and the CCSS Product and Distribution of Writing standards specify that students be able to use it, teachers can implement the **writing process** in the **writing workshop** practice outlined by numerous researchers (Atwell, 1987; Calkins, 1994; Hansen, 1987). The writing process itself and as used in writing workshop are effective tools to help second language learners (Dworin, 2006; Williams & Pilonieta, 2012) as well as English-speaking students. The writing workshop has six essential elements: (1) schedule regular, sustained writing sessions; (2) give students choices; (3) give teacher and peer feedback; (4) establish a structure; (5) build a cooperative learning community; and

(6) provide mini-lessons for direct, explicit instruction. The main premise of the writing workshop is that all writers need regular, sustained time for writing. Student writers need to be able to choose their topics and the genres. Traditionally, teachers assigned class-wide topics that may not have interested students. As for structure, many writers favor a predictable environment in which they write at the same time every day. Writing workshops also emphasize the importance of community. Teachers foster a supportive environment where students freely share their thoughts with peers without the fear of being ridiculed. Sharing ideas with an audience that extends beyond the teacher is an important aspect of writing. Teachers also need to share their expertise with students in mini-lessons.

Graves (1990) argued that accomplished authors go through five steps as they produce manuscripts: prewriting, drafting, revising, editing, and publishing. These steps are discussed below. Just because you schedule time for writing does not ensure that all students will develop good writing skills. Give extra assistance to struggling writers and teach them how to complete each of the process's five steps (Graham & Harris, 1997). Provide this help in a tutoring session or in a very small group if you can. See the Intervention activities at the end of this chapter for suggestions.

Prewriting Stage

During the **prewriting stage** of either expository or narrative text, instruct struggling writers on how to choose a topic, how to research that topic, how to brainstorm possible subtopics, how to structure their material, and how to tailor their writing to their audience.

Choosing a topic

Help students who are going to write an expository text find a topic that really interests them so they will be more likely to take ownership of their writing (Spires, Hervey, Morris, & Stelpflug, 2012). Also help students select topics that give them a chance to learn. Struggling writers often think they need to know everything about a topic in order to write about it; however, knowing too much about a topic negates the need to research it. A valuable part of writing informational text is exploring and researching new topics.

When helping young students choose a subject for a narrative text, ask them what kind of characters they want to write about. If they offer no ideas, brainstorm with them about all possible characters they could have in a story. Refer to some favorite stories for ideas. For example, if Sophia loves Norman Bridwell's *Clifford the Big Red Dog* series, suggest that she use Clifford or another dog as a character. Then the two of you can brainstorm a list of all the things Clifford could do or the problems Clifford could encounter. Next, together determine the step-by-step plot. Complete all the planning before Sophia begins to write. Struggling writers need to understand that brainstorming is an important part of writing. The Intervention section of this chapter provides other activities to help students choose a topic.

Structuring the material

Prewriting is a time to make a plan. When writing expository text, students can use a graphic organizer to create a structure for their passage. After they have chosen their topics, pose questions designed to make them consider all its aspects. Then they create a graphic organizer based on these questions, thus giving them a focus. As discussed in Chapter 9, students should choose a graphic organizer based on the organizational pattern they will use in their text to show how the information will be related. After they have created their organizer and list of questions, students read different sources to answer only those questions. Graphic organizers also keep students from copying (plagiarizing) complete paragraphs from books or the Internet by making them write phrases instead of complete sentences.

Students can also use expository frames to help them organize their material. These frames are also based on the organizational patterns of expository text as well as the signal words commonly used in the pattern (see Chapter 9). Use the expository frame activity

in the Intervention section of this chapter to help your students write informational text.

For students lacking a good sense of plot, use wordless books, such as *Carl's Afternoon in the Park* (1991) by Alexander Day, to help them structure the narrative. This book and the others listed in Appendix A.5 have no words after the first page but present a clear sequence of events that thrill most children. Ask students what is happening on each page, and help them write their answers on sticky notes as part of the prewriting process. Use wordless books with one student at a time because they often have differing ideas about the story lines (see the activity in the Intervention section).

Writing to an audience

Another aspect of prewriting is defining the intended audience. Help struggling writers understand the importance of knowing who their audience is before they write. They need to estimate the audience's background knowledge during the writing process. Good writers know that readers bring some information to the text, but that the author must explain other information explicitly. They must also decide if the passage should be formal or informal. For example, writing a letter to the president of the United States requires more formal language than texting friends. If the audience is not kept in the forefront of the writer's mind during the writing process, the writing will often lack a clear purpose.

Drafting

Students often think form is more important than content while composing a first draft (Wood-Ray, 2006). Assure them that spelling and mechanics do not matter during the **drafting** stage. Initially, you may need to engage in interactive writing with the student to keep her from becoming discouraged. By sharing the pen, students write more text in a shorter amount of time than they would by themselves. Teachers need significant patience to work with struggling writers; sit with them and ask probing questions to keep the process moving. Let them know they may find it necessary to do more research or to do more imagining. Once a writer begins the first draft, she will most likely not return to prewriting activities.

Revising

"The ability to revise is significant because it helps the writer reflect and clarify his or her thinking with the goal of improving the writing" (Dix, 2006). Struggling writers do not see the significance of **revising** and often lack the ability to do it effectively, rendering their revisions superficial. Pose questions to prompt the writer to add, delete, reword, and/or reorganize sentences or longer passages. Queries such as "How big? When? How? Why? Where? What kind? What color or shape? Whose?" will prompt the writer to add information. If she cannot answer these questions, have her go back to the prewriting stage, find the information, and then do some more drafting. Writing is recursive, requiring one to go back to previous stages occasionally.

Deleting text is often more painful than adding text, so help writers see the value of this task. Ask the writer why she included a section, or show how she has drifted from the main purpose and should delete a passage or use it in a different story or informational piece.

Introduce a writer to a thesaurus to help him see how vivid words make the piece more exciting and sophisticated. Also having the writer reread the passage to ensure that he used the correct technical terms.

Editing

At the **editing** stage, it is best to have students self-edit first (Turbill, Bean, & Fox, 2006), then have a peer edit the piece, then have the teacher edit one more time before giving the composition back to the student (Moore-Hart, 2005). A wall chart with an editing or proofing checklist helps students take ownership in analyzing various aspects of their manuscripts. Figure 11.13 is a checklist that writers can use to evaluate their own work and, later, have a peer evaluate it. Items that

students check are based on the rules that have been taught during mini-lessons. The main categories are: (1) capitalization rules, (2) punctuation rules, (3) paragraphing, and (4) spelling. You may need to go through the checklist with struggling writers first and then watch as they fill it out. It is important to teach struggling writers to become independent proofreaders.

Publishing

All students, even struggling writers, need to see their writing published and share it with an audience that extends beyond the classroom. Earlier in this chapter, I suggested that students enter writing contests so they learn to write to a distant audience. Giving younger students special stationery cards to write thank-you notes to the cafeteria workers, to parents who sponsored a skating party, or to senior citizens who supervised a field trip helps them realize that someone is going to read their note, so their writing must be correct and neat. Figure 11.14 shows thank you notes written by first graders to a student teacher on her last day in the classroom.

Consider publishing a classroom poetry book. Students contribute a poem for which they have received peer and teacher feedback. Have them verify that their poem's mechanics are correct and then neatly rewrite or type it before it is added to the class book.

You can do the same thing with informational books. Each student can research one or two aspects of a topic

figure 11.13 Checklist for proofreading (second grade).

Student _____   Date _____

Title _____

CAPITALIZATION:

_____ First words of all sentences

_____ Proper nouns (names of people and places, titles of books, musical works, etc.)

_____ Proper adjectives

PUNCTUATION:

_____ All sentences end with a period, question mark, or exclamation point.

_____ Commas

_____ Quotation marks around dialogue (what characters say)

PARAGRAPHING:

_____ Each new idea begins a new paragraph

_____ Indented for each new paragraph

_____ Only one idea in a paragraph

_____ Ideas well developed in paragraph

_____ In dialogue, each time a speaker changes, there is a new paragraph.

SPELLING:

_____ Check every word closely

_____ Use word wall when in doubt

_____ Check spelling in another book

_____ Use dictionary

Student's Signature _____

Classmate's Signature _____

figure 11.14 Thank you notes written by first graders.

Dear Miss Story,
Take you for helping us learn. And you are very very nice. My fafite theork is gingerbread man and is urse? I will vere miss you.
cathy 11-7-0 the end.
Love cathy

Dear Miss Story,
Thak you for being nis and kind to us. Thank you for the ginger bread cookies and reading to us. Thank you for helping us. We will miss you!
Love Reece

Dear Miss Story,
Thank you for being a nice teacher. Thanks for the gingerbread cookies was good. Thank you for reading books to us.
love Gabe

and then write a passage about what they have learned. They can illustrate the passage to further explain the concept. Contributing one page to a book is not a daunting task for any student. All the student-created books become a part of the classroom library and can be read often by the teacher or classmates. If there is one class book for every student by the end of the year, hold a lottery to determine who gets to keep each book.

As discussed earlier, the CCSS for writing require students to use the computer to publish their pieces. **Web 2.0** sometimes is used to refer to sites on which students can create, edit, manipulate, and collaborate online (Handsfield, Dean, & Cielocha, 2009). Students can write stories, poems, and essays and post them on blog sites and student readers from around the world can post comments. Figure 11.15 shows the opening paragraph of an 87-page story written by an eighth-grade student, along with excerpts from two student responses he received. The responses illustrate authentic writing. Notice how honest the comments are; these responders are not writing to please a teacher—they are writing to give a critique and receive clarification for their queries.

Figure 11.16 lists websites for Web 1.0 and Web 2.0 tools. As discussed earlier in this chapter, publishing beyond the boundaries of the classroom can motivate struggling writers (DeFauw, 2013).

figure 11.15 Excerpt from "Through a Dragon's Eyes by Garath Half-Elven," and student comments on the story.

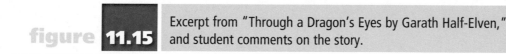

SUNDAY, OCTOBER 16, 2011, 4:34PM
Posted by: Jack

I flew over the dusty plain, watching the scene unfold beneath me. On my back, Rhovanir drew his long blade. The elaborate hilt glinted in the sunlight. He was my Rider, and he had always been there. Ever since I was a hatchling, he watched over me, the last dragon in all of Eldareht. The Elves on the battlefield below were fully engaged, their blades adorned with goblin blood. They fought side-by-side with the Men of Thelduin, attempting to stem the flow of the goblin warriors that so foully desecrated the Sacred Land. I hunger for their blood.
. . .

Add Comment (2)

COMMENTS

Posted by: Kari on Monday, October 17 , 2011, 11:32AM
I like this. It seems almost like a snippet from a larger story . . . my only complaint is the characters have odd names and I get them confused. But that is small. Overall, good job!

Posted by: Justin on Monday, October 17, 2011, 2:07PM
hmm . . . this is a good story but I'm confused about where and when it is set. Is it set in Algaesea or not? And what timeframe is it set in? I'm confused . . . .

 **11.16** Websites and online references for Web 1.0 and Web 2.0 tools.

TOOL TYPE	WEBSITE
Graphic novels and comic books	• www.scholastic.com/graphix/ includes graphic novels/comic stories that students can read and discuss with others on a discussion thread • www.plasq.com/ Offers an online space for users to develop graphic novels and comic books
Digital storytelling and video sharing	• www.VoiceThread.com A space for creating and sharing digital stories that use text, voice, and pictures and can be shared for collaboration • www.TeacherTube.com Online video streaming site. Videos can be viewed, uploaded, downloaded, and embedded into wiki pages
Mapping and webbing	• www.mind42.com • www.mindmeister.com Online collaborative mind-mapping applications • www.gliffy.com A collaborative space to create flow charts and diagrams
Collaboration	• www.docs.google.com Open source office applications for individual or collaborative use. Collaboration can be simultaneous • www.wikispaces.com • www.educationalwikis.wikispaces.com Spaces for free educator wiki development and collaboration
Blogging	• www.edublogs.org Spaces to develop and house blogs • https://www.sitebuilder.com/start/blog, https://www.websitebuilder.com/start/blog These sites allow users to create and manage their own blog using any of a selection of templates.
Social networking/ bookmarking	• www.delicious.com Spaces where you can keep all your bookmarks so they can be tagged, accessed from any computer, and shared. Diigo also has options for setting up groups (for projects, classes, etc.) and functions to highlight and place notes on bookmarked web pages • www.ning.com Online space to create a social network, including groups, messaging, and collaboration
Global classroom collaboration	• www.flatconnections.com/ Global student collaboration project
For more Web 2.0 resources and information	• www.cooltoolsforschools.wikispaces.com/ • www.teachweb2.wikispaces.com/

Source: Handsfield, L., Dean, T., Cielocha, K. (2009). Becoming critical consumers and producers of test: Teaching literacy with Web 1.0 and Web 2.0. *The Reading Teacher, 63*(1), pp. 40–50. Reprinted with permission of the International Reading Association via Copyright Clearance Center.

6 + 1 TRAIT® WRITING MODEL OF INSTRUCTION AND ASSESSMENT

Designed by the Northwest Regional Education Laboratory (NREL, 2001), **6 + 1 Trait® Writing Instruction and Assessment** is a framework for assessing, talking about, and organizing writing. Students and teachers at all levels use these traits to discuss the qualities of writing. Even primary-grade students can learn the language as they engage in the writing process. The fourth CCR Anchor Standard for Writing includes many of these writing traits, even though the 6 + 1 Writing Trait framework is not mentioned by name.

The Traits

The 6 + 1 Traits are (1) idea/content, (2) organization, (3) voice, (4) word choice, (5) sentence fluency, (6) conventions, and (+1) presentation. Because all the traits are interdependent, it is difficult to describe one without referring to another. However, the following is a brief description of each.

Idea/content

This trait focuses on the content or message of the passage. Is it a mystery story to entertain, a political essay to persuade, or an informational passage about whaling? The content must be interesting and age appropriate. It should provide well-developed and necessary details, such as clues in a mystery, reasons for a scientific phenomenon, or examples of types of jungle creatures. The content must have a clear focus. All the information in informational passages should support the whole, and all parts of a story should be important to the plot, omitting unrelated or unnecessary information. The content must be original or at least presented in a fresh way. In informational writing, readers expect the author to be credible; this means he is knowledgeable about the topic through either experience or research. Those reading a passage desire to learn something new; therefore, the writer must provide information that goes beyond the obvious.

Organization

The flow of the passage must be logical. In longer passages, the beginning paragraph typically states the purpose of the passage and must grab the reader's attention. The middle of the passage needs a logical flow. Some information is best told in a sequential manner, while other information is best told from least important to most important. The writer must know "when to slow down and elaborate, and when to pick up the pace and move on" (Northwest Regional Educational Laboratory, 2001, p. 1). The concluding paragraph must signal to the reader that it is the end of the passage.

Voice

This trait refers to the way the writer "speaks" to the reader. It is the flavor the writer gives to the passage. In expository or persuasive passages, the writer's passion for the topic becomes obvious through his or her voice, which is reflected in wit, descriptions, figures of speech, style, and word choice (the fourth trait). Voice is what distinguishes one writer from another, and it is often the trait that keeps readers coming back to a writer. Share one or two of Mo Willem's pigeon books to show students an author with a unique voice. He creates a distinct voice through his use of word bubbles and illustrations that enable the pigeon to carry on the conversation with the reader.

Word choice

This fourth trait is closely entwined with voice. Vivid nouns, verbs, and adjectives help readers visualize descriptions of objects, settings, and characters. Unique, colorful words paint pictures in the readers' minds. Good writers choose words that show rather than tell the action of the narrative. For example, instead of stating: "The young man was angry," an author writes: "Jon stormed into the room, threw his backpack on the floor, kicked over a chair and yelled, 'It was not my fault!'" In informational writing, technical terms with good descriptions help readers better understand the concept. Writers who choose words carefully do not use clichés and jargon; instead they use unique figures of speech such as metaphors, similes, personification, and onomatopoeia that bring information or scenes, characters, and action alive for the readers.

Sentence fluency

Fluent writers work at varying sentence length and use a variety of sentence types, including:

- *Simple sentence:* One independent clause or a group of words that stands by itself.
- *Compound sentence:* Two or more independent clauses connected with a semicolon or coordinating conjunction.
- *Complex sentence:* One independent and at least one dependent clause that cannot stand by itself, such as "because it rained last night."
- *Compound complex sentence:* At least two independent clauses and at least one dependent clause.

In informational text, writers use transitional words and phrases to connect thoughts within and between sentences, paragraphs, and chapters. In narrative text, dialogue is used to help reveal characters' feelings and thoughts, to show rather than tell the action, and to move the action along. When read aloud, a fluent passage is pleasant to hear.

Conventions

This sixth trait refers to the technical or mechanical part of writing. Is the paragraphing correct? Is the passage free of spelling, punctuation, capitalization, and usage errors? Mechanical errors distract readers, so passages free of mechanical errors permit readers to remain focused on the content. If the writer uses dialect for effect, the word's spelling should closely resemble its pronunciation so the reader does not have trouble figuring it out.

Presentation

The "plus 1" trait is the presentation of the passage, which refers to the formatting—the amount of white space, the width of margins, the font, the size of the print, the placement of words, and the illustrations that accompany the text. The presentation may be the first trait readers consider when they look at a passage. How small is the font? How much text is on a single page? Are the margins wide enough for making notes?

Just as the cover of a DVD attracts viewers as they select a movie, so a written passage needs eye appeal. The reader may expect to see graphs, charts, photographs, and/or illustrations to help explain an informational text. Even primary students need to know that presentation is important when writing for an audience other than just the teacher.

Teaching the 6 + 1 Traits

Every piece of writing includes all these traits. Primary grade teachers need to explain each trait during mini-lessons or guided writing sessions so students become aware of its importance. One way to introduce a trait in a mini-lesson is to choose a short passage from an age-appropriate book and discuss how the author made the passage unique and inviting. Because these traits are found in all types of passages, teachers should use examples of narrative and informational text and poetry from quality children's literature so students become conscious of how these traits are used in all types of writing. See the Intervention section for activities that teach the 6 + 1 Traits.

Assessing Writing with the 6 + 1 Traits

In order for students to develop all these traits, they must all be a part of assessment. All writing skills develop through practice, and an appropriate rubric reflects students' stages of development. The 6 + 1 Trait

rubrics provided by teachers from Sheboygan Falls, Wisconsin, can be used for informative and narrative writing (www.mshogue.com/ce9/rubrics/rubrics.htm). Instead of the point-based categories used in the samples, teachers may use qualitative categories such as *exemplary, acceptable, developing,* and *unacceptable.* You may also create your own rubrics using the template found at http://rubistar.4teachers.org.

An abbreviated version of the 6 + 1 assessment developed by the Northwest Regional Educational Laboratory is presented in Appendix C.52.

CONNECTING WRITING INSTRUCTION AND ASSESSMENT

As a pre-service or practicing teacher, you may be overwhelmed. How will you teach the writing process, provide students with writing instruction and assessment using the 6 + 1 trait framework, and cover the expectations of the CCSS Anchor 4. Appendix D.32 contains a matrix that aligns the steps of the writing process with the 6 + 1 Writing Traits, and then gives samples of the types of narrative and expository multimodal writing required by the CCSS that can be completed during each step of the writing process. Take time to study it and discuss it with your classmates. Writing instruction should excite you, not overwhelm you!

ASSESSMENT
Informal Assessment

In addition to using the 6 + 1 Traits for assessing students' writing (see Appendix C.52), teachers can use the methods of informal assessment discussed below.

Portfolios

The authentic way to document students' writing growth is through the use of portfolios. The writing portfolio includes writing attitude surveys, writing self-assessment surveys, spelling inventories completed periodically throughout the year, and samples of the student's work with scoring rubrics. Rubrics used throughout the year document growth; other rubrics are designed for a particular type of composition. The best way to assess writing growth is through students' compositions; therefore the focus of the next two sections is on developing rubrics, which is a type of informal assessment.

Assessing the writing process with rubrics

Teachers need to assess students' writing processes as well as their results. Rubrics are a great tool for helping teachers examine the crucial aspects of these processes.

In designing a rubric for the writing process, all five steps of the writing process must be considered, and rubrics must also be appropriate for the students' developmental stage. The best rubrics are those designed by teachers for their own classrooms, because they know the developmental stage of their students and what the CCSS or their state standards require for each grade level. Appendix C.53 is an example of a rubric for assessing the writing process in the primary grades, and Appendix C.54 is an example of a rubric for assessing third graders. Both may be used as springboards for teachers who have never developed scoring rubrics. Both are designed to be used over the entire year and should illustrate each student's improving skills. When you use a rubric that documents growth, you can quickly detect in which areas each student needs to improve.

Assessing writing products with rubrics

Each assignment calls for its own rubric. Narrative and informational writing are very different from each other; scoring rubrics should reflect these differences. Consider the students' developmental writing stage when developing the rubric; no teacher expects the same quality of writing from a first grader as she would from a fourth grader.

Two sample rubrics are included in Appendices C.55 and C.56. The first one is for fourth-grade story writing, the second one is for a fourth-grade research report. Figure 11.17 contains a rubric for a sixth-grade research project. This rubric states the expected performance for three levels of mastery. The rubrics in Appendices C.55 and C.56 give ratings of *excellent* to *poor* with a number assigned to each rating (e.g., *excellent* corresponds to five points). The story-writing rubric in Appendix C.57 includes detailed criteria for awarding points. Many students appreciate knowing the exact requirement for each part of the assignment and expect to be graded fairly. Providing specific criteria helps the teacher be consistent in the grading process. Appendix C.58, the Research Report Rubric, is intended for fifth- or sixth-grade students who are expected to use the Internet to gather information.

Another way to design rubrics is to weigh each component of the writing product differently. For example, in the rubric for stories you may choose to assign five possible points for characterization, five points for setting, but only two for character motivation. This may be because the class has examined vivid literary descriptions of characters and settings and your goal is for them to create similar descriptions. You may have mentioned but not emphasized character motive in class and not told students that they had to include descriptions of the characters' motives. To design a rubric with different values for each component of the story, list the possible points after each component, as in the example below.

COMPONENT	POINTS
1. Description of setting	(5 points)
2. Description of characters	(5 points)
3. Motives of characters	(2 points)

The sample sixth-grade research rubric found in Figure 11.17 focuses on conducting and writing a research report. Mr. Harmon, who designed the rubric for the first quarter, did not use his state's standards as the sole measure for assessing the research paper. He realizes that no student will be competent in all of the standards under the heading of *research* so early in the year. Therefore, he created a rubric based on the criteria set for the first research paper of the school year. It requires students to use at least two different techniques to find sources. His students already know how to use the databases in the library, so he introduces them to finding credible Internet sources. This first paper requires five sources, including one primary source, and he teaches them how to use direct quotations and citations in the exposition. He encourages his students to carefully read and analyze each source. He does not teach them how to synthesize the information, which is another part of the standards on research; he plans to do this next semester. Notice his emphasis on correct spelling.

Assessing multimedia projects with rubrics

Teachers who assign multimedia projects may use a rubric like the one found in Appendix C.59 for assessment. This rubric is designed for a group project and can be modified online to fit specific assignments. Other multimedia and classroom website rubrics are available online. Note that the rubric includes two criteria for assessing the creativity of a project: (1) attractiveness, which assesses the use of font, color, graphics, and effects to enhance the presentation, and (2) originality, which assesses the creative ideas evident in the project.

Attitude surveys

In addition to process and product, teachers also need to assess students' attitudes toward writing—how they perceive themselves as writers and their views on the process and the product. Many times students' attitudes toward writing are the greatest obstacles to their success. Appendices C.21 and C.24 include a writing attitude survey for younger students and one for older students. Another excellent survey that has been tested for reliability and validity is the Writer Self-Perception Scale (WSPS) designed by Bottomley, Henk, and Melnick (1998).

The WSPS measures the affective elements related to writing by assessing four categories of self-perception:

1. *General progress:* A student's perception of his/her past and present performance.

figure **11.17** Assessment rubric for first quarter research project, sixth grade.

STUDENT: _Char_   DATE: _November 11_

TOPIC: _Weather balloons_   TOTAL SCORE: _28_

	LEVEL OF MASTERY		
TRAIT	**TARGET (5 POINTS)**	**ACCEPTABLE (3 POINTS)**	**UNACCEPTABLE (1 POINT)**
1. Accessing information	Selected the best sources for the topic. ___	Selected some good sources for the topic. _X_	Did not select appropriate sources for the topic. ___
2. Sources used	Used 2 sources (library, database, credible Internet site) to research topic. ___	Used 1 of the 2 sources (library, database, or credible Internet site) to research topic. _X_	Used only 1 source (library, database, or Internet) to research topic but the source was not credible. ___
3. Authors used	Used as least 1 primary & 4 secondary sources to gather information. _X_	Used only 1 primary & 3 secondary sources. ___	Used 3 or fewer sources to gather information. ___
4. Note taking	Used at least 3 strategies to aid comprehension of difficult material. ___	Relied on 1 or 2 strategies to aid comprehension of difficult material. _X_	Used no organizational strategies to aid comprehension of difficult material. ___
5. Use of reference features	Used 2 or more reference features of printed text, such as citations, endnotes, & bibliographies, to locate relevant information about topic. _X_	Used at least 1 reference feature of printed text, such as citations, endnotes, & bibliographies, to locate relevant information about topic. ___	Used no reference features of printed text, such as citations, endnotes, or bibliographies, to locate relevant information about topic. ___
6. Analysis	Determined the appropriateness of an information source for the topic. ___	Determined the appropriateness of some of the information sources for the topic. _X_	Did not determine the appropriateness of any information source for the topic. ___
7. Citations	No more than 2 citation errors. ___	3 or 4 citation errors. ___	More than 4 citation errors. _X_
8. Content	Had 6 or more main ideas with fully developed supporting sentences. __	Had 4 or 5 main ideas with at least one or two supporting sentences for each idea. _X_	Had 3 or fewer main ideas with no supporting details. ___
9. Paragraphs	1 topic per paragraph & logically organized. ___	1 topic per paragraph but not logically organized. _X_	More than 1 topic per paragraph. ___
10. Capitalization	No capitalization errors. ___	1 or 2 capitalization errors. ___	More than 3 capitalization errors. _X_
11. Punctuation	No punctuation errors. ___	1 or 2 punctuation errors. ___	More than 3 punctuation errors. _X_

NOTE: THERE WILL BE ONE POINT TAKEN OFF FOR EVERY SPELLING ERROR! (Start by using your spell check!)

TEACHER'S COMMENTS:

You used some good sources and included interesting information. Concentrate on details such as spelling and punctuation, too!

2. *Observational comparison:* How the student compares him/herself to others.

3. *Social feedback:* The student's perception of others' work.

4. *Physiological state:* A student's internal feelings while he/she writes.

The scale is designed for students in grades four through six.

The WSPS is made up of 38 simple statements that are easy to read. One of the statements is general ("I think I am a good writer"), and each of the other 37 statements represents one of the five categories. The responses are based on the five-level Likert scale: "Strongly Agree," "Agree," "Undecided," "Disagree," and "Strongly Disagree." Some sample statements include:

- "I write better than other kids in my class." [observational comparison]

- "I need less help to write well than I used to." [general performance growth]

- "I choose the words I use in my writing more carefully now." [specific performance improvement]

- "My teacher thinks my writing is fine." [social feedback]

- "When I write, I feel calm." [physiological]

Each of the five areas on the WSPS has a different number of questions; the scoring guide indicates which statements belong in each category. A score in any category that is "slightly below, equal to or slightly greater than the mean indicates a normal range" (Bottomley, Henk, & Melnick, 1998, p. 294). Scores lower than this range are a cause for concern; scores higher than the normal range indicate the student has a positive self-perception of his writing.

The WSPS has been tested for validity and reliability with 964 students in grades 4, 5, and 6. Correlation among the five scales ranged from .51 to .76, showing significant relationships and scale distinctiveness. It also demonstrated strong reliability characteristics. The WSPS with scoring sheet and the directions for administering, scoring, and interpreting it are pro-

vided in Appendix C.26. It may be photocopied for classroom use.

Self-assessment instruments

Fountas and Pinnell (2001) designed a self-assessment writing and spelling instrument for grades 3 through 6. It is published in its entirety in *Guided Readers and Writers Grades 3–6: Teaching Comprehension, Genre, and Content Literacy*. This self-assessment asks the students about their writing habits, such as what kind of writing they have completed and what their favorite piece is. It also asks them what they do well as a writer and how they have improved throughout the grading period. The last questions allow the students to reflect on the mechanical aspects of writing and ask what conventions they use very well. Appendix C.60 contains a self-assessment instrument for writing and spelling.

Formal Assessment

Standardized tests such as the Iowa Test of Basic Skills, Comprehensive Test of Basic Skills, California Achievement Test, and Metropolitan Achievement Test have subtests for language, which usually means grammar. In each of these subtests, students are asked to find the segment of the sentence that has some type of a mechanical error. The error can be related to punctuation, capitalization, or usage. This type of testing assesses the student's ability to edit a product, not her ability to write. However, because writing is now generally viewed as a meaning-making process, educators realize they must assess the process as well as the product.

Many state departments of education also recognize the weakness of these standardized tests to assess students' ability to write; therefore, they have created standardized rubrics to assess students' writing. In many states teachers know the rubric benchmarks and focus their students' writing on scoring well on them. Some educators believe these students' writing now rigidly conforms to the rubric, making it "more uniform and much less interesting" (Strickland et al., 2001, p. 1).

intervention   STRATEGIES & ACTIVITIES

The strategies in this section focus on connecting reading and writing. Many struggling writers do not enjoy writing because they do not know what to write about, they see writing as a big task, and they struggle with spelling. For these students, begin with small tasks that connect reading to writing. Interactive writing activities make writing tasks manageable and less intimidating for students and give you opportunities to model writing strategies.

Interactive Writing ("Sharing the Pen")

Interactive writing is a collaborative strategy involving a teacher and student working together to create a written piece. The teacher asks a student what he would like to write about concerning an event they shared (e.g., a story they read together). The student then dictates a sentence with the teacher writing most of it. As she writes she asks the student to listen to the beginning sounds of words, which she stretches so he can distinguish them. She also invites the student to write the letters he knows. While he writes the teacher emphasizes the letter–sound relationships. As the student learns more letter–sound relationships, the teacher gradually turns the pen over to him so that he can write more, until the teacher is adding only a few unknown words.

Variation for English Learners

English learners need opportunities to engage in many writing activities. Sharing the Pen in a small group is one way they can write a passage with the help of classmates (Williams & Pilonieta, 2012). The small group can use Sharing the Pen with any type of writing; the group decides what they will write and students take turns writing the passage. The passage should be on a whiteboard or interactive whiteboard so all members can see the scribe. The students not holding the pen help the writer with spelling, punctuation, word choice, and so on.

Quick Writes (Writing on Demand)

As mentioned in the opening scenario, many students struggle with state-mandated writing tests that require them to write to a given prompt for a predetermined amount of time. Students used to the writing workshop may have a difficult time writing under those conditions, because state exams do not allow them to conference with a peer or teacher to receive feedback. All students must write and proofread their own work independently. In the opening scenario Mr. Burns used two writing strategies to prepare his students for writing on the state tests—**POW** and **TREE,** presented below—in addition to writing workshops (Mason, Benedek-Wood, & Valasa, 2010). When using these two **quick write** strategies, the teacher selects the topics and gives students 10 minutes to complete the task.

POW

POW can be used when the prompt asks students to write what they know about a certain topic after reading two or three informational texts. POW stands for

- **P**ick your ideas,
- **O**rganize your thoughts, using notes, and
- **W**rite your ideas

POW can be used when students are learning new material; it encourages them to plan their passage by making notes about their main ideas, organizing them into a logical sequence, and then using them to write the passage. Like Mr. Burns, you can collaborate with the science and social studies teachers to get short passages about a topic. Students would be required to read the short passages and then write an essay, explaining what they learned.

TREE

When students need to respond with a persuasive passage, they can use TREE. TREE stands for

- **T** = write a **topic** sentence that states your point of view;
- **R** = state the **reasons,** at least three, for your stance;
- **E** = **explain** each of the reasons with details that have been learned from the reading material; and
- **E** = **end** your passage by writing a good summary sentence.

Again, like Mr. Burns, you can present two passages with opposing points of view on a topic. Instruct students to choose one of the points of view and persuade the reader why that point of view is correct.

Read, Flip, Write

Often students are guilty of plagiarism when they first write research reports. Matson (2012) uses the Read, Flip, Write activity to teach students how to paraphrase instead of copy. This technique requires the following steps:

1. Have students discuss a good television show or movie that they recently viewed.
2. Tell them that they just paraphrased the information and then invite them to write about the movie or show.
3. Next, give students a handout containing an urban legend. For example, the tale of the vanishing hitchhiker is about a driver who picks up a young female hitchhiker, only to find out later that she died years earlier. Snopes.com, which calls itself the "definitive Internet reference source for urban legends," is a good source for these legends.
4. After the class reads and discusses the story, collect the handout and ask students to paraphrase the legend.
5. Next, give them a short informational passage to read. Instruct them to not have any writing utensil in their hands while they read.
6. Have them to flip over the paper and write down the passage's main points. Instruct students that to avoid plagiarism they need to paraphrase as they had been doing during the three summarizing exercises. Conclude by telling students that they should use the same technique when they are taking notes, especially for writing assignments.

Activities for 6 + 1 Traits of Writing

Teachers must build on what students can do, one step at a time. The best way to do this is to focus on one trait at a time and revisit traits that have already been taught. When teaching the traits to any struggling writer, whatever the student's age, begin with the first trait—ideas and content—and then emphasize subsequent traits one at a time.

Trait 1: Ideas and Content

Many students struggle with getting ideas down on paper and expressing ideas that are beyond the obvious.

For primary grades: Ask students if they have a pet, a favorite sport, or a best friend. Invite them to write four or five sentences about the topic. When they have completed the task, ask them to read their passages to you individually. After each reading, ask questions that will lead to additional information. For example, following is a student's description of his dog.

My dog is my friend. We play together. He goes with me all over. He likes me.

After listening to the passage, the teacher asks questions that will prompt the student to add details. Here is a sample of the conversation. As the student responds to the questions, the teacher records the answers on a separate piece of paper.

Teacher: It sounds like you really like your dog. What kind of dog is he?

Student: He is a lab.

Teacher: What color is he?

Student: He is brown, I think they call it chocolate.

Teacher: Is he big or small?

Student: He's really big and strong. He once licked my face and pushed me over because he is so strong. But he's not mean. He was just happy to see I was home from school.

Teacher: You wrote that you play together. Tell me some things you play.

Student: He loves it when I throw a ball and he gets it for me. I am also teaching him to catch a Frisbee. If I throw it low, he can catch it. We also play hide and seek. I hide his rubber bone, and then he finds it. Sometimes we just lie in the grass and look at the clouds.

Teacher: You wrote that he goes everywhere with you. Where are some of your favorite places to go?

Student: He likes to go walk with me and my mom. But mostly we just play in the yard together. Oh, and he loves to come in my bedroom and he sleeps there.

Teacher: You wrote that your dog liked you. What does he do that really shows you he likes you?

Student: He wags his tail when he sees me and just follows me all over the house. Oh, and he loves to lick my face. But I don't mind.

Show the student your written notes and discuss how many details he shared about his dog. Then ask the student to write about his dog again and add the details so he can share the passage with his classmates during "Author Chair" time. Most struggling writers will not resist adding details if you provide the correct spelling of all the words. Not knowing how to spell often hinders a student from writing details.

For an upper-elementary or middle school grade: Use the same approach as for younger students, but ask them to write about a favorite book character, sport hero, music star, or actor.

Trait 2: Organization

Work one-on-one with students so each gets feedback about the organization of their passage. Because organization is essential for sequential or chronological passages, invite students of any age to write in paragraph form—not numbering format—about how they prepare their favorite sandwich. Older students can write how-to procedures for more complicated tasks, perhaps connected to a hobby or sport. Have a student read her passage out loud and then ask questions that will help her rewrite the passage if necessary, using appropriate sequence.

Trait 3: Voice

This strategy can be used in grades two through middle school. Using the "Friendly Letter" strategy and the example of the letter found later in Figure 11.23, discuss with students the sentences in which Betsy asks if the Little Pigs want her to take pork chops to barbecue or if they do not eat pork. Ask students if they think those sentences reveal Betsy's sense of humor (you may need to discuss that pork is pig meat). Or do they think Betsy is being cruel by suggesting pork chops? Help students see that the rest of the letter is friendly, so the author is showing her sense of humor. Discuss how these two sentences create a "voice" for the letter because the thoughts expressed are unique. Once students understand the humor, invite them to write a letter to another fairy tale character, either inviting the character to a party or accepting an invitation to a party. Encourage students to think of creative ways to write their letters; that is, to think of one or two sentences that will set theirs apart from everyone else's. When they have finished, have each student explain which sentence he or she worked on to reveal a unique voice. Because many struggling writers are concerned only with writing the required number of sentences or paragraphs and not about giving voice to their writing, you may need to work with them individually.

Trait 4: Word Choice

Because diamante and cinquain poems are terse, they are great forms for helping writers with word choice. Using the example of the diamante poem "Pizza" or the cinquain "Novels" found in the poetry activities on pages 319–322, discuss with students what word or words they would want to change in the poem to make it better. This is an easy task for students of all ages because they have a starting poem and they get to be the "editor" who improves it. After they have made their changes, invite them to write a cinquain or a diamante of their own; both forms depend on the poet's word choice to be effective.

Trait 5: Sentence Fluency

Most struggling writers write short, simple sentences. To teach students how to combine ideas, present a short passage such as, "My cat is white. My cat also has black on it. My cat eats a lot of food. He is fat." Then invite students to be editors by helping you combine some of the ideas into a single sentence. Remind students they must keep all the author's ideas. Coach a student until she writes a sentence such as the following: "My white and black cat is fat because he eats so much." Point out that she made a more fluent sentence by using one coordinating conjunction and one subordinating conjunction. Have students reread each passage, the first with four sentences and the final with one sentence, to see if they can hear how the final passage sounds better and still contains all the ideas in the original sentences. After working with an example, have students read one of their recently written passages and consolidate the sentences without deleting any ideas.

Trait 6: Conventions

Teachers in all grades should post a large-print checklist chart somewhere in the classroom to which students can refer. The checklist could list common capitalization, punctuation, and grammar rules that are appropriate for the grade level. When you are reading a student's passage and see a mechanical error, direct her to the checklist. If you find a misspelled word, circle it so she can use resources such as word walls, dictionaries, and personalized dictionaries to correct it. You can also teach students to use spell check. The goal is for all students to become their own editors.

Trait + 1: Presentation

Students writing for an audience other than the teacher need to understand the importance of presentation. Display a short poem on the computer and instruct them how to highlight a passage and then change the font, type size, and color. Demonstrate how they can even highlight the first letter of the poem or the first letter of each line and change the size, font, and color so that the initial letter is distinctively different from the rest of the passage. Also show them how to add clip art to illustrate it. Older students can add audio (e.g., music) or video to their poems using programs such as PowerPoint, Photo Story, and Soundslides. Most students enjoy working on presentations to give their poems and other passages eye-catching appeal.

A C T I V I T Y   **Writing Interviews**   GRADES 5–8

After reading biographies about any type of American hero, invite students to write an interview. Writing interviews requires higher level thinking and a good understanding of the person they are interviewing. Here are examples of books that can be used as springboards for writing about African American heroes:

- Burleigh, R. (2007). *Stealing Home: Jackie Robinson: Against All Odds*. Illus. M. Wimmer.
- Eboch, M. M. (2008). *Jessie Owens: Young Record Breaker*. Illus. M. Henderson.
- Harness, C. (2003). *Rabble Rousers: 20 Women Who Made a Difference*.
- Harper, J. (2004). *Wilma Rudolph: Olympic Runner*. Illus. M. Henderson.
- Pinkney, A. D. (2000). *Let It Shine: Stories of Black Women Freedom Fighters*.
- Van Riper, G. (1986). *Jim Thorpe: Olympic Champion*.

If the goal is for students to learn to write interview questions, read the book or a section of it and ask students what additional information they would like to know about the hero. For example, share the story of Ida Bell Wells-Burnett from *Rabble Rousers: 20 Women Who Made a*

Difference (Harness, 2003) and ask students what questions they would ask if Ida came to their classroom. Here are a few examples:

1. How did she feel after she refused to give up her seat in the train and three men humiliated her? What exactly did they say to her?

2. How did she go about suing the railroad? Did she hire a black lawyer?

3. How did you feel when you saw the three black women dragged out of jail and then hanged? Did you attempt to stop those men?

After modeling how to write good questions, invite students to think of someone they as a class would like to interview. For example, students in the Oklahoma might like to interview an Oklahoma author/illustrator such as Mike Wimmer or Kim Doner. You may wish to contact one of these artists, explain that you are teaching students to write strong interview questions, and ask them if they would be willing to respond to questions submitted via email. If one of the individuals agrees to respond, have students write out questions they want to ask him or her. After responses are received, invite students to write a newspaper article, explaining everything they learned through the interview. Create a class newspaper for parents. Creating authentic writing projects for students generates more excitement than having them write only to fulfill an assignment.

Using Concrete Examples of Authors' Writing

GRADES 5–8   A C T I V I T Y

Help students with their narratives and poems by developing writing workshop mini-lessons in which they share effective examples from authors' published works (Baines & Kunkel, 2011). The following books include examples of many different authors' styles.

1. Two books that share various poetic forms are *Jazz ABZ* (Marsalis, 2005) and *A Kick in the Head: An Everyday Guide to Poetic Forms* (Janeczko, 2005). In *Jazz ABZ* Marsalis writes for the letter V: "her vestal vexing vigorates my soul and voids the vagrant values that restrain my heart" (n.p.). *A Kick in the Head* includes the poem "Ode," which uses vivid adjectives: Shoes are "rain-beaten, sun-beaten"; and "Villanelle" contains strong verbs such as "lurking, smirking" and "what is *plaguing* you." Descriptive words create images in a reader's mind.

2. *Hey, There, Stick Bug!* (Bulion, 2006) is a multi-genre book that features poems about different bugs and facts about them. You can use this book to demonstrate how students can write on the same topic across genres—poetry and informational text.

3. *Red Sings from Treetops: A Year in Colors* (Sidman, 2009) is another book of poems that show how authors use vivid adjectives to paint pictures in readers' minds. In "Fall" Sidman writes: "Green is tired, dusty, crisp around the edges. (In fall, / the wind feels Black: / star-spangled, full of secrets" (n.p.).

4. *City I Love* (Bennett-Hopkins, 2009) is a book of poems integrating social studies and writing. The poems take students on an international tour of cities around the world. They "travel" to New York, San Francisco, Tokyo, Cairo, Johannesburg, and Rio de Janeiro. The end pages feature a map of the world with the cities marked.

5. *Eats, Shoots and Leaves: Why, Commas Really Do Make a Difference!* (Truss, 2006) is a great book for demonstrating the importance of using commas correctly. Each double page has the same sentence punctuated two different ways to illustrate how the meaning changes when commas are moved or removed (e.g., "The student, said the teacher, is crazy" and "The student said the teacher is crazy" [pp. 19–20]).

6. David Harrison (2008) in *Pirates* uses poetry to spark students' imaginations in writing a sequence of poems that tell the story of pirates or some other person, object, or event of the sea. An example is "Through the Glass." Harrison writes: "in these waters, / let fog be our friend, / wrap us in its blanket / cold and gray as a cemetery, / cloak our secret journey home / heavy with gold for the king" (n.p.).

Guided Writing

Guided writing is based on the same format as guided reading (Fountas & Pinnell, 2001), in which you work with a small group of students who have the same writing needs. You present a concept or skill and then guide students as they apply it. The lesson is based on the needs of the group. For example, one group of students may need help with certain homophones, while another may need help with quotation marks. Some concepts taught in guided writing are listed in Figure 11.18. Guided writing differs from the traditional method of "teach and drill" because it does not follow a script or predetermined sequence. You impart what the students need to know when they need to use the skill. However, the sequence of a guided writing lesson does follow the format of traditional teaching:

1. Teach the concept.
2. Demonstrate how to use it.
3. Guide students as they practice it.
4. Expect students to use it in independent writing.

Students should keep a personal record of conventions learned in guided writing sessions so they can refer to them when they work independently (Calkins, 1994). Figure 11.19 is a log sheet for doing just that. Guided writing also helps you manage class time because you work with small groups instead of individual students.

figure 11.18 Concepts to teach in guided writing.

1. Follow capitalization rules
2. Follow punctuation rules
3. Use vivid nouns
4. Use vivid adjectives
5. Use vivid action verbs
6. Describe characters in detail (appearance, speech, dress, action)
7. Make sure pronouns–antecedents agree
8. Make sure subjects–verbs agree
9. Create clues for mysteries
10. Create flashbacks
11. Create good topic sentences
12. Add and sequencing details
13. Use transition words/signal words
14. Provide evidence
15. Cite sources
16. Synthesize information from multiple sources

figure 11.19 Sample log sheet for writing conventions.

Skills _____Marcie_____ learned in Guided Writing

SKILL	DATE
1. Don't put "and" between all ideas.	9-7
2. Instead of short sentences, use comma with "and."	9-12
3. Begin new paragraph with new idea.	9-15
4. Use "return" key to begin new paragraph.	9-16
5. Make stories become real with quotations.	9-23
6. Use verbs other than "said" in dialogue.	9-30

Mt. Plot

Creating story maps is one way to connect reading and writing. It also provides a topic to students who have "nothing to write about." Some story maps are described in Chapter 8. Mt. Plot is a story map that records main events of a story with distinct roadblocks (refer back to Figure 8.19 and see Appendix D.33 for a blank example). The plot obstacles are written going up the side of the mountain, the climax is written at the peak, and the resolution is written going down the other side.

Expository Frames (Cecil, 2015)

Expository frames help students understand expository structure by providing a systematic way to write about content they have read. This is also an effective way to introduce young students to informational writing (Cudd, 1990). Expository frames provide a scaffold for creating different ways to organize text.

1. Write a simple paragraph about a topic that lends itself to sequential ordering, using the signal words *first, next, then,* and *last.*
2. Copy the sentences onto sentence strips.
3. Review the topic and logical sequence of events with the class.
4. Have the students arrange the sentences in correct order in a pocket chart.
5. Read the completed paragraph together.
6. Have the students reorder the paragraph on their own and paste it on construction paper in paragraph form.
7. Invite the students to illustrate the details or some important part of the paragraph.

Gradually introduce a sequentially ordered expository frame for the students to complete independently, as in Figure 11.20.

figure 11.20   An expository text frame for sequence.

First, the gardener needs to prepare the ground by hoeing the soil.
Second, the gardener digs one-inch-wide rows across the garden.
After this, the gardener plants the seeds one inch apart.
Next, the gardener gently covers the seeds.
Then, he waters the garden.
Finally, he enjoys the flowers.

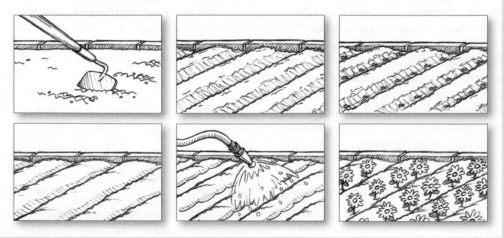

Other frames using different organizational models, such as cause/effect patterns, problem/solution patterns, and comparison/contrast patterns, are also helpful for assisting students writing expository text. Figure 11.21 is an example of a comparison/contrast pattern, and Figure 11.22 is an example of an enumeration pattern.

figure 11.21 A student's expository frame for comparison/contrast.

(Title)

Comparing Insects with Spiders

Insects differ from spiders in many ways. First, insects _fly while spiders don't_. Second, insects _don't spin webs but spiders do_. I think the easiest way to tell an insect from a spider is _to count the legs. A spider has eight legs. An insect only has six_.

Source: Nancy Cecil, *Striking a Balance: A Comprehensive Approach to Early Literacy*, 5e. Copyright © 2015 by Holcomb Hathaway (Scottsdale, AZ).

figure 11.22 A student's expository frame for enumeration.

Trees are useful in many ways. For example, _____

_____

Also, _____

In addition, _____

Finally, _____

Source: Nancy Cecil, *Striking a Balance: A Comprehensive Approach to Early Literacy*, 5e. Copyright © 2015 by Holcomb Hathaway (Scottsdale, AZ).

ACTIVITY **Sequels**   GRADES 2–6

Help a student predict what might happen to a book's characters after the end of the story. Books such as *Nana Hannah's Piano* (1996) by Barbara Bottner invite a sequel with its ending, "I'm trying out for the Little League soon. I have a new piano teacher who lives next door and likes potato dumplings." Ask the student to predict how well the team will play, to describe the new piano teacher, and to explain why the teacher likes potato dumplings. *Show and Tell* (1991) by Elvira Woodruff suggests a sequel with its illustration of a twisted fork on the final page. An older student may be able to write a sequel to Demi's *The Empty Pot* (1990) by explaining what happens when Ping becomes the new emperor. Books such as *Eloise* and *Madeline* invite students to imagine more adventures for these two characters.

ACTIVITY **Modeling Professional Writers' Picture Books**   GRADES 2–3

In the Elephant and Piggie series, Mo Willems tells the story through illustrations and speech bubbles. Invite student to write a story about two different characters, using speech bubbles and illustrations to tell the story.

After reading and sharing the funny picture book *Help Me, Mr. Mutt: Expert Answers for Dogs with People Problems* (Stevens & Stevens-Crummel, 2008), a book of response letters from disgruntled dogs, invite students to participate in a form of writing that requires higher-level thinking. In the book, dogs are writing Mr. Mutt about issues they have with humans. Invite students to think of what other issues dogs may have with humans, and have them write a complaint letter to Mr. Mutt, using a dog's point of view. Of course, students need also to write a response letter assuming the perspective of Mr. Mutt. Third graders' letters may not be as sophisticated as eighth graders' letters, but all students will need to write from a point of view that differs from their own. To extend this activity, students can give their dog complaint letter to a classmate for their Mr. Mutt response. This is another activity that you can turn into a digital or printed class book.

Writing Parodies

As stated previously, students in the intermediate grades enjoy tall tales and writing parodies of tall tales. Use the following steps to engage your students in this form of narrative writing:

1. Together with students, analyze the common elements of several tall tales. Include the following in the discussion:
   - the style is characterized by exaggeration through the use of hyperbole
   - all characters have a problem to solve
   - the main character is larger than life and superhuman
   - the plot is humorous
   - in the end, the main character solves the problem
   - the story has a lot of action
2. After the discussion, invite students in small groups to brainstorm characters they could use in a story, decide what superhuman strengths the character has, decide on the problem the main character must solve, plan a sequence of action-filled humorous events that the character experiences, and decide how the problem will be solved.
3. After planning the tall tale, invite students to write and illustrate their tales.
4. Enlist the help of the technology teacher to make the final project a multimodal presentation, including background music and photographs or illustrations. Collaborating with peers and experimenting with multiliteracies will make the task more enjoyable.
5. Have students share their presentations with other classes and parents or post on the class blog, wiki, or website.

Acrostic Poems

Acrostic poems are formed by writing a single word or short phrase vertically and using its letters to start the horizontal lines of the poem. Following is an example of an alphabet acrostic poem on spring.

> SPRING
>
> Sailing kites on a warm afternoon
> Planting young flowers
> Raking old, dead leaves
> Irises bobbing their purple faces in the breeze
> Narcissus swaying to the rhythm of the woodlands
> Setting out of school for an entire week!

After reading informational text, invite students to write an acrostic poem that conveys detailed information (Frye, Trathen, & Schlagal, 2010). Encourage students to use alliteration, assonance, and metaphors and/or to answer the five W's: *Who? What? When? Why?* and *How?*

TORNADOES

Twisting, twirling, threatening tornado

Ominous black clouds dipping down to touch earth

Rotating winds at 200 to 300 miles per hour

Nothing can withstand the tornado's force

All-time worst tornado outbreaks on May 18–20 and May 26–31, 2013

Destroying everything in its track

Organized when warm, moist ground air rushes upward to kiss cool dry air

Every continent except Antarctica can have a tornado

Spawned by giant thunderstorms called *supercells*

ACTIVITY **Cinquain Poems**

A **cinquain** is a five-line poem that follows a grammatical formula. The formula is somewhat flexible and two versions appear below. The first formula is easier for young students because they do not need to count syllables.

FORMULA 1

Line 1: a one-word subject

Line 2: two adjectives describing the subject

Line 3: three verbs that describe actions of the subject

Line 4: four words expressing a feeling or observation about the subject

Line 5: one word that renames the subject

FORMULA 2

Line 1: a one-word subject with two syllables

Line 2: four syllables describing the subject

Line 3: six syllables describing an action

Line 4: eight syllables expressing a feeling or an observation about the subject

Line 5: two syllables describing or renaming the subject

AN EXAMPLE OF FORMULA 1	AN EXAMPLE OF FORMULA 2
Connie	Novels
Humorous, kind	Thin, thick, old, new
Biking, swimming, running	Inviting me to read
Always there for me	They carry me to new places.
Friend	Best friends

ACTIVITY **Diamante**

A **diamante** is a seven-line poem that follows a formula and is written in the shape of a diamond. This poem helps students focus on parts of speech and antonyms. The formula is as follows:

Line 1: One noun subject

Line 2: Two adjectives describing the subject on line one

Line 3: Three participles (ending in "ing") that describe the subject

Line 4: Four nouns; the first two nouns relate to the subject in the first line; the third and fourth nouns relate to the antonym in line seven

Line 5: Three participles (ending in "ing") that tell about the antonym in line seven

Line 6: Two adjectives describing the antonym in line seven

Line 7: An "antonym" of line one (The term *antonym* is used loosely in this case. Many nouns do not have a true antonym and the poem will use a word that, in students' minds, contrasts with the noun in line one.)

EXAMPLE:

Pizza

Delicious, spicy

Bubbling, steaming, tantalizing

Cheese, mushrooms—scraps, litter

Molding, rotting, decaying

Smelly, yucky

Garbage

Biopoems

GRADES 4–8   A C T I V I T Y

Students in upper elementary grades who have studied famous inventors, explorers, or historical figures, can write **biopoems** (Fordham, Wellman, & Sandmann, 2002). The following is the template for the poem and an example.

Line 1: First name

Line 2: Four traits that describe the character

Line 3: Relative (brother, sister, daughter, etc.) of

Line 4: Lover of _____ (list 3 things or people)

Line 5: Who feels _____ (3 items)

Line 6: Who needs _____ (3 items)

Line 7: Who fears _____ (3 items)

Line 8: Who gives _____ (3 items)

Line 9: Who would like to see _____ (3 items)

Line 10: Resident of _____

Line 11: Last name

EXAMPLE: BIOPOEM OF BENJAMIN FRANKLIN

Benjamin

Inquisitive, precocious, practical, witty

Brother of seventeen siblings

Lover of literacy, experiments, and country

Who feels passionately about freedom of speech, science, and the Constitution

Who needs books, adventure, and humor

Who fears the British, slavery, and tariffs

Who gives the world bifocals, public hospitals, lightning rods, and public libraries

Who would like to see "truth spoken in every instance," "no one speaking ill of others," and "everyone doing good to Man"

Resident of Philadelphia

Franklin

Biopoems can also be used to encourage collaboration among classmates (Moore-Hart, 2005). Students interview each other and write a poem about their classmate, using the template below for their patterned poem.

First name
Who . . .
Relative of . . .
Lover of. . . .
Who needs . . .
Who fears . . .
Who would like to see . . .
Who attends . . .
Last name.

A C T I V I T Y **Fibbin Poems**

Fibbin poems are named after Fibonacci, an influential mathematician in the Middle Ages who popularized the number sequence that bears his name (Bintz, 2010a). Students from grades 1 through 8 often enjoy working with a pattern in poetry, such as a numerical sequence. They can write about any topic. The older students' poems will tend to be more sophisticated than younger students' poems.

The Fibbin poem follows a number sequence:

Line 1: one syllable
Line 2: one syllable
Line 3: two syllables (the sum of lines one and two)
Line 4: three syllables (the sum of lines two and three)
Line 5: five syllables (the sum of lines three and four)
Line 6: eight syllables (the sum of lines four and five)
Line 7: thirteen syllables (the sum of lines five and six)
Line 8: twenty-one syllables (the sum of lines six and seven)

and so on. After completing eight lines, students can reverse the pattern by having line nine contain twenty-one syllables, line ten contain thirteen syllables, and so on until the poem ends with the last two lines of each one syllable.

EXAMPLE:

Pete
Sprete
Athlete
Plays baseball.
Best pitcher in town!
Easily strikes out ten batters!
T'was only in his dreams that he was such a great star!

A C T I V I T Y **Friendly Letters**

This strategy teaches students the correct format for friendly letters and how to write with a particular audience in mind. It will help students develop the skills required by the fourth CCR Anchor Standard for Writing to "produce clear and coherent writing in which the development, organization, and style are appropriate to task, purpose, and audience" (NGACBP & CCSSO, CCRA for Writing, 2010, p. 41). For example, after reading *Yours Truly, Goldilocks* (1998) by Alma Flora Ada, students can write a letter to one of their favorite fairy tale characters. Figure 11.23 is a sample of a third grader's response to Pig One, Pig Two, and Pig Three's invitation to a house-warming party. The writer has been told that Goldilocks, Baby Bear, Little Red Riding Hood, and Peter Rabbit will all be attending.

figure 11.23 Response to the Three Little Pigs' invitation to a birthday picnic based on CCR Anchor Standard for Writing 4.

April 10

Dear Little Pigs,

I was happy to get your invitation to the Birthday Picnic for Goldilocks. She is one of my very best friends! I was on the same adventure through the woods when we decided to enter the little cabin. But I never ate the food, sat in the chairs, or went upstairs. When she went upstairs, I heard my mother calling me, and I remember she warned me never ever to go into a stranger's house. I ran home before the Bear family returned home.

There are three on your guest list that I have always wanted to meet. I am eager to meet Little Red Riding Hood and see her unique red cape with the hood. I have only ever seen pictures of it. I am also eager to meet Peter Rabbit; I think we may share something in common—an acute case of adventure. I am also eager to meet Baby Bear because Goldilocks reported that he is so friendly and sweet!

Please let me know if you would like me to take some pork chops to barbeque. Or don't you eat pork? If you want me to take lettuce and carrots, I can buy some garden-fresh from my neighbor Mr. Macgregor. Just let me know what you need for the picnic.

Your friend,

Betsy

If this task is daunting for a student, use an interactive approach by sharing the pen with him as he writes his letter.

Wordless Books

GRADES 2–5   ACTIVITY

Wordless books aid students who cannot think of a plot for a story because the story line is already suggested. Students can easily progress through all the steps of the writing process. First, they can "read" the pictures with you and discuss the plot. Next, they can jot down possible ideas for each page. Then, using sticky notes of different colors, they can write the first draft on each page. After that they should reread their story and make revisions, adding or deleting as necessary. Have students edit using a different color pen so marks will stand out, attending to grammar, punctuation, capitalization, and spelling. Students write the final draft on yet another set of sticky notes and share the story with their classmates. Appendix A.5 lists a number of wordless books. It is important to select a book that is appropriate for the particular student.

Classroom Alphabet Books

GRADES K–6   ACTIVITY

Wilcox and Monroe (2011) suggest that teachers integrate subject material with writing by creating class alphabet books about content area subjects. After sharing some alphabet books featuring states (e.g., *M Is for Magnolia: A Mississippi Alphabet Book* [Shoulders, 2003]; *B Is for Bluegrass: A Kentucky Alphabet Book* [Riehle, 2002]), for example, a fourth-grade class can create a math alphabet book. Each student can be given a letter of the alphabet and one vocabulary word or concept that begins with that letter. They are then instructed to explain the term and illustrate it in a creative manner. For example, A = angle; G = gallon; P = pint; Y = yard. Alphabet books can also be created for science and social studies (see the earlier discussion about creating a state alphabet book after a history unit).

You may also create class alphabet books about national parks, sea creatures, or the national monuments in Washington, D.C., by having students choose one alphabet-related aspect of the large topic, researching it, and writing one page for the class book. This activity can be adapted for grades K–2 if the books are written as a class.

ACTIVITY **Creating Brochures**   GRADES 4–8

Groups of students can create brochures about a science experiment (Duke, Purcell-Gates, Hall, & Tower, 2006). This should be an experiment they conducted in class or performed at home with a parent. The brochure should list the materials needed and the steps required to perform the experiment. Students can illustrate the steps to make them easier to follow and conclude with an explanation of the experiment's results. Teachers can laminate these brochures and keep them at the science center for other students to use.

ACTIVITY **Sentence Combining**   GRADES 2–5

Struggling writers often use only short, simple sentences. To help students learn to write extended sentences, Saddler (2005) suggests using kernel sentences in which the teacher provides a simple subject and predicate (e.g., The tree stood.). Then, the teacher models one or more of the following steps with the students. Primary students can do the first steps, but steps five through seven are intended for upper elementary students.

1. Insert adjectives and adverbs (words that answer what kind, how many, which one, whose, when, how, and where).

   My neighbor's old tall oak tree on the hill stood swaying in the wind.

2. Produce compound subjects and objects.

   The oak tree and elm tree stood erect and waved to all the children.

3. Create compound sentence with coordinating conjunction.

   The oak tree stood erect, while the weeping willow stooped over in the wind.

4. Add possessive nouns.

   My neighbor's oak tree stands at the edge of our property.

5. Create complex sentences by using subordinating conjunctions.

   Because our neighbor's oak tree stands on our property line, he allows me to climb it.

6. Add relative clauses to show relationships.

   The old oak tree that stands in my neighbor's yard is one hundred years old.

7. Add appositives.

   The oak tree, my neighbor's "friend," shades him during the hot afternoons.

Using Computers for Authentic Writing Tasks

ACTIVITY **Blogs**   GRADES 4–8

Online journals and blogs can increase the depth of your students' responses to reading. As they write entries, encourage them to (1) relate a story to their personal experiences; (2) tell how a character changes; (3) explain how a text is similar to other texts by the same author or by other authors; (4) compare how a book is similar to a movie; and (5) describe favorite passages. Blogging is a useful way to motivate reluctant writers to respond to their reading because they often enjoy using technology (Lacina & Griffith, 2012/2013; Zawilinski, 2009). Blog entries are usually short, so students are not overwhelmed attempting to compose them.

When responding to a blog, writers must acknowledge the author; explain if they agree or disagree with the posting and say why, give details, ask questions, and/or add information. Demonstrate proper etiquette to your students by following these general principles: be appropriate, polite, and avoid mechanical errors. The postings should reflect the students' grade level accurately.

First explain the mechanics of blog postings. Lacina and Griffith (2012/2013) suggest introducing blogging by using paper and pencil. Each student begins a blog on paper; after a short period of time, students move over one chair and respond to what the blogger has written. This movement continues for a couple more turns. Collect and analyze the entries in order to give feedback to the students. After you feel the students have taken on the appropriate academic register, set up an online classroom blog and invite students to dialogue with classmates about a chapter book or novel they are reading in class. Pose queries and have students respond. As students become familiar with the process and format of blogging, invite them to post their favorite poem or story so they can be read by classmates and even parents (if they are allowed access to the blog).

One website that offers teachers and students a free blog without advertisements is www.edublogs.org. The directions for setting up the blog page are very easy to follow.

Wikis
GRADES 5–8   ACTIVITY

Your students may be familiar with wikis, a type of website designed so the content can be edited by anyone. The most famous wiki is Wikipedia, the free, collaborative Internet encyclopedia. Some wikis, such as Wikispaces, however, are more geared to classroom use. Students can post information on wikis and then have others edit the post by adding or clarifying the information; or they themselves can edit a posting. For example, students in Oklahoma City can search for wiki sites about the 1995 bombing of the city's federal building. They may have information to add because they have family members who experienced the bombing, or, after visiting the Oklahoma City National Memorial and Museum, they want to add interesting facts not yet included on the site.

Blogs and wikis are great tools for teaching critical thinking skills; students must determine whether or not the information presented is factual, truthful, speculative, or erroneous. Anyone can post anything on these sites, so students must be armed with the ability to tell the difference between good and bad information.

International Pen Pals
GRADES 3–8   ACTIVITY

Writing letters to international pen pals gives students "an opportunity for authentic and meaningful writing" (Barksdale, Watson, & Park, 2007). Such letters motivate students to adhere to punctuation, capitalization, and spelling. They are invested in the content as they share their favorite foods, stories about their family and school, and details about the sports they play. International pen pals also prompt students to learn about geography, other cultures, and school settings that may be very different from their own. Students are motivated to answer their pen pal's questions and read more about their country. Of course, you will need to choose a school in which most students speak English. In many countries, English is the official language for business and education, but even many non-English-speaking countries have schools for English-speaking students from abroad. Barksdale, Watson, and Park (2007) suggest the following websites for locating pen pals.

Epals, www.epals.com

International Pen Friends, www.ipf.net.au

Connecting with Authors
GRADES 1–8   ACTIVITY

Many authors of children's and young adult literature have websites that provide age-appropriate writing activities and/or word puzzles for their readers. Some authors sponsor writing contests, while others ask readers for feedback on their latest books. Some authors correspond with students through e-mail, while others encourage readers to subscribe to their electronic newsletters. Jan Brett's website offers electronic postcards that feature her art. Students can choose a postcard, write a message, and send it to anyone in the world. These authors frequently update their sites so they stay fresh and exciting. Be sure to check them periodically to make sure the URLs still work and to share authors' new ideas with students. The following is a list of sites of popular children's authors:

Avi, www.avi-writer.com	Virginia Hamilton, www.virginiahamilton.com
Judy Blume, www.judyblume.com	Katherine Paterson, http://katherinepaterson.com/
Jan Brett, www.janbrett.com	Gary Paulsen, www.randomhousekids.com/brand/gary-paulsen/
Betsy Byars, www.betsybyars.com	
Eric Carle, www.eric-carle.com	Patricia Polacco, www.patriciapolacco.com
Tomie dePaola, www.tomie.com	J. K. Rowling, www.Pottermore.com
Mem Fox, www.memfox.net	Louis Sachar, www.louissachar.com
Gail Gibbons, www.gailgibbons.com	Jon Scieszka, www.jsworldwide.com
Dan Gutman, www.dangutman.com	Audrey Wood, www.audreywood.com

Websites often change or disappear, but most authors can also be located through a simple Google search.

ACTIVITY **Digital Storytelling**   GRADES 3–8

Digital storytelling may be the one activity that motivates struggling writers to create dynamic stories because they get to combine traditional story writing with new literacies (Sylvester & Greenridge, 2009). Most students, even reluctant writers, know how to use computers, video games, digital music players, cell phones, digital cameras, and other electronic devices. Encourage students to use their technology skills to create digital stories using either Windows Movie Maker or Apple's iMovie. Using the writing process a student begins writing a story, which eventually becomes the project's narration. After the story is complete, the author decides how to divide it into scenes and which photographs or illustrations will go along with them. Then the student finds photographs or clip art or draws illustrations to complement each page of text and scans all illustrations to get them into digital form. Next, the student records the story, using expression that conveys the story's mood and action and that will captivate the listeners. When the story is recorded error-free, the student is ready to make the movie. Some students may want to enhance their movie by adding appropriate music and/or sound effects just like a real movie. The last step is for the student to add a title frame, transitions between frames, and rolling credits that cite all the sources for their clip art, photographs, and so on. Finally, the student publishes his work by inviting peers to watch his movie either online or on an interactive whiteboard. Tools that are helpful to beginning digital storytellers include (Sylvester & Greenridge, 2009):

- A computer or tablet
- Flash drive or cloud storage to save story pieces
- Headset/microphone for recording narrative
- Digital camera, tablet, or smartphone if students want to include photographs or video
- Windows Movie Maker or Apple's iMovie
- Microsoft PowerPoint, Photo Story, or Apple Keynote to create story slides
- Audacity, an open source audio utility, for recording and editing
- For beginners, Microsoft's Photo Story website makes digital storytelling easy.

WRITING AND TECHNOLOGY

As is clear from the number of writing activities included above, computers and authentic writing tasks can and do go hand in hand. Technology tools will help your students develop the skills needed to explore online publishing outlets.

To many students and adults, word processing programs are to writing as calculators are to math. These programs, with spell checker, thesaurus, and grammar-checker capabilities, have helped many frustrated writers. However, these tools are not magical; students still need to decide on a topic or story idea, articulate those ideas, have a good understanding of the grammar and spelling of words and sentences, and be able to recognize the correct spelling from a given list.

It is imperative that young students first learn adequate keyboarding skills before they are taught how to use word processing programs. The following are a few of the keyboarding programs available online as of this writing, with prices ranging from $7.00 to $15.00. Since new and updated programs often become available, search "keyboarding software" to keep abreast of new programs.

Typing Instructor for Kids
Mavis Beacon Keyboarding Kidz
Typing Instructor Platinum 21
Disney: Mickey's Typing Adventure
Mavis Beacon Teaches Typing 18

Many struggling writers often omit the outlining and note taking or prewriting stage. Most sophisticated word processing programs help students with these tasks (for example, Don Johnston's draft builder, www.donjohnston.com/draftbuilder). Teach students to use these writing tools to save them time during the writing and revising processes.

Word processing programs are especially useful to students in the revising stage when they know how to use the copy and paste feature. (This feature is preferable to cut and paste, because it eliminates the possibility the student will press the wrong key and accidentally erase part of the composition.)

Keyboarding and word processing programs help to encourage students who have messy handwriting. They do not excuse students from practicing penmanship, but they allow students to focus on content, not handwriting, when they are composing. The two tasks should be approached separately. When teachers want students to practice penmanship, students should be permitted to copy favorite poems or environmental print in the classroom.

ReadWriteThink

The ReadWriteThink website (www.readwritethink.org) allows individuals to publish ideas, collaborate on projects, and/or carry on online conversations. The site includes a series of lessons that incorporate online writing activities for K–12 students. Example activities include an online tool that enables students to learn about and write acrostic poems, a book cover creator that allows users to design front and back book covers or full dust jackets using type and illustrations, and a story tool that enables students to create their own fractured fairy tales.

Be cautious when introducing sites that allow students to publish, collaborate, and converse online. Rely on reputable websites such as ReadWriteThink because they are created by respected organizations specifically for teachers and students.

Websites as Tools to Develop Writing Skills

Students may use the following websites to develop specific writing skills.

1. Write Express at www.rhymer.com offers a free online rhyming dictionary.
2. Bruce Lansky's site, www.gigglepoetry.com, invites students to fill in the blanks of his poems.
3. The site www.readwritethink.org (search for "graphic organizer") provides students with graphic organizers to help them develop vivid characters. The graphic organizer is divided into a character's physical appearance, actions, and reactions.
4. The five-step writing process is explained at www.funbrain.com. Students can also write their own Mad Lib stories.

Apps: Writing

Story Patch ($2.99, Grades K–3). This app allows students to create their own stories and informational texts using one of several themes. Students respond to a series of questions and can choose from over 800 included images or can import their own. Writers can create and customize characters, create informational picture books, and share their completed stories and texts.

StoryBuilder ($5.99, Grades K–4). This app helps students improve their writing skills, including paragraph formation, integration of ideas, and inference. Students can record answers to questions to help them weave together their interactive texts, both narrative and informational. Use of extensive audio clips promotes improved auditory processing for students with special needs, including autism spectrum disorders.

Pictello ($18.99, Grades K–8). This app helps students at all grade and skill levels learn narrative skills by creating talking stories and books. Each page can contain up to 10 lines of text, a picture or brief video, or recorded sound. Stories can be shared using PDF files. Available in several languages.

CONCLUDING THOUGHTS

Students must become fluent writers as well as fluent readers. As with reading, some students need special attention to develop the skills and confidence to express themselves. Teachers can better understand why particular students may not enjoy writing by administering writing attitude surveys and self-assessments.

The CCSS, national computer-based assessments, and technology have all required that students become more sophisticated writers. Students become good writers only by writing many forms of text. Most students also require mentoring in the five steps of the writing process to become proficient. When students understand this process, they know to gather information before they write. When they begin writing, they know to get their ideas down on paper before they work on revisions and mechanics. Developing writers need to feel good about their work by "publishing" their final copy and sharing it with an audience.

reflective learning

RELUCTANT WRITERS. Ms. Bryant has been teaching fifth grade for 27 years. She loves children's literature and also understands the importance of students being able to write well. Her favorite author is Avi, and she uses many of his books for read-alouds throughout the year. She has multiple copies of all his books, and students are required to read at least one of them during the school year. Many students read more than one because they, too, enjoy how he tells a story. One of Ms. Bryant's assignments at the end of the year is for students to select their favorite Avi book and focus on the book's main topic (e.g., What animal is featured in the story? In what country does the story take place? What is the major problem of the protagonist? In what period of history does the story take place?). Students must research that topic, write a report, and give an oral presentation on it. Topics taken from the books over the years have included the owls and field mice from *Poppy* (2005), the porcupines from *Ereth's Birth-*

day (2001), the Alaskan Malamute from *The Good Dog* (2004), the beavers from *Poppy and Rye* (2005), and the era of the 1400s from *Midnight Magic* (1999).

This year when Ms. Bryant presents the assignment, D.D., a reluctant writer, asks, "Why do I have to write a report when I am going to tell the class what I learned?" Ms. Bryant knows there is some truth in what he says, but she wants him to write and give an oral presentation.

questions

1. What should Ms. Bryant do to make the writing assignment authentic?

2. What type of writing assignment would give D.D.'s report a different audience?

3. What technology might Ms. Bryant include to motivate students like D.D.?

4. How should Ms. Bryant implement the new writing assignment?

12 Spelling

Use the big thinker's vocabulary. Use big, bright, cheerful words.

DAVID. J. SCHWARTZ

scenario

s. Bird, a sixth-grade language arts teacher, loves to write and wants every one of her students to become fluent writers. In the first couple weeks of school, she provides many opportunities for students to do quick writes so she can observe and assess their needs. During the quick writes, she notices that Mindy hesitates to write and that her writing is very stilted. For example, when asked to share her favorite event of the summer, she writes: "I went to kamp. It was many miles away. It was in Colordo." That is her entire composition after forty minutes of writing. Many of her other writings have also been similarly brief. Ms. Bird checks Mindy's records and finds that she is reading at grade level.

One day Ms. Bird announces a five-minute free write. The students can write whatever they want, but their pens cannot stop. When she collects their papers, she sees that Mindy has written the same sentence over and over again: "I do not like to right." This is Ms. Bird's opportunity to talk with Mindy.

During conferencing time, Ms. Bird approaches Mindy with the paper in her hand. She says, "I understand you don't like to write. Everyone has different likes and dislikes, but I am wondering if you can tell me why you don't like to write, and maybe I can help you." Mindy does not respond, so Ms. Bird asks, "Do you not know what to write about, or is there another reason?" Mindy responds, "I'm a terrible speller, and I don't want my teachers to know. I have plenty of ideas in my head, but I don't know how to spell the words. I've always been a bad speller." "Well," Ms. Bird says, "I can see how that makes writing hard for you. But I tell you what, if you come to my room during study period, I'll help you. This is something we can fix. Deal?" "A deal!" Mindy replies.

The next day Mindy comes to Ms. Bird during study period. Ms. Bird says they are going to play a game. She hands Mindy a CAFÉ sheet that has 60 boxes (see the Assessment section later in this chapter for more information). She explains that she will set the timer for ten minutes and Mindy has to fill in as many boxes as possible. Mindy can put any words in the boxes that she wants to, but she cannot use any names. She can use *mom, dad, sister,* and so on, but not their proper names. Figure 12.1 is a sample from Mindy's work.

figure 12.1 CAFÉ sheet with a sample of Mindy's words.

mum	dad	me	I	do
white	blak	gren	pink	yelo
purpel	red	blue	freind	class
lunch	carots	sanwish	grapes	milk
shool	hall	math	speling	reeding
teachure	sience	vacashun	wekends	slep
is	was	do	run	fun

As you are reading the chapter, consider the following questions:

1. Analyze Mindy's word list on the CAFÉ sheet and think about her spelling strengths and weaknesses. Do you see any pattern to her spelling?

2. What particular strategies would you use to help Mindy with her spelling?

3. How can Ms. Bird help the English learners in her class become proficient spellers?

introduction

Although spelling is secondary to composing (Alderman & Green, 2011; Newlands, 2011), it is an important skill for effective writing (Alderman & Green, 2011). As noted in previous chapters, effective readers may be poor spellers. Merely reading words does not ensure that students can spell them (Hughes & Searle, 2000; Turbill, 2000). Assigning a list of spelling words one day of the week and testing them a couple of days later does not ensure that students use, much less correctly spell, those words in their writing (Alderman & Green, 2011; Bear, Flanigan, Hayes, Invernizzi, Johnston, & Templeton, 2010; Newlands, 2011; Invernizzi, Templeton, Bear, & Johnston, 2009; Fountas & Pinnell, 2012/2013). Assigning writing projects does not ensure good spelling either because students often avoid words they cannot spell (Alderman & Green, 2011; Newlands, 2011). Therefore, teachers need to integrate spelling instruction with writing and content learning. If students are to "own" a word, they need to know its meaning, how to pronounce it, and how to spell it. As discussed in Chapter 7, the CCR Anchor Standards for Reading require students to learn technical terms associated with the content areas. New vocabulary words that appear in social studies, math, and science texts or lessons are good spelling lists to use instead of other commercial lists.

Beginning in kindergarten, many teachers display word walls of high frequency words, and they may require students to spell these words correctly when they are writing. Students then use the word walls as a resource for correct spelling. If intermediate and middle-school teachers continue to use word walls or posters to display words associated with content areas, they should also require their students to spell the posted words correctly. Having the words available for students so they can check their spelling helps them to use the words in their writing. The CCSS encourage all teachers of all subjects to view themselves as literacy teachers. They must understand that writing and spelling are a part of literacy learning, and they should encourage students to learn how to spell words that are associated with content material.

SPELLING INSTRUCTION

Good spelling instruction is "teaching children how to spell, not what to spell" (Rosencrans, 1998). The traditional technique for teaching spelling—list on Monday, test on Friday, and often forget words by Monday—does not take into account students' individual needs; one list does not fit all sizes and most often these lists are not connected to other subject areas. This technique does not challenge good spellers because they already know the words, and poor spellers memorize the words only for the test. These lists also fail to impact students' writing (Newlands, 2011). The worksheets that typically accompany such lists focus on parts of speech, definitions, using the word correctly in the sentence, or on mnemonic rules such as "when two vowels go walking, the first one does the talking." Because only 46 percent of English words are spelled phonetically (Heald-Taylor, 1998), students do not benefit from memorizing the rules and the few words that fit each rule. Instead, spelling lists should be tailored to each student's ability (Alderman & Green, 2011). For example, on Monday Ms. Bird gives a pretest of a list of words that the students encountered the previous week in the different subjects, including literature, which contains many tier 2 words. (See Chapter 7 for discussion of tier words.) Based on the pretest, she creates individual lists for each student based on his or her ability. Some students are capable of learning all twenty and may be tested on all twenty on Friday; however, a small group of students who have some learning disabilities may be given five or ten of the most important words from the list and will be tested only on those five or ten on Friday. She also challenges the gifted spellers to provide her with two to five additional words they want to learn. During the test Ms. Bird pronounces all the words, and students write only the ones they were required to learn. Teachers need to recognize all students' spelling success even if some word lists are shorter than others! Abandon competition in spelling by eliminating charts and stars for students who have perfect scores on their test. Alderman and Green (2011) argue that competition focuses on performance, when learning should focus on spelling words correctly based on internal motivation.

All students need meaningful challenges with goals that are attainable (Alderman & Green, 2011). Eliminating commercial spelling lists does not mean teachers take a laissez-faire attitude toward spelling. Rather, you can foster mastery of spelling by instilling in students a joy of learning new words and helping them to see the patterns, prefixes, and suffixes in polysyllabic words, such as *fabulous, transportation,* or *revolution.* Students need to be taught to look for patterns within words (Newlands, 2011; Rosencrans, 1998; Bear et al., 2011). Consider for example the word *photosynthesis.* Teachers need to agree with students that it is a long word, but stress that it is fun and easy one to spell if they dissect it! Most intermediate students use the word *photo* instead of *photograph* so they know how to spell the first part. The next syllable, *syn,* they may recognize from *synonym* or the musical term *syncopation.* For the last part of the word, you can point out that it consists of two words: *the* and *sis.* Put the parts together, and they can spell a very long word. Modeling how to dissect words can be a fun exercise, and students can share their own way of learning how to spell a difficult word. With younger students, you may want to begin with a compound word such as *butterfly* or *mailbox.*

Newlands (2011) provides principles for teachers to use with their own spelling and pass on to students: (1) find patterns, (2) analyze errors and correct them, (3) use a known strategy, and (4) if the first strategy does not work, try a different one. The strategies Newlands suggests are to

- visualize how the word looks,
- try different spellings and select one that looks correct,
- think of similar words such as *music* when attempting to spell *musician,*
- sound out the different syllables,
- use analogies such as thinking of *round* when attempting to spell *flounder,*
- check the word wall or other word banks, and
- ask a classmate for help.

When students begin using a word processing program, you will need to show them how to use spell check. However, even spell checkers do not guarantee that all words will be spelled correctly. Consider this verse of "Ode to the Spell Czecher" (found at www.castlemoyle.com):

I have a spelling checker.

It came with my PC.

It plane lee marks four my revue

Miss steaks aye can knot sea.

WHAT TEACHERS SHOULD KNOW ABOUT SPELLING

Teachers should be active participants in the "co-construction" process of learning to spell, based on Vygotsky's (1978) theory of the zone of proximal development. Teachers must assist students as they progress from what they know about spelling to what they do not know. This active teaching and active learning complement one another. To become an active participant, a teacher must first develop background knowledge about (1) the developmental stages of spelling, (2) the patterns of spelling, and (3) spelling and the CCSS.

Developmental Stages of Spelling

Researchers disagree on the number and names for each stage of spelling development. Chapter 11 discussed Zecker's (1999) seven stages of emergent writers. Bear et al. (2011), Gentry and Gillet (1993), Rosencrans (1998), and Ferroli and Shanahan (1987) all identify five stages of spelling but give different definitions for them. Fresch and Wheaton (1997) and Bear and Templeton (1998) identify six stages, while Sipe (2001) identifies seven. Figure 12.2 lists and explains many of these developmental stages. The various progressive stages may be similar and may overlap. Some researchers divide stages into smaller units than other researchers do. The variations are not intended to confuse you, but rather to provide all relevant information so you can better understand your struggling spellers. After you have read the section below and are familiar with the stages of spelling development, turn to the end of the chapter and complete the Reflective Learning activity, the Developmental States of Spelling.

Instructional practices for each spelling stage

This section relies on the spelling stages in Bear et al. (2008), but given the similarities in how researchers define spelling stages it should be easy to adapt them.

Emergent spelling stage. Children in this stage make scribbles or letter-like shapes and understand that writing proceeds from left to right. They need ample opportunity to "write" and adults who respond by asking the child to "read" their story or poem.

In transitioning from the pre-phonetic to phonetic stage, children begin representing their thoughts with words, and often "they use the names of the letters as cues to the sound they want to represent" (Bear et al., 2008, p. 12). To facilitate this process you can label items around the classroom and point them out. Draw attention to name cards on students'

figure 12.2   Developmental spelling stages.

BEAR, INVERNIZZI, TEMPLETON, AND JOHNSTON'S STAGES

1. Emergent: Scribbles or letter-like shapes; conventional left-to-right direction.

2. Alphabetic: Uses beginning and ending consonants and consonant blends; vowels in every word.

3. Within Word Pattern: Long vowels spelled correctly; confuses long vowel digraphs.

4. Syllables and Affixes: Uses inflectional endings correctly (double consonant with short vowel sounds); prefixes and suffixes spelled correctly.

5. Derivational Relations: Most polysyllabic words spelled correctly; unaccented vowels in derived words spelled correctly.

GENTRY AND GILLET'S STAGES

(see Figure 12.3 for sample work from the following stages)

1. Precommunicative: Random letters; scribbles; drawings; no knowledge of letter–sound relationships.

2. Semiphonetic: Realizes letters represent sounds in words; uses initial letter and ending letters of words; writes left to right; may or may not have spacing.

3. Phonetic: Hears most consonants in words.

4. Transitional: Includes vowels in each syllable; begins to use knowledge of affixes and inflectional endings.

5. Conventional: Most words spelled correctly.

FERROLI AND SHANAHAN'S STAGES

1. Preliterate: No letter–sound relationships.

2. Initial Consonant: Initial letter is correct.

3. Consonant Frame: Initial and ending consonant sounds are present.

4. Phonetic: Initial, medial, and final sounds are present.

5. Transitional: Words are spelled as they sound ("wuntz" for *once*).

ROSENCRANS'S STAGES

1. Pre-phonetic: Drawings of sticks and shapes; no letter–sound relationships.

2. Phonetic: Letter–name strategy (e.g., r = *are*); only initial and final sounds; similar sounds may be substituted (e.g., "sete" = *city*).

3. Graphophonic: Uses sound–symbol cues; uses phonic rules for letter sounds.

4. Ortho-phonic: Uses knowledge of sound–letter sequence (*qwd* is not a possible answer).

5. Morpho-phonic: Understands affixes, derivations, and structural units.

FRESCH AND WHEATON'S STAGES

1. Preliterate/Prephonetic: Scribble; aware that words are print.

2. Preliterate/Phonetic: Learns alphabet; strings letters together to spell words.

3. Letter Name: Uses environmental print as aid; learns some sight words; exchanges short vowel sounds for closest long vowel sounds; spells words as they sound (e.g., *r* for *are*).

4. Within Word: Develops sight words; use short vowels correctly; confuses long vowel digraphs (*boat* is "bote"); uses *d* for all past tense words; knows every word has vowel; internalizes rules (silent e); over-generalizes rules.

5. Syllable Juncture: Correctly doubles consonants before inflectional endings; struggles with schwa sound.

6. Derivational Constancy: Understands relationship of words, derivations, and multiple meanings.

SIPE'S STAGES

1. Scribbles: Scribble.

2. Letter-like Shapes: Mostly scribble with some letters and numbers randomly included.

3. Sequence of Letters: Understands words are more than one letter, but letters are random.

4. Encode Words with Initial Consonants: Initial consonant represents the entire word.

5. Encode Words with Initial and Ending Consonants: Both initial and ending consonants are present.

6. Encode Words with Medial Sounds: Adds the medial sound.

7. Conventional Forms: Most words are spelled correctly.

figure 12.3 Graphic examples of spelling stages.

Precommunicative:
"Grey is king on his birthday" (age 4).

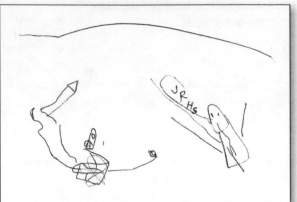

Semiphonetic:
"You are hurting us!" Grey's drawing (age 5).

Phonetic:
"Destroy" (Grey's man, age 5).

Transitional Stage: "God Loves You"
(Grey's feeling after Bible school, age 6).

Transitional:
"Half Man, Half Bat" (Grey's batman, age 6).

Conventional:
"India's Friend" (story, age 7).

desks and ask them to find other names or words that begin with the same letter, or to find the longest and shortest names in the class. Also demonstrate writing lessons by (1) writing short captions under the student's pictures, (2) spelling out the letters of each word, (3) saying each word aloud, (4) reading the caption, and finally (5) asking the child to point to each word as he reads the caption. After sharing a big book with a group, play "I spy" by asking students to point to a particular letter or word on the page. Spellers in this stage need lots of practice examining letters and hearing letter sounds.

Alphabetic spelling stage. Students in this stage are aware of the initial sounds of words. At the early alphabetic stage students often think there are always as many letters in a word as there are syllables. Thus, they spell *baby* as *bb* and *horse* as *h*. Later in the alphabetic stage they begin to write the main sounds within a word. *Baby* becomes *babe*. Give students at this stage plenty of demonstrations and chances to listen to the sounds within words.

One strategy for this stage is interactive writing. During the morning message, you can spell out the words as you write them. When you come to a familiar word, ask a student who knows the beginning letter of that word to come and write it. If you always begin the morning message with "Good morning, boys and girls," you can invite students to write the letters they know.

Within word pattern spelling stage. During this stage a teacher must help students discover patterns within words. You can begin with three-letter phonograms (word families) and write the rime of a phonogram on a flip chart and ask students to provide the onsets to create as many words as possible. You may copy poems that identify word families onto flip charts and ask students to name the word family. Also, ask students to find rhyming words (words that share the same sound but not the same letters) and identify pairs of words that rhyme. The following passage from *Guess Who's Coming, Jesse Bear* (1998) by Nancy White Carlstrom allows the teacher to draw attention to the rhyme of *whale* and *tail* despite their different spellings.

> Saturday
> Sara swims like a shark,
> Or should I say a whale?
> She says she'll nibble on a fish
> And tries to grab my tail. (unpaged)

Encourage students to spell by having them write the letters they think might be in a word and then checking the sounds of the word. When they ask if a word is correct, direct them to a page in a book or have them use sound boxes (refer back to Figure 4.6, p. 88).

In the opening scenario Mindy has trouble with a couple of word patterns, one of which is vowel digraphs, as evident in her spelling of *reeding* for *reading* and *gren* for *green*. She will benefit from learning different ways to spell the long vowel sounds such as the long /e/ spelling of double *e* (ee), *ei* (receive), *ea* (read), and so on. She also needs direct instruction on doubling consonants, given her spelling of *yellow* and *carrot*. Learning a few spelling generalizations and using the spell-check feature on a word processor will help Mindy with her writing.

Syllable and affixes spelling stage. At this stage your goal is to help students recognize chunks within words, or prefixes, suffixes, and root words, and help them spell them. Recognizing these groups of letters is far easier than listening for single letters in multisyllabic words.

Use big books to show how many words end in *ing* or *ed*. After reading a book together, play "I spy" and ask students to point to words that end with *ing* or *ed*. You may also call out a verb and ask students to write down that verb in its *ing* and *ed* forms. Later, challenge students to find other prefixes and suffixes that go along with the word.

Teachers can design an exercise using one-inch cards with prefixes in green, root words in red, and suffixes in blue. Challenge students to match three cards together (one of each color) to make words. This exercise is especially helpful for tactile learners.

Derivational relations spelling stage. Students at this stage spell most words correctly, so you might encourage them to check each other's papers for spelling errors. Students can apply simple spelling rules, such as when to double consonants before adding an *ing*. (See Appendix B.10 for a list of spelling generalizations.) Post a chart of these rules in the classroom and encourage students to check it when they have questions. During this stage students should learn how to use the spell-check feature on word processors, and they should be able to recognize the correct spelling of the word in question in a list of options.

Instructional practices for English learners' stages of spelling development

English learners pass through the same stages of spelling development as native English speakers do. Not all students develop at the same rate. Some may spend a long time in the first stage, but as their confidence increases they may pass through other stages more quickly. Students develop certain skills in each stage, and teachers can facilitate this development by providing activities based on their needs.

Emergent stage. The strategies parents use with their English-speaking toddlers are also appropriate for English learners in the emergent stage. Read to the students while pointing to words and emphasizing their sounds. Stories with rhyming words are appropriate texts; talk about the rhyming words as you read. Sharing alphabet books helps students hear initial sounds and learn names for objects. Singing songs with rhyming words is also helpful. Ebooks that highlight the text as the student listens to the passage are good activities. In addition, you can have students learn the names of everyday foods, objects, clothing, or jobs using picture cards. Give students at this stage a pencil and paper so they can "write" stories. Most often their writing will be pictures.

Letter name–alphabetic stage. If the English learners are not literate in their native language during the letter name–alphabetic stage, teach the sounds of the alphabet as you would with English-speaking students. If the English learners are literate in their native language, explain explicitly how the English alphabet differs from their native alphabet and, if possible, point out common letters in the two languages. Some languages (e.g., German, Spanish, Italian, and French) share most letters of the English alphabet; other languages have a very different alphabet. Figure 12.4 shows the Spanish alphabet, and Figure 12.5 shows the Thai consonants and the Arabic alphabet. Notice how differently the letters are shaped.

The alphabetic stage is a good time to share alphabet books that show uppercase and lowercase letters along with one or two familiar objects. Using pictures of common objects, English learners can sort the pictures first to the initial sound, then the ending sound, and finally according to the long or short vowel sound. Dominoes and any of the other strategies found at the end of Chapter 5 are also good for English learners.

Within word pattern stage. As English learners reach the within word pattern stage, they learn about the English patterns of one-syllable words and eventually multisyllabic words. One of the easiest word patterns for both native English students and English learners is the CVC pattern, because it has consistent short vowel sounds. Many word families follow this pattern: *hat, man, pen, rug, sit, pot, top, cup,* and *bed.* Other word patterns include CVVC (*road, meet*) and CVCe (*cake, hope, cane*). Words in the CVVC pattern have only one vowel sound, and in the CVCe pattern the silent *e* makes the first vowel long. As shown in the Intervention section of Chapter 5, word family flip books, word family word walls, and word family Concentration are activities that help students learn patterns within words and thus recognize more words.

Syllable and affixes stage. Simple rules to teach English learners about two-syllable words are (1) a closed syllable (one that ends in a consonant) has a short vowel sound: *cam-per, cab-in;* (2) words with double consonants in the middle of the word are divided between the two consonants, and the vowel in the first syllable is short: *but-ter, com-ment;* and (3) an open syllable (one that ends in a vowel) usually has a long sound (*o-pen, pro-vide*). Engaging students in many writing activities helps them learn the spelling patterns. Other activities include modeling how print works in shared reading (see Chapter 1), sharing the pen (see Chapter 11), and the language experience approach (see Chapter 7) (Bear et al., 2008).

figure 12.4

Spanish alphabet.

Aa, Bb, Cc, CHch, Dd, Ee, Ff, Gg, Hh, Ii, Jj, Kk, Ll, LLll, Mm, Nn, Ññ, Oo, Pp, Qq, Rr, Ss, Tt, Uu, Vv, Ww, Xx, Yy, Zz

Note: At the Tenth Congress of the Association of Spanish Language Academies, held in 1994, it was decided that for academic dictionaries, at the request of various international organizations, the *ch* and the *ll* would not be considered independent letters. The two letters come to be alphabetized in the places that correspond to them within the letter C (between -cg- and -ci-) and within the letter L (between -lk- and -lm-), respectively.

Derivational relations stage. In the derivational relations stage English learners become aware of root words, prefixes and suffixes, and the changes in words when they become different parts of speech. Among the first suffixes students learn are the inflectional endings of verbs (*singing, walking, walked, smiled*) in which the base word does not change. Next they learn inflectional endings in which the base word undergoes a slight spelling change (*hop* to *hopping, hope* to *hoping, marry* to *married*). Students also learn that prefixes have meaning. Some of the first prefixes they learn are *un-, non-, re-,* and *pre-.* They also learn how some base words change when they are used as different parts of speech (*music* becomes *musical* or *musician; nation* becomes *national; comedy* becomes *comical*). Your job is to help students understand the relationship between the spelling and the meaning of these different word forms. More strat-

figure 12.5 Sample alphabets with various scripts.

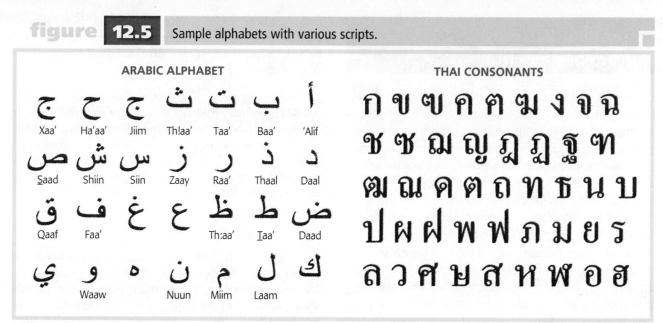

ARABIC ALPHABET

Xaa'	Ha!aa'	Jiim	Th!aa'	Taa'	Baa'	'Alif
Saad	Shiin	Siin	Zaay	Raa'	Thaal	Daal
Qaaf	Faa'		Th:aa'	Taa'	Daad	
	Waaw		Nuun	Miim	Laam	

THAI CONSONANTS

Source: Bear, Donald R.; Helman, Lori; Invernizzi, Marcia R.; Templeton, Shane; Johnston, Francine R., *Words Their Way with English Learners: Word Study for Spelling, Phonics, and Vocabulary Instruction,* 1st ed., © 2007, p. 35. Reprinted by permission of Pearson Education, Inc., Upper Saddle River, NJ.

egies for this stage are discussed in the Intervention section of Chapter 5.

Patterns of English Spelling

Orthographic patterns of words

Researchers suggest that good spellers understand orthography—letters and their sequence in words (Fountas & Pinnell, 2012/2013; Bear et al., 2011). Therefore, the purpose of explicit spelling instruction is to expand students' "knowledge of the principles of English orthography and broaden the range of strategies they use to spell unknown words" (Rymer & Williams, 2000, p. 242).

Aim to make all students word solvers who call upon their knowledge of orthographic categories at will (Fountas & Pinnell, 2012/2013). They know different spellings for the same sound and understand how words are organized. They easily identify patterns within words and make connections among words instead of memorizing whole words. Word solvers learn unknown words through:

- sound (phonemic strategy)
- vision (visual strategy)
- meaning (morphemic strategy)
- analogies (linking strategy)
- inquiry (dictionary usage) (Heald-Taylor, 1998; Fountas & Pinnell, 2006a; Zecker, 1999)

Being a word solver "is not so much about learning individual words as it is about learning how written language is organized—how written language 'works'" (Fountas & Pinnell, 2001, p. 369). "Spelling is not just memory work; it is a process of conceptual development" (Newlands, 2011).

Teaching English orthography requires that you understand some generalizations about word patterns. Appendix B.10 lists generalizations teachers must understand to help students learn to spell unknown words. These are not rules your students should memorize. Instead, they are generalizations you can point out as students solve specific spelling problems. Students need to learn to recognize word patterns, not memorize the rules!

As noted earlier, teaching students to see patterns in words or showing them how words are put together is more beneficial than having them memorize word lists. Understanding visual connections such as consonant blends, digraphs, and diphthongs aids young students as they learn word patterns. Making lists of words that follow certain patterns can be fun for students. They can keep the lists in a booklet and use them as a reference during independent writing. Appendix B.11 lists complex word patterns with a few examples. Encourage your students to see how many words they can add to each list.

Help students learn word patterns with consonant blends (e.g., *tr, gr, fl*), vowel digraphs (e.g., *oa, ie*), diphthongs (e.g., *oi* [oil]), and controlled-r sounds. Those in the later writing stages will need help with patterns based on meaning. Focusing on prefixes, suffixes, inflectional endings, and homonyms aids students in learning patterns in words as

BOX

Complex Patterns of English Spelling

Learning to spell is a complex developmental process (Newlands, 2011; Fountas & Pinnell, 2002), and teachers need to understand these complexities to help their students master the process. The English playwright George Bernard Shaw demonstrated these complexities by spelling the word *fish* "phonetically" as *ghoti*. The *gh* came from the sound in *rough,* the *o* from its sound in *women,* and the *ti* from its sound in *nation* (cited in Johnston, 2001). However, Johnston points out that (1) *gh* never calls for an /f/ sound at the beginning of a word, and (2) the *ti* for the /sh/ sound occurs only in the medial position of words. Appendix B.11 lists other complex patterns of English spelling. Understanding these patterns will help you effectively aid your students with their spelling. Remember that students do not need to memorize these patterns.

they spell. Direct instruction allows them to understand how words change when they become different parts of speech (e.g., *musical* to *musician*). Students can also have fun as they discover how accents change with different forms of words (e.g., MUS-ic, but not MUS-ic-ian).

Comparisons between English and Spanish spelling patterns

Native Spanish speakers are the fastest growing minority group in the United States and in U.S. classrooms as well, so it is to the teacher's advantage to understand the relationship between English and Spanish spelling patterns. Both English and Spanish have alphabetic foundations (phoneme–grapheme correspondence); however, the English spelling of words "does not mirror their pronunciations in a reliable fashion" (Perez-Canado, 2005). Spanish spelling is considered to have a stronger alphabetic foundation. Nevertheless, Perez-Canado (2005) believes there are similarities between the two languages, including the following:

1. One phoneme can be represented by more than one letter. For example, in Spanish the /x/ phoneme can be the letter *g* (e.g., *gente*), *j* (e.g., *joya*), or *x* (e.g., *Mexico*). (See Figure 12.6 for more examples.) In English the /k/ phoneme can be the letter *c* (e.g., *cake*) or *k* (e.g., *kite*).

2. One letter can have more than one sound. In Spanish the letter *g* can have the /g/ phoneme

(e.g., *gato*) or the /x/ sound (e.g., *gente*). (See Figure 12.6 for more examples.) In English the letter g can be the /g/ phoneme (e.g., gate) or the /j/ sound (e.g., gym).

Knowing these similarities when working with Spanish-speaking students allows you to build on their background knowledge or give analogies when explaining how some letters make more than one sound (e.g., *c* can be /k/ or /s/) and some sounds can have a number of different spellings (e.g., long /a/ as *ei* in *eight*, *ey* in *they*, or *ay* in *day*).

Spelling and the CCSS

The CCSS grade level standards include a language strand that addresses the progression of expectations for student spelling. Figure 12.7 states the standards with examples of spelling words. Notice that even in kindergarten, students are expected to spell words that they can read. Note also that second graders are expected to know how to use a dictionary to check their spelling, and fourth and fifth graders are expected to spell tier 2 and tier 3 words that are grade appropriate. In the middle grades the CCSS ELA: Language strand merely states that students are to "spell correctly" (NGACBP & CCSSO, 2010, p. 52).

GOOD VERSUS POOR SPELLERS

You will discover distinctive differences between good and poor spellers. When good spellers proofread their work, they recognize their spelling errors and correct them without seeking outside help (Hughes & Searle, 2000; Turbill, 2000). When they encounter a word they do not know how to spell, they "generate sensible written alternatives that can be compared in order to select the one that makes the most sense and 'looks right'" (Hughes & Searle, 2000, p. 205). Good spellers understand the writing process (Turbill, 2000) and know not to worry about spelling conventions during a first draft. The purpose of editing is to focus on mechanics, which includes spelling. As you work with struggling spellers, recognize what good spellers do naturally and help poor spellers do the same things. Figure 12.8 lists traits of good and poor spellers.

ASSESSMENT

Informal Assessment

As with all skills, teachers must learn what students already know about spelling and give them tasks that develop their ability and knowledge. Informal spelling instruments such as inventories and checklists are

figure 12.6 Spanish phonemes represented by more than one letter and Spanish letters associated with more than one phoneme.

PHONEME	LETTER	SPANISH	ENGLISH
/i/	i	iglesia	church
	final y	hoy	today
/b/	b	bebé	baby
	v	vaca	cow
/s/	c before e or i	cesta	basket
		cigüeña	stork
	s	sapo	toad
	x as initial letter (usually)	xilófono	xylophone
	z	zorro	fox
/k/	c before a, o, u or consonant (other than c)	casa	house
		cola	tail
		cuchillo	knife
		clase	class
		democracia	democracy
	final c (rare)	bloc	pad (of paper)
	k	kilogramo	kilogram
	qu	queso	cheese
/g/	g before a, o, or u or consonant	gato	cat
		gota	drop
		gusano	worm
		guerra	war
		guía	guide
		gramo	gram
/x/ (When speaking Spanish, English speakers often substitute /h/.)	g before e or i	gente	people
		gitano	gypsy
	j	joya	jewel
		hijo	child, son
	x in certain words with indigenous origins	México	Mexico
	x as first letter in name	Xavier	Xavier
/j/	ll	llave	key
	y (except as final y)	yeso	plaster, chalk
/ks/	cc	lección	lesson
	x other than initial	examen	exam
		extra	extra
		fax	fax
/ʃ/	x in certain words with indigenous origins	Xela (name of city in Guatemala)	Xela

Created by F. Johnson (2007). Used with permission.

figure 12.7 The CCSS ELA: Language standards with examples of spelling words.

GRADE	CCSS LANGUAGE STANDARDS	EXAMPLES
Kindergarten	CCSS.ELA-Literacy.L.K.2.d Spell simple words phonetically, drawing on knowledge of sound–letter relationships (p. 26).	*at, cat* *it, sit* *all, ball*
Grade 1	CCSS.ELA-Literacy.L.1.2.d Use conventional spelling for words with common spelling patterns and for frequently occurring irregular words (p. 26).	*sound, found* (common spelling patterns) *with, when* (frequently occurring irregular words)
	CCSS.ELA-Literacy.L.1.2.e Spell untaught words phonetically, drawing on phonemic awareness and spelling conventions (p. 26).	*clown* (*clown* is a word that a particular student wants to spell in a story, but since it is not a "word wall" word he uses knowledge of the spelling of *down* that has the same rime)
Grade 2	CCSS.ELA-Literacy.L.2.2.d Generalize learned spelling patterns when writing words (p. 26).	*cage, badge* *boy, boil*
	CCSS.ELA-Literacy.L.2.2.e Consult reference materials, including beginning dictionaries, as needed to check and correct spellings (p. 26).	Know how to look at second and third letters to find words in dictionary and to use guide words to locate words quickly.
Grade 3	CCSS.ELA-Literacy.L.3.2.d Form and use possessives (p. 28).	*girl, girl's* (singular possessive), *girls'* (plural possessive)
	CCSS.ELA-Literacy.L.3.2.e Use conventional spelling for high-frequency and other studied words and for adding suffixes to base words" (p. 28).	High-frequency or learned words: *beautiful, marvelous, science, hypothesis* Adding suffixes: *sit—sitting* *smile—smiled—smiling* *cry—cries; fly—flies* *great—greatness; happy—happiness* *truck, muck* (spelling patterns) *reuse, redo* (prefixes)
	CCSS.ELA-Literacy.L.3.2.f Use spelling patterns and generalizations in writing words (p. 28).	*hop—hopping; hope—hoping* (rules of when to double the ending consonant) *unbelievable = un+ believe+ able* (word parts)
	CCSS.ELA-Literacy.L.3.2.g Consult reference materials, including beginning dictionaries, as needed to check and correct spellings (p. 28).	
Grade 4	CCSS.ELA-Literacy.L.4.2.d Spell grade-appropriate words correctly, consulting references as needed (p. 28).	Tier 2 words: *prejudice; exotic* Tier 3 words: literature (*protagonist, antagonist, synonym, flashbacks*); science (*Mercury, hibernation*); social studies (*immigration; expedition*)
Grade 5	CCSS.ELA-Literacy.L.5.2.e Spell grade-appropriate words correctly, consulting references as needed (p. 28).	Tier 2 words: *exonerate* Tier 3 words: literature (*onomatopoeia, neologism*); science (*aerodynamics, physics*); social studies (*abolition, integration*)

Source: Standards from CCSS (2010), English Language Arts Standards, Language, Kindergarten and Grades 1–5. Washington, DC: NGACBP, CCSSO, pp. 26, 28.

figure 12.8   Traits of good and poor spellers.

GOOD SPELLERS	POOR SPELLERS
1. Pay attention to internal details of words.	1. Attempt to learn whole spelling of each word.
2. Are excellent, avid readers.	2. May be good or poor readers.
3. Are committed writers who find their voice.	3. Do not have their own writing voice.
4. Learn to spell new words when they want them in their writing.	4. Use words they know.
5. Self-monitor.	5. Do not understand self-monitoring.
6. Correct their own errors.	6. Get someone else to correct errors.
7. Quickly recognize their own errors.	7. Do not recognize their own errors.
8. Self-edit.	8. Attempt to memorize words.
9. Learn orthographic patterns within words.	9. Do not see orthographic patterns in words.
10. Learn different spellings for the same sounds.	10. Do not know different spellings for same sound.
11. Slow down when a word looks wrong.	11. Believe spelling is arbitrary.
12. Use a wide range of strategies.	12. Know no strategies.
	13. Sample only parts of words when they read.

Sources: Hughes, M., & Searle, D. (2000). Spelling and "the second 'R.'" *Language Arts, 77* (3), 201–208. / Turbill, J. (2000). Developing a spelling conscience. *Language Arts, 77*(3), 209–217. / Fresch, M. (2000). What we learned about Josh: Sorting out word sorting. *Language Arts, 77* (3), 232–240.

effective ways to determine students' spelling skills so you can plan appropriate instruction.

Spelling inventories

Templeton, Bear, Johnston, and Invernizzi (2011) have designed a developmental spelling task that assesses what students already know. The **spelling inventory** contains lists that progress from easy words (with CVC and CVCe patterns) to more difficult (multisyllabic words) that are intended as individual tests. Observe students as they spell the words if possible; often this will help you understand what students can and cannot do. The purpose of the inventory is to have students spell dictated words so you can analyze what they already know about spelling; it will also identify those who need individual help. Administer the inventory throughout the year to track your students' progress; the lists are included in Appendix C.61. To give the inventory, say a word from the list once or twice and use it in a sentence. Keep the student at ease by assuring her that she is not expected to know these words, but to write them how she thinks they are spelled. Most sets of words are presented in groups of five. When a student misses three out of five, stop the test. Remember that these tests are not intended to compare students' abilities; they are inventories to assess what a student knows about constructing words.

A student's spelling stage can be determined by how many words he spells correctly. For example, using the two inventories in Appendix C.61, the following criteria apply (Templeton et al., 2011):

SPELLED CORRECTLY	STAGE OF DEVELOPMENT
0	Emergent
1–5	Alphabetic
5–10	Within word pattern
10–15	Syllables and affixes
15–25	Derivational relations

To assess students' spelling stages, use the following guidelines:

1. In the emergent stage, students will first write the initial sound, then add the ending sound.

2. In the alphabetic stage, students correctly spell short vowel sounds and later digraphs and blends.

3. In the within word pattern stage, students can spell long vowels (including the silent *e* when the word has the CVCe pattern) and vowels that are controlled by *r*.

4. In the syllable/affixes stage, students add inflectional endings, prefixes, and suffixes. They also know when to double the consonant if they add *ed* or *ing*.

5. In the derivational stage, students are able to spell unknown words by listening for the root words and adding the correct prefixes and suffixes.

Once you understand the spelling stages, you can develop your own inventories. You can also determine a student's spelling stage by recording and analyzing the spelling of words from his independent writing tasks. The template demonstrated in Figure 12.9 is for recording and analyzing these words, using Gentry and Gillet's (1993) stages. The first step is to record the words exactly as the student spells them. List the words in the column that corresponds to the appropriate spelling stage. (Refer back to Figure 12.2 for descriptions of how words might be spelled in each stage.) Then assess how the student spelled each word in a five-word set to determine his spelling stage. Appendix C.62 has a blank form using the developmental stages of Bear et al. (2008).

CAFÉ word writing assessment

CAFÉ (Complexity, Accuracy, and Fluency Evaluation) is an assessment that evaluates students' word writing ability (Leal, 2005). It does not measure stu-dents' ability to compose; rather it measures their ability to write many words correctly (accuracy) in a given amount of time (fluency). The teacher assesses how many one-syllable and multisyllable words (complexity) students have written. This assessment can be administered to an entire class and is appropriate for any grade. Students are given a page with boxes (refer back to Figure 12.1). The number of boxes on the page varies depending on grade level. First and second graders have only 30 boxes on a page, while grades 9–12 have 90. Boxes for young students are larger to accommodate their developing fine motor skills, while the boxes for older students are smaller.

After providing the students with the CAFÉ sheet, follow these steps:

■ Give students ten minutes to fill in the boxes with only one word per box.

figure 12.9 Samples of recording students' spelling.

STUDENT Jon   GRADE K

Word	Precommunicative	Semiphonetic	Phonetic	Transitional	Conventional
1. lady	(scribble)				
2. once	abc				

STUDENT Krystal   GRADE 1

Word	Precommunicative	Semiphonetic	Phonetic	Transitional	Conventional
1. lady		ld			
2. once		wn			

STUDENT Mary B.   GRADE 2

Word	Precommunicative	Semiphonetic	Phonetic	Transitional	Conventional
1. lady			lade		
2. once			wunz		

STUDENT Kim   GRADE 3

Word	Precommunicative	Semiphonetic	Phonetic	Transitional	Conventional
1. popping				poping	
2. caught				cought	

STUDENT Cooper   GRADE 5

Word	Precommunicative	Semiphonetic	Phonetic	Transitional	Conventional
1. popping					popping
2. caught					caught

- Instruct them to write a word only once, not to use people's names, or abbreviations, or numerals (unless they spell out the word).
- Instruct them to write any words they want—words that explain what they like to do or eat, or that describe what they can smell, feel, see, or touch, or words that describe places.
- The room should be free from environmental print or the students' desks should be turned so they cannot see any words or other printed material.

Record how many words the students attempted, how many were correct, how many had one syllable, and how many had multiple syllables. This assessment will allow you to learn about the strengths and weakness of students' word-writing skills. As you carefully analyze the completed sheets, you will learn what students know about synonyms, antonyms, word families, compound words, plurals, homophones, and handwriting (Bromley, Vandenberg, & White, 2007). However, know that CAFÉ does not indicate students' composing abilities.

Formal Assessment

Standardized tests, such as the Iowa Test of Basic Skills, Comprehensive Test of Basic Skills, California Achievement Test, and Metropolitan Achievement Test have subtests for spelling. In some of these subtests, students must select the correctly spelled word from a list of four or five words. This type of testing assesses the students' ability to edit, not to spell words. However, because editing is an important step in the writing process, teachers understand that they must assess the process as well as the product. In other subtests, students must select the correct letter combination to fill in the blank in a word. This type of test assesses students' knowledge of word patterns.

intervention STRATEGIES & ACTIVITIES

Before presenting specific classroom activities, here are some general strategies that are beneficial to all students—English speakers as well as English learners.

1. Use visualization. Teach students to visualize the word in their mind by writing it in the air.

2. Divide monosyllable and multisyllable words into segments. Have students find the onset and rime or spelling patterns (CVC, CVCe, CVVC, and so on) of monosyllabic words. With multisyllable words have them segment the word into the affixes and a root or base word.

3. Focus on similarities and differences between words. For example, *hear* (action) has *ear* in the word (we need ears to hear), while *here* (location) is *there* (another location) without the letter *t*.

Keep these general strategies in mind as you use the activities in this section. The first activities focus on working with word patterns. These strategies are best taught in tutoring sessions so you can observe the student as she makes sense of patterns in words.

Magnetic Letters   GRADES 1–5   ACTIVITY

Working with magnetic letters helps students who are tactile learners and those who do not like the messiness of erasing. For students who are really weak with spelling, preselect letters and put them in a pile. First work with word families (onset and rimes) that have the CVC pattern (e.g., *at, ap, am, an,* and *up* families).

1. Select magnetic letters to spell the word and then pronounce the word.
2. Have the student pronounce the word and then you both pronounce it slowly, drawing out the sounds.
3. Mix up the three letters and ask the student to spell the word again.

4. Return the original letters to the pile and tell the student another word from the same word family.

5. For the second word, ask the student to find all three letters from the pile; she should not merely change the first letter, because it is important that she sees four or five words with the same pattern.

Much time should be given to manipulating the letters to spell new words. Have the student copy all the magnetic letter words onto a personal word wall (a sheet of paper with the rime written at the top and words listed from the bottom). An example of the *at* family is given below.

"at" family

cat

bat

fat

sat

mat

gnat

flat

This same activity can be performed with word stamps. Students in grades 3–5 can complete this activity on tablets or small dry-erase boards. Many older students also need practice with listening to the sounds within words and seeing patterns. Older students can work with the *-ight* (*light, sight*), *-ound* (*found, sound*), and *-own* (*clown, frown*) families.

ACTIVITY   **Think-Aloud on Word Patterns**   GRADES 4–5

Teach students how to look for word patterns by demonstrating think-alouds that show how a reader uses prior knowledge of word patterns to spell words; then have students sort a group of words according to their patterns and think-aloud their reasoning.

The following think-aloud is between Mr. Kingston, a fifth-grade teacher, and Toby, a student who attempts to memorize the spelling of words. Mr. Kingston is attempting to get Toby to see that learning to recognize patterns within words will make spelling easier for him. Mr. Kingston has the following words on one-inch square cards and has the cards randomly shuffled on the table: *hopped, skipping, rubbed, sitting, capping, shipped, happiness, merriment, silliest, funnier, cloudier, sunniest, windier.*

> Mr. Kingston: I would like you to sort the following words into two groups and then tell me why you grouped them into those groups.
>
> Toby: Just two groups?
>
> Mr. Kingston: Yes, just two groups.
>
> Toby: Well, "hopped" and "rubbed" both end in "ed" and "skipping," "sitting," and "capping" all end in "ing." That makes two groups, but I do not know about the others.
>
> Mr. Kingston: Just think a minute.
>
> Toby: Ah, I can put all those words into one group because you taught us that if it is a CVC word, you double the consonant before you add an ending.
>
> Mr. Kingston: Correct! I am glad you remembered that! Now look at the other words.
>
> Toby: Well, they must be the other group.
>
> Mr. Kingston: Yes, but you need to tell why they belong as a group.
>
> Toby: Well, "cloudier," "sunniest," and "windier" all have to do with weather.
>
> Mr. Kingston: Remember, we are talking about spelling patterns, not concepts.
>
> Toby: Right. Hmmm, I do not see how they belong in one group. Some end in "ier" or "est."
>
> Mr. Kingston: Correct. Do all the words have an ending?

Toby: Yeah. (A long pause and intent studying of the words.) Oh! I got it! If you took off the endings, all of these words end in "y" and you change the "y" to "i" before you add the ending. That is too cool! Is it true for all words ending in "y"?

Mr. Kingston: It is not true for all words, but it is true when you have an adjective, and you are changing the adjective to the comparative or superlative forms. Notice that all these words were adjectives. However, if a verb ends in a "y" such as "study," you keep the "y" when you add the "ing."

Toby: This will really help me in spelling. I always get confused about the spelling of the "er" and "est" words.

Mr. Kingston: I noticed that in your essays so I thought knowing this about word patterns would really help you.

Toby: It will! Thanks!

Personal Spelling Dictionary

GRADES 1–8   A C T I V I T Y

Because spelling is "a process of conceptual development" (Newlands, 2011), students are always developing their spelling skills. To individualize students' spelling growth, have them use personal dictionaries.

1. At the beginning of the year, construct the dictionaries by taking 28 legal size pieces of paper, folding them in half (width to width) and putting three staples down the middle to create a 8.5 x 7 inch booklet.

2. Next, instruct students, beginning with the first open page, to write the letters of the alphabet A–Z on the upper left-hand side of each page. Students will then have two pages for each letter of the alphabet.

3. Throughout the year, have students record their spelling word lists from each week, adding any word that you had to spell for them as they were writing.

4. As the year progresses, remind students to check their personal spelling dictionaries when they want to write a word that they know they learned, but cannot recall how to spell it.

Figure 12.10 has a sample copy of a middle school student's "L" page. Notice that most of these words are tier 2 words that the student encountered while reading novels.

figure 12.10   Sample copy of a middle-school student's personal spelling dictionary "L" page.

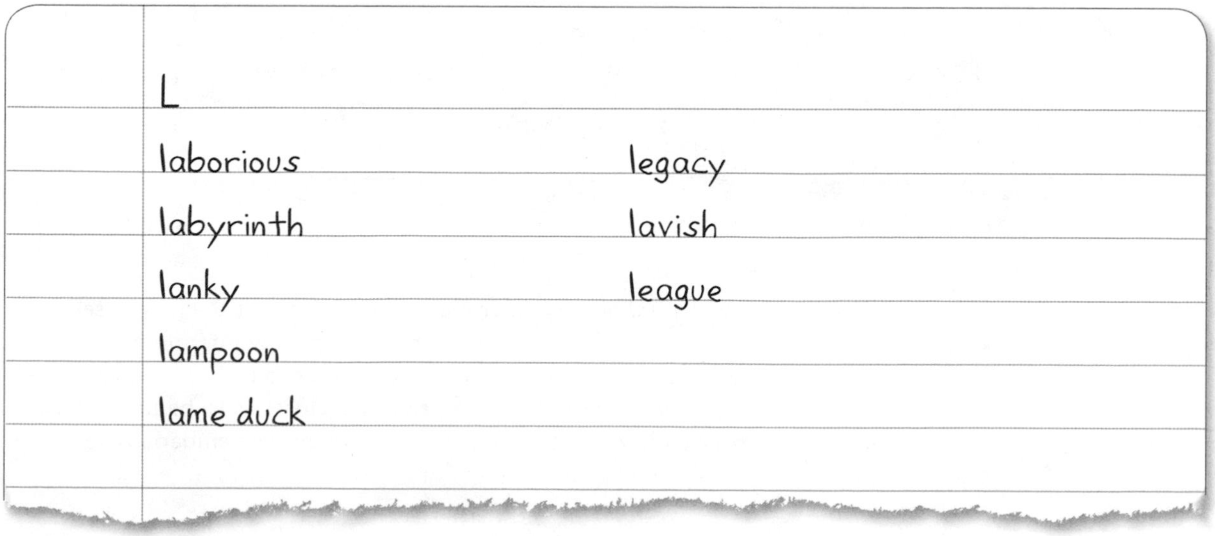

L

laborious	legacy
labyrinth	lavish
lanky	league
lampoon	
lame duck	

Foam Board Letters

You can make letter tiles from foam board purchased in a school supply or art supply store. For this activity:

1. Cut the foam board into half-inch squares.

2. Using a permanent marker, write one letter or combination of letters on each square. In addition to providing single letters to form words, see samples of tiles for forming word families in Figure 12.11.

3. Have students spell word family words or unscramble letters to make other words.

figure 12.11   Sample onset and rime letter tiles for word family activities.

C	B	F	H		S	St	L	and
M	P	S	at		Br	F	Fl	L
B	C	D	F		M	N	R	S
M	N	P	R		Fr	ight	B	F
V	an	B	H		H	M	P	R
					S	ound		

As an example of a themed word activity, after reading a book about the jungle, select animal names *(lion, tiger, elephant, kangaroo),* scramble the letters for each word, and have the student put the letters in correct order. These same foam-board letters can be used to play Scrabble, a game most children already know. Students who perceive themselves to be poor spellers benefit from playing this game with the teacher; mistakes are usually less embarrassing than when playing with peers.

Mnemonics, Memory Aids

Mnemonic strategies are unique ways to remember difficult or unusual words. For example, the sentence "George Ellen's old grandfather rode a pig home yesterday" spells *geography*. Also, it is easy to remember the difference between *dessert* and *desert* because children want two *desserts* (two *s*'s). The *c* and *s* are not confusing in *license* when one remembers that a *car* always needs to *stop* at a stop sign. (The *c* comes before the *s* in the sentence and in the word.) *Attendance* creates a command: "At ten dance!" And *capacity* is the command to "Cap a city!" Teach students how to create their own mnemonics and when to use them.

Spelling in Parts (SIP)

Some spelling problems for students are (1) alternative phonetic patterns (e.g., *education* sounds like *edukashun*), (2) spelling patterns that are less common (e.g., *ch* for the /sh/ as in *Michigan*), (3) double letters (e.g., *occur*), (4) the schwa sound that can be any vowel (e.g., *lemon, about*), and (5) commonly mispronounced words (e.g., *library*).

Powell and Aram (2008) suggest using the following **SIP (spelling in parts)** strategy to help struggling spellers. The goal of this strategy is to help students listen for and identify syllables within words. For example, if the student is struggling with *September*, write the word down and follow these steps. Have the student:

1. Clap out the syllables so he knows how many parts there are in the word. Remember: every syllable has at least one vowel.

2. Say the first syllable and circle it (e.g., Sep).

3. Pronounce the next syllable and draw a line under it (e.g., <u>tem</u>).

4. Pronounce the last syllable and draw a vertical line after it (e.g., ber/).

5. Pronounce the first syllable and write it down: S-e-p

6. Say the second syllable and write it down: *t-e-m*

7. Say the last syllable and write it down: *b-e-r*

8. Next, ask the student which syllable might cause a spelling problem and why. For example, the second syllable of *September* may sound like *tim*, instead of *tem*.

9. Discuss how the last syllable is found in three more months: *October, November,* and *December*.

Help students listen for syllables and teach them about troublesome syllables, such as *-tion* (e.g., *vacation, station, addition*) to assist them with multiple words. Teach struggling spellers to be word-pattern detectives instead of having them memorize each word independently.

Word Walls Related to Content

Displaying many posters with related words helps students learn the relationship among them and also helps them with spelling. Teachers can require students to spell correctly all words listed on one of the word walls or posters. This practice teaches students to use resources to help them spell and encourages them to use correct terminology when writing about newly learned concepts. The poster in Figure 12.12 has a list that a second-grade teacher created when the class was studying about reptiles and amphibians. As students encountered more words, they added them to the poster.

figure 12.12   Sample second grade content-related word wall.

REPTILES and AMPHIBIANS

Crocodile

Chameleon

Adder

Python

Boa Constrictor

Alligator

Salamander

Newt

Gecko

Viper   Terrapin   Bearded Dragon

SPELLING AND TECHNOLOGY
Spell Checking

Word processors are a great tool for enabling students to check their manuscripts for spelling errors; however, as noted before, spell-checkers do not identify all misspelled or incorrectly used words. Take the time to demonstrate how the spell-checker works on the word processing programs available to your students. Perhaps give a demonstration like the following.

- Type the following sentence: *The children put their unbellas in the stand.*
- Draw the students' attention to the incorrectly spelled *unbellas,* which has a red line under it.
- Put the cursor in front of the word *unbellas* and show how to correct the error.
- A screen appears with the suggested spelling. Demonstrate how to accept the suggested spelling and note how the word is changed automatically.
- Open a document with multiple misspellings. Indicate how the red lines highlight the misspellings, and show how to correct the errors again.
- Have students practice correcting the words while you watch so that you can be sure they are using the spell-checker correctly.

Once you have taught students to use the spell-checker, encourage them to type the final drafts of their work and require that all spelling be correct. However, because spell checkers do not detect errors such as *from* for *form,* or *student sin* for *students in,* students still need to proofread their work or have a peer proofread their it and circle incorrect words.

Online Resources

A number of websites feature word searches, word puzzles, and other spelling activities.

MindFun, www.mindfun.com. This helpful website builds spelling skills and allows teachers to easily create word searches.

Education Place, https://www.eduplace.com/kids/hmsv/. Hosts weekly word find puzzles on a variety of subjects.

EdHelper, www.edHelper.com. Allows teachers and students to enter word lists and have the site build word puzzles based on them.

Play Kids Games, www.playkidsgames.com. Designed for grades K–3; includes many different spelling games.

Kids Spell, www.kidsspell.com. For grades K–5; teachers can create their own spelling lists for different grades.

Fun Brain, www.funbrain.com. Features spelling games for grades K–6; user-friendly with bright graphics.

Apps: Spelling

Word Magic ($.99, Grades K–2). In this app, students view colorful pictures and try to choose the missing letter(s) to complete the word (depending on difficulty level chosen). The easy-to-use design calls for them to simply touch the correct answer. Students are reinforced for correct choices with voice response and stars. Student tracking provide a running total of correct and incorrect spellings.

Word Wagon by Duck Duck Moose ($1.99, Grades PreK–1). Based on CCSS, this award-winning app teaches letters, phonics and spelling. Kids will learn letter names, sounds and spelling of 4 and 6 letter words. Students collect stickers and earn stars (and can make various constellations).

SpellBoard ($4.99, Grades 1–12). This app allows you to create spelling lists for students in any grade and in many languages. Activities include word search, word scramble, and missing letter puzzles. Allows for multiple student profiles and sharing.

CONCLUDING THOUGHTS

S pelling is a critical skill for students' writing. When working on spelling skills, you must understand your students' developmental spelling stages and provide strategies that will help them reach the next stage. Strategies for each stage should focus on identifying patterns within words so students learn to spell groups of letters within words.

reflective learning

STAGES OF SPELLING DEVELOPMENT. Figure 12.13 has a list of misspelled words. Each word is from a different speller. For each word, decide which stage of spelling development the student is in. Then, in the third column, list a strategy you would use to help the student.

figure 12.13   Possible student misspellings of words.

SPELLED WORD/ INTENDED WORD	STAGE	SUGGESTED STRATEGY
hoping / hopping		
babe / baby		
rhime / rhyme		
rithum / rhythm		
percous / precious		
atendence / attendance		
corepes / corps		
receive / receive		
ocurance / occurrence		
neccessery / necessary		

IMPROVING SPELLING. After the first week of school, Ms. O'Nelly realizes her eighth-grade students have a wide range of spelling abilities. She is surprised to find some good readers who struggle with spelling. Others will not write a word unless it is spelled correctly; in fact, one student spends significant time attempting to find the correct spelling of a word in the dictionary. Other students select only words they know how to spell; thus, their expression of ideas is very limited. A few students write the words as they as sound; for example, *once* is spelled *wunz.*

questions

1. What instrument should Ms. O'Nelly use to assess her students' spelling?

2. What type of instruction—large group, small group, or individual—should she use?

3. What strategies should she teach the students who will not write a word unless it is spelled correctly?

4. What strategies should she teach the student who tries to find a word in the dictionary?

5. What strategies should she teach the students who use only the words they know?

6. What strategies should she teach the students who are writing words according to their sounds?

13

Identifying and Working with Students with Diverse Needs

There are two kinds of teachers: the kind that fills you with so much quail shot that you can't move, and the kind that just gives you a little prod behind and you jump to the skies.

ROBERT FROST

scenario

D r. Read, a reading professor in the education department of a university located in a large urban area, was inundated with calls from parents whose children attend a school where one of Dr. Read's former students is the principal; the parents are seeking tutors. Dr. Read calls the principal, Ms. Wilson, to find out about this sudden need for tutors. Ms. Wilson explains that the school has established a three-tier plan for its RTI (Response to Intervention). The school has just released the scores of the first benchmark assessment, and many parents are concerned that their child's score is below grade level and want to get help from a tutor. The school has decided that students below grade level after the first benchmark would receive extra small-group tutoring during the school day.

Dr. Read understands the parents' concerns and wants to help them. He decides his preservice elementary majors can gain valuable experience by tutoring the struggling readers. He tells his three Reading Diagnosis classes about the situation, and many volunteer to become tutors. He schedules a Tuesday afternoon meeting to explain what the tutors will need to do. All the preservice students are currently paired with a struggling reader from the university lab school, and he tells these new tutors that he expects the same type of lesson plan for this new program and that he will be available during tutoring hours.

Dr. Read tells Ms. Wilson that he has 16 education majors available to tutor the students with the low benchmark scores. He asks the parents to share the benchmark scores with the tutors so they can focus on the areas that will benefit the child.

A week later the 16 students come to the university reading clinic for tutoring. At the end of the first semester, they take another test at school to determine their growth. The college students are thrilled to learn that every student they tutored tested at grade level. The parents are thrilled with their children's progress and, realizing the benefits of tutoring, ask if the college students will continue to tutor their children. They say their children like the individual attention and being able to read without other classmates listening in; they also think it is "cool" to attend the university.

As you read this chapter, consider the following questions:

guiding questions

1. What other options does Ms. Wilson have in terms of providing the students with tutoring?
2. What key elements were likely part of the lesson plans Dr. Read's students used with struggling readers?
3. What adaptations to the plan would they have made for English learners?
4. If Dr. Read's students encounter a reader who stops when he does not know a word, what responses would you suggest they use with that reader?

introduction

Since 2004 when the Individuals with Disabilities Education Act (IDEA) was reauthorized, school districts have been required to use a Response to Intervention (RTI) framework for identifying students with learning disabilities and for providing instructional services. The act states that a learning disability may be present when a "child does not achieve adequately for the child's age or to meet State-approved grade-level standards . . . when provided with learning experiences and instruction appropriate for the child's age or State-approved grade-level standards" (U.S. Department of Education, 2006). IDEA 2004 means that schools are no longer required to use a severe discrepancy between a student's achievement and intellectual ability as measured solely through the use of standardized tests when determining if a student is eligible for special services. Instead, schools use the RTI framework, which identifies learning disabilities by observing how a student responds to scientific, research-based intervention. The advantage of the RTI method over the discrepancy method is that students struggling with literacy skills receive help immediately instead of waiting until they have taken a battery of tests, during which time they receive no intervention and fall further behind.

This chapter highlights details about RTI, differentiating instruction, and tutoring practices that can be used when working with students with diverse learning needs.

RESPONSE TO INTERVENTION

IDEA 2004 identified eight areas as the basis for determining if a student has a specific learning disability. Six of the areas deal with language arts: oral expression, listening comprehension, written expression, basic reading skills, fluency, and reading comprehension. IDEA 2004, however, did not provide states and districts with a prescribed method of implementing RTI. Although the specific approaches vary, the method should involve a cyclical process that begins with assessment, followed by intervention, more assessment, and more intense intervention until students are either reading and writing at grade level or receiving special services for a specific learning disability. Some states and districts have implemented a three-tier plan, while others use a five- or six-tier plan. However, "RTI is not a model to be imposed on schools, but rather a framework to help schools identify and support students before the difficulties they encounter with language and literacy become more serious" (International Reading Association, 2009a, p. 2).

The concept of RTI is for all students to "first be considered general education students" (International Reading Association, 2009a, p. 1). In order for students to be identified with a learning disability, teachers must engage in a "process that incorporates both assessment and intervention so that immediate benefits come to the student" (Mesmer & Mesmer, 2009, p. 287). The purpose is to "identify students with learning disabilities and to prevent mislabeling and over identification of students having disabilities" (Ehren, 2013, p. 451) and to catch any student that lacks or is weak in a particular skill and needs short-term explicit instruction (Lipson & Wixson, 2012).

Guiding Principles

The ILA (IRA) commission on RTI has drafted guiding principles for teachers regarding implementation of RTI.

Principle 1, Instruction. Both classroom teachers and interventionists must provide high-quality instruction backed by research-based practices. This requires all classroom teachers, from first-year to seasoned, to be highly qualified literacy teachers capable of using strategies that have been proven to increase students' literacy skills.

Principle 2, Responsive teaching and differentiation. Teachers must be able to determine if students are responding to intervention. This requires individualized kid watching; that is, teachers watching students as they use various strategies. Then, "[i]nstruction and materials selection must derive from specific student-teacher interactions" (International Reading Association, 2009a, p. 2).

Principle 3, Assessment. All teachers need to know how to assess students' literacy skills as they engage in authentic language activities.

Principle 4, Collaboration. Effective RTI requires classroom teachers to collaborate with reading specialists, speech pathologists, school psychologists, and other special education teachers. Collaboration must also involve parents so skills can be reinforced in the home.

Principle 5, Systemic and comprehensive. The school district must consider the culture of the community as administrators plan for a systemic and comprehensive RTI. The planning should include all levels of classroom teachers from pre-K through twelfth grade, reading specialists, and all other special education teachers so the students receive interventions that build from one grade level to another. Records should be comprehensive so teachers can build on interventions a student received the previous year. Accurate records eliminate time spent on reevaluating a student or offering interventions that did not prove to be useful.

Principle 6, Expertise. As stated earlier, all students deserve highly qualified teachers conversant in the latest materials and intervention practices. According to the International Reading Association, "important dimensions of teachers' expertise include their knowledge and understanding of language and literacy development, their ability to use powerful assessment tools and techniques, and their ability to translate information about student performance into instructionally relevant instructional techniques" (2009a, p. 4).

The RTI Process

As you can see, RTI requires all classroom teachers to be highly qualified to teach reading and assess reading problems so they can closely monitor how students respond to intervention. They must know which assessments to use to determine a student's ability and which interventions to use; then they must determine if that student is responding to the intervention. The following is a sample five-step RTI process:

Step 1

Because foundational skills are important for all students to become proficient readers, benchmark skills for kindergarten and first graders are determined by using such screening assessments as Dynamic Indicators of Basic Early Literacy Skills (DIBELS), Phonological Awareness Literacy Screening (PALS), or Basic Early Assessment of Reading Scope and Sequence (BEARS). These assessments measure basic early literacy skills including phonemic awareness, phonics, vocabulary, fluency, and comprehension. As students master the foundational skills of reading, students need to master the skills necessary for college and career readiness as specified in the CCSS; therefore, assessments for determining these benchmarks must focus on the higher level comprehension skills. Some of these higher level skills include comprehending complex fiction and nonfiction texts, knowing domain-specific vocabulary, citing evidence, understanding the author's perspective and the perspective not presented, and comparing and contrasting different texts on the same topic (Lipson, Chomsky-Higgins, & Kanfer, 2011; Lipson & Wixson, 2012; Wixson & Lipson, 2012). When teachers detect that students lack either the basic foundational or higher level skills, they need to provide intervention.

Even though middle-school content area teachers do not focus solely on reading skills, they "can help students develop the knowledge, reading, strategies, and thinking skills to understand and learn from increasingly complex text" (Rissman, Miller, & Torgesen, 2009, p. 13). Content area teachers must achieve three goals in their subject area: (1) help students meet graduation requirements, (2) provide appropriate instruction and intervention if necessary, and (3) provide a system that will develop continuous school improvement (Brozo, 2010; Lenski, 2012). Just like elementary teachers, middle-school teachers must assess students at the beginning of the year to determine which students are performing below grade level so they can begin intervention.

Step 2

Based on the assessment scores determined in Step 1, the student receives intervention in her areas of greatest need. Often this first round takes place in a small group of students who are weak in the same areas. Early-grade teachers often use the guided reading strategy in which the students are grouped so that reading materials are at their instructional level and not their frustration level. Middle-school teachers should differentiate their instruction in order to provide appropriate intervention (Brozo, 2010). RTI requires materials and intervention strategies to be scientifically valid and given systematically so the student has every opportunity to improve. The emphasis of RTI is to see how a student responds to intervention. This intervention does not replace the regular classroom instruction; it is an additive.

Step 3

Student progress is constantly monitored and recorded. The teacher assesses the student's progress at least weekly. For example, if DIBELS or PALS has been given as a benchmark assessment, it would be administered again to determine if the student is responding to the intervention. Middle-school subject area teachers will collaborate with the reading specialist to determine which assessment was used for the student's benchmark score so the same test can be administered again. Because middle-school teachers meet with large groups of students for a short period of time each day, the reading specialist is usually the one to administer the assessments. Regardless of the student's grade level, if she shows that she is at grade level after this assessment, she is dropped from the small group intervention. If the assessment indicates that the student is not progressing and is falling further behind her classmates, she is recommended for more intense intervention.

Step 4

More intense intervention is usually individualized or takes place in very small groups over longer periods of time. This intervention is also an additive; it does not replace general classroom instruction. The individualized attention is often from a reading interventionist. Again, the teacher or interventionist constantly monitors the student and adjusts strategies according to need.

Step 5

After a long period of time—often a year—the student's response to the intervention is assessed again. If the student is falling further below his grade level, he is considered to have a learning disability under this five-step intervention example. If the student is responding, he is not considered to have a disability and simply needs more intense intervention. During this intense intervention, a reading specialist, special education teacher, speech pathologist, and other specialists work together to give the student one-on-one instruction according to his needs. It is important that this intense instruction takes place in the setting that is most beneficial for the student. Sometimes this will be a room separate from the regular classroom; other times the reading specialist or special education teacher will work side-by-side with the student in the classroom so he receives the same curriculum as the other students. Then during individual practice time the student receives extra guidance from the specialist.

The intense intervention usually includes 30- to 40-minute tutoring sessions by the specialist on the skill(s) that the student needs in order to progress. Even in the intermediate elementary grades or middle school, the reading specialist may need to work on such basic skills as helping the student automatically recognize commonly used words such as those found in the Dolch list (see Appendix B.6) or to understand domain-specific vocabulary found in science and social studies texts. In these cases, the reading specialist may spend time with word sorts to help students understand relationship among words. As another example, if a middle-school student is struggling to comprehend informational text in a social studies book, the reading specialist may teach him how to complete simple graphic organizers so the information is easier to summarize. Some instructional recommendations for all students requiring intervention are to (1) connect learning to students' lives, (2) build student autonomy, (3) use strategic grouping, (4) use research-based cognitive strategies (Watts-Taffe et al., 2012/2013), (5) build prior knowledge, (6) build specialized vocabulary, (7) teach organizational structure of informational text by completing graphic maps, (8) pose higher-level-thinking questions, (9) teach students to compare claims across different texts and evaluate the credentials of the authors, and (10) teach students to "deconstruct complex sentences" in informational text (Lenski, 2012).

RTI and the CCSS

Wixson & Lipson (2012) note that "[b]ecause the CCSS will direct the content of the curriculum, instruction and assessment in the English language arts . . . they will most certainly have a significant impact on . . . an RTI approach" (p. 388). The RTI framework requires that some students receive intense intervention from a highly qualified reading or other specialist in order for them to develop the skills necessary for college and career reading as specified in the CCSS.

As discussed in Chapter 3, the two consortiums that are designing tests that align with the CCSS are the Partnership for Assessment and Readiness for College and Career (PARCC) and the Smarter Balanced Assessment Consortium (SBAC). As required by the CCSS, beginning in third grade, students will be assessed on the complex, higher level reading, a skill that should not be assessed with only one assessment (Lipson, Chomsky-Higgins, & Kanfer, 2011). Because

the tenth CCR Anchor Standard for Reading requires students to read complex texts independently, teachers will need to work with all students so they are reading materials at their grade level. The RTI framework is one important tool for helping students succeed and meet the rigorous standards for literacy set forth by the CCSS and new state standards based on the CCSS. As discussed throughout this text, we as educators continue to seek effective methods of individualizing instruction for diverse learners, and other principals like Ms. Wilson in the opening scenario will encourage teachers to differentiate instruction and seek tutors to help students meet the standards.

DIFFERENTIATING INSTRUCTION

Good teaching is inevitably the fine art of connecting content and kids—of doing what it takes to adapt *how* we teach so *what* we teach takes hold in the lives and minds of students" (Tomlinson & Jarvis, 2006). This type of teaching is called **differentiating instruction**.

As discussed in Chapter 1, today's classrooms are diverse; not only do teachers have English learners, but they also have students with a wide range of learning abilities and special needs (e.g., hearing impairments, emotional problems, attention deficit disorder, and gifted). Once an effective teacher understands the students' learning needs, he will prepare instruction to reach all students by modifying lessons according to these individual needs. For example, for kindergarten students who are unable to form all the letters of the alphabet, the teacher adjusts their writing center tasks by having them create one page of letters instead of six. For students who are academically gifted, the teacher can provide a blank booklet and invite them to write as much as they want. For a student who is hearing impaired, the teacher can have him sit as close as possible during read-alouds and can stand close to the student when sharing information and giving instructions at other times.

This diversity of learners prevents one lesson plan from fitting the needs of the entire class; thus teachers are responsible for modifying each lesson to fit a range of individual needs. Work should always be worthy of the student's effort (Alderman & Green, 2011; Darling-Hammond, 2006). Tasks should be manageable; for example, students with learning disabilities may receive shorter assignments so they can finish in the same amount of time as other students. These students also need clear directions. Because many students with learning disabilities can only process one directive at a time, teachers should break assignments into small tasks. After one task is completed, the teacher can give the second directive. By breaking up assignments, students taste success and become motivated to continue.

Some students may need their own space to function optimally, and the teacher will respond by setting their desks apart from the others.

Brain research indicates that all students need "emotional safety, appropriate challenges" (Theroux, 2004, p. 1), and environments in which they can construct meaning based on their previous knowledge. Teachers who provide emotional safety teach to their students' strengths and foster positive feelings in them. Because no two students have exactly the same strengths and background knowledge and no two students construct meaning in the same way, teachers need to differentiate instruction. Theroux (2004) identified four ways to differentiate instruction:

1. *Content:* Through pretesting, teachers determine which students know major concepts and which do not. Then they vary their teaching so that the students who need it receive additional instruction on the concepts while others who know the concepts do not.
2. *Process/activities:* Teachers vary strategies and activities based on students' varying knowledge and abilities.
3. *Product:* Teachers allow students to produce different products.
4. *Learning styles:* At the beginning of the year, teachers assess students' interests and learning styles so they can better understand the whole child and adapt the learning environment to accommodate individual needs.

As you can tell, the emphasis is never on teaching a set curriculum, but rather on providing an enriched environment that enables all students to build on their existing knowledge. In enriched environments, teachers (1) provide positive support, (2) encourage risk taking without fear of ridicule, (3) allow social interaction, (4) provide challenging but attainable tasks, (5) foster an atmosphere of experimentation and discovery, (6) give students choices, and (7) expect students to become active rather than passive learners (Theroux, 2004).

TUTORING

Another way to individualize instruction is through tutoring, which is one-on-one instruction. Struggling readers benefit from being tutored, and tutoring can be effective for second language learners (Otaiba & Pappamihiel, 2005). First, because instruction is based on the individual needs of the student, the reader receives instant feedback (Medcalf, Bessette, & Gibbs, 2009; Cartwright, Savage, Morgan, & Nichols, 2009; Clay, 1985; Meyer et al., 2010; Houge & Geier, 2009). Because it is tailored to the individual student, tutoring is one of the most effec-

tive forms of instruction for struggling elementary and middle-school students (Houge, Peyton, Geier, & Petrie, 2007). Most tutoring programs target students in the primary grades, because research reveals that students who are not reading by the third grade have higher chances of dropping out before graduating from high school than proficient readers (Chambers, Abrami, McWhaw, & Therrien, 2001). However, with the new requirements of the CCSS, tutoring for older students may also be necessary so they will be prepared for college and career reading and writing tasks as discussed in the previous section.

The downside to tutoring is that it is costly for school districts. One-on-one tutoring programs drain school districts' budgets, especially when they use certified teachers as tutors. A teacher who is a tutor works with one student at a time instead of 20 to 30. Even though certified teachers are more effective than uncertified tutors (Allington, 2013; Clay, 1985), many school districts seek volunteer tutors in order to save money. This often includes retired community members, college students, business leaders, and parents. All volunteers can be effective tutors, particularly if a certified teacher trains them (Johnston, Invernizzi, & Juel, 1998), but college students are most effective (Elbaum, Vaughn, Hughes, & Moody, 2000; Houge, Peyton, Geier, & Petrie, 2007). Figure 13.1 lists the major guidelines for successful tutoring programs.

figure 13.1

Guidelines for successful tutoring programs.

1. Tutors should be trained by certified reading specialists.
2. Tutors need ongoing training and feedback.
3. The student should work with the same tutor in each session.
4. Tutors must be reliable and punctual.
5. A certified specialist should be present during the tutoring sessions to answer questions and provide input.
6. Tutoring sessions need to be structured.
7. Tutors should use high-quality instructional materials.
8. The reading specialist needs to assess the tutee on a regular basis.
9. The instruction in the tutoring session must coordinate with classroom instruction.

Source: Allington, R. (2006). *What Really Matters for Struggling Readers: Designing Research-Based Programs* (2nd ed.). Boston: Pearson/Allyn & Bacon. / Invernizzi, M., Rosemary, C., Juel, C., & Richard, H. (1997). At-risk readers and community volunteers: A three-year perspective. *Scientific Studies of Reading, 1*(3), 277–300. / Wasik, B. (1998). Using volunteers as reading tutors: Guidelines for successful practice. *The Reading Teacher, 51*(7), 562–571.

Successful Tutoring Programs

Teachers may choose from many successful tutoring programs. The Howard Street Tutoring Program (Morris, 1999), developed in Chicago as an after-school program, was designed to help second- and third-grade readers. Success for All, developed by Slavin et al. (1996), is based on the premise that all students must succeed at reading in the early grades and on the principles of immediate and intensive intervention (Nunnery et al., 1999). The program is designed for first through third grades. Book Buddies, developed by Charlottesville City School, the University of Virginia, and the city of Charlottesville, Virginia, is a tutoring program for first- and second-grade struggling readers. One of the most successful tutoring programs found in schools across the United States is Reading Recovery, which was developed in New Zealand (Allington, 2013).

The Reading Recovery program was developed as an early intervention and remediation program for first graders having extreme difficulty learning to read and write (Clay, 1985; Fountas & Pinnell, 2006b). The program uses certified teachers who tutor one child for 30 minutes each day. The goal is to help struggling readers read at grade level as soon as possible, usually within 15 to 22 weeks. The student then either tests out of the program, because she has reached the reading level of her class, or she is referred to a long-term tutoring program, such as those supported by Title I. Reading Recovery uses certified teachers who are trained by certified Reading Recovery instructors. According to Allington (2013), this program is the most effective tutoring program, but it is expensive due to its specialized training, staff of certified teachers, and the use of leveled books. The recommended books are organized into fine gradients, labeled 1 through 20 for first graders. (See the discussion in Chapter 2.)

The CCSS set grade-specific standards "but do not define the intervention methods or materials necessary to support students who are well below or well above grade-level expectations" (NGACBP & CCSSO, 2010, Introduction, p. 6). In the case of first graders, Reading Recovery can help those children with "extreme literacy difficulties reach grade-level expectations by the end of first grade" (Reading Recovery Council, 2013, p. 1). Publishers of Reading Recovery books can be found at http://readingrecovery.org/rrcna/suppliers-guide.

Reading Recovery tutorial sessions are scheduled every day for 30 minutes. Each session has the following structure:

1. The student rereads two or more familiar books on an easy reading level to experience success.

2. The student rereads a book on her instructional level that was introduced in the previous session. The tutor keeps a running record of this reading to analyze and assess growth.

3. The tutor gives isolated word study instruction, often using plastic letters on a magnetic board.

4. The student writes a short story, focusing on writing for meaning and on listening for the sounds in words. Stories are only one or two sentences long. Tutor uses sound boxes to aid student in letter–sound recognition.

5. The tutor writes the story on a sentence strip and cuts the words apart. The tutee must arrange the words to construct the sentence. The tutor puts the pieces in a plastic bag and writes the sentence on the bag so the student can take it home and practice putting the pieces back together.

6. The tutor introduces a new book on the student's instructional level, and the student attempts to read the new book, which becomes the text used for the running record the following day.

Planning and Conducting the Tutoring Session

Tutors need to plan each tutoring session just as effective teachers plan for every classroom lesson. This does not mean tutors should never deviate from the plan to seize teachable moments. Whenever possible, a reading specialist or other trained tutor should observe tutoring sessions to provide feedback for the tutor. All tutors should collaborate with the classroom teacher to understand what particular skills the student lacks and what concepts are being studied in the different subject areas so the tutoring sessions can also be based on the same topics.

Lesson plans for tutoring sessions

Each tutoring session should be based on a lesson plan to ensure that it is directed toward a particular goal and that the planned activities help the student meet that goal. Figure 13.2 presents a completed form for a sample tutoring session and Appendix D.34 includes a template. The lesson plan includes (1) written objectives for each area of the tutoring session, (2) the sequence of the lesson, (3) needed materials, and (4) reflection on each area of the lesson.

Written objectives. Tutors need to reflect on the tutee's past accomplishments, current progress, and future goals to define objectives for each area of the lesson. Like all objectives, these should state what the student is expected to do with a targeted degree of accuracy.

figure **13.2**   Lesson plan for tutoring.

LESSON PLAN

TUTOR: Terri   DATE: 9-23

TUTEE: Marie   GRADE: 2

Easy Reading Objective: Marie will read <u>Bear's Cave</u> with 95% accuracy to help her meet CCSS RL 2.10.

Rereading of Last Session's Book Objective: When Marie rereads <u>Wobbly Tooth,</u> she will learn to pause when she comes to a period to help her meet CCSS RF 2.4B.

Word Study Objective: Marie will create a list of at least five words that have the /oo/ sound, as in <u>tooth,</u> to help her meet CCSS RF 2.3B.

Writing Objective: Marie will complete two sentences based on her experience of losing a loose tooth to help her meet CCSS W 2.8, spelling all words correctly.

Reading of Instructional Material Objective: When reading <u>Grandma's Bicycle,</u> Marie will use picture clues to determine unknown words to help her meet CCSS RI 2.4.

LESSON PLAN	PLANNED ACTIVITY	TIME	REFLECTION
Easy Reading	Book: <u>Bear's Cave</u>	8 min.	Marie read with 97% accuracy. She only struggled with "growled."
Rereading	Book: <u>Wobbly Tooth</u>	7 min.	She self-corrected 85% of errors. On the running record, she used visual cues more than reading for meaning.
Word Study	Materials: Dry-erase board, magnetic letters	10 min.	Her list: food, moon, broom, loose, noon. She also created a list of "oo" words that do not rhyme with <u>loose tooth:</u> book, look, cook. She liked the dry-erase board better than the magnetic letters.
Writing	Materials: Her tutoring journal	10 min.	Marie wrote 3 sen.: My dad pulls my tooth. It hurts (we used sound boxes for this word) when my dad pulls my tooth. I have six new tooths. (I explained that the plural form of tooth is teeth.)
New Reading	Book: <u>Grandma's Bicycle</u>	10 min.	She read with only 80% accuracy. She reads too fast. She needs to slow down. She told me fast reading is good reading. She liked the funny story. Her grandma rides a bicycle too.

Teachers often base the objectives on state or national (CCSS) standards. Figure 13.3 provides sample objectives for each area of the lesson. At the beginning of the school year, the tutor may write simple objectives that reflect the level of accuracy that is intended for easy reading and instructional reading. A tutor may write, "Marie will read *I Paint* with 95 percent accuracy." As the year progresses and the tutor understands the unique needs of the tutee, he should set more specific and challenging goals. For example, if the tutee is an inexpressive reader, he may write, "Marie will raise her voice at the end of each question in *I Went Walking, What Did I See?*" Or if a middle-school student is struggling to comprehend informational texts because he cannot determine the organizational structure of passages, the tutor can set an objective that the student will read different passages with different organizational structures and use graphic organizers to help in comprehending the passages.

Sequence of the lesson. As stated previously, the Reading Recovery program follows a consistent format. The major components—reading easy material, rereading a book to keep a running record, word study, writing, and new reading—are all used in the sample lesson plan that is provided in this chapter.

Research shows that effective tutorial programs have a pace that keeps tutees engaged and motivated, motivated, motivated! Students who are interested in a task will stay with the task; students who are not interested are not engaged (Houge & Geier, 2009; Meyer et al., 2010). For this reason tutoring programs should include the following elements:

1. 40-minute sessions at least twice a week.
2. Consistent format in each session:
   a. Ten minutes for easy read.
   b. Five minutes to reread the material introduced in the previous session. (Tutor keeps a running record during this reading.)
   c. Ten minutes for word study.
   d. Five to 10 minutes for writing.
   e. Ten to 15 minutes for introducing and reading new material at the tutee's instructional level.

The purpose of the easy reading is to build the tutee's reading confidence, rate, fluency, and expression. Many struggling readers read word-for-word, with no expression, and at a slow rate; they need to hear themselves read fluently to make a story exciting. These first 10 minutes are a time for struggling readers to experience success. During the rereading of the previous session's material, the tutor should keep a running record in order to analyze the percentage of words read correctly and what cueing systems the reader uses with materials at the instructional level. Chapter 3 provides detailed instructions on running records. Appendix C.11 includes a blank form to use for a running record, and Figure 3.14 provides a conversion table for quick analysis of the percentage of words read correctly. An easy text for students is one in which they make less than 1 error for every 20 words read. Students read with 99 percent accuracy if they make only 1 error for every 100 words read.

Appropriate materials. Because tutoring sessions are fast-paced, the tutor needs all necessary books and supplies at her fingertips. The lesson plan should include all the materials that will be needed, such as books, a computer, whiteboards, magnetic letters, letter stamps, salt or sand trays for writing, pencils, paper, and sentence strips. Before a session, tutors should make sure

---

figure **13.3**

Sample objectives.

EASY READING OBJECTIVES:

Sally will read *I Paint* with 95% accuracy.

When George reads *Grandma's Bicycle,* he will observe 95% of the periods with a pause.

When Juan reads *Do Whacky Do,* he will appropriately inflect his voice at the phrase, "Do Whacky Do."

REREADING OF LAST SESSION'S BOOK OBJECTIVES:

Lee will read *Bear's Cave* with 90% accuracy.

When Jon reads *Bear's Cave,* he will self-correct 80% of his errors.

WORD STUDY OBJECTIVES:

Roberto will identify 90% of the "an" family words when he plays Wordo.

Emily will correctly push and say, with 95% accuracy, the letters of these three-letter words: *hop, pup, dad, map.*

WRITING OBJECTIVES:

Heather will write the following sentence with 95% accuracy: "I like to jump rope and play ball." (Early in the semester, children can write anything about their personal lives; this is an example of such a sentence.)

Ben will compose a sentence of at least six words with 95% accuracy.

READING NEW MATERIAL OBJECTIVES:

When Virginia comes to an unknown word in *Sea Animals,* she will read to the end of the sentence to understand the context.

When reading *Making a Cake,* Marie will use picture clues to determine unknown words.

they have the materials on the list. This ensures no valuable time is wasted searching for materials.

Reflection on the lesson. An essential part of teaching is reflecting on every lesson taught. The lesson-plan form (shown in Figure 13.2) allows the tutor to reflect on each aspect of the lesson. Effective tutors reflect on what the student did well, her improvement from previous lessons, and how her attitude changed. For example, the tutor should note if the goal was reached in the easy reading section and how the tutee responded to the story. If a specific skill was taught, such as reading to the end of the sentence to figure out an unknown word, this should be noted in the reflection. If a running record was kept during the repeated reading, the tutor should note the degree of accuracy and what cueing system the tutee used. If a goal in word study or writing was not met, the tutor should reflect on why the student failed to reach the goal. Sometimes, the tutee's fatigue may be the reason. These reflections should be honest and accurate so that the tutor can plan more effectively for the next session. When preservice teachers serve as tutors, the professor can observe the session and help the tutor understand the tutee's responses.

Getting started

The first tutoring session is a time for the tutor and tutee to become acquainted.

Session 1. During the first session establish a comfortable rapport and learn about each other's interests. Having both parties complete a personal interest survey such as the one in Figure 3.25 encourages such a discussion. First the tutor and tutee discuss the tutee's interests, and then they can discuss the tutor's interests. Tutees who are at least emergent writers can "share the pen" with the tutor as they fill out the form. Tutees are encouraged to write what they can, while the tutor helps complete each thought. Sharing the pen gives the tutor an idea of the tutee's writing ability. The tutor should have a couple of books on hand that are considered below the student's reading level so he can get a quick idea of what the student can read. I have found when working with elementary students that having a simple science experiment with directions written at the intended grade level or a little below is a good ice breaker. Ask students to read the directions, write one or two hypotheses, do the experiment, and record the findings. Just observing the student reading the directions and writing a hypothesis gives the tutor some knowledge of the student's literacy skills.

Session 2. After the first session the tutor should have an idea of what books are an easy read for the tutee and select four or five from which the tutee can choose.

It is important to choose books easy enough for the tutee to experience success. During the second session, the tutor can administer one of the Reading Attitude and Writing Attitude Surveys found in Appendices C.20–24. Insight into the tutee's attitudes will pinpoint aspects of reading and writing the tutee does or does not enjoy. Often a tutee enjoys being read to but does not enjoy reading in front of peers because she is embarrassed about being a "poor" reader. The tutor can assure her they will be reading together where no one else can hear them. The Attitude Survey may also reveal that the tutee prefers informational texts over stories. The tutee's Writing Attitude Survey may indicate she thinks writing is synonymous with composing long stories. The tutor can correct this misunderstanding by having the tutee compose short lists or sentences, thereby demonstrating that writing can also be about creating short pieces. This session ends with the tutor reading a book to the tutee. Again, the book should be a repetitive text so the tutee can join in. The tutor, of course, models fluent, expressive reading.

Session 3. During this session the tutor begins to assess the tutee's reading and writing abilities. For an emergent reader, the tutor should assess his knowledge of letter names and sounds by using a chart such as the one in Appendix C.37. If the student is a beginning reader, the tutor should assess his knowledge of letter recognition, sight words, phonics, and word and passage comprehension by administering the Woodcock Tests (see Chapter 3). Conducting a miscue analysis gives the tutor an opportunity to analyze the type of miscues the reader makes most frequently. Administering the Bear, Invernizzi, Templeton, and Johnston Qualitative Spelling Inventory (2012) will aid in assessing the tutee's current level of word knowledge. (See Chapter 12 and Appendix C.61 for further information.) Assessment is an ongoing process, but it must begin early so the tutor can plan appropriate lessons.

Tutoring Sessions for English Learners

All tutors who work with second language learners must not only possess the five characteristics discussed in Chapter 14 (p. 379); they must also be culturally sensitive and understand second language acquisition. (See Chapter 1 for review of the Progressive Stages of English Language Development.) They must understand the difference between oral proficiency that most English learners acquire in two years and academic proficiency that usually takes five to seven years to acquire. Tutors must support English learners as they take active roles in the classroom, because successful social interaction leads to increased peer acceptance, which further aids academic growth (Vaughn, Elbaum, & Hughes, 1998). Tutors build English learners' confidence by accepting and reaffirming them as individuals and taking an interest in their likes and dislikes. Allow ample time for discussion during the tutoring session so the English learner becomes confident in expressing herself. This will increase her confidence in speaking with peers and foster her interactions in class activities and discussions.

Tutoring sessions for English learners and tutoring sessions for English native speakers are similar in principle, but different in format. For both, the tutor assesses the tutee's literacy skills and creates lessons based on the tutee's interests, strengths, and needs. The tutor must consider the tutee's oral English language skills, age, and native language literacy skills. Tutors working with students who know very little English and are not literate in their native language will need to spend time on oral language development. If tutees are literate in their native language, you can use this knowledge to build their English skills.

Session 1. Just like the native speaker's tutor, the English learner's tutor gets to know the tutee and make him feel comfortable during the first session. To determine the tutee's literacy skills in his native language, ask him to read concept books that are in his native language. If he cannot read the words you can assume he is not literate in his native language. Have magazines available and point to pictures, such as a slice of pizza or a glass of milk. Say the object's name, point to yourself, nod, and say "I like pizza." Then point to the tutee and ask, "Do you like pizza?" Use lots of gestures to help him understand the flow of conversation.

Magazines are excellent resources for determining a tutee's vocabulary skills, because they have many pictures of everyday objects that are not usually found in children's literature; for example, toasters, hamburgers, peanuts, lettuce, coffee pots, and so on.

Session 2. Strive to make the tutee feel safe and relaxed. During this session use the alphabet chart found in Appendix C.37 to see if the tutee knows the letter names and/or sounds. Spanish-speaking tutees may say the letters in Spanish and the sounds in Spanish. Use the picture cards found in Appendix D.5 and the bingo cards in Appendix D.6 to informally assess the tutee's oral vocabulary. Do this by placing three cards in front of her, saying one of the pictures, and pointing to the correct picture. Then place three different cards in front of her, say one object, and ask her to point to the correct card. Again, you may need to make the directions clear by using hand gestures.

Sample format for subsequent sessions

After two or three sessions of making the tutee feel comfortable and safe, use the following format. You may modify the format to meet the needs of a particular tutee, but it is important for the sessions to have a format so the tutee begins to feel comfortable with the tasks he will be asked to do. Also, a set format keeps instruction systematic. The following format is for tutees who know some words in English and are ready to begin reading and writing.

1. *Review from previous lesson.* Review words from flash cards. The tutee says the word and points to something that refers to the definition. For example, if the word is *one* he can hold up one finger. If the word is *red* he can point to something in the room that is red. This activity helps you determine whether the tutee pronounces the word correctly and knows its meaning.

2. *Phonics.* Five to 10 minutes of work with letters and their sounds. Say the name with its common sound and give at least one word that begins with that letter sound. (To review the sounds unique in English refer to Chapters 5 and 6.) Keep a record of the letters and sounds the tutee has mastered and those he is still developing.

3. *Building vocabulary.* Using alphabet books, colors and shapes, and number books, read a page and discuss the picture(s). Some books are bilingual; English and Spanish bilingual books are the most common. (See Appendices A.8 and A.9 for a short list of English–Spanish bilingual books.) Reread the page and have the tutee echo read. Next, read the page in unison. Then invite the tutee to read the page, assisting if necessary. Depending on the tutee's age, create flash cards with the words featured in the concept book. This helps him recognize words without picture clues.

4. *Sentences.* Write a short sentence featuring a vocabulary word on a sentence strip. Then (1) read the sentence to the tutee, (2) echo read with her, (3) read in unison, (4) have her read it by herself, and finally, (5) cut the sentence strip into words and have her put the pieces back in order as she reads it to you.

5. *Writing.* The tutee should write at every session. Emergent readers may write letters. When possible the tutee should dictate a sentence to the tutor. Share the pen and compose the sentence together by inviting her to write the letters and/or words she knows.

6. *Reading to the tutee.* The tutee needs to hear fluent reading. Choose a short picture book on a topic that interests her; read the text and discuss the pictures. Books with repetitive text permit the tutee to join in on repetitive lines. Rebus books for young emergent readers are good because the tutees can read the pictures while they learn directionality and the concept of space between words.

figure 13.4 Sample lesson plan for a first-grade English learner.

LESSON PLAN

TUTOR: Sarah   DATE: 9-15

TUTEE: Bonita   GRADE: 1

Review from previous lesson: Bonita will be able to read the color flash cards with 95% accuracy to help her meet CCSS RF 1.2B.

Phonics: Bonita will identify the letters B, P, H, L, and M, say their sounds, give two words that begin with each of the sounds, and use each of the words correctly in a short sentence to help her meet CCSS RF 1.2C.

Vocabulary building: After echo reading I can!/¡Yo puedo!, Bonita will independently read the book with 90% accuracy to help her meet CCSS RF 1. 3B and 1.3E.

Sentences: Bonita will identify three words from I can!/¡Yo puedo!, dictate three sentences, read the sentences each two times, and correctly put the sentences back together after they are cut apart to help her meet CCSS RF 1.1A.

Writing: Bonita will write a short sentence, using a word from her flash cards. Bonita will write a short sentence expressing her opinion about I can!/¡Yo puedo! to help her meet CCSS W 1.1.

Listening to tutor: Bonita will listen to The Little Red Hen and chime in on the phrases "Not I said the_____" to help her meet CCSS RF 1.4B.

LESSON PLAN	PLANNED ACTIVITY	TIME	REFLECTION
Review:	Color flash cards	5 min.	Bonita has difficulty pronouncing yellow and black.
Phonics:	The B, P, H, L, M cards	8 min.	She correctly identified the letters; struggled with B and P sounds; struggled with putting words into sentences.
Vocabulary:	I can!/¡Yo puedo!	8 min.	Bonita enjoyed the book and echo read it with 95% accuracy.
Sentences:	Sentence strips	8 min.	She started each sentence with I can read/play, laugh.
Writing:	Penmanship paper	5 min.	She wrote: "I lik the ball" with help hearing the sound in like.
Listening:	The Little Red Hen	7 min.	She really studied the pictures to understand the story. She had much expression with "Not I said the ___."

Each session should be relaxed, with the tutees talking a lot so they become accustomed to hearing themselves say English words. The tutors should be encouraging and speak slower than normal so the tutee can hear the space between words. Remember, they are learning language just as an infant learns it. They need to be able to distinguish one word from the next; it is easier for them to process words and their sounds when you speak slowly.

Sample lesson plan

Figure 13.4 on p. 362 offers a sample lesson plan for a first-grade English learner whose native language is Spanish and who is classified as a beginning reader. Appendix D.2 contains a template. The tutee in Figure 13.4 came to the United States in February and attended kindergarten from February through May. Notice the tutor states objectives for each part of the session.

Intervening with the Tutee During Reading

Good tutors always scaffold struggling readers as they tackle materials with challenging new words. Simply giving the word to students does not teach them a strategy, and telling them to "sound it out" may not constitute a clear direction for struggling readers. You can give a number of responses when readers come to unfamiliar words or when they give incorrect responses. Figure 13.5 lists appropriate responses for different circumstances.

Many of the instructional strategies and activities for developing phonemic awareness, word identification, comprehension, and vocabulary mentioned in this book are suitable for use in tutoring sessions. For example, the games found in the Intervention sections of the Phonemic Awareness and Word Recognition chapters are intended to be played by a struggling reader paired with an adult.

It is also helpful to log all the reading strategies a student learns and all the books read to and by him so he can be reminded to use them in new situations. You can also share these logs with classroom teachers so they understand the strategies the tutee has mastered. The classroom teacher then can remind the student of the strategy by asking, "What did you learn to do with your tutor when you come to an unknown word?" Many young students do not automatically transfer information from one setting to another. The log of learned strategies will help connect the tutoring session to the classroom.

Figures 13.6 and 13.7 contain completed log sheets. Blank forms are found in Appendices D.35 and D.36.

---

figure   13.5   Helping tutees tackle challenging words.

When a reader gets stuck on a word, always wait five seconds before intervening!

When readers lose their place or skip words:
- Have them point to each word.

When readers stop because they do not know the word:
- Have them read to the end of the sentence and ask them what would make sense.
- Have them look at the picture for clues.
- Have them read the sentence with what they think the word is and ask if that word makes sense.
- Have them check their first response with the spelling of the written word and ask them if that looks like the written word.
- If their response is incorrect, provide the correct word and ask them to read the sentence with that word to see if it makes sense.
- If there is a part of the word they know (e.g., *am* in *ham*), cover with your finger the part they do not know and ask them to read the part they do. Then ask them to try again.

When readers read words incorrectly:
- Read the sentence to the students as they have just read it and ask them if it makes sense.
- Ask them if their response matches the printed word.
- Help them find familiar elements in the printed word.
- Have them reread the sentence with the new word and ask them if that makes sense.

When readers self-correct:
- Ask them how they knew that the first response was incorrect.
- Ask them how they figured out the correct word.
- Compliment them on using the strategy!

When readers do not pause for periods:
- Read the passage back to the students and ask them if it sounds correct.
- Have them point to periods in the same manner as they point to words.

Source: Adapted from Johnston, F., Invernizzi, M., & Juel, C. (1998). *Book Buddies: Guidelines for Volunteer Tutors of Emergent and Early Readers.* New York: The Guilford Press.

figure 13.6 Log sheet for strategies.

Strategies Taught to: **Marie**   By: **Terri**

DURING EASY READ

Read phrases instead of words.
Slow down.
Raise voice with questions.
Pause for periods.
Change voice with different speakers.

DURING WORD STUDY

Words that rhyme with cat.
Learn the first 20 words of Dolch list.
Words that rhyme with sound.
Words that rhyme with Sam.
Learn 21–40 words of Dolch list.
How to add "ing" to verbs.
How to separate the onset from the rime in word families (looking for small parts within words).
How to segment sounds when writing new words.
Worked with homonyms: hear/here, dear/deer, two/too/to, four/for.

DURING WRITING

Put spaces between words.
Stop for periods.
Begin sentences with capital letters.
Make sure all sentences are complete (they make sense).
Do not connect all ideas with "and."
Capitalize people's names.
Use question marks with questions.

DURING NEW BOOK

How to read to end of sentence when encountering new words.
How to find smaller parts within one-syllable words.
How to use picture clues when encountering unknown words.
How to look at pictures to predict what will happen next.
How to fill in a story map.
How to do a cluster of facts learned in book.

figure 13.7 Log sheet for books.

BOOKS READ DURING TUTORING

Tutor: **Chan**   Tutee: **Jackson**

BOOKS READ BY TUTOR	BOOKS READ BY TUTEE*
The Remarkable Farkle McBride (J. Lithgow) 12–1	Noses (I) 12–1
Too Much Noise (A. McGovern) 12–1	Koalas (I) 12–1
If You Take a Mouse to the Movies (L. Numeroff) 12–2	Nesta (I) 12–2
Shoes from Grandpa (M. Fox) 12–2	Dragonflies (I) 12–2
The Snow Tree (C. Repchuk) 12–3	My Kite (N) 12–3
Snap: Book about Alligators & Crocodiles (M. & G. Berger) 12–4	What's Inside (N) 12–3
Seven Candles for Kwanzaa (M. Pinkney) 12–4	Mr. Wind (N) 12–4
The Most Dangerous Animals (C. C. Miller) 12–4	Thumbprint Critters (N) 12–4

* (I) = Informational; (N) = Narrative

14

Teachers, Caregivers, and the Community Working in Collaboration

Reading takes us away from home, but more important, it finds homes for us everywhere.

HAZEL ROCHMAN

scenario

It is the end of May and Mr. Blackhawk has just completed his first year of teaching second grade. He reflects on the year by compiling two lists—one of triumphs and one of trials. He lists his triumphs first and is pleased with his accomplishments. Then he begins his list of trials. At the top he writes: PARENTS. As an undergraduate he learned that teachers are responsible for working with parents and making them a part of their children's education. He never expected, however, the wide range of parents' personalities and their unpredictable reactions. In general, he has encountered six approaches from parents and caregivers: (1) those who are concerned and want to do everything to aid their child; (2) those who appear not to care in the least about their child's education and seem to not want to be bothered with school; (3) those who refuse to believe that their child has any problem with school; (4) those who cannot help their child because of a language barrier but do care about their child's progress; (5) those who are new to the United States and do not understand its educational system; and (6) those who seem to blame him for everything—these parents are frequently at the school interrupting his class.

figure 14.1

Mr. Blackhawk's model letter about his week at school.

August 27, 2015

Dear Pam,

I have had a great week at school this week. I learned many different things from my students. Alex, who spent six weeks this past summer in India visiting his grandparents, told me about the different types of food he ate. I learned that Emma is a ballerina and is going to be in the Nutcracker Suite this December. Eric knows so much about fixing dirt bikes because his dad races them. Ava told me that her family grew a fifteen-pound watermelon this summer and won the prize at the County Fair.

I made one big mistake. I forgot on Wednesday that I had recess duty so Ms. Prince, the principal, had to come get me from my room. I felt bad. She made me have bus duty that day because I forgot. I hope I never forget again.

Love,

George

P.S. My students were surprised that I have a first name!

Mr. Blackhawk decides his top priority for the summer is to research professional journals and books on working with and understanding parents. As he thumbs through some of his back issues of *The Reading Teacher,* he finds many schools and teachers have made it their priority to involve parents by giving them a simple yet effective routine for reading with their child each evening. He particularly likes Newman and Bizarri's (2012) idea of taking 30 minutes on Friday for students to write letters home to their parents, explaining what they learned and did and describing their behavior in school that week. This engages students in a fun way, and the idea might be new to parents. He suspects most parents are like anyone else—they like new ideas. He also likes that it will not take much time each week.

During the open house the first week of school, he explains to the parents what he is going to do. He asks them to let the child read the letter to them or for them to read it to the child. They are asked to sign the letter and send it back to school on Monday. He promises the parents that he will have the students add each returned, signed letter to their Friday Letter Portfolio so at the end of the year each child will have their portfolio to take home.

On the first Friday after the open house, he explains the letter format to his students and models writing a letter to his wife about his week at school and what he learned from his students (see Figure 14.1).

He decides to use the letter writing activity as an action research project. During the first weeks of school, he will obtain a benchmark of each student's spelling and their writing fluency (how many sentences they write). He will record his students' growth throughout the year.

As you are reading the chapter, consider the following questions:

1. What other information could Mr. Blackhawk include in his letter?

2. Would it be wise for Mr. Blackhawk to require the parents to write a response letter each Monday? Why or why not?

3. What other activities could Mr. Blackhawk initiate to encourage parent engagement?

introduction

Parental involvement is an important ingredient in children's education (Mui & Anderson, 2008; Oakley & Jay, 2010; Rowe & Fain, 2013). Initiatives at the local and national levels have aimed to promote parental involvement. The Goals 2000: Educate America Act states: "Every school will promote partnerships that will increase parental involvement and participation in promoting social, emotional, and academic growth of children." The National PTA has developed national standards for parental involvement programs, which charge both the school and parents with specific responsibilities. The school is responsible for (1) scheduling regular communication between home and school, (2) supporting parenting skills, and (3) involving parents in major decisions. The parents are responsible for (1) assisting in their child's learning, (2) volunteering at school, and (3) collaborating with the community to provide resources to the schools. Many local districts have also initiated school literacy programs. These programs challenge students to read books at home and to have their caregivers document it. The purpose is not only to have students read at home, but also to make literacy a family affair.

Parental involvement encompasses two basic categories: involvement at school and involvement at home. The involvement at school includes activities such as attending scheduled family–teacher conferences, attending PTA or PTO meetings, holding positions on local school boards, being part of decision-making committees, chaperoning class field trips, and volunteering on a regular basis in the classroom, on the playground, or in the library. Involvement at home includes such activities as providing breakfast for one's children, monitoring their homework, reading and writing with them, and making sure they get the proper amount of rest. Studies have shown that parental involvement at home impacts students' learning more than parental engagement at school (Southwest Educational Development Laboratory [SEDL], 2006; Michigan Department of Education, 2002). However, both affect students' grades, test scores, and attitudes (Sheldon, 2002).

This chapter focuses on (1) the importance of teachers understanding their students' home lives and any cultural differences between home and school; (2) the benefits of parental involvement; (3) attributes of engaged parents; (4) how to communicate with parents; (5) initiating parental involvement that makes a difference; (6) working with difficult parents; (7) working with community volunteers; and (8) parental involvement and technology. Remember that not all students in your classroom live with their biological parents. Instead of using the word *parent* in communications, use *caregivers*. References to parents in this chapter also refer to caregivers.

THE IMPORTANCE OF UNDERSTANDING STUDENTS' HOME LIVES

Teachers must understand their students' home lives. Many teachers work in cultural environments that differ from their own backgrounds (Hanel, Shaw, & Taylor, 2013; Mui & Anderson, 2008; Mol, Bus, DeJong, & Smeets, 2008). Different cultures sometimes emphasize different value systems and ways of communicating.

Consider that:

- Some families value cooperation. Students from such families may readily share answers with someone who does not know them.

- Some parents instruct children to lower their eyes when they are being reprimanded. These students may avoid eye contact when reprimanded.

- Some parents will never ask a child a question if they already know the answer. These students may not respond to questions if they think the teacher knows the answer.

- In some cultures children bring disgrace to the family if they complete a task incorrectly. These students may not respond in class or hand in work unless they know the answers are correct.

- In some families men expect women to defer to them. Students from these families may not accept instruction from a woman.

- In some families, reading at home does not encompass fiction and nonfiction books; it consists mostly of authentic reading, such as reading recipes, newspapers, and so on.

Be careful not to make assumptions about a student based on his neighborhood. Often teachers work in communities where the average socioeconomic status differs from their own. Consider the following situations:

- Not all poor students who live in urban areas come from homes affected by crime and drugs.
- Not all middle-class students who live in the suburbs come from homes that are free from crime and drugs.
- Some parents work long hours and have little time to spend with their children.
- Some parents work two or three jobs to keep food on the table. They may have little energy to read and write with their child when they are home.
- Some students may live with two dads or two moms.
- Some impoverished families move frequently due to circumstances beyond their control. These students may attend two or three different schools a year.
- Some children live in ethnically blended families.
- Some children live with a grandparent or another relative, or in a foster home.
- Some children live in homes where domestic employees do everything for them. They may lack practical skills.
- Some children, regardless of their class or neighborhood, live with abusive parents.
- Some children are neglected for long periods of time.
- Some parents overemphasize the importance of being popular or thin.
- Some parents who do not speak English strongly desire their children to succeed.
- Some parents will not recognize that their child has difficulty learning.

Teachers must consider all of these situations and many others when thinking about parental involvement.

Because a positive home–school connection results in higher student performance, you may want to follow these effective principles (Risko & Walker-Dalhouse, 2009).

1. Learn as much as possible about the student, his family, and the community.
2. Warmly greet parents at open houses, parent–teacher conferences, or on the street.
3. Share a student's success with her parents.
4. Ask parents what they observe about their child's literacy skills.
5. If there is a language barrier, try to find someone in the school or community to assist during conferences and to write notes home in the parents'

native language. Online resources may also be useful for this.
6. Attend community events so parents see teachers as people interested in their community.
7. Invite parents to sessions that demonstrate how parents can help their child at home, but remember that for some families such sessions will not result in a positive effect (Mol, Bus, DeJong, & Smeets, 2008).
8. Work with community groups that offer free tutoring to students in the neighborhood. Teach tutors some basic strategies, such as creating story maps or graphic organizers for informational text.
9. Research available health and social services in the community and link the agencies with the families who need them.
10. Provide parent networks to help new families who have moved into the school district.

BENEFITS OF PARENTAL INVOLVEMENT

Students benefit in a number of ways—academically, physically, socially, and emotionally—if their parents or caregivers are actively involved in their education. Studies indicate that students who are successful academically have parents who are involved in their schooling (Centers for Disease Control and Prevention, 2013; Doyle & Zhang, 2011; Hanel, Shaw, & Taylor, 2013; Newman & Bizarri, 2012). This is true of students from across the socioeconomic spectrum and from both majority and minority groups (Ho, 2002; SEDL, 2006). Their improved academic success is reflected in their daily grades and test scores. Students whose parents value learning and monitor homework also have a more positive attitude toward learning. Students whose parents discuss school with them also earn higher grades (SEDL, 2006).

Students who have academically involved parents also enjoy better physical well-being (Centers for Disease Control and Prevention, 2013). Involved parents make sure their child eats well-balanced meals; they discourage sugary snacks and provide regular meals. Involved parents who qualify for free or reduced-cost breakfast at school make sure the child is at school in time to eat it. Involved parents make sure their child gets plenty of rest. They also understand the importance of regular physical exercise; they play outside with their children and engage in sports and recreation together. Involved parents monitor the number of hours their child sits in front of the computer and the television. They are aware of the websites the child visits, the video games he plays, and the shows he watches. They often watch and discuss shows together.

Students with involved parents are socially well-adjusted (Centers for Disease Control and Prevention, 2013), because the parents model the importance of social interaction when they are involved with PTA or PTO, school-wide projects, or class field trips. Through their parents' involvement, students learn the value of contributing to society by helping others.

Students also benefit emotionally when their parents are involved in school (SEDL, 2006). When there is communication between the school and parent, the student knows that two sets of people are caring for her. Parents and teachers who have common goals for a child prevent conflict between home and school expectations. Children benefit from that stability.

Parental involvement not only improves students' performance, but it also improves parents' perception of school effectiveness (Jensen, 2006; Newman & Bizarri, 2012) and gives them ownership in the school's process. Parents involved in a school project take pride in their work. If the project is not as successful as expected, they understand it was more important to be involved than to meet their goal.

ENGAGED PARENTS

P arents become engaged when they believe that (1) they can affect/help their child's education, (2) they are important in their child's development, and (3) the school wants their help, and also when they feel comfortable helping at school (Jensen, 2006; Rasinski & Padak, 2008). Which parents are most involved in their children's school? Statistically, they are more likely to be white middle-class families (SEDL, 2006); other characteristics include parents with higher education and higher incomes, families with two parents, and parents who have ties with other parents from their child's school (Ho, 2002; Sheldon, 2002). However, demographics alone do not explain why parents become involved. Parents are inclined to become involved at school when they feel welcomed and needed by teachers and administrators (Centers for Disease Control and Prevention, 2013).

Which parents are involved in children's education at home? Race does not appear to be a factor for parental involvement at home. Parents who have ties with other adults—such as nearby relatives, parents from school, or close friends—are more involved than parents who are isolated. Urban parents have lower involvement at home than do rural or suburban parents (Sheldon, 2002). Sheldon found that when parents are connected to at least one or two parents from the same school, they become more involved in their children's education at school and at home. The social interactions give parents the opportunity to discuss mutual concerns and offer advice. Teachers and administrators must work at forming connections between parents and understanding parents' needs.

WAYS TO COMMUNICATE WITH PARENTS

T eachers should make parents feel connected to the school and understand that their involvement greatly influences their children's learning (Jensen, 2006; Kindervater, 2010; Morrow, Kuhn, & Schwanenflugel, 2006; Rasinski & Padak, 2008; White & Kim, 2008). This communication can be fostered in a number of ways—introductory letters, newsletters, flyers, memos, door hangers, progress reports, monthly calendar events, bulletin boards, parents' nooks, good news calls or emails, happy grams, portfolios with personal notes, greeting parents in the morning or after school, and family–teacher conferences (Centers for Disease Control and Prevention, 2013; Risko & Walker-Dalhouse, 2009). Schools should welcome comments and suggestions and communicate with parents not only about academics, but also health issues. Many families do not recognize that children need regular sleep routines and healthy snacks (Centers for Disease Control and Prevention, 2013).

Introductory Letters

Introductory letters from new or first-year teachers are very important to parents whether they are mailed, emailed, or sent home with students. Parents are often wary of a first-year teacher who is new to the community or building. Introductory letters give parents a brief description of a teacher's past experiences and hobbies. Sharing this information makes the teacher sound both professional and human. The letter should also include a brief description of the educational goals for the class, any school-wide initiatives for the year, a description of any new national or state standards, and a brief statement of his or her teaching philosophy. The letter can also include a list of materials that would be useful for the class throughout the year, such as empty plastic containers, old appliances for students to disassemble, materials for science experiences, or old magazines. The letter should also include important lists of materials the students are required to have for class, a telephone number and e-mail address with the best times to contact the teacher, and reminders about upcoming events. The letter should conclude with an invitation for parents to become involved at school and name some specific opportunities, such as reading and playing literacy games with the students or writing the classroom's newsletter. Figure 14.2 presents a sample letter of introduction from a fourth-grade teacher.

figure 14.2 Sample letter of introduction.

Subject: Littletown Elementary Open House!

Signature: ACAS

Dear Parents and Caregivers:

I am excited to be a new member of this community and to become a partner in your child's learning! This summer I moved to Littletown from Chicago, where I also taught fourth grade. I already have enjoyed Littletown's new library and the Children's Summer Theater program. Besides reading and going to plays, I love to take long walks and bike rides.

You may be familiar with the federal legislation that focuses on every child being ready for college and career. That is my goal, too. I love to read and want all of my students to enjoy reading materials that interest them. In order to ensure that every student at Littletown Elementary succeeds in this goal, we are embracing a new reading program this year called Soaring High with Reading. The school's goal is to have each child read at least 100 pages each week at home. Our school is encouraging parents and caregivers to listen to their child read when possible and to discuss the material with them. At Open House I will further explain this new program and answer any questions you may have.

Littletown Elementary's Open House is Tuesday, September 18, at 7 p.m. I am eager to meet each one of you and to personally encourage you to become involved at school if you can. At Open House I will have sign-up sheets for different activities—reading with students, playing word games with students, binding their books, organizing our classroom library, recording our "Soaring High with Reading" pages, and many other activities—if you are able to volunteer.

Meanwhile, please save your plastic containers, old scraps of fabric, and any broken small appliances. Our class will be needing all these materials for art and science projects.

I am looking forward to meeting you at Open House on September 18. If you are unable to come to the Open House, I would still enjoy "meeting" you by phone if you would let me know a convenient number and time to call or by email if you respond to this note. In the meantime, if you need to talk with me, you can e-mail me at bwagner@littletownschools.edu or call me at school between 8:00 and 8:20 any weekday morning.

Sincerely,
Beth Wagner

Introductory Parent–Teacher Conference

An informal introductory parent–teacher conference at the beginning of the school year is another way teachers can begin collaborating with parents. The conference is typically at school though in rare cases it may be held at the student's home. If the meeting takes place at the home, arrange for another professional to accompany you. The purpose of this conference is for you to listen to the parents and student to begin building rapport; it is an opportunity to find what the parents want to share. Find out about what the family's interests or hobbies are and what the student enjoys doing on the weekends. During conferences later in the semester, such a discussion is often not possible due to the educational matters that need to be discussed. The initial conference builds a relationship between the teacher and the parents that centers on the student and not the curriculum; it allows you to communicate a genuine interest in the

student. Later, the relationship solidifies as the teacher and parents discuss the child's academics, behavior, and social interactions in detail. The rapport established in the early conference may make any subsequent issues that arise easier to resolve.

Newsletters

Communication with parents via newsletters is often one-way—from school to home. Teachers share topics being studied in math, science, social studies, and what stories they are reading. They may describe reading and writing strategies, mention an author study, and introduce any technology the students are learning to use.

Jensen (2006) suggests teachers create newsletters that invite parents to initiate some home activities with the child, such as looking up information on particular websites or viewing certain educational television programs. Or, when the class is learning how to create timelines, use the newsletter to ask parents to assist their child in designing a timeline of the child's life highlighting events from birth to the present day. One website to share with parents when creating timelines is www.readwritethink.org/parent-afterschool-resources/activities-projects/creating-family-timelines-30287.html. If the class is studying various jobs in the community, use the newsletter to invite parents to talk about their job(s) with their child so he can tell the class about it.

When newsletters encourage parents' involvement, they feel like they are supporting their child's learning. They feel connected to the school and are much more positive about it. Students are more successful and happier when they know that teachers and parents are communicating (SEDL, 2006).

Jensen (2006) suggests the following guidelines for creating newsletters:

1. The tone of the newsletter should be warm and inviting; avoid educational jargon.

2. Use a format that is simple in design and easy to read, including bold or italic print and color for headlines.

3. Include students' work, with the permission of the parents or caregivers.

4. Always suggest websites, books, or projects that the parents can share with their child.

5. Include the topics being studied in each subject area and any new activity or project the students are doing.

6. Include a feedback section, in which parents can tear off a section or click on an email address to provide comments, ask questions, or express concerns.

7. Remember the parents whose first language is not English. Seek help translating some version of the newsletter if possible; students who speak the language may be able to assist you. Online translation websites may help, also, but beware: they tend to work best for single words or phrases.

Bulletin Boards

A bulletin board with notices of upcoming school events, field trips, fundraisers, assemblies, performances, meetings, and school pictures should be placed where parents see it when they enter the building. Important school policies, such as what happens during a tornado warning, a snowstorm, or a lockdown should also be posted on the board. Upcoming community events can also be posted. The bulletin board should be colorful and neat. Old notices should be removed and personal advertising prohibited. An online bulletin board can serve the same purpose.

Parents' Nook

A parents' nook is a special corner of the school that has books, magazines, and pamphlets that parents may borrow. The nook should include a checkout list so parents can sign out the materials. Two suggested books are Jim Trelease's *The Read-Aloud Handbook* (2013) and Margaret Read MacDonald's *The Parent's Guide to Storytelling: How to Make Up New Stories and Retell Old Favorites* (2005). The school librarian can post an annotated bibliography of new books in the school library or a recommended reading list for each grade level. The nook can also serve as the school's lost and found area and as a place for parents to exchange games, toys, or books.

Telephone Calls or Emails

Teachers usually contact parents when there is a problem with their child. However, teachers often fail to contact parents with a good report. It may be about a task with which the student struggled but now has mastered, or about a kind deed the child did for another student. All parents enjoy hearing about the positive actions and accomplishments of their child.

Happy Grams

Try communicating good behavior to parents through happy grams. Happy grams include words of praise, comments about kind acts, and reports of accomplishments. Happy grams must be honest and genuine. Parents appreciate hearing good news, and students are sure to give these notes to parents. You can design your own happy gram or use the template in Figure 14.3. Happy grams can be photocopied on bright yellow card stock paper or sent via email.

figure **14.3**

Sample happy gram.

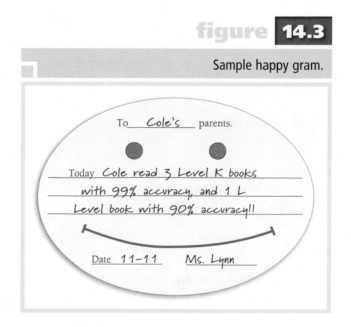

To Cole's parents.

Today Cole read 3 Level K books with 99% accuracy, and 1 L Level book with 90% accuracy!!

Date 11-11   Ms. Lynn

Weekly Student Letter to Caregivers

In the opening scenario, Mr. Blackhawk gave students 30 minutes each Friday for students to share with parents what they learned or did during the week. Recall that Mr. Blackhawk included the fact that he forgot an important duty—playground duty—and that students can likewise be honest about their shortcomings or things they do not like. Newman and Bizarri (2012) found that parents loved these letters and enjoyed watching their child's writing improve throughout the year. Collecting each signed letter and putting them in a personal letter portfolio gives each family a keepsake of the child for that particular grade. Newman and Bizarri (2012) discovered that many parents not only signed the letters, but also wrote notes back to the teacher.

Portfolios with Personal Notes

Weekly portfolios with personal notes attached to each student's work are another means of communicating with parents. The portfolio can include graded work from all the subject areas. The notes can give tips on how parents can help children practice a skill that still needs to be mastered or encourage their children to explain a concept they have learned. These handwritten notes make parents a part of their children's education; some teachers include a form that parents must sign, indicating that they have read the note. A sample of a return form is presented in Figure 14.4.

Daily Welcome

Parents appreciate seeing friendly faces at the school door when they drop their child off at school or pick her up in the afternoon. Just a brief, "How are you? Have a great day!" gives parents the assurance that their child is in caring hands. Teachers should take turns greeting those who ride the school bus as they arrive for the day. This greeting should be more than a duty; it should be a time to make children feel welcome. Parents appreciate knowing that their child is arriving in a friendly, caring atmosphere.

Family–Teacher Conference

Family–teacher conferences are important opportunities for teachers, parents, and students to exchange information about the student's education. When preparing for the conference, consider the following:

1. Schedule a time that is good for parents. Many working parents cannot come during the school day. Ask them for times and days when they will be available. Parents who have a number of children in the same building appreciate scheduling siblings' conferences around the same time.

2. Find out if the parents are able to read and/or speak English. It is important that teachers communicate clearly with these parents about the time and place of the conference. You may need to schedule an interpreter for the conference.

figure 14.4 Sample portfolio return form.

DATE: _____

DEAR _____

Thanks for reviewing and discussing the enclosed papers with your child. I am interested in your comments and questions. Please sign the form and give it to your child to return on Monday.
        Thanks again for letting me share in your child's education!

Sincerely,

- -

I reviewed and discussed _____ (child's name) work that you placed in the portfolio.

_____ I have no comments or questions.

_____ I have these comments, questions, or concerns:

SIGNATURE: _____

3. Be aware of who is coming to the conference. Not all children live with their biological parents. Children may live in a foster home, with grandparents, or with another relative. Also, be sensitive if there has been a recent death in the family, a divorce, or another difficult event.

4. Be sensitive regarding parents who live in poverty. They may not have transportation to the school and may not have a working telephone. Do not pressure the caregivers so they feel guilty or hostile. Be creative in letting these caregivers know they are an important part of the student's education.

5. Prepare for the conference by gathering samples of children's reading, writing, and other work. It is a good practice for you to record a student's reading. The parents can listen to the recording during the conference, and they can discuss the student's strengths and weaknesses.

6. Involve students. Have students help select the work they want their parents to view. Discussing concerns about children when they are present reassures them that both parents and the teacher care about their progress.

7. Arrange a clean, comfortable place for the conference. Do not sit behind your desk! The desk becomes a wall between the parents and the teacher. Also remember that student desks are not comfortable for most adults. A round table with adult-size chairs is the best setting. The room should be clean with no extra clutter.

8. Use a timer if you have conferences that run back-to-back. For example, set your cell phone to vibrate five minutes before the conference ending time. It is impolite to keep the next set of parents waiting.

9. Begin on a positive note. All parents like to hear something positive about their child. This is also a time when you can help negative parents understand that their child can do things well.

10. Have goals. Know what you want to accomplish during each conference. A few written notes can keep the conversation on track.

11. Listen to parents' concerns and questions. Parents may also have goals for the conference. It is important that you understand how parents perceive their children.

12. Don't become defensive when parents question your instructional approach or classroom policies. Many parents think they know what should be done in the classroom and disagree with how a teacher conducts her class. Give the parents plenty of time to air their concerns. If appropriate, tell them that you will consider their criticisms and suggestions.

13. Never talk about another student. Often highly competitive parents want to compare their child to classmates. Avoid mentioning the other students. Some parents may also complain about other students. Listen to what they say and reassure them that you will give their child a safe and effective learning environment.

14. Do not use jargon. The purpose of the conference is to inform the parents about their child's progress, not impress them with your knowledge.

15. End the conference with specific goals. The goals should be attainable for the child and should be goals that the parents can help the child attain. Always thank parents for coming. It is important that parents go away with valuable information and a positive feeling about the child's classroom.

Communicating with parents is an important way to get and keep them interested and involved in their children's education.

Family Literacy Programs

Studies indicate that family literacy programs have positive results on children's literacy growth (Doyle, 2009; Doyle & Zhang, 2011; Rowe & Fain, 2013; National Early Literacy Panel, 2008). Doyle and Zhang's (2011) study included two types of programs; one program included parents and their child, and the other program was for only parents. Both programs were free to the parents, including transportation and childcare. In this study, all caregivers were the parents of the children; no other guardians were involved.

In the parent-only model, the components of each session were:

1. Review of the previously shared activity and discussion among parents of their successes and struggles with the activity.
2. Introduction of a new topic.
3. Specific instructions of another activity to use at home with children.

In the parent–child model, each session included:

1. The instructor engaged the caregivers and child in a read aloud story.
2. A breakout session in which the parents learned a new activity while the child went to another room to engage in the activity that the parents were learning in the first room.
3. The parents and children came back together and engaged in the activity that the parents just learned.

Doyle and Zhang (2011) found that the program that included both the parents and child was particularly successful because parents were excited to see "the direct educational and social experiences it afforded their children" (p. 225). Parents also appreciated the free books and materials they received for use at home.

Schools that want to try this type of family literacy program should survey parents to see what times will work best for them.

PARENTAL INVOLVEMENT THAT MAKES A DIFFERENCE

When parents ask you what they can do at home to help their children, here are some specific activities you may suggest.

General Suggestions to Share with Parents

First, effective parental involvement includes a distinct style of interacting with the child. Parents need to ask about their child's day: "What did you learn?" "Did you have any problems in your subjects?" "What fun things did you do with your friends?" and "Did you have any trouble with your classmates?" Parents need to listen attentively and provide encouragement. Second, parents should provide an emotionally supportive home environment. Children need to feel safe discussing anything without fear that their parents will become angry or stop listening. Third, parents need to provide reassurance when children encounter failure. When their children are having a difficult time with reading, writing, or spelling in school, parents should encourage them to practice without resorting to pressure or ridicule. The parents' primary duty when it comes to education is helping their children understand that practice is necessary to become skillful in any task.

Boers (2002) collected a list of traits that teachers find desirable in parents. Good parents:

1. Initiate communication about their child's learning style, personality, family arrangements, extracurricular activities, and perceived school problems.
2. Monitor homework at home.
3. Create a time and place for homework and work with their child's basic reading and writing skills.
4. Demonstrate the value of learning by allowing time for homework.
5. Get involved by coming to family–teacher conferences, open houses, and other school activities.
6. Discuss school matters with their child at home.
7. Teach respect, courtesy, patience, and clean language—traits that carry over into the classroom.
8. Do not cover for their child.
9. Encourage and respect teachers.
10. Emphasize reading. They read with their child and to their child, and model reading for their child.

11. Respond to notes promptly.
12. Monitor their child's eating and sleeping habits and make sure the child comes to school clean.

Administrators can tactfully list such "Good Parenting Tips" in a newsletter that is sent home to all parents at the beginning of the year. Parents need to understand that when they perform these acts at home, they exert a positive impact on their child's education.

Suggestions for Establishing a Home–School Literacy Connection

Many parents appreciate specific advice on how to help their child become a successful reader. The following strategies have a proven track record based on studies by reading specialists, researchers, and teachers.

Reading together

Rasinski and Padak (2003, 2007) provide the following basic guidelines for teachers to facilitate parents reading with children at home or having the children read to the parent.

1. Limit the time to 10–20 minutes; remember that parents are tired and very busy.
2. Give parents options, such as reading to the child, reading with the child, or listening to the child read.
3. Provide the texts or booklists.
4. Teach parents how to select books at the child's reading level. If a child comes across more than five words on one page that he/she cannot read, the text is too hard for independent reading.
5. Encourage all types of reading.
6. Send home audio versions of the books if parents are learning English, and when possible provide a translation of the text in their native language.
7. Share one or two new strategies with parents so they stay motivated.

Recommend that parents do the following during a reading session:

1. Read a passage to the child (or they both listen to an audio version) and then discuss the story.
2. Read the passage in unison with the child, or have the child read along with the audio version.
3. Listen as the child reads the passage.
4. Choose words from the passage and write them on index cards; have the child do the same.
5. Use these cards to play different word games such as concentration or word sorts. Words can be sorted according to syllables, word patterns, or by root words.

6. Send books home with students in a plastic or canvas bag if parents have few books at home and little or no access to the public library. For parents who do not read English, you can include a portable CD/DVD or MP3 player with audiobooks and a translation of the text in their native language.

It is important that parents and children read together at home; however, they do not need to limit themselves to stories (Rasinski & Padak, 2008). Here are suggestions for how parents and children can interact with a variety of materials:

1. Read environmental print on billboards, specials in fast-food restaurants, labels on food items, and newspaper ads.
2. Read and write lists, such as recipes and birthday wish lists.
3. Read rhymes and poems and write their own version or a parody of one.
4. Sing songs and read the lyrics together.
5. Read parts of the newspaper (traditional text or online) or websites together, such as the sports section, comics, the entertainment section/movie reviews, and ads from grocery stores. Play word games found in newspapers, in magazines, or online.
6. Read mail together, including bills, so children learn how to read the amount due and the date that it is due.
7. Read from religious texts.
8. Read from songbooks or hymn books.

Kindervater (2010) conducted a study to see if using poetry, chants, and songs would strengthen the home–school connection with kindergarten students. The home–school activity described in the study included the following steps:

1. Display a poem, song, or chant on a whiteboard or large poster so the class can read it a couple of times throughout the day.
2. Point to each word as you read it chorally with the class. This helps students learn directionality of reading and also learn to identify words.
3. Use kinesthetic motions that correspond to particular sounds of the consonants (Padak & Rasinski, 2008). For example, for the /t/ sound, the students put their index finger on their thumb, as they would to indicate the "OK" gesture. When they hear the initial /t/ sound they quickly press their index finger to the thumb a couple of times and end with the index finger released from the thumb. Other consonant movements are explained in *Fast Start: Getting Ready to Read* (Padak & Rasinski, 2008).

4. After reading the poem using the kinesthetic motions, have each student take a copy of the poem home, read it with her parents, and teach them the motions. Parents are encouraged to listen to their child read the poem, read the poem in unison, or do alternate readings in which the parent reads one line and the child reads the next.

Kindervater (2010) reported that 81 percent of the kindergarten students who completed this activity with parents scored very well at the end of the year on their tests. Kindervater also reported that the parents really got involved and were excited to learn the new motions. Many reported that they would look for words in the environment and would say the word and do the motions; they found it a fun way to get their child excited about print.

Imperato (2009), a reading specialist, also used poetry to connect parents to the school. She suggested that teachers introduce a poem to students on Monday, then send a copy home in an envelope with directions glued on the front and a parent-activity sheet glued on the back. On the activity sheet, parents record what activity they did with their child that evening and the amount of time they spent on the activity. The routine took about 10 to 15 minutes each evening. Imperato (2009) gave parents the following general directions:

1. Sit side by side with your child so you can both see the text.
2. Read the poem two to four times to your child while pointing to each word.
3. Read the poem in unison with your child two to four times, again pointing to the words.
4. Have your child read the poem two to four times to you as he or she points to each word.
5. Engage in a phonemic awareness or phonics activity. If the poem uses the rime /at/, you and your child can find all the words in the poem that follow that pattern and then think of other words that come from that word family. If the poem has alliteration of the /s/, you can find all the /s/ words and then think of other words that begin with the /s/ sound.

Imperato (2009) found this activity brought good results in the first half year that the school implemented the routine with kindergarten students. In January, 66 percent of the students were nonreaders, while at the end of the year only 19 percent were nonreaders.

Summer reading programs

White and Kim (2008) were interested in connecting school to home by involving parents in their child's independent reading during the summer. They believed that when students read for enjoyment, their reading skills, such as word recognition, fluency, vocabulary, world knowledge, and comprehension, all improve. They also knew that maintaining students' motivation to read relied on providing them with books at their easy and independent reading levels. White and Kim's (2008) summer program matched students with books at their reading level. Before the students left for summer break, they were taught some basic comprehension strategies to help them as they read independently. Parents were also taught how to listen, give positive feedback to their children regarding fluency, and ask their child to retell the story. At the end of the summer the students involved in the program (in grades 3 through 5) had 1.3 additional months of school learning and their total reading scores on the Iowa Test of Basic Skills were higher than for students who were not involved in the program.

Students and parents recorded information on a postcard about each book the student. A copy of the postcard that White and Kim used is in Appendix D.37.

Word study

Teachers can encourage word study by making word puzzles, sending them home, and having the parents complete them with their children. Other game-like activities are listed in Chapter 4 (Phonemic Awareness), Chapter 6 (Word Recognition), and Chapter 7 (Vocabulary Building). After you have introduced these activities to students, send examples home so they can play them with their parents. Children have the satisfaction of teaching their parents a new game! All of these activities reinforce literacy skills.

WORKING WITH CHALLENGING PARENTS

Teachers would be living in utopia if all parents were involved in their child's education and fully supported their schools. However, three types of parental approaches pose challenges for both beginning and seasoned teachers. They are (1) parents who do not seem to value education; (2) parents who seem highly critical of everything the teacher does; and (3) parents who seem not to accept that their child is struggling in reading or writing. The first group of parents appears to avoid responsibility for any aspect of their children's education. They may not seem to care if their child learns to read and write or if their child is in school at all. The parents in the second group may frequently show up at school demanding the teacher's attention. They may appear without warning at inappropriate times, such as in the middle of class instruction. In their eyes the teacher is almost always at fault, and they frequently blame the teacher for their child's poor progress. Parents in the third group are often highly educated and have high expectations for their child. They may not accept that their child has a difficult time

with something as basic as reading and writing. All three groups of parents present different challenges.

Each of these parents is worthy of the teacher's respect. A teacher needs to remember the child when dealing with these parents, because every child deserves a fair education.

Parents Who Do Not Seem to Value Education

For students with this type of parent, provide as much extra help as possible in school because they are unlikely to receive any help at home. Pairing these students with an older, caring adult (either a retiree or a university student) or with a buddy from a middle school may help them see the importance of learning to read and write. Send home happy grams as often as possible so the parents come to see education in a more positive light. If the class presents puppet shows or readers theater for parents, encourage them to come see their child perform. Call or email these parents to schedule family–teacher conferences, encouraging them to come in and see the good work their child has completed. These parents need help changing their attitude about education; a positive teacher doing positive work may be just what they need.

Parents Who Seem Highly Critical

These parents present a totally different problem; they are negative and may attempt to control the teacher and the class. Giannetti and Sagarese (1998) present suggestions on how to transform these potential adversaries into educational partners:

1. Roll out the welcome mat when it is appropriate. When these parents come at inappropriate times, get out your calendar and ask them to schedule a time when you can give them your full attention.
2. Let them know you are an expert at what you do.
3. Show these parents a positive portrait of their children. Let them know that you too think their child has potential, but be honest!
4. Convey long-term goals you know you share with the parents. Plan with the parents some short-term goals that will help the child attain the long-term goals.
5. Reassure the parents that their child is in a physically and emotionally safe environment.
6. Be consistent.
7. Do not at any time make negative comments about other students. They will think you say negative things about their child to other parents.
8. Listen! Listen! Listen! They will eventually run out of steam!

9. Do not turn any conversation into a shouting match!

10. Ask the parents what they suggest you do with "the situation."

Parents Who Seem Not to Accept Their Child's Academic Difficulties

These parents frequently care a great deal for their child, involve him in many extracurricular activities, and set high goals for him. Use some of the same tactics here that you use with the aggressive parent:

1. Share with them the things that the child does well. Be positive about the child. Let them know that you too think their child has potential.

2. Be friendly, warm, consistent, and honest.

3. Never compare their child to another student in the class.

4. Never talk about another student.

5. Share honestly the concepts and skills with which their child struggles. Have examples of the child's work on hand to illustrate your points. Your goal is to help them understand what skills are difficult for their child. Convey that your goals are the same: the child's academic success.

6. Let them know that with extra help from them and in class, the child will succeed.

7. Set long-term goals together.

8. Also set short-term goals so they can see progress.

9. Send progress reports home regularly.

Parents are right to expect that their child's teacher cares about their child and provides a safe learning environment in which every student can succeed.

COMMUNITY VOLUNTEERS/TUTORS

Teachers can involve other members of the community besides parents in the classroom. Many volunteers are retired persons or business leaders who understand the importance of reading for success in life. Successful volunteer tutors possess the following fundamental characteristics (Otaiba & Pappamihiel, 2005):

- Meet state and district required background checks.

- Have prior experience reading to children.

- Are competent in the literacy skills they will be teaching (e.g., they understand graphophonic concepts and/or comprehension strategies) and are able to master skills taught during training.

- Have positive attitudes about working with children of many cultures and backgrounds and respect the child's developmental progress.

- Are proficient in English if they are second language learners.

Volunteers who read to students should receive training from a reading specialist about effective reading techniques. First, they need to know how to model fluent, expressive reading so the story comes alive for the listener. Reading specialists train volunteers by demonstrating expressive reading and "echo reading" (in which the tutee repeats the phrase or short sentence the volunteer has just read, using the same rate and intonation). Later the volunteers read to each other so they are comfortable reading with expression. Because students are introduced to new vocabulary words as they listen to stories, volunteers should learn how to prompt tutees to make guesses about the meaning of new words using picture and context clues. For example, when a tutee comes to an unknown word, he should be encouraged to read to the end of the sentence and ask, "Does the picture tell me what the word is? What word makes sense? Does that word sound right? Does it look right?"

Volunteers also need to be trained to encourage tutees to predict what will happen next in a story and how to discuss books without making the discussion seem like a quiz. For example, the following are two strategies that volunteers can use to help tutees make predictions. The first strategy involves discussing the cover illustration. The volunteer asks, "What do you think this book is about?" The tutee makes predictions based on the illustration. In the second strategy the volunteer and tutee preview the book by discussing all the pictures. While they discuss the pictures, the volunteer uses words that are found in the text. For example, while previewing the book *The Koalas,* from the Literacy 2000 Satellite series, the tutee may see a picture and predict that the koala is sleeping. While discussing how the koala is hanging in the tree, the volunteer uses the word *resting,* the word used in the text.

Discussions with tutees should evoke higher-level thinking, so volunteers need to learn the difference between lower-level questions in which the answer is written on the page and higher-level questions that have no simple right or wrong answers. Students then explain their answers to higher-level questions, because sometimes the answers appear to be incorrect until they explain their reasons. Good volunteers also encourage students to ask questions as they read stories. Above all, volunteers are important allies in students' literacy development, but they do not diagnose reading problems or provide instruction. Their main goal is to provide enrichment experiences without emphasizing the diagnostic and intervention aspects of reading events. They accomplish this goal by supporting students as they read and by modeling good fluent reading. Research indicates that reading to students is positively related to their reading success (Doyle & Zhang, 2011; Imperato, 2009; Kindervater, 2010; Mol & Bus, 2011; Oakley & Jay, 2010; Rowe & Fain, 2013).

As volunteers spend time listening to tutees read, they also teach them new words. They encourage tutees to work on expression, fluency, and rate by reading easy books. When a tutee reads a book that is at his or her instructional level, the volunteer and the tutee can read in unison so that the tutee does not struggle with unknown words. If possible, volunteers should record a tutee's reading and then listen to the recording with him or her, pointing out areas of improvement. This procedure permits students to evaluate their own reading. Volunteers provide encouragement and give struggling readers a chance to read without fear of being ridiculed by classmates.

Throughout this text you will find many game-like activities that build reading and writing skills. Volunteers can conduct these activities with tutees to make reading a more enjoyable experience for them. Reading specialists should explain how these activities build literacy skills so the volunteers understand their crucial role in helping a child learn to read.

CAREGIVER INVOLVEMENT AND TECHNOLOGY

Backpack Project with Audiobooks

Studies show that reading at home with children is linked to higher reading achievement (Allington, 2013; Oakley & Jay, 2010; Rowe & Fain, 2013). Other studies, however, have shown that teaching parents how to read and discuss books did not have a positive effect on children from culturally diverse families (Mol, Bus, DeJong, & Smeets, 2008); therefore, Rowe and Fain (2013) were interested in determining if providing families access to audiobooks written in English and their native language would have a positive effect on these parents. Toward that end, Rowe and Fain translated stories into the many different languages spoken in students' homes. Audiobooks with copies of English text and native translation were sent home each week in a backpack. Families were encouraged to listen to the book with the child and either to write a response in their native language or draw a response in a reader response journal. The backpack project did have a positive effect on culturally diverse parents. Some parents of English learners responded that the dual-language books and recordings made it possible for them to discuss books with their child, and that their child enjoyed sharing other books with them as well. Other parents of English learners enjoyed responding to the literature through a shared-drawing with their child, and they appreciated that they could use their native language as they labeled the drawing. They believed that this dual language project showed the teacher respected them and their language.

When providing audiobooks for reading at home, be prepared to respond to parents who think that lis-

tening to an audiobook is not reading. Do not argue with these parents, but instead send home books that are at the student's independent reading level and have the child read it to her parents.

Technology Nights

Most parents understand that computers are essential tools in the 21st century. Schools can share with parents how they use computers in the classroom. One way of doing this is to hold a technology night at the school. Students serve as teachers for the evening while the teacher monitors the activities. Each student can demonstrate for his parents how he uses the word processor for revisions, adds clip art to his story, or creates PowerPoint presentations of his research. For parents who lack computer skills, such a demonstration may be impressive. Those who are computer literate will appreciate that their child is learning to use this important tool.

On technology night, a younger student can demonstrate how she reads along with the computer. Using an interactive book, she can share how the computer helps her pronounce unknown words and provides definitions of words she does not know.

Technology Classes for Parents

Some schools are in neighborhoods where many parents do not have a computer at home. These schools can sponsor a technology class for parents on a Saturday morning or another time when most parents can attend. The instructor must know which computer programs are available to the parents in the public library so they can introduce those programs first. Then parents can go with their child to the library and use the computer together.

Technology in the Home

Teachers who work in communities where most households have computers or tablets may find it helpful to share educational websites with parents. Many children's authors have websites featuring age-appropriate activities for the author's readers, and many allow interested readers to subscribe to their free email newsletters. An activity in Chapter 11 includes a list of authors' websites.

One site that offers free narrative books is www.wegivebooks.com, sponsored by Pearson Foundation and featuring titles published by Penguin Books. After a student reads a Penguin book, the publisher donates a book to one of the organizations listed on this site that the student selects. *National Geographic* magazine offers the following site for informational reading about our social and national world: http://kids.nationalgeographic.com/.

CONCLUDING THOUGHTS

Working with parents can be one of the most challenging pieces of the teaching puzzle. However, students can benefit enormously when parents become involved in their education at school and at home. Parents can be very helpful to teachers by offering ideas and resources. It is important to remember that parents and teachers share a common goal: they want the student to succeed and remain a lifelong learner.

reflective learning

PARENT VOLUNTEERS. Mr. Moore, born and raised in a small Midwestern town, accepted his first teaching job in an large urban middle school with a diverse student population; over 50 languages are spoken in the students' homes. Like any teacher, Mr. Moore wants to make a difference in his students' lives, but the first week of school was difficult. He had trouble understanding the street lingo of his students, and he was shocked at some of their behavior in the hallways. His first inclination was to correct the students, but then he remembered an article he read just before he began his student teaching. The article was "Toward a New Mindfulness: Expectations of Home and Community Literacies" (Hanel, Shaw, & Taylor, 2013), in which the authors discuss how teachers need to recognize their own biases toward different cultures. Mr. Moore did not think he had any biases. When he recalled the article, however, he realized he was full of biases. He realized he was forming judgments about his students' language use and behaviors before he even knew them.

questions

1. What can Mr. Moore do to help him understand his students and their culture?
2. To whom can he go to help him best understand the students?

APPENDIX

Resources

A.1 NCTE/ILA Standards for the Assessment of Reading and Writing   384

A.2 Commercial Informal Reading Inventories   387

A.3 Alphabet Books   387

A.4 Poetry Collections and Mother Goose Books   387

A.5 Wordless Books   388

A.6 Wordless (or Almost Wordless) Picture Books for Content Area Learning   389

A.7 Books with Rhyme, Phonograms, Alliteration, and Other Language Play   389

A.8 Suggested Bilingual English–Spanish Concept Books   390

A.9 Suggested English–Spanish Bilingual Narrative Picture Books   391

A.10 Suggested Multicultural Picture Books   391

A.11 Audio Chapter Books   392

A.12 Software Options That Promote Comprehension and Problem Solving   392

1. The interests of the student are paramount in assessment.

Assessment experiences at all levels, whether formative or summative, have consequences for students (see standard 7). Assessments may alter their educational opportunities, increase or decrease their motivation to learn, elicit positive or negative feelings about themselves and others, and influence their understanding of what it means to be literate, educated, or successful. It is not enough for assessment to serve the well-being of students "on average"; we must aim for assessment to serve, not harm, each and every student.

2. The teacher is the most important agent of assessment.

Most educational assessment takes place in the classroom, as teachers and students interact with one another. Teachers design, assign, observe, collaborate in, and interpret the work of students in their classrooms. They assign meaning to interactions and evaluate the information that they receive and create in these settings. In short, teachers are the primary agents, not passive consumers, of assessment information. It is their ongoing, formative assessments that primarily influence students' learning. This standard acknowledges the critical role of the teacher and the consequences and responsibilities that accompany this role.

3. The primary purpose of assessment is to improve teaching and learning.

Assessment is used in educational settings for a variety of purposes, such as keeping track of learning, diagnosing reading and writing difficulties, determining eligibility for programs, evaluating programs, evaluating teaching, and reporting to others. Underlying all these purposes is a basic concern for improving teaching and learning. In the United States it is common to use testing for accountability, but the ultimate goal remains the improvement of teaching and learning. Similarly, we use assessments to determine eligibility for special education services, but the goal is more appropriate teaching and better learning for particular students. In both cases, if improved teaching and learning do not result, the assessment practices are not valid (see standard 7).

4. Assessment must reflect and allow for critical inquiry into curriculum and instruction.

Sound educational practices start with a curriculum that values complex literacy, instructional practices that nurture it, and assessments that fully reflect it. In order for assessment to allow productive inquiry into curriculum and instruction, it must reflect the complexity of that curriculum as well as the instructional practices in schools. This is particularly important because assessment shapes teaching, learning, and policy. Assessment that reflects an impoverished view of literacy will result in a diminished curriculum and distorted instruction and will not enable productive problem solving or instructional improvement. Because assessment shapes instruction, the higher the stakes of the assessment, the more important it is that it reflect this full complexity.

5. Assessment must recognize and reflect the intellectually and socially complex nature of reading and writing and the important roles of school, home, and society in literacy development.

Literacy is complex, social, and constantly changing. The literacies of students graduating from high school today were barely imaginable when they began their schooling. Outside of school, students live and will go on to work in a media culture with practices unlike those currently occurring in school (even in the setting of the school media center). Students need to acquire competencies with word processors, blogs, wikis, Web browsers, instant messaging, listservs, bulletin boards, virtual worlds, video editors, presentation software, and many other literate tools and practices. Traditional, simple definitions of literacy will not help prepare students for the literate lives of the present—let alone the future. Consequently, reading and writing cannot usefully be assessed as a set of isolated, independent tasks or events. It is critical to gather specific information about materials, tasks, and media being used with students for both instructional and assessment purposes. In addition, we need to assess how practices are used to participate in the broader media culture as well as to examine how the broader culture assigns status to some practices over others (e.g., texting as contrasted to writing paragraph summaries in language arts class).

Whatever the medium, literacy is social and involves negotiations among authors and readers around meanings, purposes, and contexts. Literate practices are now rarely solitary cognitive acts. Furthermore, literate practices differ across social and cultural contexts and across different media. Students' behavior in one setting may not be at all representative of their behavior in another. This may be particularly true of English-language learners who may lack the fluency to express themselves fully inside the classroom but may be lively contributors in their families and communities.

6. Assessment must be fair and equitable.

We live in a multicultural society with laws that promise equal rights to all. Our school communities must work to ensure that all students, as different as they are in cultural, ethnic, religious, linguistic, and economic background, receive a fair and equitable education. Assessment plays an important part in ensuring fairness and equity, first, because it is intimately related to curriculum, instruction, and learning, and second, because assessment provides a seemingly impartial way of determining who should and who should not be given access to educational institutions and resources. To be fair, then, assessment must be as free as possible of biases based on ethnic group, gender, nationality, religion, socioeconomic condition, sexual orientation, or disability. Furthermore, assessment must help us to confront biases that exist in schooling.

7. The consequences of an assessment procedure are the first and most important consideration in establishing the validity of the assessment.

Tests, checklists, observation schedules, and other assessments cannot be evaluated out of the context of their use. If a perfectly reliable and comprehensive literacy test were designed but using it took three weeks away from children's learning and half the annual budget for instructional materials, we would have to weigh these consequences against any value gained from using the test. If its use resulted in teachers building a productive learning community around the data and making important changes in their instruction, we would also have to weigh these consequences. This standard essentially argues for "environmental impact" projections, along with careful, ongoing analyses of the consequences of assessment practices. Responsibility for this standard lies with the entire school community, to ensure that assessments are not used in ways that have negative consequences for schools and students. Any assessment procedure that does not contribute positively to teaching and learning should not be used.

8. The assessment process should involve multiple perspectives and sources of data.

Perfect assessments and perfect assessors do not exist. Every person involved in assessment is limited in his or her interpretation of the teaching and learning of reading and writing. Similarly, each text and each assessment procedure has its own limitations and biases. Although we cannot totally eliminate these biases and limitations from people or tests, we can try to ensure that they are held in balance and that all stakeholders are made aware of them. The more consequential the decision, the more important it is to seek diverse perspectives and independent sources of data. For example, decisions about placement in or eligibility for specialized programs have a profound influence on a student's life and learning. Such decisions are simply too important to make on the basis of a single measure, evaluation tool, or perspective.

9. Assessment must be based in the local school learning community, including active and essential participation of families and community members.

The teacher is the primary agent of assessment and the classroom is the location of the most important assessment practices, but the most effective assessment unit is the local school learning community. First, the collective experience and values of the community can offer a sounding board for innovation and multiple perspectives to provide depth of understanding and to counter individual and cultural biases. Second, the involvement of all parties in assessment encourages a cooperative, committed relationship among them rather than an adversarial one. Third, because language learning is not restricted to what occurs in school, assessment must go beyond the school curriculum.

The local school learning community is also a more appropriate foundation for assessment than larger units such as the school district, county, state, province, or country. These larger units do not offer the relational possibilities and commitments necessary for a learning community. The distance from the problems to be solved and among the participants reduces the probability of feelings of involvement and commitment and increases the possibility that assessment will become merely a means of placing blame.

10. All stakeholders in the educational community—students, families, teachers, administrators, policymakers, and the public—must have an equal voice in the development, interpretation, and reporting of assessment information.

Each of the constituents named in this standard has a stake in assessment. Students are concerned because their literacy learning, their concepts of themselves as literate people, and the quality of their subsequent lives and careers are at stake. Teachers have at stake their understandings of their students, their professional practice and knowledge, their perceptions of themselves as teachers, and the quality of their work life and standing in the community. Families clearly have an investment in their children's learning, well-being, and educational future. The public invests money in education, in part as an investment in the future, and has a stake in maintaining the quality of that investment. The stewardship of the investment involves administrators and policymakers. Assessment is always value laden, and the ongoing participation of all parties involved in it is necessary in a democratic society. When any one perspective is missing, silenced, or privileged above others, the assessment picture is distorted.

11. Families must be involved as active, essential participants in the assessment process.

In many schools, families stand on the periphery of the school community, some feeling hopeless, helpless, and unwanted. However, the more families understand their children's progress in school, the more they can contribute to that progress. If teachers are to understand how best to assist children from cultures that are different from their own, families are a particularly important resource. Families must become, and be helped to become, active participants in the assessment process.

From *Standards for the Assessment of Reading and Writing* by the International Reading Association and the National Council of Teachers of English, Copyright ©2009 by the International Reading Association and the National Council of Teachers of English. Reprinted with permission. Visit www.ncte.org/standards/assessmentstandards for the complete standards.

A.2   Commercial Informal Reading Inventories

Bader, L. A. (2012). *Bader Reading and Language Inventory and Graded Word List* (7th ed.). Upper Saddle River, NJ: Prentice Hall.

Burns, P. & Roe, B. (2010). *Informal Reading Inventory* (12th ed.). Boston: Houghton Mifflin.

Ekwall, H. & Shanker, J. (2013). *Ekwall–Shanker Reading Inventory* (6th ed.). Boston: Allyn & Bacon.

Flynt, E. & Cooter, R. (2013). *The Flynt–Cooter Comprehensive Reading Inventory-2: Assessment of K–12 Reading Skills in English & Spanish* (2nd ed.). Upper Saddle River, NJ: Pearson.

Johns, J. (2010). *Basic Reading Inventory: Pre-Primer Through Grade Twelve and Early Literacy Assessment* (11th ed.). Dubuque, IA: Kendall/Hunt.

Leslie, L. & Caldwell, J. (2010). *Qualitative Reading Inventory-5* (5th ed.). Upper Saddle River, NJ: Pearson.

Manzo, A., Manzo, U., & McKenna, M. (1999). *Informal Reading–Thinking Inventory*. New York: Harcourt Brace College Publishers.

Wheelock, W. & Silvaroli, N. (2011). *Classroom Reading Inventory* (12th ed.). New York: McGraw-Hill.

Woods, M. & Moe, A. (2010). *Analytic Reading Inventory: Comprehensive Standards-Based Assessment for all Students including Gifted and Remedial* (9th ed.). Upper Saddle River, NJ: Pearson.

A.3   Alphabet Books

Here are a few examples of the thousands of alphabet books (search "alphabet books").

Anno, M. (1987). *Anno's Alphabet: An Adventure in Imagination*. New York: HarperCollins.

Archambault, J. (2000). *Chicka Chicka Boom Boom*. New York: Aladdin Library.

Baker, K. (2010). *LMNO Peas*. New York: Scholastic.

Baldus, P. (2002). *The Amazing Alphabet Maze Book*. Los Angeles: Price Stern Sloan.

Bataille, M. (2010). *ABC3D*. New York: Roaring Brook Press.

Carle, E. (2007). *ABC (The World of Eric Carle)*. New York: Grosset & Dunlap.

Falkenstern, L. (2014). *Professor Whiskerton Presents Steampunk ABC*. Two Lions.

Falls, C. B. & Glassman, P. (2002). *ABC Book (Books of Wonder)*. New York: Morrow Junior.

Hager-Pack, L. (2002). *A Is for Appalachia*. Louisville, KY: Harmony House.

Hillestad-Butler, D. (2000). *ABCs of Wisconsin*. Black Earth, WI: Trails Books.

Howell, T. (2003). *A is for Airplane/A es para avion* (Multilingual Edition). New York: Cooper Square.

Kontis, A. (2012). *AlphaOops!: The Day Z Went First*. New York: Candlewick.

Lawton, C. (2011). *Bugs A to Z*. New York: Scholastic.

Napier, M. (2002). *Z is for Zamboni: A Hockey Alphabet*. Chelsea, MI: Sleeping Bear Press.

Rankin, L. (1997). *The Handmade Alphabet* (sign language). New York: Picture Puffins.

Schwartz, D. M. (2009). *Q Is for Quark*. New York: Tricycle Press.

Seuss, Dr. (1963). *Dr. Seuss's ABC (I Can Read by Myself)*. New York: Random House.

Zschock, M. (2001). *Journey Around Boston from A to Z*. Beverly, MA: Commonwealth Editions.

Zschock, M. (2001). *Journey Around Cape Cod and the Islands from A to Z*. Beverly, MA: Commonwealth Editions.

Zschock, M. (2002). *Journey Around New York from A to Z*. Beverly, MA: Commonwealth Editions.

A.4   Poetry Collections and Mother Goose Books

Archer, P. (2010). *Name That Dog*. New York: Dial.

Dotlich, R. K. (2009). *Bella and Bean*. New York: Atheneum.

Doyen, D. (2009). *Once Upon a Twice*. New York: Random House.

Gossnickle Hines, A. (2003). *Pieces: A year in poems and quilts*. New York: Greenwillow.

Gossnickle Hines, A. (2011). *Peaceful Pieces: Poems and quilts about peace*. New York: Henry Holt.

Hopkins, L. B. (2010). *Sharing the Seasons.* New York: Margaret K. McElderry.

Janeczko, P. (2005). *A Poke in the I.* New York: Candlewick.

Lansky, B. (2006). *If Kids Ruled the School.* New York: Meadowbrook.

Lansky, B. (2006). *My Teacher's in Detention.* New York: Meadowbrook.

Lansky, B. (2006). *Peter, Peter Pizza Eater.* New York: Meadowbrook.

Long, S. (1999). *Sylvia Long's Mother Goose.* San Francisco, CA: Chronicle Books.

Mathers, P. (2009). *Button Up a Schertle.* New York: Harcourt Brace.

Nesbitt, K. (2001). *The Aliens Have Landed.* New York: Meadowbrook.

Nesbitt, K. (2007). *Revenge of the Lunch Ladies.* New York: Meadowbrook.

Prelutsky, J. (1994). *A Pizza the Size of the Sun.* New York: Greenwillow.

Prelutsky, J. (1999). *The 20th Century Children's Poetry Treasury.* New York: Alfred A. Knopf.

Prelutsky, J. (2005). *It's Raining Pigs and Noodles.* New York: Greenwillow.

Prelutsky, J. (2007). *Good Sports.* New York: Random House.

Prelutsky, J. (2008). *Be Glad Your Nose Is on Your Face and Other Poems.* New York: Greenwillow.

Prelutsky J. (2009). *The Swamps of Sleethe.* New York: Knopf.

Salas, L. P. (2009). *Stampede.* New York: Clarion.

Shields, C. D. (2010). *Someone Used My Toothbrush.* New York: Dutton.

Sidman, J. (2010). *Dark Emperor and Other Poems of the Night.* New York: Houghton Mifflin.

Silverstein, S. (1974). *Where the Sidewalk Ends.* New York: HarperCollins.

Silverstein, S. (1981). *A Light in the Attic.* New York: HarperCollins.

Singer, M. (2010). *Mirror, Mirror.* New York: Dutton.

Ulrich, G. (1995). *My Tooth Ith Loothe: Funny Poems to Read Instead of Doing Your Homework.* New York: Bantam Doubleday Dell Books.

Yolen, J. (2003). *Color Me a Rhyme.* Honesdale, PA: Wordsong.

Yolen, J. (2009). *In Every Tiny Grain of Sand.* Honesdale, PA: Wordsong.

Yolen, J. (2010). *An Egret's Day.* Honesdale, PA: Wordsong.

A.5   Wordless Books

Bang, M. (1980). *The Grey Lady & the Strawberry Snatcher.* New York: Four Winds.

Banyai, I. (1995). *Re-Zoom.* New York: Picture Puffin.

Banyai, I. (1995). *Zoom.* New York: Puffin.

Becker, A. (2013). *Journey.* New York: Candlewick.

Blake, Q. (1996). *Clown.* New York: Holt.

Briggs, R. (1978). *The Snowman.* New York: Random House.

Brown, C. (1989). *The Patchwork Farmer.* New York: Greenwillow.

Carle, E. (1971). *Do You Want to Be My Friend?* New York: Putnam.

Cole, H. (2012). *Unspoken: A Story from the Underground Railroad.* New York: Scholastic.

Day, A. (1985). *Good Dog, Carl.* New York: Farrar, Straus & Giroux.

Day, A. (1991). *Carl's Afternoon in the Park.* New York: Green Tiger.

dePaola, T. (1978). *Pancakes for Breakfast.* New York: Harcourt Brace.

dePaola, T. (1981). *The Hunter and the Animals.* New York: Holiday.

Drescher, H. (1987). *The Yellow Umbrella.* New York: Atheneum.

Krahn, F. (1985). *Amanda and the Mysterious Carpet.* New York: Clarion.

Lehman, B. (2007). *Rainstorm.* New York: HMH Books.

Ludy, M. (2005). *The Flower Man.* Windsor, CO: Green Pastures.

Mayer, M. (1967). *A Boy, A Dog, and A Frog.* New York: Dial.

Mayer, M. (1969). *Frog, Where Are You?* New York: Dial.

Mayer, M. (1973). *Frog on His Own.* New York: Dial.

Mayer, M. (1974). *Frog Goes to Dinner.* New York: Dial.

Mayer, M. (1976). *Ah-Choo!* New York: Dial.

Mayo, V. (1994). *The Swan.* Hauppauge, New York: Barron's Educational Series.

Pinkney, J. (2009). *The Lion and the Mouse.* New York: Little Brown Books.

Raschka, R. (2011). *A Ball for Daisy.* New York: Schwartz Press.

Schories, P. (1991). *Mouse Around.* New York: Farrar, Straus & Giroux.

Schubert, D. (no date). *Where's My Monkey?* New York: Dial.

Spier, P. (1977). *Noah's Ark.* New York: Doubleday.

Tafuri, N. (1988). *Junglewalk.* New York: William Morrow.

Thomson, B. (2010). *Chalk.* Singapore: Marshall Cavendish.

Turkle, B. (1976). *Deep in the Forest.* New York: Dutton.

Van Allsburg, C. (1982). *Ben's Dream.* Boston: Houghton Mifflin.

Wiesner, D. (2006). *Flotsam.* New York: Clarion.

Wiesner, D. (2001). *The Three Pigs.* New York: Clarion.

Wiesner, D. (2011). *Tuesday.* New York: HMH Books.

A.6   Wordless (or Almost Wordless) Picture Books for Content Area Learning

Anno, M. (1978). *Anno's Journey.* Cleveland, OH: Collins-World.

Anno, M. (1980). *Anno's Italy.* New York: Harper-Collins.

Anno, M. (1983). *Anno's U.S.A.* New York: Philomel Books.

Anno, M. (2004). *Anno's Spain.* New York: Philomel Books.

Baker, J. (1991). *Window.* New York: Greenwillow Books.

Blake, Q. (2003). *Tell Me a Picture.* Brookfield, CT: Millbrook Press.

Cole, H. (2012). *Unspoken: A Story from the Underground Railroad.* New York: Scholastic.

Collington, P. (1987). *The Angel and the Soldier Boy.* New York: Knopf.

dePaola, T. (1979). *Flicks.* San Diego, CA: Harcourt Brace.

Feelings, T. (1995). *The Middle Passage: White Ships/ Black Cargo.* New York: Dial Books.

Geisert, A. (2013). *Thunderstorm.* New York: Enchanted Lion.

Goodall, J. (1976). *An Edwardian Summer.* New York: Atheneum.

Goodall, J. (1990). *The Story of the Seashore.* New York: M. K. McElderry Books.

Gurney, J. (1998). *Dinotopia: A Land Apart from Time.* New York: HarperCollins.

Lehman, B. (2006). *Museum Trip.* Boston: Houghton Mifflin.

Louchard, A. (2001). *Little Star.* New York: Hyperion.

Raczka, B. (2006). *Unlikely Pairs: Fun with Famous Works of Art.* Minneapolis, MN: Millbrook Press.

Rockhill, D. (2005). *Ocean Whisper/Susurro del Oceano.* (E. de la Vega, Trans.). Green Bay, WI: Raven Tree Press.

Rohmann, E. (1995). *Time Flies.* New York: Scholastic.

Spier, P. (1977). *Noah's Ark.* Garden City, NY: Doubleday.

Tan, S. (2007). *The Arrival.* New York: Arthur A. Levine.

Thomson, B. (2013). *Fossil.* Two Lions.

Vincent, G. (2000). *A Day, a Dog.* New York: Front Street.

Wiesner, D. (1988). *Free Fall.* New York: Lothrop, Lee & Shepard.

Wiesner, D. (1997). *Sector 7.* New York: Clarion.

Wiesner, D. (2006). *Flotsam.* New York: Clarion.

A.7   Books with Rhyme, Phonograms, Alliteration, and Other Language Play

Andreae, G. (2001). *Giraffes Can Dance.* New York: Orchard Books.

Andreae, G. (2002). *Rumble in the Jungle.* Wilton, CT: Tiger Tales.

Andreae, G. (2004). *Cock-a-doodle-do: Barnyard hullaballoo.* Wilton, CT: Tiger Tales.

Andreae, G. (2009). *L Is for Kissing a Cool Kangaroo.* Wilton, CT: Tiger Tales.

Andreae, G. (2012). *Bustle in the Bushes*. Wilton, CT: Tiger Tales.

Beaumont, K. (2005). *Ain't Gonna Paint No More!* New York: HMH Books.

Blackstone, S. (2006). *My Granny Went to Market: A round-the-world counting rhyme*. Cambridge, MA: Barefoot Books.

Brooks, L. (2009). *Twinericks: The book of tongue-twisting limericks*. New York: Workman.

Burleigh, R. (2009). *Clang! Clang! Beep! Beep! Listen to the city*. New York: Simon & Schuster.

DeRoo, E. (2011). *The Rain Train*. New York: Candlewick.

Duncan, P. (2001). *A Noisy Warthog Word Book*. New York: Hyperion.

Fleming, C. (2012). *Oh No!* New York: Shwartz & Wade.

Floca, B. (2009). *Moonshot: The flight of Apollo 11*. New York: Atheneum.

Frazee, M. (2003). *Roller Coaster*. New York: HMH Books.

Gershator, P. (2007). *Listen, Listen*. Cambridge, MA: Barefoot Books.

Gibson, A. (2012). *Split! Splat!* New York: Scholastic.

Johnson, D. (2006). *Snow Sounds: An onomatopoeic story*. New York: HMH Books.

Judge, L. (2011). *Red Sled*. New York: Atheneum Books.

Judge, L. (2013). *Red Hat*. New York: Atheneum Books.

Lewis, K. (2006). *My Truck Is Stuck!* New York: Hyperion.

London, J. (2004). *Froggy's Day with Dad*. New York: Puffin.

MacDonald, M. R. (2010). *Too Many Fairies: A Celtic tale*. Amazon: Two Lions.

Marsalis, W. (2012). *Squeak, rumble, Whomp! Whomp! Whomp: A Sonic adventure*. New York: Candlewick.

McMullan, K. (2002). *I Stink!* New York: Harper Collins.

Mitton, T. (2001). *Down by the Cool of the Pool*. New York: Orchard Books.

Munsch, R. (2009). *No Clean Clothes*. Canada: Scholastic.

Rawlinson, J. (2006). *Fletcher and the Falling Leaves*. New York: Greenwillow.

Root, P. (2001). *Rattletrap Car*. New York: Candlewick.

Schaefer, C. L. (2011). *Who's There?* New York: Viking.

Seuss, Dr. All or most Dr. Seuss titles fit this category.

Van Genechten, G. (2010). *The Big Woods Orchestra*. Clavis.

Wallington, S. (2013). *A Day at the Lake*. Sarletta Kids.

Watson, W. (2010). *Bedtime Bunnies*. New York: Clarion.

A.8   Suggested English–Spanish Bilingual Concept Books

The first 20 books listed are by Gladys Rosa-Mendoza, published by Me+Mi Publishing, since 2000.

The Alphabet/El alfabeto

Numbers 1 2 3/Los numeros 1 2 3

Colors and Shapes/Los colores y las figures

My Family and I/Mi familia y yo

Opposites/Opuestos

The Weather/El tiempo

What Time Is It?/Que hora es?

My Body/Mi cuerpo

Jobs Around My Neighborhood/Oficios en mi vecindario

Fruits and Vegtables/Frutas y vegetales

I can!/¡Yo puedo!

When I Am/Cuando estoy

Cars, Trucks and Planes/Carros, camions y aviones

My Clothes/Mi ropa

Lupe Lupita, Where Are You?/Lupe Lupita, donde estas?

It's My Birthday!/Es mi cumpleanos!

My House/Mi casa

I Live Here! I Yo vivo aqui!

Lola

Animals at the Farm/Animales de la granja

Cisneros, S. (1997). *Hairs/Pelitos*. Dragonfly Books.

Flor Ada, A. (1997). *Gathering the Sun: An Alphabet in Spanish and English*. Rayo. (Using the Spanish alphabet, each letter is a poem about Mexican farmers and their families.)

Lomas Garza, C. (1990). *Family Pictures/Cuadros de Familia*. Children's Book Press.

Lomas Garza, C. (2000). *In My Family/En Mi Familia*. Children's Book Press.

A.9   Suggested Bilingual Spanish–English Narrative Picture Books

Ehlert, L. (1996). *Moon Rope*. New York: Voyager. A Peruvian tale of a fox and a mole trying to climb to the moon on a rope woven of grass.

Ehlert, L. (2000). *Cuckoo*. New York: Voyager. A tale with a moral: You can't tell much about a bird by looking at its feathers.

Gonzalez, L. M. (1994). *The Bossy Gallito*. New York: Scholastic. A traditional Cuban folktale.

Harris, J. (2007). *My Moon Is LeLuna: Silly Rhymes in English and Spanish*. New York: HMH Books.

Herrera, J. F. (2000). *The Upside Down Boy*. San Francisco: Children's Book Press. A young Hispanic boy adjusts to an Anglo school.

Mora, P. (2001). *Listen to the Desert*. New York: Clarion. A repetitive text in which all lines by a coyote, an owl, a dove, a toad, a snake, a fish, mice, and rain give their sound. The lines are repeated twice in English and twice in Spanish.

Moroney, L. (1998). *Baby Rattlesnake*. San Francisco: Children's Book Press. Baby rattlesnake who lives in the desert cries constantly because he does not have a rattle.

Perez, A. I. (2000). *My Very Own Room*. San Francisco: Children's Book Press. A young girl wants her own space in her home so she can read books.

Perez, A. I. (2002). *My Diary from Here to There*. San Francisco: Children's Book Press. Each entry is a little girl's true emotions about leaving her beloved Mexico. This is based on the author's life experience. The family finally gets green cards so they can join their father.

Perez, K. (2002). *First Day in Grapes*. New York: Lee & Low. Chico is about to begin his first day in Grapes—his fourth school. He stands up to some bullies and succeeds in other ways that make him sure he will like his days in Grapes.

Rohmer, H. (1993). *Uncle Nacho's Hat*. San Francisco: Children's Book Press. A Jamaican folktale about Nacho, who wears a hat full of holes.

Soto, G. (1993). *Too Many Tamales*. New York: G. P. Putnam's Sons. As part of the story, it explains how tamales are made.

Zubizarreta, R. (1994). *The Woman Who Outshone The Sun*. San Francisco: Children's Books Press. A Mexican folktale.

A.10   Suggested Multicultural Picture Books

Al Abdullah, R. (Queen Rania of Jordan) & Di Pucchio, K. (2010). *The Sandwich Swap*. Lily and Salma are best friends until one day in a lunch room Lily tells Selma that her hummus and pita sandwich looks yucky and Selma tells Lily her peanut butter and jelly sandwich looks yucky.

Bunting, E. (2001). *Jim Woo*. New York: Clarion. The first page lets readers see that the narrator is not happy like his parents are about the arrival of the new adopted baby from Korea.

Cheng, A. (2000). *Grandfather Counts*. New York: Lee & Low. On the title page readers see two sheets of paper, one with Helen spelled in English five times, the other with Helen written in Chinese. The beginning of the book has a glossary with Chinese words, the Chinese characters, the pronunciation, and the English word.

Demi. (1990). *The Empty Pot*. Boston: New York: Henry Holt. A folktale about a boy who has a magical touch with flowers and about how his honesty is rewarded.

Heo, Y. (1996). *The Green Frogs: A Korean Folktale*. Houghton Mifflin. Korean children will recognize this tale from their homeland.

Pak, S. (1999). *Dear Juno*. New York: Viking. The narrator receives a letter from his grandmother written in Korean; the boy doesn't speak Korean but finds a way to communicate with his grandmother, who doesn't speak English.

Park, L. S. (2005). *Bee-bim Bop!* New York: Clarion. Park introduces preschoolers to culinary culture of Korea.

Recorbits, H. (2003). *My Name Is Yoon*. New York: Frances Foster Books/Farrar, Straus & Giroux. A story about Yoon, who comes from Korea and longs to go back to Korea. She does not like how her name, which means Shining Wisdom, looks in English—in Korean "The symbols dance together."

Say, A. (1997). *Allison*. Boston: Houghton Mifflin. When Allison receives a kimono from her grandmother and looks into the mirror with her parents in the background, she realizes that they are not her "real" parents.

Sheth, K. (2007). *My Dadima Wears a Sari*. New York: Peachtree. A story of a young girl who explains how her grandma puts on her sari. She also tells of the activities she and her Dadima do together.

Simond, N. (2002). *Moonbeams, Dumplings and Dragon Boats*. Fairbanks, AK: Gulliver Books. Explains Chinese holidays and includes Chinese tales.

Stickler, J. (2003). *Land of Morning Calm: The Korean Culture Then and Now*. Walnut Creek, CA: Shen's Books. A picture book written for grades 5–8 about the history and politics of Korea. Each chapter's title is written using the Korean alphabet.

Tan, A. (2001). *Sagwa, the Chinese Siamese Cat*. New York: Aladdin. A folktale of a mother cat telling a story of her Chinese ancestry.

Touba, J. (1998). *Lisa Lin's Painting "Making Mooncakes."* New York: Powerkids Press. This Taiwanese artist describes her paintings of her family making mooncakes.

Yang, B. (2004). *Hannah Is My Name*. Cambridge, MA: Candlewick. The book's art is Chinese-influenced. The narrator is concerned that her name in the United States, Hannah, doesn't sound at all like her Chinese name, Na-Li, which means *beautiful*. She describes her feeling as her family waits for green cards.

A.11   Audio Chapter Books*

A Year Down Yonder by R. Peck

Bud, Not Buddy by C. P. Curtis

Out of the Dust by K. Hesse

From the Mixed-up Files of Mrs. Basil E. Frankweiler by E. L. Konigsburg

A Wrinkle in Time by M. L'Engle

The Giver by L. Lowry

Shiloh by P. R. Naylor

Island of the Blue Dolphins by S. O'Dell

Missing May by C. Rylant

Holes by L. Sachar

Brian's Return by G. Paulsen

Joey Pigza Loses Control by J. Gantos

Call It Courage by A. Sperry

Charlotte's Web by E. B. White

The Cricket in Times Square by G. Selden

Ella Enchanted by G. Carson Levine

The Fledgling by J. Langton

Hatchet by G. Paulsen

A Long Way from Chicago by R. Peck

Ramona Quimby, Age 8 by B. Cleary

The Sign of the Beaver by E. George Speare

The Watsons Go to Birmingham–1963 by C. P. Curtis

Bloomability by S. Creech

The Boxcar Children by G. C. Warner

Bunnicula: A Rabbit Tale of Mystery by D. Howe

The Amber Brown Collection I & II by P. Danziger

*Available from Bantam Books.

A.12   Software Options That Promote Comprehension and Problem Solving

Carmen San Diego (Ages 8–10)

Castle Explorer (Age 10–Adult)

Encyclopedia of Endangered Wildlife (Grades 4–6)

I Spy Junior (Ages 3–6)

I Spy Spooky Mansions (Ages 6–10)

I Spy Treasure Hunt (Ages 6–10)

Interactive Garfield Typing Pal Deluxe (Grades 1–3)

Jump Start Animal Adventures (Ages 6–10)

Kidspiration (Grades K–3)

My First Amazing World Explorer/USA (Ages 6–10)

Oregon Trail (Grades 4–6)

Oregon Trail II (Grades 4–6)

Reader Rabbit Series (Grades K–3)

Scooby Doo! Showdown in Ghost Town (Ages 5–10)

Sunburst Make a Map 3D (Grades 4–6)

Zobooma Foo: Animal Kids (Ages 3–8)

Lists and Guides

B.1	Comparison of Five Book-Leveling Systems	394
B.2	Most Common Word Families	396
B.3	Consonant Pronunciation Guide	399
B.4	Vowel Diphthongs, Digraphs, and Variants with Examples and Utility of Each	401
B.5	High-Frequency Word List	402
B.6	Dolch Word Lists	403
B.7	The Fry Phrase Lists	404
B.8	Frequently Used Suffixes and Prefixes	407
B.9	Greek and Latin Word Roots with Definitions and Examples	408
B.10	Generalizations About Word Spellings	417
B.11	Complex Patterns of English Spelling	418

B.1   Comparison of Five Book-Leveling Systems

KINDERGARTEN–FIRST GRADE

Grade Level	Lexile Rating	AR Level	DRA Level	Fountas Pinnell	Guided Reading
K	25	0–.9	A–2	A–B	A–C
1.1	50	1.1	2	C	D
1.2	75	1.2	4	C	D
1.2	100	1.2	4	D	D
1.3	125	1.3	6	E	E
1.3	150	1.3	8	E	E
1.4	175	1.4	8	F	F
1.5	200	1.5	10	F	F
1.6	225	1.6	12	F	G
1.6	250	1.6	14	G	H
1.7	275	1.7	14	G	I
1.8	300	1.8	14	H	J
1.9	325	1.9	16	I	J

SECOND GRADE

Grade Level	Lexile Rating	AR Level	DRA Level	Fountas Pinnell	Guided Reading
2	350	2	16	I	K
2.1	375	2.1	16	I	K
2.1	400	2.2	18	J	K
2.3	425	2.3	20	J	K
2.5	450	2.5	20	K	M
2.6	475	2.6	20	K	M
2.7	500	2.7	24	L	N
2.9	525	2.9	28	L	N

THIRD GRADE

Grade Level	Lexile Rating	AR Level	DRA Level	Fountas Pinnell	Guided Reading
3	550	3	28	M	N
3.2	575	3.2	28	M	N
3.3	600	3.3	30	N	O
3.5	625	3.5	34	O	O
3.7	650	3.7	36	O	P
3.9	675	3.9	38	P	P

FOURTH GRADE

Grade Level	Lexile Rating	AR Level	DRA Level	Fountas Pinnell	Guided Reading
4.1	700	4.1	38	Q	Q
4.3	725	4.3	38	Q	Q
4.5	750	4.5	40	R	R
4.7	775	4.7	42	S	S

Key: Lexile = original, not stretch; AR = accelerated reader; DRA = developmental reading assessment

FIFTH GRADE

Grade Level	Lexile Rating	AR Level	DRA Level	Fountas Pinnell	Guided Reading
5	800	5	44	T	S
5.2	825	5.2	44	U	S
5.5	850	5.5	44	U	T
5.8	875	5.8	44	V	U

SIXTH GRADE

Grade Level	Lexile Rating	AR Level	DRA Level	Fountas Pinnell	Guided Reading
6	900	6	44	W	V
6.4	925	6.4	44	X	V
6.7	950	6.7		Y	W

SEVENTH GRADE

Grade Level	Lexile Rating	AR Level	DRA Level	Fountas Pinnell	Guided Reading
7	975	7		Y	W
7.4	1000	7.4		Z	X
7.8	1025	7.8			Y

EIGHTH GRADE

Grade Level	Lexile Rating	AR Level	DRA Level	Fountas Pinnell	Guided Reading
8.2	1050	8.2			Z
8.6	1075	8.6			

Source: http://north.salkeiz.k12.or.us/sites/northsalem.drupalgardens.com/files/library_books.pdf

| **B.2** | **Most Common Word Families** |

AT	AN	AM	ALL	AND	AD
bat	ban	dam	ball	band	bad
cat	can	ham	call	hand	dad
hat	Dan	jam	fall	land	had
mat	fan	ram	hall	sand	lad
pat	man	clam	mall	brand	mad
rat	pan	cram	tall	grand	sad
sat	ran	gram	wall	stand	fad
brat	tan	slam	small	strand	pad
chat	van	swam	stall		glad
flat	clan	yam			
that	plan	wham			
	scan				
	than				

AG	AP	AB	AR	ART	
bag	cap	cab	bar	cart	
rag	lap	dab	car	dart	
sag	map	jab	far	mart	
wag	nap	nab	jar	part	
brag	rap	lab	star	tart	
flag	tap	tab		start	
drag	clap	crab		chart	
shag	flap	stab		smart	
snag	slap	grab			
tag	trap	slab			
	snap				
	wrap				
	strap				

ACK	ASH	ANK	ELL	ET	ED
back	bash	bank	bell	bet	bed
jack	cash	sank	cell	get	fed
lack	dash	tank	fell	jet	led
rack	gash	yank	sell	let	red
sack	hash	blank	tell	met	bled
tack	mash	crank	well	net	fled
black	rash	drank	shell	pet	shed
crack	sash	plank	smell	set	sled
quack	crash	prank	spell	vet	shred
shack	clash	spank	swell	wet	
snack	flash	thank	dwell	yet	
stack	smash				
track	slash				
	trash				

EN	EG	EST	ECK	IT	IG
Ben	beg	best	deck	bit	big
den	peg	nest	neck	fit	dig
hen	leg	pest	peck	hit	fig
men	keg	rest	check	kit	pig
pen		test	speck	lit	rig
then		vest	wreck	pit	wig
when		west		sit	
wren				quit	
				skit	
				spit	

IN	ILL	IP	ING	INK	ICK
bin	bill	dip	king	link	kick
fin	dill	hip	ping	mink	lick
pin	fill	lip	ring	pink	pick
tin	kill	nip	sing	rink	sick
win	mill	rip	wing	sink	tick
chin	pill	sip	bring	wink	brick
grin	will	tip	cling	blink	chick
thin	chill	zip	fling	clink	flick
twin	drill	chip	sling	drink	quick
shin	grill	clip	sting	stink	stick
skin	skill	drip	thing	think	thick
spin	spill	flip	wring	shrink	trick
	still	ship	spring		
		skip	string		
		slip			
		trip			
		whip			

OT	OP	OG	OB	OCK	ONG
cot	cop	bog	cob	dock	bong
dot	hop	dog	gob	lock	gong
got	mop	fog	job	rock	long
hot	pop	hog	mob	sock	song
jot	top	jog	rob	tock	strong
lot	drop	log	sob	block	throng
not	flop	clog	blob	flock	
pot	shop	frog	glob	frock	
blot	slop		snob	shock	
knot	stop			smock	
plot					
shot					
slot					
spot					

UT	UB	UG	UM	UN	UNG
but	cub	bug	bum	bun	hung
cut	hub	dub	gum	fun	lung
gut	rub	hug	hum	gun	rung
hut	tub	jug	chum	run	sung
nut	club	mug	drum	sun	slung
rut	grub	rug	plum	spun	strung
shut	stub	tug	scum	stun	sprung
		drug			wrung
		slug			
		snug			
		plug			

UCK	UMP	UP	UFF
buck	bump	cup	buff
duck	dump	pup	cuff
luck	hump		huff
suck	jump		muff
tuck	lump		puff
yuck	pump		fluff
cluck	plump		
pluck	stump		
stuck	thump		
truck			

B.3 Consonant Pronunciation Guide

LETTER	FORMATION	COUNTERPART	OTHER SPELLINGS	OTHER SOUNDS	VOICED	VOICELESS
B Bat Cab	Lips are lightly pressed together. A puff of breath opens the lips to create sound.	P	silent in final position (*comb, lamb*)		+	
C Soft as in Cent	Edge of tongue touches toward top of mouth near upper teeth. Hissing sound comes when breath strikes teeth.	Z		/K/	+	
C Hard as in Cut	Back part of tongue is raised. Breath erupts through mouth.	/g	k	/s/		+
D Dog Bed	Front of tongue is in back of upper front teeth. Jaws are slightly open.	T			+	
F Fun Leaf	Lower lip is under upper teeth. Breath moves out between teeth and lower lips to create sound.	V	gh (*laugh*) ph (*phone*) lf (*half*) ft (*often*)	/v/ of		+
G Gate Dog	Back part of tongue is raised and pressed against lower part of front teeth.	/K/	gh (*ghost*) gue (*plague*) x (*excite*)	/j/ (*gym*) silent (*gnat*) ng (*sing*) gh = f (*rough*)	+	
H Hat	It is made with a simple breath.		silent (*heir*) (*ghost*) (*rhyme*) (*exhaust*)			+
J Jeep	Lips are slightly rounded, stick out. Teeth are together with tongue pressed against them.	ch	d (*educate*) di (*soldier*) dg (*bridge*) de (*grandeur*)		+	
K Keep Book	Back part of tongue is raised. Breath erupts through the mouth.	/g/	ck (*sock*) c (*cat*) q (*queen*) k (*except*)	silent when followed by n (*know*)		+
L Leaf Bail	Front of the tongue is behind the upper front teeth while allowing vibrating breath to emerge.	None	None	None	+	
M Milk Drum	Lips are lightly pressed together. Lips vibrate when breath passes through sinuses.		mb (*lamb*) lm (*calm*) mn (*column*)		+	

LETTER	FORMATION	COUNTERPART	OTHER SPELLINGS	OTHER SOUNDS	VOICED	VOICELESS
N Nut Run	Tongue is pressed tightly against upper teeth. Breath passes through sinuses.		gn *(gnat)* kn *(knee)* pn *(pneumonia)* mn *(mnemonic)*		+	
P Pet Soup	Lips are closed and pressed together. Sound comes when breath quickly passes through lips.	B	ph *(diptheria)*	silent when followed by *n, s, t* ph = /f/		+
Q Queen Bouquet	Back part of tongue is raised. Breath erupts through mouth.	/g/	always followed by u, except in *Iraq*	/kw/ *(quite)* /k/ *(bouquet)*		+
R Run Four	Tip of tongue is raised toward the top of mouth with jaw slightly open.		wr *(wren)* rhy *(rhythm)* rps *(corps)*		+	
S Sun Bus	Edges of tongue touch the jaws near the sockets of upper teeth. Hissing sound comes when breath strikes teeth.		c *(city)* ps *(psychology)* z *(waltz)*	/z/ *(dogs)* /sh/ *(sugar)* /zh/ *(pleasure)*		+
T Ten Tent	Mouth is slightly open. Tongue is pressed against inside of upper palate.	D	th *(thyme)* bt *(debt)* ed *(talked)* ght *(light)* tw *(two)* pt *(receipt)*	silent after *f & s* *(often, listen)* silent with quet *(bouquet)* ch *(natural)* sh *(question)*		+
V Van Five	Lower lip is slightly under the upper teeth.	F	f *(of)* ph *(Stephen)* lv *(half)*		+	
W We	Lips closed, but not pressed together. Vibrating the vocal chords produces sound.	Wh	ju *(marijuana)* ou *(Ouija)*	silent in *wr*	+	
Y Yo-yo	With teeth separated, sides of tongue are pressed against upper teeth.		i *(onion)* e *(azalea)* j *(hallelujah)*	/i/ *(fly)* /e/ *(happy)* ay *(day)* /i/ *(lymph)*	+	
Z Zip Quiz	Edges of tongue touch the jaws near sockets of the teeth.	S	s *(does)* ss *(scissors)* x *(xylophone)* sc *(discern)* cz *(czar)* si *(business)* sp *(raspberry)*	/s/ *(pretzel)*	+	

B.4 Vowel Diphthongs, Digraphs, and Variants with Examples and Utility of Each

VOWELS	EXAMPLES	UTILITY
aw	law	100%
oy	boy	98%
oi	oil	98%
ay	day	96%
ew	dew	95%
au	haul	94%
oa	road	94%
ee	fleet	86%
ai	rain	74%
oo	moon	59%
oo	foot	36%
ey	key (long /e/)	58%
ey	they (long /a/)	20%
ea	leaf (long /e/)	51%
ea	bread (short /e/)	26%
ie	chief (long /e/)	51%
ie	lie (long /i/)	17%
ie	ancient (schwa)	15%
ow	know (long /o/)	50%
ow	now (/ou/)	48%
ei	eight (long /a/)	40%
ei	receive (long /e/)	26%
ei	foreign (short /i/)	13%
ei	seismic (long /i/)	11%

B.5   High-Frequency Word List

about	don't	it	phone	they're
after	down	it's	play	thing
all	drink	joke	presents	this
am	each	jump	pretty	those
an	eat	junk	question	time
and	family	kick	rain	to
animal	father	know	ride	too
are	favorite	like	right	trip
as	first	line	run	truck
at	fly	little	said	two
be	for	long	sale	up
because	friend	look	saw	us
been	from	made	school	use
best	fun	mail	see	very
big	get	make	she	want
black	girl	many	sister	was
boy	give	me	slow	way
brother	go	more	skate	we
bug	good	mother	small	went
but	green	my	snap	were
by	gym	name	so	what
call	had	new	some	when
can	has	nice	sports	where
can't	have	night	stop	which
car	he	no	street	who
caught	her	not	talk	why
children	here	now	teacher	will
city	him	of	tell	with
clock	his	off	than	won
coat	house	old	thank	won't
come	how	on	that	would
could	hurt	one	the	write
crash	I	or	their	you
day	if	other	them	your
did	in	out	then	zoo
didn't	into	over	there	
do	is	people	they	

Source: From Cunningham, Patricia M., *Phonics They Use: Words for Reading and Writing,* 3rd Ed. Copyright © 2000, pp. 63, 94. Reprinted by permission of Pearson Education, Inc., Upper Saddle River, NJ.

B.6   Dolch Word Lists

EASIER 110			HARDER 110		
a	go	over	about	hurt	small
after	going	play	again	just	start
all	good	put	always	keep	take
am	green	ran	any	kind	tell
an	had	red	ask	laugh	thank
and	has	ride	ate	let	that
are	have	round	because	light	their
around	he	run	been	live	them
as	help	said	before	long	then
at	her	saw	best	many	there
away	here	see	better	much	these
be	him	she	both	must	they
big	his	so	bring	myself	think
black	I	some	buy	never	those
blue	if	soon	clean	new	today
brown	in	stop	could	now	together
but	into	ten	cut	off	try
by	is	the	does	once	upon
call	it	this	done	only	us
came	its	three	draw	open	use
can	jump	to	drink	or	very
carry	know	too	eight	our	walk
cold	like	two	every	own	want
come	little	under	fall	pick	warm
did	look	up	far	please	wash
do	made	was	five	pull	were
down	may	went	found	read	when
eat	me	what	four	right	where
fast	my	who	full	say	which
find	no	will	gave	seven	white
fly	not	with	goes	shall	why
for	of	yellow	got	show	wish
from	old	yes	grow	sing	work
funny	on	you	hold	sit	would
get	one	your	hot	six	write
give	out		how	sleep	

B.7   Phrases and Short Sentences for
Repeated Reading Practice (the Fry Phrase Lists)

These phrases contain the words from the Fry Instant Word List (1980), which represent some of the most common words students encounter in their reading. The complete list of 300 words contains approximately two-thirds of all the words students encounter in their reading. Repeated reading of a few phrases per week gives students practice reading high-frequency words and developing fluency and general proficiency. These phrases may be written on sentence strips, transparencies, or a chart for use in a literacy center or small group instructional setting.

FIRST 100 WORDS

The people	Look for some people.	Write it down.
By the water	So there you are.	Who will make it?
You and I	A long time	What will they do?
He called me.	Have you seen it?	We had their dog.
What did they say?	One more time	When would you go?
No way	All day long	A number of people
One or two	It's about time.	How long are they?
More than the other	Up in the air	Come and get it.
How many words?	Which way?	Part of the time
This is a good day.	He has it.	Can you see?
Sit down.	If we were older	Now and then
But not me	It's no use.	Go find her.
Not now	With his mom	At your house
From my room	As big as the first	It's been a long time.
Will you be good?	When will we go?	Give them to me.
Then we will go.	From here to there	Now is the time.
An angry cat	More people	May I go first?
Write your name.	Go down.	This is my cat.
That dog is big.	Did you like it?	Get on the bus.
Two of us	When did they go?	Did you see it?
The first word	She said to go.	How did they get it?
I like him.	Each of us	Number two
Out of the water	What are these?	Look up.
We were here.	There was an old man.	All or some
Could you go?	It may fall down.	A long way to go
We like to write.	See the water	For some of your people
Into the water	But not for me	The other people

SECOND 100 WORDS

Over the river	A good man	My new place
After the game	Another great sound	Most of the animals
Take a little.	Our best things	Give it back.
Just the same	Only a little	My last name
It's only me.	That's very good	I know why.
Think before you act.	Three years ago	Mother says to now.
Live and play.	Where are you?	I need help.
Try your best.	I work too much.	Move over.
Any old time	We found it here.	Through the line
Study and learn	Right now	Kind of nice
Mother means it.	Spell your name.	Same time tomorrow
The good American	Tell the truth.	Change your clothes.
A little boy	Play it again.	The following day
Back off.	We came home.	Give it away.
We want to go.	Answer the phone.	Show us around.
Turn the page.	Form two lines.	The air is warm.
A small house also	Read my letters.	Another old picture
It's still here.	Write one sentence.	Where in the world
Set it up.	We need more.	Put it there.
I study in school.	Where does it end?	I'm an American.
I don't feel well.	Such a mess	My home is large.
Point it out.	It turned out well.	Right now
Read the sentence.	It's a small world.	This must be it.
Big and small	Hand it over.	Home sweet home
Such a big house	Around the clock	The men asked for help.
Show and tell	A different land	You must be right.
They went here.	Tell the truth.	Get to the point.
Good and plenty	Because we should.	Help me out.
Even the animals	It turned out well.	It's your place.
I think so.	Good things	Read the book.

THIRD 100 WORDS

Near the car	Stay a while.	Between the lines
A few good men	My own father	Don't open the door.
In the country	You might be right.	Add it up.
It seemed too good.	Read every story.	Along the way
Below the water	Next time	Plants and flowers
It's hard to open.	Will it last?	Something good
Keep it up.	For example	Plant the trees.
In the beginning	Light the fire.	Those other people
The light in your eyes	A group of friends	In my head
We got together	Under the earth	We left it here.
We saw the food.	Both children	Close the door.
It's my life.	The big city	Always be kind.
We started the fire.	Read the paper.	It never happened.
Run for miles.	A good thought	Once upon a time.
Do it often.	Is it really true?	We walked four miles.
It's time to eat.	Until the end	Let me carry it.
A second later	Near the sea	Stop the music.
Talk to my father.	Read your book.	The young face
Sing your song.	The long list	State your case.
My family	I miss you.	I cut myself.
A very important person	Above the clouds	On my side
Watch the game.	I took the car.	The peaceful Indians
So far so good.	Without a care	The young girl
I like being on the team.	My feet hurt.	The tall mountains
The dark night	Next to me	A good idea
A few children	It began to grow.	A long life
Watch the river.	A group of Indians	White clouds
He started to cry.	Too soon	I hear the sea.
Leave it to me.	An important idea	I hear the waves.
The first day of school	Almost enough	Almost four miles

From *THE FLUENT READER: ORAL READING STRATEGIES FOR BUILDING WORD RECOGNITION, FLUENCY, AND COMPREHENSION* by Timothy Rasinski. Scholastic, Inc./Teaching Resources. Copyright ©2003 by Timothy V. Rasinski. Reprinted by permission.

B.8 Frequently Used Suffixes and Prefixes

SUFFIXES	COMMON MEANING	EXAMPLE
s, es	plural	boys, churches
ed	past tense	walked
ing	verb form/present participle	smiling
ly	characteristic of	quickly
er, or	person connected with	printer, editor
ion, tion	act, process	transportation
ation, ition	process of, condition of, result of	action
ible, able	can be done	edible
al, ial	having characteristics of	denial
y	characterized by	discovery
ness	state of, condition of	happiness
ity, ty	state of	responsibility
ment	action or process	management
ic	having characteristics of	heroic
ous, eous	possessing the qualities of	courageous
ious	full of	glorious
en	made of, resembling	forgotten
er	comparative	happier
ive, ative, itive	adjective form of noun	expensive
ful	full of	playful
less	without	helpless
est	superlative	homeliest

PREFIXES	COMMON MEANING	EXAMPLE
un	not, opposite	unhappy
re	again	redo
in, im, ir, ill	not	impossible
dis	not, opposite of	disagree
en, em	cause to	encourage
non	not	nonliving
in, im	in or into	invade
over	too much	overzealous
mis	wrongly	mislead
sub	under	submerge
pre	before	prelude
inter	between, among	interstate
fore	before	foreground
de	opposite of	decompose
trans	across	transport
super	above	supercede
semi	half	semicircle
anti	against	antisocial
mid	middle	midway
under	too little	underweight

B.9   Greek and Latin Word Roots with Definitions and Examples

ROOT	MEANING	EXAMPLES
acer, acid, acri	bitter, sour, sharp	acerbic, acidity, acrid, acrimony
acu	sharp	acute, acupuncture, accurate
ag, agi, ig, act	do, move, go	agent, agenda, agitate, navigate, ambiguous, action
ali, allo, alter	other	alias, alibi, alien, alloy, alter, alter ego, altruism
alt(us)	high, deep	altimeter, altitude
am, amor	love, liking	amiable, amorous, enamored
anni, annu, enni	year	anniversary, annually, centennial
anthrop	man	anthropology, misanthrope, philanthropy
anti(co)	old	antique, antiquated, antiquity
arch	chief, first, rule	archangel, architect, archaic, monarchy, matriarchy, patriarchy, Archeozoic era
aster, astr	star	aster, asterisk, asteroid, astronomy, astronaut
aud, aus	hear, listen	audiology, auditorium, audio, audition, auscultate
aug, auc	increase	augur, augment, auction
auto, aut	self	automobile, autograph, automatic
belli	war	rebellion, belligerent, casus belli, bellicose
bibl	book	Bible, bibliography, bibliomania
bio	life	biology, biometrics, biome, biosphere
brev	short	abbreviate, brief
cad, cas	to fall	cadaver, cadence, cascade
calor	heat	calorie, caloric, calorimeter
cap, cip, cept	take	capable, intercept, forceps, capture, except, reciprocate
capit, capt	head	decapitate, capital, captain, caption
carn	flesh	carnivorous, incarnate, reincarnation, carnal
caus, caut	burn, heat	caustic, cauldron, cauterize
cause, cuse, cus	cause, motive	because, excuse, accusation
ced, ceed, cede, cess	move, yield, go, surrender	procedure, proceed, cede, concede, recede, precede, accede, success
cenetri	center	concentric, centrifugal, centripetal, eccentric
chrom	color	chrome, chromosome, polychrome, chromatic
chron	time	chronology, chronometer, synchronize

ROOT	MEANING	EXAMPLES
cide, cise	cut down, kill	homicide, exorcise, germicide, incision, scissors
cit	call, start	incite, citation, cite
civ	citizen	civic, civil, civilian, civilization
clam, claim	cry out	exclamation, clamor, proclamation, reclamation, acclaim
clud, clus, claus	shut	include, conclude, recluse, claustrophobia, occlusion, occult
cognoac, gnosi	know	recognize, prognosis, cognoscenti, incognito, agnostic
cord, cor, cardi	heart	cordial, concord, discord, courage, encourage
corp	body	corporation, corporal punishment, corpse, corpulent, corpus luteum
cosm	universe, world	cosmos, microcosm, cosmopolitan, cosmonaut
crat, cracy	rule	autocrat, aristocrat, theocracy, technocracy
crea	create	creature, recreation, creation
cred	believe	creed, credo, credence, credit, credulous, incredulous, incredible
cresc, cret, crease, cru	rise, grow	crescendo, concrete, increase, decrease, accrue
crit	separate, choose	critical, criterion, hypocrite
cur, curs	run	current, concurrent, concur, incur, recur, occur, courier, precursor, cursive
cura	care	curator, curative, manicure
cycl, cyclo	wheel, circular	Cyclops, unicycle, bicycle, cyclone, cyclic
deca	ten	decade, decalogue, decathlon, decahedron
dem	people	democracy, demography, epidemic
dent, dont	tooth	dental, denture, orthodontist, periodontal
derm	skin	hypodermic, dermatology, epidermis, taxidermy
dict	say, speak	dictation, dictionary, dictate, dictator, Dictaphone, edict, predict, verdict, contradict, benediction
doc, dokein	teach	doctrine, indoctrinate, document, dogma, dogmatic
domin	master	dominate, dominion, predominant, domain
don	give	donate, condone
dorm	sleep	dormant, dormitory
dox	opinion, praise	orthodox, heterodox, paradox, doxology

(continued)

ROOT	MEANING	EXAMPLES
drome	run, step	syndrome (run together), hippodrome (place where horses run)
duc, duct	lead	induce, seduce (lead aside), produce, reduce
dura	hard, lasting	durable, duration, endure
dynam	power	dynamo, dynamic, dynamite, hydrodynamics
endo	within	endorse, endocardial, endoskeletal, endoskeleton, endosperm
equi	equal	equinox, equilibrium, equipoise
erg	work	energy, erg, allergy, ergometer, ergograph, ergophobia
fac, fact, fic, fect	do, make	factory, fact, manufacture, amplification, confection
fall, fals	deceive	fallacy, falsify, fallacious
fer	bear, carry	ferry, coniferous, fertile, defer, infer, refer, transfer
fid, fide, feder(is)	faith, trust	confidante, fidelity, confident, infidelity, infidel, federal, confederacy, semper fi
fila, fili	thread	filigree, filament, filter, filet, filibuster
fin	end, ended, finished	final, finite, finish, confine, fine, refine, define, finale
fix	fix	fix, fixation, fixture, affix, prefix, suffix
flex, flect	bend	flex, reflex, flexible, flexor, inflexibility, reflect, deflect
flu, fluc, fluv	flowing	influence, fluid, flue, flush, fluently, fluctuate
form	form, shape	form, uniform, conform, formulary, perform, formal, formula
fort, forc	strong	fort, fortress, fortify, forte, fortitude
fract, frag	break	fracture, infraction, fragile, fraction, refract
gam	marriage	bigamy, monogamy, polygamy
gastr(o)	stomach	gastric, gastronomic, gastritis, gastropod
gen	birth, race, produce	genesis, genetics, eugenics, genealogy, generate, genetic, antigen, pathogen
geo	earth	geometry, geography, geocentric, geology
germ	vital part	germination, germ, germane
gest	carry, bear	congest, gestation
gloss, glot	tongue	glossary, polyglot, epiglottis
glu, glo	lump, bond, glue	glue, agglutinate, conglomerate
grad, gress	step, go	grade, gradual, graduate, progress, graduated, egress
graph, gram	write, written	graph, graphic, autograph, photography, graphite, telegram

ROOT	MEANING	EXAMPLES
grat	pleasing	congratulate, gratuity, grateful, ingrate
grav	heavy, weighty	grave, gravity, aggravate, gravitate
greg	herd	gregarious, congregation, segregate, gregarian
hypn	sleep	hypnosis, hypnotherapy
helio	sun	heliograph, heliotrope, heliocentric
hema, hemo	blood	hemorrhage, hemoglobin, hemophilia, hemostat
here, hes	stick	adhere, cohere, cohesion, inherent, hereditary
hetero	different	heterogeneous, heterosexual, heterodox
homo	same	homogeneous, homonym, homogenize
hum, human	earth, ground, man	humus, exhume, humane
hydr, hydra, hydro	water	dehydrate, hydrant, hydraulic, hydraulics, hydrogen, hydrophobia
ignis	fire	ignite, igneous, ignition
ject	throw	deject, inject, project, eject, interject
join, junct	join	adjoining, enjoin, juncture, conjunction, injunction, conjunction
juven	young	juvenile, rejuvenate
lau, lav, lot, lut	wash	launder, lavatory, lotion, ablution, dilute
leg	law	legal, legislate, legislature, legitimize
levi	light	alleviate, levitate, levity
liber, liver	free	liberty, liberal, liberalize, deliverance
liter	letters	literary, literature, literal, alliteration, obliterate
loc, loco	place	locality, allocate, locomotion
log, logo, ology	word, study, speech	catalog, prologue, dialogue, logogram (symbol representing a word), zoology
loqu, locut	talk, speak	eloquent, loquacious, colloquial, circumlocution
luc, lum, lus, lun	light	translucent, luminary, luster, luna (moon goddess)
macr, macer	lean	emaciated, meager
magn	great	magnify, magnificent, magnanimous, magnate, magnitude, magnum
man	hand	manual, manage, manufacture, manacle, manicure, manifest, maneuver, emancipate
mand	command	mandatory, remand, mandate

(continued)

ROOT	MEANING	EXAMPLES
mania	madness	mania, maniac, kleptomania, pyromania
mar, mari, mer	sea, pool	marine, marsh, maritime, mermaid
matri	mother	matrimony, maternal, matriarchate, matron
medi	half, middle, between, halfway	mediate, medieval, Mediterranean, mediocre, medium
mega	great	megaphone, megalopolis, megacycle (a million cycles), megaton
mem	remember	memo, commemoration, memento, memoir, memorable
meter	measure	meter, voltammeter, barometer, thermometer
micro	small	microscope, microfilm, microcard, microwave, micrometer
migra	wander	migrate, emigrant, immigrate
mit, miss	send	emit, remit, submit, admit, commit, permit, transmit, omit, intermittent, mission, missile
mob, mot, mov	move	mobile, motionless, motor
mon	warn, remind	monument, admonition, monitor, premonition
mor, mort	mortal, death	mortal, immortal, mortality, mortician, mortuary
morph	form	amorphous, dimorphic, metamorphosis, morphology
multi	many, much	multifold, multilingual, multiped, multiply
nat, nasc	to be from, to spring forth	innate, natal, native, renaissance
neo	new	Neolithic, nouveau riche, neologism, neophyte, neonate
neur	nerve	neuritis, neuropathic, neurologist, neural, neurotic
nom	law, order	autonomy, astronomy, gastronomy, economy
nomen, nomin	name	nomenclature, nominate, ignominious
nov	new	novel, renovate, novice, nova, innovate
nox, noc	night	nocturnal, equinox, noctilucent
numer	number	numeral, numeration, enumerate, innumerable
numisma	coin	numismatics
oligo	few, little	Oligocene, oligosaccharide, oligotrophic, oligarchy
omni	all, every	omnipotent, omniscient, omnipresent, omnivorous
onym	name	anonymous, pseudonym, antonym, synonym
oper	work	operate, cooperate, opus

ROOT	MEANING	EXAMPLES
ortho	straight, correct	orthodox, orthodontist, orthopedic, unorthodox
pac	peace	pacifist, pacify, pacific ocean
paleo	old	Paleozoic, Paleolithic, paleomagnetism, paleopsychology
pan	all	Pan-American, pan-African, panacea, pandemonium (place of all the demons)
pater, patr	father	paternity, patriarch, patriot, patron, patronize
path, pathy	feeling, suffering	pathos, sympathy, antipathy, apathy, telepathy
ped, pod	foot	pedal, impede (get feet in a trap), pedestrian, centipede, tripod, podiatry, antipode
pedo	child	orthopedic, pedagogue, pediatrics
pel, puls	drive, urge	compel, dispel, expel, repel, propel, pulse, impulse, pulsate, compulsory, expulsion, repulsive
pend, pens, pond	hang, weigh	pendant, pendulum, suspend, appendage, pensive
phage	eat	macrophage, bacteriophage
phil	love	philosophy, philanthropy, philharmonic, bibliophile
phlegma	inflammation	phlegm, phlegmatic
phobia, phobos	fear	phobia, claustrophobia, acrophobia, aquaphobia, ergophobia
phon	sound	phonograph, phonetic, symphony, homophone, euphonious
photo	light	photograph, photoelectric, photogenic, photosynthesis
plac, plais	please	placid, placebo, placate, complacent
plu, plur, plus	more	plural, pluralist, plus
pneuma, pneumon	breath	pneumatic, pneumonia
pod (see ped)		
poli	city	metropolis, police, politics, Indianapolis, megalopolis, acropolis
poly	many	polysaccharide, polyandrous, polytheistic
pon, pos, pound	place, put	postpone, component, opponent, proponent, expose, impose, deposit, posture, position, expound, impound
pop	people	population, populous, popular
port	carry	porter, portable, transport, report, export, import, support, transportation
portion	part, share	portion, proportion

(continued)

ROOT	MEANING	EXAMPLES
pot	power	potential, potentate, impotent
prehendere	seize, grasp	apprehend, comprehend, comprehensive, prehensile
prim, prime	first	primacy, prima donna, primitive, primary, primal, primeval
proto	first	prototype, protocol, protagonist, protozoan, Proterozoic, protoindustrial
psych	mind, soul	psyche, psychiatry, psychology, psychosis
punct	point, dot	punctual, punctuation, puncture, acupuncture, punctuation
reg, recti	straighten	regiment, regular, rectify, correct, direct, rectangle
ri, ridi, risi	laughter	deride, ridicule, ridiculous, derision, risible
rog, roga	ask	prerogative, interrogation, derogatory
rupt	break	rupture, interrupt, abrupt, disrupt, ruptible
sacr, sanc, secr	sacred	sacred, sacrosanct, sanction, consecrate, desecrate
salv, salu	safe, healthy	salvation, salvage, salutation
sat, satis	enough	satient (giving pleasure, satisfying), saturate, satisfy
sci, scientia	know	science, conscious, omniscient, cognoscenti
scope	see, watch	telescope, microscope, kaleidoscope, periscope, stethoscope
scrib, script	write	scribe, scribble, inscribe, describe, subscribe, prescribe, manuscript
sed, sess, sid	sit	sediment, session, obsession, possess, preside, president, reside, subside
sen	old	senior, senator, senile
senescere	to grow old	senescence, evanescent
sent, sens	feel	sentiment, consent, resent, dissent, sentimental, sense, sensation, sensitive, sensory, dissension
sequ, secu, sue	follow	sequence, consequence, sequel, subsequent, prosecute, consecutive, second, ensue, pursue
serv	save, serve	servant, service, subservient, servitude, preserve, conserve, reservation, deserve, conservation, observe
sign, signi	sign, mark, seal	signal, signature, design, insignia, significant
simil, simul	like, resembling	similar, assimilate, simulate, simulacrum, simultaneous
sist, sta, stit	stand	assist, persist, circumstance, stamina, status, state, static, stable, stationary, substitute
solus	alone	solo, soliloquy, solitaire, solitude

ROOT	MEANING	EXAMPLES
solv, solu	loosen	solvent, solve, absolve, resolve, soluble, solution, resolution, resolute, dissolute
somnus	sleep	insomnia, somnambulist
soph	wise	sophomore (wise fool), philosophy, sophisticated
spec, spect, spic	look	specimen, specific, spectator, spectacle, aspect, speculate, inspect, respect, prospect, retrospective, introspective, expect, conspicuous
sphere	ball, sphere	sphere, stratosphere, hemisphere, spheroid
spir	breath	spirit, conspire, inspire, aspire, expire, perspire, respiration
string, strict	draw tight	stringent, strict, restrict, constrict, boa constrictor
stru, struct	build	construe (build in the mind, interpret), structure, construct, instruct, obstruct, destruction, destroy
sume, sump	take, use, waste	consume, assume (to take, to use), sump, pump, presumption (to take or use before knowing all the facts)
tact, tang, tag, tig, ting	touch	tactile, contact, intact, intangible, tangible, contagious, contiguous
tele	far	telephone, telegraph, telegram, telescope, television, telephoto, telecast, telepathy
tempo	time	tempo, temporary, extemporaneously, contemporary, pro tem, temporal
ten, tin, tain	hold	tenacious, tenant, tenure, untenable, detention, retentive, content, pertinent, continent, obstinate, contain, abstain, pertain, detain
tend, tent, tens	stretch, strain	tendency, extend, intend, contend, pretend, superintend, tender, extent, tension, pretense
terra	earth	terrain, terrarium, territory, terrestrial
test	to bear witness	testament, detest, testimony, attest
the, theo	God, a god	monotheism, polytheism, atheism, theology
therm	heat	thermometer, theorem, thermal, thermos bottle, thermostat, hypothermia
thesis, thet	place, put	antithesis, hypothesis, synthesis, epithet
tom	cut	atom (not cuttable), appendectomy, tonsillectomy, dichotomy, anatomy
tort, tors	twist	torture (twisting to inflict pain), retort, extort (twist out), distort, contort, torsion, tortuous, torturous
tox	poison	toxic, intoxicate, antitoxin

(continued)

ROOT	MEANING	EXAMPLES
tract, tra	draw, pull	tractor, attract, traction, subtract, tractable, abstract (to draw away), subtrahend (the number to be drawn away from another)
trib	pay, bestow	tribute, contribute, attribute, retribution, tributary
turbo	disturb	turbulent, disturb, turbid, turmoil
typ	print	type, prototype, typical, typography, typewriter, typology, typify
ultima	last	ultimate, ultimatum
umber, umbraticum	shadow	umbra, penumbra, (take) umbrage, adumbrate
uni	one	unicorn, unify, university, unanimous, universal
vac	empty	vacate, vacuum, evacuate, vacation, vacant, vacuous
vale, vali, valu	strength, worth	equivalent, valiant, validity, evaluate, value, valor
ven, vent	come	convene, intervene, venue, convenient, avenue, circumvent, invent, convent, venture, event, advent, prevent
ver, veri	true	very, aver, verdict, verity, verify, verisimilitude
vert, vers	turn	avert, divert, invert, introvert, convertible, reverse, controversy, versatile
vic, vicis	change, substitute	vicarious, vicar, vicissitude
vict, vinc	conquer	victor, evict, convict, convince, invincible
vid, vis	see	video, evident, provide, providence, visible, revise, supervise, vista, visit, vision
viv, vita, vivi	alive, life	revive, survive, vivid, vivacious, vitality, vivisection
voc	call	vocation, avocation, convocation, invocation, evoke, provoke, revoke, advocate, provocative, vocal
vol	will	malevolent, benevolent, volunteer, volition
volcan	fire	volcano, vulcanize, Vulcan
volvo	turn about, roll	revolve, voluble (easily turned about or around or talkative), voluminous, convolution
vor	eat greedily	voracious, carnivorous, herbivorous, omnivorous, devour
zo	animal	zoo (short for zoological garden), zoology, zoomorphism (attributing animal form to god), zodiac (circle of animal constellations), protozoan

B.10   Generalizations About Word Spellings

1. Every syllable has a vowel sound.

2. Blends and digraphs always stay together (e.g., *fa-ther*, not *fat-her*).

3. Syllables ending with a vowel have a long sound. Pattern = CV

4. Syllables ending with a consonant have short vowel sounds. Pattern = CVC

5. Inflectional endings are usually separate syllables (e.g., *play-ing*).

6. Prefixes are usually separate syllables (e.g., *re-turn*).

7. The consonant before a final *le* is part of the last syllable (e.g., *dou-ble, a-ble*).

8. When words end in silent *e*, the *e* is dropped before adding the ending (e.g., *giving, having, hoping*).

9. When words end in *y*, change *y* to *i* before adding the suffix, unless the ending is *ing* (e.g., *married, marrying*).

10. When words have a CVC pattern, double the final consonant before adding an ending that begins with a vowel (*sit, sitting; hop, hopping*).

11. The letter *q* is followed by *u* (exception: *Iraq*).

12. The final *e* remains on root word when suffix begins with a consonant (e.g., *lately*).

13. When singular noun has a consonant before *y*, the *y* is changed to *i* to form plural (e.g., *babies*).

14. When singular noun has a vowel before *y*, only the *s* is added to form plural (e.g., *boys*).

15. The letter *i* before *e* except after *c* or when digraph sounds like the long /a/ sound (e.g., *receive, eight*).

16. In one-syllable words with the pattern CVCe (*cape*), the vowel is long.

17. In one-syllable words with the pattern CVVC (*road*), one vowel is usually long.

18. In one-syllable words with the patterns CVC (*hop*) the vowel is short.

19. In two-syllable words with pattern CVC-CV (*rabbit*), the vowel is short in the first syllable.

Sources: Bear, D., Invernizzi, M., Templeton, F., & Johnston, F. (2011). *Words their way: Word study for phonics, vocabulary and spelling instruction* (5th ed.). Upper Saddle River, NJ: Merrill.

Fountas, I. & Pinnell, G. S. (2001). *Guided readers and writers: Grades 3–6: Teaching comprehension, genre and content literacy.* Portsmouth, NH: Heinemann.

Heald-Taylor, B. G. (1998). Three paradigms of spelling instruction in grades 3–6. *The Reading Teacher, 51*(5), 404–413.

B.11 Complex Patterns of English Spelling

1. "gh" in *sigh, light, night*, etc. serves as a marker for the long /i/ sound.

2. double consonants mark short vowels (*hill, pass, butter, silly*).

3. "ck" at end of word makes vowel short (*truck, clock*).

4. "tch" at end of word makes vowel short (*match, itch*).

5. "ch" at end of word makes vowel short when there is only one vowel (*rich, such*); when the word has a vowel digraph, the vowel is long (*teach, coach*).

6. "ge" at the end of a word makes the "soft" g sound (*orange, ledge, ridge, sponge*).

7. "ge" within a word makes the "soft" g sound (*dungeon, pigeon, angel*).

8. "ce" at the end of a word gives c the /s/ sound (*prince, dance*).

9. "c" at the end of word calls for the /k/ sound (*magic, picnic*).

10. "c" followed by *e, i, y* makes a "soft" c (*city, cent, cycle*).

11. "c" followed by *a, o, u* makes a /k/ sound (*cat, cot, cut*).

12. initial "g" followed by *a, o, u* makes a "hard" g (*gate, goat, gut*).

13. initial "g" followed by *y* makes a "soft" g (*gym*).

14. initial "g" followed by *i* or *e* is often inconsistent (*give, get, giant, gem*).

15. the "k" in "kn" at the beginning of words is silent (*know, knee*).

16. the "g" in "gn" at beginning of words is silent (*gnaw, gnat*).

17. When long /u/ sound is at end of a word, it is spelled "oo" (*zoo*), "ew" (*few*), or "ue" (*blue*). The one is exception is *you*.

Source: Johnston, F. R. (Dec 2000/Jan 2001). Spelling exceptions: Problems or possibilities? *The Reading Teacher, 54*(4), 372–378. Reprinted with permission of Francine R. Johnston and the International Reading Association via Copyright Clearance Center. All rights reserved.

Assessment Devices

C.1 DeFord Theoretical Orientation to Reading Profile   421

C.2 Checklist for Assessing Students' Multiple Intelligences   422

C.3 Applying the Fry Readability Formula   425

C.4 Concepts of Print Checklist   427

C.5 Concepts of Writing Checklist   428

C.6 Miscue Analysis Grid   429

C.7 Grandma's Garden Student Story   430

C.8 Miscue Analysis Grid for Grandma's Garden   432

C.9 Johnny's Birthday Student Story   434

C.10 Miscue Analysis Grid for Johnny's Birthday   436

C.11 Running Record Form   438

C.12 Blank Checklist for Assessing Progress for Use with Any Standards   439

C.13 Checklist for Observations of Progress Toward the CCSS ELA CCR Anchor Standards for Reading   440

C.14 Observational Checklist of Literacy Habits: Early Emergent Literacy Stage   442

C.15 Observational Checklist of Literacy Habits: Emergent Literacy Stage   443

C.16 Observational Checklist of Literacy Habits: Beginning Reading and Writing Stage   444

C.17 Observational Checklist of Literacy Habits: Nearly Fluent Stage   445

C.18 Observational Checklist of Literacy Habits: Fluent Reading and Writing Stage   446

C.19 Personal Interest Survey   447

C.20 Reading Attitude Survey for Primary Students   448

C.21 Writing Attitude Survey for Primary Students   450

C.22 Scoring Sheet for Attitude Surveys   452

C.23 Reading Attitude Survey for Older Students   453

C.24 Writing Attitude Survey for Older Students   454

C.25 Reader Self-Perception Scale   455

C.26 Writer Self-Perception Scale   457

C.27 Reading Log for Primary Students   460

C.28 Reading Log for Intermediate Students   461

C.29 Reading Reflection Log   462

C.30 Quick Phonemic Awareness Assessment Device   463

C.31 Pre-Assessment for Phonemic Awareness   464

C.32 Post-Assessment for Phonemic Awareness   468

C.33 Checklist for Phonemic Awareness for Primary Grades   472

C.34 Checklist for Progress Toward the CCSS ELA Reading: Foundational Skills Phonological Awareness Standards for Kindergarten   473

C.35 Checklist for Progress Toward the CCSS ELA Reading: Foundational Skills Phonological Awareness Standards for Grade 1   474

C.36 Phonics, Word Recognition, and Fluency Checklist Based on the CCSS ELA Reading: Foundational Skills Standards for Grade 3   475

C.37 Checklist of Known Letter Names and Sounds   476

C.38 Phonics Mastery Survey   478

C.39 Scoring Sheet for Word or Phrase Lists   481

C.40 Vocabulary Growth Checklist Based on the CCSS ELA Standards for Language for Grade 8   482

C.41 Rubric for Narrative Reading Comprehension Based on the CCSS ELA Reading: Literature Standards for Grade 5   483

C.42 Interest Inventory for Informational Texts   484

C.43 Observation Checklist of Student's Informational Text Reading   485

C.44 Rubric for Informational Text Comprehension Based on the CCSS ELA Reading: Informational Texts Standards for Grade 6   486

C.45 Informational Text Reading Rubric   487

C.46 Checklist of Basic Online Skills   488

C.47 Fluency Questions for Self-Evaluation   489

C.48 Fluency Checklist   490

C.49 Fluency Checklist for Narrative Text   491

C.50 Oral Reading Fluency Rubric   492

C.51 Student Checklist for Evaluating the Presentation of an Argument   493

C.52 6 + 1 Trait® Writing Assessment   494

C.53 Rubric for Assessing the Writing Process of Writers in Primary Grades   496

C.54 Rubric for Assessing the Writing Process of Third Graders   498

C.55 Rubric for Writing Stories for Grade 4   500

C.56 Rubric for Writing a Research Paper for Grade 4   501

C.57 Rubric for Story Writing   502

C.58 Research Report Rubric for Grades 5/6   503

C.59 Multimedia Group Project Rubric   505

C.60 Writing and Spelling Self-Assessment   506

C.61 Bear, Invernizzi, Templeton, & Johnston, Qualitative Spelling Inventory   507

C.62 Recording and Analyzing Spelling   508

C.1   DeFord Theoretical Orientation to Reading Profile (p. 12)

SA = strongly agree, SD = strongly disagree.

SA . . . SD

1. A child needs to be able to verbalize the rules of phonics in order to ensure proficiency in processing new words. 1 2 3 4 5

2. An increase in reading errors is usually related to a decrease in comprehension. 1 2 3 4 5

3. Dividing words into syllables according to rules is a helpful instructional practice for reading new words. 1 2 3 4 5

4. Fluency and expression are necessary components of reading that indicate good comprehension. 1 2 3 4 5

5. Materials for early reading should be written in natural language without concern for short, simple words and sentences. 1 2 3 4 5

6. When children do not know a word, they should be instructed to sound out its parts. 1 2 3 4 5

7. It is good practice to allow children to edit a text into their own dialect when they are learning to read. 1 2 3 4 5

8. The use of a glossary or dictionary is necessary for determining the meaning and pronunciation of new words. 1 2 3 4 5

9. Reversals (e.g., saying "saw" for "was") are significant problems in the teaching of reading. 1 2 3 4 5

10. It is good practice to correct a child as soon as she makes an oral reading mistake. 1 2 3 4 5

11. It is important for a word to be repeated a number of times after it has been introduced to ensure that it will become a part of sight vocabulary. 1 2 3 4 5

12. Paying close attention to punctuation marks is necessary to understanding story content. 1 2 3 4 5

13. The repetition of words and phrases is a sign of an ineffective reader. 1 2 3 4 5

14. Being able to label words according to grammatical function (nouns, verbs, etc.) is useful in proficient reading. 1 2 3 4 5

SA . . . SD

15. When encountering an unknown word, the reader should be encouraged to guess about its meaning and go on. 1 2 3 4 5

16. Young readers need to be introduced to the root forms of words (*run, long*) before they are asked to read inflected forms (*running, longest*). 1 2 3 4 5

17. It is necessary for a child to know the letters of the alphabet in order to learn to read. 1 2 3 4 5

18. Flash card drills with sight words is an unnecessary form of practice in reading instruction. 1 2 3 4 5

19. The ability to use accent patterns in multi-syllable words (*pho' to graph, pho to' gra phy,* and *pho to gra' phic*) should be developed as part of reading instruction. 1 2 3 4 5

20. Controlling text through consistent spelling patterns ("The fat cat ran back. The fat cat sat on a hat.") is an effective means of learning to read. 1 2 3 4 5

21. Formal instruction in reading is necessary to ensure the adequate development of all the skills used in reading. 1 2 3 4 5

22. Phonics analysis is the most important form of analysis used when encountering new words. 1 2 3 4 5

23. Children's initial experiences with print should focus on meaning more than precise graphic representation. 1 2 3 4 5

24. Word shapes (word configuration) should be taught to aid in word recognition. 1 2 3 4 5

25. It is important to teach skills in relation to other skills. 1 2 3 4 5

26. If a child says "house" for the written word *home,* this response should be left uncorrected. 1 2 3 4 5

27. It is not necessary to introduce new words before they appear in the reading text. 1 2 3 4 5

28. Some problems in reading are caused by readers dropping the inflectional endings from words (e.g., *jumps, jumped*). 1 2 3 4 5

Source: DeFord, D. (1985, Spring). Validating the Construct of Theoretical Orientation in Reading Instruction. *Reading Research Quarterly, 20* (3), 351–367. Reprinted with permission of Diane E. DeFord and the International Reading Association via Copyright Clearance Center. All rights reserved.

| **C.2** | Checklist for Assessing Students' Multiple Intelligences (p. 29) |

Name of Student: _____

Check items that apply:

LINGUISTIC INTELLIGENCE

- ○ writes better than average for age
- ○ spins tall tales or tells jokes and stories
- ○ has a good memory for names, places, dates, or trivia
- ○ spells words accurately (or if preschool, does developmental spelling that is advanced for age)
- ○ enjoys word games
- ○ enjoys reading books
- ○ appreciates nonsense rhymes, puns, tongue twisters
- ○ enjoys listening to the spoken word (stories, commentary on the radio, talking books)
- ○ has a good vocabulary for age
- ○ communicates to others in a highly verbal way

  OTHER LINGUISTIC ABILITIES:

LOGICAL–MATHEMATICAL INTELLIGENCE

- ○ asks a lot of questions about how things work
- ○ enjoys working or playing with numbers
- ○ enjoys math class (or if preschool, enjoys counting and doing other things with numbers)
- ○ finds math and computer games interesting (or if no exposure to computers, enjoys other math or science games)
- ○ enjoys playing chess, checkers, or other strategy games
- ○ enjoys working on logic puzzles or brainteasers (or if preschool, enjoys hearing logical nonsense)
- ○ enjoys putting things in categories, hierarchies, or other logical patterns
- ○ likes to do experiments in science class or in free play
- ○ shows interest in science-related subjects
- ○ does well on Piagetian-type assessments of logical thinking

  OTHER LOGICAL-MATHEMATICAL ABILITIES:

SPATIAL INTELLIGENCE

- ○ reports clear visual images
- ○ reads maps, charts, and diagrams more easily than text (or if preschool, enjoys looking at more than text)
- ○ daydreams a lot
- ○ enjoys art activities
- ○ good at drawings
- ○ likes to view movies, slides, or other visual presentations

- ○ enjoys doing puzzles, mazes, or similar visual activities
- ○ builds interesting three-dimensional constructions (e.g., LEGO buildings)
- ○ gets more out of pictures than words while reading
- ○ doodles on workbooks, worksheets, or other materials
  OTHER SPATIAL ABILITIES:

BODILY–KINESTHETIC INTELLIGENCE

- ○ excels in one or more sports (or if preschool, shows physical prowess advanced for age)
- ○ moves, twitches, taps, or fidgets while seated for a long time in one spot
- ○ cleverly mimics other people's gestures or mannerisms
  loves to take things apart and put them back together again
- ○ puts his/her hands all over something he/she's just seen
- ○ enjoys running, jumping, wrestling, or similar activities (or if older, will show these interests in a more "restrained" way—e.g., running to class, jumping over a chair)
- ○ shows skill in a craft (e.g., woodworking, sewing, mechanics) or good fine-motor coordination in other ways
- ○ has a dramatic way of expressing herself/himself
- ○ reports different physical sensations while thinking or working
- ○ enjoys working with clay or other tactile experiences (e.g., fingerpainting)
  OTHER BODILY-KINESTHETIC ABILITIES:

MUSICAL INTELLIGENCE

- ○ tells you when music sounds off-key or disturbing in some other way
- ○ remembers melodies of songs
- ○ has a good singing voice
- ○ plays a musical instrument or sings in a choir or other group (or if preschool, enjoys playing percussion instruments and/or singing in a group)
- ○ has a rhythmic way of speaking and/or moving
- ○ unconsciously hums to himself/herself
- ○ taps rhythmically on the table or desk as he/she works
- ○ sensitive to environmental noises (e.g., rain on the roof)
- ○ responds favorably when a piece of music is put on
- ○ sings songs that he/she has learned outside of the classroom
  OTHER MUSICAL ABILITIES:

INTERPERSONAL INTELLIGENCE

- ○ enjoys socializing with peers
- ○ seems to be a natural leader
- ○ gives advice to friends who have problems
- ○ seems to be street-smart
- ○ belongs to clubs, committees, organizations, or informal peer groups
- ○ enjoys informally teaching other kids
- ○ likes to play games with other kids

○ has two or more close friends

○ has a good sense of empathy or concern for others

○ others seek out his/her company

OTHER INTERPERSONAL ABILITIES:

INTRAPERSONAL INTELLIGENCE

○ displays a sense of independence or a strong will

○ has a realistic sense of his/her abilities and weaknesses

○ does well when left alone to play or study

○ marches to the beat of a different drummer in his/her style of living and learning

○ has an interest or hobby that he/she doesn't talk much about

○ has a good sense of self-direction

○ prefers working alone to working with others

○ accurately expresses how he/she is feeling

○ is able to learn from his/her failures and successes in life

○ has good self-esteem

OTHER INTRAPERSONAL ABILITIES:

NATURALISTIC INTELLIGENCE

○ talks a lot about favorite pets, or preferred spots in nature, during class sharing

○ likes field trips in nature, to the zoo, or to a natural history museum

○ shows sensitivity to nature formations (e.g., while walking outside with the class, will notice mountains, clouds; or if in an urban environment, may show this ability in sensitivity to popular culture "formations" such as sneakers or automobile styles)

○ likes to water and tend to the plants in the classroom

○ likes to hang around the gerbil cage, the aquarium, or the terrarium in class

○ gets excited when studying about ecology, nature, plants, or animals

○ speaks out in class for the rights of animals, or the preservation of planet earth

○ enjoys doing nature projects, such as bird watching, butterfly or insect collections, tree study, or raising animals

○ brings to school bugs, flowers, leaves, or other natural things to share with classmates or teachers

○ does well in topics at school that involve living systems (e.g., biological topics in science, environmental issues in social studies)

OTHER NATURALISTIC ABILITIES:

C.3   Applying the Fry Readability Formula (p. 33)

DIRECTIONS

1. Randomly select three 100-word passages from a book or an article. The three passages should be from the beginning, middle, and end of the book.

2. Count the number of syllables in each passage and find the average number of syllables of the three passages. For example, the sample passage below has 145 syllables.

3. Count the number of sentences, estimating length of the fraction of the last sentence to the nearest one-tenth. For example, the sample passage has eight complete sentences. The 100th word of the passage is the 6th word of the 9th sentence, which is not the end of the sentence. To find the fraction of the last sentence in the passage, divide the number of words in the 9th sentence through the 100th word (6) by the number of words in the entire sentence (16) and round to the nearest tenth (6/16 = .375 or .4). The total number of sentences for this passage would be 8.4 sentences.

   After finding the number of sentences in each 100-word passage, find the average number for the three passages.

4. On the Fry Readability Graph, plot the average number of syllables and the average number of sentences for the three passages to get the estimated reading level of the book.

SAMPLE PASSAGE

(Sample Passage from Boyle, D. [1998]. *Coral reef hideaway: The story of a clown anemonefish.* New York: Scholastic.)

3 1 1 1 1 1 1 1 1   1   1   2 1 1 1
Percula's mate cleans the rock. If they get the chance, some wrasses will eat the

5   1 1   1 1 1 2   2 1 1 1 1   3
anemonefish eggs when they are laid. Before twilight the rock is clean. Percula's

1 1 1 1   4   1 1 2   1 1 1   1 1
mate rests near the anemone mouth as darkness falls. Now sharks, jacks and

4   1 2 1 3 1   2 1 1 1 1   3
barracudas swarm around the shadowy reef, snapping up blue tangs and parrotfish

1 1 1 1 1 1 1   2   2   3   1 1 1 1 1
that have stayed too long in their daytime waters. Percula and her mate are safe

1 1 4 1 1 2 1 1 2 2 1 2   1 1 1
in the anemone. As the nearly full moon rises over the lagoon, the reef's night

2   1 1 2 1 3   1 1 2 2   1
creatures emerge. Like thousands of miniature stars, the coral itself blooms.

3 1 3   1 1 2
Squirrelfish and soldierfish leave the sheltered (100th word) crevices and hunt

along the bottom for worms and crabs.

NOTE:

1. Scores falling in the gray areas of the graph are invalid. If this occurs, another sample must be taken.

2. A word is defined as a group of symbols with a space on either side. Acronyms (ILA), dates (2004), initials (J.), titles (Jr.), and symbols (&) each count as one word.

3. With numerals, acronyms, initials, titles, and symbols, each symbol within them is one syllable. For example, 2004 = 4 syllables; ILA = 3 syllables; J. = 1 syllable.

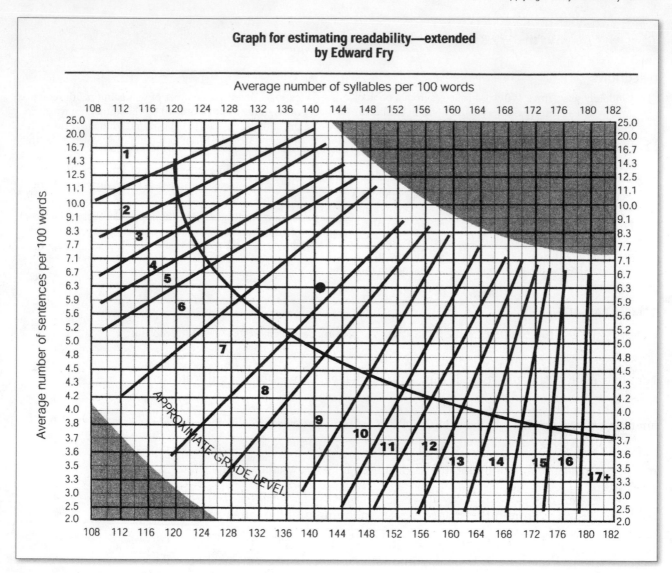

Graph for estimating readability—extended by Edward Fry

Source: Fry, E. B. (2002). Readability Versus Leveling. *The Reading Teacher, 56*(3), 286–291.

EXAMPLE:

The readability level indicated on the graph above is based on three samples with the following syllable and word counts:

	Syllables	Sentences
First hundred words	124	6.6
Second hundred words	141	5.5
Third hundred words	<u>158</u>	<u>6.8</u>
Average	141	6.3

Readability seventh grade (see dot plotted on graph)

Source: Fry, E. B. (2002). Readability Versus Leveling. *The Reading Teacher, 56*(3), 286–291.

C.4   Concepts of Print Checklist (p. 46)

Student: _____   Date: _____

	YES	NO
1. Knows which is the front of the book.	○	○
2. Holds a book correctly.	○	○
3. Knows that the words, not the print, are what is read when asked, "Where do I start to read?"	○	○
4. Knows that one reads from the top of the page to the bottom.	○	○
5. Knows that one reads the left-hand page and then the right-hand page. Can point to where to go after completing the left-hand page.	○	○
6. Knows the return sweep concept (where to go when he/she reaches the end of a line).	○	○
7. Is able to point from word to word.	○	○
8. Knows the difference between		
a word	○	○
a letter	○	○
a sentence	○	○
9. Knows letter order is important and different in each word (recognizes the misspelled words).	○	○
10. Is able to identify the first and last letters in words.	○	○
11. Knows the purpose of		
a period	○	○
question mark	○	○
exclamation mark	○	○

Source: Los Angeles County Office of Education. (2000). *Kindergarten and Grade One Reading: Basic to Success.* Retrieved from http://teams.lacoe.edu/documentation/classrooms/patti/K-1/teacher/assessment/print/concepts.html.

C.5 Concepts of Writing Checklist (p. 47)

Student: _____   Date: _____

	YES	NO
1. Understands that writing carries a message.	○	○
2. Understands that what is spoken can be written down.	○	○
3. Sees the unique differences between letters.	○	○
4. Has learned to embellish letters while retaining their identities.	○	○
5. Enjoys producing patterns in writing.	○	○
6. Combines or arranges elements of print in an inventive manner.	○	○
7. Writes from left to right and from top to bottom.	○	○
8. Can distinguish differences between the shapes, meanings, and sounds in letters and words.	○	○
9. Understands that a space is needed between words.	○	○
10. Understands that letters construct words.	○	○

Source: Adapted from Clay, M. (2006). *Principles and Concepts of Early Writing.* www.learningtowrite.ecsd.net/principles%20 and%20concepts.htm.

C.6 Miscue Analysis Grid (p. 49)

TEXT	Substitution	Mispronun-ciation	Insertion	Omission	Repeats	Self-correction	Syntax unacceptable	Meaning disrupted
TOTAL MISCUES:								

Notes:

Grandma's Garden

"Megan, today we are going to Grandma's house. She wants us to help her pick vegetables in the garden."

"Goodie! I love to visit Grandma, and help her in her garden. She has such beautiful flowers."

When they got to Grandma's house, she was standing on the porch, waving to them. Megan went running to Grandma and gave her a big hug. "We are here to help you pick vegetables, Grandma."

"Super! I need help picking the beans and the peas. Here is a basket for you, one for your mom, and one for me. And here is a sun hat for you, one for your mom, and one for me. I do not want you to get a sun burn."

In the garden, they began to pick the beans. Megan filled her basket first. Grandma gave her another basket. "Now you can fill this one with peas," Grandma said.

After all the baskets were filled, Grandma said, "Now let's see if the carrots are big enough to pick."

Grandma took Megan to the row of carrots. "Here they are," Grandma announced.

"I don't see any carrots," Megan said.

"You cannot see them, but watch." Grandma took a bunch of green tops and pulled straight up.

"Wow!" said Megan, "That is magic! May I eat this big carrot?"

"Of course, but first help me pick two more: one for your mom and one for me. Then we will wash them and enjoy them," Grandma said.

And that is just what they did. They washed the carrots and went to sit in the porch swing to eat their big, fat carrot.

C.8 Miscue Analysis Grid for Grandma's Garden (p. 49)

TEXT (Level 2.2, 275 words)	Substitution	Mispronunciation	Insertion	Omission	Repeats	Self-correction	Syntax unacceptable	Meaning disrupted
"Megan, today we are going to Grandma's house. She								
wants us to help her pick vegetables in the garden."								
"Goodie! I love to visit Grandma, and help her in her								
garden. She has such beautiful flowers." When they got								
to Grandma's house, she was standing on the porch,								
waving to them. Megan went running to Grandma and								
gave her a big hug. "We are here to help you pick								
vegetables, Grandma." "Super! I need help picking beans								
and peas. Here is a basket for you, one for your mom,								
and one for me. And here is a sun hat for you, one for								
your mom, and one for me. I do not want you to get a sun								
burn." In the garden, they began to pick the beans.								
Megan filled her basket first. Grandma gave her another								
basket. "Now you can fill this one with peas," Grandma								
said. After all the baskets were filled, Grandma said,								
"Now let's see if the carrots are big enough to pick."								

TEXT	Substitution	Mispronun-ciation	Insertion	Omission	Repeats	Self-correction	Syntax unacceptable	Meaning disrupted
Grandma took Megan to the row of carrots. "Here they								
are," Grandma announced. "I don't see any carrots,"								
Megan said. "You cannot see them, but watch." Grandma								
took a bunch of green tops and pulled straight up.								
"Wow!" said Megan, "That is magic! May I eat this big								
carrot?" "Of course, but first help me pick two more:								
one for your mom and one for me. Then we will wash								
them and enjoy them," Grandma said. And that is just								
what they did. They washed the carrots and went								
to sit in the porch swing to eat their big, fat carrot.								
TOTAL MISCUES:								

Johnny's Birthday

"Get up, Johnny! It's your birthday! I have a great day planned for us!" Johnny jumped out of bed and ran downstairs.

"What did you make for breakfast?"

"Your favorite—pancakes with chocolate chips and peanut butter!"

"They are the best, Dad!" Johnny said as he finished his third pancake. "What are we going to do today?" Johnny asked.

"We are going to the zoo to see the baby elephant."

"GREAT! I love the zoo! Can I go to the petting pen after we see the baby elephant?"

"Of course! I love to pet the goats!"

At the zoo, Dad and Johnny first went to the baby elephant.

"Look, Dad, the baby is eating a melon. It looks so funny to see him eat with his trunk."

After the baby elephant finished the melon, Dad said, "Let's take a train ride. It will take us past the zebras, the giraffes, and the tigers." They hopped on the train.

"Look at that giraffe eat the leaves off the tree! The giraffes are so tall!"

"The zebras look like a horse with stripes," Dad laughed.

"And look at the tiger yawn! What a big mouth!" Johnny exclaimed.

After they rode past all the animals, they got off the train at the petting pen. "Now I can pet the animals! This is my favorite part of the zoo!" Johnny remarked. They petted the goats, sheep, and baby bunnies.

After they petted all the animals, Dad said, "I'm hungry! How about a hot dog?"

"I am hungry too! I love hot dogs!" They found a big tree to sit under as they enjoyed their hot dogs. After they finished their hot dogs, they went back to the car.

"This was the best birthday yet! Thanks, Dad, for taking me to the zoo."

"I had a great day too, Johnny! I love doing things with you!"

C.10 Miscue Analysis Grid for Johnny's Birthday (p. 49)

TEXT (Level 1.8, 316 words)	Substitution	Mispronunciation	Insertion	Omission	Repeats	Self-correction	Syntax unacceptable	Meaning disrupted
"Get up, Johnny! It's your birthday! I have a great day								
planned for us!" Johnny jumped out of bed and ran								
downstairs. "What did you make for breakfast?"								
"Your favorite—pancakes with chocolate chips and								
peanut butter!" "They are the best, Dad!" Johnny said as								
he finished his third pancake. "What are we going to do								
today?" Johnny asked. "We are going to the zoo to see								
the baby elephant." "GREAT! I love the zoo! Can I go								
to the petting pen after we see the baby elephant?"								
"Of course! I love to pet the goats!" At the zoo, Dad and								
Johnny first went to the baby elephant. "Look, Dad, the								
baby is eating a melon. It looks so funny to see him eat								
with his trunk." After the baby elephant finished the								
melon, Dad said, "Let's take a train ride. It will take								
us past the zebras, the giraffes, and the tigers."								
They hopped on the train. "Look at that giraffe eat								

TEXT	Substitution	Mispronun-ciation	Insertion	Omission	Repeats	Self-correction	Syntax unacceptable	Meaning disrupted
the leaves off the tree! The giraffes are so tall!" "The								
zebras look like a horse with stripes," Dad laughed.								
"And look at the tiger yawn! What a big mouth!"								
Johnny exclaimed. After they rode past all the animals,								
they got off the train at the petting pen. "Now I can								
pet the animals! This is my favorite part of the zoo!"								
Johnny remarked. They petted the goats, sheep, and								
baby bunnies. After they petted all the animals,								
Dad said, "I'm hungry! How about a hot dog?"								
"I am hungry too! I love hot dogs!" They found a								
big tree to sit under as they enjoyed their hot dogs.								
After they finished their hot dogs, they went back								
to the car. "This was the best birthday yet!								
Thanks, Dad, for taking me to the zoo." "I had a great								
day too, Johnny! I love doing things with you!"								
TOTAL MISCUES:								

C.11 Running Record Form (p. 54)

Student: _____   Date: _____

Teacher: _____   Reading Level: _____

Story: _____

Number of Errors: _____   Percentage: _____

Running Words: _____   Level for Student: Easy, Instructional, Frustration

Comments:

TEXT	ANALYSIS			
	Number		System Used	
	E	SC	E	SC
Page				

C.12   **Blank Checklist for Assessing Progress for Use with Any Standards** (p. 58)

Teacher: _____   Date: _____

+ = always   X = sometimes   O = seldom/never

STANDARD	STUDENTS																

C.13   Checklist for Observations of Progress Toward the CCSS ELA CCR
Anchor Standards for Reading (p. 58)

Name: _____   Grade: _____

STANDARDS	CONTEXT	DATE OBSERVED	CONTEXT	DATE OBSERVED	CONTEXT	DATE OBSERVED
CCSS.ELA-Literacy.CCRA.R.1 Read closely to determine what the text says explicitly and to make logical inferences from it; cite specific textual evidence when writing or speaking to support conclusions drawn from the text.						
CCSS.ELA-Literacy.CCRA.R.2 Determine central ideas or themes of a text and analyze their development; summarize the key supporting details and ideas.						
CCSS.ELA-Literacy.CCRA.R.3 Analyze how and why individuals, events, or ideas develop and interact over the course of a text.						
CCSS.ELA-Literacy.CCRA.R.4 Interpret words and phrases as they are used in a text, including determining technical, connotative, and figurative meanings, and analyze how specific word choices shape meaning or tone.						
CCSS.ELA-Literacy.CCRA.R.5 Analyze the structure of texts, including how specific sentences, paragraphs, and larger portions of the text (e.g., a section, chapter, scene, or stanza) relate to each other and the whole.						
CCSS.ELA-Literacy.CCRA.R.6 Assess how point of view or purpose shapes the content and style of a text.						
CSS.ELA-Literacy.CCRA.R.7 Integrate and evaluate content presented in diverse media and formats, including visually and quantitatively, as well as in words.						

STANDARDS	CONTEXT	DATE OBSERVED	CONTEXT	DATE OBSERVED	CONTEXT	DATE OBSERVED
CCSS.ELA-Literacy.CCRA.R.8 Delineate and evaluate the argument and specific claims in a text, including the validity of the reasoning as well as the relevance and sufficiency of the evidence.						
CCSS.ELA-Literacy.CCRA.R.9 Analyze how two or more texts address similar themes or topics in order to build knowledge or to compare the approaches the authors take.						
CCSS.ELA-Literacy.CCRA.R.10 Read and comprehend complex literary and informational texts independently and proficiently.						

*The standards used in this checklist are the CCSS English Language Arts Standards, College and Career Readiness Anchor Standards for Reading (Washington, DC: NGACBP, CCSSO, 2010. p. 13.). Any state standards could be used, and the checklist can be made grade-level specific using state standards or the grade-level specific CCSS.

C.14   Observational Checklist of Literacy Habits: Early Emergent Literacy Stage (p. 58)

Student: _____   Grade: _____

Teacher: _____

− = Behavior not observed   + = Behavior observed   X = Progressing

			DATES		
EARLY EMERGENT LITERACY STAGE:					
1. Shows pleasure in read-alouds.					
2. Can retell stories in sequence.					
3. Uses book language in retellings.					
4. Likes to make up stories.					
5. Holds books correctly.					
6. Recognizes environmental print (e.g., cereals, cookies).					
7. Pretends to read.					
8. Scribbles messages.					
9. Writes some letters correctly.					
10. Has phonemic awareness.					

C.15   Observational Checklist of Literacy Habits: Emergent Literacy Stage (p. 58)

Student: _____   Grade: _____

Teacher: _____

− = Behavior not observed   + = Behavior observed   X = Progressing

	DATES				
EMERGENT LITERACY STAGE:					
1. "Reads" top to bottom of page.					
2. "Reads" front to back of book.					
3. "Reads" left to right.					
4. Recognizes nonstandard English.					
5. Enjoys jokes.					
6. Enjoys alliteration.					
7. Hears rhyming words.					
8. Knows difference between words and letters.					
9. Matches words with voice when reading.					
10. Knows, title, author, and illustrator of books.					
11. Recognizes letters in random order.					
12. Matches uppercase with lowercase letters.					
13. Recognizes name in print.					
14. Can write most letters.					
15. Uses phonemic awareness when writing.					
16. Can name initial and ending letter sounds of words.					
17. Shows interest in writing stories, notes, etc.					

C.16 Observational Checklist of Literacy Habits: Beginning Reading and Writing Stage (p. 58)

Student: _____   Grade: _____

Teacher: _____

− = Behavior not observed   **+** = Behavior observed   **X** = Progressing

	DATES				
BEGINNING READING AND WRITING STAGE:					
1. Self-corrects nonstandard English.					
2. Can paraphrase what others say.					
3. Can summarize a story.					
4. Participates in discussion.					
5. Enjoys nonsense and silly poems.					
6. Recognizes all letters in random order.					
7. Recognizes many sight words.					
8. Uses phonics to pronounce new words.					
9. Understands concepts of onset and rime.					
10. Reads own writing.					
11. Chooses to write independently.					
12. Word-by-word reading.					
13. Sounds out words instead of guessing.					
14. Lip-voicing movements in silent reading.					
15. Finger-points at every word.					
16. Uses spelling that reflects phonics knowledge.					
17. Uses word processing when writing.					
18. Uses all five steps of writing process.					
19. Adequate reading rate.					
20. Adequate vocabulary knowledge.					

C.17 Observational Checklist of Literacy Habits: Nearly Fluent Stage (p. 58)

Student: _____   Grade: _____

Teacher: _____

− = Behavior not observed   + = Behavior observed   X = Progressing

NEARLY FLUENT LITERACY STAGE:	DATES				
1. Uses oral standard English.					
2. Uses new vocabulary words correctly.					
3. Listens and questions speaker.					
4. Appreciates symbolic language.					
5. Uses structural analysis to determine unknown words.					
6. Uses context clues.					
7. Reads with 90% accuracy in grade-level materials.					
8. Self-corrects.					
9. Understands stories read to him/her that are above his/her grade level.					
10. Reads/comprehends a variety of genres.					
11. Prefers to read silently.					
12. Aware of own purpose for reading.					
13. Understands expository text structures.					
14. Beginning to synthesize information from a variety of sources.					
15. Can interpret simple graphs.					
16. Can locate information online.					
17. Writes good stories.					
18. Writes good paragraphs.					
19. Uses word processing tools to revise and edit work.					
20. Uses five steps of writing process.					
21. Uses vivid language when writing.					

C.18 Observational Checklist of Literacy Habits: Fluent Reading and Writing Stage (p. 58)

Student: _____   Grade: _____

Teacher: _____

− = Behavior not observed   + = Behavior observed   X = Progressing

	DATES				
FLUENT READING AND WRITING STAGE:					
1. Enjoys readers theater.					
2. Enjoys giving speeches in front of class.					
3. Understands the elements of stories.					
4. Understands differences in genres.					
5. Uses effective strategies when reading.					
6. Can self-correct when reading.					
7. Enjoys reading during free time.					
8. Knows where to locate information.					
9. Uses writing to persuade.					
10. Can edit classmates' work.					
11. Can edit own writing.					
12. Self-checks spelling and grammar.					
13. Revises own work when necessary.					
14. Recognizes authors' style and techniques in writing.					
15. Attempts to copy a writer's style.					

C.19 Personal Interest Survey (p. 64)

Name: _____ Grade: _____ Date: _____

Write more than one item for each category if more than one item interests you. Explain why for each response. For example, why do you enjoy football?

1. My favorite foods are _____

2. My favorite eating places are _____

3. My favorite snacks are _____

4. My favorite TV shows are _____

5. My favorite TV characters are _____

6. My favorite movies are _____

7. My favorite actors are _____

8. My favorite video games are _____

9. The best book I ever read was _____

10. My favorite music group is _____

11. My favorite song is _____

12. My favorite sport is _____

13. My favorite school subject is _____

14. I know I am very good at _____

15. When I am alone, I like to _____

16. My favorite thing to do with my friends is _____

17. My least favorite thing to do by myself is _____

18. My favorite thing to do on Saturday and Sunday is _____

19. The thing I fear most is _____

20. If I had a million dollars, I would _____

From *Literacy Assessment and Intervention for Classroom Teachers* (4th ed.), by Beverly DeVries. Copyright ©2015 by Holcomb Hathaway, Publishers, Scottsdale, AZ.

C.20 **Reading Attitude Survey for Primary Students** (p. 66)

Name: _____   Grade: _____   Date: _____

1. How I feel when the teacher reads to me.

2. How I feel when classmates read in class.

3. How I feel when asked to read aloud in class.

4. How I feel when asked to read aloud just for my teacher.

5. How I feel when I read stories to my family.

6. How I feel when I read to myself.

7. How I feel during independent reading.

8. How I feel about reading mystery stories.

9. How I feel about listening to my teacher read mystery stories.

10. How I feel about reading funny stories.

11. How I feel about listening to my teacher read funny stories.

12. How I feel about reading scary stories.

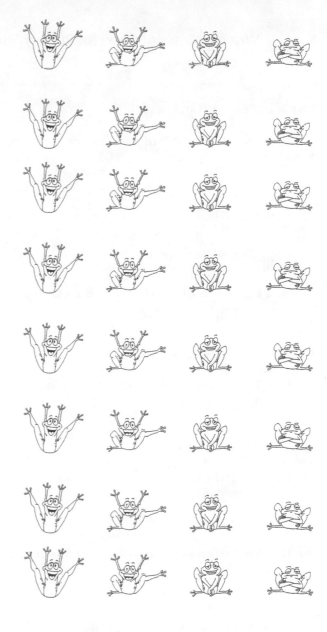

13. How I feel about listening to my teacher read scary stories.

14. How I feel about reading poetry.

15. How I feel about listening to my teacher read poetry.

16. How I feel about reading informational books about sports.

17. How I feel about reading informational books about spiders, snakes, and other creatures.

18. How I feel about reading informational books on places to visit.

19. How I feel about reading stories on the computer.

20. How I feel about finding information on the computer.

See C.22, "Scoring Sheet for Attitude Surveys."

C.21   **Writing Attitude Survey for Primary Students** (p. 66)

Name: _____   Grade: _____   Date: _____

Pretest or Posttest (Circle one)

1. How I feel when asked to write a story.

2. How I feel when asked to write riddles.

3. How I feel when asked to write about my favorite
    sport or pet.

4. How I feel when asked to write to my favorite
    author.

5. How I feel when asked to write a poem.

6. How I feel when asked to write about myself.

7. How I feel when asked to write a thank-you note.

8. How I feel when asked to write in front of my
    classmates.

9. How I feel when I write on a dry-erase board.

10. How I feel when I write on the computer.

11. How I feel when I write *with* classmates.

12. How I feel when I write with my teacher.

13. How I feel about writing science reports.

14. How I feel when asked to check for mistakes in my writing.

15. How I feel about my spelling ability.

16. How I feel when asked to change something in my writing.

17. How I feel when my story or poem or article is posted for my classmates to read.

18. How I feel when my teacher reads my poem, story, or article to the class.

19. How I feel if I do not have to write in school.

20. How I feel if I have more time to write in school.

See C.22, "Scoring Sheet for Attitude Surveys."

C.22   Scoring Sheet for Attitude Surveys (p. 66)

Student: _____   Grade: _____   Pretest Date: _____

Teacher: _____   Posttest Date: _____

Scoring Guide:

   Happy character = 4 points

   "Somewhat" happy character = 3 points

   Neutral character = 2 points

   Unhappy character = 1 point

ITEMS: PRETEST

1. _____   2. _____   3. _____   4. _____   5. _____

6. _____   7. _____   8. _____   9. _____   10. _____

11. _____   12. _____   13. _____   14. _____   15. _____

16. _____   17. _____   18. _____   19. _____   20. _____

TOTAL: _____

Comments:

ITEMS: POSTTEST

1. _____   2. _____   3. _____   4. _____   5. _____

6. _____   7. _____   8. _____   9. _____   10. _____

11. _____   12. _____   13. _____   14. _____   15. _____

16. _____   17. _____   18. _____   19. _____   20. _____

TOTAL: _____

Comments:

C.23 Reading Attitude Survey for Older Students (p. 66)

Student: _____ Grade: _____ Date: _____

Pretest or Posttest (Circle one)

Respond to the statement by circling SL for Strongly Like, L for Like, O for Okay, DL for Dislike, and SD for Strongly Dislike.

1.	Completing research on the Internet.	SL	L	O	DL	SD
2.	Reading my science text.	SL	L	O	DL	SD
3.	Reading my history text.	SL	L	O	DL	SD
4.	Reading informational texts online.	SL	L	O	DL	SD
5.	Reading informational books for a report.	SL	L	O	DL	SD
6.	Reading realistic fiction.	SL	L	O	DL	SD
7.	Reading historical fiction.	SL	L	O	DL	SD
8.	Reading poetry.	SL	L	O	DL	SD
9.	Reading a funny book.	SL	L	O	DL	SD
10.	Reading the comics in a newspaper.	SL	L	O	DL	SD
11.	Reading the sports section of a newspaper.	SL	L	O	DL	SD
12.	Reading a sports magazine online.	SL	L	O	DL	SD
13.	Listening to classmates read.	SL	L	O	DL	SD
14.	Listening to my teacher read.	SL	L	O	DL	SD
15.	Reading in front of my peers.	SL	L	O	DL	SD
16.	Reading on the weekend.	SL	L	O	DL	SD
17.	Learning to become a better reader.	SL	L	O	DL	SD

Answer the following questions. Be honest in your responses.

1. Do you consider yourself a good reader? Explain.

_____

2. Do you like to help other classmates with their reading problems? Explain.

_____

3. What is the hardest thing for you to do in reading?

_____

4. What do you do best as a reader?

_____

From *Literacy Assessment and Intervention for Classroom Teachers* (4th ed.), by Beverly DeVries. Copyright ©2015 by Holcomb Hathaway, Publishers, Scottsdale, AZ.

C.24   Writing Attitude Survey for Older Students (p. 66)

Student: _____   Grade: _____   Date: _____

Pretest or Posttest (Circle one)

Respond to the statement by circling SL for Strongly Like, L for Like, O for Okay, DL for Dislike, and SD for Strongly Dislike.

1. Writing a story for class.	SL	L	O	DL	SD
2. Writing about my science project.	SL	L	O	DL	SD
3. Writing a history or other report.	SL	L	O	DL	SD
4. Writing a persuasive essay.	SL	L	O	DL	SD
5. Writing poetry.	SL	L	O	DL	SD
6. Writing lyrics for a song.	SL	L	O	DL	SD
7. Writing letters and notes to friends.	SL	L	O	DL	SD
8. Writing in a personal diary or journal.	SL	L	O	DL	SD
9. Writing in a dialogue journal with your teacher.	SL	L	O	DL	SD
10. Writing a script for a play or readers theater.	SL	L	O	DL	SD
11. Writing jokes or other funny material.	SL	L	O	DL	SD
12. Writing scary stories or mysteries.	SL	L	O	DL	SD
13. Prewriting in writing workshop.	SL	L	O	DL	SD
14. Writing my first draft in writing workshop.	SL	L	O	DL	SD
15. Revising and editing in writing workshop.	SL	L	O	DL	SD
16. Having other classmates read my story or report.	SL	L	O	DL	SD
17. Helping classmates edit their work.	SL	L	O	DL	SD
18. Having other classmates edit my work.	SL	L	O	DL	SD
19. Using a word processor for writing.	SL	L	O	DL	SD
20. Using paper and pen or pencil for writing.	SL	L	O	DL	SD
21. Writing in my spare time.	SL	L	O	DL	SD
22. Writing e-mails to friends.	SL	L	O	DL	SD
23. Texting a friend.	SL	L	O	DL	SD
24. Writing information for web pages.	SL	L	O	DL	SD

Answer the following questions honestly.

1. I think I am a (good or not-so-good) writer because

_____

2. I wish I could write like my favorite author because

_____

3. The hardest thing for me to do in writing is

_____

C.25 Reader Self-Perception Scale (p. 66)

Listed below are statements about reading. Please read each statement carefully. Then circle the letters that show how much you agree or disagree with the statement. Use the following:

SA = Strongly Agree
A = Agree
U = Undecided
D = Disagree
SD = Strongly Disagree

Example: I think pizza with pepperoni is best.   SA   A   U   D   SD

If you are *really positive* that pepperoni pizza is best, circle SA (Strongly Agree).
If you *think* that it is good but maybe not great, circle A (Agree).
If you *can't decide* whether or not it is best, circle U (Undecided).
If you *think* that pepperoni pizza is not all that good, circle D (Disagree).
If you are *really positive* that pepperoni pizza is not very good, circle SD (Strongly Disagree).

[GPR]	1. I think I am a good reader.	SA	A	U	D	SD
[SF]	2. I can tell that my teacher likes to listen to me read.	SA	A	U	D	SD
[SF]	3. My teacher thinks that my reading is fine.	SA	A	U	D	SD
[OC]	4. I read faster than other kids.	SA	A	U	D	SD
[PS]	5. I like to read aloud.	SA	A	U	D	SD
[OC]	6. When I read, I can figure out words better than other kids.	SA	A	U	D	SD
[SF]	7. My classmates like to listen to me read.	SA	A	U	D	SD
[PS]	8. I feel good inside when I read.	SA	A	U	D	SD
[SF]	9. My classmates think that I read pretty well.	SA	A	U	D	SD
[PR]	10. When I read, I don't have to try as hard as I used to.	SA	A	U	D	SD
[OC]	11. I seem to know more words than other kids when I read.	SA	A	U	D	SD
[SF]	12. People in my family think I am a good reader.	SA	A	U	D	SD
[PR]	13. I am getting better at reading.	SA	A	U	D	SD
[OC]	14. I understand what I read as well as other kids do.	SA	A	U	D	SD
[PR]	15. When I read, I need less help than I used to.	SA	A	U	D	SD
[PS]	16. Reading makes me feel happy inside.	SA	A	U	D	SD
[SF]	17. My teacher thinks I am a good reader.	SA	A	U	D	SD
[PR]	18. Reading is easier for me than it used to be.	SA	A	U	D	SD
[PR]	19. I read faster than I could before.	SA	A	U	D	SD
[OC]	20. I read better than other kids in my class.	SA	A	U	D	SD
[PS]	21. I feel calm when I read.	SA	A	U	D	SD
[OC]	22. I read more than other kids.	SA	A	U	D	SD
[PR]	23. I understand what I read better than I could before.	SA	A	U	D	SD
[PR]	24. I can figure out words better than I could before.	SA	A	U	D	SD

[PS]	25.	I feel comfortable when I read.	SA	A	U	D	SD
[PS]	26.	I think reading is relaxing.	SA	A	U	D	SD
[PR]	27.	I read better now than I could before.	SA	A	U	D	SD
[PR]	28.	When I read, I recognize more words than I used to.	SA	A	U	D	SD
[PS]	29.	Reading makes me feel good.	SA	A	U	D	SD
[SF]	30.	Other kids think I'm a good reader.	SA	A	U	D	SD
[SF]	31.	People in my family think I read pretty well.	SA	A	U	D	SD
[PS]	32.	I enjoy reading.	SA	A	U	D	SD
[SF]	33.	People in my family like to listen to me read.	SA	A	U	D	SD

The Reader Self-Perception Scale Scoring Sheet

Student name: _____

Teacher: _____   Grade: _____   Date: _____

Scoring key:

  5 = Strongly Agree (SA)
  4 = Agree (A)
  3 = Undecided (U)
  2 = Disagree (D)
  1 = Strongly Disagree (SD)

SCALES

General Perception (GPR)	Progress (PR)	Observational Comparison (OC)	Social Feedback (SF)	Physiological States (PS)
1. _____	10. _____	4. _____	2. _____	5. _____
	13. _____	6. _____	3. _____	8. _____
	15. _____	11. _____	7. _____	16. _____
	18. _____	14. _____	9. _____	21. _____
	19. _____	20. _____	12. _____	25. _____
	23. _____	22. _____	17. _____	26. _____
	24. _____		30. _____	29. _____
	27. _____		31. _____	32. _____
	28. _____		33. _____	
Raw scores	_____ of 45	_____ of 30	_____ of 45	_____ of 40

Score interpretation	PR	OC	SF	PS
High	44+	26+	38+	37+
Average	39	21	33	31
Low	34	16	27	25

C.26   Writer Self-Perception Scale (p. 66)

Listed below are statements about writing. Please read each statement carefully. Then circle the letters that show how much you agree or disagree with the statement. Use the following scale:

SA = Strongly Agree
A = Agree
U = Undecided
D = Disagree
SD = Strongly Disagree

Example: I think Batman is the greatest super hero.   SA   A   U   D   SD

If you are *really positive* that Batman is the greatest, circle SA (Strongly Agree).

If you *think* that Batman is good but maybe not great, circle A (Agree).

If you *can't decide* whether or not Batman is the greatest, circle U (Undecided).

If you *think* that Batman is not all that great, circle D (Disagree).

If you are *really positive* that Batman is not the greatest, circle SD (Strongly Disagree).

[OC]	1. I write better than other kids in my class.	SA	A	U	D	SD
[PS]	2. I like how writing makes me feel inside.	SA	A	U	D	SD
[GPR]	3. Writing is easier for me than it used to be.	SA	A	U	D	SD
[OC]	4. When I write, my organization is better than the other kids in my class.	SA	A	U	D	SD
[SF]	5. People in my family think I am a good writer.	SA	A	U	D	SD
[GPR]	6. I am getting better at writing.	SA	A	U	D	SD
[PS]	7. When I write, I feel calm.	SA	A	U	D	SD
[OC]	8. My writing is more interesting than my classmates' writing.	SA	A	U	D	SD
[SF]	9. My teacher thinks my writing is fine.	SA	A	U	D	SD
[SF]	10. Other kids think I am a good writer.	SA	A	U	D	SD
[OC]	11. My sentences and paragraphs fit together as well as my classmates' sentences and paragraphs.	SA	A	U	D	SD
[GPR]	12. I need less help to write well than I used to.	SA	A	U	D	SD
[SF]	13. People in my family think I write pretty well.	SA	A	U	D	SD
[GPR]	14. I write better now than I could before.	SA	A	U	D	SD
[GPR]	15. I think I am a good writer.	SA	A	U	D	SD
[OC]	16. I put my sentences in a better order than the other kids.	SA	A	U	D	SD
[GPR]	17. My writing has improved.	SA	A	U	D	SD
[GPR]	18. My writing is better than before.	SA	A	U	D	SD
[GPR]	19. It's easier to write well now than it used to be.	SA	A	U	D	SD

[GPR] 20. The organization of my writing has really improved.   SA   A   U   D   SD

[OC] 21. The sentences I use in my writing stick to the topic more than the ones the other kids use.   SA   A   U   D   SD

[SPR] 22. The words I use in my writing are better than the ones I used before.   SA   A   U   D   SD

[OC] 23. I write more often than other kids.   SA   A   U   D   SD

[PS] 24. I am relaxed when I write.   SA   A   U   D   SD

[SPR] 25. My descriptions are more interesting than before.   SA   A   U   D   SD

[OC] 26. The words I use in my writing are better than the ones other kids use.   SA   A   U   D   SD

[PS] 27. I feel comfortable when I write.   SA   A   U   D   SD

[SF] 28. My teacher thinks I am a good writer.   SA   A   U   D   SD

[SPR] 29. My sentences stick to the topic better now.   SA   A   U   D   SD

[OC] 30. My writing seems to be more clear than my classmates' writing.   SA   A   U   D   SD

[SPR] 31. When I write, the sentences and paragraphs fit together better than they used to.   SA   A   U   D   SD

[PS] 32. Writing makes me feel good.   SA   A   U   D   SD

[SF] 33. I can tell that my teacher thinks my writing is fine.   SA   A   U   D   SD

[SPR] 34. The order of my sentences makes better sense now.   SA   A   U   D   SD

[PS] 35. I enjoy writing.   SA   A   U   D   SD

[SPR] 36. My writing is more clear than it used to be.   SA   A   U   D   SD

[SF] 37. My classmates would say I write well.   SA   A   U   D   SD

[SPR] 38. I choose the words I use in my writing more carefully now.   SA   A   U   D   SD

Writer Self-Perception Scale Scoring Sheet

Student name: _____

Teacher: _____ Grade: _____ Date: _____

Scoring key:

    5 = Strongly Agree (SA)

    4 = Agree (A)

    3 = Undecided (U)

    2 = Disagree (D)

    1 = Strongly Disagree (SD)

SCALES

General Progress (GPR)	Specific Progress (SPR)	Observational Comparison (OC)	Social Feedback (SF)	Physiological States (PS)
3. _____	22. _____	1. _____	5. _____	2. _____
6. _____	25. _____	4. _____	9. _____	7. _____
12. _____	29. _____	8. _____	10. _____	24. _____
14. _____	31. _____	11. _____	13. _____	27. _____
15. _____	34. _____	16. _____	28. _____	32. _____
17. _____	36. _____	21. _____	33. _____	35. _____
18. _____	38. _____	23. _____	37. _____	
19. _____		26. _____		
20. _____		30. _____		

Raw scores

_____ of 40   _____ of 35   _____ of 45   _____ of 35   _____ of 30

Score interpretation	GPR	SPR	OC	SF	PS
High	39+	34+	37+	32+	28+
Average	35	29	30	27	22
Low	30	24	23	22	16

C.27   **Reading Log for Primary Students** (p. 66)

Books I Have Read

Name: _____   Grade: _____

Circle the face that best shows how you feel about the book.

BOOK	AUTHOR/ILLUSTRATOR	COMMENTS
		☺ ☺ ☹
		☺ ☺ ☹
		☺ ☺ ☹
		☺ ☺ ☹
		☺ ☺ ☹
		☺ ☺ ☹
		☺ ☺ ☹
		☺ ☺ ☹
		☺ ☺ ☹
		☺ ☺ ☹
		☺ ☺ ☹
		☺ ☺ ☹
		☺ ☺ ☹
		☺ ☺ ☹
		☺ ☺ ☹

C.28 **Reading Log for Intermediate Students** (p. 66)

Books I Have Read

Name: _____   Grade: _____   Quarter: 1 2 3 4

BOOK	AUTHOR	GENRE	DATE STARTED/ ENDED	COMMENTS

My favorite book I read this quarter was _____

because _____

From *Literacy Assessment and Intervention for Classroom Teachers* (4th ed.), by Beverly DeVries. Copyright ©2015 by Holcomb Hathaway, Publishers, Scottsdale, AZ.

C.29 **Reading Reflection Log** (p. 68)

My Thoughts About My Reading

Name: _____ Grade: _____ Quarter: 1 2 3 4

1. The informational books I read were about

_____

_____

_____

2. The novels I read were mostly: realistic, historical, biographies, autobiographies, mysteries, science fiction, fantasy, folktales.

3. My favorite author is _____

_____

4. The best book I read was _____

_____

5. When I dislike a book, I _____

_____

6. My favorite place to read is _____

_____

7. My reading habits at home are _____

_____

8. I do not enjoy reading books about _____

_____

9. The book I recommended to my friends was _____

_____

10. After I read a book, I like to _____

_____

C.30 Quick Phonemic Awareness Assessment Device (p. 80)

A high correlation exists between the ability to recognize spoken words as a sequence of individual sounds and reading achievement. Explicit instruction can increase the phonemic awareness of children. To assist in determining the level of phonemic awareness of each child in your class, the following assessment items may be utilized. *Use as many samples as necessary to determine mastery.*

Assessment 1. Isolation of beginning sounds. Ask the child what the first sound of selected words is.

"What is the first sound in *dog*?"

Assessment 2. Deletion of initial sound. Read a word and ask the child to say it without the first sound.

"Say the word *cat.* Say *cat* without the /k/."

Assessment 3. Segmentation of phonemes. Ask the child to say the separate sounds of the word being read.

"What are the two sounds in the word *go*?"

Assessment 4. Blending of phonemes. Slowly read the individual sounds of a word and ask the child to tell what the word is.

"What word am I saying? /d/ /o/ /g/"

Assessment 5. Phoneme manipulation. Read a word and ask the child to replace the initial sound with another. Have the child say the new word.

"In the word *fan,* the first sound is an /f/. If you replace the /f/ with an /m/, how would you say the new word?"

Source: Cecil, N. L. (2015). *Striking a Balance: A Comprehensive Approach to Early Literacy* (5th ed.). Scottsdale, AZ: Holcomb Hathaway. Used with permission.

Name: _____   Date: _____

NOTE: The teacher will check "Yes" if the child can do the task, and "No" if the child cannot do the task. It is good to give one example to the child so they fully understand the task they are asked to perform. Examples are provided.

Syllabicating Words

Practice: "Words have different syllables. Some words have one syllable such as *hand* (clap once). *Mitten* has two syllables: mit- (clap once) ten (clap once). *Celebrate* has three syllables: cel- (clap once) e (clap once) brate (clap once). Clap and tell me how many syllables *table* has (   ). How about *shop* (   ) and *wandering* (   )."

	YES	NO
1. Clap each time you hear a syllable in the following word:		
Sally	○	○
Bob	○	○
Kimberly	○	○
Mary	○	○
John	○	○

TOTAL CORRECT _____

Distinguishing Initial Sounds

Practice: "Many words begin with the same sound. *Pig* and *penny* both begin with the /p/ sound. Tell me two words that begin with the same sound as *wind* (   ), *tent* (   ), and *jump* (   )."

	YES	NO
2. Name two other words that begin with the same sound as the word:		
cat	○	○
Sally	○	○
bed	○	○
milk	○	○
fat	○	○

TOTAL CORRECT _____

Distinguishing Rime and Rhyme

Practice: "Rhyming words sound the same at the end. I can rhyme three words: *sad, bad, glad*. Tell me a word that rhymes with *pin* (   ), *round* (   ), and *cup* (   )."

		YES	NO
3.	Tell me if the two words rhyme.		
	sand – hand	○	○
	big – pig	○	○
	rule – milk	○	○
	fair – farm	○	○
	bat – hat	○	○

TOTAL CORRECT   _____

Distinguishing Oddity

Practice: "Sometimes in a group of three words, two words will begin with the same sound, but the other word will begin with a different sound. For example, with the three words *fox, fur,* and *tree, tree* does not begin with the same sound as *fox* and *fur*. Tell me which word begins with a different sound: *juice, milk, mom* (   ), *wind, weather, sun* (   ), *big, funny, fat* (   )."

		YES	NO
4.	Tell me which word does not begin with the same sound as the other two words:		
	hat – man – hot	○	○
	leg – lips – nose	○	○
	man – money – nose	○	○
	dog – tag – time	○	○
	big – pull – push	○	○

TOTAL CORRECT   _____

Blending Onset with Rime

Practice: "Many one-syllable words have two parts that can be blended together. For example, I can put a /b/ sound in front of *ug* and get *bug*. I want you to put an /m/ sound in front of /at/ and say the new word (   ); now put /s/ in front of /and/ (   ); now put /m/ in front of /eat/ (   )."

		YES	NO
5.	I am going to give you two parts of a word. I want you to blend the two parts together to make a word:		
	/s/ + at	○	○
	/k/ + ake	○	○
	/b/ + ug	○	○
	/j/ + ump	○	○
	/n/ + ight	○	○

TOTAL CORRECT   _____

Blending Letter Sounds

Practice: "Words are made up of individual sounds. For example, if I put /m/ + /u/ + /g/ together, I get *mug*. I want you to put these three sounds together: /f/ + /u/ + /n/ (   ). Now add /b/ + /u/ + /g/ (   ). Now add /s/ + /i/ + /t/ (   )."

		YES	NO
6. I am going to give you three sounds. I want you to blend the sounds together and say the word:			
	/c/ + /u/ + /t/	○	○
	/f/ + /a/ + /n/	○	○
	/b/ + /i/ + /g/	○	○
	/h/ + /o/ + /t/	○	○
	/l/ + /e/ + /g/	○	○

TOTAL CORRECT _____

Segmenting Sounds in Words

Practice: "I can hear sounds in words. For example, when I say *bit*, I hear /b/ + /i/ + /t/. Tell me what sounds do you hear in *cat* (   ), in *fan* (   ), and in *ham* (   )."

		YES	NO
7. I want you to tell me what three sounds you hear in each word:			
	sad (/s/ + /a/ + /d/)	○	○
	pop	○	○
	bun	○	○
	him	○	○
	hen	○	○

TOTAL CORRECT _____

Manipulating Initial Sounds in Words

Practice: "I can change a sound in a word to make a new word. For example, in the word *land*, I can change the /l/ to /s/ and get *sand*. Tell me what new word you get when you change one letter for another. In the word *round,* change the /r/ to /s/ (   ). In the word *light*, change the /l/ to /n/ (   ). In *frown*, change the /fr/ to /cl/ (   )."

		YES	NO
8. I am going to say a word; then I will ask you to change one sound to make a new word:			
	fan – change /f/ to /m/	○	○
	hut – change /h/ to /c/	○	○
	right – change /r/ to /n/	○	○
	meat – change /m/ to /n/	○	○
	fat – change /f/ to /b/	○	○

TOTAL CORRECT _____

Deleting Initial Sounds of Words

Practice: "With some words, I can take off the initial sound and get a new word. For example if I take /b/ off of *beat,* I get *eat.* Tell me what word you get when you take /m/ off of *man* (   ); /f/ off of *fit* (   )."

	YES	NO
9. I am going to say a word; then I will ask you to take off a sound and give me the new word:		
late – take off the /l/	○	○
sand – take off the /s/	○	○
ham – take off the /h/	○	○
fat – take off the /f/	○	○
land – take off the /l/	○	○

TOTAL CORRECT _____

GRAND TOTAL CORRECT _____

It is important to look at each section to determine strengths and weaknesses because each question is a different task. In each section, five correct responses indicate that the child has mastered the skill. Three or four correct responses indicate that the child is developing the skill, and only one or two correct responses indicate that the child has difficulty with the task.

GENERAL COMMENTS:

C.32   Post-Assessment for Phonemic Awareness (p. 80)

Name: _____   Date: _____

NOTE: The teacher will check "Yes" if the child can do the task, and "No" if the child cannot do the task. It is good to give one example to the child so they fully understand the task they are asked to perform. Examples are provided.

Syllabicating Words

Practice: "Words have different syllables. Some words have one syllable such as *hand* (clap once). *Mitten* has two syllables: mit- (clap once) ten (clap once). *Celebrate* has three syllables: cel- (clap once) e (clap once) brate (clap once). Clap and tell me how many syllables *table* has (   ). How about *shop* (   ) and *wandering* (   )."

	YES	NO
1. Clap each time you hear a syllable in the following words:		
Peter	○	○
Jane	○	○
Nathaniel	○	○
Joe	○	○
Molly	○	○

TOTAL CORRECT _____

Distinguishing Initial Sounds

Practice: "Many words begin with the same sound. *Pig* and *penny* both begin with the /p/ sound. Tell me two words that begin with the same sound as *wind* (   ), *tent* (   ), and *jump* (   )."

	YES	NO
2. Name two other words that begin with the same sound as the word:		
coat	○	○
snake	○	○
banana	○	○
money	○	○
fish	○	○

TOTAL CORRECT _____

Distinguishing Rime and Rhyme

Practice: "Rhyming words sound the same at the end. I can rhyme three words: *sad, bad, glad*. Tell me a word that rhymes with *pin* (   ), *round* (   ), and *cup* (   )."

	YES	NO
3. Tell me if the two words rhyme.		
clock – block	○	○
fan – man	○	○
drink – doughnut	○	○
zoo – child	○	○
light – night	○	○

TOTAL CORRECT _____

Distinguishing Oddity

Practice: "Sometimes in a group of three words, two words will begin with the same sound, but the other word will begin with a different sound. For example, with the three words *fox, fur,* and *tree, tree* does not begin with the same sound as *fox* and *fur*. Tell me which word begins with a different sound: *juice, milk, mom* (   ), *wind, weather, sun* (   ), *big, funny, fat* (   )."

	YES	NO
4. Tell me which word does not begin with the same sound as the other two words:		
milk – man – nuts	○	○
lamp – hut – house	○	○
clock – meat – mouse	○	○
snake – goat – smile	○	○
sun – fun – friend	○	○

TOTAL CORRECT _____

Blending Onset with Rime

Practice: "Many one-syllable words have two parts that can be blended together. For example, I can put a /b/ sound in front of *ug* and get *bug*. I want you to put an /m/ sound in front of /at/ and say the new word (   ); now put /s/ in front of /and/ (   ); now put /m/ in front of /eat/ (   )."

	YES	NO
5. I am going to give you two parts of a word. I want you to blend the two parts together to make a word:		
/f/ + *un*	○	○
/l/ + *ight*	○	○
/r/ + *ug*	○	○
/s/ + *and*	○	○
/b/ + *ump*	○	○

TOTAL CORRECT _____

Blending Letter Sounds

Practice: "Words are made up of individual sounds. For example, if I put /m/ + /u/ + /g/ together, I get *mug*. I want you to put these three sounds together: /f/ + /u/ + /n/ (   ). Now add /b/ + /u/ + /g/ (   ). Now add /s/ + /i/ + /t/ (   )."

                                                  YES   NO

6. I am going to give you three sounds. I want you to blend the sounds together and say the word:

	YES	NO
/f/ + /a/ + /t/	○	○
/r/ + /u/ + /g/	○	○
/p/ + /i/ + /g/	○	○
/p/ + /o/ + /t/	○	○
/m/ + /a/ + /n/	○	○

TOTAL CORRECT _____

Segmenting Sounds in Words

Practice: "I can hear sounds in words. For example, when I say *bit*, I hear /b/ + /i/ + /t/. Tell me what sounds do you hear in *cat* (   ), in *fan* (   ), and in *ham* (   )."

7. I want you to tell me what three sounds you hear in each word:

	YES	NO
pen = /p/ + /e/ + /n/	○	○
Dad	○	○
top	○	○
sun	○	○
fin	○	○

TOTAL CORRECT _____

Manipulating Initial Sounds in Words

Practice: "I can change a sound in a word to make a new word. For example, in the word *land*, I can change the /l/ to /s/ and get *sand*. Tell me what new word you get when you change one letter for another. In the word *round*, change the /r/ to /s/ (   ). In the word *light*, change the /l/ to /n/ (   ). In *frown*, change the /fr/ to /cl/ (   )."

8. I am going to say a word; then I will ask you to change one sound to make a new word:

	YES	NO
man – change /m/ to /f/	○	○
cut – change /c/ to /h/	○	○
might – change /m/ to /s/	○	○
cake – change /c/ to /b/	○	○
hat – change /h/ to /f/	○	○

TOTAL CORRECT _____

Deleting Initial Sounds of Words

Practice: "With some words, I can take off the initial sound and get a new word. For example if I take /b/ off of *beat*, I get *eat*. Tell me what word you get when you take /m/ off of *man* (   ); /f/ off of *fit* (   )."

                                              YES   NO

9. I am going to say a word; then I will ask you to take off a sound and give me the new word:

	YES	NO
fan – take off /f/	○	○
band – take off /b/	○	○
meat – take off /m/	○	○
Sam – take off /s/	○	○
rat – take off /r/	○	○

TOTAL CORRECT _____

GRAND TOTAL CORRECT _____

It is important to look at each section to determine strengths and weaknesses because each question is a different task. In each section, five correct responses indicate that the child has mastered the skill. Three or four correct responses indicate that the child is developing the skill, and only one or two correct responses indicate that the child has difficulty with the task.

GENERAL COMMENTS:

C.33 Checklist for Phonemic Awareness for Primary Grades (p. 81)

(Based on the Seven Dimensions)

Teacher: _____ Date: _____

+ = always   X = sometimes   O = seldom/never

DIMENSION	STUDENTS																	
1. Ability to hear syllables within words																		
2. Ability to hear initial sounds or recognize alliteration																		
3. Ability to hear rhyming words																		
4. Ability to distinguish oddity																		
5. Ability to blend words orally																		
6. Ability to segment words:																		
• Drop beginning sound																		
• Drop ending sound																		
7. Ability to manipulate sounds orally to create new words																		

C.34 Checklist for Progress Toward the CCSS ELA Reading: Foundational Skills Phonological Awareness Standards for Kindergarten (p. 81)

Teacher: _____   Date: _____

+ = always   X = sometimes   O = seldom/never

STANDARD   STUDENTS

1. Recognize and produce rhyming words.

2. Count, pronounce, blend, and segment syllables in spoken words.

3. Blend and segment onsets and rimes of single-syllable spoken words.

4. Isolate and pronounce the initial, medial, vowel, and final sounds (phonemes) in three-phoneme (consonant–vowel–consonant, or CVC) words.*

5. Add or substitute individual sounds (phonemes) in simple, one-syllable words to make new words.

*This does not include CVCs ending with /l/, /r/, or /x/.)

Standards based on the National Governors Association Center for Best Practices and Council of Chief State School Officers, 2010, p. 15.

| **C.35** | **Checklist for Progress Toward the CCSS ELA Reading: Foundational Skills Phonological Awareness Standards for Grade 1** (p. 81) |

Teacher: _____   Date: _____

+ = always   X = sometimes   O = seldom/never

STANDARD	STUDENTS																		
1. Distinguish long form short vowel sounds in spoken single-syllable words.																			
2. Orally produce single-syllable words by blending sounds (phonemes).																			
3. Isolate and pronounce initial, medial vowel, and final sounds (phonemes) in spoken single-syllable words.																			
4. Segment spoken single-syllable words into their complete sequence of individual sounds (phonemes).																			

Standards based on the National Governors Association Center for Best Practices and Council of Chief State School Officers, 2010, p. 15.

C.36 Phonics, Word Recognition, and Fluency Checklist Based on the CCSS ELA Reading: Foundational Skills Standards for Grade 3 (p. 110)

Teacher: _____ Date: _____

+ = always   X = sometimes   O = seldom/never

STANDARD	STUDENTS

CCSS.ELA-Literacy.RF.3.3 Know and apply grade-level phonics and word analysis skills in decoding words.

CCSS.ELA-Literacy.RF.3.3.a Identify and know the meaning of the most common prefixes and derivational suffixes.

CCSS.ELA-Literacy.RF.3.3.b Decode words with common Latin suffixes.

CCSS.ELA-Literacy.RF.3.3.c Decode multisyllable words.

CCSS.ELA-Literacy.RF.3.3.d Read grade-appropriate irregularly spelled words.

CCSS.ELA-Literacy.RF.3.4 Read with sufficient accuracy and fluency to support comprehension.

CCSS.ELA-Literacy.RF.3.4.a Read grade-level text with purpose and understanding.

CCSS.ELA-Literacy.RF.3.4.b Read grade-level prose and poetry orally with accuracy, appropriate rate, and expression on successive readings.

CCSS.ELA-Literacy.RF.3.4.c Use context to confirm or self-correct word recognition and understanding, rereading as necessary.

Standards from National Governors Association Center for Best Practices & Council of Chief State School Officers (2010). Washington, DC: NGACBP, CCSSO, p. 17.

C.37 Checklist of Known Letter Names and Sounds (p. 110)

Student: _____   Date: _____

LETTER	UPPERCASE NAME	LOWERCASE NAME	SCRIPT NAME	SOUND	WORD WITH INITIAL SOUND	WORD WITH ENDING SOUND
K						
N						
E						
J						
A						
T						
B						
S						
I						
M						
O						
D						
C						
Y						
G						
V						
Z						
P						
F						

Photocopy this page, cut apart the cards, and enlarge each card (200% will double the size) for use with children.

Master Card of Letters

K	N	E	J	A	T
B	S	I	M	R	H
L	W	X	Q	O	D
C	Y	G	V	Z	P
U	F				

k	n	e	j	a	t
b	s	i	m	r	h
l	w	x	q	o	d
c	y	g	v	z	p
u	f				

Master Card of Script Letters

K	N	E	J	A	T
B	S	I	M	R	H
L	W	X	Q	O	D
C	Y	G	V	Z	P
U	F				

k	n	e	j	a	t
b	s	i	m	r	h
l	w	x	q	o	d
c	y	g	v	z	p
u	f				

From *Literacy Assessment and Intervention for Classroom Teachers* (4th ed.), by Beverly DeVries. Copyright ©2015 by Holcomb Hathaway, Publishers, Scottsdale, AZ.

Instructions: Before administering this survey, reproduce letters and words on 3- × 5-inch cards in large, lowercase letters, so the child can see them with ease. This survey should be administered to one child at a time. Use a separate sheet to document each child's progress. In the first section, stop if the child makes more than 10 errors. For every other section, stop when child makes five or more errors. When sounds are incorrect, write the sound the child makes above the word.

1. Consonant Sounds

Show the child one card at a time, featuring lowercase consonant letters. Ask the child to tell you what sound the letter makes. On the assessment sheet, circle the letter if an incorrect sound is given. Write the incorrect sound the child gives on top of the letter.

— —

p b m w f v t s d r j h z n l y k c g

If the child is not able to identify at least 10 sounds, terminate this assessment.

2. Rhyming Words

Ask the child to read the following words and to say three words that rhyme with each of them. Nonsense words are acceptable.

1. be _____

2. go _____

3. say _____

4. do _____

5. make _____

6. will _____

7. get _____

8. blink _____

9. tan _____

10. bug _____

3. CVC Words

Ask the child to read the following short-vowel, CVC nonsense words. There are four examples of each short vowel sound. Indicate which vowel sounds were read correctly and which were not.

1. nid _____
2. gat _____
3. bul _____
4. rup _____
5. sen _____
6. nat _____
7. det _____
8. rit _____
9. nup _____
10. nop _____

11. wat _____
12. vin _____
13. lom _____
14. hap _____
15. yub _____
16. pem _____
17. dom _____
18. kud _____
19. wom _____
20. zet _____

4. Consonant Blends

Ask the child to read the following words and nonsense words that contain beginning or ending consonant blends (or both). Indicate any blends the child says incorrectly.

1. blithe _____
2. clog _____
3. plush _____
4. flounce _____
5. frisk _____
6. dwelt _____
7. skig _____
8. crass _____
9. trek _____
10. swap _____

11. trink _____
12. brind _____
13. scup _____
14. stint _____
15. smeat _____
16. spole _____
17. gluck _____
18. brame _____
19. dredge _____
20. lasp _____

5. Consonant Digraphs

Have the child read the following nonsense words containing consonant digraphs. Indicate any digraphs the child says incorrectly.

1. shan _____
2. thort _____
3. phrat _____
4. chib _____
5. phant _____
6. yeth _____
7. rosh _____
8. lotch _____
9. gresh _____
10. chass _____

11. scord _____
12. squean _____
13. sling _____
14. sprill _____
15. strug _____
16. splom _____
17. squim _____
18. throbe _____

6. Long Vowel Sounds

Have the child read the following nonsense words that contain long vowel sounds. There are four examples of each long vowel sound. Indicate which vowels are read correctly and which are not.

1. stope _____
2. kade _____
3. fede _____
4. gride _____
5. blude _____
6. kroan _____
7. jaike _____
8. theade _____
9. smight _____
10. dreud _____

11. ploan _____
12. tayne _____
13. sheed _____
14. vied _____
15. trewd _____
16. whade _____
17. strean _____
18. blipe _____
19. roke _____
20. krume _____

7. Other Vowel Sounds

Have the child read the following nonsense words that contain variant vowel sounds. Indicate vowel sounds the child reads incorrectly.

1. nook (oo) _____
2. krouse (ou, ow) _____
3. sar (ar) _____
4. moil (oi) _____
5. noy (oy) _____
6. thirl (ir, er, ur) _____
7. floom (oo) _____

8. gorn (or) _____
9. chaw (aw, au) _____
10. zout (ou) _____
11. larm (ar) _____
12. groil (oi) _____
13. nirl (ir, er, ur) _____

_____

8. Number of Word Parts (Syllables)

Ask the child to read the following words and count the number of word parts or syllables in each word. (Correct answers are in parentheses.)

1. retention (3) _____
2. ride (1) _____
3. panic (2) _____
4. carnival (3) _____
5. monster (2) _____

6. contaminate (4) _____
7. computer (3) _____
8. antagonist (4) _____
9. guess (1) _____
10. consider (3) _____

Source: Cecil, N. L. (2015). *Striking a Balance: A Comprehensive Approach to Early Literacy* (5th ed.). Scottsdale, AZ: Holcomb Hathaway. Used with permission.

C.39 Scoring Sheet for Word or Phrase Lists (p. 130)

Student: _____   Grade: _____

+ = yes   − = no

WORDS/PHRASES	BEGINNING OF YEAR	1ST QUARTER	2ND QUARTER	3RD QUARTER	4TH QUARTER

C.40 Vocabulary Growth Checklist Based on the CCSS ELA Standards for Language for Grade 8 (p. 157)

Teacher: _____   Date: _____

+ = always   X = sometimes   O = seldom/never

STANDARD	STUDENTS																	
1. Can determine meaning of domain-specific words.																		
2. Can determine meaning of tier two (academic) words, appropriate for eighth grade.																		
3. Understands figurative language in texts.																		
4. Can identify rich word choices in texts.																		
5. Can explain how word choice affects tone.																		
6. Identifies and understands allusions.																		
7. Understands analogies.																		

Standards based on the National Governors Association Center for Best Practices and Council of Chief State School Officers, 2010, p. 53.

C.41   Rubric for Narrative Reading Comprehension Based on the CCSS ELA Reading: Literature Standards for Grade 5 (p. 191)

TRAIT	TARGET (4–5 points)	ACCEPTABLE (2–3 points)	UNACCEPTABLE (0–1 point)	SCORE
CCSS RL.5.1	Quotes accurately from a text when explaining what the text says explicitly and when drawing inferences from the text.	With the assistance of an adult, quotes accurately from a text when explaining what the text says explicitly and when drawing inferences from the text.	Cannot quote accurately from a text when explaining what the text says explicitly and when drawing inferences from the text.	
CCSS RL.5.2	Determines a theme of a story, drama, or poem from details in the text, including how characters in a story or drama respond to challenges or how the speaker in a poem reflects upon a topic; summarize the text.	With the assistance of an adult, determines a theme of a story, drama, or poem from details in the text, including how characters in a story or drama respond to challenges or how the speaker in a poem reflects upon a topic; summarize the text.	Cannot determine a theme of a story, drama, or poem from details in the text, including how characters in a story or drama respond to challenges or how the speaker in a poem reflects upon a topic; summarize the text.	
CCSS RL.5.3	Compares and contrasts two or more characters, settings, or events in a story or drama drawing on specific details in the text (e.g. how characters interact).	With the assistance of an adult, compares and contrasts two or more characters, settings, or events in a story or drama drawing on specific details in the text (e.g. how characters interact).	Cannot compare and contrast two or more characters, settings, or events in a story or drama drawing on specific details in the text (e.g. how characters interact).	
CCSS RL.5.4	Determines the meaning of words and phrases as they are used in a text, including figurative language such as metaphors and similes.	With the assistance of an adult, determines the meaning of words and phrases as they are used in a text, including figurative language such as metaphors and similes.	Cannot determine the meaning of words and phrases as they are used in a text, including figurative language such as metaphors and similes.	
CCSS RL.5.5	Explains how a series of chapters, scenes, or stanzas fits together to provide the overall structure of a particular story, drama, or poem.	With the assistance of an adult, explains how a series of chapters, scenes, or stanzas fits together to provide the overall structure of a particular story, drama, or poem.	Cannot explain how a series of chapters, scenes, or stanzas fits together to provide the overall structure of a particular story, drama, or poem.	
CCSS. RL 5.6	Describes how a narrator's or speaker's point of view influences how events are described.	With the assistance of an adult, describes how a narrator's or speaker's point of view influences how events are described.	Cannot describe how a narrator's or speaker's point of view influences how events are described.	
CCSS. RL 5.7	Analyzes how visual and multi-media elements contribute to the meaning, tone, or beauty of a text (e.g. graphic novel, multimedia presentation of fiction, folktale, myth, poem).	With the assistance of an adult, analyzes how visual and multimedia elements contribute to the meaning, tone, or beauty of a text (e.g. graphic novel, multimedia presentation of fiction, folktale, myth, poem).	Cannot analyze how visual and multimedia elements contribute to the meaning, tone, or beauty of a text (e.g. graphic novel, multimedia presentation of fiction, folktale, myth, poem).	
CCSS. RL 5.9	Compares and contrasts stories in the same genre (e.g. mysteries and adventure stories) on their approaches to similar themes and topics.	With the assistance of an adult, compares and contrasts stories in the same genre (e.g. mysteries and adventure stories) on their approaches to similar themes and topics.	Cannot compare and contrast stories in the same genre (e.g. mysteries and adventure stories) on their approaches to similar themes and topics.	
CCSS. RL 5.10	By the end of the year, reads and comprehends literature, including stories, dramas, and poetry at the high end of the grades 4—5 text complexity band independently and proficiently.	By the end of the year, with the assistance of an adult, reads and comprehends literature, including stories, dramas, and poetry at the high end of the grades 4—5 text complexity band independently and proficiently.	By the end of the year, cannot read and comprehend literature, including stories, dramas, and poetry at the high end of the grades 4—5 text complexity band independently and proficiently.	
			TOTAL SCORE:	

Standards from National Governors Association Center for Best Practices (NGACBP) & Council of Chief State School Officers (CCSSO). (2010). English Language Arts Standards, Reading: Literature, Grade 5. Washington D.C.: National Governors Association Center for Best Practices, Council of Chief State School Officers, p. 12.

C.42 | Interest Inventory for Informational Texts (p. 219)

THINGS THAT INTEREST ME

All of these questions are about your interests! You can list more than one thing for each question.

Name: _____   Date: _____

1. What is your favorite subject in school?

   _____

2. What subject that is not offered in school do you wish you could study?

   _____

3. What is your favorite sport?

   _____

4. What is your favorite TV program?

   _____

5. Who is your favorite athlete?

   _____

6. Who is your favorite actor/actress?

   _____

7. On Saturday, what is your favorite thing to do?

   _____

8. What type of music do you like?

   _____

9. What do you want to be when you grow up?

   _____

10. What is your favorite book?

    _____

11. If you could hop on a magic carpet, where in the world would you like to go?

    _____

12. If you could live in "another time," what time would it be? In the future? In the past?

    _____

13. What subject would you like to read about when we are working together?

    _____

C.43 Observation Checklist of Student's Informational Text Reading (p. 234)

Student: _____   Grade: _____

BEHAVIOR	Most of the time	Sometimes	Seldom	Never
BEFORE READING				
1. Determines purpose for reading	○	○	○	○
2. Predicts by reading headings	○	○	○	○
3. Skims to get overview of passage	○	○	○	○
4. Checks how long the passage is	○	○	○	○
5. Relates prior knowledge to passage	○	○	○	○
DURING READING				
1. Does not omit unknown words	○	○	○	○
2. Attempts to pronounce new words	○	○	○	○
3. Decodes new words easily	○	○	○	○
4. Does not use finger or other object to keep place	○	○	○	○
5. Does not insert words	○	○	○	○
6. Reads punctuation correctly	○	○	○	○
7. Rereads if comprehension breaks down	○	○	○	○
8. Connects reading material to prior knowledge	○	○	○	○
9. Reads figures, pictures, etc.	○	○	○	○
10. Looks up unknown words in glossary	○	○	○	○
11. Does not mouth words when reading silently	○	○	○	○
12. Does not have difficult time staying on task during silent reading	○	○	○	○
AFTER READING				
1. Summarizes in logical order	○	○	○	○
2. Retells main points	○	○	○	○
3. Retells information not found in text	○	○	○	○
4. Relates information to prior knowledge	○	○	○	○
5. Interprets text correctly	○	○	○	○
6. Makes inferences	○	○	○	○
7. Shows signs of critical thinking	○	○	○	○
8. Asks questions about material	○	○	○	○
9. Desires to know more about topic	○	○	○	○

COMMENTS

C.44   Rubric for Informational Text Comprehension Based on the CCSS ELA Reading: Informational Text Standards for Grade 6 (p. 232)

Student: _____   Total Score: _____   Grading Period   1   2   3   4

Level of Mastery

STANDARD	TARGET (4–5 POINTS)	ACCEPTABLE (2–3 POINTS)	UNACCEPTABLE (0–1 POINT)	SCORE
Citing evidence.	Always cites evidence to support analysis of what the text says explicitly as well as inferences drawn from the text.	Cites evidence to support analysis of what the text says explicitly but cannot cite evidence from inferences drawn from the text.	Struggles to cite evidence to support analysis of what the text says.	
Determining central theme.	Always determines a central idea and how it is conveyed through particular details; provides a summary of the text distinct from personal opinions or judgments.	Can usually determine a central idea and how it is conveyed through particular details; however, struggles to provide a summary of the text distinct from personal opinions or judgments.	Cannot determine the central theme and struggle to provide a summary of the text.	
Analyzing details.	Analyzes in detail how a key individual, event, or idea is introduced, illustrated, and elaborated in a text.	Gives brief analysis of how a key individual, event, or idea is introduced, illustrated, and elaborated in a text.	Struggles in analysis of key details.	
Determining meaning of words.	Determines the meaning of words and phrases as they are used in a text, including figurative, connotative, and technical meanings.	Determines the meaning of most words as used in a text, but struggles with figurative, connotative, and some technical meanings.	Struggles with meaning of words as used in a text.	
Understanding overall structure of text.	Analyzes how a particular sentence, paragraph, chapter, or section fits into the overall structure of a text and contributes to the development of the ideas.	Analyzes how a particular sentence and paragraph contributes to the small section of the text, but struggles to understand how they fit into the overall structure.	Cannot explain how a particular sentence, paragraph, chapter, or section fits into the overall structure of a text.	
Determining point of view.	Determines an author's point of view or purpose in a text and explains how it is conveyed in the text.	Determines author's point of view or purpose, but struggles to explain how it is conveyed in the text.	Cannot determine the author's point of view.	

Standards based on National Governors Association Center for Best Practices & Council of Chief State School Officers (2010). Washington, DC: NGACBP, CCSSO, pp. 38–39.

C.45 Informational Text Reading Rubric (p. 234)

Name _____   Date _____

3 POINTS	2 POINTS	1 POINT	0 POINTS	SCORE
Always establishes purpose for reading.	Usually establishes purpose for reading.	Seldom sets purpose for reading.	Never sets purpose for reading.	
Analyzes large bank of academic and domain-specific terms with ease.	Analyzes most academic and domain-specific words with ease.	Analyzes a few academic and domain-specific terms.	Cannot analyze new academic and domain-specific terms.	
Integrates relevant text information with background knowledge to comprehend passage.	Integrates some background knowledge with text information to comprehend passage.	Integrates little background knowledge with text information to comprehend passage.	Cannot integrate background knowledge with text information.	
Readily makes accurate inferences about information in passage.	Most inferences are accurate about information in passage.	Makes a few accurate inferences about information in passage.	Cannot make accurate inferences about information in passage.	
Uses multiple fix-up strategies when comprehension breaks down.	Uses some fix-up strategies when comprehension breaks down.	Uses one or two different strategies when comprehension breaks down.	Uses no strategies when comprehension breaks down.	
Readily builds up relationships between larger units of text.	Builds up relationships between larger units of text.	Can build up some relationships between larger units of text.	Cannot build up relationships between larger units of text.	
Can readily create appropriate graphic organizer of text.	Can create appropriate graphic organizer of text.	With prompting from teacher, can create appropriate graphic organizer of text.	Cannot create an appropriate graphic organizer of text.	
Can synthesize information from at least four sources.	Can synthesize information from at least three sources.	Can synthesize information from at least two sources.	Cannot synthesize information from various sources.	
Easily chooses key terms for Internet use.	Can choose some key terms for Internet use.	With prompting from teacher, can choose key terms for Internet use.	Cannot choose key terms for Internet use.	
Can use search engines on the Internet and effectively choose helpful sites.	Can use search engines on the Internet when given enough time.	Can use search engines on the Internet when given large blocks of time.	Cannot use search engines effectively.	
Can readily identify author or organization of Internet material.	Can identify author or organization of Internet material when given enough time.	Can identify author or organization of Internet material when given large blocks of time.	Cannot identify author or organization of Internet material.	
Can readily determine if information on Internet sites is accurate by comparing it to background knowledge or other sources.	Can determine if information on Internet sites is accurate by comparing it to background knowledge.	With prompting from teacher, can determine if information on Internet site is accurate.	Cannot determine if Internet information is accurate.	
Can effectively and in a timely manner scan passages to find key dates, names, terms, and other information.	Can effectively scan passages to find key dates, names, and terms.	Can scan passages to find key dates and names.	Cannot scan passages to find key dates, names, or terms.	
Can effectively skim text and pictures to gather main idea of passage to determine if he/she wants to read passage.	Can skim text and pictures to gather main idea of passage to determine if he/she wants to read passage.	Can skim pictures to gather main idea of passage.	Cannot skim text to gather main idea.	

TOTAL SCORE: _____ /42
(Acceptable score is 34 or 80%)

C.46   Checklist of Basic Online Skills (p. 254)

Student: _____   Date: _____

	YES	NO
1. Has skills to locate materials.	○	○
2. Is able to identify important questions.	○	○
3. Knows how to use search engines and how to select words.	○	○
4. Knows how to refine search words so they are as specific as possible.	○	○
5. Knows how to read and evaluate the short descriptions found in search engine results.	○	○
6. Uses only the sites that address the topic.	○	○
7. Is able to evaluate the author's authority.	○	○
8. Understands the importance of the "back" button.	○	○
9. Is able to read and comprehend the text.	○	○
10. Takes notes from the sites.	○	○
11. Is able to synthesize material from the various sites.	○	○
12. Cites sources correctly.	○	○

Source: Adapted from Henry, L. (2006). Searching for an answer: The critical role of new literacies while reading on the Internet. *The Reading Teacher, 59*(7), 614–626.

C.47 Fluency Questions for Self-Evaluation (p. 270)

Name: _____   Date: _____

○ Did my reading sound like real speech, like people talking? Would someone listening understand what the author meant from my reading?

○ Did I easily pronounce the words correctly?

○ Did I make many mistakes in my reading? When I made a mistake that changed the meaning, did I go back and change it?

○ Did I read with good expression? Did I vary my volume when appropriate to express meaning?

○ Was I reading loudly enough?

○ Did I change speed when necessary, especially when I wanted to stress certain parts?

○ Did I have an appropriate rate when I read out loud?

○ Did I group the words correctly?

○ Did I pay attention to periods to make my voice go down?

○ Did I pause for commas?

○ Did my voice go up for question marks?

○ Did I sound excited for exclamation marks?

○ Did I emphasize any words that needed it?

Answer the following two questions in one or two sentences:

What is best about my reading?

What should I work on to make my reading even better?

Source: Adapted from Rasinski (2003) and Cecil (2011).

C.48   Fluency Checklist (p. 270)

Name: _____   Grade: _____

Evaluator: _____

CHARACTERISTIC	DATE	DATE	DATE	DATE
STAGE 1				
Rate: Word-by-word reading with many pauses				
Prosody: No phrasing				
Prosody: Omits punctuation				
Automaticity: Sounds out letter by letter; ignores chunks in words				
Expression: Lacks expression				
STAGE 2				
Rate: Some two- or three-word phrases with many pauses				
Prosody: Aware of some end marks (periods, question marks)				
Automaticity: Begins to recognize chunks within monosyllabic words (onsets and rimes)				
Expression: Lacks expression				
STAGE 3				
Rate: Appropriate most of the time				
Prosody: Attentive to end marks and commas				
Automaticity: Recognizes chunks within words and inflectional endings				
Expression: Beginning to recognize dialogue				
STAGE 4				
Rate: Varies speed with difficulty of text				
Prosody: Attentive to all punctuation, good phrasing				
Automaticity: Recognizes syllables				
Expression: Appropriate for dialogue and mood				

C.49 Fluency Checklist for Narrative Text (p. 271)

Name: _____ Date: _____

Story: _____ Number of words: _____

Time it took to read: _____ WPM: _____

TRAIT	YES	NO
1. Stopped for periods	○	○
2. Raised voice for question marks	○	○
3. Read with excitement for exclamation marks	○	○
4. Made slight pause for commas	○	○
5. Read phrases correctly	○	○
6. Changed voice for different characters (watched quotation marks)	○	○
7. Changed volume for different moods	○	○
8. Changed rate for different moods	○	○
9. Paused for ellipses	○	○
10. Emphasized italicized words	○	○

C.50   Oral Reading Fluency Rubric (p. 271)

Rate the reader's fluency in each of the four categories below. Choose the appropriate score in each category and write the number of points on that line. Add all four scores for Total Score.

ORAL READING

____ (5 pts.) Reading is fluent, confident, and accurate.

____ (4 pts.) Reading is fluent and accurate for the most part, but reader occasionally falters or hesitates.

____ (3 pts.) Reader lacks confidence at times, and reading is characterized by frequent pauses, miscues, and hesitations.

____ (2 pts.) Reader consistently lacks confidence and occasionally lapses into word-by-word reading with frequent meaning-violating miscues.

____ (1 pt.) Reader demonstrates largely word-by-word reading with little or no inflection and numerous meaning-violating miscues, some of which may be nonwords.

INTONATION

____ (5 pts.) Intonation consistently supports meaning of the text.

____ (4 pts.) Intonations are largely meaningful but may include exaggerations or inflections inappropriate for the text.

____ (3 pts.) Intonation is characterized by some joining of words into meaningful phrases, but this element often breaks down when the reader encounters difficulties.

____ (2 pts.) Intonation is largely flat with lack of enthusiasm.

____ (1 pt.) Intonation is almost completely absent.

PUNCTUATION

____ (5 pts.) Reader demonstrates a natural use of and appreciation for punctuation.

____ (4 pts.) Reader demonstrates a solid use of punctuation as an aid to intonation.

____ (3 pts.) Reaction to punctuation marks results in pauses that are inappropriately long or short.

____ (2 pts.) Punctuation is occasionally ignored and meaning may be distorted.

____ (1 pt.) Reader demonstrates frequent ignoring of punctuation.

PACING

____ (5 pts.) Pacing is rapid but smooth and unexaggerated.

____ (4 pts.) Reading is well paced with only occasional weakness in response to difficulties with the text.

____ (3 pts.) Pacing is relatively slow and markedly slower (or markedly faster) when reader encounters difficult text.

____ (2 pts.) Pacing is either very slow or inappropriately fast.

____ (1 pt.) Pacing is painfully slow and halting.

____ **TOTAL SCORE**

Source: Applegate, Mary D.; Quinn, Kathleen B.; Applegate, Anthony J., *Critical Reading Inventory, The: Assessing Student's Reading and Thinking,* 2nd ed., © 2008, p. 78. Adapted by permission of Pearson Education, Inc., Upper Saddle River, NJ.

C.51   Student Checklist for Evaluating the Presentation of an Argument (p. 296)

EVALUATING THE POWER OF MY ARGUMENT

Introducing My Persuasive Claim and the Counterclaim(s)

____ My clearly stated claim is . . .

____ My authority of my claim has been established by . . .

____ The counterclaim to my claim is . . .

Supporting My Claim and Refuting the Counterclaim

____ Evidence is included to support my claim. The evidence is . . .

____ I have refuted the counterclaim using the following evidence or reasoning . . .

____ The knowledge concerns and questions of the intended audience have been addressed by . . .

____ The formalness of tone matches my familiarity with the audience. My tone is . . .

Illustrating Language Power

____ Rhetorical questions have been asked. These are . . .

____ Power verbs and adjectives have been included. These include . . .

____ An unforgettable power phrase has been included. It is . . .

Summing Up

____ My claim or position is clearly presented, developed, and supported as shown in lines . . .

____ A powerful punchy conclusion reinforces the authority and clout of the original claim. It is . . .

Source: Adapted from D. Lapp and S. Fisher (2012). Persuasion = Stating and arguing claims well. *Journal of Adolescent & Adult Literacy, 55*(7), pp. 641–644.

C.52 **6 + 1 Trait® Writing Assessment** (p. 307)

Name: _____   Date: _____

SCORING CONTINUUM

WOW! Exceeds expectations

5 *Strong* Shows control and skill in this trait; many strengths present

4 *Effective* On balance, the strengths outweigh the weaknesses; a small amount of revision is needed

3 *Developing* Strengths and need for revision are about equal; about halfway home

2 *Emerging* Need for revision outweighs strengths; isolated moments hint at what the writer has in mind

1 *Not Yet* A bare beginning; writer not yet showing any control

Circled number shows where you are on the continuum for each trait.

IDEAS

⑤ This paper is clear and focused. It holds the reader's attention. Relevant anecdotes and details enrich the central theme.

③ The writer is beginning to define the topic, even though development is still basic or general.

① As yet, the paper has no clear sense of purpose or central theme. To extract meaning from the text, the reader must make inferences based on sketchy or missing details. The writing reflects more than one of the problems.

ORGANIZATION

⑤ The organization enhances and showcases the central idea or theme. The order, structure, or presentation of information is compelling and moves the reader through the text.

③ The organizational structure is strong enough to move the reader through the text without too much confusion.

① The writing lacks a clear sense of direction. Ideas, details, or events seem strung together in a loose or random fashion; there is no identifiable internal structure. The writing reflects more than one of the problems.

VOICE

⑤ The writer speaks directly to the reader in a way that is individual, compelling, and engaging. The writer crafts the writing with an awareness and respect for the audience and the purpose for writing.

③ The writer seems sincere, but not fully engaged or involved. The writing has discernable purpose, but is not compelling.

① The writer seems indifferent to the topic and the content. The writing lacks purpose and audience engagement.

WORD CHOICE

(5) Words convey the intended message in a precise, interesting, and natural way. The words are powerful and engaging.

(3) The language is functional, even if it lacks much energy. It is easy to figure out the writer's meaning on a general level.

(1) The writer demonstrates a limited vocabulary or has not searched for words to convey specific meaning.

SENTENCE FLUENCY

(5) The writing has an easy flow, rhythm, and cadence. Sentences are well built, with strong and varied structure that invites expressive oral reading.

(3) The text hums along with a steady beat, but tends to be more pleasant or business-like than musical, more mechanical than fluid.

(1) The reader has to practice quite a bit in order to give this paper a fair interpretive reading. The writing reflects more than one of the problems.

CONVENTIONS

(5) The writer demonstrates a good grasp of standard writing conventions (e.g., spelling, punctuation, capitalization, grammar, usage, paragraphing) and uses conventions effectively to enhance readability. Errors tend to be so few that just minor touch-ups would get this piece ready to publish.

GRADES 7 AND UP ONLY: The writing is sufficiently complex to allow the writer to show skill in using a wide range of conventions. For writers at younger ages, the writing shows control over those conventions that are grade age appropriate.

(3) The writer shows reasonable control over a limited range of standard writing conventions. Conventions are sometimes handled well and enhance readability; at other times, errors are distracting and impair readability.

(1) Errors in spelling, punctuation, capitalization, usage, and grammar and/or paragraphing repeatedly distract the reader and make the text difficult to read. The writing reflects more than one of the problems.

PRESENTATION (Optional)

(5) The form and presentation of the text enhances the ability of the reader to understand and connect with the message. It is pleasing to the eye.

(3) The writer's message is understandable in this format.

(1) The reader receives a garbled message due to problems relating to the presentation of the text.

C.53   Rubric for Assessing the Writing Process of Writers in Primary Grades (p. 308)

Name: _____   Grade: _____

Scores: Consistently present = 5, Sometimes present = 3, Not present = 0

COMPETENCY		DATES/SCORES			
PREWRITING	DATES:				
1. Generates own writing ideas.					
2. Reflects on idea before writing.					
3. Self-starter.					
4. Shares ideas with others.					
5. Draws before writing.					
DRAFTING					
1. Writes without worry about mechanics.					
2. Writes in various formats.					
3. Forms letters correctly.					
4. Uses invented spelling.					
5. Shows awareness of letter–sound relationships.					
6. Generates many ideas.					
7. Stories have beginning, middle, and end.					
8. Informational texts have supporting details for each main point.					
9. Opinion pieces have strong supporting points or reasons.					
10. Writes independently.					
11. Completes a passage.					
REVISING					
1. Rereads passage.					
2. Adds to passage.					
3. Deletes sections.					
4. Reads passage to peers.					
5. Reads ideas to others.					
6. Listens to others read.					

COMPETENCY		DATES/SCORES			
EDITING	**DATES:**				
1. Looks at spelling patterns.					
2. Checks and corrects letter formation.					
3. Self-edits.					
4. Rewrites passage to make "clean" copy.					
5. Seeks help from teacher.					
6. Seeks help from peers.					
7. Helps peers with their editing.					
PUBLISHING					
1. Willing to share in author's chair.					
2. Willing to share written copy with others.					
3. Enjoys listening to others' stories.					
TOTAL:					

TEACHER'S COMMENTS:

From *Literacy Assessment and Intervention for Classroom Teachers* (4th ed.), by Beverly DeVries. Copyright ©2015 by Holcomb Hathaway, Publishers, Scottsdale, AZ.

C.54 Rubric for Assessing the Writing Process of Third Graders (p. 308)

Student: _____

Teacher: _____

Scores: 0 = Never 1 = Seldom 2 = Sometimes 3 = Usually 4 = Always

STRATEGY		DATES/SCORES			
PREWRITING	DATES:				
1. Researches books, magazines, websites, or _____ (other).					
2. Brainstorms ideas on graphic organizers.					
3. Shares ideas with classmate(s).					
4. Makes notes and cites sources.					
5. Plans for a particular audience.					
6. Makes good use of time.					
7. Records ideas through writing/drawing.					
8. Plans purpose.					
DRAFTING					
1. Uses plans and resources.					
2. Writes consistently, without over-deleting.					
3. Takes risk with new genre.					
4. Knows audience.					
5. Writes without worrying about mechanics.					
6. Stays on task.					
7. Demonstrates good keyboarding skills.					
REVISING					
1. Deletes material.					
2. Conducts more research.					
3. Reorganizes material.					
4. Seeks comments from peers.					
5. Seeks comments from teacher.					
6. Is willing to rewrite.					
7. Focuses on good word choice.					
8. Uses word processor to make revisions.					

STRATEGY		DATES/SCORES			
EDITING	DATES:				
1. Self-checks spelling.					
2. Self-checks punctuation.					
3. Self-checks usage.					
4. Self-checks legibility.					
5. Self-checks for any plagiarism.					
PUBLISHING					
1. Puts text in neat, final form, including references.					
2. Shares with class.					
3. Shares with wider community.					
4. Uses computer for publishing.					
TOTAL:					

TEACHER'S COMMENTS:

C.55   **Rubric for Writing Stories for Grade 4** (p. 308)

Name: _____   Date: _____

Scores: Excellent = 5   Fair = 3   Poor = 0

COMPETENCY	EXCELLENT	FAIR	POOR
1. Setting description	○	○	○
2. Character description	○	○	○
3. Actions of characters	○	○	○
4. Dialogue of characters	○	○	○
5. Motives of characters	○	○	○
6. Story starter	○	○	○
7. Plot with roadblocks	○	○	○
8. Climax to plot	○	○	○
9. Resolution to plot	○	○	○
10. Choice of adjectives	○	○	○
11. Choice of verbs	○	○	○
12. Choice of nouns	○	○	○
13. Use of figurative speech	○	○	○
14. Quotation marks	○	○	○
15. Spelling	○	○	○
16. Punctuation	○	○	○
17. Paragraphing	○	○	○
18. Standard usage	○	○	○
19. Presentation	○	○	○

TEACHER'S COMMENTS: TOTAL _____

C.56 Rubric for Writing a Research Paper for Grade 4 (p. 308)

Name: _____   Date: _____

Scores: Excellent = 5   Fair = 3   Poor = 0

COMPETENCY	EXCELLENT	FAIR	POOR
1. Used books to get information.	○	○	○
2. Used video to get information.	○	○	○
3. Used Internet to get information.	○	○	○
4. Interviewed others for information.	○	○	○
5. Wrote interesting introduction.	○	○	○
6. Developed ideas with explanations, details, or examples.	○	○	○
7. Organized information within paragraphs.	○	○	○
8. Good organization within report.	○	○	○
9. Used descriptive language, specific nouns.	○	○	○
10. Included new, interesting information.	○	○	○
11. Used writing conventions such as:			
Capitalization	○	○	○
Correct usage	○	○	○
Correct spelling	○	○	○
Paragraph indentation	○	○	○
Correct paragraphing	○	○	○
12. Included citations.	○	○	○
13. Wrote complete sentences.	○	○	○
14. Summarized ideas at end.	○	○	○
15. Included references in correct format.	○	○	○
16. Presented in neat format.	○	○	○

TOTAL _____

TEACHER'S COMMENTS:

C.57 Rubric for Story Writing (p. 308)

Title: _____

Name: _____ Date: _____

3 POINTS	2 POINTS	1 POINT	0 POINTS	SCORE
Title is creative, relates to action, and sparks interest in readers.	Title is related to action.	Title does not relate to action.	No title was given.	
Evidence of prewriting with descriptive setting and characters, with sequence of plot.	Evidence of some prewriting with names of characters and some events of plot.	Little evidence of prewriting with only names of characters.	No evidence of prewriting.	
Many vivid descriptive words to paint a picture of time and place of action.	Some descriptive words to explain time and place of action.	Few descriptive words to explain time and place of action.	No descriptive words to explain time and place of action.	
Many vivid, descriptive words to paint a picture of characters' physical appearance and actions.	Some descriptive words to explain characters' physical appearance and actions.	Characters are named, but reader knows little about their physical appearance.	Most characters do not have names; they are identified as "the boy" or "the girl."	
Characters come to life through appropriate amount of dialogue.	There is dialogue, but characters do not come to life.	There is very little dialogue and it is difficult to distinguish who is speaking.	There is no dialogue.	
The story comes to life through vivid action verbs (active voice). The story's action creates mood.	The story has active voice, but the verbs are not vivid.	The story shifts from active to passive voice.	The story is told in passive voice.	
The main character's problem is revealed at the beginning of the story with many roadblocks to make the plot exciting.	It is clear what the main character's problem is, but the plot lacks an appropriate number of roadblocks.	It is not clear what is the main character's problem, and there are only two insignificant roadblocks.	There is no clear problem because there are no roadblocks.	
The plot has a clear climax with an appropriate resolution.	The plot has a clear climax, but the resolution is too long.	The plot has somewhat of a clear climax, but there is no resolution.	There is no climax; thus no resolution.	
Original illustrations are detailed, colorful, attractive, and relate to the text on the page.	Original illustrations are somewhat detailed and colorful, but do not always relate to the text.	Original illustrations somewhat relate to the text. They lack color and details.	Illustrations are not present, or they are merely stick figures.	
All of the written requirements (number of pages, font size, font style, amount of text on pages) are present.	The required font size and style and the number of pages are present.	The required font size and font style are present.	The required font size is present.	
Uses many transition words from one event to the next.	Uses transition words for main roadblocks or setting changes.	Uses transition words, but some are inappropriate.	Transitions are missing.	
The story contains many creative details, figures of speech, and other vivid words that contribute to the readers' enjoyment. Author's imagination is unique.	The story contains a few creative details and vivid words that contribute readers' enjoyment. Author has good imagination.	The details and word choice distract from the story.	There are no creative details or vivid word choice. The story lacks imagination.	
The story contains no spelling, punctuation, capitalization, or grammar errors.	The story contains no more than two of the following errors: spelling, punctuation, capitalization, or grammar.	The story contains no more than three of the following errors: spelling, punctuation, capitalization, or grammar.	The story contains four or more of the following errors: spelling, punctuation, capitalization, or grammar.	

From _Literacy Assessment and Intervention for Classroom Teachers_ (4th ed.), by Beverly DeVries. Copyright ©2015 by Holcomb Hathaway, Publishers, Scottsdale, AZ.

TOTAL SCORE: _____ /39
(Acceptable score is 31 or 80%).

C.58 Research Report Rubric for Grades 5/6 (p. 308)

Title: _____

Name: _____ Date: _____

3 POINTS	2 POINTS	1 POINT	0 POINTS	SCORE
All sources (text and graphics) are accurately cited in the required format.	All sources are documented, but not in the required format.	At least one source is not documented, but others are in required format.	Two or more sources are not documented or some sources are not in required format.	
Notes are organized in a neat, orderly fashion.	Notes are recorded legibly and are somewhat organized.	Notes are recorded.	There are no notes.	
Graphic organizer or out line has been completed and shows clear, logical relationships between all topics and subtopics.	Graphic organizer or outline has been completed and shows all main topics with a few subtopics.	Graphic organizer or out-line has been completed, showing only main topics.	Graphic organizer or outline has not been completed.	
At least three articles or books and at least three Internet sources were used.	At least two articles or books and at least three Internet sources were used.	At least two articles or books and at least two Internet sources were used.	Only one article or book and only one Internet source were used.	
In the introductory paragraph, the main concept and subtopics are clearly stated.	Introduces main concept, but does not let readers know subtopics at the beginning of the paper.	Readers need to infer the main concept.	An introductory paragraph is missing.	
Report is logically organized, using headings, illustrations, and/ or multimedia where appropriate.	Report is logically organized, using a few headings and illustrations.	Report is logically organized but includes no heading or illustrations.	Report is not logically organized.	
In an engaging manner, the report presents facts, definitions, details, and quotations to support subtopics.	The report includes facts, definitions, details, and quotations to support subtopics.	Report includes facts and details, but does not include necessary definitions or quotations.	Report is lacking necessary facts and details; topic is not well developed.	
Uses transition and connecting words in paragraphs and between paragraphs so that ideas are easy to follow.	Uses transition and connecting words within paragraphs.	Transition and connecting words are missing in paragraphs and between paragraphs.	Sentences are simple with no connecting words.	
Uses a variety of domain-specific words that are assoc-iated with the topic, and defines them when appropriate.	Uses some domain-specific words associated with the topic.	Uses only one or two domain-specific words.	No domain-specific words are used throughout the paper.	
Student had three peers and teacher read report for content. Student accepted suggestions readily.	Student had two peers and teacher read report for content. Student accepted most suggestions.	Student had one peer and teacher read report for content. Student did not readily accept suggestions.	Student had no peer read report for content.	
Student had three peers edit the report. Student accepted suggestions readily.	Students had two peers edit the report. Student accepted only some of the suggestions.	Student had one peer edit the report. Student accepted few suggestions.	Student had no peer edit the report.	
Finished product was neatly prepared and shared and posted on the bulletin board or online.	Finished product was neatly prepared and shared orally OR posted on the bulletin board or online.	Finished product was somewhat neat. Student posted it on the bulletin board.	Student did not share his/her report in any manner.	

Finished product had title page, page numbers, table of contents, and reference page.	Finished product was missing one of the following: title page, page numbers, table of contents, or reference page.	Finished product was missing two of the following: title page, page numbers, table of contents, or reference page.	Finished product was missing three or more of the following: title page, page numbers, table of contents, or reference page.	
The report contained no spelling, punctuation, capitalization, or grammar errors.	The report contained no more than one of the following errors: punctuation, spelling, capitalization, or grammar.	The report contained no more than two of the following errors: spelling, punctuation, capitalization, or grammar.	The report contained more than three of the following errors: spelling, punctuation, capitalization, or grammar.	
The report was well organized with all paragraphs correctly constructed.	The report was well organized with only one paragraph not correctly constructed.	The report was organized with only two paragraphs not correctly constructed.	There was no clear organization to the report. It lacked well-constructed paragraphs.	
The topic was age appropriate and interesting.	The topic was age appropriate and somewhat interesting.	The topic was age appropriate with only a few new pieces of information.	The topic was age appropriate, but contained no new information.	

TOTAL SCORE: _____ /45
(Acceptable score is 36 or 80%).

From *Literacy Assessment and Intervention for Classroom Teachers* (4th ed.), by Beverly DeVries. Copyright ©2015 by Holcomb Hathaway, Publishers, Scottsdale, AZ.

C.59 Multimedia Group Project Rubric (p. 308)

Name: _____   Date: _____

CATEGORY	4	3	2	1
Sources POINTS _____	Source information collected for all graphics, facts and quotes. All documented in desired format.	Source information collected for all graphics, facts and quotes. Most documented in desired format.	Source information collected for graphics, facts and quotes, but not documented in desired format.	Very little or no source information was collected.
Permissions POINTS _____	All permissions to use graphics "borrowed" from web pages or scanned from books have been requested, received, printed and saved for future reference.	All permissions to use graphics "borrowed" from web pages or scanned from books have been requested and received.	Most permissions to use graphics "borrowed" from web pages or scanned from books have been requested and received.	Permissions were not requested for several graphics "borrowed" from web pages or scanned from books.
Attractiveness POINTS _____	Makes excellent use of font, color, graphics, effects, etc. to enhance the presentation.	Makes good use of font, color, graphics, effects, etc. to enhance to presentation.	Makes use of font, color, graphics, effects, etc. but occasionally these detract from the presentation content.	Use of font, color, graphics, effects etc. but these often distract from the presentation content.
Rough Draft POINTS _____	Rough draft brought on due date. Student shares with peer and extensively edits based on peer feedback.	Rough draft brought on due date. Student shares with peer and peer makes edits.	Provides feedback and/or edits for peer, but own rough draft was not ready for editing.	Rough draft not ready for editing and student did not participate in reviewing draft of peer.
Requirements POINTS _____	All requirements are met and exceeded.	All requirements are met.	One requirement was not completely met.	More than 1 requirement was not completely met.
Content POINTS _____	Covers topic in-depth with details and examples. Subject knowledge is excellent.	Includes essential knowledge about the topic. Subject knowledge appears to be good.	Includes essential information about the topic but there are 1 or 2 factual errors.	Content is minimal OR there are several factual errors.
Organization POINTS _____	Content is well organized using headings or bulleted lists to group related material.	Uses headings or bulleted lists to organize, but the overall organization of topics appears flawed.	Content is logically organized for the most part.	There was no clear or logical organizational structure, just lots of facts.
Originality POINTS _____	Product shows a large amount of original thought. Ideas are creative and inventive.	Product shows some original thought. Work shows new ideas and insights.	Uses other people's ideas (giving them credit), but there is little evidence of original thinking.	Uses other people's ideas, but does not give them credit.
Mechanics POINTS _____	No misspellings or grammatical errors.	Three or fewer misspellings and/or mechanical errors.	Four misspellings and/or grammatical errors.	More than 4 errors in spelling or grammar.
Workload TOTAL POINTS _____	The workload is divided and shared equally by all team members.	The workload is divided and shared fairly by all team members, though workloads may vary from person to person.	The workload was divided, but one person in the group is viewed as not doing his/her fair share of the work.	The workload was not divided OR several people in the group are viewed as not doing their fair share of the work.

Source: Created using http://rubistar.4teachers.org.

From *Literacy Assessment and Intervention for Classroom Teachers* (4th ed.), by Beverly DeVries. Copyright ©2015 by Holcomb Hathaway, Publishers, Scottsdale, AZ.

C.60 Writing and Spelling Self-Assessment (p. 310)

Name: _____

Circle: First quarter   Second quarter   Third quarter   Fourth quarter

1. I started _____ different writing projects this quarter.

2. I completed _____ writing projects this quarter.

3. I wrote the following genres (poem, mystery, adventure story, autobiography, informational composition, opinion pieces or arguments, or any other genre).

    _____

    _____

    _____

    _____

4. My favorite writing was _____

    because _____

5. My most difficult piece to write was _____

    because _____

6. How did you share your writing with others? _____

    _____

7. What did you do when you did not know how to spell a word? _____

    _____

8. Do you think you are a good or poor writer? _____

    Why do you think that? _____

9. What did you learn as a writer this quarter? _____

    _____

10. What is the hardest part of writing? _____

    _____

TEACHER'S COMMENTS:

C.61   Bear, Invernizzi, Templeton, & Johnston Qualitative Spelling Inventory (p. 341)

ONE

SET #1

| 1. bed | 2. ship | 3. when | 4. lump | 5. float |

SET #2

| 1. train | 2. place | 3. drive | 4. bright | 5. shopping |

SET #3

| 1. spoil | 2. serving | 3. chewed | 4. carries | 5. marched |

SET #4

| 1. shower | 2. cattle | 3. favor | 4. ripen | 5. cellar |

SET #5

| 1. pleasure | 2. fortunate | 3. confident | 4. civilize | 5. opposition |

TWO

SET #1

| 1. net | 2. trip | 3. crime | 4. dump | 5. then |

SET #2

| 1. chain | 2. forest | 3. trail | 4. soap | 5. reaches |

SET #3

| 1. preparing | 2. popping | 3. cattle | 4. caught | 5. inspection |

SET #4

| 1. comparing | 2. topping | 3. battle | 4. fought | 5. intention |

SET #5

| 1. rupture | 2. stellar | 3. treasure | 4. confident | 5. tempest |

Source: Bear, Donald R.; Invernizzi, Marcia R.; Templeton, Shane; Johnston, Francine R., *Words their way: Word study for phonics, vocabulary, and spelling instruction.* Top: 4th ed., © 2006, p. 35. Bottom: 2nd ed., © 2000, p. 294. Reprinted by permission of Pearson Education, Inc. Upper Saddle River, NJ.

C.62 Recording and Analyzing Spelling (p. 342)

Student: _____   Grade: _____

Word	Emergent	Alphabetic	Within Word Pattern	Syllables + Affixes	Derivational Relations
1.					
2.					
3.					
4.					
5.					
6.					
7.					
8.					
9.					
10.					

TEACHER'S COMMENTS:

Instruction Materials

D.1 Qualitative Dimensions of Text Complexity (Chapter 2)   511

D.2 Lesson Plan for English Learners (Chapter 13)   512

D.3 Directions for Creating Game Boards and Picture/Word Cards (Chapter 4)   513

D.4 How Many Syllables in the Zoo? Game Board and Picture Cards (Chapter 4)   514

D.5 Remember the Beginning Sound Picture Cards (Chapter 4)   517

D.6 Initial Sound Picture Bingo Cards (Chapter 4)   530

D.7 Toss the Cube Art (Chapter 4)   540

D.8 Go Fish Picture Cards (Chapter 4)   549

D.9 Humpty Dumpty Game Board and Picture Cards (Chapter 4)   556

D.10 Listen for the Initial Consonant Blend Sound Game Board and Picture Cards (Chapter 5)   561

D.11 Word Dominoes (Chapter 5)   567

D.12 Concentration Word Cards (Chapter 5)   571

D.13 Blank Bingo Card (Chapter 5)   575

D.14 Listen for the Vowel Sound Board and Game Pieces (Chapter 5)   576

D.15 Dolch List Bingo Word Cards (Chapter 6)   582

D.16 Templates for Morphology Rummy Cards (Chapter 6)   588

D.17 Vocabulary Bookmark Template (Chapter 7)   590

D.18   Cognate Sort (Chapter 7)   591

D.19   Multiple Meaning Racetrack Board (Chapter 7)   592

D.20   Questions to Consider When Previewing Features of Historical Fiction Picturebooks (Chapter 8)   593

D.21   Text Mapping Form (Chapter 8)   594

D.22   Narrative E-Book Evaluation Form (Chapter 8)   595

D.23   Textbook and Trade Book Evaluation Checklist (Chapter 9)   596

D.24   Template for a Chart Comparing Multiple Sources for a Topic (Chapter 9)   598

D.25   Template for a K-T-W-L-E Chart (Chapter 9)   599

D.26   Informational E-Text Evaluation Form (Chapter 9)   600

D.27   Record, Check, Chart (Chapter 10)   601

D.28   Fluency Log (Chapter 10)   602

D.29   Readers Theater Sample Script (Chapter 10)   603

D.30   Graphic Organizer for an Argument (Chapter 11)   605

D.31   Graphic Organizer for Prewriting an Argumentative Essay (Chapter 11)   606

D.32   Matrix Aligning Elements of Writing Instruction and Assessment (Chapter 11)   607

D.33   Mt. Plot (Chapter 11)   608

D.34   Lesson Plan for Tutors (Chapter 13)   609

D.35   Log Sheet of Strategies (Chapter 13)   610

D.36   Log Sheet of Books Read (Chapter 13)   611

D.37   Postcard for Children Reading Books with Oral Reading and Comprehension Scaffolding (Chapter 14)   612

D.1   Qualitative Dimensions of Text Complexity (p. 34)

LEVELS OF MEANING (LITERARY TEXTS) OR PURPOSE (INFORMATIONAL TEXTS)

- Single level of meaning → Multiple levels of meaning
- Explicitly stated purpose → Implicit purpose, may be hidden or obscure

STRUCTURE

- Simple → Complex
- Explicit → Implicit
- Conventional → Unconventional (chiefly literary texts)
- Events related in chronological order → Events related out of chronological order (chiefly literary texts)
- Traits of a common genre or subgenre → Traits specific to a particular discipline (chiefly informational texts)
- Simple graphics → Sophisticated graphics
- Graphics unnecessary or merely supplementary to understanding the text → Graphics essential to understanding the text and may provide information not otherwise conveyed in the text

LANGUAGE CONVENTIONALITY AND CLARITY

- Literal → Figurative or iconic
- Clear → Ambiguous or purposefully misleading
- Contemporary, familiar → Archaic or otherwise unfamiliar
- Conversational → General academic or otherwise unfamiliar
- Conversational → General academic and domain-specific

KNOWLEDGE DEMANDS: LIFE EXPERIENCES (LITERARY TEXTS)

- Simple theme → Complex or sophisticated themes
- Single themes → Multiple themes
- Common, everyday experiences or clearly fantastical situations → Experiences distinctly different from one's own
- Single perspective → Multiple perspectives
- Perspective(s) like one's own → Perspective(s) unlike or in opposition to one's own

KNOWLEDGE DEMANDS: CULTURAL/LITERARY KNOWLEDGE (CHIEFLY LITERARY TEXTS)

- Everyday knowledge and familiarity with genre conventions required → Cultural and literary knowledge useful
- Low intertextuality (few if any references/allusions to other texts) → High intertextuality (many references/allusions to other texts)

KNOWLEDGE DEMANDS: CONTENT/DISCIPLINE KNOWLEDGE (CHIEFLY INFORMATIONAL TEXTS)

- Everyday knowledge and familiarity with genre conventions required → Extensive, perhaps specialized discipline-specific knowledge required
- Low intertextuality (few if any references to/citations of other texts) → High intertextuality (many references to/citations of other texts)

Sources: Adapted from ACT, Inc. (2006). *Reading between the lines: What the ACT reveals about college readiness in reading.* Iowa City, IA: Author. / Carnegie Council on Advancing Adolescent Literacy. (2010). *Time to act: An agenda for advancing adolescent literacy for college and career success.* New York: Carnegie Corporation of New York. / Chall, J.S., Bissex, G. L., Conrad, S. S., & Harris-Sharples, S. (1996). *Qualitative assessment of text difficulty: A practical guide for teachers and writers.* Cambridge, UK: Brookline Books. / Hess, K., & Biggam, S. (2004). A discussion of "increasing text complexity." Published by the New Hampshire, Rhode Island, and Vermont departments of education as part of the New England Common Core Assessment Program (NECAP). Retrieved from www.nciea.org/publications/TextComplexity_KH05.pdf.

D.2   Lesson Plan for English Learners (p. 363)

Tutor: _____   Date: _____

Tutee: _____   Grade: _____

Review from previous lesson:

Phonics:

Vocabulary building:

Sentences:

Writing:

Listening to tutor:

LESSON PLAN	PLANNED ACTIVITY	TIME REFLECTION
Review:		
Phonics:		
Vocabulary:		
Sentences:		
Writing:		
Listening:		

D.3   **Directions for Creating Game Boards and Picture/Word Cards** (pp. 87, 112)

To assemble:

- Create a front title page.

- Glue the title on the front of a colored file folder.

- Copy the game board from appendix or create your own. Decorate the game board. Glue the game board inside the file folder.

- Reproduce the pictures for the various activities on plain stock card paper and the word cards on colorful stock paper. Laminate them and cut them out so that they can be stacked in a deck.

- Using the directions given in the chapter Intervention sections, copy or create a sheet of directions. Glue the directions and an envelope to store playing pieces on the back of the folder.

D.4   How Many Syllables in the Zoo? Game Board and Picture Cards (pp. 87, 112)

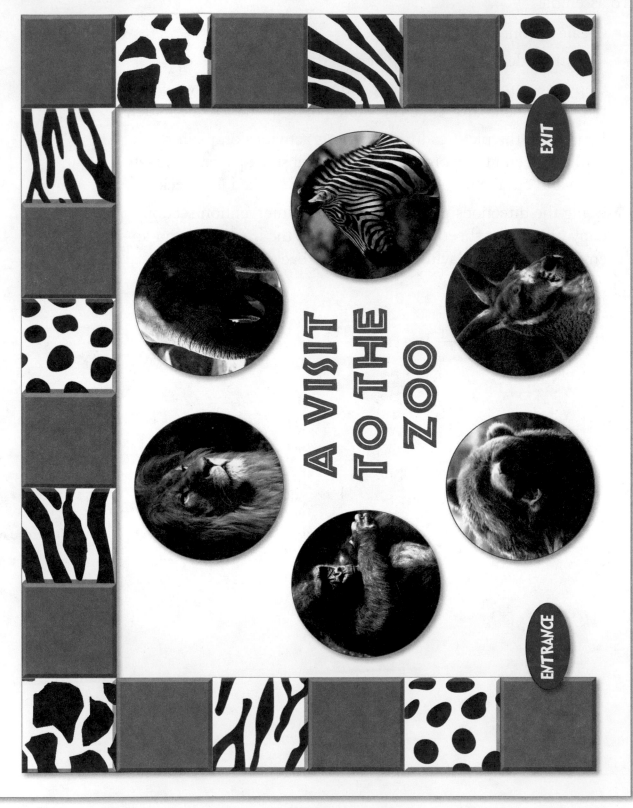

EXIT

A VISIT TO THE ZOO

ENTRANCE

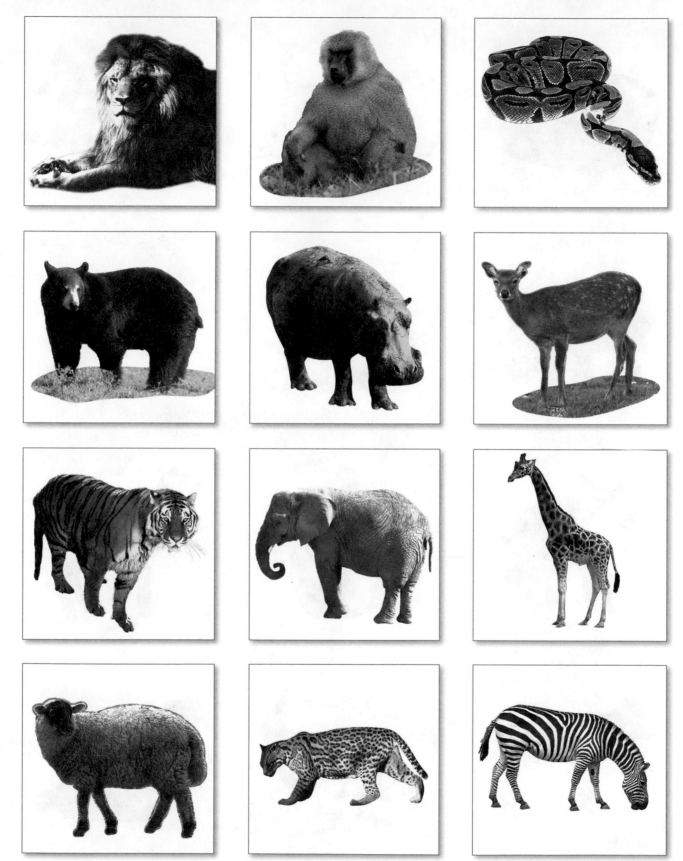

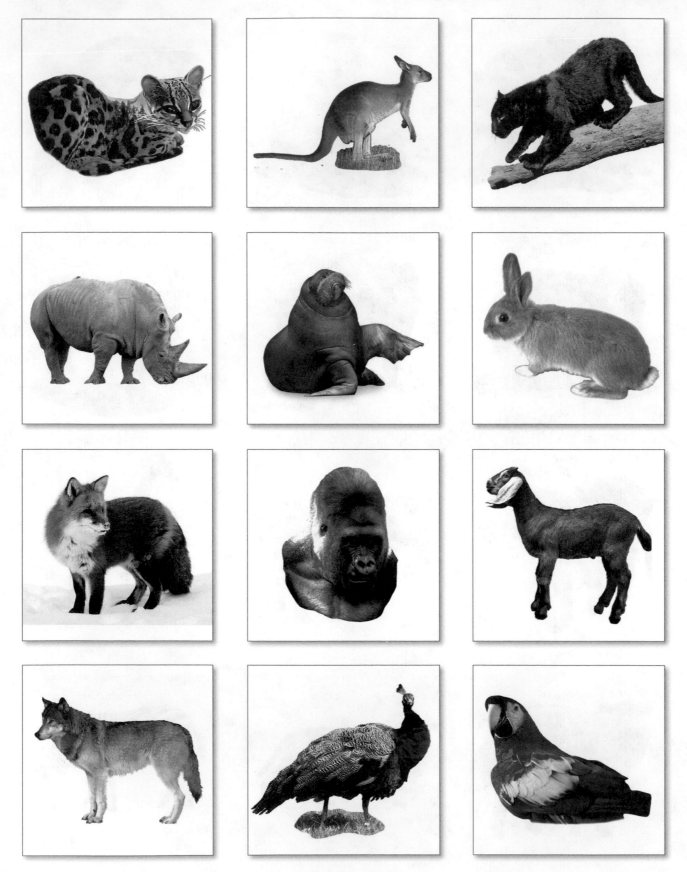

D.5   Remember the Beginning Sound Picture Cards (pp. 74, 91–93)

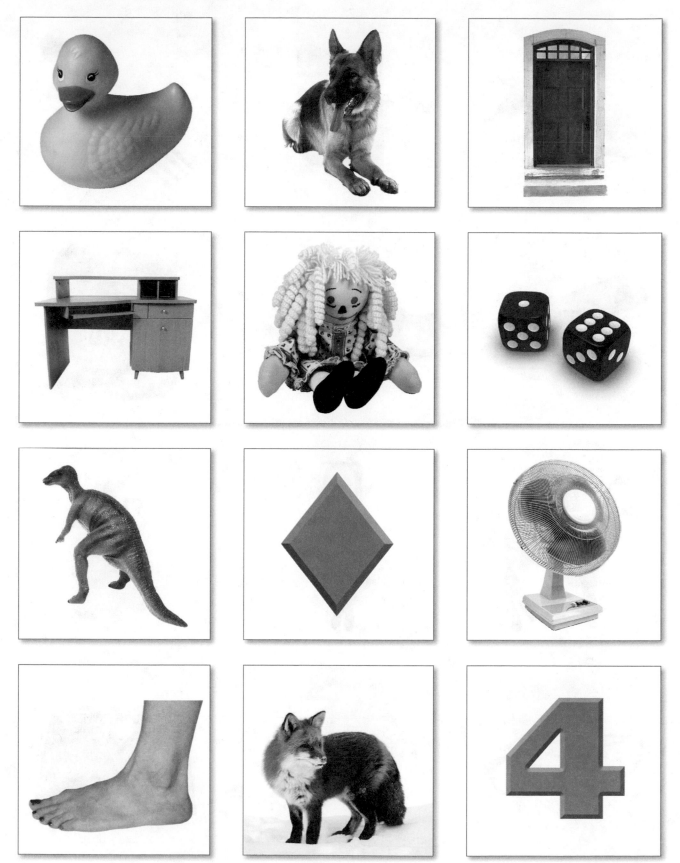

From *Literacy Assessment and Intervention for Classroom Teachers* (4th ed.), by Beverly DeVries. Copyright ©2015 by Holcomb Hathaway, Publishers, Scottsdale, AZ.

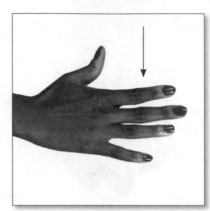

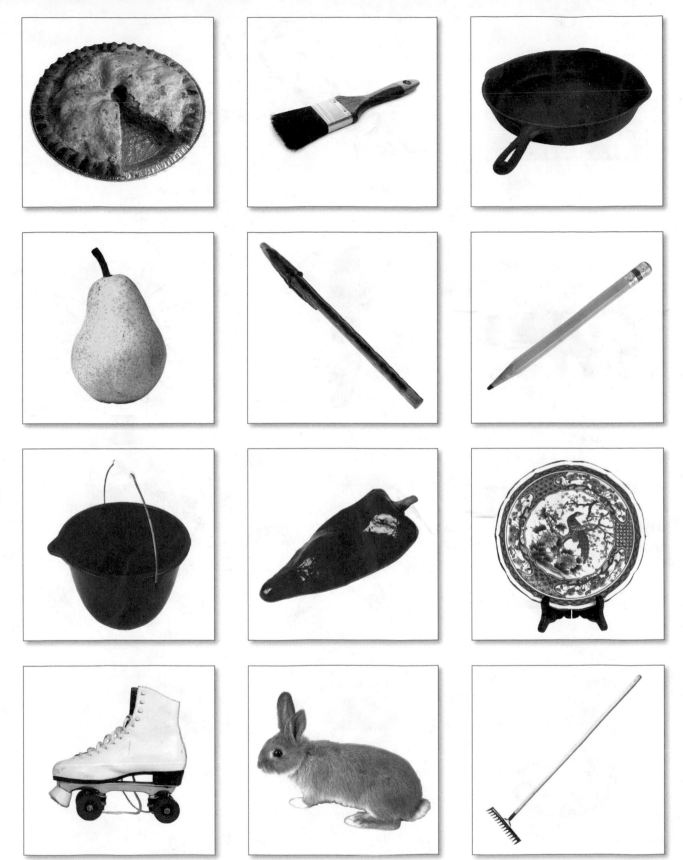

From *Literacy Assessment and Intervention for Classroom Teachers* (4th ed.), by Beverly DeVries. Copyright ©2015 by Holcomb Hathaway, Publishers, Scottsdale, AZ.

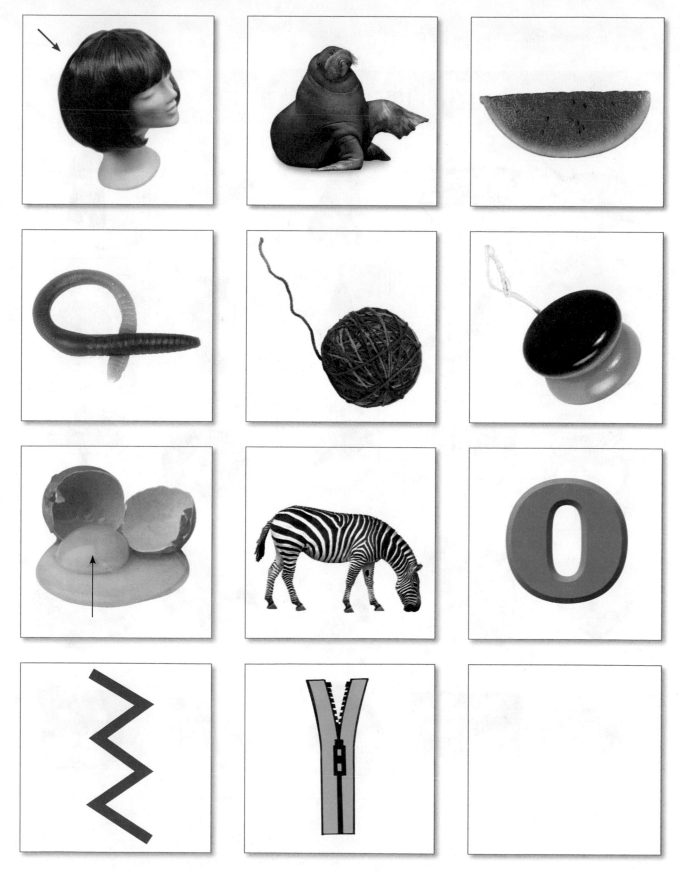

D.6   Initial Sound Picture Bingo Cards (pp. 89, 361)

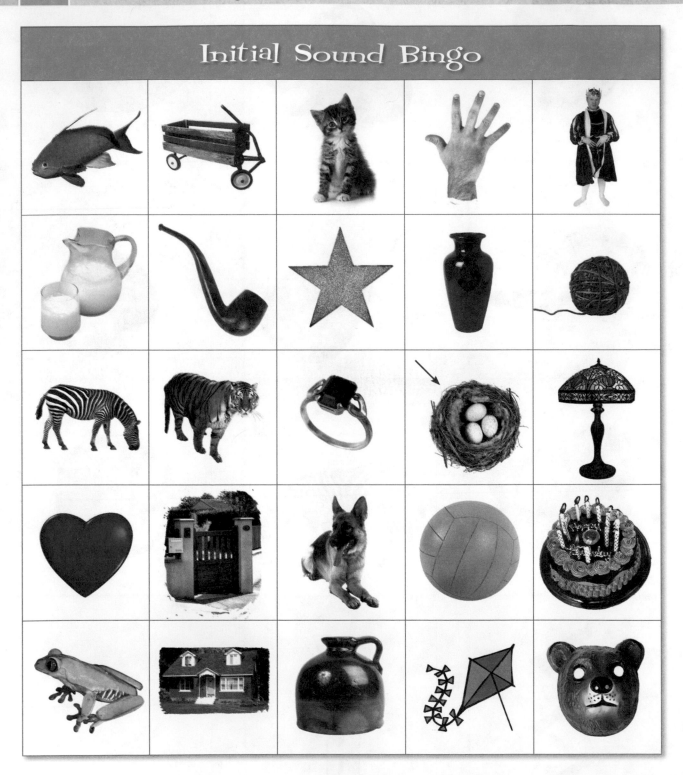

Initial Sound Bingo

Initial Sound Bingo

Initial Sound Bingo

Initial Sound Bingo

Initial Sound Bingo

Initial Sound Bingo

Initial Sound Bingo

Initial Sound Bingo

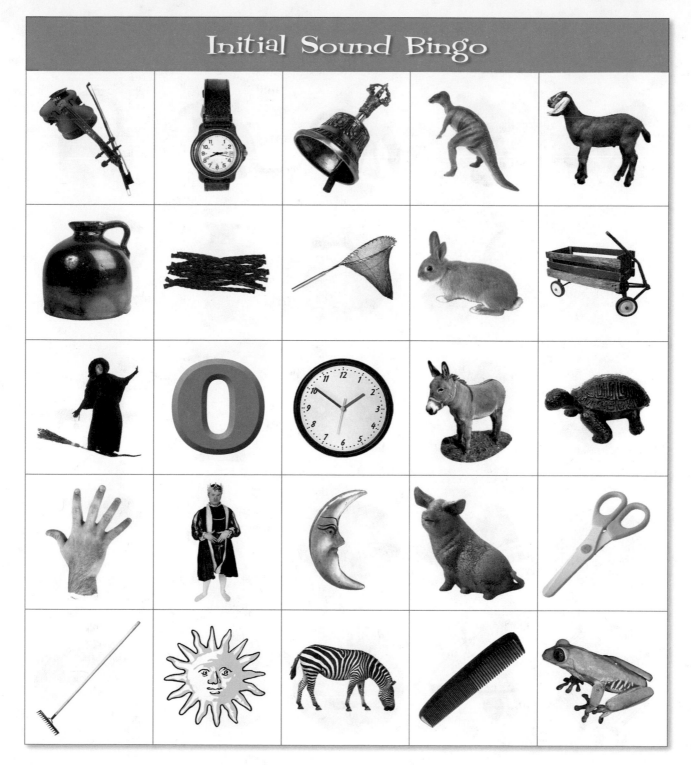

Initial Sound Bingo

Initial Sound Bingo

D.7   **Toss the Cube Art** (p. 90, 140, 171)

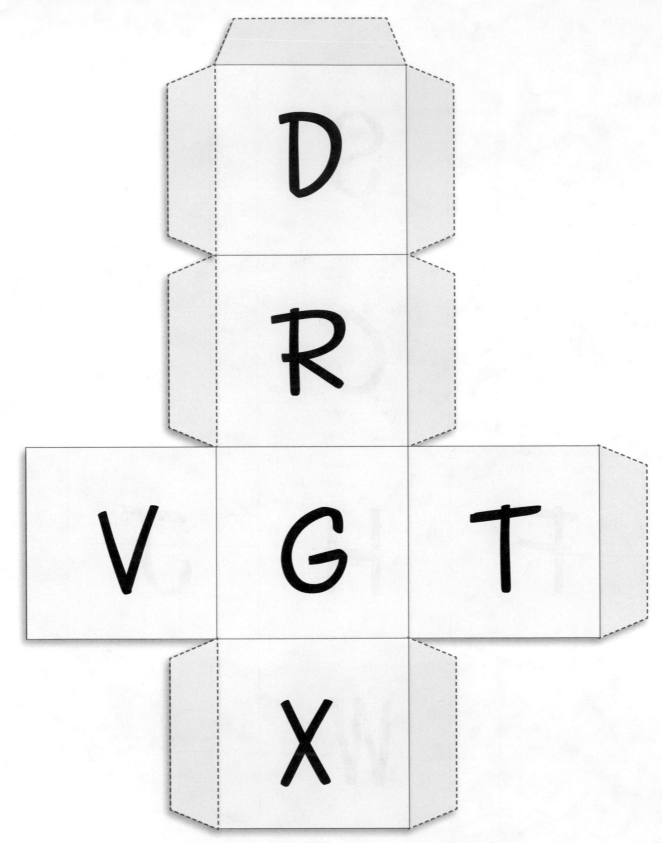

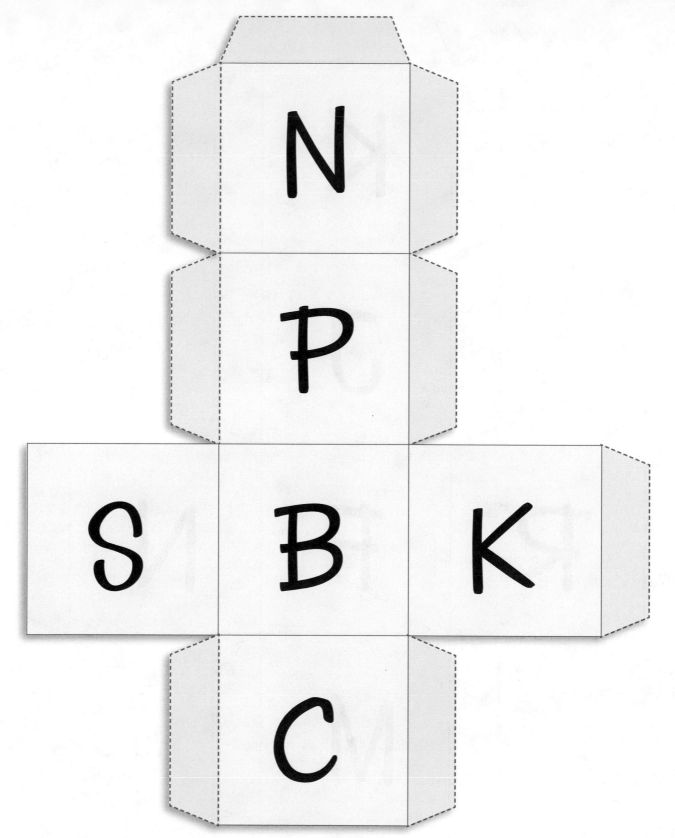

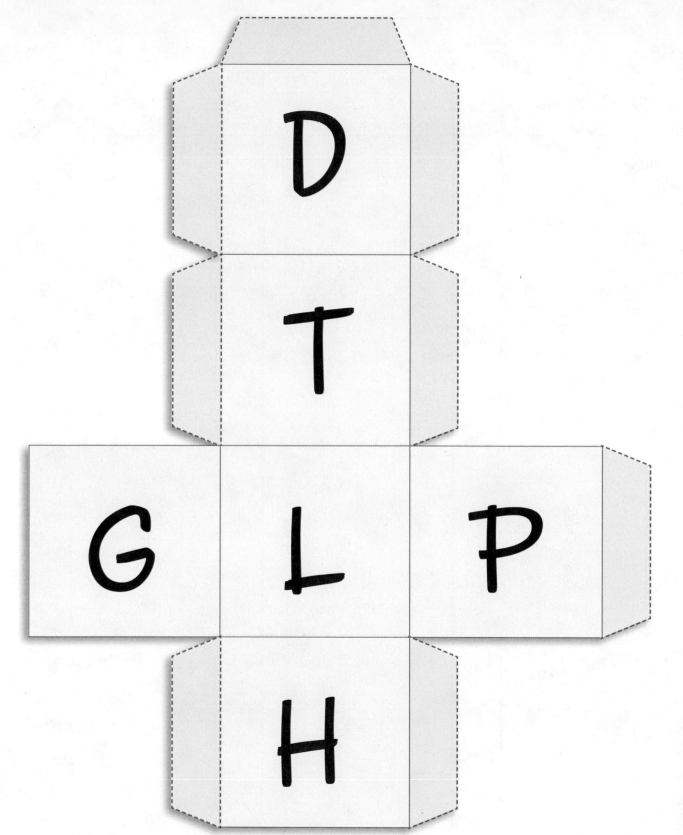

D.8   **Go Fish Picture Cards** (p. 90)

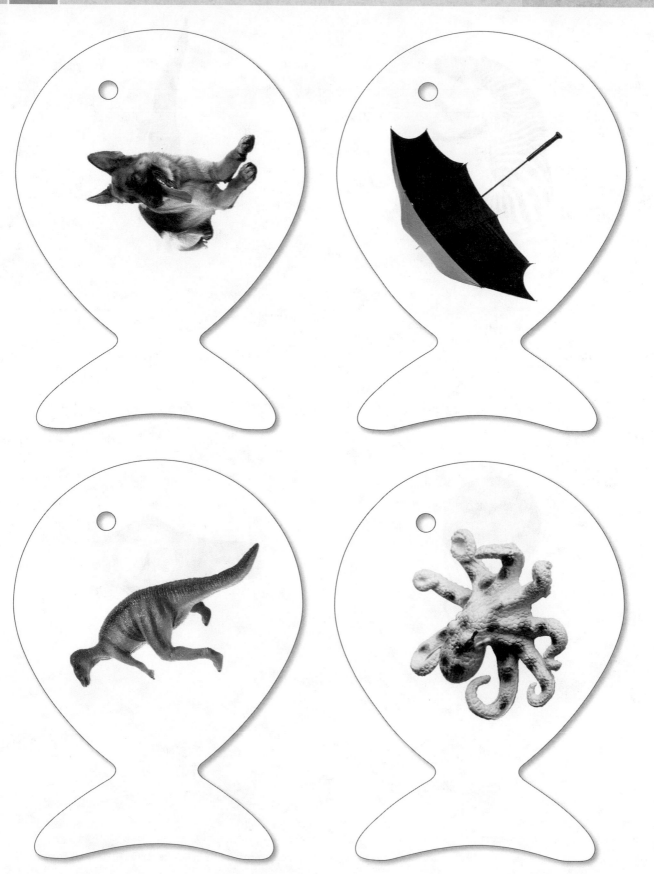

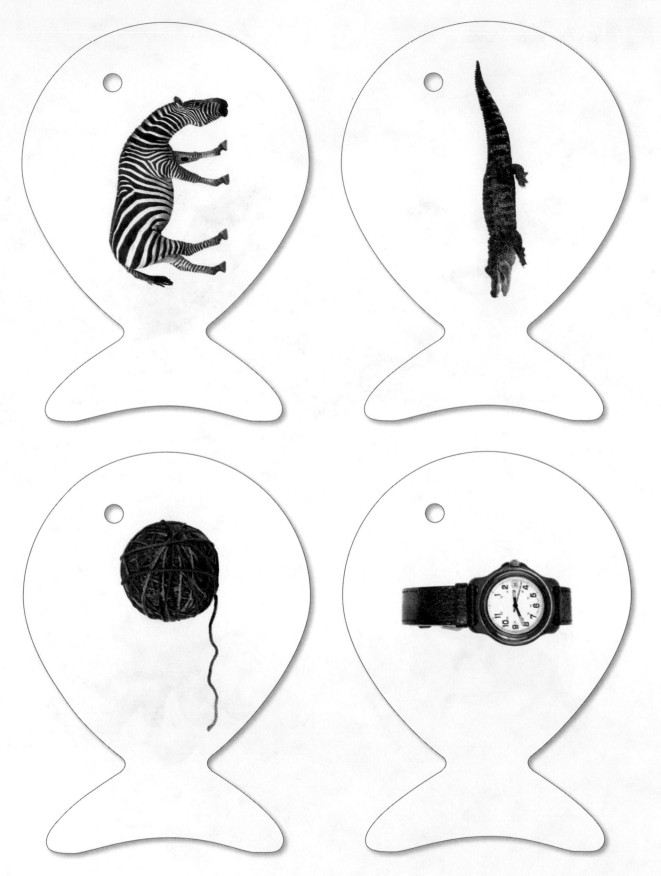

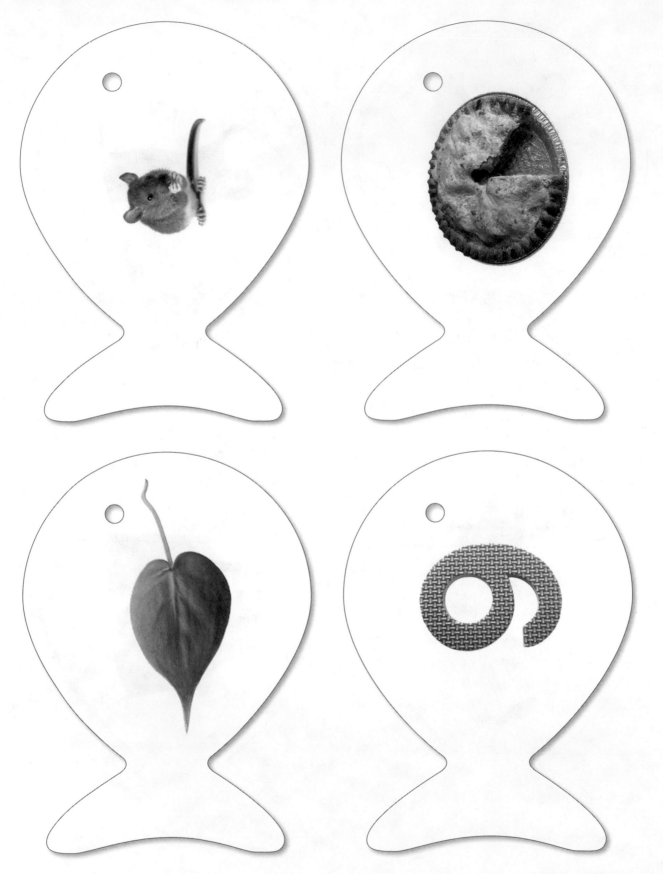

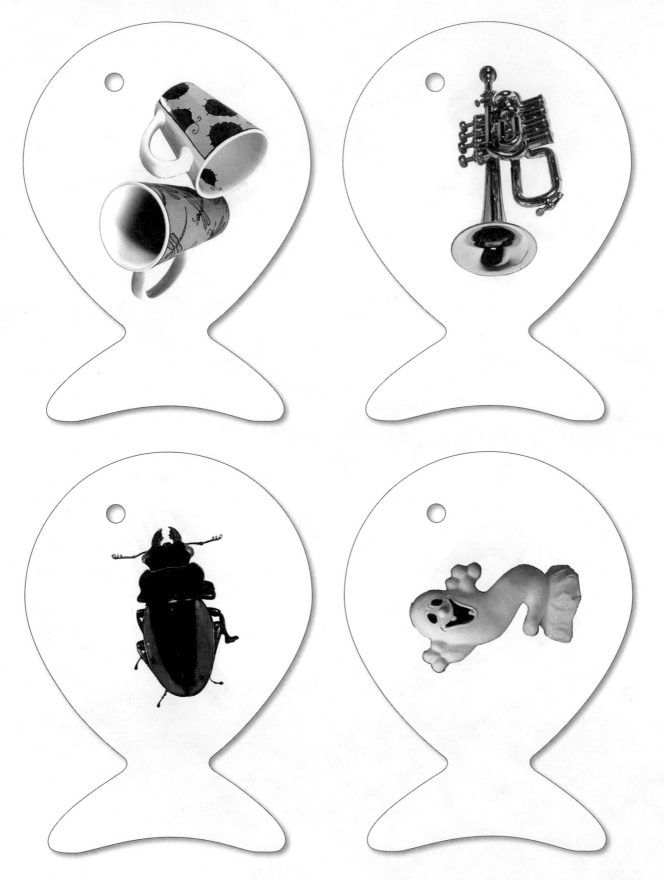

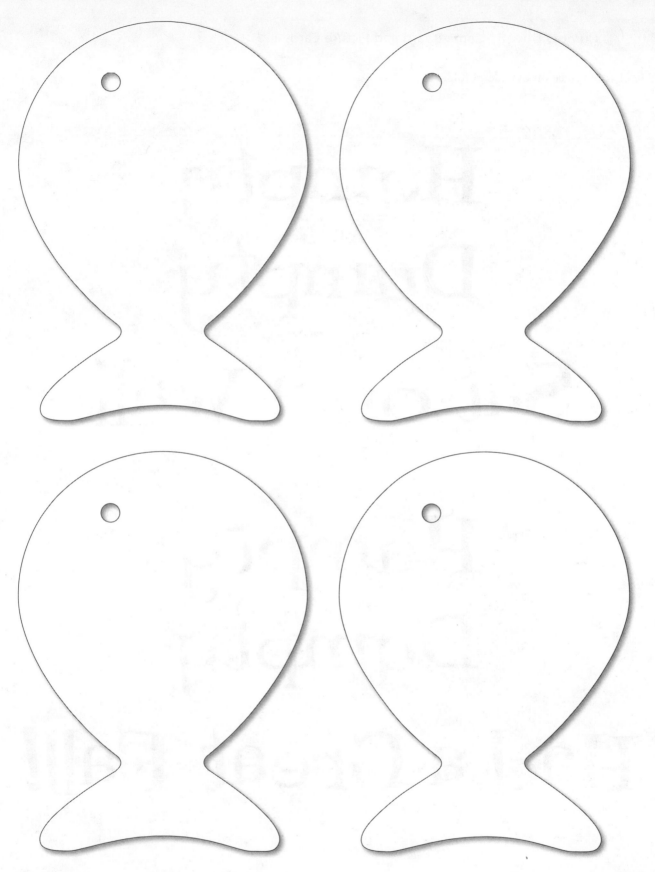

D.9   Humpty Dumpty Game Board and Picture Cards (p. 91)

Folder title (place on outside of folder)

Humpty Dumpty Sat on a Wall

Humpty Dumpty Had a Great Fall!

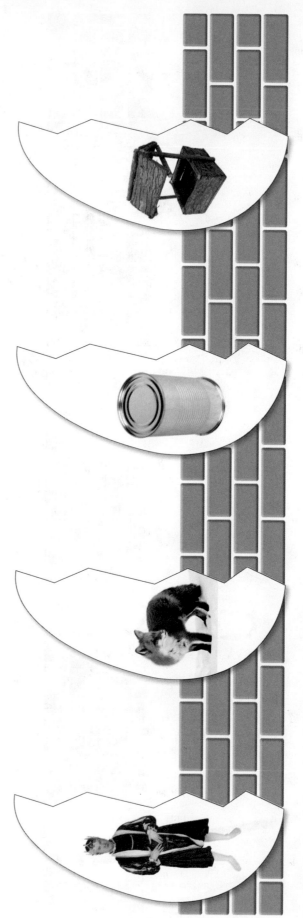

From *Literacy Assessment and Intervention for Classroom Teachers* (4th ed.), by Beverly DeVries. Copyright ©2015 by Holcomb Hathaway, Publishers, Scottsdale, AZ.

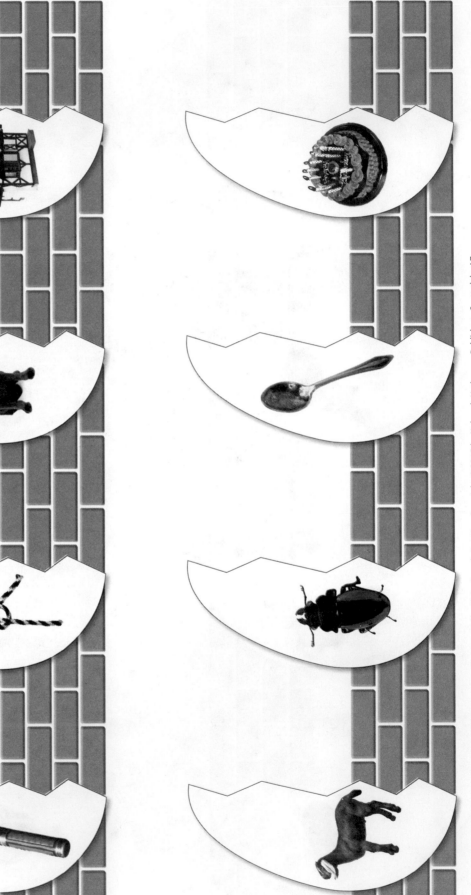

D.10 Listen for the Initial Consonant Blend Sound Game Board and Picture Cards (p. 112)

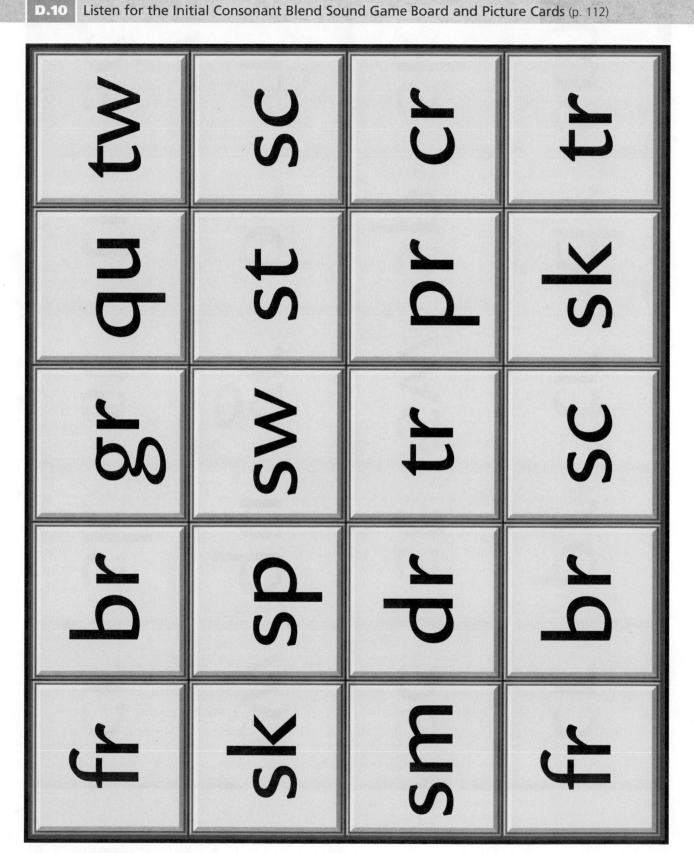

tw	sc	cr	tr
qu	st	pr	sk
gr	sw	tr	sc
br	sp	dr	br
fr	sk	sm	fr

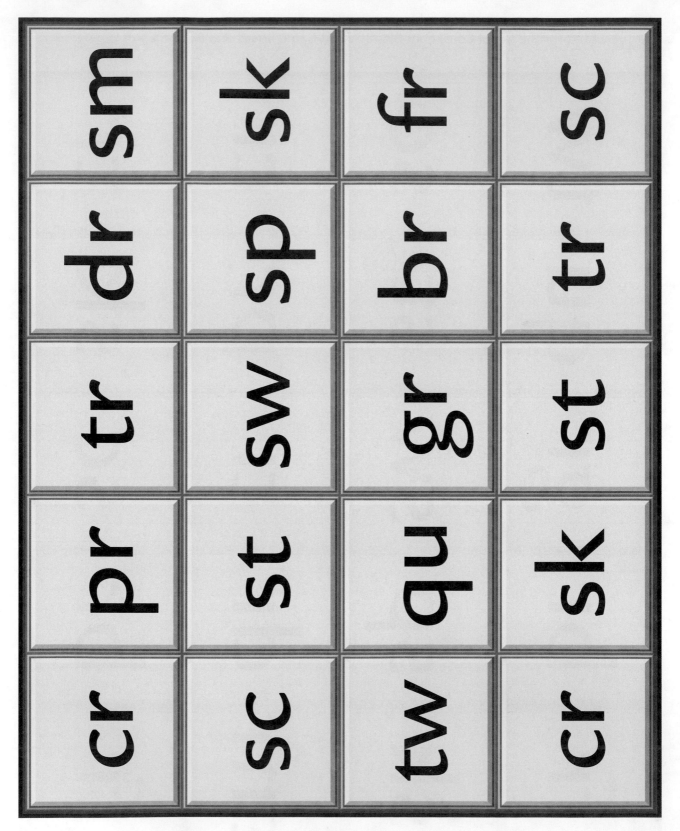

sm	sk	fr	sc
dr	sp	br	tr
tr	sw	gr	st
pr	st	qu	sk
cr	sc	tw	cr

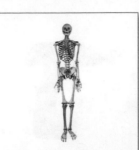

D.11   Word Dominoes (p. 113)

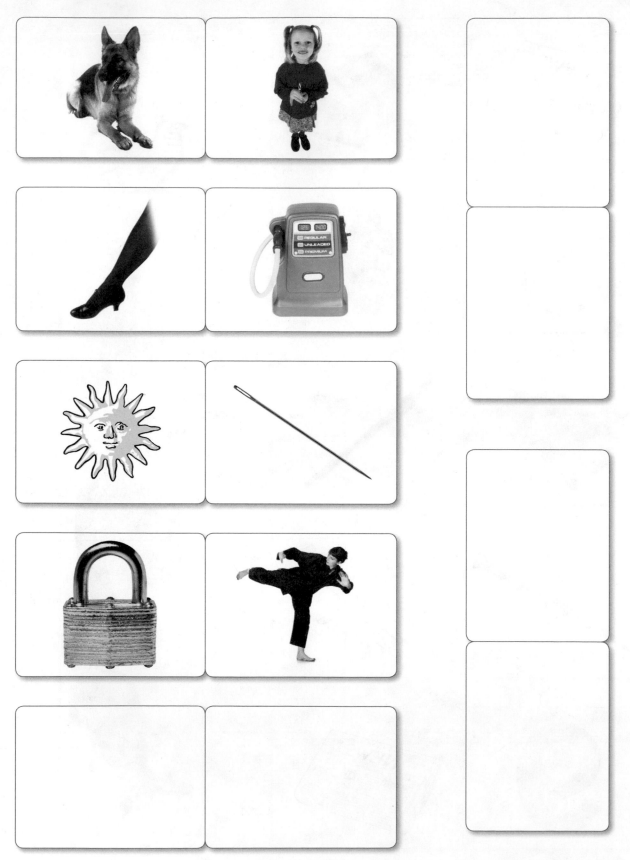

D.12 **Concentration Word Cards*** (pp. 115, 118)

*Game pieces on this page are based on *Sheep Out to Eat* by Nancy Shaw (1992).

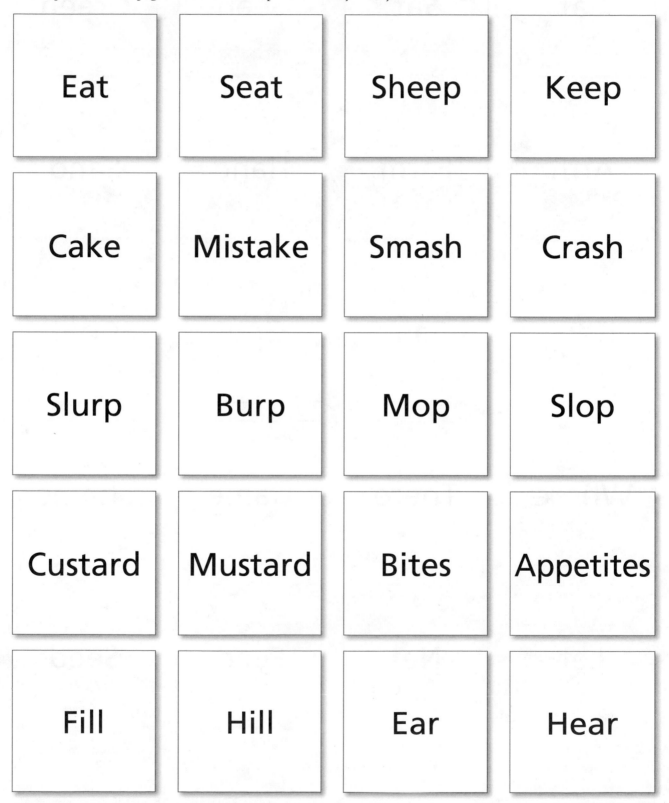

Eat	Seat	Sheep	Keep
Cake	Mistake	Smash	Crash
Slurp	Burp	Mop	Slop
Custard	Mustard	Bites	Appetites
Fill	Hill	Ear	Hear

Cat	Sat	Seen	Green
Arm	Farm	Hand	Sand
Ham	Sam	Goat	Coat
Where	There	Game	Shame
Let	Net	Feed	Seed

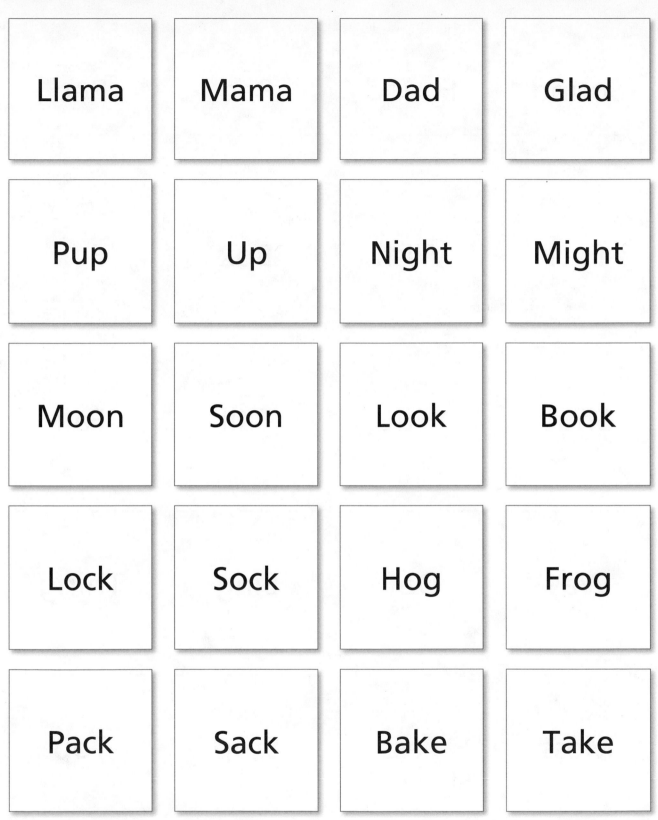

Llama	Mama	Dad	Glad
Pup	Up	Night	Might
Moon	Soon	Look	Book
Lock	Sock	Hog	Frog
Pack	Sack	Bake	Take

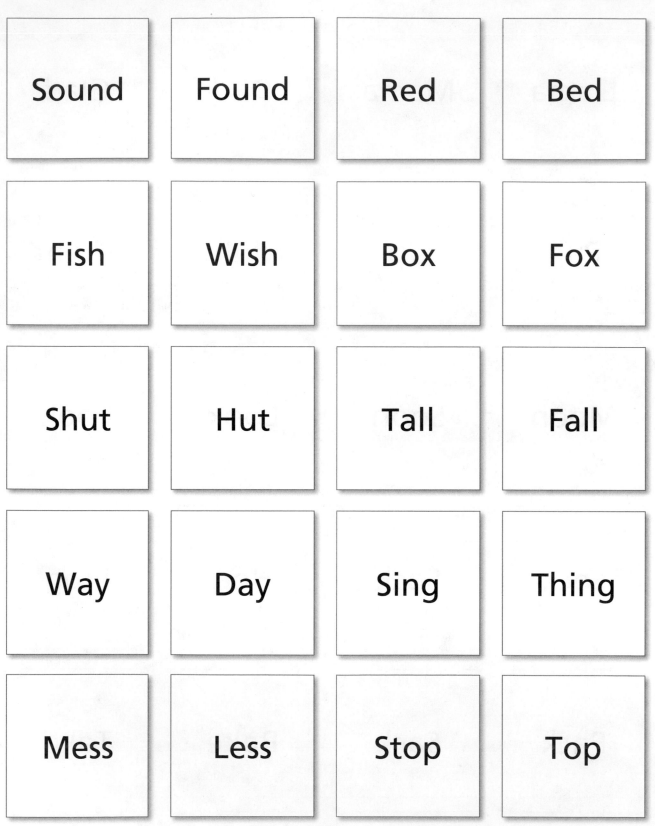

Sound	Found	Red	Bed
Fish	Wish	Box	Fox
Shut	Hut	Tall	Fall
Way	Day	Sing	Thing
Mess	Less	Stop	Top

D.13   **Blank Bingo Card** (p. 116)

B	I	N	G	O

D.14   Listen for the Vowel Sound Game Board and Game Pieces (p. 117)

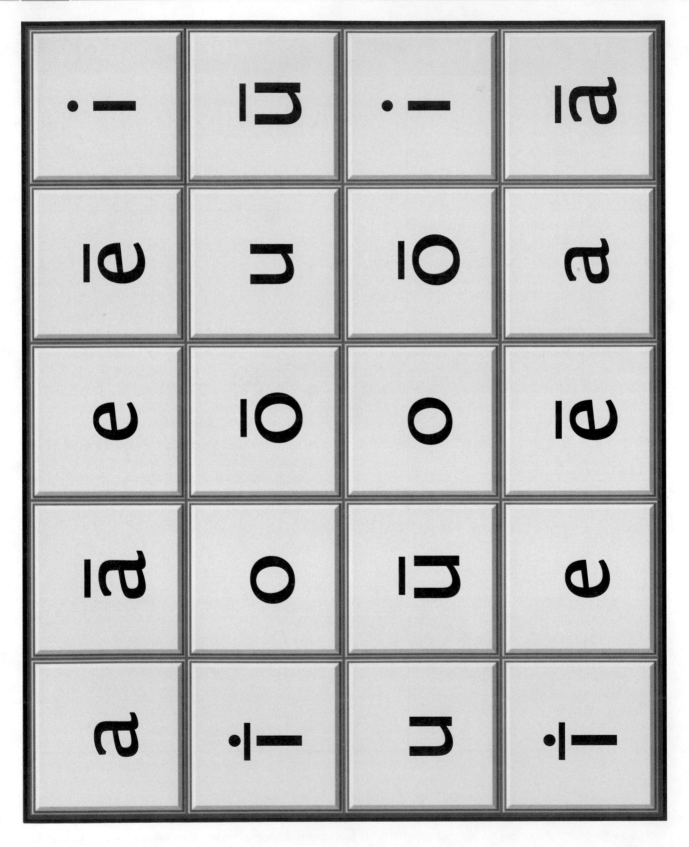

From *Literacy Assessment and Intervention for Classroom Teachers* (4th ed.), by Beverly DeVries. Copyright ©2015 by Holcomb Hathaway, Publishers, Scottsdale, AZ.

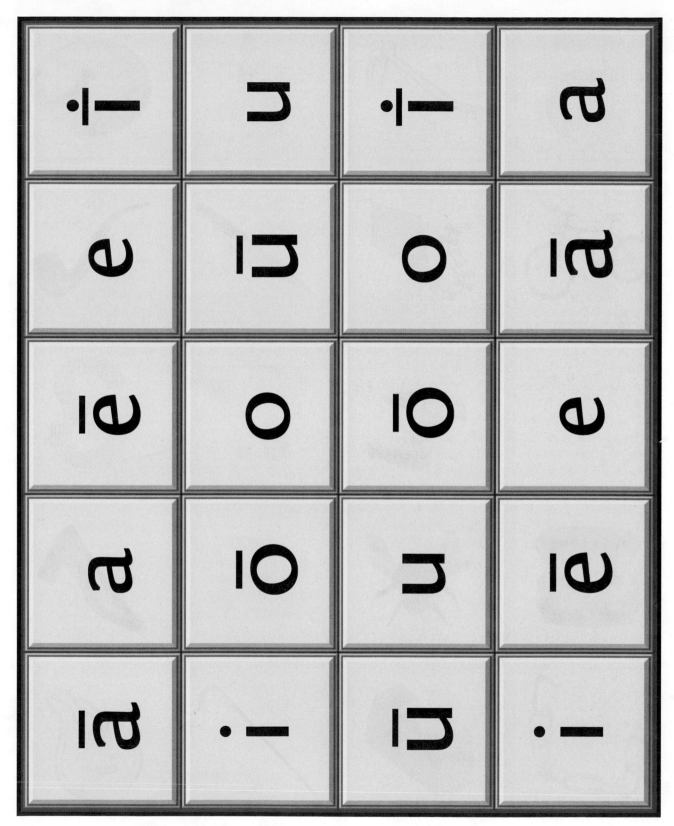

B	I	N	G	O
a	after	all	am	an
and	are	around	as	at
away	be	big	black	blue
brown	but	by	call	came
can	carry	cold	come	did

B	I	N	G	O
go	going	good	green	had
has	have	he	help	her
here	him	his	hurt	I
if	in	into	is	it
its	jump	know	like	little

B	I	N	G	O
look	over	play	put	ran
red	ride	round	run	said
saw	see	she	so	some
soon	stop	ten	the	this
three	to	too	two	under

B	I	N	G	O
up	about	again	any	ask
ate	because	been	before	best
better	both	bring	buy	clean
could	cut	does	done	draw
drink	eight	every	fall	far

B	I	N	G	O
hurt	just	keep	kind	laugh
let	light	live	long	many
much	must	myself	never	new
now	off	once	only	open
or	our	own	pick	please

B	I	N	G	O
small	start	take	tell	thank
that	their	them	then	there
these	they	think	those	today
together	try	upon	us	use
very	walk	want	warm	wish

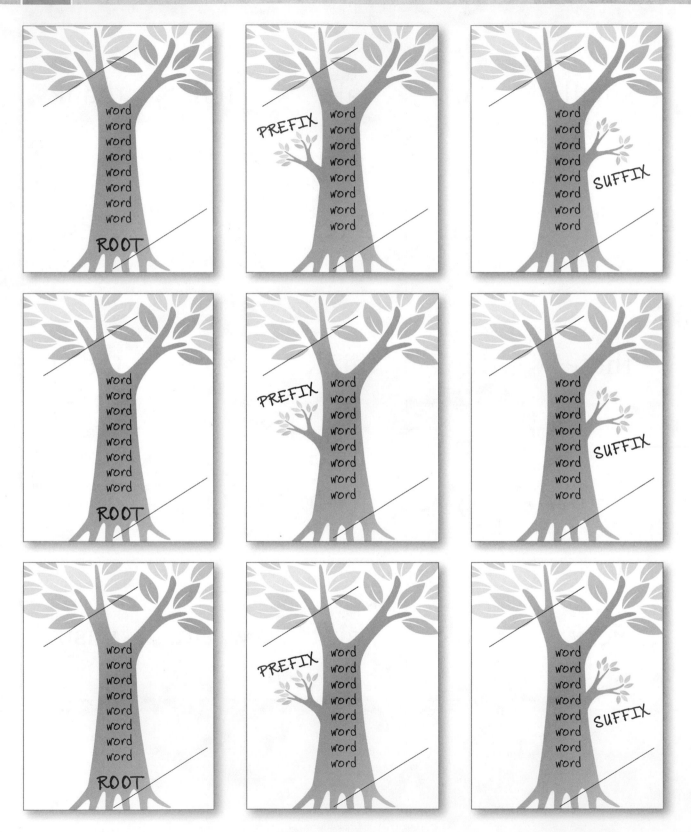

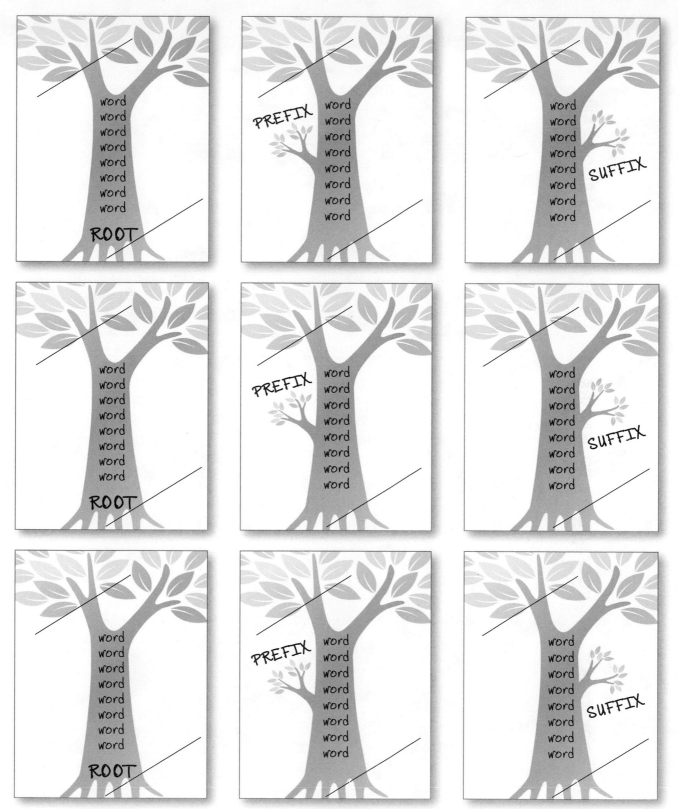

D.17 Vocabulary Bookmark Template (p. 159)

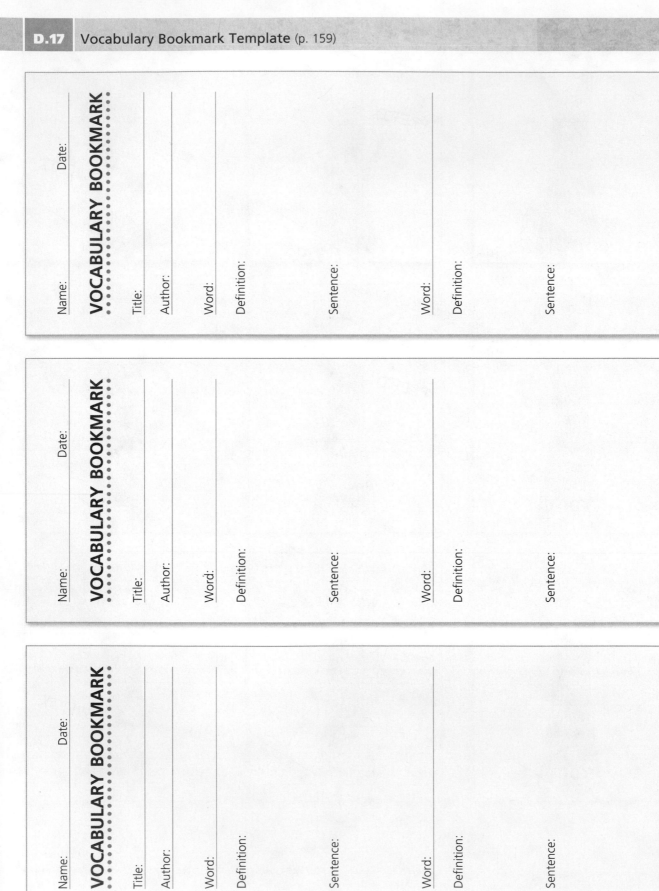

VOCABULARY BOOKMARK

Name: _____ Date: _____

Title: _____

Author: _____

Word: _____

Definition: _____

Sentence: _____

Word: _____

Definition: _____

Sentence: _____

VOCABULARY BOOKMARK

Name: _____ Date: _____

Title: _____

Author: _____

Word: _____

Definition: _____

Sentence: _____

Word: _____

Definition: _____

Sentence: _____

VOCABULARY BOOKMARK

Name: _____ Date: _____

Title: _____

Author: _____

Word: _____

Definition: _____

Sentence: _____

Word: _____

Definition: _____

Sentence: _____

D.18 **Cognate Sort** (p. 169)

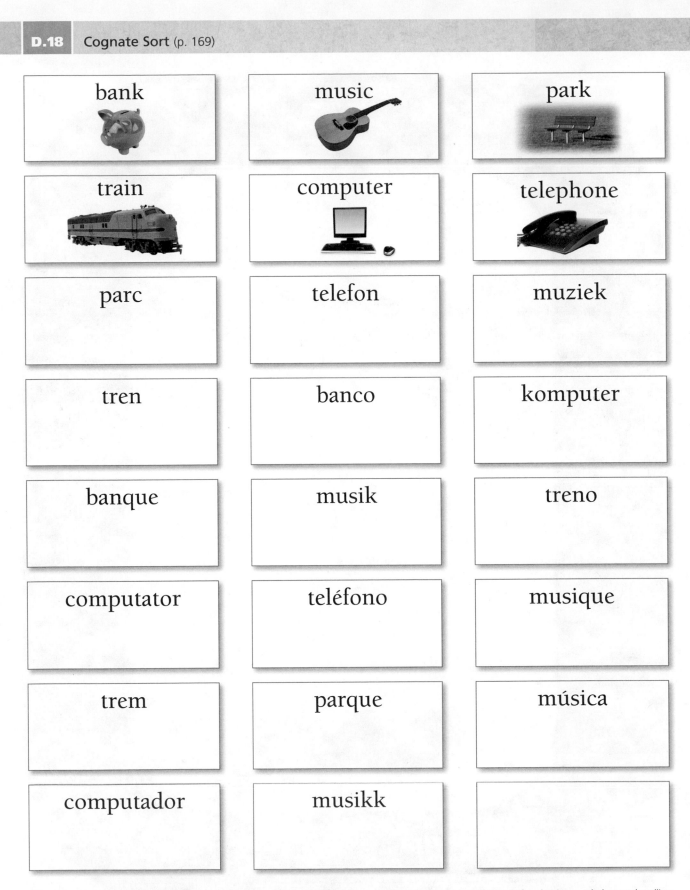

bank	music	park
train	computer	telephone
parc	telefon	muziek
tren	banco	komputer
banque	musik	treno
computator	teléfono	musique
trem	parque	música
computador	musikk	

Bear, D. R., Helman, L., Templeton, S., Invernizzi, M., Johnston, F. (2007). *Words their way with English learners: Word study for phonics, vocabulary, and spelling instruction* (4th ed.). Upper Saddle River, NJ: Pearson.

D.19   Multiple Meaning Racetrack Board (p. 169)

Flat tire—Back three spaces

Yellow flag—Back one space

Pass all other cars—Advance one space

START

Finish Line

Need gas—Back two spaces

D.20 **Questions to Consider When Previewing Features of Historical Fiction Picturebooks** (pp. 187, 208)

COVER

- What do you notice on the cover of the picture book?
- What are the most important features on the cover?
- What is the title of the book? What does this title mean to you?
- Has the book won any awards? Are they displayed on the cover?
- What colors dominate the cover design?
- What is in the foreground? What is in the background? What is the significance of the placement?
- Are there any visual images in the background to consider?
- What historical clues are provided for you on the cover?

CHARACTER REPRESENTATION

- Are any characters represented on the cover?
- Is the character looking at you? How does this affect you?
- If the character is looking at you, what might he/she be demanding from you?
- Is the character looking away or at someone or something else? How does this affect you?
- Is this the character a historical figure or fictional? How do you know?

SETTING

- What setting is portrayed on the cover and other illustrations?
- When do you think this story is taking place?
- What visual and textual clues are provided on the cover, jacket, and within the authors' note?
- How is setting important to the genre of historical fiction?
- How is color, texture, and motif used to represent the setting of the story?

ILLUSTRATION STYLE

- Are the illustrations realistic, folk art, surreal, or impressionistic?
- How might the style of illustration add to the mood or theme of the book?
- Is the style representative of the historical era? What does the style do for your understanding?

END PAGES

- What do you notice about the end pages?
- Do the end pages contain a visual narrative?
- Do the end pages contribute to the visual continuity of the picture book?
- Do the end pages represent the historical era in any way?

BOOK JACKET

- What information is contained in the front and back book jacket?
- How does the jacket information help to establish historical background information for the story?
- How does this information help you to understand the story?
- What clues are given about the historical facts and fictional aspects being presented?

TITLE PAGE

- What information is included on the title page?
- Was a visual image included on the title page?
- What historical significance might this image have?
- Is the image within the story? If so, what is the significance?
- If the image is not within the story, what symbolic meaning does it hold?

D.21   Text Mapping Form (p. 198)

TITLE: _____

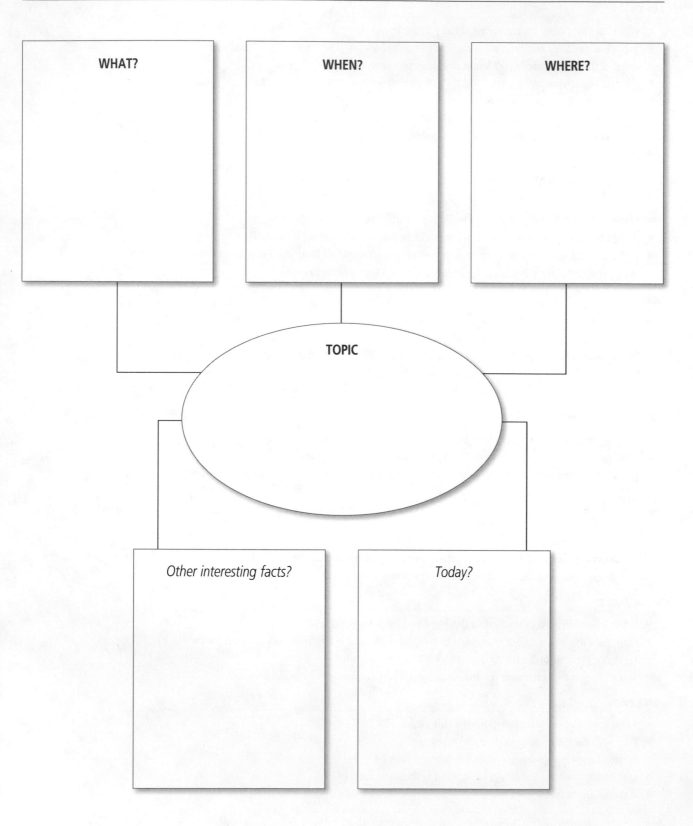

WHAT?

WHEN?

WHERE?

TOPIC

Other interesting facts?

Today?

D.22   Narrative E-Book Evaluation Form (p. 209)

Book Title _____   Copyright Date _____

Publisher _____   Grade Levels _____

Evaluator _____   Date _____

Scores: 3 = Superior   2 = Adequate   1 = Poor   0 = Not included

DESCRIPTOR	SCORE: 3	2	1	0
Written documentation with instructions.	○	○	○	○
Minimal download time.	○	○	○	○
Child-friendly installation.	○	○	○	○
Easy-to-follow instructions on screen.	○	○	○	○
Easy-to-comprehend verbal instructions.	○	○	○	○
Easy to quit at any point.	○	○	○	○
Verbal how-to-quit instructions.	○	○	○	○
Appropriate font size.	○	○	○	○
Appropriate amount of print on page.	○	○	○	○
Highlighted text correlates with computer voice.	○	○	○	○
Appropriate rate of computer's reading.	○	○	○	○
Appropriate fluency of computer's voice.	○	○	○	○
Easy-to-turn-off computer's voice.	○	○	○	○
User can click on words for pronunciation.	○	○	○	○
User can click on word for definition.	○	○	○	○
Music complements story.	○	○	○	○
Animations augment characters' actions.	○	○	○	○
Animations/music augment story's mood.	○	○	○	○
Hot spots are congruent with story line.	○	○	○	○
Appropriate open-ended, exploratory features.	○	○	○	○

Total Score _____ /60

Source: Adapted from Shamir, A., & Korat, O. (2006). How to select CD-ROM storybooks for young children. *The Reading Teacher, 59*(6), 532–543.

D.23 Textbook and Trade Book Evaluation Checklist (pp. 228, 229)

Rate the statements below, using the following rating system:

5 = Excellent

4 = Good

3 = Adequate

2 = Poor

1 = Unacceptable

NA = Not applicable

Further comments may be written in the space provided.

Book Title: _____

Publisher: _____

Copyright date: _____

FORMAT – EYE APPEAL

_____ A.　Photographs

_____ B.　Photographs that include different races and both sexes

_____ C.　Colorful charts and diagrams

_____ D.　White spaces on page

_____ E.　No two side-by-side pages of ALL text

_____ F.　Appropriate size of text for grade level

_____ G.　Appropriate text font for grade level

FORMAT – STRUCTURE

_____ A.　Detailed table of contents

_____ B.　Glossary

_____ C.　Index

_____ D.　Main headings in larger type

_____ E.　Subheadings in different font/size

_____ F.　New vocabulary in boldface or italics

_____ G.　Definitions of new vocabulary in margins

_____ H.　Appropriate captions under photographs and illustrations

_____ I.　Important facts repeated in illustrations and diagrams

_____ J.　Important facts highlighted in separate boxes

_____ K.　Pre-chapter questions—literal, inferential, and critical

_____ L.　Pre-chapter organizers

_____ M.　End-of-chapter questions—literal, inferential, and critical

TEXT

_____ A. Readability appropriate for intended grade

_____ B. New vocabulary explained adequately

_____ C. Appropriate assumption of reader's vocabulary

_____ D. Appropriate assumption of reader's background knowledge

_____ E. Information logically presented

_____ F. Important new information restated through visual aids

_____ G. Clear explanation of new concepts

_____ H. Text is not so oversimplified that relationships among ideas are not clear

_____ I. Appropriate in-depth presentation of information

_____ J. Information presented in a non-encyclopedic manner

_____ K. Sentence structure grammatically correct

_____ L. Appropriate use of conjunctions so relationships among ideas are clear

_____ M. Good pronoun usage

_____ N. Active voice

EXTENSION OF INFORMATION

_____ A. Lists of books where students can get more information

_____ B. Lists of websites where students can get more information

_____ C. Suggestions for outside projects

_____ D. In science texts, good description of appropriate step-by-step experiments

STRENGTHS OF BOOK:

_____

_____

_____

_____

WEAKNESSES OF BOOK:

_____

_____

_____

_____

Recommended for use by _____ (Child's name)

by _____ (Teacher's name)

D.24 Template for a Chart Comparing Multiple Sources for a Topic (p. 237)

TOPIC	FACTS	SOURCES	PAGE #/URL

D.25   Template for a K-T-W-L-E Chart (p. 247)

Name: _____   Date: _____

Topic: _____

K	T	W	L	E

D.26 Informational E-Text Evaluation Form (p. 255)

	YES	NO

AUTHOR CREDIBILITY

- Is the author/source or producer stated? ○ ○
- Is the authority or expertise of the individual or group that created this site stated? ○ ○
- Is there a way to contact the author or supply feedback? ○ ○

ACCURACY AND RELIABILITY

- Is the information accurate? ○ ○
- Is the information current? Is a date of publication provided? Is the resource updated frequently? ○ ○
- Is the information presented in an objective, balanced manner? ○ ○
- Does the text follow basic rules of grammar, spelling, and composition? ○ ○
- Are the sources of information stated? Can the information be verified? ○ ○
- Does the information support something already known or learned from another source? ○ ○

SCOPE

- Is the primary purpose of the site (e.g., advertising, information) clear? ○ ○
- Is the material covered adequately? ○ ○
- Is it interactive enough to make students think? ○ ○
- Is it clear whether the information is factual or opinion? ○ ○
- Does the site contain original information (as opposed to being simply links to other sites)? ○ ○

FORMAT AND NAVIGATION

- Can you find your way around and easily locate a particular page from any other page? ○ ○
- Does it take only a few links to get to something useful? ○ ○
- Is the arrangement of links uncluttered? ○ ○
- If there are links to other sites, do they work? ○ ○
- Do pages of the site load quickly? ○ ○
- Can nonmembers still have access to part of the site? ○ ○
- Do illustrations, video, or audio add value to the site? ○ ○
- Do the multimedia, graphics, and art serve a function? ○ ○
- Is the quality of the multimedia or graphic images good? Do these images enhance the content? ○ ○
- Are the individual web pages concise (e.g., not excessive scrolling)? ○ ○
- Is the site easily browsable or searchable? ○ ○

Source: Adapted from Cecil, N. L., Gipe, J. P., & Merrill, M. (2014). *Literacy in Grades 4–8: Best Practices for a Comprehensive Program* (3rd ed.). Scottsdale, AZ: Holcomb Hathaway.

D.27   Record, Check, Chart (p. 274)

Name: _____   Grade: _____

STORY	1ST READING ERRORS	2ND READING ERRORS	3RD READING ERRORS	TEACHER COMMENTS
1.				
2.				
3.				
4.				
5.				
6.				
7.				
8.				
9.				
10.				

TEACHER'S GENERAL COMMENTS:

D.28 **Fluency Log** (p. 275)

Books I Can Read

BY _____

TITLE	AUTHOR	PARENTS' COMMENTS	DATE	NUMBER OF TIMES READ
1.				
2.				
3.				
4.				
5.				
6.				
7.				

THE STORY OF THE THREE CATS WHO LOST THEIR HATS

Narrator 1: You have all heard the story of the three kittens who lost their mittens, well . . .

Narrator 2: Those sweet little kittens grew up to be quite the adventuresome cats.

Narrator 1: This is the story of those three cats who lost their hats.

Flat Cat, Fat Cat, Pat Cat: Oh Mother, dear, see here! See here! Our hats we have lost!

Mother: Oh no, not again! How did this happen?

Flat Cat: Well, you see, I was touring down Route 66 in my BMW convertible and all was going well until I turned the curve and the Oklahoma wind came swooping down the plain and ripped my hat right off my head!

Narrator 1: And that's the truth! I saw it with my own two eyes!

Mother: *(glaring at Fat Cat)* And I suppose you were riding with him.

Fat Cat: Oh no, not at all!

Mother: Well, then, how did you lose your hat?

Fat Cat: Well, I too was cruising Route 66 on my Harley.

Mother: Your what?

Fat Cat: My Harley.

Mother: Who is Harley?

Narrator 2: *(addressing audience)* You must understand that Mother does not believe any cat should get from point A to point B any way other than prowling on all four paws.

Fat Cat: Like I was saying, I was cruising down Route 6 on my Harley, you know Mom, a motorcycle, and I too turned the curve and the Oklahoma wind came rushing down the plain and ripped my hat off my head!

Narrator 1: And that is the truth! I saw it happen with my own two eyes! That wind just swooped down and lifted Fat Cat's hat right off his head!

Mother: Oh dear, oh dear! What can we do?

Narrator 2: The third cat, Pat Cat, is standing with a smirk on her face.

Mother: *(looking at Pat Cat)* Now tell me, how did you lose your hat? Which one of your brothers were you riding with?

Pat Cat: Neither! I was flying my biplane over Route 66 when I spotted two hats! I recognized them as Flat Cat's and Fat Cat's hats! I slowed my engine, swooped down low, and snatched hat 1 and hat 2. Here they are!

Fat Cat and Flat Cat: Our hats we have found!

Mother: Pat Cat, but you still did not tell me how you lost your hat?

Narrator 1: Pat Cat puts her paw to her head.

Pat Cat: Oh No! I must have been so excited about seeing and catching their hats, I did not realize that mine must have blown off!

Narrator 1: Just then . . .

Narrator 2: Pat Cat's hat came fluttering down right on top of Pat Catís head!

Narrator 1: And Flat Cat, Fat Cat and Pat Cat

Narrator 2: And don't forget Mother

Narrator 1 and Narrator 2: Were happy once again!

D.30 Graphic Organizer for an Argument (pp. 246, 296)

Position of Reader: Thesis:			Counter Position: Thesis:
Reason #1	**Reason #2**	**Reason #3**	
Supporting Details	**Supporting Details**	**Supporting Details**	
Reader's Conclusion:			
Sources:			

D.31   Graphic Organizer for Prewriting an Argumentative Essay (p. 296)

After reading the two sources provided* and at least three other sources on the topic, write an opinion piece, state your point of view, and state the reasons (logically presented) for and the evidence that supports your point of view. Use the following table to take and organize notes. Remember: All direct quotes must be in quotation marks and quoted accurately. Also remember to watch sources in the address bar as you click on different links.

INFORMATION/FACTS (STATED IN YOUR OWN WORDS)	DIRECT EVIDENCE (QUOTE)	PAGE NUMBER	SOURCE (PUT NUMBER OF SOURCES THAT YOU LIST ON THE BOTTOM OF THE TABLE)	POSSIBLE ORDER FOR USING INFORMATION IN WRITING	GIVE CREDENTIALS OF THE AUTHOR OR ORGANIZATION

*Teacher provides two sources for this assignment.

D.32   Matrix Aligning Elements of Writing Instruction and Assessment (p. 307)

Matrix Connecting Writing Process (CCSS W.5), 6 + 1 Writing Trait (CCSS W.3), Narrative Text (CCSS W.3), and Multiliteracies Presentation (CCSS W.2 & W.6)

WRITING PROCESS (CCSS W.5)	6 + 1 TRAIT WRITING (CCSS W.3)	NARRATIVE (CCSS W. 1-2.3)	INFORMATIONAL MULTI-LITERACIES PRESENTATION (CCSS W.2 & 6)
Brainstorming	Content/Idea	Particular Theme? Sequel to story? New story for familiar character? New version of fairy tale? New fable based on established moral? Comic strip? Humorous? Serious? Script for skit or readers theater? All-bubble story (such as Mo Willems)?	Ask compelling questions. Ask questions based on writer's curiosity. Question has social importance. Content of question aligns with the standard course of study.

Drafting	Organization	Establishing:
		    setting
		    protagonist
		    antagonist
		    plot (flashback, roadblocks, climax)
		    point-of-view
		    style
		    theme
			Gather and analyze information.
			 Teach about .org and .com.
			 Creatively synthesize.
			 Create storyboard.
			 Select images/pictures.
			 Learn copyright laws.
			 Check credentials of site and author.

Revising	Voice	Supports theme? Critical literacy? (leads to action) Humorous?	Rearrange storyboard. Choose music to fit content. Uniquely arrange images/pictures.
	Word Choice	Vivid figurative speech Vivid verbs, adjectives	Vivid language in script. Author's stance is clearly articulated. Appropriate images for audience.
	Sentence Fluency	Simple sentence (S), compound sentence (CD), complex sentence (CX), compound–complex sentence (CD–CX)	Natural flow from one image to the next (iMovie, Movie Maker, PowerPoint, Key Note).
Editing	Conventions	Punctuation, capitalization, spelling, paragraphing,	Peer, self, and expert evaluation on the following: **Intellectual quality:** (a) clear purpose, (b) synthesis and construction of ideas, (c) curriculum connections, (d) clear beginning and ending, (e) and sources cited appropriately. **Aesthetic and technical quality:** (a) image quality, (b) editing/transitions, (c) audio (music and dialogue), and (d) creativity/originality.
Publishing	Presentation	How does student share it? Orally? Written? Online?	Publish on school website or share with world at edublogs.org; or www.watchknow.org/default.aspx.

Sources: DeVries, B. (2015). *Literacy Assessment & Intervention for Classroom Teachers.* Scottsdale, AZ: Holcomb Hathaway. / Northwest Regional Education Laboratory (1998/1999). 6 + 1 Trait Writing Assessment and Instruction. Available: http://educationnorthwest.org. / Spire, Hervey, Morris, Stelpflug (2012). Energizing inquiry through video projects. *Journal of Adolescent & Adult Literacy, 55*(6), 483–494.

END

MIDDLE

BEGINNING

D.34 Lesson Plan for Tutors (p. 357)

Tutor: _____ Date: _____

Tutee: _____ Grade: _____

Easy Reading Objective:

Rereading of Last Session's Book Objective:

Word Study Objective:

Writing Objective:

Reading of Instructional Materials Objective:

LESSON PLAN	PLANNED ACTIVITY	TIME	REFLECTION

D.35 **Log Sheet of Strategies** (p. 363)

STRATEGIES TAUGHT TO _____ BY _____

DURING EASY READ

DURING WRITING

DURING WORD STUDY

DURING NEW BOOK

BOOKS READ DURING TUTORING

Tutor: _____   Tutee: _____

BOOKS READ BY TUTOR	DATE	BOOKS READ BY TUTEE	DATE

D.37   Postcard for Children Reading Books with
Oral Reading and Comprehension Scaffolding (p. 378)

Student: _____   Date: _____

1. What's the title of your book? _____

2. Did you finish reading this book?   ○ Yes   ○ No, I stopped on page _____ .

3. How many times did you read this book?   ○ Didn't finish   ○ 1 time   ○ 2 times   ○ 3 times.

4. What did you do to better understand this book? (check all that apply)

    ○ I reread parts of this book.

    ○ I made predictions about this book.

    ○ I asked questions about this book.

    ○ I made connections (text-to-text, text-to-self).

    ○ I summarized parts of the book.

5. After you read the book, tell someone in your family what the book was about. Pick a part of the book to read aloud two times. Ask him or her how you improved the second time you read the section and ask for his or her signature. (check all that apply)

    ○ Did I read more smoothly?

    ○ Did I know more words?

    ○ Did I read with more expression?

6. Family member's signature: _____

    Optional comment about this student's reading:

Source: T.G. White & J.S. Kim (2008). Teacher and parent scaffolding of voluntary summer reading. *The Reading Teacher 62*(2), p. 120. Reprinted with permission of the INTERNATIONAL READING ASSOCIATION via Copyright Clearance Center.

references

Acha, J. (2009). The effectiveness of multimedia programs in children's verbal learning. *British Journal of Educational Technology, 40*(1), 23–31.

Ada, A. F. (1998). *Yours truly, Goldilocks.* New York: Atheneum Books.

Adams, M. J. (1990). *Beginning to read: Thinking and learning about print.* Cambridge, MA: MIT Press.

Adams, M., Foorman, B., Lundberg, I., & Beeler, T. (2013). Phonemic activities for the preschool or elementary classroom. Retrieved from http://www.readingrockets.org/article.

Adler, D. (1990). *A picture book of Benjamin Franklin.* New York: A Trumpet Club Special Edition.

Afflerbach, P., Cho, B-Y, Kim, J-Y, Crassas, M. E., & Doyle, B. (2013). Reading: What else matters besides strategies and skills? *The Reading Teacher, 66*(60), 440–448.

Afflerbach, P., & VanSledright, B. (2001). Hath! Doth! What? Middle graders reading innovative history text. *Journal of Adolescent & Adult Literacy, 44*(8), 696–708.

Ahlberg, J. (1986). *The jolly postman. New York*: Scholastic.

Alderman, G., & Green, S. (2011). Fostering lifelong spellers through meaningful experiences. *The Reading Teacher, 64*(8), 599–605.

Allington, R. (1983). Fluency: The neglected goal. *The Reading Teacher, 36,* 556–561.

Allington, R. (2002). What I've learned about effective reading instruction: From a decade of studying exemplary elementary classroom teachers. *Phi Delta Kappan, 83*(10), 740–747.

Allington, R. (2006). *What really matters for struggling readers: Designing research-based programs* (2nd ed.). Boston: Pearson/Allyn & Bacon.

Allington, R. (2011). *What really matters for struggling readers: Designing research-based programs* (3rd ed.). Boston: Allyn & Bacon.

Allington, R. (2013). What really matters when working with struggling readers. *The Reading Teacher, 66*(7), 520–530.

Allington, R., Johnston, P., & Day, J. (2002). Exemplary fourth-grade teachers. *Language Arts, 79*(6), 462–466.

Allyn, P. (2014). *The power to persuade: Opinion and argument: A staircase to standards, success for English language arts.* Boston: Pearson.

Alyousef, H. S. (2005). Teaching reading comprehension to ESL/EFL learners. *The Reading Matrix, 5*(2), 142–153.

Ambruster, B. (1996). Considerate text. In D. Lapp, J. Flood, & N. Farnan (Eds.), *Content area reading and learning: Instructional strategies* (2nd ed.), pp. 47–58. Boston: Allyn & Bacon.

Ames, C. (1992). Classrooms: Goals, structures and students motivation. *Journal of Educational Psychology, 84*(3), 261–271.

Anders, P., & Lloyd, C. (1996). The significance of prior knowledge in the learning of new content-specific ideas. In D. Lapp, J. Flood, & N. Farnan (Eds.), *Content area reading and learning: Instructional strategies* (2nd ed.), pp. 323–338. Boston: Allyn & Bacon.

Anderson, K. (2012, Sept. 24). Wikipedia's writing—tests show it's too sophisticated for its audience. The Scholarly Kitchen. Retrieved from http://scholarlykitchen.sspnet.org/2012/09/24/wikipedias-writing-tests-show-its-too-sophisticated-for-its-audience/

Anderson, L. H. (2008). *Chains.* New York: Simon & Schuster.

Anderson, N., & Briggs, C. (2011). Reciprocity between reading and writing strategic processing as common ground. *The Reading Teacher, 64*(7), 546–549.

Anderson, R. (2013). Role of the reader's schema in comprehension, learning, and memory. In D. Alvermann, N. Unrau, & R. Ruddell (Eds.), *Theoretical models and processes of reading* (pp. 476–488). Newark, DE: International Reading Association.

Anthony, H., & Raphael, T. (1996). Using questioning strategies to promote students' active comprehension of content area material. In D. Lapp, J. Flood, & N. Farnan (Eds.), *Content area reading and learning: Instructional strategies* (2nd ed.), pp. 307–322. Boston: Allyn & Bacon.

Applegate, A. J., & Applegate, M. D. (2010). A study of thoughtful literacy and the motivation to read. *The Reading Teacher, 64*(4), 226–234.

Applegate, K. (2011). *The one and only Ivan.* New York: HarperCollins.

Applegate, M. D., Quinn, K. B., Applegate, A. J. (2008). *The critical reading inventory: Assessing student's reading and thinking* (2nd ed.). Upper Saddle River, NJ: Pearson.

Armstrong, T. (2000). *Multiple intelligences in the classroom* (2nd ed.). Alexandria, VA: Association for Supervision and Curriculum Development.

Armstrong, T. (2004). Making the words roar. *Educational Leadership, 61*(6), 78–81.

Ashby, J., Dix, H., Bontrager, M., Dey, R., & Archer, A. (2013). Phonemic awareness contributes to text reading fluency: Evidence from eye movements. *School Psychology Review, 42*(2), 157–170.

Asher, J. (1982). *Learning another language through actions.* Los Gatos, CA: Sky Oaks Productions.

Ashton-Warner, S. (1963). *Teacher.* New York: Simon & Schuster.

Atwell, N. (1987). *In the middle.* Portsmouth, NH: Heinemann.

August, D., Carlo, M., Dressler, C., & Snow, C. (2005). The critical role of vocabulary development for English language learners. *Learning Disabilities Research and Practice, 20*(1), 50–57.

August, D., & Shanahan, T. (2006). *Developing literacy in second-language learners.* Report of the National Panel on Language minority children and youth. Mahwah, NJ: Erlbaum.

Avi. (1999). *Midnight magic.* New York: Scholastic.

Avi. (2001). *Ereth's birthday.* New York: HarperTrophy.

Avi. (2004). *The good dog.* New York: Aladdin.

Avi. (2005) *Poppy.* New York: Simon & Schuster.

Avi. (2005). *Poppy and Rye.* New York: HarperTrophy.

Avi. (2006). *Poppy's return.* New York: HarperTrophy.

Avi (2012). *City of Orphans* (Rev. ed.). New York: Scholastic.

Back, K. (2009). The characteristics of effective teachers. *Teaching and Learning Online.* Retrieved from www.edu-book.com/the-characteristics-of-effective-teachers/8690.

Bagert, B. (1997). *The gooch machine: Poems for children to perform.* Honesdale, PA: Boyds Mills Press.

Bagert, B. (1999). *Rainbows, head lice and pea-green tile.* Gainesville, FL: Maupin House.

Bagert, B. (2006). *Hormone jungle: Coming of age.* Gainesville, FL: Maupin House.

Bailey-Beard, D. (1995). *The pumpkin man from Piney Creek.* New York: Simon & Schuster.

Bailey-Beard, D. (1998). *The flimflam man.* New York: Farrar, Straus & Giroux.

Baines, L., & Kunkel, A. (2011). Sparking students enthusiasm for writing in the secondary classroom—Yes, it's possible. *Journal of Adolescent and Adult Literacy, 55*(3), 244–247.

Banyai, I. (1995). *Zoom.* New York: Puffin.

Barksdale, M. A., Watson, C., & Park, E. S. (2007). Pen pal letter exchanges: Taking first steps toward developing cultural understandings. *The Reading Teacher, 61*(1), 58–68.

Barrett, J., & Barrett, R. (1978). *Cloudy with a chance of meatballs.* New York: Atheneum Books.

Barry, A. (1998). The evolution of reading tests and other forms of educational assessment. *Clearing House, 71*(4), 231–236.

Baumann, J. F., Kame'enui, E. J., & Ash, G. E. (2003). Research on vocabulary instruction: Voltaire redux. In J. Flood, D. Lapp, J. R. Squire, & J. M. Jensen (Eds.), *Handbook on teaching the English language arts* (2nd ed.), pp. 752–785. Mahwah, NJ: Erlbaum.

Baumann, J. F., Ware, D., & Carr-Edwards, E. (2007). "Bumping into spicy, tasty words that catch your tongue": A formative experiment on vocabulary instruction. *The Reading Teacher, 61*(2), 108–122.

Beall, P. C., & Nipp, S. H. (2005). *Wee sing children's songs and fingerplay with CD.* New York: Price Stern Sloan.

Bear, D., Flanigan, K., Hayes, L., Invernizzi, M., Johnston, F., & Templeton, S. (2010). *Words their way with struggling readers: Word study for reading, vocabulary, and spelling instruction. Grades 4–12.* New York: Pearson.

Bear, D., Helman, L., Templeton, S., Invernizzi, M., & Johnston, F. (2007). *Words their way with English learners: Word study for phonics, vocabulary, and spelling instruction* (4th ed.). Upper Saddle River, NJ: Pearson.

Bear, D., Invernizzi, M., Templeton, S., & Johnston, F. (2008). *Words their way: Word study for phonics, vocabulary, and spelling instruction.* Upper Saddle River, NJ: Pearson/Prentice Hall.

Bear, D., Invernizzi, M., Templeton, S., & Johnston, F. (2011). *Words their way: Word study for phonics, vocabulary, and spelling instruction* (5th ed.). Upper Saddle River, NJ: Prentice Hall.

Bear, D., & Templeton, S. (1998). Exploration in developmental spelling: Foundations for learning and teaching phonics, spelling and vocabulary. *The Reading Teacher, 52*(3), 222–242.

Beauchat, K. A., Blamey, K., & Walpole, S. (2009). Building preschool children's language and literacy one storybook at a time. *The Reading Teacher, 63*(1), 26–39.

Beck, A. (2005). A place for critical literacy. *Journal of Adolescent and Adult Literacy, 48*(5), 392–400.

Beck, I. L., & McKeown, M. (2001). Text talk: Capturing the benefits of read-aloud experiences for younger children. *The Reading Teacher, 55*(1), 10–21.

Beck, I. L., McKeown, M. G., & Kucan, L. (2002). *Bringing words to life: Robust vocabulary instruction.* New York: Guilford.

Beck, I., McKeown, M., & Kucan, K. (2013). *Bringing words to life: Robust vocabulary instruction* (2nd ed.). New York: Guilford.

Beck, L. (2006). *A children's treasury of lullabies.* New York: Sterling.

Beckman-Anthony, A. (2008). Output strategies for English-language learners: Theory to practice. *The Reading Teacher, 61*(6), 472–482.

Behrman, E. H. (2006). Teaching about language, power and text: A review of classroom practices that support critical literacy. *Journal of Adolescent and Adult Literacy, 49*(6), 490–498.

Bemelmans, L. (1986). *Madeline and the gypsies.* New York: Viking.

Berninger, V. & Wolf, B. (2009). *Teaching students with dyslexia and dysgraphia: Lessons from teaching and science.* Baltimore: Brooks.

Bennett, J. (Ed.). (1987). *Noisy poems.* Oxford, New York: Oxford University Press.

Bennett-Hopkins, L. (2009). *City I love.* Illus. by M. Hall. New York: Abrams Books for Young Readers.

Berger, M., & Berger, G. (2003). *Sharks*. New York: Scholastic.

Biancarosa, G., & Snow, C. E. (2004). Reading next—A vision for action and research in middle and high school literacy. A report to Carnegie Corporation of New York. Washington, D.C.: Alliance for Excellence in Education.

Bintz, W. (2010a). Fibbin with poems across the curriculum. *The Reading Teacher, 63*(6), 509–513.

Bintz, W. (2010b). Singing across the curriculum. *The Reading Teacher, 63*(8), 683–686.

Bintz, W. (2011). Writing parodies across the curriculum. *The Reading Teacher, 64*(7), 511–514.

Blachowicz, C. I., Fisher, P., & Watts-Taffe, S. (2011). Vocabulary questions from the classroom. *Reading Research Quarterly, 47*(4), 524–539.

Blachowicz, C., & Fisher, P. (2005a). *Teaching vocabulary in all classrooms* (3rd ed.). Upper Saddle River, NJ: Merrill.

Blachowicz, C., & Fisher, P. (2005b). Vocabulary lessons. *Educational Leadership, 61*(6), 66–69.

Black, L. (2006). *A children's treasury of songs*. New York: Sterling.

Blevins, W. (2001). *Teaching phonics and word study in the intermediate grades*. New York: Scholastic.

Blevins, W. (2006). *Phonics from A to Z: A practical guide* (2nd ed.). New York: Scholastic.

Bloodgood, J. W., & Pacifici, L. C. (2004). Bringing word study in intermediate classrooms. *The Reading Teacher, 58*(3), 250–263.

Bluestein, A. (2010). Unlocking text features for determining importance in expository text: A strategy for struggling readers. *The Reading Teacher, 63*(7), 597–600.

Blum, I., Koskinen, P., Bhartiya, P., & Hluboky, S. (2010). Thinking and talking about books: Using prompts to stimulate discussion. *The Reading Teacher, 62*(6), 495–499.

Boers, D. (2002). What teachers need of parents. *Education Digest, 67*(8), 37–41.

Borgia, L., & Owles, C. (2011, Fall). Using the reading and writing connection to aid comprehension. *Illinois Reading Council Journal*. Retrieved from http://www.illinois-readingcouncil.org/.

Bos, C. S., & Vaughn, S. (2011). *Strategies for teaching students with learning and behavior problems* (8th ed.). Boston: Allyn & Bacon.

Bottner, B. (1996). *Nana Hannah's piano*. Boston: Houghton Mifflin.

Bottomley, D., Henk, W., & Melnick, S. (1998). Assessing children's views about themselves as writers using the Writer Self-Perception Scale. *The Reading Teacher, 51*(4), 286–296.

Bouchereau-Bauer, E., & Manyak, P. (2008). Creating language-rich instruction for English-language learners. *The Reading Teacher, 62*(2), 176–178.

Brabham, E., Buskist, C., Henderson, S. C., Paleologos, T., & Bough, N. (2012). Flooding vocabulary gaps to accelerate word learning. *The Reading Teacher, 65*(8), 523–533.

Branley, F. (1997). *Down comes the rain* (Illustrated ed.). New York: HarperTrophy.

Branley, F. (1999). *Flash, crash, rumble and roll* (Reprint ed.). New York: HarperTrophy.

Brett, J. (1989). *The mitten*. New York: G. P. Putnam's Sons.

Brett, J. (1991). *Berlioz the bear*. New York: G. P. Putnam's Sons.

Brett, J. (1995). *Armadillo rodeo*. New York: G. P. Putnam's Sons.

Brett, J. (2002). *Daisy comes home*. New York: Putnam Juvenile.

Brewer, P. (2003). *You must be joking! Lots of cool jokes, plus 17 1/2 tips for remembering, telling, and making up your own jokes*. Battle Creek, MI: Cricket.

Bromley, K., Vandenberg, A., & White, J. (2007). What can we learn from the word writing CAFÉ? *The Reading Teacher, 61*(4), 284–295.

Brown, K. (1999/2000). What kind of text—For whom and when? Textual scaffolding for beginning readers. *The Reading Teacher, 53*(4), 292–308.

Brown, S., & Kappes, L. (2012). Implementing the CCSS: A primer on "close reading of text." *Aspen Institute Education and Society Program*. Retrieved from www.aspeninstitute.org/education.

Broyles, N. (2012/2013). Closing in on close reading. *Educational Leadership, 70*(4), 36–41.

Brozo, W. G. (2010). Response to intervention or responsive instruction? Challenges and possibilities of response to intervention for adolescents. *Journal of Adolescent and Adult Literacy, 53*(4), 277–281.

Brozo, W. G., & Flynt, S. E. (2008). Motivating students to read in the content classroom: Six evidence-based principles. *The Reading Teacher, 62*(2), 172–174.

Bruner, J. (1960). *The process of education*. Cambridge, MA: Harvard University Press.

Buchanan, J. (1997). *Gratefully yours*. New York: Puffin Books.

Buehner, C. (2002). *Snowmen at night*. Illus. M. Buehner. New York: Dial.

Bulion, L. (2006). *Hey, there, stick bug!* Illus. by L. Evans. Watertown, MA: Charlesbridge.

Bunting, E. (1990). *In the haunted house*. New York: Trumpet Club Special Edition.

Buros Institute. (2002). *Reading*. Retrieved from www.unl.edu/buros/index13.html

Cabell, S., Tortorelli, L., & Gerde, H. (2013). How do I write? *The Reading Teacher, 66*(8), 650–659.

Cahill, M. A., & Gregory, A. (2011). Putting the fun back into fluency instruction. *The Reading Teacher, 65*(2), 127–131.

Calkins, L. M. (1994). *The art of teaching writing* (Rev. ed.). Portsmouth, NH: Heinemann.

Calkins, L., Montgomery, K., Santman, D., & Falk, B. (1998). *A teacher's guide to standardized reading tests*. Portsmouth, NH: Heinemann.

Calo, K., Woodlard-Ferguson, T., & Koitz, E. (2013). Fluency idol: Using pop culture to engage students and boost fluency skills. *The Reading Teacher, 66*(6), 432–508.

Camilli, G., & Wolfe, P. (2004). Research on reading: A cautionary tale. *Educational Leadership, 61*(6), 26–29.

Campbell-Ernst, L. (1995). *Little Red Riding Hood: A newfangled prairie tale*. Illus. by L. Campbell-Ernst. New York: Aladdin Paperbacks.

Canizares, S., & Reid, M. (1998). *Who lives in the rainforest?* New York: Scholastic.

Carbo, M. (1978). Teaching reading with talking books. *The Reading Teacher, 32*, 267–273.

Carbo, M. (1996a). Recorded books raise reading skills. *Education Digest, 61*(9), 59.

Carbo, M. (1996b). Selecting the "right" reading method. *Teaching PreK–8, 27*(1), 84.

Carbo, M. (1996c). Whole language or phonics? Use both! *Education Digest, 61*(6), 60–63.

Carbo, M. (1997). Four key questions to evaluate reading programs. *Education Digest, 62*(5), 64–68.

Carbo, M. (1998). *Reading styles: High rapid reading gains with diverse learners.* Syosset, NY: National Reading Styles Institute.

Carbo, M. (2007). *Becoming a great teacher of reading: Achieving high rapid reading gains with powerful, differentiated strategies.* New York: Corwin Press.

Carlo, M., August, D., McLaughlin, B., Snow, C., Dressler, C., Lippman, D., Lively, T., & White, C. (2004). Closing the gap: Addressing the vocabulary needs of English language learners in bilingual and mainstream classrooms. *Reading Research Quarterly, 39*(2), 188–215.

Carlstrom, N. (1998). *Guess Who's Coming, Jesse Bear.* New York: Aladdin.

Carney, E. (2010). *National Geographic Readers: Bats.* Washington, DC: National Geographic Society.

Carrell, P. (2010). Three components of background knowledge in reading comprehension. *Learning Language, 33*(2), 183–203.

Cartwright, K., Savage, D., Morgan, K., & Nichols, B. (2009). Literacy partners programs: In-school tutoring in a school-university partnership. In J. C. Richards & C. A. Lassonde (Eds.), *Literacy tutoring that works,* pp. 56–89. Newark, DE: IRA.

Cauley, L. B. (1992). *Clap your hands.* New York: Scholastic.

Cavanaugh, T. (2007, Spring). Technology and phonological awareness. *Florida Reading Quarterly, 43*(3). Retrieved from http://www.flreads.org/Publications/quarterly/samples/phonological.

Cecil, N. L. (2015). *Striking a balance: A comprehensive program for early literacy* (5th ed.). Scottsdale, AZ: Holcomb Hathaway.

Cecil, N., Gipe, J., & Merrill, M. (2014). *Literacy in grades 4–8: Best practices* (3rd ed.). Scottsdale, AZ: Holcomb Hathaway.

Celenza, A. H. (2000). *The farewell symphony.* Watertown, WA: Charlesbridge Publishing.

Center for Public Education (2013). How many English learners are in our schools? Retrieved from www.centerforpubliceducation.org

Center for Public Education (2010). What is the racial and ethnic makeup of our school(s)? Retrieved from www.centerforpubliceducation.org

Centers for Disease Control and Prevention (2013). *Parent engagement: Strategies for involving parents in school health.* Atlanta, GA: U.S. Department of Health and Human Services.

Cerullo, M. (1999). *Dolphins: What they can teach us.* New York: Scholastic.

Cervetti, G., Pardales, M. J., & Damico, J. S. (2001). A tale of differences: Comparing the traditions, perspectives, and educational goals of critical reading and critical literacy. *Reading Online, 4*(9). Retrieved from www.readingonline.org/articles/cervetti/

Chall, J. S. (1983). *Learning to read: The great debate* (Rev. ed.). New York: McGraw-Hill.

Chall, J. S., & Jacobs, V. A. (2003). Poor children's fourth-grade slump. *American Educator, 27*(1), 14–15, 44.

Chambers, B., Abrami, P., McWhaw, K., & Therrien, M. (2001). Developing a computer-assisted tutoring program to help children at risk learn to read. *Educational Research and Evaluation, 7*(2–3), 223–239.

Chandler-Olcott, K. (2009). Tale of two tasks: Editing in the era of digital literacies. *Journal of Adolescent & Adult Literacy, 53*(1), 71–74.

Childress, K. (2011). *What does research say about the benefits of reading aloud to children?* Retrieved from http://www.appstate.edu/~koppenhaverd/rcoe/s11/5710/question1/kathleenchildress.pdf.

Ciardiello, A. (1998). Did you ask a good question today? Alternative cognitive and metacognitive strategies. *Journal of Adolescent & Adult Literacy, 42*(3), 210–220.

Ciardiello, A. V. (2004). Democracy's young heroes: An instructional model of critical literacy practices. *The Reading Teacher, 58*(2), 138–147.

Ciardiello, A. V. (2010). "Talking Walls": Presenting a case for social justice poetry in literacy education. *The Reading Teacher, 63*(6), 464–473.

Clarke, L., & Whitney, E. (2009). Walking in their shoes: Using multiple-perspective texts as a bridge to critical literacy. *The Reading Teacher, 62*(6), 530–535.

Clay, M. (1985). *The early detection of reading difficulties* (3rd ed.). Portsmouth, NH: Heinemann.

Clay, M. (1991). *Becoming literate: The construction of inner control.* Portsmouth, NH: Heinemann.

Clay, M. (1993a). *Sand.* Portsmouth, NH: Heinemann.

Clay, M. (1993b). *Stones.* Portsmouth, NH: Heinemann.

Clay, M. (1993c). *Reading Recovery: A guidebook for teachers in training.* Portsmouth, NH: Heinemann.

Clay, M. (2000a). *Follow me, moon.* Portsmouth, NH: Heinemann.

Clay, M. (2000b). *No shoes.* Portsmouth, NH: Heinemann.

Clay, M. (2000c). *Running records for classroom teachers.* Portsmouth, NH: Heinemann.

Clay, M. (2006). *Marie Clay's principles and concepts of early writing.* Retrieved from www.learning towrite.ecsd.net/principles%20and %20concepts.htm

Coffey, H. (2010). Critical literacy. LEARN NC: University of North Carolina at Chapel Hill School of Education. Retrieved from www.learnc.org/lp/pages/4437

Cohen, C. L. (2000). *How many fish?* Illus. S. D. Schindler. New York: HarperCollins.

Coiro, J. (2009). Rethinking reading assessment in a digital age: How is reading comprehension different and where do we turn now. *Educational Leadership, 66*, 59–63.

Coiro, J., & Moore, D. (2012). New literacies and adolescent learners: An interview with Julie Coiro. *Journal of Adolescent and Adult Literacy, 55*(6), 551–553.

Cole, J., & Calmenson, S. (Eds.). (1990). *Ready . . . set . . . read!* New York: Doubleday.

Common Core State Standards Initiative, Mission Statement. (n.d.). Available: http://www.corestandards.org/.

Cooper, J. D. (2006). *Literacy: Helping children construct meaning* (6th ed.). Boston: Houghton Mifflin.

Cooper, J. D., Kiger, N., Robinson, M., & Slansky, J. (2012). *Literacy: Helping students construct meaning.* Belmont, CA: Wadsworth, Cengage Learning.

Cooter, R. B., & Perkins, J. H. (2011). Much done much yet to do. *The Reading Teacher, 64*(8), 563.

Correia, M. P. (November, 2011). Fiction vs. informational texts: Which will kindergartners choose? *Young Children, 66*(6), 110–114. Retrieved from www.naeyc.org/files.

Coulman, V. (2001). *When pigs fly.* Montreal: Lobster Press.

Couric, K. (2000). *The brand new kid.* New York: Doubleday.

Cudd, E. (1990). The paragraph frame: A bridge from narrative to expository text. In N. L. Cecil (Ed.), *Literacy in the 90s: Readings in the language arts.* Dubuque, IA: Kendall/Hunt.

Cummins, J. (1979). Cognitive/academic language proficiency, linguistic interdependence, the optimum age question, and some other matters. *Working Papers on Bilingualism, 19,* 121–129.

Cummins, J. (1981). Age on arrival and immigrant second language learning in Canada: A reassessment. *Applied Linguistics, 2,* 132–149.

Cummins, S., & Quiroa, R. (2012). Teaching for writing expository responses to narrative text. *The Reading Teacher, 65*(6), 381–386.

Cunningham, J., Cunningham, P., Hoffman, J., & Yopp, H. (1998). *Phonemic awareness and the teaching of reading: A position statement from the Board of Directors of the International Reading Association.* Newark, DE: IRA.

Cunningham, P. (2004). *Phonics they use: Words for reading and writing* (4th ed.). New York: Allyn & Bacon.

Cunningham, P. (2012). *Phonics they use: Words for reading and writing* (5th ed.). New York: Pearson.

Curtis, C. P. (1995). *The Watsons go to Birmingham 1963.* New York: Scholastic.

Curtis, C. P. (1999). *Bud, not Buddy.* New York: Scholastic.

Curtis, C. P. (2007). *Elijah of Buxton.* New York: Scholastic.

Curtis, C. P. (2012). *The Mighty Miss Malone.* New York: Wendy Lamb Books.

Dale, E., O'Rourke, J., & Bamman, H. (1971). *Techniques of teaching vocabulary.* Palo Alto, CA: Field Educational Publication.

Daly, N. (2006). *Pretty Salma: A Little Red Riding Hood story from Africa.* Illus. N. Daly. New York: Clarion Books.

Danziger, P. (2001). *A is for Amber: It's Justin time, Amber Brown.* New York: G. P. Putnam's Sons.

Darling-Hammond, L. (2006). If they'd only do their work. *Educational Leadership, 63*(50), 8–13.

Davey, B. (1983). Think aloud: Modeling the cognitive processes of reading comprehension. *Journal of Reading, 27,* 44–47.

Davis, J. (2011). *You are my sunshine.* Illus. C. Church. New York: Cartwheel Books.

Day, A. (1991). *Carl's afternoon in the park.* New York: Farrar, Straus & Giroux.

Deeney, T. (2010). One-minute fluency measures: Mixed messages in assessment and instruction. *The Reading Teacher, 63*(6), 440–450.

DeFauw, D. (2013). Ten writing opportunities to "teach to the text." *The Reading Teacher, 66*(7), 569–573.

DeFord, D. E. (1985). Validating the construct of theoretical orientation in reading instruction. *Reading Research Quarterly, 20,* 351–367.

DeKonty-Applegate, M., Applegate, A., & Modla, V. (2009). "She's my best reader; she just can't comprehend": Studying the relationship between fluency and comprehension. *The Reading Teacher, 62*(6), 512–521.

DeKonty-Applegate, M., Quinn, K. B., & Applegate, A. J. (2008). *The critical reading inventory: Assessing students' reading and thinking* (2nd ed.). Upper Saddle River, NJ: Pearson.

DeMauro, L. (1990). *Bats.* New York: Trumpet Club.

Demi. (1990). *The empty pot.* New York: Henry Holt.

dePaola, T. (1981). *Now one foot, now the other.* New York: Putnam Juvenile.

dePaola, T. (1984). *Clouds* (Reprint ed.). New York: Holiday House.

dePaola, T. (1997). *Strega Nona.* New York: G. P. Putnam's Sons.

dePaola, T. (1999). *26 Fairmount Avenue.* New York: G. P. Putnam's Sons.

Deuker, C. (2007). *Runner.* New York: HMH Books for Young Readers.

DiCamillo, K. (2003). *The tale of Despereaux.* New York: Candlewick Press.

Dickinson, D. K., & Porche, M. (2011). Relations between language experiences in preschool classrooms and children's kindergarten and fourth-grade language and reading ability. *Child Development, 82*(3), 870–886.

Dillon, L. (2002). *Rap a tap tap: Here's Bojangles.* New York: Blue Sky Press.

Dix, S. (2006). I'll do it my way: Three writers and their revision practices. *The Reading Teacher, 59*(6), 566–573.

Dolch, E. W. (1948). *Problems in reading.* New York: The Garrard Press.

Dombey, H. (2011). Distorting the process of learning to read: The "light touch" phonics test for six year olds. *Education Review, 23*(2), 23–34.

Donavan, C., & Smolkin, L. (2011). Supporting informational writing in elementary grades. *The Reading Teacher, 64*(6), 406–416.

Doty, D., Popplewell, S., & Byers, G. (2001). Interactive CD-ROM storybooks and young readers' reading. *Journal of Research on Computing in Education, 33*(4), 374–385.

Dowhower, S. (1999). Supporting a strategic stance in the classroom: A comprehension framework for helping teachers help students to be strategic. *The Reading Teacher, 52*(7), 672–688.

Doyle, A. (2009). *A family literacy program with varying participation structures: Effects on parent and child learning.* University of Toronto. DAI 2010-99070-23.

Doyle, A., & Zhang, J. (2011). Participation structure impacts on parent engagement in family literacy programs. *Early Childhood Education Journal, 39*(3), 223–233.

Dozier, C., Garnett, S., & Tabatabai, S. (2011). Responsive teaching through conversation. *The Reading Teacher, 64*(8), 636–638.

Drew, S. V. (2012/2013). Open up the ceiling on Common Core State Standards: Preparing students for 21st-century literacy—now. *Journal of Adolescent and Adult Literacy, 56*(4), 321–330.

Drucker, M.J. (2003). What reading teachers should know about ESL learners. *The Reading Teacher, 57*(1), 22–29.

Duffy-Hester, A. (1999). Teaching struggling readers in elementary school classrooms: A review of classroom reading programs and principles for instruction. *The Reading Teacher, 52*(5), 480–495.

Duke, N. (2003). Reading to learn from the very beginning: Informational books in early childhood. *Young Children, 58*(2), 14–20. Retrieved from www.Earlychildhoodconnection.com/documents/informationBooks.pdf.

Duke, N. K., Purcell-Gates, V., Hall, L., & Tower, C. (2006). Authentic literacy activities for developing comprehension and writing. *The Reading Teacher, 60*(4), 344–355.

Dunn, C. M., & Dunn, L. M. (1997). *Peabody picture vocabulary test* (3rd ed.). Circle Pines, MN: American Guidance Service.

Dworin, J. (2006). The family stories project: Using funds of knowledge for writing. *The Reading Teacher, 59*(6), 510–519.

Earle, A. (1995). *Zipping, zapping, zooming bats*. Illus. H. Cole. New York: HarperCollins.

Echevarria, J., & Short, D. (2007). The sheltered instruction observation protocol (SIOP). Retrieved from www.siopinstitute.net

Edmunds, K. M., & Bauserman, K. L. (2006). What teachers can learn about reading motivation through conversation with children. *The Reading Teacher, 59*(5), 414–424.

Edwards, P. D. (1996). *Some smug slug*. New York: HarperTrophy.

Ehren, B. (2013). Expanding pockets of excellence in RTI. *The Reading Teacher, 66*(6), 440–453.

Ehri, L. C., Dreyer, L. G., Flugman, B., & Gross, A. (2007). Reading rescue: An effective tutoring intervention model for language minority students who are struggling readers in first grade. *American Educational Research Journal, 44*(2), 414–448.

Ehri, L. C., Numes, S. R., Willows, D. M., Schuster, B. V., Yaghoub-zadeh, Z., & Shanahan, T. (2001). Phonemic awareness instruction helps children learn to read: Evidence from the National Reading Panel's meta-analysis. *Reading Research Quarterly, 36*(3), 250–287.

Ekwall, E., & Shanker, J. (1999). *Ekwall/Shanker reading inventory* (4th ed.). Boston: Allyn & Bacon.

Elbaum, B., Vaughn, S., Hughes, M. T., & Moody, S. M. (2000). How effective are one-on-one tutoring programs in reading for elementary students at risk for reading failure? A meta-analysis of the intervention research. *Journal of Educational Psychology, 92*(4), 605–619.

Elkonin, D. B. (1973). U.S.S.R. In J. Downing (Ed.), *Comparative reading*, pp. 551–579. New York: Macmillan.

Engelbreit, M. (2005). *Mary Engelbreit's Mother Goose: One hundred best-loved verses*. Illus. M. Engelbreit. New York: HarperCollins.

Erskine, K. (2010). *Mockingbird*. New York: Philomel Books.

Falwell, C. (1998). *Word wizard*. New York: Clarion Books.

Fargeon, E. (1987). Jazz-man. In J. Bennett (Ed.), *Noisy poems*. Oxford, New York: Oxford University Press.

Farndon, J. (2000). *All about planet earth*. New York: Anness Publishing.

Fenton, M. B. (2001). *Bats*. New York: Checkmark Books.

Ferreiro, E., & Teberosky, A. (1982). *Literacy before schooling* (K. G. Castro, Trans.). Portsmouth, NH: Heinemann. (Original work published in 1979.)

Ferroli, L., & Shanahan, T. (1987). Kindergarten spelling: Explaining its relation to first grade reading. In J. E. Readence & R. S. Baldwin (Eds.), *Research in literacy: Merging perspectives* (36th yearbook of the National Reading Conference), pp. 93–99. Rochester, NY: National Reading Conference.

Fezell, G. (2012). Robust vocabulary instruction in a readers' workshop. *The Reading Teacher, 66*(3), 233–242.

Fiderer, A. (1999). *40 rubrics and checklists to assess reading and writing*. New York: Scholastic.

Finn, C. E. (2013). Text complexity grade bands and Lexile bands. *The Lexile Framework for Reading*. Retrieved from http://lexile.com.

Fisher, D., & Frey, N. (2012). Close reading in the elementary schools. *The Reading Teacher, 66*(3), 179–188.

Fisher, D., Frey, N., & Lapp, D. (2008). Shared readings: Modeling comprehension, vocabulary, text structure and text features for older readers. *The Reading Teacher, 61*(7), 548–556.

Fitzgerald, J., & Noblit, G. (1999). About hopes, aspirations, and uncertainty; First-grade English-language learners' emergent reading. *Journey of Literacy Research, 31*, 133–182.

Flanigan, K., Templeton, S., & Hayes, L. (2012). What's in a word? Using content vocabulary to generate growth in general vocabulary knowledge. *Journal of Adolescent and Adult Literacy 56*(2), 132–140.

Fleischman, P. (1985). *I am phoenix: Poems for two voices*. New York: HarperTrophy.

Fleischman, P. (1988). *Joyful noise: Poems for two voices*. New York: Harper & Row.

Fleischman, P. (2000). *Big talk: Poems for four voices*. Cambridge, MA: Candlewick Press.

Flood, J., Lapp, D., & Fisher, D. (2005). Neurological impress method plus. *Reading Psychology, 26*(2), 147–160.

Flynt, E. S., & Brozo, W. (2008). Developing academic language: Got words? *The Reading Teacher, 61*(6), 500–502.

Flynt, E., & Cooter, R. (2003). *Flynt–Cooter reading inventory for the classroom* (5th ed.). Upper Saddle River, NJ: Prentice Hall.

Flynt, E. S., & Cooter, R. B., Jr. (2005). Improving middle-grades reading in urban schools: The Memphis comprehension framework. *The Reading Teacher, 58*(8), 774–780.

Fordham, N., Wellman, D., & Sandmann, A. (2002). Taming the text: Engaging and supporting students in social studies readings. *Social Studies, 93*(4), 149–159.

Fountas, I. C., & Pinnell, G. S. (2001). *Guiding readers and writers: Teaching comprehension, genre, and content literacy.* Portsmouth, NH: Heinemann.

Fountas, I. C., & Pinnell, G. S. (2002). *Phonics and spelling minilessons: Buddy study system.* Portsmouth, NH: Heinemann.

Fountas, I. C., & Pinnell, G. S. (2002). *Words matter: Teaching phonics and spelling in the reading/writing classroom.* Portsmouth, NH: Heinemann.

Fountas, I. C., & Pinnell, G. S. (2003). *Phonics lessons: Letters, words, and how they work (Grade 1).* Portsmouth, NH: Heinemann.

Fountas, I. C., & Pinnell, G. S. (2006a). *Guiding readers and writers, grades 3–6: Teaching comprehension, genre, and content literacy.* Portsmouth, NH: Heinemann.

Fountas, I. C., & Pinnell, G. S. (2006b). *Guided reading: Good first teaching for all children.* Portsmouth, NH: Heinemann.

Fountas, I. C., and Pinnell, G. S. (2007). *Guiding readers and writers: Teaching comprehension, genre, and content literacy.* Portsmouth, NM: Heinemann Educational Books.

Fountas, I. C., & Pinnell, G. S. (2008). *When readers struggle: Teaching that works.* Portsmouth, NH: Heinemann.

Fountas, I. C., & Pinnell, G. S. (2012/2013). Guided reading: The romance and the reality. *The Reading Teacher 66*(4), 268–284

Fountas, I. C., & Pinnell, G. S. (2013). Guided reading: The romance and the reality. *The Reading Teacher, 66*(4), 268–284.

Fox, D., Weissman, D., Wilkins, S. (2010). *The great family songbook: A treasury of favorite show tunes, singalongs, pop songs, and blues.* New York: Black Dog & Leventhal Publishers.

Fox, M. (1987). *Hattie and the fox.* New York: Scholastic.

Fresch, M. J. (2000). What we learned from Josh: Sorting out word sorting. *Language Arts, 77*(3), 232–240.

Fresch, M. J., & Wheaton, A. (1997). Sort, search, and discover: Spelling in the child-centered classroom. *The Reading Teacher, 51*(1), 20–31.

Fry 1000 instant words. Retrieved from http://www.unique teachingresources.com/Fry-1000-Instant-Words.html

Fry, E. (1977). Fry's readability graph: Clarifications, validity, and extension to level 17. *Journal of Reading, 21,* 242–252.

Fry, E. (2002). Readability versus leveling. *The Reading Teacher, 56*(3), 286–291.

Fry, E. B., & Kress, J. E. (2006). *The Reading Teacher's book of lists* (5th ed.). San Francisco: Jossey-Bass.

Frye, E., Trathen, W., & Schlagal, B. (2010). Extending acrostic poetry into content learning: A scaffolding framework. *The Reading Teacher, 63*(7), 591–596.

Gambrell, L. (2011). Seven rules of engagement: What's most important to know about motivation to read. *The Reading Teacher, 65*(3), 172–178.

Garan, E. M. (2002). *Resisting reading mandates: How to triumph with the truth.* Portsmouth, NH: Heinemann.

Gardner, H. (1983). *Frames of mind: The theory of multiple intelligences.* New York: Basic Books.

Gardner, H. (1993). *Multiple intelligences: The theory into practice.* New York: Basic Books.

Gates, L., & Yale, I. (2011). A logical letter-sound system in five phonic generalizations. *The Reading Teacher, 64*(5), 330–339.

Gentry, J. R. (1982). An analysis of developmental spelling in GNYS at WRK. *The Reading Teacher, 36,* 192–200.

Gentry, J. R. (2007). *Breakthrough in beginning reading and writing: The evidence-based approach to pinpointing students' needs and delivering targeted instruction.* New York: Scholastic.

Gentry, J. R., & Gillet, J. W. (1993). *Teaching kids to spell.* Portsmouth, NH: Heinemann.

George, W. (1989). *Box turtle at Long Pond.* New York: A Trumpet Club Special Edition.

Giannetti, C., & Sagarese, M. (1998). Turning parents from critics to allies. *Educational Leadership, 55*(8), 40–42.

Gibbons, G. (1992). *Weather words and what they mean.* New York: Holiday House.

Gibbons, G. (1993). *Weather forecasting* (Reprint ed.). New York: Aladdin.

Gibbons, G. (1998). *Soccer.* Illus. G. Gibbons. New York: Holiday House.

Gibbons, G. (2000). *Baseball.* Illus. G. Gibbons. New York: HarperCollins.

Gibbons, G. (2000). *Basketball.* Illus. G. Gibbons. New York: Holiday House.

Gibbons, G. (2000). *Bats.* Illus. G. Gibbons. New York: Holiday House.

Gibbons, G. (2000). *Football.* Illus. G. Gibbons. New York: HarperCollins.

Gibbons, G. (2002). *Polar bears.* Illus. by M. Lloyd. New York: Holiday House.

Gill, S. R. (2009). What teachers need to know about the "new" nonfiction. *The Reading Teacher, 63*(4), 260–267.

Gillet, J. W., & Temple, C. (2004). *Understanding reading problems: Assessment and instruction* (6th ed.). New York: Allyn & Bacon.

Gilpin, R., & Pratt, L. (2008). *The Usborne big book of science things to make and do.* Tulsa, OK: EDC.

Gipe, J. (2013) *Multiple Paths to Literacy: Assessment and Differentiated Instruction for Diverse Learners, K12* (8th ed.). Upper Saddle River, NJ: Pearson.

Glazer, T. (1973). *Eye Winker, Tom Tinker, Chin Chopper.* New York: Doubleday.

Goals 2000: Educate America Act. Retrieved from http://lamar.colostate.edu/~hillger/laws/goals-2000.html

Goldish, M. (1993). *Step inside the rain forest.* New York: MacMillan.

Goodman, K. S. (1969). Analysis of oral reading miscues: Applied psycholinguistic. *Reading Research Quarterly, 5*(1), 9–30.

Goodman, Y. (1972/1997). Reading diagnosis—qualitative or quantitative? *The Reading Teacher, 50*(7), 534–538.

Goodman, K. (1996). *Ken Goodman: On reading.* Portsmouth, NH: Heinemann.

Goodman, Y. (1996). *Notes from a kidwatcher: Selected writings of Yetta M. Goodman.* Portsmouth, NH: Heinemann.

Goodman, Y., & Burke, C. L. (1972). *Reading miscue inventory: Procedures for diagnosis and evaluation.* New York: MacMillan.

Goodman, Y., & Marek, A. (1996). *Retrospective miscue analysis: Revaluing readers and reading.* Katonah, NY: Richard C. Owen.

Goodman, Y., Watson, D., & Burke, C. (1987). *Reading miscue inventory: Alternative procedures* (2nd ed.). Katonah, NY: Richard C. Owen.

Goodman, Y., Watson, D., & Burke, C. (1996). *Reading strategies: Focus on comprehension* (2nd ed.). Katonah, NY: Richard C. Owen.

Goodwin, A., Lipsky, M., & Ahn, S. (2012). Word detectives: Using units of meaning to support literacy. *The Reading Teacher, 65*(7), 461–470.

Graham, S., & Harris, K. (1997). It can be taught, but it does not develop naturally: Myths and realities in writing instruction. *School Psychology Review, 26*(3), 414–425.

Graham, S., & Hebert, M. (2010). Writing to read and evidence how writing can improve reading. *A Carnegie Corporation Time to Act Report.* Washington, DC: Alliance for Excellent Education.

Graves, D. (1990, July 27). The process-writing model. Paper presented at OKTAWL Conference, Norman, OK.

Graves, D. (1991). *Build a literate class.* Portsmouth, NH: Heinemann.

Graves, D. (1994). *A fresh look at writing.* Portsmouth, NH: Heinemann.

Graves, M. F., & Watts-Taffe, S. (2002). The place of word consciousness in a research-based vocabulary program. In A. Farstrup & S. Samuels (Eds.), *What research has to say about reading instruction* (3rd ed.), pp. 140–165. Newark, DE: IRA.

Graves, M. F., & Watts-Taffe, S. (2008). For the love of words: Fostering word consciousness in young readers. *The Reading Teacher, 62*(3), 185–193.

Gravett, E. (2008). *Little Mouse's big book of fears.* New York: Simon & Schuster.

Gregory, A., & Cahill, M. A. (2010). Kindergartners can do it, too! Comprehension strategies for young readers. *The Reading Teacher, 63*(6), 515–521.

Greil, A. (2013). Benjamin Franklin went to France. Retrieved from http://www.buyjumpropes.net/Jump_Rope_Rhymes.

Griffith, L. W., & Rasinski, T. (2004). A focus on fluency: How one teacher incorporated fluency with her reading curriculum. *The Reading Teacher, 58*(2), 126–137.

Grout, D. J. (1964). *A history of Western music.* New York: W. W. Norton.

Guarino, D. (1989). *Is your mama a llama?* New York: Scholastic.

Guccione, L. (2011). Integrating literacy and inquiry for English learners. *The Reading Teacher, 64*(8), 567–577.

Gunning, T. (2001). *Building words: A resource manual for teaching word analysis and spelling strategies.* Boston: Allyn & Bacon.

Guthrie, J. T., & Davis, M. H. (2003). Motivating struggling readers in middle school through an engagement model of classroom practice. *Reading & Writing Quarterly, 19,* 59–89.

Gwynne, F. (1988). *The king who rained.* New York: Aladdin.

Gwynne, F. (1999). *A little pigeon toad.* New York: Aladdin.

Hadaway, N., Vardell, S., & Young, T. (2001). Scaffolding oral language development through poetry for students learning English. *The Reading Teacher, 54*(8), 796–807.

Hal Leonard Corp. (2004). *The big book of nursery rhymes and children' songs.* Milwaukee, WI: Hal Leonard Corporation.

Hall, E. (2006). Learning styles—is there an evidence base from this popular idea? *Education Review, 19*(1), 49–56.

Hall, K. (1995). *A bad, bad day.* New York: Scholastic.

Handsfield, L., Dean, T., & Cielocha, K. (2009). Becoming critical consumers and producers of text: Teaching literacy with Web 1.0 and Web 2.0. *The Reading Teacher, 63*(1), 40–50.

Hanel, E. C., Shaw, S., & Taylor, T. S. (2013). Toward a new mindfulness: Exploration of home and community literacies. *Language Arts, 90*(6), 428–440.

Hanf, M. B. (1971). Mapping: A technique for translating reading into thinking. *Journal of Reading, 14,* 225–230, 270.

Hannus, M., & Hyona, J. (1999). Utilization of illustrations during learning of science textbook passages among low- and high-ability children. *Contemporary Educational Psychology, 24*(2), 95–123.

Hansen, J. (1987). *When writers read.* Portsmouth, NH: Heinemann.

Harris, K., Graham, S., Friedlander, B., & Laud, L. (2013). Bring powerful writing strategies into your classroom: Why and how. *The Reading Teacher, 66*(7), 538–542.

Harris, T., & Hodges, R. (Eds.). (1995). *The literacy dictionary: The vocabulary of reading and writing.* Newark, DE: IRA.

Harrison, D. (2008). *Pirates.* Illus. by D. Burr. Honesdale, PA: Wordsong.

Hart, B., & Risley, T. R. (2003). The early catastrophe: The 30 million word gap. *American Education, 27*(1), 4–9.

Harvey, S., & Goudvis, A. (2007). *Strategies that work: Teaching comprehension for understanding and engagement* (2nd ed.). Portland, ME: Stenhouse Publishers.

Harvey, S., & Goudvis, A. (2013). Comprehension at the core. *The Reading Teacher, 66*(6), 432–439.

Harvey, T. (1998). The curse of the foul-smelling armpit. In B. Lansky (Ed.), *Miles of smiles: Kids pick the funniest poems, Book #3,* pp. 66–67. New York: Meadowbrook Press.

Hasbrouck, J., & Tindal, G. (2006). Oral reading fluency norms: A valuable assessment tool for reading teachers. *The Reading Teacher, 59*(7), 636–644.

Haskins, J. (1995). *The day Fort Sumter was fired on: A photo history of the Civil War.* New York: Scholastic.

Heald-Taylor, B. G. (1998). Three paradigms of spelling instruction in grades 3 to 6. *The Reading Teacher, 51*(5), 404–412.

Heath, S. B. (2004). The children of Trackton's children: Spoken and written language in social change. In R. B. Ruddell & N. J. Unrau (Eds.), *Theoretical models and processes of reading,* pp. 187–209. Newark, DE: IRA.

Heilmann, J., Miller, J., & Dunaway, C. (2010). Properties of the narrative scoring scheme using narrative retells in young school-age children. *American Journal of Speech-Language Pathology, 19,* 154–166.

Heller, R. (1987). *A cache of jewels.* New York: Grosset & Dunlap.

Heller, R. (1989). *Many luscious lollipops.* New York: Grosset & Dunlap.

Helman, L., Bear, D., Invernizzi, S., & Templeton, S. (2008). *Words their way: Emergent sorts for Spanish-speaking English learners.* Upper Saddle River, NJ: Pearson/Prentice Hall.

Helman, L., Bear, D. R., Templeton, S., Invernizzi, M., & Johnston, F. (2011). *Words their way with English learners: Word study for phonics, vocabulary, and spelling* (2nd ed.). New York: Prentice Hall.

Helman, L. A. (2004). Building on the sound system of Spanish: Insights from the alphabetic spellings of English-language learners. *The Reading Teacher, 57*(5), 452–460.

Helman, L. A., & Burns, M. K. (2008). What does oral language have to do with it? Helping young English-language learners acquire a sight word vocabulary. *The Reading Teacher, 62*(1), 14–19.

Henk, W. A., & Melnick, S. A. (1995). The Reader Self-Perception Scale (RSPS): A new tool for measuring how children feel about themselves as readers. *The Reading Teacher, 48,* 470–482.

Henkes, K. (1991). *Chrysanthemum.* New York: Greenwillow Books.

Henkes, K. (1995). *Julius: The baby of the world.* New York: Greenwillow Books.

Henkes, K. (1996). *Lily's purple plastic purse.* New York: Greenwillow Books.

Henkes, K. (2006). *Lily's big day.* New York: Greenwillow Books.

Henry, L. (2006). Searching for an answer: The critical role of new literacies while reading on the Internet. *The Reading Teacher, 59*(7), 614–626.

Hesse, K. (1998). *Just juice.* New York: Scholastic.

Hesse, K. (1999). *Come on, rain!* New York: Scholastic.

Hessell, J. (1989). *Secret soup.* Crystal Lake, IL: Rigby.

Heubach, K. (December, 1995). Integrating literature into fourth-grade social studies curriculum: The effects on student learning and attitude. Paper presented at the meeting of the National Reading Conference, New Orleans, LA.

Hiebert, E. (1999). Text matters in learning to read. *The Reading Teacher, 52*(6), 552–566.

Hiebert, E. (2013). Supporting the students' movement up the staircase of text complexity. *The Reading Teacher 66*(6), 459–468.

Hindes, M. (2007). Readability and comprehension. Guidance Channel Online. Retrieved from www.csapmodel programs.com/default.aspx?M=a&index-628&cat=29

Ho, B. (2002). Application of participatory action research to family school intervention. *School Psychology Review, 31*(1), 106–122.

Holdaway, D. (1979). *The foundations of literacy.* Sydney, Australia: Ashton Scholastic.

Holdaway, D. (1986). The structure of natural language as a basis for literacy instruction. In M. L. Sampson (Ed.), *The pursuit of literacy: Early reading and writing.* Dubuque, IA: Kendall/Hunt.

Hollenbeck, A., & Saternus, K. (2013). Mind the comprehension iceberg: Avoiding titanic mistakes with the Common Core State Standards. *The Reading Teacher, 66*(7), 558–568.

Holt, K. W. (1998). *Mister and me.* New York: G. P. Putnam's Sons.

Houge, T., & Geier, C. (2009). Delivering one-to-one tutoring in literacy via videoconferencing. *Journal of Adolescent & Adult Literacy, 53*(2), 154–163.

Houge, T., Peyton, D., Geier, C., & Petrie, B. (2007). Adolescent literacy tutoring: Face-to-face and via webcam technology. *Reading Psychology, 28*(3), 283–300.

Hughes, J., King, A., Perkins, P., & Fuke, V. (2011). Adolescents and "autographics": Reading and writing coming-of-age graphic novels. *Journal of Adolescent and Adult Literacy, 54*(8), 601–612.

Hughes, M., & Searle, D. (2000). Spelling and "the second 'R.'" *Language Arts, 77*(3), 203–208.

Hurley, S. R., & Blake, S. (2000). Assessment in the content areas for students acquiring English. In S. R. Hurley & J. V. Tinajero (Eds.), *Literacy assessment of second language learners,* pp. 84–103. Boston: Allyn & Bacon.

Hurst, C. (2000). Guided reading can strengthen comprehension skills. *Teaching PreK–8, 31*(2), 70–72.

Illingworth, M. (2000). *Real-life math problem solving: 40 exciting, classroom-tested problems with annotated solutions.* New York: Scholastic.

Imperato, F. (2009). Getting parents and children off to a strong start in reading. *The Reading Teacher, 63*(4), 342–344.

International Reading Association (1997). *The role of phonics in reading instruction.* Newark, DE: Author.

International Reading Association (2000). All about assessment. *Reading Today, 18*(2), 34.

International Reading Association (2001). *Second-language literacy instruction: A position statement of the International Reading Association.* Newark, DE: Author.

International Reading Association (2002). Educators meet to discuss early childhood literacy issues. *Reading Today, 20*(1), 1.

International Reading Association (2003). International Reading Association's summary of the (U.S.) National Reading Panel Report. Retrieved from www.reading.org/advocacy/nrp/chapter2.html

International Reading Association (2009a). IRA commission on RTI: Working draft of guiding principles. Retrieved from www.reading.org

International Reading Association (2009b). New literacies and 21st-century technologies: Position statement 1067. Retrieved from www.reading.org/libraries/position_statements_and resolutions/ps1067_newliteracies21century.sflb.asbx.

International Reading Association (2009c). Response to Intervention: Guiding principles for educators from the International Reading Association. Newark, DE: IRA.

International Reading Association (2010). Alphabiography. Retrieved from www.ReadWriteThink.org

International Reading Association and The National Association for the Education of Young Children (1998). Learning to read and write: Developmentally appropriate practices for young children. *Young Children, 53*(4), 30–46.

International Reading Association and The National Council of Teachers of English (1996). *Standards for the English language arts.* Newark, DE: International Reading Association & Urbana, IL: National Council of Teachers of English.

Invernizzi, M., Rosemary, C., Juel, C., & Richard, H. (1997). At-risk readers and community volunteers: A three-year perspective. *Scientific Studies of Reading, 1*(3), 279–300.

Invernizzi, M., Templeton, S., Bear, D., & Johnston, F. (2009). *Words their way letter and picture sorts for emergent spellers* (2nd ed.). New York: Pearson.

Iorio, N., (2005). *Bats!* New York: HarperCollins.

Ivey, G., & Baker, M. (2004). Phonics instruction for older students? Just say, "No." *Educational Leadership, 61*(1), 35–39.

Ivey, G., & Fisher, D. (2005). Learning from what doesn't work. *Educational Leadership, 63*(2), 8–14.

Jackman, H. (1999). *Sing me a story! Tell me a song!* Thousand Oaks, CA: Corwin Press.

Jacobson, J., Thrope, L., Fisher, D., Lapp, D., Frey, N., & Flood, J. (2001). Cross-age tutoring: A literacy improvement approach for struggling adolescent readers. *Journal of Adolescent & Adult Literacy, 44*(6), 528–537.

Janeczko, P. (2005). *A kick in the head: An everyday guide to poetic forms.* Illus. by C. Raschka. Cambridge, MA: Candlewick Press.

Jensen, D. (2006). Using newsletters to create home-school connections. *The Reading Teacher, 60*(2), 186–193.

Jeunesse, G., & Verdet, J-P. (2005). *First discovery: The universe.* Illus. D. Grant. New York: Scholastic.

Johns, J. (2007). Monitoring progress in fluency: Possible unintended consequences. *Reading Today, 24*(6), 18.

Johnson-Higgins, J. (2002). Multicultural children's literature: Creating and applying an evaluation tool in response to the needs of urban educators. New Horizons of Learning. Retrieved from http://newhorizons.org/strategies/multicultural/higgins.htm

Johnston, F. (2001). Spelling exceptions: Problems or possibilities? *The Reading Teacher, 54*(4), 372–378.

Johnston, F., Invernizzi, M., & Juel, C. (1998). *Book buddies: Guidelines for volunteer tutors of emergent readers.* New York: The Guilford Press.

Johnston, P., Ivey, G., & Faulkner, A. (2011/2012). Talking in class: Remembering what is important about classroom talk. *The Reading Teacher, 65*(4), 232–237.

Johnston, R., Bear, D., & Invernizzi, M. (2005). *Words their way: Word sorts for derivational relations spellers.* New York: Prentice Hall.

Jones, C. (2002). *Every girl tells a story.* New York: Simon & Schuster.

Jongsma, K. (1999/2000). Vocabulary and comprehension strategy development. *The Reading Teacher, 53*(4), 310–313.

Jongsma, K. (2000). Teaching—aids & devices—book review. *The Reading Teacher, 54*(1), 80–83.

Joosse, B. (1991). *Mama, do you love me?* New York: Scholastic.

Juel, C., & Deffes, R. (2004). Making words stick. *Educational Leadership, 61*(6), 30–34.

Kamil, M. L., Mosenthal, P. B., Pearson, P. D., & Barr, R. (Eds.) (2000). *Handbook of reading research* (3rd ed.). Mahwah, NJ: Erlbaum.

Kara-Soteriou, J., Zawilinski, L., & Henry, L. (2007). Children's books and technology in the classroom: A dynamic combo for supporting the writing workshop. *The Reading Teacher, 60*(7), 698–707.

Karchmer, R. (2001). The journey ahead: Thirteen teachers report how the Internet influences literacy and literacy instruction in the K–12 classrooms. *Reading Research Quarterly, 36*(4), 442–466.

Karchmer-Klein, R. & Shinas, V. H. (2012). Guiding principles for supporting new literacies in your classroom. *The Reading Teacher, 65*(5), 288–293.

Kaufman, M. (2002). Putting it all together: From one first-grade teacher to another. *The Reading Teacher, 55*(8), 722–726.

Keating, F. (2001). *Will Rogers.* Illus. by M. Wimmer. San Diego, CA: Silver Whistle/Harcourt, Inc.

Keehn, S. (2003).The effect of instruction and practice through Readers Theatre on young readers' oral reading fluency. *Reading Research and Instruction, 42*(4), 40–61.

Kelley, M., & Clausen-Grace, N. (2009). Facilitating engagement by differentiating independent reading. *The Reading Teacher, 63*(4), 313–318.

Kesler, T. (2012). Writing with voice. *The Reading Teacher, 66*(1), 25–30.

Khanduri, K. (1992). *Polar wildlife.* Illus. by I. Jackson. New York: Scholastic.

Kieffer, M. J., & Lesaux, N. (2007). Breaking down words to build meaning: Morphology, vocabulary, and reading comprehension in the urban classroom. *The Reading Teacher, 61*(2), 134–144.

Kindervater, T. (2010). Models of parent involvement. *The Reading Teacher, 63*(7), 610–612.

Kinerk, R. (2003). *Clorinda.* Illus. S. Kellogg. New York: Aladdin.

Kinney, A. (2012). Loops, lyrics and literacy: Songwriting as a site of resistance for an urban adolescent. *Journal of Adolescent and Adult Literacy, 55*(5), 395–404.

Kinniburgh, L., & Shaw, E. L. (2009). Using question-answer-relationships to build reading comprehension in science. *Science Activities, 45*(4), 19–26.

Kirk, D. (1999). *Miss Spider's new car.* New York: Scholastic Press. (Board book)

Kletzien, S. B. (1991). Strategy used by good and poor comprehenders reading expository text of differing levels. *Reading Research Quarterly, 26,* 67–86.

Koskinen, P., Blum, I., Bisson, S., Phillips, S., Creamer, T., & Baker, T. (1999). Shared reading, books, and audiotapes: Supporting diverse students in school and at home. *The Reading Teacher, 52*(5), 430–444.

Krashen, S. (1981). *Second language acquisition and second language learning.* Oxford, England: Pergamon.

Krashen, S. (2004/2005). Skyrocketing scores: An urban legend. *Educational Leadership, 62*(4), 37–39.

Krashen, S., & Brown, C. L. (2005). The ameliorating effects of high socioeconomic status: A secondary analysis. *Bilingual Research Journal, 29*(1), 185–196.

Kucan, L. (2012). What is most important to know about vocabulary. *The Reading Teacher, 65*(6), 360–366.

Kuhlman, N. (2005). The language assessment conundrum: What tests claim to assess and what teachers need to know. *The ELL Outlook.* Retrieved from www.coursecrafters.com/ELLp Outlook/2005/mar_apr/ELLOutlook ITIArticle1.htm

L'Engle, M. (1962). A wrinkle in time. New York: Farrar Straus & Giroux.

Labadie, M., Wetzel, M. M., & Rogers, R. (2012). Opening spaces for critical literacy. *The Reading Teacher, 66*(2), 117–127.

LaBerge, D., & Samuels, S. (1974). Toward a theory of automatic information processing in reading. *Cognitive Psychology 6*(2), 293–323.

Lacina, J., & Griffith, R. (2012/2013). Blogging as a means of crafting writing. *The Reading Teacher, 66*(4), 316–320.

Lamoreaux, L., & Lee, D. M. (1943). *Learning to read through experiences.* New York: Appleton-Century-Crofts.

Lane, H. S., & Pullen, P. (2004). *Phonological awareness assessment and instruction: A sound beginning.* Boston: Allyn & Bacon.

Langeland, D. (1997). *Octopus' den.* New York: Scholastic.

Lansky, B. (2000). *If pigs could fly . . . and other deep thoughts.* Illus. S. Carpenter. Minnetonka, MN: Meadowbrook Press.

Lansky, B. (2009). *My dog ate my homework!* New York: Meadowbrook Press.

Lansky, B. (Ed.). (1998). *Miles of smiles: Kids pick the funniest poems, book #3.* New York: Meadowbrook Press.

Lapp, D., & Fisher, D. (2012). Persuasion = stating and arguing claims well. *Journal of Adolescent and Adult Literacy, 55*(7), 641–648.

Lapp, D., Fisher, D., & Johnson, K. (2010). Text mapping plus: Improving comprehension through supported retellings. *Journal of Adolescent & Adult Literacy, 53*(5), 323–426.

Larkin, R. B. (2001). Can we act it out? *The Reading Teacher, 54*(5), 478–481.

Lauber, P. (1986). *Volcano: The eruption and healing of Mount St. Helens.* New York: Bradbury Press.

Leal, D. (2005). The word writing CAFÉ: Assessing student writing for complexity, accuracy, and fluency. *The Reading Teacher, 59*(4), 340–350.

Lehr, F., Osborn, J., & Heibert, E. (2005). *A focus on vocabulary.* Pacific Resources for Education and Learning. Retrieved from www.tasaliteracy.com/rpe/instruction/vocab.html

Lenhart, A., Madden, M., Smith, A., Purcell, K., Zickuhr, D., & Rainie, L. (2011). Teens, kindness, and cruelty on social network sites. *Pew Internet and the American Life Project.* Retrieved from www.pewinternet.org.

Lenski, S. (2012). What RTI means for content area teachers. *Journal of Adolescent and Adult Literacy 55*(4), 276–285.

Lenski, S. D., Ehlers-Zavala, F., Daniel, M. C., & Sun-Irminger, X. (2006). Assessing English-language learners in the mainstream classroom. *The Reading Teacher, 60*(1), 24–34.

Lepthien, E. (1997). *A true book: Sea turtles.* Illus. by E. Lepthien. New York: Children's Press.

Leu, D. J., Kinzer, J., Coiro, J., Castek, J., & Henry, L. (2013). New literacies: A dual-level theory of the changing nature of literacy, instruction, and assessment. In D. Alvermann, N. Unrau, and R. Ruddell (Eds.), *Theoretical models and processes of reading* (pp. 1150–1181). Newark, DE: IRA.

Lewin, L. (2009). *Teaching comprehension with questioning strategies that motivate middle school readers.* New York: Scholastic.

Lewis, J. P. (2012). *National Geographic book of animal poetry: 200 poems with photographs that squeak, soar, and roar.* Washington, DC: National Geographic.

Lewis, M. (1986). *Hooked on Caldecott Award winners! 60 crossword puzzles based on the Caldecott Gold Medal books.* New York: The Center for Applied research Education.

Lewis, P. (1990). *A hippopotamustn't.* New York: Dial Books for Young Readers.

Lewison, M., Flint, A. S., & Van Sluys, K. (2002). Taking on critical literacies: The journey of newcomers and novices. *Language Arts, 79,* 382–392.

Lies, B. (2006). *Bats at the beach.* New York: HMH Books.

Lies, B. (2008). *Bats at the library.* Boston: Houghton Mifflin.

Lies, B. (2010). *Bats at the ballroom.* Boston: Houghton Mifflin.

Lindeen, C. (2005). *Jellyfish.* Mankato, MN: Capstone Press.

Lipson, M., Chomsky-Higgins, P., & Kanfer, J. (2011). Diagnosis: The missing ingredient in RTI assessments. *The Reading Teacher 65*(3), 203–208.

Lipson, M., & Wixson, K. (2012). To what intervention are students responding? *The Reading Teacher, 66*(2), 111–115.

Lloyd, C. (2003). Song lyrics as text to develop critical literacies. *Reading Online, 6*(10). Retrieved from www.readingonline.org/articles/lloyd

Lobel, A. (1983). *The book of pigericks.* New York: Harper & Row.

Los Angeles County Office of Education. (2000). *Kindergarten and grade one reading: Basic to success.* Retrieved from http://teams.lacoe.edu/Documentation/classrooms/patti/k-1/teacher/assessment/print/concept

Low, A. (1993). *The popcorn shop.* Illus. by P. Hammel. New York: Scholastic.

MacDonald, M. (1995). *The old woman who lived in a vinegar bottle*. Little Rock, AR: August House.

MacDonald, M. R. (2005). *The parent's guide to storytelling: How to make up new stories and retell old favorites* (2nd ed.). Little Rock, AR: August House.

MacLachlan, P. (1982). *Mama one, mama two*. New York: HarperCollins.

MacLulich, C. (1996). *Frogs*. New York: Scholastic.

Malock, B., & Horsey, M. (2013). Living inquiry: Learning from and about informational texts in second-grade classrooms. *The Reading Teacher, 66*(6), 475–486.

Manning, M. (2001). Characterization. *Teaching PreK–8, 31*(8), 84–87.

Manning, M. L. (2002). Revisiting developmentally appropriate middle level schools. *Childhood Education, 78*(4), 225–227.

Manyak, P. C., & Bouchereau-Bauer, E. (2009). English vocabulary instruction for English learners. *The Reading Teacher, 63*(2), 174–176.

Marcell, B. (2011/2012). Putting fluency on a fitness plan: Building fluency is meaning-making muscles. *The Reading Teacher, 65*(4), 242–249.

Marcell, B., & Ferraro, C. (2013). So long robot reader: A superhero intervention plan for improving fluency. *The Reading Teacher, 66*(8), 607–614.

Marinak, B., & Gambrell, L. (2009). Building world knowledge: Motivating children to read and enjoy informational text. Retrieved from http://www.readingrockets.org/article/33920.

Marino-Weisman, D., & Hansen, L. (Sept./Oct. 2007). Strategies for teaching social studies to English-language learners at the elementary level. *Social Studies,* 180–184.

Markle, S. (1996). *Outside and inside sharks*. New York: Aladdin Paperbacks.

Marsalis, W. (2005). *Jazz ABZ*. Illus. by P. Rogers. Cambridge, MA: Candlewick.

Martens, P. (1998). Using retrospective miscue analysis to inquire: Learning from Michael. *The Reading Teacher, 52*(2), 176–180.

Martin, B. (1996). *Brown Bear, Brown Bear, what do you see?* Illus. E. Carle. New York: Henry Holt.

Martin, B., Jr., & Archambault, J. (1998). *Here are my hands.* New York: Henry Holt.

Marzano, R., & Pickering, D. (2010). *Building academic vocabulary*. Alexandria, VA: Association for Supervision Development.

Maslow, A. (1987). *Motivation and personality* (3rd ed.). New York: Harper & Row.

Mason, J. A., Stahl, S. A., Au, K. H., & Herman, P. A. (2003). Reading: Children's developing knowledge of words. In J. Flood, D. Lapp, J. R. Squire, & J. M. Jensen (Eds.), *Handbook of research on reading of the English language arts* (2nd ed.), pp. 914–930. Mahwah, NJ: Erlbaum.

Mason, L., Benedek-Wood, E., & Valasa, L. (2010). Teaching low-achieving students to self-regulate: Persuasive quick writes responses. *Journal of Adolescent and Adult Literacy, 53*(4), 303–312.

Mass, W. (2005). *Twice upon a time: Rapunzel: The one with all the hair.* Illus. by W. Mass. New York: Scholastic.

Matson, S. (2012) Read, flip, write. *Journal of Adolescent and Adult Literacy, 56*(2), 109.

May, F. (2001). *Unraveling the seven myths of reading: Assessment and intervention practices for counteracting their effects.* Boston: Allyn & Bacon.

McBratney, S. (1994). *Guess how much I love you*. New York: Scholastic.

McCarthy, P. (2008). Using sound boxes systematically to develop phonemic awareness. *The Reading Teacher, 62*(4), 346–349.

McCormick, S. (2010). *Instructing students who have literacy problems* (6th ed.). Upper Saddle River, NJ: Prentice Hall.

McGee, L., & Schickedanz, J. (2007). Repeated interactive read-alouds in preschool and kindergarten. *The Reading Teacher, 60*(8), 742–751.

McKenna, M., & Cournoyer-Picard, M. (2006). Revisiting the role of miscue analysis in effective teaching. *The Reading Teacher, 60*(4), 378–380.

McKenna, M. C., & Kear, D. J. (1990). Measuring attitude toward reading: A new tool for teachers. *The Reading Teacher, 43*, 626–639.

McKeown, M. G., & Beck, I. (2004). Direct and rich vocabulary instruction. In J. F. Baumann & E. J. Kame'enui (Eds.), *Vocabulary instruction,* pp. 13–27. New York: Guilford.

McLaughlin, M. (2012). Reading comprehension: What every teacher needs to know. *The Reading Teacher, 65*(7), 432–440.

McLaughlin, M., & DeVoogd, G. (2004). Critical literacy as comprehension: Expanding reader response. *Journal of Adolescent & Adult Literacy, 48*(1), 52–62.

McTigue, E., Thornton, E., & Wiese, P. (2013). Authentication projects for historical fiction: Do you believe it? *The Reading Teacher, 66*(6), 495–505.

McTigue, R. M., & Flowers, A. (2011). Science visual literacy: Learners' perceptions and knowledge of diagrams. *The Reading Teacher, 64*(8), 578–589.

Medcalf, N., Bessette, K., & Gibbs, D. (2009). Everyone wins: A school–higher education partnership for reading improvement. In J. C. Richards & C. A. Lassonde (Eds.), *Literacy tutoring that works,* pp. 96–107. Newark, DE: IRA.

Medearis, M., & Medearis, A. (2005). *Daisy and the Doll.* Illus. by L. Johnson. Lebanon, NH: University Press of New England.

Mesmer, E., & Mesmer, H. A. (2009). Response to intervention (RTI): What teachers of reading need to know. *The Reading Teacher, 62*(4), 280–290.

Meyer, B., Wijekumar, K., Middlemiss, W., Highly, K., et al. (2010). Web-based tutoring of the structure strategy with or without elaborated feedback or choice for fifth- and seventh-grade readers. *Reading Research Quarterly, 45*(1), 62–92.

Meyer, K. W. (2010). A collaborative approach to reading workshop in middle years. *The Reading Teacher, 63*(6), 501–507.

Michigan Department of Education (2002). What research says about parent involvement in children's education. Retrieved from www.michigan.gov/documents/final_parent_involvement_fact_sheet_14732_7.pdf

Micucci, C. (2003). *The life and times of the ant*. Boston: Houghton Mifflin.

Miller, W. (1988). *Reading teacher's complete diagnosis and correction manual*. New York: Center for Applied Research in Education.

Mills, K. (2009). Floating on a sea of talk: Reading comprehension through speaking and listening. *The Reading Teacher, 63*(4), 325–329.

Mist, R. (2008). *Mercury and Venus: Become a space explorer*. Laguna Hills, CA: QEB Publishing.

Moats, L. (1995). *Spelling, development, disability, and instruction*. Baltimore: York Press.

Mohr, K. A. J. (2003). Children's choices: A comparison of book preferences between Hispanic and non-Hispanic first-graders. *Reading Psychology 24*(2), 163–176.

Mokhtari, K., Hutchinson, A., & Edwards, P. (2010). Organizing instruction for struggling readers in tutorial settings. *The Reading Teacher, 64*(4), 287–290.

Mol, S. E., & Bus, A. G. (2011). To read or not to read: A meta-analysis of print exposure from infancy to early adulthood. *Psychological Bulletin 137*(2), 261–296.

Mol, S. E., Bus, A. G., DeJong, M. T., & Smeets, D. J. H., (2008). Added value of dialogic parent-child book readings: A meta-analysis. *Early Education and Development 19*(1), 7–16.

Molfese, V. J., Modglin, A., & Molfese, D. L. (2003). The role of environment in the development of reading skills. A longitudinal study of preschool and school-age measures. *Journal of Learning Disabilities, 36*, 59–67.

Montelong, J., Herter, R. J., Ansaldo, R., & Hatter, N. (2010). A lesson cycle for teaching expository reading and writing. *Journal of Adolescent and Adult Literacy, 53*(8), 656–666.

Moore, D. W., & Moore, S. A. (1986). Possible sentences. In E. K. Dishner, T. W. Bean, J. E. Readence, & D. W. Moore (Eds.), *Reading in the content areas,* pp. 174–178. Dubuque, IA: Kendall Hunt.

Moore, D., & Hinchman, K. (2006). *Teaching adolescents who struggle with reading: Practical strategies*. Boston: Pearson.

Moore, R., & Aspegren, C. (2001). Reflective conversations between two learners: Retrospective miscue analysis. *Journal of Adolescent & Adult Literacy, 44*(6), 492–504.

Moore-Hart, M. (2005). A writers' camp in action: A community of readers and writers. *The Reading Teacher, 59*(4), 326–338.

Morgan, H., & York, K. (2009). Examining multiple perspectives with creative think-alouds. *The Reading Teacher, 63*(4), 307–311.

Morgan, S. (2005). *Penguins*. Laguna Hills, CA: QEB Publishing.

Morgan, S. (2005). *Snakes*. Laguna Hills, CA: QEB Publishing.

Morgan, S. (2006). *Owls*. Laguna Hills, CA: QEB Publishing.

Morris, D. (1999). *The Howard Street Tutoring manual: Teaching at-risk readers in the primary grades*. New York: Guilford Press.

Morris, D., & Nelson, L. (1992). Supported oral reading with low-achieving second graders. *Reading Research and Instruction, 31,* 49–63.

Morrow, L. M., Kuhn, M., & Schwanenflugel, P. J. (2006). The family fluency program. *The Reading Teacher, 60*(4), 322–333.

Mosenthal, J. (1994). Text structure. In A. Purves, L. Papa, & J. Jordan (Eds.), *Encyclopedia of English studies and languages arts,* pp. 1201–1203. New York: Scholastic.

Moss, L. (1995). *Zin! Zin! Zin! A violin*. New York: Scholastic.

Moustafa, M., & Maldonado-Colon, E. (1999). Whole-to-parts phonics instruction: Building on what children know to help them know more. *The Reading Teacher, 52*(5), 448–456.

Mouza, C. (2005). Using technology to enhance early childhood learning: The 100 days of school project. *Educational Research & Evaluation, 11*(6), 513–528.

Muhammad, G. (2012). Creating spaces for black adolescent girls to "Write it out!" *Journal of Adolescent and Adult Literacy, 56*(3), 203–211.

Mui, S., & Anderson, J. (2008). At home with the Johars: Another look at family literacy. *The Reading Teacher, 67*(3), 234–243.

Murphy, S. (1995). Revisioning reading assessment: Remembering to learn from the legacy of reading tests. *Clearing House, 68*(4), 235–239.

Nagy, W. E., & Herman, P. A. (1987). Breadth and depth of vocabulary knowledge: Implications for acquisition and instruction. In M. G. McKeown & M. E. Curtis (Eds.), *The nature of vocabulary acquisition,* pp. 19–35. Hillsdale, NJ: Lawrence Erlbaum.

Nagy, W. E., & Scott, J. A. (2004). Vocabulary processes. In R. Ruddell & N. Unrau (Eds.), *Theoretical models and processes of reading* (5th ed.), pp. 574–593. Newark, DE: IRA.

Nagy, W., & Scott, J. (2013). Vocabulary processes. In D. Alvermann, N. Unrau, & R. Ruddell (Eds.), *Theoretical models and processes of reading* (pp. 458–475). Newark, DE: International Reading Association.

National Assessment Governing Board (2008). *Reading Framework for the 2009 National Assessment of Educational Progress*. Washington, DC: Government Printing Office. Retrieved from www.nagb.org/publications/frameworks/reading09.pdf.

National Center for Education Statistics (2005). Fast facts. Retrieved from http://nces.ed.gov/fastfacts/

National Center for Education Statistics (2010). Fast facts. Retrieved from http://nces.ed.gov/fastfacts/

National Center for Education Statistics (2012, September). *The nation's report card: Writing*. Retrieved from http://nces.ed.gov/nationsreportcard/pubs/main2011/2012470.aspx

National Center for Education Statistics (2013). *The condition of education 2013: English learners*. Retrieved from http://nces.ed.gov/programs/coe/indicator_cgf.asp.

National Clearinghouse for English Language Acquisition (2010). Standards and assessments. Retrieved from www.ncela.gwu.edu/assessment

National Council of Teachers of English. (1996). Standards for the English language arts. Retrieved from www.ncte.org/standards

National Council of Teachers of English (2005). *Position statement on multimodal literacies.* Retrieved from www.ncte.org/positions/statements/multimodalliteracies.

National Council of Teachers of English (2006). Taking a look at NAEP reading results. *The Council Chronicle, 15*(3), 1.

National Early Literacy Panel (2008). *Developing Early Literacy: Report of the National Early Literacy Panel.* Online: http://lincs.ed.gov/publications/pdf/NELPReport09.pdf.

National Governors Association Center for Best Practices (NGACBP) & Council of Chief State School Officers (CCSSO). (2010). Common Core State Standards for English language arts & literacy in history/social studies, science, and technical subjects. Washington, DC: NGACBP, CCSSO.

National Institute for Literacy (2006). *What is scientifically based research?* Jessup, MD: U.S. GPO.

National Institute of Child Health and Human Development (2000). *Report of the National Reading Panel: Teaching children to read.* Washington, DC: National Institute for Literacy.

National Reading Panel (2000). *Report of the subgroups.* Washington, DC: National Institute of Child Health and Human Development. Retrieved from www.nationalreadingpanel.org/Publications/subgroups.htm

Ness, M. (2009). Laughing through rereadings: Using joke books to build fluency. *The Reading Teacher, 62*(8), 691–694.

Neuman, S., & Roskos, K. (2012). More than teachable moments: Enhancing oral vocabulary instruction in your class. *The Reading Teacher, 66*(6), 63–68.

Newlands, M. (2011). Intentional spelling: Seven steps to eliminate guessing. *The Reading Teacher, 64*(7), 531–534.

Newman, T., & Bizarri, S. (2012). Friday letters: Connecting students, teachers, and families through writing. *The Reading Teacher, 65*(4), 275–280.

NGA & CCSSO (2010). Common Core State Standards for English Language Arts & Literacy in history/social studies, science, and technical subjects. *Common Core State Standards Initiative: Preparing America's Students for College & Career.* Online: www.corestandards.org.

Nieto, S. (1996). *Affirming diversity: The sociopolitical context for multicultural education* (2nd ed.). White Plains, NY: Longman.

Nilsen, A. P., & Nilsen, D. L. F. (2004). *Vocabulary Plus K–8.* New York: Pearson.

No Child Left Behind Act of 2001. Summary and overview. Retrieved from www.ed.gov/nclb/overview/Intro/Index.html

Noble, T. H. (1992). *The day Jimmy's boa ate the wash.* Illus. S. Kellogg. New York: Puffin.

North Central Association for Accreditation and School Improvement (2010, February). Characteristics of good readers. Retrieved from wwww.ncacasi.org.

Northwest Regional Educational Laboratory (2001). *6 + 1 Trait(r) rubrics (aka scoring guides).* Retrieved from http://educationnorthwest.org/resource/464

Nunnery, J., Ross, S., Smith, L., Slavin, R., Hunter, P., & Stubbs, J. (1999). *An assessment of Success for All program component configuration effects on the reading achievement of at-risk first grade students.* Baltimore: Center for Research on the Education of Students Placed at Risk, Johns Hopkins University.

O'Connor, R. E., Bell, K. M., Harty, K. R., Larkin, L. K., Sackor, S. M., & Zigmond, N. (2002). Teaching reading to poor readers in the intermediate grades: A comparison of text difficulty. *Journal of Educational Psychology, 94*(3), 474–485.

O'Connor, R. E., White, A., & Swanson, H. (2007). Repeated reading versus continuous reading: Influences on reading fluency and comprehension. *Exceptional Children, 74*(1), 31–46.

O'Loughlin, J., & Haynes, J. (2004). Organizing and assessing in the content area classrooms. *Everything ESL.* Retrieved from www.everythingesl.net

O'Neill, M. (1961). *Hailstones and halibut bones.* New York: John Walker.

Oakhill, J., & Patel, S. (1991). Can imagery training help children who have comprehension problems? *Journal of Research in Reading, 14,* 106–115.

Oakley, G., & Jay, J. (2010). "Making time" for reading: Factors that influence the success of multimedia reading in the home. *The Reading Teacher, 62*(3), 246–255.

Ogle, D. (1986). K-W-L: A teaching model that develops active reading of expository text. *The Reading Teacher, 39*(7), 564–570.

Ogle, D., & Correa-Kovtun, A. (2010). Supporting English-language learners and struggling readers in content literacy with the "Partner Reading and Content, Too" routine. *The Reading Teacher, 63*(7), 532–543.

Oliver, K., Wilcox, B., & Eldredge, J. L. (2000). Effect of difficulty levels on second-grade delayed readers using dyad reading. *Journal of Education Research, 94*(2), 113–120.

Olson, K. M. (2001). *Chinese immigrants 1850–1900.* Bloomington, IN: Capstone Press.

Olson, M., & Gee, T. (1991). Content reading instruction in the primary grades: Perceptions and strategies. *The Reading Teacher, 45,* 298–307.

Opie, I. (Ed.). (1996). *My very first Mother Goose.* Cambridge, MA: Candlewick Press.

Oster, L. (2001). Using the think-aloud for reading instruction. *The Reading Teacher, 55*(1), 64–70.

Otaiba, S., & Pappamihiel, N. E. (2005, July/August). Guidelines for using volunteer literacy tutors to support reading instruction for English language learners. *Teaching Exceptional Children, 37*(6), 6–11.

Oxford University Press (2013). *Concise Oxford English Dictionary* (12th ed.). Retrieved from http://www.oxforddictionaries.com/us.

Pacheo, M., & Goodwin, A. (2013). Putting two and two together: Middle school students' morphological problem-solving strategies for unknown words. *Journal of Adolescent and Adult Literacy, 56*(7), 541–553.

Padak, N., & Rasinski, T. (2008). *Fast start: Getting ready to read.* New York: Scholastic.

Paige, D. (2011). "That sounded good!" Using whole-class choral reading to improve fluency. *The Reading Teacher, 64*(6), 435–438.

Palmer, R., & Stewart, R. (1997). Nonfiction trade books in content area instruction: Realities and potential. *Journal of Adolescent & Adult Literacy, 40*(8), 630–642.

Pappas, T. (1991). *Math talk: Mathematical ideas in poems for two voices.* San Carlos, CA: Wide World Publishing/Tetra.

Paquette, K. R., Fello, S., & Renck-Jalongo, M. (2007). The talking drawings strategy: Using primary children's illustrations and oral language to improve comprehension of the expository text. *Early Childhood Education Journal, 35*(1), 65–70.

Park, L. S. (2001). *A single shard.* New York: Clarion Books.

Parks, R. (1999). *I am Rosa Parks.* Illus. by J. Haskins & W. Clay. New York: Puffin.

Parsons, S., & Ward, A. (2011). The case for authentic tasks in content literacy. *The Reading Teacher, 64*(6), 462–465.

Patent, D. H. (2002). *The Lewis and Clark trail: Then and now.* Photographs by W. Muno. New York: Dutton Children's Books.

Paterson, K. (1991). *Lyddie.* New York: Lodestar Books.

Patterson, E., Schaller, M., & Clemens, J. (2008). A closer look at interactive writing. *The Reading Teacher, 61*(6), 496–497.

Pearson, P. D., & Fielding, L. (1991). Comprehension instruction. In R. Barr, M. Kamil, P. Mosenthal, & P. D. Pearson (Eds.), *Handbook of reading research* (Vol. 2), pp. 815–860. New York: Longman.

Peck, R. (1998). *A long way from Chicago.* New York: Puffin.

Peck, R. (2000). *A year down yonder.* New York: Dial Books for Young Readers.

Peck, R. (2013). *The mouse with the question mark tail.* Illus. K. Murphy. New York: Dial Books for Young Readers.

Peebles, J. (2007). Incorporating movement with fluency instruction: A motivation for struggling readers. *The Reading Teacher, 60*(6), 578–581.

Perez-Canado, M. (2005). English and Spanish spelling: Are they really different? *The Reading Teacher, 58*(6), 522–530.

Piaget, J., & Inhelder, B. (1969). *The psychology of the child* (H. Weaver, Trans.). New York: Basic Books.

Pinnell, G. S. (1999). Word solving: Investigating the properties of words. In I. C. Fountas & G. S. Pinnell (Eds.), *Voices on word matters: Learning about phonics and spelling in the literacy classroom,* pp. 3–12. Portsmouth, NH: Heinemann.

Pinnell, G. S. (2006). Every child a reader: What one teacher can do. *The Reading Teacher, 60*(1), 78–83.

Pinnell, G. S., & Fountas, I. C. (2001). *Guiding readers and writers.* Portsmouth, NH: Heinemann.

Pinnell, G. S., & Fountas, I. C. (2007). *Continuum of literacy learning: Grades K–2.* Portsmouth, NH: Heinemann.

Piston, W. (1962). *Harmony* (3rd ed.). New York: W. W. Norton.

Polacco, P. (1987). *Meteor!* New York: Philomel Books.

Polacco, P. (2001). *Mr. Lincoln's Way.* New York: Philomel Books.

Polacco, P. (2002). *Luba and the Wren.* New York: Penguin.

Pollard-Durodola, S., Gonzalez, D., Simons, D., Davis, M., Simmons, M., & Nava-Walichowski, M. (2011/2012). Using knowledge networks to develop preschoolers content vocabulary. *The Reading Teacher, 65*(4), 265–274.

Powell, D., & Aram, R. (2008). Spelling in parts: A strategy for spelling and decoding polysyllabic words. *The Reading Teacher, 61*(70), 567–570.

Powers, J. (1988). *Henny Penny.* New York: Checkerboard Press.

Prelutsky, J. (1983). *Zoo doings: Animal poems.* New York: Trumpet Club Special Edition.

Prelutsky, J. (1984). *The new kid on the block.* New York: Greenwillow Books.

Prelutsky, J. (1990a). *Beneath a blue umbrella.* New York: Greenwillow Books.

Prelutsky, J. (1990b). *Something big has been here.* New York: Greenwillow Books.

Prelutsky, J. (1994). *A pizza the size of the sun.* New York: Greenwillow Books.

Prelutsky, J. (Ed.). (1999). *20th century children's poetry treasury.* New York: Alfred A. Knopf.

Puccelli, M., & Paez, M. (2007). Narrative and vocabulary development of bilingual children from kindergarten to first grade: Developmental changes and associations among English and Spanish skills. *Language, Speech and Hearing Services in Schools, 38,* 235–236.

RAND Reading Study Group (2002). *Reading for understanding: Toward an R & D program in reading comprehension.* Santa Monica, CA: RAND.

Rankin-Erickson, J., & Pressley, M. (2000). A survey of instructional practices of special education teachers nominated as effective teachers of literacy. *Learning Disabilities Research & Practice, 15*(4), 206–225.

Ransom, K., Santa, C. M., Williams, C., & Farstrup, A. (1999). *Using multiple methods of beginning reading instruction: A position statement of the International Reading Association.* Newark, DE: IRA.

Raphael, T. E. (1986). Teaching question–answer relationships. *The Reaching Teacher, 39*(7), 516–520.

Raphael, T. E., & Au, K. H. (2005). QAR: Enhancing comprehension and test taking across grades and content areas. *The Reading Teacher, 59*(3), 206–221.

Rasinski, T. V. (2000). Speed does matter in reading. *The Reading Teacher, 54*(2), 146–151.

Rasinski, T. V. (2003). *The fluent reader.* New York: Scholastic.

Rasinski, T. V. (2005a). *Word ladders.* New York: Scholastic.

Rasinski, T. V. (2005b). *Daily word ladders.* New York: Teaching Resources.

Rasinski, T. V. (2012). Why reading fluency should be hot! *The Reading Teacher, 65*(8), 516–522.

Rasinski, T. V., & Lenhart, L. (2007). Explorations of fluent readers. *Reading Today, 25*(3), 18.

Rasinski, T. V., & Padak, N. (2003). *Effective reading strategies: Teaching children who find reading difficult* (3rd ed.). Upper Saddle River, NJ: Prentice Hall.

Rasinski, T. V., & Padak, N. (2004). Beyond consensus— beyond balance: Toward a comprehensive literacy curriculum. *Reading and Writing Quarterly, 20,* 91–102.

Rasinski, T. V., & Padak, N. D. (2005). Fluency beyond the primary grades: Helping adolescent readers. *Voices from the Middle, 13,* 34–41.

Rasinski, T. V., & Padak, N. D. (2007). *Evidence-based instruction in reading: A professional development guide to comprehension.* Boston: Allyn & Bacon.

Rasinski, T. V., & Padak, N. D. (2008). Beyond stories. *The Reading Teacher, 61*(70), 582–584.

Rasinski, T. V., Padak, N., Linek, W., & Sturtevant, E. (1994). Effects of fluency development on urban second-grade readers. *Journal of Educational Research, 87*(3), 158–165.

Rasinski, T. V., Padak, N. D., Newton, R. M., & Newton, E. (2008). *Greek & Latin roots: Keys to building vocabulary.* Huntington Beach, CA: Shell Education.

Rasinski, T. V., Padak, N., & Newton, R. (2013). *Starting with prefixes and suffixes.* Huntington Beach, CA: Shell Education.

Read, S. (2005). First and second graders writing informational text. *The Reading Teacher, 59*(1), 36–44.

Read, S. (2010). A model for scaffolding writing instruction: IMSCI. *The Reading Teacher, 64*(1), 47–52.

Reading Recovery Council (2013). Reading Recovery and Common Core State Standards. Online: http://www.acpl.lib.in.us/children/recovery_titleab.html.

Reedy, D. (2011). Misconceptions about teaching reading: Is it only about phonics? *Education Review, 24*(2), 50–60.

Reutzel, D. R., & Cooter, R. (2011). *Strategies for reading assessment and instruction: Helping every child succeed* (4th ed.). Upper Saddle River, NJ: Merrill.

Reutzel, D. R., & Hollingsworth, P. (1993). Effects of fluency training on second graders' reading comprehension. *Journal of Educational Research, 86,* 325–331.

Rhodes, C. (2002). Mindful reading: Strategy training that facilitates transfer. *Journal of Adolescent and Adult Literacy, 45*(6), 498–513.

Richards, J. (2006). Question, connect, transform (QCT): A strategy to help middle school students engage critically with historical fiction. *Reading & Writing Quarterly, 22,* 193–198.

Richards, M. (2000). Be a good detective: Solve the case of oral reading fluency. *The Reading Teacher, 53*(7), 534–539.

Richardson, J., Morgan, R., & Fleener, C. (2011). *Reading to learn in the content areas* (8th ed.). Belmont, CA: Wadsworth.

Richek, M. A. (2005). Words are wonderful: Interactive, time-efficient strategies to teach meaning vocabulary. *The Reading Teacher, 58*(5), 414–423.

Richek, M. A., Caldwell, J. S., Jennings, J. H., & Lerner, J. W. (2006). *Reading problems: Assessment and teaching strategies* (5th ed.). Boston: Allyn & Bacon.

Riehle, M. A. M. (2002). *B is for bluegrass: A Kentucky alphabet book.* Chelsea, MI: Sleeping Bear Press.

Risko, V. J., & Walker-Dalhouse, D. (2009). Parents and teachers: Talking with or past one another—or not talking at all? *The Reading Teacher, 62*(5), 442–444.

Risko, V. J., & Walker-Dalhouse, D. (2010). Making the most of assessments to inform instruction. *The Reading Teacher, 63*(5), 420–422.

Rissman, L. M., Miller, D. H., & Torgesen, J. K. (2009). *Adolescent literacy walk-through for principals: A guide for instructional leaders.* Portsmouth, NH: RMC Research Corp. Center on Intervention.

Roessel, D., & Rampersad, A. (1994). *Poetry for young people: Langston Hughes.* New York: Scholastic.

Rose, D., Parks, M., Androes, K., & McMahon, S. (2000). Imagery-based learning: Improving elementary students' reading comprehension with drama techniques. *Journal of Educational Research, 94*(1), 55–64.

Rosenbloom, J., & Artell, M. (1999). *The little giant book of tongue twisters.* New York: Sterling.

Rosencrans, G. (1998). *The spelling book: Teaching children how to spell, not what to spell.* Newark, DE: IRA.

Rosing, N. (2006). *The world of the polar bear.* Photographs by N. Rosing. Richmond, ON: Firefly Books.

Roskos, K., & Neuman, S. (2012). Formative assessment: Simply, no additives. *The Reading Teacher, 65*(9), 534–538.

Rossell, C. (2004/2005). Teaching English through English. *Educational Leadership, 62*(4), 32–36.

Routman, R. (2002). *Reading essential: The specifics you need to teach reading well.* Portsmouth, NH: Heinemann.

Rowe, D., & Fain, J. G. (2013). The family backpack project: Responding to dual language texts through family journals. *Language Arts, 90*(6), 402–416.

Rubin, R., & Carlan, V. G. (2005). Using writing to understand bilingual children's literacy development. *The Reading Teacher, 58*(8), 728–732.

Ruddell, R. (1964). A study of cloze comprehension technique in relation to structurally controlled reading material. *Proceedings of the International Reading Association, 9,* 298–303.

Rylant, C. (1987). *Henry and Mudge in the green time.* New York: Trumpet Club.

Rymer, R., & Williams, C. (2000). "Wasn't that a spelling word?": Spelling instruction and young children's writing. *Language Arts, 77*(3), 241–249.

Saddler, B. (2005). Sentence combining: A sentence level writing intervention. *The Reading Teacher, 58*(5), 468–471.

Salley, C. (2006). *Epossumondas saves the day.* New York: HMH Books for Young Readers.

Samuels, S. J. (1979/1997). The method of repeated readings. *The Reading Teacher, 50*(5), 376–381.

Santoro, L. E., Chard, D., Howard, L., & Baker, S. (2008). Making the very most of classroom read-alouds to promote comprehension and vocabulary. *The Reading Teacher, 61*(5), 396–408.

Savage, H. (2001). *Sound it out: Phonics in a balanced reading program.* Boston: McGraw Hill.

SBAC (2011). Appendix B: Grade Level Tables for All Claims and Assessment Targets and Item Types. http://www.smarterbalanced.org/wordpress/wp-content/uploads/2011/12/ELA-Literacy-Content-Specifications.pdf

Scarella, R. (2003). *Accelerating academic English: A focus on English language learners.* Oakland, CA: Regents of University of California.

Schiefele, U. A., Krapp, A., & Winteler, A. (1992). Interest as a predictor of academic achievement: A meta-analysis of research. In K. A. Renniger, S. Hidi, & A. Krapp (Eds.), *In the role of interest and development* (pp. 183–211). Hillsdale, NJ: Erlbaum.

Schmidt, R., Rozendal, M., & Greenman, G. (2002). Reading instruction in the inclusion classroom. *Remedial and Special Education, 23*(3), 130–140.

Schneider, R. (1993). *That's not all!* Grand Haven, MI: School Zone.

Schreiber, A. (2009). *National Geographic readers: Penguins.* Washington, DC: National Geographic Society.

Schulman, M. B., & Payne, C. D. (2000). *Guided reading: Making it work. New York*: Scholastic.

Scieszka, J. (1995). *The true story of the three little pigs. Illus.* by L. Smith. New York: Puffin.

Sciezka, J. (2006). *Guys write for guys read: Boys favorite authors write about being boys.* New York: Viking Books.

Scillian, D. (2003). *S is for Sooner.* Illus. K. Radzinski. Ann Arbor, MI: Sleeping Bear Press.

SEDL (Southwest Educational Development Laboratory) (2006). Importance of family and community involvement continues to grow. *SEDL Letter, 28*(3). Retrieved from http://www.sedl.org/pubs/sedl-letter/v18n03/index.html

Serafini, F. (2011). Expanding perspectives for comprehending visual images in multimodal texts. *Journal of Adolescent and Adult Literacy 54*(5), 342–350.

Seuss, Dr. (1957). *The cat in the hat.* New York: Random House.

Seuss, Dr. (1960). *Green eggs and ham.* New York: Random House.

Seuss, Dr. (1975). *Oh, the thinks you can think.* New York: Random House Books for Young Readers.

Seuss, Dr. (1978). *I can read with my eyes shut.* New York: Random House Books for Young Readers.

Shamir, A., & Korat, O. (2006) How to select CD-ROM storybooks for young children: The teacher's role. *The Reading Teacher, 59*(6), 532–543.

Shanahan, T. (2012). *What is close reading?* Retrieved from http://www.shsnahanonliteracy.com/2012/06/what-is-close-reading.html.

Shanahan, T., & Shanahan, S. (1997). Character perspective charting: Helping children to develop a more complete conception of story. *The Reading Teacher, 50*(8), 668–677.

Shanker, J. L., & Ekwall, E. E. (2002). *Locating and correcting reading difficulties* (8th ed.). Upper Saddle River, NJ: Prentice Hall.

Shaughnessy, M. (2010). An interview with Dan Willingham: Reading comprehension. *EducationNews.org.* Retrieved from www.ednews.org/articles/an-interview-with-dan-willingham-reading-comprehension.html

Shaw, N. (1992). *Sheep out to eat.* New York: A Trumpet Club Special Edition.

Sheldon, S. (2002). Parents' social networks and beliefs as predictors of parent involvement. *The Elementary School Journal, 102*(4), 301–316.

Shenton, A., & Beautyman, W. (2012). The provision of topic choice as a motivational strategy. *Education Journal, 142,* 11–14.

Short, D., & Echevarria, J. (2004/2005). Teacher skills to support English language learners. *Educational Leadership, 62*(4), 8–13.

Shoulders, M. (2003). *M is for magnolia: A Mississippi alphabet book.* Chelsea, MI: Sleeping Bear Press.

Showers, P. (1961). *The listening walk.* New York: HarperTrophy.

Sidman, J. (2009). *Red sings from treetops: A year in colors.* Illus. P. Zagarenski. Boston: Houghton Mifflin Books for Children.

Siebert, D. (2001). *Mississippi.* New York: HarperCollins.

Silverstein, S. (1974). *Where the sidewalk ends.* New York: HarperCollins.

Silverstein, S. (1981). *A light in the attic.* New York: HarperCollins.

Simon, S. (1989). *Whales.* New York: Scholastic.

Simon, S. (1992). *Storms* (Reprint ed.). New York: HarperTrophy.

Simon, S. (2001). *Tornadoes.* New York: HarperTrophy.

Simon, S. (2002). *Hurricanes.* New York: HarperTrophy.

Sipe, L. (2001). Invention, convention, and intervention: Invented spelling and the teacher's role. *The Reading Teacher, 55*(3), 264–273.

Slavin, R. E., Madden, N. A., Dolan, L. J., Wasik, B. A., Rose, S. M., Smith, L. J., et al. (1996). Success for All: A summary of research. *Journal of Education for Students Placed at Risk, 1*(1), 41–76.

Smith, F. (1978). *Reading without nonsense.* New York: Teachers College Press.

Smith, F. (2005). *Reading without nonsense* (4th ed.). New York: Teachers College Press.

Smith, M., Walker, B., & Yellin, D. (2004). From phonological awareness to fluency in each lesson. *The Reading Teacher, 58*(3), 302–307.

Smith, N. B. (1965). *American reading instruction.* Newark, DE: IRA.

Snow, C., Burns, M., & Griffin, P. (Eds.). (1998). *Preventing reading difficulties in young children.* Washington, DC: National Academies Press.

Soares, L. B., & Wood, K. (2010). A critical literacy perspective for teaching and learning social studies. *The Reading Teacher, 63*(6), 486–494.

Sox, A., & Rubinstein-Avila, E. (2009, September). WebQuests for English-language learners: Essential elements for design. *Journal of Adolescent & Adult Literacy, 53*(1), 38–48.

Spence, L. (2009). Developing multiple literacies in a website project. *The Reading Teacher 62*(7), 542–597.

Spence, L. (2010). Generous reading: Seeing students through their writing. *The Reading Teacher, 63*(8), 634–642.

Spires, H., Hervey, L., Morris, G., & Stelpflug, C. (2012). Energizing project-based inquiry: Middle-grade students read, write, and create videos. *Journal of Adolescent and Adult Literacy, 55*(6), 483–494.

Staal, L. (2000). The story face: An adaptation of story mapping that incorporates visualization and discovery learning to enhance reading and writing. *The Reading Teacher, 54*(1), 26–31.

Stahl, K. D. (2011). Applying new visions of reading development in today's classroom. *The Reading Teacher, 65*(1), 52–56.

Stahl, S. (1998). Saying the "P" word: Nine guidelines for exemplary phonics instruction. In R. Allington (Ed.), *Teaching struggling readers* (pp. 208–216). Newark, DE: IRA.

Stahl, S., & Kuhn, M. (1995). Does whole language or instruction matched to learning styles help children learn to read? *School Psychology Review, 24*(3), 393–404.

Stanley, J. (1992). *Children of the Dust Bowl: The true story of the school at Weedpatch Camp.* New York: A Trumpet Club Special Edition.

Stanovich, K. E. (1991). Word recognition: Changing perspectives. In R. Barr, M. L. Kamil, P. Mosenthal, & P. D. Pearson (Eds.), *Handbook of reading research, Vol. 2,* pp. 418–452. Hillsdale, NJ: Erlbaum.

Staudt, D. H. (2009). Intensive word study and repeated reading improves reading skills for two students with learning disabilities. *The Reading Teacher, 63*(2), 142–151.

Steele, P. (1994). *I wonder why castles had moats and other questions about long ago.* New York: Kingfisher Books.

Stein, D. E. (2010). *Interrupting chicken.* Illus. D. E. Stein. New York: Candlewick.

Stephens, K. (2008). A quick guide to selecting great informational books for young children. *The Reading Teacher, 61*(6), 488–490.

Sterling-Honig, A. (2007). Oral language development. *Early Child Development and Care, 177*(6 & 7), 581–613.

Stevens-Crummel, S. (2012). *Sherlock Bones and the missing cheese.* Illus. D. Donohue. Seattle, WA: Two Lions.

Stirling, I. (1999). *Polar Bears.* Photographs by I. Stirling. Ann Arbor, MI: University of Michigan Press.

Strickland, D., Bodino, A., Buchan, K., Jones, K., Nelson, A., & Rosen, M. (2001). Teaching writing in a time of reform. *Elementary School Journal, 101,* 385–398.

Stricklin, K. (2011). Hand-on reciprocal teaching: A comprehension technique. *The Reading Teacher, 64*(8), 620–625.

Sturges, P. (1999). *The Little Red Hen makes a pizza.* New York: Puffin Books.

Swanson, P., & De La Paz, S. (1998). Teaching effective comprehension strategies to students. *Intervention in School & Clinic, 33*(4), 209–219.

Swartz, R. J., & Parks, S. (1994). *Infusing the teaching of critical and creative thinking into elementary instruction: A lesson design handbook.* Pacific Grove, CA: Critical Thinking Press & Software.

Sweeny, S. (2010). Writing for the instant messaging and text messaging generation: Using new literacies to support writing instruction. *Journal of Adolescent and Adult Literacy, 54*(2), 121–130.

Sylvester, R., & Greenidge, W. (2009). Digital storytelling: Extending the potential for struggling writers. *The Reading Teacher, 63*(4), 284–295.

Symons, S., & Pressley, M. (1993). Prior knowledge affects text search success and extraction of information. *Reading Research Quarterly, 28*(3), 250–259.

Taylor, B., Pressley, M., & Pearson, D. (2000). *Research-supported characteristics of teachers and schools that promote reading achievement.* Ann Arbor, MI: Center for the Improvement of Early Reading Achievement (CIERA).

Teachers of English to Speakers of Other Languages (2006). TESOL revises pre-K–12 English language proficiency standards. Retrieved from www.tesol.org/s_tesol/sec_document.asp?CID=1186 & DID=5349

Temple, C., Nathan, R., & Temple, C. (2012). *The beginnings of writing* (4th ed.). Upper Saddle River, NJ: Pearson.

Templeton, S., Bear, D., Johnston, F., & Invernizzi, M. (2011). *Words their way: Word study for phonics, vocabulary, and spelling instruction* (5th ed.). New York: Pearson.

Tempo, F. (1993). *Origami magic.* New York: Scholastic.

Terban, M. (1988). *Guppies in tuxedos.* New York: Clarion Books.

Terban, M. (2007). *Eight ate: A feast of homonym riddles.* New York: Scholastic.

Theroux, P. (2004). *Enhance learning.* Retrieved from http://members.shaw.ca/priscillatheroux/differentiating.html

Thoermer, A. & Williams, L. (2012). Using digital text to promote fluent readers. *The Reading Teacher, 65*(7), 441–445.

Thomas, J. (2012). Language play for infants: Man in the moon for male caregivers. *Australasian Public Libraries and Information Services, 25*(2), 71–75.

Tomlinson, C. A., & Jarvis, J. (2006). Teaching beyond the book. *Educational Leadership, 64*(1), 16–21.

Tompkins, G. (2002). *Language arts: Content and teaching strategies.* Upper Saddle River, NJ: Merrill.

Topping, K., & Ehly, S. (1998). *Peer assisted learning.* Mahwah, NJ: Lawrence Erlbaum.

Townsend, D. (2009). Building academic vocabulary in after-school settings: Games for growth with middle school English-language learners. *Journal of Adolescent and Adult Literacy, 53*(3), 242–251.

Trelease, J. (2013). *The read-aloud handbook.* New York: Penguin Books.

Tresselt, A. (1964). *The mitten.* Illus. by Yaroslava. New York: Lothrop, Lee & Shepard.

Truss, L. (2006). *Eats, shoots and leaves: Why, commas really do make a difference!* Illus. by B. Timmons. New York: Putnam.

Turbill, J. (2000). Developing a spelling conscience. *Language Arts, 77*(3), 209–217.

Turbill, J., Bean, W., & Fox, M. (2006). *Writing instruction K–6: Understanding process, purpose, audience.* New York: Richard C. Owen.

Turkle, B. (1976). *Deep in the forest.* New York: Dutton.

Twain, M. (1882). *The prince and the pauper.* Franklin, NC: Franklin Press.

U.S. Department of Education (2006). Building the Legacy: IDEA 2004. Retrieved from http://idea.ed.gov/explore/view/p/,root,dynamic,TopicalBrief,23.

U.S. Office of Education (1977). Assistance to states for education for handicapped children: Procedures for evaluating specific learning disabilities. *Federal Register, 42,* G1082–G1085.

Ulrich, G. (1995). *My tooth ith loothe: Funny poems to read instead of doing your homework.* South Holland, IL: A Yearling Book.

Valencia, S., Smith, A., Reece, A., Li, M., et al. (2010). Oral reading fluency assessment: Issues of construct, criterion, and consequential validity. *Reading Research Quarterly, 45*(3), 270–291.

Van Allen, R. (1976). *Language experiences in education.* Boston: Houghton Mifflin.

Van Allsburg, C. (1988). *Two bad ants.* Boston: Houghton Mifflin.

VanNess, A., Murnen, T., & Bertelsen, C. (2013). Let me tell you a secret: Kindergartners can write. *The Reading Teacher, 66*(7), 574–585.

Vardell, S. M., Hadaway, N. L., & Young, T. A. (2006). Matching books and readers: Selecting literature for English learners. *The Reading Teacher, 59*(8), 734–741.

Vaughn, S., Elbaum, J. S., & Hughes, M. T. (1998). Social outcomes for students with and without disabilities in inclusive classrooms. *Journal of Disabilities, 31*(5), 428–436.

Vaughn, S., et al. (2000). Fluency and comprehension interventions for third-grade students. *Remedial and Special Education, 21*(6), 325–335.

Vaughn, S., Mathes, P. G., Linan-Thompson, S., & Francis, D. (2005). Teaching English language learners at risk for reading disabilities to read: Putting research into practice. *Learning Disabilities Research & Practice, 20*(1), 58–67.

Vellutino, R. (1991). Introduction to three studies on reading acquisition: Convergent findings on theoretical foundations of code-oriented versus whole-language approaches to reading instruction. *Journal of Educational Psychology, 83*(4), 437–444.

Vygotsky, L. (1962). *Thought and language* (E. Hanfmann & G. Vaka, Eds. & Trans.). Cambridge, MA: MIT Press.

Vygotsky, L. (1978). *Mind in society: The development of higher psychological processes.* Cambridge, MA: Harvard University Press.

Wagner, K., & Racine, S. (2008). *Everything kids astronomy book.* Avon, MA: Adams Media.

Walker, B. (2004). *Diagnostic teaching of reading: Techniques for instruction and assessment* (5th ed.). Upper Saddle River, NJ: Prentice Hall.

Wall, H. (2008). Interactive writing beyond the primary grades. *The Reading Teacher, 62*(2), 149–152.

Wallace, B. (1988). *Beauty.* New York: A Minstrel Book.

Walton, R. (2011). *Once there was a bull . . . (frog): Adventures in compound words* (Rev. ed.). Layton, UT: Gibbs Smith Education.

Wasik, B. (1998). Using volunteers as reading tutors: Guidelines for successful practices. *The Reading Teacher, 51*(7), 562–571.

Wasik, B. (2006). Building vocabulary one word at a time. *Young Children, 61*, 70–78.

Wasik, B., & Iaunote-Campbell, C. (2012/2013). Developing vocabulary through purposeful, strategic conversations. *The Reading Teacher, 66*(4), 321–332.

Watkins, S. (1997). *Green snake ceremony.* San Francisco: Council Oak Books.

Watt, F. (1993). *Earthquakes and volcanoes.* New York: Scholastic.

Watts-Taffe, S., Laster, B., Broach, L., Marinak, B., Connor, C. M., & Walker-Dalhouse, D. (2012/2013). Differentiated instruction. *The Reading Teacher, 66*(4), 303 –314.

Weaver, C. (2002). *Reading process and practice* (3rd ed.). Portsmouth, NH: Heinemann.

Weber, R. (1991). Linguistic diversity: Reading in American society. In R. Barr, M. L. Kamil, P. B. Mosenthal, & P. D. Pearson (Eds.), *Handbook of reading research (Vol. 2)*, pp. 97–110. White Plains, NY: Longman.

Weinstein, S. (2002). The writing on the wall: Attending to students' self-motivated literacy. *English Education, 35*(1), 21–45.

Weitzman, I. (2006). *Jokelopedia: The biggest, best, silliest, dumbest joke book ever.* New York: Workman.

White, A. L., & Swanson, A. H. L. (2007). Intensive word study and repeated reading improves reading skills for two students with learning disabilities. *The Reading Teacher, 63*(2), 141–151.

White, E. B. (1952). *Charlotte's web.* Illus. G. Williams. New York: HarperCollins.

White, T. G., & Kim, J. S. (2008). Teacher and parent scaffolding of voluntary summer reading. *The Reading Teacher, 62*(2), 116–125.

Wiesner, D. (1988). *Freefall.* New York: Clarion Books.

Wiesner, D. (1991). *Tuesday.* New York: Clarion Books.

Wiesner, D. (1997). *Sector 7.* New York: Clarion Books.

Wiesner, D. (2001). *The three pigs.* New York: Clarion Books.

Wiesner, D. (2006). *Flotsam.* New York: Clarion Books.

Wilcox, B., & Monroe, E. (2011). Integrating writing and math. *The Reading Teacher, 64*(7), 521–529.

Wiles, D. (2005). *Freedom Summer.* Illus. J. Lagarigue. New York: Aladdin.

Wilfong, L. (2009). Textmasters: Bringing literature circles to textbook reading across the curriculum. *Journal of Adolescent and Adult Literacy, 53*(2), 164–171.

Wilkinson, T. (1994). *Bison for kids.* Minnetonka, MN: NorthWord.

Williams, B. (2004). *Albert's impossible toothache.* New York: Candlewick.

Williams, C., & Pilonieta, P. (2012). Using interactive writing instruction with kindergartners and first-grade English language learners. *Early Childhood Education Journal, 40*, 145–150.

Williams, K. T. (1997). *Expressive vocabulary test.* Circle Pines, MN: American Guidance Service.

Williams, L. (1986). *The little old lady who was not afraid of anything.* New York: HarperTrophy.

Williams, S. (1996). *I went walking.* Illus. J. Vivas. New York: HMH Books for Young Readers.

Winn, P., Graham, L., & Prock, L. (1993). A model of poor readers' text-based inferencing: Effects of explanatory feedback. *Reading Research Quarterly, 28*(1), 52–64.

Winter, P. (1976). *The bear and the fly.* New York: Crown.

Wixson, K., & Lipson, M. (2012). Perspectives on RTI: Relations between the CCSS and RTI in literacy and language. *The Reading Teacher, 65*(6), 387–391.

Wolf, M. K., Crossen, A. C., & Resnick, L. B. (2004). Classroom talk for rigorous reading comprehension and instruction. *Reading Psychology, 26*(1), 27–53.

Wolsey, T., Lapp, D., & Fisher, D. (2012). Students' and teachers' perceptions: An inquiry into academic writing. *Journal of Adolescent and Adult Literacy, 55*(8), 714–724.

Wood, C., Mustian, A., & Ya-yu, L. (2013). Effects of supplemental computer-assisted reciprocal peer tutoring on kindergarteners' phoneme segmentation fluency. *Education and treatment of children, 35*(1), 33–48.

Wood, J. (1990). *Caves: Facts and stories and activities.* New York Scholastic.

Wood-Ray, K. (2006). *Study driven: A framework for planning units of study in the writing workshop.* Portsmouth, NH: Heinemann.

Woodruff, E. (1991). *Show and tell.* New York: A Trumpet Club Special Edition.

Woodson, J. (2001). *The other side.* Illus. E. B. Lewis. New York: Putnam & Sons.

Wray, D., Medwell, J., Fox, R., & Poulson, L. (2000). The teaching of practices of effective teachers of literacy. *Educational Review, 52*(1), 75–85.

Yaden, D. B., Tam, A., Madrigal, P., Grassell, D., Massa, J., Altamirano, L. S., et al. (2000). Early literacy for inner-city children: The effects of reading and writing interventions in English and Spanish during the preschool years. *The Reading Teacher, 54*(2), 186–190.

Yellin, D., Blake, M., & DeVries, B. (2008). *Integrating the language arts* (4th ed.). Scottsdale, AZ: Holcomb Hathaway.

Yin (2001). *Coolies.* New York: Penguin Books for Young Readers.

Yoder, E., & Yoder, N. (2010). *One minute mysteries: 65 short mysteries you solve with math!* Washington, DC: Science, Naturally!

Yolen, J. (1992). *Encounter.* Illus. by D. Shannon. Orlando, FL: Voyager Books/Harcourt.

Yopp, H. K. (2005). A test for assessing phonemic awareness in young children. In S. J. Barrentine & S. M. Stokes (Eds.), *Reading assessment,* pp. 262–271. Newark, DE: IRA.

Yopp, H. K., & Yopp, R. H. (2000). Supporting phonemic awareness development in the classroom. *The Reading Teacher, 54*(2), 130–143.

Yopp, R. H., & Yopp, H. K. (2007). Ten important words plus: A strategy for building word knowledge. *The Reading Teacher, 61*(2), 157–160.

Young, C., & Rasinski, T. (2009). Implementing readers theatre as an approach to classroom fluency instruction. *The Reading Teacher, 63*(1), 4–13.

Youngs, S., & Serafini, F. (2011). Comprehension strategies for reading historical fiction picture books. *The Reading Teacher, 65*(2), 115–126.

Zawilinski, L. (2009). HOT blogging: A framework for blogging to promote higher order thinking. *The Reading Teacher, 62*(8), 650–661.

Zecker, L. B. (1999). Different texts, different emergent writing forms. *Language Arts, 76*(6), 483–490.

Zhang, C. (2013, March). Effects of instruction on ESL students' synthesis writing. *Journal of Second Language Writing, 22*(1), 51–67.

Zipke, M. (2008). Teaching metalinguistic awareness and reading comprehension with riddles. *The Reading Teacher, 62*(2), 128–137.

Zumbrum, S., & Krause, K. (2012). Conversations with leaders: Principles of effective writing instruction. *The Reading Teacher, 65*(7), 346–353.

author index

Acha, J., 172
Ada, A., 322
Adams, M., 5, 96
Adler, D., 32, 222, 242
Afflerbach., P., 27, 28, 175, 213
Ahlberg, J., 140
Alcott, L. M., 55
Alderman, G., 22, 25, 26, 331, 332, 355
Allington, R., 9, 21, 22, 24, 25, 26, 27, 30, 31, 34, 35, 46, 175, 208, 246, 261, 262, 264, 265, 268, 274, 277, 356, 357, 380
Allyn, P., 294
Alyousef, H. S., 12
Armbruster, B., 229
Ames, C., 25
Anders, P., 219
Anderson, L. H., 180
Anderson, N., 285, 286
Anderson, R., 3
Anthony, H., 248, 249
Applegate, A. J., 22, 23, 177, 186, 271, 488
Applegate, K., 178, 271
Applegate, M. D., 177, 186, 271, 488
Arlington, J., 238
Armstrong, T., 29, 30, 31, 147, 424
Ashby, J., 78
Asher, J., 163
Ashton-Warner, S., 162
Atwell, N., 301
August, D., 126, 147, 155, 218
Avi, 166

Bagert, B., 90, 136, 137, 278
Back, K., 175
Bailey-Beard, D., 48
Baines, L., 315
Banks, K., 154
Banyai, I., 136

Barksdale, M. A., 325
Barrett, J., 200, 299
Barry, A., 41
Baumann, J., 147, 159
Beall, P., 82, 87
Bear, D., 75, 79, 88, 100, 103, 105, 106, 107, 109, 111, 127, 128, 129, 133, 169, 288, 331, 332, 336, 337, 341, 360, 417, 503, 587
Beauchat, K. A., 150
Beck, I., 4, 5, 82, 148, 177, 185, 194, 201
Beckman-Anthony, A., 188
Behrman, E. H., 4
Bemelman, L., 103
Bennett, J., 83, 152, 154, 278, 315
Bennett-Hopkins, L., 315
Berger, G., 229
Biancarosa, G., 127
Bintz, W., 231, 322
Blachowicz, C., 147, 154, 157, 175, 176
Black, L., 82
Blevins, W., 39, 75, 76, 77, 105, 106, 127, 134, 198, 199, 342, 407
Bloodgood, J. W., 133, 141
Bluestein, A., 249
Blum, I., 204
Blume, J., 326
Boers, D., 376
Borgia, L., 285, 286, 299
Bos, C., 223
Bottner, B., 318
Bottomley, D., 66, 308, 310, 454, 455
Bouchereau-Bauer, E., 11
Brabham, E., 149, 156, 159
Branley, F., 231
Brett, J., 85, 136, 207, 267
Brewer, P., 276
Bridwell, N., 241
Bromley, K., 343

Brown, K., 180, 202
Brown, S., 178, 179, 188
Browning, C. R., 195
Broyles, N., 179
Brozo, W. G., 22, 24, 35, 354
Bruner, J., 3
Buchanan, J., 184
Buehner, C., 108
Bulion, L., 315
Bunting, E., 85
Burleigh, R., 314
Burns, P., 130

Cabell, S., 285, 286, 291
Cahill, M. A., 182, 183, 266, 269
Calkins, L., 44, 316
Calo, K., 266, 269, 277
Camilli, G., 100
Campbell-Ernst, L., 183
Canizares, S., 223
Carbo, M., 9, 28, 29, 200, 274
Carle, E., 326, 387, 388
Carlo, M., 151, 156
Carlstrom, N., 272, 335
Carney, E., 300
Carrell, R. L., 26
Cartwright, K., 356
Cauley, L., 6
Cavanaugh, T., 76, 78
Cecil, N., 78, 80, 110, 270, 318, 437, 459, 476, 596
Celenza, A., 206
Center for Public Education, 9
Centers for Disease Control and Prevention, 370, 371
Cerullo, M., 223, 228, 244
Cervetti, G., 4
Chaffin, J., 131
Chall, J., 5, 127
Chambers, B., 356
Chandler-Olcott, K., 17

Childress, K., 148
Church, C. J. 82
Ciardiello, A., 186, 251
Clarke, L., 202
Clay, M., 28, 30, 46, 51, 123, 190, 291, 356, 357, 428
Cleary, B., 154
Coffey, H., 4, 5
Cohen, C. L., 108
Coiro, J., 16, 17, 255
Cole, J., 84
Container Recycling Institute, 296, 297
Cooper, J., 58, 147, 181, 205, 438, 439, 440, 441, 442
Cooter, R. B., 24, 25, 30, 186
Correia, M. P., 213
Coulman, V., 108
Couric, K., 181
Cudd, E., 317
Cummins, J., 9, 285
Cummins, S., 298
Cunningham, J., 76, 79, 85
Cunningham, P., 6, 100, 103, 105, 106, 107, 108, 109, 118, 125, 126, 288, 402
Curtis, C. P., 161, 162, 178

Dahl, M., 276
Dahl, R., 178
Dale, E., 157
Daly, N., 183
Danziger, P., 56, 185
Darling-Hammond, L., 22, 355
Davey, B., 250
Dawson, N., 86
Day, A., 302
Deeney, T., 260, 261, 262, 268, 269
DeFauw, D., 287, 299, 304
DeFord, D., 12, 13, 421
Deforest, J., 416
DeGross, M., 154
DeKonty-Applegate, M., 177, 186, 260, 268
Demi, 162, 318
dePaola, T., 150, 165, 184, 200, 231
Department of Environmental Conservation, 297
Deuker, C., 365
Defelice, C., 365
DiCamillo, K., 154
Dickinson, D. K., 148
Dillon, L., 108
Dix, S., 302
Dolch, E., 125, 403, 578
Dombey, H., 100, 103

Donavan, C., 299
Doty, D., 179, 208
Dowhower, S., 179
Doyle, A., 175, 370, 375, 379
Dozier, C., 24, 27
Drew, S. V., 16
Drucker, M. J., 11, 12
Duke, N., 212, 213, 324
Duffy-Hester, A., 179
Dunn, R., 158
Dworin, J., 285, 301

Earle, A., 300
Eboch, M. M., 314
Echevarria, J., 11
Edmunds, K. M., 22, 24, 25
Edwards, P. D., 150, 154
Ehren, B., 353
Ehri, L., 25, 79
Elbaum, B., 356
Elkonin, D., 88
Elliot, R., 276
Engelbreit, M., 83
Environmental Media Association, 297
Erskine, K., 181

Falwell, C., 154
Farndon, J., 250
Fenton, M. B., 300
Ferreiro, E., 293
Ferroli, L., 332
Fezell, G., 149, 151, 161
Fiderer, A., 59
Finn, C. E., 31
Fisher, D., 175, 176, 177, 178, 185, 186, 228, 236, 298
Fitzgerald, J., 9
Flanigan, K., 148, 152, 177
Fleischman, P., 280
Fleming, D., 208
Floca, B., 328
Flood, J., 177, 268
Florian, D., 84, 280
Flynt, E., 151, 186, 194, 236
Fordham, N., 321
Foresman, S., 225, 226, 227
Fountas, I. C., 27, 28, 30, 32, 33, 35, 100, 105, 134, 135, 182, 183, 194, 262, 267, 288, 291, 310, 316, 337, 357, 394–395, 417, 486
Fox, D., 82
Fox, M., 118
Frasier, D., 154, 155
Fresch, M., 332, 341
Fry, E., 33, 125, 126, 404, 425–426

Frye, E., 292, 319

Gambrell, L., 24, 25, 26
Garan, E. M., 189
Gardner, H., 29
Gates, L., 105, 108
Gentry, J., 293, 332, 342
George, W., 242, 243
Giannetti, C., 378
Gibbons, G., 231, 237, 238, 298, 300
Gill, S., 225
Gillet, J., 55, 191, 193
Gilpin, R., 239
Gipe, J., 219, 437, 596
Glazer, T., 82
Glick, S., 195
Goldish, M., 135
Goldstein, B. A., 77
Goodman, K., 6, 12, 48, 190
Goodman, Y., 6, 46, 48, 51, 190
Goodwin, A., 149, 152, 175
Graham, S., 285, 286, 301
Graves, M. F., 149, 151, 155, 301
Gravett, E., 154, 155
Gregory, A., 182, 183, 203, 213
Griffith, L. W., 268
Grout, D. J., 146
Gross, E. B., 195
Guarino, D., 76
Guccione, L., 176
Gunning, T., 125
Guthrie, J. T., 25
Gwynne, F., 154

Hadaway, N., 82, 86
Hall, E., 28
Hall, K., 116
Hal Leonard Corp., 82
Handsfield, L., 304, 305
Hanel, E. C., 369, 370, 381
Hannus, M., 215
Hanf, M., 242
Hansen, J., 301
Harness, C., 314, 315
Harper, J., 314
Harris, A., 39, 131, 285
Harris, K., 286
Harris, T., 51, 261
Harrison, D., 315
Hart, B., 148
Harvey, S., 175, 186, 190, 215
Harvey, T., 150
Harwood, J., 277
Hasbrouck, J. E., 262, 263
Haskins, J., 279, 280
Heald-Taylor, B., 331, 337, 417

Heath, S. B., 126
Heilmann, J., 147
Heller, R., 150, 154
Helman, L.A., 44, 77, 105, 106, 126, 337
Henk, W., 66, 452, 454, 455
Henkes, K., 177, 179, 298
Henry, L., 254
Hesse, K., 54, 266, 267, 273
Hessell, J., 274
Heubach, K., 242
Hiebert, E., 32, 103, 108
Hill, L., 86
Hindes, M., 225
Ho, B., 370, 371
Holdaway, D., 6, 162
Hollenbeck, A., 175
Holt, K., 184, 265
Houge, T., 356, 359, 365
Hughes, C., 238
Hughes, J., 300
Hughes, M., 331, 338, 341
Hurley, S. R., 63
Hurst, C., 179

Illingworth, M., 240
Imperato, F., 377, 379
International Reading Association, 9, 15, 16, 21, 40, 75, 78, 79, 100, 107, 113, 125, 126, 193, 353, 384
Invernizzi, M., 331, 337, 356
Iorio, N., 300
IRA/NAEYC, 40, 193, 386
Ivey, G., 100, 175

Jackman, H., 82
Jacobs, F., 127
Jacobson, J., 189
Janeczko, P., 315
Jensen, D., 371, 372
Jeunesse, G., 138
Johns, J., 387, 390
Johnson, F., 185, 186, 339
Johnson-Higgins, J., 189
Johnston, F., 337, 356, 363, 418
Johnston, P., 23, 24, 34, 35
Johnston, R., 104
Jones, C., 299
Jongsma, K., 81, 190
Joosse, B., 281
Juel, C., 147, 148

Kamil, M. L., 189
Kara-Soteriou, J., 292
Karchmer, R., 254, 255

Karchmer-Klein, R., 16, 217
Kaufman, M., 5
Keating, F., 260
Keehn, S., 177
Keep America Beautiful, 297
Kelley, M., 24
Kerr, J., 195
Kesler, T., 86, 294
Khanduri, K., 238
Kieffer, M. J., 125, 128
Kiger, N., 58, 181, 438, 439, 440, 441, 442
Kindervater, T., 371, 377, 379
Kinerk, R., 85
King-Smith, D., 33
Kinney, A., 287
Kinniburgh, L., 248, 249
Kipling, R., 49, 50
Kirk, D., 85
Kletzien, S., 219
Koskinen, P., 274
Krashen, S., 9, 11, 155
Krinitz, E. N., 195
Ksypka, H., 83
Kucan, L., 147, 148, 149, 151, 152, 156, 160, 177, 185
Kuhlman, N., 63
Kuhn, M., 29, 371

L'Engle, M., 178
Labadie, M., 4, 187
LaBerge, D., 264
Lacina, J., 324, 325
Lamoreaux, L., 162
Lane, H. S., 79
Langeland, D., 252
Lansky, B., 84, 87, 90, 100, 115, 116, 278
Lapp, D., 177, 185, 186, 198, 265, 295, 298, 489
Larkin, R. B., 279
Lauber, P., 224, 228
Leal, D., 342
Lehr, F., 151
Lenhart, A., 300
Lenski, S. D., 63, 64, 355
Lepthien, E., 239
Leu, D. J., 16
Levenson, G. 86
Lewin, L., 186
Lewis, J. P., 84
Lewis, M., 166
Lewis, P., 278
Lewison, M., 4
Lies, B., 300
Lindeen, C., 294

Lipson, M., 353, 354, 355
Lithgow, J., 364
Lloyd, C., 4, 5
Lobel, A., 278
London, J., 390
Los Angeles County Office of Education, 46, 427
Low, A., 200

Macaruso, P., 119
MacDonald, M., 180, 267, 373
MacLachlan, P., 185, 199
MacLulich, C., 223
Maestro, G., 154
Malock, B., 212, 213
Manning, M., 9, 179
Manyak, P. C., 151, 155
Marcell, B., 260, 261, 262, 266, 268, 269, 276, 278
Marinak, B., 213, 220
Marino-Weisman, D., 230
Markle, S., 223
Marsalis, W., 315
Martens, P., 190
Martin, B., 115, 299
Marzano, R., 151
Maslow, A., 4
Mason, L., 150, 284, 292, 311
Mass, W., 185
Matson, S., 312
May, F., 181
McBratney, S., 141
McCarthy, P., 88
McCormick, S., 3, 234
McGee, L., 196
McGovern, A., 364
McKissack, P., 208
McKenna, M., 66, 124
McKeown, M., 177, 185, 227
McLaughlin, M., 175, 180, 187, 190, 236, 254
McTigue, E., 213, 215, 238
Medcalf, N., 356
Medearis, M., 239
Mesmer, E., 15, 353
Meyer, B., 253, 356
Michigan Department of Education, 369
Michigan Department of Treasury, 296, 297
Micucci, C., 238
Miller, W., 41
Mills, K., 185, 230
Mist, R., 217
Moats, L., 103
Mohr, K. A. J., 213

Mokhtari, K., 39
Mol, S. E., 369, 370, 379, 380
Molfese, V. J., 125
Montelong, J., 246
Moore, D., 260, 279
Moore, R., 190
Moore-Hart, M., 303, 321
Morgan, H., 4
Morgan, S., 247, 257
Morris, D., 277, 357
Morrow, L. M., 371
Mosenthal, J., 242
Moss, L., 85, 281
Moustafa, M., 103
Mouza, C., 17
Muhammad, G., 287
Mui, S., 369
Murphy, S., 44

Nagy, W., 149, 150, 177
National Assessment Governing Board, 213
National Association for the Education of Young Children, 75
National Center for Education Statistics, 9, 13, 26, 285, 286
National Clearinghouse for English Language Acquisition, 43
National Council of Teachers of English, 300, 384
National Early Literacy Panel, 375
National Geographic, 277, 380
National Governors Association Center for Best Practices, 14, 16, 31, 33, 34, 58, 60, 80, 107, 109 128, 147, 149, 175, 176, 177, 178, 183, 193, 214, 216, 221, 233, 237, 246, 268, 269, 285, 293, 294, 298, 300, 322, 323, 338, 357
National Institute for Literacy, 14
National Institute of Child Health and Human Development, 13
National Reading Panel, 260
NEA Today, 179
Nelson, M., 86
Nesbitt, K., 83, 388
Ness, M., 276
Neufeld, P., 221
Neuman, S., 151
Newlands, M., 331, 332, 337, 345
Newman, T., 369, 370, 371, 374
Nieto, S., 186
Nilsen, A. P., 126
Nipp, S., 87
Noble, T. H., 177, 299

Northwest Regional Education Library, 306, 490, 490, 491, 602
Novick, M., 154
Numeroff, L., 364
Nunnery, J., 357

O'Connor, R. E., 25, 268
O'Loughlin, J., 43
O'Neill, M., 278
Oakhill, J., 219
Oakley, G., 379, 380
Ogle, D., 230, 246
Oklahoma State Department of Education, 435
Oliver, K., 277
Olson, M., 229, 238
Opie, I., 87
Oster, L., 179, 199
Otaiba, S., 9, 10, 356, 379
Oxford University Press, 147

Pacheo, M., 128, 148, 149, 152
Padak, N., 166, 177, 377
Paige, D., 266, 269, 276, 278
Palmer, R., 229
Pappas, T., 280
Paquette, K., 233
Parish, P., 154
Park, L., 185
Parks, R., 175, 179, 239
Parsons, S., 24, 25, 27, 35
Patent, D. H., 215
Paterson, K., 206
Patterson, E., 24
Patz, N., 86
Paulsen, G., 164, 326, 392
Pearson, P., 202
Peck, R., 161, 178
Peebles, J., 281
Perez-Canado, M., 106, 293, 338
Piaget, J., 3, 107
Pinkney, A. D., 314
Pinkney, J., 86, 389
Pinkney, M., 364
Pinnell, G., 123, 133, 182, 183, 286, 331, 337, 394–395, 417, 486
Piston, W., 145
Polacco, P., 195, 205
Pollard-Durodola, S., 149
Powell, D., 347
Powers, J., 85
Prelutsky, J., 83, 84, 150, 278, 280
Profita, C., 297
Puccelli, M., 147, 156

RAND Reading Study Group, 127, 212

Rankin-Erickson, J., 23
Ransom, K., 76
Raphael, T., 248, 253
Rappaport, D., 86
Rasinski, T., 7, 119, 125, 126, 129, 131, 132, 133, 150, 151, 166, 177, 260, 261, 262, 266, 268, 269, 270, 275, 276, 277, 278, 371, 376, 377, 406
Read, S., 286
Reading Recovery Council, 357
Reedy, D., 103
Reutzel, D. R., 5, 105, 274
Rhodes, C., 175
Richards, J., 186, 206
Richards, M., 266
Richardson, J., 218, 219, 229, 253
Richek, M., 147, 170, 189, 218
Riehle, M. A. M., 323
Risko, V. J., 39, 370
Rissman, L. M., 354
Roessel, D., 278
Root, B., 67
Rosa-Mendoza, G., 390
Rose, D., 175, 179
Rosenbloom, J., 113, 277
Rosencrans, G., 331, 332
Rosing, N., 237, 238
Roskos, K., 39, 40, 46
Rossell, C., 9
Routman, R., 5, 6
Rowe, D., 375, 379, 380
Rowling, J. K., 326
Rubin, R., 285, 292, 293
Rubin, S. G., 195
Ruddell, R., 55
Rylant, C., 276, 392
Rymer, R., 337

Sachar, L., 326, 392
Saddler, M., 324
Salley, C., 183, 299
Samuels, S. J., 277
Santoro, L. E., 179, 181, 182, 238, 239
Sanders, N., 86
Savage, H., 6
SBAC, 40, 355
Scarella, R., 294
Schiefele, U. A., 213
Schmidt, R., 23
Schneider, R., 116
Schotter, R., 154
Schulman, M., 53
Scieszka, J., 185, 299
Scillian, D., 298
Serafini, F., 187, 208, 589

Seuss, Dr., 6, 85, 114
Shamir, A., 209, 593
Shanahan, T., 181, 206
Shanker, J., 48, 125, 130
Shaughnessy, M., 26
Shaw, C., 248, 249, 369, 370, 381
Shaw, N., 115, 567
Sheldon, S., 369, 371
Shenton, A., 22, 24
Shepard, L., 131
Short, D., 9
Shoulders, M., 323
Showers, P., 163
Sidman, J., 86, 177, 315
Siebert, D., 86
Silvaroli, N., 130
Silverstein, S., 278
Simon, S., 3, 222, 231
Sipe, L., 332
Slavin, R., 357
Smedley, M., 296, 297
Smith, F., 77, 123
Smith, M., 100, 115
Snow, C., 149
Soares, L. B., 186, 231
Southwest Educational Development
    Laboratory, 369
Sox, A., 17
Spence, L., 17, 288, 293
Spinelli, J., 195
Spires, H., 300, 302
Scholastic, 241
Staal, L., 183, 184, 204
Stahl, K. D., 260, 261, 262, 268, 269
Stahl, S., 29, 100
Standards for the English Language
    Arts, 271, 340
Stanley, J., 224, 242, 245
Stanovich, K., 5
Staudt, D. H., 151
Steele, P., 223, 228
Stein, D. E., 179
Stephens, K., 225
Sterling-Honig, A., 153
Stevens, J. 191, 319
Stevens-Crummel, S., 154, 208
Strickland, 310
Stricklin, K., 175, 213, 246
Sturges, P., 67

Swanson, P., 177, 186
Swartz, R. J., 221
Sweeny, S., 286, 295
Sylvester, R., 16, 326
Symons, S., 219

Taylor, B., 82, 86
Teachers of English to Speakers of
    Other Languages, 43
Temple, C., 55, 191, 193
Templeton, S., 177, 332, 337, 341
Tempo, F., 240
Terban, M., 154, 166, 277
Theroux, P., 22, 23, 356
Thoermer, A., 208
Thomas, J., 82
Tolkien, J. R. R., 32
Tomlinson, C.A., 22, 355
Tompkins, G., 224
Topping, K., 273
Townsend, D., 147, 151, 155, 170, 171
Trelease, J., 373
Tresselt, A., 207
Truss, L., 315
Turbill, J., 303, 331, 338, 341
Turkle, B., 162
Twain, M., 178

Ulrich, G., 83
U.S. Department of Education, 261,
    352

Valencia, S., 261, 262, 268
Van Allen, R., 162
Van Allsburg, C., 238
VanNess, A., 286, 291
Van Riper, G., 314
Vardell, S., 188, 231
Vaughn, S., 11, 87, 156, 179, 190,
    229, 279, 360
Vellutino, R., 5
Vygotsky, L., 3, 17, 155, 253, 291, 332

Wagner, K., 239
Walker, B., 27, 28
Wall, H., 291
Wallace, B., 150
Walton, R., 140
Wasik, B., 125, 126, 148, 356

Watkins, S., 178
Watt, F., 228, 242, 244
Watts-Taffe, S., 175, 176
Weaver, C., 5, 6, 49
Weber, R., 9
Weinstein, S., 287
Weitzman, I., 277
Wells, R., 87, 294
White, A. L., 177
White, E. B., 178
White, T. G., 371, 377, 378, 609
Wiese, J., 238
Wiesner, D., 162, 166, 201
Wilcox, B., 323
Wiles, D., 184, 208
Wilfong, L., 236, 237
Wilkinson, T., 222
Williams, B., 239
Williams, C., 285, 291, 311
Williams, K. T., 158
Williams, L., 206, 266
Williams, S., 299
Winn, P., 219
Winter, P., 162
Wixson, K., 354, 355
Wolf, M., 230
Wolf, S., 125
Wolsey, T., 294
Wood, C., 78, 96, 186, 228, 251
Wood, J., 224
Wood-Ray, K., 302
Woodruff, E., 200, 318
Woodson, J., 178, 208
Wray, D., 23

Yaden, D. B., 11
Yellin, D., 8
Yin, C., 238
Yoder, E., 240
Yolen, J., 202
Yopp, H., 75, 76, 80, 150
Young, A., 278
Youngs, S., 589

Zawilinski, L., 324
Zecker, L., 287, 288, 332, 337
Zhang, C., 285
Zipke, M., 153, 169
Zumbrum, S., 287

subject index

A Is for Amber, 56
Academic vocabulary, 15, 148 (*see also* Domain-specific vocabulary)
Academic writing, 294
Accelerated Reader Program, 31, 33, 193
Accent, 101
Acceptance needs, 4
Accomplishments log, 68–70
Accuracy, fluency and, 261, 264
Achievement goal theory, 25
Achievement tests, 42–44
Acronyms, 154
Acrostic poems, writing, 319–320
Action Jeopardy, 171
Active learning, 240
Activities:
    collaborative, 170–171
    comprehension, 193–208, 236–254
    directions for, 513
    emergent writing, 291–292
    fluency, 272–281
    initial consonant sounds, 112–113
    initial sounds, 88–90
    materials/resources for, 514–592
    onset and rime, 93, 114–115, 140
    phonemic awareness, 86–96
    phonics, 111–119
    reading comprehension, 193–208, 236–254
    receptive/expressive vocabularies, 135–136
    rhyme, 115–116
    rime, 114–115
    sounds within words, 117–119
    Spanish/English concept books, 89
    spelling, 343–350
    vocabulary building, 159–171
    word patterns, 116–117
    word recognition, 133–143
    writing, 310–327

Adequate yearly progress, 22
Advocates, language arts teachers as, 218
Affixes, 101, 140–141 (*see also* Prefixes; Suffixes)
    frequently used, 407
    spelling stage, 335, 336
    teaching to English learners, 129
    Word Study, activity, 140–141
African Americans, 9, 210
    heroes, 314
    integration and, 4
    literature and, 178, 184
    writing by girls, 287
Age, leveling books for, 31
AIMS Standard Reading Assessment Passages, 272
Aimsweb, 45
All About Planet Earth, 250
Allington, Richard, and effective teachers, 21–22
Alliteration, 76, 82–86
    activity, 113
    books with, 389–390
Allophones, 104
Alphabet:
    Arabic, 337
    books, 323–324, 387
    sound booklets, 89
    Spanish, 336
Alphabetic spelling stage, 113, 333, 335, 336, 341
Alphabiography activity, 113
Alternate Writing, activity, 197
America Reads Challenge Act, 13
Analogies, activity, 165–166
Analogy phonics, 108
Analysis, structural, *see* Structural analysis
Analysis, visual, *see* Visual analysis
Analytic phonics, 101, 108

Analytical learning style, 28–29
Anchor standards, CCR, *see* CCRA
And This Is the Rest of the Story, activity, 200
Anecdotal records, 56–57
Antonyms, 153, 154
Appositive phrase, 153
Apps:
    assessment, 70
    fluency, 282
    informational text, 256
    narrative text, 209–210
    phonemic awareness, 96
    phonics, 120
    spelling, 349
    vocabulary, 172
    word recognition, 144
    writing, 327
Arabic alphabet, 337
Argument/persuasion, 221–222
    checklist evaluation, 298, 493
    essay example, 297
    graphic organizer for, 242, 245, 246, 296, 605, 606
    writing and, 294–298
Armadillo Rodeo, 136
Articulation, of vowel sounds, 105
Assessment, 38–71 (*see also* Diagnostic tests; Formal assessment; Informal assessment)
    6 + 1 Trait, writing, 307, 494–495
    authentic, 46
    blank checklist, 439
    blank running record, 438
    categories of, 39
    computer programs and, 193
    defining, 39–40
    DeFord theoretical orientation to reading, 421
    devices/tools, 419–508
    formal, 41–45

formative, 40
Fry readability formula, 425–426
informal instruments, 45–63 (*see also* Informal assessment)
informational text comprehension and, 232–235
matrix of, 45
miscue analyses, 48–51
NCTE/IRA standards, 384–386
next generation, 40
of background knowledge, 233–234 (*see also* Background knowledge; Prior knowledge)
of emergent reading/writing, 46–47
of fluency, 270–272
of foundational reading skills, 45
of oral reading, 44–45
of phonemic awareness and, 80–81
of phonemic awareness, 463–468
of readers' growth, 234
of reading comprehension, 190–193
personal philosophy, forming, 2–18
phonics and, 109–111
reliability of, 41
retrospective miscue analysis, 51
RTI and, 353
self-, 66–70
spelling, 338, 341–343
standardized test scores, 42
standards for, 40–41
summative, 40
technology and, 70
validity of, 41
vocabulary and, 156–158
word recognition and, 128–133
writing and spelling, 506
Assonance, 82–86
Attitude survey, 66, 308, 310
reading and writing, 448–454
Audience, writing to, 302
Audio chapter books, 392
Audiobooks, 220, 380
English learners and, 12
teacher-made, 200–201
Authentic assessment, 46
Authors:
intent, 185–186, 202–203
word choice and, 216
writing to, 325–326
Automatic information processing theory, 264
Automaticity, 124
fluency and, 262, 264

Babe the Gallant Pig, 32

Background knowledge, 3, 12, 16, 26, 34, 123, 126, 131, 179, 249
assessment and, 54–55, 233–234
connecting to texts, 183–185, 218, 219, 220
Backpack project, 380
Bad, Bad Day, A, 116
Bandwagon, 222
Base, 101
Basic Early Assessment of Reading, 45, 80, 111, 354
Scope and Sequence, 354
Basic Elementary Reading Vocabulary, 131
Bats, informational writing and, 300–301
BEAR, 45, 80, 111
BEARS, 354
Bear, Invernizzi, Templeton, Johnston Qualitative Spelling Inventory, 360, 507
Bear, Invernizzi, Templeton, Johnston spelling stages, 333
Bear's Cave, 358
Beauty, 150
Beetle Bop, 208
Beginning readers, traits of, 47
Beginning Sound, picture cards, 517–529
Ben's Dream, 136
Berlioz the Bear, 85–86
Best-work portfolios, 63
Big Talk, 280
Bilingual:
concept books, 89, 390–391
narrative picture books, 391
Bilingual students (*see also* English learners), writing stages of, 292–293
Bingo:
blank card, 575
Dolch List, 137, 582–587
initial sound, 89, 530–539
materials for, 530–539, 575, 582–587
morphology, 160
short vowel, 116–117
Biopoems, writing, 321–322
Bison for Kids, 222, 227
Blending:
activities, 92–93
assessing, 132
onset with rime, 140
polysyllabic words, 127
Blends, 76–77, 101
consonant, 112

Blogging, 304, 305
activity, 324–325
Bob Books, 6
Book (*see also* Books):
Buddies, 357
-leveling systems, comparison, 394–395
logs, 66, 67
Bookmarks, vocabulary, 159, 590
Books to Remember Series, 108
Books (*see also* Texts):
alphabet, 323–324, 387
audio, 12, 200–201, 392
bilingual, 89, 390–391
concept, 89, 390
content area learning, 389
ebooks, 208–209
flip, 114–115
interactive, 380
language play and, 389–390
leveled, 31–33
log sheet for, 364
Mother Goose, 387–388
multicultural, 189, 391–392
picture, 136, 187, 391–392
poetry, 387–388
wordless, 136, 162, 201, 323, 388–389
Brand New Kid, The, 181–182, 182–183
Brochures, creating, 324
Brown Bear, Brown Bear, 299
Bud, Not Buddy, 161–162
Buddy reading, 8, 23, 74
Bulletin boards, parents and, 373
Bush, George W., 13
Butterfly, The, 195

Cache of Jewels, A, 150
CAFÉ assessment, 330, 342–343
California Achievement Tests–Reading, 42, 158, 310, 343
California Critical Thinking Test, 235
California Test of Mental Maturity, 41
Cam Jansen and the Mystery of the Monster Movie, 32
Camtesia, 255
Capitalization, 303
Carbo Recorded Book Method, 274
Card stacking, 222, 245
Caregivers, and educators, 367–381 (*see also* Parents)
Cat in the Hat, The, 6, 114–115
Categorizing, activity, 164
Cause/effect, 222, 224
graphic organizer for, 242, 244
Caves, 224, 228, 251

CCRA, language, 147, 159, 160
  vocabulary and, 149
CCRA, reading, 176, 221, 237–238, 246
  vocabulary and, 147
CCRA, writing, 285, 293–301, 322
CCSS, 13–14, 15 (see also CCRA; Standards)
  as basis for assessment, 40
  checklist for phonics instruction, 58, 109
  checklist for vocabulary growth, 158
  checklist for word recognition skills, 58, 130
  concerns about, 2
  criterion-referenced tests and, 43
  fluency and, 268–269, 271
  informational text and, 59–60, 213–214, 232
  Lexile leveling, 31
  mission of, 213
  narrative text and, 176
  phonemic awareness and, 79–80
  phonics and, 107
  reading, 80, 107, 109, 128, 177, 178, 179, 183–184, 192–193, 216
  reading informational texts and, 59–60
  RTI and, 355
  rubric for reading informational text, 59–60, 232
  rubric measuring fluency, 271
  spelling and, 331, 338, 340
  state-designed criterion-referenced tests, 43
  text complexity and, 33–34
  text selection and, 29
  tutoring and, 357, 358
  vocabulary growth and, 149, 158
  word categories and, 148
  word recognition and, 128
  writing and, 285, 293–301
  writing informational text, 298–299
Center for Public Education, 155
Chains, 180–181
Change Hen to Fox, activity, 118–119
Chapter books, audio, 392
Character Perspective Chart, activity, 206–207
Character Sketch, activity, 208
Chart:
  comparing multiple sources, 598
  K-T-W-L-E, template, 599
  record and check, 601

Checklist(s), 57–58
  activity, 251
  argument presentation, 493
  argument writing, 298
  assessing multiple intelligence, 422–424
  basic online skills, 488
  blank, 439
  CCRA, 440–441
  concepts of print, 427
  concepts of writing, 428
  fluency, 270, 490–491
  foundational reading skills, 473, 474
  informational reading, 485
  known letter names and sounds, 476–477
  letter–sound relationships, 476–477
  literacy habits, 442–446
  phonemic awareness, 81, 472
  phonics, word recognition, and fluency, third grade, 475
  phonics assessment and, 109–110
  proofreading, 303
  reading, 440–441, 473, 474, 485
  textbook evaluation, 596–597
  tradebook evaluation, 596–597
  vocabulary assessment and, 157–158, 482
  word recognition assessment, 129, 130
  writing, 298, 428, 493
Children of the Dust Bowl, 224, 242, 245
Children's Choices, 224
Children's literature, 84–86
Children's Progress Academic Assessment (CPAA), 45
Choral reading, 11, 279–281
Chronology, 221, 222
  graphic organizer for, 242–243
Chrysanthemum, 177
Chunks, recognizing within words, 264
Cinquains, writing, 320
Citing evidence, theme of CCSS, 15
City of Orphans, 166
Civil War, 253
Clap Your Hands, 6
Clarity, of language, 178
Classic literature, levels of meaning in, 178178
Classification, 223
  graphic organizer for, 242, 243
Classroom Reading Inventory (Silvaroli & Wheelock), 130

Classroom(s):
  activity in, 20–21
  assessment in, see Assessment
  strategies used in, chart, 8
  diverse students in, 26 (see also Diversity; English learners)
  instruction, see Instruction; Teaching
Clay, Marie, 46, 51
Clifford the Big Red Dog, 241
Clinton, Bill, 13
Clorinda, 85
Close reading, 15, 215–216
  theme of CCSS, 15
Closed syllable, 101
Clouds, 165
Clown activity, 91
Cloze tests, 54–56, 131, 191
  activity, 139
  informational text and, 232
  vocabulary and, 157
Cluster, consonant, 101, 104
COCA, 255–256
Cognate Picture Cards, activity, 169
Cognate sort, materials, 591
Cognitive processes, 286
Collaboration, 8
  activities, 170–171, 253
  RTI and, 353
  social networking and, 17
  writing and, 305
College and Career Readiness Anchor Standards, see CCRA (see also CCSS)
Come on, Rain, 273
Comic books, 305
Common Core State Standards, see CCSS
Communication:
  multimodal, 16 (see also New literacies)
  with parents, 368–369, 371–376
Community, reading comprehension and, 220
Community volunteers, 379–380
Comparison, book-leveling systems, 394–395
Comparison/contrast, 222, 223–224
  expository frame for, 318
  graphic organizer for, 242, 244
Competition, reading and, 23
Complexity, of texts, 15, 33–34, 177–178
Compound word, 101, 140
Comprehending Visual Images, activity, 208

Comprehension:
  activities for, 193–208, 236–254
  assessment of, 190–193, 236–254
  critical literacy and, 186–188
  decoding and, 176–177
  environmental factors, 219–220
  factors affecting, 217–220
  factors within reader, 217–219
  factors within text, 220
  fluency and, 177, 260–261, 268
    (*see also* Fluency)
  of complex text, 215–217
  of informational text, 211–257 (*see also* Informational text)
  of narrative text, 174–210 (*see also* Narrative text)
  pairing fiction and nonfiction texts, 238–239
  reading rate and, 282
  reciprocal theory, 268
  rubric, informational text, 486
  rubric, narrative text, 483
  school as factor in, 220
  self-monitoring, 182
  software promoting, 392
  strategies for informational text, 214–217
  strategies for narrative text, 179–186
  technology and, 208–210, 254–256
  vocabulary and, 177 (*see also* Vocabulary)
Comprehensive approach to reading, 6–9
Comprehensive Test of Basic Skills, 158
Computer programs, assessment and, 193 (*see also* Apps; Technology; Websites)
Computers, writing and, 324–327
"Concentration" activities, 115
  materials, 571–574
Concept books, 89, 390
Concepts of Comprehension Assessment, 255–256
Concepts of print, checklist, 427
Conclusions, drawing, 185
Conferences, 8
  family–teacher, 372, 374–375
Considerate vs. inconsiderate styles, 229
Consonant(s):
  blends, 112, 337
  cluster, 101, 104
  digraphs, 102, 104
  fricative, 102
  generalizations, 104
  initial sounds, activities, 112–113

  nasal, 102
  plosive, 102
  pronunciation guide, 399–400
  sounds, 75
  spelling patterns, 104
  Thai, 337
Constrained skills, 261–262
Constructivist theory, 3
Content area learning, wordless books, 389 (*see also* Informational text)
Content:
  differentiating instruction and, 356
  6 + 1 traits and, 306, 312–313
Context, 34, 108–109
Context clues, 125, 126
  activity, 139
  assessing, 131
  vocabulary instruction and, 153
Controlled-r sounds, 337
Conventional spelling stage, 288, 290
Conventions, 6 + 1 traits and, 307, 314
Cook-a-Doodle-Doo, 191
Cornell Critical Thinking Test, 235
Council of Chief State School Officers, 13–14 (*see also* CCSS)
CPAA, 45
Criterion-referenced tests, 42–44
Critical:
  questions, 199
  reading, 4 (*see also* Comprehension)
  thinking, writing and, 286
Critical literacy, 4–5, 231, 235
  reading comprehension and, 186–188
  reflective learning, 210
  themes, 186–187
  theory, 4–5
Crossword Puzzle, activity, 166–167
Cueing systems, 28, 53, 123–124
CVC pattern, 103, 110, 116, 117, 341, 343
CVCe pattern, 103, 117, 341, 343
CVVC pattern, 103, 343
CWPM, *see* WCPM

Daily welcome, 374
Daisy Comes Home, 267
Day Jimmy's Boa Ate the Wash, The, 177
Decoding, 102, 103 (*see also* Phonemic awareness)
  reading comprehension and, 176–177
Deep in the Forest, 162
Deep reading, 269

Definition Concentration, activity, 167–168
DeFord Theoretical Orientation to Reading Profile, 12–13, 421
Deleting, activities, 77, 94–95
Demographics, of U. S. students, 9
Derivational relations spelling stage, 333, 335, 336
Derivational suffixes, 102
Description, 221, 222–223
  expository frame for, 318
  graphic organizer for, 242, 243
Developmental Reading Assessment, Second Edition, Plus, 45
Diagnostic Reading Scales, 44, 111, 133
Diagnostic tests, 44–45, 158, 272
Diagrams, 215 (*see also* Graphic organizers)
Diamante, writing, 320–321
Diaries, 213
DIBELS, 45, 80, 111, 354
Dick and Jane series, 6
Dictionary usage, 113, 337, 345
Differentiating instruction, 355–356
  gifted students, 365
  RTI, *see* Response to intervention
Digital storytelling, 305, 326
Digraphs, 105
  consonant, 5, 102, 104, 479
  vowel, 5, 102, 105, 337, 401
Diphthongs, vowel, 102, 105, 401
Directed Listening–Thinking activity (DL-TA), 197
Directed Reading–Thinking activity (DR-TA), 197–198
Directions, for creating game boards, 513
Disfluency, 261, 262 (*see also* Fluency)
Diversity in learners, 9–12, 26 (*see also* English learners)
  identifying students' needs, 14–15, 351–366
DLM's Word Radar, 131
Dolch Basic Sight Vocabulary, 126, 129, 403
  apps for, 144
  Bingo, activity, 137, 582–587
Dolphins: What They Can Teach Us, 223
Domain-specific vocabulary, 148, 215, 227–228
  activity, 138–139
  theme of CCSS, 15
Dominoes activity, 113, 567–570
Dr. Seuss, 85, 265
DRA2+, 45

Drafting, 302
Durrell Analysis of Reading Difficulties, 44, 111, 133, 158, 272
Dust Bowl, 224, 245
Dynamic Indicators of Basic Early Literacy Skills, *see* DIBELS

Early production stage, of language development, 10
easyCBM, 45
Eats, Shoots and Leaves, 315
Ebooks, 8, 220, 227
    English learners and, 12
    evaluation form, 595
    reading comprehension and, 208–209
Echo reading, 272–273
Editing, 303
Education for All Handicapped Children Act, 15
Education, parents who don't value, 378
Educationwise Public Library, 220
Effective teachers, reading comprehension strategies, 186
Ekwall/Shanker Reading Inventory, 48
Electronic portfolios, 63
Electronic texts, *see* Ebooks
Elementary and Secondary Education Act of 1966, 13
Elijah from Boston, 162
Email, writing, 325–326
    to parents, 373
Emergent readers, 47, 360
Emergent spelling stage, 332, 333, 335, 336, 341
Emergent writing, stages of, 288–293 (*see also* Writing)
Empty Pot, The, 162
Encoding, 102, 103
Encounter, 202–203
Engagement, student, 20–21, 24
English:
    as symbolic language, 288
    compared to Spanish, 106
    development of, 9–10
    layers of spelling, 103
    phonemes, and in other languages, 77–78
    semantic complexities of, 152, 153
    spelling patterns in, 104–106, 337–338
    standards for language proficiency, 43
    –Spanish bilingual concept books, 390

English Language Arts, CCSS, *see* CCSS
English learners, 9–12
    consonant sounds and, 104
    criterion-referenced tests for, 43–44
    effective practices for, 11–12
    fluency instruction and, 270
    graphophonic system, 106
    I + 1 theory, 11
    informal assessment for, 63–64
    informational text and, 229–231
    Japanese, 77, 78, 256
    lesson plan, 362, 363, 512
    magazine for Spanish speakers, 241
    narrative texts and, 188–189
    observation of, 63
    phonemic awareness and, 77–78
    proficiency standards, 158
    RTI and, *see* Response to intervention
    sharing the pen activity, 311
    sheltered instruction and, 11
    sight words and, 144
    social networking and, 17
    stages of spelling development, 335–337
    TPR approach, 11
    tutoring sessions for, 360–363
    vocabulary learning and, 148, 155–156
    vowel sounds and, 104–105
    word sorting with pictures, 112
    word study and, 128, 129
    writing and, 285
    writing stages of, 292–293
Enumeration, 221, 222–223
    expository frame for, 318
    graphic organizer for, 242, 243
Environmental factors, 219–220
Environmental print, 377
E-Pals, 8
Epistemic knowledge, 26, 27, 28
Epossumondas Saves the Day, 183
ESA Word List, 131
Esteem needs, 4
E-text evaluation, form, 600
Euphemisms, 154
Evaluative questions, 199, 226
Every Day Lasts a Year, 194
Everything Kids Astronomy Book, 239–240
Example of Meaning, activity, 160–161
Examples, concrete, 315
Existential intelligence, 29, 30
Experience, 149–150, 184–185, 218 (*see also* Background knowledge)

Explicit instruction, vocabulary, 151–154
Expository frames, 302, 317–318
Expository text, *see* Informational text
Expression, in reading, 266–267
Expressive language art, 286
Expressive vocabulary, 125
    activities, 135–136, 158
Expressiveness, 261 (*see also* Fluency)
Extrinsic rewards, reading and, 23

Fairmount Avenue, 150
Farewell Symphony, The, 206–207
Features, text, 225–227
Ferroli and Shanahan's spelling stages, 333
Fibbin poems, 322
Fiction (*see also* Narrative text):
    historical, 187
    pairing with nonfiction, 238–239
Figurative Speech, activity, 161–162
First Discovery: The Universe, 138
Flash cards, 6, 137–138
Flimflam Man, The, 184
Flip books, 114–115
Flotsam, 162
Fluency, 259–282
    activities, 272–281
    assessment of, 270–272
    automaticity, 124, 262, 264
    Carbo Recorded-Book Method, 274
    CCSS and, 268–269
    checklists, 490, 491
    choral reading, 279–281
    components of, 261–268
    comprehension and, 260–261, 268
    defined, 260–262
    development lesson, 275–276
    dyad reading, 277
    echo reading, 272–273
    expression and, 266–267
    Idol, activity, 277–278
    instruction and, 268–270
    intervention, 272–281
    log, 602
    NAEP scale, 261
    norms based on WCPM, 263
    oral recitation lesson, 274
    phrasing/prosody, *see* Phrasing
    preview-pause-prompt-praise strategy, 273
    punctuation and, 267
    questions for self-evaluation, 489
    readers theater, 278–279
    reading comprehension and, 177
    reading rate, 261 (*see also* Rate)

reciprocal theory, 268
record check, chart activity, 274–275
repeated readings, 277
research related to, 269
rubric for oral reading, 492
sentence, 306–307
supported-reading strategy, 277
technology and, 282
traits of vs. disfluency, 261
tutoring activities, 272–275
Foam board letters, 346
Follow Me, Moon (Clay) assessment, 46
Formal assessment, 41–45
achievement tests, 42–44
criterion-referenced tests, 42–44
defined, 39
diagnostic tests, 44–45
norm-referenced tests, 42
of comprehension, 234–235
of fluency, 272
of informational text comprehension, 234–235
of reading comprehension, 193
of writing, 310
phonics and, 111
vocabulary and, 158
word recognition and, 132–133
Formative assessments, 40
Foundational reading skills, assessment of, 45
Foundational Skills Reading Standards, 128, 129
Fountas & Pinnell Reading Record, app, 70
Fountas and Pinnell Leveled Books, 33
Fourth-grade slump, 212
"Fractured Fairy Tales," 209
Franklin, Benjamin, 222
Freedom Summer, 184, 208
Freefall, 162
Fresch and Wheaton's spelling stages, 333
Fricative consonant, 102
Frogs, 223
Frustration reading level, 30, 48
Fry Phase List (Instant Word List), 125, 129, 130, 143, 404–406
Fry Readability formula, 33, 425–426

Game boards/game pieces, 513, 514–592
Gardner, Howard, 29
Gates-MacGinitie Reading Tests, 42, 158, 235

Gates-McKillop-Horowitz Tests, 44, 111, 133, 158
Gentry and Gillet's spelling stages, 333, 342
George Washington's Breakfast, 32
Gestalt, language, 159
Gifted students, 18, 365
Gilmore Oral Reading tests, 44, 133
Glittering generalities, 222, 245
Global:
learning style, 29
pen pals, 325
publishing, 305
Glossary, 226
Go Fish, activity, 90, 549–555
Goals, similar for reading and writing, 286
Goals 2000: Educate America Act, 369
Goal-setting, logs, 68–70
Goin' Places, 208
GRADE, 45
Grade equivalent scores, 42
Grade, leveling books for, 31
Grades, reading levels of, 3
Gradient leveling, 32
"Grandma's Garden," 54, 190, 430–431
miscue analysis grid, 432–433
running record for, 54
Grapheme, 101, 102
Graphic component of writing, 287–288
Graphic novels, 305
Graphic organizers, 215, 218, 221, 302
activities, 204–205, 242–246
argument, 242, 245, 246, 296, 605, 606
English learners and, 230
persuasive writing and, 242, 245, 246, 296, 605, 606
prewriting argumentative essay, 606
samples, 195, 242–246
word web, 138–139
Graphics, 225 (*see also* Graphic organizers)
informational text and, 215
Graphophonic component of writing, 288
Graphophonic cueing system, 34, 53, 101, 124
Gray Oral Reading Test, 44, 133, 272
Green Eggs and Ham, 6, 85
Green Snake Ceremony, 178
Group intelligence tests, 41

Group Reading Assessment and Diagnostic Evaluation, 45
Grouping words, fluency and, 261
Groups, small, *see* Small groups
Growth portfolios, 62–63
Guess How Much I Love You, 141
Guess Who's Coming, Jesse Bear, 273
Guess Who's Coming to Dinner, Jesse Bear, 335
Guided reading, 8, 32, 134–135
Guided Reading: Good First Teaching for All Children, 32, 135
Guided writing, 316
Guides, and lists, 393–418
Guppies in Tuxedos: Funny Eponyms, 166

Happy Grams, 373
Harry Potter series, 182
Henkes, Kevin, 179
Henny Penny, 85, 204
Here Are My Hands, 115
Heteronyms, 124
Hierarchy, 223
of human needs, 4
High-frequency words, 126, 331, 402
Historical fiction, picture books, 187, 593
Hobbit, The, 32
Holocaust, reading unit on, 194–195
Home, technology in, 380
Home life, students', 369–370
Homographs, 124
Homonyms, 124, 154
Homophone Rummy, 141
Homophones, 154
Hooked on Caldecott Award Winners! 166
Hormone Jungle: Coming of Age, 136
How Many Fish?, 108
Howard Street Tutoring Program, 357
Human needs, hierarchy of, 4
Humpty Dumpty board game, 91, 556–560

I + 1 theory, 11
I Can Read With My Eyes Shut!, 265
I Show U, 255
I Wonder Why Castles Had Moats, 223, 228
IDEA, 14–15, 26, 260, 352
Idea/content, 6 + 1 traits and, 306, 312–313
Idioms, books emphasizing, 154
In the Haunted House, 85
In the Tall, Tall Grass, 208

Independent reading, 7, 8, 20, 25, 34, 51, 134, 159, 175, 186, 212, 213
   level, 30, 35, 48
Index, 226
Individual intelligence tests, 41
Individualized instruction, need for, 352–353 (*see also* Differentiating instruction; Response to intervention; Tutoring)
Individuals with Disabilities Education Act (IDEA), 14–15, 26, 260, 352
Inference training, 248
Inferences, making, 181–182
Inferential:
   questions, 199, 226
   reading, developing, 201
   thinking, 248
Inflectional endings, 102
Informal assessment, 45–64 (*see also* Anecdotal records; Checklists; Cloze tests; Informal reading inventories; Miscue analysis; Running records)
   cloze procedure, *see* Cloze tests
   defined, 39
   inventories for, 387
   maze technique, 56, 157, 191, 230, 231, 232
   of comprehension, 232–234
   of fluency, 270–271
   of phonemic awareness, 80
   of reading comprehension, 190–193
   of reading interests, 233–234
   of spelling, 338, 341–343
   of writing, 307–310
   phonics and, 109–111
   rubrics, *see* Rubrics
   running records, *see* Running records
   vocabulary and, 156–158
   word recognition and, 128–132
Informal reading inventories, 47–48, 190, 387
   informational text and, 232
   phonics and, 111
   word recognition and, 130
Informal Reading Inventory, 130
Information, knowledge of general, 26
Information communication technologies, 217
Informational literacy, 16
Informational reading vs. literary reading, 15
Informational report writing, 298–299
Informational text, 24
   activities for, 236–254

analysis of, 224–229
answering questions, 248–249, 253–254
assessing comprehension, 232–235
CCSS and, 15, 213–214, 298–299
chart for citing sources, 237–238
checklist, 485
checklist activity, 251
comprehension of, 211–257
comprehension rubric, 486
comprehension strategies, 214–217
critical literacy and, 231, 235
dramatizing, 254
English learners and, 229–231
e-text evaluation form, 600
graphic organizer activity, 242–246
inference training, 248
kindergarteners and, 213–214
K-T-W-L-E activity, 246–247
learning logs, 252–253
organizational structure of, 221–224
persuasion and, 221–222
PReP, 249–250
QARs and, 248–249
reading rubric, 487
ReQuest activity, 251
research report rubric, 308, 309
scanning activity, 252
selecting for English learners, 231
survey activity, 249
technical vocabulary and, 215, 227–228
technology and, 254–255
think-aloud for, 250
websites, 255
word choice and, 216
wordless books, 389
writing and CCSS, 298–299
young students and, 213–214
Initial consonant sound, game 561–566
Initial sounds, 76, 88–90
   bingo, 89, 530–539
Insertions, 48, 49
Instruction:
   comprehension strategies, 186
   differentiated, *see* Differentiating instruction
   explicit, of vocabulary, 151–154
   fluency and, *see* Fluency
   for spelling stages, 332–336, 341
   for struggling readers, 12–13
   multiple intelligences and, 29, 30
   tools/materials for, 509–612
   vocabulary, *see* Vocabulary
Instructional reading level, 30, 48

Instruments, assessment, *see* Assessment
Intelligence tests, 41
Intelligences, multiple, 29, 30
Intent, author's, 185–186, 202–203
Interactive writing, 8, 11, 311
Interest inventory/survey, 233–234, 360, 447, 484
Interests, comprehension and, 218–219
Intermediate fluency language stage, 10
International Literacy Association, 78–79, 119, 209
   Standards for Assessment of Reading and Writing, 40, 384–386
   qualities of effective teachers, 21
Internet:
   checklist of skills, 488
   E-Pals and 8
   publishing and, 304, 305
   vocabulary building and, 150
Interpersonal intelligence, 29, 30
Interrupting Chicken, 179
Intervention, strategies (*see also* Activities):
   for comprehension, 193–207, 236–254
   for fluency, 272–281
   for phonemic awareness, 86–95
   for phonics, 111–118
   for spelling, 343–350
   for struggling readers, 12–13
   for vocabulary, 159–170
   for word recognition, 133–142
   for writing, 310–327
Interviews, writing, 314–315
Intrapersonal intelligence, 29, 30
Intrinsic motivation, for reading, 24–26
Introductory letters to parents, 368–369, 371–372
Inventories:
   Bear, Invernizzi, Templeton, & Johnston Qualitative Spelling, 507
   informal reading, 47–48, 190, 387
   interest, *see* Interest inventory
   spelling, 111, 341–342
   TORP, 12–13
Iowa Silent Reading Test, 44, 158
Iowa Test of Basic Skills, 42, 111, 158, 235, 310, 343
IQ, 41
IRA, *see* International Reading Association
i-Ready, 45

IRIs, 47–48, 190, 387
Istation, 193
It's Justin Time, Amber Brown, 185

James Madison Test of Critical
    Thinking, 235
"Johnny's Birthday," 434–437
Johns Hopkins, 217
Jokes, telling, activity, 276–277
Jolly Postman, The, 140
Journal:
    learning log, 252–253
    writing, 7, 8, 18, 189, 206, 324, 380
Joyful Noise, 280
Julius: The Baby of the World, 174, 179
Jump rope jingles, 84
Jungle Book, The, 50
Just Juice, 54, 267

Key words, 221–222
Keyboarding software, 327
Kinesthetic intelligence, 29, 30
Knowledge (*see also* Prior knowledge)
    demands, 34
    epistemic, 26, 27, 28
    literary, 183
    rhetorical, 126
    student, 26–28
    world, 184
K-T-W-L-E chart, 233, 246–247, 599

Language:
    concepts, books for, 154
    concepts, instruction in, 153–154
    development of, 9–10, 82 (*see also*
        Phonemic awareness; Phonics)
    I + 1 theory, 11
    play, 81–86, 389–390
    systems, 28
    text complexity and, 34, 178
Language arts (*see also* Reading;
    Writing):
    CCSS and, 14 (*see also* CCSS)
    receptive vs. expressive, 286
Language Assessment Scales–Oral,
    43–44, 63
Language Assessment Scales–Reading/
    Writing, 43–44, 63
Language experience approach, 8,
    11–12, 64
    activities for, 162–164
Language Gestalts, activity, 159
Languages, phonemes in various, 77–78
LAS–O, 43–44, 63
LAS–R/W, 43–44, 63
Latin word roots, 408–416

LEA, *see* Language experience approach
Learners, diverse, 9–12 (*see also*
    English learners)
Learning:
    active, 240
    collaborative, *see* Collaboration
    disability, 15
    experience, components of, 21–35
    logs, activity, 252–253
    styles, 28–29, 356, 422–424
    theories, literacy and, 3–5
Lesson cycle, activity, 246
Lesson plan:
    for English learners, 362, 363, 512
    for tutoring session, 357, 358, 359,
        362, 363, 609
Letter names checklist, 476–477
Letter–sound relationships, checklist,
    476–477
Letter-name stage, 333, 336
Letters, 213 (*see also* Consonants;
    Vowels)
    associating with sounds, 264
    foam board, 346
    magnetic, 343–344
    names and sounds, checklist of,
        110
    silent, 102
Letters, writing, 322–323
    introductory to parent, 368–369,
        371–372
Leveled books, 31–33
Lewis and Clark, 216, 254
Lexical and Structural Riddles,
    activity, 169–170
Lexile Band reading scale, 31–32, 33,
    40, 228–229
Libraries for the Blind, 12
Library of Congress, 255
Life experience, 149, 184–185 (*see*
    also Prior knowledge)
Lilly's Big Day, 179
Lilly's Purple Plastic Purse, 179
Lindamood-Bell Auditory Conceptual-
    ization Test, 80
Linguistic:
    approach to reading, 6
    awareness games, 79
    intelligence, 29, 30
Linking strategy, 337
Listen for the Vowel Sound, 576–581
Listening, 14, 40, 42, 74, 81–82, 96,
    117
    directed listening–thinking activity,
        197
    for syllables, 87–88

for initial sounds, 88–90, 112–113
    (*see also* Phonemic awareness)
for onset, rime, and rhyme, 114–116
vocabulary, 44, 125, 177
Listening Walk, activity, 163
Listing, organizational, 223
Lists, and guides, 393–418
Literacies, new, 16–17, 217
Literacy, 2–3
    as event, 20–35
    assessment, 38–71 (*see also*
        Assessment)
    club, 8
    critical, 4–5, 231, 235
    family, 375–378 (*see also* Parents)
    independent tasks, 35
    learning theories related to, 3–5
    new, 16–17, 217
    personal philosophy, 2–18
    self-perception scales, 73
    skills, 27
    student knowledge of, 26–28
Literal questions, 199, 226
Literary knowledge, 183
Literary reading vs. informational
    reading, 15
Literature:
    children's, 84–86
    multiple levels of meaning in, 178
    theme of CCSS, 15
Little Men, 55
Little Mouse's Big Book of Fears, 155
Little Old Lady Who Was Not Afraid of
    Anything, The, 206
Little Red Riding Hood, 183
Log(s):
    accomplishment, 68–70
    book, 66, 67
    fluency, 602
    goal-setting, 68–70
    reading, 610, 611
    reflection, 68, 69
    skill, 66, 68
    tutoring strategies, 363, 364
Logical-mathematical intelligence, 29,
    30
Long Way from Chicago, A, 162
Lower socioeconomic groups, reading
    scores of, 13
Luba and the Wren, 205
Lyddie, 206

Madeline and the Gypsies, 103
Magazines, read-alouds and, 241
Magical E!, activity, 117
Magnetic letters, activity, 343–344

Mama One, Mama Two, 199
Manipulating, activities, 77, 95–96
Many Luscious Lollipops, 150
Mapping, 198, 242, 305
Marek, Ann, 51
Mary Engelbreit's Mother Goose, 83
Maslow's hierarchy, 4
Mastery orientation, 25
Match the Word, activity, 137
Matching Game, activity, 171
Materials, for instruction, 509–612
Math, games, activity, 239–240
Max's Dragon Shirt, 295
Maze tests, 56, 157, 191
    text and, 230–232
Meaning (*see also* Comprehension):
    English spelling, 103
    of narrative text, 178
    text complexity and, 33, 177
Meaning, Structure, Visual (MSV), 53
Media literacy, 16
Memory, aids to, 347
Memphis Comprehension Framework,
    194–195
Metacognition, 26, 27–28
Metropolitan Achievement Tests, 42,
    111, 158, 235, 310, 343
Mighty Miss Malone, The, 178
Miles of Smiles, 83
Milkweed, 194
Mime, 223
Mini-lessons, 8, 301, 303, 315
Minorities, reading scores of, 13
Miscue analysis, 12, 48–51, 190, 429
    during tutoring, 360
    for fluency, 270
    grid for "Grandma's Garden,"
        432–433
    grid for "Johnny's Birthday,"
        436–437
    informational text and, 232
    retrospective, 51, 270–271
    scoring, 50–51
Mispronunciations, 48, 49
Miss Alaineus: A Vocabulary Disaster,
    155
Miss Spider's New Car, 85
Mississippi, 86
Mister and Me, 265
Mitten, The, 207
Mnemonics activity, 347
Mockingbird, 181
Modeling:
    a think-aloud, 295
    close reading, 215–216
    dissecting words, 332

professional picture books, 318
    teachers, 103–104
Models, reading, 5–9
    part-to-whole, 5–6
Monosyllabic words, 125, 126–127,
    140
Morning message, 8, 335
Morphemes, 125, 127, 337
Morphology, 127–128, 141–143, 149
    Rummy, activity, 141–143, 588–589
    Tic-Tac-Toe, activity, 160
Mother Goose books, 387–388
Motivation, 22–26, 212, 213
Mouse with the Question Mark Tail,
    The, 178
Moving the Tiles, activity, 95
Mr. Lincoln's Way, 199
Mt. Plot, 205, 317, 608
Multicultural books, 189, 391–392
Multimedia project rubric, 308, 505
Multimodal communication, 16
Multimodal text, 299–301
Multiple intelligences, 29, 30, 422–424
Multiple Meaning Racetrack, 169
Multiple Perspectives, activity,
    202–203
Music Puzzlers, activity, 170
Music, activity, 87
Musical intelligence, 29, 30
My Dog Ate My Homework!, 90, 116
"My Grandma's Teeth," 265
"My Tooth Ith Loothe," 83
My Very First Mother Goose, 87
Mystery word, activity, 114

NAEP, 261
NAEYC, 78–79
Name calling, 222
Narrative ebook evaluation, 595
Narrative picture books, bilingual, 391
Narrative text, 174–210
    choosing, 188–189
    close reading of, 177–179
    comprehension of, 174–210 (*see*
        also Comprehension)
    for English learners, 188–189
    graphic organizers for, 204–205
        (*see also* Graphic organizers)
    rubrics, 191–193, 483 (*see also*
        Rubrics)
    student interest in, 24
    writing and CCSS, 299
NASA, 217
Nasal consonant, 102
National Assessment of Educational
    Progress, 261

National Association for the Education
    of Young Children, 78–79
National Center for Education
    Statistics, 13, 26
National Council of Teachers of
    English, 119, 209, 255
    multimodal writing and, 300
    Standards for Assessment of
        Reading and Writing, 40,
        384–386
National Geographic Book of Animal
    Poetry, 84
National Geographic Kids, 227
National Governors Association for
    Best Practices, 13–14 (*see also*
    CCSS)
National Institute for Literacy, 14
National Reading Panel Report, 13,
    79, 260
Naturalistic intelligence, 29, 30
NCTE, *see* National Council of
    Teachers of English
Needs, hierarchy of, 4
Nelson–Denny Reading Test, 44, 158
Neologisms, 154
New literacies, 16–17, 217
Newbridge, 201
Newsletters, 372–373
Next generation assessments, 40
No Child Left Behind Act, 13, 14
No Shoes, 46
Noh plays, 223
Noisy Poems, 83, 152
Nonfiction (*see also* Informational text):
    award-winning books, 224
    pairing with fiction, 238–239
Nonsense words, 82–86
Noread, 220
Norm-referenced tests, 42
Northwest Regional Education
    Laboratory, 306
Now One Foot, Now the Other, 184, 185
Nursery rhymes, 82

Objectives, tutoring, 357, 359
Observational checklist of literacy
    habits:
    beginning reading and writing
        stage, 444
    early emergent literacy stage, 442
    emergent literacy stage, 443
    fluent reading and writing stage,
        446
    nearly fluent stage, 445
    of student's informational text
        reading, 485

Octopus' Den, 252
Odd-Card Out!, activity, 92
Oddity, 76, 91–92
"Ode to the Spell Czecher," 332
Old Woman Who Lived in a Vinegar Bottle, The, 180, 205
Omissions, 48, 49
Once There Was a Bull...(frog), 140
One and Only Ivan, The, 178
Online:
    comprehension assessments, 254–255
    publishing, 304, 305
    reading, 213
    research project, 8
Onomatopoeia, 82–86, 154
Onset, 6, 102, 108, 132
    activities for, 93, 114–115, 140
Open syllable, 102
Open-ended questions, 23–24
Opinion writing, 294–298 (*see also* Persuasion)
Oral reading, 35
    assessment of, 44–45
    comprehension scaffolding, 612
    fluency rubric, 492
    fluency scale, 261
    rate, 261 (*see also* Fluency)
    running record of, 51–54
Oral recitation lesson (ORL), 274
Orbis Pictus Award, 224
ORCAs, 254–255
Organization, 6 + 1 traits and, 306, 313
Organizational:
    patterns, sequence for teaching, 224
    structure, of informational text, 221–224
Origami, 240
Origin of Words, activity, 166
Orthographic representation, of words, 149
Orthography, 337–338
Other Side, The, 178, 208
Outside and Inside Sharks, 223
Oxymoron, 154

Painting Mental Pictures, activity, 203
PALS, 354
Paragraphing, 303
Paraprofessionals, 365
PARCC, 40, 41, 235, 284, 355
    rubrics and, 60, 61–62
    state-designed criterion-referenced tests, 43

Parents:
    as partners to teachers, 367–381
    as volunteers, 381
    benefits of involvement, 370–371
    conferencing with, 372, 374–375
    critical, 378–379
    engaged, 371
    family literacy programs and, 375–376
    newsletters to, 372–373
    reading to children, 376–377
    suggestions for involving, 376–378
    technology classes for, 380
    telephone calls to, 373
    ways to communicate with, 356–361
    working with challenging, 378–379
Parodies, writing, 319
Parsing phrases, 265–266 (*see also* Prosody)
Partner Reading and Content Too, 241
Partnership for Assessment and Readiness for College and Career, *see* PARCC
Part-to-whole reading model, 5–6
Patterns:
    of English spelling, 103, 418, 337–338
    word, 116–117
PBSKids.org, 119
Peabody Picture Vocabulary Test, 41, 158
Pedagogical features, 225–227
Pen pals, 325
Percentile ranking scores, 42
Performance orientation theory, 25
Personal interest surveys, 64–65
Personalized Flash Cards, activity, 137–138
Personalized Word-Part Dictionaries, activity, 141
Persuasion (argument), 221–222
    checklist evaluation, 298, 493
    essay example, 297
    graphic organizer for, 242, 245, 246, 296, 605, 606
    writing and, 294–298
Philosophy:
    regarding assessment, 2–18
    TORP and, 12–13
Phonemes, 102 (*see also* Phonemic awareness)
    common, 75
    defined, 75
    English vs. other languages, 77–78
    Spanish, 339

Phonemic awareness, 74–97, 102
    activities/strategies for, 86–96
    assessment of, 80–81, 463–468
    checklist for, 81
    defined, 75–76
    English learners and, 77–78
    in the CCSS, 79–80
    necessity of, 78–79
    pre-assessment of, 464–467
    post-assessment of, 468–471
    proficient reading and, 78–79
    sounds of language and, 81–86
    technology and, 96
    what teachers should know, 78–80
Phonemic strategy, 337
Phonetic spelling stages, 333, 334, 335
Phonetic stage, bilingual writers, 292
Phonetics, 102
Phonics, 100–120
    activities/strategies for, 111–119
    analogy, 108
    analytic, 101, 108
    approach to reading, 5–6
    assessment and, 109–111
    CCSS and, 107, 109
    commercial programs, 5
    defined, 75, 101
    English learners and, 77–78, 361
    explicit instruction of, 114
    glossary, 101–102
    in context, 108
    mastery survey, 478–480
    instruction of, 103–109
    programs for, 108
    synthetic, 102, 108
    teacher modeling and, 103–104
    technology and, 119–120
    texts for, 108
Phonics Criterion Test, 111, 235
Phonics Mastery Survey, 110
Phonograms, 6, 102, 108, 335
    books with, 389–390
Phonological awareness, 75, 102
Phonological Awareness Literacy Screening, 354
Phonological representation, of words, 149
Phrases and Short Sentences for Repeated Reading Practice list, 125
Phrasing, 261, 264–267
Physiological needs, 4
Pictello, 327
Pictionades, activity, 171
Picture Book of Benjamin Franklin, A, 222

Picture books, 136
  bilingual, 391
  historical fiction, 187, 593
  modeling, 318
  multicultural, 391–392
Picture cards, materials for, 514–529,
    549–566
  beginning sound, 517–529
  directions, 513
  Go Fish, 549–555
  How Many Syllables in the Zoo?,
    514–516
  Humpty Dumpty, 556–560
  initial consonant sound, 561–566
Picture clues, 126
Picture Puzzlers, activity, 170
Pictures:
  expressive vocabulary and, 136
  painting mental, 203
Plagiarism, 312
Plain folk, 222
Plosive consonant, 102
Poetry, 82–84
  acrostic, 319–320
  biopoems, 321–322
  cinquain, 320
  collections, 387–388
  diamante, 320–321
  echo reading and, 272–273
  fibbin poems, 322
  identifying rhyme in, 90
  informational books in, 86
  parents reading, 377
  party, activity, 270–271
  phrasing and, 265
  rich language of, 150, 152, 177
  Yankee Doodle, 116
Polysyllabic words, 125, 127
  activities, 140–143
Pop Off the Beads!, activity, 94
Portfolio Assessment Kit, 63
Portfolio Builder for PowerPoint, 63
Portfolios, 60, 62–63
  parents and, 374
  writing assessment and, 307–310
Portmanteaus, 154
Possible Sentences, activity, 165
Postcard, for oral reading scaffolding,
    612
POW strategy, 284, 311
PPP strategy, 273
Pragmatic component of writing, 288
Pragmatic cueing system, 28, 124
PRC2, 241
Precommunicative stage, bilingual
    writers, 292

Predictable text, 108, 115–116
Predicting, 179–181
Prefixes, 133, 337
  frequently used, 407
  poster, 152
Pre-Language Assessment Scales,
    43–44
Prelutsky, Jack, 83, 84, 150
PReP, activity, 249–250
Prephonetic spelling stage, 333
Preproduction, language development
    and, 10
Pre-reading questions, 226
Prescriptive Reading Performance
    Test, 111
Presentation, 6 + 1 traits and, 307,
    314
*Pretty Salma: A Little Red Riding Hood
    Story from Africa,* 183
Preview-pause-prompt-praise strategy,
    273
Prewriting stage, 301–302
Primary sources, 213
Print size, 225
Prior knowledge, 3, 12, 16, 26, 34,
    123, 126, 131, 179, 213, 218,
    223, 249
  assessment and, 54–55, 233–234
  author's assumption of, 228
  connecting to texts, 183–185, 218,
    219, 220
  informational texts and, 228
Problem solving, software and, 392
Problem/solution, 222, 224
  graphic organizer for, 242, 245
Process, differentiating, 356 (*see also*
    Differentiating instruction)
Productive language stage, 10
Professor Garfield, 256
Projects, online research, 8
Pronunciation guide, consonant,
    399–400
Proofreading, 303
Propaganda, 222
Prosody, 261, 264–267
PTA/PTO, 369
Publishers, audiobooks, 201
Publishing, 303–305
Punctuation, 267, 303
Puns, 154
Puppets, 8, 92
Purpose, setting a, 181 (*see also*
    Argument)
Puzzles, 166–167, 170

QARs, 248–249, 253

QCT, activity, 253–254
Qualitative analysis:
  of miscue analysis, 51
  of running records, 52–54
Qualitative dimensions of text com-
    plexity, 33–34, 177–178, 511
Qualitative Spelling Inventories, 111
Quantitative analysis:
  of miscue analysis, 50–51
  of running records, 52
Quantitative dimension of text
    complexity, 33, 177
Question Builder, app, 256
Question Connect Transform activity,
    206, 253–254
Question–answer relationships, 248–
    249, 253
Questioning:
  reciprocal, 198
  technique, activity, 246
Questions:
  activity, 248–249, 253–254
  higher-level, 194
  in textbooks, 226–227
  open ended, 23–24, 188
  pre-reading, 226
  types of, 196
Quick Phonemic Awareness Assess-
    ment Device, 80, 463
Quick Writes, 284, 311–312, 330

Rabble Rousers, 314–315
Race Track, activity, 592
Rap a Tap Tap, 108
Rate, fluency and, 261, 262–264, 282
Read, flip, write, activity, 312
Readability, 227–228
  calculations, 33
  formulas, 33, 425–426
  levels, 29–31, 48
Read-alouds, 177, 194, 196, 240–241
Reader Self-Perception Scale, 66,
    455–456
Readers (*see also* Reading):
  becoming proficient, 78–79
  considerations, text complexity
    and, 34
  cultural/literary demands placed
    on, 178
  interests/attitudes, 218–219
  internal factors and comprehension,
    217–219
  metacognition and, 27–28
  past experiences of, 178
  phonics and, 5–6
  skilled vs. struggling, 189

skilled vs. unskilled re informational text, 219
struggling, 12–13, 104, 123, 154,
356 (*see also* Differentiating
instruction; Response to intervention; Struggling readers;
Tutoring)
traits of emergent/beginning, 47
use of cueing systems, 123–124
Readers theater, 8, 266, 267
fluency activities, 278–279
sample script, 603–604
websites, 278–279
Reading (*see also* Comprehension;
Fluency):
aloud to children, 376–377 (*see
also* Read-alouds)
approaches, 5–9
as a competition, 23–24
assessment of, *see* Assessment
attitude surveys, 360, 448–449, 453
(*see also* Interest inventories)
before/during/after strategies,
179–186
buddy, 8, 23, 74, 277
CCRA checklist, 440–441 (*see also*
Checklists; Rubrics)
choral, 11, 279–281
comprehension, *see* Comprehension
comprehensive approach to, 6–9
confidence and, 22–23
context, *see* Context; Context clues
critical, 4 (*see also* Critical literacy)
dyad, 277
echo, 272–273
emerging, 46–47
English learners and, *see* English
learners
Fluency Monitor, 271 (*see also*
Fluency)
guided, *see* Guided reading
independent, *see* Independent
reading
inferential, 201
informational text, *see* Informational text
lack of interest in, 30, 31
leveled books and, 31–33
levels, 3, 29–31, 48
literary vs. informational, 15
miscues, *see* Miscue analysis
models, 5–9
motivation and, 22–26
narrative text, 174–210 (*see also*
Narrative text)
new literacies and, *see* New literacies

oral, *see* Oral reading
proficiency, 22–23
rate, 261, 262–264
reforms, 13–16
repeated, *see* Repeated reading
rubrics, *see* Rubrics
scores, 13
shared, 6, 8, 12
silent, 25, 35, 44, 47, 190, 232,
256, 263
skills, 176–179 (*see also* Comprehension; Decoding; Fluency;
Vocabulary)
summer programs, 377–378
text selection and, 29–34
tutors and, *see* Tutoring
vocabulary and, *see* Vocabulary
workshop, 8, 253
writing and, 285–286 (*see also*
Writing)
Reading Inventory (Shanker & Ekwall),
130
Reading logs:
for intermediate students, 461
for primary students, 460
reflection, 462
Reading Recovery, 32, 357, 359
ReadWriteThink.org, 119, 143, 209,
327
Ready . . . Set . . . Read, 84
Receptive language art, 286
Receptive vocabulary, 125, 129,
135–136
Reciprocal Questioning, 198–199
Reciprocal theory, 268
Record and check chart, 274–275, 601
Records, anecdotal, 56–57
Red Sings from Treetops, 177
Reflection logs, 68, 69
Reflective thinking, 23–24
Reforms, in reading instruction, 13–16
Regionalisms, 154
Reliability, 41
Renaissance Learning, 31
Repeated Interactive Read-Aloud, 196
Repeated reading, 6, 125
activity, 201–202, 277
Fry phrase list and, 125
Repetitions, 48, 49
ReQuest, activity, 251
Research report rubrics, 308, 309,
503–504
Response to Intervention, 14–16, 260,
352–355, 365, 366
Retelling, 185, 190, 196
with Puppets, 206

Retrospective miscue analysis (RMA),
190, 270–271 (*see also* Miscue
analysis)
Revising, 302–303
Rhetorical knowledge, 126
Rhyme, 76, 82, 102, 108
activities, 87, 90–91, 115–116
books with, 389–390
Rhythm walks, activity, 281
Riddles, activities, 169–170
Rime, 6, 76, 102, 108
activities for, 93, 114–115, 140
visual analysis and, 132
Roots, word, 141, 408–416
Rosa Parks, 32
Rosencran's spelling stages, 333
RTI, *see* Response to intervention
Rubrics, 59–60
for fluency, 271
for informational text comprehension, 232–233, 486, 487
for multimedia projects and, 308,
505
for oral reading fluency, 492
for reading comprehension, 191–193,
232–233, 483, 486, 487
for research reports, 308, 309,
503–504
for story writing, 500, 502
writing assessment and, 307–310,
496, 498–499
Rummy cards, morphology, 588–589
Runner, 365
Running records, 51–57, 132, 190, 270
blank form, 438
informational texts and, 232

S Is for Sooner, 298
Safety needs, 4
Sand (Clay) assessment, 46
SBAC, 40, 43, 235, 355
Scaffolding, 3–4, 363, 612
Scanning, activity, 252
Scavenger hunts, 255
Schema, 126
Scholastic:
audiobooks and, 12, 143, 201
Electronic Portfolio, 63
Phonemic Awareness Kit, 80
Phonics Inventory, 111
Reading Inventory, 32, 33, 193
Schoolyard Safari, activity, 163
Schwa, 102
Science, 217, 253
experiments, activities, 162, 239–240
Scientifically based research, 14

Scores:
    in reading, 13
    types of, 42
    rubrics as guides, 59–60 (*see also*
        Rubrics)
    scoring sheets, 452, 481
Scoring miscues, *see* Miscue analysis
Script, readers theater, 603–604
Sector 7, 162
Segmenting, activity, 77, 93
Self-actualization, 4
Self-assessment, 66–70, 506
    instruments, for writing, 308, 310
Self-consciousness, reading and,
    22–23
Self-correction, 49, 52, 53, 54, 268,
    269, 273, 363 (*see also* Miscue
    analysis)
Self-efficacy, 27, 28
Self-monitoring, 182
Semantic:
    component of writing, 288
    cueing system, 28, 53, 124
    gradient word chart, 156
    representation, 149
Semiphonetic writing stage, 333, 334,
    342
    bilingual writers, 292, 293
Sentence combining, 324
Sentence fluency, 6 + 1 traits and, 306,
    314
Sentences, simple/compound/
    complex, 306
Sequels, writing, 318
Sequence, 221–222
    expository frame for, 317
    graphic organizer for, 242–243
Serafini, Frank, 187
SES, 155
Share time, 8
Shared reading, 6, 8, 12
Sharing the pen, 311
Sharks, 229–230
Sheltered instruction, 11
Sherlock Bones and the Missing Cheese,
    208
Short vowels, 102
Sibert Medal, 224
Sight vocabulary, 125, 126, 130–131
    activities, 137–139
Sight words, 6, 123, 125–126, 264
    activities, 136–137
    assessing, 129–130
Silent letters, 102
Silent reading, 25, 35, 44, 47, 190,
    232, 256, 263

Silent stage, of language development,
    10
Single Shard, A, 185
Sipay Word Analysis Test, 44, 111
Sipe's spelling stages, 333
6 + 1 Trait Writing Assessment, 284,
    285, 306–307, 494–495
    activities for, 312–314
Skill logs, 66, 68
Skilled readers, qualities of, 189
Skills, 26 (*see also* Phonics; Reading;
    Vocabulary; Writing)
    constrained, 261–262
    new literacies and, 16–17, 217
Slosson Intelligence Test (SIT), 41
Small groups, activities for, 134,
    170–171
    fluency activities for, 275–281
Smarter Balanced Assessment Consor-
    tium, 40, 235, 355
Snakes, 257
Snowmen at Night, 108
Social networking, 17, 305
Social studies, 218
Software, comprehension and, 392
    readability formulas and, 33
Solving Mysteries, activity, 208
Some Smug Slug, 150
Songs, 82, 87
Sorting with words, activity, 118
Sound boxes, 88
Sounds, of language, 81–86
    articulation of vowel, 105
    beginning, 88–90 (*see also* Initial
        sounds)
    blending, 76–77, 93
    children and, activity, 92, 94–95
    deleting, 94–95
    initial, 76, 88–90
    manipulating, 77, 95–96
    segmenting, 93
    within words, activities, 117–119
Sources, citing, 237–238, 296, 598
"Spaghetti, Spaghetti," 280
Spanish:
    alphabet, 336
    compared to English, 106
    –English bilingual books, 89, 391
    magazines for, 241
    phonemes, 77–78, 339
    spelling patterns, 338
    vowel sounds in, 106
Spatial intelligence, 29, 30
Speaking, CCSS, 14
Speech, figurative, 161–162
Speech reading, 276

Spell checking, 349
Spelling, 329–350
    apps, 349
    assessment of, 338, 341–343
    CCSS and, 338, 340
    chart summarizing stages, 333
    developmental stages of, 332–336,
        341, 349–350
    diphthongs and, 105
    English and Spanish patterns
        compared, 338
    English learners and, 335–337
    explicit instruction, 331–332
    generalizations about, 417
    good vs. poor, 338, 341
    graphic examples of stages, 334
    high-frequency patterns, 106
    inventories, 341–342, 507
    layers in English, 103
    lists, 331–332
    morphemic strategy and, 337
    patterns, 104–106, 337–338, 341,
        343, 418
    phonemic strategy and, 337
    proofreading and, 303
    recording and analyzing, 508
    recording students', 342
    self-assessment, 506
    standards and, 338, 340
    technology and, 349
    tutoring and, 360
    visual connections, 337
    vowel sounds and, activity, 118
Spelling in Parts activity, 347
Spin the Discussion, activity, 204
Stages:
    of language development, 9–10
    of spelling, 332–336, 341,
        349–350
    of writing development, 288–293
Stance, critical, 187–188
Standard scores, 42
Standardized tests, 39, 41, 42, 111,
    234–235
Standards:
    Common Core, *see* CCSS
    English language proficiency, 43
    English learner proficiency, 158
    fluency and, 268–269
    for assessment, 40–41
    informational text and, 213–214
        (*see also* Informational text)
    RTI and, 355
    spelling and, 331
    tutoring and, 357, 358
    writing and, 285, 293–301

Stanford Achievement Tests, 42, 111, 158, 235

Stanford Diagnostic Reading Test, 44, 111, 158, 272

Stanford-Binet Intelligence Scale, 41

Stanine scores, 42

Step Inside the Rain Forest, 135

Stones (Clay) assessment, 46

Storms, 231

Story:
elements of, 183, 185
map, 205
writing, rubric, 502

StoryBuilder, 327

Story Face strategy, 183, 184

Story Patch, 327

Story-poem, 217

Storytelling, digital, 326

Strategies:
comprehension, 179–186, 193–208, 236–254
fluency, 272–281
log sheet, 364, 610
phonemic awareness and, 86–96
phonics, 111–119
spelling, 343–350
Story Face, 183, 184
vocabulary building, 159–171
word recognition, 133–143
word-learning, 152
writing, 310–327

Stretch Lexile band, 31, 40 (*see also* Lexile band)

Structural analysis, 215, 127–128
activities, 140–143
assessment of, 132

Structure, text complexity and, 33–34, 177–178

Struggling readers, 123
consonant sounds and, 104
dominoes activity, 113
limited vocabulary, 148
philosophy of instruction for, 12–13
qualities of, 189
reading comprehension strategies for, 179–186
vocabulary and, 154–155
vowel sounds and, 104

Students:
as component of learning experience, 26–29
assessment of, *see* Assessment
confidence of 22–23
context of reading, 34
critical reading and, 4, 187–188 (*see also* Critical literacy)

diverse needs of, *see* Differentiating instruction; RTI
engaged in reading/writing, 21
English learners, *see* English learners
home life of, 369–370 (*see also* Parents)
inferential thinking and, 181–182
knowledge of, 26–28
lack of interest in reading, 24
survey of, 64–66, 448–454 (*see also* Interest inventories; Surveys)

Subheadings, 225

Substituting sounds, 77

Substitutions, 48, 49

Success for All, 357

Suffixes, 102, 133, 337
frequently used, 407

Summative assessment, 40

Summer reading programs, 377–378

Sundance, publisher, 201

Supported-reading, 277

Surveys:
phonics mastery, 478–480
attitude, 66, 448–454
for phonics assessment, 110
personal interest, 64–65, 447
using during tutoring, 360

Sustained silent reading, 25, 35

Syllable and affixes stage, 333, 335, 336

Syllables, 76, 101, 102
activities emphasizing, 87–88
recognizing within words, 264
teaching to English learners, 129

Symbols, visual, 187

Synonyms, 153, 154
Concentration, activity, 167–168

Syntactic component of writing, 288

Syntactic cueing system, 28, 53, 123–124

Syntax, of words, 149

Synthetic phonics, 102, 108

Systems, book-leveling, 394–395

Table of contents, 225, 249

Talking drawings, 233

Task, as component of learning experience, 34–35

Task considerations, text complexity and, 34

Taxonomy of Reading Miscues, 48

Teacher modeling, *see* Modeling

Teacher-Made Audiobooks, activity, 200–201

Teachers:
anecdotal records and, 56–57

as component of learning experience, 21–26
as literacy advocates, 218
caregivers and, 367–381 (*see also* Parents)
checklists and, *see* Checklists
communication with parents, 367–369
comprehensive approach to reading and, 7–9
considering reading task, 34–35
critical literacy and, *see* Critical literacy
effective, 9, 11–12, 21–22, 23, 107
English learners, *see* English learners
inferential thinking and, 181–182
knowledge of phonemic awareness, 78–80
knowledge of phonics, 103–107
knowledge of vocabulary, 147–149
knowledge of word recognition, 123–128
language play and, 81–86
metacognition and, 28
modeling, *see* Modeling
personal philosophy of, 12–13
responsibility of, 35
text selection and, 29–34
vocabulary instruction, 151–154, 155, 156 (*see also* Vocabulary)
whole-part-whole reading model and, 6

Teachers of English to Speakers of Other Languages (TESOL), 43

Teaching (*see also* Teachers):
multiple intelligences and, 29, 30
personal philosophy, 12–13

Technical words, 148, 227–228
activity, 138–139

Technological literacy, 16

Technology:
assessment and, 70, 193
classes for parents, 380
comprehension and, 208–210, 254–255
fluency and, 282
informational texts and, 254–255
nights, 380
phonemic awareness and, 96
phonics and, 119–120
spelling and, 349
tutoring and, 365
vocabulary, 171–172
word recognition and, 143–144
writing and, 324–327

Telephone calls, to parents, 373
Telling jokes, activity, 276–277
Templates:
    K-T-W-L-E, chart, 599
    morphology rummy cards,
        588–589
    multiple sources chart, 598
    vocabulary bookmark, 590
Terms, defining, 225, 227–228 (*see
    also* Vocabulary)
TESOL, 43
Test of Phonological Awareness, 80
Test scores, types of, 42
Testimonials, 222
Testing of Reading Fluency, 272
Tests (*see also* Assessment):
    achievement, 42–44
    cloze, 54–56
    criterion-referenced, 42–44
    diagnostic, 44–45, 158, 272
    informal assessment, 45–63
    intelligence, 41
    maze, 56, 157, 191, 231, 232
    norm-referenced, 42
    oral reading, 44–45
    standardized, 39, 41, 42, 111,
        234–235
Text:
    as component of learning experience,
        29–34
    complexity of, 15, 33–34, 177–178
    informational, 211–257 (*see also*
        Informational text)
    mapping, 198, 594
    nonlinear, 16–17
    predictable, 108
    qualitative dimensions of complexity,
        511
Textbook, evaluation checklist,
    596–597
Textmasters, activity, 236–238
Texts (*see also* Books):
    background knowledge, *see* Back-
        ground knowledge
    complexity of, 177–178
    connections to text/world/self,
        183–185
    considerate vs. inconsiderate styles,
        229
    features, 225–227
    guidelines for selecting, 31
    informational, 224–229 (*see also*
        Informational text)
    readability of, 228–229
    selecting appropriate levels, 31–33
    survey of features, 249

technical vocabulary in, 227–228
    (*see also* Vocabulary)
    writing style, 227–229
Text-Talk, activity, 201
Thai consonants, 337
Thank you notes, activity, 304
That's Not All!, 116
The Bear and the Fly, 162
The Day Fort Sumter Was Fired On, 280
The Story of Friedl Dicker-Brandeis, 194
The Three Pigs, 162
Theories, learning, 3–5
Think-alouds, 8, 28, 191
    for narrative text, 199–200
    for informational text, 250
    modeling, 295
    word patterns and, 344–345
Thinking, inferential, 181–182, 194
Three little pigs, letter, 323
Tic-Tac-Toe, morphology, 160
Tier one words, 148
Tier three words, 148, 151
Tier two words, 148, 151–152
Time frame, 221, 222
Time magazine, 219
Timeline, 242
Tone, word choice and, 216
Tongue twisters, 84, 90
Topic, choosing a, 302
Tornadoes, 231
Toss the Cube, 90, 140, 540–548
Total physical response, 11, 163–164
Tradebook, evaluation checklist,
    596–597
Transfer, persuasion and, 222
Transitional stage, bilingual writers,
    292
TREE strategy, 284, 311
*True Story of the Three Little Pigs as
    Told by A. Wolf, The,* 185
Tuesday, 162, 166, 201
Tutoring, 356–365
    activities, 272–275
    appropriate materials for, 359–360
    English learners and, 360–363, 512
    guidelines for successful, 356
    lesson plans for, 357, 358, 359,
        362, 363, 512, 609
    log sheet for books read, 364
    planning and conducting, 357–360
    reflection on lesson, 360
    science and, 240
    successful programs, 357
    technology and, 365
    volunteer, 379–380
    written objectives for, 357, 359

Twice Upon a Time: Rapunzel, 185, 186
Two Cube Game, activity, 171

Unconstrained skills, 262
Under the Same Sky, 365
Unscramble the Sentence, activity,
    137
Unscramble the Word, activity, 138
Usborne Big Book of Science, 239

Validity, 41
Venn Diagrams, activity, 207
Vicarious experience, vocabulary and,
    149–150
Visual:
    activity, 140
    analysis, 126–127, 132, 136, 140
    appeal, texts and, 225
    literacy, 16
    symbols, 187
    system, 53
Visualizing, 182–183
Vocabulary:
    academic, 14, 15, 229
    activities/strategies for, 135–136,
        159–171
    assessment and, 129–131, 156–158
    bookmarks, activity, 159, 590
    books emphasizing, 154
    building, 146–172
    categories of words, 148
    checklists and, 157–158
    comprehension and, 177
    context clues and, 153
    development, 148
    diagnostic tests for, 158
    domain-specific, 15, 227–228
    domain specific vs. academic, 15
    English learners and, 155–156,
        230, 361
    explicit instruction, 151–154
    growth checklist, 482
    increasing, 149–156
    language experience approach,
        162–164
    limited, students', 156
    listening, 44, 125, 177
    morphology and, 127–128
    poetry and, 150, 152
    reading and, 147–148
    receptive and expressive, 125
    reflective learning on, 172
    struggling readers and, 154–155
    technical, 215, 227–228
    technology and, 171–172
    tutoring and, 361, 363

what teachers should know, 147–149
Voice, 6 + 1 traits and, 306, 313
Volcano, 224
Volunteers:
    community, 379–380
    parents as, 381
Vowel:
    articulation of sounds, 105
    digraphs, 105, 110, 337, 401
    diphthongs, 105, 401
    generalizations about, 106
    listening to sounds, activity, 117
    r-controlled, 102
    schwa, 102
    short, 102
    short, bingo, 116–117
    sounds, 75, 104–105, 106
    sounds in Spanish, 106
    spelling and, activity, 118
    spelling patterns, 104–105, 106
    variants, 401
Vygotsky, Lev, 3, 155

Watsons Go to Birmingham, 1963,
    161–162
WCPM, 260–261, 262–263, 282
Weather Forecasting, 231
Weather Words and What They Mean,
    231
Web 2.0, 304, 305
Webbing, 305
WebQuest, 17
Websites:
    assessment, 64, 70, 158
    author, 326
    for assessing English learners, 64,
        158
    for Caldecott winners, 208
    for creating puzzles, 166
    for free e-texts, 209
    for games boards, 171
    for miscue analysis/running
        records, 190
    informational text, 255
    phonemic awareness, 96
    phonics, 119–120
    readers theater, 278–279
    spelling and, 349
    using the Fry phrase list, 130
    vocabulary growth, 158
    word recognition, 143–144
    writing contests, 287
    writing skills, 327
    writing/publishing, 305
Wechsler Intelligence Scales, 41
Wee Sing, 87

Whales, 222
What If?, activity, 200
When Hitler Stole Pink Rabbit, 194
When Pigs Fly, 108
Who Lives in the Rain Forest?, 223
Whole word approach, 102
Whole-part-whole reading model, 6
Wide reading, 269
Wiesner, David, 162, 166
Wikipedia, 17
Wikis, 325
Will Rogers, 260
Within word pattern spelling stage,
    333, 335, 336, 341
Wobbly Tooth, The, 27, 358
Woodcock Reading Mastery Test, 44,
    111, 158, 272
    tutoring and, 360
Word (*see also* Words):
    Box, activity, 161
    cards, directions, 513
    dominoes, materials, 567–570
    Expert Cards, activity, 170
    families, 396–398
    frequency, 32
    hierarchies, instruction in, 153
    identification, *see* Word recognition
    knowledge, *see* Vocabulary
    ladders activity, 119
    processing, 327
    recognition, *see* Word recognition
    roots, 141, 408–416
    solvers, 337
    sorts, 110–111
    study, at home, 378
    web, 138–139
Word choice:
    author's, 216
    6 + 1 traits and, 306, 313–314
Word families, 6, 76
    activity, 114
    concentration activity, 115
    most common, 396–398
Word lists:
    Dolch, *see* Dolch Basic Sight
        Vocabulary
    Fry phrase, *see* Fry phrase list
    high-frequency, 126, 331, 402
Word patterns (*see also* Spelling
        patterns):
    activities for, 116–117
    English learners and, 337–338
    think-aloud on, 344–345
Word recognition, 122–144
    activities/strategies for, 133–143
    assessment of, 128–133

CCSS and, 128
components of, 123, 124–128
cueing systems and, 123–124
technology and, 143–144
what teachers should know, 123–128
Word walls, 8, 112–113, 114, 138
    content-related, 347–348
Wordless books, 136, 162, 323,
    388–389
    for developing inferential reading,
        201
    modeling, 318
Words:
    analysis of, 125, 126–128
    blending, 127
    categories of, 148
    compound, 101, 140
    correct per minute, 260–261,
        262–263, 282
    decoding/encoding, 103, 176–177
        (*see also* Phonics)
    features of, 148–149
    find the mystery, activity, 114
    high frequency, 126, 331, 402
    language gestalts and, 159
    mono- and polysyllabic, 125,
        126–127
    morphemic structure of, 125
    multiple meanings of, 124
    nonsense, 82–86
    origin of, 166
    personalized dictionary, 113
    recognizing common, 264
    recognizing meanings of, 264
    rhyming, 91, 108 (*see also* Rhymes)
    root, 141, 408–416
    segmenting, 77
    semantic gradient chart, 156
    sight, *see* Sight words
    sorting with pictures, 112
    sorts, activity, 118
    sounds within, activities, 117–119
    spelling patterns of, 106 (*see also*
        Spelling)
    structural analysis, 127–128
    unscrambling activity, 138
    visual analysis, *see* Visual analysis
Working portfolios, 62
Workshop, writing, 8, 284, 285, 292,
    298, 301, 311, 315
World knowledge, 184
World War II, discussion questions
    for, 194
Writer Self-Perception Scale (WSPS),
    66, 308, 310, 457–459
Writers, reluctant, 328

Writing, 283–328
    academic, 294
    alternate, 197
    and spelling self-assessment, 506
    apps, 327
    arguments, *see* Arguments
    assessment of, 40, 307–310, 607
        (*see also* Rubrics)
    attitude surveys and, 308, 310, 360,
        450–451, 454
    audience and, 302
    authentic tasks, 315, 324–326
    bilingual English learners and,
        292–293
    brochures, 324
    CCSS and, 14, 285, 293–301
    CCSS and informational text,
        298–299
    CCSS and narrative text, 299
    checklists, *see* Checklists
    choosing a topic, 302
    components of, 287–288
    comprehensive approach to, 7
    computers and, 286, 324–327
    concrete examples and, 315
    conventional stage, 288, 290,
        291–292
    conventions, 314
    copying stage, 288, 290
    drafting, 302
    drawing stage, 288, 289, 291
    editing, 303
    email, 325–326
    emergent, 46–47, 288–293
    English learners and, 292–293, 361
    expository frames and, 302, 317–318
    guided, 316
    in kindergarten, 286
    informational texts and, 227–229,
        298–299
    instruction and assessment matrix,
        607
    interactive, 8, 11, 311
    intervention, 310–327
    interviews, 314–315
    invented spelling stage, 288, 290,
        291
    journal, 7, 8, 18, 189, 206, 324, 380
    letter strings, 288, 289
    letter-like forms, 288, 289
    letters, 322–323, 368–369
    Mt. Plot activity, 317
    multimodal text and, 299–301
    on demand, 311
    parodies, 319
    poetry, *see* Poetry
    prewriting stage, 301–302
    primary grades' rubric, 496
    process, 301–305
    publishing, 303–305
    reading and, 285–286
    reluctant writers, 328
    research report, *see* Research report
        rubrics
    revising, 302–303
    rubrics for assessing, 307–310,
        496–504
    scribbling stage, 288, 289
    self-assessment, 506
    sentence combining activity, 324
    sequels, 318
    6 + 1 Trait model, 306–307
    standards for assessment, 40
    structuring the material, 302
    technology and, 324–327
    third grade, rubric, 498–499
    to authors, 325–326
    tutoring objectives, 359
    wordless books and, 323
    workshop, 8, 284, 285, 292, 298,
        301, 311, 315

Yankee Doodle Poetry, activity, 116
YouTube, 16

Zin! Zin! Zin! A Violin, 85, 281
Zip test, 157
Zone of proximal development, 3–4
Zoo activity, 87–88
Zoo Doings: Animal Poems, 83

TUTORING AND TECHNOLOGY

I t is "estimated that 70 percent of adolescents—students in grades 4–12—have difficulty reading in some manner and require direct, explicit instructional interventions to expand their word recognition, decoding, reading fluency and comprehension skills" (Houge & Geier, 2009, p. 154). Many of these students do not live near a university with a research-based literacy tutoring program. However, most attend schools that have appropriate software programs and Internet access that allow face-to-face tutoring through videoconferencing. Many teacher education programs have videoconferencing capabilities. Houge and Geier (2009) completed a research study with 61 adolescents (grades 4–12) who were experiencing problems with word recognition, decoding, fluency, and comprehension. The purpose of the study was to determine if tutoring via videoconference resulted in higher reading scores. Students received 16 one-hour sessions of individual tutoring by a university student in a teacher education program. Each tutor received instruction in administrating and interpreting assessment instruments and strategies that focused on word identification, vocabulary, comprehension, and fluency. The study indicated that tutoring via video-conference did improve students' comprehension and fluency as shown on the growth from the pre-test to the post-test (Houge & Geier, 2009).

As the CCSS are implemented, the need for tutors for K–12 students is likely to grow. Tutors may benefit from instruction using videoconferencing to teach strategies that will help K–12 students do close readings with complex texts; compare and contrast text on the same topic; write argumentative, narrative, and informational passages; and research and synthesize information gathered from multiple sources.

CONCLUDING THOUGHTS

A ll teachers need to understand all the implications of RTI and how they will implement it in their classrooms. They also need to understand how and when they and their students need help to meet RTI mandates. For educators to meet the goals set by the CCSS, they must tap the resources of their communities by drawing on paraprofessionals, preservice teachers, and technology for tutoring. For tutors to be effective they must be trained and supervised by reading specialists. They need to implement appropriately structured programs and use appropriate materials. The goal of all of tutoring is to help struggling readers and writers to gain the literacy skills they will need in college and/or their careers.

reflective learning

DIFFERENTIATING INSTRUCTION: GIFTED STUDENTS. Mr. Kasai has just completed his first year of teaching seventh-grade language arts at a school in a low socioeconomic neighborhood. His classes were diverse, each with three to four students who were English learners. Most students came from single-parent homes in which the parent worked one or two jobs to support the family. During the year, he observed that three of his academically gifted students were bored by daily assignments; in fact, they usually failed to hand them in. He did notice that when they were discussing the novels *Under the Same Sky* (DeFelice, 2003), about social inequality, and *Runner* (Deuker, 2007) about a teen who lives in poverty on a boat with his alcoholic father, these students became very engaged in the reading and discussion. Mr. Kasai also noticed that they enjoyed research on the topics they were able to choose. They also loved to collaborate on gathering research and on creating multimodal presentations.

At the end of the year, Mr. Kasai wished he had given the three gifted students a bigger challenge in every assignment. He is determined to find resources throughout the summer that will challenge all his students in the next year. But he does not know where to go for ideas. He needs your help.

Throughout this text much emphasis is placed on individualizing learning for all students, but too often we focus on struggling readers, when the students who are academically gifted are not challenged. Together with your classmates answer the following questions. Use these ideas challenge your future students when the time comes.

questions

1. Who are some educators/researchers besides Joseph Renzulli who focus on the gifted student?

2. What resources, books, and websites can you recommend to Mr. Kasai?

3. What specific projects (find at least 20) would you recommend to Mr. Kasai to increase the motivation and engagement of his gifted students?

RTI, ENGLISH LEARNERS, AND TUTORING. Miss Thomas is a first-year teacher in an urban school in the city where she attended college. During her four years at the university, she observed in this school and volunteered to read to the students. She is thrilled to teach second grade at school because she wants to make a difference in children's lives. She knows her students' success in life will hinge on their receiving a good education and developing a love of learning. She has enough experience to understand that school and learning must be interesting and fun.

However, after two weeks she is overwhelmed by the mandates of RTI and the needs of her students. Many are native Spanish speakers who have been in the United States less than two years. Through informal observation, she finds that many do not know the letter names or their sounds. The school has two reading specialists: one whose main job is to assess the students, and the other who is a reading intervention teacher providing small group instruction. Miss Thomas, however, does not understand whether she or the reading specialists are responsible for making sure students who need intense intervention as mandated by RTI receive it. She knows her students need more help than small group instruction will offer, but is unsure about of her students' tier or step in the RTI process.

questions

1. Where should Miss Thomas go for help?
2. Should she approach the reading specialists about the problem?
3. Should she go to the reading specialists with an idea or a plan?
4. If the school has no funds to pay for outside help, where can she go?
5. If the school chooses to use tutors, should the reading specialists train the tutors?
6. What lesson format should the tutors follow?
7. Where should the students receive the extra help?
8. What materials will the school need to provide for the tutors?
9. When should the tutors work with the students? Should the students miss the literacy instruction in class? Should the tutors tutor while the class has reading?